Europe
Europa

ATLAS ROUTIER et TOURISTIQUE
TOURIST and MOTORING ATLAS
STRASSEN- und REISEATLAS
TOERISTISCHE WEGENATLAS
ATLANTE STRADALE e TURISTICO
ATLAS DE CARRETERAS y TURÍSTICO
ATLAS RODOVIÁRIO e TURÍSTICO

CW00339982

II

Sommaire

Contents / Inhaltsübersicht / Inhoud / Sommario / Sumario / Sumário

II - VII

IV - VII Légende / Key to maps / Zeichenerklärung / Verklaring van detekens / Legenda / Signos conventionales

VIII Plaques d'immatriculation par pays
International vehicle registration plates / Internationale Autokennzeichen / Nationaliteitssticker van de auto's / Sigle automobilistiche internazionali / Matrículas automóvilisticas por país / Chapas de matrícula por país

1 - 19

Europe / Europa **1:3 700 000**

20 - 205

Europe / Europa **1:1 000 000**

20 - 21 Tableau d'assemblage / Key to road map / Seitennübersicht / Overzichtskaarten / Quadro d'insieme / Mapa índice / Tabela de montagem

22 - 37 Irlande / Ireland / Irland / Ierland / Irlanda
Royaume-Uni / United Kingdom / Vereinigtes Königreich / Verenigd Koninkrijk / Regno Unito / Reino Unido

38 - 55 France / Frankreich / Francia / França
Monaco / Mónaco

56 - 75 Espagne / Spain / Spanien / Spanje / Spagna / España / Espanha
Portugal / Portogallo
Andorre / Andorra

76 - 79 Pays-Bas / Netherlands / Niederlande / Nederland / Paesi Bassi / Países Bajos / Países Baixos
Belgique / Belgium / Belgien / België / Belgio / Bélgica
Luxembourg / Luxemburg / Lussemburgo / Luxemburgo

80 - 99 Allemagne / Germany / Deutschland / Duitsland / Germania / Alemania / Alemanha
République tchèque / Czech Republic / Tschechische Republik / Tsjechische Republiek / Repubblica Ceca / República Checa
Autriche / Austria / Österreich / Oostenrijk / Áustria
Liechtenstein / Listenstaine
Suisse / Switzerland / Schweiz / Zwitserland / Svizzera / Suiza / Suiça

100 - 115 Italie / Italy / Italien / Italië / Italia / Itália
Saint-Marin / San Marino / São Marinho
Vatican / Vatikan / Vaticaan / Vaticano
Malte (1:500 000) / Malta

116 - 133 Pologne / Poland / Polen / Polonia / Polónia
Hongrie / Hungary / Ungarn / Hongarije / Ungheria / Hungría / Hungria
République slovaque / Slovak Republic / Slowakische Republik / Slowakije / Repubblica Slovacca / República Eslovaca

Eslovénia / Eslovenia / Slovenië / Slowenien / Slovenia / **Slovénie**   134 - 139
Croácia / Croacia / Croazia / Croatië / Kroatien / Croatia / **Croatie**
Bosnien und Herzegowina / Bosnia and Herzegovina / **Bosnie-Herzégovine**
Bósnia-Herzegovina / Bosnia y Herzegovina / Bosnia-Erzegovina / Bosnië en Herzegovina
Montenegro / **Monténégro**

Sérvia / Servië / Serbien / Serbia / **Serbie**   140 - 145
Republiek Macedonië / Republik Mazedonien / Republic of Macedonia / **République de Macédoine**
República da Macedónia / República de Macedonia / Repubblica di Macedonia
Albânia / Albanië / Albanien / Albania / **Albanie**

Roménia / Rumanía / Roemenië / Rumänien / Romania / **Roumanie**   146 - 173
Bulgária / Bulgaria / Bulgaria / Bulgarije / Bulgarien / Bulgaria / **Bulgarie**
Grécia / Grecia / Griekenland / Griechenland / Greece / **Grèce**

Chipre / Cipro / Zypern / Cyprus / **Chypre (1:700 000)**   174 - 175

Noruega / Norvegia / Noorwegen / Norwegen / Norway / **Norvège (1:1 500 000)**   176 - 199
Islândia / Islandia / Islanda / IJsland / Island / Iceland / **Islande (1: 2 800 000)**
Suécia / Suecia / Svezia / Zweden / Schweden / Sweden / **Suède (1:1 500 000)**
Finlândia / Finlandia / Finnland / Finland / **Finlande (1:1 500 000)**
Dinamarca / Danimarca / Denemarken / Dänemark / Denmark / **Danemark (1:1 500 000)**

Estónia / Estland / Estonia / **Estonie (1:1 000 000)**   200 - 205
Letónia / Letonia / Lettonia / Letland / Lettland / Latvia / **Lettonie (1:1 000 000)**
Lituânia / Lituania / Litouwen / Litauen / Lithuania / **Lituanie (1:1 000 000)**

206 - 264

Índice / Indice / Register / **Index**

265 - 341

Pianta di città / Stadsplattegronden / Stadtpläne / Town plans / **Plans de ville**
Planos de ciudades / Plantas de Cidade

342 - 351

Conduire en Europe   342- 344
Conducir en Europa / Guidare in Europa / Autorijden in Europa / Autofahren in Europa / Driving in Europe /
Conduzir na Europa

Automóvel clube / Club del Automóvil / Automobielclub / Automobil Club / **Automobile Club**   345

Tableau des distances   346- 347
Quadro de distâncias / Cuadro de distancias / Tabella delle distanze / Afstandstabel / Entfernungstabelle / Distances

Europe des 28   348- 351
Europa dos 28 / Europa de los 28 / Europa dei 28 / Het Europa van de 28 / Europa der 28 / 28 EU Member States

Back of the guide: key to map pages / En fin d'atlas : tableau d'assemblage
Achter in het boek: overzichtskaart / Am Ende des Buches: Übersich
No final do volume : tabela de montagem / Al final del volumen : mapa índice / Alla fine del volume: quadro d'insieme

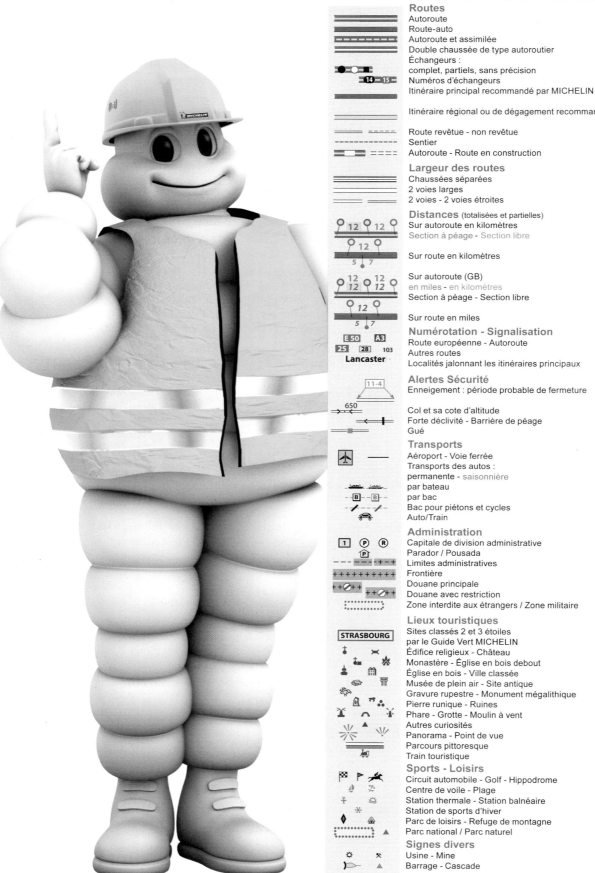

Légende

Routes
Autoroute
Route-auto
Autoroute et assimilée
Double chaussée de type autoroutier
Échangeurs :
complet, partiels, sans précision
Numéros d'échangeurs
Itinéraire principal recommandé par MICHELIN

Itinéraire régional ou de dégagement recommandé par MICHELIN

Route revêtue - non revêtue
Sentier
Autoroute - Route en construction

Largeur des routes
Chaussées séparées
2 voies larges
2 voies - 2 voies étroites

Distances (totalisées et partielles)
Sur autoroute en kilomètres
Section à péage - Section libre

Sur route en kilomètres

Sur autoroute (GB)
en miles - en kilomètres
Section à péage - Section libre

Sur route en miles

Numérotation - Signalisation
Route européenne - Autoroute
Autres routes
Localités jalonnant les itinéraires principaux

Alertes Sécurité
Enneigement : période probable de fermeture

Col et sa cote d'altitude
Forte déclivité - Barrière de péage
Gué

Transports
Aéroport - Voie ferrée
Transports des autos :
permanente - saisonnière
par bateau
par bac
Bac pour piétons et cycles
Auto/Train

Administration
Capitale de division administrative
Parador / Pousada
Limites administratives
Frontière
Douane principale
Douane avec restriction
Zone interdite aux étrangers / Zone militaire

Lieux touristiques
Sites classés 2 et 3 étoiles
par le Guide Vert MICHELIN
Édifice religieux - Château
Monastère - Église en bois debout
Église en bois - Ville classée
Musée de plein air - Site antique
Gravure rupestre - Monument mégalithique
Pierre runique - Ruines
Phare - Grotte - Moulin à vent
Autres curiosités
Panorama - Point de vue
Parcours pittoresque
Train touristique

Sports - Loisirs
Circuit automobile - Golf - Hippodrome
Centre de voile - Plage
Station thermale - Station balnéaire
Station de sports d'hiver
Parc de loisirs - Refuge de montagne
Parc national / Parc naturel

Signes divers
Usine - Mine
Barrage - Cascade

Key | Zeichenerklärung

Roads | Straßen

Motorway	Autobahn
Motorway: single carriageway	Autostraße
Motorway (unclassified)	Autobahn oder Schnellstraße
Dual carriageway with motorway characteristics	Schnellstraße mit getrennten Fahrbahnen
Interchanges:	Anschlussstellen:
complete, limited, not specified	Voll - bzw. Teilanschluss, ohne Angabe
Interchange numbers	Interchange numbers / Anschlussstellennummern
Recommended MICHELIN main itinerary	Von MICHELIN empfohlene Hauptverkehrsstraße
Recommended MICHELIN regional itinerary	Von MICHELIN empfohlene Regionalstraße
Road surfaced - unsurfaced	Straße mit Belag - ohne Belag
Footpath	Pfad
Motorway/Road under construction	Autobahn/Straße im Bau

Road widths | Straßenbreiten

Dual carriageway	Getrennte Fahrbahnen
2 wide lanes	2 breite Fahrspuren
2 lanes - 2 narrow lanes	2 Fahrspuren - 2 schmale Fahrspuren

Distances (total and intermediate) | Entfernungen (Gesamt- und Teilentfernungen)

On motorway in kilometers	Auf der Autobahn in Kilometern
Toll roads - Toll-free section	Mautstrecke - Mautfreie Strecke
On road in kilometers	Auf der Straße in Kilometern
On motorway (GB)	Auf der Autobahn (GB)
in miles - in kilometers	in Meilen - in Kilometern
Toll roads - Toll-free section	Mautstrecke - Mautfreie Strecke
On road in miles	Auf der Straße in Meilen

Numbering - Signs | Nummerierung - Wegweisung

European route - Motorway	Europastraße - Autobahn
Other roads	Sonstige Straßen
Destination on primary route network **Lancaster**	Richtungshinweis auf der empfohlenen Fernverkehrsstraße

Safety Warnings | Sicherheitsalerts

Snowbound, impassable road during the period shown	Eingeschneite Straße: voraussichtl. Wintersperre
Pass and its height above sea level	Pass mit Höhenangabe
Steep hill - Toll barrier	Starke Steigung - Mautstelle
Ford	Furt

Transportation | Verkehrsmittel

Airport - Railway	Flughafen - Bahnlinie
Transportation of vehicles:	Autotransport: ganzjährig
year-round - seasonal	saisonbedingte Verbindung
by boat	per Schiff
by ferry	per Fähre
Ferry (passengers and cycles only)	Fähre für Personen und Fahrräder
Motorail	Autoreisezug

Administration | Verwaltung

Administrative district seat	Verwaltungshauptstadt
Parador / Pousada	Parador / Pousada
Administrative boundaries	Verwaltungsgrenzen
National boundary	Staatsgrenze
Principal customs post	Hauptzollamt
Secondary customs post	Zollstation mit Einschränkungen
Restricted area for foreigners / Military property	Sperrgebiet für Ausländer / Militärgebiet

Sights | Sehenswürdigkeiten

2- and 3-star MICHELIN Green Guide sites	Sehenswürdigkeiten mit 2 und 3 Sternen im Grünen Reiseführer MICHELIN
Religious building - Historic house, castle	Sakral-Bau - Schloss, Burg
Monastery - Stave church	Kloster - Stabkirche
Wooden church - Listed historic town	Holzkirche - denkmalgeschützter Stadtteil
Open air museum - Antiquities	Freilichtmuseum - Antike Fundstätte
Rock carving - Prehistoric monument	Felsbilder - Vorgeschichtliches Steindenkmal
Rune stone - Ruins	Runenstein - Ruine
Lighthouse - Cave - Windmill	Leuchtturm - Höhle - Windmühle
Other places of interest	Sonstige Sehenswürdigkeit
Panoramic view - Viewpoint	Rundblick - Aussichtspunkt
Scenic route	Landschaftlich schöne Strecke
Tourist train	Museumseisenbahn-Linie

Sport & Recreation Facilities | Sport - Freizeit

Racing circuit - Golf course - Horse racetrack	Rennstrecke - Golfplatz - Pferderennbahn
Sailing - Beach	Yachthafen - Badestrand
Spa - Seaside resort	Thermalbad - Seebad
Ski resort	Skigebiet
Recreation ground - Mountain refuge hut	Erholungspark - Schutzhütte
National park / Nature park	Nationalpark / Naturpark

Other signs | Sonstige Zeichen

Factory - Mine	Fabrik - Bergwerk
Dam - Waterfall	Staudamm - Wasserfall

Verklaring van de tekens / Legenda

Wegen / Strade

Autosnelweg	Autostrada
Autoweg	Strada-auto
Autosnelweg of gelijksoortige weg	Autostrada, strada di tipo autostradale
Gescheiden rijbanen van het type autosnelweg	Doppia carreggiata di tipo autostradale
Aansluitingen:	Svincoli:
volledig, gedeeltelijk, zonder aanduiding	completo, parziale, imprecisato
Afritnummers	Svincoli numerati
Hoofdweg	Itinerario principale raccomandato da MICHELIN
Regionale weg	Itinerario regionale raccomandato da MICHELIN
Verharde weg - onverharde weg	Strada rivestita - non rivestita
Pad	Sentiero
Autosnelweg - Weg in aanleg	Autostrada - Strada in costruzione

Breedte van de wegen / Larghezza delle strade

Gescheiden rijbanen	Carreggiate separate
2 brede rijstroken	2 corsie larghe
2 rijstroken - 2 smalle rijstroken	2 corsie - 2 corsie strette

Afstanden (totaal en gedeeltelijk) / Distanze (totali e parziali)

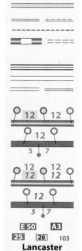

Op autosnelwegen in kilometers	Su autostrada in chilometri
Gedeelte met tol - Tolvrij gedeelte	Tratto a pedaggio - Tratto esente da pedaggio
Op andere wegen in kilometers	Su strada in chilometri
Op autosnelwegen (GB) in mijlen - in kilometers	Su autostrada (GB) in miglia - in chilometri
Gedeelte met tol - Tolvrij gedeelte	Tratto a pedaggio - Tratto esente da pedaggio
Op andere wegen in mijlen	Su strada in miglia

Wegnummers - Bewegwijzering / Numerazione - Segnaletica

Europaweg - Autosnelweg	Strada europea - Autostrada
Andere wegen	Altre strade
Plaatsen langs een hoofdweg met bewegwijzering	Località delimitante gli itinerari principali

E 50 A3 25 28 103 Lancaster

Hindernissen / Ostacoli

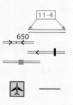

Sneeuw: vermoedelijke sluitingsperiode	Innevamento: probabile periodo di chiusura
Bergpas en hoogte boven de zeespiegel	Passo ed altitudine
Steile helling - Tol	Forte pendenza - Casello
Wad	Guado

Vervoer / Trasporti

Luchthaven - Spoorweg	Aeroporto - Ferrovia
Vervoer van auto's:	Trasporto auto:
het hele jaar - tijdens het seizoen	tutto l'anno - stagionale
per boot	su traghetto
per veerpont	su chiatta
Veerpont voor voetgangers en fietsers	Traghetto per pedoni e biciclette
Autotrein	Auto/treno

Administratie / Amministrazione

Hoofdplaats van administratief gebied	Capoluogo amministrativo
Parador / Pousada	Parador / Pousada
Administratieve grenzen	Confini amministrativi
Staatsgrens	Frontiera
Hoofddouanekantoor	Dogana principale
Douanekantoor met beperkte bevoegdheden	Dogana con limitazioni
Terrein verboden voor buitenlanders / Militair gebied	Zona vietata agli stranieri / Zona militare

Bezienswaardigheden / Mete e luoghi d'interesse

STRASBOURG

Locaties met 2 en 3 sterren volgens de Groene Gids van MICHELIN	Siti segnalati con 2 e 3 stelle dalla Guida Verde MICHELIN
Kerkelijk gebouw - Kasteel	Edificio religioso - Castello
Klooster - Stavkirke (houten kerk)	Monastero - Chiesa in legno di testa
Houten kerk - Onder monumentenzorg geplaatste stad	Chiesa in legno - Citta' classificata
Openluchtmuseum - Overblijfsel uit de Oudheid	Museo all'aperto - Sito antico
Rotstekening - Megaliet	Incisione rupestre - Monumento megalitico
Runensteen - Ruïne	Pietra runica - Rovine
Vuurtoren - Grot - Molen	Faro - Grotta - Mulino a vento
Andere bezienswaardigheden	Altri luoghi d'interesse
Panorama - Uitzichtpunt	Panorama - Vista
Schilderachtig traject	Percorso pittoresco
Toeristentreintje	Trenino turistico

Sport - Recreatie / Sport - Divertimento

Autocircuit - Golfterrein - Renbaan	Circuito automobilistico - Golf - Ippodromo
Kampeerterrein - Jachthaven - Strand	Campeggio - Centro velico - Spiaggia
Kuuroord - Badplaats	Stazione termale - Stazione balneare
Wintersportplaats	Sport invernali
Recreatiepark - Berghut	Parco divertimenti - Rifugio
Nationaal park / Natuurpark	Parco nazionale / Parco naturale

Diverse tekens / Simboli vari

Fabriek - Mijn	Fabbrica - Miniera
Stuwdam - Waterval	Diga - Cascata

Signos convencionales

Legenda

Carreteras	**Estradas**
Autopista	Auto-estrada
Carretera	Rota-automovilística
Autopista, Autovía	Auto-estrada ou similar
Autovía	Estrada com 2 faixas de rodagem do tipo auto-estrada
Accesos:	Nós:
completo, parcial, sin precisar	completo - parciais - sem precisão
Números de los accesos	Número de nós
Itinerario principal recomendado por MICHELIN	Itinerário principal recomendado pela MICHELIN
Itinerario regional recomendado por MICHELIN	Itinerário regional recomendado pela MICHELIN
Carretera asfaltada - sin asfaltar	Estrada asfaltada - não asfaltada
Sendero	Atalho
Autopista - Carretera en construcción	Auto-estrada - Estrada em construção

Ancho de las carreteras	**Largura das estradas**
Calzadas separadas	Faixas de rodagem separadas
Dos carriles anchos	Com 2 vias largas
Dos carriles - Dos carriles estrechos	Com 2 vias - Com 2 vias estreitas

Distancias (totales y parciales)	**Distâncias** (totais e parciais)
En autopista en kilómetros	Em auto-estrada em quilómetros
Tramo de peaje - Tramo libre	Em secção com portagem - sem portagem
En carretera en kilómetros	Em estrada em quilómetros
En autopista (GB)	Em auto-estrada (GB)
en millas - en kilómetros	em milhas - em quilómetros
Tramo de peaje - Tramo libre	Em secção com portagem - sem portagem
En carretera en millas	Em estrada em milhas

Numeración - Señalización	**Numeração - Sinalização**
Carretera europea - Autopista	Estrada Europeia - Auto-estrada
Otras carreteras	Outras estradas
Localidades situadas nos principais itinerários	Localidades situadas nos principais itinerários

Alertas Seguridad	**Obstáculos**
Nevada: Período probable de cierre	Nevadas: período provável de encerramento
Puerto y su altitud	Passagem de montanha - Altitude
Pendiente Pronunciada - Barrera de peaje	Forte declive - Portagem
Vado	Vau

Transportes	**Transportes**
Aeropuerto - Línea férrea / Aeroporto - Via férrea	Aeroporto - Via férrea
Transporte de coches: todo el año - de temporada	Transporte de automóveis:
	permanente - temporal
por barco	por barco
por barcaza	por barcaça
Barcaza para el paso de peatones y vehículos dos ruedas	Barcaça para peões e ciclos
Auto-tren	Auto/trem

Administración	**Administração**
Capital de división administrativa	Capital de divisão administrativa
Parador / Pousada	Parador / Pousada
Limites administrativos	Limites administrativos
Frontera	Fronteira
Aduana principal	Alfândega principal
Aduana con restricciones	Alfândega com restrições
Zona prohibida a los extranjeros / Propiedad militar	Zona proibida aos estrangeiros / Zona militar

Curiosidades	**Curiosidades**
Lugares clasificados con 2 y 3 estrellas por la Guía Verde MICHELIN	Lugares classificados com 2 e 3 estrelas pelo Guia Verde MICHELIN
Edificio religioso - Castillo	Edifício religioso - Castelo
Monasterio - Iglesia de madera	Mosteiro - Antiga igreja de madeira
Iglesia de madera - Ciudad clasificada	Igreja de madeira - cidade classificada
Museo al aire libre - Zona de vestigios antiguos	Museu ao ar livre - Zona de vestígios antigos
Grabado rupestre - Monumento megalítico	Gravura rupestre - Monumento megalítico
Piedra rúnica - Ruinas	Pedra rúnica - Ruínas
Faro - Cueva - Molino de viento	Farol - Gruta - Moínho de Vento
Otras curiosidades	Outras curiosidades
Vista panorámica - Vista parcial	Panorama - Vista
Recorrido pintoresco	Percuso pitoresco
Tren turístico	Caminho de ferro turístico

Deportes - Ocio	**Desportos - Ocio**
Circuito automovilístico - Golf - Hipódromo	Circuito automobilístico - Golfe - Hipódromo
Vela - Playa	Centro de Vela - Praia
Estación termal - Aguas termales	Termas - Águas termais
Área de esquí	Estação de esqui
Zona recreativa - Refugio de montaña	Parque de recreio - Refúgio de montanha
Parque nacional - Parque natural	Parque nacional - Parque natural

Signos diversos	**Signos diversos**
Fábrica - Mina	Fábrica - Mina
Presa - Cascada	Barragem - Cascada

Pays
Countries - Ländern - Landen - Paesi - Países

(FIN) Plaques d'immatriculation par pays

International vehicle registration plates / Internationale Autokennzeichen / Nationaliteitssticker van de auto's / Sigle automobilistiche internazionali / Matrículas automóvilisticas por país / Chapas de matrícula por país.

(A) Österreich
Autriche / Austria / Oostenrijk / Áustria

(AL) Shqipëria
Albanie / Albania / Albanien
Albanië / Albânia

(AND) Andorra
Andorre

(B) Belgique, België, Belgien
Belgium / Belgio / Bélgica

(BG) Bălgarija
Bulgarie / Bulgaria / Bulgarien
Bulgarije / Bulgária

(BIH) Bosna i Hercegovina
Bosnie-Herzégovine
Bosnia and Herzegovina
Bosnien und Herzegowina
Bosnië en Herzegovina
Bosnia-Erzegovina
Bosnia y Herzegovina
Bósnia-Herzegovina

(BY) Belarus', Biełaruś
Biélorussie / Bielorussia / Weißrussland
Belarus / Bielorrusia / Bielorrússia

(CH) Schweiz, Suisse, Svizzera
Switzerland / Zwitserland
Suiza / Suiça

(CY) Kýpros, Kibris
Chypre / Cyprus / Zypern / Cipro / Chipre

(CZ) Česká Republika
République tchèque
Czech Republic
Tschechische Republik
Tsjechische Republiek
Repubblica Ceca
República Checa

(D) Deutschland
Allemagne / Germany / Duitsland
Germania / Alemania / Alemanha

(DK) Danmark
Danemark / Denmark / Dänemark
Denemarken / Danimarca / Dinamarca

(E) España
Espagne / Spain / Spanien / Spanje
Spagna / Espanha

(EST) Eesti
Estonie / Estonia / Estland / Estónia

(F) France
Frankreich / Francia / França

(FIN) Suomi, Finland
Finlande / Finnland / Finlandia /
Finlândia

(FL) Liechtenstein
Listenstaine

(GB) United Kingdom
Royaume-Uni
Vereinigtes Königreich
Verenigd Koninkrijk
Regno Unito
Reino Unido

(GR) Elláda
Grèce / Greece / Griechenland
Griekenland / Grecia / Grécia

(H) Magyarország
Hongrie / Hungary / Ungarn / Hongarije
Ungheria / Hungría / Hungria

(HR) Hrvatska
Croatie / Croatia / Kroatien / Kroatië
Croazia / Croacia / Croácia

(I) Italia
Italie / Italy / Italien / Italië / Itália

(IRL) Ireland,Éire
Irlande
Irland
Ierland
Irlanda

(IS) Ísland
Islande / Iceland / Island / IJsland
Islanda / Islandia / Islândia

(L) Luxembourg, Luxemburg, Lëtzebuerg
Lëtzebuerg / Lussemburgo / Luxemburgo

(LT) Lietuva
Lituanie / Lithuania / Litauen / Litouwen
Lituania / Lituânia

(LV) Latvija
Lettonie / Latvia / Lettland / Letland
Lettonia / Letonia / Letónia

(M) Malta
Malte

(MC) Monaco
Mónaco

(MD) Moldova
Moldavie / Moldawien / Moldavië /

(MK) Makedonija
République de Macédoine / Republic
of Macedonia / Republik Mazedonien /
Republiek Macedonië / Repubblica di
Macedonia / República de Macedonia /
República da Macedónia

(MNE) Crna Gora
Monténégro
Montenegro

(N) Norge
Norvège / Norway / Norwegen
Noorwegen / Norvegia / Noruega

(NL) Nederland
Pays-Bas
Netherlands
Niederlande
Paesi Bassi
Países Bajos
Países Baixos

(P) Portugal
Portogallo

(PL) Polska
Pologne / Poland / Polen / Polonia
Polónia

(RO) România
Roumanie / Romania / Rumänien
Roemenië / Rumanía / Roménia

(RSM) San Marino
Saint-Marin / São-Marinho

(RUS) Rossija
Russie / Russia / Russland / Rusland
Rusia / Rússia

(S) Sverige
Suède / Sweden / Schweden / Zweden
Svezia / Suecia / Suécia

(SK) Slovenská Republika
République slovaque
Slovak Republic
Slowakische Republik
Slowakije
Repubblica Slovacca
República Eslovaca

(SLO) Slovenija
Slovénie
Slovenia
Slowenien
Slovenië
Eslovenia
Eslovénia

(SRB) Srbija
Serbie / Serbia / Serbien / Servië / Sérvia

(TR) Türkiye
Turquie / Turkey / Türkei / Turkije
Turchia / Turquía / Turquia

(UA) Ukraïna
Ukraine
Oekraïne
Ucraina
Ucrania
Ucrânia

(V) Vaticano
Vatican / Vatikan / Vaticaan

EUROPE

1: 3 700 000

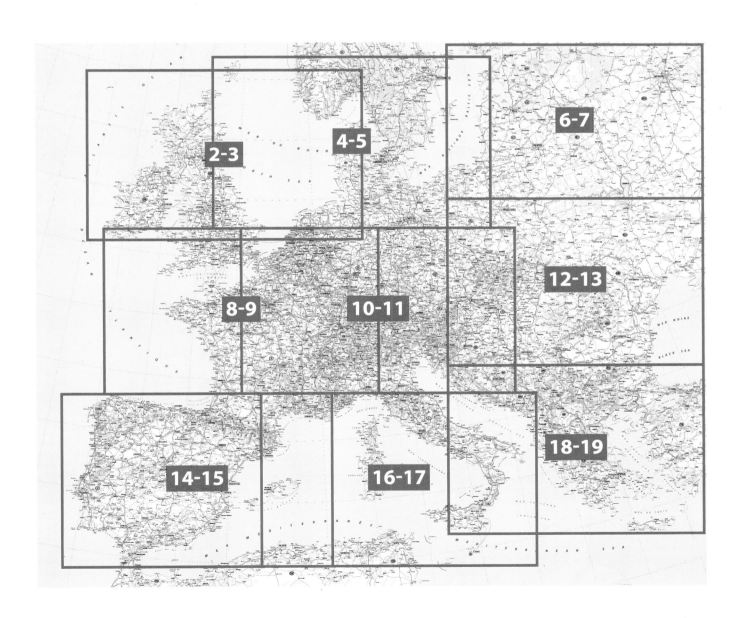

Sognefjorden
Sogndalsfjøra
Balestrand
Lavik
Brekke
Gudvangen
Flåm
Voss
Bergen
Osterøy
Dale
Kinsarvik
Hardangerjøkulen
Rosendal
Odda
Hardangervidda
Tysnesøy
Stord
Svortland
Bømlo
Ølen
Sand
Sauda
Hovden
Haugesund
Karmøy
Hjelmelandsvågen
Skudeneshavn
Stavanger
Sandnes
Svartevatn
Tonstad
Egersund
Flekkefjord
Farsund
Lindesnes
Mandal
Kristiansand

Vangsnes
Lærdalsøyri
Borgund
Gol
Fagernes
Dokka
Randsfjorden
Geilo
Nesbyen
Uvdal
Nore og Uvdal
Rødberg
Rjukan
Gausta
Drammen
Kongsberg
Åmot
Heddal
Notodden
Brunkeberg
Norsjø
Skien
Sandefjord
Porsgrunn
Larvik
Kragerø
Åmli
Evje
Arendal
Grimstad

MER DU NORD
NORTH SEA

Banff
Fraserburgh
Keith
Peterhead
Aberdeen
Stonehaven
Montrose
Arbroath
St Andrews
North Berwick
Haddington
Berwick-upon-Tweed
Coldstream
Jedburgh
Alnwick
Blyth
South Shields
Newcastle upon Tyne
Tynemouth
Gateshead
Sunderland
Durham
Hartlepool
Darlington
Middlesbrough
Whitby
Thirsk
Scarborough
Fountains
Skipton
Bradford
Leeds
Halifax
Huddersfield
Wakefield
Bridlington
Hartlepool
York
Kingston-upon-Hull
Scunthorpe
MANCHESTER
Stockport
Sheffield
Chesterfield
Doncaster
Grimsby
Humber River
Louth
Stoke-on-Trent
Mansfield
Skegness
Derby
Nottingham
Boston
Loughborough
Grantham
The Wash
King's Lynn
Leicester
Stamford
Wisbech
Cromer
Great Yarmouth
Northampton
Kettering
Huntingdon
Ely
Thetford
Lowestoft
Cambridge
Bury St Edmunds

Hanstholm
Thisted
Nykøbing Mors
Struer
Skive
Viborg
Holstebro
Ringkøbing
Herning
Skjern
Silkeborg
Varde
Blåvands Huk
Esbjerg
Ribe
Rømø
Sylt
Westerland
Tønder
Husum
Sankt Peter-Ording
Helgoland
Deutsche Bucht
Cuxhaven
Wilhelmshaven
Bremerhaven
Norden
Wangerooge
Nordenham
Aurich
Leer
Delfzijl
Emden
Oldenburg
Bad Zwischenahn
Leeuwarden
Groningen
Harlingen
Sneek
Assen
Cloppenburg
Den Helder
Heerenveen
Emmen
Alkmaar
Meppel
Zwolle
Osnabrück
AMSTERDAM
Haarlem
Lelystad
Almelo
Hengelo
Enschede
Haarlem
Het Loo
Deventer
Apeldoorn
Rhine
Keukenhof
Leiden
Scheveningen

75 km

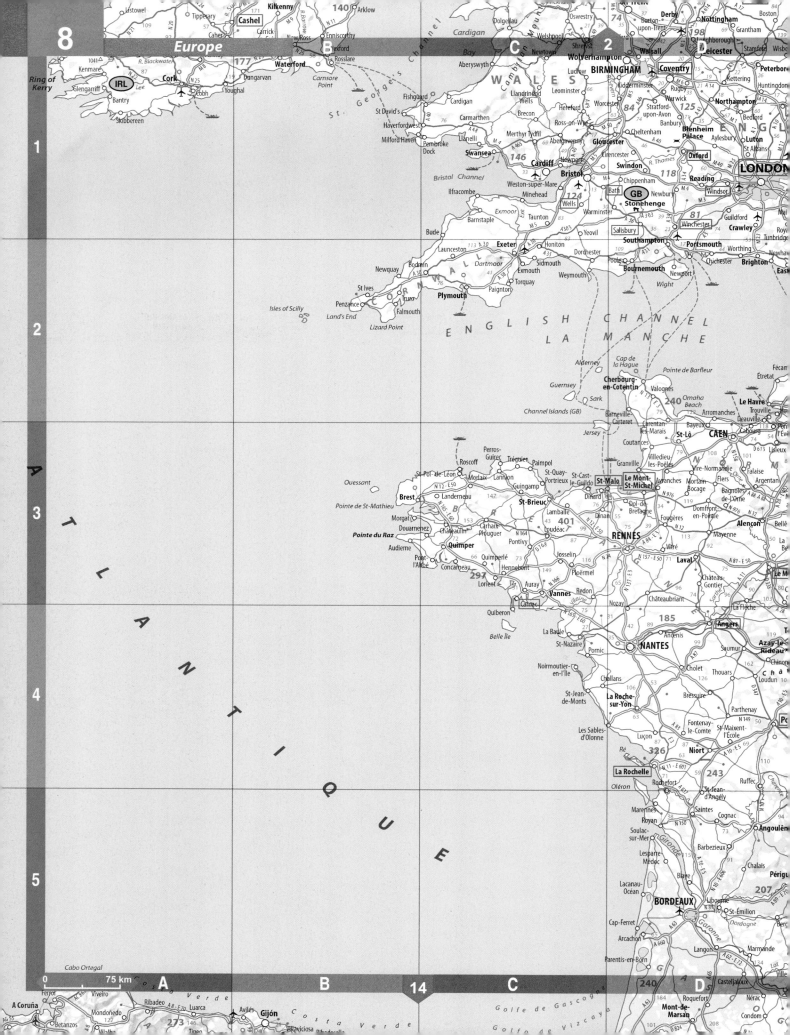

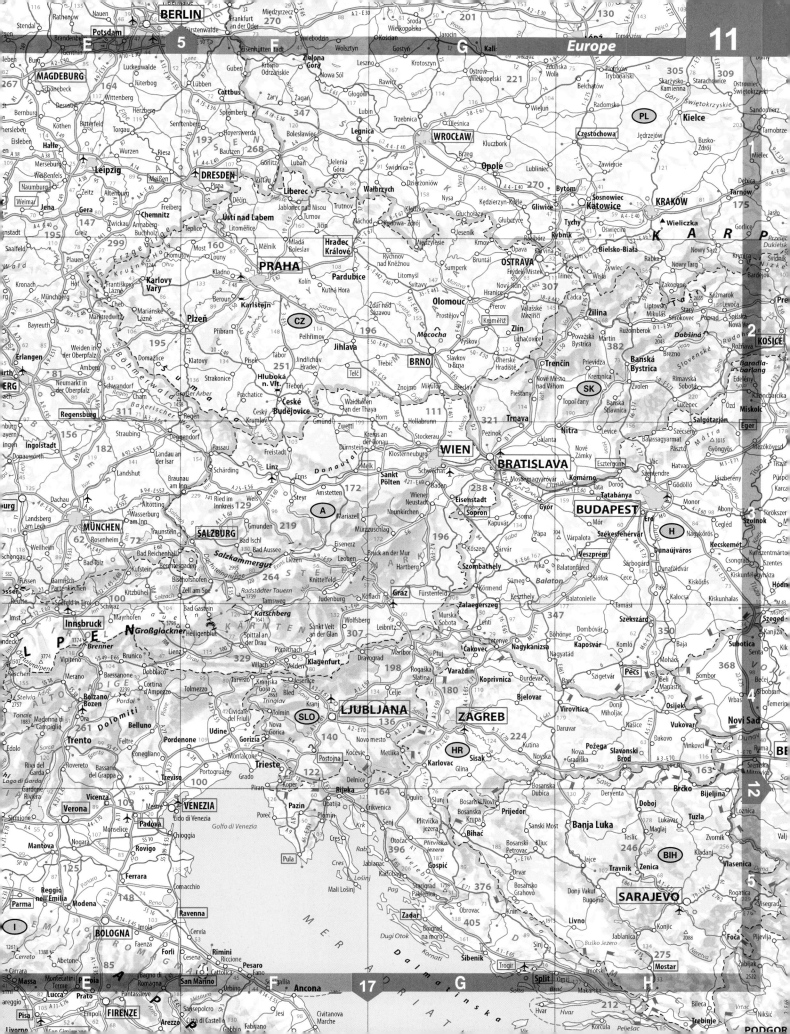

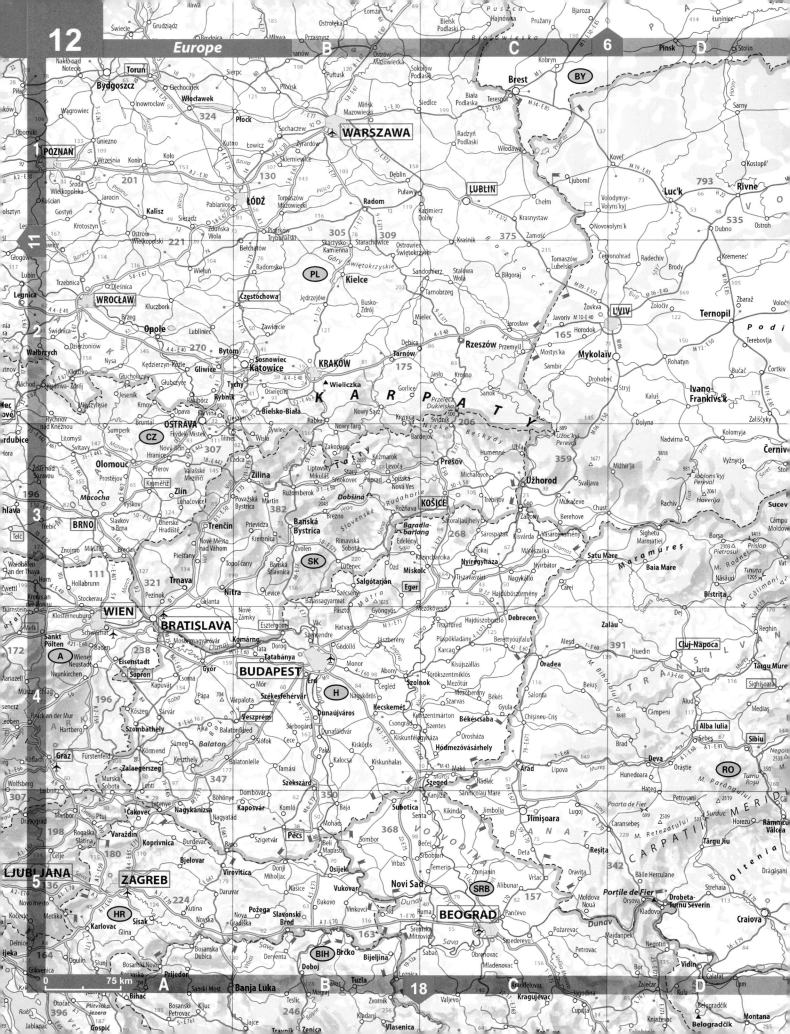

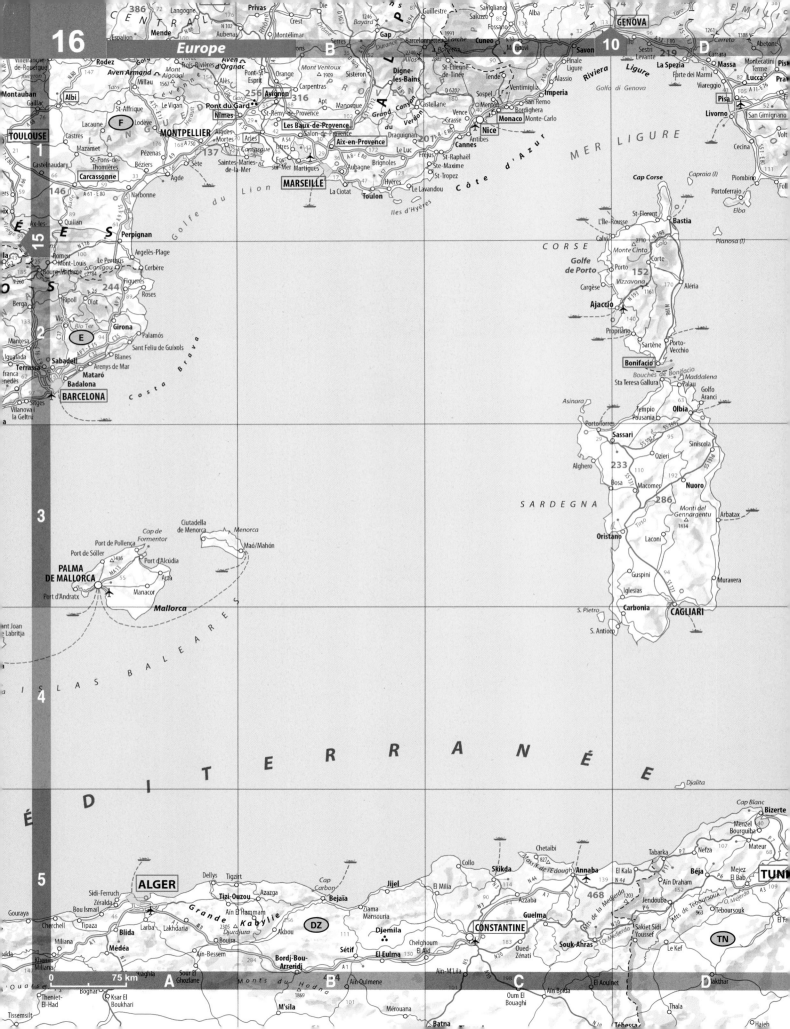

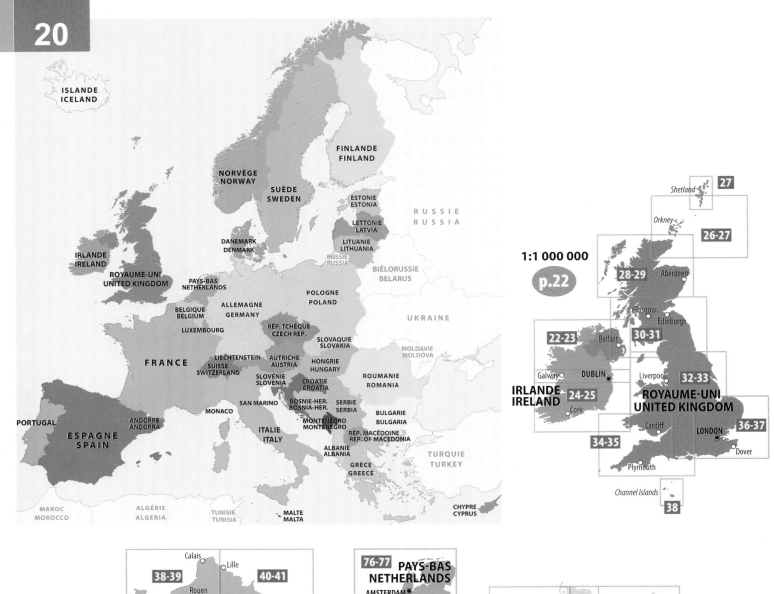

ISLANDE
ICELAND

NORVÈGE
NORWAY

SUÈDE
SWEDEN

FINLANDE
FINLAND

RUSSIE
RUSSIA

ESTONIE
ESTONIA

LETTONIE
LATVIA

DANEMARK
DENMARK

LITUANIE
LITHUANIA

RÚSSIE
RUSSIA

BIÉLORUSSIE
BELARUS

IRLANDE
IRELAND

ROYAUME-UNI
UNITED KINGDOM

PAYS-BAS
NETHERLANDS

ALLEMAGNE
GERMANY

POLOGNE
POLAND

UKRAINE

BELGIQUE
BELGIUM

LUXEMBOURG

RÉP. TCHÈQUE
CZECH REP.

SLOVAQUIE
SLOVAKIA

MOLDAVIE
MOLDOVA

FRANCE

LIECHTENSTEIN
SUISSE
SWITZERLAND

AUTRICHE
AUSTRIA

HONGRIE
HUNGARY

ROUMANIE
ROMANIA

SLOVÉNIE
SLOVENIA

CROATIE
CROATIA

SAN MARINO

BOSNIE-HER.
BOSNIA-HER.

SERBIE
SERBIA

BULGARIE
BULGARIA

PORTUGAL

ANDORRE
ANDORRA

MONACO

MONTÉNÉGRO
MONTENEGRO

RÉP. MACÉDOINE
REP. OF MACEDONIA

ESPAGNE
SPAIN

ITALIE
ITALY

ALBANIE
ALBANIA

GRÈCE
GREECE

TURQUIE
TURKEY

MAROC
MOROCCO

ALGÉRIE
ALGERIA

TUNISIE
TUNISIA

MALTE
MALTA

CHYPRE
CYPRUS

1:1 000 000

p.22

Shetland

27

Orkney

26-27

28-29

Aberdeen

22-23

Belfast

30-31

Glasgow

Edinburgh

IRLANDE
IRELAND

Galway

24-25

DUBLIN

Liverpool

32-33

ROYAUME-UNI
UNITED KINGDOM

Cork

Cardiff

34-35

LONDON

36-37

Plymouth

Dover

Channel Islands

38

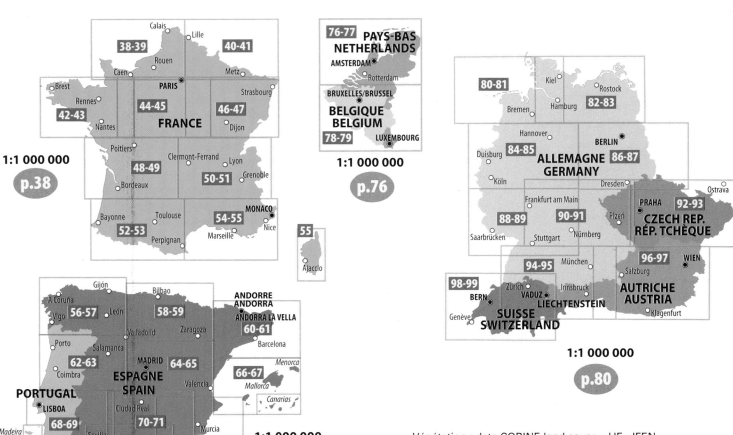

Calais

Lille

38-39

40-41

Rouen

Caen

Metz

Brest

PARIS

Strasbourg

Rennes

42-43

44-45

Dijon

Nantes

FRANCE

46-47

Poitiers

Clermont-Ferrand

Lyon

1:1 000 000

48-49

50-51

Grenoble

p.38

Bordeaux

Bayonne

Toulouse

54-55

MONACO

52-53

Perpignan

Marseille

Nice

55

Ajaccio

76-77

PAYS-BAS
NETHERLANDS

AMSTERDAM

Rotterdam

BRUXELLES/BRUSSEL

BELGIQUE
BELGIUM

78-79

LUXEMBOURG

1:1 000 000

p.76

80-81

Kiel

Rostock

Bremen

Hamburg

82-83

Hannover

84-85

BERLIN

86-87

Duisburg

ALLEMAGNE
GERMANY

Köln

Dresden

Ostrava

Frankfurt am Main

PRAHA

92-93

88-89

90-91

Plzeň

CZECH REP.
RÉP. TCHÈQUE

Saarbrücken

Stuttgart

Nürnberg

96-97

WIEN

94-95

München

Salzburg

98-99

Zürich

VADUZ

Innsbruck

AUTRICHE
AUSTRIA

BERN

LIECHTENSTEIN

Genève

SUISSE
SWITZERLAND

Klagenfurt

1:1 000 000

p.80

Gijón

Bilbao

ANDORRE
ANDORRA

A Coruña

56-57

León

58-59

ANDORRA LA VELLA

Vigo

60-61

Valladolid

Zaragoza

Barcelona

Porto

62-63

Salamanca

MADRID

64-65

Menorca

Coimbra

ESPAGNE
SPAIN

66-67

Mallorca

Valencia

PORTUGAL

Canarias

LISBOA

Ciudad Real

Madeira

68-69

70-71

Murcia

1:1 000 000

Sevilla

Granada

72-73

p.56

74-75

Gibraltar(GB)

Végétation : data CORINE land cover - UE - IFEN

EUROPE / EUROPA

Tableaux d'assemblage détaillés

Detailed key to road map
Detaillierte Seitenübersicht
Gedetailleerde overzichtskaarten
Quadro d'insieme dettagliato
Mapa índice detallado
Tabela de montagem detalhado

178
p.178 REYKJAVÍK Akureyri ISLANDE ICELAND
1:2 800 000

194 Føroyar
1:1 500 000
p.176

176-177 Tromsø
179
180-181 Bodø
Rovaniemi
182-183 Luleå
184-185 Oulu
186-187
SUÈDE SWEDEN
FINLANDE FINLAND
Trondheim Umeå Vaasa Kuopio
Ålesund
NORVÈGE NORWAY
188-189
Tampere Lahti
190-191
192-193
Bergen
OSLO Uppsala Turku
HELSINKI
Skien Karlstad
Stavanger
194-195 **196-197** STOCKHOLM
Gotland
Aalborg Göteborg
DANEMARK DENMARK
198-199 Kalmar
Öland
Esbjerg KØBENHAVN Malmö
Bornholm

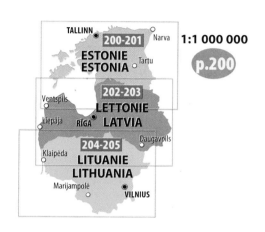

TALLINN Narva
200-201
ESTONIE ESTONIA Tartu
1:1 000 000
p.200
Ventspils **202-203**
LETTONIE LATVIA
Liepāja RĪGA Daugavpils
Klaipėda **204-205**
LITUANIE LITHUANIA
Marijampolė
VILNIUS

Gdańsk Olsztyn
116-117 **118-119** Białystok
Szczecin
POLOGNE POLAND
Poznań WARSZAWA
120-121 Łódź
Wrocław **122-123** Lublin
Katowice Kraków
124-125 **126-127**
1:1 000 000 SLOVAQUIE SLOVAKIA Košice
p.116 BRATISLAVA **132-133**
Győr BUDAPEST Debrecen
128-129 HONGRIE HUNGARY **130-131**
Szeged
Pécs

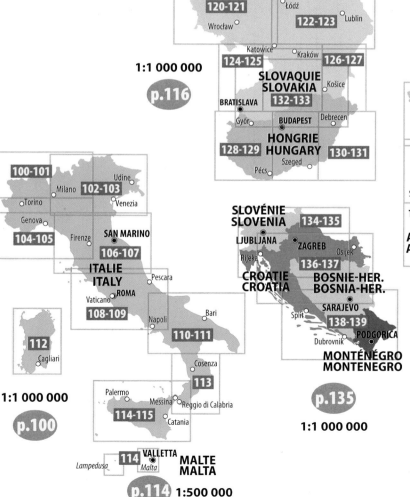

100-101 Udine
Milano **102-103**
Torino Venezia
Genova
104-105 Firenze SAN MARINO
106-107
ITALIE ITALY Pescara
Vaticano ROMA
108-109 Napoli Bari
110-111
112 Cosenza
Cagliari **113**
1:1 000 000 Palermo
p.100 Messina Reggio di Calabria
114-115 Catania

SLOVÉNIE SLOVENIA
134-135
LJUBLJANA ZAGREB Osijek
Rijeka **136-137**
CROATIE CROATIA BOSNIE-HER. BOSNIA-HER.
SARAJEVO
Split **138-139**
PODGORICA
Dubrovnik
MONTÉNÉGRO MONTENEGRO
p.135
1:1 000 000

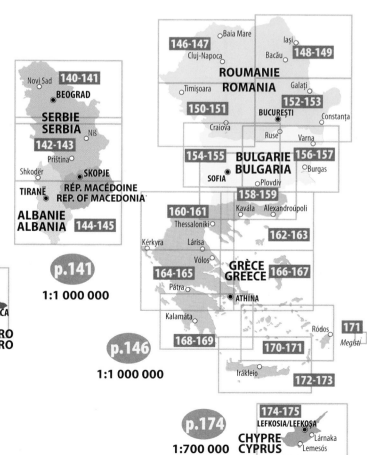

Novi Sad **140-141**
BEOGRAD
SERBIE SERBIA
Niš
142-143 Priština
Shkodër SKOPJE
TIRANË RÉP. MACÉDOINE REP. OF MACEDONIA
ALBANIE ALBANIA **144-145**
p.141
1:1 000 000

Baia Mare Iași
146-147 **148-149**
Cluj-Napoca Bacău
ROUMANIE ROMANIA
Timișoara Galați
150-151 **152-153**
BUCUREȘTI Constanța
Craiova
Ruse Varna
154-155 BULGARIE BULGARIA **156-157**
SOFIA Plovdiv Burgas
158-159
160-161 Kavála Alexandroúpoli
Thessaloníki
162-163
Kérkyra Lárisa
GRÈCE GREECE **166-167**
Vólos
164-165 Pátra
ATHÍNA
Kalamáta
Ródos **171**
168-169 **170-171** Megísti
p.146
1:1 000 000 Irákleio
172-173

174-175
p.174 LEFKOSIA/LEFKOŞA
CHYPRE CYPRUS Lárnaka
Lemesós
1:700 000

Lampedusa
114 VALLETTA MALTE MALTA
Malta
p.114 1:500 000

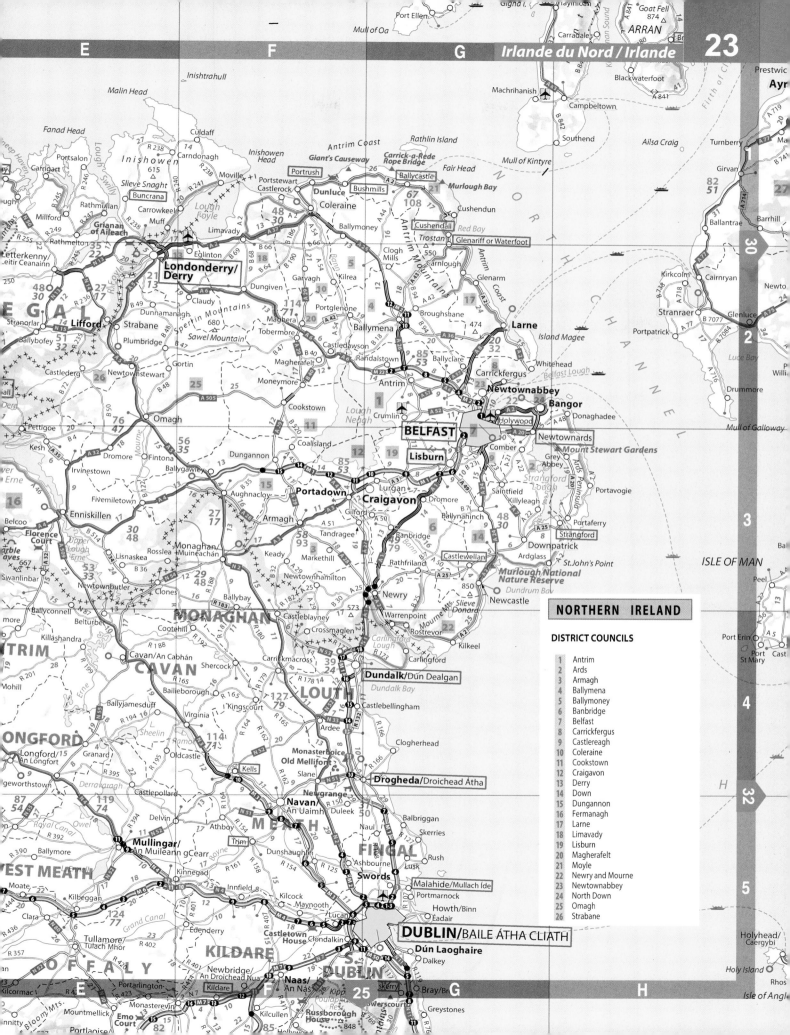

NORTHERN IRELAND

DISTRICT COUNCILS

1 Antrim
2 Ards
3 Armagh
4 Ballymena
5 Ballymoney
6 Banbridge
7 Belfast
8 Carrickfergus
9 Castlereagh
10 Coleraine
11 Cookstown
12 Craigavon
13 Derry
14 Down
15 Dungannon
16 Fermanagh
17 Larne
18 Limavady
19 Lisburn
20 Magherafelt
21 Moyle
22 Newry and Mourne
23 Newtownabbey
24 North Down
25 Omagh
26 Strabane

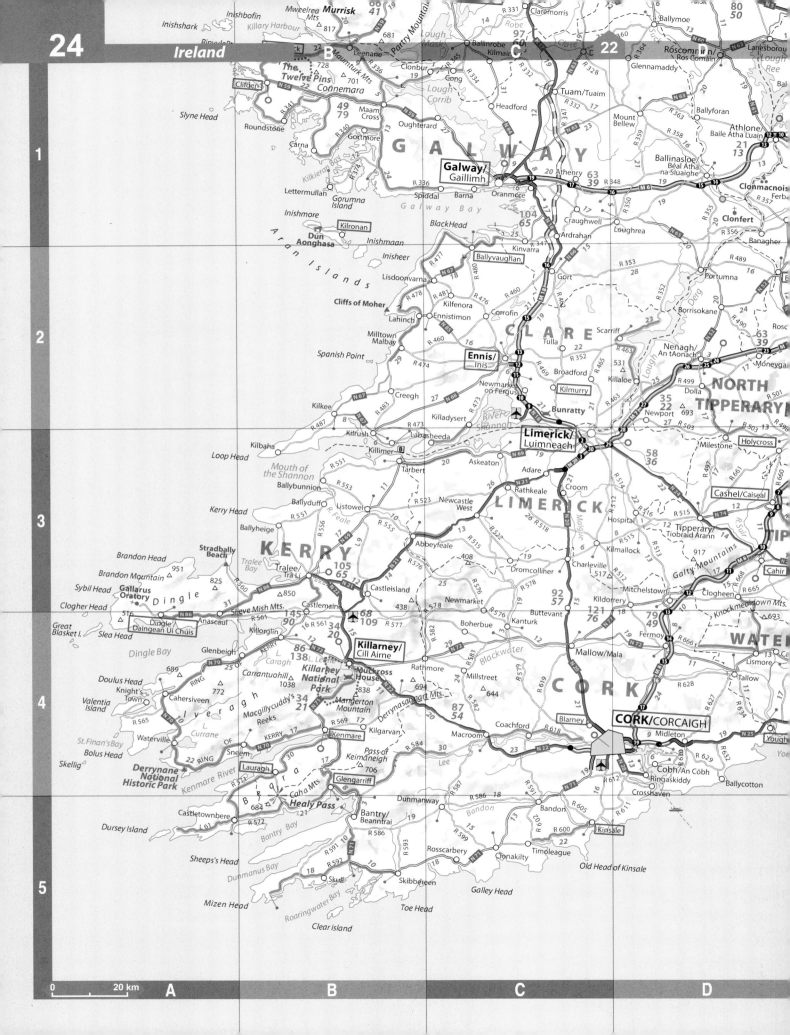

SCOTLAND

UNITARY AUTHORITIES

1 Aberdeen City
2 Aberdeenshire
3 Angus
4 Argyll and Bute
5 Clackmannanshire
   City of Edinburgh
   City of Glasgow
8 Dumfries and Galloway
9 Dundee City
10 East Ayrshire
11 East Dunbartonshire
12 East Lothian
13 East Renfrewshire
14 Falkirk
15 Fife
16 Highland

17 Inverclyde
18 Midlothian
19 Moray
20 North Ayrshire
21 North Lanarkshire
22 Orkney Islands
23 Perth and Kinross
24 Renfrewshire
25 Scottish Borders
26 Shetland Islands
27 South Ayrshire
28 South Lanarkshire
29 Stirling
30 West Dunbartonshire
31 West Lothian
32 Na H-Eileanan Siar (Western Isles)

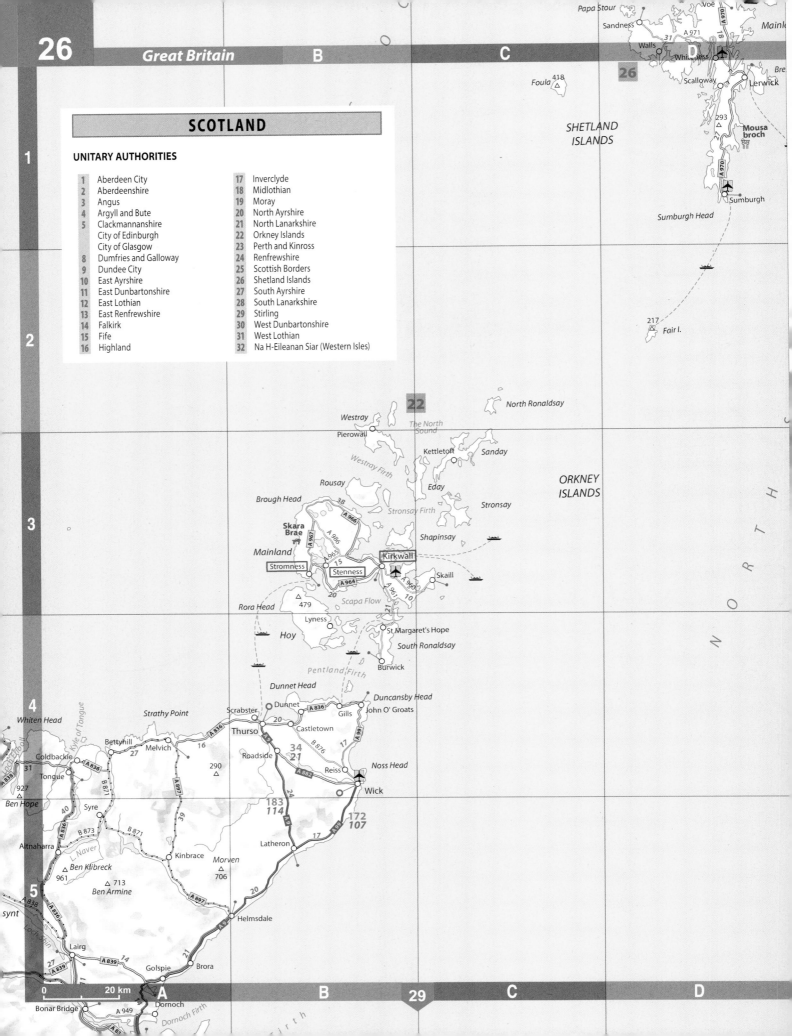

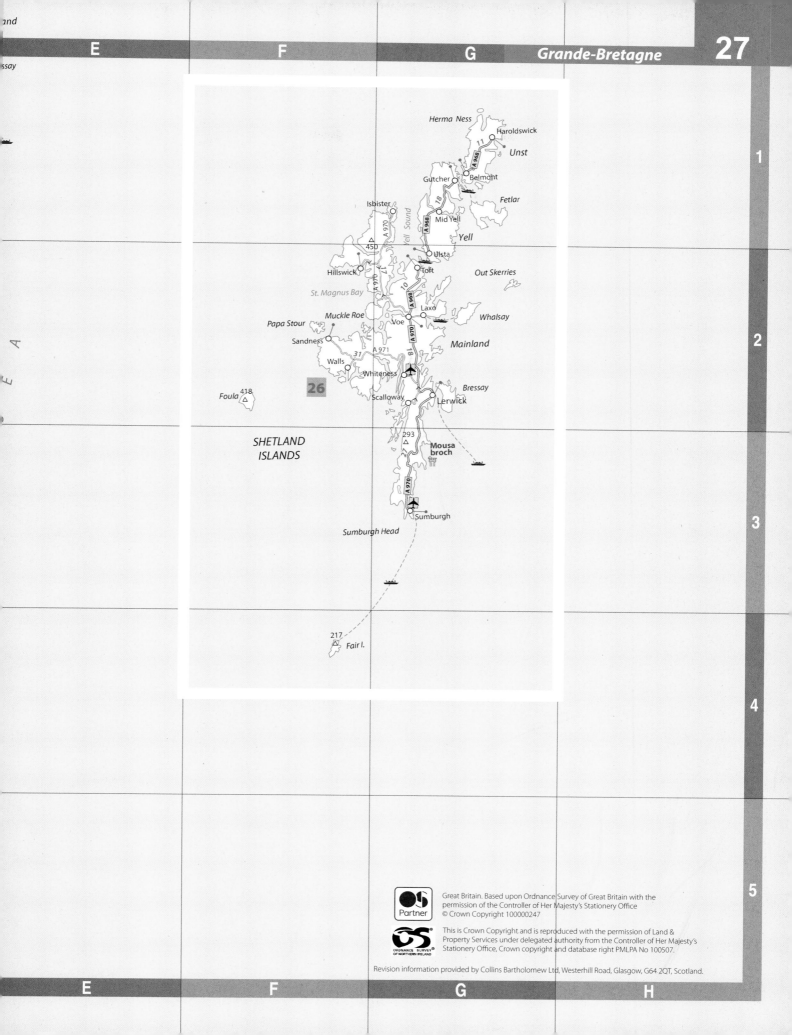

Herma Ness

Haroldswick

A 968 11

Unst

Gutcher Belmont

Fetlar

18

A 968

Isbister

Yell Sound

Mid Yell

Yell

A 970

△ 450

A 970 17

Ulsta

Out Skerries

Hillswick

Toft

10

St. Magnus Bay

A 968

Laxo

Whalsay

Muckle Roe

Voe

Papa Stour

A 970

Mainland

Sandness

A 971

18

Walls

31

A 971

Whiteness

Bressay

26

Scalloway

Lerwick

Foula 418 △

△ 293

27

Mousa broch

SHETLAND ISLANDS

A 970

Sumburgh

Sumburgh Head

217
△ Fair I.

A B C D

1

2

3

4

5

LEWIS

Butt of Lewis
Port of Ness

Barvas
A 857
16
A 857
A 858
Carloway
292
12
Broad Bay
Portnaguran
Stornoway
Tiumpan Head
24
A 858
A 866
Garynahine
Eye Peninsula
36
574
A 859
572
Kebock Head

Flannan I.

NA H - EILEANAN
SIAR
32
Rubha Réidh
(WESTERN
ISLES)

Rubha Còigeach

THE MINCH

Kinlochbe
Scourie
A 894
Eddrachillis
Bay
A 837
19
Lochinver
849
Coigach
743
A 835
Ull

Hushinish
B 887
Clisham
799
Tarbert
A 859
24

West Loch Tarbert

Toe Head
Harris
Leverburgh
Rodel
Renish Point

Laide
29
A 832
Inverewe
Gardens
15
Dundonnell
1062
A 832
Falls of N
Sgurr N
Gairloch
980
Loch Maree
20
Wester Ross
9
Kinlochewe
A 896
Liathach
1054
10
Torridon
19
A 896
Glen Carron
896
24
A 896
Lochcarron
Stromeferry
A 890
15
118

Gruinard
Bay
Loch Broom

Loch Torridon
Shieldaig

North Uist
Otternish
Tigharry
25
A 865
A 865
Lochmaddy
A 865
347
Balivanich
13
Benbecula
Creagorry

South Uist
620
22
Daliburgh
A 865
Lochboisdale

Sound of Monach

Sound of Harris

Sound of Barra

OUTER HEBRIDES

Watersnish
Point
Dunvegan
Head
Dunvegan
A 850
21
Idrigill Point
Loch Bracadale

Trotternish
Peninsula
A 855
Uig
Staffin
34
The Storr
719
16
A 855
22
Portree
Bracadale
84
52
Sconser
9
444
Sligachan
SKYE
The Cuillins
993
Elgol
B 8083
14
Ardvasar

Loch
Snizort
Rona
Sound of Raasay
Raasay
Inner Sound
Scalpay
Kyle of Lochalsh
Broadford
17
A 87
Kyleakin
Kylerhea
Isleornsay
7

Dornie
Eilean Donan Castle
Shiel Bridge
Glenelg
A' Chràl
1120
32
A 87
50
80

SEA OF
THE HEBRIDES

Canna

Barra
383
Bayhirivagh
888
Castlebay

Mingulay

Barra Head

Rhum
812

Cuillin Sound

Muck

Eigg
Sound of Rhum

Mallaig
Arisaig
19
Loch Morar
882

Sound of Sleat
Loch Nevis
1040
Loch Quoich
Sgurr na Ciche

A 830
76
46
Glenfinnan
27
Loch Shiel
888
A 861
9
F

Loch Arkaig
Cale
Co

Coll
Arinagour

Tiree
Scarinish

Sanna Beach
Kilchoan
B 8007
528

Dervaig
A 8073
Tobermory
10
Salen
L. Tuath
Ulva
Staffa
MULL
Ben More
966
Iona
Flionnphort
18
Bunessan

Coll

Salen
A 861
Strontian
13
A 861
Loch Sunart
19
B 884
Lochaline
Sound of Mull
Craignure
17
Lismore

Sanna Beach

Corran
Inchree
Onich
Ballach
Kentallen
Portnacroish
27
Achnacroish
46
74
Connel
Oban
Taynuilt
Kerrera
Firth of Lorn
Seil
Kilninver
A 819

Ben
Cruachan
1126
18

30

St. Kilda

0
20 km
A B C D

4

DUNDEE
Angus
51 Carnoustie
32 Monifieth
9 Tayport
Newport-on-Tay Toddon Ness
Leuchars

Newburgh
Auchtermuchty
Cupar
St. Andrews
Fife Ness
Falkland
Crail
Glenrothes
15
Anstruther
Leven
Pittenweem
Methil
Saint Monans
Kirkcaldy
Buckhaven
Elie
Cowdenbeath
Burntisland
Kinross
Lochgelly
Inverkeithing
North Berwick
FORTH BRIDGE
Leith
Aberlady
Dunbar
Prestonpans
East
S. Queensferry
Musselburgh
Linton
90
Livingston
Tranent
Haddington
56
Cockburnspath
Loanhead Dalkeith
St Abb's Head
EDINBURGH
Lammermuir Hills
St Abb's Head
RosslynChapel
535
National Nature Reserve
Penicuik
Eyemouth
Linton
Duns
Berwick-upon-Tweed
Peebles
Lauder
Greenlaw
Holy Island
Innerleithen
Galashiels
Earlston
Mellerstain
Coldstream
Belford
Bamburgh Castle
Melrose
Abbey
Kelso
100
Broad Law
Dryburgh
Newtown
63
Selkirk
St Boswells
Wooler
Hawick
Jedburgh
The Cheviot
Alnwick
Carter Bar
Northumberland
Warkworth
The Cheviot Hills
Rothbury
Amble
Moffat
National Park
Felton
Kielder Resr.
Langholm
Otterburn
48
Ashington
Newbiggin-by-the-Sea
Lockerbie
169 Morpeth
105
Blyth
Canonbie
Bedlington
Belsay
Seaton Delaval
Annan
NEWCASTLE
Whitley Bay
Gretna
Chollerford
UPON TYNE
Tynemouth
Bowness-
Greenhead
Hadrian's Wall
Jarrow
South Shields
on-Solway
Housesteads
Prudhoe
Carlisle
Hexham
Gateshead
SUNDERLAND
55
Corbridge
Stanley
Washington
34
Thursby
Consett
Chester-
Seaham
Wigton
Lanchester
le-Street
Houghton-le-Spring
Aspatria
Durham
55
Horden
Bothel
34
CrossFell
Crook
Spennymoor
Peterlee
Cockermouth
893
Wolsingham
Hartlepool
Skiddaw
Penrith
Bishop Auckland
Sedgefield
Keswick
Middleton-
Newton
Redcar
in-Teesdale
W. Auckland
Aycliffe
Billingham
Marske-by-the-Sea
Appleby
Barnard Castle
Stockton-
Saltburn-by-the-Sea
Lake
Brough
Bowes
Darlington
on-Tees
Brotton
District
Shap
Richmond
MIDDLESBROUGH
Whitby
Coniston
Kirkby
Eaglescliffe
National
Stephen
Northallerton
North York
Park
Tebay
Reeth
Moors
Kendal
Leyburn
Bedale
National
Sedbergh
Thirsk
Park
Hawes
Rievaulx
Scalby
Whernside
Yorkshire
Swale
Abbey
Kirkby
736
Helmsley
Pickering
Scarboro
Lonsdale
Dales
66
Ingleton
National
41
Ripon
Easingwold
Malton
Morecambe
Settle
Pateley
Boroughbridge
Norton
Lancaster
Threshfield
Bridge
Knaresborough
YORK
Heysham
Long
Preston
Bolton Priory
Harrogate

WALES

UNITARY AUTHORITIES

1	Anglesey/Sir Fôn	12	Merthyr Tydfil/Merthyr Tudful
2	Blaenau Gwent	13	Monmouthshire/Sir Fynwy
3	Bridgend/Pen-y-bont ar Ogwr	14	Neath Port Talbot/Castell-nedd Phort Talbot
4	Caerphilly/Caerffili	15	Newport/Casnewydd
5	Cardiff/Caerdydd	16	Pembrokeshire/Sir Benfro
6	Carmarthenshire/Sir Gaerfyrddin	17	Powys
7	Ceredigion	18	Rhondda Cynon Taff/Rhondda Cynon Taf
8	Conwy	19	Swansea/Abertawe
9	Denbighshire/Sir Ddinbych	20	Torfaen/Tor-faen
10	Flintshire/Sir y Fflint	21	Vale of Glamorgan/Bro Morgannwg
11	Gwynedd	22	Wrexham/Wrecsam

0   20 km

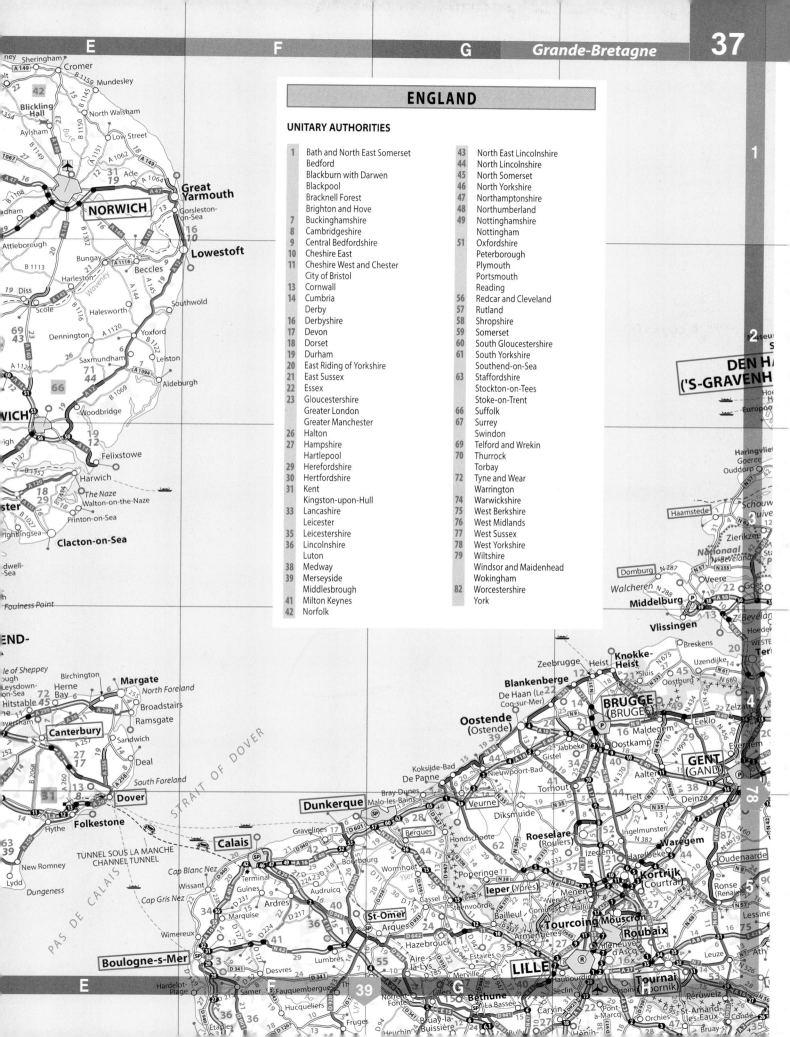

ENGLAND

UNITARY AUTHORITIES

1	Bath and North East Somerset	43	North East Lincolnshire
	Bedford	44	North Lincolnshire
	Blackburn with Darwen	45	North Somerset
	Blackpool	46	North Yorkshire
	Bracknell Forest	47	Northamptonshire
	Brighton and Hove	48	Northumberland
7	Buckinghamshire	49	Nottinghamshire
8	Cambridgeshire		Nottingham
9	Central Bedfordshire	51	Oxfordshire
10	Cheshire East		Peterborough
11	Cheshire West and Chester		Plymouth
	City of Bristol		Portsmouth
13	Cornwall		Reading
14	Cumbria	56	Redcar and Cleveland
	Derby	57	Rutland
16	Derbyshire	58	Shropshire
17	Devon	59	Somerset
18	Dorset	60	South Gloucestershire
19	Durham	61	South Yorkshire
20	East Riding of Yorkshire		Southend-on-Sea
21	East Sussex	63	Staffordshire
22	Essex		Stockton-on-Tees
23	Gloucestershire		Stoke-on-Trent
	Greater London	66	Suffolk
	Greater Manchester	67	Surrey
26	Halton		Swindon
27	Hampshire	69	Telford and Wrekin
	Hartlepool	70	Thurrock
29	Herefordshire		Torbay
30	Hertfordshire	72	Tyne and Wear
31	Kent		Warrington
	Kingston-upon-Hull	74	Warwickshire
33	Lancashire	75	West Berkshire
	Leicester	76	West Midlands
35	Leicestershire	77	West Sussex
36	Lincolnshire	78	West Yorkshire
	Luton	79	Wiltshire
38	Medway		Windsor and Maidenhead
39	Merseyside		Wokingham
	Middlesbrough	82	Worcestershire
41	Milton Keynes		York
42	Norfolk		

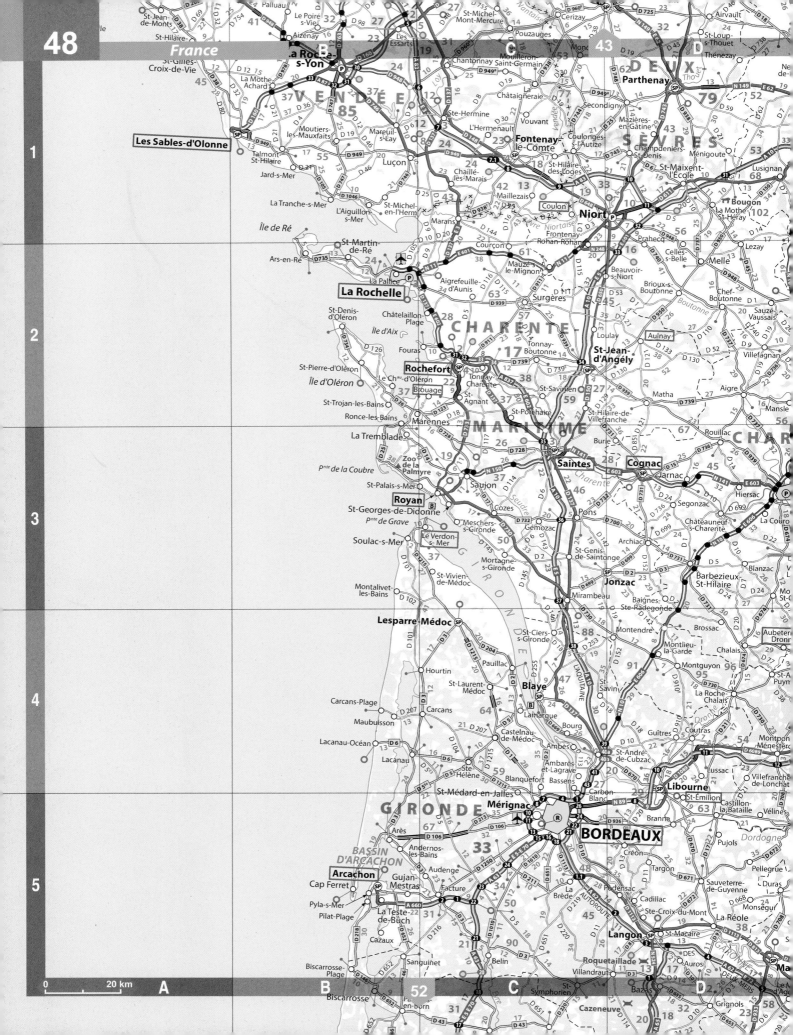

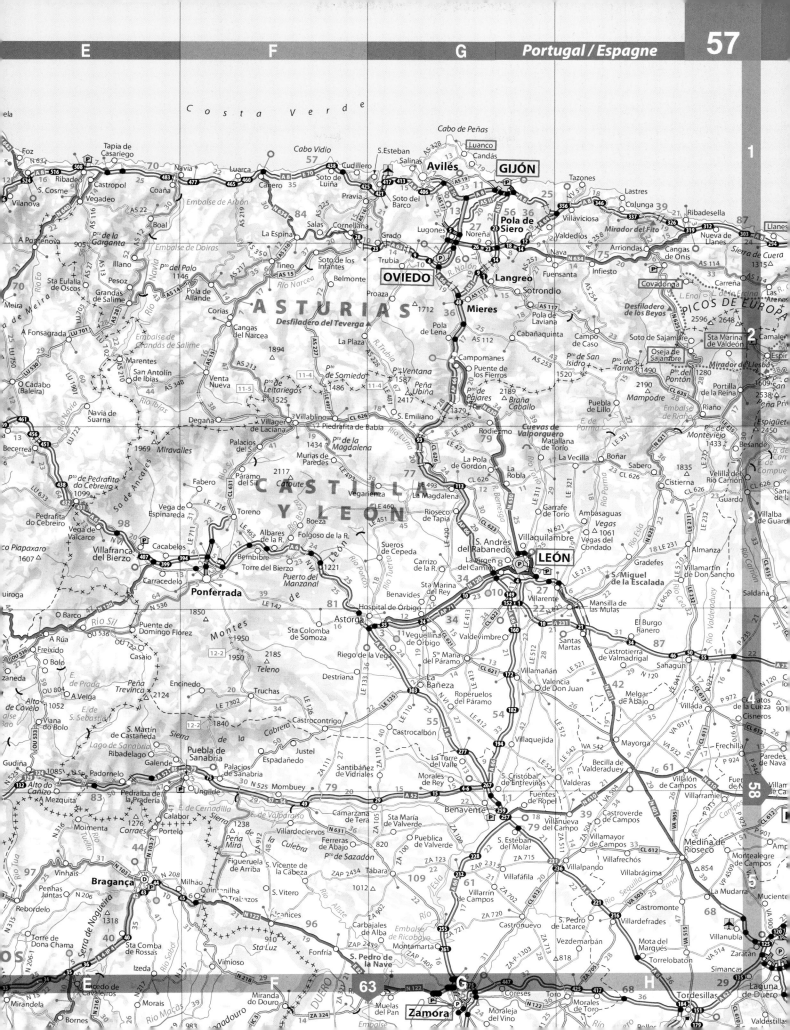

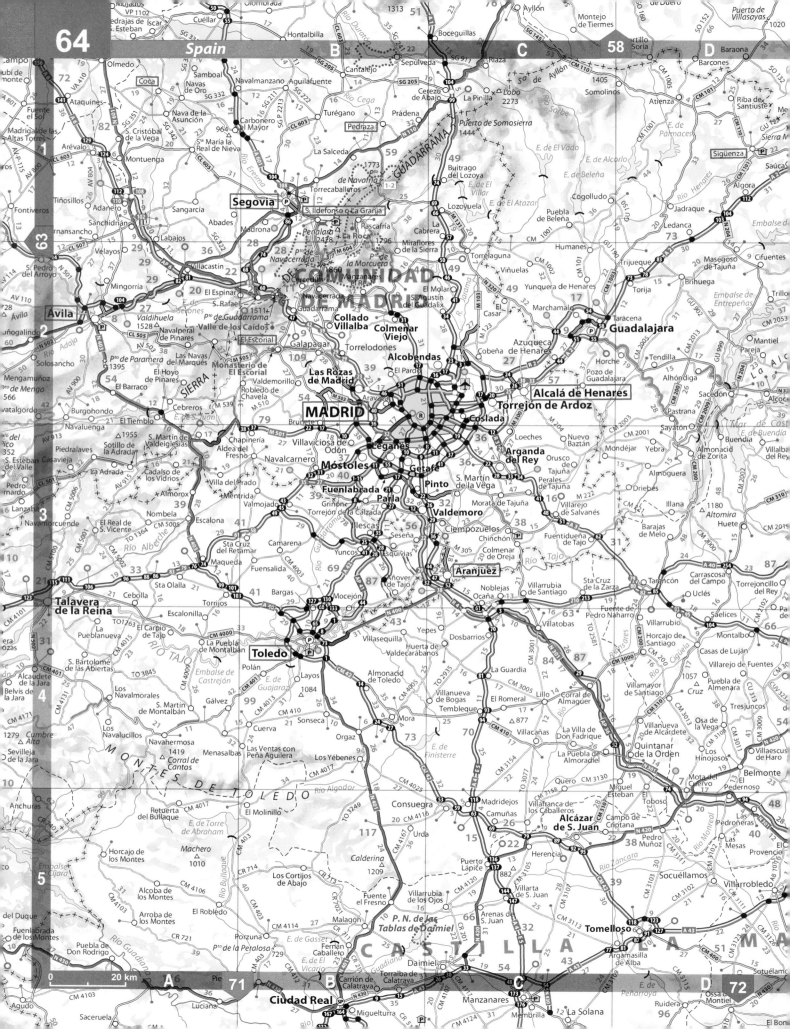

MADEIRA

OCÉANO

ILHA DO
PORTO SANTO

Vila
Baleira

ATLÁNTICO

ARQUIPÉLAGO
DA MADEIRA

Porto Moniz
Santana
Ribeira Brava
Funchal
ILHA DA MADEIRA

Desertas

0   50 km

1/2 750 000

A   B   C   D

1

37

2

76-77
PAYS-BAS
NETHERLANDS
AMSTERDAM ●
○ Rotterdam

BRUXELLES/BRUSSEL
●
BELGIQUE
BELGIUM
LUXEMBOURG ●
78-79

3

'outh

toft

4

5

0   20 km

Nationaal
Park Duinen
Van Texel
De Koog
Te
Den Burg
Den Helder
De
Oev
24 54
N 249 N 9
44 NOOR
N 248
Schagen 48
N 245 78 29
N 241
Bergen HOLLA
Bergen aan Zee N 507
Egmond aan Zee
N 512 **Alkmaar**
23 N 244 90
Beverwijk **Purmerend** 10
IJmuiden Wormerveer
Bloemendaal Zaanstad **AMST**
HAARLEM A
Zandvoort 22 16
Heemstede **Amstelveen**
Hillegom Bu
Keukenhof Aalsmeer Hilvers
Noordwijk aan Zee Lisse
Sassenheim A44 ED Uithoorn N 201 37
Katwijk aan Zee 207
Wassenaar **Leiden** UTR
Museum Beelden aan Zee Alphen
Scheveningen Voorschoten a/d Rijn **UTRECH**
DEN HAAG N11
('S-GRAVENHAGE) **Zoetermeer** Bodegraven Woerden
Hoek van Boskoop E25 N210
Holland 5 **Delft** N228
Europoort **Gouda** Vianen
Schiedam Schoonhoven
Maassluis A20 43 Krimpen N 210
Brielle **ROTTERDAM**
Vlaardingen Kinderdijk A15 Leerda
Haringvlietdam Gorinchen
Goeree **Spijkenisse** 39 20
Ouddorp **Hellevoetsluis** Oud **Zwijndrecht**
Beijerland N 287
Haamstede **Dordrecht** Sliedrecht
N 215 's-Gravendeel N.P. De
Schouwen Middelharnis Biesbosch
Duiveland Overflakkee 90 Geertruidenberg N 283
Zierikzee N 59 Willemstad 75 Oosterhout N 59 Wa
Domburg N 287 18 N 59 NOORD-BRA
Nationaal Steenbergen Oudenbosch **Breda**
W'cheren Park Stavenisse Etten-Leur
Middelburg Goes Oosterschelde Tholen N 256
N 288 Bergen op A58 Roosendaal
Vlissingen Z Zoom Gilze Goirl

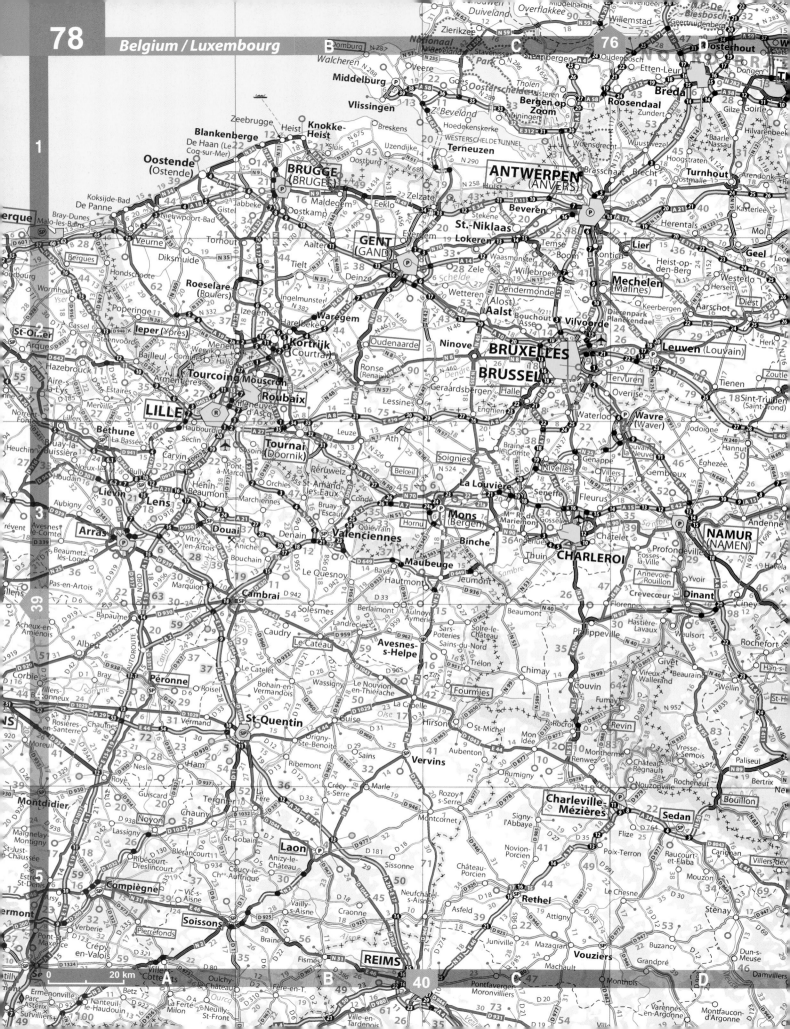

80-81

Kiel

Rostock

Bremen   Hamburg   82-83

Hannover   BERLIN

Duisburg   84-85   86-87

ALLEMAGNE
GERMANY

Köln

Dresden

Frankfurt am Main   PRAHA   92-93

88-89   90-91   Plzeň   Ostrava

CZECH REP.
RÉP. TCHÈQUE

Saarbrücken   Stuttgart   Nürnberg

München   96-97   WIEN

94-95   Salzburg

98-99   Zürich   VADUZ   Innsbruck   **AUTRICHE**
BERN   **AUSTRIA**

Genève   **LIECHTENSTEIN**

Klagenfurt

SUISSE
SWITZERLAND

N   O   R   D   Z   E   E

Ostfriesi

Norderney

Juist

Waddeneilanden   Norddeich

Borkum   Nord

Schiermonnikoog   **N.P. Niedersächsisch**
Wattenmeer

Ameland   Schiermonnikoog

Hollum   Buren   Eemshaven   Krummhörn

Oosterend   Nes   Uithuizen

West-
Terschelling   *Terschelling*   45   N 363   N 46   33   N 33

Holwerd   Anjum   N 361   N.P.   Delfzijl

Oost-
Vlieland   Dokkum   14   N 366   Zoutkamp   Winsum   Bedum   N 996   25   Emde

Vlieland   N 357   30   11   52   *Van Starkenborgh*   15   **GRONINGEN**

Nationaal   N 393   66   52   **GRONINGEN**
Park Duinen   **Leeuwarden**   14   N 355   Burgum   Nieuwesch
Van Texel   Harlingen/ 34   20   N 31   21   22   N 369   33   35   40   16

De Koog   Harns   Franeker   N 384   20   N 31   20   15   Haren   Hoogezand   57

Texel   10   N 359   29   28   25   26   A7   57   Eelde   15   57

Den Burg   15   A7   Bolsward   **N.P. de**   35   **N.P. Beek**
Den Helder   17   18   12   **Alde Feanen**   Drachten   Roden   N 919   **en Esdorpent schap**

Den   Workum   Sneek/Snits   **FRYSLÂN**   Norg   N 858   35   **Drentsche Aa**   Vlagtwedde
Oever   A7   21   43   N 392   Gorredijk   N 380   42   30   Oude
Afsluitdijk   22   Jonger kanaal   A28   Pekela

54   A7   **Heerenveen**   A7   12   Smilde   16   N 378   N 857   Ter Apel
N 99   14   13   N 928   Wolvega   A28   **Assen**   **Stadskanaal**
Stavoren   Sloten   39   N 353   **N.P.**   23   **DRENTHE**   N 366
44   N 248   Lemmer   **Dwingelderveld**   Oranjekan   27   Börger   Musselkanaal   N 391
Schagen   48   *IJsselmeer*   N 359   N 855   31   28   N 374   N 381   Ter Apel
N 245   29   67   Beilen   408
78   Medemblik   Steenwijk   13   **Hoogeveen**   43   **Emmen**
Bergen   Enkhuizen   Giethoorn   47   26   52
Bergen aan Zee   N 302   *Noord-Oost-Polder*   Meppel   48   Coevorden
HOLLAND   Urk   77   N 333   24   20   N 34   N 377   45
Alkmaar   Hoorn   N 331   Emmen heim   Twist
0   20 km   102   N 506   N 352   N 762   N 331   Dedemsvaart   Emlichheim
N 23   90   Markermeer   IJsselmuiden   N 377   53
Edam

1

2

...ceglie **Molfetta**
SS 16BIS 46
6 Giovinazzo
14 10
A 14 11 9 8
Terlizzi 12 9
SP 231 **Bitonto**
BARI
9 Mola di Bari
21
Capurso
Modugno 5
Palo del Colle
Bitetto SP 90 SP 111 35
Sannicandro di Bari Adelfia SP 240
SP 108 SP 68 Casamassima SP 121
46 Rutigliano
38 SP 89 Turi SP 120
SP 145 Conversano 16
SP 236 Acquaviva SP 102 SP 237
Cassano delle Murge delle Fonti SP 106 **Monopoli**
SP 151 12 Sammichele 104
di Bari Castellana
SP 79 Putignano Grotte Torre
SP 236 **Altamura** Noci 21 Canne
12 66 **Gioia** Fasano
SP 235 del Colle Alberobello
Santeramo 14 Locorotondo 113
in Colle SP 377 Cisternino E 55
17 67 **Martina Franca** SS 172 Ostuni
SS 271 Mottola 19 Ceglie SS 581 38
SS 230 VIA APPIA Massapica
Matera 54 SS 7 Massafra 23 Francavilla
Laterza Castellaneta Grottaglie Fontana 64
Miglionico 20 Palagiano 14 26
29 Montescaglioso 39 45 Oria
SS 7 35 5 3 4 S. Giorgio 17 Sava
Bernalda SS 106 **TARANTO** Jonico Manduria
22 Lido di SS 7 Avetrana
Metaponto SS 106
Lido Silvana SS 174
Pisticci 25 Lido di Metaponto SP 122 72 **PUGLIA**
SS 598 SS 103
18 Scanzano Jonico
Tursi
Policoro SS 106
SS 653
...raro 34

5

Carovigno
S. Vito dei Normanni
SS 16 APPIA **Brindisi**
SP 81
Tuturano 41
Latiano Mesagne S. Pietro
SP 51 Vernotico
SP 75 SP 51 Torchiarolo
SP 68 Squinzano 48
82 S. Donaci Trepuzzi 38 Surbo
S. Pancrazio 44 Campi S. Cataldo
Salentino Salentina 12
Monteroni P S. Caldo
di Lecce **Lecce**
SS 101 Leverano 25 SP 20 Melendugno
Copertino 34 Alimini Grande
PortoCesareo SP 359 17 Alimini Piccolo
SP 112 Martano 22 SP 48
Nardò 11 SP 47 Galatina 10 45
Galatone 26 Maglie SS 16 Otranto
83 SP 361 68 S. Cesarea Terme
Gallipoli Casarano SP 362 SP 363
Parabita 43 SP 374 Tricase
SP 215 SP 65 Ugento SP 91
Gagliano del Capo

Marina di Leuca
Capo S.
a di Leuca

GOLFO
DI TARANTO

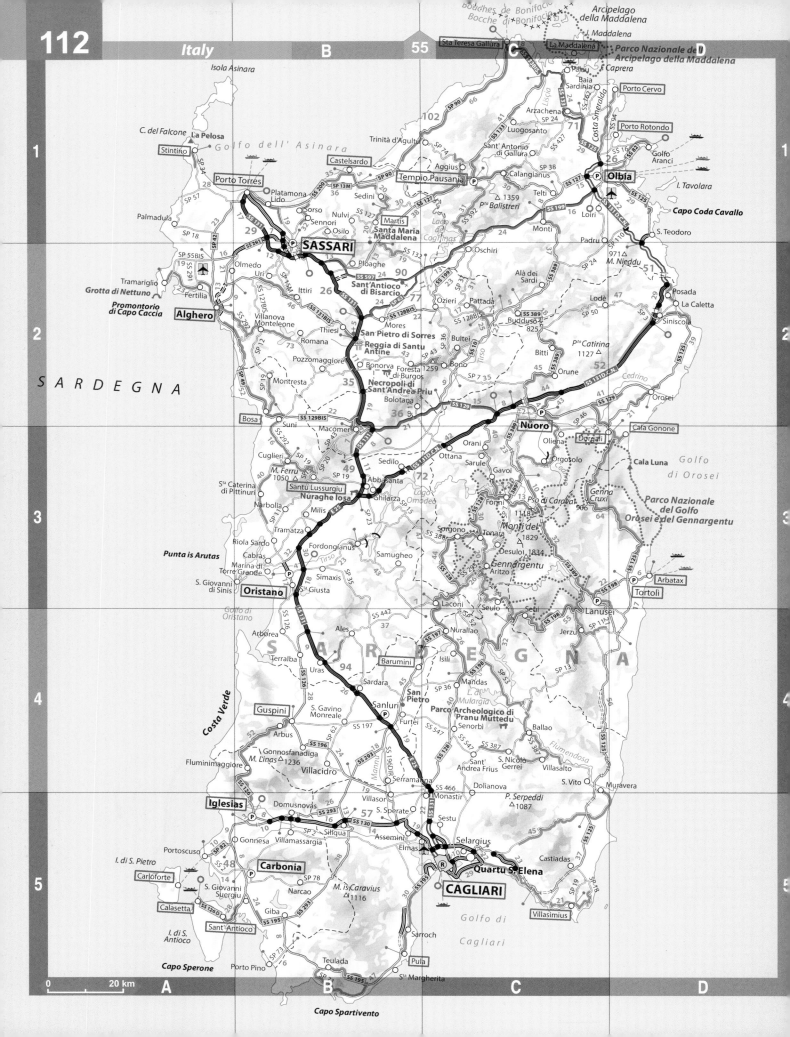

1

I. di Ustica

M A R E   T I R

2

S I C I L I A

Capo Gallo
6 30 Sferracavallo Mondello
S. Vito lo Capo   Cinisi 44 Capaci 606 M. Pellegrino
Golfo di   63   Carini   **PALERMO**
Castellammare   Monreale   R   Soluto
Torre dell'Impiso   Castellammare 26 E90 17 **BAGHERIA**
Erice SP20 SP 16   del Golfo 24 SS 13 Casteldaccia 54
Trapani SP 16 34   9 E90 16 Partinico SS 624 Altavilla A 19 Ter
Paceco 53 Fulgatore A 29 6 Misilmeri Milicia Trabia 47 Ime
Isole 42 Segesta Alcamó 80   Marineo SP 5 SS 118 Caccamo
Egadi 50 Calatafimi SS 119 S. Cipirello R⁰ Busambra Villafrati Montemaggiore
I. Maréttimo 36 SP 8 41 57 1613 Corleone Roccapalumba Belsite
I. Favignana **Marsala** Salemi 6 A 29 28 SS 118 Prizzi Lercara Torto
SS 188 SP 50 Sᵗᵃ Ninfa SS 119 SS 188C Friddi SS 118
SS 115 Partanna Belice Chiusa Sclafani SS 118
3 Castelvetrano SS 188 Sᵗᵃ Margherita SS 188
22 3 di Belice Sambuca S. Stefano Quisquina
Mazara 25 di Sicilia Alessandria
del Vallo 21 Caltabellotta della Rocca Casteltermini
Campobello SP 56 Menfi SP 37 Ribera S. Biagio
di Mazara 22 SS 386 Platani Platani
Selinunte Marinella SP 79 **Sciacca** Aragona
Raffadali 70 SP 17
Spiaggia SP 3
Capo Bianco **Agrigento**
Porto Empedocle 6 P Favar

4

MALTA

Ras Zebbug Marsalforn
San Dimitri Ta'Pinu Ramla Bay
Gharb Xaghra San Blas Bay
Dwejra Point Ggantija Nadur Ras ti-Qala
Victoria/Rabat Xewkija Qala *BAHAR MEDITERRAN*
Xlendi Mgarr
GOZO Comino
(Kammuna) I. di Linosa
Armier Bay
Cirkewwa Mellieha
St Paul's Bay
Mellieha Bugibba
10 Sliema
Golden Mosta 25 15
Bay Naxxar **VALLETTA**
MALTA Mgarr Zebbigh Attard Vittoriosa / Birgu
Bahrija Mdina 9 Zabbar
Rabat Verdala Palace Tarxien Marsaskala
Siggiewi Zejtun St Thomas Bay
Ras id Dawwara Dingli Ghar Marsaxlokk
Dingli Cliffs Dalam *Isole Pelagie*
Zurrieq Birzebbuga
Hagar Qim Blue Grotto *Marsaxlokk Bay*
Filfla I. di Lampedusa

5

Pantelleria SP54
Tracino
Montana Grande △ 836
Isola di Pantelleria

I. di Linosa

Isole Pelagie

Lampedusa
I. di Lampedusa

0   5   10 km
0   5 miles

0   20 km
A   B   C   D

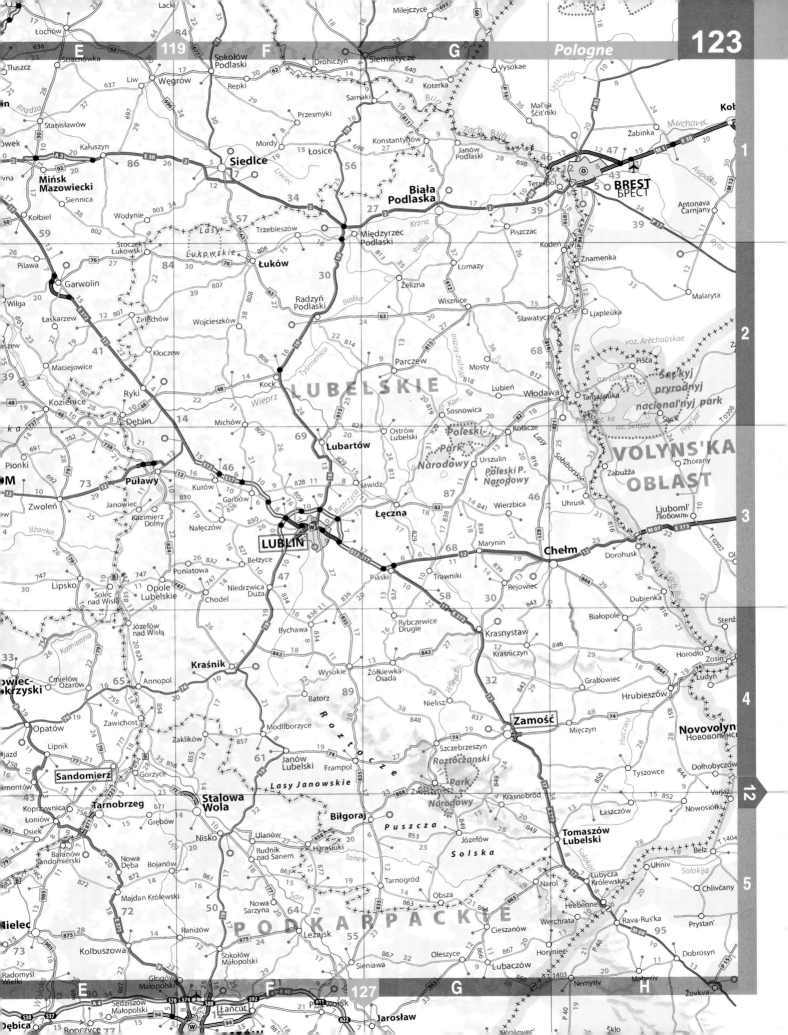

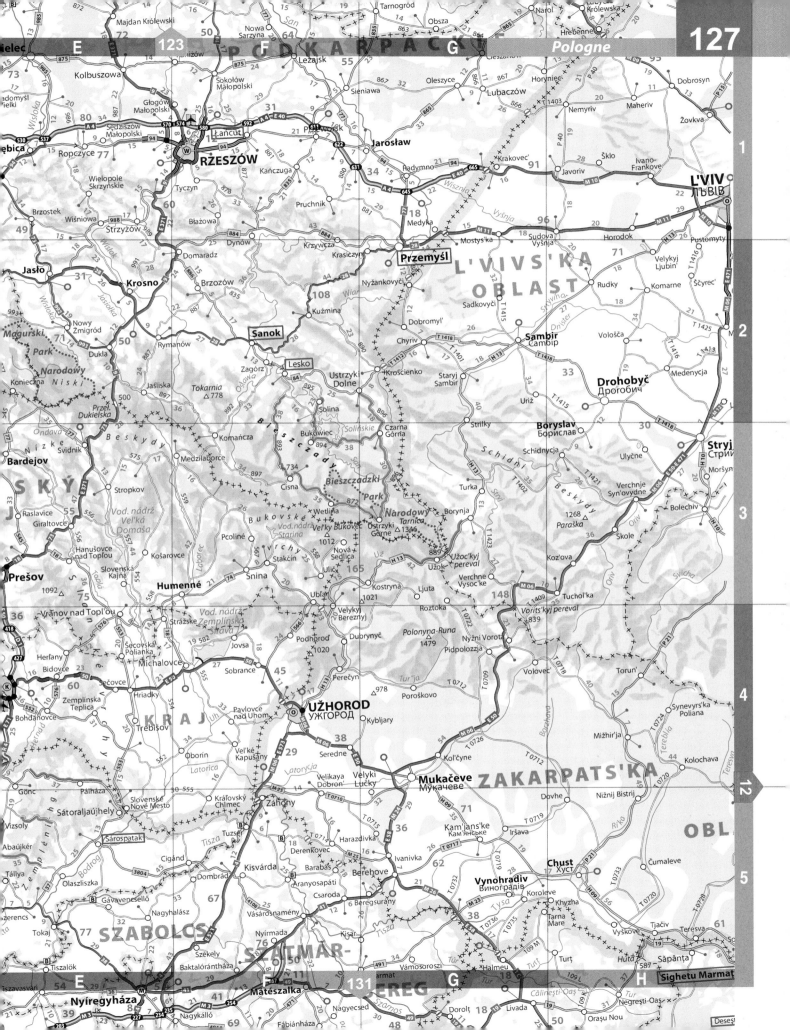

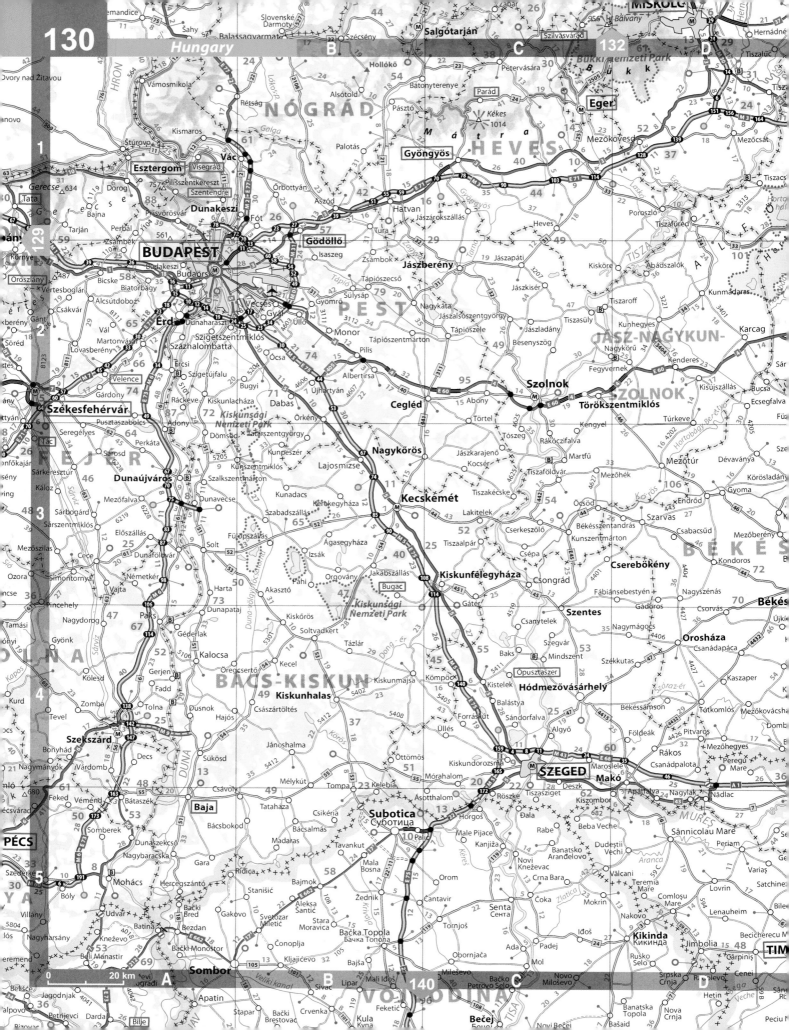

124

OLOMOUCKÝ

Olomouc

Prostějov

Přerov

ZLÍNSKÝ

Zlín

OSTRAVA

Frýdek-Místek

BIELSKO-BIAŁA

Karviná

Havířov

Český Těšín

Čadca

Žilina

ŽILINSKÝ KRAJ

Martin

Považská Bystrica

Ružomberok

TATRANSKÝ NÁRO

Uherské Hradiště

TRENČIANSKY KRAJ

Trenčín

Nové Mesto nad Váhom

Prievidza

Banská Bystrica

BANSKOBYS

Piešťany

Partizánske

Zvolen

Detva

Topoľčany

TRNAVSKÝ KRAJ

Trnava

Nitra

Levice

BRATISLAVSKÝ KRAJ

BRATISLAVA

NITRIANSKY KRAJ

Šaľa

Nové Zámky

Balassagyarmat

NÓGRÁD

Hegyeshalom

Mosonmagyaróvár

Komárno

GYŐR

Esztergom

Vác

Dunakeszi

GYŐR-MOSON-SOPRON

KOMÁROM-ESZTERGOM

Tatabánya

BUDAPEST

Gödöllő

130

0 20 km

A **B** **C** **D**

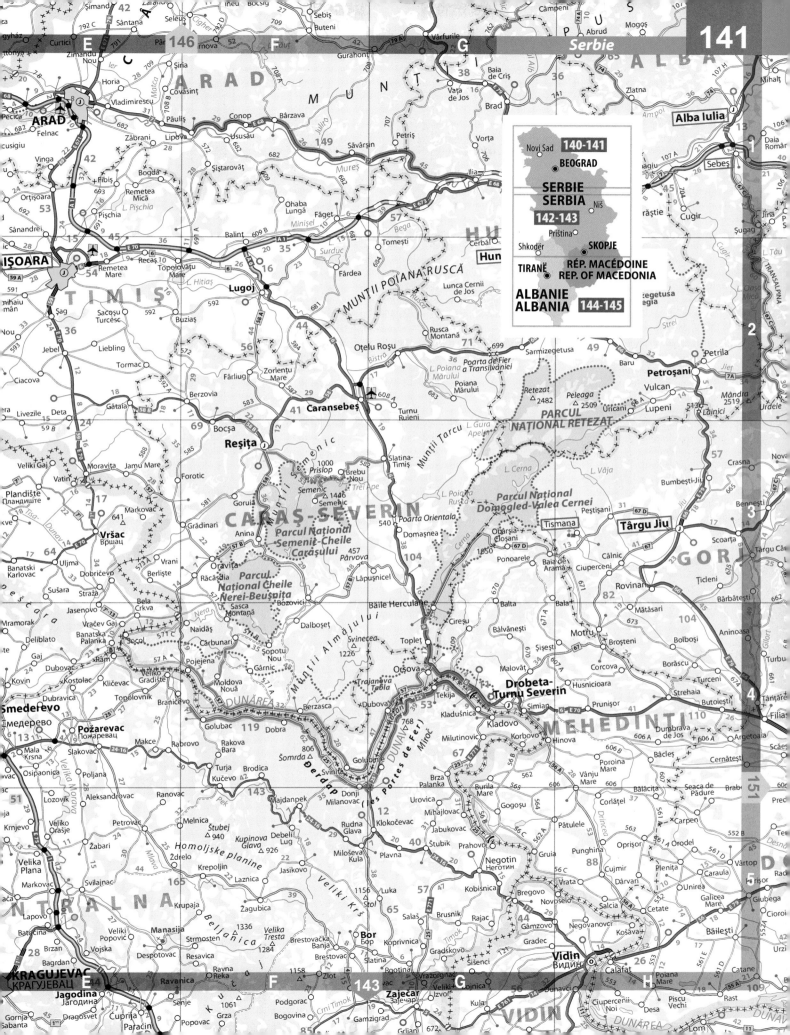

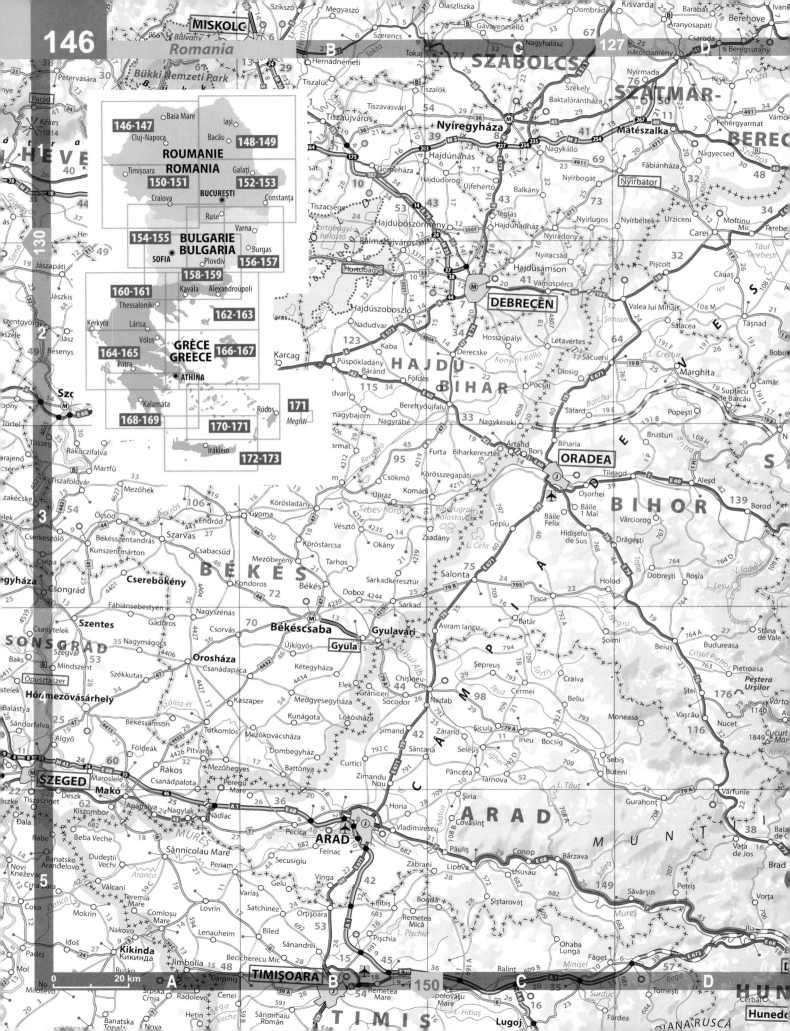

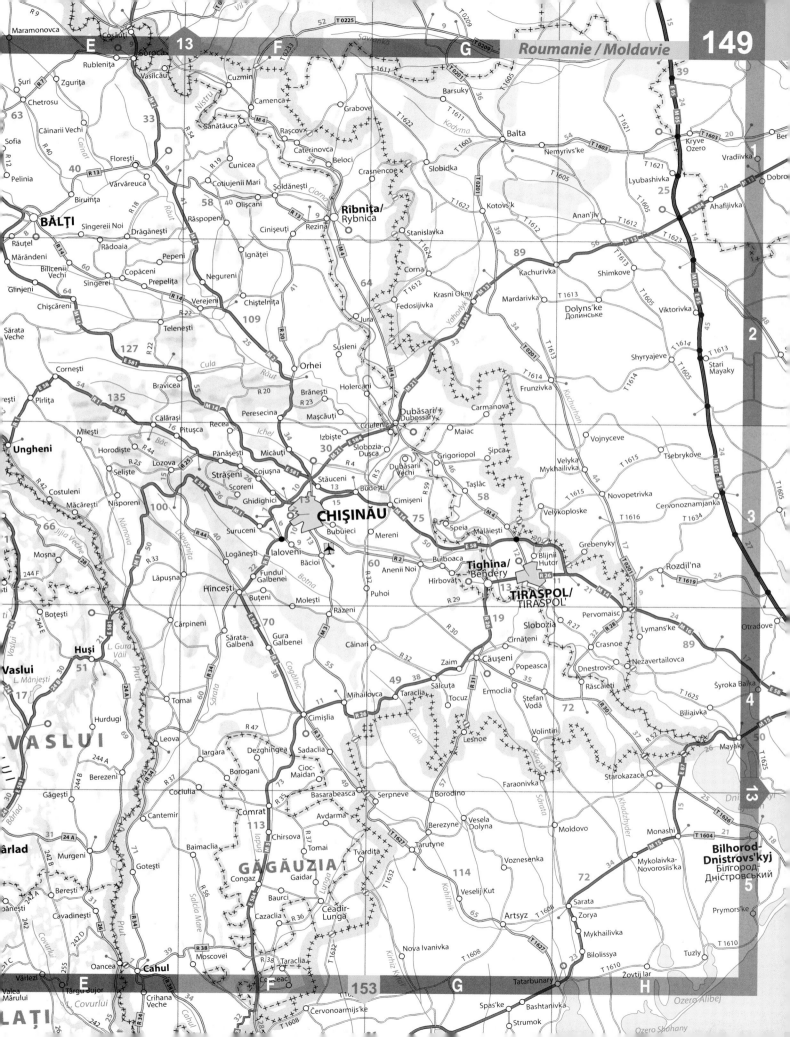

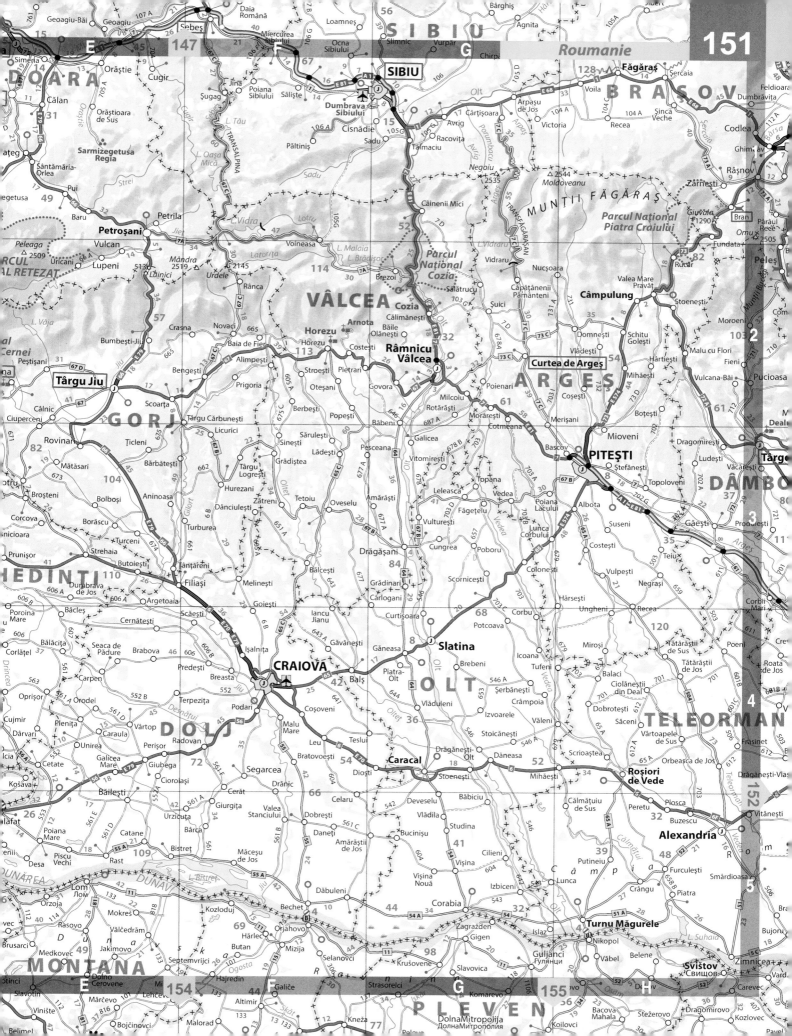

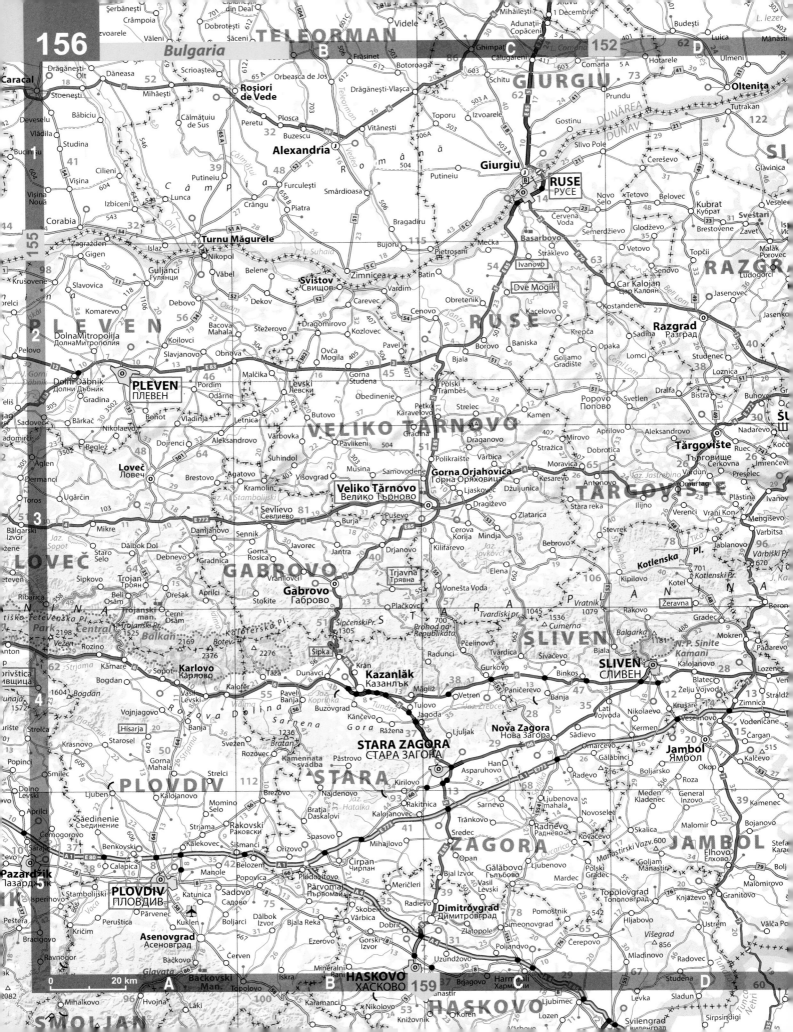

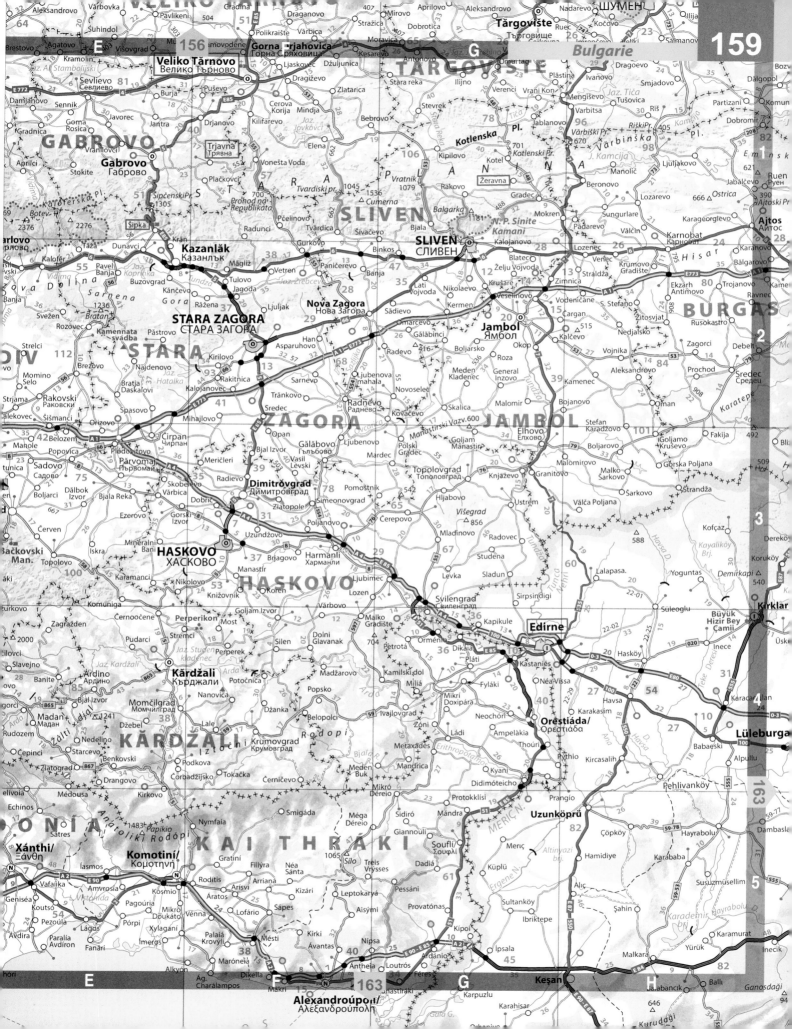

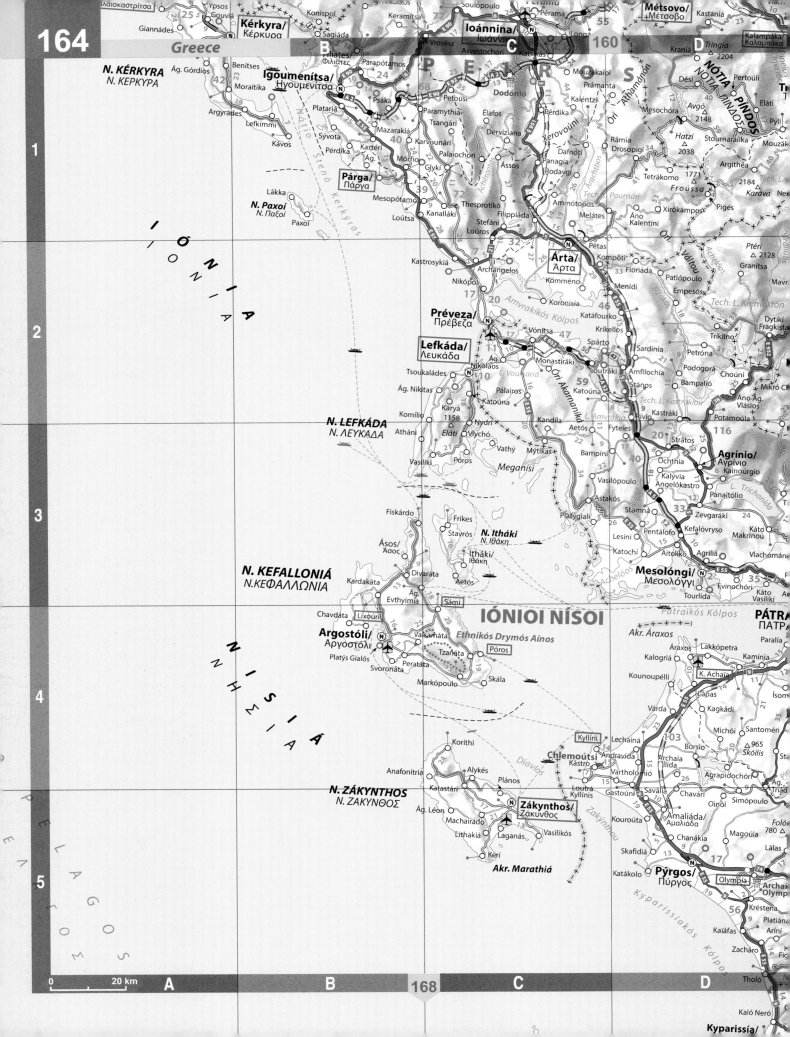

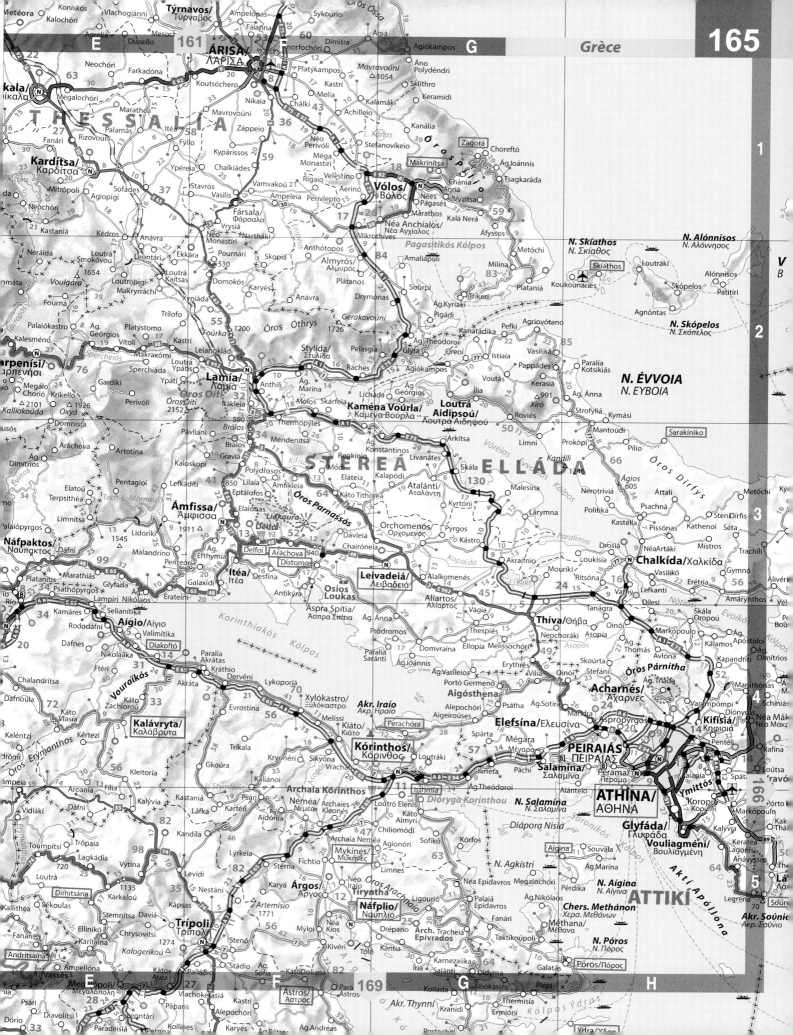

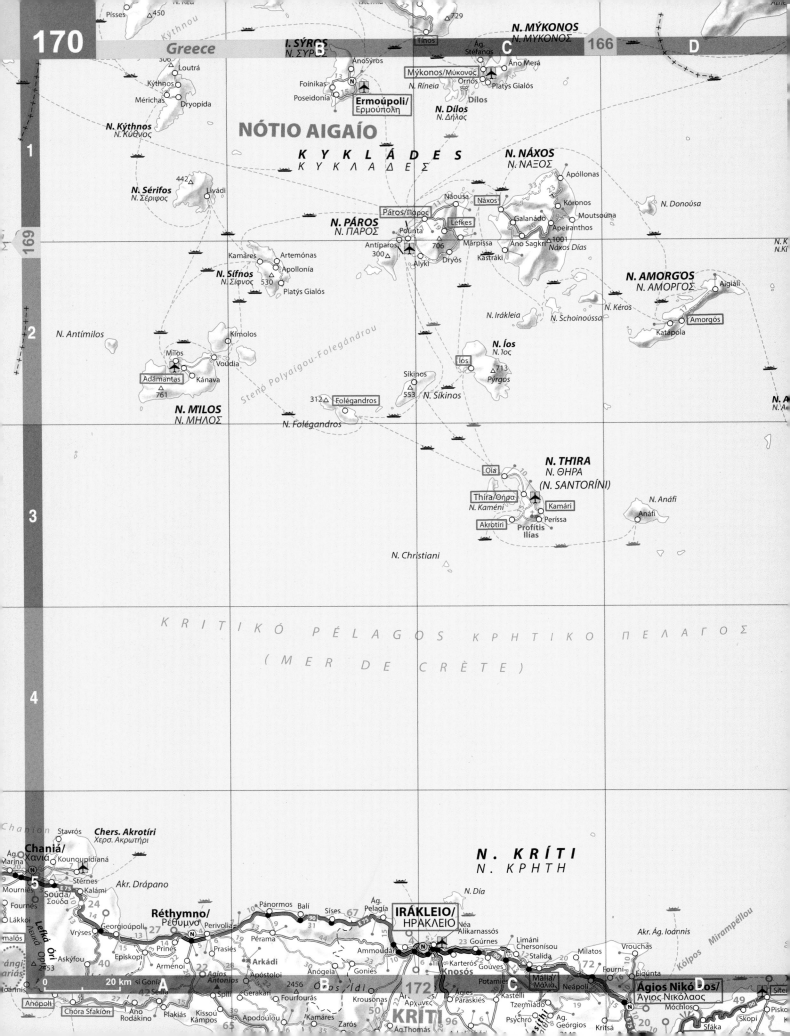

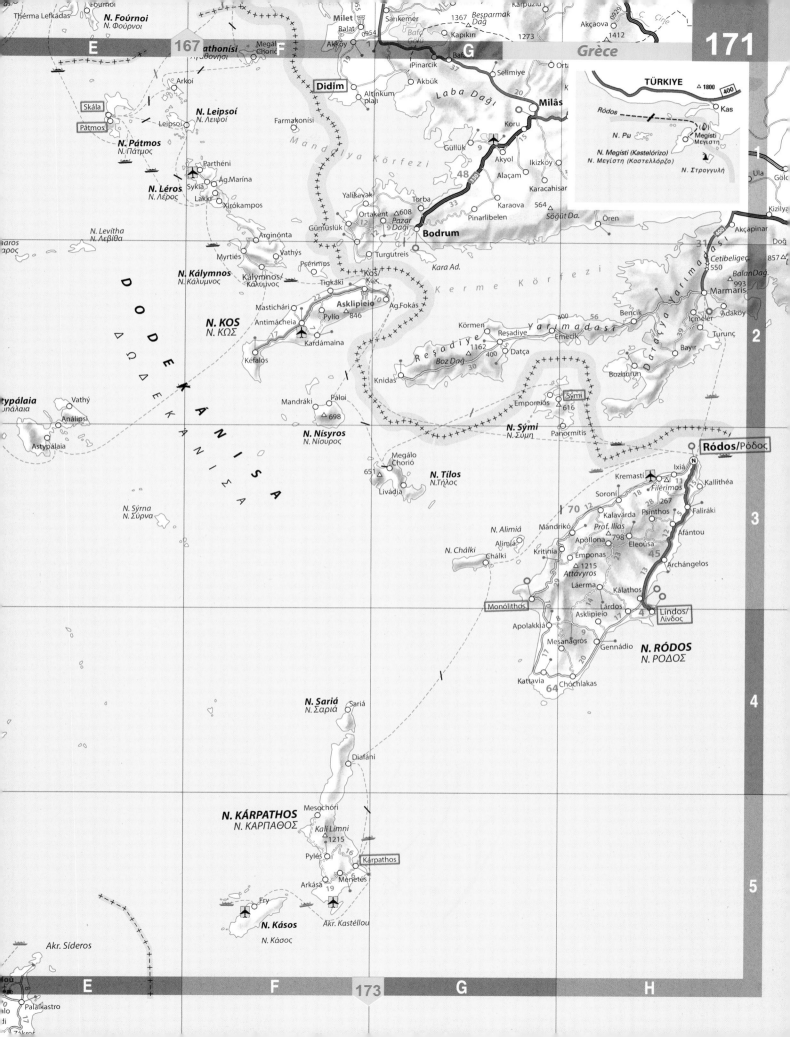

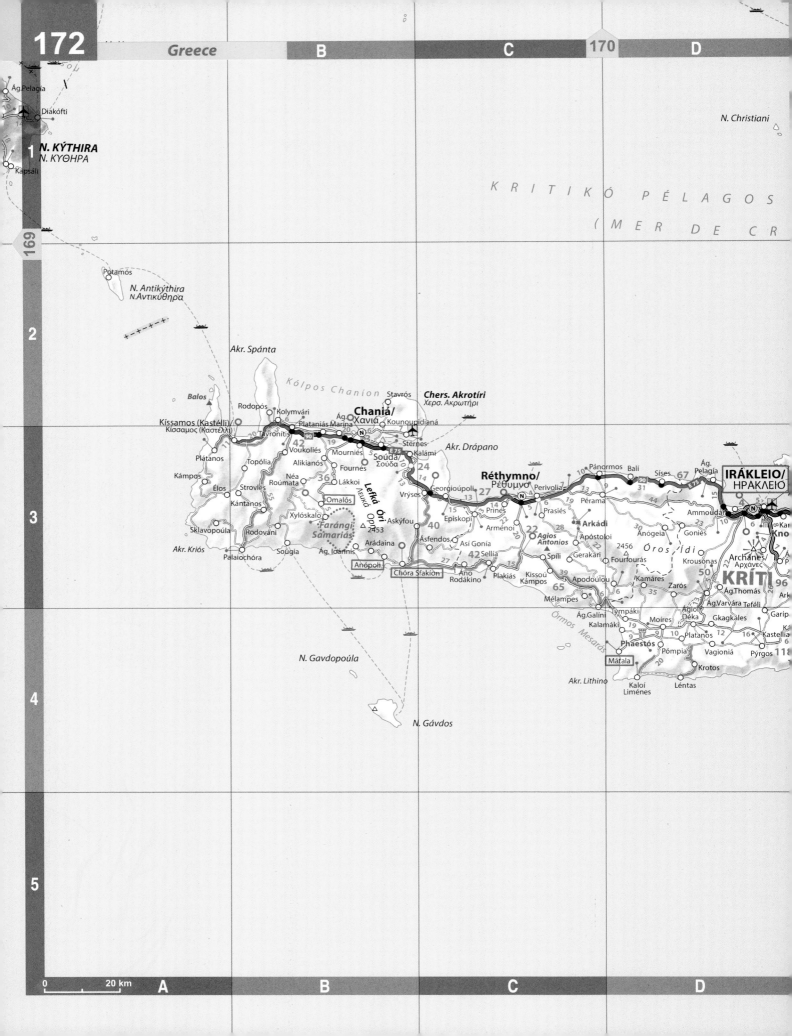

A | B | C | D

N. KÝTHIRA
N. ΚΥΘΗΡΑ

Ág.Pelagía
Diakófti
Kapsáli

N. Christiani

K R I T I K Ó   P É L A G O S
(M E R   D E   C R

Potamós
N. Antikýthira
N.Αντικύθηρα

Akr. Spánta

Kólpos Chaníon

Balos

Rodopós
Kolymvári
Stavrós
Chers. Akrotíri
Χερσ. Ακρωτήρι

Kíssamos (Kastélli)
Kíσσαμος (Καστέλλι)
Tavronítis
Plataniás Marina
Ág.
Chaniá/
Χανιά
Kounoupidianá

Plátanos
Topólia
Alikianós
Voukoliés
Mourniés
Fournés
Soúda/
Σούδα
Stérnes
Kalámi
Akr. Drápano

Akr. Drápano

Réthymno/
Ρέθυμνο
Pánormos
Bali
Síses
Ág.
Pelagía
IRÁKLEIO/
ΗΡΑΚΛΕΙΟ

Kámpos
Élos
Strovlés
Néa
Roúmata
Lákkoi
Lefká Óri
Λευκά
Όρι
Georgioúpoli
Vrýses
Perivólia
Prinés
Prasiés
Pérama
Ammoudár
N
Kno

Kántanos
Sklavopoúla
Omalós
Xylóskalo
**Farángi
Samariás**
Askýfou
Episkopi
Arménoi
Arkádi
Anógeia
Goniés
Ág.
Pelagía
Krí

Rodováni
Soúgia
Ág. Ioánnis
Arádaina
Anópoli
Ásfendos
Asi Goniá
Sellía
**Agios
Antonios**
Apóstoloi
Gerakári
Spíli
Fourfourás
2456
Óros Ídi
Krousónas
Kamáres
Zarós
Archánes/
Αρχάνες
Teféli
Garíp

Akr. Kríos
Palaiochóra
Chóra Sfakíon
L.Áno
Rodákino
Plakiás
Kissoú
Kámpos
Apodoúlou
Mélampes
Ág.Galíni
Tympáki
Moíres
Agíoi
Déka
Ág.Varvára
Gkagkáles
Ká
Kastellia

N. Gavdopoúla
Órmos Mesarás
Kalamáki
Platános
Vagioniá
Pýrgos
118
Phaestós
Pómpia
Krotos
Mátala
Akr. Lithino
Kaloí
Liménes
Léntas

N. Gávdos

A | B | C | D

0   20 km

1

Cape Apostolos Andreas

136 △ ✛ **Apostolos
Andreas**
Panagia Afendrika ✛
191 △

Rizokarpaso
Panagia Eleosa ✛
241 △ ○

Aigialousa ○ 383 △
Agios ○ K A R P' A S I A
Andronikos ○
Vothylakas ○

Eptakomi ○ 166 △ Leonarisso ○

2

Davlos ○ 330 △ Komi ○ 64
Kantara ✈
724 △ Patriki ○
Akanthou ○ Agios Theodoros ○

740 ○ △ *Cape Elaia*

Agios ○
Amvrosios Kalograia ○ 91 △
△ **Antifonitis** Lapathos ○
Charkeia ○ 819 Gypsou ○ Trikomo ○ *Ammochostos Bay*

740 △ Lefkonoiko ○
Kythrea ● Marathovounos ○ Milia ○
Neo Chorio ○ Peristerona ○
Exo ○ Limnia ○
Metochi 61 Genagra ○ Agios Sergios ○
Palaikythro ○ 47 Stylloi ○ ✛ **Salamis**
Angastina ○ E903 ○ **Apostolos Varnavas**
Pediaios Prastio ○ ○ Tuzla

3

Afanteia ○
Askeia ○ Vatili ○ Acheritou ○
Tymvou ○ 140 Lysi ○ **AMMÓCHOSTOS / GAZIMAĞUSA**
Tremetousia ○ Kontea ○ Kalopsida ○ **FAMAGUSTA**
Arsos ○ Makrasyka ○ 45 Deryneia ○
Achna ○ Avgorou ○ Frenaros ○ Paralimni ○
Potamia ○ Athienou ○ 28 20 Liopetri ○ 174 △
350 Troulloi ○ Pyla ○ Xylotymvou ○ Sotira ○
Lympia ○ Voroklini ○ Ormideia ○ 25
B2 6 Xylofagou ○ **Agía Napa**
20 Aradippou ● 58 59 B3 48 *Cape Gkreko*
72 Livadia ○ 19
Pyrga ○ *Larnaka Bay* *Cape Pyla*
Kalo Chorio ○
Stavrovouni B5 **LÁRNAKA**
Dromolaxia ○
Anglisides ○ Kiti ○ × ✈
Anafotida ○ Perivolia ○ **Panagia Angeloktistos**
Mazotos ○ *Cape Kiti*

4

M E D I T E R R A N E A N   S E A

5

▬▬ Ligne de démarcation - Green Line

E   F   G

A U S T H A V E T

Knivskjellodden   **Nordkapp**
Gjesvær   11-5
35
Skarsvåg
E69
Magerøya
Honningsvåg
Kåfjord
B
105
Porsangerhalvøya
Repvåg

Russenes
23   E6
Skaidi
58   64   E6   42   Børselv   81

Lakselv
Skuov 'gilraš 'sa
Vuorji   1024

N M A R K

93   92
Karasjok
18
92

Finnmarksvidda

Øvre Anarjokka
nasjonalpark
Noarvaš   536

Naltijärvi

Lemmenjoen
kansallispuisto

31
Nunnanen
Peltovuoma

E   F   181   G   H

Mehamn   868   Gamvik
18
894
Kjøllefjord   28
Kifjord
Sandfjellet   486

Veidnesklubben
Kalak
Lebesby
Ifjord   22
Vestertana
211
Ifjordfjellet
98
11-5   88
Sirma

Duolbbadasgai 'sa
668
890
Leirpollskogen

Rustefjelbma
17   Varangerbotn
Tana Bru
Skipagurra
Nuorgam   26
Polmak
71
970
48   70
E6 E75   32

Levajok   970
Utsjoki
Deatnu
104
Nuvvos-Ailigas   535
Kevo
113
E75
Valjok
Teno   970   541
Kuivi
Paistunturit   619
Kevon
luonnonpuisto
552
Ruohtir
101
E75

Karigasniemi
72   92
642
516   Nuhppir
Is 'kuras
520   Muotkatunturit
64
590
Koarvikodds

62   9553
Angeli
Otsamo   418
36
575
Menesjärvi
Lemmenjoki
Maarestatunturit

599
Viipustunturit   955
Tupalaki   400

Repojoki
71
Kuttura   9694

957   996   Pokka

Berlevåg
Store
Molvik   Kongsfjord
890   60   **Båtsfjord**
33   Syltefjord   Hamningberg
891   11-5
Varangerhalvøya
nasjonalpark
11-5   **Vardø**
Varangerhalvøya   E75
Falkefjellet   76   Kiberg
548   125
49   Vestre Jakobselv
E75   **Vadsø**
Nesseby   F
Varangerfjorden   Hurtigruten
26   E6
Bugøynes
81   124
Skogerøya
Korgåsen   400
886
Villavaara   Grense
344   Jakobselv
Neiden   **Kirkenes**   63
893   Hesseng   12-5   448
10   Boris Gleb
883   Viksjøfjell
Bjørnevatn   Pečeng
32   E105   67   88   21   A 138
Svanvik   885   Zapol'arnyj
177   Nikel   P 10
Sevettijärvi   650   Petsamontunturit
52   971
Partakko   Nyrud
Vasikkaselkä   Øvre Pasvik
nasjonalpark
Pasvikelva   P 12
40
Kaamanen
INARIJÄRVI
Sikovuono   Ukonselkä   Nellim
26   **Inari**
Akku   Veskoniemi
39   327   950   Sarmitunturit   411
Akujärvi   51
Ivalo
Törmänen   Lutto
Ivalojoki   Ávvil   91
Saariselkä   Raja Jooseppi
Jorn Njuhtshoaiv   715
Urho Kekkosen
kansallispuisto
Kakslauttanen
32   Saariselkä   718
Sokosti
Nattaset   633
544   Talkkunapää   Korvatunturi
483
181   Sompion
luonnonpuisto

1

2

3

4

5

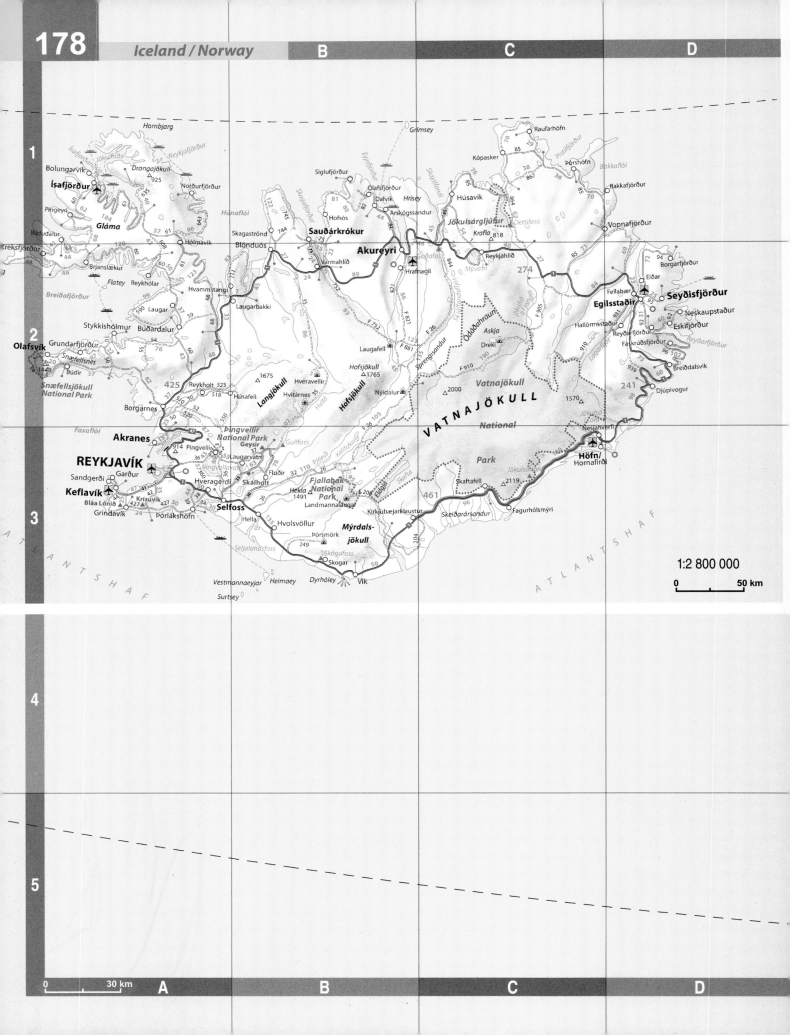

1

2

3

N O R S K E H A V E T

Valøya

Vikna

Foslandet
Statland

Hurtigruten

Flatanger

N

4

Osen

Roan

715

44

Harsvik

723

66

Åfjord

715

Follafoss

720

Verran

755

Mosvik

Frøya

716

Sistranda

Opphaug

Botngård

710

720

Leksvik

755

Levange

Titran

Flatval

Ørlandet

Brekstad

30

Kjerringvåg

Ansnes

Rissa

718

Valset

755

Frosta

Åsen

93

Fillan

Stjørnfjorden

Hitra

Sandstad

Agdenes

714

Rørvik

717

23

Skatval

Dyrnes

669

Forsnes

38

713

Sunde

Selbekken

Flakk

Stjørdal

Smøla

Nerdvika

Trondheimsleia

Snillfjord

680

TRONDHEIM

Malvik

Hegra

705

Edøya

Korsvoll

Aure

Kyrksæterøra

714

Orkanger

710

42

Heimdal

Hommelvik

Leira

Vinsternes

Arasvika

165

E39

Buvika

Klæbu

5

Kristiansund

Hurtigruten

Tustna

Tømmervåg

Halsa

Hannset

68

71

46

Skaun

Melhus

Selbu

Bremsnes

Averøya

64

Frei

9

Svorkmo

708

SØR

663

Kvernes

Kanestraum

65

39

Rindal

65

701

Løkken

53

Bud

Fræna

670

Eide

666

Skei

65

Meldal

700

Støren

Gauldalen

Steinshamn

663

64

665

Surnadalsøra

Trollheimen

Rønnebu

156

Sandøya

Aukra

Hollingsholm

666

Tingvoll

Kvanne

Todalsøra

Berkåk

662

Molde

40

Eidsvåg

69

Kårvatn

122

Haltdålen

A

64

B

188

C

Blåhø

1672

D

Valderøya

Søvik

659

Vatne

Rødven

Afarnes

660

Isfjorden

Eresfjord

Sunndalsøra

Ulsberg

TRØNDELA

Ålesund

Skodje

70

Tresfjord

660

Blåøret

0   30 km

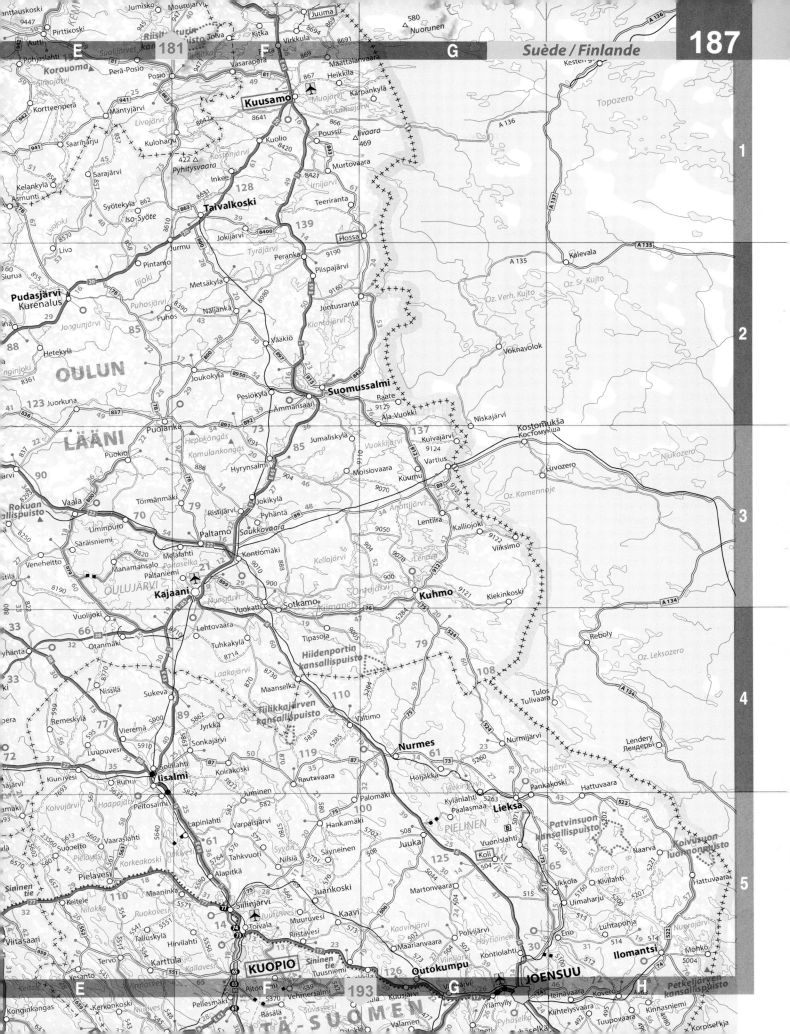

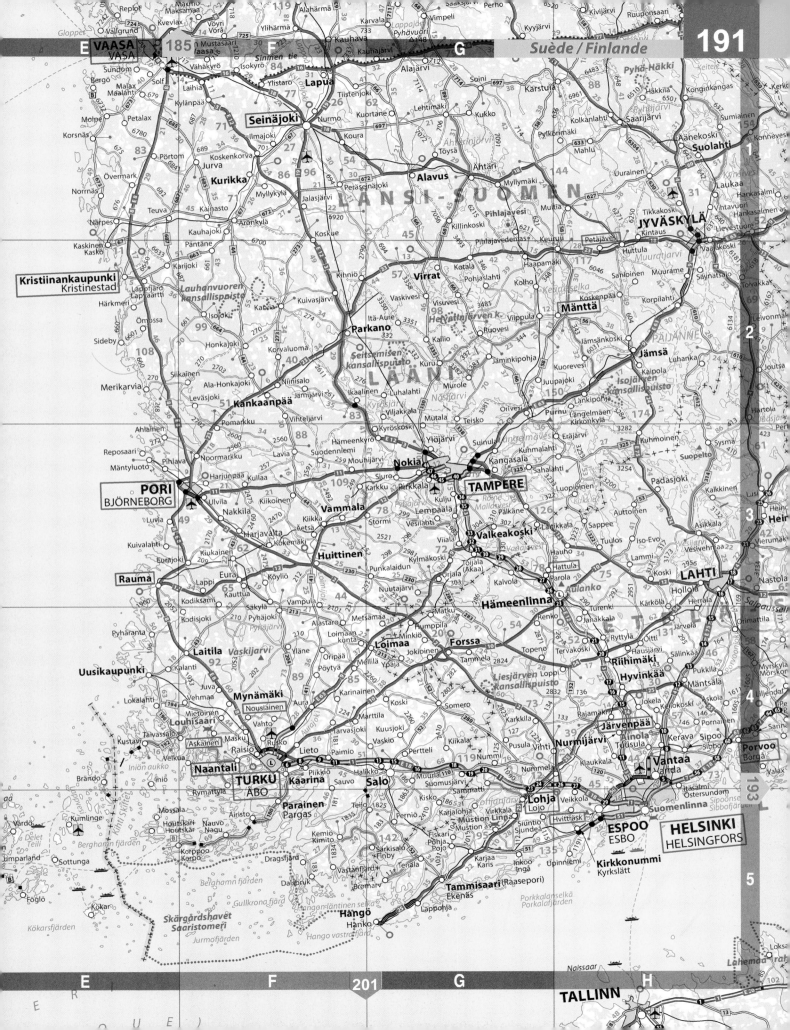

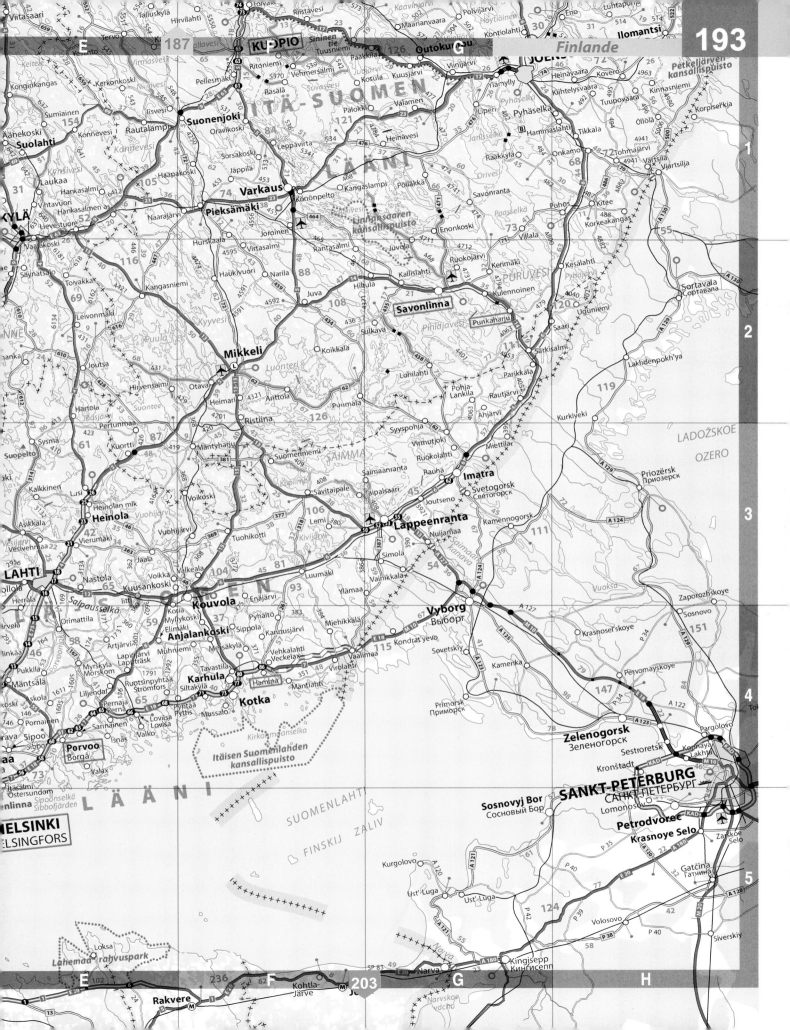

Åkrehamn
Kopervik
Tysvær
Nedstrand
Ryfylke
Setesdalsheiene
Eidsborg
Lifjell
Notodden
Hedda
Karmøy
Jelsa
Vindsvik
Byklehei
Bykle
Seljord
Kviteseid
Skudeneshavn
Mortavika
Judaberg
Hjelmeland
Rygnestad
188
Bø
Kvitsøy
Rennesøy
Vikevåg
Tau
Valle
Vrådal
Lunde
Ulefoss
Randaberg
Jørpeland
ROGALAND
Helle
Fyresdal
Treungen
Porsgru
STAVANGER
Prekestolen
Lysefjorden
Rysstad
AUST-
Drangedal
Herre
Sola
Hommersåk
Oanes
Forsand
AGDER
Sandnes
Lauvvik
Oltedal
Svartevath
Bygland
Treungen
Kleppe
Ålgård
Dirdal
VEST-
Grendi
Dølemo
Amli
Kragerø
Bryne
Jæren
AGDER
Byglandsfjord
Vegårshei
Nærbø
Tonstad
Åseral
Evje
Søndeled
Øysang
Varhaug
Bjerkreim
Risnes
Hornnes
Risør
Brusand
Dalane
150
Kvinesdal
Eiken
Iveland
Blakstad
Tvedestrand
Sirevåg
Moi
Sira
Hægebostad
Hægeland
Rykene
Eydehavn
Hellvik
Egersund
Hauge
Kvinesdal
Hægeland
Vennesla
Arendal
Åna Sira
Flekkefjord
Feda
Konsmo
Birkeland
Vik
Grimstad
Vestbygda
Apta
Alleen
Lyngdal
Nodeland
Lillesand
Farsund
Vigeland
Søgne
Høllen
116
Skalevik
Kristiansand
Lindesnes
Mandal

SKAGERRAK

Hirtsha

Hjørrin

FØROYAR
FÆRØERNE
(DK)

NORÐOYAR

Løkken
Jammerbugten
Brønderslev
Blokhus
Pandrup
Aabybro
Hanstholm
94
Frøstrup
Fjerritslev
Brovst
Vidareidi
Tjørnuvik Eiði
882
Gjógv Kunoy
Øyntdartfjørður
Viðoy
Svínoy
Nørre
Vorupør
Thy
AALBORG
Streymoy
790
Eysturoy
Borðoy
Hvalvik
Leirvik
Klaksvik
Thisted
Løgstør
Nibe
Vestmanna
Hvalvik
Eiði
Mykines
722
Vágar
58
Toftir
Hurup
Nykøbing
Mors
Sørvágur
Thyborøn
Torshavn
Salling
Breum
Aars
Kirkjubøur
Skopun
Sandoy
Skive
88
Hvalpsund
Hobro
Sandur
479
Rødding
Møldrup
17 Skalavik
Lemvig
Struer
Vinderup
Viborg
Suðuroyarfjørður
Holstebro
Torsminde
Ulfborg
Bjerringbro
Hvalba
Tvøroyri
Ringkøbing
Avium
Karup
Kjellerup
Hadsten
Hammel
610
Suðuroy
Herning
Videbæk
Silkeborg
Galten
Famjin
Ikast
Kibæk
Vagur
Sumba
Hvide Sande
Skjern
Tarm
Sønder
Felding Brande
Snede
Skanderborg
Nørre Nebel
Ølgod
Give
Nørre
Snede
Tørring

0   30 km   A

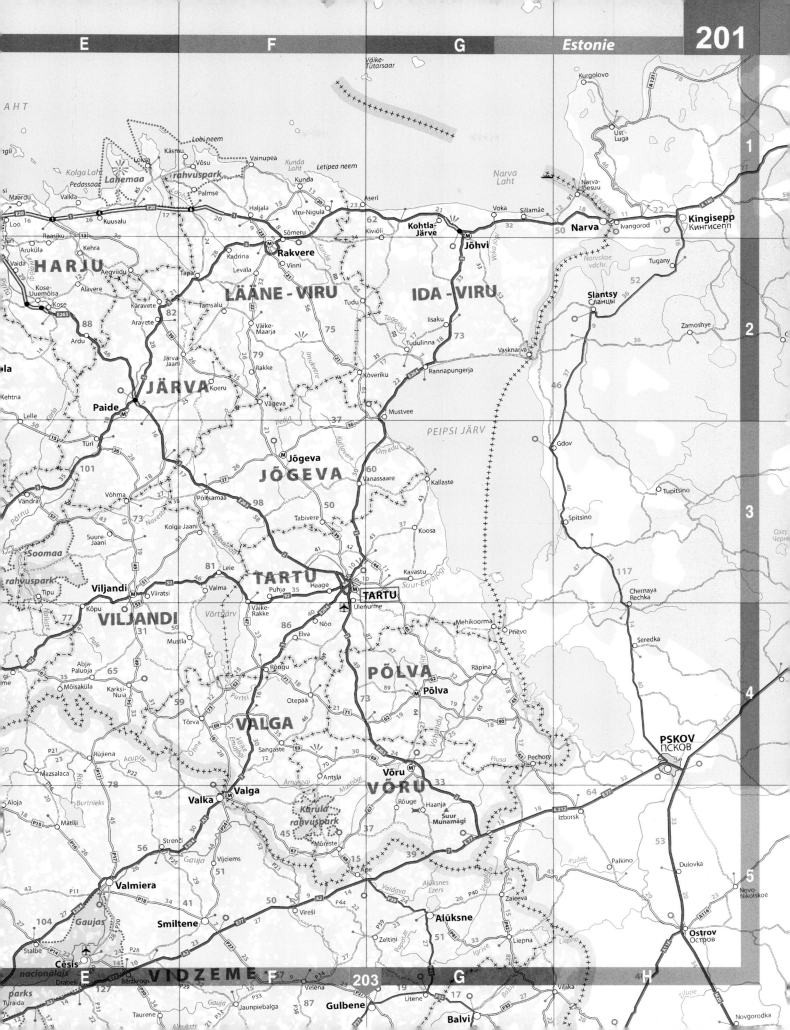

Index / Register / Indice / Índice

Localité / Place / Ort / Plaatsen
Località / Localidad / Localidade

Numéro de page / Page number / Seitenzahl / Paginanummer
Numero di pagina / Número de página / Número da página

Sites touristiques isolés / Outlying touristic attractions
Abgelegen Sehenswürdigkeiten
Afgelegen toeristische sites / Siti turistici isolati
Sitios turísticos aislados / Locais isolados de interesse

Aachen *(D)* .... 84 **B 5**
Voroneţ (RO).......... 148 **B 2**

Coordonnées de carroyage / Grid coordinates Koordinate-
nangabe / Verwijstekens ruitsysteem
Coordinate riferite alla quadrettatura /
Coordenadas en los mapas / Referência da quadrícula

Pays / Country / Land / Paesi / País

A Österreich, Austria	**CZ** Česká republika	**GR** Elláda/Ελλάς	**M** Malta	**RO** România
AL Shqipëria, Albania	**D** Deutschland	**H** Magyarország, Hungary	**MC** Monaco	**RSM** San Marino
AND Andorra	**DK** Danmark	**HR** Hrvatska, Croatia	**MD** Moldova	**RUS** Rossija/Россия
B Belgique, België	**E** España	**I** Italia	**MK** Makedonija/Македонија	**S** Sverige
BG Balgarija/България	**EST** Eesti	**IRL** Ireland, Éire	**MNE** Crna Gora, Montenegro	**SK** Slovenská republika
BIH Bosna i Hercegovina	**F** France	**IS** Ísland	**N** Norge	**SLO** Slovenija
BY Belarus'/Беларусь	**FIN** Suomi, Finland	**L** Luxembourg, Lëtzebuerg	**NL** Nederland	**SRB** Srbija/Србија
CH Schweiz, Suisse, Svizzera	**FL** Liechtenstein	**LT** Lietuva	**P** Portugal	**TR** Türkiye
CY Kýpros, Kıbrıs	**GB** United Kingdom	**LV** Latvija	**PL** Polska	**UA** Ukraïna/Україна

1 Decembrie *(RO)* ...... 152 **B 4**

A
A Barrela *(E)* .... 56 **D 3**
A Cambra *(E)* .... 56 **C 2**
A Cañiza *(E)* .... 56 **C 4**
A Coruña *(E)* .... 56 **C 1**
A Estrada *(E)* .... 56 **C 3**
A Fonsagrada *(E)* .... 57 **E 2**
A Guarda *(E)* .... 56 **B 5**
A Gudiña *(E)* .... 57 **E 4**
A Laracha *(E)* .... 56 **B 2**
A Merca *(E)* .... 56 **C 4**
A Mezquita *(E)* .... 57 **E 5**
A Pobra de Trives *(E)* .. 57 **E 4**
A Pobra
  do Caramiñal *(E)* ..... 56 **B 3**
A Pontenova *(E)*........ 57 **E 2**
A Ramallosa *(E)* .... 56 **B 4**
A Rúa *(E)*............... 57 **E 4**
A Veiga *(E)* .... 57 **E 4**
Aabybro *(DK)* .... 194 **D 4**
Aachen *(D)* .... 84 **B 5**
Aakirkeby *(DK)*........ 199 **G 4**
Aalborg *(DK)*......... 194 **D 4**
Aalen *(D)* .... 89 **G 4**
Aalestrup *(DK)* .... 194 **D 5**
Aalsmeer *(NL)*.........76 **D 4**
Aalst (Alost) *(B)* .... 78 **C 2**
Aalten *(NL)* .... 77 **F 5**
Aalter *(B)* .... 78 **B 2**
Äänekoski *(FIN)* ...... 191 **H 1**
Aapajärvi *(FIN)* .... 181 **F 4**
Aarau *(CH)* .... 98 **D 2**
Aarberg *(CH)*........... 98 **C 2**
Aarburg *(CH)* .... 98 **D 2**
Aarhus *(DK)* .... 194 **D 5**
Aars *(DK)* .... 194 **D 4**
Aarschot *(B)* .... 78 **D 2**
Aavasaksa *(FIN)* ...... 185 **F 1**
Abades *(E)* .... 64 **A 1**
Abadiño *(E)*............ 58 **D 1**
Abádszalók *(H)* .... 129 **H 2**
Abaliget *(H)*........... 128 **D 5**
Abanilla *(E)* .... 73 **E 2**
Abano Terme *(I)*....... 103 **E 4**
Abaújkér *(H)* .... 127 **E 5**
Abbadia
  San Salvatore *(I)*..... 106 **D 5**
Abbasanta *(I)* ....112 **B 3**
Abbeville *(F)*........... 39 **G 3**
Abbey Town *(GB)* ......31 **E 4**

Abbeyfeale *(IRL)* .... 24 **B 3**
Abbeyleix *(IRL)* .... 25 **E 2**
Abbiategrasso *(I)* ...... 101 **E 4**
Abborrträsk *(S)* .... 184 **D 2**
Abbots Bromley *(GB)*.... 32 **D 4**
Abbotsbury *(GB)*........ 38 **A 1**
Abcoude *(NL)*...........76 **D 4**
Abejar *(E)*............... 58 **D 4**
Abejuela *(E)* .... 65 **G 4**
Abela *(P)*............... 68 **B 3**
Abelvær *(N)*........... 183 **E 3**
Abenberg *(D)* .... 90 **D 4**
Abenójar *(E)* .... 70 **C 2**
Åbenrå *(DK)* .... 198 **B 4**
Abensberg *(D)*..........91 **F 5**
Aberaeron *(GB)* .... 32 **A 5**
Aberdare / Aberdare *(GB)*. 35 **E 1**
Aberdaron *(GB)* .... 32 **A 4**
Aberdaugleddau /
  Milford Haven *(GB)*.... 25 **H 5**
Aberdeen *(GB)*.......... 29 **H 4**
Aberdovey *(GB)* .... 32 **B 5**
Aberfeldy *(GB)* .... 29 **F 5**
Aberfoyle *(GB)* .... 30 **C 1**
Abergavenny *(GB)* ..... 35 **E 1**
Abergele *(GB)*........... 32 **B 3**
Abergwaun /
  Fishguard *(GB)* .... 25 **H 4**
Aberlady *(GB)*...........31 **E 1**
Abermaw *(GB)* .... 32 **B 4**
Aberporth *(GB)* .... 34 **C 1**
Abersoch *(GB)* .... 32 **A 4**
Abertawe /
  Swansea *(GB)* .... 34 **D 2**
Abertillery *(GB)* .... 35 **E 1**
Aberystwyth *(GB)*...... 32 **A 5**
Abetone *(I)* .... 105 **G 3**
Abiego *(E)* .... 59 **H 4**
Abington *(GB)*.......... 35 **H 1**
Abington *(GB)* .... 30 **D 3**
Abisko *(S)*............. 180 **A 3**
Abja-Paluoja *(EST)* ..... 201 **E 4**
Abla *(E)*................. 71 **F 5**
Ablis *(F)*................. 45 **E 2**
Abondance *(F)*...........51 **G 1**
Aboyne *(GB)* .... 29 **G 4**
Abrantes *(P)* .... 62 **C 5**
Abreschviller *(F)* ....47 **G 1**
Abriès *(F)*...............51 **G 5**

Abrud *(RO)* .... 147 **E 5**
Abtenau *(A)*............ 96 **C 3**
Åby *(S)*................ 197 **E 2**
Acâş *(RO)* .... 147 **E 2**
Acâţari *(RO)*........... 147 **G 4**
Acceglio *(I)* .... 104 **B 2**
Accettura *(I)*...........110 **D 4**
Acciaroli *(I)* ....110 **B 5**
Accous *(F)* .... 52 **C 4**
Accrington *(GB)*........ 32 **D 2**
Acebo *(E)* .... 63 **E 4**
Acedo *(E)* .... 59 **E 2**
Acehúche *(E)* .... 63 **E 4**
Acerno *(I)*.............110 **B 4**
Acerra *(I)*............. 109 **H 5**
Aceuchal *(E)* .... 69 **F 2**
Acharnés /
  Αχαρνές *(GR)* .... 165 **H 4**
Acheritou *(CY)* .... 175 **F 3**
Achern *(D)*............. 88 **D 5**
Acheux-
  en-Amiénois *(F)* ...... 39 **H 3**
Achílleio *(GR)* .... 165 **F 1**
Achim *(D)*..............81 **G 5**
Achna *(CY)*........... 175 **E 3**
Achnacroish *(GB)* ..... 28 **D 5**
Achnasheen *(GB)* ..... 28 **D 3**
Aci Castello *(I)* ....115 **G 3**
Aci Trezza *(I)*..........115 **G 3**
Acireale *(I)*............115 **G 3**
Acle *(GB)* .... 37 **E 1**
Acqualagna *(I)* .... 107 **F 3**
Acquapendente *(I)*..... 107 **E 5**
Acquasanta Terme *(I)* .. 107 **G 5**
Acquasparta *(I)* .... 107 **F 5**
Acquaviva
  delle Fonti *(I)* ....111 **E 3**
Acqui-Terme *(I)* .... 104 **D 2**
Acri *(I)*.................113 **G 2**
Ács *(H)*................ 128 **D 1**
Ada *(SRB)* .... 140 **C 2**
Adak *(S)* .... 184 **C 2**
Adámantas *(GR)* ...... 169 **H 4**
Adamclisi *(RO)* .... 153 **E 5**
Adamuz *(E)* .... 70 **C 4**
Adâncata *(RO)* .... 148 **B 2**
Adanero *(E)* .... 64 **A 1**
Adapazarı *(TR)* ....19 **H 1**
Adare *(IRL)* .... 24 **C 3**
Adaševci *(SRB)* .... 137 **H 3**
Adelboden *(CH)* .... 98 **C 4**

Adelfia *(I)* ....111 **E 3**
Adelsheim *(D)* .... 89 **F 3**
Ademuz *(E)* .... 65 **G 3**
Adenau *(D)* .... 88 **C 1**
Adjud *(RO)* .... 148 **D 5**
Admont *(A)*............ 97 **E 3**
Adolfsström *(S)* ...... 183 **H 1**
Adony *(H)*............ 129 **E 3**
Adorf *(D)*..............91 **F 2**
Adra *(E)*................75 **G 3**
Adradas *(E)* .... 59 **E 5**
Adrall *(E)*............... 60 **C 2**
Adrano *(I)*.............115 **F 3**
Adria *(I)*.............. 103 **E 5**
Adunaţii-
  Copăceni *(RO)* ...... 152 **B 4**
Adutiškis *(LT)* .... 205 **H 3**
Aegviidu *(EST)* .... 201 **E 2**
Ænes *(N)*............. 188 **B 4**
Ærǿskøbing *(DK)*..... 198 **C 4**
Aerinó *(GR)* .... 165 **F 1**
Ærǿskøbing *(DK)*..... 198 **C 4**
Aetópetra *(GR)*....... 160 **C 5**
Aetós (Floriná) *(GR)* ... 160 **D 3**
Aetós (Itháki) *(GR)*. ... 164 **C 3**
Aetós
  (Etolia-Arkanía) *(GR)* . 164 **C 3**
Äetsä *(FIN)* .... 191 **F 3**
Afanteia *(CY)* .... 175 **E 3**
Afántou *(GR)* .... 171 **H 3**
Affi *(I)* .... 101 **H 4**
Afjord *(N)* .... 182 **D 4**
Aflenz Kurort *(A)* ..... 97 **F 3**
Afumaţi *(RO)*......... 152 **B 4**
Afyssos *(GR)* .... 165 **G 1**
Áfytos *(GR)* .... 161 **H 5**
Agaete *(E)* ....67 **G 5**
Agás *(RO)*............ 148 **B 4**
Agasegyháza *(H)*....... 129 **F 3**
Agatovo *(BG)* .... 159 **E 1**
Agay *(F)* .... 55 **G 3**
Agazzano *(I)* .... 101 **F 5**
Agde *(F)*............... 54 **A 3**
Agen *(F)* .... 53 **E 1**
Åger *(E)*............... 60 **B 3**
Agerbæk *(DK)* .... 198 **B 3**
Aggius *(I)*.............112 **C 1**
Aggsbach *(A)* .... 97 **F 1**
Aggsbach-Dorf *(A)*..... 97 **F 1**
Aggtelek *(H)* .... 126 **D 5**
Aghia *(GR)* .... 164 **B 1**
Aghíreşu *(RO)* .... 147 **E 3**
Agiá *(GR)* .... 161 **F 5**

Agía Ánna
  (Évvoia) (GR)........ 165 **H 2**
Agía Ánna
  (Voiotía) (GR) .... 165 **G 4**
Agía Efthymía *(GR)*.... 165 **F 3**
Agía Evthymía *(GR)* ... 164 **C 3**
Agía Fotiá *(GR)*....... 173 **E 4**
Agía Galíni *(GR)* ...... 172 **C 4**
Agía Kyriakí (Dytikí Make-
  donía) *(GR)* .... 160 **D 4**
Agía Kyriakí (
  Magnesia) *(GR)*...... 165 **G 2**
Agía Kyriakí
  (Sámos) (GR) .... 167 **F 5**
Agia Marína *(CY)*......174 **D 3**
Agía Marína
  (Aígina) (GR) .... 165 **H 5**
Agía Marína
  (Attikí-Peiraiás) (GR).. 166 **B 4**
Agía Marína
  (Nótio Aigaío) (GR) .. 171 **F 1**
Agía Marína
  (Stereá Elláda) (GR)... 165 **F 2**
Agía Marína (Kríti) *(GR)*. 172 **B 3**
Agia Napa *(CY)*....... 175 **F 3**
Agía Paraskeví
  *(Anatolikí Makedonía
  kai Thráki) (GR)*....... 162 **B 3**
Agía Paraskeví
  (Ípeiros) (GR) .... 160 **C 4**
Agía Paraskeví
  (Vóreio Aigaío) (GR) .. 167 **F 2**
Agía Pelagía
  (Attikí) (GR) .... 169 **E 5**
Agía Pelagía (Kríti) *(GR)* 170 **B 5**
Agía Sofía *(GR)* .... 168 **D 2**
Agía Sotíra *(GR)* ...... 165 **H 4**
Agía Triáda (GR) ...... 172 **D 4**
Agía Triáda
  (Attikí) (GR) .... 165 **H 4**
Agía Triáda
  (Dytikí Elláda) (GR).. 164 **D 5**
Agía Triáda (Kentrikí
  Makedonía) *(GR)* ..... 161 **G 4**
Agía Varvára *(CY)* .....174 **D 4**
Agía Varvára *(GR)* ..... 172 **D 3**
Agíasma *(GR)* .... 162 **C 3**
Agiásos *(GR)* .... 167 **F 2**
*Agios Georgios
  Alamanos (CY)*........174 **C 4**

Agiófyllo *(GR)*.......... 160 **D 5**
Ágioi Anárgyroi *(GR)* ... 168 **D 3**
Ágioi Apóstoloi
  (Attikí) (GR) .... 165 **H 4**
Ágioi Apóstoloi
  (Stereá Elláda) (GR)... 166 **B 3**
Ágioi Theódoroi (Dytikí
  Makedonía) *(GR)* ..... 160 **D 5**
Ágioi Theódoroi
  (Pelopónnisos) (GR).. 165 **G 4**
Ágioi Theódoroi
  (Thessalía) (GR) ..... 165 **G 2**
Agiókampos
  (Stereá Elláda) (GR).. 165 **G 2**
Agiókampos
  (Thessalía) (GR) ..... 161 **G 5**
Agionóri *(GR)* .... 165 **G 5**
Agiopigí *(GR)* .... 165 **E 1**
Agios Amvrosios *(CY)* .. 175 **E 2**
Ágios Andréas *(GR)* .... 168 **D 2**
Agios Andronikos *(CY)* . 175 **F 2**
Agios Athanasios *(CY)*...174 **E 4**
Ágios Athanásios
  (Pélla) (GR) .... 161 **E 3**
Ágios Athanásios
  (Thessaloníki) (GR) ... 161 **F 3**
Ágios Charálampos *(GR)*. 162 **D 3**
Ágios Dimítrios
  (Attiki) (GR) .... 166 **B 4**
Ágios Dimítrios
  (Dytikí Elláda) (GR)... 165 **E 3**
Ágios Dimítrios
  (Pelopónnisos) (GR).. 169 **E 3**
Ágios Dimítrios
  (Stereá Elláda) (GR).. 166 **B 4**
Agios Dometios *(CY)*....174 **D 3**
Ágios Efstrátios *(GR)* .. 166 **C 1**
Ágios Epiktitos *(CY)*....174 **D 2**
Ágios Fokás *(GR)* ..... 171 **G 2**
Ágios Geórgios
  (Iónia Nisiá) (GR) .... 165 **G 2**
Agios Georgios
  (Keryneia) (CY) ....174 **D 2**
Ágios Geórgios
  (Kríti) *(GR)* .... 173 **E 2**
Agios Georgios
  (Páfos) (CY) ....174 **B 4**
Ágios Geórgios
  (Stereá Elláda) (GR) .. 165 **G 2**
*Agios Georgios
  Alamanos (CY)*........174 **C 4**
Ágios Germanós *(GR)* .. 160 **D 3**

Ágios Górdios (GR)..... 164 A 1
Agios Ilerion (CY) ....174 D 3
Ágios Ioánnis (Kríti) (GR) .... 172 B 3
Agios Ioannis (Lefkoşa) (CY) ...174 D 3
Ágios Ioánnis (Magnisía) (GR)....... 165 G 1
Agios Ioannis (Óros Ólimbos) (CY) ...174 C 4
Ágios Ioánnis (Pelopónnisos) (GR) .. 169 E 4
Ágios Ioánnis (Voiotía) (GR) .... 165 G 4
Ágios Konstantínos (GR). 165 G 3
Ágios Kosmás (Anatolikí Makedonía kai Thráki) (GR) .... 162 C 2
Ágios Kosmás (Dytikí Makedonía) (GR)..... 160 D 4
Ágios Léon (GR)...... 164 C 5
Ágios Márkos (GR) ... 161 G 2
Agios Neofytos (CY).....174 B 4
Ágios Nikítas (GR)...... 164 C 2
Ágios Nikólaos / Άγιος Νικόλαος (Kríti) (GR) . 173 E 3
Ágios Nikólaos (Attikí) (GR) .... 165 G 5
Ágios Nikólaos (Dytikí Elláda) (GR) ... 164 C 2
Ágios Nikólaos (Ípeiros) (GR)........ 160 B 5
Ágios Nikólaos (Kentrikí Makedonía) (GR)..... 161 H 4
Ágios Nikólaos (Lakonía) (GR)....... 168 D 3
Ágios Nikólaos (Messinía) (GR)...... 168 D 3
Ágios Nikólaos (Stereá Elláda) (GR) .. 165 E 3
Ágios Panteleímonas (GR).. 161 E 4
Ágios Pétros (GR) ..... 168 D 2
Ágios Pródromos (GR). 161 H 4
Agios Sergios (CY) ... 175 F 3
Ágios Stéfanos (Attikí) (GR) .... 165 H 4
Ágios Stéfanos (Nótio Aigaío) (GR) ... 170 C 1
Agios Theodoros (Karpasia) (CY) ..... 175 F 2
Agios Theodoros (Larnaka) (CY)...174 D 4
Ágios Theódoros (Óros Ólimbos) (CY) ...174 C 4
Agios Therapon (CY)...174 C 4
Ágios Thomás (Kríti) (GR). 172 D 3
Ágios Thomás (Stereá Elláda) (GR) .. 165 H 4
Ágios Vasileios (CY)...174 D 3
Ágios Vasíleios (Thessaloníki) (GR) .. 161 G 3
Ágios Vasíleios (Voiotía) (GR) .... 165 G 4
Ágioi Déka (GR) ... 172 D 4
Agira (I)...........115 F 3
Aglangia (Aglantzia) (CY).174 D 3
Åglen (BG) .... 155 F 2
Aglona (LV) .... 203 G 4
Agnita (RO) .... 147 G 5
Agnone (I)........... 109 G 3
Agnóntas (GR) ..... 165 H 2
Agoitz (E) .... 59 F 2
Agolada (E) .... 56 C 3
Agon-Coutainville (F) .. 38 B 5
Agordo (I) .... 103 E 2
Agost (E)............ 73 F 2
Ágra (GR) .... 167 E 2
Agramunt (E) ...... 60 B 3
Agrapidochóri (GR) .. 164 D 4
Agrate Brianza (I) ... 101 E 4
Ágreda (E)........ 59 E 4
Agreliá (GR) ...... 161 E 5
Agriá (GR) .... 165 G 1
Agrigento (I)........114 D 4
Agriliá (GR) .... 164 D 3
Agrínio / Αγρίνιο (GR) .. 164 D 3

Agriovótano (GR) ...... 165 G 2
Agropoli (I) ....110 B 5
Agros (CY) ....174 C 4
Aguadulce (E)........ 70 B 5
Aguadulce (E).......75 H 3
Aguaviva (E) .... 65 H 1
Agudo (E) .... 70 B 1
Águeda (P)........... 62 B 3
Aguiar (P)............ 68 C 3
Aguiar da Beira (P) ...... 62 D 2
Águila, cueva del (E) .. 63 H 4
Aguilafuente (E) .... 64 B 1
Aguilar (E) .... 70 C 5
Aguilar de Campóo (E) .. 58 B 2
Aguilar del Alfambra (E). 65 G 2
Águilas (E) .... 71 H 5
Agurain / Salvatierra (E). 59 E 2
Ahaus (D)............ 84 C 2
Åheim (N)........... 188 B 1
Ahigal (E) .... 63 F 4
Ahjärvi (FIN) .... 193 G 2
Ahlainen (FIN) ..... 191 E 3
Ahlbeck (D)......... 83 G 3
Ahlen (D)........... 84 D 3
Ahlhorn (D).........81 F 5
Ahrensbök (D) ...... 82 B 3
Ahrensburg (D)...... 82 B 4
Ahrweiler (D)........ 84 C 5
Ähtäri (FIN) .... 191 G 1
Ahtopol (BG)........ 157 F 5
Ahun (F)............ 49 G 2
Åhus (S) .... 199 G 3
Ahvenselkä (FIN).... 181 F 4
Aiani (GR).......... 161 E 4
Aiánteio (GR) .... 165 H 4
Aichach (D) .... 95 F 1
Aidenbach (D) ...... 96 B 1
Aidone (I)...........115 E 4
Aïdónia (GR) .... 165 F 5
Aigeiroúses (GR) .... 165 G 4
Aigen im Mühlkreis (A) .. 96 D 1
Aigiáli (GR) .... 170 D 2
Aigialousa (CY) ..... 175 G 2
Aigiés (GR)......... 168 D 4
Aígina (GR) .... 165 H 5
Aigínio (GR)........ 161 F 4
Aígio / Αίγιο (GR)... 165 E 4
Aigle (CH).......... 98 C 4
Aignan (F) .... 52 D 2
Aignay-le-Duc (F) ...... 46 C 3
Aigósthena (GR) . 165 G 4
Aigre (F)............ 48 D 2
Aigrefeuille-d'Aunis (F).. 48 C 2
Aigrefeuille-sur-Maine (F)....... 43 F 5
Aiguablava (E)........61 F 2
Aiguebelette-le-Lac (F) .51 E 3
Aiguebelle (F)........51 F 3
Aigueperse (F)....... 50 A 2
Aigues-Mortes (F)..... 54 B 2
Aiguilles (F).........51 G 5
Aiguillon (F) .... 52 D 1
Aigurande (F)........ 49 G 1
Ailefroide (F)........51 F 4
Aillant-sur-Tholon (F) .. 45 G 3
Ailly-le-Haut-Clocher (F). 39 G 3
Ailly-sur-Noye (F) .... 39 H 4
Aimargues (F)....... 54 C 2
Aime-la-Plagne (F).....51 G 3
Ainaži (LV) .... 202 D 1
Ainhoa (F) .... 52 A 3
Ainola (FIN) .... 191 H 4
Ainsa (E) .... 60 A 2
Ainsdale (GB) ...... 32 C 2
Ainzón (E) .... 59 F 4
Airaines (F) .... 39 G 3
Airasca (I).......... 100 B 5
Airdrie (GB)........ 30 D 2
Aire-sur-la-Lys (F) .... 39 H 2
Aire-sur-l'Adour (F)... 52 C 2
Airisto (FIN) .... 191 F 5
Airolo (CH) .... 99 E 4
Airvault (F) .... 43 H 5
Aistere (LV) .... 202 A 3
Aisými (GR)........ 163 E 3
Aiterhofen (D).......91 G 5
Aitolikó (GR) ...... 164 D 3

Aitrach (D) .... 95 E 2
Aiud (RO) .... 147 F 5
Aix-en-Othe (F) .... 45 G 2
Aix-en-Provence (F)... 55 E 2
Aix-les-Bains (F)........51 E 3
Aixe-sur-Vienne (F) ... 49 F 3
Aizenay (F)........... 43 F 5
Aizkraukle (LV)....... 203 E 4
Aizpute (LV) .... 202 A 3
Ajaccio (F) .... 55 G 5
Ajaureforsen (S)....... 183 H 2
Ajdanovac (SRB) ..... 143 E 2
Ajdovščina (SLO)...... 134 B 3
Ajka (H) .... 128 C 3
Ajo (E) .... 58 C 1
Ajos (FIN) .... 185 G 2
Ajtos / Айтос (BG).... 159 H 1
Akademija (LT)....... 205 E 4
Akaki (CY) ....174 D 3
Akanthou (CY) ...... 175 E 2
Äkäsjokisuu (FIN).... 180 D 4
Äkäslompolo (FIN) ... 180 D 4
Akasztó (H) .... 129 F 3
Aken (D) .... 86 B 3
Akriní (GR) .... 161 E 4
Akrogiáli (GR)....... 161 H 3
Akropótamos (GR) ... 162 B 3
Akrotiri (CY) ....174 C 5
Akrotíri (GR) .... 170 C 3
Aksakovo (BG) ...... 157 F 2
Akujärvi (FIN) ...... 177 G 5
Akureyri (IS) .... 178 C 2
Ål (N) .... 188 D 4
Ala (I) .... 101 H 3
Alà dei Sardi (I).......112 C 2
Ala di Stura (I)....... 100 B 4
Ala-Honkajoki (FIN) ... 191 F 2
Ala-Vuokki (FIN) .... 187 G 3
Alacant / Alicante (E).... 73 F 2
Alaejos (E) .... 63 H 1
Alagna Valsesia (I)..... 100 C 3
Alagón (E) .... 59 G 4
Alahärmä (FIN) ..... 185 F 5
Alaior (E) ....67 H 2
Alajärvi (FIN) ...... 191 G 1
Alakylä (FIN) .... 180 D 4
Alalkomenés (GR) ... 165 G 3
Alameda (E) .... 70 C 5
Alamillo (E) .... 70 B 2
Alaminos (CY) ...... 175 E 4
Alampra (CY) ....174 D 4
Alanäs (S) .... 183 G 4
Alandroal (P)........ 69 E 2
Alange (E) .... 69 G 2
Alanís (E) .... 69 G 3
Alanta (LT) .... 205 G 3
Alapitkä (FIN) ...... 187 F 5
Alar del Rey (E) ..... 58 A 3
Alaraz (E) .... 63 H 2
Alarcón (E) .... 65 E 4
Alaşehir (TR)........19 H 3
Alassio (I).......... 104 C 3
Alastaro (FIN) ...... 191 F 4
Alatoz (E) .... 65 G 5
Alatri (I) .... 109 F 3
Alavere (EST) .... 201 E 2
Alavieska (FIN) ..... 185 G 4
Alavus (FIN)........ 191 G 1
Alba (I) .... 104 C 2
Alba Adriatica (I)..... 107 H 5
Alba de Tormes (E).... 63 G 2
Alba Iulia (RO) ...... 147 F 5
Albacete (E)......... 71 H 1
Albacken (S) .... 190 B 1
Älbæk (DK) .... 195 E 3

Albaida (E) .... 73 F 1
Albaladejo (E)........... 71 F 2
Albalate de Cinca (E) .. 60 A 3
Albalate de las Nogueras (E).... 65 E 3
Albalate del Arzobispo (E)..... 65 H 1
Alban (F)............. 53 H 2
Albánchez (E)......... 71 G 5
Albano di Lucania (I) ...110 D 4
Albano Laziale (I) ..... 109 E 3
Albarca (E) .... 60 B 4
Albarracín (E)........ 65 F 2
Albatana (E) .... 71 H 2
Albatera (E) .... 73 F 2
Albena (BG) .... 157 G 2
Albenga (I)........... 104 C 3
Albens (F)............51 E 2
Alberga (S)........... 197 E 1
Albergaria-a-Velha (P).. 62 B 2
Alberic (E) .... 65 H 5
Albernoa (P) .... 68 C 4
Alberobello (I) ....111 F 3
Albersdorf (D) ....81 G 3
Albert (F) .... 39 H 3
Albertirsa (H) .... 129 F 2
Albertkázmérpuszta (H). 128 C 1
Albertville (F) ....51 F 3
Albeşti-Paleologu (RO). 152 B 3
Albestroff (F).........41 F 5
Albi (F) .... 53 G 2
Albina (I) .... 100 C 4
Albinia (I) .... 108 B 1
Albino (I) .... 101 F 3
Albissola Marina (I).... 104 D 3
Albocàsser (E) .... 66 A 1
Alboloduy (E) .... 72 B 5
Albolote (E) .... 70 D 5
Albona / Labin (HR) . 134 B 4
Alborea (E) .... 65 G 5
Albota (RO) .... 151 H 3
Albox (E)............ 71 G 5
Albstadt-Ebingen (D) .. 94 C 2
Albstadt-Tailfingen (D).. 89 F 5
Albufeira (P) .... 68 C 5
Albujón (E) .... 73 E 3
Albuñol (E).......... 75 G 3
Alburquerque (E) .... 69 E 1
Alby (S) .... 190 A 1
Alby-sur-Chéran (F) ...51 F 2
Alcácer do Sal (P) .... 68 B 2
Alcáçovas (P) .... 68 C 2
Alcadozo (E) .... 71 G 2
Alcafozes (E) .... 63 E 4
Alcains (P)........... 62 D 4
Alcalá de Guadaíra (E). 69 G 5
Alcalá de Henares (E).. 64 C 2
Alcalá de la Selva (E) .. 65 H 2
Alcalá de los Gazules (E)..74 B 4
Alcalá de Xivert (E) .. 66 A 1
Alcalá del Júcar (E) ... 65 F 5
Alcalá del Río (E) .... 69 G 5
Alcalá la Real (E) .... 70 D 5
Alcalfar (E)...........67 H 2
Alcamo (I) ....114 C 3
Alcampell (E) .... 60 A 3
Alcanar (E) .... 66 B 1
Alcanede (P) .... 62 A 5
Alcanena (P) .... 62 B 5
Alcanhões (P) .... 62 B 5
Alcaníces (E) .... 57 F 5
Alcañiz (E) .... 60 A 5
Alcántara (E) .... 63 E 5
Alcantarilha (P) ..... 68 C 5
Alcantarilla (E) ...... 73 E 3
Alcaracejos (E) ...... 70 B 3
Alcaraz (E) .... 71 F 2
Alcaria Ruiva (P)..... 68 D 4
Alcarràs (E) .... 60 B 4
Alcaudete (E) .... 70 D 5
Alcaudete de la Jara (E). 63 H 5
Alcázar de San Juan (E). 64 D 4
Alceda (E) .... 58 B 1
Alcester (GB) .... 32 D 5
Alcira / Alzira (E) .... 65 H 5
Alcoba de los Montes (E). 64 A 5

Alcobaça (P) .... 62 A 5
Alcobendas (E)........ 64 C 2
Alcocer (E) .... 64 D 2
Alcochete (P) .... 68 B 2
Alcoi / Alcoy (E) ..... 73 F 1
Alcolea (E) .... 70 C 4
Alcolea de Cinca (E)... 60 A 3
Alcolea del Pinar (E).. 65 E 1
Alcolea del Río (E)...... 69 G 4
Alconchel (E) .... 69 E 2
Alcorisa (E) .... 65 H 1
Alcossebre (E) .... 66 A 2
Alcoutim (P) .... 68 D 5
Alcover (E) .... 60 C 4
Alcoy / Alcoi (E) ..... 73 F 1
Alcsútdoboz (H) ..... 129 E 2
Alcubierre (E) .... 59 H 4
Alcubilla de Avellaneda (E) ..... 58 C 5
Alcublas (E) .... 65 H 4
Alcúdia (E) ....67 F 2
Alcudia de Guadix (E) .. 71 E 5
Alcuéscar (E) .... 69 G 1
Aldea del Cano (E) ... 69 F 1
Aldea del Fresno (E)... 64 B 3
Aldea del Rey (E)..... 70 D 2
Aldea Quintana (E) ... 70 B 4
Aldeacentenera (E) ... 63 G 5
Aldeanueva de Ebro (E). 59 E 3
Aldeanueva de la Vera (E) .... 63 G 4
Aldeanueva del Camino (E) ...... 63 G 3
Aldeburgh (GB) ...... 37 E 2
Aldeia da Ponte (P)... 63 E 3
Aldeia Gavinha (P) ... 68 B 1
Aldershot (GB) ...... 35 H 2
Aldinci (MK) .... 145 F 1
Aledo (E) .... 71 H 4
Aleksa Šantić (SRB).... 137 H 1
Aleksandrovac (Kruševac) (SRB) ..... 143 E 2
Aleksandrovac (Požerevac) (SRB) .....141 E 5
Aleksandrovo (Jambol) (BG) ...... 159 H 2
Aleksandrovo (Loveč) (BG)........ 156 A 3
Aleksandrovo (Tårgovište) (BG)...... 156 D 3
Aleksandrów Kujawski (PL)........117 H 5
Aleksandrów Łódzki (PL)......... 122 B 2
Aleksin (RUS) ....7 G 3
Aleksinac / Алексинац (SRB) .... 143 F 2
Alektora (CY) ....174 C 5
Ålen (N)............ 189 F 1
Alençon (F) .... 44 B 2
Alenquer (P) .... 68 B 1
Alepochóri (Attikí) (GR) .... 165 G 4
Alepochóri (Pelopónnisos) (GR).. 168 D 2
Aléria (F) .... 55 H 4
Alès (F) .... 54 B 1
Ales (I) ....112 B 4
Aleşd (RO) .... 146 D 3
Alessandria (I) ...... 100 D 5
Alessandria della Rocca (I)........114 C 4
Ålesund (N) .... 188 C 1
Alexándreia / Αλεξάνδρεια (GR) ... 161 F 3
Alexandria (GB) ..... 30 C 1
Alexandria (RO) ..... 151 H 5
Alexandroúpoli / Αλεξανδρούπολη (GR). 163 E 3
Alexandru Vlahuţă (RO). 148 D 4
Alf (D) .... 88 C 1
Alfajarín (E) .... 59 G 5
Alfambra (E)........ 65 G 2
Alfambra (P) .... 68 B 5
Alfândega da Fé (P) .. 63 E 1
Alfaro (E) .... 59 F 4

Alfarràs (E) .... 60 B 3
Alfatar (BG) .... 152 D 5
Alfaz del Pí / L'Alfàs del Pí (E) .... 66 A 5
Alfedena (I) .... 109 G 3
Alfeizerão (P) .... 62 A 5
Alfeld (Hildesheim) (D).. 85 G 2
Alfeld (Nürnberger Land) (D).91 E 4
Alfonsine (I)........... 107 E 1
Alford (Aberdeen) (GB).. 29 G 4
Alford (Lincoln) (GB) .... 33 G 3
Alfreton (GB) .... 33 E 3
Alfta (S) .... 190 A 3
Algaida (E)...........67 F 3
Algar (E) ....74 B 3
Algar de Palancia (E) .. 65 H 4
Ålgård (N) .... 194 B 1
Algarinejo (E) .... 70 C 5
Algarrobo (E) ....75 E 3
Algatocín (E).........74 C 4
Algeciras (E) ....74 C 5
Algemesí (E) .... 65 H 5
Alghero (I)..........112 B 2
Alginet (E) .... 65 H 5
Algodonales (E).......74 C 3
Algora (E).......... 64 D 1
Algoz (P)........... 68 C 5
Algyő (H) .... 129 G 4
Alhama de Almería (E).. 72 B 5
Alhama de Aragón (E).. 59 E 5
Alhama de Granada (E)..75 F 3
Alhama de Murcia (E) .. 71 H 4
Alhambra (E) .... 71 E 2
Alhaurín el Grande (E)..74 D 3
Alhóndiga (E)........ 64 D 2
Alì Terme (I)........115 G 2
Alià (E) .... 63 H 5
Alia (I) ....114 D 3
Aliaga (E) .... 65 H 2
Aliaguilla (E) .... 65 G 4
Alíartos / Αλίαρτος (GR). 165 G 3
Alibunar (SRB).......141 E 3
Alicante / Alacant (E).. 73 F 2
Alicún de Ortega (E) ... 71 E 4
Alife (I) .... 109 G 4
Alijó (P) .... 62 D 1
Álika (GR) .... 168 D 4
Alikianós (GR)....... 172 B 3
Alimiá (GR) .... 171 G 3
Alimpeşti (RO) ...... 151 F 2
Alingsås (S) .... 195 G 3
Alinyà (E) .... 60 C 2
Alise-Ste-Reine (F) ... 46 C 4
Aliseda (E) .... 63 E 5
Alistráti (GR) .... 162 B 2
Alivéri (GR) .... 166 B 3
Alizava (LT) .... 205 F 1
Aljezur (P) .... 68 B 5
Aljucén (E) .... 69 F 1
Aljustrel (P) .... 68 C 4
Alkmaar (NL).........76 D 3
Alkyón (GR) .... 162 D 3
Allaire (F) .... 43 E 5
Allanche (F) .... 50 A 4
Alland (A) .... 97 G 2
Allariz (E) .... 56 B 4
Alleen (N) .... 194 B 2
Alleghe (I) .... 103 E 2
Allègre (F) .... 50 B 4
Allensbach (D) ...... 94 C 3
Allentsteig (A) ...... 92 D 3
Allepuz (E) .... 65 H 2
Allersberg (D).........91 E 4
Allershausen (D) ..... 95 G 1
Alleuze, château d' (F) . 50 A 4
Allevard (F) ....51 F 3
Allinge (DK) .... 199 G 4
Alloa (GB) .... 30 D 1
Allonnes (F) .... 43 H 4
Alloza (E) .... 65 H 1
Allstedt (D) .... 86 A 4
Almacelles (E) ...... 60 A 3
Almáchar (E).........75 E 3

A
B
C
D
E
F
G
H
I
J
K
L
M
N
O
P
Q
R
S
T
U
V
W
X
Y
Z

A

Almada (P).............. 68 A 2
Almadén (E) .... 70 B 2
Almadén de la Plata (E). . 69 G 4
Almadenejos (E) .... 70 B 2
Almagro (E)............. 70 D 2
Almajano (E)............ 59 E 4
Almancil (P)........... 68 C 5
Almansa (E) .... 73 E 1
Almanza (E)............ 57 H 3
Almaraz (E) .... 63 G 4
Almargen (E)...........74 D 3
Almarza (E)............ 58 D 4
Almassora /
  Almazora (E) .... 66 A 2
Almazán (E)........... 58 D 5
Almazora /
  Almassora (E) .... 66 A 2
Almedinilla (E) .... 70 D 5
Almeida (P)........... 63 E 2
Almeida de Sayago (E) . . 63 F 1
Almeirim (P)........... 68 B 1
Almelo (NL)........... 77 G 4
Almenar (E)........... 60 B 3
Almenar de Soria (E) .... 59 E 5
Almenara (E)........... 66 A 3
Almendral (E)........... 69 E 2
Almendralejo (E)........... 69 F 2
Almere-Stad (NL) ...... 77 E 4
Almería (E)........... 72 B 5
Almerimar (E)...........75 H 3
Almese (I)........... 100 B 5
Älmhult (S) .... 195 H 5
Almodôvar (P) .... 68 C 4
Almodóvar
  del Campo (E) .... 70 C 2
Almodóvar del Pinar (E) . 65 F 4
Almodóvar del Río (E)... 70 B 4
Almogía (E)...........74 D 3
Almoguera (E)........... 64 D 3
Almoharín (E)........... 69 G 1
Almonacid
  de la Sierra...........59 F 5
Almonacid de Toledo (E). 64 B 4
Almonacid de Zorita (E) . 64 D 3
Almonaster la Real (E).... 69 E 4
Almonte (E)........... 69 F 5
Almoradí (E)........... 73 E 3
Almorox (E)........... 64 A 3
Almourol, castelo de (P). 62 B 4
Almudévar (E)........... 59 H 4
Almuñécar (E)...........75 F 3
Almuradiel (E) .... 71 E 2
Almyró (GR)........... 168 C 3
Almyropótamos (GR) .. 166 B 4
Almyrós / Αλμυρός (GR). 165 F 2
Alness (GB) .... 29 E 3
Alnö (S)........... 190 B 2
Alnwick (GB)...........31 G 3
Aloja (LV)........... 203 E 1
Alona (CY)...........174 D 4
Alónia (GR)........... 161 F 4
Alónnisos (GR)........... 165 H 2
Álora (E)...........74 D 3
Alosno (E)........... 69 E 4
Alozaina (E)...........74 D 3
Alp (E)........... 60 D 2
Alpalhão (P)........... 62 D 5
Alpbach (A)........... 95 G 3
Alpe-d'Huez (F)...........51 F 4
Alpedrinha (P)........... 62 D 4
Alpera (E)........... 72 D 1
Alphen aan den Rijn (NL).76 D 4
Alpiarça (P)........... 68 B 1
Alpignano (I)........... 100 C 5
Alpirsbach (D) .... 89 E 5
Alpua (FIN)........... 185 H 3
Alqueva (P)........... 68 D 3
Als (DK)........... 195 E 5
Alsasua / Altsasu (E)... 59 E 2
Alsdorf (D)........... 84 B 5
Alsėdžiai (LT)........... 204 C 1
Alsen (S)........... 183 F 5
Alsfeld (D)........... 85 F 5
Alsleben (D)........... 86 B 3
Alsóörs (H)........... 128 D 3
Alsótold (H)........... 129 F 1
Alstahaug (N)........... 183 F 1

Alston (GB) ....31 F 4
Alt Ruppin (D) .... 83 E 5
Alta (N)...........176 D 3
Altamura (I)...........111 E 3
Altastenberg (D) .... 85 E 4
Altaussee (A) .... 96 C 3
Altavilla Milicia (I)...........114 D 2
Altdöbern (D)........... 87 E 3
Altdorf (CH) .... 99 E 3
Altdorf
  bei Nürnberg (D)....91 E 4
Altea (E) .... 66 A 5
Altedo (I)........... 106 D 1
Altena (D)........... 84 D 4
Altenahr (D)........... 84 C 5
Altenau (D)........... 85 H 3
Altenberg (D)........... 86 D 5
Altenberge (D)........... 84 D 2
Altenburg (D)........... 86 C 4
Altenholz (D)...........81 H 2
Altenhundem (D)........... 85 E 4
Altenkirchen (D) .... 83 F 1
Altenkirchen
  in Westerwald (D).... 84 D 5
Altenmarkt
  an der Alz (D) ...... 95 H 2
Altenmarkt bei
  Sankt Gallen (A)... 97 E 3
Altenmarkt
  im Pongau (A) ...... 96 C 3
Altenstadt (D)........... 95 E 2
Altensteig (D)........... 89 E 5
Altentreptow (D)........... 83 F 3
Altenwalde (D)...........81 F 3
Alter do Chão (P)........... 68 D 1
Altglashütten (D) ...... 94 B 2
Altheim (A)........... 96 C 2
Althofen (A)........... 97 E 4
Altimir (BG)........... 155 E 2
Altkirch (F)...........47 G 3
Altlandsberg (D)........... 86 D 1
Altlengbach (A)........... 97 G 2
Altmünster (A)........... 96 C 2
Altnaharra (GB) .... 26 A 5
Alto Campoo (E) .... 58 A 2
Alton (GB)........... 35 H 3
Altopascio (I)........... 105 G 4
Altorricón (E)........... 60 A 3
Altötting (D)........... 95 H 2
Altrincham (GB)........... 32 D 3
Altsasu / Alsasua (E)..... 59 E 2
Altshausen (D)........... 94 D 2
Altstätten (CH)........... 99 G 2
Altura (E)........... 65 H 4
Altweilnau (D)........... 89 E 1
Altzola (E)........... 59 E 1
Alūksne (LV)........... 203 G 2
Aluniş (RO)........... 147 H 3
Alustante (E)........... 65 F 2
Alva (P)........... 62 B 4
Alvaiázere (P)........... 62 B 4
Alvalade (P)........... 68 C 3
Alvdal (N)........... 189 F 2
Älvdalen (S)........... 189 H 3
Alverca do Ribatejo (P). . 68 B 1
Alvesta (S)........... 195 H 5
Alvignac (F)........... 49 G 5
Alvito (P)........... 68 C 3
Älvkarleby (S)........... 190 B 4
Alvor (P)........... 68 B 5
Älvros (S)........... 190 A 2
Älvsbyn (S)........... 185 E 2
Alwernia (PL)........... 125 F 1
Alykés (GR)........... 164 C 4
Alykí (GR)........... 170 C 2
Alyth (GB)........... 29 F 5
Alytus (LT)........... 205 E 5
Alzenau
  in Unterfranken (D) .. 89 F 1
Alzey (D)........... 88 D 2
Alzira / Alcira (E)........... 65 H 5
Alzon (F)........... 54 A 2
Alzonne (F)........... 53 G 3
Amadora (P)........... 68 A 2
Åmål (S)........... 195 G 1
Amalfi (I)........... 109 H 5

Amaliáda /
  Αμαλιάδα (GR)....... 164 D 5
Amaliápoli (GR)........... 165 G 2
Amance (F)...........47 E 3
Amancey (F)...........47 E 5
Amandola (I)........... 107 G 5
Amantea (I)...........113 B 3
Amara (RO)........... 152 D 3
Amarante (P)........... 62 C 1
Amárantos (GR)........... 160 C 4
Amărăşti (RO)........... 151 G 3
Amărăştii de Jos (RO) . . 151 G 5
Amareleja (P)........... 69 E 3
Amares (P)........... 56 C 5
Amargeti (CY)...........174 B 4
Amárynthos (GR)........... 165 H 3
Amatrice (I)........... 107 G 5
Amay (B)........... 79 E 3
Ambarès-et-Lagrave (F). 48 C 4
Ambasaguas (E)........... 57 H 3
Ambazac (F)........... 49 F 2
Amberg (D)...........91 F 4
Ambérieu-en-Bugey (F).51 E 2
Ambert (F)........... 50 B 3
Ambierle (F)........... 50 B 2
Amble (GB)...........31 G 3
Ambleside (GB)...........31 E 5
Amboise (F)........... 44 C 4
Ambra (I)........... 106 D 4
Ambrières-les-Vallées (F). 43 H 2
Ameixial (P)........... 68 C 5
Amelia (I)........... 108 D 1
Amélie-
  les-Bains-Palalda (F).. 53 H 5
Amelinghausen (D) .....81 H 5
Amer (E)...........61 E 2
Amerongen (NL)........... 77 E 5
Amersfoort (NL)........... 77 E 4
Amersham (GB)........... 36 B 4
Amesbury (GB)........... 35 G 3
Amfíkleia (GR)........... 165 F 3
Amfilochía (GR)........... 164 D 2
Amfípoli (GR)........... 161 H 3
Amfissa / Άμφισσα (GR). 165 F 3
Amiens (F)........... 39 H 3
Amilly (F)........... 45 F 3
Åmli (N)........... 194 D 1
Amlwch (GB)........... 32 A 3
Ammanford (GB)........... 34 D 1
Ämmänsaari (FIN)........... 187 F 2
Ammarnäs (S)........... 183 H 1
Ammochóri (GR)........... 160 D 3
Ammóchostos / Gazimağusa
  (Famagusta) (CY)..... 175 F 3
Ammótopos (GR)........... 164 C 1
Ammoudára (GR)........... 170 B 5
Ammoudáres (GR)........... 173 E 4
Ammoulianí (GR)........... 162 B 4
Amorbach (D)........... 89 F 2
Amorebieta (E)........... 58 D 1
Amorgós (GR)........... 170 D 2
Åmot (N)........... 188 C 5
Åmot (N)........... 189 F 2
Åmot (S)........... 189 E 5
Åmot (S)........... 190 B 4
Åmotfors (S)........... 189 G 5
Amou (F)........... 52 B 2
Ampelákia (GR)........... 161 F 5
Ampeleía (GR)........... 165 F 1
Ampelikou (CY)...........174 C 3
Ampelónia (GR)........... 168 C 2
Ampelónas (GR)........... 161 F 5
Ampezzo (I)........... 103 G 2
Ampfing (D)........... 95 H 2
Amphion (F)...........51 F 1
Amplepuis (F)........... 50 C 2
Amposta (E)........... 60 B 5
Ampthill (GB)........... 36 C 3
Ampudia (E)........... 58 B 3
Ampuero (E)........... 58 C 1
Amriswil (CH)........... 99 F 1
Amsele (S)........... 184 D 3
Amstelveen (NL)...........76 D 4
Amsterdam (NL)...........76 D 4
Amstetten (A)........... 97 E 2
Amurrio (E)........... 58 D 2
Amusco (E)........... 58 A 4

Amvrosía (GR) .... 162 D 2
Amygdaleónas (GR).... 162 B 3
Amýntaio (GR)........... 161 E 3
Amzacea (RO)........... 153 F 5
An Cabhán /
  Cavan (IRL) .... 23 E 4
An Cóbh / Cobh (IRL) .. 24 D 4
An Droichead Nua /
  Newbridge (IRL) ...... 25 F 2
An Longfort /
  Longford (IRL) ...... 23 E 4
An Muileann gCearr /
  Mullingar (IRL) ...... 23 E 5
An Nás / Naas (IRL).... 25 F 1
An tAonach /
  Nenagh (IRL)........ 24 D 2
An Uaimh / Navan (IRL). 23 F 5
Åna Sira (N) .... 194 B 2
Anadia (P) .... 62 B 3
Anáfi (GR)........... 170 D 3
Anafonítria (GR)........... 164 C 4
Anafotida (CY)........... 175 E 4
Anagni (I)........... 109 E 3
Análipsi
  (Nótio Aigaío) (GR)... 171 E 3
Análipsi
  (Pelopónnisos) (GR).. 168 C 3
Anan''iv (UA)...........13 F 2
Anárgyroi (GR)........... 161 E 3
Anarita (CY)...........174 B 4
Anascaul (IRL)........... 24 A 4
Änäset (S)........... 185 E 4
Anatolí (GR)........... 173 E 4
Anávatos (GR)........... 167 E 3
Anávra (Kardítsa) (GR).. 165 E 2
Anávra (Magnisía) (GR). 165 F 2
Anávyssos (GR)........... 165 H 5
Ancenis (F)........... 43 G 4
Ancerville (F)........... 46 D 1
Anchuras (E)........... 63 H 5
Ancona (I)........... 107 G 3
Ancy-le-Franc (F)........... 45 H 3
Anda (N)........... 188 C 2
Andalo (I)........... 101 H 3
Åndalsnes (N)........... 188 D 1
Andebu (N)........... 195 E 1
Andelot (F)........... 46 D 2
Andenes (N)........... 179 G 1
Andenne (B)........... 78 D 3
Anderlues (B)........... 78 C 3
Andermatt (CH)........... 99 E 3
Andernach (D)........... 88 D 1
Andernos-les-Bains (F). . 48 B 5
Anderstorp (S)........... 195 G 4
Andoain (E)........... 59 E 1
Andocs (H)........... 128 D 4
Andorno Micca (I)........... 100 C 4
Andorra (E)........... 65 H 1
Andorra la Vella (AND) . . 60 C 1
Andosilla (E)........... 59 E 3
Andover (GB)........... 35 G 2
Andrășești (RO)........... 152 D 3
Andratx (E)...........67 E 3
Andravída (GR)........... 164 D 4
Andrespol (PL)........... 122 B 2
Andretta (I)...........110 C 3
Andria (I)...........110 D 3
Andrijevica (MNE)........... 139 H 4
Andrioniškis (LT)........... 205 F 2
Andrítsaina (GR)........... 164 D 5
Ándros (GR)........... 166 C 5
Andrychów (PL)........... 125 F 2
Andrzejówka (PL)........... 125 H 3
Andselv (N)...........176 B 4
Andújar (E)........... 70 D 4
Anduze (F)........... 54 B 1
Aneby (S)........... 195 H 3
Anet (F)........... 39 G 5
Angastina (CY)........... 175 E 3
Ånge (S)........... 183 F 5
Ängelholm (S)........... 195 G 5
Angeli (FIN)........... 177 H 5
Angelochóri (GR)........... 161 F 3
Angelókastro (GR) ...... 164 D 3

Anger (A) .... 97 F 3
Angera (I)........... 100 D 3
Angermünde (D)........... 83 G 5
Angern
  an der March (A). ... 97 H 1
Angers (F) .... 43 H 4
Angerville (F) .... 45 E 2
Anghiari (I)........... 107 E 3
Angísta (GR)........... 162 B 3
Angítis (GR)........... 162 B 2
Anglès (E)...........61 E 2
Anglès (F)........... 53 H 3
Angles-sur-l'Anglin (F) . . 49 F 1
Anglesola (E)........... 60 B 3
Anglet (F)........... 52 A 3
Anglisides (CY)........... 175 E 4
Anglure (F)........... 45 G 1
Angoulême (F)........... 48 D 3
Angri (I)........... 109 H 5
Angüés (E)........... 59 H 4
Anguiano (E)........... 58 D 3
Anguillara Veneta (I) .. 103 E 5
Aniane (F)........... 54 B 2
Aniche (F)........... 40 A 2
Anina (RO)........... 150 C 2
Aninoasa (RO)........... 151 E 3
Anizy-le-Château (F).. 40 A 4
Anjalankoski (FIN)........... 193 F 4
Anjum (NL)........... 77 F 2
Ankaran (SLO)........... 134 A 3
Ankarsrum (S)........... 197 E 3
Anklam (D)........... 83 G 3
Ankum (D)........... 84 D 1
Ånn (S)........... 183 E 5
Annaberg (A)........... 97 F 2
Annaberg-Buchholz (D). 86 C 5
Annaburg (D)........... 86 C 3
Annan (GB)........... 31 E 4
Anndalsvågen (N)........... 183 E 2
Annecy (F)...........51 F 2
Annemasse (F)...........51 F 2
Annevoie-Rouillon (B) . . 78 D 3
Annonay (F)........... 50 D 4
Annone Veneto (I) .... 103 F 3
Annopol (PL)........... 123 E 4
Annot (F)........... 55 F 1
Annweiler am Trifels (D). 88 D 2
Áno Ágios Vlásios (GR) . 164 D 2
Áno Kalentíni (GR)........... 164 D 1
Áno Kallinikí (GR)........... 160 D 3
Áno Kómi (GR)........... 161 E 4
Áno Merá (GR)........... 170 C 1
Áno Polydéndri (GR)........... 165 G 1
Áno Poróia (GR)........... 161 G 2
Áno Rodákino (GR)........... 172 C 3
Áno Sagkrí (GR)........... 170 C 1
Áno Sýros (GR)........... 169 H 2
Áno Viánnos (GR)........... 173 E 4
Áno Vrontoú (GR)........... 161 H 2
Anógeia (GR)........... 170 B 5
Anogyra (CY)...........174 C 4
Ánoixi (GR)........... 160 D 5
Anópoli (GR)........... 172 B 3
Ansbach (D)........... 89 H 3
Anse (F)........... 50 D 2
Ansedonia (I)........... 108 B 2
Ansião (P)........... 62 B 4
Ansnes (N)........... 182 C 4
Ansó (E)........... 59 G 2
Anstruther (GB)...........31 E 1
Antartikó (GR)........... 160 D 3
Antas (E)........... 71 H 5
Antegnate (I)........... 101 F 4
Antequera (E)...........74 D 3
Anterselva di Mezzo /
  Antholz Mittertal (I) . 103 E 1
Antheia (GR)........... 163 E 3
Anthí (GR)........... 161 H 3
Anthíli (GR)........... 165 F 2
Antholz Mittertal /
  Anterselva di Mezzo . 103 E 1
Anthótopos (GR)........... 165 F 2
Anthochóri (GR)........... 162 B 2
Antibes (F)........... 55 G 2
Antikýra (GR)........... 165 F 3
Antimácheia (GR)........... 171 F 2

AntInbhear Mór /
  Arklow (IRL) .... 25 G 2
Antinítsa (GR)........... 165 F 2
Antíparos (GR)........... 170 B 2
Antírrio (GR)........... 165 E 3
Ántissa (GR)........... 167 E 2
Antnäs (S)........... 185 E 2
Anton (BG)........... 158 D 1
Antonin (PL)........... 121 G 3
Antonovo (BG)........... 156 C 3
Antraigues (F)........... 50 C 5
Antrain (F)........... 43 F 2
Antrim (GB)........... 23 G 2
Antrodoco (I)........... 109 E 2
Antsla (EST)........... 201 F 4
Anttola (FIN)........... 193 F 2
Antwerpen (Anvers) (B) . 78 C 1
Anykščiai (LT)........... 205 F 2
Anzano di Puglia (I)...........110 C 3
Anzio (I)........... 109 E 4
Anzola d'Ossola (I)........... 100 D 3
Anzy-le-Duc (F)........... 50 B 1
Aosta / Aoste (I) ...... 100 B 3
Aoste / Aosta (I) ...... 100 B 3
Apahida (RO)........... 147 F 3
Apátfalva (H)........... 129 H 5
Apatin (SRB)........... 137 H 1
Apatovac (HR)........... 135 F 2
Ape (LV)........... 203 G 2
Apecchio (I)........... 107 F 3
Apeíranthos (GR)........... 170 C 1
Apeldoorn (NL)........... 77 F 4
Apen (D)...........81 E 5
Apidiá (GR)........... 168 D 3
Apodoúlou (GR)........... 172 D 3
Apolakkiá (GR)........... 171 G 4
Apold (RO)........... 147 H 5
Apolda (D)........... 86 A 4
Apollon Ylatis,
  sanctuary of (CY) ....174 C 5
Apóllona (GR)........... 171 H 3
Apóllonas (GR)........... 170 C 1
Apollonía (GR)........... 169 H 3
Apollonía (GR)........... 161 H 3
Apostolache (RO)........... 152 B 2
Apóstoloi (GR)........... 172 C 3
Apostolos Andreas (CY). 175 H 1
Apostolos Varnavas (CY). 175 F 3
Apostolove (UA)...........13 H 2
Äppelbo (S)........... 189 H 4
Appenweier (D)........... 88 D 5
Appenzell (CH)........... 99 F 2
Appiano / Eppan (I) .... 101 H 2
Appingedam (NL)........... 77 G 2
Appleby (GB)...........31 F 4
Apremont,
  parc floral d' (F) ..... 45 F 5
Aprica (I)........... 101 G 3
Apricena (I)...........110 C 1
Aprilci (Loveč) (BG)..... 159 E 1
Aprilci (Pazardžik) (BG). 158 D 2
Aprília (I)........... 109 E 3
Aprilovo (BG)........... 156 D 3
Apt (F)........... 54 D 2
Apta (N)........... 194 B 2
Aquileia (I)........... 103 G 3
Arabba (I)........... 103 E 2
Aracena (E)........... 69 F 4
Aráchova
  (Dytikí Elláda) (GR) ... 165 E 3
Aráchova
  (Stereá Elláda) (GR)... 165 F 3
Araci (RO)........... 152 A 1
Aračinovo (MK)........... 143 F 5
Arad (RO)........... 146 B 5
Arádaina (GR)........... 172 B 3
Aradippou (CY)........... 175 E 4
Aragona (I)...........114 D 4
Arahal (E)........... 69 H 5
Aramits (F)........... 52 B 3
Aranda de Duero (E) .... 58 B 5
Aranđelovac /
  Аранђеловац (SRB).. 140 D 5
Aranjuez (E)........... 64 C 3
Arantzazu (E)........... 59 E 2
Aranyosapáti (H)........... 127 F 5

A B C D E F G H I J K L M N O P Q R S T U V W X Y Z

209

Aras de los Olmos (E) 65 G3
Arasluokta (S) 179 H4
Arasvika (N) 182 C5
Áratos (GR) 162 D2
Aravaca (E) 64 B2
Aravete (EST) 201 E2
Aravissós (GR) 161 F3
Áraxos (GR) 164 D4
Arazede (P) 62 B3
Arbatax (I) 112 D3
Arbeca (E) 60 B4
Arbesbach (A) 97 E1
Arboga (S) 197 E1
Arbois (F) 47 E5
Arbon (CH) 99 F2
Arbore (RO) 148 B2
Arborea (I) 112 B4
Arborio (I) 100 D4
Arbrå (S) 190 B3
Arbroath (GB) 29 G5
Arbúcies (E) 61 E3
Arbus (I) 112 B4
Arc-en-Barrois (F) 46 D3
Arcachon (F) 48 B5
Arčar (BG) 151 E5
Arce (I) 109 F3
Arcen (NL) 79 F1
Arcevia (I) 107 F3
Archaía Epídavros (GR) 165 G5
Archaía Ílida (GR) 164 D4
Archaía Kórinthos (GR) 165 G5
Archaía Neméa (GR) 165 F5
Archaía Olympía (GR) 164 D5
Archaíes Kleonés (GR) 165 F5
Archánes / Αρχάνες (GR) 172 D3
Archángelos (Ípeiros) (GR) 164 C2
Archángelos (Nótio Aigaío) (GR) 171 H3
Archena (E) 72 D3
Archiac (F) 48 D3
Archidona (E) 75 E2
Arcidosso (I) 106 D5
Arcis-sur-Aube (F) 45 H2
Arco (I) 101 H3
Arco de Baúlhe (P) 62 C1
Arcos (E) 58 B3
Arcos de Jalón (E) 65 E1
Arcos de la Frontera (E) 74 B3
Arcos de Valdevez (P) 56 C5
Arcusa (E) 60 A2
Arcyz (UA) 13 F3
Ardales (E) 74 D3
Årdalstangen (N) 188 D3
Ardánio (GR) 163 E3
Ardara (IRL) 22 D2
Ardberg (GB) 30 A2
Ardee (IRL) 23 F4
Ardentes (F) 49 G1
Ardentinny (GB) 30 C1
Ardes (F) 50 A3
Ardez (CH) 99 H3
Ardglass (GB) 23 H3
Ardino / Ардино (BG) 162 D1
Ardisa (E) 59 G3
Ardlussa (GB) 30 B1
Ardmore (IRL) 25 E4
Ardrahan (IRL) 24 C1
Ardres (F) 39 G1
Ardrishaig (GB) 30 B1
Ardrossan (GB) 30 C2
Ardu (EST) 201 E2
Arduaine (GB) 30 B1
Ardud (RO) 147 E2
Ardvasar (GB) 28 C4
Åre (S) 183 F5
Areeta (E) 58 D1
Arenas de Iguña (E) 58 B1
Arenas de San Juan (E) 64 C5
Arenas de San Pedro (E) 63 H4
Arendal (N) 194 D2
Arendonk (B) 78 D1
Arendsee (D) 82 D5
Arenys de Mar (E) 61 E3
Arenzano (I) 104 D3
Areópoli (GR) 168 D4
Ares (E) 56 C1
Arès (F) 48 B5
Ares (N) 194 A1
Aréthousa (GR) 161 H3
Arévalo (E) 64 A1
Arez (P) 62 C5
Arezzo (I) 107 E4
Argaka (CY) 174 B2
Argaki (CY) 174 C3
Argamasilla de Alba (E) 64 D5
Argamasilla de Calatrava (E) 70 D2
Arganda del Rey (E) 64 C3
Arganil (P) 62 C3
Argelès-Gazost (F) 52 D4
Argelès-sur-Mer (F) 54 A5
Argent-sur-Sauldre (F) 45 E4
Argenta (I) 107 E1
Argentan (F) 43 H1
Argentat (F) 49 G4
Argente (E) 65 G2
Argentière (F) 51 G2
Argenton-Château (F) 43 H5
Argenton-sur-Creuse (F) 49 G1
Argentona (E) 61 E3
Argentré-du-Plessis (F) 43 G3
Argetoaia (RO) 151 E3
Argithéa (GR) 164 D1
Árgos / Άργος (GR) 165 F5
Árgos Orestikó (GR) 160 D4
Argostóli / Αργοστόλι (GR) 164 B4
Arguedas (E) 59 F4
Argueil (F) 39 G4
Arguellite (E) 71 G3
Arguis (E) 59 H3
Argyrádes (GR) 164 B1
Ariano Irpino (I) 110 B3
Ariano nel Polesine (I) 103 E5
Aribe (E) 59 F2
Aridaía (GR) 161 E3
Arieşeni (RO) 146 D4
Arija (E) 58 B2
Arild (S) 195 F5
Arilje (SRB) 139 H1
Arinagour (GB) 28 C5
Aríni (GR) 164 D5
Ariño (E) 65 H1
Arinthod (F) 51 E1
Ariogala (LT) 205 E3
Arisaig (GB) 28 D4
Arísti (GR) 160 C5
Aristoménis (GR) 168 C3
Arísvi (GR) 162 D2
Aritzo (I) 112 C3
Ariza (E) 59 E5
Årjäng (S) 195 F1
Arjeplog (S) 184 C1
Arjona (E) 70 D4
Arkádi (GR) 170 B5
Arkalochóri (GR) 173 E3
Arkása (GR) 171 F5
Arkítsa (GR) 165 G3
Arklow / An tInbhear Mór (IRL) 25 G2
Arkoi (GR) 171 E1
Arlanc (F) 50 B3
Arlanzón (E) 58 C3
Arlempdes (F) 50 B5
Arles (F) 54 C2
Arles-sur-Tech (F) 53 H5
Arlesheim (CH) 98 D1
Arlon (Aarlen) (B) 79 E5
Arma di Taggia (I) 104 C4
Armação de Pêra (P) 68 C5
Armadale (GB) 30 D2
Armagh (GB) 23 F3
Armamar (P) 62 D1
Armenistís (GR) 167 E5
Arménoi (GR) 170 A5
Armentières (F) 40 A1
Armilla (E) 75 F2
Armólia (GR) 167 E4
Arnac-Pompadour (F) 49 F3
Arnaía (GR) 161 H4
Arnay-le-Duc (F) 46 C5
Arnedillo (E) 59 E3
Arnedo (E) 59 E3
Arnes (E) 60 A5
Årnes (N) 189 F5
Arnhem (NL) 77 F5
Arni (I) 105 G4
Árnissa (GR) 161 E3
Arnoldstein (A) 96 D5
Arnota (RO) 151 F2
Arnsberg (D) 85 E4
Arnstadt (D) 86 A5
Arnstein (D) 89 G2
Aroanía (GR) 165 E5
Aroche (E) 69 E4
Arona (I) 100 D3
Aroniádika (GR) 169 E5
Aronkylä (FIN) 191 F1
Åros (N) 189 E5
Arosa (CH) 99 G3
Arouca (P) 62 C2
Årøysund (N) 195 E1
Arpajon (F) 45 E1
Arpaşu de Jos (RO) 151 G1
Arpela (FIN) 185 G1
Arquata del Tronto (I) 107 G5
Arques (F) 39 H1
Arques-la-Bataille (F) 39 F3
Arquillos (E) 71 E3
Arrabal (E) 56 B4
Arracourt (F) 47 F1
Arraiolos (P) 68 C2
Arras (F) 39 H2
Arrasate / Mondragon (E) 58 D2
Arreau (F) 52 D4
Arrecife (E) 67 H4
Arredondo (E) 58 C1
Arrens (F) 52 C4
Arrianá (GR) 163 E2
Arrigorriaga (E) 58 D1
Arriondas (E) 57 H2
Arroba de los Montes (E) 64 A5
Arrochar (GB) 30 C1
Arromanches (F) 38 D4
Arronches (P) 69 E1
Arroyo de la Luz (E) 63 E5
Arroyo de San Serván (E) 69 F2
Arroyo del Ojanco (E) 71 F3
Arroyomolinos de León (E) 69 F3
Arroyomolinos de Montánchez (E) 69 G1
Arruda dos Vinhos (P) 68 B1
Ars (F) 41 E5
Ars-en-Ré (F) 48 B2
Arsié (I) 103 E3
Arsiero (I) 102 D3
Arskógssandur (IS) 178 C1
Arsos (Lemesos) (CY) 174 C4
Arsos (Lysi) (CY) 175 E3
Årsunda (S) 190 B4
Arsy (F) 39 H4
Artà (E) 67 G2
Árta / Άρτα (GR) 164 C2
Arta Terme (I) 103 G2
Artà, coves d' (E) 67 G2
Artajona (E) 59 F3
Ártánd (H) 131 E2
Artea (E) 58 D1
Arteixo (E) 56 C2
Artemisía (GR) 168 C3
Artemónas (GR) 169 H3
Artena (I) 109 E3
Artenay (F) 45 E3
Artern (D) 86 A4
Artés (E) 60 D3
Artesa de Segre (E) 60 B3
Arth (CH) 99 E2
Arth (D) 95 G1
Arthurstown (IRL) 25 F4
Arties (E) 60 B1
Artjärvi (FIN) 193 E4
Artotína (GR) 165 E3
Artstetten (A) 97 F1
Artziniega (E) 58 C1
Arucas (E) 67 G5
Arudy (F) 52 C3
Aruküla (EST) 201 E2
Arundel (GB) 38 D1
Árvi (GR) 173 E4
Arvidsjaur (S) 184 D2
Arvika (S) 189 G5
Årviksand (N) 176 C3
Arzachena (I) 112 C1
Arzacq-Arraziguet (F) 52 C3
Arzano (F) 42 C3
Aržano (HR) 138 C2
Arzberg (D) 91 F3
Arzignano (I) 102 D4
Arzúa (E) 56 C2
As (B) 79 E2
Aš (CZ) 91 F2
As Neves (E) 56 C4
As Pontes de García Rodríguez (E) 56 D1
Åsa (S) 195 F4
Asamati (MK) 145 E2
Åsarna (S) 189 H1
Åsarp (S) 195 G3
Ascain (F) 52 A3
Ascha (D) 91 G5
Aschach an der Donau (A) 96 D1
Aschaffenburg (D) 89 F2
Aschau im Chiemgau (D) 95 H3
Aschbach-Markt (A) 97 E2
Ascheberg (Coesfeld) (D) 84 D3
Ascheberg (Plön) (D) 82 B3
Aschersleben (D) 86 A3
Asciano (I) 106 D4
Ascó (E) 60 B4
Ascoli Piceno (I) 107 H5
Ascoli Satriano (I) 110 C3
Ascona (CH) 99 E4
Åse (N) 179 G2
Åseda (S) 197 E4
Åsele (S) 184 B4
Åsen (N) 182 D5
Asenovgrad / Асеновград (BG) 159 E3
Åseral (N) 194 C2
Aseri (EST) 201 F1
Asfeld (F) 40 B4
Ásfendos (GR) 172 C3
Åsgårdstrand (N) 195 E1
Asgata (CY) 174 D4
Ashbourne (GB) 33 E4
Ashbourne (IRL) 23 F5
Ashburton (GB) 34 D4
Ashby de la Zouch (GB) 33 E4
Ashford (GB) 37 E5
Ashington (GB) 31 G3
Ashton-under-Lyne (GB) 32 D3
Así Gonía (GR) 172 C3
Asiago (I) 103 E3
Asikkala (FIN) 191 H3
Asín (E) 59 G3
Asipovičy (BY) 7 E4
Ask (N) 189 F5
Askainen (FIN) 191 F4
Askeaton (IRL) 24 C3
Askeia (CY) 175 E3
Askersund (S) 196 D2
Askim (N) 195 F1
Asklipieío (GR) 171 H4
Asklipieío (GR) 171 F2
Askola (FIN) 191 H4
Askós (GR) 161 H3
Askvoll (N) 188 B2
Askýfou (GR) 170 A5
Asmunti (FIN) 185 H1
Asola (I) 101 G5
Asolo (I) 103 E3
Asomáton (GR) 172 C3
Asomatos Keryneias (CY) 174 D3
Asopía (GR) 165 H4
Asopós (GR) 169 E4
Ásos / Άσος (GR) 164 B3
Ásotthalom (H) 129 G5
Aspang-Markt (A) 97 G3
Aspatria (GB) 31 E4
Aspe / Asp (E) 73 E2
Asperg (D) 89 F4
Aspet (F) 53 E4
Áspra Spítia / Άσπρα Σπίτια (GR) 165 F3
Aspres-sur-Buëch (F) 51 E5
Áspro (GR) 161 F3
Asprópyrgos (GR) 165 H4
Asprovalta (GR) 161 H3
Asse (B) 78 C2
Assemini (I) 112 C5
Assen (NL) 77 G3
Assens (DK) 198 C4
Assergi (I) 109 F2
Assisi (I) 107 F4
Assmannshausen (D) 88 D2
Ássos (GR) 164 C1
Astaffort (F) 53 E1
Astakós (GR) 164 C3
Asten (A) 96 D2
Astérix, parc (F) 39 H5
Asti (I) 100 D5
Astorga (E) 57 G4
Åstorp (S) 199 E3
Astromeritis (CY) 174 D3
Ástros / Άστρος (GR) 168 D2
Astudillo (E) 58 A4
Astypálaia (GR) 171 E3
Asūne (LV) 203 H5
Asvestochóri (GR) 160 C5
Aszód (H) 129 F1
Aszófő (H) 128 D3
Atalánti / Αταλάντη (GR) 165 G3
Ataquines (E) 64 A1
Atašiene (LV) 203 F4
Ateca (E) 59 F5
Atella (I) 110 C3
Atessa (I) 109 H2
Ath (Aat) (B) 78 B3
Atháni (GR) 164 C3
Athboy (IRL) 23 F5
Athenry (IRL) 22 C5
Atherstone (GB) 33 E5
Athienou (CY) 175 E3
Athína / Αθήνα (GR) 165 H4
Athlone / Baile Átha Luain (IRL) 22 D5
Athy (IRL) 25 F2
Atid (RO) 147 H4
Atienza (E) 64 D1
Atina (I) 109 G3
Atios (E) 56 C1
Atouguia da Baleia (P) 62 A5
Ätran (S) 195 G4
Atri (I) 107 H5
Atsiki (GR) 162 D5
Atsítsa (GR) 166 B2
Áttali (GR) 165 H3
Attard (M) 114 C5
Attendorn (D) 84 D4
Attersee (A) 96 C2
Attigliano (I) 108 D1
Attigny (F) 40 C4
Attleborough (GB) 33 H4
Attnang (A) 96 C2
Åtvidaberg (S) 197 E3
Atzeneta del Maestrat (E) 66 A2
Au in der Hallertau (D) 95 G1
Aua (D) 85 G5
Aub (D) 89 G3
Aubagne (F) 55 E3
Aubange (B) 79 E5
Aubenas (F) 50 C5
Aubenton (F) 40 B3
Aubergenville (F) 39 G5
Auberive (F) 46 D3
Aubeterre-sur-Dronne (F) 48 D4
Aubigny (F) 39 H2
Aubigny-sur-Nère (F) 45 E4
Aubin (F) 49 H5
Aubonne (CH) 98 B4
Aubrac (F) 50 A5
Aubusson (F) 49 H2
Auce (LV) 202 C4
Auch (F) 53 E2
Auchencairn (GB) 30 D4
Auchterarder (GB) 30 D1
Auchtermuchty (GB) 31 E1
Audenge (F) 48 C5
Audeux (F) 47 E4
Audierne (F) 42 B2
Audincourt (F) 47 G4
Audlem (GB) 32 D4
Audley End (GB) 36 D3
Audru (EST) 200 D3
Audruicq (F) 39 G1
Audun-le-Roman (F) 41 E4
Audun-le-Tiche (F) 41 E4
Aue (D) 86 C5
Auer / Ora (I) 101 H2
Auerbach (D) 86 C5
Auerbach in der Oberpfalz (D) 91 E3
Auffach (A) 95 H3
Aughnacloy (GB) 23 F3
Aughrim (IRL) 25 F2
Augsburg (D) 89 H5
Augusta (I) 115 G4
Augustenborg (DK) 198 C4
Augustów (PL) 119 G2
Augustusburg (D) 86 D5
Aukan (N) 182 B5
Aukra (N) 182 A5
Aukštadvaris (LT) 205 F4
Aulanko (FIN) 191 H3
Auletta (I) 110 C4
Aulla (I) 105 F3
Aullène (F) 55 H5
Aulnay (F) 48 D2
Aulnoye-Aymeries (F) 40 B3
Ault (F) 39 G3
Aulus-les-Bains (F) 53 F4
Auma (D) 86 B5
Aumale (F) 39 G3
Aumetz (F) 41 E4
Aumont-Aubrac (F) 50 A5
Aunay-sur-Odon (F) 38 C5
Auneau (F) 44 D2
Auneuil (F) 39 G4
Auning (DK) 195 E5
Aups (F) 55 F2
Aura (FIN) 191 F4
Auray (F) 42 D3
Aurdal (N) 189 E3
Aure (N) 182 C5
Aurec-sur-Loire (F) 50 C4
Aurich (D) 81 E4
Aurignac (F) 53 E3
Aurillac (F) 49 H5
Auritz / Burgete (E) 59 F2
Aurland (N) 188 C3
Auron (F) 55 G1
Auronzo di Cadore (I) 103 F2
Auros (F) 48 D5
Ausonia (I) 109 F4
Aussa-Corno (I) 103 G4
Außernbrünst (D) 96 C1
Austbygd (N) 188 D5
Auterive (F) 53 F3
Authon-du-Perche (F) 44 C2
Autol (E) 59 E3
Autrans (F) 51 E4
Autrey-lès-Gray (F) 47 E4
Autti (FIN) 181 F5
Auttoinen (FIN) 191 H3
Autun (F) 45 H5
Auvillar (F) 53 E1
Auxerre (F) 45 G3
Auxi-le-Château (F) 39 G2
Auxonne (F) 46 D4
Auzances (F) 49 H2
Auzon (F) 50 A3
Availles-Limouzine (F) 49 E2
Avaldsnes (N) 188 A5
Avallon (F) 45 H4
Ávantas (GR) 163 E3
Avaviken (S) 184 C2
Avdimou (CY) 174 C5
Ávdira (GR) 162 C3

A B C D E F G H I J K L M N O P Q R S T U V W X Y Z

A
B
C
D
E
F
G
H
I
J
K
L
M
N
O
P
Q
R
S
T
U
V
W
X
Y
Z

Avebury (GB) .... 35 G 2
Aveiras de Cima (P) ..... 68 B 1
Aveiro (P) .... 62 B 2
Avellino (I) .... 109 H 5
Aven Armand (F) .... 54 A 1
Aven d'Orgnac (F) ...... 54 C 1
Aversa (I) .... 109 G 5
Avesnes-le-Comte (F) ... 39 H 2
Avesnes-sur-Helpe (F) .. 40 B 3
Avesta (S) .... 190 B 5
Avetrana (I) .... 111 G 4
Avezzano (I) .... 109 F 2
Avgerinós (GR) .... 160 D 4
Avgorou (CY) .... 175 F 3
Aviano (I) .... 103 F 3
Aviemore (GB) .... 29 F 4
Avigliana (I) .... 100 B 5
Avigliano (I) .... 110 C 4
Avignon (F) .... 54 C 2
Ávila (E) .... 64 A 2
Avilés (E) .... 57 G 1
Avintes (P) .... 62 B 1
Avión (E) .... 56 C 4
Avioth (F) .... 40 D 4
Avis (P) .... 68 D 1
Avize (F) .... 40 B 5
Avlákia (GR) .... 167 G 5
Avlés (GR) .... 161 E 4
Avlí (GR) .... 162 B 3
Avliótes (GR) .... 160 A 5
Avlona (CY) .... 174 D 3
Avlóna (GR) .... 165 H 4
Avlonári (GR) .... 166 B 3
Avlum (DK) .... 194 C 5
Avola (I) .... 115 G 4
Avonmouth (GB) .... 35 F 2
Avord (F) .... 45 F 5
Avoriaz (F) .... 51 G 2
Avram Iancu (RO) ..... 146 C 4
Avranches (F) .... 43 F 1
Avren (BG) .... 157 F 3
Avrig (RO) .... 151 G 1
Avtovac (BIH) .... 139 F 3
Ax-les-Thermes (F) ..... 53 G 4
Axams (A) .... 95 F 4
Axat (F) .... 53 G 4
Axintele (RO) .... 152 C 3
Axiochóri (GR) .... 161 F 3
Axioúpoli (GR) .... 161 F 3
Axminster (GB) .... 35 E 3
Ay (F) .... 40 B 5
Ayamonte (E) .... 68 D 5
Aydın (TR) .... 19 G 3
Ayerbe (E) .... 59 G 3
Aylesbury (GB) .... 35 H 1
Ayllón (E) .... 58 C 5
Aylsham (GB) .... 37 E 1
Ayna (E) .... 71 G 2
Ayora (E) .... 65 G 5
Ayr (GB) .... 30 C 3
Ayvalık (TR) .... 19 G 4
Aywaille (B) .... 79 E 3
Azaila (E) .... 59 H 5
Azambuja (P) .... 68 B 1
Azanja (SRB) .... 140 D 5
Azaruja (P) .... 68 D 2
Azay-le-Ferron (F) ..... 44 C 5
Azay-le-Rideau (F) .... 44 B 4
Azinheira dos Barros (P). 68 C 3
Azkoitia (E) .... 59 E 1
Aznalcázar (E) .... 69 F 5
Aznalcóllar (E) .... 69 F 5
Azpeitia (E) .... 59 E 1
Azuaga (E) .... 69 G 3
Azuara (E) .... 65 G 1
Azuel (E) .... 70 C 3
Azuga (RO) .... 152 A 2
Azuqueca
  de Henares (E) ...... 64 C 2
Azzano Decimo (I) .... 103 F 3
Azzurra, grotta (I) ...... 110 A 4

B

Baad (A) .... 95 E 4
Baal (D) .... 84 B 4
Baamonde (E) .... 56 D 2
Baarle-Nassau (NL) ...... 78 D 1

Baarn (NL) .... 77 E 4
Babadag (RO) .... 153 F 3
Babelsberg (D) .... 86 C 1
Babenhausen (Darmstadt -
  Dieburg) (D) ...... 89 F 2
Babenhausen
  (Unterallgaü) (D) ...... 95 E 2
Bäbeni
  (Râmnicu Vâlcea) (RO). 151 G 3
Băbeni (Zalău) (RO) .... 147 E 2
Babiak (PL) .... 118 D 2
Babimost (PL) .... 120 D 1
Babin Kal (SRB) .... 143 G 2
Babin Most (SRB) ...... 143 E 4
Babin Potok (HR) .... 134 D 5
Babina Greda (HR) .... 137 G 2
Babino Polje (HR) ...... 138 D 4
Babljak (MNE) .... 139 G 3
Babno Polje (SLO) .... 134 C 3
Babócsa (H) .... 128 C 5
Baborów (PL) .... 124 D 1
Baboszewo (PL) .... 118 D 5
Babrujsk (BY) .... 7 E 4
Babušnica (SRB) .... 143 G 3
Bač (SRB) .... 137 H 2
Bacău (RO) .... 148 C 4
Baccarat (F) .... 47 F 2
Baceno (I) .... 100 D 2
Băceşti (RO) .... 148 D 4
Bacharach (D) .... 88 D 1
Bachmač (UA) .... 7 F 5
Bačina (SRB) .... 143 E 1
Bačka Palanka (SRB) ... 140 B 3
Bačka Topola /
  Бачка Топола (SRB) .. 140 B 2
Bäckaskog (S) .... 199 G 3
Backe (S) .... 183 H 4
Bäckebo (S) .... 197 E 5
Bäckefors (S) .... 195 F 2
Bački Bred (SRB) ...... 137 H 1
Bački Brestovac (SRB) .. 137 H 1
Bački Monoštor (SRB) .. 137 H 1
Bački Petrovac (SRB) .. 140 B 3
Backnang (D) .... 89 F 4
Bačko Gradište (SRB) .. 140 C 2
Bačko Novo Selo (SRB) . 137 H 2
Bačko
  Petrovo Selo (SRB) .. 140 C 2
Bačkovo (BG) .... 151 E 5
Bačkovski
  manastir (BG) .... 162 C 1
Bâcleş (RO) .... 151 E 4
Bacoli (I) .... 109 G 5
Bacova Mahala (BG) ... 156 B 2
Bacqueville
  -en-Caux (F) ...... 39 F 3
Bácsalmás (H) .... 129 F 5
Bácsbokod (H) .... 129 F 5
Bad Aibling (D) .... 95 G 2
Bad Arolsen (D) .... 85 F 4
Bad Aussee (A) .... 96 D 3
Bad Bederkesa (D) .... 81 G 4
Bad Bentheim (D) ...... 84 C 1
Bad Bergzabern (D) .... 88 D 4
Bad Berka (D) .... 86 A 5
Bad Berleburg (D) .... 85 E 4
Bad Berneck
  im Fichtelgebirge (D) .. 91 E 3
Bad Bertrich (D) .... 88 C 1
Bad Bevensen (D) ...... 82 B 5
Bad Bibra (D) .... 86 A 4
Bad Blankenburg (D) .... 86 A 5
Bad Bodenteich (D) .... 82 C 5
Bad Brambach (D) .... 91 F 2
Bad Bramstedt (D) .... 81 H 3
Bad Brückenau (D) .... 89 G 1
Bad Buchau (D) .... 94 D 2
Bad Camberg (D) .... 89 E 1
Bad Deutsch-
  Altenburg (D) .... 97 H 1
Bad Doberan (D) .... 82 D 3
Bad Driburg (D) .... 85 F 3
Bad Düben (D) .... 86 C 3
Bad Dürkheim (D) .. 89 E 3
Bad Dürrenberg (D) ...... 86 B 4
Bad Dürrheim (D) .... 94 B 2

Bad Eisenkappel (A) ..... 97 E 5
Bad Elster (D) .... 91 F 2
Bad Ems (D) .... 88 B 1
Bad Endorf (D) .... 95 H 2
Bad Essen (D) .... 85 E 2
Bad Fallingbostel (D) .... 81 H 5
Bad Frankenhausen (D) . 86 A 4
Bad Freienwalde (D) .... 83 G 5
Bad Friedrichshall (D) ... 89 F 3
Bad Gandersheim (D) .. 85 G 3
Bad Gastein (A) .... 96 C 4
Bad Gleichenberg (A) .. 97 G 4
Bad Godesberg (D) ...... 84 C 5
Bad Gottleuba (D) .... 87 E 5
Bad Griesbach
  im Rottal (D) .... 96 C 1
Bad Grönenbach (D) ... 95 E 2
Bad Grund (D) .... 85 H 3
Bad Hall (A) .... 96 D 2
Bad Harzburg (D) .... 85 H 3
Bad Herrenalb (D) .... 89 E 4
Bad Hersfeld (D) .... 85 G 5
Bad Hindelang (D) .... 95 E 3
Bad Hofgastein (A) .... 96 C 4
Bad Homburg
  vor der Höhe (D) .... 89 E 1
Bad Honnef (D) .... 84 C 5
Bad Hönningen (D) .... 84 C 5
Bad Iburg (D) .... 85 E 2
Bad Ischl (A) .... 96 C 3
Bad Karlshafen (D) .... 85 F 3
Bad Kissingen (D) .... 89 G 1
Bad Kleinen (D) .... 82 D 3
Bad König (D) .... 89 F 2
Bad Königshofen
  im Grabfeld (D) .... 89 H 1
Bad Kösen (D) .... 86 B 4
Bad Kötzting (D) .... 91 G 5
Bad Kreuznach (D) .... 88 D 2
Bad Krozingen (D) .... 94 A 2
Bad Laasphe (D) ...... 85 E 5
Bad Langensalza (D) .. 85 H 4
Bad Lauchstädt (D) .... 86 B 4
Bad Lausick (D) .... 86 C 4
Bad Lauterberg (D) .... 85 H 3
Bad Leonfelden (A) .... 96 D 1
Bad Liebenstein (D) .... 85 H 5
Bad Liebenwerda (D) .... 86 D 3
Bad Liebenzell (D) .... 89 E 4
Bad Lippspringe (D) .... 85 F 3
Bad Meinberg (D) .... 85 F 2
Bad Mergentheim (D) .... 89 G 3
Bad Mitterndorf (A) .... 96 D 3
Bad Münder
  am Deister (D) ...... 85 F 2
Bad Münster
  am Stein (D) .... 88 D 2
Bad Münstereifel (D) .... 84 C 5
Bad Muskau (D) ...... 87 F 3
Bad Nauheim (D) .... 89 E 1
Bad Nenndorf (D) .... 85 F 2
Bad Neuenahr (D) .... 84 C 5
Bad Neustadt
  an der Saale (D) .... 89 G 1
Bad Oeynhausen (D) .. 85 F 2
Bad Oldesloe (D) .... 82 B 3
Bad Orb (D) .... 89 F 1
Bad Peterstal (D) .... 89 E 5
Bad Pyrmont (D) .... 85 F 2
Bad Radkersburg (A) ... 97 G 5
Bad Ragaz (CH) .... 99 F 3
Bad Rappenau (D) .... 89 F 3
Bad Reichenhall (D) .... 96 B 3
Bad Rippoldsau (D) .... 89 H 1
Bad Rodach (D) .... 89 H 1
Bad Rothenfelde (D) .... 85 E 2
Bad Saarow (D) .... 87 E 1
Bad Sachsa (D) .... 89 E 1
Bad Säckingen (D) .... 94 A 3
Bad Salzdetfurth (D) .... 85 G 2
Bad Salzschlirf (D) .... 85 F 5
Bad Salzuflen (D) .... 85 F 2
Bad Salzungen (D) .... 85 H 5
Bad Sankt Leonhard
  im Lavanttal (A) ..... 97 E 4
Bad Saulgau (D) .... 94 D 2

Bad Schallerbach (A) .... 96 D 2
Bad Schandau (D) ...... 87 E 4
Bad Schmiedeberg (D) .. 86 C 3
Bad Schönborn (D) .... 89 E 3
Bad Schussenried (D) ... 94 D 2
Bad Schwalbach (D) .... 88 D 1
Bad Schwartau (D) .... 82 C 3
Bad Segeberg (D) ...... 82 B 3
Bad Soden (D) .... 89 F 1
Bad Soden
  am Taunus (D) ...... 89 E 1
Bad Sooden-
  Allendorf (D) .... 85 G 4
Bad Staffelstein (D) ..... 91 E 3
Bad Sulza (D) .... 86 A 4
Bad Sülze (D) .... 83 E 3
Bad Tatzmannsdorf (A).. 97 G 3
Bad Tennstedt (D) ...... 85 H 4
Bad Tölz (D) .... 95 G 3
Bad Urach (D) .... 89 F 5
Bad Vilbel (D) .... 89 E 1
Bad Vöslau (A) .... 97 G 2
Bad Waldsee (D) ...... 94 D 2
Bad Wiessee (D) .... 95 G 3
Bad Wildungen (D) .... 85 F 4
Bad Wilsnack (D) .... 82 D 5
Bad Wimpfen (D) .... 89 F 3
Bad Windsheim (D) .... 89 H 3
Bad Wörishofen (D) .... 95 E 2
Bad Wurzach (D) .... 94 D 2
Bad Zurzach (CH) .... 99 E 1
Bad Zwischenahn (D) .... 81 F 5
Badacsonytomaj (H) ... 128 C 3
Badajoz (E) .... 69 E 2
Badalona (E) .... 60 D 4
Badalucco (I) .... 113 C 4
Badljevina (HR) .... 135 G 4
Badolato (I) .... 113 C 4
Badolatosa (E) .... 70 C 5
Badonviller (F) .... 47 G 1
Badovinci (SRB) .... 140 B 4
Bae Colwyn /
  Colwyn Bay (GB) .... 32 B 3
Baena (E) .... 70 C 4
Baeza (E) .... 71 E 4
Bagà (E) .... 60 D 2
Bâgé-le-Châtel (F) .... 50 D 1
Bagenalstown (IRL) ... 25 F 3
Bagenkop (DK) .... 198 C 4
Bagheria (I) .... 114 D 2
Bagn (N) .... 189 E 4
Bagnacavallo (I) .... 107 E 1
Bagnara Calabra (I) .... 115 H 2
Bagnères-
  de-Bigorre (F) .... 52 D 4
Bagnères-
  de-Luchon (F) .... 53 E 4
Bagni del Masino (I) .... 101 F 2
Bagni di Lucca (I) .... 105 G 4
Bagno a Ripoli (I) .... 105 H 4
Bagno di Romagna (I) . 107 E 3
Bagnoles-de-l'Orne (F).. 43 H 2
Bagnoli del Trigno (I) . 109 H 3
Bagnolo Mella (I) .... 101 G 4
Bagnols-les-Bains (F) .. 50 B 5
Bagnols-sur-Cèze (F) .. 54 C 1
Bagnoregio (I) .... 107 E 5
Bagod (H) .... 128 B 3
Bagolino (I) .... 101 G 3
Bagrationovsk (RUS) .... 5 H 4
Bagrdan (SRB) .... 141 E 5
Bahrija (M) .... 114 B 5
Baia (Suceava) (RO) ... 148 B 2
Baia (Tulcea) (RO) .... 153 F 3
Baia de Aramă (RO) ... 150 D 2
Baia de Arieş (RO) .... 147 E 4
Baia de Criş (RO) .... 146 D 5
Baia de Fier (RO) .... 151 F 2
Baia Mare (RO) .... 147 F 2
Baia Sardinia (I) .... 112 D 1

Baia Sprie (RO) .... 147 F 2
Baiano (I) .... 109 H 5
Baião (P) .... 62 C 1
Băicoi (RO) .... 152 B 3
Baiersbronn (D) .... 89 E 5
Baignes-
  Sainte-Radegonde (F). 48 D 3
Baigneux-les-Juifs (F) ... 46 C 4
Băile 1 Mai (RO) .... 146 C 3
Băile Felix (RO) .... 146 C 3
Băile Herculane (RO) .. 150 D 3
Băile Olăneşti (RO) .... 151 G 2
Băile Tuşnad (RO) .... 148 B 5
Băileşti (RO) .... 151 E 5
Bailieborough (IRL) .... 23 F 4
Bailleul (F) .... 39 H 1
Bain-de-Bretagne (F).... 43 F 3
Bains-les-Bains (F) ...... 47 F 3
Baio (E) .... 56 B 2
Baiona (E) .... 56 B 4
Bais (F) .... 43 H 2
Baişoara (RO) .... 147 E 4
Baisogala (LT) .... 205 E 2
Baja (H) .... 129 E 5
Bajánsenye (H) .... 128 B 3
Bajgora (SRB) .... 143 G 4
Bajina Bašta (SRB) .... 139 G 1
Bajlovo (BG) .... 158 C 2
Bajmok (SRB) .... 140 B 1
Bajna (H) .... 129 E 1
Bajram Curri (AL) ...... 142 C 4
Bajša (SRB) .... 140 B 2
Bajzë (AL) .... 142 B 5
Bak (H) .... 128 B 3
Bakar (HR) .... 134 B 4
Bakarac (HR) .... 134 C 4
Bakewell (GB) .... 33 E 3
Bakkafjörður (IS) .... 178 D 1
Bakonybél (H) .... 128 D 2
Bakonycsernye (H) .... 128 D 2
Bakonygyepes (H) .... 128 C 2
Bakonykoppány (H) .. 128 D 2
Bakonysárkány (H) .... 128 D 2
Bakonyszombathely (H). 128 D 2
Baks (H) .... 129 G 4
Baktakék (H) .... 126 D 5
Baktalórántháza (H) .... 131 F 1
Bakvattnet (S) .... 183 F 4
Bala (GB) .... 32 B 4
Bala (RO) .... 150 D 3
Bălăbăneşti (RO) .... 149 E 5
Bălăceanu (RO) .... 152 D 2
Bălaci (RO) .... 151 H 4
Bălăciţa (RO) .... 151 E 3
Balaguer (E) .... 60 B 3
Bălan (RO) .... 148 B 4
Balanegra (E) .... 75 G 3
Balaruc-les-Bains (F) .. 54 B 3
Balassagyarmat (H) ... 126 B 5
Balástya (H) .... 129 G 4
Balatonakali (H) .... 128 D 3
Balatonalmádi (H) .... 128 D 3
Balatonboglár (H) .... 128 C 3
Balatonederics (H) .... 128 D 3
Balatonfőkajár (H) .... 128 D 3
Balatonföldvár (H) .... 128 D 3
Balatonfüred (H) .... 128 D 3
Balatonfűzfő (H) .... 128 D 3
Balatonkenese (H) .... 128 D 3
Balatonkeresztúr (H) .. 128 C 3
Balatonlelle (H) .... 128 D 3
Balatonszemes (H) .... 128 D 3
Balatonvilágos (H) .... 128 D 3
Bălăuşeri (RO) .... 147 G 4
Balazote (E) .... 71 G 2
Balbieriškis (LT) .... 205 E 4
Balbigny (F) .... 50 C 3
Balbriggan (IRL) .... 23 G 5
Balcani (RO) .... 148 C 4
Bălceşti (RO) .... 151 F 3

Baldock (GB) .... 36 C 3
Baldone (LV) .... 202 D 3
Bale (HR) .... 134 A 4
Baleal (P) .... 62 A 5
Baleizão (P) .... 68 D 3
Balerma (E) .... 75 H 3
Balestrand (N) .... 188 C 3
Bălgarevo (BG) .... 157 G 2
Bălgarovo (BG) .... 157 E 4
Bălgarski Izvor (BG) .... 158 D 1
Balí (GR) .... 170 B 5
Balikesir (TR) .... 19 G 2
Bälinge (S) .... 190 C 5
Balingen (D) .... 89 E 5
Balinţ (RO) .... 150 C 1
Balivanich (GB) .... 28 B 3
Balkány (H) .... 131 F 1
Ballachulish (GB) .... 28 D 5
Ballaghaderreen (IRL) .. 22 D 4
Ballangen (N) .... 179 H 3
Ballantrae (GB) .... 23 H 1
Ballao (I) .... 112 C 4
Ballater (GB) .... 29 G 4
Ballaugh (GB) .... 30 C 5
Ballenstedt (D) .... 86 A 3
Balleroy (F) .... 38 C 5
Ballerup (DK) .... 199 E 3
Ballina /
  Béal an Átha (IRL) .... 22 C 3
Ballinamore (IRL) .... 23 E 4
Ballinasloe / Béal Átha
  na Sluaighe (IRL) ..... 22 D 5
Ballingarry (IRL) .... 25 E 3
Ballinrobe (IRL) .... 22 C 4
Ballintubber (IRL) .... 22 C 4
Ballobar (E) .... 60 A 3
Ballon-Saint Mar (F) ... 44 B 2
Ballsh (AL) .... 144 C 3
Ballstad (N) .... 179 F 3
Ballybay (IRL) .... 23 F 4
Ballybofey (IRL) .... 23 E 2
Ballybunnion (IRL) .... 24 B 3
Ballycastle (GB) .... 23 G 1
Ballycastle (IRL) .... 22 C 3
Ballyclare (IRL) .... 23 G 2
Ballyconnell (IRL) .... 23 E 4
Ballycotton (IRL) .... 24 D 4
Ballycroy (IRL) .... 22 B 4
Ballyduff (IRL) .... 24 B 3
Ballyforan (IRL) .... 22 D 5
Ballygawley (GB) .... 23 F 3
Ballyhaunis (IRL) .... 22 C 4
Ballyheige (IRL) .... 24 B 3
Ballyjamesduff (IRL) .... 23 E 4
Ballymahon (IRL) .... 23 E 5
Ballymena (GB) .... 23 G 2
Ballymoe (IRL) .... 22 D 4
Ballymoney (GB) .... 23 F 1
Ballymore (IRL) .... 23 E 5
Ballymote (IRL) .... 22 D 4
Ballynahinch (GB) .... 23 G 3
Ballysadare (IRL) .... 22 D 3
Ballyshannon (IRL) .... 22 D 3
Ballyvaughan (IRL) .... 24 C 2
Balmaseda (E) .... 58 C 1
Balmazújváros (H) ..... 131 E 1
Balme (I) .... 100 B 4
Balmoral Castle (GB) .... 29 G 4
Balneario
  de Panticosa (E) .... 59 H 2
Balninkai (LT) .... 205 G 3
Baloteşti (RO) .... 152 B 3
Baloži (LV) .... 202 D 3
Balş (RO) .... 151 F 4
Balsareny (E) .... 60 D 3
Balsicas (E) .... 73 E 3
Balsorano Nuovo (I) .. 109 F 3
Bålsta (S) .... 197 E 1
Balsthal (CH) .... 98 D 2
Balta (UA) .... 13 F 2
Balta Albă (RO) .... 152 D 2
Baltanás (E) .... 58 B 4
Baltar (E) .... 56 D 5
Bălţi (MD) .... 13 E 3
Baltijsk (RUS) .... 5 H 4
Baltinglass (IRL) .... 25 F 2

Baltoji Vokė (LT)....... 205 G4
Baltrum (D).............81 E3
Bălvăneşti (RO)....... 150 D3
Balvi (LV)............. 203 G2
Bamberg (D)........... 89 H2
Bamburgh Castle (GB)..31 G4
Bampalió (GR)........ 164 D2
Bampíni (GR)......... 164 D3
Bampton (GB)......... 35 E3
Bana (H)............. 128 D1
Banagher (IRL)........ 24 D1
Banatska Palanka (SRB).141 E4
Banatska Topola (SRB). 140 D2
Banatski
  Brestovac (SRB)..... 140 D4
Banatski Dvor (SRB).. 140 D2
Banatski Karlovac (SRB).141 E3
Banatsko
  Aranđelovo (SRB).... 140 C1
Banatsko
  Karađorđevo (SRB). 140 D2
Banatsko
  Novo Selo (SRB).... 140 D3
Banbridge (GB)........ 23 G3
Banbury (GB)......... 35 H1
Banchory (GB)........ 29 H4
Band (RO)............ 147 G4
Bande (E)............ 56 C4
Bandırma (TR)........19 G2
Bandol (F)............. 55 E3
Bandon (IRL)......... 24 C5
Băneasa (RO)......... 153 C5
Banff (GB)............ 29 G3
Bangor (IRL).......... 22 B3
Bangor (Gwynedd) (GB). 32 A3
Bangor
  (North Down) (GB)... 23 G2
Bangsund (N)......... 183 E3
Banica (BG).......... 154 D3
Banie (PL)............116 B4
Banie Mazurskie (PL)...119 F2
Baniska (BG)......... 156 C2
Banite (BG).......... 162 C1
Banja (SRB).......... 139 G2
Banja (SRB).......... 140 D5
Banja (Burgas) (BG).. 157 F4
Banja (Plovdiv) (BG)... 159 E2
Banja (Sliven) (BG)... 159 F2
Banja Koviljača (SRB). 137 H4
Banja Luka (BIH)..... 135 G5
Banja Vrućica (BIH)... 137 F4
Banjani (SRB)........ 140 C4
Banjska (SRB)........ 142 D3
Bankeryd (S)......... 195 H3
Bankja (BG).......... 158 B1
Bannalec (F).......... 42 C3
Bañolas / Banyoles (E)..61 E2
Bañón (E)............ 65 G1
Banon (F)............ 55 E1
Baños de Cerrato (E)... 58 A4
Baños de la Encina (E)... 70 D3
Baños
  de la Fuensanta (E).. 71 G4
Baños de Molgas (E)... 56 D4
Baños
  de Montemayor (E)... 63 G3
Banova Jaruga (HR).... 135 F4
Bánovce
  nad Bebravou (SK).. 132 B3
Banovići (BIH)........ 137 G4
Bansin (D)........... 83 G3
Banská Bystrica (SK)... 132 D3
Banská Štiavnica (SK). 132 C3
Bansko (MK)......... 145 H1
Bansko / Банско (BG)... 161 H1
Bantry / Beanntraí (IRL).. 24 B5
Banyalbufar (E).......67 E2
Banyeres de Mariola (E). 73 E1
Banyoles / Bañolas (E)..61 E2
Banyuls-sur-Mer (F)... 54 A5
Bapaume (F).......... 40 A3
Baqueira (E)........... 60 B1
Bar (MNE)........... 139 F5
Bar (UA).............13 E2
Bar-le-Duc (F)........ 46 D1
Bar-sur-Aube (F)...... 46 C2
Bar-sur-Seine (F)..... 45 H2

Barabás (H)........... 127 F5
Baraći (BIH).......... 137 E4
Bărăganul (RO)....... 152 D3
Barajas de Melo (E)... 64 D3
Barajevo (SRB)....... 140 D4
Barakaldo (E)......... 58 D1
Baralla (E)............ 57 E3
Baranavičy (BY)........6 D5
Báránd (H)...........131 E2
Barane (SRB)......... 142 D4
Baranów
  Sandomierski (PL)... 123 E5
Baraolt (RO).......... 148 A5
Baraona (E).......... 64 D1
Baraque de Fraiture (B).. 79 E4
Baraque Michel (B)... 79 F3
Baraqueville (F)...... 53 H1
Barbadillo
  del Mercado (E)..... 58 C4
Barban (HR).......... 134 B4
Barbarano
  Vicentino (I)........ 103 E4
Barbarušince (SRB)... 143 G4
Barbastro (E)......... 60 A3
Barbat na Rabu (HR). 134 C5
Barbate (E)............74 B4
Bărbăteşti (RO)....... 151 F3
Barbazan (F)......... 53 E4
Barberino
  di Mugello (I)....... 105 H4
Barbezieux-
  Saint-Hilaire (F)... 48 D3
Barbizon (F).......... 45 F2
Barbotan-
  les-Thermes (F)... 52 D2
Barby (D)............ 86 B2
Bârca (RO)........... 151 F5
Barca de Alva (P)..... 63 E2
Barcarrota (E)........ 69 E2
Barcellona Pozzo
  di Gotto (I).........115 G2
Barcelona (E)......... 60 D4
Barcelonnette (F).....51 G5
Barcelos (P).......... 56 B5
Barchfeld (D)......... 85 H5
Barcin (PL)...........117 G5
Barcis (I)............ 103 F3
Barcones (E)......... 64 D1
Barcs (H)............ 128 C5
Barczewo (PL)........118 D3
Bardal (N)........... 183 E4
Bardejov (SK)........ 133 G2
Bardi (I)............. 105 F2
Bardineto (I)......... 104 C3
Bardo (PL)........... 121 E5
Bardolino (I)......... 101 H4
Bardonecchia (I)..... 100 A5
Bare (SRB).......... 139 H3
Barèges (F).......... 52 D4
Barentin (F)......... 39 F4
Barenton (F)......... 43 G1
Barfleur (F).......... 38 C4
Bargas (E)........... 64 B4
Bârghiş (RO)......... 147 G5
Bargoed (GB)......... 35 E4
Bargteheide (D)...... 82 B3
Bari (I)..............111 E3
Barić Draga (HR)..... 136 B4
Barisciano (I)........ 109 F2
Barjac (F)............ 54 C1
Barjols (F)........... 55 E2
Bârkač (BG)......... 156 A2
Bârlad (RO)......... 149 E5
Barlby (GB)......... 33 E2
Barletta (I)...........110 D2
Barlinek (PL).........116 C5
Barlovento (E)........67 E4
Barmstedt (D)........81 H3
Barna (IRL).......... 22 C5
Barnard Castle (GB)..31 G5
Bärnau (D)...........91 G3
Barneveld (NL)....... 77 E5
Barneville-Carteret (F). 38 B4
Barnsley (GB)........ 33 E2
Barnstaple (GB)...... 34 D3

Barnstorf (D)........... 85 E1
Barntrup (D).......... 85 F2
Barovo (MK)......... 145 G2
Barqueiro (P)......... 62 B4
Barr (F)...............47 G2
Barracas (E)......... 65 H3
Barrachina (E)........ 65 G1
Barranco Velho (P)... 68 C5
Barrancos (P)........ 69 E3
Barranda (E)......... 71 G3
Barre-des-Cévennes (F). 54 B1
Barrea (I)............ 109 G3
Barreiro (P).......... 68 A2
Barrême (F).......... 55 F1
Barrhead (GB)........ 30 C2
Barrhill (GB)......... 30 C3
Barri / Barry (GB).... 35 E2
Barrow-in-Furness (GB). 32 C1
Barruecopardo (E).... 63 E2
Barruelo de Santullán (E). 58 A2
Barry / Barri (GB).... 35 E2
Bârsana (RO)........ 147 F1
Barsinghausen (D).... 85 F2
Barstyčiai (LT)....... 204 C1
Bârta (LV)........... 202 A4
Barth (D)............ 83 E2
Barton-upon-
  Humber (GB)...... 33 F2
Bartoszyce (PL).......118 D2
Baru (RO)........... 151 E1
Barumini (I)..........112 C4
Baruth (D).......... 86 D2
Barutin (BG)......... 162 B1
Barvas (GB)......... 28 B1
Barwice (PL).........117 E3
Barysaŭ (BY)..........6 D4
Bârzava (RO)........ 146 C5
Barzio (I)............ 101 F3
Bas-en-Basset (F).... 50 C4
Bašaid (SRB)........ 140 D2
Basarbovo
  manastir (BG)...... 152 B5
Bàscara (E)...........61 E2
Baschi (I)........... 107 E5
Basconcillos del Tozo (E). 58 B2
Bascov (RO)......... 151 H3
Basel (CH)........... 98 D1
Baselga di Pinè (I).... 101 H3
Basigo de Bakio (E)... 58 D1
Basildon (GB)....... 36 D4
Basingstoke (GB).... 35 H2
Baška (HR).......... 134 C5
Baška Voda (HR).... 138 C2
Baške Oštarije (HR).. 136 B4
Basovizza (I)......... 103 H4
Bassano del Grappa (I). 103 E3
Bassens (F).......... 48 C5
Bassum (D)..........81 F5
Båstad (S).......... 195 G5
Bastasi (BIH)........ 136 D4
Bastelica (F)......... 55 H4
Bastia (F)........... 55 H3
Bastida (E)......... 58 D3
Bastogne
  (Bastenaken) (B)... 79 E4
Bastuträsk (S)...... 184 D3
Bäta (BG).......... 158 C2
Bata (BG).......... 157 F4
Batajnica (SRB)..... 140 C4
Batak (BG)......... 162 B1
Batalha (P)......... 62 B5
Batanovci (BG)..... 158 A2
Batăr (RO)......... 146 C4
Bátaszék (H)....... 129 E5
Baté (H)........... 128 D4
Batea (E)......... 60 A5
Bath (GB)......... 35 F2
Bathgate (GB)..... 30 D2
Batin (BG)......... 156 C2
Batina (HR)....... 137 H1
Batočina (SRB).....141 E5
Batorz (PL)....... 123 F4
Båtsfjord (N)...... 177 G2

Batsí (GR)........... 166 C5
Battaglia Terme (I)... 103 E5
Battenberg (D)....... 85 E4
Battice (B)........... 79 E3
Battipaglia (I)........110 B4
Battle (GB).......... 36 D5
Battonya (H)......... 130 D4
Batz-sur-Mer (F)..... 43 E4
Baud (F)............ 42 D3
Baugé-en-Anjou (F)... 43 H4
Baugy (F)........... 45 F5
Baume-les-Dames (F)...47 F4
Baumholder (D)..... 88 C2
Bauska (LV)........ 202 D4
Bautzen (D)........ 87 E4
Bavanište (SRB).... 140 D4
Bavay (F)........... 40 B2
Baveno (I).......... 100 D3
Bayerisch Eisenstein (D). 91 H5
Bayeux (F)......... 38 C5
Bayhirivagh (GB)... 28 B4
Bayındır (TR).......19 G3
Bayon (F)...........47 F2
Bayreuth (D).......91 E3
Bayrischzell (D).... 95 G3
Baza (E)............ 71 F5
Bazas (F)........... 52 C1
Bazilionai (LT)...... 204 D2
Bazoches-sur-Hoëne (F). 44 C2
Bazoches, château de (F). 45 G4
Bazzano (I)......... 105 H3
Bcie / Buje (HR)... 134 A4
Beaconsfield (GB)... 36 B4
Béal an Átha /
  Ballina (IRL)...... 22 C3
Béal Átha na Sluaighe /
  Ballinasloe (IRL)... 22 D5
Beaminster (GB)... 38 A1
Beanntraí / Bantry (IRL). 24 B5
Beariz (E)......... 56 C3
Beas (E)........... 69 E5
Beas de Segura (E)... 71 F3
Beasain (E)........ 59 E2
Beattock (GB)...... 31 E3
Beaucaire (F)...... 54 C2
Beaufort (F)........51 E1
Beaufort (F)........51 H4
Beaufort-en-Vallée (F). 43 H4
Beaugency (F)...... 44 D3
Beaujeu (F)........ 50 C2
Beaulieu (F)........ 55 H2
Beaulieu (GB)...... 38 C1
Beaulieu-
  sur-Dordogne (F)... 49 G4
Beaumaris (GB).... 32 A3
Beaumesnil (F)..... 39 E5
Beaumetz-lès-Loges (F). 39 H2
Beaumont (F)...... 78 C4
Beaumont (F)...... 49 E5
Beaumont (F)...... 39 H5
Beaumont-
  de-Lomagne (F)... 53 E2
Beaumont-
  du-Périgord (F)... 49 E5
Beaumont-Hague (F). 38 B4
Beaumont-le-Roger (F). 39 F5
Beaumont-sur-Sarthe (F). 44 A2
Beaune (F)......... 46 D5
Beaune-la-Rolande (F). 45 E3
Beaupréau-
  en-Mauges (F)... 43 G4
Beaurainville (B).... 78 D4
Beaurepaire (F).... 50 D4
Beaurepaire-
  en-Bresse (F)..... 50 D1
Beauvais (F)...... 39 G4
Beauvoir-sur-Mer (F). 43 E5
Beauvoir-sur-Niort (F). 48 D2
Beba Veche (RO).. 146 A5
Bebington (GB).... 32 C3
Bebra (D)......... 85 G4
Bebrovo (BG)..... 159 F1
Beccles (GB)...... 37 E2
Becedas (E)....... 63 G3
Beceite (E)....... 60 A5
Bečej / Бечеj (SRB).. 140 C2

Becerreá (E)........... 57 E3
Bécherel (F).......... 43 F2
Bechet (RO)......... 151 F5
Bechhofen (D)....... 89 H3
Becicherecu Mic (RO). 146 B5
Bečići (MNE)........ 139 F5
Becilla
  de Valderaduey (E). 57 H4
Beckenried (CH)..... 99 E3
Beckington (GB).... 35 F2
Beckum (D)........ 85 E3
Beclean (RO)....... 147 G3
Bečov nad Teplou (CZ)..91 G3
Becsehely (H)...... 128 B4
Becsvölgye (H)..... 128 B3
Bedale (GB).........31 G5
Bédarieux (F)...... 54 A2
Beddgelert (GB).... 32 A4
Bedford (GB)....... 33 F5
Bedlington (GB).....31 G3
Bedmar (E)........ 71 E4
Bedonia (I)........ 105 F3
Bedum (NL)........ 77 G2
Bedwas (GB)....... 35 E2
Bedworth (GB).... 33 E5
Będzin (PL)........ 122 B5
Beeford (GB)....... 33 F1
Beelitz (D)........ 86 C2
Beerfelden (D)..... 89 E3
Beeskow (D)....... 87 E2
Beesten (D)....... 84 D1
Beetzendorf (D).... 86 A1
Beg-Meil (F)....... 42 B3
Bégard (F)......... 42 D1
Begejci (SRB)...... 140 D2
Begleż (BG)........ 156 A3
Begov Han (BIH)... 137 F4
Begues (E)........ 60 D4
Begur (E)...........61 F2
Behobia (E)........ 59 F1
Behringersmühle (D)..91 E3
Beiarn (N)......... 179 F5
Beidaud (RO)...... 153 F3
Beilen (NL)....... 77 F3
Beilngries (D)......91 E5
Beisfjord (N)....... 179 H3
Beith (GB)......... 30 C2
Beitostølen (N)..... 188 D3
Beiuş (RO)......... 146 D4
Beja (P)........... 68 D3
Béjar (E)........... 63 G3
Békés (H)..........131 E3
Békéscsaba (H).....131 E3
Békéssámson (H)... 129 H4
Békésszentandrás (H). 129 H3
Bel (E)............ 66 A1
Bela Crkva (SRB)... 140 B5
Bela Crkva (SRB)....141 E4
Bělá nad Radbuzou (CZ)..91 G4
Bela Palanka (SRB).. 143 G2
Bela pod Pradědem (CZ). 93 E2
Bélâbre (F)........ 49 F1
Belalcázar (E)...... 69 H2
Belanovce (MK).... 143 F5
Belanovica (SRB)... 140 D5
Bélavár (H)........ 128 C5
Belcaire (F)........ 53 G4
Belceşti (RO)...... 148 D2
Bełchatów (PL)..... 122 B3
Belchite (E)....... 59 G5
Belčišta (MK)...... 145 E2
Belcoo (B)......... 23 E3
Bele Vode (SRB)... 139 H2
Belec (HR)........ 135 E2
Belecke (D)....... 85 E3
Beled (H)......... 128 C2
Belegiš (SRB)..... 140 D3
Belej (HR)....... 134 B5
Belenci (BG)..... 158 C1
Belene (BG)..... 151 H5
Belev (RUS)........7 G3
Belfast (GB)....... 23 G3
Belford (GB).......31 G2
Belforte all'Isauro (I). 107 F3
Belgern (D)....... 86 D3
Belgodère (F)..... 55 H3

Belgorod (RUS)..........7 H5
Belgun (BG)......... 157 G2
Beli Iskăr (BG)...... 158 B2
Beli Manastir (HR)... 137 G1
Beli Osăm (BG)..... 158 B1
Beli Potok (SRB).... 143 F2
Belianes (E)........ 60 B4
Belica (BG)......... 161 H1
Belimel (BG)....... 154 C2
Belin (F)........... 48 C5
Beliş (RO).......... 147 E4
Belišće (HR)........ 135 H3
Beliu (RO).......... 146 C4
Beljakovce (MK).... 143 F5
Beljina (SRB)....... 140 D5
Bell-lloc d'Urgell (E)... 60 B3
Bellac (F)........... 49 F2
Bellagio (I)......... 101 E3
Bellano (I)......... 101 E3
Bellaria (I)......... 107 F2
Bellcaire d'Urgell (E)... 60 B3
Belle-Isle-en-Terre (F)... 42 C1
Bellegarde (F)...... 54 C2
Bellegarde (F)...... 45 E3
Bellegarde-
  en-Marche (F).... 49 H2
Bellegarde-
  sur-Valserine (F)...51 E2
Bellême (F)........ 44 C2
Bellencombre (F)... 39 F4
Bellerive-sur-Allier (F). 50 A2
Belleville (F)....... 50 D2
Belley (F)...........51 E3
Bellinzona (CH).... 99 F4
Bello (E)........... 65 F1
Bellpuig (E)........ 60 B3
Belluno (I)......... 103 F3
Bellver (I)..........67 E3
Bellver de Cerdanya (E). 60 D2
Bélmez (E)......... 69 H3
Belmont (GB)...... 27 G1
Belmont (F)........ 50 C2
Belmont-sur-Rance (F). 53 H2
Belmonte (E)...... 57 F2
Belmonte (E)...... 64 D4
Belmonte (P)...... 62 D3
Belmullet (IRL).... 22 B3
Belo Brdo (SRB)... 142 D2
Belo Polje (SRB)... 142 D4
Belœil (B)......... 78 B3
Belogradčik (BG)... 150 D5
Beloljin (SRB)..... 143 E2
Belopolci (BG)..... 163 E1
Belorado (E)...... 58 C3
Beloslav (BG)..... 157 F3
Belotinci (BG)..... 154 C2
Belovec (BG)..... 152 C5
Belovo (BG)..... 158 C3
Belozem (BG)..... 159 E3
Belpech (F)....... 53 G3
Belper (GB)....... 33 E4
Belsay (GB)........31 G3
Belsh (AL)........ 144 C3
Beltinci (SLO)..... 135 E1
Belturbet (IRL).... 23 E4
Belušić (SRB)..... 143 E1
Belvedere Marittimo (I).113 B1
Belver de Cinca (E).. 60 A3
Belvès (F)......... 49 F5
Belvís de la Jara (E)... 63 H5
Belvoir Castle (GB)... 33 F4
Belz (F)........... 42 D3
Belzig (D)......... 86 C2
Bełżyce (PL)...... 123 F3
Bembibre (E)...... 57 F3
Bemposta (P)..... 62 C5
Benabarre (E)..... 60 A2
Benaguasil (E).... 65 H4
Benahadux (E).... 72 B5
Benalmádena (E)...74 D3
Benalmádena-
  Costa (E).........74 D4
Benalúa de Guadix (E).. 71 E5
Benalúa de las Villas (E). 70 D5
Benamargosa (E)...75 E3
Benamaurel (E).... 71 F4

A B C D E F G H I J K L M N O P Q R S T U V W X Y Z

A B C D E F G H I J K L M N O P Q R S T U V W X Y Z

Benamejí (E) ... 70 C 5
Benaoján (E) ... 74 C 3
Benasal (E) ... 66 A 1
Benasque (E) ... 60 A 1
Benavente (E) ... 57 G 5
Benavente (P) ... 68 B 1
Benavides (E) ... 57 G 3
Bendorf (D) ... 88 D 1
Benediktbeuern (D) ... 95 G 3
Benešov (CZ) ... 92 B 3
Benešov nad Ploučnicí (CZ) ... 87 E 5
Bénévent-l'Abbaye (F) ... 49 G 2
Benevento (I) ... 109 H 4
Benfeld (F) ... 47 H 2
Benfleet (GB) ... 36 D 4
Bengeşti (RO) ... 151 F 2
Bengtsfors (S) ... 195 F 1
Beničanci (HR) ... 135 H 3
Benicarló (E) ... 66 B 1
Benicàssim (E) ... 66 A 2
Benidorm (E) ... 66 A 5
Benifaió (E) ... 65 H 5
Benissa (E) ... 66 A 5
Benítses (GR) ... 164 A 1
Benkovac (HR) ... 136 C 5
Benkovski (Dobrič) (BG) ... 157 F 2
Benkovski (Kărdžali) (BG) ... 162 D 2
Benkovski (Plovdiv) (BG) ... 158 D 3
Benneckenstein (D) ... 85 H 3
Bénodet (F) ... 42 B 3
Benquerencia de la Serena (E) ... 69 H 2
Bensberg (D) ... 84 C 4
Bensersiel (D) ... 81 E 4
Bensheim (D) ... 89 E 2
Bentley (GB) ... 33 E 2
Beočin (SRB) ... 140 C 3
Beograd / Београд (SRB) ... 140 D 4
Bera (E) ... 59 F 1
Berane (MNE) ... 139 H 3
Berat (AL) ... 144 C 3
Berazino (BY) ... 7 E 4
Berbegal (E) ... 60 A 3
Berberana (E) ... 58 C 2
Berbeşti (RO) ... 151 F 2
Berceto (I) ... 105 F 3
Berching (D) ... 91 E 5
Berchtesgaden (D) ... 96 B 3
Berck-Plage (F) ... 39 G 2
Berdyčiv (UA) ... 13 E 1
Bere Regis (GB) ... 38 A 1
Beregsurány (H) ... 127 G 5
Bereguardo (I) ... 101 E 4
Berehove (UA) ... 12 C 3
Berek (HR) ... 135 F 3
Beremend (H) ... 129 E 5
Bereşti (RO) ... 149 E 5
Beret (E) ... 60 B 1
Berettyóújfalu (H) ... 131 E 2
Berezeni (RO) ... 149 E 4
Berezivka (UA) ... 13 G 3
Berg (A) ... 97 H 2
Berg (N) ... 183 E 2
Berg (S) ... 189 H 1
Berga (D) ... 86 A 3
Berga (E) ... 60 D 2
Bergama (TR) ... 19 G 3
Bergamo (I) ... 101 F 4
Bergara (E) ... 59 E 1
Bergby (S) ... 190 B 4
Bergedorf (D) ... 81 H 4
Bergen (D) ... 188 B 4
Bergen (NL) ... 76 D 3
Bergen (Celle) (D) ... 81 H 5
Bergen (Rügen) (D) ... 82 C 5
Bergen aan Zee (NL) ... 76 D 3
Bergen auf Rügen (D) ... 83 F 2
Bergen op Zoom (NL) ... 78 C 1
Bergerac (F) ... 49 E 3
Berggießhübel (D) ... 87 E 5
Bergheim (D) ... 84 C 4
Bergisch Gladbach (D) ... 84 C 4

Bergnäset (S) ... 185 E 2
Bergneustadt (D) ... 84 D 4
Bergö (FIN) ... 191 E 1
Bergsjö (S) ... 190 B 2
Bergsviken (S) ... 185 E 2
Bergues (F) ... 39 H 1
Bergün / Bravuogn (CH) ... 99 G 3
Berhida (H) ... 128 D 3
Beringel (P) ... 68 C 3
Beringen (B) ... 78 D 2
Berja (E) ... 72 A 5
Berka (D) ... 85 G 5
Berkåk (N) ... 189 E 1
Berkeley Castle (GB) ... 35 F 1
Berkhamsted (GB) ... 36 B 3
Berkheim (D) ... 95 E 2
Berkhof (D) ... 85 G 1
Berkovica (BG) ... 154 D 3
Berkovići (BIH) ... 139 E 3
Berlaimont (F) ... 40 B 3
Berlanga (E) ... 69 G 3
Berlanga de Duero (E) ... 58 D 5
Berlebeck (D) ... 85 F 2
Berlevåg (N) ... 177 G 1
Berlin (D) ... 86 D 1
Berlişte (RO) ... 150 B 2
Bermeo (E) ... 58 D 1
Bermillo de Sayago (E) ... 63 F 1
Bern (CH) ... 98 C 3
Bernartice (CZ) ... 92 A 4
Bernalda (I) ... 111 E 4
Bernau am Chiemsee (D) ... 95 H 3
Bernau bei Berlin (D) ... 86 D 1
Bernau im Schwarzwald (D) ... 94 B 3
Bernaville (F) ... 39 H 3
Bernay (F) ... 39 E 5
Bernburg (D) ... 86 B 3
Berndorf (A) ... 97 G 2
Berne (D) ... 81 F 5
Bernhardsthal (A) ... 93 G 4
Bernkastel-Kues (D) ... 88 C 2
Bernsdorf (D) ... 87 E 3
Bernstein (A) ... 97 G 3
Beronovo (BG) ... 159 H 1
Beroun (CZ) ... 92 A 3
Berovo (MK) ... 145 H 1
Berra (I) ... 103 E 5
Berre-l'Étang (F) ... 54 D 3
Beršad' (UA) ... 13 F 2
Bersenbrück (D) ... 84 D 1
Bertamiráns (E) ... 56 B 3
Bertești de Jos (RO) ... 153 E 3
Bertinoro (I) ... 107 E 2
Bertrix (B) ... 78 D 4
Berwang (A) ... 95 F 3
Berwick-upon-Tweed (GB) ... 31 F 2
Beryslav (UA) ... 13 H 2
Berzasca (RO) ... 150 C 3
Bērzaune (LV) ... 203 F 3
Berzence (H) ... 128 C 4
Berzocana (E) ... 63 G 5
Berzovia (RO) ... 150 C 1
Bērzpils (Bierzpiļs) (LV) ... 203 G 3
Besalú (E) ... 61 E 2
Besançon (F) ... 47 E 4
Besande (E) ... 57 H 3
Besenyszög (H) ... 129 G 2
Beška (SRB) ... 140 C 3
Besigheim (D) ... 89 F 4
Besse-et-Saint-Anastaise (F) ... 50 A 3
Besse-sur-Issole (F) ... 55 F 3
Bessèges (F) ... 54 B 1
Bessines-sur-Gartempe (F) ... 49 F 2
Betancuria (E) ... 67 H 5
Betanzos (E) ... 56 C 2
Betelu (E) ... 59 E 2
Bétera / Bètera (E) ... 65 H 4
Bethesda (GB) ... 32 B 3
Béthune (F) ... 39 H 2
Bettna (S) ... 197 F 2

Bettola (I) ... 105 F 2
Bettolle (I) ... 107 E 4
Bettyhill (GB) ... 26 A 4
Betws-y-Coed (GB) ... 32 B 3
Betz (F) ... 40 A 5
Betzdorf (D) ... 84 D 5
Beuil (F) ... 55 G 1
Beuron (D) ... 94 C 2
Beuzeville (F) ... 39 E 4
Bevagna (I) ... 107 F 5
Beveren (B) ... 78 C 1
Beverley (GB) ... 33 F 2
Beverstedt (D) ... 81 G 4
Beverungen (D) ... 85 F 3
Beverwijk (NL) ... 76 D 4
Bewdley (GB) ... 32 D 5
Bex (CH) ... 98 C 4
Bexhill (GB) ... 36 D 5
Beynac-et-Cazenac (F) ... 49 F 5
Beynat (F) ... 49 G 4
Bezas (E) ... 65 G 3
Bezdan (SRB) ... 137 H 1
Bežков (RUS) ... 7 F 1
Béziers (F) ... 54 A 3
Bezmisth (AL) ... 145 E 3
Béznar (E) ... 75 F 3
Biała (PL) ... 121 F 5
Biała Piska (PL) ... 119 F 3
Biała Podlaska (PL) ... 123 G 1
Biała Rawska (PL) ... 122 C 2
Białaszewo (PL) ... 119 F 3
Białe Błota (PL) ... 117 G 4
Białobrzegi (PL) ... 122 D 2
Białogard (PL) ... 116 D 2
Białogóra (PL) ... 117 G 1
Białopole (PL) ... 123 H 4
Białowieża (PL) ... 119 H 5
Biały Bór (PL) ... 117 E 3
Białystok (PL) ... 119 G 4
Biancavilla (I) ... 115 F 3
Bianco (I) ... 115 H 2
Biandrate (I) ... 100 D 4
Biar (E) ... 73 E 1
Biarritz (F) ... 52 A 3
Biasca (CH) ... 99 F 4
Biasteri (E) ... 58 D 3
Biatorbágy (H) ... 129 E 2
Bibbiena (I) ... 107 E 3
Biberach an der Riß (D) ... 94 D 2
Biberach im Kinzigtal (D) ... 88 D 5
Bibinje (HR) ... 136 B 5
Bibione (I) ... 103 G 4
Bibury (GB) ... 35 G 1
Bicaj (AL) ... 142 D 5
Bicaz (RO) ... 148 B 3
Bicaz-Chei (RO) ... 148 B 4
Bicester (GB) ... 35 H 1
Bichl (D) ... 95 G 3
Bicske (H) ... 129 E 2
Bidache (F) ... 52 B 3
Bidart (F) ... 52 A 3
Biddenden (GB) ... 36 D 5
Bideford (GB) ... 34 D 3
Bidovce (SK) ... 133 G 3
Biebelried (D) ... 89 G 2
Biecz (PL) ... 127 E 2
Biedenkopf (D) ... 85 E 5
Biel / Bienne (CH) ... 98 C 2
Bielawa (PL) ... 121 E 5
Bielefeld (D) ... 85 E 2
Biella (I) ... 100 C 4
Bielsa (E) ... 60 A 1
Bielsk (PL) ... 118 C 5
Bielsk Podlaski (PL) ... 119 G 5
Bielsko-Biała (PL) ... 125 F 2
Bienne / Biel (CH) ... 98 C 2
Bientina (I) ... 105 G 4
Bienvenida (E) ... 69 G 3
Bierdzany (PL) ... 121 G 4
Bierné (F) ... 43 H 3
Biertan (RO) ... 147 G 5
Bieruń (PL) ... 125 F 1
Bierutów (PL) ... 121 F 4
Biescas (E) ... 59 H 2
Biesenthal (D) ... 83 G 5

Bietigheim-Bissingen (D) ... 89 F 4
Bieżuń (PL) ... 118 C 4
Biga (TR) ... 19 G 2
Biggar (GB) ... 30 D 2
Biggleswade (GB) ... 36 C 3
Bignasco (CH) ... 99 E 4
Bihać (BIH) ... 135 E 5
Biharia (RO) ... 146 C 3
Biharkeresztes (H) ... 131 E 2
Biharnagybajom (H) ... 131 E 2
Bijele Poljane (MNE) ... 139 F 4
Bijeljani (BIH) ... 139 E 3
Bijeljina / Бијељина (BIH) ... 137 H 3
Bijelo Brdo (HR) ... 137 H 2
Bijelo Polje (MNE) ... 139 G 3
Bila Cerkva (UA) ... 13 F 1
Bilbao (E) ... 58 D 1
Bilbor (RO) ... 148 A 3
Bildudalur (IS) ... 178 A 1
Bileća (BIH) ... 139 E 3
Bilecik (TR) ... 19 H 2
Biled (RO) ... 146 B 5
Biłgoraj (PL) ... 123 G 5
Bilhorod-Dnistrovs'kyj (UA) ... 13 G 3
Bílina (CZ) ... 86 D 5
Bilisht (AL) ... 145 E 3
Biljača (SRB) ... 143 F 4
Biljanovac (SRB) ... 142 D 2
Bilje (HR) ... 137 H 1
Billerbeck (D) ... 84 C 2
Billericay (GB) ... 36 D 4
Billingham (GB) ... 31 G 4
Billingshurst (GB) ... 36 C 5
Billom (F) ... 50 A 3
Billund (DK) ... 198 B 3
Bilopillja (UA) ... 7 G 5
Bílovec (CZ) ... 93 G 3
Bilto (N) ... 176 C 4
Bilzen (B) ... 79 E 2
Binaced (E) ... 60 A 3
Binasco (I) ... 101 E 4
Binche (B) ... 78 C 3
Binéfar (E) ... 60 A 3
Bingen am Rhein (D) ... 88 D 2
Bingham (GB) ... 33 F 4
Bingley (GB) ... 32 D 2
Bingsjö (S) ... 190 A 4
Binic (F) ... 42 D 1
Binkos (BG) ... 159 G 2
Binn Éadair / Howth (IRL) ... 23 G 5
Binz (D) ... 83 F 2
Bioče (MNE) ... 139 G 4
Biograd na moru (HR) ... 136 B 5
Bionaz (I) ... 100 B 3
Biosca (E) ... 60 C 3
Bira (RO) ... 148 C 3
Birchington (GB) ... 37 E 4
Biri (N) ... 189 F 3
Birkeland (N) ... 194 C 2
Birkenfeld (D) ... 88 C 2
Birkenhead (GB) ... 32 C 3
Birkenwerder (D) ... 86 D 1
Birkerød (DK) ... 199 E 3
Birkfeld (A) ... 97 F 3
Birmingham (GB) ... 32 D 5
Birr (IRL) ... 24 D 2
Biržai (LT) ... 205 F 1
Birżebbuga (M) ... 114 C 5
Bisaccia (I) ... 110 C 3
Biscarrosse (F) ... 52 B 1
Biscarrosse-Plage (F) ... 48 B 5
Bisceglie (I) ... 111 E 3
Bischofsgrün (D) ... 91 F 3
Bischofsheim an der Rhön (D) ... 89 G 1
Bischofshofen (A) ... 96 C 3
Bischofswerda (D) ... 87 E 4
Bischofswiesen (D) ... 96 B 3
Bischofszell (CH) ... 99 F 2
Bischwiller (F) ... 41 H 5
Bisenti (I) ... 109 G 1
Bishop Auckland (GB) ... 31 G 4
Bishop's Castle (GB) ... 32 C 5

Bishop's Stortford (GB) ... 36 C 3
Bisignano (I) ... 113 B 2
Bisko (HR) ... 138 B 2
Biskupice Radłowskie (PL) ... 125 H 1
Biskupiec (Iława) (PL) ... 118 B 3
Biskupiec (Olsztyn) (PL) ... 118 D 2
Biskupin (PL) ... 117 F 5
Bismark (D) ... 86 A 1
Bismo (N) ... 188 D 2
Bispgården (S) ... 190 B 1
Bispingen (D) ... 81 H 5
Bistra (BG) ... 156 D 2
Bistret (RO) ... 151 E 5
Bistrica (BG) ... 158 B 2
Bistrica (MNE) ... 139 G 3
Bistrica (SRB) ... 139 G 3
Bistrica ob Sotli (SLO) ... 134 D 2
Bistrița (RO) ... 147 G 3
Bisztynek (PL) ... 118 D 2
Bitburg (D) ... 88 B 2
Bitche (F) ... 41 G 5
Bitetto (I) ... 111 E 3
Bitola (MK) ... 145 F 2
Bitonto (I) ... 111 E 3
Bitterfeld (D) ... 86 B 3
Bitti (I) ... 112 C 2
Bixad (RO) ... 148 B 5
Bizau (A) ... 94 D 4
Bizovac (HR) ... 137 G 1
Bjal Izvor (Kărdžali) (BG) ... 162 D 1
Bjal Izvor (Stara Zagora) (BG) ... 159 F 3
Bjala (Ruse) (BG) ... 156 C 2
Bjala (Sliven) (BG) ... 159 G 1
Bjala (Varna) (BG) ... 157 F 3
Bjala Reka (BG) ... 159 E 3
Bjala Slatina / Бяла Слатина (BG) ... 155 E 2
Bjaroza (BY) ... 6 C 5
Bjästa (S) ... 184 C 5
Bjelovar (HR) ... 135 F 3
Bjerkreim (N) ... 194 B 1
Bjerkvik (N) ... 176 A 5
Bjerringbro (DK) ... 194 D 5
Bjørkelangen (N) ... 189 F 5
Björkliden (S) ... 180 A 3
Björklinge (S) ... 190 C 5
Björköby (FIN) ... 185 E 5
Björksele (S) ... 184 C 3
Bjorli (N) ... 188 D 1
Björna (S) ... 184 C 5
Björsäter (S) ... 197 E 3
Bjurholm (S) ... 184 D 4
Bjursås (S) ... 190 A 4
Bjuv (S) ... 199 E 3
Blå Jungfrun nationalpark (S) ... 197 F 4
Blace (SRB) ... 143 E 2
Blachownia (PL) ... 121 H 5
Blackburn (GB) ... 32 D 2
Blackpool (GB) ... 32 C 2
Blackwater (IRL) ... 25 F 3
Blackwaterfoot (GB) ... 23 H 1
Blaenau Ffestiniog (GB) ... 32 B 4
Blaenavon (GB) ... 35 E 1
Blagaj (BIH) ... 138 D 3
Blagnac (F) ... 53 F 2
Blagoevgrad / Благоевград (BG) ... 158 B 3
Blåhammaren (S) ... 183 E 5
Blain (F) ... 43 F 4
Blainville (F) ... 47 F 1
Blair Atholl (GB) ... 29 F 5
Blairgowrie (GB) ... 29 G 5
Blaj (RO) ... 147 F 5
Blakeney (GB) ... 33 H 4
Blakstad (N) ... 194 D 2
Blâmont (F) ... 47 F 1
Blanca (E) ... 71 H 3
Blândești (RO) ... 148 C 2
Blanes (E) ... 61 E 3
Blangy-le-Château (F) ... 39 E 5
Blangy-sur-Bresle (F) ... 39 G 3

Blankenberge (B) ... 78 B 1
Blankenburg (D) ... 86 A 3
Blankenhain (D) ... 86 A 5
Blankenheim (D) ... 88 B 1
Blanquefort (F) ... 48 C 4
Blansko (CZ) ... 93 E 4
Blanzac (F) ... 48 D 3
Blanzy (F) ... 50 C 1
Blarney (IRL) ... 24 C 4
Blåskovo (BG) ... 157 E 3
Blatec (BG) ... 159 G 2
Blatná (CZ) ... 92 A 4
Blatnica (BIH) ... 137 F 4
Blato (HR) ... 138 C 2
Blattniksele (S) ... 184 C 2
Blaubeuren (D) ... 89 G 3
Blaufelden (D) ... 89 G 3
Blaustein (D) ... 89 G 5
Blaye (F) ... 48 C 4
Blaževo (SRB) ... 143 E 2
Błażowa (PL) ... 127 F 1
Bleckede (D) ... 82 C 4
Bled (SLO) ... 134 B 2
Bleiburg (A) ... 97 E 5
Bleicherode (D) ... 85 H 3
Bleik (N) ... 179 G 1
Bléneau (F) ... 45 F 3
Blenheim Palace (GB) ... 35 H 1
Blénod (F) ... 41 E 5
Blérancourt (F) ... 40 A 4
Bléré (F) ... 44 C 3
Blesle (F) ... 50 A 4
Bletchley (GB) ... 35 H 1
Bletterans (F) ... 47 E 5
Blexen (D) ... 81 F 4
Blickling Hall (GB) ... 37 E 1
Blieskastel (D) ... 88 C 3
Bligny (F) ... 46 C 5
Blinisht (AL) ... 144 C 1
Blinja (HR) ... 135 E 4
Bliznaci (BG) ... 157 F 3
Bliznak (BG) ... 157 E 5
Bloemendaal (NL) ... 76 D 4
Blois (F) ... 44 D 4
Blokhus (DK) ... 194 D 4
Blomberg (D) ... 85 F 2
Blönduós (IS) ... 178 B 2
Błonie (PL) ... 122 D 1
Blonville-sur-Mer (F) ... 38 D 4
Blosenberg (D) ... 91 F 2
Bloškapolica (SLO) ... 134 B 3
Błotnowola (PL) ... 122 D 5
Blovice (CZ) ... 91 H 4
Bludenz (A) ... 94 D 4
Blumberg (Schwarzwald-Baar) (D) ... 94 B 3
Blumberg arnim (D) ... 86 D 1
Blyth (GB) ... 31 G 3
Bø (N) ... 194 D 1
Bø (N) ... 179 F 2
Bo' Ness (GB) ... 30 D 1
Boal (E) ... 57 E 1
Boan (MNE) ... 139 G 3
Boara Pisani (I) ... 103 E 5
Bobbio (I) ... 105 E 2
Bòbbio Pèllice (I) ... 100 B 5
Bobigny (F) ... 39 H 5
Bobingen (D) ... 89 H 5
Böblingen (D) ... 89 F 4
Boblitz (D) ... 87 E 2
Bobolice (PL) ... 117 E 3
Boboševo (BG) ... 158 A 3
Boboszów (PL) ... 124 B 1
Bobota (RO) ... 146 D 2
Bobov dol (BG) ... 158 A 2
Bobrovycja (UA) ... 13 F 1
Bobrowniki (PL) ... 119 H 4
Bobrynec' (UA) ... 13 G 2
Bocac (BIH) ... 137 E 4
Bocairent (E) ... 73 F 1
Boceguillas (E) ... 58 C 5
Bochnia (PL) ... 125 H 1
Bocholt (D) ... 84 C 2
Bochov (CZ) ... 91 G 2
Bochum (D) ... 84 C 3
Bockenem (D) ... 85 G 2

Böckstein (A) .... 96 C 4
Bockum-Hövel (D) ..... 84 D 3
Bocognano (F) ..... 55 H 4
Bocşa (RO) .... 150 C 2
Bocsig (RO) .... 146 C 4
Böda (S) .... 197 F 4
Boda (N) .... 190 A 4
Bodafors (S) .... 195 H 4
Bodajk (H) .... 128 D 2
Bođani (SRB) .... 137 H 2
Bodegraven (NL) ...... 76 D 5
Boden (S) .... 185 E 1
Bodenmais (D) .... 91 H 5
Bodenwerder (D) ..... 85 G 2
Bodenwöhr (D) .... 91 H 4
Bodeşti (RO) .... 148 C 3
Bodiam Castle (GB) ... 36 D 5
Bodman (D) .... 94 C 3
Bodmin (GB) .... 34 C 4
Bodø (N) .... 179 F 4
Bodrum (TR) .... 19 G 4
Bodzanów (PL) .... 118 C 5
Bodzanowice (PL) ..... 121 H 4
Bodzentyn (PL) .... 122 D 4
Boechout,
 omein van (B) .... 78 C 2
Boecillo (E) .... 58 A 5
Boëge (F) .... 51 F 2
Boën-sur-Lignon (F.) .. 50 B 3
Boeza (E) .... 57 F 3
Boffalora (I) .... 101 E 4
Bogádmindszent (H) .. 128 D 5
Bogarra (E) .... 71 G 2
Bogatić (SRB) .... 140 B 4
Bogatynia (PL) .... 120 B 4
Bogda (RO) .... 146 C 5
Bogdan (BG) .... 158 D 2
Bogdanci (BG) .... 156 D 2
Bogdanci (MK) .... 145 H 2
Bogdand (RO) .... 147 E 2
Bogdaniec (PL) .... 116 C 5
Bogë (AL) .... 142 C 4
Bogen (D) .... 91 G 5
Bogen (N) .... 176 A 5
Bogense (DK) .... 198 C 3
Bogetići (MNE) ...... 139 F 4
Bognanco (I) .... 100 D 3
Bognor Regis (GB) .... 38 D 1
Bogodol (BIH) .... 138 D 2
Bogojevo (SRB) ...... 137 H 2
Bogomila (MK) .... 145 F 1
Bogomolje (HR) ...... 138 C 3
Bogorodica (MK) ..... 145 H 2
Bogorovo (BG) .... 152 D 5
Bögöte (H) .... 128 C 3
Bogovina (SRB) ...... 143 F 1
Boguszów Gorce (PL) . 120 D 4
Bogutovac (SRB) ..... 142 D 2
Bohain-
 en-Vermandois (F) .... 40 A 3
Bohdanovce (SK) .... 133 G 3
Boherbue (IRL) .... 24 C 4
Bohinjska
 Bistrica (SLO) ...... 134 B 2
Böhlen (D) .... 86 C 4
Böhmenkirch (D) ..... 89 G 5
Bohmte (D) .... 85 E 1
Bohoduchiv (UA) ...... 7 H 5
Böhönye (H) .... 128 C 4
Bohot (BG) .... 156 A 2
Bohumín (CZ) .... 93 G 2
Bohuslav (UA) .... 13 F 1
Boiro (E) .... 56 B 3
Bois-d'Amont (F) ...... 51 F 1
Boitzenburg (D) ...... 83 F 4
Bóixols (E) .... 60 C 2
Boizenburg (D) ...... 82 C 4
Bojadła (PL) .... 120 D 2
Bojano (I) .... 109 H 4
Bojanovo (BG) .... 159 G 2
Bojanów (PL) .... 123 E 5
Bojanowo (PL) .... 121 E 2
Bojčinovci (BG) ...... 154 D 2
Bor / Бор (SRB) ...... 141 F 5
Bojden (DK) .... 198 C 4
Bojkovice (CZ) .... 93 F 4
Bojnica (BG) .... 150 D 5
Bojnik (SRB) .... 143 F 3

Bol (HR) .... 138 B 2
Bøla (N) .... 183 E 4
Bolaños de Calatrava (E) . 70 D 2
Bolbec (F) .... 39 E 4
Bolboşi (RO) .... 151 E 3
Bolchov (RUS) .... 7 G 3
Boldeşti-Scăeni (RO) .. 152 B 3
Bolesław (PL) .... 122 D 5
Bolesławiec (PL) ..... 120 C 3
Boleszkowice (PL) ..... 116 B 5
Bolhrad (UA) .... 13 F 4
Borek Wielkopolski (PL) . 121 F 2
Boliden (S) .... 184 D 3
Bolintin-Vale (RO) ... 152 B 4
Boliqueime (P) .... 68 C 5
Boljanići (MNE) ...... 139 G 2
Boljarci (BG) .... 159 E 3
Boljarovo (BG) .... 159 H 3
Boljarsko (BG) .... 159 G 2
Boljevac (SRB) .... 143 F 1
Boljevci (SRB) .... 140 C 4
Boljkovci (SRB) ...... 139 H 1
Boljuni (BIH) .... 138 D 3
Bolkesjø (N) .... 188 D 5
Bolków (PL) .... 120 D 4
Bollebygd (S) .... 195 G 3
Bollène (F) .... 54 C 1
Bollnäs (S) .... 190 B 3
Bollstabruk (S) ...... 190 C 1
Bollullos
 de la Mitación (E) .... 69 G 5
Bollullos Par
 del Condado (E) ...... 69 F 5
Bolochovo (RUS) .... 7 G 3
Bologna (I) .... 106 D 1
Bologne (F) .... 46 D 2
Bologoje (RUS) .... 7 E 1
Bolotana (I) .... 112 C 2
Bolsena (I) .... 107 E 5
Bolsward (NL) .... 77 E 3
Boltaña (E) .... 60 A 2
Boltenhagen (D) ..... 82 C 3
Boričje (MNE) .... 139 F 3
Borino (BG) .... 162 B 1
Borja (E) .... 59 F 4
Borken (D) .... 84 C 2
Borkenes (Kvæfjord) (N) . 179 G 2
Borki (PL) .... 122 D 5
Borkum (D) .... 80 D 4
Bormes-
 les-Mimosas (F) ...... 55 F 3
Bormio (I) .... 101 G 2
Born am Darß (D) .... 83 E 2
Borna (D) .... 86 C 4
Bornes (P) .... 63 E 1
Bornheim (D) .... 81 H 3
Börnicke (D) .... 86 C 1
Bornos (E) .... 74 B 3
Borod (RO) .... 146 D 3
Boroşneu Mare (RO) .. 152 B 1
Boroughbridge (GB) .. 33 E 1
Borovan (BG) .... 155 E 2
Borovci (BG) .... 154 D 3
Borovec (BG) .... 158 B 2
Boroviči (RUS) .... 7 E 1
Borovnica (SLO) ..... 134 B 3
Borovo (BG) .... 156 C 2
Borovo (HR) .... 137 H 2
Borovsk (RUS) .... 7 G 2
Borre (N) .... 195 E 1
Borriana (E) .... 66 A 2
Borriol (E) .... 66 A 2
Borris (IRL) .... 25 F 3
Borrisokane (IRL) .... 24 D 2
Borş (RO) .... 146 C 3
Borşa (RO) .... 147 G 2
Borsec (RO) .... 148 A 3
Børselv (N) .... 177 E 2
Borsfa (H) .... 128 B 4
Borsh (AL) .... 144 C 5
Bórsio (GR) .... 164 D 4
Borský Mikuláš (SK) .. 132 A 3
Bort-les-Orgues (F) ... 49 H 3
Börtnan (S) .... 189 H 1
Boryspil' (UA) .... 13 F 1
Borzna (UA) .... 7 F 5
Borzonasca (I) ...... 105 E 3

Borca (RO) .... 148 B 3
Borča (SRB) .... 140 D 4
Borcea (RO) .... 153 E 4
Borci (BIH) .... 139 E 2
Bordeaux (F) .... 48 C 5
Bordei Verde (RO) .... 152 D 2
Bordères-Louron (F) .. 52 D 4
Bordesholm (D) .... 81 H 3
Bordighera (I) .... 104 C 4
Bore (I) .... 105 F 2
Borello (I) .... 107 E 2
Borensberg (S) ...... 197 E 2
Borgå / Porvoo (FIN) . 193 E 4
Borgafjäll (S) .... 183 G 3
Borgarfjörður (IS) ... 178 D 2
Borgarnes (IS) .... 178 A 2
Börger (D) .... 81 E 5
Borger (NL) .... 77 G 3
Borghetto
 Santo Spirito (I) .... 104 D 3
Borghetto
 Val Tidone (I) ...... 101 F 5
Borgholm (S) .... 197 F 5
Borgholzhausen (D) ... 85 E 2
Borghorst (D) .... 84 D 2
Borgia (I) .... 113 C 3
Borgo
 San Dalmazzo (I) .... 104 B 3
Borgo San Lorenzo (I) . 106 D 2
Borgo Tufico (I) ..... 107 G 4
Borgo Val di Taro (I) . 105 F 3
Borgo Valsugana (I) .. 102 D 3
Borgone Susa (I) .... 100 B 5
Borgonovo
 Val Tidone (I) ...... 101 F 5
Borgorose (I) .... 109 F 2
Borgosesia (I) ...... 100 D 3
Borgsjö (S) .... 190 A 1
Borgvattnet (S) ..... 183 H 5
Boričje (MNE) .... 139 F 3
Borino (BG) .... 162 B 1
Borja (E) .... 59 F 4

Bosa (I) .... 112 B 2
Bosanci (HR) .... 134 D 4
Bosanci (RO) .... 148 B 2
Bosanska Dubica /
 Kosarska Dubica (BIH) . 135 F 4
Bosanska Gradiška /
 Gradiška (BIH) ...... 135 G 4
Bosanska
 Kostajnica (BIH) .... 135 F 4
Bosanska Krupa (BIH) . 135 E 5
Bosanska Rača (BIH) .. 137 H 3
Bosanski (BIH) ...... 135 G 5
Bosanski Novi /
 Novi Grad (BIH) ..... 135 E 5
Bosanski
 Petrovac (BIH) ...... 136 D 4
Bosanski Šamac /
 Šamac (BIH) .... 137 G 3
Bosansko
 Grahovo (BIH) ...... 136 D 5
Bosansko
 Petrovo Selo (BIH) .. 137 G 4
Bősárkány (H) .... 128 C 1
Bosco (I) .... 107 F 4
Bosco Chiesanuova (I) . 101 H 4
Bosilegrad (SRB) .... 143 G 4
Bosiljevo (HR) .... 134 D 4
Bosiljevo (HR) ...... 134 D 4
Boskoop (NL) .... 76 D 5
Boskovice (CZ) ...... 93 E 4
Bošnjace (SRB) ...... 143 F 3
Bošnjaci (HR) .... 137 H 3
Bossolasco (I) ...... 104 C 2
Bossòst (E) .... 60 B 1
Boştanj (SLO) .... 134 D 2
Boston (GB) .... 33 G 4
Bošulja (BG) .... 158 C 2
Boţeşti (Piteşti) (RO) . 151 H 2
Boţeşti (Vaslui) (RO) . 149 E 4
Botevgrad /
 Ботевград (BG) ..... 158 C 1
Bothel (GB) .... 31 E 4
Boticas (P) .... 56 D 5
Botiza (RO) .... 147 G 2
Botley (GB) .... 38 C 1
Botngård (N) .... 182 D 4
Botoroaga (RO) ...... 152 A 4
Botoš (SRB) .... 140 D 3
Botoşani (RO) .... 148 C 2
Botsmark (S) .... 184 D 4
Bottrop (D) .... 84 C 3
Botun (MK) .... 145 E 2
Bouaye (F) .... 43 F 5
Boucau (F) .... 52 A 2
Bouchain (F) .... 40 A 2
Boudry (CH) .... 98 B 3
Bouges, château de (F) . 44 D 5
Boughton House (GB) . 33 F 5
Bouillon (B) .... 78 D 5
Bouilly (F) .... 45 H 2
Boulay-Moselle (F) .... 41 F 5
Boulogne-sur-Gesse (F) . 53 E 3
Boulogne-sur-Mer (F) . 39 G 1
Bouloire (F) .... 44 C 3
Bourbon-
 l'Archambault (F) .... 50 A 1
Bourbonne-
 les-Bains (F) .... 47 E 3
Bourbourg (F) .... 39 H 1
Bourbriac (F) .... 42 D 1
Bourdeaux (F) .... 50 D 5
Bourdeilles (F) ...... 49 E 4
Bourg (F) .... 48 C 4
Bourg-Achard (F) .... 39 F 4
Bourg-Argental (F) ... 50 C 4
Bourg-de-Péage (F) .. 50 D 4
Bourg-de-Visa (F) .... 53 E 1
Bourg-en-Bresse (F) .. 50 D 2
Bourg-Lastic (F) ..... 49 H 3
Bourg-Madame (F) ... 53 G 5
Bourg-Saint-Andéol (F) . 54 C 1
Bourg-Saint-Maurice (F) . 51 G 3
Bourganeuf (F) ...... 49 G 2
Bourges (F) .... 45 E 5

Bourgneuf-en-Retz (F) . 43 E 5
Bourgoin-Jallieu (F) .. 50 D 3
Bourgueil (F) .... 44 B 4
Bourmont (F) .... 47 E 2
Bourne (GB) .... 33 F 4
Bournemouth (GB) .... 38 B 1
Bouro (P) .... 56 C 5
Boussac (F) .... 49 H 1
Boussens (F) .... 53 E 3
Bouxwiller (F) .... 41 G 5
Bouzonville (F) .... 41 F 4
Bova Marina (I) ...... 115 H 2
Bovalino Marina (I) .. 115 H 2
Bovan (SRB) .... 143 F 2
Bovec (SLO) .... 134 A 2
Bóveda (E) .... 56 D 3
Bøverdal (N) .... 188 D 2
Boves (F) .... 39 H 3
Boves (I) .... 104 B 3
Bovey Tracey (GB) .... 34 D 4
Bovolone (I) .... 101 H 5
Bowes (GB) .... 31 F 5
Bowness-
 on-Solway (GB) ...... 31 E 4
Bowness-on-
 Windermere (GB) .... 31 E 5
Boxholm (S) .... 196 D 3
Boxmeer (NL) .... 79 F 1
Boxtel (NL) .... 79 E 1
Boyle (IRL) .... 22 D 4
Božaj (MNE) .... 139 G 5
Božava (HR) .... 136 A 5
Bozdoğan (TR) .... 19 H 3
Bozel (F) .... 51 G 3
Bozen / Bolzano (I) .. 102 D 2
Boži dar (CZ) .... 91 G 2
Božica (SRB) .... 143 G 4
Bozouls (F) .... 53 H 1
Bozovici (RO) .... 150 C 3
Božuriște (BG) ...... 158 B 1
Bozüyük (TR) .... 19 H 2
Bozzolo (I) .... 101 G 5
Bra (I) .... 104 C 2
Brabova (RO) .... 151 E 4
Bracadale (GB) .... 28 C 3
Bracciano (I) .... 108 D 2
Bračevci (HR) .... 135 H 4
Brachlewo (PL) ...... 117 H 3
Bracieux (F) .... 44 D 4
Bracigovo (BG) ...... 158 D 3
Bräcke (S) .... 190 A 1
Brackenheim (D) ..... 89 F 4
Brackley (GB) .... 35 H 1
Bracknell (GB) .... 35 H 2
Brackwede (D) .... 85 E 2
Brad (RO) .... 146 D 5
Bradashesh (AL) .... 144 C 2
Brădeanu (RO) ...... 152 C 3
Bradford (GB) .... 33 E 2
Bradford-on-Avon (GB) . 35 F 2
Bradina (RO) .... 139 E 1
Bradvari (BG) .... 152 D 5
Bradwell-on-Sea (GB) . 36 D 3
Braemar (GB) .... 29 F 4
Braga (P) .... 56 B 5
Bragadiru
 (Alexandria) (RO) ... 152 A 5
Bragadiru
 (Bucureşti) (RO) .... 152 B 4
Bragança (P) .... 57 E 5
Brahestad /
 Raahe (FIN) .... 185 G 3
Brăila (RO) .... 153 E 2
Braine (F) .... 40 B 4
Braine-le-Comte (B) .. 78 C 3
Braintree (GB) .... 36 D 3
Brake (D) .... 81 F 4
Brakel (D) .... 85 F 3
Bräkne-Hoby (S) .... 199 G 2
Brállos (GR) .... 165 F 3
Brallo di Pregola (I) . 105 E 2
Brampton (GB) .... 31 E 4
Bran (RO) .... 151 H 1

Brancaleone Marina (I) . 115 H 2
Brancion (F) .... 50 D 1
Brand (A) .... 94 B 2
Brand-Erbisdorf (D) .. 86 D 5
Brandbu (N) .... 189 E 4
Brande (DK) .... 198 B 2
Brande-
 Hörnerkirchen (D) .... 81 H 3
Brandenburg (D) ..... 86 C 1
Brandis (D) .... 86 C 4
Brändo (FIN) .... 191 E 4
Brandon (GB) .... 33 H 5
Brăneşti (RO) .... 152 C 4
Branice (PL) .... 124 D 1
Braničevo (SRB) ..... 141 F 4
Braniewo (E) .... 48 D 5
Brañosera (E) .... 58 A 2
Brańsk (PL) .... 119 G 5
Br'ansk (RUS) .... 7 F 4
Brańszczyk (PL) ..... 119 E 5
Brantôme-
 en-Périgord (F) ...... 49 E 4
Braskereidfoss (N) ... 189 F 4
Braslaŭ (BY) .... 6 D 3
Braşov (RO) .... 152 A 1
Brassac (F) .... 53 H 2
Brassac-les-Mines (F) . 50 A 3
Brasschaat (B) .... 78 D 1
Bratislava (SK) ...... 132 A 4
Bratja Daskalovi (BG) . 159 E 2
Bratovoeşti (RO) ..... 151 F 4
Brattvåg (N) .... 188 C 1
Bratunac (BIH) ...... 140 B 5
Braubach (D) .... 88 D 1
Braunau am Inn (A) .. 96 B 2
Braunfels (D) .... 85 E 5
Braunlage (D) .... 85 H 3
Braunsbedra (D) ..... 86 B 4
Braunschweig (D) .... 85 H 2
Braunton (GB) .... 34 D 3
Bravães (P) .... 56 B 5
Bravuogn / Bergün (CH) . 99 G 3
Bray (F) .... 39 H 3
Bray / Bré (IRL) ...... 25 G 2
Bray-Dunes (F) .... 39 H 1
Bray-sur-Seine (F) .... 45 G 2
Brazatortas (E) ...... 70 C 2
Brbinj (HR) .... 136 B 5
Brčko (BIH) .... 137 H 3
Brđani (SRB) .... 139 H 1
Bré / Bray (IRL) ...... 25 G 2
Brea de Aragón (E) ... 59 F 5
Breasta (RO) .... 151 F 4
Breaza (RO) .... 152 A 2
Brebeni (RO) .... 151 G 4
Brebu Nou (RO) ..... 150 C 2
Brécey (F) .... 43 G 3
Brechin (GB) .... 29 G 5
Brecht (B) .... 78 D 1
Břeclav (CZ) .... 93 E 5
Brecon (GB) .... 35 E 1
Breda (E) .... 61 E 3
Breda (NL) .... 78 D 1
Bredbyn (S) .... 184 C 5
Bredelar (D) .... 85 F 3
Bredstedt (D) .... 81 G 2
Bree (B) .... 79 E 2
Breganze (I) .... 103 E 4
Bregenz (A) .... 94 D 3
Bregovo (BG) .... 150 D 4
Bréhal (F) .... 38 B 5
Brehna (D) .... 86 B 3
Breiðdalsvik (IS) .... 178 D 2
Breil-sur-Roya (F) .... 55 H 1
Breisach am Rhein (D) . 94 A 2
Breitengüßbach (D) .. 89 H 2
Breitungen (D) .... 85 H 5
Breivikbotn (N) ...... 176 D 2
Brekke (N) .... 188 B 3
Brekken (N) .... 189 G 1
Brekkvasselv (N) .... 183 F 3
Brekstad (N) .... 182 C 4
Brela (HR) .... 138 C 2
Bremen (D) .... 81 G 5
Bremerhaven (D) ...... 81 F 4
Bremervörde (D) ...... 81 G 4
Bremsnes (N) .... 182 B 5

A
B
C
D
E
F
G
H
I
J
K
L
M
N
O
P
Q
R
S
T
U
V
W
X
Y
Z

A B C D E F G H I J K L M N O P Q R S T U V W X Y Z

Brenes (E)............... 69 G 5
Brenica (BG) .... 155 E 2
Brennilis (F)............. 42 C 2
Breno (I) .... 101 G 3
Brénod (F).............51 E 2
Brentwood (GB) .... 36 D 4
Brescia (I)............... 101 G 4
Breskens (NL) .... 78 B 1
Bresles (F) .... 39 H 4
Bressanone / Brixen (I) . 103 E 1
Bressuire (F) .... 43 H 5
Brest (BY)................12 C 1
Brest (F) .... 42 B 2
Brestanica (SLO) ...... 134 D 2
Brestovac (SRB) .... 143 F 3
Brestovac (SRB).......141 F 4
Brestovac (SRB) ....143 F 3
Brestovac (Rijeka) (HR). 134 B 4
Brestovac
   (Slavonski Brod) (HR). 135 G 4
Brestovačka Banja (SRB).141 F 5
Brestovene (BG) .... 152 C 5
Brestovo (BG) .... 159 E 1
Brețcu (RO) .... 148 B 5
Bretenoux (F) .... 49 G 5
Breteuil (F)............. 39 H 4
Breteuil-sur-Iton (F) .... 44 C 1
Bretten (F)............. 89 E 4
Breuil Cervinia (I) ...... 100 C 3
Breum (DK) .... 194 D 5
Brevik (N) .... 195 E 1
Breza (BIH) .... 137 G 5
Brežđe (SRB)........... 140 C 5
Brézé, château de (F)... 43 H 5
Brežice (SLO)........... 134 D 3
Brezna (SRB) .... 142 D 2
Breznica (HR) .... 135 E 2
Breznica
   Đakovačka (HR) .....135 H 4
Březnice (CZ) .... 92 A 4
Breznik (BG) .... 158 A 1
Brezno (SK) .... 132 D 3
Brezoi (RO) .... 151 G 2
Brezolles (F) .... 44 C 1
Brezová
   pod Bradlom (SK) .... 132 C 2
Brezovica (SRB) ...... 143 E 5
Brezovo (BG) .... 159 E 2
Brezovo Polje (BIH) .... 137 H 3
Briançon (F)............51 G 4
Briare (F)............. 45 F 4
Bribirske Mostine (HR) . 136 C 5
Bricquebec-
   en-Cotentin (F) ...... 38 B 4
Brides-les-Bains (F)...... 51 F 3
Bridge of Allan (GB) .... 30 D 1
Bridgend /
   Pen-y-bont (GB) .... 34 D 2
Bridgend (Islay) (GB) .. 30 A 2
Bridgnorth (GB)........ 32 D 5
Bridgwater (GB)........ 35 E 4
Bridlington (GB) .... 33 G 1
Bridport (GB)........... 38 A 1
Brie-Comte-Robert (F) .. 45 F 1
Briec (F) .... 42 B 2
Brielle (NL)...........76 C 5
Brienne-le-Château (F).. 46 C 2
Brienon (F)............ 45 G 3
Brienz (CH) .... 98 D 3
Brienza (I)...............110 C 4
Briey (F)..............41 E 4
Brig (CH) .... 98 D 4
Brigg (GB) .... 33 F 2
Brighouse (GB)........ 33 E 2
Brightlingsea (GB) ..... 37 E 3
Brighton (GB).......... 38 D 1
Brignogan-Plages (F) .. 42 B 1
Brignoles (F)........... 55 F 3
Brihuega (E)........... 64 D 2
Briksdal (N) .... 188 C 2
Brilon (D)............. 85 E 4
Brinches (P)............ 68 D 3
Brindisi (I)...............111 G 4
Brinon-sur-Beuvron (F).. 45 G 4
Brioni (HR) .... 134 A 5
Brionne (F)............. 39 E 5
Brioude (F)............. 50 A 4

Brioux-
   sur-Boutonne (F)...... 48 D 2
Briouze (F).............. 43 H 1
Brisighella (I)........... 107 E 2
Brissac-Quincé (F)..... 43 H 4
Brissago (CH) .... 99 E 5
Bristol (GB) .... 35 F 2
Brive-la-Gaillarde (F) ... 49 G 4
Briviesca (E)............ 58 C 3
Brixham (GB) .... 35 E 4
Brixen / Bressanone (I) . 103 E 1
Brixlegg (A)............. 95 G 3
Brjagovo (BG).......... 163 E 1
Brjanslækur (IS)........ 178 A 2
Brka (BIH)............. 137 H 3
Brna (HR) .... 138 C 3
Brnaze (HR) .... 138 B 2
Brno (CZ) .... 93 E 4
Bro (S) .... 197 F 1
Broadford (GB)......... 28 C 4
Broadford (IRL) .... 24 C 2
Broadstairs (GB) .... 37 E 4
Broadway (GB) .... 35 G 1
Broager (DK).......... 198 C 4
Broby (S).............. 199 F 2
Brocēni (LV)........... 202 B 3
Broch of Mousa (GB) ... 26 D 1
Brod (BIH) .... 139 F 2
Brod na Kupi (HR) ..... 134 C 4
Brod Prizrenski (SRB).. 142 D 5
Brodarevo (SRB) ...... 139 G 3
Brodica (SRB)...........141 F 4
Brodick (GB) .... 30 B 2
Brodnica (PL).......... 118 B 4
Brodowe Łąki (PL).....119 E 4
Brody (UA)..............12 D 2
Brody
   (Starachowice) (PL)... 122 D 4
Brody
   (Zielona Gora) (PL) ... 120 B 2
Broglie (F) .... 39 E 5
Brohl-Lützing (D) ...... 84 C 5
Brok (PL)..............119 F 5
Brolio (I)............. 106 D 4
Brolo (I)...............115 F 2
Bromarv (FIN) .... 191 G 5
Brome (D) .... 85 H 1
Bromölla (S) .... 199 G 3
Bromsgrove (GB)....... 32 D 5
Bromyard (GB)......... 32 D 5
Bronchales (E) .... 65 F 2
Brønderslev (DK)....... 194 D 4
Broni (I).............. 101 E 5
Brønnøysund (N)....... 183 E 2
Brøns (DK) .... 198 B 4
Bronte (I)..............115 F 3
Bronzani Majdan (BIH) . 135 F 5
Broons (F) .... 43 E 2
Brora (GB) .... 26 A 5
Brösarp (S)............ 199 F 3
Brossac (F)............. 48 D 4
Brøstadbotn (N) ......176 A 4
Broșteni (Drobeta-Turnu
   Severin) (RO) .... 151 E 3
Broșteni
   (Suceava) (RO) ..... 148 A 3
Broto (E) .... 59 H 2
Brotton (GB) .... 31 H 4
Brøttum (N)........... 189 F 3
Brou (F) .... 50 D 2
Brou (F)............... 44 D 2
Brouage (F)............ 48 C 2
Broughshane (GB) ..... 23 G 2
Broughton-
   in-Furness (GB) ...... 31 E 5
Broumov (CZ).......... 87 H 5
Brovst (DK) .... 194 D 4
Brownhills (GB) .... 32 D 4
Brozas (E) .... 63 E 5
Bruay-la-Buissière (F) .. 39 H 2
Bruay-sur-l'Escaut (F) .. 40 A 2
Bruchsal (D)............ 89 E 4
Brück (D)............. 86 C 2
Bruck an der
   Großglocknerstraße (A).96 B 4
Bruck an der Leitha (A) .. 97 H 2

Bruck an der Mur (A) .... 97 F 3
Bruck
   in der Oberpfalz (D)....91 F 4
Brückl (A)............. 97 E 5
Bruckmühl (D) .... 95 G 2
Brudzeń Duży (PL).....118 B 5
Brüel (D)............. 82 D 3
Brués (E)............. 56 C 3
Brugg (CH) .... 99 E 2
Brügge (D)............ 84 D 4
Brugge (Bruges) (B) .... 78 B 1
Brühl (D)............. 84 C 5
Bruksvallarna (S)....... 189 G 1
Brûlon (F)............. 43 H 3
Brumath (F)............ 41 H 5
Brummen (NL).......... 77 F 5
Brumov (CZ)........... 93 G 4
Brumunddal (N) .... 189 F 4
Bruneck / Brunico...... 103 E 1
Brunete (E)............ 64 B 3
Brunflo (S) .... 190 A 1
Brunico / Bruneck (I) ... 103 E 1
Bruniquel (F)........... 53 F 1
Brunkeberg (N) .... 188 D 5
Brunnen (CH) .... 99 E 3
Brunsbüttel (D) .... 81 G 3
Brunssum (NL) .... 79 F 2
Bruntál (CZ)............ 93 F 2
Brus (SRB) .... 143 E 2
Brusand (N)........... 194 A 1
Brušane (HR) .... 136 B 4
Brusarci (BG) .... 151 E 5
Brusasco (I) .... 100 C 5
Brusnik (SRB) ....141 G 5
Brusno (SK) .... 132 D 3
Brussel / Bruxelles ..... 78 C 2
Brusson (I).............. 100 C 3
Brusturi (RO).......... 146 D 3
Brusy (PL)..............117 F 3
Bruton (GB) .... 35 F 3
Bruvno (HR) .... 136 C 4
Bruxelles / Brussel (B) .. 78 C 2
Bruyères (F)............47 F 2
Brwinów (PL) .... 122 D 1
Bryne (N) .... 194 A 1
Brynmawr (GB) .... 35 E 1
Brza Palanka (SRB).....141 G 4
Brzan (SRB) ....141 E 5
Brzeće (SRB) .... 143 E 2
Brzeg (PL) .... 121 F 4
Brzeg Dolny (PL)....... 121 E 3
Brześć Kujawski (PL) ...118 B 5
Brzesko (PL).......... 125 H 1
Brzeszcze (PL) .... 125 F 1
Brzeziny (PL).......... 122 B 2
Brzostek (PL).......... 127 E 1
Brzozów (PL).......... 127 F 2
Buarcos (P) .... 62 B 3
Buavåg (N)............ 188 A 5
Bubry (F) .... 42 D 3
Bučač (UA)..............12 D 2
Buccheri (I)..............115 F 4
Bucchianico (I)......... 109 G 2
Bucecea (RO) .... 148 C 1
Buchen (D) .... 89 F 3
Buchenwald (D)........ 86 A 4
Buchholz in
   der Nordheide (D) ....81 H 4
Buchloe (D) .... 95 F 2
Buchlovice (CZ)........ 93 F 4
Buchs (CH) .... 99 F 2
Buchy (F) .... 39 F 4
Bučin Prohod (BG) ..... 158 B 1
Bucine (I)............. 106 D 4
Bucinişu (RO) .... 151 G 5
Buciumi (RO) .... 147 E 3
Bučje (SRB) .... 143 G 1
Bückeburg (D) .... 85 F 2
Buckfastleigh (GB) ..... 34 D 4
Buckhaven (GB).......31 E 1
Buckie (GB) .... 29 G 3
Buckingham (GB) ...... 35 H 1
Buckow (GB) .... 87 E 1
Bückwitz (D) .... 83 E 5
Bucsa (H) .... 130 D 2

Bucsu (H) .... 128 B 2
București (RO) .... 152 B 4
Bud (N) .... 182 A 5
Buda (RO).............. 152 C 1
Budakeszi (H) .... 129 E 2
Budaörs (H).......... 129 E 2
Budapest (H).......... 129 F 2
Búðardalur (IS)........ 178 A 2
Buddusò (I)...............112 C 2
Bude (GB)............. 34 C 3
Büdelsdorf (D)........ 81 H 2
Budești (RO) .... 152 C 4
Budimlić Japra (BIH) ... 135 E 5
Büdingen (D) .... 89 F 1
Budinščina (HR)........ 135 E 2
Búðir (IS)............. 178 A 2
Budleigh Salterton (GB). 35 E 4
Budrio (I) .... 106 D 1
Budureasa (RO) ...... 146 D 4
Budva (MNE)........... 139 F 5
Budyně nad Ohří (CZ).. 92 A 2
Budziszów Wielki (PL).. 121 E 4
Budzyń (PL)...........117 E 5
Buen Amor (E) .... 63 G 2
Buenache de Alarcón (E). 65 E 4
Buenavista
   de Valdavia (E) .... 58 A 3
Buendía (E)............ 64 D 3
Bueu (E).............. 56 B 4
Buftea (RO) .... 152 B 4
Bugac (I).............. 129 G 3
Bugeat (F)............. 49 G 3
Bugibba (M)...........114 C 5
Bugojno (BIH)......... 137 E 5
Bugøynes (N) .... 177 G 3
Bugyi (H) .... 129 F 2
Bühl (D).............. 88 D 4
Buhovci (BG).......... 156 D 2
Buhuși (RO).......... 148 C 4
Builth Wells (GB) .... 32 B 5
Buis-les-Baronnies (F)... 54 D 1
Buitrago del Lozoya (E). 64 C 1
Bujalance (E)........... 70 C 4
Bujanovac (SRB) ...... 143 F 4
Bujaraloz (E) .... 59 H 5
Buje / Bcie (HR) .... 134 A 5
Bujoru (RO) .... 152 A 5
Bük (H) .... 128 B 2
Buk (PL)..............121 G 1
Bukinje (BIH)......... 137 G 4
Bükkösd (H).......... 128 D 5
Bukova Gora (BIH) .... 138 C 2
Bukovi (SRB).......... 139 H 1
Bukowiec (PL)......... 127 F 3
Bukowno (PL)......... 122 B 5
Bülach (CH) .... 99 E 1
Bulair (BG) .... 159 F 2
Buldan (TR)............19 H 3
Bulgnéville (F).........47 E 2
Bullas (E)............. 71 H 3
Bulle (CH) .... 98 C 3
Büllingen (B) .... 79 F 3
Bully (F).............. 39 H 2
Bultei (I)...............112 C 2
Bumbești-Jiu (RO).... 151 F 4
Bun Dobhráin /
   Bundoran (IRL)...... 22 D 3
Buna (BIH) .... 138 D 3
Bunclody (IRL) .... 25 F 3
Buncrana (IRL) .... 23 E 1
Bunde (D).............81 E 5
Bünde (D)............ 85 E 2
Bundoran /
   Bun Dobhráin (IRL).... 22 D 3
Bunessan (GB) .... 30 A 1
Bungay (GB) .... 37 E 2
Bunić (HR) .... 134 D 5
Bunmahon (IRL) ...... 25 E 4
Buñol (E).............. 65 H 5
Bunratty Castle (IRL)... 24 C 2
Buntingford (GB)....... 36 C 3
Buñuel (E) .... 59 F 4
Buonabitàcolo (I)....... 110 C 5
Buonalbergo (I)........ 110 B 3
Buonconvento (I) ...... 106 D 4
Buonfornello (I)........ 114 D 3

Burbáguena (E) .... 65 F 1
Bureå (S) .... 185 E 3
Burela (E) .... 56 D 1
Buren (D) .... 85 E 3
Buren (NL).............. 77 F 2
Burfjord (N) ....176 C 2
Burford (GB) .... 35 G 1
Burg (D) .... 86 B 2
Burg auf Fehmarn (D) .. 82 C 2
Burg Stargard (D) ..... 83 F 4
Burgas / Бургас (BG) .. 157 F 4
Burgau (D)............ 89 H 5
Burgbernheim (D) ..... 89 H 3
Burgdorf (CH) .... 98 D 2
Burgdorf (D)........... 85 G 1
Bürgel (D)............ 86 B 5
Burgess Hill (GB) ...... 38 D 1
Burgete / Auritz (E)..... 59 F 2
Burggrub (D) ....91 E 2
Burghasungen (D) ..... 85 F 4
Burghausen (D) .... 96 B 2
Burgkunstadt (D) ....91 E 2
Burglengenfeld (D)......91 F 5
Burgohondo (E)........ 64 A 2
Burgos (E)............ 58 B 3
Burgsinn (D) .... 89 G 1
Burgstädt (D) .... 86 C 5
Burgsteinfurt (D) ...... 84 D 2
Burgsvik (S)........... 197 G 4
Burguillos del Cerro (E).. 69 F 3
Burgum (NL).......... 77 F 2
Burgwedel (D) .... 85 G 1
Burhaniye (TR).........19 G 3
Burie (F) .... 48 D 3
Burila Mare (RO) ...... 150 D 4
Burja (BG)............ 159 E 1
Burjassot / Burjasot (E).. 65 H 4
Burkau (D) .... 87 E 4
Burnham-
   on-Crouch (GB) ...... 36 D 4
Burnham-on-Sea (GB)... 35 E 2
Burnley (GB) .... 32 D 2
Burntisland (GB) ....31 E 1
Buronzo (I) .... 100 D 4
Burrel (AL) .... 144 C 1
Burry Port (GB)........ 34 D 2
Bursa (TR)..............19 G 2
Burscheid (D) .... 84 C 4
Bürstadt (D) .... 89 E 2
Burton-upon-Trent (GB). 33 E 3
Burträsk (S) .... 185 E 3
Burwick (GB) .... 26 B 4
Bury (GB) .... 32 D 2
Bury
   Saint Edmunds (GB)... 33 H 5
Busalla (I) .... 105 E 2
Busca (I) .... 104 B 2
Buševec (HR) .... 135 E 3
Bushat (AL) .... 142 B 5
Bushmills (GB) .... 23 F 1
Busko-Zdrój (PL) ...... 122 D 5
Busovača (BIH)........ 137 F 5
Bussang (F)............47 G 3
Bussière-Badil (F) ..... 49 E 3
Bussolengo (I) .... 101 H 4
Bussum (NL).......... 77 E 4
Busseto (I) .... 101 F 5
Busto Arsizio (I) ...... 101 E 4
Busto de Bureba (E) ... 58 C 3
Büsum (D)............81 G 3
Butan (BG) .... 151 F 5
Buteni (RO) .... 146 C 4
Butera (I)..............115 E 4
Butjadingen-
   Burhave (D)...........81 F 4
Butoiești (RO) .... 151 E 3
Butovo (BG).......... 156 B 2
Buttermere (GB).........31 E 5
Buttevant (IRL) .... 24 C 4
Buttstädt (D).......... 86 A 4
Butzbach (D) .... 89 E 1
Bützow (D)............ 82 D 3
Buxtehude (D)...........81 H 4

Buxy (F) .... 50 C 1
Buzançais (F) .... 44 D 5
Buzancy (F) .... 40 D 4
Buzău (RO) .... 152 C 2
Buzescu (RO) .... 151 H 5
Buzet / Pinguente (HR). 134 B 4
Bużiaş (RO) .... 150 C 1
Bužim (BIH) .... 135 E 5
Buzovgrad (BG) ...... 159 E 2
Bychaŭ (BY)............7 E 4
Bychawa (PL) .... 123 F 4
Byczyna (PL) .... 121 G 4
Bydgoszcz (PL)........117 G 4
Bygdeå (S) .... 185 E 4
Bygdin (N) .... 188 D 3
Bygdsiljum (S) .... 185 E 4
Bygland (N) .... 194 C 1
Byglandsfjord (N) ..... 194 C 2
Bykle (N).............. 188 C 5
Bylderup-Bov (DK)..... 198 B 4
Byrkjelo (N)........... 188 C 2
Byske (S) .... 185 E 3
Bystřice nad
   Pernštejnem (CZ) ..... 92 D 4
Bystřice pod
   Hostýnem (CZ)........ 93 F 4
Bystrzyca Kłodzka (PL). 124 B 1
Bytča (SK)............ 132 C 2
Bytom (PL)............ 121 H 5
Bytom Odrzański (PL).. 120 D 2
Bytów (PL)............117 F 2
Byxelkrok (S)........... 197 F 4

C

Cabañaquinta (E) .... 57 G 2
Cabanes (E)............ 66 A 2
Cabeceiras de Basto (P) . 62 C 1
Cabeço de Vide (P)..... 68 D 1
Cabella Ligure (I)....... 105 E 2
Cabeza del Buey (E).... 69 H 2
Cabezas Rubias (E)..... 69 E 4
Cabezón de la Sal (E)... 58 B 1
Cabezón de Pisuerga (E). 58 A 5
Cabezuela del Valle (E) .. 63 G 4
Cabo de Gata (E) ...... 72 C 5
Cabourg (F)............ 38 D 5
Cabra (E).............. 70 C 5
Cabra del Sto Cristo (E) . 71 E 4
Cabras (I)...............112 B 3
Cabreiros (E) .... 56 D 1
Cabrerets (F).......... 49 G 5
Cabrillas (E) .... 63 F 2
Cacabelos (E) .... 57 E 3
Čačak / Чачак (SRB) .. 139 H 1
Caccamo (I)............114 D 3
Cacela Velha (P)....... 68 D 5
Cáceres (E)............ 63 F 5
Cachafeiro (E).......... 56 C 3
Cachopo (P)........... 68 D 5
Čačinci (HR)........... 135 H 3
Cádabo (O Baleira) (E).. 57 E 2
Cadalso
   de los Vidrios (E) ..... 64 A 3
Cadaqués (E)...........61 F 2
Cadaval (P)............ 62 A 5
Čađavica (BIH)........ 137 E 4
Čadca (SK)............ 132 C 1
Cadelbosco di Sopra (I). 105 G 2
Cadenabbia (I)......... 101 E 3
Cadenberge (D)...........81 G 3
Cadenet (F)............ 54 D 2
Cádiar (E) .... 72 A 5
Cadillac (F)............ 48 D 5
Cadipietra / Steinhaus (I).103 E 1
Cádiz (E)..............74 A 4
Cadouin (F)............ 49 F 5
Caen (F) .... 38 D 5
Caerdydd / Cardiff (GB) . 35 E 2
Caerffili / Caerphilly (GB). 35 E 2
Caerfyrddin /
   Carmarthen (GB)...... 34 C 1
Caergybi /
   Holyhead (GB)........ 32 A 3
Caernarfon (GB) .... 32 A 3
Caerphilly /
   Caerffili (GB) .... 35 E 2

Caersws (GB) .... 32 B 5
Cafasan (AL) .... 144 D 2
Cagli (I) .... 107 F 3
Cagliari (I) ....112 C 5
Čaglin (HR) .... 135 H 4
Cagnano Varano (I) .....110 C 1
Cagnes-sur-Mer (F) ..... 55 G 2
Caher (IRL) .... 24 D 3
Cahersiveen (IRL) ...... 24 A 4
Cahors (F) .... 53 F 1
Cahul (MD) ....13 F 4
Caianello (I) .... 109 G 4
Caiazzo (I) .... 109 H 4
Câinenii Mici (RO) ..... 151 G 1
Caión (E) .... 56 B 1
Cairnryan (GB) .... 23 H 2
Cairo Montenotte (I) ... 104 D 3
Caiseal / Cashel (IRL) .. 24 D 3
Caisleán an Bharraigh /
  Castlebar (IRL) ...... 22 C 4
Caistor (GB) .... 33 F 2
Cajarc (F) .... 53 G 1
Čajetina (SRB) .... 139 G 1
Čajniče (BIH) .... 139 F 2
Cajvana (RO) .... 148 B 2
Čakovec (HR) .... 135 E 2
Cakran (AL) .... 144 C 3
Çal (TR) ....19 H 3
Cala en Porter (E) ......67 H 2
Cala Gonone (I) ....112 D 3
Cala Rajada (E) ....67 G 2
Calabor (E) .... 57 E 5
Calaceite (E) .... 60 A 5
Calacuccia (F) .... 55 H 4
Calaf (E) .... 60 C 3
Calafat (RO) .... 151 E 5
Calafell (E) .... 60 C 4
Calafort Ros Láir / Rosslare
  Harbour (IRL) .... 25 F 4
Calahonda (E) ....75 G 3
Calahorra (E) .... 59 E 3
Calais (F) .... 39 G 1
Calamocha (E) .... 65 G 1
Cälan (RO) .... 151 E 1
Calañas (E) .... 69 E 4
Calanda (E) .... 65 H 1
Calangianus (I) ....112 C 1
Calapica (BG) .... 158 D 3
Călăraşi (MD) ....13 F 3
Călăraşi (RO) .... 152 D 4
Calasetta (I) ....112 A 5
Calasparra (E) .... 71 H 4
Calatafimi (I) ....114 C 3
Calatañazor (E) .... 58 D 5
Calatayud (E) .... 59 F 5
Calatorao (E) .... 59 F 5
Calau (D) .... 87 E 3
Calbe (D) .... 86 B 2
Calcena (E) .... 59 F 5
Caldaro / Kaltern (I) ... 101 H 2
Caldarola (I) .... 107 G 4
Caldas da Rainha (P) ... 62 A 5
Caldas de Reis (E) ..... 56 B 3
Caldelas (E) .... 56 C 5
Caldelas das Taipas (P) . 62 C 1
Caldes de Boí (E) ...... 60 B 1
Caldes de Malavella (E)..61 E 3
Caldes de Montbui (E) .. 60 D 3
Caldirola (I) .... 105 E 2
Calella (E) ....61 E 3
Calella de Palafrugell (E) .61 F 2
Calenzana (F) .... 55 G 3
Calera de León (E)...... 69 F 3
Calera y Chozas (E)..... 63 H 4
Caleruega (E) .... 58 C 4
Càlig (E) .... 66 A 1
Călimăneşti (RO) ...... 151 G 2
Calitri (I) ....110 C 3
Calizzano (I) .... 104 C 3
Callac (F) .... 42 C 2
Callan (IRL) .... 25 E 3
Callander (GB) .... 30 D 1
Callas (F) .... 55 F 2
Callington (GB) .... 34 C 4
Callosa de Segura (E) ... 73 E 3
Callosa d'En Sarrià (E) .. 66 A 5
Călmăţuiu de Sus (RO) . 151 H 5

Calmbach (D) .... 89 E 4
Calne (GB) .... 35 G 2
Câlnic (RO) .... 151 E 2
Calolziocorte (I) ...... 101 F 3
Calonge (E) ....61 F 3
Calp (E) .... 66 A 5
Caltabellotta (I) ....114 C 3
Caltagirone (I) ....115 F 4
Caltanissetta (I) ....115 E 4
Caltavuturo (I) ....114 D 3
Călugăreni
  (Bucureşti) (RO) ..... 152 B 4
Călugăreni
  (Ploieşti) (RO) ...... 152 C 2
Caluso (I) .... 100 C 4
Calvi (F) .... 55 G 3
Calvörde (D) .... 86 A 1
Calw (D) .... 89 E 4
Calzada de Calatrava (E). 70 D 2
Calzada
  de Valdunciel (E) ..... 63 G 2
Camaiore (I) .... 105 G 4
Camaldoli,
  convento di (I) .... 107 E 3
Camaleño (E) .... 58 A 1
Camâr (RO) .... 146 D 2
Camarasa (E) .... 60 B 3
Cămăraşu (RO) .... 147 G 4
Camarena (E) .... 64 B 3
Camarès (F) .... 53 H 2
Camaret-sur-Mer (F) ... 42 B 2
Camarillas (E) .... 65 G 2
Camariñas (E) .... 56 A 2
Camarzana de Tera (E).. 57 G 5
Camas (E) .... 69 G 5
Cambados (E) .... 56 B 3
Cambas (P) .... 62 C 4
Camberley (GB) .... 35 H 2
Cambil (E) .... 71 E 4
Cambo-les-Bains (F) ... 52 A 3
Camborne (GB) .... 34 B 5
Cambrai (F) .... 40 A 3
Cambremer (F) .... 38 D 5
Cambridge (GB) .... 33 G 5
Cambrils (E) .... 60 C 5
Camburg (D) .... 86 B 4
Camelford (GB) .... 34 C 4
Camerino (I) .... 107 G 4
Camigliatello Silano (I) ..113 C 2
Caminha (P) .... 56 B 5
Caminomorisco (E)..... 63 F 3
Caminreal (E) .... 65 F 1
Camogli (I) .... 105 E 3
Campagna (I) ....110 B 4
Campagne-
  lès-Hesdin (F) .... 39 G 2
Campan (F) .... 52 D 4
Campana (I) ....113 C 2
Campanario (E) .... 69 H 2
Campanas (E) .... 59 F 2
Campaspero (E) ...... 58 B 5
Campbello /
  El Campello (E) ...... 73 F 2
Câmpeni (RO) .... 147 E 4
Campi Bisenzio (I) ..... 105 H 4
Campi Salentina (I) .....111 G 4
Câmpia Turzii (RO) .... 147 F 4
Campiglia
  Marittima (I) .... 106 C 4
Campillo (E) .... 72 B 5
Campillo
  de Altobuey (E) ...... 65 F 4
Campillo de Aragón (E). 65 F 1
Campillo de Arenas (E). 70 D 5
Campillo de Llerena (E). 69 G 2
Campillos (E) ....74 D 2
Câmpina (RO) .... 152 B 2
Campione (I) .... 101 E 3
Campitello Matese (I) .. 109 H 4
Campli (I) .... 107 H 5
Campo (E) .... 60 A 2
Campo da Feira (E) .... 56 C 2
Campo de Caso (E) .... 57 H 2
Campo de Criptana (E) . 64 C 5
Campo del Hospital (E). 56 D 1
Campo di Giove (I) .... 109 G 2
Campo Ligure (I) ...... 104 D 2

Campo Maior (P) ...... 69 E 1
Campo Tures /
  Sand in Taufers (I) ... 103 E 1
Campobasso (I) .... 109 H 3
Campobello
  di Licata (I) ....114 D 4
Campobello
  di Mazara (I) ....114 C 3
Campodonico (I) ...... 107 F 4
Campoformido (I) ..... 103 G 3
Campogalliano (I) ..... 105 H 2
Campomanes (E) ..... 57 G 2
Campomarino (I) ....110 B 1
Campora
  San Giovanni (I) ......113 B 3
Camporrobles (E)...... 65 F 4
Campos (E) ....67 F 3
Camposampiero (I) .... 103 E 4
Camprodon (E) .... 60 D 2
Câmpulung (RO) ...... 151 H 2
Câmpulung
  Moldovenesc (RO) ... 148 A 2
Câmpuri (RO) .... 148 C 5
Camucia (I) .... 107 E 4
Camuñas (E) .... 64 C 5
Cañada de
  Benatanduz (E) ...... 65 H 2
Canal San Bovo (I) .... 103 E 3
Canales (E) .... 58 D 4
Canals (E) .... 73 F 1
Cañamero (E) .... 63 H 5
Canas de Senhorim (P) . 62 C 3
Cañaveral (E) .... 63 F 5
Cañaveral de León (E) . 69 F 3
Cañaveras (E) .... 65 E 3
Canazei (I) .... 103 E 2
Cancale (F) .... 43 F 1
Cancarix (E) .... 71 H 3
Cancon (F) .... 49 E 5
Candanchú (E) .... 59 H 2
Candás (E) .... 57 G 1
Candasnos (E) .... 60 A 4
Candé (F) .... 43 G 4
Candela (I) ....110 C 3
Candelario (E) .... 63 G 3
Candeleda (E) .... 63 H 4
Candes-Saint-Martin (F). 43 H 4
Canelli (I) .... 104 D 2
Canelobres,
  coves dels (E) .... 73 F 2
Canero (E) .... 57 F 1
Canet de Mar (E) ....61 E 3
Canet-Plage (F) .... 54 A 4
Cañete (E) .... 65 F 3
Cañete
  de las Torres (E) ..... 70 C 4
Cañete la Real (E) ......74 D 3
Canfranc-Estación (E) .. 59 H 2
Cangas (E) .... 56 B 4
Cangas de Onís (E) .... 57 H 2
Cangas del Narcea (E) .. 57 F 2
Canha (P) .... 68 B 2
Canicatti (I) ....114 B 5
Canicattini Bagni (I) .....115 G 5
Caniles (E) .... 71 F 5
Canino (I) .... 108 C 1
Canisy (F) .... 38 C 5
Cañizal (E) .... 63 H 1
Canjáyar (E) .... 72 B 5
Cannero Riviera (I) ....61 E 1
Cannes (F) .... 55 G 2
Canneto (I) .... 105 G 5
Cannich (GB) .... 28 D 3
Cannobio (I) .... 100 D 3
Cannock (GB) .... 32 D 4
Canonbie (GB) ....31 E 4
Canosa di Puglia (I) ....110 D 3
Cansano (I) .... 109 G 2
Cantalapiedra (E) ..... 63 H 2
Cantalejo (E) .... 64 B 1
Cantalpino (E) .... 63 H 2
Cantanhede (P) .... 62 B 3
Cantavieja (E) .... 65 H 2
Čantavir (SRB) .... 140 C 1
Canterbury (GB) ...... 37 E 4
Cantillana (E) .... 69 G 4

Cantoira (I) .... 100 B 4
Cantoral (E) .... 58 A 2
Cantoria (I) .... 71 G 5
Cantù (I) .... 101 E 3
Canvey Island (GB) .... 36 D 4
Cany-Barville (F) ...... 39 E 3
Caorle (I) .... 103 G 4
Caorso (I) .... 101 F 5
Cap Ferret (F) .... 48 B 5
Capaccio (I) ....110 B 4
Capaci (I) ....114 C 2
Capalbio (I) .... 108 C 1
Caparde (BIH) .... 137 H 4
Caparroso (E) .... 59 F 3
Căpăţânenii
  Pământeni (RO) ...... 151 G 2
Capbreton (F) .... 52 A 2
Capdenac-Gare (F).... 49 G 5
Capel Curig (GB) ...... 32 B 3
Capellades (E) .... 60 C 3
Capendu (F) .... 53 H 3
Capestang (F) .... 54 A 3
Capestrano (I) .... 109 F 2
Capileira (E) .... 72 A 5
Capistrello (I) .... 109 F 3
Čapljina (BIH) .... 138 D 3
Capmany (E) ....61 E 1
Capo Bianco,
  Spiaggia (I) ....114 C 4
Capo d'Orlando (I) .....115 F 2
Capodistria /
  Koper (SLO) .... 134 A 3
Cappelle sul Tavo (I) ... 109 G 2
Cappoquin (IRL) ...... 24 D 4
Capracotta (I) .... 109 G 3
Capri (I) ....110 A 4
Capriati a Volturno (I) . 109 G 4
Captieux (F) .... 52 C 1
Capua (I) .... 109 G 4
Capurso (I) ....111 E 3
Capvern (F) .... 52 D 4
Car Kalojan /
  Цар Калоян (BG)..... 156 D 2
Cara Droma Rúisc / Carrick-
  on-Shannon (IRL) .... 22 D 4
Caracal (RO) .... 151 G 4
Caracuel
  de Calatrava (E) ..... 70 D 2
Caraman (F) .... 53 F 3
Caramanico Terme (I) .. 109 G 2
Caramulo (P) .... 62 C 3
Caransebeş (RO) ..... 150 D 1
Carantec (F) .... 42 C 1
Caraula (RO) .... 151 E 4
Caravaca de la Cruz (E). 71 H 3
Carbajales de Alba (E).. 57 G 5
Carballiño (E) .... 56 C 4
Carballo (E) .... 56 B 2
Carbon-Blanc (F)...... 48 C 5
Carboneras (E) .... 72 C 5
Carboneras
  de Guadazaón (E) .... 65 F 4
Carbonero el Mayor (E). 64 A 1
Carbonia (I) ....112 B 5
Carbonin /
  Schluderbach (I) ..... 103 F 2
Carbonne (F) .... 53 F 3
Carbunari (RO) .... 150 C 3
Carcaboso (E) .... 63 F 4
Carcabuey (E) .... 70 C 5
Carcagente /
  Carcaixent (E) .... 65 H 5
Carcaixent /
  Carcagente (E) ...... 65 H 5
Carcans (F) .... 48 C 4
Carcans-Plage (F) ..... 48 B 4
Carcare (I) .... 104 D 3
Carcassonne (F) ...... 53 H 3
Carcastillo (E) .... 59 F 3
Carcès (F) .... 55 F 3
Cardedeu (E) ....61 E 3
Cardeña (E) .... 70 C 3
Cardenete (E) .... 65 F 4
Cardiff / Caerdydd (GB) . 35 E 2
Cardigan (GB) .... 34 C 1
Cardona (E) .... 60 C 3

Carei (RO) .... 146 D 1
Carentan les Marais (F). . 38 C 4
Carev Brod (BG) ...... 157 E 2
Carev Dvor (MK) ..... 145 E 2
Carevdar (HR) .... 135 F 2
Carevec (BG) .... 156 B 2
Carevo (BG) .... 157 F 5
Čargan (BG) .... 159 G 2
Cargèse (F) .... 55 G 4
Carhaix-Plouguer (F) .. 42 C 2
Caria (P) .... 62 D 3
Cariati (I) ....113 D 2
Caričin Grad (SRB) .... 143 F 3
Carignan (F) .... 40 D 4
Carignano (I) .... 100 C 5
Carina (MK) .... 145 E 3
Cariñena (E) .... 59 G 5
Carini (I) ....114 C 2
Cariño (E) .... 56 D 1
Carinola (I) .... 109 G 4
Carisbrooke Castle (GB). 38 C 1
Carisio (I) .... 100 D 4
Cârjoaia (RO) .... 148 C 2
Carlet (E) .... 65 H 5
Cârlibaba (RO) .... 147 H 2
Carling (F) ....41 F 5
Carlingford (IRL) ..... 23 G 4
Carlisle (GB) ....31 E 4
Carloforte (I) ....112 A 5
Carlogani (RO) .... 151 G 4
Carlow /
  Ceatharlach (IRL) .... 25 F 2
Carloway (GB) .... 28 B 1
Carluke (GB) .... 30 D 2
Carmagnola (I) .... 100 C 5
Carmaux (F) .... 53 G 1
Carmona (E) .... 69 H 5
Carna (IRL) .... 22 B 5
Carnac (F) .... 42 D 3
Carndonagh (IRL) .... 23 E 1
Carnew (IRL) .... 25 F 3
Carnforth (GB) ....31 E 5
Carni (I) .... 103 G 2
Carnikava (LV) .... 202 D 3
Carnlough (GB) ...... 23 G 2
Carnon-Plage (F)...... 54 B 3
Carnota (E) .... 56 B 3
Carnoustie (GB) ...... 29 G 5
Carnwath (GB) .... 30 D 2
Carolles (F) .... 43 F 1
Carovigno (I) ....111 G 4
Carpaneto
  Piacentino (I) .... 101 F 5
Carpegna (I) .... 107 F 3
Carpen (RO) .... 151 E 4
Carpenedolo (I) ...... 101 G 4
Carpentras (F) .... 54 D 1
Carpi (I) .... 105 H 2
Carpignano Sesia (I) .. 100 D 4
Carpineti (I) .... 105 G 3
Carpineto Romano (I) . 109 E 3
Cârpiniş (RO) .... 150 B 1
Carpinone (I) .... 109 G 3
Carquefou (F) .... 43 F 4
Carqueiranne (F)...... 55 F 3
Carracedelo (E) ...... 57 E 3
Carradale (GB) .... 30 B 2
Carral (E) .... 56 C 2
Carrapateira (P) ...... 68 B 5
Carrara (I) .... 105 F 3
Carrascosa
  del Campo (E)........ 64 D 3
Carrazeda de Ansiães (P). 62 D 1
Carrazedo
  de Montenegro (P) ... 56 D 5
Carrbridge (GB) ...... 29 E 4
Carregado (P) .... 68 B 1
Carregal do Sal (P) ... 62 C 3
Carreña (E) .... 58 A 1
Carrick-on-Shannon / Cara
  Droma Rúisc (IRL) .... 22 D 4
Carrick-on-Suir (IRL) .. 25 E 3
Carrickfergus (GB) .... 23 G 2
Carrickmacross (IRL) .. 23 F 4

Carrigart (IRL) .... 23 E 1
Carrió (E) .... 56 C 2
Carrión de Calatrava (E). 70 D 1
Carrión de los Condes (E). 58 A 3
Carrizo de la Ribera (E) . 57 G 3
Carro (F) .... 54 D 3
Carrouges (F) .... 43 H 1
Carrowkeel (IRL) ..... 23 F 1
Carrù (I) .... 104 C 2
Carry-le-Rouet (F) ..... 54 D 3
Carsoli (I) .... 109 E 2
Cartagena (E) .... 73 E 4
Cártama (E) ....74 D 3
Cartaxo (P) .... 68 B 1
Cartaya (E) .... 69 E 5
Carteret (F) .... 38 B 4
Cârţişoara (RO) ...... 151 G 1
Carviçais (P) .... 63 E 1
Carvin (F) .... 40 A 2
Carvoeiro (P) .... 68 B 5
Casa Branca (P) ...... 68 D 1
Casa Branca (P) ...... 68 B 3
Casabermeja (E) ....75 E 3
Casacalenda (I) ...... 109 H 3
Casaio (E) .... 57 E 4
Casalarreina (E) ...... 58 D 3
Casalbordino (I) ...... 109 H 2
Casalbuttano (I) ...... 101 F 5
Casale Monferrato (I) . 100 D 5
Casale sul Sile (I) ..... 103 F 4
Casalecchio di Reno (I) . 105 H 3
Casalmaggiore (I) .... 101 G 5
Casalpusterlengo (I) .. 101 F 5
Casamari,
  abbazia di (I) .... 109 F 3
Casamassima (I) ....111 E 3
Casamicciola Terme (I) . 109 G 5
Casar de Cáceres (E).. 63 F 5
Casarabonela (E) ......74 D 3
Casarano (I) ....111 H 5
Casares (E) ....74 C 4
Casares de las Hurdes (E). 63 F 3
Casariche (E) .... 70 B 5
Casarsa (I) .... 103 G 3
Casas de Don Pedro (E). 69 H 1
Casas de
  Fernando Alonso (E). 65 E 5
Casas de Juan Núñez (E). 65 F 5
Casas de Luján (E) .... 64 D 4
Casas de Miravete (E) . 63 G 5
Casas del Puerto (E)... 72 D 2
Casas Ibáñez (E)...... 65 F 5
Casas Nuevas (E) ..... 72 D 3
Casasimarro (E) ...... 65 E 5
Casatejada (E) .... 63 G 4
Casavieja (E) .... 64 A 3
Cascais (P) .... 68 A 2
Cascante (E) .... 59 F 4
Cascia (I) .... 107 G 5
Casciana Terme (I) .... 105 G 5
Cascina (I) .... 105 G 4
Casei (I) .... 101 E 5
Caselle in Pittari (I) .....110 C 5
Caselle Torinese (I) ... 100 C 5
Caserta (I) .... 109 G 4
Casetas (E) .... 59 G 4
Cashel / Caiseal (IRL) .. 24 D 3
Casicas
  del Río Segura (E) ... 71 F 3
Casillas de Coria (E) .. 63 E 4
Casimcea (RO) .... 153 F 3
Casina (I) .... 105 G 3
Casinos (E) .... 65 H 4
Čáslav (CZ) .... 92 C 3
Casnewydd /
  Newport (GB) .... 35 E 2
Casola in Lunigiana (I).. 105 G 3
Casoli (I) .... 109 G 2
Casoria (I) .... 109 G 5
Caspe (E) .... 60 A 4
Cassà de la Selva (E)...61 E 3
Cassagnes-Bégonhès (F). 53 H 1
Cassano allo Ionio (I) ..113 C 1
Cassano delle Murge (I) .111 E 3
Cassel (F) .... 39 H 1
Cassino (I) .... 109 G 4
Cassis (F) .... 55 E 3

Castalla (E)............. 73 E 1
Castanet-Tolosan (F) .... 53 F 3
Castanheira de Pêra (P) . 62 C 4
Castasegna (CH) .... 99 F 4
Casteggio (I) .... 101 E 5
Castejón (E)............. 59 F 4
Castejón
  de Monegros (E) .. 59 H 5
Castejón de Sos (E)...... 60 A 1
Castejón
  de Valdejasa (E) ..... 59 G 4
Castel del Monte (I) .. 109 F 2
Castel del Rio (I)........ 106 D 2
Castel di Sangro (I).... 109 G 3
Castel Gandolfo (I).... 109 E 3
Castel Madama (I)...... 109 E 3
Castel San Giovanni (I) . 101 F 5
Castel San Lorenzo (I) ..110 C 4
Castel
  San Pietro Terme (I) . 106 D 1
Castel Volturno (I)...... 109 G 5
Castelbuono (I).......115 E 3
Casteldaccia (I) ....114 D 2
Casteldelfino (I)....... 104 B 2
Castelfidardo (I)........ 107 G 4
Castelfiorentino (I)...... 105 H 5
Castelfranco Emilia (I) .. 105 H 2
Castelfranco
  in Miscano (I) ....110 B 3
Castelfranco Veneto (I). 103 E 4
Casteljaloux (F) ...... 52 D 1
Castell de Ferro (E)......75 G 3
Castellabate (I).........110 B 5
Castellammare
  del Golfo (I).......114 C 2
Castellammare
  di Stabia (I) .... 109 H 5
Castellamonte (I) ...... 100 C 4
Castellana Grotte (I)....111 F 3
Castellane (F) .... 55 F 2
Castellaneta (I).........111 E 4
Castellar de la Muela (E). 65 F 2
Castellar de Santiago (E). 71 E 2
Castellar
  de Santisteban (E)... 71 E 3
Castellar del Vallès (E).. 60 D 3
Castell'Arquato (I)...... 101 F 5
Castelldans (E)........ 60 B 4
Castelldefels (E)....... 60 D 4
Castelleone (I) .... 101 F 4
Castellfollit
  de la Roca (E) ....61 E 2
Castellina in Chianti (I) . 105 H 5
CastellNedd /
  Neath (GB)............ 34 D 2
Castelló de la Plana / Castellón
  de la Plana (E)...... 66 A 2
Castelló de Rugat (E).... 73 F 1
Castello del Lago (I)... 109 H 4
Castelló d'Empúries (E)...61 F 2
Castello Tesino (I) .... 103 E 3
Castellolí (E) .... 60 D 3
Castellote (E) ...... 65 H 1
Castellterçol (E) ...... 60 D 3
Castelluccio (I) .... 107 G 5
Castelmassa (I).......... 101 H 5
Castelmauro (I) .... 109 H 3
Castelmoron-sur-Lot (F). 53 E 1
Castelnau-de-Médoc (F) 48 C 4
Castelnau-
  de-Montmiral (F)...... 53 G 2
Castelnau-Magnoac (F). 53 E 3
Castelnau-Montratier (F). 53 F 1
Castelnau-
  Rivière-Basse (F) ..... 52 D 2
Castelnaud,
  château de (F) .... 49 F 5
Castelnaudary (F)....... 53 G 3
Castelnovo ne' Monti (I). 105 G 3
Castelnuovo
  Berardenga (I) ...... 106 D 4
Castelnuovo
  Bocca d'Adda (I)..... 101 F 5
Castelnuovo
  della Daunia (I).......110 B 2
Castelnuovo
  di Garfagnana (I)..... 105 G 3

Castelnuovo di Porto (I). 108 D 2
Castelnuovo Scrivia (I) . 101 E 5
Castelo Branco (P) ..... 62 D 4
Castelo de Paiva (P).... 62 C 2
Castelo de Vide (P)..... 62 D 5
Castelraimondo (I) ..... 107 G 4
Castelrotto (I) .... 103 E 2
Castelsardo (I) ....112 B 1
Castelsarrasin (F)....... 53 F 1
Castelserás (E) .... 65 H 1
Casteltermini (I).......114 D 3
Castelvecchio
  Subequo (I)......... 109 F 2
Castelvetrano (I).......114 B 3
Castets (F) .... 52 B 2
Castiadas (I)...........112 C 5
Castiglion Fiorentino (I). 107 E 4
Castiglioncello (I) ...... 105 G 5
Castiglione d'Adda (I) . 101 F 5
Castiglione dei Pepoli (I).105 H 3
Castiglione del Lago (I) . 107 E 4
Castiglione
  della Pescaia (I) ...... 106 C 5
Castiglione
  delle Stiviere (I) ...... 101 G 4
Castiglione
  in Teverina (I) .... 107 E 5
Castiglione
  Messer Marino (I) .... 109 H 3
Castiglione Olona (I) .... 101 E 3
Castilblanco (I) .... 70 B 1
Castilblanco
  de los Arroyos (E) ..... 69 G 4
Castilleja del Campo (E). 69 F 5
Castilléjar (E) .... 71 F 4
Castillejo
  de Martín Viejo (E) ... 63 E 2
Castillo de Calatrava la Nueva,
  convento de (E) ...... 70 D 2
Castillo de Loarre (E).... 59 H 3
Castillo de Locubín (E) .. 70 D 5
Castillon-
  en-Couserans (F)...... 53 E 4
Castillon-la-Bataille (F).. 48 D 5
Castillonnès (F) ...... 49 E 5
Castilruiz (E) .... 59 E 4
Castions di Strada (I) ... 103 G 3
Castle Douglas (GB).... 30 D 4
Castlebar / Caisleán an
  Bharraigh (IRL)...... 22 C 4
Castlebay (GB)......... 28 B 4
Castlebellingham (IRL).. 23 F 4
Castleblayney (IRL).... 23 F 4
Castlecomer (IRL)...... 25 E 2
Castledawson (GB)..... 23 F 2
Castlederg (GB)....... 23 E 2
Castledermot (IRL)..... 25 F 2
Castleford (GB)....... 33 E 2
Castleisland (IRL)..... 24 B 3
Castlemaine (IRL)..... 24 B 4
Castlepollard (IRL) .... 23 E 4
Castlerea (IRL) ...... 22 D 4
Castlerock (GB)...... 23 F 1
Castletown
  (Highland) (GB) .... 26 B 4
Castletown
  (Isle of Man) (GB)... 32 A 1
Castletown House (IRL). 23 F 5
Castletownbere (IRL)... 24 A 5
Castlewellan (GB).... 23 G 3
Castrejón
  de Trabancos (E) .... 63 H 1
Castres (F) .... 53 G 2
Castries (F) .... 54 B 2
Castril (E) .... 71 F 4
Castrillo de la Reina (E). 58 C 4
Castrillo de Villavega (E). 58 A 3
Castro (E) .... 56 D 2
Castro Daire (P)....... 62 C 2
Castro del Río (E)....... 70 C 4
Castro Marim (P)...... 68 D 5
Castro-Urdiales (E).... 58 C 1
Castro Verde (P)...... 68 C 4
Castrocalbón (E)..... 57 G 4
Castrocaro Terme (I) ... 107 E 2
Castrocontrigo (E)..... 57 F 4

Castrojeriz (E).......... 58 B 3
Castromonte (E) .... 57 H 5
Castronuevo (E)........ 57 G 5
Castronuño (E)......... 63 H 1
Castropol (E)........... 57 E 1
Castrop-Rauxel (D)..... 84 C 3
Castroreale (I).........115 G 2
Castroreale Terme (I)....115 G 2
Castrotierra
  de Valmadrigal (E) ... 57 H 4
Castroverde (E) .... 56 D 2
Castroverde
  de Campos (E) ...... 57 H 5
Castrovillari (I).........113 B 1
Castuera (E)........... 69 H 2
Catane (RO)........... 151 E 5
Catania (I) ....115 G 3
Catanzaro (I)..........113 C 3
Catanzaro Lido (I) ......113 C 3
Câțcău (RO)........... 147 F 3
Catenanuova (I)........115 F 3
Čatež ob Savi (SLO) .... 134 D 3
Cathair na Mart /
  Westport (IRL)........ 22 B 4
Čatići (BIH)...........137 G 5
Catignano (I).......... 109 G 2
Catoira (E) .... 56 B 3
Catral (E) .... 73 E 2
Cattenom (F)...........41 E 4
Cattolica (I) .... 107 F 2
Catus (F) .... 49 F 5
Căuaș (RO)........... 146 D 2
Caudebec-en-Caux (F).. 39 E 4
Caudete (E) .... 73 E 1
Caudiel (E) .... 65 H 3
Caudry (F) .... 40 A 3
Caulnes (F) .... 43 E 2
Caulonia (I)...........113 C 4
Caumont-l'Éventé (F) ... 38 C 5
Caunes-Minervois (F) ... 53 H 3
Căușeni (MD).........13 F 3
Caussade (F) .... 53 F 1
Cauterets (F)......... 52 C 4
Cava de' Tirreni (I)...... 109 H 5
Cavadinești (RO) ...... 149 E 5
Cavaglià (I)........... 100 C 4
Cavaillon (F) .... 54 D 2
Cavalaire-sur-Mer (F).... 55 F 3
Cavalese (I) .... 102 D 2
Cavalière (F) .... 55 F 3
Cavan /
  An Cabhán (IRL)....... 23 E 4
Cavarzere (I) .... 103 E 5
Cavazzo Carnico (I)..... 103 G 2
Çavdarhisar (TR).......19 H 2
Cavezzo (I)........... 105 H 2
Cavnic (RO)........... 147 F 2
Cavo (I) .... 106 B 5
Cavour (I) .... 100 B 5
Cavtat (RO)........... 139 E 4
Cayeux-sur-Mer (F)..... 39 G 3
Caylus (F) .... 53 G 1
Cayres (F) .... 50 B 5
Cazalla de la Sierra (E)... 69 G 4
Cazals (F) .... 49 F 5
Căzănești (RO)........ 152 D 3
Cazaubon (F) .... 52 D 1
Cazaux (F) .... 48 B 5
Cazeneuve,
  château de (F) .... 52 C 1
Cazères (F) .... 53 E 3
Cazin (BIH)........... 135 E 5
Čazma (HR)........... 135 F 3
Cazorla (E) .... 71 F 4
Cea (E) .... 56 C 3
Ceadîr-Lunga (MD)....13 F 4
Ceahlău (RO).......... 148 B 3
Ceatharlach /
  Carlow (IRL)....... 25 F 2
Cebolla (E) .... 64 A 4
Cebreros (E) .... 64 A 2
Cece (H) .... 129 E 3
Cecina (I) .... 105 G 5

Ceclavín (E) .... 63 E 4
Cedeira (E) .... 56 C 1
Cedillo (E) .... 62 D 5
Cedrillas (E) .... 65 G 2
Cedynia (PL)...........116 B 5
Cefalù (I) ....115 E 2
Cegléd (H) .... 129 G 2
Ceglie Messapica (I)....111 F 4
Cehegín (E) .... 71 H 3
Cehu Silvaniei (RO)..... 147 E 2
Čejč (CZ) .... 93 E 5
Čelákovice (CZ) ...... 92 B 2
Celano (I) .... 109 F 2
Celanova (E) .... 56 C 4
Celarevo (SRB) .... 140 B 3
Celaru (RO) .... 151 F 5
Čelebić (BIH) .... 136 D 5
Čelebići (BIH) .... 139 F 2
Čelić (BIH) .... 137 H 3
Čelinac (BIH) .... 135 G 5
Celje (SLO) .... 134 D 2
Cella (E) .... 65 G 2
Celldömölk (H) .... 128 C 2
Celle (D) .... 85 G 1
Celle Ligure (I) ...... 104 D 3
Celles-sur-Belle (F) ..... 48 D 2
Čelopeci (MK).......... 145 E 1
Celorico da Beira (P).... 62 D 3
Celorico de Basto (P) ... 62 C 1
Čemerno (BIH) .... 139 F 3
Cencenighe
  Agordino (I)......... 103 E 2
Cenei (RO) .... 150 A 1
Cenicero (E) .... 58 D 3
Cenovo (BG) .... 156 C 2
Censeau (F) ....47 F 5
Čenta (SRB) .... 140 D 3
Centelles (E) .... 60 D 3
Cento (I) .... 105 H 2
Centuripe (I) ....115 F 3
Cepagatti (I) .... 109 G 2
Čepan (AL) .... 144 D 4
Čepelare (BG) .... 162 C 1
Čepin (HR) .... 137 G 2
Čepinci (BG) .... 162 C 2
Čepinski Martinci (HR). 137 G 2
Ceppo (I) .... 107 G 5
Ceprano (I) .... 109 F 3
Čeralije (HR) .... 135 G 3
Cerăt (RO) .... 151 F 5
Cerbăl (RO) .... 150 D 1
Cerbère (F) .... 54 A 5
Cercal (P) .... 68 B 4
Cercal (P) .... 68 B 1
Cercedilla (E) .... 64 B 2
Cerchiara di Calabria (I) .113 C 1
Cerdedo (E) .... 56 C 3
Cerdeira do Côa (P) .... 63 E 3
Cerea (I) .... 101 H 5
Cerença (BG) .... 156 D 2
Čerepovo (BG) .... 159 G 3
Céres (I) .... 100 B 4
Čereševo (BG) .... 152 C 5
Ceresole Reale (I) ...... 100 B 4
Céret (F) .... 53 H 5
Cerezo de Abajo (E) .... 64 C 1
Cerezo de Riotirón (E)... 58 C 3
Cergy (F) .... 39 G 5
Cerignola (I) ....110 D 3
Cérilly (F) .... 50 A 1
Cerisiers (F) .... 45 G 2
Cerisy-la-Salle (F) ..... 38 C 5
Cerizay (F) .... 43 G 5
Čerkasy (UA)...........13 G 1
Cerknica (SLO) .... 134 B 3
Cerkno (SLO) .... 134 B 2
Čerkovna (BG) .... 156 D 3
Cerkwica (PL)..........116 C 2
Cerler (E) .... 60 A 1
Cermei (RO) .... 146 C 4
Cerna (HR) .... 137 G 2
Cerna (RO) .... 153 F 2
Černá v Pošumaví (CZ). 92 A 5
Cernătești (RO) .... 151 E 4
Cernavodă (RO) .... 153 E 4

Cernay (F) ....47 G 3
Černi Osăm (BG) .... 158 D 1
Černičevo (BG) .... 163 E 2
Černihiv (UA) ....7 F 5
Cernik (HR) .... 135 G 4
Černivci (UA)...........13 E 3
Cernobbio (I) .... 101 E 3
Černogorovo (BG) ..... 158 D 2
Černolik (BG) .... 152 D 5
Černomorec (BG) ...... 157 F 4
Černoočene (BG) ...... 162 D 1
Cerova Korija (BG) ..... 159 F 1
Cerovo (BG) .... 158 B 1
Cerreto Sannita (I) ..... 109 H 4
Cerrigydrudion (GB) ... 32 B 4
Certaldo (I) .... 105 H 5
Certeju de Sus (RO) .... 147 E 5
Cervatos (I) .... 58 B 2
Cervatos de la Cueza (E). 58 A 3
Červen (BG) .... 162 C 1
Červen brjag /
  Червен бряг (BG) ... 155 E 3
Červena Voda (BG) ..... 152 B 5
Červená Voda (CZ) ..... 93 E 2
Červenci (BG) .... 157 E 2
Červený Kostelec (CZ).. 87 H 5
Cervera (E) .... 60 C 3
Cervera
  de la Cañada (E)...... 59 F 5
Cervera de Pisuerga (E). 58 A 2
Cervera
  del Río Alhama (E) ... 59 E 4
Cerveteri (I) .... 108 D 2
Cervia (I) .... 107 F 2
Cervień (BY)...........6 D 4
Cervignano del Friuli (I). 103 G 3
Cervinara (I) .... 109 H 5
Cervione (F) .... 55 H 4
Cervo (E) .... 56 D 1
Červonohrad (UA) .....12 D 2
Cesana Torinese (I)..... 100 A 5
Cesarica (HR) .... 136 B 4
Cesarò (I) ....115 F 3
Cesena (I) .... 107 E 2
Cesenatico (I) .... 107 F 2
Cēsis (LV) .... 203 E 2
Česká Kamenice (CZ) ... 87 E 5
Česká Lípa (CZ) ...... 87 F 5
Česká Skalice (CZ) ..... 87 H 5
Česká Třebová (CZ) .... 92 D 3
České Budějovice (CZ) . 92 B 5
České Velenice (CZ) .... 92 B 5
Český Brod (CZ) ...... 92 B 2
Český Krumlov (CZ) ... 92 A 5
Český Těšín (CZ) ...... 93 G 3
Çeşme (TR) ....19 G 3
Cespedosa
  de Tormes (E) ...... 63 G 3
Cessalto (I) .... 103 F 4
Čestimensko (BG) ..... 152 D 5
Cesvaine (LV) .... 203 F 3
Cetate (RO) .... 151 E 4
Cetatea de Baltă (RO) .. 147 G 5
Cetina (E) .... 65 E 1
Cetinje (MNE) .... 139 F 4
Cetraro (I) ....113 B 2
Ceuta (E) ....74 C 5
Ceutí (E) .... 72 D 3
Ceva (I) .... 104 C 3
Cevico de la Torre (E)... 58 A 4
Čevo (MNE) .... 139 F 4
Ceyrat (F) .... 50 A 3
Ceyzériat (F) .... 50 D 2
Chabanais (F) .... 49 E 2
Chabeuil (F) .... 50 D 5
Chablis (F) .... 45 G 3
Chabotterie,
  logis de la (F)........43 F 5
Chabris (F) .... 44 D 4
Chagny (F) .... 46 D 5
Chailland (F) .... 43 G 2
Chaillé-les-Marais (F)... 48 C 1
Chairóneia (GR) .... 165 G 4
Chalabre (F) .... 53 G 4
Chalain, lac de (F).......51 E 1

Chalais (F) .... 48 D 4
Chalamont (F) .... 50 D 2
Chalampé (F) ....47 H 3
Chalandrítsa (GR) ..... 165 E 4
Chalindrey (F) .... 46 D 3
Chalkeió (GR) .... 167 E 4
Chálki
  (Nótio Aigaío) (GR) .. 171 G 3
Chálki (Thessalía) (GR) . 165 F 1
Chalkiádes (GR) .... 165 F 1
Chalkída / Χαλκίδα (GR) 165 H 3
Chalkidóna (GR) ...... 161 F 3
Challans (F) .... 43 E 5
Challes-les-Eaux (F) .....51 F 3
Chalon-sur-Saône (F) .. 46 D 5
Chalonnes-sur-Loire (F). 43 G 4
Châlons-
  en-Champagne (F)... 40 C 5
Châlus (F) .... 49 F 3
Cham (D) ....91 G 4
Chambéry (F) ....51 E 3
Chambley (F) ....41 E 5
Chambly (F) .... 39 H 5
Chambon-sur-Lac (F) ... 50 A 3
Chambon-
  sur-Voueize (F) ...... 49 H 2
Chambord (F)........... 44 D 4
Chamonix-
  Mont-Blanc (F).......51 F 3
Champ de Bataille,
  château du (F) .... 39 F 5
Champagnac-
  de-Belair (F) .... 49 E 3
Champagne-Mouton (F). 49 E 2
Champagnole (F) ....47 E 5
Champdeniers-
  Saint-Denis (F) ...... 48 D 1
Champeaux (F) .... 43 F 2
Champeix (F) .... 50 A 3
Champéry (CH) .... 98 B 4
Champex (CH) .... 98 C 5
Champlitte (F) ....47 E 5
Champlon (B) .... 79 E 4
Champoluc (I) .... 100 C 3
Champorcher (I) ...... 100 C 4
Champs-
  sur-Tarentaine (F) .... 49 H 4
Champs, château de (F). 45 F 1
Champtoceaux (F) ..... 43 F 4
Chamrousse (F) ....51 E 4
Chamusca (P) .... 62 B 5
Chanac (F) .... 54 A 1
Chanákia (GR) .... 164 D 5
Chanas (F) .... 50 D 4
Chandrás (GR) .... 173 F 4
Chandria (CY)...........174 C 2
Chaniá /
  Χανιά (Kríti) (GR) ..... 172 B 3
Chánia
  (Pelopónnisos) (GR) .. 168 D 3
Chánia (Thessalía) (GR). 165 G 1
Chaniótis (GR) .... 161 H 5
Chantada (E) .... 56 D 3
Chantelle (F) .... 50 A 2
Chantemerle (F) ....51 G 4
Chantilly (F) .... 39 H 5
Chantonnay (F) .... 48 C 1
Chaource (F) .... 45 H 3
Chapel-en-le-Frith (GB) . 32 D 3
Chapinería (E) .... 64 B 3
Charavgí (GR) .... 161 E 4
Charbonnières (F)...... 50 D 3
Chard (GB) .... 35 E 3
Charenton-du-Cher (F).. 49 H 1
Charkeia (CY) .... 175 E 2
Charkiv (UA)...........7 H 5
Charleroi (B) .... 78 C 3
Charlestown (IRL) ..... 22 C 4
Charleville (IRL) ...... 24 C 3
Charleville-Mézières (F). 40 C 3
Charlieu (F) .... 50 C 2
Charlottenberg (S) .... 189 G 5
Charly-sur-Marne (F) ... 40 A 5
Charmes (F) ....47 F 2
Charny-Orée
  de Puisaye (F)......... 45 F 3
Charny-sur-Meuse (F) .. 40 D 5

Charokopeió (GR) ...... 168 C 3
Charolles (F) .... 50 C 1
Chârost (F)................ 45 E 5
Charquemont (F) .....47 G 4
Charroux (F) .... 49 E 2
Chartres (F) .... 44 D 2
Chasseneuil-
　sur-Bonnieure (F) .. 49 E 3
Chastleton House (GB) .. 35 G 1
Château-Arnoux-
　Saint-Auban (F) .... 55 E 1
Château-Chinon (F) .... 45 H 5
Château-d'Oex (CH) .. 98 C 4
Château-du-Loir (F) .... 44 B 3
Château-Gaillard (F)... 39 F 5
Château-Gontier (F)... 43 G 3
Château-la-Vallière (F) .. 44 B 4
Château-Landon (F) .... 45 F 2
Château-Porcien (F).... 40 C 4
Château-Queyras (F) ..51 G 5
Château-Regnault (F).. 40 C 3
Château-Renard (F) .... 45 F 3
Château-Renault (F).... 44 C 4
Château-Salins (F)...... 41 F 5
Château-Thierry (F) .... 40 A 5
Châteaubourg (F) ...... 43 F 3
Châteaubriant (F) ...... 43 F 3
Châteaudun (F) .... 44 D 3
Châteaugiron (F)....... 43 F 3
Châteaulin (F)........... 42 B 2
Châteaumeillant (F) .. 49 H 1
Châteauneuf-
　de-Randon (F) .... 50 B 5
Châteauneuf-
　d'Ille-et-Vilaine (F) .. 43 F 1
Châteauneuf-du-Faou (F). 42 C 2
Châteauneuf-du-Pape (F). 54 C 1
Châteauneuf-
　en-Thymerais (F) ...... 44 D 2
Châteauneuf-la-Forêt (F) . 49 G 3
Châteauneuf-
　les-Bains (F).......... 50 A 2
Châteauneuf-
　sur-Charente (F) ...... 48 D 3
Châteauneuf-
　sur-Cher (F) .... 45 E 5
Châteauneuf-
　sur-Loire (F) .... 45 E 3
Châteauneuf-
　sur-Sarthe (F) .... 43 H 3
Châteauponsac (F)...... 49 F 2
Châteaurenard (F) ..... 54 D 2
Châteauroux (F)........ 44 D 5
Châteauvillain (F) ...... 46 D 3
Châtel (F)................51 G 1
Châtel-Guyon (F) ..... 50 A 2
Châtel-Montagne (F) .. 50 B 2
Châtel-Saint-Denis (CH) . 98 B 4
Châtel-sur-Moselle (F)..47 F 2
Châtelaillon-Plage (F).. 48 C 2
Châtelaudren (F)........ 42 D 1
Châteldon (F)........... 50 B 2
Châtelet (B)............. 78 C 3
Châtellerault (F)......... 44 C 5
Châtelus-Malvaleix (F).. 49 G 2
Châtenois (F)............47 E 2
Chatham (GB)........... 36 D 4
Châtillon (I)............. 100 C 3
Châtillon-Coligny (F)... 45 F 3
Châtillon-en-Bazois (F).. 45 G 5
Châtillon-en-Diois (F) ...51 E 5
Châtillon-
　sur-Chalaronne (F) .... 50 D 2
Châtillon-sur-Indre (F) .. 44 D 5
Châtillon-sur-Loire (F).. 45 F 3
Châtillon-sur-Marne (F) .. 40 B 5
Châtillon-sur-Seine (F).. 46 C 3
Chatsworth House (GB) .. 33 E 3
Chatteris (GB)........... 33 G 5
Chaudes-Aigues (F)..... 50 A 5
Chauffailles (F)......... 50 C 2
Chaufour-
　lès-Bonnières (F)...... 39 G 5
Chaulnes (F)............ 39 H 3
Chaumergy (F)...........47 E 5
Chaumont (F)........... 46 D 2
Chaumont-en-Vexin (F). 39 G 5

Chaumont-sur-Loire (F) . 44 D 4
Chauny (F).............. 40 A 4
Chaussin (F)............. 47 E 5
Chauvigny (F)........... 49 E 1
Chavári (GR)........... 164 D 5
Chavdáta (GR) .... 164 B 4
Chaves (P) .... 56 D 5
Chazelles (F) .... 50 C 3
Cheb (CZ)................91 F 3
Chęciny (PL) .... 122 C 4
Cheia (RO) .... 152 B 2
Cheimarros (GR) ...... 161 G 2
Cheles (E) .... 69 E 2
Chełm (PL) .... 123 H 3
Chełmno (PL).......... 117 G 4
Chełmża (PL).......... 117 H 4
Cheltenham (GB) ...... 35 G 1
Chelva (E)................ 65 G 4
Chemillé-en-Anjou (F) .. 43 G 4
Chemin (F)............... 46 D 5
Chemnitz (D) .... 86 C 5
Chênehutte-
　Trèves-Cunault (F) .. 43 H 4
Chénérailles (F) .... 49 H 2
Chenonceaux (F) ...... 44 D 5
Chepstow (GB)........... 35 F 2
Chera (E)................. 65 G 4
Cherbourg-
　en-Cotentin (F) ...... 38 B 4
Chéroy (F) .... 45 F 2
Cherson (UA)............13 G 3
Cheshunt (GB).......... 36 C 3
Cheste (E)................ 65 H 4
Chester (GB)............ 32 C 3
Chester-le-Street (GB)...31 G 4
Chesterfield (GB)........ 33 E 3
Chevagnes (F) .... 50 B 1
Cheverny,
　château de (F) ...... 44 D 4
Chevillon (F)............ 46 D 2
Chevreuse (F) .... 45 E 1
Chiampo (I)............ 101 H 4
Chianciano Terme (I) .. 107 E 4
Chiaramonte Gulfi (I)..115 F 5
Chiaravalle (I) .... 107 G 3
Chiaravalle Centrale (I) ..113 C 4
Chiari (I)............... 101 F 4
Chiasso (CH) .... 99 F 5
Chiavari (I)............. 105 E 3
Chiavenna (I) .... 101 F 2
Chichester (GB)......... 38 C 1
Chiclana
　de la Frontera (E)...74 B 4
Chieming (D) .... 95 H 2
Chieri (I) .... 100 C 5
Chiesa
　in Valmalenco (I) ..... 101 F 2
Chiesina Uzzanese (I) .. 105 G 4
Chieti (I) .... 109 G 2
Chiliomódi (GR)....... 165 G 5
Chillon (CH) .... 98 C 4
Chimay (B)............. 78 C 4
Chinchilla
　de Monte Aragón (E) .. 71 H 1
Chinchón (E)........... 64 C 3
Chinon (F)............. 44 B 5
Chiochiş (RO) .... 147 G 3
Chioggia (I) .... 103 F 5
Chíos / Xíoς (GR) ..... 167 E 4
Chipiona (E).............74 A 3
Chippenham (GB)........ 35 G 2
Chipping
　Campden (GB)....... 35 G 1
Chipping Norton (GB)... 35 G 1
Chipping Sodbury (GB).. 35 F 2
Chirivel (E)............. 71 G 4
Chirpăr (RO)........... 147 G 5
Chişinău (MD).............13 F 3
Chişineu-Criş (RO) .... 146 C 4
Chitila (RO) .... 152 B 4
Chiusa / Klausen (I) ... 103 E 2
Chiusa di Pesio (I) .... 104 C 3
Chiusa Sclafani (I).....114 C 3
Chiusaforte (I) .... 103 G 2
Chiusi (I)............... 107 E 5

Chiva (E)................. 65 H 4
Chivasso (I) .... 100 C 5
Chlapowo (PL)......... 121 F 1
Chlemoútsi (GR) ...... 164 C 4
Chlewiska (PL) .... 122 D 3
Chlorakas (CY).........174 B 4
Chlum u Třeboně (CZ) .. 92 B 5
Chlumec
　nad Cidlinou (CZ) .... 92 C 2
Chmel'nyc'kyj (UA).......13 E 2
Chmielnik (PL) .... 122 D 5
Chmil'nyk (UA)............13 E 2
Choceň (CZ) .... 92 D 2
Chóchlakas (GR) ...... 171 H 4
Chochołów (PL)........ 125 G 3
Chocianów (PL) .... 120 D 3
Chociwel (PL)..........116 C 4
Chocz (PL).............. 121 G 2
Chodecz (PL) .... 121 H 1
Chodel (PL) .... 123 F 3
Chodov (CZ).............91 G 2
Chodzież (PL)...........117 E 5
Chojna (PL)............116 B 5
Chojnice (PL)...........117 F 3
Chojniki (BY)..............7 E 5
Chojnów (PL) .... 120 D 3
Cholet (F)............... 43 G 5
Chollerford (GB).........31 F 3
Chołm (RUS)...............7 E 2
Chomutov (CZ).......... 91 H 2
Chóra
　(Pelopónnisos) (GR) .. 168 C 3
Chóra
　(Vóreio Aigaío) (GR) .. 167 G 5
Chóra Sfakíon (GR) ... 172 B 3
Choreftó (GR)......... 165 G 1
Chorges (F)...............51 F 5
Chorin, kloster (D) .... 83 G 5
Chorley (GB) .... 32 C 2
Chorol (UA)...............13 G 1
Chorzele (PL)..........118 D 4
Chorzów (PL) .... 122 A 5
Choszczno (PL)..........116 C 4
Chotěboř (CZ) .... 92 C 3
Chotyn (UA)..............13 E 2
Choumnikó (GR) ...... 161 H 3
Chouni (GR) .... 164 D 2
Chouto (GR) .... 68 C 1
Chrást (CZ) .... 92 B 3
Christchurch (GB)....... 38 B 1
Christiani (GR) .... 168 B 3
Christiansfeld (DK).... 198 B 3
Chrudim (CZ) .... 92 C 3
Chrýsafa (GR) .... 168 D 3
Chrysí Aktí (GR)....... 162 C 3
Chrysí Ammoudiá (GR).. 162 C 3
Chrysoúpoli (GR)...... 162 C 3
Chrysovítsi (GR)....... 165 E 5
Chrzanów (PL) .... 125 F 1
Chur / Coira (CH) ...... 99 G 3
Church Stretton (GB)... 32 C 5
Chust (UA)................12 D 3
Chynów (PL) .... 122 D 2
Ciacova (RO) .... 150 B 1
Cicciano (I)............. 109 H 5
Ćićevac (SRB) .... 143 E 1
Ćićevo (BIH) .... 139 E 4
Cidones (E) .... 58 D 4
Ciechanów (PL).........118 D 5
Ciechanowiec (PL) ....119 G 5
Ciechocinek (PL).......117 H 5
Ciempozuelos (E) ..... 64 C 3
Cieplice (PL) .... 120 C 4
Cieszanów (PL) .... 123 G 5
Cieszyn (PL) .... 125 F 2
Cieza (E) .... 71 H 3
Ciężkowice (PL) ...... 125 H 2
Cifuentes (E)........... 64 D 2
Cigánd (H) .... 127 F 5
Cigliano (I) .... 100 C 4
Cilavegna (I) .... 100 D 4
Cilibia (RO) .... 152 D 2
Cilieni (RO) .... 151 G 5
Ćilipi (HR) .... 139 E 4
Cill Airne /
　Killarney (IRL) .... 24 B 4

Cill Chainnigh /
　Kilkenny (IRL) .... 25 E 3
Cill Mhantáin /
　Wicklow (IRL) .... 25 G 2
Cillas (E) .... 65 F 1
Cilleros (E) .... 63 E 4
Cilleruelo de Bezana (E). 58 B 2
Cimişlia (MD) ....13 F 3
Cinctorres (E) .... 65 H 2
Ciney (B) .... 78 D 3
Cinfães (P) .... 62 C 2
Cingoli (I) .... 107 G 4
Cinigiano (I) .... 106 D 5
Cinisi (I)................114 C 2
Cínovec (CZ)............ 86 D 5
Cintegabelle (F)........ 53 F 2
Cintruénigo (E) .... 59 F 4
Ciocăneşti (RO) ...... 152 D 4
Ciolăneştii
　din Deal (RO) .... 151 H 4
Ciorăşti (RO) .... 152 D 2
Cioroiaşi (RO) .... 151 E 4
Ciprovci (BG) .... 154 C 3
Círák (H) .... 128 C 2
Cirencester (GB) ...... 35 G 1
Cireşu (RO) .... 150 D 3
Cirey-sur-Vezouze (F) ...47 G 1
Ciria (E) .... 59 E 5
Cirié (I) .... 100 C 4
Cirò (I).................113 D 2
Cirò Marina (I) ....113 D 2
Čirpan / Чирпан (BG) .. 159 E 3
Cislău (RO) .... 152 C 2
Cisna (PL) .... 127 F 3
Cisnădie (RO) .... 151 G 1
Cisneros (E) .... 58 A 3
Cista Mala (HR) ...... 136 C 5
Cista Provo (HR) ...... 138 C 2
Cisterna di Latina (I).. 109 E 3
Cisternino (I)...........111 F 4
Cisterna (E) .... 57 H 3
Čitluk (BIH) .... 138 D 3
Città della Pieve (I)... 107 E 5
Città di Castello (I) ... 107 E 4
Città Sant' Angelo (I).. 109 G 1
Cittadella (I) .... 103 E 4
Cittaducale (I) .... 109 E 2
Cittanova (I)............115 H 2
Cittanova d'Istria /
　Novigrad (HR) .... 134 A 4
Cittareale (I) .... 107 G 5
Ciucea (RO) .... 147 E 3
Ciucurova (RO)........ 153 F 3
Ciudad Real (E)......... 70 D 1
Ciudad Rodrigo (E).... 63 F 3
Ciuperceni (RO) ...... 151 E 3
Ciupercenii Noi (RO) .. 151 E 5
Ciutadella
　de Menorca (E).......67 G 2
Cividale del Friuli (I) .. 103 G 3
Civita Castellana (I)... 108 D 2
Civitanova Marche (I) . 107 H 4
Civitavecchia (I)....... 108 C 2
Civitella del Tronto (I).. 107 H 5
Civitella Roveto (I) ... 109 F 3
Civray (F) .... 49 E 2
Cjurupyns'k (UA).........13 G 3
Clacton-on-Sea (GB) .. 37 E 3
Clairvaux-les-Lacs (F) ...51 E 1
Clamecy (F)............ 45 G 4
Clamouse,
　grotte de (F) .... 54 A 2
Clandon Park (GB) .... 36 C 4
Claonaig (GB).......... 30 B 2
Clapham (GB)...........31 F 5
Clara (IRL) .... 23 E 5
Clare (GB).............. 33 H 5
Claremorris (IRL) ..... 22 C 4
Claudy (GB) .... 23 F 2
Clausthal-Zellerfeld (D) .. 85 H 3
Claut (I) .... 103 F 2
Clavière (I) .... 100 A 5
Clay Cross (GB)......... 33 E 3
Claye (F)................ 39 H 5
Clécy (F) .... 38 D 5
Cleethorpes (GB) ...... 33 G 2
Clefmont (F)............47 E 2
Coldbackie (GB)........ 26 A 4

Cléguérec (F) .... 42 D 2
Clejani (RO) .... 152 B 4
Clelles (F)................51 E 5
Clères (F) .... 39 F 4
Clermont (F) .... 39 H 4
Clermont-
　en-Argonne (F) ...... 40 D 5
Clermont-Ferrand (F) .. 50 A 3
Clermont-l'Hérault (F).. 54 A 2
Clerval (F)...............47 F 4
Clervaux (L) .... 79 E 4
Cléry-Saint-André (F)... 44 D 3
Cles (I) .... 101 H 2
Clevedon (GB) .... 35 E 2
Cleveleys (GB) .... 32 C 2
Clifden (IRL) .... 22 B 5
Clisson (F) .... 43 F 5
Clitheroe (GB).......... 32 D 2
Clogh Mills (GB)........ 23 G 2
Cloghan (IRL) .... 22 D 5
Clogheen (IRL) .... 24 D 3
Clogherhead (IRL) .... 23 G 4
Clonakilty (IRL) .... 24 C 5
Clonbur (IRL) .... 22 C 5
Clondalkin (IRL)........ 23 F 5
Clones (IRL) .... 23 E 3
Clonmacnoise (IRL) ... 22 D 5
Clonmel /
　Cluain Meala (IRL) .. 25 E 3
Cloppenburg (D)........81 F 5
Clovelly (GB) .... 34 C 3
Cloyes-sur-le-Loir (F).. 44 D 3
Cluain Meala /
　Clonmel (IRL) .... 25 E 3
Cluj-Napoca (RO) ..... 147 F 4
Clun (GB) .... 32 C 5
Cluny (F)............... 50 C 1
Cluses (F) ....51 F 2
Clusone (I) .... 101 F 3
Clydebank (GB) .... 30 C 2
Ćmielów (PL) .... 123 E 4
Coachford (IRL) .... 24 C 4
Coalisland (GB) .... 23 F 3
Coalville (GB) .... 33 E 4
Coaña (E) .... 57 E 1
Coarnele Caprei (RO)... 148 D 2
Coatbridge (GB) ...... 30 D 2
Cobadin (RO) .... 153 F 5
Cobeña (E) .... 64 C 2
Cobh / An Cóbh (IRL)... 24 D 4
Coburg (D).............. 90 D 2
Coca (E)................. 64 A 1
Cocconato (I) .... 100 C 5
Cocentaina (E) .... 73 F 1
Cochem (D).............. 88 C 1
Cockburnspath (GB)....31 F 2
Cockermouth (GB) .....31 E 5
Cocora (RO)........... 152 D 3
Codăeşti (RO) .... 149 E 3
Code (LV) .... 202 D 4
Codevigo (I) .... 103 E 5
Codigoro (I) .... 107 E 1
Codlea (RO) .... 152 A 1
Codognè (I)............ 103 F 3
Codogno (I) .... 101 F 4
Codos (E) .... 59 F 5
Codroipo (I) .... 103 G 3
Coesfeld (D) .... 84 C 2
Coevorden (NL)........ 77 G 3
Cofrentes (E) .... 65 G 5
Cogealac (RO) .... 153 F 3
Cogeces del Monte (E).. 58 D 3
Cognac (F) .... 48 D 3
Cogne (I) .... 100 B 4
Cogolin (F).............. 55 F 3
Cogolludo (E) .... 64 C 1
Coimbra (P) .... 62 B 3
Coín (E).................74 D 3
Coira / Chur (CH) ...... 99 G 3
Cojocna (RO) .... 147 F 4
Čoka (SRB) .... 140 C 1
Col (SLO) .... 134 B 3
Colares (P) .... 68 A 1
Colchester (GB)........ 36 D 3

Colditz (D)............... 86 C 4
Coldstream (GB)........31 F 3
Coleford (GB) .... 35 F 1
Coleraine (GB) .... 23 F 1
Colfiorito (I) .... 107 F 5
Colico (I) .... 101 F 3
Coligny (F).............. 50 D 1
Colinas (E) .... 69 G 5
Colindres (E) .... 58 C 1
Colintraive (GB) .... 30 B 2
Coll de Nargó (E) ..... 60 C 2
Collado de Tallante (E) .. 73 E 4
Collado Villalba (E) .... 64 B 2
Colle di Val d'Elsa (I).. 105 H 5
Colle Isarco /
　Gossensaß (I) .... 102 D 1
Colle Sannita (I) ...... 109 H 4
Colleferro (I) .... 109 E 3
Collesalvetti (I)........ 105 G 5
Collesano (I)...........114 D 3
Colli a Volturno (I).... 109 G 3
Collinée (F) .... 43 E 2
Collio (I) .... 101 G 3
Collioure (F) .... 54 A 5
Collobrières (F) .... 55 F 3
Collodi (I) .... 105 G 4
Collonges (I)............51 E 2
Collonges-la-Rouge (F) . 49 G 4
Colmar (F)...............47 G 2
Colmars (F) .... 55 F 1
Colmenar (E)............75 E 3
Colmenar de Oreja (E).. 64 C 3
Colmenar Viejo (E) .... 64 B 2
Colnabaichin (GB)...... 29 G 4
Colne (GB) .... 32 D 2
Colobraro (I)...........111 E 5
Cologna Veneta (I) .... 102 D 4
Cologne (F).............. 53 E 2
Colombey-les-Belles (F).47 E 1
Colombey-
　les-Deux-Églises (F) ... 46 D 2
Colombres (E) .... 58 A 1
Colomera (E)............ 70 D 5
Coloneşti (RO) .... 151 G 3
Colònia de Sant Jordi (E).67 F 3
Colorno (I) .... 101 H 4
Colosimi (I) ....113 C 3
Colunga (E) .... 57 H 1
Colwyn Bay /
　Bae Colwyn (GB) .... 32 B 3
Coma-ruga (E) .... 60 C 4
Comacchio (I)......... 107 E 1
Čomakovci (BG) ...... 155 E 3
Comana (RO) .... 152 B 4
Comana de Jos (RO).. 147 H 5
Comăneşti (RO) ...... 148 C 4
Comarnic (RO)........ 152 A 2
Combarro (E) .... 56 B 3
Combe Martin (GB) ... 34 D 3
Combeaufontaine (F)...47 E 3
Comber (GB) .... 23 G 3
Combloux (F)...........51 F 2
Combourg (F)........... 43 F 2
Combronde (F) .... 50 A 2
Comeglians (I) .... 103 G 2
Comillas (E) .... 58 A 1
Comines (F) .... 40 A 1
Comiso (I) ....115 F 5
Comloşu Mare (RO) .. 146 A 3
Commentry (F) .... 49 H 2
Commercy (F)...........47 E 1
Como (I) .... 101 E 3
Cómpeta (E) ....75 E 3
Compiègne (F)......... 40 A 4
Comporta (P) .... 68 B 2
Comps-sur-Artuby (F).. 55 F 2
Comrat (MD).............13 F 3
Comunanza (I) .... 107 G 5
Concarneau (F) .... 42 C 3
Concha (E) .... 58 C 1
Conches-en-Ouche (F).. 39 F 5
Concordia
　sulla Secchia (I) ..... 101 H 5
Condat (F).............. 50 A 4
Condé (F)............... 40 B 2
Condé-en-Brie (F)....... 40 B 5

A B C D E F G H I J K L M N O P Q R S T U V W X Y Z

Condé-en-Normandie (F)..... 38 D 5
Condeixa-a-Nova (P).... 62 B 4
Condom (F)............. 52 D 2
Condrieu (F)............ 50 D 3
Conegliano (I)........... 103 F 3
Conev (BG)............. 157 F 3
Conflans-en-Jarnisy (F)...41 E 5
Confolens (F).......... 49 E 2
Cong (IRL)............ 22 C 5
Congleton (GB)......... 32 D 3
Congosto de Valdavia (E). 58 A 2
Congresbury (GB)....... 35 F 2
Conil de la Frontera (E)...74 B 4
Conisbrough (GB)....... 33 E 3
Coniston (GB)...........31 E 5
Conlie (F)............. 43 H 2
Conliège (F)............51 E 1
Connel (F)............ 28 D 5
Connerré (F).......... 44 C 3
Conop (RO)........... 146 C 5
Čonoplja (SRB)........ 137 H 1
Conques-en-Rouergue (F) ... 49 H 5
Conquista (E)........... 70 C 3
Conselice (I)........... 107 E 1
Conselve (I)........... 103 E 5
Consett (GB)...........31 G 4
Constância (P)......... 62 B 5
Constanţa (RO)........ 153 F 4
Constantina (E)........ 69 H 4
Consuegra (E)......... 64 C 5
Consuma (I)........... 106 D 3
Contarina (I)........... 103 F 5
Conthey (CH)......... 98 C 4
Contigliano (I)......... 109 E 2
Contin (GB)........... 29 E 3
Contres (F)............ 44 D 4
Contrexéville (F)........47 E 2
Contursi Terme (I)......110 C 4
Conty (F)............. 39 H 4
Conversano (I)..........111 F 3
Conwy (GB)........... 32 B 3
Cookstown (GB)....... 23 F 2
Cootehill (IRL)........ 23 F 4
Čop (UA)..............12 C 3
Copalnic-Mănăştur (RO) ... 147 F 2
Cope (E)............. 71 H 5
Copertino (I)..........111 G 5
Copparo (I)........... 103 E 5
Copşa Mică (RO)...... 147 G 5
Corabia (RO).......... 151 G 5
Coral Bay (CY)........174 B 4
Corato (I).............111 E 3
Coray (F)............ 42 C 2
Čorbadžijsko (BG)..... 162 D 2
Corbeil-Essonnes (F)... 45 E 1
Corbie (F)............. 39 H 3
Corbigny (F).......... 45 G 4
Corbii Mari (RO)....... 152 A 4
Corbola (I)........... 103 E 5
Corbridge (GB)........31 F 4
Corbu (Constanţa) (RO) . 153 F 4
Corbu (Slatina) (RO).... 151 G 4
Corby (GB)........... 33 F 5
Corcaigh / Cork (IRL)... 24 C 4
Corcieux (F)...........47 G 2
Corconte (E)......... 58 B 2
Corcova (RO)......... 151 E 3
Corcubión (E)......... 56 A 2
Cordes-sur-Ciel (F).... 53 G 1
Córdoba (E)........... 70 B 4
Cordobilla de Lácara (E). 69 F 1
Corduente (E)......... 65 E 1
Corella (E)........... 59 F 4
Coreses (E)........... 63 G 1
Corfe Castle (GB)....... 38 B 1
Cori (I).............. 109 E 3
Coria (E)............. 63 F 4
Coria del Río (E)...... 69 G 5
Corias (E)............ 57 F 2
Corigliano Calabro (I) ...113 C 1
Corinaldo (I)......... 107 G 3
Coripe (E)............74 C 3
Cork / Corcaigh (IRL).... 24 C 4

Corlăţel (RO).......... 151 E 4
Corlay (F)............ 42 D 2
Corleone (I)...........114 C 3
Corleto Perticara (I)....110 D 4
Cormatin (F).......... 50 C 1
Cormeilles (F)........ 39 E 5
Cormery (F).......... 44 C 4
Cormons (I)........... 103 H 3
Cornago (E).......... 59 E 4
Cornellana (E)........ 57 F 1
Corneşti (RO)......... 147 F 3
Corniglio (I)......... 105 G 3
Cornimont (F).........47 G 3
Čornobyl' (UA)..........7 F 5
Čornomors'ke (UA).....13 H 3
Cornu Luncii (RO)..... 148 B 2
Cornuda (I)........... 103 E 3
Cornus (F)............ 54 A 2
Corod (RO).......... 152 D 1
Çorovodë (AL)........ 144 D 4
Corps (F).............51 F 5
Corral de Almaguer (E).. 64 C 4
Corralejo (P)...........67 H 5
Corrales del Vino (E)... 63 G 1
Corran (GB).......... 28 D 5
Corredoiras (E)....... 56 C 2
Correggio (I)......... 105 H 2
Corrèze (F)........... 49 G 4
Corridonia (I)......... 107 G 4
Corrofin (IRL)........ 24 C 2
Corsham (GB)........ 35 F 2
Čortanovci (SRB)..... 140 C 3
Corte (F)............. 55 H 4
Corte de Peleas (E).... 69 F 2
Cortegada (E)........ 56 C 4
Cortegana (E)........ 69 E 4
Cortemaggiore (I)..... 101 F 5
Cortemilia (I)......... 104 D 2
Corteolona (I)........ 101 E 5
Cortes (E)............ 59 F 4
Cortes de Aragón (E)... 65 G 1
Cortes de Baza (E).... 71 F 4
Cortes de la Frontera (E)..74 C 3
Cortijos Nuevos (E)..... 71 F 3
Cortina d'Ampezzo (I).. 103 E 2
Čortkiv (UA)...........12 D 2
Cortona (I)........... 107 E 4
Coruche (P).......... 68 B 1
Corund (RO)......... 147 H 4
Corvara in Badia (I)... 103 E 2
Corvera (E)........... 73 E 3
Corwen (GB)......... 32 B 4
Cosenza (I)...........113 B 2
Coşereni (RO)........ 152 C 3
Coşeşti (RO)......... 151 H 2
Cosham (GB)........ 38 C 1
Coslada (E).......... 64 C 2
Cosne-Cours-sur-Loire (F). 45 F 4
Cosne-d'Allier (F)..... 50 A 1
Coşoveni (RO)........ 151 F 4
Cossato (I)........... 100 D 4
Cossé-le-Vivien (F).... 43 G 3
Cossonay (CH)....... 98 B 3
Costa da Caparica (P).. 68 A 2
Costa de Santo André (P). 68 B 3
Costache Negri (RO)... 153 E 1
Costeşti (Buzău) (RO).. 152 C 2
Costeşti (Piteşti) (RO).. 151 H 3
Costeşti (Râmnicu Vâlcea) (RO). 151 F 2
Costigliole d'Asti (I)... 100 D 5
Costineşti (RO)....... 153 F 5
Coswig (Meißen Radebeul) (D). 86 D 4
Coswig Anhalt-Zerbst) (D)........ 86 C 2
Coteşti (RO).......... 152 D 1
Cotignac (F).......... 55 F 2
Cotmeana (RO)....... 151 G 2
Cottbus (D)........... 87 E 3
Coţuşca (RO)........ 148 C 1
Couches (F).......... 46 C 5
Couço (P)............ 68 C 1
Coucy-le-Château-Auffrique (F)...... 40 A 4
Couhé (F)............ 49 E 1

Couilly-Pont-aux-Dames (F).. 40 A 5
Couiza (F)............ 53 G 4
Coulanges-la-Vineuse (F). 45 G 3
Coulanges-sur-Yonne (F). 45 G 4
Coulommiers (F)....... 45 F 1
Coulon (F)............ 48 C 1
Coulonges-sur-l'Autize (F).. 48 C 1
Coupar Angus (GB).... 29 F 5
Couptrain (F)......... 43 H 2
Cour-Cheverny (F).... 44 D 4
Courances, château de (F)....... 45 E 2
Courchevel (F).........51 G 3
Courçon (F).......... 48 C 2
Courmayeur (I)....... 100 B 3
Cournon-d'Auvergne (F)... 50 A 3
Courpière (F)......... 50 B 3
Cours (F)............ 50 C 2
Coursan (F).......... 54 A 3
Coursegoules (F)..... 55 G 2
Courseulles-sur-Mer (F) . 38 D 4
Courson-les-Carrières (F) .... 45 G 4
Courtenay (F)........ 45 F 3
Courthézon (F)....... 54 D 1
Courtomer (F)........ 44 B 1
Courtown (IRL)....... 25 G 3
Courville-sur-Eure (F) ... 44 D 2
Coussey (F)...........47 E 2
Coutances (F)........ 38 B 5
Coutras (F)........... 48 D 4
Couvin (B)........... 78 C 4
Covadonga (E)....... 57 H 2
Covarrubias (E)....... 58 C 4
Covăsinţ (RO)........ 146 C 5
Covasna (RO)........ 152 B 1
Coventry (GB)........ 33 E 5
Covilhã (P).......... 62 D 3
Cowbridge (GB)....... 35 E 2
Cowdenbeath (GB).....31 E 1
Cowes (GB).......... 38 C 1
Cowfold (GB)......... 36 C 5
Cozes (F)............ 48 D 3
Cozia (RO)........... 151 G 2
Cozieni (RO)......... 152 C 2
Crăcăoani (RO)....... 148 B 3
Craco (I).............111 E 4
Crăieşti (RO)......... 147 G 4
Craigavon (GB)....... 23 G 3
Craigellachie (GB).... 29 G 3
Craighouse (GB)...... 30 A 2
Craignure (GB)....... 28 D 5
Crail (GB)............31 F 1
Crailsheim (D)........ 89 G 4
Craiova (RO)......... 151 F 4
Craiva (RO).......... 146 C 4
Crâmpoia (RO)....... 151 G 4
Crângu (RO)......... 151 H 5
Cranborne (GB)....... 38 B 1
Cranleigh (GB)....... 36 C 4
Craon (F)............ 43 G 3
Craonne (F).......... 40 B 4
Craponne-sur-Arzon (F). 50 B 4
Crasna (RO)......... 151 F 2
Crato (P)............ 68 D 1
Craughwell (IRL)..... 22 C 5
Čravarica (BG)....... 158 A 3
Craven Arms (GB).... 32 C 5
Crawinkel (D)........ 85 H 5
Crawley (GB)........ 36 C 5
Creagorry (GB)....... 28 B 3
Crécy-en-Ponthieu (F).. 39 G 2
Crécy-la-Chapelle (F)... 40 A 5
Crécy-sur-Serre (F).... 40 B 4
Crediton (GB)........ 34 D 3
Creegh (IRL)......... 24 B 2
Creeslough (IRL)..... 23 E 1
Creglingen (D)....... 89 G 3
Creil (F)............. 39 H 5
Crema (I)............ 101 F 4
Crémieu (F).......... 50 D 3
Cremona (I).......... 101 F 5

Créon (F)............ 48 D 5
Crepaja (SRB)........ 140 D 3
Crépy-en-Valois (F).... 40 A 5
Cres (HR)............ 134 B 5
Crescentino (I)....... 100 C 5
Crespino (I)......... 103 E 5
Crest (F)............ 50 D 5
Cresta (CH).......... 99 F 4
Créteil (F)........... 45 E 1
Creully (F).......... 38 D 4
Creußen (D)...........91 E 3
Creutzwald (F)........41 E 5
Creuzburg (D)........ 85 H 4
Crevacuore (I)....... 100 D 3
Crevalcore (I)........ 105 H 2
Crèvecœur-le-Grand (F). 39 G 4
Crèvecœur, château de (B)........ 78 D 3
Crevedia Mare (RO)... 152 A 4
Crevillent / Crevillente (E) . 73 E 2
Crewe (GB)........... 32 D 3
Crewkerne (GB)....... 38 A 1
Crianlarich (GB)...... 30 C 1
Criccieth (GB)........ 32 A 4
Crickhowell (GB)...... 35 E 1
Cricklade (GB)........ 35 G 2
Crieff (GB)........... 30 D 1
Criel-sur-Mer (F)..... 39 F 3
Crikvenica (HR)...... 134 C 4
Crimmitschau (D)..... 86 C 5
Crinan (GB).......... 30 B 1
Criquetot-l'Esneval (F) .. 39 E 4
Crissolo (I)......... 104 B 2
Cristuru Secuiesc (RO) . 147 H 5
Crivitz (D)........... 82 D 4
Crkvice (MNE)....... 139 F 4
Crkvice (SRB)........ 142 D 4
Črmošnjice (SLO)..... 134 C 3
Crna Bara (SRB)...... 140 C 1
Crna Bara (SRB)...... 140 B 4
Črna na Koroškem (SLO). 134 C 1
Crna Trava (SRB)..... 143 G 3
Crnac (HR).......... 135 H 3
Crni Guber (BIH)..... 137 H 5
Crni Lug (BIH)....... 136 D 5
Crni Lug (RO)........ 134 C 5
Črni Vrh (SLO)....... 134 B 2
Crnjelovo Donje (BIH).. 137 H 3
Črnkovci (HR)....... 135 H 3
Črnomelj (SLO)...... 134 C 3
Crocq (F)............ 49 H 2
Crolly (IRL)......... 22 D 1
Cromarty (GB)....... 29 F 3
Cromer (GB)......... 37 E 1
Crook (GB)...........31 G 4
Croom (IRL)......... 24 C 3
Cross Hands (GB)..... 34 D 1
Crosshaven (IRL)..... 24 D 4
Crossmaglen (GB).... 23 F 4
Crossmolina (IRL).... 22 C 3
Crotone (I)..........113 D 3
Crowborough (GB).... 36 D 5
Crowland (GB)....... 33 G 4
Crowle (GB)......... 33 F 2
Croyde (GB)......... 34 D 3
Croydon (GB)........ 36 C 4
Crozant (F).......... 49 G 1
Crozon (F)........... 42 B 2
Crucea (RO)......... 153 F 4
Cruden Bay (GB)..... 29 H 3
Crudgington (GB)..... 32 D 4
Crumlin (GB)........ 23 G 2
Crumlin (IRL)........ 23 G 4
Cruseilles (F)........51 F 2
Crussol, château de (F).. 50 D 4
Cruz da Légua (P).... 62 A 5
Cruzamento de Pegões (P)...... 68 B 2
Crveni Grm (BIH)..... 138 D 3
Crvenka (SRB)....... 140 B 2
Crymmych (GB)...... 34 C 1
Csabacsűd (H)....... 129 H 3
Csabrendek (H)...... 128 C 3
Csákberény (H)....... 129 E 2
Csákvár (H).......... 129 E 2
Csanádapáca (H)..... 129 H 4
Csanádpalota (H)..... 129 H 4
Csanytelek (H)....... 129 G 4

Csaroda (H).......... 127 F 5
Császár (H).......... 128 D 2
Császártöltés (H)..... 129 F 4
Csávoly (H).......... 129 F 5
Csém (H)............ 134 B 5
Csépa (H)........... 129 G 3
Cserebökény (H)..... 129 H 3
Cserkeszőlő (H)...... 129 G 3
Csesztreg (H)........ 128 B 3
Csetény (H)......... 128 D 2
Csikéria (H)......... 129 F 5
Csökmő (H)..........131 E 3
Csokonyavisonta (H).. 128 C 5
Csömend (H)........ 128 C 4
Csongrád (H)........ 129 G 3
Csopak (H).......... 128 D 3
Csor (H)............ 128 D 2
Csorna (H).......... 128 C 1
Csorvás (H)......... 129 H 4
Csót (H)............ 128 C 2
Csurgó (H).......... 128 C 4
Cuacos de Yuste (E)... 63 G 4
Cualedro (E)......... 56 D 5
Cuba (P)............ 68 D 3
Cubel (E)............ 65 F 1
Cuckfield (GB)....... 36 C 5
Cudalbi (RO)........ 153 E 1
Cudillero (E)......... 57 F 1
Čudovo (RUS)..........6 D 1
Cuéllar (E).......... 58 A 5
Cuenca (E).......... 65 E 3
Cuers (F)............ 55 F 3
Cuerva (E).......... 64 B 4
Cuevas de San Clemente (E)... 58 C 4
Cuevas de San Marcos (E)..... 70 C 5
Cuevas del Almanzora (E).. 71 H 5
Cuevas del Becerro (E)..74 D 3
Cuevas del Campo (E)... 71 F 4
Cuevas del Valle (E)... 63 H 3
Cugir (RO).......... 151 E 1
Cuglieri (I)..........112 B 3
Cuijk (NL)........... 77 E 5
Cuiseaux (F)..........51 E 1
Cuisery (F).......... 50 D 1
Cujmir (RO)......... 151 E 4
Culan (F)............ 49 H 1
Culdaff (IRL)........ 23 F 1
Culemborg (NL)...... 77 E 5
Cúllar Baza (E)...... 71 F 4
Cullen (GB)......... 29 F 3
Cullera (E).......... 66 A 4
Cullompton (GB)..... 35 E 3
Culoz (F)............51 E 2
Culross (GB)......... 30 D 1
Cuma, acropoli di (I) . 109 G 5
Cumbernauld (GB).... 30 D 2
Cumbres Mayores (E) .. 69 F 3
Cumiana (I)......... 100 B 5
Cumnock (GB)....... 30 D 3
Cumpăna (RO)....... 153 F 4
Cuneo (I)........... 104 B 3
Cungrea (RO)........ 151 G 3
Cunlhat (F).......... 50 B 3
Čunski (HR)......... 134 B 5
Cuntis (E)........... 56 B 3
Cuorgnè (I)......... 100 C 4
Cupar (GB)...........31 E 1
Cupello (I)........... 109 H 2
Cupramontana (I).... 107 G 4
Čuprene (BG)........ 154 C 2
Ćuprija (SRB)........ 143 E 1
Čurek (BG).......... 158 C 1
Curia (I)............ 62 B 3
Curtea de Argeş (RO).. 151 G 2
Curtici (RO)......... 146 B 4
Curtişoara (RO)...... 151 G 4
Curtis (E)........... 56 C 2
Čurug (SRB)......... 140 C 2
Cusano Mutri (I)..... 109 H 4
Cushendall (GB)..... 23 G 1
Cushendun (GB)..... 23 G 1
Cusset (F)........... 50 B 2
Cutro (I)............113 D 3

Cuxhaven (D)...........81 F 3
Cvikov (CZ)......... 87 F 5
Čvrstec (HR)........ 135 F 3
Cwmbrân (GB)....... 35 E 2
Cybinka (PL)........ 120 B 1
Cysoing (F).......... 40 A 2
Czacz (PL).......... 121 E 2
Czajków (PL)........ 121 G 3
Czaplinek (PL).......116 D 3
Czarna Białostocka (PL)....119 G 4
Czarna Dąbrówka (PL) ..117 E 2
Czarna Górna (PL)..... 127 G 3
Czarna Woda (PL)....117 G 3
Czarnków (PL).......117 E 5
Czchów (PL)........ 125 H 2
Czechowice-Dziedzice (PL).... 125 F 1
Czempiń (PL)....... 121 E 1
Czerniejewo (PL)..... 121 F 1
Czersk (PL)..........117 G 3
Czerwin (PL)........119 E 4
Czerwińsk nad Wisłą (PL)....... 122 C 1
Czerwionka-Leszczyny (PL).... 125 E 1
Częstochowa (PL).... 121 H 4
Człopa (PL)..........116 D 3
Człuchów (PL).......117 F 3
Czosnów (PL)....... 122 D 1
Czyżew-Osada (PL) ....119 F 5

D

D. Ljubata (SRB)...... 143 G 4
Dabar (HR).......... 134 D 5
Dabas (H)........... 129 F 2
Dąbie (Koło) (PL).... 121 H 2
Dąbie (Szczecin) (PL)..116 B 4
Dabilje (MK)........ 145 H 1
Dăbnica (BG)........ 161 H 1
Dabo (F).............47 G 1
Dabromani (BIH)..... 139 E 4
Dąbrowa Białostocka (PL).......119 H 3
Dąbrowa Górnicza (PL). 122 B 5
Dąbrowa Tarnowska (PL).... 125 H 1
Dăbuleni (RO)....... 151 F 5
Dachau (D).......... 95 G 2
Dačice (CZ)......... 92 C 5
Dadiá (GR).......... 163 E 2
Dáfnes (GR)......... 165 E 4
Dáfni (Achaïa) (GR)... 165 E 5
Dáfni (Ágio Óros) (GR).. 162 B 4
Dáfni (Aitolo-Arkananía) (GR). 165 E 4
Dafnotí (GR)........ 164 C 1
Dafnoúla (GR)....... 165 E 4
Dagali (N).......... 188 D 4
Dagda (LV)......... 203 H 4
Dagebüll-Kirche (D)...81 G 1
Dagenham (GB)..... 36 C 4
Dahlen (D).......... 86 C 4
Dahlenburg (D)..... 82 C 5
Dahme (Teltow Fläming) (D) .. 82 C 2
Dahme Ostholstein) (D) . 86 D 2
Dahn (D)............ 88 D 3
Daia Română (RO) ... 147 F 5
Daimiel (E)......... 64 C 5
Daimonía (GR)...... 169 E 4
Daimús (E)......... 66 A 4
Đakovica / Gjakovë (SRB). 142 D 4
Đakovo (HR)........ 137 G 2
Dal (N)............. 189 F 5
Đala (SRB)......... 140 C 1
Dalbeattie (GB)..... 30 D 4
Dălbok Dol (BG)..... 158 D 1
Dălbok Izvor (BG)... 159 E 3
Dalboşeţ (RO)....... 150 C 3
Dalby (S)........... 199 F 3
Dale (N)............ 188 B 2
Dale (N)............ 188 B 4
Dalen (N).......... 188 B 4
Dalen (N).......... 188 D 4
Daleszyce (PL)...... 122 D 4
Dălgopol (BG)....... 157 E 3

Dali (CY) ... 175 E3
Dalías (E) ... 75 H3
Daliburgh (GB) ... 28 B4
Dalj (HR) ... 137 H2
Dalkeith (GB) ... 31 E2
Dalkey (IRL) ... 23 G5
Dalmally (GB) ... 30 C1
Dalmellington (GB) ... 30 C3
Dalry (GB) ... 30 C2
Dals Långed (S) ... 195 G2
Dalsbruk (FIN) ... 191 F5
Dalsjöfors (S) ... 195 G3
Dalton-in-Furness (GB) ... 31 E5
Dalvík (IS) ... 178 C1
Dalwhinnie (GB) ... 29 E4
Damaskiniá (GR) ... 160 D4
Damazan (F) ... 52 D1
Damelevières (F) ... 47 F1
Damgan (F) ... 43 E4
Damjanovo (BG) ... 159 E1
Dammartin-en-Goële (F) ... 39 H5
Damme (D) ... 85 E1
Damnjane (SRB) ... 142 D5
Dampierre (F) ... 47 E4
Dampierre-sur-Salon (F) ... 47 E4
Dampierre, château de (F) ... 45 E1
Damville (F) ... 39 F5
Damvillers (F) ... 40 D4
Dănciulești (RO) ... 151 E4
Dăneasa (RO) ... 151 G4
Daneți (RO) ... 151 F5
Dangé-Saint-Romain (F) ... 44 C5
Dângeni (RO) ... 148 C1
Danilovgrad (MNE) ... 139 F4
Dannemarie (F) ... 47 G3
Dannenberg (D) ... 82 C5
Daoulas (F) ... 42 B2
Darabani (RO) ... 148 C1
Darány (H) ... 128 C5
Darbénai (LT) ... 204 B1
Darda (HR) ... 137 G1
Dardesheim (D) ... 85 H2
Darfo-Boario Terme (I) ... 101 G3
Dargilan, grotte de (F) ... 54 A1
Dargun (D) ... 83 E3
Darlington (GB) ... 31 E5
Darłowo (PL) ... 117 E1
Dărmănești (RO) ... 148 C3
Darmstadt (D) ... 89 E2
Darney (F) ... 47 E2
Daroca (E) ... 65 F1
Darque (P) ... 56 B5
Dartford (GB) ... 36 D4
Dartmouth (GB) ... 35 E4
Daruvar (HR) ... 135 G3
Dărvari (RO) ... 151 E4
Darwen (GB) ... 32 D2
Dărzciems (LV) ... 202 C3
Daržyno (PL) ... 117 F1
Dasburg (D) ... 88 B1
Dasing (D) ... 95 F1
Dasochóri (GR) ... 162 C3
Dassel (D) ... 85 G3
Dassow (D) ... 82 C3
D'at'kovo (RUS) ... 7 F4
Datteln (D) ... 84 D3
Daudzese (LV) ... 203 E4
Daugai (LT) ... 205 F5
Daugailiai (LT) ... 205 G2
Daugavpils (LV) ... 203 G5
Daun (D) ... 88 C1
Dava (GB) ... 29 F3
Daventry (GB) ... 33 E5
Daviá (GR) ... 165 E5
Dávleia (GR) ... 165 F3
Davlos (CY) ... 175 F2
Davor (HR) ... 135 G4
Davos (CH) ... 99 G3
Dawlish (GB) ... 35 E4
Dax (F) ... 52 B2
De Bilt (NL) ... 77 E5
De Haan (Le Coq-sur-Mer) (B) ... 78 B1
De Koog (NL) ... 76 D2
De Panne (B) ... 78 A1

Deal (GB) ... 37 E4
Dealu (RO) ... 152 A3
Dealu Morii (RO) ... 148 D5
Deauville (F) ... 39 E4
Deba (E) ... 59 E1
Debar (MK) ... 144 D1
Debarska Banja Banjišta (MK) ... 144 D1
Debeli Lug (SRB) ... 141 F5
Debeljača (SRB) ... 140 D3
Debelt (BG) ... 157 E4
Debnevo (BG) ... 159 E1
Dębica (PL) ... 127 E1
Dęblin (PL) ... 123 E2
Dębnica Kaszubska (PL) ... 117 F2
Dębno (Myślibórz) (PL) ... 116 B5
Dębno (Nowy Targ) (PL) ... 125 G2
Debovo (BG) ... 156 A2
Debrc (SRB) ... 140 C4
Debrecen (H) ... 131 E2
Debrznica (PL) ... 117 F3
Debrzno (PL) ... 117 F3
Dečani (SRB) ... 139 H4
Decazeville (F) ... 49 H5
Děčín (CZ) ... 87 E5
Decize (F) ... 45 G5
Decs (H) ... 129 E4
Deda (RO) ... 147 H3
Dedemsvaart (NL) ... 77 F4
Degaña (E) ... 57 F2
Degerfors (S) ... 195 H1
Degerndorf am Inn (D) ... 95 H3
Deggendorf (D) ... 91 G5
Degracias (P) ... 62 B4
Dehesa de Montejo (E) ... 58 A2
Deià (E) ... 67 E2
Deidesheim (D) ... 89 E3
Deinze (B) ... 78 B2
Deiva Marina (I) ... 105 F3
Dej (RO) ... 147 H3
Deje (S) ... 195 G1
Dekov (BG) ... 156 B2
Delčevo (MK) ... 143 H5
Delden (NL) ... 77 G4
Deleitosa (E) ... 63 G5
Delémont (CH) ... 98 C2
Deléria (GR) ... 161 F5
Delfoí (GR) ... 165 F3
Delfoí (GR) ... 165 F3
Delft (NL) ... 76 C5
Delfzijl (NL) ... 77 G2
Delia (I) ... 114 D4
Delianuova (I) ... 115 H2
Deliblato (SRB) ... 141 E4
Deliceto (I) ... 110 C3
Delimeđe (SRB) ... 139 H4
Delitzsch (D) ... 86 B3
Delle (F) ... 47 G4
Delme (F) ... 41 F5
Delmenhorst (D) ... 81 F5
Delnice (HR) ... 134 C4
Delsbo (S) ... 190 B2
Deltebre (E) ... 60 B5
Delvin (IRL) ... 23 F5
Delvináki (GR) ... 160 C5
Delvine (AL) ... 144 D5
Demandice (SK) ... 132 C4
Demänovská Dolina (SK) ... 132 D2
Demidov (RUS) ... 7 E3
Demir Kapija (MK) ... 145 G1
Demirci (TR) ... 19 G3
Demmin (D) ... 83 F3
Demoiselles, grotte des (F) ... 54 B2
Den Burg (NL) ... 76 D2
Den Haag ('s-Gravenhage) (NL) ... 76 C5
Den Helder (NL) ... 76 D3
Den Oever (NL) ... 77 E3
Denain (F) ... 40 A2
Denbigh / Dinbych (GB) ... 32 B3
Dendermonde (B) ... 78 C2
Denekamp (NL) ... 77 G4
Dénia / Denia (E) ... 66 A5

Denkendorf (D) ... 91 E5
Dennington (GB) ... 37 E2
Denny (GB) ... 30 D1
Derby (GB) ... 33 E4
Derecske (H) ... 131 E2
Dereköy (TR) ... 19 F1
Derenburg (D) ... 85 H3
Dermanci (BG) ... 155 E3
Dermbach (D) ... 85 G5
Derneburg (D) ... 85 G2
Derry / Londonderry (GB) ... 23 E2
Derrynane National Historic Park (IRL) ... 24 A4
Deruta (I) ... 107 F5
Dervaig (GB) ... 28 C5
Derval (F) ... 43 F3
Dervéni (GR) ... 165 F4
Derventa (BIH) ... 135 H5
Dervíziana (GR) ... 164 C1
Deryneia (CY) ... 175 F3
Desa (RO) ... 151 E5
Desborough (GB) ... 33 F5
Descartes (F) ... 44 C5
Desenzano (I) ... 101 G4
Deşeşti (RO) ... 147 F1
Desfína (GR) ... 165 F3
Dési (GR) ... 164 D1
Desimirovac (SRB) ... 140 D5
Desio (I) ... 101 E4
Deskáti (GR) ... 161 E5
Despotovac (SRB) ... 141 E5
Despotovo (SRB) ... 140 B2
Dessau (D) ... 86 B3
Destné v Orlických horách (CZ) ... 92 D2
Destriana (E) ... 57 F4
Desulo (I) ... 112 C3
Desvres (F) ... 39 G2
Deszk (H) ... 129 G4
Deta (RO) ... 150 B1
Detmold (D) ... 85 F2
Dettelbach (D) ... 89 G2
Dettifoss (IS) ... 178 C1
Detva (SK) ... 132 D3
Deurne (NL) ... 79 E1
Deutsch Wagram (A) ... 97 H1
Deutschkreutz (A) ... 97 H3
Deutschlandsberg (A) ... 97 F5
Deva (RO) ... 147 E5
Dévaványa (H) ... 129 H3
Devecser (H) ... 128 C3
Devene (BG) ... 154 D3
Deventer (NL) ... 77 F4
Deveselu (RO) ... 151 G5
Devil's Bridge (GB) ... 32 B5
Devin / Девин (BG) ... 162 B1
Devizes (GB) ... 35 G2
Devnja (BG) ... 157 F3
Dewsbury (GB) ... 33 E2
Deza (E) ... 59 E5
Dezzo di Scalve (I) ... 101 G3
Dhermi (AL) ... 144 C4
Diafáni (GR) ... 171 F4
Diakófti (GR) ... 169 E5
Diakoftó (GR) ... 165 E4
Diamante (I) ... 113 B1
Diano Marina (I) ... 104 C4
Diásello (GR) ... 161 E5
Diavolítsi (GR) ... 168 C2
Dicmo (HR) ... 138 B2
Dicomano (I) ... 106 D3
Didim (TR) ... 19 G4
Dídyma (GR) ... 169 E2
Die (F) ... 51 E5
Dieburg (D) ... 89 F2
Diedorf (D) ... 85 H4
Diego Álvaro (E) ... 63 H3
Diekirch (L) ... 79 F5
Diemelstadt (D) ... 85 F3
Diepholz (D) ... 85 E1
Dieppe (F) ... 39 F3
Dierdorf (D) ... 84 D5
Dieren (NL) ... 77 F5
Diesdorf (D) ... 85 H1
Dießen am Ammersee (D) ... 95 F2

Diest (B) ... 78 D2
Dietenheim (D) ... 95 E2
Dietfurt an der Altmühl (D) ... 91 E5
Dietikon (CH) ... 99 E2
Dietmannsried (D) ... 95 E3
Dietzenbach (D) ... 89 E2
Dieulefit (F) ... 50 D5
Dieulouard (F) ... 41 E5
Dieuze (F) ... 41 F5
Dieveniškės (LT) ... 205 G5
Diez (D) ... 88 D1
Diezma (E) ... 71 E4
Differdange (L) ... 79 E5
Dignano (I) ... 103 G3
Dignano / Vodnjan (HR) ... 134 A5
Digne-les-Bains (F) ... 55 F1
Digoin (F) ... 50 B1
Dijon (F) ... 46 D4
Dikanäs (S) ... 183 H2
Díkella (GR) ... 163 E3
Diksmuide (B) ... 78 A2
Diktynaíon (GR) ... 172 B2
Dílesi (GR) ... 165 H4
Dillenburg (D) ... 85 E5
Dillingen (D) ... 88 B3
Dillingen an der Donau (D) ... 89 H5
Dímari (GR) ... 162 C2
Dímitra (GR) ... 161 F5
Dimitrítsi (GR) ... 161 H3
Dimitrovgrad (SRB) ... 143 H3
Dimitrovgrad / Димитровград (BG) ... 159 F3
Dimitsána (GR) ... 165 F5
Dimovo (BG) ... 150 D5
Dinami (I) ... 115 H1
Dinan (F) ... 43 E2
Dinant (B) ... 78 D4
Dinard (F) ... 43 E1
Dinbych / Denbigh (GB) ... 32 B3
Dinbych-y-pysgod / Tenby (GB) ... 34 C2
Dingelstädt (D) ... 85 H4
Dingle (IRL) ... 24 A4
Dingle (S) ... 195 F2
Dingli (M) ... 114 C5
Dingolfing (D) ... 95 H1
Dingwall (GB) ... 29 E3
Dinjiška (HR) ... 136 B4
Dinkelsbühl (D) ... 89 H4
Dinklage (D) ... 85 E1
Dinslaken (D) ... 84 C3
Dío (GR) ... 161 F4
Dióni (GR) ... 162 D3
Diónysos (GR) ... 165 H4
Diorios (CY) ... 174 D3
Diosig (RO) ... 146 C2
Dioşti (RO) ... 151 G4
Dippoldiswalde (D) ... 86 D5
Dirdal (N) ... 194 B1
Disentis / Mustér (CH) ... 99 E3
Disneyland Resort Paris (F) ... 39 H5
Diss (GB) ... 33 H5
Dissen am Teutoburger Wald (D) ... 85 E2
Dístomo (GR) ... 165 F3
Dístrato (GR) ... 160 C5
Ditrău (RO) ... 148 A4
Ditzingen (D) ... 89 F4
Diva Slatina (BG) ... 154 C3
Divača (SLO) ... 134 B3
Divaráta (GR) ... 164 B3
Divčibare (SRB) ... 139 H1
Dives (F) ... 38 D4
Divič (BIH) ... 137 H4
Divjakë (AL) ... 144 B2
Divljana (SRB) ... 143 G2
Divonne-les-Bains (F) ... 51 F1
Divuša (HR) ... 135 E4
Djulino (BG) ... 157 F3
Djúpivogur (IS) ... 178 D2
Djupvik (N) ... 176 C3
Djurås (S) ... 190 A4

Długosiodło (PL) ... 119 E5
Dmitrov (RUS) ... 7 G2
Dniprodzeržyns'k (UA) ... 13 H1
Dnipropetrovs'k (UA) ... 13 H1
Dno (RUS) ... 6 D2
Dobanovci (SRB) ... 140 C4
Dobărsko (BG) ... 158 B3
Dobbiaco / Toblach (I) ... 103 F1
Dobczyce (PL) ... 125 G1
Dobel (D) ... 89 E4
Dobele (LV) ... 202 C3
Döbeln (D) ... 86 D4
Doberlug-Kirchhain (D) ... 86 D3
Döbern (D) ... 87 F3
Dobersberg (A) ... 92 C5
Dobiegniew (PL) ... 116 D5
Dobiesławice (PL) ... 122 D5
Dobieszczyn (PL) ... 116 B3
Doboj (BIH) ... 135 H5
Dobošnica (BIH) ... 137 G4
Doboz (H) ... 131 E3
Dobra (RO) ... 152 B3
Dobra (RO) ... 147 E5
Dobra (Szczecin) (PL) ... 116 C3
Dobra (Turek) (PL) ... 121 H2
Dobrčane (SRB) ... 143 F4
Dobre Miasto (PL) ... 118 D2
Dobrešti (Craiova) (RO) ... 151 F5
Dobrešti (Oradea) (RO) ... 146 D3
Dobri Do (SRB) ... 143 E3
Döbriach (A) ... 96 C5
Dobrič (BG) ... 159 F3
Dobrič / Добрич (BG) ... 157 F2
Dobrica (SRB) ... 140 D3
Dobričevo (SRB) ... 141 E3
Dobrin (BG) ... 153 E5
Dobrinja (BIH) ... 139 H1
Dobříš (CZ) ... 92 A3
Dobrljin (BIH) ... 135 E4
Dobrna (SLO) ... 134 D2
Dobro (BIH) ... 139 E2
Dobrodzień (PL) ... 121 G5
Dobromir (BG) ... 157 E2
Dobroplodno (BG) ... 157 E2
Dobrošinci (MK) ... 145 H1
Dobroteşti (RO) ... 151 H4
Dobrotica (BG) ... 156 D3
Dobrovnik (SLO) ... 135 E1
Dobrun (BIH) ... 139 G1
Dobruš (BY) ... 7 F5
Dobruševo (MK) ... 145 F2
Dobruška (CZ) ... 92 D2
Dobrzany (PL) ... 116 C4
Dobrzyń nad Wisłą (PL) ... 118 B5
Dobrzyniewo Duże (PL) ... 119 G4
Docksta (S) ... 190 C1
Dodóni (GR) ... 164 C1
Doesburg (NL) ... 77 F5
Doetinchem (NL) ... 77 F5
Doganović (SRB) ... 143 E5
Dogliani (I) ... 104 C2
Doïráni (GR) ... 161 G2
Dojrenci (BG) ... 156 A3
Dokani (BIH) ... 137 G4
Dokka (N) ... 189 E4
Dokkum (NL) ... 77 F2
Doksy (CZ) ... 87 F5
Dol-de-Bretagne (F) ... 43 F1
Dole (F) ... 47 E5
Dølemo (N) ... 194 C2
Dolenci (MK) ... 145 E2
Dolenjavas (SLO) ... 134 C3
Dolenjske Toplice (SLO) ... 134 C3
Dolga Vas (SLO) ... 135 F1
Dolgellau (GB) ... 32 B4
Dolhasca (RO) ... 148 C2
Dołhobyczów (PL) ... 123 H4
Doliana (GR) ... 160 C5
Dolianova (I) ... 112 C5
Dolíchi (GR) ... 161 E5
Doljani (HR) ... 136 C4
Dolla (IRL) ... 24 D2
Döllach (A) ... 96 B4
Dollar (GB) ... 30 D1
Dolle (D) ... 86 A1

Dolna Banja (BG) ... 158 C2
Dolna Dikanja (BG) ... 158 B2
Dolna Mitropolija / Долна Митрополия (BG) ... 156 A2
Dolná Strehová (SK) ... 132 D4
Dolni Dăbnik / Долни Дъбник (BG) ... 156 A2
Dolní Dvořiště (CZ) ... 96 D1
Dolni Glavanak (BG) ... 163 E1
Dolní Lipka (CZ) ... 93 E2
Dolni Lom (BG) ... 154 C2
Dolní Poustevna (CZ) ... 87 E4
Dolno Cerovene (BG) ... 154 D2
Dolno Kamarci (BG) ... 158 C1
Dolno Kosovrasti (MK) ... 144 D1
Dolno Levski (BG) ... 158 D2
Dolno Ujno (BG) ... 158 A2
Dolný Kubín (SK) ... 132 D2
Dolo (I) ... 103 E4
Dolores (E) ... 73 E2
Dolovo (SRB) ... 140 D4
Dolsk (PL) ... 121 E2
Dolyna (UA) ... 12 D2
Domaradz (PL) ... 127 F2
Domart-en-Ponthieu (F) ... 39 H3
Domaševo (BIH) ... 139 E3
Domaşnea (RO) ... 150 D2
Domažlice (CZ) ... 91 G4
Dombås (N) ... 189 E2
Dombasle (F) ... 47 F1
Dombegyház (H) ... 131 E4
Dombóvár (H) ... 128 D4
Dombrád (H) ... 127 F5
Domburg (NL) ... 78 B1
Domène (F) ... 51 E4
Doméniko (GR) ... 161 E5
Domèvre-en-Haye (F) ... 41 E5
Domfront en Poiraie (F) ... 43 G1
Dömitz (D) ... 82 C5
Domme (F) ... 49 F5
Dommitzsch (D) ... 86 C3
Domnești (București) (RO) ... 152 B4
Domnești (Pitești) (RO) ... 151 H2
Domnista (GR) ... 165 E3
Domodedovo (RUS) ... 7 G2
Domodossola (I) ... 100 D3
Domokós (GR) ... 165 F2
Dompierre (F) ... 47 F2
Dompierre-sur-Besbre (F) ... 50 B1
Domrémy (F) ... 47 E2
Dömsöd (H) ... 129 F3
Domusnovas (I) ... 112 B5
Domvraína (GR) ... 165 G4
Domžale (SLO) ... 134 C2
Don Benito (E) ... 69 E2
Doña María Ocaña (E) ... 72 B5
Doña Mencía (E) ... 70 C5
Donaghadee (GB) ... 23 H2
Donaueschingen (D) ... 94 B2
Donauwörth (D) ... 89 H4
Donawitz (A) ... 97 E3
Doncaster (GB) ... 33 E2
Donegal / Dún na nGall (IRL) ... 22 D2
Doneztebe / Santesteban (E) ... 59 F1
Dongen (NL) ... 78 D1
Donges (F) ... 43 E4
Donington (GB) ... 33 G4
Donja Bebrina (HR) ... 135 H5
Donja Brezna (MNE) ... 139 F3
Donja Bukovica (MNE) ... 139 F3
Donja Šatornja (SRB) ... 140 D5
Donje Crniljevo (SRB) ... 140 B5
Donje Dragovlje (SRB) ... 143 G3
Donje Ljupče (SRB) ... 143 E5
Donji Andrijevci (HR) ... 135 H5
Donji Barbeš (SRB) ... 143 F3
Donji Kazanci (BIH) ... 136 D5
Donji Lapac (HR) ... 136 C4
Donji Lukavac (BIH) ... 139 E1
Donji Malovan (BIH) ... 137 E5
Donji Miholjac (HR) ... 135 H3
Donji Milanovac (SRB) ... 141 F5

A B C D E F G H I J K L M N O P Q R S T U V W X Y Z

Donji Muć (HR) .... 138 B 2
Donji Rujani (BIH) ...*136 D 5
Donji Slatina (SRB) ..... 143 F 3
Donji Stajovac (SRB) .. 143 G 4
Donji Stupnik (HR) ... 135 E 3
Donji Vakuf (BIH) ..... 137 E 5
Donji Vijačani (BIH) ... 135 G 5
Donnemarie-
Dontilly (F) ...... 45 F 2
Donnersbachwald (A) ... 96 D 3
Dønnes (N) .... 183 F 1
Donostia-
San Sebastián (E) ..... 59 E 1
Donzenac (F) ...... 49 G 4
Donzère (F) .... 54 C 1
Donzy (F) .... 45 F 4
Doorn (NL) .... 77 E 5
Dopiewo (PL) ...... 121 E 1
Dora (CY) ....174 C 4
Đorce Petrov (MK) .. 143 E 5
Dorchester (GB) .... 38 A 1
Dordives (F) ...... 45 F 2
Dordrecht (NL) ....76 D 5
Dorfen (D) .... 95 H 2
Dorfmark (D) .....81 H 5
Dorgali (I) ....112 D 3
Dório (GR) ...... 168 C 2
Dorkáda (GR) ...... 161 G 3
Dorking (GB) .... 36 C 4
Dormagen (D) ..... 84 C 4
Dormans (F) ...... 40 B 5
Dorna Candrenilor (RO) . 147 H 2
Dornbirn (A) ...... 94 D 3
Dornburg (D) ...... 86 B 4
Dorndorf (D) ..... 85 G 5
Dornes (F) .... 50 A 1
Dorneşti (RO) ...... 148 B 1
Dornie (GB) .... 28 D 4
Dornoch (GB) ..... 29 F 2
Dornstetten (D) .... 89 E 5
Dornum (D) .....81 E 4
Dorobanţu (RO) .... 152 D 4
Dorog (H) ...... 129 E 1
Dorogobuž (RUS) ....7 F 3
Dorohoi (RO) ...... 148 B 1
Dorohusk (PL) ...... 123 H 3
Dorolţ (RO) ...... 147 E 1
Dorotea (S) ...... 183 H 4
Dörpstedt (D) .....81 G 2
Dorsten (D) ...... 84 C 3
Dortan (F) ....51 E 1
Dortmund (D) ..... 84 D 3
Dorum (D) .....81 F 4
Dörzbach (D) ..... 89 G 3
Dos Hermanas (E) ... 69 G 5
Dosbarrios (E) ...... 64 C 4
Dospat (BG) ...... 162 B 1
Douai (F) .... 40 A 2
Douarnenez (F) ..... 42 B 2
Doucier (F) ....51 E 1
Doudeville (F) ..... 39 F 4
Doué-la-Fontaine (F) .... 43 H 4
Douglas
(Isle of Man) (GB) ..... 30 C 5
Douglas (South
Lanarkshire) (GB) .... 30 D 2
Doulaincourt (F) ..... 46 D 2
Doulevant-
le-Château (F) ..... 46 D 2
Doullens (F) ...... 39 H 3
Doune (GB) ...... 30 D 1
Dourdan (F) ...... 45 E 2
Dourgne (F) ...... 53 G 3
Doůsk (BY) ....7 E 4
Douvaine (F) ....51 F 1
Douvres-
la-Délivrande (F) ... 38 D 4
Dover (GB) ...... 37 E 5
Dovre (N) ...... 189 E 2
Dovreskogen (N) ...... 189 E 2
Downham Market (GB) .. 33 G 4
Downpatrick (GB) ... 23 G 3
Dowra (IRL) ...... 22 D 3
Doxáto (GR) ...... 162 B 2
Dozulé (F) .... 38 D 5
Drabeši (LV) ...... 203 D 2
Dračevo (MK) ...... 143 F 5

Drach, coves del (E) ...67 G 3
Drachten (NL) .... 77 F 2
Dragalevci (BG) ...... 158 B 2
Dragalina (RO) ...... 152 D 4
Dragalovci (BIH) ...... 135 H 5
Dragaš / Dragaš (SRB) .. 142 D 5
Dragaši (MNE) ...... 139 G 2
Drăgeşti (RO) ...... 146 C 3
Draginac (SRB) ...... 140 B 5
Draginje (SRB) ...... 140 C 5
Dragiževo (BG) ...... 159 F 1
Dragočaj (BIH) ...... 135 F 5
Dragoevo (BG) ...... 159 H 1
Dragoevo (MK) ...... 145 G 1
Dragoman (BG) ...... 158 A 1
Dragomireşti
(Baia Mare) (RO) ... 147 G 2
Dragomireşti
(Ploieşti) (RO) ...... 151 H 3
Dragomirna (RO) ... 148 B 2
Dragomirovo (BG) .... 156 B 2
Dragoni (I) ...... 109 G 4
Dragør (DK) ...... 199 E 3
Dragoš (MK) ...... 145 F 3
Dragoş Vodă (RO) ... 152 D 4
Dragosloveni (RO) .... 148 C 5
Dragosvet (SRB) ...... 143 E 1
Dragović (HR) ...... 135 G 4
Dragovištica (BG) .... 158 A 2
Dragozetići (HR) .... 134 B 4
Dragsfjärd (FIN) .... 191 F 5
Dragsvik (N) ...... 188 C 3
Draguignan (F) ...... 55 F 2
Drăguşeni (RO) ...... 148 C 3
Drahovce (SK) ...... 132 B 3
Dralfa (BG) ...... 156 D 2
Dráma / Δράμα (GR) .. 162 B 2
Drammen (N) ...... 189 E 5
Drangedal (N) ...... 194 D 1
Drangovo (BG) ...... 162 D 2
Drănic (RO) ...... 151 F 5
Dranske (D) ...... 83 F 1
Drasenhofen (A) .... 93 E 5
Dravograd (SLO) .... 134 C 1
Drawsko
Pomorskie (PL) ....116 D 3
Draženov (CZ) ....91 G 4
Draževac (SRB) .... 140 C 4
Drebkau (D) ...... 87 E 3
Drenovac (SRB) ...... 143 F 4
Drenovci (HR) ...... 137 H 3
Drenovec (BG) ...... 151 E 5
Drenovo (MK) ...... 145 F 1
Drépano (Dytikí
Makedonía) (GR) .... 161 E 4
Drépano
(Pelopónnisos) (GR) .. 165 G 5
Dresden (D) ...... 86 D 4
Dreux (F) ...... 44 D 1
Drezdenko (PL) ....116 D 3
Drežnik Grad (HR) .... 134 D 5
Driebergen-
Rijsenburg (NL) ..... 77 E 5
Driebes (E) .... 64 D 3
Drienica (SK) ...... 133 G 2
Driffield (GB) ...... 33 F 1
Drinjača (BIH) ...... 137 H 4
Drinovci (BIH) ...... 138 C 2
Drisht (AL) ...... 142 C 5
Drjanovo (BG) ...... 159 F 1
Drlače (SRB) ...... 139 G 1
Drnholec (CZ) ...... 93 E 5
Drniš (HR) ...... 136 C 5
Drnje (HR) ...... 135 F 2
Drnovo (SLO) ...... 135 E 2
Drøbak (N) ...... 189 E 5
Drobeta-
Turnu Severin (RO) .. 150 D 3
Drobin (PL) ....118 C 5
Drochia (MD) ....13 E 3
Drochtersen (D) ....81 G 4

Drogheda /
Droichead Átha (IRL) . 23 G 4
Drohiczyn (PL) ...... 123 F 1
Drohobyč (UA) ....12 C 2
Droichead Átha /
Drogheda (IRL) ...... 23 G 4
Droitwich (GB) ...... 32 D 5
Dromcolliher (IRL) ... 24 C 3
Dromolaxia (CY) ...... 175 E 4
Dromore
(Banbridge) (GB) ..... 23 G 3
Dromore (Omagh) (GB) . 23 E 3
Dronero (I) ...... 104 B 2
Dronfield (GB) ...... 33 E 3
Dronninglund (DK) ... 195 E 4
Dronten (NL) ...... 77 E 4
Dropla (BG) ...... 157 G 2
Drosáto (GR) ...... 161 G 2
Drosendorf Stadt (A) .. 92 C 5
Drosiá (GR) ...... 165 H 3
Drosopigí (Dytikí
Makedonía) (GR) ..... 160 D 3
Drottningholms
slott (S) ...... 197 G 1
Droué (F) ...... 44 C 3
Drouseia (CY) ......174 B 4
Drugnia (PL) ...... 122 D 4
Drugovci (BIH) ...... 137 F 5
Drulingen (F) ....41 G 5
Drumeva (BG) ...... 157 E 3
Drumkeeran (IRL) ...... 22 D 3
Drumlanrig Castle (GB) . 30 D 3
Drummore (GB) ...... 23 H 2
Drumnadrochit (GB) ... 29 E 3
Drumshanbo (IRL) ..... 22 D 4
Drusenheim (F) ....41 H 5
Druskininkai (LT) .... 205 E 5
Druten (NL) ...... 77 E 5
Družbo (BG) ...... 154 D 3
Drvar (BIH) ...... 136 D 4
Drvenik (HR) ...... 138 C 3
Dryburgh Abbey (GB) ...31 F 2
Drygały (PL) ....119 F 3
Drymen (GB) ...... 30 C 1
Drymónas (GR) ...... 165 G 2
Drymós (GR) ...... 161 G 2
Dryopída (GR) ...... 169 G 2
Dryós (GR) ...... 170 C 2
Dubăsari (MD) ....13 F 3
Duben (D) ...... 86 D 2
Dubí (CZ) ...... 86 D 5
Dubienka (PL) ...... 123 H 3
Dublin /
Baile Átha Cliath (IRL) . 23 G 5
Dubna (RUS) ....7 F 1
Dubňany (CZ) ...... 93 E 5
Dubnica
nad Váhom (SK) .... 132 B 2
Dubno (UA) ....12 D 1
Duboćke (MNE) ...... 139 F 3
Duboka (SRB) ...... 140 D 3
Dubona (SRB) ...... 140 D 4
Duboštica (BIH) ...... 137 G 4
Dubova (RO) ...... 150 D 3
Dubovac (SRB) ....141 E 4
Dubovsko (BIH) ...... 135 E 5
Dubrava
(Pelješac Otoc) (HR) .. 138 D 3
Dubrava (Zagreb) (HR) . 135 F 3
Dubrava Stara (BIH) .. 135 G 5
Dubrave (Brčko) (BIH) . 137 G 3
Dubrave (Tuzla) (BIH) . 137 G 4
Dubravica (SRB) ....141 E 4
Dubrovnik (HR) ...... 139 E 4
Ducey-Les Chéris (F) .... 43 G 1
Duchcov (CZ) ...... 86 D 5
Ducherow (D) ...... 83 G 3
Duchovščina (RUS) ....7 E 3
Duclair (F) ...... 39 F 4
Dudince (SK) ...... 132 C 4
Dudley (GB) ...... 32 D 5
Dudweiler (D) ...... 88 C 2
Dueñas (E) ...... 58 A 4
Duesund (N) ...... 188 B 3

Dufftown (GB) .... 29 G 3
Duga Poljana (SRB) .... 139 H 2
Duga Resa (HR) ...... 134 D 4
Dugi Rat (HR) ...... 138 B 2
Dugo Selo (HR) ...... 135 E 3
Duingt (F) ....51 F 2
Duino (I) ...... 103 H 4
Duisburg (D) ...... 84 C 3
Dukat (SRB) ...... 143 G 4
Dukla (PL) ...... 127 E 2
Dūkštas (LT) ...... 205 H 2
Dulceşti (RO) ...... 148 C 3
Duleek (IRL) ...... 23 F 5
Dulje (SRB) ...... 143 E 4
Dülken (D) ...... 84 B 4
Dülmen (D) ...... 84 C 3
Dulnain Bridge (GB) ... 29 F 4
Đulovac (HR) ...... 135 G 3
Dulovo (BG) ...... 152 D 5
Dumbarton (GB) ...... 30 C 2
Dumbrava de Jos (RO) . 151 E 3
Dumbrăveni
(Constanţa) (RO) .... 153 E 5
Dumbrăveni
(Suceava) (RO) ...... 148 B 2
Dumbrăveni
(Focşani) (RO) ...... 152 D 1
Dumbrăviţa (RO) ...... 152 A 1
Dumbría (E) ...... 56 B 2
Dumfries (GB) ...... 30 D 3
Dumitra (SRB) ...... 143 G 3
Dumitra (RO) ...... 147 G 3
Dún Dealgan /
Dundalk (IRL) ...... 23 F 4
Dún Laoghaire (IRL) ... 23 G 5
Dun-le-Palestel (F) .... 49 G 2
Dún na nGall /
Donegal (IRL) ...... 22 D 2
Dun-sur-Auron (F) .... 45 F 5
Dun-sur-Meuse (F) .... 40 D 4
Dunaföldvár (H) ...... 129 E 3
Dunaharaszti (H) ...... 129 F 2
Dunajská Streda (SK) .. 132 A 4
Dunakeszi (H) ...... 129 F 1
Dunapataj (H) ...... 129 F 4
Dunaszekcső (H) ...... 129 E 5
Dunaújváros (H) ...... 129 E 3
Dunavci
(Stara Zagora) (BG) .. 159 E 2
Dunavci (Vidin) (BG) .. 150 D 5
Dunavecse (H) ...... 129 E 3
Dunbar (GB) ....31 F 1
Dunblane (GB) ...... 30 D 1
Dundaga (LV) ...... 202 B 2
Dundalk /
Dún Dealgan (IRL) ... 23 F 4
Dundee (GB) ...... 29 G 5
Dundonnell (GB) ...... 28 D 2
Dunfanaghy (IRL) ...... 23 E 1
Dunfermline (GB) ....31 E 1
Dungannon (GB) ...... 23 F 3
Dungarvan (IRL) ...... 25 E 4
Dungiven (GB) ...... 23 F 2
Dungloe (IRL) ...... 22 D 2
Dunje (MK) ...... 145 F 2
Dunkeld (GB) ...... 29 F 5
Dunkerque (F) ...... 39 H 1
Dunluce Castle (GB) ... 23 F 1
Dunmanway (IRL) ...... 24 C 5
Dunmore (IRL) ...... 22 C 5
Dunmore East (IRL) ... 25 F 4
Dunnamanagh (GB) ... 23 E 2
Dunoon (GB) ...... 30 C 2
Duns (GB) ....31 F 2
Dunshaughlin (IRL) ... 23 F 5
Dunstable (GB) ...... 36 C 3
Dunster (GB) ...... 35 E 3
Dunvegan (GB) ...... 28 C 3
Dupnica
Дупница (BG) ...... 158 B 2
Đurakovac (SRB) .... 142 D 4
Durango (E) ...... 58 D 1
Durankulak (BG) .... 153 F 5
Duras (F) ...... 48 D 5
Dürău (RO) ...... 148 B 3
Durban-Corbières (F) ... 53 H 4

Durbuy (B) .... 79 E 3
Dúrcal (E) ....75 F 3
Đurđevac (HR) ...... 135 F 2
Đurđevića Tara (MNE) ... 139 G 3
Đurđevik (BIH) ...... 137 G 4
Düren (D) ...... 84 B 5
Durham (GB) ....31 G 4
Durlach (D) ...... 89 E 4
Durlas / Thurles (IRL) ... 24 D 3
Đurmanec (HR) ...... 135 E 2
Dürnkrut (A) ...... 97 H 1
Dürnstein (A) ...... 97 F 1
Durrës (AL) ...... 144 B 2
Durrow (IRL) ...... 25 E 2
Dursley (GB) ...... 35 F 4
Durtal (F) ...... 43 H 3
Duruelo de la Sierra (E).. 58 B 4
Dušanovo (BIH) ...... 137 H 4
Dusina (BIH) ...... 137 F 5
Dusnok (H) ...... 129 E 4
Düsseldorf (D) ...... 84 C 4
Duszniki (PL) ...... 121 E 1
Duszniki-Zdrój (PL) .... 120 D 5
Duved (S) ...... 183 F 5
Duži (Mostar) (BIH) .... 138 D 3
Duži (Trebinje) (BIH) .. 139 E 4
Dve Mogili (BG) ...... 156 C 2
Dverberg (N) ...... 179 G 1
Dvor (HR) ...... 135 E 5
Dvorovi (BIH) ...... 137 H 3
Dvory nad Lužnicí (CZ) .. 92 B 5
Dvory
nad Žitavou (SK) .... 132 B 4
Dvůr Králové
nad Labem (CZ) ...... 87 G 5
Dynów (PL) ...... 127 F 2
Dyrnes (N) ...... 182 B 5
Dyrráchi (GR) ...... 168 C 3
Dytikí Fragkísta (GR) .. 164 D 2
Dywity (PL) ....118 D 3
Džanka (BG) ...... 163 E 1
Džebel (BG) ...... 162 D 2
Dżep (SRB) ...... 143 G 3
Dziadkowice (PL) ....119 G 5
Działdowo (PL) ....118 C 4
Działoszyce (PL) ...... 122 C 5
Działoszyn (PL) ...... 121 H 4
Dzierzgoń (PL) ....118 B 2
Dzierżoniów (PL) ...... 121 E 5
Dziwnów (PL) ....116 C 2
Dziwnówek (PL) ....116 C 2
Dzjaržynsk (BY) ....6 D 4
Džuljunica (BG) ...... 159 F 1
Džumajlija (MK) ...... 145 F 1
Džurkovo (BG) ...... 162 C 1
Džurovo (BG) ...... 158 C 1
Dźwierzuty (PL) ....118 D 3
Dźwirzyno (PL) ....116 C 2

E

Eaglescliffe (GB) ....31 G 5
Earith (GB) ...... 33 G 5
Earlston (GB) ....31 F 2
Easingwold (GB) ....31 H 5
Easky (IRL) ...... 22 C 3
East Dereham (GB) .... 33 H 4
East Grinstead (GB) ... 36 C 5
East Kilbride (GB) ...... 30 D 2
East Linton (GB) ....31 F 1
Eastbourne (GB) ...... 37 E 5
Eastleigh (GB) ...... 38 C 1
Eaux-Bonnes (F) ...... 52 C 4
Eauze (F) ...... 52 D 2
Ebbw Vale /
Glyn Ebwy (GB) ..... 35 E 1
Ebeleben (D) ...... 85 H 4
Ebeltoft (DK) ...... 195 E 5
Eben im Pongau (A) ... 96 C 3
Ebenfurth (A) ...... 97 G 2
Ebensee (A) ...... 96 C 2
Eberbach (D) ...... 89 F 3
Eberbach, kloster (D) ...88 D 1
Ebermannstadt (D) .....91 E 3
Ebern (D) ...... 89 H 1

Ebersbach (D) .... 87 F 4
Ebersberg (D) ...... 95 G 2
Eberstein (A) ...... 97 E 5
Eberswalde (D) ...... 83 G 5
Ebmath (D) .....91 F 2
Eboli (I) ......110 B 4
Ebrach (D) ...... 89 H 2
Ebreichsdorf (A) ...... 97 G 2
Ébreuil (F) ...... 50 A 2
Ebstorf (D) ...... 82 B 5
Eccleshall (GB) ...... 32 D 4
Eceabat (TR) ....19 F 2
Echallens (CH) ...... 98 B 3
Echínos (GR) ...... 162 C 2
Echt (NL) ...... 79 E 2
Echte (D) ...... 85 G 3
Echternach (L) ...... 79 F 5
Écija (E) ...... 70 B 5
Ečka (SRB) ...... 140 D 3
Eckartsberga (D) ...... 86 A 4
Eckernförde (D) ....81 H 2
Eckerö (FIN) ...... 190 D 5
Écommoy (F) ...... 44 B 3
Écos (F) ...... 39 G 5
Écouché-les-Vallées (F).. 43 H 1
Écouen, château d' (F) .. 39 H 5
Écueillé (F) ...... 44 D 5
Écsegfalva (H) ...... 129 H 2
Ed (S) ...... 195 F 2
Edam (NL) ....76 D 4
Edane (S) ...... 195 G 1
Ēdas (LV) ...... 202 B 3
Ede (NL) ...... 77 E 5
Edelény (H) ...... 126 D 5
Edenderry (IRL) ...... 23 F 5
Edenkoben (D) ...... 88 D 3
Édessa / Έδεσσα (GR) . 161 E 3
Edgeworthstown (IRL) .. 23 E 5
Edinburgh (GB) ....31 E 2
Edineţ (MD) ....13 E 3
Edirne (TR) ....19 F 1
Edland (N) ...... 188 C 5
Edolo (I) ...... 101 G 3
Edremit (TR) ....19 G 2
Edsåsdalen (S) ...... 183 F 5
Edsbro (S) ...... 190 C 5
Edsbyn (S) ...... 190 A 3
Edsele (S) ...... 183 H 5
Eeklo (B) ...... 78 B 1
Eelde (NL) ...... 77 G 2
Eemshaven (NL) ...... 77 G 2
Eferding (A) ...... 96 D 1
Efkarpía (Kilkís) (GR) .... 161 H 3
Efkarpía
(Thessaloníki) (GR) .... 161 G 2
Eforie Nord (RO) ...... 153 F 5
Egeln (D) ...... 86 A 2
Eger (H) ...... 129 H 1
Egersund (N) ...... 194 B 2
Egervár (H) ...... 128 B 3
Egeskov (DK) ...... 198 C 4
Egeskov (DK) ...... 198 C 4
Egestorf (D) ....81 H 5
Egg (A) ...... 94 D 3
Eggenburg (A) ...... 92 D 5
Eggenfelden (D) ...... 96 B 1
Eggesin (D) ...... 83 G 3
Eggum (N) ...... 179 F 3
Éghezée (B) ...... 78 D 3
Egiertowo (PL) ....117 G 2
Egilsstaðir (IS) ...... 178 D 2
Egkomi
(Ammóchostos) (CY) . 175 F 3
Egkomi (Lefkoşa) (CY) ...174 C 4
Égletons (F) ...... 49 G 3
Eglinton (GB) ...... 23 F 2
Egloffstein (D) ....91 E 3
Egluciems (LV) ...... 203 H 3
Egmond aan Zee (NL) ...76 D 4
Egremont (GB) ...... 30 D 5
Egtved (DK) ...... 198 B 3
Egüés (E) ...... 59 F 2
Éguzon (F) ...... 49 G 1
Ehingen (D) ...... 89 G 5
Ehra (D) ...... 85 H 1
Ehrang (D) ...... 88 B 2
Ehrenberg (D) ...... 89 G 1

Ehrenhausen (A) .... 97 F 5
Ehrwald (A) .... 95 F 4
Eibar (E) .... 58 D 1
Eibenstock (D) .... 86 C 5
Eichstätt (D) ....91 E 5
Eiðar (IS) .... 178 D 2
Eide (N) .... 182 B 5
Eidet (N) .... 179 F 3
Eidfjord (N) .... 188 C 4
Eiði (Færøerne) (DK).... 194 A 4
Eidkjosen (N) ....176 B 4
Eidsborg (N) .... 188 C 5
Eidsbugarden (N) ..... 188 D 3
Eidsdal (N) .... 188 C 1
Eidsfoss (N) .... 189 E 5
Eidsvåg (N) .... 188 D 1
Eidsvoll (N) .... 189 F 4
Eidsvollsbygningen (N) . 189 F 4
Eikelandsosen (N)..... 188 B 4
Eiken (N) .... 194 C 2
Eikesdal (N) ....61 F 1
Eilean Donan Castle (GB). 28 C 4
Eilenburg (D) .... 86 C 3
Eilsleben (D) .... 86 A 2
Einbeck (D) .... 85 G 3
Eindhoven (NL) .... 79 E 1
Einsiedeln (CH) ...... 99 E 2
Eisenach (D) .... 85 H 4
Eisenberg (D) .... 86 B 4
Eisenerz (A) .... 97 E 3
Eisenhüttenstadt (D).... 87 F 2
Eisenstadt (A) .... 97 H 2
Eisfeld (D) .... 89 H 1
Eišiškės (LT) .... 205 F 5
Eisleben Lutherstadt (D). 86 A 3
Eislingen (D) .... 89 G 4
Eitorf (D) .... 84 D 5
Eivissa / Ibiza (E) .. 66 D 4
Ejea de los Caballeros (E). 59 G 4
Ejulve (E) .... 65 H 2
Ekenäs /
  Tammisaari (FIN) .. 191 G 5
Ekkára (GR) .... 165 E 2
Ekshärad (S) .... 189 H 5
Eksjö (S) .... 195 H 4
Ekzarh Antimovo (BG). . 159 H 2
El Algar (E) .... 73 E 4
El Almendro (E) .... 69 E 5
El Alquián (E) .... 72 C 5
El Astillero (E) ...... 58 B 1
El Barco de Ávila (E) .. 63 G 3
El Barraco (E) .... 64 A 2
El Bodón (E) .... 63 F 3
El Bonillo (E) .... 71 F 1
El Bosque (E) ....74 C 4
El Burgo (E) ....74 D 3
El Burgo de Osma (E) .. 58 D 5
El Burgo Ranero (E) ... 57 H 4
El Cabaco (E) .... 63 F 3
El Campello /
  Campello (E) ...... 73 E 2
El Campo
  de Peñaranda (E) .. 63 H 2
El Cañigral (E) .... 65 F 3
El Carpio (E) .... 70 C 4
El Carpio
  de Tajo (E) .... 64 A 4
El Casar (E) .... 64 C 2
El Castell
  de Guadalest (E) .. 66 A 5
El Castellar (E) ...... 65 G 2
El Castillo
  de las Guardas (E) . 69 F 4
El Centenillo (E) ..... 70 D 3
El Cerro de Andévalo (E). 69 E 4
El Coronil (E) ....74 C 2
El Cubillo (E) .... 65 F 3
El Cubo
  de Don Sancho (E) . 63 F 2
El Cubo
  de Tierra del Vino (E) . 63 G 1
El Cuervo (E) ....74 B 3
El Ejido (E) ....75 H 3
El Escorial (E) .... 64 B 2
El Espinar (E) .... 64 B 2
El Fondó de les Neus (E) . 73 E 2

El Formigal (E) .... 59 H 2
El Grado (E) .... 60 A 2
El Grau de Castelló (E).. 66 A 2
El Grau de València (E) . 65 H 4
El Hoyo de Pinares (E) . 64 A 2
El Madroño (E) .... 69 F 4
El Masnou (E) ....61 E 4
El Molar (E) .... 64 C 2
El Molinillo (E) ...... 64 B 5
El Moral (E) .... 71 G 4
El Pardo (E) .... 64 B 2
El Pedernoso (E) ...... 64 D 5
El Pedroso (E) .... 69 G 4
El Perelló (E) .... 65 H 5
El Perelló (E) .... 60 B 5
El Picazo (E) .... 65 E 5
El Pinell de Brai (E) . 60 B 5
El Pinós (E) .... 73 E 2
El Pobo de Dueñas (E) .. 65 F 2
El Pont d'Armentera (E) . 60 C 4
El Pont de Suert (E) .. 60 B 2
El Port de la Selva (E).61 F 1
El Port de Llançà (E) ..61 F 1
El Port de Sagunt (E) . 66 A 3
El Portal (E) ....74 B 3
El Prat de Llobregat (E). 60 D 4
El Provencio (E) ...... 64 D 5
El Puente (E) .... 58 C 1
El Puente
  del Arzobispo (E)... 63 H 5
El Puerto
  de Sta María (E) ...74 A 3
El Real de la Jara (E) . 69 G 4
El Real de San Vicente (E). 64 A 3
El Robledo (E) .... 64 A 5
El Rocío (E) .... 69 F 5
El Romeral (E) .... 64 C 4
El Rompido (E) .... 69 E 5
El Ronquillo (E) ...... 69 G 4
El Royo (E) .... 58 D 4
El Rubio (E) .... 70 B 5
El Saler (E) .... 65 H 5
El Salobral (E) .... 71 G 2
El Saucejo (E) ....74 C 2
El Serrat (AND) .... 60 C 1
El Soplao (E) .... 58 A 1
El Tiemblo (E) .... 64 A 2
El Toboso (E) .... 64 D 4
El Vendrell (E) .... 60 C 4
El Villar de Arnedo (E) . 59 E 3
El Viso (E) .... 70 B 2
El Viso del Alcor (E). . 69 G 5
Élafos (GR) .... 164 C 1
Elaiochóri (GR) ...... 162 B 3
Elaiochória (GR) ..... 161 G 4
Elaiónas (GR) .... 165 F 3
Elassóna /
  Ελασσόνα (GR) ..... 161 E 5
Eláteia (GR) .... 165 F 3
Eláti (Dytikí
  Makedonía) (GR) ... 161 E 5
Eláti (Thessalía) (GR) . 164 D 1
Elatoú (GR) .... 165 E 3
Elbasan (AL) .... 144 C 2
Elbeuf (F) .... 39 F 5
Elbigenalp (A) .... 95 E 4
Elbingerode (D) ...... 85 H 3
Elbląg (PL) ....118 B 2
Elburg (NL) .... 77 F 4
Elche / Elx (E) .... 73 E 2
Elche de la Sierra (E) . 71 G 3
Elda (E) .... 73 E 2
Eldena (D) .... 82 D 5
Elefsína /
  Ελευσίνα (GR)...... 165 H 4
Eleftherés (GR) ...... 162 B 3
Eléfthero (GR) .... 160 C 5
Eleftherochóri (GR) ... 160 D 5
Eleftheroúpoli /
  Ελευθερούπολη (GR). 162 B 3
Eleja (LV) .... 202 D 4
Elek (H) ....131 E 4
Elektrėnai (LT) ...... 205 F 4
Elemir (SRB) .... 140 C 2
Elena (BG) .... 159 F 1
Eleoúsa (GR) .... 171 H 3
Elgå (N) .... 189 G 2

Elgin (GB)............. 29 F 3
Elgoibar (E) .... 59 E 1
Elgol (GB)............. 28 C 4
Elhovo Елхово (BG)... 159 G 3
Eliá (GR) .... 168 D 4
Elie (GB)..............31 E 1
Elimäki (FIN) .... 193 E 4
Elin Pelin /
  Елин Пелин (BG).... 158 B 2
Elisejna (BG) .... 158 B 1
Elizondo (E)........... 59 F 1
Ełk (PL) ....119 F 2
Ellesmere (GB)........ 32 C 4
Ellesmere Port (GB) ... 32 C 3
Ellingen (D) ....91 E 5
Ellinikó (GR) .... 165 E 5
Ellon (GB)............ 29 H 3
Ellopía (GR) .... 165 G 4
Ellös (S) .... 195 F 3
Ellrich (D) .... 85 H 3
Ellwangen (D) ....89 G 4
Elmas (I) ....112 C 5
Elmshorn (D)...........81 H 3
Elne (F) .... 54 A 5
Elnesvågen (N)........ 182 B 5
Elorrio (E) .... 58 D 1
Élos (GR) .... 172 A 3
Előszállás (H)........ 129 E 3
Eloúnta (GR) .... 173 E 3
Éloyes (F) ....47 F 2
Elphin (IRL) .... 22 D 4
Els Monjós (E) .... 60 D 4
Elsdorf (D) .... 84 B 4
Elsendorf (D).......... 95 G 1
Elsfleth (D) ....81 F 5
Elšica (BG) .... 158 C 2
Elsterberg (D) .... 86 B 5
Elsterwerda (D) ...... 86 D 3
Eltisley (GB) .... 33 G 5
Eltmann (D) .... 89 H 2
Eltz (D) .... 88 C 1
Elva (EST) .... 201 F 4
Elvanfoot (GB) .... 30 D 3
Elvas (P) .... 69 E 1
Elvekrok (N)........... 188 C 2
Elven (F) .... 43 E 3
Elverum (N)........... 189 F 4
Elx / Elche (E) .... 73 E 2
Ely (GB).............. 33 G 5
Elzach (D) .... 94 B 2
Elze (D) .... 85 G 2
Embid (E) .... 65 F 1
Embid de Ariza (E) .... 59 E 5
Embrun (F)............ .51 F 5
Embūte (LV) .... 202 B 4
Emden (D) .... 80 D 4
Emet (TR) ....19 H 2
Emlichheim (D) .... 84 C 1
Emmaboda (S) .... 197 E 5
Emmaste (EST)......... 200 B 3
Emmeloord (NL) .... 77 E 3
Emmen (NL) .... 77 G 3
Emmendingen (D) ...... 94 A 2
Emmerich (D) .... 84 B 2
Emo Court (IRL) .... 25 E 2
Empa (CY) ....174 B 4
Empesós (GR) .... 164 D 2
Empoli (I) .... 105 H 4
Emporeiós
  (Nótio Aigaío) (GR) . 171 G 2
Emporeiós
  (Vóreio Aigaío) (GR) . 167 E 4
Empúries (E)...........61 F 2
Encamp (AND) .... 60 C 1
Encausse-
  les-Thermes (F) ... 53 E 4
Encinas de Abajo (E) .. 63 G 2
Encinasola (E)........ 69 E 4
Encinedo (E) .... 57 F 4
Encs (H) .... 126 D 5
Endriejavas (LT) ..... 204 C 2

Endrinal (E) .... 63 G 3
Endrőd (H) .... 129 H 3
Enego (I) .... 103 E 3
Enese (H) .... 128 C 1
Enfesta (E) .... 56 C 2
Engelberg (CH) .... 99 E 3
Engelhartszell (A) .... 96 C 1
Engelskirchen (D) ..... 84 D 4
Engen (D) .... 94 C 2
Engerdal (N) .... 189 G 2
Enghien (B) .... 78 C 3
Engstingen (D)........ 89 F 5
Enguera (E) .... 73 E 1
Enguídanos (E) .... 65 F 4
Enkhuizen (NL) .... 77 E 3
Enköping (S) .... 197 F 1
Enna (I) ....115 E 3
Ennepetal (D).......... 84 D 4
Ennezat (F) .... 50 A 2
Engerdal (N) .... 189 G 2
Enniscorthy /
  Inis Córthaidh (IRL). 25 F 3
Enniskerry (IRL) ...... 25 G 2
Enniskillen (GB) ...... 23 E 3
Ennistimon (IRL) ...... 24 C 2
Enns (A) .... 96 D 2
Eno (FIN) .... 187 H 5
Enonkoski (FIN) ...... 193 G 1
Enontekiö (FIN) ....176 D 5
Enschede (NL) .... 77 G 4
Ensisheim (F).........47 G 3
Entlebuch (CH)........ 98 D 3
Entraygues-
  sur-Truyère (F) ... 49 H 5
Entre-os-Rios (P) ..... 62 C 1
Entrevaux (F)......... 55 G 1
Entrèves (I) .... 100 B 3
Entroncamento (P)..... 62 B 5
Envermeu (F) .... 39 F 3
Enviken (S) .... 190 A 4
Enying (H) .... 128 D 3
Enzklösterle (D) ...... 89 E 5
Epe (NL) .... 77 F 4
Épernay (F) .... 40 B 5
Épernon (F) .... 44 D 1
Épila (E) .... 59 G 5
Épinac (F) .... 46 C 5
Épinal (F) ....47 F 2
Episkopí (Attikí) (GR) . 169 F 2
Episkopí (Lasíthi) (GR). . 173 F 4
Episkopi (Lemesós) (CY).174 C 5
Episkopí (Páfos) (CY) ..174 B 4
Episkopí
  (Réthymno) (GR) ... 170 A 5
Eppan / Appiano (I) .. 101 H 2
Epping (GB) .... 36 C 3
Eppingen (D) .... 89 F 3
Epsom (GB)............ 36 C 4
Eptachóri (GR) .... 160 D 4
Eptakomi (CY) .... 175 F 2
Eptálofos (GR) .... 165 F 3
Epworth (GB) .... 33 F 2
Eraclea (I) .... 103 F 4
Eraclea Mare (I) ..... 103 F 4
Eräjärvi (FIN) .... 191 H 3
Erateiní (GR) .... 165 E 3
Erátyra (GR) .... 160 D 4
Erba (I)............. 101 E 3
Erbach (D) .... 89 F 2
Erbalunga (F) .... 55 H 3
Erbendorf (D).........91 F 3
Erbërge (LV) .... 203 E 4
Ercolano (I) .... 109 G 5
Ercsi (H)............. 129 E 2
Érd (H) .... 129 E 2
Erdek (TR) ....19 G 2
Erdevik (SRB) .... 140 B 3
Erding (D)............ 95 G 2
Erdut (HR) .... 137 H 2
Eremitu (RO) .... 147 H 4
Eresfjord (N) .... 188 D 1
Eresós (GR) .... 167 E 2
Erétria (GR) .... 165 H 5
Erezée (B) .... 79 E 4
Erfde (D) ....81 G 2

Erftstadt (D) .... 84 C 5
Erfurt (D) .... 86 A 4
Ergates (CY) ....174 D 3
Ērgļi (LV) .... 203 F 3
Ergoldsbach (D)....... 95 H 1
Erice (I) ....114 B 2
Ericeiras (P) .... 68 A 1
Ericksberg (S) .... 197 E 2
Eriksmåle (S) .... 197 E 5
Erimi (CY) ....174 C 5
Erkelenz (D).......... 84 B 4
Erkner (D) .... 86 D 1
Erla (E) .... 59 G 4
Erlangen (D) ....91 E 4
Erlsbach (A) .... 95 H 5
Ermenonville (F)...... 39 H 5
Ermidas-Aldeia (P) .... 68 C 3
Ermióni (GR) .... 169 E 2
Ermoúpoli /
  Ερμούπολη (GR) .... 169 H 2
Ermsleben (D) .... 86 A 3
Erndtebrück (D)......... 85 E 4
Ernée (F) .... 43 G 2
Ernei (RO)............ 147 G 4
Ernestinovo (HR) ..... 137 G 2
Ernstbrunn (A) .... 97 G 1
Erquy (F) .... 43 E 1
Erratzu (E) .... 59 F 1
Erronkari (E) .... 59 G 2
Ersekë (AL) .... 144 D 4
Erstein (F)............47 H 2
Ervenik (HR) .... 136 C 5
Ervidel (P) .... 68 C 3
Ervy-le-Châtel (F) .... 45 H 3
Erwitte (D) .... 85 E 3
Erythrés (GR) .... 165 G 4
Eržvilkas (LT) .... 204 D 3
es Caló (E) .... 66 D 5
es Mercadal (E) ....67 H 2
Esbjerg (DK) .... 198 B 3
Esblada (E) .... 60 C 4
Esbo / Espoo (FIN) ... 191 H 5
Escairón (E) .... 56 D 3
Escalada (E) .... 58 B 2
Escalante (E) .... 58 C 1
Escaldes-
  Engordany (AND) ... 60 C 1
Escalona (E) .... 64 A 3
Escalonilla (E) ...... 64 A 4
Escalos de Cima (P) ... 62 D 4
Escatrón (E) .... 59 H 5
Esch (D) .... 89 E 1
Esch-sur-Alzette (L) .. 79 E 5
Esch-sur-Sûre (L) ..... 79 E 4
Eschede (D) .... 85 H 1
Eschenbach
  in der Oberpfalz (D) ....91 F 3
Eschershausen (D) .... 85 G 2
Eschwege (D) .... 85 G 4
Eschweiler (D) .... 84 B 5
Escombreras (E)....... 73 E 4
Escorihuela (E)....... 65 G 2
Escullar (E) .... 71 F 5
Escurial (E) .... 69 G 1
Esens (D) ....81 E 4
Esguevillas
  de Esgueva (E) .... 58 A 5
Esher (GB) .... 36 C 4
Eskifjörður (IS) ..... 178 D 2
Eskilstuna (S) .... 197 F 1
Eskoriatza (E)........ 58 D 2
Eslarn (D) ....91 G 4
Eslohe (D) .... 85 E 4
Eslöv (S) .... 199 F 3
Esmoriz (P) .... 62 B 2
Espadañedo (E) .... 57 F 4
Espalion (F) .... 50 A 2
Esparreguera (E) ...... 60 D 3
Esparros, gouffre d' (F). 52 D 4
Espedal (N) .... 189 E 3
Espejo (E) .... 70 C 4
Espejón (E) .... 58 D 5
Espelette (F) .... 52 A 3
Espelkamp (D) .... 85 E 1
Espelúy (E) .... 70 D 3
Espenschied (D) .... 88 D 1
Espera (E) ....74 B 3

Espiel (E)............ 70 B 3
Espinama (E) .... 58 A 1
Espinho (P) .... 62 B 2
Espinilla (E) .... 58 B 2
Espinosa de Cerrato (E). 58 B 4
Espinosa
  de los Monteros (E) ... 58 C 2
Espolla (E) ....61 F 1
Espoo / Esbo (FIN) ... 191 H 5
Esporles (E) ....67 G 2
Espot (E) .... 60 B 1
Esquedas (E) .... 59 H 3
Esquivias (E) .... 64 B 3
Esse (FIN) .... 185 F 5
Essen (Cloppenburg) (D). 84 C 3
Essen (Essen) (D) .... 84 D 1
Essenbach (D) .... 95 H 1
Esslingen am Neckar (D). 89 F 4
Essoyes (F)........... 46 C 3
Estación de Salinas (E) ..75 E 2
Estadilla (E) .... 60 A 2
Estagel (F) .... 53 H 4
Estaing (F) .... 49 H 5
Estaires (F) .... 39 H 2
Estarreja (P) .... 62 B 2
Estavayer-le-Lac (CH) . 98 B 3
Este (I) .... 103 E 5
Estella (E) .... 59 E 2
Estepa (E) .... 70 B 5
Estepona (E) ....74 C 4
Esteras de Medinaceli (E). 65 E 1
Esternay (F) .... 45 G 1
Esterri d'Àneu (E) .... 60 B 1
Estissac (F) .... 45 G 2
Estói (P) .... 68 C 5
Estoril (P) .... 68 A 2
Estrées-Saint-Denis (F) . 39 H 4
Estremoz (P) .... 68 D 2
Esztergom (H) .... 129 E 2
Étables-sur-Mer (F) ... 42 D 1
Étain (F) ....41 E 5
Étampes (F) .... 45 E 2
Étang-sur-Arroux (F) .. 45 H 5
Étaples (F) .... 39 G 2
Étel (F) .... 42 D 3
Etne (N) .... 188 B 5
Étrépagny (F) .... 39 G 5
Étretat (F) .... 39 E 4
Etropole /
  Етрополе (BG) ..... 158 C 1
Ettelbruck (L) .... 79 F 5
Etten-Leur (NL) ...... 78 D 1
Ettenheim (D) .... 88 D 5
Ettington (GB) .... 33 E 5
Ettlingen (D) .... 89 E 4
Etxarri-Aranatz (E) ... 59 E 2
Eu (F) .... 39 G 3
Eugénie-les-Bains (F).. 52 C 2
Eupen (B) .... 79 F 3
Eura (FIN) .... 191 F 3
Eurajoki (FIN) .... 191 F 3
Euratsfeld (A) .... 97 E 2
Europa-Park (D) ...... 88 D 5
Euskirchen (D) .... 84 C 5
Eußenhausen (D) ...... 89 H 1
Eutin (D) .... 82 C 3
Evangelismós (GR) .... 161 F 5
Évaux-les-Bains (F) ... 49 H 2
Évdilos (GR).......... 167 F 5
Evendorf (D)...........81 H 5
Evenskjær (Skånland) (N). 179 G 2
Evergem (B) .... 78 B 2
Everöd (S)............ 199 F 3
Evertsberg (S)........ 189 H 3
Evesham (GB) .... 35 G 1
Évian (F).............51 F 1
Evijärvi (FIN) .... 185 G 5
Evinochóri (GR) ...... 164 D 3
Évisa (F) .... 55 G 4
Evje (N) .... 194 C 2
Évlalo (GR) .... 162 C 3
Evolène (CH) .... 98 C 5
Évora (P) .... 68 D 2
Évoramonte (P) .... 68 D 2
Évran (F) .... 43 F 2
Évrecy (F) .... 38 D 5

222

E

Évreux (F) . . . . 39 F 5
Évron (F) . . . . 43 H 2
Evropós (GR) . . . . 161 F 3
Evrostína (GR) . . . . 165 F 4
Évry (F) . . . . 45 E 1
Evrychou (CY) . . . . 174 C 3
Évzonoi (GR) . . . . 161 F 2
Exaplátanos (GR) . . . . . 161 E 3
Excideuil (F) . . . . 49 F 4
Exeter (GB) . . . . 35 E 4
Exmes (F) . . . . 44 B 1
Exmouth (GB) . . . . 35 E 4
Exo Metochi (CY) . . . . 175 C 3
Exochí (GR) . . . . 161 H 2
Exter (D) . . . . 85 F 2
Eydehavn (N) . . . . 194 D 2
Eye (GB) . . . . 33 G 4
Eyemouth (GB) . . . . . . 31 F 2
Eyguières (F) . . . . 54 D 2
Eygurande (F) . . . . 49 H 3
Eymet (F) . . . . 49 E 5
Eymoutiers (F) . . . . . . 49 G 3
Ezcaray (E) . . . . 58 D 3
Eczároz (E) . . . . 59 G 2
Èze (F) . . . . 55 H 2
Ezernieki
  (Bukmuiža) (LV) . . . . 203 H 4
Ezerovo (BG) . . . . 159 E 3
Ezine (TR) . . . . 19 F 2

F

Faak (A) . . . . 96 D 5
Fabara (E) . . . . 60 A 4
Fabero (E) . . . . 57 F 3
Fábiánháza (H) . . . . . . 131 F 1
Fabianki (PL) . . . . 117 H 5
Fåborg (DK) . . . . 198 C 4
Fabriano (I) . . . . 107 F 4
Fábricas de Riópar (E) . . 71 G 2
Fabro (I) . . . . 107 E 5
Făcăeni (RO) . . . . 153 E 3
Facinas (E) . . . . 74 B 4
Facture (F) . . . . 48 C 5
Fadd (H) . . . . 129 E 4
Faenza (I) . . . . 107 E 2
Faeto (I) . . . . 110 B 2
Fafe (P) . . . . 62 C 1
Făgăraș (RO) . . . . 151 H 1
Fågelfors (S) . . . . 197 E 4
Fagernes (N) . . . . 176 B 4
Fagernes (N) . . . . 189 E 3
Fagersta (S) . . . . 190 A 5
Făget (RO) . . . . 146 B 5
Făgețelu (RO) . . . . 151 G 3
Fagurhólsmýri (IS) . . . 178 C 3
Fairford (GB) . . . . 35 G 1
Fakenham (GB) . . . . . . 33 H 4
Fakija (BG) . . . . 159 H 3
Fakovici (BIH) . . . . 139 G 1
Fakse (DK) . . . . 199 E 4
Fakse Ladeplads (DK) . 199 E 4
Falaise (F) . . . . 38 D 5
Falakró (GR) . . . . 162 B 2
Fálanna (GR) . . . . 161 F 5
Falásarna (GR) . . . . . . 172 A 3
Falcade (I) . . . . 103 E 2
Falces (E) . . . . 59 F 3
Falconara Marittima (I) . 107 G 4
Falcone (I) . . . . 115 F 2
Falerna (I) . . . . 113 B 3
Faliráki (GR) . . . . 171 H 3
Falkenberg (D) . . . . . . 86 D 3
Falkenberg (S) . . . . . . 195 F 5
Falkensee (D) . . . . 86 C 1
Falkenstein (D) . . . . . . 91 F 2
Falkirk (GB) . . . . 30 D 1
Falkland (GB) . . . . 31 E 1
Falköping (S) . . . . 195 G 3
Fallersleben (D) . . . . . 85 H 1
Fällfors (S) . . . . 185 E 2
Falmouth (GB) . . . . . . 34 B 5
Falset (E) . . . . 60 B 4
Falsterbo (S) . . . . 199 E 4
Fălticeni (RO) . . . . 148 B 2
Falun (S) . . . . 190 A 4

Fameck (F) . . . . 41 E 4
Famjin (Færøerne) (DK) . 194 A 5
Fanári (Anatolikí Makedonía
  kai Thráki) (GR) . . . . 162 D 3
Fanári (Attikí) (GR) . . . 165 G 5
Fanári (Dytikí
  Elláda) (GR) . . . . 165 E 5
Fanári (Thessalía) (GR) . 165 E 1
Fanefjord (DK) . . . . . . 199 E 4
Fanjeaux (F) . . . . 53 G 3
Fano (I) . . . . 107 G 3
Fanós (GR) . . . . 161 F 2
Fara Novarese (I) . . . . 100 D 4
Faraoani (RO) . . . . 148 C 4
Fårbo (S) . . . . 197 E 4
Fårdea (RO) . . . . 150 C 1
Fareham (GB) . . . . 38 C 1
Fårevejle (DK) . . . . . . 198 D 3
Färgelanda (S) . . . . . . 195 F 2
Färila (S) . . . . 190 A 2
Farindola (I) . . . . 109 G 1
Faringdon (GB) . . . . . . 35 G 2
Farini (I) . . . . 105 F 2
Färjestaden (S) . . . . . . 197 E 5
Farkadóna (GR) . . . . . . 165 E 1
Farkasgyepű (H) . . . . . 128 C 2
Farkaždin (SRB) . . . . . 140 D 3
Farlete (E) . . . . 59 H 5
Fårliug (RO) . . . . 150 C 1
Farmakonísi (GR) . . . . 171 F 1
Farnborough (GB) . . . . 35 H 2
Farnese (I) . . . . 108 C 1
Farnham (GB) . . . . 35 H 2
Faro (P) . . . . 68 C 5
Fårösund (S) . . . . 197 G 3
Farra d'Alpago (I) . . . . 103 F 3
Fársala / Φάρσαλα (GR) . 165 F 1
Farsø (DK) . . . . 194 D 4
Farsund (N) . . . . 194 B 2
Farum (DK) . . . . 199 E 3
Fasano (I) . . . . 111 F 3
Fáskrúðsfjörður (IS) . . 178 D 2
Fastiv (UA) . . . . 13 F 1
Fatež (RUS) . . . . 7 G 4
Fátima (P) . . . . 62 B 5
Fatmomakke (S) . . . . . 183 G 3
Faucogney-
  et-la-Mer (F) . . . . 47 F 3
Faulquemont (F) . . . . . 41 F 5
Fauquembergues (F) . . 39 G 2
Făurei (Brăila) (RO) . . . 152 D 2
Făurei
  (Piatra-Neamț) (RO) . . 148 C 3
Fauske (N) . . . . 179 G 4
Fauville-en-Caux (F) . . 39 E 4
Fåvang (N) . . . . 189 E 3
Favara (E) . . . . 65 H 5
Favara (I) . . . . 114 D 4
Faverges (F) . . . . 51 F 3
Faverney (F) . . . . 47 E 3
Faversham (GB) . . . . . 37 E 4
Fawley (GB) . . . . 38 C 1
Fay-sur-Lignon (F) . . . 50 C 4
Fayence (F) . . . . 55 G 2
Fayl-Billot (F) . . . . 47 E 3
Fayón (E) . . . . 60 A 4
Fécamp (F) . . . . 39 E 3
Feces de Abaixo (E) . . 56 D 5
Feda (N) . . . . 194 B 2
Fegyvernek (H) . . . . . . 129 H 2
Fehérgyarmat (H) . . . . 131 G 1
Fehrbellin (D) . . . . 83 E 5
Fehring (A) . . . . 97 G 4
Feked (H) . . . . 129 E 5
Feketić (SRB) . . . . 140 C 2
Felanitx (E) . . . . 67 F 3
Feld am See (A) . . . . . 96 D 5
Feldafing (D) . . . . 95 F 2
Feldbach (A) . . . . 97 G 4
Feldberg (D) . . . . 83 F 4
Feldberger Hof (D) . . . 94 B 2
Feldioara (RO) . . . . . . 152 A 1
Feldkirch (A) . . . . 94 D 4
Feldkirchen
  in Kärnten (A) . . . . . . 96 D 5
Feldru (RO) . . . . 147 G 2

Felgueiras (P) . . . . 62 C 1
Felixstowe (GB) . . . . . 37 E 3
Fellabær (IS) . . . . 178 D 2
Fellbach (D) . . . . 89 F 4
Felletin (F) . . . . 49 H 2
Fellingsbro (S) . . . . . . 197 E 3
Felnac (RO) . . . . 146 B 5
Felton (GB) . . . . 31 G 3
Feltre (I) . . . . 103 E 3
Fene (E) . . . . 56 C 1
Fener (I) . . . . 103 E 3
Fénétrange (F) . . . . . . 41 G 5
Feolin Ferry (GB) . . . . 30 A 2
Ferbane (IRL) . . . . 23 E 5
Ferdinandovac (HR) . . 135 G 2
Ferdinandshof (D) . . . 83 G 3
Fère-Champenoise (F) . 45 H 1
Fère-en-Tardenois (F) . 40 B 5
Ferentino (I) . . . . 109 F 3
Féres (GR) . . . . 163 E 3
Feričanci (HR) . . . . . . 135 H 4
Ferizaj /
  Uroševac (SRB) . . . . . 143 E 4
Ferlach (A) . . . . 96 D 5
Fermo (I) . . . . 107 H 4
Fermoselle (E) . . . . . . 63 F 1
Fermoy (IRL) . . . . 24 D 4
Fernán Caballero (E) . . 64 B 5
Fernán Núñez (E) . . . . 70 B 4
Ferney-Voltaire (F) . . . 51 F 1
Ferrandina (I) . . . . 111 E 4
Ferrara (I) . . . . 106 D 1
Ferreira (E) . . . . 56 D 1
Ferreira do Alentejo (P) . 68 C 3
Ferreira do Zêzere (P) . 62 B 5
Ferreras (P) . . . . 68 C 5
Ferreras de Abajo (E) . . 57 F 5
Ferreries (E) . . . . 67 H 2
Ferreruela
  de Huerva (E) . . . . . . 65 G 1
Ferrette (F) . . . . 47 G 4
Ferriere (I) . . . . 105 F 2
Ferrières-
  en-Gâtinais (F) . . . . . 45 F 3
Ferrol (E) . . . . 56 C 1
Fertilia (I) . . . . 112 A 2
Fertőd (H) . . . . 128 B 1
Fertőszentmiklós (H) . . 128 B 1
Fetești (RO) . . . . 153 E 4
Fethard (IRL) . . . . 25 E 3
Fetsund (N) . . . . 189 F 5
Feucht (D) . . . . 91 E 4
Feuchtwangen (D) . . . 89 H 3
Feurs (F) . . . . 50 C 3
Feyzin (F) . . . . 50 D 3
Fiamignano (I) . . . . . . 109 E 2
Fiano Romano (I) . . . . 108 D 2
Fiastra (I) . . . . 107 G 5
Fibiș (RO) . . . . 146 B 5
Ficarolo (I) . . . . 102 D 5
Fíchtio (GR) . . . . 165 F 5
Fidenza (I) . . . . 101 F 5
Fieberbrunn (A) . . . . . 95 H 3
Fieni (RO) . . . . 152 A 2
Fier (AL) . . . . 144 C 3
Fiera di Primiero (I) . . 103 E 3
Fierbinți-Târg (RO) . . . 152 C 3
Fiesole (I) . . . . 105 H 4
Figaró (E) . . . . 60 D 3
Figeac (F) . . . . 49 G 5
Figline Valdarno (I) . . . 106 D 3
Figueira da Foz (P) . . . 62 B 3
Figueira
  de Castelo Rodrigo (P) . 63 E 2
Figueiró dos Vinhos (P) . 62 C 4
Figueres (E) . . . . 61 E 2
Figueruela de Arriba (E) . 57 F 5
Fikardou (CY) . . . . 174 D 4
Filadelfia (I) . . . . 113 C 3
Filákovo (SK) . . . . 133 E 4
Fília (Dytikí Elláda) (GR) . 165 E 5
Fília (Vóreio Aigaío) (GR) . 167 E 2
Filiași (RO) . . . . 151 F 3
Filiátes / Φιλιάτες (GR) . 160 B 5

Filiatrá / Φιλιατρά (GR) . 168 B 3
Filipeștii
  de Pădure (RO) . . . . . 152 B 3
Filipów (PL) . . . . 119 G 2
Filippiáda (GR) . . . . . . 164 C 1
Fílippoi (GR) . . . . 162 B 3
Filipstad (S) . . . . 189 H 5
Fillan (N) . . . . 182 C 4
Felsőszölnök (H) . . . . . 128 A 3
Fillýra (GR) . . . . 162 D 2
Filottrano (I) . . . . 107 G 4
Finale Emilia (I) . . . . . 105 H 2
Finale Ligure (I) . . . . . 104 D 3
Fiñana (E) . . . . 71 F 5
Finby / Särkisalo (FIN) . 191 G 5
Finchingfield (GB) . . . . 36 D 3
Finja (S) . . . . 199 F 3
Finneidfjord (N) . . . . . 183 F 1
Finnentrop (D) . . . . . . 84 D 4
Finnsnes (Lenvik) (N) . . 176 A 4
Finow (D) . . . . 83 G 5
Finowfurt (D) . . . . 83 G 5
Finspång (S) . . . . 197 E 2
Finsterau (D) . . . . 91 H 5
Finsterwalde (D) . . . . . 86 D 3
Finström (FIN) . . . . . . 190 D 5
Fintona (GB) . . . . 23 E 3
Fintown (IRL) . . . . 22 D 2
Fionnphort (GB) . . . . . 30 A 1
Fiorenzuola d'Arda (I) . 101 F 5
Firenze (I) . . . . 105 H 4
Firenzuola (I) . . . . 106 D 2
Firminy (F) . . . . 50 C 3
Firmo (I) . . . . 113 B 1
Fischamend Markt (A) . . 97 H 2
Fischbach (D) . . . . 91 E 4
Fischbeck (D) . . . . 86 B 1
Fischen im Allgäu (D) . 95 E 3
Fishbourne (GB) . . . . . 38 C 1
Fishguard /
  Abergwaun (GB) . . . . 25 H 4
Fiskárdo (GR) . . . . 164 B 3
Fiskari (FIN) . . . . 191 G 5
Fisterra (E) . . . . 56 A 2
Fitero (E) . . . . 59 F 4
Fitjar (N) . . . . 188 A 4
Fiuggi (I) . . . . 109 F 3
Fiumicino (I) . . . . 108 D 3
Fivemiletown (GB) . . . 23 E 3
Fivizzano (I) . . . . 105 G 3
Fjærland (N) . . . . 188 C 2
Fjällåsen (S) . . . . 180 A 4
Fjällbacka (S) . . . . 195 E 1
Fjällnäs (S) . . . . 189 G 1
Fjärdhundra (S) . . . . . 190 B 5
Fjätervålen (S) . . . . . . 189 G 2
Fjelie (DK) . . . . 199 E 4
Fjerritslev (DK) . . . . . . 194 D 4
Fjerze (AL) . . . . 142 C 5
Flå (N) . . . . 189 E 4
Fladungen (D) . . . . . . 85 G 5
Flaine (F) . . . . 51 G 2
Flakk (N) . . . . 182 D 5
Flåm (N) . . . . 188 C 3
Flămânzi (RO) . . . . . . 148 C 2
Flampourári (GR) . . . . 160 C 5
Flampourési (GR) . . . . 161 E 5
Flámpouro (GR) . . . . . 161 H 3
Flattnitz (A) . . . . 96 D 4
Flatval (N) . . . . 182 C 4
Fléchères,
  château de (F) . . . . . . 50 D 2
Fleckenstein,
  château de (F) . . . . . . 41 H 5
Fleetwood (GB) . . . . . . 32 C 2
Flekkefjord (N) . . . . . . 194 B 2
Flen (S) . . . . 197 F 2
Flensburg (D) . . . . 81 G 1
Flers (F) . . . . 43 H 1
Flesberg (N) . . . . 188 D 5
Fleurance (F) . . . . 53 E 2
Fleurier (CH) . . . . 98 B 3
Fleurus (B) . . . . 78 C 4
Fleury (F) . . . . 45 F 2
Fleury-sur-Andelle (F) . 39 F 4
Flims-Waldhaus (CH) . . 99 F 3
Flint (GB) . . . . 32 C 3

Flisa (N) . . . . 189 G 4
Flix (E) . . . . 60 B 4
Flixecourt (F) . . . . 39 G 3
Flize (F) . . . . 40 C 4
Floda (S) . . . . 190 A 4
Flogny (F) . . . . 45 H 3
Flöha (D) . . . . 86 C 5
Flor da Rosa (P) . . . . . 62 D 5
Florac-Trois-Rivières (F) . 54 A 1
Florence Court (GB) . . 23 E 3
Florennes (B) . . . . 78 C 4
Florensac (F) . . . . 54 A 3
Florenville (B) . . . . 78 D 5
Florești (MD) . . . . 13 F 3
Florești
  (Cluj-Napoca) (RO) . . 147 F 4
Florești (Ploiești) (RO) . 152 B 3
Floriáda (GR) . . . . 164 D 2
Floridia (I) . . . . 115 G 4
Flórina / Φλώρινα (GR) . 160 D 3
Floro (N) . . . . 188 B 2
Flörsheim-
  Dalsheim (D) . . . . . . 89 E 2
Flötningen (S) . . . . 189 G 2
Fluðir (IS) . . . . 178 B 3
Flüelen (CH) . . . . 99 E 3
Flühli (CH) . . . . 98 D 3
Flumet (F) . . . . 51 F 2
Fluminimaggiore (I) . . 112 B 4
Flums (CH) . . . . 99 F 2
Foča (BIH) . . . . 139 F 2
Foça (TR) . . . . 19 G 3
Foce Verde (I) . . . . 109 E 4
Fochabers (GB) . . . . . . 29 G 3
Fockbek (D) . . . . 81 H 2
Focșani (RO) . . . . 152 D 1
Focuri (RO) . . . . 148 D 2
Foeni (RO) . . . . 150 A 1
Foggia (I) . . . . 110 C 2
Föglö (FIN) . . . . 191 E 5
Fohnsdorf (A) . . . . 97 E 4
Foiano della Chiana (I) . 107 E 4
Foini (CY) . . . . 174 C 4
Foínikas (GR) . . . . 169 H 2
Foinikoúntas (GR) . . . . 168 C 3
Foix (F) . . . . 53 F 4
Fojnica (Mostar) (BIH) . 139 E 3
Fojnica (Zenica) (BIH) . 137 F 5
Földeák (H) . . . . 129 H 4
Foldereid (N) . . . . 183 E 3
Földes (H) . . . . 131 E 2
Foleá (GR) . . . . 162 B 3
Folégandros (GR) . . . . 169 H 4
Folgaria (I) . . . . 101 H 3
Folgoso de la Ribera (E) . 57 F 3
Foligno (I) . . . . 107 F 5
Folkestone (GB) . . . . . 37 E 5
Follafoss (N) . . . . 182 D 4
Folldal (N) . . . . 189 E 2
Follebu (N) . . . . 189 E 3
Follina (I) . . . . 103 E 3
Föllinge (S) . . . . 183 G 5
Follonica (I) . . . . 106 C 5
Folmava (CZ) . . . . 91 G 4
Fombellida (E) . . . . . . 58 B 4
Fompedraza (E) . . . . . 58 B 5
Fondevila (E) . . . . 56 C 5
Fondi (I) . . . . 109 F 4
Fondo (I) . . . . 101 H 2
Fonfría (E) . . . . 57 F 5
Fonfría (E) . . . . 65 G 1
Fonn (N) . . . . 188 C 2
Fonni (I) . . . . 112 C 3
Fonollosa (E) . . . . 60 C 3
Font-Romeu-
  Odeillo-Via (F) . . . . . 53 G 5
Fontaine (F) . . . . 47 G 3
Fontaine-
  de-Vaucluse (F) . . . . . 54 D 2
Fontaine-Française (F) . 46 D 4
Fontaine-Henry,
  château de (F) . . . . . . 38 D 5
Fontaine-le-Dun (F) . . 39 F 3
Fontainebleau (F) . . . . 45 F 2
Fontanigorda (I) . . . . . 105 E 2
Fontenay-le-Comte (F) . 48 C 1
Fontenay-Trésigny (F) . 45 F 1

Fontevraud-
  l'Abbaye (F) . . . . 43 H 5
Fontgombault (F) . . . . 49 F 1
Fontibre (E) . . . . 58 B 2
Fontiveros (E) . . . . 63 H 2
Fontoy (F) . . . . 41 E 4
Fontvieille (F) . . . . 54 C 2
Fonyód (H) . . . . 128 C 3
Fonz (E) . . . . 60 A 3
Fonzaso (I) . . . . 103 E 3
Foppolo (I) . . . . 101 F 3
Forbach (F) . . . . 41 F 5
Forcall (E) . . . . 65 H 2
Forcalquier (F) . . . . . . 55 E 2
Forcarei (E) . . . . 56 C 3
Forchheim (D) . . . . . . 91 E 3
Førde (N) . . . . 188 B 2
Førde (N) . . . . 188 B 5
Förderstedt (D) . . . . . . 86 A 2
Fordingbridge (GB) . . . 38 B 1
Fordon (PL) . . . . 117 G 4
Fordongianus (I) . . . . . 112 B 3
Forenza (I) . . . . 110 D 3
Foresta di Burgos (I) . . 112 C 2
Føresvik (N) . . . . 188 A 5
Forfar (GB) . . . . 29 G 5
Forges-les-Eaux (F) . . . 39 G 4
Forio (I) . . . . 109 G 5
Forlì (I) . . . . 107 E 2
Forlì del Sannio (I) . . . 109 G 3
Forlimpopoli (I) . . . . . 107 E 2
Formazza (I) . . . . 100 D 2
Formby (GB) . . . . 32 C 2
Formerie (F) . . . . 39 G 4
Formia (I) . . . . 109 F 4
Formigine (I) . . . . 105 H 2
Fornaci di Barga (I) . . . 105 G 4
Fornells (E) . . . . 67 H 1
Forni Avoltri (I) . . . . . . 103 F 2
Forni di Sopra (I) . . . . 103 F 2
Forni di Zoldo (I) . . . . 103 F 2
Fornos de Algodres (P) . . 62 D 3
Fornovo di Taro (I) . . . 105 G 2
Forotic (RO) . . . . 150 B 2
Forráskút (H) . . . . 129 G 4
Forres (GB) . . . . 29 F 3
Forsa (S) . . . . 190 B 3
Forsand (N) . . . . 194 B 1
Forserum (S) . . . . 195 H 3
Forshaga (S) . . . . 195 G 1
Forsnes (N) . . . . 182 C 5
Forssa (FIN) . . . . 191 G 4
Forst (D) . . . . 87 F 3
Fort Augustus (GB) . . . 28 D 4
Fort-Mahon-Plage (F) . 39 G 2
Fort William (GB) . . . . 28 D 5
Forte dei Marmi (I) . . . 105 G 4
Forth (D) . . . . 91 E 4
Fortrose (GB) . . . . 29 E 3
Fortuna (E) . . . . 73 E 2
Fortuneswell (GB) . . . . 38 A 2
Forvik (N) . . . . 183 F 2
Fos (F) . . . . 53 E 4
Fos-sur-Mer (F) . . . . . . 54 D 3
Foslandsosen (N) . . . . 183 E 3
Fosnavåg (N) . . . . 188 B 1
Fossacesia (I) . . . . 109 H 2
Fossano (I) . . . . 104 C 2
Fossbakken (N) . . . . . . 176 A 5
Fosses-la-Ville (B) . . . . 78 D 3
Fossombrone (I) . . . . . 107 F 3
Fót (H) . . . . 129 F 1
Foteiná (GR) . . . . 161 F 4
Foteinó (GR) . . . . 161 E 5
Fotolívos (GR) . . . . . . 162 B 2
Fouesnant (F) . . . . 42 B 3
Foug (F) . . . . 47 E 1
Fougères (F) . . . . 43 G 2
Fougerolles (F) . . . . . . 47 F 3
Fouras (F) . . . . 48 C 2
Fourchambault (F) . . . 45 F 5
Fourfourás (GR) . . . . . 172 D 3
Fourmies (F) . . . . 40 B 3
Fourná (GR) . . . . 165 E 2
Fournels (F) . . . . 50 A 5
Fournés (GR) . . . . 172 B 3
Fourní (GR) . . . . 173 E 3

Foúrnoi (GR) 167 F5
Fours (F) 45 G5
Foústani (GR) 161 F2
Fowey (GB) 34 C4
Foxford (IRL) 22 C4
Foyers (GB) 29 E4
Foz (E) 57 E1
Foz do Arelho (P) 62 A5
Foz Giraldo (P) 62 D4
Frabosa Soprana (I) 104 C3
Fraddon (GB) 34 C4
Fraga (E) 60 A4
Fragkádes (GR) 160 C5
Frailes (E) 70 D5
Fraize (F) 47 G2
Fram (SLO) 134 D1
Frammersbach (D) 89 F1
Frampol (PL) 123 F4
Francavilla al Mare (I) 109 G1
Francavilla di Sicilia (I) 115 G3
Francavilla Fontana (I) 111 G4
Francavilla in Sinni (I) 110 D5
Francofonte (I) 115 F4
Francorchamps (B) 79 E3
Frändefors (S) 195 F2
Franeker (NL) 77 E2
Frangy (F) 51 E2
Frankenberg (Mittweida) (D) 86 C5
Frankenberg (Waldeck) Frankenberg (D) 85 F4
Frankenburg am Hausruck (A) 96 C2
Frankenmarkt (A) 96 C2
Frankenstein (D) 88 D3
Frankenthal (D) 89 E3
Frankfurt am Main (D) 89 E1
Frankfurt an der Oder (D) 87 E1
Františkovy Lázně (CZ) 91 F2
Frantsila / Rantsila (FIN) 185 H3
Frasassi, grotte di (I) 107 G4
Frascati (I) 109 E3
Frascineto (I) 113 B1
Frasdorf (D) 95 H1
Fraserburgh (GB) 29 H3
Frasin (RO) 148 B2
Frăsinet (RO) 151 H4
Frătăuții Noi (RO) 148 B1
Fratel (P) 62 C5
Fratta Polesine (I) 103 E5
Frauenfeld (CH) 99 F1
Frauenkirchen (A) 97 H2
Frauenstein (D) 86 D5
Frechen (D) 84 C5
Frechilla (E) 58 A4
Freckenhorst (D) 84 D2
Fredensborg (DK) 199 E3
Fredericia (DK) 198 C3
Frederikshavn (DK) 195 E4
Frederikssund (DK) 199 E3
Frederiksværk (DK) 199 E3
Fredrika (S) 184 C4
Fredriksberg (S) 189 H5
Fredrikstad (N) 195 F1
Fregenal de la Sierra (E) 69 F3
Fregene (I) 108 D3
Freiberg (D) 86 D5
Freiburg (D) 81 G3
Freiburg im Breisgau (D) 94 A2
Freihung (D) 91 F4
Freilassing (D) 96 B2
Freilingen (D) 84 D5
Freising (D) 95 G1
Freistadt (A) 96 D1
Freital (D) 86 D4
Freixedas (P) 63 E2
Freixido (E) 57 E4
Freixo de Espada à Cinta (P) 63 E2
Fréjus (F) 55 G3
Frenaros (CY) 175 F3
Frenchpark (IRL) 22 D4
Frenštát pod Radhoštěm (CZ) 93 E2
Freren (D) 84 D1
Freshford (IRL) 25 E3
Freshwater (GB) 38 B1

Fresnay-sur-Sarthe (F) 43 H2
Fresne-Saint-Mamès (F) 47 E4
Fresnes-en-Woëvre (F) 41 E5
Fresno Alhándiga (E) 63 G2
Freudenberg (Main-Tauber) (D) 89 F2
Freudenberg (Siegen Wittgenstein) (D) 84 D5
Freudenstadt (D) 89 E5
Frévent (F) 39 H2
Freyburg (D) 86 B4
Freyenstein (D) 83 E4
Freyming-Merlebach (F) 41 F5
Freyung (D) 91 H5
Frías (E) 58 C2
Frías de Albarracín (E) 65 F3
Fribourg (CH) 98 C3
Fridingen an der Donau (D) 94 C2
Friedberg (A) 97 G3
Friedberg (Aichach-Friedberg) (D) 95 F1
Friedberg (Wetteraukreis) (D) 89 E1
Friedeburg (D) 81 E4
Friedersdorf (D) 86 D1
Friedland (Göttingen) (D) 85 G4
Friedland (Mecklenburg-Strelitz) (D) 83 F4
Friedrichroda (D) 85 H5
Friedrichshafen (D) 94 D3
Friedrichskoog (D) 81 G3
Friedrichsort (D) 81 H2
Friedrichstadt (D) 81 G2
Friedrichsthal (D) 88 C3
Friesach (A) 97 E4
Friesack (D) 86 C1
Friesoythe (D) 81 E5
Frigiliana (E) 75 F3
Frihetsli (N) 176 B5
Fríkes (GR) 164 C3
Frinton-on-Sea (GB) 37 E3
Friol (E) 56 D2
Fristad (S) 195 G3
Fritsla (S) 195 G4
Fritzlar (D) 85 F4
Frizington (GB) 31 E5
Frodsham (GB) 32 C3
Frogner (N) 189 F5
Frohburg (D) 86 C4
Frohnleiten (A) 97 F4
Froissy (F) 39 H4
Froitzheim (D) 84 B5
Frombork (PL) 118 C1
Frome (GB) 35 F2
Fromentine (F) 43 E5
Frómista (E) 58 A3
Frontenay-Rohan-Rohan (F) 48 C2
Frontenhausen (D) 95 H1
Frontignan (F) 54 B3
Fronton (F) 53 F2
Frosinone (I) 109 F3
Frosolone (I) 109 H3
Frösön (S) 183 G5
Frosta (N) 188 D5
Frostavallen (S) 199 F3
Frøstrup (DK) 194 D4
Frouard (F) 47 E1
Frövi (S) 197 E1
Fruges (F) 39 H2
Frutigen (CH) 98 D3
Fry (GR) 171 F5
Furtwangen im Schwarzwald (D) 94 B2
Frýdek-Místek (CZ) 93 G3
Frýdlant (CZ) 87 F4
Frýdlant nad Ostravicí (CZ) 93 G3
Frygnowo (PL) 118 C3
Fryšták (CZ) 93 F4
Ftelíá (GR) 162 B2
Ftéri (GR) 165 E4
Fucecchio (I) 105 H4
Fuencaliente (E) 70 C4
Fuencaliente de la Palma (E) 67 E5

Fuendejalón (E) 59 F4
Fuendetodos (E) 59 G5
Fuengirola (E) 74 D4
Fuenlabrada (E) 64 B3
Fuenlabrada de los Montes (E) 70 B1
Fuenmayor (E) 58 D3
Fuensalida (E) 64 B3
Fuensanta (E) 57 H2
Fuensanta de Martos (E) 70 D4
Fuente Álamo (E) 71 H2
Fuente Alamo de Murcia (E) 73 E3
Fuente de Cantos (E) 69 F3
Fuente de Pedro Naharro (E) 64 D4
Fuente de Piedra (E) 74 D2
Fuente del Maestre (E) 69 F2
Fuente el Fresno (E) 64 B5
Fuente el Sol (E) 63 H1
Fuente Obejuna (E) 69 H3
Fuente Palmera (E) 69 H4
Fuentecén (E) 58 B5
Fuenteguinaldo (E) 63 E3
Fuentelapeña (E) 63 H1
Fuentepinilla (E) 58 D5
Fuentes de Andalucía (E) 69 H5
Fuentes de Ayódar (E) 65 H3
Fuentes de Ebro (E) 59 H5
Fuentes de León (E) 69 F3
Fuentes de Nava (E) 58 A4
Fuentes de Oñoro (E) 63 E3
Fuentes de Ropel (E) 57 G5
Fuentes de Valdepero (E) 58 A4
Fuentesaúco (E) 63 G1
Fuentidueña (E) 58 B5
Fuentidueña de Tajo (E) 64 C3
Fuerte del Rey (E) 70 D4
Fügen (A) 95 G4
Fuglebjerg (DK) 198 D4
Fulda (D) 85 G5
Fulga de Jos (RO) 152 C3
Fulgatore (I) 114 B3
Fulnek (CZ) 93 F3
Fülöpszállás (H) 129 F3
Fulpmes (A) 95 F4
Fumay (F) 40 C3
Fumel (F) 49 F5
Funäsdalen (S) 189 G1
Funchal (P) 68 A5
Fundão (P) 62 D4
Fundata (RO) 151 H1
Fundeni (RO) 152 C4
Fundulea (RO) 152 C4
Funes / Villnöß (I) 103 E2
Furadouro (P) 62 B2
Furci (I) 109 H2
Furculești (RO) 151 H5
Furnace (GB) 30 B1
Fürstenau (D) 84 D1
Fürstenberg (D) 83 F5
Fürstenfeld (A) 97 G4
Fürstenfeldbruck (D) 95 F2
Fürstenlager (D) 89 E2
Fürstenwalde (D) 87 E1
Fürstenwerder (D) 83 F4
Fürstenzell (D) 96 C1
Furta (H) 131 E2
Furtei (I) 112 B4
Fürth (D) 91 E4
Furth im Wald (D) 91 G4
Furudal (N) 190 A3
Furuflaten (N) 176 B4
Fuscaldo (I) 113 B2
Fuschl am See (A) 96 C3
Fuseta (P) 68 D5
Fushë-Arrëz (AL) 142 C5
Fushë Kosovë / Kosovo Polje (SRB) 143 E4
Fushë-Krujë (AL) 144 C1
Fushë-Muhur (AL) 144 D1

Fusignano (I) 107 E1
Füssen (D) 95 E3
Fustiñana (E) 59 F4
Futog (SRB) 140 C3
Futuroscope, parc du (F) 49 E1
Füzesgyarmat (H) 131 E2
Fužine (HR) 134 C4
Fylakí (GR) 163 F1
Fylí (GR) 165 H4
Fyllia (CY) 174 D3
Fýllo (GR) 165 E1
Fynshav (DK) 198 C4
Fyresdal (N) 194 C1
Fyteíes (GR) 164 D3

G

Gaal (A) 97 E4
Gabare (BG) 155 E3
Gabarret (E) 52 D2
Gabčíkovo (SK) 132 A5
Gabela (BIH) 138 D3
Gaber (BG) 158 A1
Gabicce Mare (I) 107 F2
Gąbin (PL) 122 B1
Gabrovka (SLO) 134 C2
Gabrovo / Габрово (BG) 159 E1
Gacé (F) 44 B1
Gacko (BIH) 139 E3
Gäddede (S) 183 F3
Gadebusch (D) 82 C4
Gádor (E) 72 B5
Gádoros (H) 129 H3
Gadžin Han (SRB) 143 F2
Găești (RO) 151 H3
Gaeta (I) 109 F4
Gagarin (RUS) 7 F2
Găgești (RO) 149 E5
Gaggenau (D) 89 E4
Gagliano del Capo (I) 111 H5
Gagnef (S) 190 A4
Gagyvendégi (H) 126 D5
Gaigalava (Bikova) (LV) 203 G3
Gaildorf (D) 89 G4
Gailey (D) 32 D4
Gaillac (F) 53 G2
Gaillimh / Galway (IRL) 22 C5
Gaillon (F) 39 F5
Gainsborough (GB) 33 F3
Gairloch (GB) 28 D3
Gaj (SRB) 141 E4
Gakovo (SRB) 137 H1
Gălăbinci (BG) 159 G2
Gălăbovo / Гълъбово (BG) 159 F3
Galambok (H) 128 C4
Galan (F) 52 D3
Galanádo (GR) 170 C1
Galanta (SK) 132 B4
Galapagar (E) 64 B2
Galaroza (E) 69 F4
Galashiels (GB) 31 E2
Galata (CY) 174 C4
Galatádes (GR) 161 F3
Galatás (GR) 165 H5
Galați (RO) 153 E2
Galatina (I) 111 H5
Galatone (I) 111 H5
Galaxídi (GR) 165 F3
Galdakao (E) 58 D1
Gáldar (E) 67 G5
Galeata (I) 107 E2
Galende (E) 57 E4
Galera (E) 71 F4
Gâlgău (RO) 147 F2
Galiče (BG) 155 E2
Galicea (RO) 151 G3
Galicea Mare (RO) 151 E4
Galičnik (MK) 144 D1
Galini (CY) 174 C3
Galipsós (GR) 162 B3
Galisteo (E) 63 F4
Gallardon (F) 44 D2

Gallareto (I) 100 C5
Gallargues (F) 54 B2
Galliate (I) 100 D4
Gallikós (GR) 161 G3
Gallipoli (I) 111 G5
Gallneukirchen (A) 96 D1
Gällö (S) 190 A1
Gallspach (A) 96 C2
Gallur (E) 59 F4
Galluzzo certosa (I) 105 H4
Galston (GB) 30 C2
Galten (DK) 194 D5
Galtür (A) 95 E4
Galveias (P) 68 C1
Gálvez (E) 64 A4
Galway / Gaillimh (IRL) 22 C5
Gamaches (F) 39 G3
Gambarie (I) 115 H2
Gaming (A) 97 E2
Gamleby (S) 197 E3
Gammelstaden (S) 185 E2
Gammertingen (D) 89 F5
Gams (A) 99 F2
Gamvik (N) 177 H1
Gamzigrad (SRB) 143 G1
Gâmzovo (BG) 150 D4
Ganacker (D) 95 H1
Gándara (E) 56 C1
Ganderkesee (D) 81 F5
Gandesa (E) 60 A5
Gandia (E) 66 A4
Gandino (I) 101 F3
Gandria (CH) 99 F5
Ganges (F) 54 B2
Gangi (I) 115 E3
Gangkofen (D) 95 H1
Gänserndorf (A) 97 H1
Gánt (H) 129 E2
Gañuelas (E) 71 H4
Gap (F) 51 F5
Gara (H) 129 F5
Garaballa (E) 65 F4
Garbów (PL) 123 F3
Garching an der Alz (D) 95 H2
Garcia (E) 60 B4
Garciaz (E) 63 G5
Garda (I) 101 H4
Gârdani (RO) 147 E2
Gardanne (F) 55 E3
Gårdby (S) 197 F5
Gardeja (PL) 117 H3
Gardelegen (D) 86 A1
Gardermoen (N) 189 F5
Gardíki (GR) 165 E2
Garding (D) 81 G2
Gardjönäs (S) 183 H2
Gardna Wielka (PL) 117 F1
Gärdnäs (S) 183 G4
Gardone Riviera (I) 101 G4
Gardone Val Trompia (I) 101 G4
Gardony (H) 129 E2
Garður (IS) 178 A3
Garešnica (HR) 135 F3
Garessio (I) 104 C3
Garforth (GB) 33 E2
Gargaliáni / Γαργαλιάνοι (GR) 168 B3
Garganta la Olla (E) 63 G4
Gargnano (I) 101 G4
Gargnäs (S) 184 C2
Gargždai (LT) 204 B2
Garípa (GR) 173 E4
Garlasco (I) 101 E5
Garliava (LT) 205 E4
Garlin (F) 52 C2
Garlstorf (D) 81 H5
Gärmen (BG) 161 H1
Garmisch-Partenkirchen (D) 95 F3
Gârnic (RO) 150 C3
Garoza (LV) 202 D3

Garpenberg (S) 190 B5
Garphyttan nationalpark (S) 196 D1
Garraf (E) 60 D4
Garrafe de Torío (E) 57 G3
Garray (E) 59 E4
Garrel (D) 81 F5
Garriguella (E) 61 F2
Garrovillas de Alconétar (E) 63 E5
Garrucha (E) 71 H5
Gars am Kamp (A) 97 F1
Gartow (D) 82 D5
Gartz (D) 83 H4
Garvagh (GB) 23 F2
Garvão (P) 68 C4
Garve (GB) 28 E3
Garwolin (PL) 123 E2
Garynahine (GB) 28 C2
Garz (D) 83 F2
Gaschurn (A) 94 D4
Gassino Torinese (I) 100 C5
Gastoúni (GR) 164 D5
Gata (E) 63 E3
Gata de Gorgos (E) 66 A5
Gătaia (RO) 150 B1
Gatčina (RUS) 6 D1
Gatehouse of Fleet (GB) 30 D4
Gátér (H) 129 G3
Gateshead (GB) 31 G4
Gattinara (I) 100 D4
Gattorna (I) 105 E3
Gaucín (E) 74 C4
Gaulstad (N) 183 E4
Gaupne (N) 188 C2
Gaurė (LT) 204 D3
Gautegiz-Arteaga (E) 58 D1
Gauting (D) 95 G2
Găvănești (RO) 151 F4
Gavardo (I) 101 G4
Gavarnie (F) 52 D4
Gávavencsellő (H) 127 E5
Gavi (I) 104 D2
Gavião (P) 62 C5
Gavirate (I) 100 D3
Gävle (S) 190 B4
Gavoi (I) 112 C3
Gavray (F) 38 B5
Gavrilov-Jam (RUS) 7 G1
Gávrio (GR) 166 C5
Gåvsta (S) 190 C5
Gåxsjö (S) 183 G5
Gazimağusa / Ammóchostos (Famagusta) (CY) 175 F3
Gazzuolo (I) 101 G5
Gdańsk (PL) 117 H2
Gdov (RUS) 6 C1
Gdów (PL) 125 G1
Gdynia (PL) 117 H1
Geaune (F) 52 C2
Gebesee (D) 85 H4
Gebze (TR) 19 G1
Géderlak (H) 129 E4
Gedern (D) 89 F1
Gediz (TR) 19 H2
Gedser (DK) 198 D5
Geel (B) 78 D2
Geertruidenberg (NL) 76 D5
Geesthacht (D) 82 B4
Gefell (D) 91 F2
Gefrees (D) 91 F3
Géfyra (Kentrikí Makedonía) (GR) 161 F3
Géfyra (Pelopónnisos) (GR) 169 E4
Gehren (D) 86 A5
Geilenkirchen (D) 84 B4
Geilo (N) 188 D4
Geiranger (N) 188 C1
Geirangerfjorden (N) 188 C1
Geisa (D) 85 G5
Geiselhöring (D) 91 G5
Geisenfeld (D) 95 G1
Geisenhausen (D) 95 H1
Geising (D) 86 D5
Geisingen (D) 94 B2

A B C D E F G H I J K L M N O P Q R S T U V W X Y Z

Geislingen an der Steige (D) 89 G5
Geismar (D) 85 G4
Geisnes (N) 183 E3
Geithain (D) 86 C4
Gela (I) 115 E5
Geldern (D) 84 B3
Geldrop (NL) 79 E1
Geleen (NL) 79 E2
Gelibolu (TR) 19 F2
Gelnhausen (D) 89 F1
Gelsa (E) 59 H5
Gelsdorf (D) 84 C5
Gelse (H) 128 B4
Gelsenkirchen (D) 84 C3
Gelting (D) 81 H1
Gelu (RO) 146 B5
Gelvonai (LT) 205 F3
Gembloux (B) 78 D3
Gemeaux (F) 46 D4
Gemenele (RO) 153 E2
Gémenos (F) 55 E3
Gemert (NL) 79 E1
Gemlik (TR) 19 G2
Gemona del Friuli (I) .. 103 G2
Gémozac (F) 48 C3
Gemünd (D) 84 B5
Gemünden (D) 88 D2
Gemünden (Wohra) (D) .. 85 F4
Gemünden am Main (D) 89 G1
Genagra (CY) 175 E3
Genappe (B) 78 C3
Gençay (F) 49 E1
General Inzovo (BG) ... 159 E4
General Toševo (BG) ... 153 E5
Generalski Stol (HR) .. 134 D4
Genève (CH) 98 A4
Geniséa (GR) 162 C3
Genk (B) 79 E2
Genlis (F) 46 D4
Gennádio (GR) 171 H4
Gennep (NL) 79 F1
Gennes (F) 43 H4
Génolhac (F) 54 B1
Genova (I) 105 E3
Gent (Gand) (B) ... 78 B2
Genthin (D) 86 B1
Gentioux-Pigerolles (F) . 49 G3
Genzano di Lucania (I) ..110 D3
Genzano di Roma (I) ... 109 G3
Geoagiu (RO) 147 E5
Geoagiu-Băi (RO) 147 E5
Georgianoí (GR) 161 H4
Georgioúpoli (GR) .. 170 A5
Georgítsi (GR) 168 D3
Gepiu (RO) 146 C3
Gera (D) 86 B5
Geraardsbergen (B) .. 78 C2
Gerabronn (D) 89 G3
Gerace (I) 113 C4
Gerakári (GR) 172 C3
Gerakaroú (GR) 161 G3
Gérakas (GR) 169 E4
Geráki / Γεράκι (GR) .. 168 D3
Gerakiní (GR) 161 H4
Gérardmer (F) 47 G2
Geras (A) 92 C5
Gerbéviller (F) 47 F1
Gerbstedt (D) 86 A3
Gerena (E) 69 G5
Gerês (P) 56 C5
Geretsried (D) 95 G2
Gérgal (E) 72 B5
Geri (CY) 175 E3
Geringswalde (D) ... 86 C4
Gerjen (H) 129 E4
Gerlos (A) 95 H4
Gérmas (GR) 160 D4
Germasogeia (CY) .. 174 D4
Germering (D) 95 F2
Germersheim (D) .. 89 E3
Gernrode (D) 86 A3
Gernsbach (D) 89 E4
Gernsheim (D) 89 E3
Gerola Alta (I) 101 F3
Gerolakkos (CY) ... 174 D3

Geroliménas (GR) 168 D4
Gerolstein (D) 88 B1
Gerolzhofen (D) 89 H2
Geroplátanos (GR) ... 161 H4
Geroskipou (CY) ... 174 B4
Gerovo (HR) 134 C3
Gersau (CH) 99 E3
Gersfeld (D) 89 G1
Gerstetten (D) 89 G5
Gersthofen (D) 89 H5
Gerswalde (D) 83 G5
Gerviškės (LT) 205 G5
Geseke (D) 85 E3
Gesualdo (I) 110 B3
Geta (FIN) 190 D5
Getafe (E) 64 B3
Gettorf (D) 81 H2
Getxo (E) 58 D1
Gevelsberg (D) 84 D4
Gevgelija (MK) 145 H2
Gevrey-Chambertin (F) . 46 D4
Gex (F) 51 F1
Geyve (TR) 19 H1
Gföhl (A) 97 F1
Ghedi (I) 101 G4
Gheorgheni (RO) 148 A4
Gherla (RO) 147 F3
Ghilarza (I) 112 B3
Ghimbav (RO) 152 A1
Ghimpaţi (RO) 152 B4
Ghisonaccia (F) 55 H4
Ghisoni (F) 55 H4
Gialia (CY) 174 B3
Giannádes (GR) 160 A5
Giannitsá / Γιαννιτσά (GR) 161 F3
Giannítsi (GR) 166 B4
Giannoúli (GR) 163 E2
Giardini-Naxos (I) .. 115 G3
Giarratana (I) 115 F5
Giarre (I) 115 G3
Giat (F) 49 H3
Giaveno (I) 100 B5
Giba (I) 112 B5
Gibostad (N) 176 A4
Gibraleón (E) 69 E5
Giby (PL) 119 G2
Gic (H) 128 B4
Gideå (S) 184 D5
Gidle (PL) 122 B4
Gieboldehausen (D) .. 85 G3
Gieczno (PL) 121 E4
Giedraičiai (LT) ... 205 F3
Gien (F) 45 F3
Giengen an der Brenz (D).. 89 H5
Giens (F) 55 F4
Giera (RO) 150 B1
Gießen (D) 85 E5
Giethoorn (NL) ... 77 F3
Gifhorn (D) 85 H1
Gigen (BG) 151 G5
Giglio Porto (I) ... 108 B2
Gignac (F) 54 A2
Gijón (E) 57 G1
Gilău (RO) 147 E4
Gilching (D) 95 F2
Gilford (GB) 23 G3
Gilleleje (DK) 199 E2
Gillhov (S) 190 A1
Gillingham (Dorset) (GB) .. 35 F3
Gillingham (Kent) (GB) .. 36 D4
Gills (GB) 26 B4
Gilze (NL) 78 D1
Gimenells (E) 60 A3
Gimo (S) 190 C5
Gimont (F) 53 E2
Gingst (D) 83 F2
Ginosa (I) 111 E4
Ginzling (A) 95 G4
Gioia del Colle (I) .. 111 E4
Gioia Tauro (I) ... 115 H4
Giolou (CY) 174 B4
Giovinazzo (I) ... 111 E3

Girifalco (I) 113 C3
Girkalnis (LT) 204 D3
Girne / Kerýneia (CY) ..174 D2
Giromagny (F) ... 47 G3
Girona (E) 61 E2
Gironella (E) 60 D2
Girov (RO) 148 C3
Girvan (GB) 30 C3
Gisburn (GB) ... 32 D2
Gislaved (S) 195 G4
Gisors (F) 39 G5
Gissi (I) 109 H2
Gistel (B) 78 A1
Gittun (S) 184 C1
Giubega (RO) ... 151 G5
Giuliaviana (I) ... 107 H5
Giulvăz (RO) ... 150 B1
Giurgeni (RO) ... 153 E3
Giurgiţa (RO) ... 151 F5
Giurgiu (RO) ... 152 B5
Give (DK) 198 B3
Givet (F) 40 C3
Givors (F) 50 D3
Givry (F) 46 D5
Givry-en-Argonne (F).. 40 D5
Giżałki (PL) 121 F2
Gizycko (PL) 119 E2
Gjakovë / Đakovica (SRB) 142 D4
Gjendesheim (N) .. 188 D3
Gjerde (N) 188 C2
Gjermundshavn (N) .. 188 B4
Gjesvær (N) 177 E1
Gjilani / Gnjilane (SRB) . 143 F4
Gjirokastër (AL) ... 144 D5
Gjøra (N) 189 E1
Gjorm (AL) 144 C4
Gjov (Færøerne) (DK). .. 194 A4
Gjøvik (N) 189 F4
Gjuesevo (BG) ... 158 A2
Gkagkáles (GR) .. 172 D4
Gkoritsá (GR) ... 168 D3
Gkoúra (GR) 165 F4
Gladbeck (D) ... 84 C3
Gladenbach (D) .. 85 E5
Gladstad (N) 183 E2
Glamis (GB) 29 G5
Glamis Castle (GB) .. 29 G5
Glamoč (SRB) ... 137 E5
Glamsbjerg (DK) .. 198 C4
Glan-Münchweiler (D) .. 88 D3
Glandorf (D) 84 D2
Glanshammar (S) .. 197 E1
Glarus (CH) 99 F3
Glasgow (GB) ... 30 D2
Glastonbury (GB) .. 35 F3
Glauchau (D) ... 86 C5
Glava (S) 195 G1
Glavanovci (BG) .. 158 A1
Glavatičevo (BIH) .. 139 E2
Glavice (BIH) ... 136 D5
Glavičice (BIH) .. 137 H4
Glavinica (BG) .. 152 C5
Glavnik (SRB) ... 143 E3
Głębock (PL) 118 C1
Gledić (SRB) ... 143 E1
Glein (N) 183 F1
Gleisdorf (A) ... 97 F4
Glenamoy (IRL) .. 22 B3
Glenariff or Waterfoot (GB) .. 23 G2
Glenarm (GB) ... 23 G2
Glenbeigh (IRL) .. 24 B4
Glencolumbkille (IRL) . 22 D2
Glendalough (IRL) .. 25 F2
Glenelg (GB) 28 D4
Glenfinnan (GB) .. 28 D4
Glengarriff (IRL) .. 24 B4
Glenluce (GB) 30 C4
Glenmaddy (IRL) .. 22 D5
Glenrothes (GB) .. 31 E1
Glenties (IRL) ... 22 D2
Glina (HR) 135 E4
Glina (RO) 152 B4
Glinojeck (PL) ... 118 D5
Gliwice (PL) 122 A5
Globočica (SRB) .. 143 E5

Glodeni (RO) 147 G4
Glodževo (BG) 152 C5
Gloggnitz (A) 97 G3
Głogów (PL) 120 D2
Głogów Małopolski (PL) . 127 F1
Głogówek (PL) ... 121 G5
Glomfjord (N) 179 F5
Glommersträsk (S) .. 184 D2
Głoska (PL) 121 E3
Glossop (GB) 32 D3
Gloucester (GB) .. 35 F1
Głowaczów (PL) .. 123 E2
Główczyce (PL) .. 117 F1
Głowno (PL) 122 B2
Głożan (SRB) ... 140 B3
Gložene (BG) 158 C1
Głubczyce (PL) .. 124 D1
Głuchołazy (PL) .. 124 C1
Glücksburg (D) .. 81 H1
Glückstadt (D) ... 81 G3
Glumso (DK) ... 198 D4
Glusci (SRB) 140 B4
Głuszyca (PL) ... 120 D5
Glýfa (GR) 165 G2
Glyki (GR) 164 C1
Glyn Ebwy / Ebbw Vale (GB) .. 35 E1
Gmünd (A) 92 B5
Gmund am Tegernsee (D) .. 95 G3
Gmünd in Kärnten (A) .. 96 C4
Gmunden (A) ... 96 D2
Gnarp (S) 190 B2
Gneisenaustadt Schildau (D) .. 86 C3
Gnesta (S) 197 F2
Gniechowice (PL) .. 121 E4
Gniew (PL) 117 H3
Gniewkowo (PL) .. 117 G5
Gniezno (PL) ... 121 F1
Gnisvärd (S) 197 G4
Gnjilane / Gjilani (SRB) . 143 F4
Gnoien (D) 83 E3
Gnosjö (S) 195 G4
Goce Delčev / Гоце Делчев (BG) 161 H1
Goch (D) 84 B3
Godalming (GB) .. 36 B5
Godby (FIN) 190 D5
Godeč (BG) 158 B1
Godelheim (D) .. 85 F3
Goderville (F) ... 39 E4
Godmanchester (GB).. 33 G5
Gödöllő (H) 129 E5
Godovič (SLO) .. 134 B2
Gödre (H) 128 D4
Godziszewo (PL) .. 117 H2
Goes (NL) 78 C1
Gogești (RO) 151 F4
Gogolin (PL) 121 G5
Gogoşu (RO) ... 150 D4
Goirle (NL) 78 D1
Góis (P) 62 C4
Goisern (A) 96 C3
Goito (I) 101 G5
Gokčanica (SRB) .. 142 D2
Gol (N) 188 D4
Gola (H) 135 F2
Gołańcz (PL) 117 F5
Golčův Jeníkov (CZ) . 92 C3
Golczewo (PL) ... 116 C3
Gołdap (PL) 119 F1
Goldberg (D) 82 D4
Goldenstedt (D) .. 81 F5
Golega (P) 62 B5
Golemo Selo (SRB) .. 143 F4
Goleniów (PL) ... 116 C3
Goleš (SRB) 143 G4
Golfe-Juan (F) ... 55 G2

Golfo Aranci (I) 112 D1
Golina (PL) 121 G1
Goljam Izvor (BG) .. 163 E1
Goljam Manastir (BG) . 159 G3
Goljamo Gradište (BG) . 156 C2
Goljamo Kruševo (BG).. 159 H3
Göllersdorf (A) ... 97 G1
Golling an der Salzach (A) .. 96 C3
Golnik (SLO) ... 134 B2
Golpejas (E) 63 G2
Golspie (GB) ... 26 A5
Golßen (D) 86 D2
Golub-Dobrzyń (PL) ...117 H4
Golubac (SRB) ...141 F4
Golubinje (SRB) ...141 G4
Golubovci (MNE) .. 139 G5
Golubovec (HR) ... 135 E2
Gołuchów (PL) ... 121 G2
Gołymin-Ośrodek (PL) ..118 D5
Golzow (D) 86 C2
Gómara (E) 59 E5
Gomáti (GR) 161 H4
Gombrèn (E) 60 D2
Gomecello (E) ... 63 G2
Gommern (D) ... 86 B2
Gönc (H) 127 E5
Goncelin (F) 51 F3
Gondomar (E) ... 56 B4
Gondomar (P) ... 62 B1
Gondrecourt-le-Château (F) .. 46 D2
Gonfaron (F) ... 55 F3
Gönen (TR) 19 G2
Goniądz (PL) ... 119 G3
Goniés (GR) 170 B5
Gonnesa (I) 112 B5
Gónnoi (GR) 161 F5
Gonnosfanadiga (I) .. 112 B4
Gönyű (H) 128 D1
Goole (GB) 33 F2
Goor (NL) 77 G4
Goppenstein (CH) .. 98 D4
Göppingen (D) .. 89 G4
Gor (E) 71 F5
Gor. Tlamino (SRB) .. 143 G4
Gora (HR) 135 E4
Góra (PL) 121 E3
Góra Kalwaria (PL) .. 122 D2
Goražde (BIH) .. 139 F2
Görbeháza (H) .. 131 E1
Görcsöny (H) ... 128 D5
Gördalen (S) ... 189 G3
Gordes (F) 54 D2
Gorenjavas (SLO) .. 134 B2
Gorey (GB) 38 B4
Gorey (IRL) 25 G3
Görgeteg (H) ... 128 C5
Gorgonzola (I) .. 101 F4
Gorgopótamos (GR) . 160 C4
Gorgota (RO) ... 152 B3
Gorica (BIH) ... 138 C2
Gorica (MK) ... 145 E2
Goričan (HR) ... 135 E2
Gorinchem (NL) .. 76 D5
Gorizia (I) 103 H3
Górka (PL) 125 H1
Górki (PL) 122 D3
Gorlice (PL) 126 D2
Görlitz (D) 87 F4
Gorna Bešovica (BG) . 155 E3
Gorna Koznica (BG) .. 158 A2
Gorna Kremena (BG) . 155 E3
Gorna Mahala (BG) .. 158 D2
Gorna Malina (BG) .. 158 C1
Gorna Orjahovica / Горна Оряховица (BG) . 159 E4
Gorna Rosica (BG) .. 159 E1
Gorna Studena (BG) .. 156 B2
Gornja Grabovica (BIH) . 138 D2
Gornja Kamenica (SRB). 143 G2
Gornja Klina (SRB) .. 142 D3
Gornja Ljuboviđa (SRB) . 140 B5
Gornja Ploča (HR) .. 136 C4
Gornja Radgona (SLO) . 135 E1
Gornja Sabanta (SRB) . 143 E1
Gornja Slatina (BIH) .. 137 G3

Gornja Toponica (SRB) . 143 F2
Gornja Tuzla (BIH) 137 H4
Gornje Jelenje (HR) ... 134 C4
Gornje Ratkovo (BIH) .. 137 E4
Gornje Selo (HR) 138 B2
Gornje Vratno (HR) ... 135 E2
Gornji Grad (SLO) ... 134 C2
Gornji Kneginec (HR). . 135 E2
Gornji Kokoti (MNE) .. 139 G4
Gornji Kosinj (HR) ... 134 D5
Gornji Lapac (HR) ... 136 C4
Gornji Milanovac / Горњи Милановац (SRB) 142 D1
Gornji Petrovci (SLO) .. 135 E1
Gornji Podgradci (BIH) . 137 E4
Gornji Rajić (HR) ... 135 F4
Gornji Ravno (BIH) .. 137 E5
Gornji Srb (HR) 136 C4
Gornji Vakuf (BIH) ... 137 F5
Górno (PL) 122 D4
Gorno Orizari (MK) .. 145 F1
Goro (I) 107 E1
Górowo Iławeckie (PL) . 118 D2
Gorredijk (NL) 77 F3
Gorron (F) 43 G2
Gorska Poljana (BG) .. 159 H3
Gorski Izvor (BG) ... 159 G4
Gorsleston-on-Sea (GB) . 37 H1
Gort (IRL) 24 C2
Gorteen (IRL) 22 D4
Gortin (GB) 23 E2
Gortmore (IRL) ... 22 B5
Goruia (RO) 150 C2
Görzke (D) 86 B2
Gorzkowice (PL) .. 122 B3
Gorzów Śląski (PL) .. 121 G4
Gorzów Wielkopolski (PL) ..116 C5
Gorzyce (PL) 123 E4
Gorzyń (PL) 120 D1
Gosaldo (I) 103 E2
Gosau (A) 96 C3
Göschenen (CH) .. 99 E3
Gościno (PL) 116 D2
Gosforth (GB) 31 E5
Goslar (D) 85 H2
Gosławice (PL) ... 121 G1
Gospić (HR) 136 B4
Gospođinci (SRB) .. 140 C3
Gosport (GB) 38 C1
Gossau (CH) 99 F2
Gosselies (B) 78 C3
Gossensaß / Colle Isarco (I) .. 102 D1
Gößl (A) 96 D3
Gößnitz (D) 86 C5
Gößweinstein (D) .. 91 E3
Gostinu (RO) 152 B5
Gostivar (MK) ... 145 E1
Göstling an der Ybbs (A) .. 97 E2
Gostomia (PL) ... 117 E4
Gostyń (PL) 121 E2
Gostynin (PL) ... 122 B1
Göteborg (S) 195 F3
Götene (S) 195 G2
Gotha (D) 85 H5
Göttingen (D) ... 85 G3
Götzis (A) 94 D4
Gouarec (F) 42 C2
Gouda (NL) 76 D5
Gouménissa (GR) .. 161 F3
Goumois (F) 47 G4
Gourdon (F) 49 G5
Gourin (F) 42 C2
Gournay-en-Bray (F) . 39 G4
Goúrnes (GR) ... 170 C5
Gourock (GB) ... 30 C1
Gourri (CY) 174 D4
Gouveia (P) 62 B3
Goúves (GR) 170 C5
Gouviá (GR) 160 A5
Gouzon (F) 49 H2
Govedari (HR) ... 138 D4
Govora (RO) 151 G2
Goworowo (PL) .. 119 E5
Gozd Martuljek (SLO) . 134 A1

Gozdnica (PL) . . . . 120 C 3
Gozdowice (PL) . . . . . . .116 B 5
Gozzano (I) . . . . 100 D 3
Graal-Müritz (D) . . . . 83 E 2
Graben (D) . . . . 89 E 3
Grabenstätt (D) . . . . 95 H 2
Grabovac (HR) . . . . 138 C 2
Grabovci (SRB) . . . . 140 C 4
Grabow (D) . . . . 82 D 4
Grabów (PL) . . . . 121 H 2
Grabów
nad Prosna (PL) . . . . . 121 G 3
Grabowiec (PL) . . . . 123 H 4
Gračac (HR) . . . . 136 C 4
Gračanica (BIH) . . . . 135 H 5
Gračanica
(Priština) (SRB) . . . . . 143 E 4
Gračanica
(Valjevo) (SRB) . . . . . 140 B 5
Graçay (F) . . . . 45 E 5
Grächen (CH) . . . . 98 D 4
Gradac (HR) . . . . 138 D 3
Gradac (MNE) . . . . 139 F 2
Gradac (SRB) . . . . 142 D 2
Gradačac (BIH) . . . . 137 G 3
Gradara (I) . . . . 107 F 3
Gradec (HR) . . . . 135 F 3
Gradec (Sliven) (BG) . . . 159 G 1
Gradec (Vidin) (BG) . . . . 150 D 5
Gradefes (E) . . . . 57 H 3
Gradevo (BG) . . . . 161 G 1
Gradina (HR) . . . . 135 G 3
Gradina (SRB) . . . . 143 H 3
Gradina (Pleven) (BG) . . 156 A 2
Gradina
(Veliko Tărnovo) (BG) . 156 B 3
Grădinari (Reşiţa) (RO) . 151 G 3
Grădinari (Slatina) (RO) . 150 C 2
Gradisca d'Isonzo (I) . . . 103 H 3
Gradiška / Bosanska
Gradiška (BIH) . . . . . . 135 G 4
Gradište (BG) . . . . 157 E 2
Gradište (HR) . . . . 135 H 4
Gradište (MK) . . . . 143 F 5
Grădiştea (RO) . . . . 151 F 3
Gradnica (BG) . . . . 159 E 1
Grado (E) . . . . 57 G 2
Grado (I) . . . . 103 G 4
Gradsko (MK) . . . . 145 F 1
Gradskovo (SRB) . . . . . .141 G 5
Graewo (PL) . . . . .119 F 3
Gräfelfing (D) . . . . 95 G 2
Grafenau (D) . . . . .91 H 5
Gräfenberg (D) . . . . .91 E 4
Gräfenhainichen (D) . . . . 86 C 3
Grafenwöhr (D) . . . . 91 E 1
Grafing bei München (D) . 95 G 2
Gragnano (I) . . . . 109 H 5
Grahovo (MNE) . . . . 139 F 4
Grahovo (SLO) . . . . 134 A 2
Graiguenamanagh (IRL) . 25 E 3
Grain (GB) . . . . 36 D 4
Grainau (D) . . . . 95 F 3
Grajvoron (RUS) . . . . .7 H 5
Gram (DK) . . . . 198 B 3
Gramada (BG) . . . . 150 D 5
Gramat (F) . . . . 49 G 5
Grămeşti (RO) . . . . 148 B 1
Grametten (A) . . . . 92 C 5
Grammichele (I) . . . . 115 F 4
Gramsh (AL) . . . . 144 D 3
Gramzow (D) . . . . 83 G 4
Gran (N) . . . . 189 E 4
Gran Tarajal (E) . . . . .67 H 5
Granada (E) . . . . 70 D 5
Granadilla de Abona (E) . .67 F 5
Granard (IRL) . . . . 23 E 4
Grancey-le-Château (F) . 46 D 3
Grand
Bourgtheroulde (F) . . . 39 F 4
Grand-Champ (F) . . . . . . 42 D 3
Grand-Couronne (F) . . . . 39 F 4
Grand-Fougeray (F) . . . . 43 F 4
Grandas de Salime (E) . . 57 E 2
Grandcamp-Maisy (F) . . . 38 C 4
Grândola (P) . . . . 68 B 3
Grandpré (F) . . . . 40 C 4

Grandrieu (F) . . . . 50 B 5
Grandson (CH) . . . . 98 B 3
Grandvilliers (F) . . . . 39 G 4
Grañén (E) . . . . 59 H 4
Grange-over-Sands (GB) .31 E 5
Grangemouth (GB) . . . . . 30 D 1
Granges-sur-Vologne (F) .47 F 2
Grängesberg (S) . . . . . . 190 A 5
Grániceri (RO) . . . . 146 B 4
Granítis (GR) . . . . 162 B 2
Granitovo (BG) . . . . 159 G 3
Granítsa (GR) . . . . 164 D 2
Granja (P) . . . . 69 E 3
Granja
de Torrehermosa (E) . . 69 H 3
Gränna (S) . . . . 195 H 3
Granollers (E) . . . . .61 E 3
Granön (S) . . . . 184 D 4
Grantham (GB) . . . . 33 F 4
Grantown-on-Spey (GB) . 29 F 3
Granville (F) . . . . 38 B 5
Granvin (N) . . . . 188 C 4
Graševo (BG) . . . . 162 B 1
Grasleben (D) . . . . 86 A 2
Grasmere (GB) . . . . .31 E 5
Grassano (I) . . . . .110 D 4
Grasse (F) . . . . 55 G 2
Gråsten (DK) . . . . 198 C 4
Grästorp (S) . . . . 195 G 2
Gratangen (N) . . . . .176 A 5
Gratini (GR) . . . . 162 D 2
Gratkorn (A) . . . . 97 F 4
Graulhet (F) . . . . 53 G 2
Graus (E) . . . . 60 A 2
Grávalos (E) . . . . 59 E 4
Gravdal (N) . . . . 179 F 3
Grave (NL) . . . . 77 E 5
Gravedona (I) . . . . 101 E 3
Gravelines (F) . . . . 39 H 1
Gravellona-Toce (I) . . . . 100 D 3
Gravesend (GB) . . . . 36 D 4
Graviá (GR) . . . . 165 F 3
Gravina in Puglia (I) . . . .111 E 3
Gray (F) . . . . .47 E 4
Grays (GB) . . . . 36 D 4
Graz (A) . . . . 97 F 4
Grazalema (E) . . . . .74 C 3
Grazzanise (I) . . . . 109 G 4
Grčak (SRB) . . . . 143 E 2
Grdelica (SRB) . . . . 143 G 3
Great Dunmow (GB) . . . . 36 D 3
Great Malvern (GB) . . . . . 35 F 1
Great Torrington (GB) . . . 34 D 3
Great Yarmouth (GB) . . . 37 E 1
Grebbestad (S) . . . . 195 F 2
Grebnik (SRB) . . . . 142 D 4
Grębów (PL) . . . . 123 E 5
Greccio (I) . . . . 109 E 4
Greci (RO) . . . . 153 E 2
Greding (D) . . . . .91 E 5
Greenhead (GB) . . . . . . .31 F 4
Greenlaw (GB) . . . . .31 F 2
Greenock (GB) . . . . 30 C 2
Greenodd (GB) . . . . .31 E 5
Greggio (I) . . . . 100 D 4
Gregolímano (GR) . . . . . 165 G 2
Greifenburg (A) . . . . 96 C 5
Greiffenberg (D) . . . . 83 G 5
Greifswald (D) . . . . 83 F 3
Grein (A) . . . . 97 E 1
Greiz (D) . . . . 86 B 5
Grenå (DK) . . . . 195 E 5
Grenade (F) . . . . 53 F 2
Grenade-sur-l'Adour (F) . 52 C 2
Grenchen (CH) . . . . 98 C 2
Grendi (N) . . . . 194 C 1
Grenoble (F) . . . . .51 E 4
Grense Jakobselv (N) . . .177 H 3
Gréoux-les-Bains (F) . . . 55 F 2
Gresse-en-Vercors (F) . .51 E 4
Gressoney-la-Trinité (I) . 100 C 3
Gressoney-
Saint-Jean (I) . . . 100 C 3

Gresten (A) . . . . 97 E 2
Grésy-sur-Isère (F) . . . . .51 F 3
Gretna (GB) . . . . .31 E 4
Greußen (D) . . . . 86 A 4
Greve (DK) . . . . 199 E 3
Greve in Chianti (I) . . . . 105 H 5
Greven (D) . . . . 84 D 2
Grevená / Γρεβενά (GR) . 160 D 5
Grevenbroich (D) . . . . . . 84 B 4
Grevenbrück (D) . . . . 84 D 4
Greveníti (GR) . . . . 160 C 5
Grevenmacher (L) . . . . . 79 F 5
Grevesmühlen (D) . . . . . 82 C 3
Grey Abbey (GB) . . . . . . 23 H 3
Greystones (IRL) . . . . . . 25 G 2
Grez-en-Bouère (F) . . . . 43 H 3
Grezzana (I) . . . . 101 H 4
Griebenow (D) . . . . 83 F 3
Gries am Brenner (A) . . . 95 G 4
Gries im Sellrain (A) . . . 95 F 4
Grieskirchen (A) . . . . 96 D 2
Griffen (A) . . . . 97 E 5
Grigiškės (LT) . . . . 205 F 4
Grignan (F) . . . . 54 D 1
Grigno (I) . . . . 103 E 3
Grignols (F) . . . . 52 D 1
Grimaldi (I) . . . . .113 B 3
Grimaud (F) . . . . 55 F 3
Grimma (D) . . . . 86 C 4
Grimmen (D) . . . . 83 F 3
Grimsbu (N) . . . . 189 E 2
Grimstad (N) . . . . 194 D 2
Grindaheim (N) . . . . 188 D 3
Grindavík (IS) . . . . 178 A 3
Grindelwald (CH) . . . . . . 98 D 3
Grindsted (DK) . . . . 198 B 3
Griñón (E) . . . . 64 B 3
Gripsholms slott (S) . . . . 197 F 1
Grisignano di Zocco (I) . 103 E 4
Grisolles (F) . . . . 53 F 2
Grisslehamn (S) . . . . . . 190 C 5
Grivița (RO) . . . . 152 D 3
Grk (BIH) . . . . 135 H 5
Grljan (SRB) . . . . 143 G 1
Grnča (SRB) . . . . 137 H 4
Grøa (N) . . . . 188 D 1
Grobina (LV) . . . . 202 A 4
Gröbming (A) . . . . 96 D 3
Grocka (SRB) . . . . 140 D 4
Gröditz (D) . . . . 86 D 3
Grodków (PL) . . . . 121 F 5
Grodzisk
Mazowiecki (PL) . . . . . 122 D 1
Grodzisk
Wielkopolski (PL) . . . . 121 E 1
Groenlo (NL) . . . . 77 G 5
Grohotno (BG) . . . . 162 B 1
Groitzsch (D) . . . . 86 B 4
Groix (F) . . . . 42 C 3
Grójec (PL) . . . . 122 D 2
Grömitz (D) . . . . 82 C 3
Gromnik (PL) . . . . 125 H 2
Gronau (D) . . . . 84 C 2
Grong (N) . . . . 183 E 3
Grönhögen (S) . . . . 199 H 2
Gröningen (D) . . . . 86 A 2
Groningen (NL) . . . . 77 G 2
Grönskåra (S) . . . . 197 G 2
Gropello Cairoli (I) . . . . 101 E 5
Groscavallo (I) . . . . 100 B 4
Grosio (I) . . . . 101 G 2
Groß-Enzersdorf (A) . . . . 97 H 1
Groß-Gerau (D) . . . . 89 E 2
Groß Gerungs (A) . . . . . . 97 E 1
Groß Reken (D) . . . . 84 C 3
Groß Schönebeck (D) . . 83 F 5
Groß-Siegharts (A) . . . . . 92 C 5
Groß-Umstadt (D) . . . . . 89 F 2
Großbreitenbach (D) . . . 86 A 5
Großenhain (D) . . . . 86 D 4
Großenkneten (D) . . . . . .81 H 5
Grosseto (I) . . . . 106 C 5
Großhabersdorf (D) . . . . 89 H 3
Großheubach (D) . . . . . . 89 F 2

Großpetersdorf (A) . . . . . 97 G 3
Großraming (A) . . . . 97 E 2
Großräschen (D) . . . . . . 87 E 3
Großröhrsdorf (D) . . . . . . 87 E 4
Großschönau (D) . . . . . . 87 F 4
Großweil (D) . . . . 95 F 3
Großwitzeetze (D) . . . . . 82 C 5
Grostenquin (F) . . . . .41 F 5
Grosuplje (SLO) . . . . . . 134 C 2
Grotli (N) . . . . 188 D 2
Grötlingbo (S) . . . . 197 G 4
Grottaglie (I) . . . . .111 F 4
Grottaminarda (I) . . . . . .110 B 3
Grottammare (I) . . . . 107 H 5
Grotteria (I) . . . . .113 C 4
Grövelsjön (S) . . . . 189 G 2
Grovfjord (N) . . . . .176 A 5
Grozdjovo (BG) . . . . 157 F 3
Grubišno Polje (HR) . . . 135 G 3
Gruda (HR) . . . . 139 E 4
Grude (BIH) . . . . 138 D 2
Grudusk (PL) . . . . .118 D 4
Grudziądz (PL) . . . . .117 H 4
Gruia (RO) . . . . 150 D 4
Gruissan (F) . . . . 54 A 4
Gruiu (RO) . . . . 152 B 3
Grums (S) . . . . 195 G 1
Grünau im Almtal (A) . . . 96 D 2
Grünberg (D) . . . . 85 F 5
Grünburg (A) . . . . 96 D 2
Grundarfjörður (IS) . . . . 178 A 2
Grundforsen (S) . . . . . . 189 G 3
Grundlsee (A) . . . . 96 D 3
Grundsund (S) . . . . 195 F 3
Grundtjärn (S) . . . . 184 B 5
Grünstadt (D) . . . . 89 E 3
Grünwald (D) . . . . 95 G 2
Grupčin (MK) . . . . 143 E 5
Gruta (PL) . . . . .117 H 4
Grūtas (LT) . . . . 205 E 5
Grütas (LT) . . . . 205 E 5
Gruyères (CH) . . . . 98 C 3
Gruž (SRB) . . . . 142 D 1
Gumiel de Izán (E) . . . . . 58 B 4
Gruzdžiai (LT) . . . . 204 D 1
Grybów (PL) . . . . 125 H 2
Grycksbo (S) . . . . 190 A 4
Gryfice (PL) . . . . .116 C 3
Gryfino (PL) . . . . .116 B 4
Gryfów Śląski (PL) . . . . . 120 C 4
Gryllefjord
(Torsken) (N) . . . . . . .176 A 4
Grythyttan (S) . . . . 195 H 1
Grza (SRB) . . . . 143 F 1
Gstaad (CH) . . . . 98 C 4
Gstadt am Chiemsee (D). 95 H 2
Guadahortuna (E) . . . . . . 71 E 5
Guadalajara (E) . . . . 64 C 2
Guadalaviar (E) . . . . 65 F 2
Guadalcanal (E) . . . . 69 G 3
Guadalupe (E) . . . . 63 H 5
Guadarrama (E) . . . . 64 B 2
Guadassuar (E) . . . . 65 H 5
Guadiaro (E) . . . . .74 C 4
Guadix (E) . . . . 71 E 5
Gualdo Tadino (I) . . . . . 107 F 4
Guarda (P) . . . . 62 D 3
Guardamar
del Segura (E) . . . . . . 73 F 3
Guardia Sanframondi (I). 109 H 4
Guardiagrele (I) . . . . 109 G 2
Guardo (E) . . . . 58 A 2
Guareña (E) . . . . 69 G 2
Guarromán (E) . . . . 70 D 3
Guastalla (I) . . . . 101 G 5
Gubbio (I) . . . . 107 F 4
Guben (D) . . . . 87 F 2
Guberevac (SRB) . . . . . 142 D 1
Gubin (PL) . . . . 120 B 2
Guča (SRB) . . . . 139 H 1
Guča Gora (BIH) . . . . . . 137 F 4
Gudavac (BIH) . . . . 135 E 5
Gudhjem (DK) . . . . 199 G 4
Gudow (D) . . . . 82 C 4
Gudvangen (N) . . . . 188 C 3
Gudžiūnai (LT) . . . . 205 E 2
Guebwiller (F) . . . . .47 G 3
Guéméné-Penfao (F) . . . 43 F 3
Guémené-sur-Scorff (F) . 42 D 2

Güeñes (E) . . . . 58 C 1
Guer (F) . . . . 43 E 3
Guérande (F) . . . . 43 E 4
Guéret (F) . . . . 49 G 2
Guérigny (F) . . . . 45 G 5
Guerri de la Sal (E) . . . . 60 B 2
Guéthary (F) . . . . 52 A 3
Gueugnon (F) . . . . 50 B 1
Gugești (RO) . . . . 152 D 1
Güglingen (D) . . . . 89 F 4
Guglionesi (I) . . . . 109 H 3
Guía de Isora (E) . . . . . .67 F 5
Guichen (F) . . . . 43 F 3
Guidonia (I) . . . . 109 E 2
Guignes (F) . . . . 45 F 1
Guijo de Granadilla (E) . . 63 F 4
Guijuelo (E) . . . . 63 G 3
Guildford (GB) . . . . 36 C 4
Guillaumes (F) . . . . 55 G 1
Guillena (E) . . . . 69 G 5
Guillestre (F) . . . . .51 G 5
Guillon (F) . . . . 45 H 4
Guilvinec (F) . . . . 42 B 3
Güímar (E) . . . . .67 F 5
Guimarães (P) . . . . 62 C 1
Guimiliau (F) . . . . 42 C 1
Guînes (F) . . . . 39 G 1
Guingamp (F) . . . . 42 D 1
Guipavas (F) . . . . 42 B 1
Guisborough (GB) . . . . .31 H 5
Guiscard (F) . . . . 40 A 4
Guise (F) . . . . 40 B 3
Guissona (E) . . . . 60 C 3
Guist (GB) . . . . 33 H 4
Guîtres (F) . . . . 48 C 4
Gujan-Mestras (F) . . . . . 48 B 5
Gulbene (LV) . . . . 203 G 2
Guljanci / Гуляици (BG) . 151 G 5
Gullfoss (IS) . . . . 178 B 3
Gullspång (S) . . . . 195 H 2
Gummersbach (D) . . . . . 84 D 4
Gundelfingen
an der Donau (D) . . . . 89 H 5
Gundelsheim (D) . . . . . . 89 F 3
Gunnarn (S) . . . . 184 C 3
Gunnarsbyn (S) . . . . . . 185 E 1
Gunnarskog (S) . . . . . . 189 G 5
Gunten (A) . . . . 98 B 3
Günterode (D) . . . . 85 G 4
Guntín de Pallares (E) . . 56 D 3
Günzburg (D) . . . . 89 H 5
Gunzenhausen (D) . . . . 89 H 4
Gura Humorului (RO) . . 148 B 2
Gura Teghii (RO) . . . . . 152 C 1
Gurahonţ (RO) . . . . 146 D 5
Gurk (A) . . . . 96 D 4
Gurkovo (BG) . . . . 159 F 2
Gurrea de Gállego (E) . . 59 G 4
Gusev (RUS) . . . . .6 B 4
Gusinje (MNE) . . . . 139 H 4
Guspini (I) . . . . .112 B 4
Güssing (A) . . . . 97 G 4
Güstrow (D) . . . . 83 E 3
Gutcher (GB) . . . . 27 G 1
Gutenstein (A) . . . . 97 G 2
Gütersloh (D) . . . . 85 E 2
Gutkowo (PL) . . . . .118 D 3
Gützkow (D) . . . . 83 F 3
Guyhirn (GB) . . . . 33 G 4
Guzet-Neige (F) . . . . 53 F 4
Gvardejsk (RUS) . . . . . . .6 B 4
Gvarv (N) . . . . 194 D 1
Gvozd (HR) . . . . 135 E 4
Gvozd (MNE) . . . . 139 F 3
Gy (F) . . . . .47 E 4
Gyál (H) . . . . 129 F 2
Gyékényes (H) . . . . 128 B 4
Gymnó (GR) . . . . 165 H 3
Gyoma (H) . . . . 129 H 3
Gyömrő (H) . . . . 129 F 2
Gyöngyös (H) . . . . 129 G 1
Gyönk (H) . . . . 129 E 4
Győr (H) . . . . 128 C 1
Gypsou (CY) . . . . 175 E 3

Gysinge (S) . . . . 190 B 5
Gýtheio / Γύθειο (GR) . . 168 D 4
Gyula (H) . . . . 131 E 4
Gyulafirátót (H) . . . . 128 D 2
Gyulakeszi (H) . . . . 128 C 3
Gyulavári (H) . . . . 131 E 4

H

Haag (A) . . . . 97 E 2
Haag am Hausruck (A) . . 96 C 2
Haag in Oberbayern (D) . 95 H 2
Haage (EST) . . . . 201 F 3
Haaksbergen (NL) . . . . . 77 G 5
Haamstede (NL) . . . . . . .76 C 5
Haapajärvi (FIN) . . . . . . 185 H 4
Haapakoski (FIN) . . . . . 193 F 1
Haapamäki (FIN) . . . . . 185 H 5
Haapamäki (FIN) . . . . . 191 G 2
Haapavesi (FIN) . . . . . . 185 H 4
Haapsalu (EST) . . . . . . 200 C 2
Haar (D) . . . . 95 G 2
Haarby (DK) . . . . 198 C 4
Haaren (D) . . . . 85 E 3
Haarlem (NL) . . . . .76 D 4
Habartice (CZ) . . . . 87 F 4
Habay-la-Neuve (B) . . . . 79 E 5
Habo (S) . . . . 195 H 3
Habovka (SK) . . . . 132 D 2
Håbu (N) . . . . 195 E 1
Hachenburg (D) . . . . 84 D 5
Hachmühlen (D) . . . . 85 F 2
Hackås (S) . . . . 189 H 1
Hadamar (D) . . . . 88 D 1
Haddington (GB) . . . . . . .31 E 1
Haddon Hall (GB) . . . . . . 33 E 3
Hadersdorf
am Kamp (A) . . . . 97 F 1
Haderslev (DK) . . . . 198 B 4
Hadjač (UA) . . . . .7 G 5
Hadleigh (GB) . . . . 33 H 5
Hadmersleben (D) . . . . . 86 A 2
Hadsten (DK) . . . . 194 D 5
Hadsund (DK) . . . . 194 D 5
Hadžići (BIH) . . . . 137 G 5
Hadžidimovo (BG) . . . . 161 H 1
Hægebostad (N) . . . . . . 194 C 2
Hægeland (N) . . . . 194 C 2
Haganj (HR) . . . . 135 F 3
Hagen (D) . . . . 84 D 4
Hagen
im Bremischen (D) . . .81 F 4
Hagenow (D) . . . . 82 C 4
Hagetmau (F) . . . . 52 C 2
Hagfors (S) . . . . 189 H 5
Häggdånger (S) . . . . . . 190 C 1
Haggenås (S) . . . . 183 G 5
Hagondange (F) . . . . . . .41 E 4
Haguenau (F) . . . . .41 H 5
Hahnbach (D) . . . . .91 E 1
Haigerloch (D) . . . . 89 E 5
Hailsham (GB) . . . . 36 D 5
Hailuoto / Karlö (FIN) . . 185 G 3
Hainburg
an der Donau (A) . . . . 97 H 1
Hainfeld (A) . . . . 97 F 2
Hainichen (D) . . . . 86 D 4
Hajdúböszörmény (H) . .131 E 1
Hajdučica (SRB) . . . . . .141 E 3
Hajdúdorog (H) . . . . . . .131 E 1
Hajdúhadház (H) . . . . . .131 E 1
Hajdúnánás (H) . . . . . . .131 E 1
Hajdúsámson (H) . . . . . .131 E 1
Hajdúszoboszló (H) . . . .131 E 2
Hajnówka (PL) . . . . .119 H 5
Hajós (H) . . . . 129 F 4
Hajredin (BG) . . . . 154 D 2
Hajsyn (UA) . . . . .13 F 2
Hajvoron (UA) . . . . .13 E 2
Hakkas (S) . . . . 180 B 5
Häkkilä (FIN) . . . . 191 H 1
Hălăuceşti (RO) . . . . . . 148 C 3
Halbe (D) . . . . 86 D 2
Halberstadt (D) . . . . 86 A 2
Halden (N) . . . . 195 F 1
Haldensleben (D) . . . . . . 86 A 2
Halesowen (GB) . . . . 32 D 5

A
B
C
D
E
F
G
H
I
J
K
L
M
N
O
P
Q
R
S
T
U
V
W
X
Y
Z

Halesworth (GB) .... 37 E 2
Halhjem (N) .... 188 B 4
Halifax (GB) .... 32 D 2
Halikko (FIN) .... 191 G 4
Haljala (EST) .... 201 F 1
Halju (S) .... 180 C 3
Hall in Tirol (A) .... 95 G 4
Halle (B) .... 78 C 2
Halle (D) .... 86 B 3
Halle (Saale) (D) .... 85 E 2
Halle-Neustadt (D) ...... 86 B 3
Hällefors (S) .... 189 H 5
Hälleforsnäs (S) .... 197 E 1
Hallein (A) .... 96 B 3
Hällekis (S) .... 195 G 2
Hallenberg (D) .... 85 E 4
Hallencourt (F) .... 39 G 3
Hällesjö (S) .... 190 B 1
Hällevadsholm (S) ...... 195 F 2
Hällnäs (S) .... 184 D 4
Hallörmsstaður (IS) .... 178 D 2
Hallsberg (S) .... 196 D 1
Hallstadt (D) .... 89 H 2
Hallstahammar (S) ...... 197 E 1
Hallstatt (A) .... 96 C 3
Hallstavik (S) .... 190 C 5
Halluin (F) .... 40 A 1
Halmeu (RO) .... 147 E 1
Halmstad (S) .... 195 G 5
Hals (DK) .... 195 E 4
Halsa (N) .... 182 B 5
Hälsingtuna (S) .... 190 B 3
Halsskov (DK) .... 198 D 4
Halstead (GB) .... 36 D 3
Halsteren (NL) .... 78 C 1
Halsua (FIN) .... 185 G 5
Haltdålen (N) .... 189 F 1
Haltern am See (D) ...... 84 C 3
Halver (D) .... 84 D 4
Ham (F) .... 40 A 4
Hamar (N) .... 189 F 4
Hamarøy (N) .... 179 G 3
Hamburg (D) .... 81 H 4
Hambye, abbaye de (F) .. 38 C 5
Hamdorf (D) .... 81 H 2
Hämeenkyrö (FIN) ...... 191 G 3
Hämeenlinna (FIN) ..... 191 H 3
Hämelerwald (D) .... 85 G 1
Hameln (D) .... 85 F 2
Hamersleben (D) .... 86 A 2
Hamilton (GB) .... 30 D 2
Hamina (FIN) .... 193 F 4
Hamm (D) .... 84 D 3
Hammarland (FIN) ...... 190 D 5
Hammarstrand (S) ...... 190 B 1
Hammaslahti (FIN) ..... 193 H 1
Hammel (DK) .... 194 D 5
Hammelburg (D) .... 89 G 1
Hammerdal (S) .... 183 G 5
Hammerfest (N) .... 176 D 2
Hamningberg (N) .... 177 H 2
Hamoir (B) .... 79 E 3
Hamra (S) .... 190 A 3
Hamra national park (S) . 190 A 2
Hamre (N) .... 194 C 2
Hamzali (MK) .... 145 H 1
Hamzići (BIH) .... 138 D 2
Han Asparuhovo (BG) ... 159 F 2
Han-Pijesak (BIH) ...... 137 H 5
Han-sur-Lesse (B) .... 78 D 4
Hanau (D) .... 89 F 1
Handlová (SK) .... 132 C 3
Hanerau-
  Hademarschen (D) ..... 81 G 3
Hangö / Hanko (FIN) ... 191 G 5
Hangu (RO) .... 148 B 3
Hani i Hotit (AL) .... 142 B 5
Hankamäki (FIN) .... 187 F 5
Hankasalmen as (FIN) .. 193 E 1
Hankasalmi (FIN) .... 193 E 1
Hankensbüttel (D) ...... 85 H 1
Hanko / Hangö (FIN) ... 191 G 5
Hann-Münden (D) ...... 85 G 4
Hannover (D) .... 85 G 1
Hannut (B) .... 78 D 3
Hansnes (N) .... 176 B 3
Hanstedt (D) .... 81 H 5

Hanstholm (DK) .... 194 C 4
Hanušovce
  nad Topľou (SK) ..... 133 G 2
Hanušovice (CZ) .... 93 E 2
Haparanda (S) .... 185 G 1
Haradok (BY) .... 7 E 3
Harads (S) .... 185 E 1
Haraldshaugen (N) ..... 188 A 5
Harasiuki (PL) .... 123 F 5
Harburg (D) .... 81 H 4
Harburg (Schwaben) (D) . 89 H 4
Hardbakke (N) .... 188 A 3
Hardegg (A) .... 92 D 5
Hardegsen (D) .... 85 G 3
Hardelot-Plage (F) ...... 39 G 2
Hardenberg (NL) .... 77 G 4
Harderwijk (NL) .... 77 E 4
Hardeshøj (DK) .... 198 C 4
Hardheim (D) .... 89 F 2
Hardwick Hall (GB) .... 33 E 3
Hareid (N) .... 188 C 1
Harelbeke (B) .... 78 B 2
Haren (D) .... 80 D 5
Haren (NL) .... 77 G 2
Harewood (GB) .... 33 E 2
Haría (E) .... 67 H 4
Harjavalta (FIN) .... 191 F 3
Harjunpää (FIN) .... 191 F 3
Härkmeri (FIN) .... 191 E 2
Härkány (H) .... 128 D 5
Hårlau (RO) .... 148 C 2
Hårlec (BG) .... 151 F 5
Harlech (GB) .... 32 A 4
Harlesiel (D) .... 81 E 3
Harleston (GB) .... 37 E 2
Harlingen / Harns (NL) .. 77 E 2
Harlow (GB) .... 36 C 3
Harmånger (S) .... 190 B 2
Harmanli /
  Хармани (BG) ...... 163 E 1
Härnösand (S) .... 190 C 1
Harns / Harlingen (NL) .. 77 E 2
Haro (E) .... 58 D 3
Harold Hillier
  Gardens (GB) .... 35 G 3
Haroldswick (GB) .... 27 G 1
Háromfa (H) .... 128 C 5
Haroué (F) .... 47 E 2
Harøysund (N) .... 182 A 5
Harpenden (GB) .... 36 C 3
Harplinge (S) .... 195 G 5
Harpstedt (D) .... 81 F 5
Harrachov (CZ) .... 87 G 5
Harrogate (GB) .... 33 E 1
Härryda (S) .... 195 F 3
Harsefeld (D) .... 81 H 4
Hårsești (RO) .... 151 H 4
Hârşova (RO) .... 153 E 3
Harsprånget (S) .... 180 A 5
Harstad (N) .... 179 G 2
Harsvik (N) .... 182 D 4
Harta (H) .... 129 F 3
Hartberg (A) .... 97 G 3
Hartha (D) .... 86 C 4
Hârtiești (RO) .... 151 H 2
Hartlepool (GB) .... 31 G 4
Hartmannsdorf (D) ..... 86 C 5
Hartola (FIN) .... 193 E 2
Harwich (GB) .... 37 E 3
Harzgerode (D) .... 86 A 3
Haselünne (D) .... 84 D 1
Haskovo / Хасково (BG) . 162 D 1
Haslach an der Mühl (A) . 96 D 1
Haslach im Kinzigtal (D) . 88 D 5
Hasle (DK) .... 199 G 4
Haslemere (GB) .... 35 H 3
Haslev (DK) .... 199 E 4
Haßfurt (D) .... 89 H 2
Hässleholm (S) .... 199 F 3
Hastière-Lavaux (B) ..... 78 D 4
Hastings (GB) .... 36 D 5
Hasvik (N) .... 176 C 2
Haté (CZ) .... 92 D 5

Haţeg (RO) .... 151 E 1
Hatfield (GB) .... 36 C 3
Hatherleigh (GB) .... 34 D 3
Hattem (NL) .... 77 F 4
Hattfjelldal (N) .... 183 F 2
Hattingen (D) .... 84 C 3
Hattula (FIN) .... 191 G 3
Hattuvaara (FIN) .... 187 H 5
Hattuvaara (FIN) .... 187 H 5
Hatvan (H) .... 129 G 1
Hatvik (N) .... 188 B 4
Haubourdin (F) .... 40 A 2
Hauge (N) .... 194 B 2
Haugesund (N) .... 188 A 5
Hauho (FIN) .... 191 H 3
Haukeligrend (N) .... 188 C 5
Haukipudas (FIN) ...... 185 H 2
Haukivuori (FIN) .... 193 F 2
Haunstetten (D) .... 95 F 2
Haus (A) .... 96 B 3
Hausach (D) .... 88 D 5
Hausham (D) .... 95 G 3
Hausjärvi (FIN) .... 191 H 4
Haut-Kœnigsbourg,
  château du (F) .... 47 G 2
Hautajärvi (FIN) .... 181 G 5
Hautefort (F) .... 49 F 4
Hauterives (F) .... 50 D 4
Hauteville-Lompnes (F) .. 51 E 2
Hautmont (F) .... 40 B 2
Havant (GB) .... 35 G 4
Havârna (RO) .... 148 C 1
Havelange (B) .... 78 D 3
Havelberg (D) .... 82 D 5
Haverfordwest /
  Hwlffordd (GB) ...... 25 H 5
Haverhill (GB) .... 33 H 5
Haverö (S) .... 190 A 2
Havířov (CZ) .... 93 G 3
Havlíčkův Brod (CZ) .... 92 C 3
Havneby (DK) .... 198 B 4
Havøysund (N) .... 177 E 1
Havraň (CZ) .... 91 H 2
Hawes (GB) .... 31 F 5
Hawick (GB) .... 31 E 3
Hawkhurst (GB) .... 36 D 5
Hay-on-Wye (GB) .... 35 E 1
Hayange (F) .... 41 E 4
Hayle (GB) .... 34 B 5
Haywards Heath (GB) ... 36 C 5
Hazebrouck (F) .... 39 H 1
Headford (IRL) .... 22 C 5
Heanor (GB) .... 33 E 4
Héas (F) .... 52 D 4
Heathfield (GB) .... 36 D 5
Heby (S) .... 190 B 5
Hechingen (D) .... 89 F 5
Hecho (E) .... 59 G 2
Hechtel (B) .... 79 E 2
Hecklingen (D) .... 86 A 3
Hedal (N) .... 188 D 4
Heddal (N) .... 188 D 5
Hédé-Bazouges (F) ..... 43 F 2
Hede (S) .... 189 H 1
Hedemora (S) .... 190 A 5
Hedenäset (S) .... 185 F 1
Hédervár (H) .... 128 C 1
Hedeviken (S) .... 189 H 1
Hedon (GB) .... 33 G 2
Heemstede (NL) .... 76 D 4
Heerde (NL) .... 77 F 4
Heerenveen (NL) .... 77 F 3
Heerlen (NL) .... 79 F 2
Heeze (NL) .... 79 E 1
Hegge (N) .... 188 D 3
Hegra (N) .... 182 D 5
Hegyeshalom (H) ...... 128 C 1
Hegyhátsál (H) .... 128 B 3
Heia (N) .... 176 B 4
Heide (D) .... 81 G 2
Heidelberg (D) .... 89 E 3
Heidenau (D) .... 87 E 4
Heidenheim
  an der Brenz (D) ...... 89 G 5
Heidenreichstein (A) .... 92 C 5
Heikendorf (D) .... 81 H 2
Heikkila (FIN) .... 187 F 1

Heilbronn (D) .... 89 F 3
Heiligenberg (D) .... 94 C 3
Heiligenblut (A) .... 96 B 4
Heiligenhafen (D) .... 82 C 2
Heiligenkirchen (D) ..... 85 F 2
Heiligenkreuz
  im Lafnitztal (A) ...... 97 G 4
Heiligenstadt (D) .... 85 G 4
Heilsbronn (D) .... 89 H 3
Heimari (FIN) .... 193 F 2
Heimdal (N) .... 182 D 5
Heimertingen (D) .... 95 E 2
Heinävaara (FIN) ...... 193 H 1
Heinävesi (FIN) .... 193 G 1
Heinola (FIN) .... 193 E 3
Heinolan mlk (FIN) ..... 193 E 3
Heinsberg (D) .... 84 B 4
Heist (B) .... 78 B 1
Heist-
  op-den-Berg (B) ...... 78 D 2
Hel (PL) .... 117 H 1
Heldburg (D) .... 89 H 1
Heldrungen (D) .... 86 A 4
Helechal (E) .... 69 H 2
Helensburgh (GB) .... 30 C 1
Hella (IS) .... 178 B 3
Helle (N) .... 188 C 3
Helle (N) .... 194 C 1
Hellendoorn (NL) .... 77 F 4
Hellesylt (N) .... 188 C 1
Hellevoetsluis (NL) ...... 76 C 5
Hellín (E) .... 71 H 2
Hellvik (N) .... 194 B 2
Helmbrechts (D) .... 91 F 2
Helmond (NL) .... 79 E 1
Helmsdale (GB) .... 26 B 5
Helmsley (GB) .... 31 H 5
Helmstadt (D) .... 89 G 2
Helmstedt (D) .... 86 A 2
Helsa (D) .... 85 G 4
Helshan (AL) .... 142 D 5
Helsinborg (S) .... 199 E 3
Helsinge (DK) .... 199 E 3
Helsingfors /
  Helsinki (FIN) .... 191 H 5
Helsingør (DK) .... 199 E 3
Helsinki /
  Helsingfors (FIN) .... 191 H 5
Helston (GB) .... 34 B 5
Heltermaa (EST) .... 200 C 2
Hemau (D) .... 91 F 5
Hemavan (S) .... 183 G 1
Hemel Hempstead (GB) . 36 C 3
Hemer (D) .... 84 D 4
Hemmoor (D) .... 81 G 4
Hemnes (N) .... 189 F 5
Hemnesberget (N) ..... 183 F 1
Hemsedal (N) .... 188 D 3
Hendaye (F) .... 52 A 3
Hengelo (NL) .... 77 G 4
Hengersberg (D) .... 91 H 5
Hénin-Beaumont (F) .... 40 A 2
Henley (GB) .... 33 E 5
Henley-on-Thames (GB). 35 H 2
Henneberg (D) .... 89 H 1
Hennebont (F) .... 42 D 3
Hennef (D) .... 84 C 5
Hennigsdorf (D) .... 86 D 1
Henningsvær (N) .... 179 F 3
Henrichemont (F) .... 45 F 4
Henstedt-Ulzburg (D) ... 81 H 3
Henstridge (GB) .... 38 A 1
Hepoköngäs (FIN) ..... 187 F 3
Heppenheim (D) .... 89 E 2
Heraclea (MK) .... 145 F 2
Herbault (F) .... 44 D 4
Herbertingen (D) .... 94 D 2
Herbignac (F) .... 43 E 4
Herbolzheim (D) .... 88 D 5
Herborn (D) .... 89 E 5
Herbrechtingen (D) ..... 89 G 5
Herbstein (D) .... 85 F 5
Herceg Novi (MNE) .... 139 E 4
Hercegovac (HR) ...... 135 F 3
Hercegovacka
  Goleša (SRB) .... 139 G 2
Hercegszántó (H) ...... 129 E 5
Higuera de la Sierra (E) . 69 F 4

Hereford (GB) .... 35 F 1
Herencia (E) .... 64 C 5
Herend (H) .... 128 D 2
Herentals (B) .... 78 D 2
Herford (D) .... 85 E 2
Héricourt (F) .... 47 F 3
Heringsdorf (D) .... 83 G 3
Herisau (CH) .... 99 F 2
Hérisson (F) .... 49 H 1
Hérisson,
  cascades du (F) .... 51 E 1
Herk-de-Stad (B) .... 78 D 2
Herľany (SK) .... 133 G 3
Herleshausen (D) .... 85 G 4
Hermagor (A) .... 96 C 5
Hermannsburg (D) ...... 81 H 5
Hermansverk (N) ...... 188 C 3
Heřmanův Městec (CZ). 92 C 3
Herment (F) .... 49 H 3
Hermeskeil (D) .... 88 C 2
Hermigua (E) .... 67 F 5
Hermsdorf (D) .... 86 B 5
Hernádnémeti (H) ..... 126 D 5
Hernani (E) .... 59 E 1
Hernansancho (E) ...... 64 A 2
Herne (D) .... 84 C 3
Herne Bay (GB) .... 37 E 4
Herning (DK) .... 194 C 5
Heroldsberg (D) .... 91 E 4
Herrala (FIN) .... 191 H 4
Herre (N) .... 194 D 1
Herrenberg (D) .... 89 F 5
Herrenchiemsee (D) .... 95 H 2
Herrera (E) .... 70 B 5
Herrera de Alcántara (E). 62 D 5
Herrera
  de los Navarros (E) ... 65 G 1
Herrera de Pisuerga (E) . 58 A 3
Herrera del Duque (E) .. 70 B 1
Herreruela (E) .... 63 E 5
Herrestad (S) .... 195 F 2
Herrieden (D) .... 89 H 3
Herrljunga (S) .... 195 G 3
Herrnburg (D) .... 82 C 3
Herrnhut (D) .... 87 F 4
Herrsching
  am Ammersee (D) .... 95 F 2
Herrskog (S) .... 190 C 1
Hersbruck (D) .... 91 E 4
Herselt (B) .... 78 D 2
Herstal (B) .... 79 E 3
Herstedt (D) .... 86 A 3
Herten (D) .... 84 C 3
Hertford (GB) .... 36 C 3
Hervás (E) .... 63 G 3
Herzberg (D) .... 86 D 3
Herzberg am Harz (D) .. 85 H 3
Herzogenaurach (D) .... 89 H 3
Herzsprung (D) .... 83 E 5
Hesdin (F) .... 39 G 2
Hesel (D) .... 81 E 4
Hesseng (N) .... 177 H 3
Hessisch Lichtenau (D). 85 G 4
Hessisch Oldendorf (D) . 85 F 2
Hetekylä (FIN) .... 185 H 2
Hetin (SRB) .... 140 D 2
Hettange-Grande (F).... 41 E 4
Hettstedt (D) .... 86 A 3
Heubach (D) .... 89 G 4
Heuchin (F) .... 39 H 2
Heves (H) .... 129 G 1
Hévíz (H) .... 128 C 2
Hevlín (CZ) .... 92 D 5
Hexham (GB) .... 31 F 4
Heyrieux (F) .... 50 D 3
Heysham (GB) .... 32 C 1
Hidcote
  Manor Garden (GB) ... 35 G 1
Hidișelu de Sus (RO) .. 146 C 3
Hieflau (A) .... 97 E 3
Hiersac (F) .... 48 D 3
Hietaniemi (FIN) ...... 181 G 4
High Wycombe (GB) .... 35 H 2
Higham Ferrers (GB) ... 33 F 5
Higuera
  de la Serena (E) ...... 69 G 2

Higuera de Vargas (E) ... 69 E 2
Higuera la Real (E) ...... 69 F 3
Higueruela (E) .... 71 H 1
Híjar (E) .... 65 H 1
Hilchenbach (D) .... 85 E 4
Hildburghausen (D) ..... 89 H 1
Hilden (D) .... 84 C 4
Hilders (D) .... 85 G 5
Hildesheim (D) .... 85 G 2
Hillegom (NL) .... 76 D 4
Hillerød (DK) .... 199 E 3
Hillesøy (N) .... 176 A 4
Hillswick (GB) .... 27 D 3
Hilpoltstein (D) .... 91 E 5
Hiltula (FIN) .... 193 G 2
Hilvarenbeek (NL) ...... 78 D 1
Hilversum (NL) .... 77 E 4
Himanka (FIN) .... 185 G 4
Hîncești (MD) .... 13 F 3
Hinckley (GB) .... 33 E 5
Hindhead (GB) .... 35 H 3
Hinojares (E) .... 71 F 4
Hinojosa de Duero (E).. 63 E 2
Hinojosa del Duque (E).. 69 H 2
Hinova (RO) .... 150 D 3
Hintersee (D) .... 83 G 4
Hinterstoder (A) .... 96 D 3
Hintertux (A) .... 95 G 4
Hinterweidenthal (D) ... 88 D 3
Hirschau (D) .... 91 F 4
Hirschberg (D) .... 91 F 2
Hirschegg (A) .... 95 E 4
Hirsingue (F) .... 47 G 3
Hirson (F) .... 40 B 3
Hirtshals (DK) .... 195 E 4
Hirvasvaara (FIN) ..... 181 G 5
Hirvensalmi (FIN) ..... 193 E 2
Hirvilahti (FIN) .... 187 F 5
Hirwaun (GB) .... 35 E 1
Hisarja (BG) .... 158 D 2
Histria (RO) .... 153 F 3
Hitchin (GB) .... 36 C 3
Hitrino (BG) .... 157 E 2
Hitzacker (D) .... 82 C 5
Hjartdal (N) .... 188 D 5
Hjellestad (N) .... 188 B 4
Hjelmeland (N) .... 194 B 1
Hjerkinn (N) .... 189 E 2
Hjo (S) .... 195 H 3
Hjørring (DK) .... 195 E 4
Hlebine (HR) .... 135 F 2
Hlinsko (CZ) .... 92 D 3
Hljabovo (BG) .... 159 G 3
Hlobyne (UA) .... 13 G 1
Hlohovec (SK) .... 132 B 3
Hlubočky (CZ) .... 93 F 3
Hluboká
  nad Vltavou (CZ) .... 92 B 3
Hluchiv (UA) .... 7 G 3
Hlučín (CZ) .... 93 G 2
Hluk (CZ) .... 93 F 5
Hlýbokaje (BY) .... 6 D 4
Hnúšťa (SK) .... 133 E 3
Hobro (DK) .... 194 D 5
Höchberg (D) .... 89 G 2
Hochdorf (CH) .... 99 E 2
Hochfelden (F) .... 41 E 5
Hochspeyer (D) .... 88 D 3
Höchst
  im Odenwald (D) ..... 89 F 2
Höchstadt
  an der Aisch (D) ...... 89 H 2
Höchstädt
  an der Donau (D) ..... 89 H 5
Hockenheim (D) .... 89 E 3
Hoddesdon (GB) .... 36 C 3
Hodenhagen (D) .... 85 G 1
Hódmezővásárhely (H). 129 H 4
Hodnanes (N) .... 188 B 4
Hodnet (D) .... 32 C 4
Hodonín (CZ) .... 93 E 5
Hodoš (SLO) .... 135 E 1
Hodovo (BIH) .... 138 D 3
Hoedekenskerke (NL) .. 78 C 1
Hoek van Holland (NL).. 76 C 5
Hoemsbu (N) .... 188 D 1
Hof (D) .... 91 F 2

Hofgeismar *(D)* .... 85 F 3
Hofheim
   in Unterfranken *(D)* ... 89 H 1
Hofles *(N)* .... 183 E 3
Höfn/Hornafirði *(IS)* ... 178 D 3
Hofolding *(D)* .... 95 G 2
Hofors *(S)* .... 190 B 4
Hofsós *(IS)* .... 178 B 1
Höganäs *(S)* .... 199 E 2
Høgebru *(N)* .... 188 C 2
Hoghilag *(RO)* .... 147 G 5
Höglekardalen *(S)*. ..... 183 F 5
Högsäter *(S)* .... 195 F 2
Högsby *(S)* .... 197 E 4
Hohen-Landin *(D)* ...... 83 G 5
Hohenau
   an der March *(A)* ..... 93 E 5
Hohenberg *(A)*. .... 97 F 2
Hohenems *(A)* .... 94 D 4
Hohengandern *(D)* ..... 85 G 4
Hohenlimburg *(D)* ...... 84 D 4
Hohenlinden *(D)* .... 95 G 2
Hohenlockstedt *(D)*....81 H 3
Hohenmölsen *(D)*...... 86 B 4
Hohenpeißenberg *(D)* .. 95 F 3
Hohenseeden *(D)* ...... 86 B 2
Hohenstein-Ernstthal *(D)*. 86 C 5
Hohentauern *(A)*. .... 97 E 3
Hohenwestedt *(D)* ....81 H 3
Hohenzollern (D) .... 89 F 5
Højer *(DK)* .... 198 B 4
Hokksund *(N)* .... 189 E 5
Hokstad *(N)*............ 182 D 4
Hol *(N)* .... 188 D 4
Hola Prystan' *(UA)* .....13 G 3
Holbæk *(DK)* .... 198 D 3
Holbeach *(GB)* .... 33 G 2
Holdorf *(D)* .... 85 E 1
Holešov *(CZ)* .... 93 F 4
Holguera *(E)* .... 63 F 4
Holíč *(SK)* .... 132 A 3
Holice *(CZ)*............. 92 D 2
Höljäkkä *(FIN)*.......... 187 G 4
Höljes *(S)* .... 189 G 4
Holkham Hall (GB)..... 33 H 4
Hollabrunn *(A)* .... 97 G 1
Hollád *(H)*. .... 128 C 4
Høllen *(N)* .... 194 B 2
Hollenstedt *(D)* ....81 H 4
Hollfeld *(D)* ....91 E 3
Hollingsholm *(N)*. ...... 182 A 5
Hollola *(FIN)* .... 191 H 3
Hollum *(NL)*. .... 77 E 3
Hollywood *(IRL)* .... 25 F 2
Holm *(N)*. .... 183 E 2
Holm *(S)* .... 190 B 1
Hólmavik *(IS)* .... 178 A 1
Holmec *(SLO)* .... 134 C 1
Holmen *(N)* .... 189 E 4
Holmestrand *(N)* .... 195 E 1
Holmfirth *(GB)* .... 33 E 2
Holmön *(S)* .... 185 E 4
Holmsund *(S)* .... 184 D 5
Holod *(RO)* .... 146 C 3
Holstebro *(DK)*. .... 194 C 5
Holsted *(DK)* .... 198 B 3
Holsworthy *(GB)* .... 34 C 3
Holt *(GB)* .... 33 H 4
Holwerd *(NL)* .... 77 F 2
Holycross *(IRL)* .... 24 D 3
Holyhead /
   Caergybi *(GB)*........ 32 A 3
Holywell /
   Treffynnon *(GB)*...... 32 C 3
Holywood *(GB)* .... 23 G 2
Holzappel *(D)* .... 88 D 1
Holzgau *(A)* .... 95 E 4
Holzkirchen *(D)* .... 95 G 2
Holzminden *(D)*......... 85 F 3
Homberg (Efze) *(D)* .... 85 F 4
Homberg
   (Niederrhein) *(D)*. ..... 84 C 3
Homberg (Ohm) *(D)* .... 85 F 4
Homburg *(D)* .... 88 C 3
Homiel *(BY)* ....7 F 5
Hommelstø *(N)* .... 183 F 2
Hommelvik *(N)* .... 182 D 5

Hommersåk *(N)* .... 194 B 1
Homorod *(RO)* .... 147 H 5
Hondarribia *(E)* .... 59 F 1
Hondschoote *(F)* .... 39 H 1
Hönebach *(D)*........... 85 G 5
Hønefoss *(N)*. .... 189 E 5
Honfleur *(F)*............. 39 E 4
Høng *(DK)* .... 198 D 3
Honiton *(GB)* .... 35 E 3
Honkajoki *(FIN)* .... 191 F 2
Honningsvåg *(N)*. .... 177 E 1
Honrubia *(E)* .... 65 E 4
Honrubia de la Cuesta *(E)*. 58 B 5
Hontalbilla *(E)* .... 58 B 5
Hontianske Nemce *(SK)*. 132 C 4
Hontoria del Pinar *(E)* .. 58 C 4
Hoogeveen *(NL)* .... 77 F 3
Hoogezand *(NL)* .... 77 G 2
Hoogstraten *(B)*. .... 78 D 1
Höör *(S)* .... 199 F 3
Hoorn *(NL)*. .... 77 E 3
Hopârta *(RO)* .... 147 F 5
Hopetoun House (GB)..31 E 1
Hopfgarten-Markt *(A)*... 95 H 3
Hopperstad *(N)* .... 188 C 3
Hora Svatého
   Šebestiána *(CZ)*...... 86 D 5
Horažďovice *(CZ)*......91 H 4
Horb am Neckar *(D)*... 89 E 5
Hörby *(S)* .... 199 F 3
Horcajo de los Montes *(E)*. 64 A 5
Horcajo de Santiago *(E)*. 64 D 4
Horcajo Medianero *(E)*.. 63 H 3
Horche *(E)*. .... 64 D 2
Horden *(GB)* ....31 G 4
Hořejší Kunčice *(CZ)*.... 93 F 3
Horezu (RO) .... 151 F 2
Horezu (RO) .... 151 F 2
Horgen *(CH)* .... 99 E 2
Horgoš *(SRB)* .... 140 C 1
Horia (Arad) *(RO)*. ..... 146 B 5
Horia (Tulcea) *(RO)*. .... 153 F 2
Hořice *(CZ)* .... 92 C 2
Horki *(BY)*. ....7 E 4
Horley *(GB)* .... 36 C 5
Horn *(A)* .... 92 C 5
Horn *(D)*. .... 94 C 3
Horn (-Bad Meinberg) *(D)*. 85 F 3
Horná Mariková *(SK)*... 132 C 2
Horná Streda *(SK)*...... 132 B 3
Hornachos *(E)*. .... 69 G 2
Hornachuelos *(E)* ...... 69 H 4
Hornafirði / Höfn. .... 85 E 5
Hornberg *(D)* .... 89 E 5
Hornburg *(D)* .... 85 H 2
Horncastle *(GB)* .... 33 G 3
Horndal *(S)* .... 190 B 5
Horneburg *(D)*. ....81 H 4
Hörnefors *(S)* .... 184 D 5
Horní Benešov *(CZ)*.... 93 F 2
Horní Lideč *(CZ)* .... 93 G 4
Horní Počernice *(CZ)*... 92 B 2
Horní Slavkov *(CZ)*......91 G 2
Hornindal *(N)* .... 188 C 2
Hørning *(DK)*. .... 198 C 2
Hornnes *(N)*. .... 194 C 2
Hornos *(E)* .... 71 F 3
Hornoy-le-Bourg *(F)* ... 39 G 3
Hornsea *(GB)*. .... 33 G 2
Hornu *(B)*. .... 78 B 3
Hörnum *(D)*. ....81 F 1
Horodło *(PL)*........... 123 H 4
Horodnja *(UA)*..........7 F 5
Horodok *(UA)*..........12 C 2
Horodyšče *(UA)*.........13 F 1
Hořovice *(CZ)* .... 92 A 3
Horsens *(DK)* .... 198 C 3
Horsham *(GB)*. .... 36 C 5
Hørsholm *(DK)*. .... 199 E 3
Horšovský Týn (CZ) .....91 G 4
Horst *(D)*. .... 82 C 4
Horstmar *(D)*. .... 84 D 2
Horten *(N)* .... 195 E 1
Hortezuela *(E)* .... 58 D 5
Hortobágy *(H)*. .... 131 E 1
Horyniec *(PL)*.......... 123 H 5
Hösbach *(D)* .... 89 F 2

Hospental *(CH)* .... 99 E 3
Hospital *(IRL)* .... 24 D 3
Hospital de Órbigo *(E)* .. 57 G 4
Hossa *(FIN)* .... 187 G 1
Hossegor *(F)*. .... 52 A 2
Hosszúpályi *(H)* ....131 E 2
Hostalric *(E)*. ....61 E 3
Hostinné *(CZ)*. .... 87 G 5
Hotagen *(S)* .... 183 F 4
Hotarele *(RO)* .... 152 C 4
Hoting *(S)*. .... 183 H 4
Hotton *(B)*. .... 79 E 4
Houdain *(F)* .... 39 H 2
Houdan *(F)* .... 44 D 1
Houeillès *(F)* .... 52 D 1
Houffalize *(B)* .... 79 E 4
Houghton-
   le-Spring *(GB)*........31 G 4
Houlgate *(F)* .... 38 D 4
Hourtin *(F)*. .... 48 C 4
Houtskär /
   Houtskari *(FIN)*...... 191 E 5
Houtskari /
   Houtskär *(FIN)* ...... 191 E 5
Hov *(DK)*. .... 198 C 3
Hovden *(N)*. .... 188 C 5
Hove *(GB)*. .... 38 D 1
Hovet *(N)* .... 188 D 4
Hovmantorp *(S)*. .... 196 D 5
Høvringen *(N)*. .... 189 E 2
Howden *(GB)* .... 33 F 2
Howth / Binn Éadair *(IRL)*. 23 G 5
Höxter *(D)* .... 85 F 3
Hoya *(D)*. ....81 G 5
Høyanger *(N)* .... 188 B 3
Hoyerswerda *(D)*. ...... 87 E 3
Hoylake *(GB)* .... 32 C 3
Høylandet *(N)*. .... 183 E 3
Hoym *(D)*. .... 86 A 3
Hoyos *(E)*. .... 63 E 4
Hrabrovo *(BG)* .... 157 F 2
Hradec Králové *(CZ)*.... 92 C 2
Hrádek *(CZ)*. .... 92 D 5
Hrádek nad Nisou *(CZ)*.. 87 F 5
Hrafnagil *(IS)*. .... 178 C 2
Hranice *(CZ)* ....91 F 2
Hranice *(CZ)* .... 93 F 3
Hrasnica *(BIH)* .... 137 G 5
Hrastnik *(SLO)* .... 134 C 2
Hrastovlje *(SLO)*. ...... 134 A 3
Hrebenne *(PL)* .... 123 H 5
Hřensko *(CZ)*. .... 87 E 5
Hriadky *(SK)* .... 133 G 3
Hriňová *(SK)* .... 132 D 3
Hrodna *(BY)* ....6 C 5
Hronov *(CZ)*. .... 87 H 5
Hrtkovci *(SRB)* .... 140 C 4
Hrubieszów *(PL)* ...... 123 H 4
Hrušovany
   nad Jevišovkou *(CZ)*... 92 D 5
Hrvace *(HR)* .... 136 D 5
Hrvatska Dubica *(HR)* . 135 F 4
Hrvatska Kostajnica *(HR)*. 135 F 4
Hückeswagen *(D)*. ..... 84 C 4
Hucknall *(GB)* .... 33 E 3
Hucqueliers *(F)* .... 39 G 2
Huddersfield *(GB)*. ..... 33 E 2
Hude *(D)*. ....81 F 5
Hyde *(GB)*. .... 32 D 3
Hyen *(N)*. .... 188 B 2
Hyères *(F)*. .... 55 F 3
Hyltebruk *(S)*. .... 195 G 4
Hyrynsalmi *(FIN)*. ...... 187 F 3
Hythe *(GB)*. .... 37 E 5
Hyvinkää *(FIN)* .... 191 H 4
Hyypiö *(FIN)* .... 181 F 5

I

Ianca *(RO)* .... 152 D 2
Iancu Jianu *(RO)* ...... 151 F 4
Iara *(RO)* .... 147 F 4
Iaşi *(RO)* .... 148 D 3
Iasmos *(GR)* .... 162 D 2
Ibănești *(RO)*. .... 147 H 4
Ibbenbüren *(D)*. .... 84 D 2
Ibestad *(N)*. ....176 A 5
Ibi *(E)* .... 73 F 1

Huétor Santillán *(E)* .... 71 E 5
Huétor Tájar *(E)* .... 70 D 5
Hüfingen *(D)*. .... 94 B 2
Huftarøy *(N)* .... 188 A 4
Huittinen *(FIN)* .... 191 F 3
Huizen *(NL)* .... 77 E 4
Hulín *(CZ)*. .... 93 F 4
Hulst *(NL)*. .... 78 C 1
Hultsfred *(S)* .... 197 E 4
Humac *(BIH)* .... 138 D 3
Humada *(E)*. .... 58 B 2
Humanes *(E)* .... 64 C 2
Humanes de Mohernando *(E)*. ... 64 C 2
Humenné *(SK)* .... 133 H 2
Humpolec *(CZ)* .... 92 C 4
Humppila *(FIN)* .... 191 G 4
Hundested *(DK)* .... 199 E 3
Hundorp *(N)* .... 189 E 3
Hunedoara *(RO)* ...... 151 E 1
Hünfeld *(D)* .... 85 G 5
Hungerford *(GB)* ...... 35 G 2
Hunnebostrand *(S)*..... 195 F 2
Hunspach *(F)* ....41 H 5
Hunstanton *(GB)* ...... 33 H 4
Huntingdon *(GB)* ...... 33 G 5
Huntly *(GB)* .... 29 G 3
Hurbanovo *(SK)*. ...... 132 B 5
Hurdal *(N)* .... 189 F 4
Hurdugi *(RO)* .... 149 E 4
Hurezani *(RO)* .... 151 F 3
Huriel *(F)* .... 49 H 1
Hurskaala *(FIN)* .... 193 F 1
Hürth *(D)* .... 84 C 5
Hurup *(DK)* .... 194 C 4
Húsafell *(IS)*. .... 178 B 2
Húsavík *(IS)* .... 178 C 1
Husavik *(N)* .... 188 A 4
Husbands Bosworth *(GB)*. 33 F 5
Hushinish *(GB)*. .... 28 B 2
Huşi *(RO)* .... 149 E 4
Huskvarna *(S)* .... 195 H 3
Husnes *(N)*. .... 188 B 5
Husnicioara *(RO)*. ...... 150 D 3
Hüsten *(D)* .... 84 D 3
Hustopeče *(CZ)* .... 93 E 5
Husum *(D)*. ....81 G 2
Husum *(S)* .... 184 D 5
Hutovo *(BIH)*. .... 138 D 3
Hüttenberg *(A)* .... 97 E 4
Hüttlingen *(D)* .... 94 C 4
Hüttschlag *(A)*. .... 96 C 4
Huttula *(FIN)* .... 191 H 2
Huttwil *(CH)* .... 98 D 2
Huy *(B)*. .... 78 D 3
Hvalba (Færøerne) *(DK)*. 194 A 5
Hvaler *(N)*. .... 195 E 1
Hvalpsund *(DK)*. .... 194 D 5
Hvalvík
   (Færøerne) *(DK)*. ..... 194 A 4
Hvammstangi *(IS)*. ..... 178 B 2
Hvar *(HR)* .... 138 B 3
Hveragerði *(IS)*. .... 178 B 3
Hvidbjerg *(DK)*. .... 194 C 5
Hvide Sande *(DK)*. ..... 194 C 5
Hvittingfoss *(N)*. .... 195 E 1
Hvitträsk *(FIN)* .... 191 H 5
Hvojna *(BG)*. .... 162 C 1
Hvolsvöllur *(IS)*. .... 178 B 3
Hwlffordd /
   Haverfordwest *(GB)*... 25 H 5

Ibiza / Eivissa *(E)* ...... 66 D 4
Iclod *(RO)* .... 147 F 3
Ičnja *(UA)*..............7 F 5
Icoana *(RO)* .... 151 G 4
Icod de los Vinos *(E)*...67 F 5
Idaío Ántro *(GR)*. ...... 172 D 3
Idanha-a-Nova *(P)* ..... 62 D 4
Idar-Oberstein *(D)* ..... 88 C 2
Iðoš *(SRB)*. .... 140 C 2
Idre *(S)*. .... 189 G 2
Idrija *(SLO)* .... 134 B 2
Idro *(I)* .... 101 G 3
Idstein *(D)* .... 89 E 1
Iecava *(LV)* .... 202 D 4
Ieper (Ypres) *(B)*. ...... 78 A 2
Ierápetra *(GR)*. .... 173 E 4
Ierissós /
   Ιερισσός *(GR)*. .... 161 H 4
Iernut *(RO)* .... 147 G 4
If, château d' *(F)* ...... 54 D 3
Ifjord *(N)*. .... 177 F 2
Ifta *(D)* .... 85 G 4
Ig *(SLO)* .... 134 C 2
Igal *(H)* .... 128 C 4
Igalo *(MNE)* .... 139 E 4
Iggesund *(S)* .... 190 B 3
Ightham Mote (GB) .... 36 D 4
Iglesias *(I)* ....112 B 5
Igls *(A)* .... 95 G 4
Ignalina *(LT)* .... 205 H 3
Igoumenítsa /
   Ηγουμενίτσα *(GR)*.... 164 B 1
Igrane *(HR)* .... 138 C 3
Igualada *(E)* .... 60 C 3
Iharosberény *(H)* ...... 128 C 4
Ihtiman *(BG)* .... 158 C 2
Ii / Ijo *(FIN)* .... 185 H 2
Iisaku *(EST)* .... 201 G 2
Iisalmi *(FIN)* .... 187 E 4
Iisvesi *(FIN)* .... 193 E 1
Iitti *(FIN)* .... 193 E 3
IJmuiden *(NL)*...........76 D 4
Ijo / Ii *(FIN)*. .... 185 H 2
IJsselmuiden *(NL)*. ...... 77 F 4
IJzendijke *(NL)* .... 78 B 1
Ikaalinen *(FIN)* .... 191 F 2
Ikast *(DK)* .... 194 D 5
Ikervár *(H)*. .... 128 B 2
Ikšķile *(LV)* .... 202 D 3
Ilandža *(SRB)*. .... 140 D 3
Ilava *(SK)* .... 132 B 2
Iława *(PL)*. ....118 C 3
Ilche *(E)*. .... 60 A 3
Ilchester *(GB)*. .... 38 A 1
Ilfracombe *(GB)*. ...... 34 D 3
Ílhavo *(P)*. .... 62 B 3
Ília *(P)*. .... 165 G 2
Ilia *(RO)* .... 146 D 5
Ilidža *(BIH)*. .... 137 G 5
Ilija Blaškovo *(BG)*. .... 157 E 3
Ilijaš *(BIH)*. .... 137 G 5
Ilijno *(BG)*. .... 159 G 1
Iliókastro *(GR)* .... 169 E 2
Ilirska Bistrica *(SLO)* ... 134 B 3
Ilişeşti *(RO)*. .... 148 B 2
Ilkeston *(GB)*. .... 33 E 4
Ilkley *(GB)*. .... 33 E 2
Illana *(E)* .... 64 D 3
Illano *(E)*. .... 57 E 2
Illar *(E)* .... 72 B 5
Ille-sur-Têt *(F)*. .... 53 H 5
Illertissen *(D)* .... 94 C 4
Illescas *(E)* .... 64 B 3
Illhaeusern *(F)*. ....47 G 2
Illičivs'k *(UA)*. ....13 G 3
Illiers-Combray *(F)* ..... 44 D 2
Illingen *(D)* .... 89 F 4
Illmitz *(A)* .... 97 H 2
Illora *(E)* .... 70 D 5
Illueca *(E)* .... 59 F 5
Ilmajoki *(FIN)* .... 191 F 1
Ilmenau *(D)* .... 85 H 5
Ilminster *(GB)* .... 35 E 3
Ilok *(HR)* .... 140 B 3
Ilomantsi *(FIN)* .... 187 H 5
Iłów *(PL)* .... 122 C 1

Iłowa *(PL)* .... 120 C 3
Ilsenburg *(D)* .... 85 H 3
Ilsfeld *(D)* .... 89 F 4
Ilūkste *(LV)* .... 203 F 5
Iłża *(PL)* .... 122 D 3
Imatra *(FIN)* .... 193 G 3
Ímeros *(GR)* .... 162 D 3
Immenstaad
   am Bodensee *(D)*..... 94 C 3
Immenstadt im Allgäu *(D)*. 95 E 3
Immingham *(GB)* ...... 33 G 3
Immingham Dock *(GB)*.. 33 G 2
Imola *(I)* .... 107 E 2
Imotski *(HR)* .... 138 C 2
Imperia
   (Porto Maurizio) *(I)* ... 104 C 4
Imphy *(F)* .... 45 G 5
Impruneta *(I)* .... 105 H 4
Imrenčevo *(BG)* .... 156 D 3
Imst *(A)* .... 95 F 4
Inari *(FIN)* .... 177 F 4
Inca *(E)* ....67 F 2
Inchnadamph *(GB)*. .... 28 D 2
Inchree *(GB)*. .... 28 D 5
Incisa in Val d'Arno *(I)* .. 106 D 3
Indal *(S)*. .... 190 B 1
Ineia *(CY)*. ....174 B 4
Ineu *(RO)* .... 146 C 4
Infesta *(E)*. .... 56 B 3
Infiesto *(E)*. .... 57 H 2
Ingå / Inkoo *(FIN)* ..... 191 G 5
Ingelmunster *(B)*. ...... 78 B 2
Ingleton *(GB)*. ....31 F 5
Ingolstadt *(D)* .... 95 G 1
Ingrandes *(F)*. .... 43 G 4
Ingwiller *(F)*. ....41 G 5
Inhulec' *(UA)*. ....13 G 2
Iniesta *(E)* .... 65 F 5
Iniö *(FIN)* .... 191 E 4
Inis / Ennis *(IRL)* ...... 24 C 2
Inis Córthaidh /
   Enniscorthy *(IRL)*..... 25 F 3
Inishcrone *(IRL)* .... 22 C 3
Inkee *(FIN)* .... 187 F 1
Inkoo / Ingå *(FIN)* ..... 191 G 5
Innbygda *(N)* .... 189 G 3
Inndyr *(N)*. .... 179 F 5
Innellan *(GB)*. .... 30 C 2
Innerleithen *(GB)* ......31 E 2
Innfield *(IRL)* .... 23 F 5
Innhavet *(N)* .... 179 G 3
Innichen /
   San Candido *(I)* ...... 103 F 1
Inning am Ammersee *(D)*. 95 F 2
Innsbruck *(A)* .... 95 G 4
Innset *(N)*. ....176 B 5
Innvik *(N)* .... 188 C 2
Inoijا / Иньија *(SRB)* ... 140 C 3
Inowłódz *(PL)* .... 122 C 3
Inowrocław *(PL)* ....117 G 5
Ins *(CH)*. .... 98 C 3
Insel Hiddensee *(D)* .... 83 F 2
Ińsko *(PL)* ....116 D 4
Însurăţei *(RO)* .... 153 E 3
Interlaken *(CH)*. .... 98 D 3
Întorsura Buzăului *(RO)*. 152 B 1
Inveraray *(GB)*. .... 30 C 1
Inverbervie *(GB)*. ...... 29 G 5
Inverewe Gardens (GB).. 28 D 2
Invergarry *(GB)*. .... 28 E 4
Invergordon *(GB)*. ..... 29 F 3
Inverkeithing *(GB)* .....31 E 1
Invermoriston *(GB)*. .... 28 E 4
Inverness *(GB)*. .... 29 E 3
Inverurie *(GB)*. .... 29 H 4
Inzell *(D)* .... 96 B 3
Ioánnina / Ιωάννινα *(GR)*. 160 C 3
Ion Corvin *(RO)* ...... 153 E 4
Íos *(GR)* .... 170 C 2
Iphofen *(D)* .... 89 H 2
Ipsala *(TR)* ....19 F 2
Ipswich *(GB)*. .... 37 E 3
Iraío *(GR)* .... 167 G 5
Irákleia (Dytikí
   Makedonía) *(GR)* ..... 165 G 2
Irákleia (Kentrikí
   Makedonía) *(GR)* ..... 161 G 2

Irákleio / Ηράκλειο (GR) . 170 C5
Irdning (A) 96 D3
Iregszemcse (H)........ 128 D3
Íria (GR)................. 165 G5
Irig (SRB)............... 140 C3
Ironbridge (GB) 32 D4
Irschenberg (D) 95 G3
Irsina (I)................110 D4
Irun (E) 59 F1
Irurtzun (E) 59 F2
Irvine (GB) 30 C2
Irvinestown (GB) 23 E3
Is-sur-Tille (F) 46 D4
Isaba (E) 59 G2
Isaccea (RO) 153 F2
Ísafjörður (IS) 178 A1
Isalnița (RO) 151 F4
Isane (N) 188 B2
Isaszeg (H) 129 F2
Isbister (GB)............ 27 G1
Iscar (E)................. 58 A5
Ischgl (A) 95 E4
Ischia (I) 109 G5
Ise (N) 195 F1
Iselle (I) 100 D2
Iseo (I) 101 G4
Iserlohn (D)............ 84 D4
Isernia (I) 109 G3
Isfjorden (N)........... 188 D1
Ishëm (AL) 144 C1
Isigny-sur-Mer (F) 38 C4
Isili (I)..................112 C4
Iskra (BG) 162 D1
Iskrec (BG) 158 B1
Isla (E) 58 C1
Isla Cristina (E) 68 D5
Islaz (RO) 151 G5
Isle of Whithorn (GB) ... 30 C4
Isleornsay (GB) 28 D4
Ismaning (D) 95 G2
Isnäs (FIN) 193 E4
Isny im Allgäu (D) 95 E3
Iso-Evo (FIN) 191 H3
Isojoki (FIN) 191 F2
Isokylä (FIN) 181 F5
Isokyrö (FIN) 191 F1
Isola 2000 (F) 55 G1
Isola del Gran
    Sasso d'Italia (I) 109 F1
Isola del Liri (I) 109 F3
Isola della Scala (I) 101 H5
Isola di Capo Rizzuto (I) .113 D3
Ísoma (GR)............. 164 D4
Isona (E)................ 60 B2
Isorella (I).............. 101 G4
Isperih / Исперих (BG) . 152 C5
Isperihovo (BG)........ 158 D3
Ispica (I)...............115 F5
Issigeac (F)............. 49 E5
Issoire (F) 50 A3
Issoudun (F) 45 E5
Issy-l'Évêque (F) 50 B1
Istán (E)................74 D4
İstanbul (TR)............19 G1
Istarske Toplice (HR) ... 134 A4
Istebna (PL) 125 E2
Istérnia (GR) 166 D5
Istha (D) 85 F4
Isthmía (GR) 165 G5
Istiaía (GR) 165 G2
Istibanja (MK) 143 G5
Istok (SRB) 142 D4
Istres (F) 54 B2
Isturitz et d'Oxocelhaya,
    grottes d' (F) 52 B3
Itä-Aure (FIN) 191 G2
Itäsalmi /
    Östersundom (FIN)... 191 H5
Itéa / Ιτέα
    (Stereá Elláda) (GR)... 165 F3
Itéa (Flórina) (GR)...... 160 D3
Itéa (Grevená) (GR)..... 161 E5
Itéa (Thessalía) (GR)... 165 E1
Itháki / Ιθάκη (GR)..... 164 C3
Ithómi (GR) 168 C3
Itri (I) 109 F4
Ittiri (I)................112 B2

Itzehoe (D) 81 H3
Ivacevičy (BY).........6 D5
Ivajlovgrad (BG)....... 163 E1
Ivalo (FIN) 177 G5
Ivančice (CZ)........... 92 D4
Ivančići (BIH)........... 137 G5
Ivančna Gorica (SLO) .. 134 C3
Ivanec (HR) 135 E2
Ivanić Grad (HR) 135 E3
Ivanjica (SRB) 139 H2
Ivanjska (BIH)........... 135 F5
Ivanka pri Dunaji (SK) .. 132 A4
Ivankovo (HR)........... 137 G2
Ivano-Frankivs'k (UA) ...12 D2
Ivanovo (RUS)...........7 H1
Ivanovo (Ruse) (BG) ... 152 B5
Ivanovo (Šumen) (BG).. 159 H1
Ivanska (HR) 135 F3
Ivanski (BG)............ 157 E3
Iveşti (RO) 152 D1
Ívira (GR) 161 H3
Ivrea (I) 100 C4
Ivry-la-Bataille (F) 39 G5
Ixworth (GB) 33 H5
Izbica Kujawska (PL)... 121 H1
Izbiceni (RO) 151 G5
Izeda (P)................ 63 E1
Izegem (B) 78 B2
Izernore (F)............51 E2
Izmaïl (UA).............13 F4
İzmir (TR)..............19 G3
İzmit (TR)..............19 H1
Iznalloz (E) 71 E5
İznik (TR)..............19 H2
Izola / Isola (SLO) 134 A3
Izsák (H) 129 E3
Izvoarele (Giurgiu) (RO). 152 B5
Izvoarele (Slatina) (RO). 151 G4
Izvor (BG).............. 158 A2
Izvor (Jagodina) (SRB).. 143 F1
Izvor (Kičevo) (MK) 145 E1
Izvor (Veles) (MK) 145 F1
Izvor (Vranje) (SRB)... 143 G4
Izvoru (RO) 152 C2
Izvoru Berheciului (RO). 148 D4

J

Jaala (FIN) 193 E3
Jabălčevo (BG) 159 H1
Jabbeke (B)............ 78 B1
Jablan Do (BIH) 139 E4
Jablanac (HR) 134 C5
Jablanica (BG) 158 C1
Jablanica (BIH).......... 138 D2
Jablanovo (BG) 159 G1
Jablonec nad Nisou (CZ). 87 F5
Jablonica (SK).......... 132 A3
Jabłonka (PL)........... 125 G2
Jabłonna (PL)........... 122 D1
Jablonné v
    Podještědí (CZ) 87 F5
Jabłonowo
    Pomorskie (PL).......117 H4
Jablunkov (CZ)......... 93 H3
Jabugo (E).............. 69 F4
Jabuka (E).............. 69 F4
Jabuka (Beograd) (SRB). 140 D4
Jabuka (Prijepolje) (SRB). 139 G2
Jabukovac (HR)......... 135 E4
Jabukovac (SRB).......141 G5
Jaca (E)................ 59 H3
Jáchymov (CZ)..........91 G2
Jade (D)................81 F4
Jäder (S)............... 197 F1
Jadraque (E)........... 64 D1
Jaén (E)................ 70 D4
Jagoda (BG) 159 F2
Jagodina /
    Јагодина (SRB)... 143 E1
Jagodnjak (HR) 137 G1
Jagsthausen (D)........ 89 F3
Jahorina (BIH) 139 F2
Jahotyn (UA)............13 F1

Jajce (BIH) 137 E4
Jakabszállás (H) 129 F3
Jakimovo (BG) 151 E5
Jäkkvik (S) 183 H1
Jakobstad /
    Pietarsaari (FIN)..... 185 F5
Jakoruda (BG).......... 158 C3
Jakovo (BG)............ 161 G1
Jakšić (HR) 135 G4
Jakubovik (SRB) 143 G3
Jakuszyce (PL) 120 C4
Jalasjärvi (FIN) 191 F1
Jaligny-sur-Besbre (F) .. 50 B1
Jalovik Izvor (SRB)..... 143 G2
Jambol / Ямбол (BG)... 159 G2
Jamena (SRB) 137 H3
Jämijärvi (FIN) 191 F2
Jäminkipohja (FIN) 191 G2
Jamnička Kiselica (HR) . 135 E3
Jämsä (FIN) 191 H2
Jämsänkoski (FIN) 191 H2
Jamu Mare (RO) 150 B2
Jana (BG) 158 B1
Janakkala (FIN) 191 H4
Janče (MK)............ 144 D1
Janderup (DK) 198 B3
Janikowo (PL)..........117 G5
Janja (BIH) 137 H3
Janjevo (SRB) 143 F3
Janjina (HR)............ 138 D3
Jánoshalma (H) 129 F4
Jánosháza (H) 128 C2
Jánossomorja (H) 128 C1
Janów (PL).............. 122 B4
Janów Lubelski (PL).... 123 F4
Janów Podlaski (PL).... 123 G1
Janowiec (PL)........... 123 E3
Janowiec
    Wielkopolski (PL)....117 F5
Jantra (BG) 159 E1
Janville (F) 45 E2
Janzé (F)................ 43 F3
Jäppilä (FIN) 193 F1
Jaraba (E) 65 F1
Jarafuel (E)............. 65 G5
Jaraicejo (E)............ 63 G5
Jaraíz de la Vera (E).... 63 G4
Jarak (SRB)............ 140 C4
Jarandilla de la Vera (E). 63 G4
Järbo (S)............... 190 B4
Jarcevo (RUS)...........7 F3
Jard-sur-Mer (F)........ 48 B1
Jardins d'Orsan (F)..... 49 H1
Jaren (N)............... 189 E4
Jargeau (F)............. 45 E3
Jarkovac (SRB) 140 D3
Jarmen (D)............. 83 F3
Jarmenovci (SRB) 140 D5
Järna (S) 197 F1
Järna (S) 189 H4
Jarnac (F)............... 48 D3
Jarnages (F)............. 49 G2
Jarny (F)................41 E5
Jarocin (PL) 121 F2
Jaroměř (CZ)........... 92 C2
Jaroměřice
    nad Rokytnou (CZ).... 92 D4
Jaromierz (PL)..........117 H3
Jaroslavl' (RUS).........7 G1
Jarosław (PL)........... 127 G1
Jarosławiec (PL)........117 E1
Jarošov
    nad Nežárkou (CZ)... 92 B4
Järpen (S).............. 183 F5
Jarrow (GB)............31 G4
Järva-Jaani (EST)....... 201 F1
Järvakandi (EST)....... 200 D3
Järvelä (FIN) 191 H4
Järvenpää (FIN)........ 191 H4
Järvsö (S).............. 190 B3
Jaša Tomić (SRB)...... 140 D2
Jasenak (BIH).......... 134 C4
Jasenica (BIH) 135 E5
Jasenkovo (BG) 157 E2

Jasenovac (HR) 135 F4
Jasenovec (BG) 156 D2
Jasenovo (SRB).........141 E4
Jasenovo (SRB) 139 H2
Jasień (PL) 120 E2
Jasika (SRB) 143 E2
Jasikovo (SRB).........141 F5
Jašiūnai (LT) 205 G4
Jašliska (PL) 127 E2
Jasło (PL) 127 E2
Jasna Poljana (BG) 157 F5
Jasov (SK).............. 133 F3
Jastarnia (PL)..........117 H1
Jastrebarsko (HR)...... 134 D3
Jastrowie (PL)..........117 E4
Jastrzębia Góra (PL)....117 G1
Jastrzębie Zdrój (PL) .. 125 E1
Jászalsószentgyörgy (H). 129 G2
Jászapáti (H) 129 G2
Jászárokszállás (H) 129 G1
Jászberény (H) 129 G2
Jászkarajenő (H) 129 G3
Jászkisér (H) 129 G2
Jászladány (H) 129 G2
Jaunay-Clan (F) 49 E1
Jaunbērze (LV) 202 C3
Jaunjelgava (LV) 203 E3
Jaunmārupe (LV)....... 202 D3
Jaunpiebalga (LV)...... 203 F2
Jausiers (F).............51 G5
Jávea / Xàbia (E) 66 A5
Jávenitz (D)............ 86 A1
Javor (BG).............. 159 E1
Javoriv (UA)............12 C2
Javorník (CZ)........... 93 E2
Javron (F).............. 43 H2
Jawidz (PL) 123 F3
Jawor (PL) 120 D4
Jaworzno (PL).......... 125 F1
Jaworzyna Śląska (PL).. 121 E4
Jebel (RO) 150 B1
Jedburgh (GB)..........31 F3
Jedlina-Zdrój (PL) 120 D5
Jedlińsk (PL) 122 D3
Jednorožec (PL).........119 E4
Jędrzejów (PL) 122 C5
Jedwabne (PL).........119 F4
Jedwabno (PL)..........118 D3
Jeesiö (FIN) 181 E4
Jefremov (RUS).........7 H3
Jegălia (RO) 153 E4
Jegorjevsk (RUS).......7 G2
Jegun (F)............... 52 D2
Jegunovce (MK) 143 E5
Jēkabpils (LV) 203 F4
Jektevik (N) 188 B4
Jelah (BIH) 137 F4
Jelašca (BIH) 139 F2
Jelec (RUS).............7 H3
Jelenia Góra (PL) 120 D4
Jelgava (LV) 202 D3
Jelling (DK) 198 C3
Jelsa (HR) 138 B3
Jelsa (N) 188 B5
Jelšava (SK) 133 E3
Jelsi (I) 109 H3
Jemnice (CZ) 92 C5
Jena (D) 86 A5
Jenbach (A) 95 G4
Jennersdorf (A) 97 G4
Jeppo (FIN) 185 F5
Jerez de la Frontera (E)..74 B3
Jerez de los Caballeros (E). 69 F3
Jérica (E)............... 65 H3
Jerichow (D) 86 B1
Jerpoint Abbey (IRL) ... 25 E3
Jerte (E)............... 63 G4
Jerxheim (D)........... 85 H2
Jerzu (I)................112 D4
Jerzwałd (PL)..........118 C3

Jesolo (I)............... 103 F4
Jessen (D) 86 C3
Jessheim (N) 189 F5
Jeßnitz (D) 86 B3
Jetzelsdorf (A) 92 D5
Jeumont (F)............ 40 B2
Jevenstedt (D) 81 H2
Jever (D)...............81 E4
Jevíčko (CZ)........... 93 E3
Jevišovice (CZ)........ 92 D5
Jevnaker (N) 189 E4
Jezerane (HR) 134 C5
Jezerce (SRB) 143 E4
Jezero (BIH) 137 E4
Ježevica (SRB) 139 H1
Ježewo (PL) 117 G4
Jeziorany (PL)..........118 D2
Ježów (PL) 122 C2
Jibert (RO) 147 H5
Jibou (RO) 147 E2
Jičín (CZ) 87 G5
Jieznas (LT) 205 E4
Jihlava (CZ) 92 C4
Jilava (RO) 152 B4
Jilavele (RO) 152 C3
Jilemnice (CZ) 87 G5
Jílové u Prahy (CZ) 92 B3
Jimbolia (RO) 150 A1
Jimena (E) 71 E4
Jimena de la Frontera (E) .74 C4
Jina (RO) 151 F1
Jindřichovice (CZ).......91 G2
Jindřichův Hradec (CZ).. 92 B4
Jirkov (CZ)............. 86 D5
Jirlău (RO) 152 D2
Joachimsthal (D)....... 83 G5
Jockfall (S) 180 C5
Jódar (E) 71 E4
Jodoigne (B) 78 D3
Joensuu (FIN) 193 G1
Jõgeva (EST) 201 F3
Johanngeorgenstadt (D).91 G2
John O' Groats (GB) 26 B4
Johnstone (GB) 30 C2
Johovac (BIH) 135 H5
Jõhvi (EST)............ 201 G1
Joigny (F) 45 G3
Joinville (F) 46 D2
Jokela (FIN) 191 H4
Jokijärvi (FIN) 187 F1
Jokikylä (FIN) 187 F3
Jokioinen (FIN) 191 G4
Jokkmokk (S) 180 A5
Jökulsárlón (IS) 178 C3
Joloskylä (FIN) 185 H2
Jonava (LT) 205 F3
Jondal (N) 188 B4
Joniškėlis (LT) 205 E1
Joniškis (LT) 205 G3
Joniškis (LT) 205 E1
Jönköping (S) 195 H3
Jonzac (F) 48 D3
Jordanów (PL) 125 G2
Jordbro (S) 197 G1
Jormlien (S) 183 F3
Jörn (S) 184 D3
Joroinen (FIN) 193 F1
Jørpeland (N) 194 B1
Jørstadmoen (N) 189 E3
Jošanica (SRB) 143 F1
Jošanička Banja (SRB). 142 D2
Jošavka (BIH) 135 G5
Josipdol (HR) 134 D4
Josipovac (HR) 137 G1
Josselin (F) 43 E3
Jouarre (F) 40 A5
Joué-lès-T. (F) 44 C4
Jougne (F).............47 F5
Joukokylä (FIN) 187 F2
Joutsa (FIN) 193 E2
Joutseno (FIN) 193 G3
Joutsijärvi (FIN) 181 F5

Jovsa (SK)............. 133 H3
Joyeuse (F) 50 C5
Józefów
    (Warszawa) (PL)... 123 G5
Józefów (Zamość) (PL) . 122 D1
Józefów
    nad Wisłą (PL)... 123 E4
Juan-les-Pins (F) 55 G2
Juankoski (FIN) 187 F5
Jüchen (D) 84 B4
Juchnov (RUS)..........7 F3
Juchnowiec
    Kościelny (PL).......119 G4
Judaberg (N)........... 194 B1
Judenau (A)............ 97 G1
Judenburg (A) 97 E4
Juelsminde (DK) 198 C3
Jugon-les-Lacs (F) 43 E2
Jugorje (SLO) 134 D3
Juillac (F).............. 49 F4
Juist (D).............. 80 D3
Jukkasjärvi (S) 180 B3
Jülich (D) 84 B4
Jullouville (F) 43 F1
Jumaliskylä (FIN) 187 F3
Jumeaux (F) 50 A3
Jumièges (F) 39 F4
Jumilhac-le-Grand (F).. 49 F3
Jumilla (E) 71 H2
Juminen (FIN) 187 F5
Jumisko (FIN) 181 F5
Jundola (BG) 158 C3
Juneda (E) 60 B4
Junik (SRB) 139 H4
Juniville (F) 40 C4
Junosuando (S) 180 C4
Junsele (S) 183 H5
Juntusranta (FIN) 187 G2
Juodupė (LT) 205 F2
Juoksenki (FIN) 180 D5
Juorkuna (FIN) 187 E2
Jurata (PL)............117 H1
Jurbarkas (LT) 204 D3
Jüri (EST) 200 D2
Jurilovca (RO) 153 G3
Jūrkalne (LV) 202 A3
Jūrmala (LV) 202 D3
Jurmu (FIN) 187 F2
Juromenha (P) 69 E2
Jurva (FIN) 191 F1
Jussey (F) 47 E3
Justel (E) 57 F4
Juta (H) 128 D4
Jüterbog (D) 86 C2
Jutrosin (PL) 121 F3
Juuka (FIN) 187 G5
Juuma (FIN) 181 G5
Juupajoki (FIN) 191 G2
Juva (FIN) 191 F4
Juva (FIN) 193 F2
Juvigny-le-Tertre (F) .. 43 G1
Juvigny-
    sous-Andaine (F)...... 43 H2
Juvola (FIN) 193 G2
Juzennecourt (F) 46 D2
Jūžintai (LT) 205 G2
Jyderup (DK) 198 D3
Jyrkkä (FIN) 187 F4
Jyväskylä (FIN) 191 H2

K

Kaakamo (FIN) 185 G1
Kaamanen (FIN)....... 177 F4
Kaaresuvanto (FIN).....176 D5
Kaarina (FIN) 191 F4
Kaatsheuvel (NL)....... 78 D1
Kaavi (FIN) 187 F5
Kaba (H)...............131 E2
Kåbdalis (S) 184 D1
Kableškovo (BG) 157 F4
Kać (SRB) 140 C3
Kačanik (SRB) 143 E4
Kačarevo (SRB) 140 D4
Kacelovo (BG) 156 C2
Kachovka (UA)..........13 H2
Kačikol (SRB) 143 E4
Kadaň (CZ).............91 H2

Kadarkút (H) 128 C4
Kadrifakovo (MK) 145 G1
Kadrina (EST) 201 F2
Kadzidło (PL) 119 E4
Kåfjord (N) 177 E1
Kaga (S).............. 197 E2
Kåge (S) 185 E3
Kagkádi (GR)............. 164 D4
Kaharlyk (UA)..........13 F1
Kahla (D)................ 86 A5
Kaïáfas (GR).............. 164 D5
Kailbach (D) 89 F3
Käina (EST) 200 B3
Kainasto (FIN)........... 191 F1
Kaindorf (A)............. 97 G4
Kainoúrgio (GR)........ 164 D3
Kaipola (FIN) 191 H2
Kairala (FIN)............ 181 F4
Kaiserslautern (D)...... 88 D3
Kaisheim (D).......... 89 H4
Kajaani (FIN) 187 F3
Kajnardža (BG)......... 152 D5
Kakanj (BIH) 137 G5
Kakaviá (GR) 160 B5
Kakí Thálassa (GR) 166 B5
Kakopetria (CY).........174 C4
Kakslauttanen (FIN)... 177 G5
Kalá Nerá (GR) 165 G1
Kalajoki (FIN) 185 G4
Kalak (N)............... 177 F2
Kalamáki (Kríti) (GR).. 172 D4
Kalamáki
  (Thessalía) (GR)....... 165 F1
Kalamáta /
  Καλαμάτα (GR)....... 168 C3
Kalámi (Kríti) (GR)..... 170 A5
Kalámi
  (Vóreio Aigaío) (GR) .. 167 G5
Kalamítsi (GR)......... 162 B5
Kalamiótissa (GR)...... 170 D3
Kálamos (GR) 165 H4
Kalamotí (GR) 167 E4
Kalándra (GR) 161 H5
Kalanti (FIN) 191 E4
Kalapódi (GR)......... 165 G3
Kälarne (S) 190 B1
Kálathos (GR) 171 H3
Kalavárda (GR) 171 H3
Kalavasos (CY).........174 D4
Kalávryta /
  Καλάβρυτα (GR) 165 E4
Kal'azin (RUS)..........7 G1
Kalbe (D) 86 A1
Kalce (SLO) 134 B3
Kalčevo (BG) 159 G2
Káld (H).............. 128 C2
Kałęczyn (PL)..........119 E3
Kalekovec (BG) 158 D3
Kaléntzi
  (Dytikí Elláda) (GR) ... 165 E4
Kaléntzi (Ípeiros) (GR).. 164 C1
Kalérgo (GR) 166 B4
Kalesija (BIH)........... 137 H4
Kalesméno (GR)......... 165 E2
Kalety (PL) 121 H5
Kali (HR) 136 B5
Kaliánoi (GR)........... 165 F5
Kaliningrad (RUS).........5 H4
Kalinkavičy (BY)..........7 E5
Kalinovnik (BIH)........ 139 E2
Kalinowo (PL)..........119 G2
Kaliráchi (GR) 160 D5
Kalisz (PL)............ 121 G2
Kalisz Pomorski (PL).....116 D4
Kalix (S).............. 185 F1
Kalkar (D)............. 83 G4
Kalkkinen (FIN)........ 191 H3
Kall (S).............. 183 F5
Kallaste (EST) 201 G3
Källby (FIN) 185 F5
Källby (S) 195 G2
Kallepeia (CY)..........174 B4
Kalli (EST)............ 200 D3
Kallimasiá (GR)........ 167 E4
Kallinge (S) 199 G4
Kallio (FIN) 191 G2
Kalliojoki (FIN)....... 187 G3

Kallipéfki (GR) 161 F5
Kallislahti (FIN)....... 193 G2
Kallithéa
  (Dytikí Elláda) (GR) ... 165 E5
Kallithéa (Kentrikí
  Makedonía) (GR) 161 H5
Kallithéa
  (Nótio Aigaío) (GR) ... 171 H3
Kallithéa
  (Pelopónnisos) (GR) ... 168 C3
Kallmünz (D)............91 F5
Kalloní (GR)............. 167 F2
Kalmar (S)............... 197 E5
Kalna (SRB) 143 G2
Kalnik (H)............ 135 F2
Kaló Chorió (GR) 173 E3
Kalo Chorio
  (Larnaka) (CY)....... 175 E4
Kalo Chorio (Lefka) (CY).174 C3
Kalo Chorio
  (Lemesos) (CY)........174 D4
Kalo Chorio
  Kapouti (CY)...........174 D3
Kaló Neró (GR) 168 C2
Kalochóri (GR) 161 E5
Kalocsa (H) 129 F4
Kalofer (BG)............ 159 E2
Kalograia (CY) 175 E2
Kalogriá (GR) 164 D4
Kaloí Liménes (GR) 172 D4
Kalojan (GR) 157 E2
Kalojanovec (BG) 159 F2
Kalojanovo
  (Plovdiv) (BG) 158 D2
Kalojanovo
  (Sliven) (BG)......... 159 G2
Kalókastro (GR) 161 H3
Kalopanagiotis (CY).....174 C4
Kalopsida (CY) 175 F3
Kaloskopí (GR) 165 F3
Kalotina (BG)........... 158 A1
Káloz (H)............. 129 E3
Kalpáki (GR).............. 160 C5
Kals
  am Großglockner (A)... 95 H4
Kalsdorf bei Graz (A) ... 97 F4
Kaltanėnai (LT)......... 205 G3
Kaltbrunn (CH)........... 99 F2
Kaltenkirchen (D)........81 H3
Kaltennordheim (D)..... 85 G5
Kaltern / Caldaro (I) ... 101 H2
Kaluga (RUS)...........7 G3
Kalugerovo (BG) 158 C2
Kalundborg (DK)....... 198 D3
Kaluš (UA) 12 D2
Kałuszyn (PL) 123 E1
Kalvarija (LT)........... 204 D4
Kalvehave (DK) 199 E4
Kalvene (LV) 202 A3
Kälviä (FIN) 185 F4
Kalvola (FIN) 191 G3
Kalvträsk (S) 184 D3
Kalwaria
  Zebrzydowska (PL)... 125 F1
Kálymnos /
  Κάλυμνος (GR) 171 F2
Kalyvári (GR) 166 C4
Kalýves (GR) 162 C3
Kalývia (Achaïa) (GR) ... 165 E5
Kalývia (Aitolía-
  Akarnanía) (GR) 164 D3
Kalývia (Attikí) (GR) ... 165 H5
Kalývia Varikoú (GR) ... 161 F4
Kám (H)............. 128 B3
Kamajai (LT) 205 G2
Kamáres
  (Dytikí Elláda) (GR) ... 165 E4
Kamáres (Kríti) (GR) ... 172 D3
Kamáres
  (Nótio Aigaío) (GR) ... 169 H3
Kamári (GR) 170 C3
Kamariótissa (GR)..... 162 D4
Kamedulów,
  klasztor (PL).........119 G2
Kapitan
  Dimitrovo (BG) 153 E5

Kamen (BG)............ 156 C2
Kamen (D)............. 84 D3
Kaména Voúrla / Καμένα
  Βούρλα (GR) 165 F3
Kamenari (MNE) 139 F4
Kamenec (BG) 159 H2
Kamenica (MK) 143 H5
Kamenica (SRB) 140 C5
Kamenice
  nad Lipou (CZ)....... 92 B4
Kameno (BG) 157 E4
Kamensko
  (Daruvar) (HR) 135 G4
Kamensko (Split) (HR) .. 138 C2
Kamenz (D)............. 87 E4
Kamień Krajeński (PL)...117 F3
Kamień Pomorski (PL)...116 C2
Kamieniec
  Ząbkowicki (PL)..... 121 E5
Kamienna Góra (PL)... 120 D4
Kamieńsk (PL)........ 122 B3
Kamilski dol (BG)...... 163 E1
Kaminaria (CY).........174 C4
Kamínia
  (Dytikí Elláda) (GR) ... 164 D4
Kamínia
  (Vóreio Aigaío) (GR) .. 162 D5
Kamjanec'-
  Podil's'kyj (UA).......13 E2
Kam'janka (UA).........13 G1
Kam'janka
  Dniprovs'ka (UA)......13 H2
Kamnik (SLO) 134 C2
Kamp-Bornhofen (D)... 88 D1
Kamp-Lintfort (D)...... 84 B3
Kampánis (GR) 161 G3
Kampen (D)............81 F1
Kampen (NL) 77 F4
Kampiá (GR) 167 E3
Kampochóri (GR) 161 F3
Kampos (CY)...........174 C3
Kámpos (Kríti) (GR) ... 172 A3
Kámpos
  (Pelopónnisos) (GR) ... 168 C3
Kanal (SLO) 134 A2
Kanália (GR) 165 G1
Kanalláki (GR)......... 164 C1
Kanatádika (GR)....... 165 G2
Kánava (GR) 169 H4
Kančevo (BG) 159 F2
Kańczuga (PL) 127 F1
Kandel (D)............. 89 E4
Kandern (D)............. 94 A3
Kandersteg (CH)....... 98 D4
Kandíla
  (Dytikí Elláda) (GR) ... 164 C3
Kandíla
  (Pelopónnisos) (GR) ... 165 F5
Kandıra (TR)...........19 H1
Kandrše (SLO).......... 134 C2
Kanestraum (N) 182 B5
Kanfanar (HR)......... 134 A4
Kangasala (FIN) 191 G3
Kangaslampi (FIN) 193 F1
Kangasniemi (FIN) 193 E2
Kangosjärvi (FIN)...... 180 D3
Kaniv (UA).............13 F1
Kanjiža (SRB)......... 140 C1
Kankaanpää (FIN)..... 191 F2
Kannonkoski (FIN).... 185 H5
Kannus (FIN).......... 185 G4
Kannusjärvi (FIN) 193 F4
Kántanos (GR)......... 172 B3
Kanturk (IRL).......... 24 C4
Kaolinovo (BG)........ 157 E2
Kaona (SRB) 142 D1
Kaonik (BIH) 137 F5
Kaonik (SRB).......... 143 F2
Kapandríti (GR)........ 165 H4
Kapari (CY)............174 C3
Kapčiamiestis (LT)..... 205 E5
Kapellskär (S)......... 197 G1
Kapfenberg (A) 97 F3

Kaplice (CZ)............ 92 B5
Kaposfő (H) 128 C4
Kaposszekcső (H) 128 D4
Kaposvár (H)........... 128 D4
Kapp (N).............. 189 F4
Kappel (D)............ 88 C2
Kappeln (D)............81 H1
Kaprun (A)............. 96 B4
Kapsáli (GR) 169 E5
Kápsas (GR)............ 165 F5
Kapsoúri (GR) 166 C4
Kapuvár (H)........... 128 C1
Karabiga (TR)...........19 G2
Karaburun (TR).........19 G3
Karačev (RUS)...........7 G4
Karageorgievo (BG)... 159 H1
Karamanci (BG)....... 162 D1
Karan (SRB) 139 H1
Karanovo (BG) 159 H2
Karapelit (BG).......... 157 F2
Karasjok (N)........... 177 E4
Karasu (TR)............19 H1
Karats (S)............ 180 A5
Karavas (GR) 174 D2
Karavás (GR) 169 E5
Karavete (EST) 201 E2
Karavostasi (CY).......174 C3
Kårböle (S) 190 A2
Karcag (H) 129 H2
Kardakáta (GR) 164 B3
Kardam (BG) 153 E5
Kardámaina (GR) 171 F2
Kardámyla (GR) 167 E3
Kardamýli (GR) 168 C3
Kardiá (GR) 161 G4
Karditsa /
  Καρδίτσα (GR) 165 E1
Kárdla (EST) 200 B2
Kárdžali /
  Кърджали (BG) 162 D1
Karesuando (S).........176 D5
Karfás (GR)............ 167 E4
Kargowa (PL) 120 D2
Karhukangas (FIN) 185 H3
Karhula (FIN) 193 F4
Karianí (GR) 162 B3
Karigasniemi (FIN) 177 F4
Karijoki (FIN) 191 E1
Karinainen (FIN) 191 F4
Karis / Karjaa (FIN) ... 191 G5
Karítaina (GR) 165 E5
Karjaa / Karis (FIN) ... 191 G5
Karjalohja (FIN) 191 G5
Karkaloú (GR) 165 E5
Karkkila (FIN) 191 F3
Karkku (FIN) 191 F3
Kärkölä (LT) 204 D2
Kärkölä (FIN) 191 H4
Karksi-Nuia (EST)..... 201 E4
Karleby / Kokkola (FIN). 185 F4
Karlevi (S)............ 197 E5
Karlino (PL)...........116 D2
Karlivka (UA)...........13 H1
Karló / Hailuoto (FIN).. 185 G3
Karlobag (HR) 136 B4
Karlova Studánka (CZ) .. 93 E2
Karlovac (HR) 134 D4
Karlovási /
  Καρλοβάσι (GR) 167 F5
Karlovo / Карлово (BG). 158 D2
Karlovy Vary (CZ)......91 G2
Karlsborg (S) 195 H2
Karlsburg (D) 83 F3
Karlsfeld (D) 95 G2
Karlshamn (S) 199 G3
Karlshuld (D).......... 95 F1
Karlskoga (S).......... 195 H1
Karlskrona (S) 199 H3
Karlsruhe (D)........... 89 E4
Karlstad (S) 195 G1
Karlstadt (D).......... 89 G2
Karlštejn (CZ)......... 92 A3
Karlstift (A) 97 E1
Karmélava (LT) 205 E3
Karmi (CY)............174 D2

Karnezaíika (GR) 165 G5
Karnobat /
  Карнобат (BG)....... 159 H2
Karolinka (CZ) 93 G4
Karow (D)............ 83 E4
Karpacz (PL) 120 D4
Kärpänkylä (FIN) 187 G1
Kárpathos (GR) 171 F5
Karpenísi /
  Καρπενήσι (GR) 165 E2
Karperí (GR) 161 G2
Kärsämäki (FIN) 185 H4
Kärsava (LV) 203 H3
Karsin (PL)...........117 G3
Karstädt (D)........... 82 D5
Karstula (FIN) 191 H1
Kartal (TR)............19 G1
Kartena (LT).......... 204 C2
Kartéri (Ípeiros) (GR) ... 164 B1
Kartéri
  (Pelopónnisos) (GR) ... 165 F5
Karterós (GR) 170 C5
Karttula (FIN) 187 E5
Kartuzy (PL)...........117 G2
Karungi (S)........... 185 G1
Karunki (FIN) 185 G1
Karup (DK) 194 D5
Karvala (FIN) 185 G5
Karvia (FIN) 191 F2
Karviná (CZ) 93 G2
Karvoskylä (FIN) 185 H4
Karvounári (GR) 164 B1
Karwia (PL)...........117 G1
Karyá (Iónia Nisiá) (GR). 164 C2
Karyá
  (Pelopónnisos) (GR) .. 165 F5
Karyés / Καρυές
  (Ágio Óros) (GR)..... 162 B4
Karyés
  (Pelopónnisos) (GR) .. 168 D2
Karyés
  (Stereá Elláda) (GR) ... 165 F2
Kašalj (SRB) 142 D3
Kašin (RUS)...........7 F1
Kašina (HR) 135 E3
Kašira (RUS)...........7 G2
Kaskinen / Kaskö (FIN) . 191 E2
Kaskö / Kaskinen (FIN) . 191 E2
Käsmu (EST) 201 F1
Káspakas (GR) 162 D5
Kašperské Hory (CZ) ...91 H5
Kaspičan (BG) 157 E2
Kassándreia (GR) 161 H5
Kassel (D)............. 85 G4
Kassiópi (GR) 160 B5
Kastaniá
  (Kardítsa) (GR) 165 E1
Kastaniá (Kentrikí
  Makedonía) (GR) 161 E4
Kastaniá
  (Pelopónnisos) (GR) ... 165 F5
Kastaniá (Tríkala) (GR) . 160 D5
Kastaniés (GR) 163 F1
Kastanítsa (GR) 165 E5
Kaštel Stari (HR)...... 138 B2
Kaštel Žegarski (HR)... 136 C5
Kastelholms slott (FIN). 190 D5
Kastellaun (D) 88 D1
Kastélli (GR) 173 E3
Kasterlee (B) 78 D1
Kastl (D)............91 F4
Kastorf (D)........... 82 B3
Kastoria /
  Καστοριά (GR) 160 D4
Kastráki
  (Dytikí Elláda) (GR) ... 164 D3
Kastráki
  (Nótio Aigaío) (GR) ... 170 C2
Kastrí
  (Pelopónnisos) (GR) ... 168 D2
Kastrí
  (Stereá Elláda) (GR) ... 165 E2
Kastrí (Thessalía) (GR). 165 F1
Kástro (GR) 165 H2

Kástro
  (Dytikí Elláda) (GR) ... 164 C4
Kástro
  (Stereá Elláda) (GR) ... 165 G3
Kastrosykiá (GR) 164 C2
Kaszaper (H)........... 129 H4
Katáfourko (GR) 164 D2
Katáfyto (GR) 161 H2
Katákolo (GR) 164 D5
Katápola (GR) 170 D2
Katastári (GR) 164 C5
Kateríni / Κατερίνη (GR). 161 F4
Kathenoí (GR).......... 165 H3
Kathikas (CY) 174 B4
Katići (SRB) 139 H2
Kätkäsuvanto (FIN)... 180 C3
Katlanovo (MK) 143 F5
Katlanovska Banja (MK). 143 F5
Katlenburg (D)......... 85 G3
Káto Achaïa (GR) 164 D4
Káto Almyrí (GR) 165 G5
Káto Aséa (GR) 168 D2
Kato Deftera (CY) 174 D4
Káto Dikomo (CY) 174 D3
Káto Dolianá (GR) 168 D2
Káto Figáleia (GR) 165 E5
Káto Glykóvrysi (GR).. 168 D3
Kato Kastellianá (GR).. 173 E4
Káto Kleinés (GR) 160 D3
Kato Lakatameia (CY) ...174 D3
Káto Makrinoú (GR) ... 164 D3
Káto Nevrokópi (GR) .. 161 H2
Kato Polemidia (CY)....174 C5
Kato Pyrgos (CY).......174 C3
Káto Tithoréa (GR) 165 F3
Káto Vasilikí (GR)...... 164 D3
Káto Vérga (GR) 168 C3
Káto Vérmio (GR) 161 E4
Káto Vlasía (GR) 165 E4
Káto Vrontoú (GR) 161 H2
Káto Zachloroú (GR) ... 165 E4
Kato Zodeia (CY)......174 C3
Katochi (GR) 164 D3
Katokopia (CY).........174 D3
Katoúna
  (Dytikí Elláda) (GR) ... 164 C2
Katoúna
  (Iónia Nisiá) (GR) ... 164 C2
Katowice (PL) 122 A5
Katrineholm (S) 197 E2
Katsikás (GR) 164 C1
Kattavia (GR).......... 171 G4
Katunci (BG) 161 H2
Katunica (BG).......... 159 E3
Katwijk aan Zee (NL) ...76 D4
Kąty Wrocławskie (PL). 121 E4
Katyčiai (LT)........... 204 C3
Kaub (D)............. 88 D1
Kaufbeuren (D) 95 E2
Kauhajärvi (FIN) 191 G1
Kauhajoki (FIN) 191 F1
Kauhava (FIN) 185 F5
Kaukonen (FIN) 180 D4
Kaunas (LT).......... 205 E4
Kaupanger (N) 188 C3
Kaustinen (FIN) 185 G5
Kautokeino (N)........176 D4
Kauttua (FIN) 191 F3
Kavadarci (MK)....... 145 G1
Kavajë (AL)........... 144 C2
Kavála / Καβάλα (GR).. 162 B3
Kavarna (BG).......... 157 G2
Kavastu (EST) 201 G3
Kävlinge (S).......... 199 F3
Kávos (GR) 164 B1
Kavoúsi (GR) 173 F3
Käyla (FIN) 181 G5
Kaysersberg-
  Vignoble (F) 47 G2
Kazafani (CY) 174 D2
Kažani (MK).......... 145 E2
Kazanlăk /
  Казанлък (BG) 159 E2
Kazárma (GR) 168 C3
Kazimierz Dolny (PL) .. 123 E3
Kazimierza Wielka (PL). 122 C5
Kazincbarcika (H) 126 D5

A B C D E F G H I J **K** L M N O P Q R S T U V W X Y Z

Kazlų Rūda *(LT)* .... 205 E 4
Kcynia *(PL)* ....117 F 5
Kdyně *(CZ)* ....91 G 4
Kéa *(GR)* .... 166 B 5
Keadew *(IRL)* .... 22 D 4
Keady *(GB)* .... 23 F 3
Kebnekaise *(S)* .... 180 A 3
Kecel *(H)* .... 129 F 4
Kechrókampos *(GR)* ... 162 C 2
Kecskemét *(H)* .... 129 G 3
Kėdainiai *(LT)* .... 205 E 3
Kédros *(GR)* .... 165 E 2
Kędzierzyn-Koźle *(PL)* .. 121 G 5
Keel *(IRL)* .... 22 B 4
Keerbergen *(B)* .... 78 D 2
Kéfalos *(GR)* .... 171 F 2
Kefalóvryso
  (Dytikí Elláda) *(GR)* ... 164 D 3
Kefalóvryso
  (Ípeiros) *(GR)* .... 160 C 5
Kefalóvryso
  (Pelopónnisos) *(GR)* ... 168 C 3
Kefalóvryso
  (Thessalía) *(GR)* .... 161 E 5
Keflavík *(IS)* .... 178 A 3
Ķegums *(LV)* .... 203 E 3
Kehl *(D)* .... 88 D 5
Kehra *(EST)* .... 201 E 2
Kehtna *(EST)* .... 200 D 2
Keighley *(GB)* .... 32 D 2
Keila *(EST)* .... 200 D 2
Ķeipene *(LV)* .... 203 E 3
Keitele *(FIN)* .... 187 E 5
Keith *(GB)* .... 29 G 3
Kelankylä *(FIN)* .... 185 H 1
Kelberg *(D)* .... 88 C 1
Kelbra *(D)* .... 86 A 3
Kelcyrë *(AL)* .... 144 D 4
Kelebia *(H)* .... 129 F 5
Kelefá (GR) .... 168 D 4
Kelheim *(D)* ....91 F 5
Kellinghusen *(D)* ....81 H 3
Kellokoski *(FIN)* ...... 191 H 4
Kells *(IRL)* .... 23 F 4
Kelmė *(LT)* .... 204 D 2
Kelokedara *(CY)* ......174 B 4
Kelso *(GB)* ....31 F 2
Kelujärvi *(FIN)* .... 181 F 4
Kemberg *(D)* .... 86 C 3
Kembs *(F)* ....47 H 3
Kemeneshőgyész *(H)* .. 128 C 2
Kémes *(H)* .... 128 D 5
Kemi *(FIN)* .... 185 G 1
Kemijärvi *(FIN)* .... 181 F 5
Keminmaa *(FIN)* ...... 185 G 1
Kemiö / Kimito *(FIN)* .. 191 F 5
Kemnath *(D)* ....91 F 3
Kempele *(FIN)* .... 185 H 3
Kempen *(D)* .... 84 B 3
Kempenich *(D)* .... 88 C 1
Kempten *(D)* .... 95 E 3
Kendal *(GB)* ....31 F 5
Kenderes *(H)* .... 129 H 2
Kengyel *(H)* .... 129 H 3
Kenilworth *(GB)* .... 33 E 5
Kenmare *(IRL)* .... 24 B 4
Kennacraig *(GB)* ...... 30 B 2
Kentallen *(GB)* .... 28 D 5
Kentrikó *(GR)* .... 161 G 2
Kenzingen *(D)* .... 94 A 2
Kępice *(PL)* ....117 E 2
Kępno *(PL)* .... 121 G 3
Kerameia *(GR)* .... 167 F 2
Keramídi *(GR)* .... 165 G 1
Keramítsa *(GR)* ...... 160 B 5
Kéramos *(GR)* .... 167 E 3
Keramotí *(GR)* .... 162 C 3
Kerasiá *(GR)* .... 165 G 2
Kerasiés *(GR)* .... 161 E 3
Keratéa *(GR)* .... 166 B 5
Keratokampos *(GR)* .. 173 E 4
Kerava *(FIN)* .... 191 H 4
Kerdalo, jardins de (F) ... 42 D 1
Kerekegyháza *(H)* .... 129 F 3
Kerí *(GR)* .... 164 C 5
Kerimäki *(FIN)* .... 193 G 2
Kerken *(D)* .... 84 B 3

Kerkonkoski *(FIN)* ...... 193 E 1
Kerkrade *(NL)* .... 79 F 2
Kérkyra / Κέρκυρα *(GR)* . 160 B 5
Kermen *(BG)* .... 159 G 2
Kernascléden *(F)* ....42 C 2
Kerpen *(D)* .... 84 C 5
Kerta *(H)* .... 128 C 2
Kerteminde *(DK)* ..... 198 C 3
Kértezi *(GR)* .... 165 E 4
Keryneia / Girne *(CY)* ....174 D 2
Kerzers *(CH)* .... 98 C 3
Kesälahti *(FIN)* ...... 193 H 2
Keşan *(TR)* ....19 F 2
Kesarevo *(BG)* .... 156 C 3
Kesh *(GB)* .... 23 E 3
Kestilä *(FIN)* .... 185 H 3
Keswick *(GB)* ....31 E 4
Keszthely *(H)* .... 128 C 3
Kétegyháza *(H)* ....131 E 4
Kętrzyn *(PL)* ....119 E 2
Kettering *(GB)* .... 33 F 5
Kettletoft *(GB)* ...... 26 C 3
Kettwig *(D)* .... 84 C 4
Kęty *(PL)* .... 125 F 1
Ketzin *(D)* .... 86 C 1
Keuruu *(FIN)* .... 191 H 2
Kevelaer *(D)* .... 84 B 3
Kevo *(FIN)* .... 177 F 3
Keynsham *(GB)* ...... 35 F 2
Kežmarok *(SK)* .... 133 F 2
Kiáto / Κιάτο *(GR)* .... 165 F 4
Kibæk *(DK)* .... 194 C 5
Kiberg *(N)* .... 177 H 2
Kičevo *(BG)* .... 157 F 2
Kičevo *(MK)* .... 145 E 1
Kidderminster *(GB)* ... 32 D 5
Kidlington *(GB)* ...... 35 H 1
Kidsgrove *(GB)* ...... 32 D 3
Kidwelly *(GB)* .... 34 C 1
Kiefersfelden *(D)* ...... 95 H 3
Kiekinkoski *(FIN)* ..... 187 G 3
Kiel *(D)* ....81 H 2
Kielce *(PL)* .... 122 D 4
Kiental *(CH)* .... 98 D 3
Kierinki *(FIN)* .... 181 E 4
Kietrz *(PL)* .... 124 D 1
Kietz *(D)* .... 87 E 1
Kiev = Kyïv *(UA)* ....13 F 1
Kifisiá / Κηφισιά *(GR)* ... 165 H 4
Kifjord *(N)* .... 177 F 1
Kihelkonna *(EST)* .... 200 B 3
Kihlanki *(FIN)* .... 180 C 4
Kihniö *(FIN)* .... 191 F 2
Kiihtelysvaara *(FIN)* .. 193 H 1
Kiikala *(FIN)* .... 191 G 4
Kiikka *(FIN)* .... 191 F 3
Kiikoinen *(FIN)* ...... 191 F 3
Kiiminki / Kiminge *(FIN)* .. 185 H 2
Kiiskilä *(FIN)* .... 185 G 4
Kiistala *(FIN)* .... 180 D 3
Kijevo *(HR)* .... 136 D 5
Kijevo *(SRB)* .... 142 D 4
Kikinda / Кикинда *(SRB)*. 140 D 2
Kikół *(PL)* ....117 H 5
Kil *(S)* .... 195 G 1
Kilafors *(S)* .... 190 B 3
Kilbaha *(IRL)* .... 24 B 3
Kilbeggan *(IRL)* ...... 23 E 5
Kilbirnie *(GB)* .... 30 C 2
Kilbotn *(N)* .... 179 G 2
Kilchoan *(GB)* .... 28 C 5
Kilcock *(IRL)* .... 23 F 5
Kilcormac *(IRL)* .... 25 E 2
Kilcreggan *(GB)* ..... 30 C 1
Kilcullen *(IRL)* .... 25 F 2
Kildare *(IRL)* .... 25 F 2
Kildorrery *(IRL)* .... 24 D 4
Kilfenora *(IRL)* .... 24 C 2
Kilgarvan *(IRL)* ...... 24 B 4
Kilifarevo *(BG)* ...... 159 F 1
Kilija *(UA)* ....13 F 4
Kilingi-Nõmme *(EST)*. 201 E 4
Kilkee *(IRL)* .... 24 B 2
Kilkeel *(GB)* .... 23 G 4
Kilkenny /
  Cill Chainnigh *(IRL)* .... 25 E 3
Kilkhampton *(GB)* ...... 34 C 3

Kilkís / Κιλκίς *(GR)* .... 161 G 3
Killadysert *(IRL)* .... 24 C 3
Killaloe *(IRL)* .... 24 D 2
Killarney /
  Cill Airne *(IRL)* ...... 24 B 4
Killashandra *(IRL)* .... 23 E 4
Killenaule *(IRL)* ...... 25 E 3
Killimer *(IRL)* .... 24 B 3
Killin *(GB)* .... 29 E 5
Killinkoski *(FIN)* ..... 191 G 1
Killorglin *(IRL)* .... 24 B 4
Killybegs *(IRL)* ...... 22 D 2
Killyleagh *(GB)* ...... 23 G 3
Kilmaine *(IRL)* .... 22 C 5
Kilmallock *(IRL)* ..... 24 C 3
Kilmarnock *(GB)* ..... 30 C 2
Kilmartin *(GB)* .... 30 B 1
Kilmore Quay *(IRL)* .. 25 F 4
Kilmurry *(IRL)* .... 24 C 2
Kilninver *(GB)* .... 30 B 1
Kilnsea *(GB)* .... 33 G 2
Kilpisjärvi *(FIN)* ....176 C 4
Kilrea *(GB)* .... 23 F 2
Kilronan *(IRL)* .... 22 B 5
Kilrush *(IRL)* .... 24 B 3
Kilsyth *(GB)* .... 30 D 1
Kiltealy *(IRL)* .... 25 F 3
Kiltimagh *(IRL)* ...... 22 C 4
Kilwinning *(GB)* ...... 30 C 2
Kılyos *(TR)* ....19 G 1
Kiminge / Kiiminki *(FIN)*. 185 H 2
Kimito / Kemiö *(FIN)* .. 191 F 5
Kímolos *(GR)* .... 169 H 4
Kimry *(RUS)* ....7 F 1
Kimstad *(S)* .... 197 E 2
Kinbrace *(GB)* .... 26 A 5
Kincardine *(GB)* ..... 30 D 1
Kindberg *(A)* .... 97 F 3
Kindelbrück *(D)* ...... 86 A 4
Kinéta *(GR)* .... 165 G 4
Kingisepp *(RUS)* ....6 C 1
King's Lynn *(GB)* .... 33 G 4
Kingsbridge *(GB)* .... 34 D 5
Kingscourt *(IRL)* ..... 23 F 4
Kingston *(GB)* .... 36 C 4
Kingston
  upon Hull *(GB)* ..... 33 F 2
Kingswear *(GB)* ..... 35 E 4
Kington *(GB)* .... 32 C 5
Kingussie *(GB)* ...... 29 F 4
Kinloch Rannoch *(GB)* .. 29 F 5
Kinlochbervie *(GB)* ... 28 E 1
Kinlochewe *(GB)* .... 28 D 3
Kinna *(S)* .... 195 G 4
Kinnasniemi *(FIN)* ... 193 H 1
Kinnegad *(IRL)* ...... 23 F 5
Kinnitty *(IRL)* .... 25 E 2
Kinnula *(FIN)* .... 185 H 5
Kinross *(GB)* ....31 E 1
Kinsale *(IRL)* .... 24 C 5
Kinsarvik *(N)* .... 188 C 4
Kintai *(LT)* .... 204 B 2
Kintaus *(FIN)* .... 191 H 2
Kintore *(GB)* .... 29 H 4
Kinvarra *(IRL)* .... 24 C 2
Kipilovo *(BG)* .... 159 G 1
Kipinä *(FIN)* .... 185 H 2
Kípoi (Anatolikí Makedonía
  kai Thráki) *(GR)* ..... 163 F 3
Kípoi (Ípeiros) *(GR)* .. 160 C 5
Kipoureío *(GR)* ...... 160 D 5
Kirchbach
  in Steiermark *(A)* ... 97 F 4
Kirchberg *(D)* .... 86 C 5
Kirchberg (Hunsrück) *(D)*. 88 C 2
Kirchberg am Wagram *(A)*. 97 G 1
Kirchberg
  an der Pielach *(A)* ... 97 F 3
Kirchberg in Tirol *(A)* .. 95 H 3
Kirchdorf
  an der Krems *(A)* .... 96 D 2
Kirchenlamitz *(D)* ....91 F 2
Kirchenthumbach *(D)* ...91 F 3
Kirchhain *(D)* .... 85 G 5
Kirchheim *(D)* .... 85 G 5
Kirchheim am Neckar *(D)*. 89 F 4
Kirchheim unter Teck *(D)*. 89 F 5

Kirchheimbolanden *(D)*. 88 D 2
Kirchhundem *(D)* ..... 85 E 4
Kirchlengern *(D)* ..... 85 E 2
Kirchschlag in
  der Buckligen Welt *(A)*. 97 G 3
Kirilovo *(BG)* .... 159 E 2
Kiriši *(RUS)* ....6 D 1
Kırıkağaç *(TR)* ....19 G 3
Kirkby Lonsdale *(GB)* ..31 F 5
Kirkby Stephen *(GB)* ...31 F 5
Kirkcaldy *(GB)* ....31 E 1
Kirkcolm *(GB)* .... 23 H 2
Kirkcudbright *(GB)* ... 30 D 4
Kirkebygden *(N)* ..... 195 F 1
Kirkenær *(N)* .... 189 G 4
Kirkenes *(N)* .... 177 H 3
Kirkham *(GB)* .... 32 C 2
Kírki *(GR)* .... 163 E 3
Kirkintilloch *(GB)* .... 30 D 2
Kirkjubæjarklaustur *(IS)*. 178 C 3
Kirkjubøur
  (Færøerne) *(DK)* ..... 194 A 5
Kirkkonummi /
  Kyrkslätt *(FIN)* .... 191 H 5
Kırklareli *(TR)* ....19 F 1
Kirkonkylä /
  Längelmäen *(FIN)* ... 191 H 2
Kirkovo *(BG)* .... 162 D 2
Kirkwall *(GB)* .... 26 B 3
Kirn *(D)* .... 88 D 2
Kirov *(RUS)* ....7 F 3
Kirovohrad *(UA)* ....13 G 2
Kirriemuir *(GB)* ...... 29 G 5
Kirtorf *(D)* .... 85 F 5
Kiruna *(S)* .... 180 A 3
Kiržač *(RUS)* ....7 G 1
Kisa *(S)* .... 197 E 3
Kisač *(SRB)* .... 140 C 3
Kisar *(H)* .... 127 G 5
Kisbér *(H)* .... 128 D 2
Kiseljak (Bijeljina) *(BIH)*. 137 H 4
Kiseljak (Sarajevo) *(BIH)*. 137 G 4
Kiseljak (Tuzla) *(BIH)* .. 137 G 4
Kishajmás *(H)* .... 128 D 5
Kisielice *(PL)* ....117 H 3
Kisko *(FIN)* .... 191 G 5
Kisköre *(H)* .... 129 H 2
Kiskőrös *(H)* .... 129 F 4
Kiskundorozsma *(H)* .. 129 G 4
Kiskunfélegyháza *(H)*. 129 G 3
Kiskunhalas *(H)* ..... 129 F 4
Kiskunlacháza *(H)* ... 129 F 2
Kiskunmajsa *(H)* ..... 129 G 4
Kismaros *(H)* .... 129 F 1
Kíssamos (Kastélli) / Κίσσαμος
  (Καστέλλι) *(GR)* ... 172 B 3
Kißlegg *(D)* .... 94 D 3
Kissonerga *(CY)* ....174 B 4
Kissoú Kámpos *(GR)* .. 172 C 3
Kistanje *(HR)* .... 136 C 5
Kistelek *(H)* .... 129 G 4
Kisújszállás *(H)* ..... 129 H 2
Kisvárda *(H)* .... 127 F 5
Kiszkowo *(PL)* .... 121 F 1
Kiszombor *(H)* .... 129 H 4
Kitee *(FIN)* .... 193 H 1
Kiten *(BG)* .... 157 F 5
Kiti *(CY)* .... 175 E 4
Kitka *(FIN)* .... 181 G 5
Kitros *(GR)* .... 161 F 4
Kittelfjäll *(S)* .... 189 H 1
Kittsee *(A)* .... 97 H 2
Kitzbühel *(A)* .... 95 H 3
Kitzingen *(D)* .... 89 G 2
Kiukainen *(FIN)* ..... 191 F 3
Kiuruvesi *(FIN)* ...... 187 E 4
Kiutaköngäs (FIN) ... 181 G 5
Kivéri *(GR)* .... 165 G 5
Kivijärvi *(FIN)* .... 185 H 5
Kivilahti *(FIN)* .... 187 H 5
Kiviöli *(EST)* .... 201 G 2
Kivitaipale *(FIN)* ..... 181 E 5
Kivotós *(GR)* .... 160 D 4
Kizári *(GR)* .... 160 D 4

Kjøllefjord *(N)* .... 177 F 1
Kjøpsvik *(N)* .... 179 G 3
Kjustendil /
  Кюстендил *(BG)* .... 158 A 2
Kladanj *(BIH)* .... 137 G 4
Kladnica *(BG)* .... 158 B 2
Kladnice *(HR)* .... 138 B 2
Kladno *(CZ)* .... 92 A 2
Kladovo *(SRB)* ....141 G 4
Kladušnica *(SRB)* ....141 G 4
Klæbu *(N)* .... 182 D 5
Klagenfurt *(A)* .... 96 D 5
Klaipėda *(LT)* .... 204 B 2
Klakegg *(N)* .... 188 C 2
Klaksvík (Færøerne) *(DK)*. 194 B 4
Klana *(HR)* .... 134 B 4
Klanac *(HR)* .... 134 D 5
Knole (D) .... 36 D 4
Knosós (GR) .... 170 C 5
Klanxbüll *(D)* ....81 G 1
Klašnice *(BIH)* ...... 135 G 5
Klässbol *(S)* .... 195 G 1
Klášterec nad Ohří *(CZ)* .91 H 2
Klatovy *(CZ)* ....91 H 4
Klaukkala *(FIN)* ...... 191 H 4
Klausen / Chiusa *(I)*. 103 G 2
Klazienaveen *(NL)* ..... 77 G 3
Kłecko *(PL)* ....117 F 5
Kleczew *(PL)* .... 121 G 1
Kleinhaugsdorf *(A)* ... 92 D 5
Kleinkirchheim *(A)* ... 96 D 5
Kleisoúra *(GR)* ...... 160 D 4
Kleitoría *(GR)* .... 165 E 4
Klembów *(PL)* .... 122 D 1
Klenovica *(HR)* ...... 134 C 4
Kleppe *(N)* .... 194 A 1
Kleppestø *(N)* .... 188 B 4
Kleszczele *(PL)* ....119 H 5
Kleve *(D)* .... 84 B 3
Kličevac *(SRB)* ....141 E 4
Klimavičy *(BY)* ....7 F 4
Klimontów *(PL)* ...... 123 E 4
Klimpfjäll *(S)* .... 183 G 3
Klin *(RUS)* ....7 F 2
Klina *(SRB)* .... 142 D 4
Klinča Sela *(HR)* ..... 134 D 3
Klingenbach *(A)* ..... 97 H 2
Klingenthal *(D)* ....91 G 2
Klintehamn *(S)* ...... 197 G 4
Klippan *(S)* .... 199 F 3
Klippen *(S)* .... 183 G 1
Klirou *(CY)* ....174 D 3
Klis *(HR)* .... 138 B 2
Klisura *(BG)* .... 158 B 2
Klisura *(SRB)* .... 143 G 3
Klitten *(D)* .... 87 F 3
Klixbüll *(D)* ....81 G 1
Kljajićevo *(SRB)* ..... 137 H 1
Ključ *(BIH)* .... 136 D 4
Kłobuck *(PL)* .... 121 H 4
Kłoczew *(PL)* .... 123 E 2
Kłodawa *(PL)* .... 121 H 1
Kłodzko *(PL)* .... 121 E 5
Kløfta *(N)* .... 189 F 5
Klokkarvik *(N)* .... 188 A 4
Klokočevac *(SRB)* ....141 G 5
Klos *(AL)* .... 144 C 1
Kloštar Ivanić *(HR)* .. 135 E 3
Klösterle *(A)* .... 95 E 4
Klosterneuburg *(A)* ... 97 G 1
Klosters *(CH)* .... 99 G 3
Kloten *(CH)* .... 99 E 2
Klötze *(D)* .... 86 A 1
Klöverträsk *(S)* ...... 185 E 2
Klövsjö *(S)* .... 189 H 1
Kluczbork *(PL)* ...... 121 G 4
Kluczewo *(PL)* ....116 D 3
Kluki *(PL)* ....117 F 1
Klukowa Huta *(PL)* ....117 G 2
Klupe *(BIH)* .... 137 F 4
Klütz *(D)* .... 82 C 3
Knäred *(S)* .... 195 G 5
Knaresborough *(GB)* . 33 E 1
Knarvik *(N)* .... 188 B 4
Kneža *(BG)* .... 155 G 2
Knežak *(SLO)* .... 134 B 3
Kneževi Vinogradi *(HR)*. 137 H 1
Kneževo *(HR)* .... 137 G 1

Kneževo /
  Skender Vakuf *(BIH)* .. 137 E 4
Knežica *(BIH)* .... 135 F 4
Knežina *(BIH)* .... 137 H 5
Knić *(SRB)* .... 142 D 1
Knighton *(GB)* .... 32 C 5
Knight's Town *(IRL)* .. 24 A 4
Knin *(HR)* .... 136 C 5
Knittelfeld *(A)* .... 97 E 4
Knivsta *(S)* .... 197 F 1
Knižovnik *(BG)* ...... 162 D 1
Knjaževac /
  Књажевац *(SRB)* .... 143 G 2
Knjaževo *(BG)* .... 159 G 3
Knokke-Heist *(B)* ..... 78 B 1
Knole *(D)* .... 36 D 4
Knosós *(GR)* .... 170 C 5
Knurów *(PL)* .... 122 A 5
Knutsford *(GB)* ...... 32 D 3
Knyszyn *(PL)* ....119 G 4
Kobarid *(SLO)* .... 134 A 2
Kobeljaky *(UA)* ....13 G 1
København *(DK)* ..... 199 E 3
Kobern *(D)* .... 88 D 1
Kobišnica *(SRB)* ......141 G 5
Koblenz *(D)* .... 88 D 1
Kobryn *(BY)* ....12 C 1
Kobylanka *(PL)* ....116 C 4
Kobylin *(PL)* .... 121 F 2
Kobyłka *(PL)* .... 122 D 1
Kocan *(BG)* .... 162 B 1
Kočani *(MK)* .... 143 G 5
Koceljeva *(SRB)* ..... 140 C 5
Kočerin *(BIH)* .... 138 D 2
Kočerinovo *(BG)* ..... 158 B 3
Kočevje *(SLO)* .... 134 C 3
Kochel am See *(D)* ... 95 F 3
Kock *(PL)* .... 123 F 2
Kočmar *(BG)* .... 152 D 5
Kočovo *(BG)* .... 156 D 3
Kocs *(H)* .... 128 D 1
Kocsér *(H)* .... 129 G 2
Kocsola *(H)* .... 128 D 4
Kodeń *(PL)* .... 123 H 2
Kodiksami *(FIN)* ..... 191 F 4
Kodisjoki *(FIN)* ...... 191 F 4
Kodovjat *(AL)* .... 144 D 3
Koeru *(EST)* .... 201 F 2
Kofinou *(CY)* .... 175 E 4
Köflach *(A)* .... 97 F 4
Køge *(DK)* .... 199 E 3
Kohila *(EST)* .... 200 D 2
Kohtla-Järve *(EST)* ... 201 G 1
Koikkala *(FIN)* .... 193 F 2
Koíla *(GR)* .... 161 E 4
Koíli *(GR)* .... 169 E 2
Koilani *(CY)* ....174 C 4
Koilovci *(BG)* .... 156 A 2
Koínyra *(GR)* .... 162 C 5
Koirakoski *(FIN)* ..... 187 F 4
Koivu *(FIN)* .... 185 G 1
Kojetín *(CZ)* .... 93 F 4
Kojnare *(BG)* .... 155 E 3
Kökar *(FIN)* .... 191 E 5
Kokava nad
  Rimavicou *(SK)* .... 133 E 3
Kokemäki *(FIN)* ...... 191 F 3
Kokin Brod *(SRB)* .... 139 H 2
Kokkála *(GR)* .... 168 D 4
Kokkári *(GR)* .... 167 G 5
Kókkino Neró *(GR)* .. 161 G 5
Kokkinotrimithia *(CY)* .174 D 3
Kokkola / Karleby *(FIN)*. 185 F 5
Koksijde-Bad *(B)* ..... 78 A 1
Kola *(BIH)* .... 135 F 5
Kołacze *(PL)* .... 123 G 3
Kolari *(FIN)* .... 180 D 4
Kolari *(SRB)* .... 140 D 4
Kolárovo *(BG)* .... 161 G 2
Kolárovo *(SK)* ...... 132 B 5
Kolašin *(MNE)* .... 139 G 3
Kölbäck *(S)* .... 197 E 1
Kolåsen *(S)* .... 183 F 4
Kołbacz *(PL)* ....116 C 4
Kołbaskowo *(PL)* ......116 B 4
Kolbermoor *(D)* ...... 95 H 3
Kołbiel *(PL)* .... 123 E 1

Kolbuszowa (PL) 123 E5
Kolby Kås (DK) 198 C3
Kolchikó (GR) 161 G3
Kołczewo (PL)...........116 B2
Kołczygłowy (PL) 117 F2
Kolding (DK) 198 C3
Kölesd (H) 129 E4
Kolga-Jaani (EST) 201 F3
Kolho (FIN) 191 G2
Koli (FIN) 187 G5
Kolín (CZ) 92 C3
Kolindrós (GR) 161 F4
Kolka (LV) 202 B1
Kolkanlahti (FIN) 191 H1
Kölleda (D)............. 86 A4
Kollínes (GR) 168 D2
Köln (D).............. 84 C4
Kolno (PL) 119 F3
Koło (PL) 121 H1
Kołobrzeg (PL)..........116 D2
Kolomna (RUS)..........7 G2
Kolomyja (UA) 12 D3
Kolonowskie (PL) 121 G5
Kolossi (CY)...........174 C5
Koloveč (CZ) 91 H4
Kolovrat (SRB) 139 G2
Kolpino (RUS) 6 D1
Kolsva (S) 197 E1
Koluszki (PL) 122 B2
Koluvere (EST) 200 D2
Kolvereid (N) 183 E3
Kolymvári (GR) 172 B2
Koma tou Gialou (CY) .. 175 F2
Komádi (H) 131 E3
Komagfjord (N).........176 D3
Komańcza (PL) 127 F3
Kómanos (GR) 161 E4
Komarevo (BG) 156 A2
Komárno (SK) 132 B5
Komárom (H) 128 D1
Komi (CY) 175 F2
Kómi (GR) 167 E4
Komílio (GR) 164 C3
Komin (HR) 135 E2
Kómito (GR) 166 C4
Komiža (HR) 138 A3
Komló (H) 128 D5
Kömlőd (H) 128 D2
Komméno (GR) 164 C2
Komniná (Anatolikí Makedonía kai Thráki) (GR)...... 162 C2
Komniná (Dytikí Makedonía) (GR) 161 E3
Komninádes (GR) 160 D4
Komorane (SRB) 143 E4
Komorniki (PL) 121 E1
Komotiní / Κομοτηνή (GR) . 162 D2
Kömpöc (H)............ 129 G4
Kompóti (GR) 164 C2
Komulankongäs (FIN).. 187 F3
Komunari (BG) 157 E3
Komuniga (BG) 162 D1
Konak (SRB)........... 140 D3
Konakovo (RUS).........7 F1
Končanica (HR) 135 G3
Kondolovo (BG) 157 F5
Kondoros (H) 129 H3
Kondrić (HR) 135 H4
Køng (DK) 198 D4
Köngernheim (D) 89 E2
Konginkangas (FIN) 191 H1
Kongsberg (N) 189 E5
Kongsfjord (N) 177 G1
Kongsvinger (N) 189 F5
Konice (CZ) 93 E3
Koniecpol (PL) 122 B4
Konieczna (PL) 127 E2
Königs Wusterhausen (D)... 86 D1
Königsbrück (D)........ 87 E4
Königsbrunn (D)....... 89 H5
Königsee (D).......... 86 A5
Königsfeld im Schwarzwald (D)... 94 B2
Königslutter am Elm (D). 85 H2
Königssee (D).......... 96 B3

Königstein (D) 87 E4
Königstein im Taunus (D). 89 E1
Königswiesen (A) 97 E1
Königswinter (D) 84 C5
Konin (PL) 121 G1
Koniskós (GR) 161 E5
Korneuburg (A) 97 G1
Konispol (AL) 144 D5
Kónitsa (GR) 160 C5
Kõnnu (EST) 201 F3
Konjavo (BG) 158 A2
Konjevrate (HR) 136 C5
Konjic (BIH) 139 E2
Konjsko (BIH) 139 E4
Könnern (D) 86 B3
Konnevesi (FIN) 193 E1
Könönpelto (FIN) 193 F1
Konopište (MK) 145 G2
Konopiště (CZ) 92 B3
Konotop (UA) 7 G5
Końskie (PL) 122 C3
Konsko (MK) 145 G2
Konstancin-Jeziorna (PL) 122 D1
Konstantinovy Lázně (CZ) 91 G3
Konstantynów (PL).... 123 G1
Konstantynów Łódzki (PL) 122 B2
Konstanz (D) 94 C3
Kontea (CY) 175 E3
Kontemenos (CY) 174 D3
Kontiás (GR) 162 D5
Kontich (B)............. 78 C2
Kontiolahti (FIN) 187 G5
Kontiomäki (FIN) 187 F3
Kontopoúli (GR) 162 D5
Konttajärvi (FIN) 180 D5
Konz (D) 88 B2
Koosa (EST) 201 G3
Kopanós (GR) 161 E4
Kópasker (IS) 178 C1
Köpenick (D).......... 86 D1
Koper / Capodistria (SLO) 134 A3
Kopervik (N) 188 A5
Kopidlno (CZ) 92 C2
Kopiec (PL)...........119 G3
Köping (S) 197 E1
Köpingsvik (S) 197 F3
Koplik (AL) 142 B5
Köpmanholmen (S) 184 C5
Koporiće (SRB) 143 E3
Koppang (N) 189 F3
Kopparberg (S) 190 A5
Kopperby (D) 81 H1
Koprivlen (BG) 161 H1
Koprivna (BIH) 135 H5
Koprivnica (HR) 135 F2
Koprivštica / Копривщица (BG) . 158 D2
Koprzywnica (PL) 123 E5
Kõpu (EST) 201 E4
Korakou (CY) 174 C3
Korbach (D) 85 F4
Korbevac (SRB) 143 G4
Korbielów (PL) 125 F2
Korbovo (SRB) 141 G4
Korçë (AL) 145 E3
Korčula (HR) 138 C3
Koren (BG) 163 E1
Korenica (HR) 134 D5
Korfantów (PL) 121 F5
Kórfos (GR) 165 G5
Korgen (N) 183 F1
Koria (FIN) 193 E4
Korinós (GR) 161 F4
Korinthos / Κόρινθος (GR).... 165 G4
Korisós (GR) 160 D4
Korissía (GR) 166 B5
Korita (BIH) 139 E3
Korita (HR) 138 D4
Korita (MNE) 139 G4
Koriten (BG) 153 E5
Kórithi (GR) 164 C4
Koritnik (SRB) 142 D2

Korkeakangas (FIN) 193 H1
Korkeakoski (FIN)..... 187 E5
Kormakitis (CY) 174 C2
Körmend (H) 128 B3
Kornica (BG) 161 H1
Kórnik (PL) 121 F1
Kornos (CY) 174 D4
Kornwestheim (D) 89 F4
Környe (H) 129 E2
Koromačno (HR) 134 B5
Koróni / Κορώνη (GR) . 168 C3
Koronisía (GR) 164 C2
Kóronos (GR) 170 C1
Koronoúda (GR) 161 G3
Koronowo (PL) 117 G4
Koropí / Κορωπί (GR).. 165 H5
Körösladány (H) 130 D3
Körösszegapáti (H)......131 E3
Köröstarcsa (H) 130 D3
Korosten' (UA) 13 E1
Korostyšiv (UA) 13 E1
Korpilahti (FIN) 191 H2
Korpilombolo (S)...... 180 C5
Korpo / Korppoo (FIN) . 191 F5
Korppoo / Korpo (FIN) . 191 F5
Korsberga (S) 196 D4
Korsholm / Mustasaari (FIN) 185 E5
Korsnäs (FIN) 191 E1
Korsør (DK) 198 D4
Korsun'-Ševčenkivs'kyj (UA) ...13 F1
Korsze (PL)............119 E2
Kortesjärvi (FIN) 185 F5
Kórthio (GR) 166 C5
Kortrijk (Courtrai) (B) 78 B2
Korttenperä (FIN) 185 H1
Korvala (FIN) 181 E5
Korvaluoma (FIN) 191 F2
Korycin (PL)...........119 G3
Koryfási (GR) 168 B3
Kos / Κως (GR) 171 F2
Kosančić (SRB) 143 F3
Kosanica (MNE) 139 G3
Košarovce (SK) 133 H2
Kosarska Dubica / Bosanska Dubica (BIH) 135 F4
Košava (BG) 151 E4
Kościan (PL) 121 E2
Kościelec (PL) 121 H1
Kościerzyna (PL) 117 G2
Kose (EST) 201 E2
Kose-Uuemõisa (EST) . 201 E2
Kosel (MK) 145 E2
Koserow (D) 83 G3
Košice (SK) 133 G3
Kosjerić (SRB) 139 H1
Koška (HR) 135 H4
Koskenkorva (FIN) 191 F1
Koskenpää (FIN) 191 H2
Koski (FIN) 191 G4
Koski (FIN) 191 F2
Koskue (FIN) 191 F2
Kosmás (GR) 168 D3
Kósmio (GR) 162 D2
Kosovo Polje / Fushë Kosovë (SRB) . 143 E4
Kosovska Kamenica (SRB) ... 143 F4
Kosovska Mitrovica / Kosovska Mitrovicë 143 E3
Kosovska Mitrovicë / Kosovska Mitrovica 143 E3
Kosów Lacki (PL) 119 F5
Kössen (A) 95 H3
Kósta (GR) 165 G5
Kostandenec (BG) 156 C2
Kostandovo (BG) 158 C3
Kostanjevac (HR) 134 D3
Kostanjevica na Krki (SLO) 134 D3
Kostelec nad Černými Lesy (CZ).. 92 B3
Kostelec nad Orlicí (CZ). 92 D2

Kostenec (BG).......... 158 C2
Koster (S) 195 F2
Kosti (BG) 157 F5
Kostinbrod (BG) 158 B1
Kostolac (SRB).........141 E4
Kostomłoty (PL) 121 E4
Kostopil' (UA) 12 D1
Kostrzyn (PL) 121 F1
Kostrzyn nad Odrą (PL)..116 B5
Kosturino (MK) 145 H1
Kosula (FIN) 193 F1
Koszalin (PL) 116 D2
Kőszeg (H) 128 B2
Koszyce (PL) 125 H1
Kotala (GR) 181 G4
Kotala (FIN) 191 G2
Kótas (GR) 160 D3
Kotel (BG) 159 G1
Koterka (PL) 123 G1
Köthen (D) 86 B3
Kotka (FIN) 193 F4
Kotor (MNE) 139 F4
Kotor-Varoš (BIH) 137 E4
Kotoriba (HR) 135 F2
Kotorsko (BIH) 135 H5
Kotovs'k (UA) 13 F2
Kotraža (SRB) 139 H1
Kótronas (GR) 168 D4
Köttsjön (S) 183 H5
Koufália (GR) 161 F3
Koufós (GR) 161 H5
Kouklia (CY) 174 B5
Koukounariés (GR) 165 H2
Kouloúra (GR) 161 F4
Kounoupélli (GR) 164 D4
Kounoupidianá (GR) .. 170 A5
Koura (FIN) 191 F1
Kourion (CY) 174 C5
Kouroúta (GR) 164 D5
Koutsó (GR) 162 C3
Koutsóchero (GR) 165 F1
Koutsourás (GR) 173 F4
Kouvola (FIN) 193 F3
Kovačevci (Pernik) (BG). 158 A2
Kovačevci (Sofia-Grad) (BG).....158 B2
Kovačevica / Ковачевица (BG) 161 H1
Kovačevo (BG) 159 G2
Kovačica (SRB) 140 D3
Kovel' (UA) 12 D1
Kõveriku (EST) 201 F2
Kovero (FIN) 193 H1
Kovilj (SRB) 140 C3
Kovin (SRB) 141 E4
Kovrov (RUS)..........7 H1
Kowal (PL) 118 B5
Kowalewo Pomorskie (PL)...117 H4
Kowary (PL) 120 D4
Köyliö (FIN) 191 F3
Kozáni / Κοζάνη (GR) . 161 E4
Kozarac (BIH) 135 F5
Kozarac (HR) 137 G1
Kozel'sk (RUS) 7 G3
Kozica (HR) 138 C3
Koziegłowy (PL) 121 H5
Kozienice (PL) 123 E2
Kozina (SLO) 134 B3
Kozjatyn (UA) 13 E1
Kozloduj (BG) 151 F5
Kozlovec (BG) 156 B2
Kozluk (BIH) 137 H4
Koźmin Wielkopolski (PL) ... 121 F2
Kożuchów (PL) 120 C2
Kragenæs (DK) 198 D4
Kragerø (N) 194 D1
Kragujevac / Крагујевац (SRB) ... 143 E1
Kraište (BG) 161 H1
Krajan (AL) 142 C5
Krajenka (PL) 117 E4
Krajišnik (SRB) 140 D2
Krajkovac (SRB) 143 F2
Krajnik Dolny (PL)...116 B4

Krakės (LT) 205 E3
Krakhella (N) 188 B3
Kraków (PL) 125 G1
Krakow am See (D) ... 83 E4
Kraljevica (HR) 134 B4
Kraljevo / Краљево (SRB) ... 142 D1
Král'ovec (CZ) 87 H5
Kralovice (CZ) 91 H3
Kráľovský Chlmec (SK) . 133 H3
Kralupy nad Vltavou (CZ). 92 A2
Kramfors (S) 190 C1
Kramolin (BG) 159 E1
Kramsk (PL) 121 G1
Krän (BG) 159 E2
Kranenburg (D) 84 B3
Krani (MK) 145 E3
Kranídi (GR) 169 E2
Kranj (SLO) 134 B2
Kranjska Gora (SLO) .. 134 A1
Kranovo (BG) 153 E5
Krape (Lobe) (LV) 203 E3
Krapina (HR) 135 E2
Krapinske Toplice (HR). 135 E2
Krapkowice (PL) 121 G5
Krasen (BG) 153 E5
Krašić (HR) 134 D3
Krasiczyn (PL) 127 G2
Kráslava (LV) 203 G5
Kraslice (CZ) 91 G2
Krásná Lípa (CZ) 87 E4
Kraśniczyn (PL) 123 G4
Kraśnik (PL) 123 F4
Krasno Polje (HR) 134 C5
Krasnobród (PL) 123 G5
Krásnohorské Podhradie (SK) ... 133 F3
Krasnohrad (UA) 13 H1
Krasnopol (PL)...........119 G2
Krasnosielc (PL)...........119 E4
Krasnovo (BG) 158 D2
Krasnyj Cholm (RUS) ...7 F1
Krasnystaw (PL) 123 G4
Krasocin (PL) 122 C4
Kráthio (GR) 165 F4
Krátigos (GR) 167 F2
Kratovo (MK) 143 G5
Kratovska Stena (SRB).. 139 H1
Krauchenwies (D) 94 C3
Krautheim (D) 89 G3
Kravaře (CZ) 93 F2
Kravarsko (HR) 135 E3
Krefeld (D) 84 B4
Krekenava (LT) 205 E2
Kremastí (Nótio Aigaío) (GR) ... 171 H3
Kremastí (Pelopónnisos) (GR) .. 169 E3
Kremenčuk (UA) 13 G1
Kremenec' (UA) 12 D2
Kremenica (MK) 145 F3
Kremmen (D) 86 C1
Kremna (SRB) 139 G1
Kremnica (SK) 132 C3
Krems an der Donau (A). 97 F1
Kremsmünster (A) ... 96 D2
Krepča (BG) 156 C2
Krepoljin (SRB)...........141 F5
Kreševo (BIH) 137 F5
Kresna (BG) 161 G1
Krestcy (RUS) 7 E1
Kréstena (GR) 164 D5
Kretinga (LT) 204 B2
Kreuth (D) 95 G3
Kreuzlingen (CH) 99 F1
Kreuztal (D) 84 D4
Kričim (BG) 158 D3
Krieglach (A) 97 F3
Kriens (CH) 99 E3
Krikello (GR) 165 E2
Kríkellos (GR) 164 D2
Krimml (A) 95 H4

Krimpen aan den IJssel (NL) 76 D5
Krinídes (GR) 162 B3
Kristdala (S) 197 E4
Kristiansand (N) 194 C2
Kristianstad (S) 199 F3
Kristiansund (N) 182 B5
Kristiinankaupunki / Kristinestad (FIN) ... 191 E2
Kristineberg (S) 184 C3
Kristinehamn (S) 195 H1
Kristinehov (S) 199 F3
Kristinestad / Kristiinankaupunki (FIN) ... 191 E2
Kritinía (GR) 171 H3
Kritou Tera (CY) 174 B4
Kritsá (GR) 173 E3
Kriukai (LT) 205 E1
Kriva Feja (SRB) 143 G4
Kriva Palanka (MK) .. 143 G5
Kriváň (SK) 132 D3
Krivodol (BG) 154 D3
Krivogaštani (MK) ... 145 F2
Krivolak (MK) 145 G1
Křižanov (CZ) 92 D4
Križevci (HR) 135 F2
Krk (HR) 134 B5
Krnjača (SRB) 140 D4
Krnjak (HR) 134 D4
Krnjeuša (BIH) 135 E5
Krnjevo (SRB).........141 E5
Krnov (CZ) 93 F2
Krobia (PL) 121 E2
Kroczyce (PL) 122 B5
Krokeide (N) 188 B4
Krokek (S) 197 E2
Krokialaukis (LT) 205 E4
Krokom (S) 183 G5
Kroksjö (S) 184 C3
Krolevec' (UA)..........7 G5
Kroměříž (CZ) 93 F4
Kronach (D)...........91 E2
Kronborg Slot (DK) .. 199 E3
Kronoby / Kruunupyy (FIN) ... 185 F5
Kronštadt (RUS)..........6 C1
Kröpelin (D)........... 82 D3
Kropp (D).............81 H2
Kroppenstedt (D) 86 A2
Krościenko (PL) 127 G2
Krościenko nad Dunajcem (PL). 125 H2
Krosna (LT)........... 205 E5
Krośniewice (PL) 121 H1
Krosno (PL) 127 F2
Krosno Odrzańskie (PL). 120 C2
Krotos (GR)...........172 D4
Krotoszyn (PL) 121 F2
Krousónas (GR) 172 D3
Krška vas (SLO) 134 C3
Krško (SLO) 134 C3
Krstac (MNE) 139 F3
Krstinja (HR) 134 D4
Kruë i Fushës (AL) ... 142 C5
Kruiningen (NL) 78 C1
Krujë (AL) 144 C4
Krumbach (D) 89 H5
Krummhörn (D) 80 D4
Krumovgrad (BG) 163 E2
Krumovo Gradište (BG). 159 H2
Krumpendorf am Wörther See (A) ... 96 B3
Krün (D) 95 F3
Kruonis (LT) 205 F4
Kruopiai (LT) 204 D1
Krupá (CZ)...........91 H2
Krupa na Vrbasu (BIH). 137 E4
Krupac (BIH) 137 G5
Krupac (SRB) 143 H3
Krupaja (SRB)..........141 F5
Krupište (MK) 143 G5
Krupnik (BG) 161 G1
Kruså (DK) 198 B4
Krušare (BG) 159 G2

A B C D E F G H I J **K** L M N O P Q R S T U V W X Y Z

Krušari (BG) 153 E5
Kruščica (BIH) 137 F5
Kruśedol (SRB) 140 C3
Kruševac / Крушевац (SRB) 143 E4
Kruševec (BG) 157 F5
Kruševica (SRB) 140 D5
Kruševo (MK) 145 E2
Krušovene (BG) 151 G5
Kruszwica (PL) 117 G5
Krute (MNE) 139 G5
Kruunupyy / Kronoby (FIN) .. 185 F2
Krýa Vrýsi (GR) 161 F3
Kryčaŭ (BY) 7 E4
Krynica (PL) 125 H2
Krynica Morska (PL)..118 B1
Krynki (PL) 119 H4
Kryonéri (Korinthia) (GR). 165 F4
Kryonéri (Messinía) (GR). 168 C2
Kryopigi (GR) 161 H5
Krystallopigi (GR) 160 D3
Kryvyj Rih (UA).........13 G2
Krzepice (PL)......... 121 H4
Krzeszowice (PL) 125 F1
Krzeszyce (PL) 116 C5
Krzynowłoga Mała (PL) .118 D4
Krzywcza (PL)........ 127 F2
Krzywiń (PL) 121 E2
Krzyż Wielkopolski (PL).116 D5
Książ Wielkopolski (PL). 121 F2
Küblis (CH) 99 G3
Kubrat / Кубрат (BG) .. 152 C5
Kučevište (MK) 143 F5
Kučevo (SRB) 141 F5
Kuchl (A) 96 C3
Kućište (HR) 138 C3
Kućište (SRB) 139 H4
Kuçovë (AL) 144 C3
Kudirkos Naumiestis (LT). 204 D4
Kudowa-Zdrój (PL) 120 D5
Kufstein (A) 95 H3
Kühlungsborn (D)....... 82 D3
Kuhmalahti (FIN) 191 H3
Kuhmo (FIN) 187 G3
Kuhmoinen (FIN)..... 191 H3
Kuivajärvi (FIN) 187 G3
Kuivalahti (FIN) 191 E3
Kuiviniemi (FIN) 185 G2
Kuivasjärvi (FIN) 191 F2
Kuivastu (EST) 200 C3
Kukës (AL) 142 D5
Kukko (FIN) 191 G1
Kuklen (BG) 158 D3
Kukljica (HR) 136 B5
Kukujevci (SRB) 137 H3
Kukulje (BIH) 135 G5
Kula (BG) 150 D5
Kula (TR) 19 H3
Kula / Кула (SRB) 140 B2
Kuldiga (LV) 202 B3
Kulen Vakuf (BIH) 136 C4
Kulennoinen (FIN) 193 G2
Kuliai (LT) 204 C2
Kulina (SRB) 143 F2
Kulju (FIN) 191 G3
Kullaa (FIN) 191 F3
Kulmbach (D) 91 E3
Kuloharju (FIN) 187 F1
Külsheim (D)......... 89 G2
Kultakero (FIN) 181 F4
Kumane (SRB) 140 C2
Kumanovo (MK) 143 F5
Kumla (S) 196 D1
Kumlinge (FIN) 191 E5
Kummavuopio (S)....176 C5
Kumrovec (HR)...... 134 D2
Kunadacs (H) 129 F3
Kunágota (H) 130 D4
Kunda (EST)......... 201 F1
Kungälv (S) 195 F3
Kungsbacka (S) 195 F4
Kungshamn (S) 195 F2
Kungsör (S) 197 E1
Kunhegyes (H) 129 H2
Kunmadaras (H)..... 129 H2
Kunpeszér (H)....... 129 F3

Kunrau (D) 86 A1
Kunszentmárton (H) ... 129 G3
Kunszentmiklós (H) 129 F3
Künzelsau (D)......... 89 G3
Kuolio (FIN) 187 F1
Kuopio (FIN) 187 F5
Kuorevesi (FIN) 191 H2
Kuortane (FIN) 191 G1
Kuortti (FIN) 193 E3
Kup (H) 128 C2
Kupferzell (D) 89 G3
Kupinovo (SRB) 140 C4
Kupiškis (LT) 205 F2
Kupres (BIH) 137 E5
Kurbnesh (AL) 144 C1
Kurd (H) 128 D4
Kurenalus / Pudasjärvi (FIN) 187 E2
Kuressaare (EST) 200 B4
Kurikka (FIN) 191 F1
Kuřim (CZ) 93 E4
Kurów (PL) 123 F3
Kuršėnai (LT) 204 D1
Kursk (RUS) 7 G4
Kursu (FIN) 181 F5
Kuršumlija (SRB) 143 E3
Kuršumlijska Banja (SRB). 143 E3
Kurtakko (FIN) 180 D4
Kurtuvėnai (LT) 204 D2
Kuru (FIN) 191 G2
Kurzętnik (PL)........118 C4
Kusadak (SRB) 140 D5
Kuşadası (TR) 19 G3
Kusel (D) 88 C3
Küsnacht (CH) 99 E2
Küssnacht am Rigi (CH). 99 E2
Kustavi (FIN) 191 E4
Kütahya (TR) 19 H2
Kutas (H) 128 C4
Kutina (HR) 135 F4
Kutjevo (HR) 135 H4
Kutná Hora (CZ) 92 C3
Kutno (PL) 122 B1
Kuttanen (FIN) 176 D5
Kuttura (FIN) 177 F5
Kúty (SK) 132 A3
Kuumu (FIN) 187 G3
Kuusalu (EST) 201 E1
Kuusamo (FIN) 187 F1
Kuusankoski (FIN) ... 193 F3
Kuusjärvi (FIN) 193 G1
Kuusjoki (FIN) 191 G4
Kuvšinovo (RUS) 7 F2
Kužiai (LT) 204 D1
Kuzma (SLO) 135 E1
Kuzmin (SRB) 140 B3
Kuźnia Raciborska (PL). 125 E1
Kuźnica (PL) 119 H3
Kuźnica (PL) 127 F2
Kv. Sarafovo (BG) 157 F4
Kvænangsbotn (N)..... 176 C4
Kværndrup (DK) 198 C4
Kvalsund (N) 176 D2
Kvam (N) 189 E2
Kvanndal (N) 188 C4
Kvędarna (LT) 204 C2
Kvernes (N) 182 B5
Kvevlax (FIN) 185 E5
Kvikkjokk (S) 179 H5
Kvinesdal (N) 194 B2
Kviteseid (N) 194 D1
Kwidzyn (PL).........117 H3
Kyani (GR) 163 F2
Kybartai (LT) 204 D4
Kyïv = Kiev (UA).......13 F1
Kyjov (SK) 93 E5
Kykkos (CY)........174 C4
Kylänlahti (FIN) 187 G5
Kylänpää (FIN) 191 F1
Kyle of Lochalsh (GB).. 28 C4
Kyleakin (GB) 28 C4
Kylerhea (GB) 28 C4
Kylestrome (GB) 28 E1
Kyllburg (D) 88 B1
Kyllíni (GR) 164 C4
Kylmäkoski (FIN) ... 191 G3
Kylmälä (FIN) 185 H3

Kymási (GR)........... 165 H3
Kými (GR) 166 B3
Kyparíssi (GR) 169 E3
Kyparissía / Κυπαρισσία (GR)..... 168 B2
Kypárissos (GR) 165 F1
Kyperounta (CY)....174 C4
Kyra (CY)............174 D3
Kyritz (D) 83 E5
Kyrksæterøra (N)....... 182 C5
Kyrkslätt / Kirkkonummi (FIN) .. 191 H5
Kyröskoski (FIN) 191 G3
Kyrtóni (GR) 165 G3
Kyselka (CZ) 91 G2
Kýthira (GR) 169 E5
Kýthnos (GR) 169 G2
Kythrea (CY) 175 E3
Kyyjärvi (FIN) 185 G5
Kómi (GR) 166 D5

L

La Adrada (E) 64 A3
La Alberca (E) 63 F3
La Alberca de Záncara (E). 65 E4
La Alberguería de Argañán (E)........ 63 E3
La Albuera (E) 69 E2
La Aldea de San Nicolás (E) 67 G5
La Algaba (E) 69 G5
La Almarcha (E) 65 E4
La Almunia de Doña Godina (E) 59 F5
La Antilla (E) 69 E5
La Azohía (E) 73 E4
La Bañeza (E) 57 G4
La Barca de la Florida (E).74 B3
La Barthe-de-Neste (F).. 52 D4
La Bassée (F)......... 39 H2
La Bastide-Clairence (F). 52 B3
La Bastide-de-Sérou (F). 53 F4
La Bâtie-Neuve (F)....51 F5
La Baule (F) 43 E4
La Bégude-de-Mazenc (F). 50 D5
La Bérarde (F)........ 51 F4
La Bisbal de Falset (E) .. 60 B4
La Bisbal d'Empordà (E).. 61 F2
La Bonneville-sur-Iton (F). 39 F5
La Bourboule (F) 49 H3
La Bóveda de Toro (E) ... 63 H1
La Brède (F).......... 48 C5
La Bresse (F) 47 G3
La Cabrera (E)......... 64 C1
La Calahorra (E) 71 E5
La Caletta (I) 112 C4
La Calzada de Oropesa (E) 63 H4
La Campana (E) 69 H5
La Canourgue (F) 54 A1
La Capelle (F) 40 B3
La Carlota (E) 70 B4
La Carolina (E) 70 D3
La Cavalerie (F) 54 A2
La Chaise-Dieu (F) ... 50 B4
La Chambre (F) 51 F3
La Chapelle- d'Angillon (F) 45 E4
La Chapelle- de-Guinchay (F)...... 50 D2
La Chapelle- en-Valgaudémar (F)....51 F4
La Chapelle- en-Vercors (F)........51 E4
La Charité-sur-Loire (F).. 45 F5
La Chartre-sur-le-Loir (F). 44 C3
La Châtaigneraie (F) .. 48 C1
La Châtre (F) 49 G1
La Chaux-de-Fonds (CH). 98 B2
La Chèze (F) 42 D2
La Ciotat (F) 55 E3
La Clayette (F) 50 C1
La Clusaz (F) 51 F2
La Codosera (E) 69 E1
La Coronada (E) 69 H1
La Côte-Saint-André (F). 50 D3
La Couronne (F)...... 48 D3

La Courtine (F).......... 49 H3
La Couvertoirade (F) ... 54 A2
La Crau (F) 55 F3
La Croix-Valmer (F)... 55 F3
La Cumbre (E) 63 F5
La Cure (F) 51 F1
La Espina (E) 57 F1
La Féclaz (F) 51 F3
La Fère (F) 40 A4
La Ferté-Alais (F) 45 E2
La Ferté-Bernard (F).. 44 C2
La Ferté-en-Ouche (F). 44 C1
La Ferté-Gaucher (F).. 45 G1
La Ferté-Macé (F) ... 43 H1
La Ferté-Milon (F)... 40 A5
La Ferté- Saint-Aubin (F). 45 E3
La Ferté- sous-Jouarre (F)... 40 A5
La Ferté-Vidame (F).. 44 C1
La Flèche (F) 43 H3
La Font de la Figuera (E). 73 E1
La Fregeneda (E) 63 E2
La Frontera (E) 65 E2
La Fuente de San Esteban (E) ... 63 F2
La Gacilly (F) 43 E3
La Garde-Freinet (F).. 55 F3
La Garriga (E) 60 D3
La Gineta (E) 65 E5
La Granadella (E)..... 60 B4
La Grand-Combe (F) .. 54 B1
La Grand-Croix (F) .. 50 C3
La Grande-Motte (F).. 54 B3
La Granjuela (E) 69 H3
La Grave (F)..........51 F4
La Guardia (E) 64 C4
La Guardia de Jaén (E). 70 D4
La Guerche- de-Bretagne (F)..... 43 G3
La Guerche- sur-l'Aubois (F)...... 45 F5
La Haye-du-Puits (F).. 38 B4
La Haye-Pesnel (F) .. 43 F1
La Hermida (E) 58 A1
La Herradura (E) 75 F4
La Horcajada (E) 63 G3
La Horra (E) 58 B5
La Iglesuela del Cid (E).. 66 A1
La Jana (E) 66 A1
La Javie (F) 55 F1
La Jonquera (E) 61 E1
La Laguna (E) 67 F5
La Latte, fort (F)...... 43 E1
La Léchère (F)........51 F3
La Línea de la Concepción (E) ..74 C4
La Londe-les-Maures (F). 55 F3
La Losa (E) 71 F4
La Loupe (F) 44 C2
La Louvière (B) 78 C3
La Luisiana (E) 69 H5
La Machine (F) 45 G5
La Maddalena (I) 112 C1
La Magdalena (E) 57 G3
La Malène (F) 54 A1
La Manga del Mar Menor (E)..... 73 E4
La Mesa Roldán (E) .. 72 C5
La Molina (E) 60 D2
La Mongie (F) 52 D4
La Mothe-Achard (F).. 48 B1
La Mothe-Saint-Héray (F). 48 D1
La Motte-Chalancon (F). 51 E5
La Motte-du-Caire (F). 55 E1
La Mudarra (E) 57 H5
La Muela (E) 59 G5
La Mure (F) 51 E4
La Napoule (F) 55 G2
La Nava de Ricomalillo (E). 63 H5
La Nava de Santiago (E). 69 F1
La Neuve-Lyre (F) ... 39 E5
La Neuveville (CH) ... 98 C2
La Nuez de Arriba (E). 58 B3
La Oliva (E) 67 H5
La Orotava (E) 67 F5
La Paca (E) 71 H4

La Pacaudière (F) 50 B2
La Pallice (F) 48 B2
La Palma del Condado (E). 69 F5
La Petite-Pierre (F)....41 G5
La Pinilla (E) 64 C1
La Plagne (F)..........51 G3
La Plaza (E) 57 F2
La Pobla de Benifassà (E). 66 A1
La Pobla de Lillet (E) .. 60 D2
La Pobla de Massaluca (E). 60 A4
La Pobla de Segur (E).. 60 C2
La Pobla de Vallbona (E). 65 H4
La Pobla Llarga (E) ... 65 H5
La Pobla Tornesa (E) .. 66 A2
La Pola de Gordón (E). 57 G3
La Porta (F) 55 H3
La Primaube (F) 53 H1
La Puebla de Almoradiel (E) .. 64 C4
La Puebla de Cazalla (E). 69 H5
La Puebla de Híjar (E).. 65 H1
La Puebla de los Infantes (E)... 69 H4
La Puebla de Montalbán (E) 64 A4
La Puebla de Valverde (E). 65 G3
La Puebla del Río (E).. 69 G5
La Pueblanueva (E) ... 64 A4
La Puerta de Segura (E). 71 F3
La Rábita (E) 75 G3
La Rambla (E) 70 B4
La Réole (F) 48 D5
La Rinconada (E) 69 G5
La Rivière-Thibouville (F). 39 E5
La Robla (E) 57 G3
La Roca de la Sierra (E). 69 F1
La Roca del Vallès (E)..61 E3
La Roche-Bernard (F).. 43 E4
La Roche-Canillac (F). 49 G4
La Roche-Chalais (F).. 48 D4
La Roche-Derrien (F).. 42 D1
La Roche-en-Ardenne (B). 79 E4
La Roche-Guyon (F).. 39 G5
La Roche-Posay (F)... 44 C5
La Roche-sur-Foron (F).51 F2
La Roche-sur-Yon (F).. 48 B1
La Rochefoucauld (F).. 49 E3
La Rochelle (F)....... 48 B2
La Rochepot (F)...... 45 H5
La Rochette (F) 51 F3
La Roda (E) 65 E5
La Roda de Andalucía (E). 70 B5
La Roquebrussanne (F). 55 E3
La Roque-Gageac (F).. 49 F5
La Rosière 1850 (F)....51 G3
La Salceda (E) 64 B1
La Salvetat-Peyralès (F). 53 G1
La Salvetat-sur-Agout (F). 53 H2
La Seca (E) 63 H1
La Selva del Camp (E).. 60 C4
La Sénia (E) 66 A1
La Seu d'Urgell (E) ... 60 C2
La Seyne (F) 55 E3
La Solana (E) 71 E1
La Souterraine (F) ... 49 G2
La Spezia (I) 105 F3
La Sterza (I) 105 G5
La Suze-sur-Sarthe (F). 43 H3
La Teste-de-Buch (F).. 48 B5
La Thuile (I) 100 B3
La Torre del Valle (E) .. 57 G4
La Torre d'En Besora (E). 66 A1
La Tour-d'Auvergne (F). 49 H3
La Tour-du-Pin (F)....51 E3
La Tour-Fondue (F) .. 55 F4
La Toussuire (F) 51 F4
La Tranche-sur-Mer (F). 48 B1
La Tremblade (F) 48 B3
La Trimouille (F) 49 F1
La Trinité (F) 42 D3
La Trinité-Porhoët (F). 43 E2
La Turballe (F) 43 E4
La Turbie (F) 55 H2
La Unión (E) 73 E4
La Vall d'Uixó / Vall de Uxó (E) .. 65 H4
La Vecilla (E) 57 H3

La Vellés (E)............ 63 G2
La Verpillière (F) 50 D3
La Vila Joiosa (E) 66 A5
La Vilella Baixa (E) .. 60 B4
La Villa (I) 103 E2
La Villa de Don Fadrique (E)..... 64 C4
La Villedieu-du-Clain (F). 49 E1
La Virgen del Camino (E). 57 G3
La Voulte-sur-Rhône (F). 50 D5
La Wantzenau (F)......47 H1
La Yesa (E) 65 H4
Laa an der Thaya (A) .. 92 D5
Laage (D) 83 E3
Laagri (EST) 200 D2
Läätsa (EST) 200 B4
Labajos (E)........... 64 A2
Labanoras (LT) 205 G3
Labasheeda (IRL) 24 C3
Labastide-Murat (F).. 49 G5
Labastide-Rouairoux (F). 53 H3
L'Aber-Wrac'h (F) .. 42 B1
Labin / Albona (HR) .. 134 B4
Labinot-Fushë (AL)... 144 D2
Łabiszyn (PL) 117 G5
Lábod (H) 128 C5
Laboe (D) 81 H2
Labouheyre (F) 52 B1
Labrit (F) 52 C1
Labruguière (F) 53 G3
Labudnjaca (SRB) .. 137 H2
Laç (AL) 144 C1
Lacanau (F) 48 B4
Lacanau-Océan (F)... 48 B4
Lacapelle-Marival (F). 49 G5
Laćarak (SRB) 140 B4
Lacave, grottes de (F).. 49 G5
Lacedonia (I).........110 C3
Lachanás (GR) 161 G3
Łąck (PL) 122 B1
Łącko (PL) 125 H2
Läckö (S) 195 G2
Laconi (I) 112 C4
Lacq (F) 52 C3
Lacu Roșu (RO) 148 B4
Lacu Sărat (RO) 153 E2
Lad (H) 128 C5
Ląd (PL) 121 G1
Ladbergen (D) 84 D1
Lądek-Zdrój (PL) ... 121 E5
Lădești (RO) 151 F3
Ládi (GR) 163 F2
Ladispoli (I) 108 D3
Ladoeiro (P) 62 D4
Lærdal (N) 188 C3
Láerma (GR) 171 H3
Laferté-sur-Amance (F). 47 E3
Laffrey (F) 51 E4
Láfka (GR) 165 F5
Lafrançaise (F) 53 F1
Lagan (S) 195 H5
Laganás (GR) 164 C5
Lagartera (E) 63 H4
Lage (D) 85 F2
Laggan (GB) 29 E4
Lagká (Pelopónnisos) (GR).. 168 D4
Lagkáda (Vóreio Aigaío) (GR). 167 E3
Lagkadás (GR) 161 G3
Lagkádia (GR) 165 E5
Lagkadíkia (GR) ... 161 G3
Lagnieu (F) 51 E2
Lagny (F) 39 H5
Lago (I)............113 E2
Lagoa (P) 68 B5
Lagoaça (P) 63 E1
Lagonegro (I).........110 D5
Lágos (GR) 162 D3
Lagos (P) 68 B5
Lagoudera (CY).....174 C4
Łagów (Świebodzin) (PL) .. 120 D5
Lagrasse (F)......... 53 H4
Laguarres (E) 60 A2

Laguarta (E) .... 59 H 3
Laguépie (F) .... 53 G 1
Laguiole (F) .... 50 A 5
Laguna de Duero (E) .... 58 A 5
Lagyná (GR) .... 161 G 3
Lahiguera (E) .... 70 D 4
Lahinch (IRL) .... 24 B 2
Lahnstein (D) .... 88 D 1
Laholm (S) .... 195 G 5
Lahr (D) .... 88 D 5
Lahti (FIN) .... 191 H 3
Laichingen (D) .... 89 G 5
Laide (GB) .... 28 D 2
L'Aigle (F) .... 44 C 1
Laignes (F) .... 45 H 3
Laigueglia (I) .... 104 C 4
L'Aiguillon-sur-Mer (F) .. 48 B 1
Laihia (FIN) .... 191 F 1
Laiküla (EST) .... 200 D 3
Laïliás (GR) .... 161 H 2
Laimbach
am Ostrong (A) ...... 97 E 1
Laimjala (EST) .... 200 C 3
Laimoluokta (S)....... 180 A 3
Lainate (I) .... 101 E 4
Lairg (GB) .... 26 A 5
Laissac-
Sévérac-l'Eglise (F) ... 53 H 1
Laïsta (GR) .... 160 C 5
Laisvall (S) .... 183 H 1
Laitikkala (FIN) .... 191 G 3
Laitila (FIN) .... 191 F 4
Laižuva (LT) .... 204 D 1
Lajkovac (SRB) .... 140 C 5
Lajosmizse (H) .... 129 F 3
Lakavica (MK) .... 145 G 1
Läki (BG) .... 162 C 1
Lakitelek (H) .... 129 G 3
Lákka (GR) .... 164 B 1
Lakki (GR) .... 171 F 1
Lákkoi (GR) .... 172 B 3
Lákkoma (GR) .... 162 D 4
Lakkópetra (GR) .... 164 D 4
Lakócsa (H) .... 128 D 5
Lakselv (N) .... 177 E 3
Laktaši (BIH) .... 135 G 5
Lálas (GR) .... 164 D 5
Lalbenque (F) .... 53 F 1
L'Alcora (E) .... 65 H 3
L'Alcúdia (E) .... 65 H 5
L'Alcúdia de Crespins (E) . 73 F 1
L'Aldea (E) .... 60 B 5
Lale (BG) .... 162 D 1
L'Alfàs del Pi /
Alfaz del Pí (E)...... 66 A 5
Laliki (PL) .... 125 F 2
Lalín (E) .... 56 C 3
Lalinac (SRB) .... 143 F 2
Lalinde (F) .... 49 E 5
Lalm (N) .... 189 E 2
Lalouvesc (F) .... 50 C 4
Lalueza (E) .... 59 H 4
Lam (D) .... 91 H 5
Lama dei Peligni (I) ... 109 G 2
Lamalou-les-Bains (F) .. 54 A 2
Lamarche (F) .... 47 E 2
Lamarque (F) .... 48 C 4
Lamastre (F) .... 50 C 4
Lambach (A) .... 96 D 2
Lamballe (F) .... 43 E 2
Lambesc (F) .... 54 D 2
Lambrecht (D) .... 88 D 3
Lamego (P) .... 62 C 1
L'Ametlla de Mar (E)..... 60 B 5
Lamía / Λαμία (GR) ... 165 F 2
Lamlash (GB) .... 23 H 1
Lammhult (S) .... 195 H 4
Lammi (FIN) .... 191 H 3
Lamotte-Beuvron (F)... 45 E 4
Lampaul (F) .... 42 A 1
Lámpeia (GR) .... 165 E 5
Lampertheim (D) .... 89 E 2
Lampeter (GB) .... 34 D 1
Lampíri (GR) .... 165 E 4
L'Ampolla (E) .... 60 B 5
Lámpou Mýloi (GR) ... 167 F 2
Lamstedt (D) .... 81 G 4

Lamure-sur-Azergues (F) . 50 C 2
Lana (I) .... 101 H 2
Lanaja (E) .... 59 H 4
Lanaken (B) .... 79 E 2
Lanark (GB) .... 30 D 2
Lancaster (GB) .... 32 C 1
Lanciano (I) .... 109 G 2
Łańcut (PL) .... 127 F 1
Landau an der Isar (D)... 95 H 1
Landau in der Pfalz (D) .. 88 D 3
Landeck (A) .... 95 E 4
Landerneau (F) .... 42 B 1
Landete (E) .... 65 G 4
Landévennec (F) .... 42 B 2
Landivisiau (F) .... 42 B 1
Landivy (F) .... 43 G 2
Landquart (CH) .... 99 G 3
Landrecies (F) .... 40 B 3
Landriano (I) .... 101 E 4
Landsberg (D) .... 86 B 3
Landsberg am Lech (D) . 95 F 2
Landshut (D) .... 95 H 1
Landskrona (S) .... 199 E 3
Landstuhl (D) .... 88 D 3
Landverk (S) .... 183 E 5
Lanersbach (A) .... 95 G 4
Längelmäen /
Kirkonkylä (FIN) ... 191 H 2
Langelsheim (D) .... 85 H 2
Langen (Cuxhaven) (D) ..81 F 4
Langen (Offenbach) (D) . 89 E 2
Langenargen (D) .... 94 D 3
Langenau (D) .... 89 G 5
Langenberg (D) .... 86 B 5
Langenbruck (D) .... 95 G 1
Langenburg (D) .... 89 G 3
Langenfeld (A) .... 95 F 4
Langenfeld (D) .... 84 C 4
Langenhagen (D) .... 85 G 1
Langenhahn (D) .... 84 D 5
Langenlois (A) .... 97 F 1
Langenthal (CH) .... 98 D 2
Langenwang (A) .... 97 F 3
Langenzenn (D) .... 89 H 3
Langeoog (D) .... 81 E 3
Långeserud (S) .... 195 G 1
Langeskov (DK) .... 198 C 3
Langesund (N) .... 195 E 1
Langevåg (N) .... 188 C 1
Langevåg (N) .... 188 A 5
Langfjord (N) ....176 D 2
Langhirano (I) .... 105 G 2
Langholm (GB) .... 31 E 3
Langnau
im Emmental (CH) .. 98 D 3
Langogne (F) .... 50 B 5
Langon (F) .... 48 D 5
Langport (GB) .... 35 F 3
Langreo (E) .... 57 G 2
Langres (F) .... 46 D 3
Langrune-sur-Mer (F) .. 38 D 4
Långsele (S) .... 183 H 5
Långshyttan (S) .... 190 A 4
Långträsk (S) ....184 D 2
Lanjarón (E) .... 75 F 3
Lanke (D) .... 83 F 5
Länkipohja (FIN) .... 191 H 2
Lanmeur (F) .... 42 C 1
Lannemezan (F) .... 52 D 3
Lannilis (F) .... 42 B 1
Lannion (F) .... 42 C 1
Lanouaille (F) .... 49 F 4
Lans-en-Vercors (F) .....51 E 4
Lanškroun (CZ) .... 93 E 3
Lanta (F) .... 53 G 2
Lantejuela (E) .... 69 H 5
Lantosque (F) .... 55 G 1
Lanvollon (F) .... 42 D 1

Lanzahíta (E) .... 63 H 4
Lanzo Torinese (I) ...... 100 B 4
Laon (F) .... 40 B 4
Lapalisse (F) .... 50 B 2
Lápas (GR) .... 164 D 4
Lapathos (CY) .... 175 F 3
Laperdiguera (E) .... 60 A 3
Lapinjärvi /
Lappträsk (FIN) ...... 193 E 4
Lapinlahti (FIN) .... 187 F 5
Lapithos (CY) ....174 D 2
Lapleau (F) .... 49 H 4
Laplume (F) .... 53 E 1
Lapoutroie (F) .... 47 G 2
Lapovo (SRB) .... 141 E 5
Lappajärvi (FIN) .... 185 G 5
Lappalaisten-
Kesätuvat (FIN) ... 177 E 5
Lappea (FIN) .... 180 D 4
Lappeenranta (FIN) ... 193 G 3
Lappfjärd /
Lapväärtti (FIN) ... 191 E 2
Lappfors (FIN) .... 185 F 5
Lappi (FIN) .... 191 F 3
Lappohja (FIN) .... 191 G 5
Lappträsk (S) .... 185 F 1
Lappträsk /
Lapinjärvi (FIN) ...... 193 E 4
Lapua (FIN) .... 191 F 1
Lăpușnicel (RO) ...... 150 C 2
Lapväärtti /
Lappfjärd (FIN) ...... 191 E 2
Łapy (PL)........119 G 4
L'Aquila (I) .... 109 F 2
Laragh (IRL) .... 25 G 2
Laragne-Montéglin (F) .. 55 E 1
L'Arbresle (F) .... 50 C 2
Lärbro (S) .... 197 G 3
Larche (D) ....51 G 5
Larche (F) .... 49 F 4
Larderello (I) .... 105 H 5
Lárdos (GR) .... 171 H 4
Laredo (E) .... 58 C 1
Laren (N) .... 77 E 4
Largentière (F) .... 50 C 5
L'Argentière-la-Bessée (F)51 G 5
Largs (GB) .... 30 C 2
Larino (I) .... 109 H 3
Lárisa / Λάρισα (GR) ... 165 F 1
Larmor-Plage (F) .... 42 C 3
Lárnaka (CY) .... 175 E 4
Larnakas Lapithou (CY) .174 D 3
Larne (GB) .... 23 G 2
Larochette (L) .... 79 F 5
Laroles (E) .... 72 A 5
Laroque-d'Olmes (F)... 53 G 4
Laroque-Timbaut (F) ... 53 E 1
Laroquebrou (F) .... 49 H 4
Larraga (E) .... 59 E 3
Larsmo (FIN) .... 185 F 4
Laruns (F) .... 52 C 4
Larv (S) .... 195 G 3
Larvik (N) .... 195 E 1
Lárymna (GR) .... 165 G 3
Las Arenas (E) .... 58 A 1
Las Cabezas
de San Juan (E) .....74 B 3
Las Caldas de Besayas (E). 58 B 1
Las Mesas (E) .... 64 D 5
Las Mestas (E) .... 63 F 4
Las Minas (E) .... 71 H 3
Las Navas
de la Concepción (E) .. 69 H 4
Las Navas
del Marqués (E) ...... 64 A 2
Las Negras (E) .... 72 C 5
Las Pajanosas (E) .... 69 G 4
Las Palmas
de Gran Canaria (E) ....67 G 5
Las Pedroñeras (E) .... 64 D 5
Las Pedrosas (E) .... 59 G 4
Las Rozas de Madrid (E). 64 B 2
Las Veguillas (E) .... 63 G 2
Las Ventas
con Peña Aguilera (E) . 64 B 4
Las Vertientes (E) .... 71 G 4
Las Viñas (E) .... 70 D 3

Lasalle (F) .... 54 B 1
Lasarte-Oria (E) .... 59 E 1
Låsby (DK) .... 194 D 5
Laxe (E) .... 56 B 2
Lascaux, grotte de (F) .. 49 F 4
Łasin (PL)........117 H 4
Łask (PL) .... 121 H 3
Łaskarzew (PL) .... 123 E 2
Laško (SLO) ....134 D 2
Lassan (D) .... 83 G 3
Lassay-les-Châteaux (F) . 43 H 2
Lassigny (F) .... 40 A 4
Lastovo (HR) .... 138 C 4
Lastra a Signa (I) .... 105 H 4
Lastres (E) .... 57 H 1
Lastrup (D) ....81 E 5
Lastva (BIH) .... 139 E 4
Lašva (BIH) .... 137 F 5
Laterza (I) .... 111 E 4
Latisana (I) .... 103 G 3
Lathen (D) ....81 E 5
Latheron (GB) .... 26 B 5
Lati Vojvoda (BG) ...... 159 G 2
Latiano (I) .... 111 G 4
Latikberg (S) ....183 H 3
Latina (I) .... 109 E 4
Latour-de-France (F) ... 53 H 4
Latronico (I) ....110 D 5
Latronquière (F) .... 49 G 5
Lauchhammer (D) ...... 86 D 3
Lauder (GB) ....31 E 2
Laudio / Llodio (E) ...... 58 D 1
Lauenau (D) .... 85 F 2
Lauenburg (D) .... 82 B 4
Lauenstein (D) .... 87 E 5
Lauf an der Pegnitz (D)..91 E 4
Laufen (CH) .... 98 C 2
Laufen (D) .... 96 B 2
Laufenburg (D) .... 94 B 3
Lauffen am Neckar (D) . 89 F 4
Laugar (IS) .... 178 A 2
Laugarbakki (IS) .... 178 B 2
Laugarvatn (IS) .... 178 B 3
Laugharne (GB) .... 34 D 1
Lauingen (D) .... 89 H 5
Láujar de Andarax (E) ... 72 B 5
Laukaa (FIN) .... 191 H 1
Laukuva (LT) .... 204 C 2
Launceston (GB) .... 34 C 4
Laupheim (D) .... 89 G 5
Lauragh (IRL) .... 24 B 4
Laurana / Lovran (HR) ... 134 B 4
Laureana di Borrello (I) ..115 H 1
Laurencekirk (GB) .... 29 G 5
Lauria (I) .... 110 D 5
Laurière (F) .... 49 G 2
Laurenzana (I) ....110 D 4
Lauro (I) .... 110 C 4
Lausanne (CH) .... 98 B 4
Lauta (D) .... 87 E 3
Lautenthal (D) .... 85 H 4
Lauterbach (D) .... 85 F 5
Lauterbourg (F) ....41 H 5
Lauterbrunnen (CH)..... 98 D 3
Lauterecken (D) .... 88 D 2
Lauvik (N) .... 194 B 1
Lauvuk (N) .... 194 B 1
Lauzerte (F) .... 53 F 1
Lauzun (F) .... 49 E 5
Lavacolla (E) .... 56 C 2
Lavagna (I) .... 105 E 3
Laval (F) .... 43 G 3
Lavamünd (A) .... 97 E 5
Lavangen (N) ....176 A 5
Lavardac (F) .... 52 D 1
Lavaur (F) .... 53 G 2
Lavelanet (F) .... 53 G 4
Lavello (I) ....110 C 3
Lavelsloh (D) .... 85 F 1
Lavenham (GB) .... 33 H 5
Laveno (I) .... 100 D 3
Lavéra (F) .... 54 C 3
Lavia (FIN) .... 191 F 3
Laviano (I) ....110 C 4
Lavik (N) .... 188 B 3
Lavinio-Lido di Enea (I). 108 D 4
Lavis (I) .... 101 H 3
Lavit-de-Lomagne (F)... 53 E 2
Lavoûte-Chilhac (F) ... 50 B 4

Lavre (P) .... 68 C 2
Lávrio / Λαύριο (GR) ... 166 B 5
Laxå (S) .... 195 H 2
Laxe (DK) .... 194 D 5
Laxey (GB) .... 32 C 1
Laxford Bridge (GB) ... 28 D 1
Laxo (GB) .... 27 G 2
Layos (E) .... 64 B 4
Laza (E) .... 56 D 4
Lazarev Krst (MNE) ...... 139 F 4
Lazarevac /
Лазаревац (SRB) ... 140 C 5
Lazarevo (SRB) .... 140 D 3
Lazaropole (MK) .... 144 D 1
Lazdijai (LT) .... 205 E 5
Lazise (I) .... 101 H 4
Lázně Bohdaneč (CZ) ... 92 C 2
Lázně Kynžvart (CZ).....91 G 3
Laznica (SRB) .... 141 F 5
Łazy (Koszalin) (PL).....116 D 2
Łazy (Zawiercie) (PL) ... 122 B 5
Le Bar-sur-Loup (F) ... 55 F 3
Le Beausset (F) .... 55 E 3
Le Bec-Hellouin (F) ... 39 E 5
Le Bény-Bocage (F) ... 38 C 5
Le Biot (F) ....51 F 1
Le Blanc (F) .... 49 F 1
Le Bleymard (F) .... 50 B 5
Le Boréon (F) .... 55 G 1
Le Boulou (F) .... 53 H 5
Le Bourg-d'Oisans (F) ...51 F 4
Le Bourget-du-Lac (F) ..51 E 3
Le Bousquet-d'Orb (F) .. 54 A 2
Le Bugue (F) .... 49 F 5
Le Buisson-
de-Cadouin (F)....... 49 F 5
Le Cap-d'Agde (F) ...... 54 A 3
Le Cateau (F) .... 40 B 3
Le Catelet (F) .... 40 A 3
Le Caylar (F) .... 54 A 2
Le Chambon-
Feugerolles (F)....... 50 C 3
Le Chambon-
sur-Lignon (F)....... 50 C 4
Le Château-d'Oléron (F). 48 B 2
Le Chatelard (F) ....51 F 3
Le Châtelet (F) .... 49 H 1
Le Châtelet-en-Brie (F) .. 45 F 2
Le Chesne (F) .... 40 C 4
Le Cheylard (F) .... 50 C 5
Le Conquet (F) .... 42 A 2
Le Creusot (F) .... 45 H 5
Le Croisic (F) .... 43 E 4
Le Crotoy (F) .... 39 G 3
Le Donjon (F) .... 50 B 1
Le Dorat (F) .... 49 F 2
Le Faou (F) .... 42 B 2
Le Faouët (F) .... 42 C 2
Le Folgoët (F) .... 42 B 1
Le Fossat (F) .... 53 F 3
Le Fousseret (F) .... 53 E 3
Le Grand-Bornand (F)...51 F 2
Le Grand-Bourg (F) ... 49 G 2
Le Grand-Lemps (F) ...51 E 3
Le Grand-Lucé (F) ...... 44 C 3
Le Grand-Pressigny (F) .. 44 C 5
Le Grand-Serre (F) ...... 50 D 4
Le Grau-du-Roi (F) ...... 54 B 3
Le Havre (F) .... 39 E 4
Le Hohwald (F) ....47 G 2
Le Lauzet-Ubaye (F) ...51 F 5
Le Lavandou (F) .... 55 F 3
Le Lion-d'Angers (F) ... 43 H 3
Le Lioran (F) .... 50 A 4
Le Locle (CH) .... 98 B 2
Le Loroux-Botterau (F). 43 F 4
Le Louroux-
Béconnais (F) .... 43 G 4
Le Luc (F) .... 55 F 3
Le Lude (F) .... 44 B 4
Le Malzieu-Ville (F)...... 50 A 5
Le Mans (F) .... 44 B 4
Le Markstein (F) ....47 G 3
Le Mas-d'Agenais (F) ... 52 D 1
Le Mas-d'Azil (F) .... 53 F 3
Le Massegros (F) .... 54 A 1
Le Mayet-
de-Montagne (F)...... 50 B 2

Le Mêle-sur-Sarthe (F) .. 44 B 2
Le Merlerault (F) .... 44 B 2
Le Monastier-
sur-Gazeille (F)....... 50 B 4
Le Monêtier (F) ....51 F 4
Le Mont-Dore (F) .... 50 A 3
Le Mont-Saint-Michel (F). 43 F 1
Le Montet (F) .... 50 A 1
Le Muy (F) .... 55 F 3
Le Neubourg (F) .... 39 F 5
Le Nouvion-
en-Thiérache (F) ...... 40 B 3
Le Palais (F) .... 42 D 4
Le Péage-
de-Roussillon (F)...... 50 D 3
Le Pellerin (F) .... 43 F 4
Le Perthus (F) .... 53 H 5
Le Poiré-sur-Vie (F) ... 43 F 5
Le Pont-de-Beauvoisin (F).51 E 3
Le Pont-de-Claix (F) ...51 E 4
Le Pont-de-Montvert (F). 54 B 1
Le Pontet (F) .... 54 D 2
Le Pouldu (F) .... 42 C 3
Le Pouliguen (F) .... 43 E 4
Le Pouzin (F) .... 50 D 5
Le Puy-en-Velay (F) .... 50 B 4
Le Quesnoy (F) .... 40 B 2
Le Rozier (F) .... 54 A 1
Le Russey (F) ....47 F 4
Le Sauze (F) .... 55 F 1
Le Teil (F) .... 50 D 5
Le Teilleul (F) .... 43 G 2
Le Theil (F) .... 44 C 2
Le Thillot (F) ....47 F 4
Le Touquet-
Paris-Plage (F) ...... 39 G 2
Le Touvet (F) ....51 F 3
Le Trayas (F) .... 55 G 2
Le Tréport (F) .... 39 F 3
Le Val-André (F) .... 43 E 1
Le Val-d'Ajol (F) ....47 F 4
Le Verdon-sur-Mer (F)... 48 C 3
Le Vigan (F) .... 54 B 2
Le Vivier-sur-Mer (F) .... 43 F 1
Leadenham (GB) .... 33 F 3
Łeba (PL)........117 F 1
Lebach (D) .... 88 C 3
Lebane (SRB) .... 143 F 2
Lebedyn (UA) .... 7 G 5
Lébény (H) .... 128 C 1
Lebesby (N) .... 177 F 2
Lębork (PL)........117 G 1
Lebrija (E) ....74 B 3
Lebus (D) .... 87 E 1
Lecce (I) .... 111 H 4
Lecco (I) .... 101 F 3
Lécera (E) .... 65 H 1
Lećevica (HR) ....138 B 2
Lech (A) .... 95 E 4
Lechainá (GR) .... 164 D 4
Lechinţa (RO) .... 147 G 3
Lechlade (GB) .... 35 G 1
Léchovo (GR) .... 160 D 3
Leciñena (E) .... 59 H 4
Leck (D) ....81 G 1
Lectoure (F) .... 53 E 2
Łęczna (PL) .... 123 G 3
Łęczyca (PL) .... 121 H 2
Ledaña (E) .... 65 F 5
Ledanca (E) .... 64 D 1
Ledbury (GB) .... 35 F 1
Ledeč nad Sázavou (CZ). 92 C 3
Ledesma (E) .... 63 G 2
Lédignan (F) .... 54 B 2
Ledmore (GB) .... 28 D 2
Lednice (CZ) .... 93 E 5
Lednogora (PL) .... 121 F 1
Leeds (GB) .... 33 E 2
Leek (GB) .... 32 D 3
Leenane (IRL) .... 22 B 4
Leer (D) ....81 E 4
Leerdam (NL) ....76 D 3
Lees (E) .... 60 B 1
Leese (D) .... 85 F 1
Leeuwarden (NL) .... 77 F 2
Lefka (CY) ....174 C 3
Lefkáda / Λευκάδα (GR) . 164 C 2

A B C D E F G H I J K **L** M N O P Q R S T U V W X Y Z

Lefkádia (GR) 161 E3
Lefkadíti (GR) 165 E3
Lefkantí (GR) 165 H3
Léfkes (GR) 170 C1
Lefkímmi (GR) 164 B1
Lefkonoiko (CY) 175 E3
Lefkopigí (GR) 161 E4
Lefkoşa / Lefkosía (Nicosia) (CY) .174 D3
Lefkosía / Lefkoşa (Nicosia) (CY) .174 D3
Legan (D) 81 H2
Leganés (E) 64 B3
Legé (F) 43 F5
Legionowo (PL) 122 D1
Legnago (I) 101 H5
Legnano (I) 101 E4
Legnica (PL) 120 D4
Legrad (HR) 135 F2
Legrená (GR) 166 B5
Léguevin (F) 53 F2
Legutio (E) 58 D2
Lehčevo (BG) 154 D2
Lehliu-Gară (RO) 152 C4
Lehmden (D) 81 F4
Lehnin (D) 86 C1
Lehrberg (D) 89 H3
Lehre (D) 85 H2
Lehrte (D) 85 G1
Lehtimäki (FIN) 191 G1
Lehtovaara (FIN) 181 E4
Lehtovaara (FIN) 187 F4
Leianokládi (GR) 165 F2
Leibnitz (A) 97 F5
Leicester (GB) 33 E4
Leiden (NL) 76 D4
Leie (EST) 201 F3
Leigh (GB) 32 D3
Leighton Buzzard (GB) 35 H1
Leikanger (N) 188 C3
Leiknes (N) 179 G3
Leinefelde (D) 85 H4
Leinì (I) 100 C5
Leipalingis (LT) 205 E5
Leipheim (D) 89 G5
Leipsoí (GR) 171 F1
Leipzig (D) 86 B4
Leira (N) 182 B5
Leira (N) 189 E3
Leirbotn (N) 176 D3
Leiria (P) 62 B4
Leiro (E) 56 C4
Leirpollskogen (N) 177 G2
Leirvåg (N) 188 A3
Leirvik (N) 188 B3
Leirvik (N) 188 B3
Leirvik (Færøerne) (DK) 194 A4
Leisnig (D) 86 C4
Leiston (GB) 37 E2
Leith (GB) 31 E1
Leitir Ceanainn / Letterkenny (IRL) 23 E2
Leitza (E) 59 E2
Leitzkau (D) 86 B2
Leivadeiá / Λειβαδειά (GR) 165 G3
Leivadítis (GR) 162 C2
Leivonmäki (FIN) 193 E2
Leka (N) 183 E2
Lekáni (GR) 162 C2
Łękawica (PL) 125 F2
Lekeitio (E) 58 D1
Lekenik (HR) 135 E3
Leknes (N) 179 F3
Łęknica (PL) 120 B3
Leksand (S) 190 A4
Leksvik (N) 182 D4
Lekunberri (E) 59 E2
Leland (N) 183 F1
Leleasca (RO) 151 G3
Lelis (PL) 119 E4
Leliūnai (LT) 205 G2
Lelle (EST) 201 E3
Lelów (PL) 122 B4
Lelystad (NL) 77 E3
Lelystad Haven (NL) 77 E4
Lembach (F) 41 H5

Lembeye (F) 52 D3
Lemesós (Limassol) (CY) .174 D5
Lemförde (D) 85 E1
Lemgo (D) 85 F2
Lemi (FIN) 193 F3
Lemithou (CY) 174 C4
Lemland (FIN) 190 D5
Lemmenjoki (FIN) 177 F5
Lemmer (NL) 77 E3
Lempäälä (FIN) 191 G3
Lempdes-sur-Allagnon (F) 50 A4
Lemvig (DK) 194 C5
Lenart v Slovenskih Goricah (SLO) 135 E1
Lenauheim (RO) 146 A5
Lencloître (F) 44 B5
Lend (A) 96 B4
Lendava (SLO) 135 F1
Lendinara (I) 103 E5
Lengefeld (D) 86 D5
Lengenfeld (D) 86 C5
Lengerich (D) 84 D2
Lenggries (D) 95 G3
Lengyeltóti (H) 128 C3
Lenhovda (S) 196 D5
Lenk (CH) 98 C5
Lenkimai (LT) 204 B1
Lennestadt (D) 85 E4
Lens (F) 39 H2
Lensahn (D) 82 C2
Léntas (GR) 172 D4
Lentföhrden (D) 81 H3
Lenti (I) 128 B4
Lentiira (FIN) 187 G3
Lenting (D) 91 E5
Lenzburg (CH) 98 D2
Lenzen (D) 82 D5
Lenzerheide Valbella (CH) 99 G3
Lenzkirch (D) 94 B2
Leoben (A) 97 F3
Leobersdorf (A) 97 G2
Leogang (A) 96 B3
Leominster (GB) 32 C5
León (E) 57 G3
Léon (F) 52 B2
Leonarisso (CY) 175 F2
Leonberg (D) 89 F4
Léoncel (F) 50 D4
Leonessa (I) 109 E1
Leonforte (I) 115 E3
Leonídio / Λεωνίδιο (GR) 169 E3
Leontári (Pelopónnisos) (GR) 168 C2
Leontári (Thessalía) (GR) 165 E2
Leopoldsburg (B) 79 E2
Leopoldsdorf im Marchfelde (A) 97 H1
Lepe (E) 69 E5
Lepetani (MNE) 139 F4
Lepiel (BY) 6 D4
L'Épine (F) 40 C5
Lepoglava (HR) 135 E2
Leposavić (SRB) 142 D3
Lépoura (GR) 166 B3
Leppäjärvi (FIN) 176 D5
Leppävirta (FIN) 193 F1
Lepşa (RO) 148 C5
Lepsény (H) 128 D3
Leptokaryá (Anatolikí Makedonía kai Thráki) (GR) 163 E2
Leptokaryá (Kentrikí Makedonía) (GR) 161 F5
Lercara Friddi (I) 114 D3
Léré (F) 45 F4
Lerici (I) 105 F3
Lerín (E) 59 E3
Lerma (E) 58 B4
Lermoos (A) 95 F4
Lerum (S) 195 F3
Lerwick (GB) 26 D1
Les Abrets-en-Dauphiné (F) 51 E4
Les Aix-d'Angillon (F) 45 F5
Les Andelys (F) 39 F5
Les Arcs (F) 51 G3

Les Arcs (F) 55 F3
Les Baux-de-Provence (F) 54 C2
Les Bézards (F) 45 F3
Les Borges Blanques (E) 60 B4
Les Bouchoux (F) 51 E1
Les Cabannes (F) 53 F4
Les Contamines-Montjoie (F) 51 G2
Les Coves de Vinromà (E) 66 A1
Les Deux-Alpes (F) 51 F4
Les Diablerets (CH) 98 C4
Les Écharmeaux (F) 50 C2
Les Échelles (F) 51 E3
Les Essarts (F) 43 F5
Les Eyzies-de-Tayac (F) 49 F5
Les Gets (F) 51 G2
Les Herbiers (F) 43 G5
Les Houches (F) 51 G2
Les Issambres (F) 55 G3
Les Lecques (F) 55 E3
Les Llosses (E) 60 D2
Les Matelles (F) 54 B2
Les Mées (F) 55 E1
Les Menuires (F) 51 F3
Les Ollières (F) 50 C5
Les Pieux (F) 38 B4
Les Planches-en-Montagne (F) 51 E1
Les Ponts-de-Cé (F) 43 H4
Les Riceys (F) 45 H3
Les Rosiers-sur-Loire (F) 43 H4
Les Rousses (F) 51 F1
Les Sables-d'Olonne (F) 48 B1
Les Settons (F) 45 H5
Les Trois-Épis (F) 47 G2
Les Trois-Moutiers (F) 43 H5
Les Useres (E) 66 A2
Les Vans (F) 54 B1
Les Vignes (F) 54 A1
Lešak (SRB) 142 D3
Lešani (MK) 145 E2
Lešć (HR) 134 D4
Lesce (SLO) 134 B2
Lescar (F) 52 C3
L'Escarène (F) 55 H2
Lescun (F) 52 C4
Lesencetomaj (H) 128 C3
Leshnicë (AL) 144 D3
Lesičovo (BG) 158 C2
Lesina (I) 110 C1
Lesíni (GR) 164 D3
Lesja (N) 188 D2
Lesjöfors (S) 189 H5
Lesko (PL) 127 F2
Leskovac / Лесковац (SRB) 143 F3
Leskovik (AL) 144 D4
Leskovo (BG) 153 E5
Leśna (PL) 120 C4
Lesneven (F) 42 B1
Lešnica (SRB) 137 H4
Lesparre-Médoc (F) 48 C4
Lespezi (RO) 148 C2
L'Espluga de Francolí (E) 60 C4
L'Espunyola (E) 60 D2
Lessay (F) 38 B5
Lessebo (S) 196 D5
Lessines (B) 78 B2
L'Estartit (E) 61 F2
Lestelle-Bétharram (F) 52 C3
Lestijärvi (FIN) 185 G5
Lestkov (CZ) 91 G3
Leszno (Poznań) (PL) 121 E2
Leszno (Warszawa) (PL) 122 C1
Létavértes (H) 131 F2
Letchworth (GB) 36 C3
Letenye (H) 128 B4
Letino (I) 109 G4
Letmathe (D) 84 D4
Letnica (BG) 156 B2
Letschin (D) 87 E1
Letterfrack (IRL) 22 B4
Letterkenny / Leitir Ceanainn (IRL) 23 E2
Lettermullan (IRL) 22 B5

Letur (E) 71 G3
Letuš (SLO) 134 C2
Letymvou (CY) 174 B4
Letzlingen (D) 86 A1
Leu (RO) 151 F4
Leuchars (GB) 31 E1
Leukerbad (CH) 98 D4
Leuna (D) 86 B4
Leutenberg (D) 86 A5
Leutershausen (D) 89 H3
Leutkirch im Allgäu (D) 94 D3
Leutschach (A) 97 F5
Leuven (Louvain) (B) 78 D2
Leuze-en-Hainaut (B) 78 B3
Levajok (N) 177 F3
Levala (EST) 201 F2
Levanger (N) 183 E4
Levanjska Varoš (HR) 135 H4
Levanto (I) 105 F3
Levásjoki (FIN) 191 F2
Leven (East Riding of Yorks.) (GB) 33 F2
Leven (Fife) (GB) 31 E1
Levens (F) 55 G2
Levens Hall (GB) 31 E5
Leverano (I) 111 G4
Leverburgh (GB) 28 B2
Leverkusen (D) 84 C4
Levet (F) 45 E5
Levi (FIN) 180 D3
Levice (SK) 132 C4
Levico Terme (I) 101 H3
Levídi (GR) 165 E5
Levie (F) 55 H5
Levier (F) 47 F5
Levka (BG) 163 F1
Levoča (SK) 133 F2
Levroux (F) 44 D5
Levski / Левски (BG) 156 B2
Lewes (GB) 36 C5
Leyburn (GB) 31 G5
Leyland (GB) 32 C2
Leysdown-on-Sea (GB) 37 E4
Leysin (CH) 98 C4
Leżajsk (PL) 123 F5
Lézardrieux (F) 42 D1
Lézat-sur-Lèze (F) 53 F3
Lezay (F) 48 D2
Lezhë (AL) 144 C1
Lézignan-Corbières (F) 53 H3
Ležimir (SRB) 140 B3
Lezoux (F) 50 A3
Lezuza (E) 71 G1
Liljanovo (BG) 161 H1
L'gov (RUS) 7 G4
L'Hermenault (F) 48 C2
L'Hospitalet de l'Infant (E) 60 B5
Libáň (CZ) 92 B2
Liberec (CZ) 87 F5
Libochovice (CZ) 92 A2
Libofshë (AL) 144 C3
Libourne (F) 48 D5
Librazhd (AL) 144 D2
Librilla (E) 71 H4
Licata (I) 114 D4
Licciana Nardi (I) 105 F3
Lich (D) 85 F5
Lichádra (GR) 165 G2
Lichfield (GB) 33 E4
Lichoslavl' (RUS) 7 F1
Lichtenberg (D) 91 E2
Lichtenfels (D) 91 E2
Lichtenstein (D) 86 C5
Lichtenvoorde (NL) 77 F5
Lički Jesenica (HR) 134 D5
Lički Osik (HR) 136 B4
Ličko Lešće (HR) 134 D5
Licurici (RO) 151 F3
Licze (PL) 117 H3
Lida (BY) 6 C5
Liden (S) 190 B1
Lidhult (S) 195 G5
Lidköping (S) 195 G2
Lido degli Estensi (I) 107 E1
Lido delle Nazioni (I) 107 E1
Lido di Camaiore (I) 105 G4

Lido di Classe (I) 107 F2
Lido di Jesolo (I) 103 F4
Lido di Metaponto (I) 111 G4
Lido di Ostia (I) 108 D3
Lido di Savio (I) 107 F2
Lido di Spina (I) 107 E1
Lido di Torre Mileto (I)...110 C1
Lido di Venezia (I) 103 F4
Lido Silvana (I) 111 F4
Lidoríki (GR) 165 G3
Lidzbark (PL) 118 C4
Lidzbark Warmiński (PL).118 D2
Liebenwalde (D) 83 F5
Lieberose (D) 87 E2
Liebling (RO) 150 B1
Liège (Luik) (B) 79 E3
Lieksa (FIN) 187 G5
Lielvārde (LV) 203 E3
Lienz (A) 96 B5
Liepāja (LV) 202 A4
Liepas (Mežamuiža) (LV) 203 F4
Liepna (LV) 203 G2
Lier (B) 78 D2
Liérganes (E) 58 B1
Liernais (F) 45 H4
Liestal (CH) 98 D2
Liești (RO) 152 D1
Lieto (FIN) 191 F4
Liétor (E) 71 G2
Lieurey (F) 39 E5
Lievestuore (FIN) 193 E1
Liévin (F) 39 H2
Liezen (A) 96 D3
Liffol-le-Grand (F) 47 E2
Lifford (IRL) 23 E2
Liffré (F) 43 F2
Lignano Sabbiadoro (I). 103 G4
Lignières (F) 49 H1
Ligny-en-Barrois (F) 46 D1
Ligny-le-Châtel (F) 45 G3
Ligourió (GR) 165 G5
Ligueil (F) 44 C5
Lihula (EST) 200 C3
Liikasenvaara (FIN) 181 G5
Lijeva Rijeka (MNE) 139 G4
Lijevi Dubravčak (HR) 135 E3
Likenäs (S) 189 G4
Lilaía (GR) 165 F3
Liland (N) 176 A5
L'Île-Bouchard (F) 44 B5
L'Île-Rousse (F) 55 G2
Lilienfeld (A) 97 F2
Liljendal (FIN) 193 E4
Lilla Edet (S) 195 F3
Lillby (F) 185 F5
Lille (F) 40 A2
Lillebonne (F) 39 E4
Lillehammer (N) 189 E3
Lillerød (DK) 199 E3
Lillers (F) 39 H2
Lillesand (N) 194 C2
Lillestrøm (N) 189 F5
Lillhärdal (S) 189 H2
Lillholmsjön (S) 183 G5
Lillo (E) 64 C4
Lillögda (S) 184 C4
Lima (S) 189 H4
Limáni Chersonísou (GR) 170 C5
Limáni Géraka (GR) 169 E4
Limavady (GB) 23 F2
Limbach-Oberfrohna (D). 86 C5
Limburg an der Lahn (D). 88 D1
Limbaži (LV) 203 E2
Limenária (GR) 162 C3
Limenás (GR) 167 E4
Limerick / Luimneach (IRL) 24 C3
Limingen (N) 183 F2
Limingo / Liminka (FIN). 185 H3
Liminka / Limingo (FIN). 185 H3
Liminpuro (FIN) 185 H4
Limljani (MNE) 139 F5
Límnes (GR) 165 G5
Límni (GR) 165 G3
Limnia (CY) 175 F3

Limnítsa (GR) 165 E3
Limoges (F) 49 F3
Limogne-en-Quercy (F) 53 G1
Limone Piemonte (I) 104 D3
Limonest (F) 50 D2
Limours-en-Hurepoix (F) 45 E1
Limoux (F) 53 G4
Lin (AL) 144 D2
Linares (E) 70 D3
Linares de Mora (E) 65 H3
Linares de Riofrío (E) 63 G3
Linariá (GR) 166 C2
Lincoln (GB) 33 F3
Lindås (N) 188 B3
Lindau (D) 94 D3
Linden (BG) 161 H2
Linden (D) 89 H1
Lindenberg im Allgäu (D) 94 D3
Linderhof (D) 95 F3
Lindern (D) 81 E5
Lindesberg (S) 197 E1
Lindesnes (N) 194 B2
Lindö (S) 197 E2
Líndos / Λίνδος (GR) 171 H4
Lindoso (P) 56 C5
Lindow (D) 83 F5
Lindsdal (S) 197 E5
Lingbo (S) 190 B4
Linge (N) 188 C3
Lingen (D) 84 D1
Linghem (S) 197 E2
Linguaglossa (I) 115 G3
Linken (D) 83 G4
Linköping (S) 197 E2
Linkuva (LT) 205 E1
Linlithgow (GB) 30 D1
Linnamäe (EST) 200 C2
Linsell (S) 189 H2
Linslade (GB) 35 H1
Linthal (CH) 99 F3
Linyola (E) 60 B3
Linz (A) 96 D1
Linz am Rhein (D) 84 C5
Lion-sur-Mer (F) 38 D4
Lioni (I) 110 B3
Liopetri (CY) 175 F3
Lipar (SRB) 140 B2
Lipari (I) 115 F1
Liperi (FIN) 193 G1
Lipiany (PL) 116 C5
Lipica (SLO) 134 A3
Lipik (HR) 135 G4
Lipki Wielkie (PL) 116 C5
Lipkovo (MK) 143 F5
Lipljan (SRB) 143 E4
Lipnica (Chojnice) (PL) 117 F2
Lipnica (Toruń) (PL) 117 H4
Lipnik (CZ) 123 E4
Lipník nad Bečvou (CZ) . 93 F3
Lipno (PL) 117 H5
Lipno nad Vltavou (CZ).. 96 C1
Lipova (RO) 146 C5
Lipová-Lázně (CZ) 93 E2
Lipovac (HR) 137 H3
Lippstadt (D) 85 E3
Lipsk (PL) 119 H3
Lipsko (PL) 123 E3
Lipszczany (PL) 119 H3
Liptovský Hrádok (SK).. 133 F2
Liptovský Mikuláš (SK) . 132 D2
Ļipuški (LV) 203 H4
Liqenas (AL) 145 E3
Liria / Llíria (E) 65 H4
Lis (AL) 144 C1
Lisac (BIH) 137 F5
Lisboa (P) 68 A2
Lisburn (GB) 23 G3
Lisdoonvarna (IRL) 24 C2
Lisewo (PL) 117 H4
Lisieux (F) 39 E5
Liskeard (GB) 34 C4
Lisków (PL) 121 G2
L'Isle-Adam (F) 39 H5
L'Isle-d'Abeau (F) 50 D3
L'Isle-de-Noé (F) 52 D2
L'Isle-en-Dodon (F) 53 E3

L'Isle-Jourdain (F) ...... 49 E 2
L'Isle-Jourdain (F) ...... 53 E 2
L'Isle-sur-la-Sorgue (F) .. 54 D 2
L'Isle-sur-le-Doubs (F)...47 F 4
L'Isle-sur-Serein (F) .... 45 H 4
Lisle-sur-Tarn (F) ...... 53 G 2
Lismore (IRL)............ 24 D 4
Lisnaskea (GB) .... 23 E 3
Lišnja (BIH) .... 135 G 5
Lisovići (BIH) .... 137 G 4
Lispeszentadorján (H). 128 B 4
Lisse (NL) ....76 D 4
Listowel (IRL)........... 24 B 3
Lit (S) .... 183 G 5
Lit-et-Mixe (F)......... 52 B 1
Litakovo (BG) .... 158 C 1
Litene (LV) .... 203 G 2
Liteni (RO) .... 148 C 2
Lithakiá (GR) .... 164 C 5
Lithínes (GR) .... 173 F 4
Lithótopos (GR) .... 161 G 2
Litija (SLO) .... 134 C 2
Litke (H) .... 126 B 5
Litóchoro /
  Λιτόχωρο (GR) ... 161 F 5
Litoměřice (CZ) ...... 87 E 5
Litomyšl (CZ) .... 92 D 3
Litovel (CZ) .... 93 E 3
Litschau (A) .... 92 B 5
Littlehampton (GB) ... 38 D 1
Littleport (GB) .... 33 G 5
Litvínov (CZ) .... 86 D 5
Liu (EST) .... 200 D 4
Liudvinavas (LT) ...... 205 E 4
Livada (RO) .... 147 E 1
Livade (HR) .... 134 A 4
Livaderó (GR) .... 162 B 2
Livadhe (AL) .... 144 D 5
Livádi
  (Nótio Aigaío) (GR) ... 169 H 3
Livádi (Thessalía) (GR).. 161 E 4
Livadia (CY) .... 175 E 4
Livádia (GR) .... 171 G 3
Livadiá (GR) .... 161 G 2
Livadochóri (GR) ..... 162 D 5
Livanátes (GR) .... 165 G 3
Līvāni (LV) .... 203 F 4
Livari (MNE) .... 139 G 5
Livarot (F.)........... 39 E 5
Livera (CY) .... 174 C 2
Liverdun (F.).......... 47 E 1
Livernon (F.)........... 49 G 5
Liverpool (GB) .... 32 C 3
Livezile (Bistrița) (RO) .. 147 G 3
Livezile
  (Timișoara) (RO). 150 B 1
Livigno (I) .... 101 G 2
Livingston (GB) .... 30 D 2
Livno (BIH)........... 137 E 5
Livny (RUS)...........7 H 4
Livo (FIN) .... 185 H 2
Livold (SLO) .... 134 C 3
Livorno (I) .... 105 G 5
Livorno Ferraris (I) ... 100 C 4
Livron-sur-Drôme (F)... 50 D 5
Liw (PL) .... 123 E 1
Lixoúri (GR) .... 164 B 4
Lizard (GB)............ 34 B 5
Lizy (F.)............... 40 A 5
Lizzano in Belvedere (I). 105 H 3
Ljeskove Vode (BIH)... 135 H 5
Ljig (SRB) .... 140 C 5
Ljubaništa (MK) ...... 145 E 3
Ljubašivka (UA).........13 F 2
Ljuben (BG) .... 158 D 2
Ljuben Karavelovo (BG). 157 F 2
Ljubenova mahala (BG). 159 F 2
Ljubenovo (BG) ...... 159 F 3
Ljubija (BIH) .... 135 F 5
Ljubimec (BG) .... 163 E 1
Ljubinje (BIH) .... 139 E 3
Ljubiš (SRB) .... 139 H 2
Ljubljana (SLO)....... 134 B 2
Ljubno ob Savinji (SLO). 134 C 2
Ljubojno (MK) .... 145 E 3
Ljuboml' (UA)..........12 C 1

Ljubovija (SRB)......... 140 B 5
Ljubuški (BIH) .... 138 D 3
Ljugarn (S) .... 197 G 4
Ljuljak (BG) .... 159 F 2
Ljuljakovo (BG)....... 159 H 1
Ljungby (S) .... 195 H 5
Ljungbyhed (S) ...... 199 F 3
Ljungdalen (S) .... 189 G 1
Ljungsbro (S) .... 197 E 2
Ljungskile (S) .... 195 F 3
Ljusdal (S) .... 190 B 2
Ljusne (S) .... 190 B 3
Ljuta (BIH) .... 139 E 2
Ljutići (MNE) .... 139 G 3
Ljutoglav (SRB) ...... 142 D 5
Ljutomer (SLO) ...... 135 E 1
Ljutribrod (BG) ...... 158 C 1
Llagostera (E) ....61 E 3
Llan Ffestiniog (GB) .. 32 B 4
Llanberis (GB) .... 32 A 3
Llançà (E) ....61 F 1
Llandeilo (GB) .... 34 D 1
Llandovery (GB) ...... 34 D 1
Llandrindod Wells (GB). 32 B 5
Llandudno (GB)....... 32 B 3
Llandysul (GB) .... 34 C 1
Llanelli (GB) .... 34 D 2
Llanerchymedd (GB) .. 32 A 3
Llanes (E) .... 58 A 1
Llanfairfechan (GB) ... 32 B 3
Llanfyllin (GB)........ 32 C 4
Llangadog (GB) ...... 34 D 1
Llangefni (GB) .... 32 A 3
Llangollen (GB) ...... 32 C 4
Llangurig (GB) .... 32 B 5
Llanidloes (GB) ...... 32 B 5
Llanrhystud (GB) ..... 32 A 5
Llanrwst (GB) .... 32 B 3
Llanwrtyd Wells (GB).... 34 D 1
Llavorsí (E) .... 60 C 1
Lleida (E) .... 60 B 3
Llera (E).............. 69 G 3
Llerena (E) .... 69 G 3
Lles de Cerdanya (E) .. 60 C 2
Llessui (E) .... 60 B 2
Llíria / Liria (E). ..... 65 H 4
Llívia (E) .... 60 D 1
Llodio / Laudio (E) .. 58 D 1
Lloret de Mar (E) .....61 E 3
Llucmajor (E) ....67 F 3
Llynclys (GB)......... 32 C 4
Lnáře (CZ) .... 92 A 4
Lniano (PL)...........117 G 3
Loamneș (RO)........ 147 F 5
Loanhead (GB)........31 E 2
Loano (I) .... 104 D 3
Löbau (D) .... 87 F 4
Löbejün (D) .... 86 B 3
Lobenstein (D)........ 91 E 2
Lobez (D) ....116 D 3
Löbnitz (D) .... 83 E 2
Lobón (E) .... 69 F 2
Loburg (D) .... 86 B 2
Łobżenica (PL)........117 F 4
Loch Garman /
  Wexford (IRL) .... 25 F 3
Lochaline (GB) .... 28 D 5
Lochboisdale (GB) .... 28 B 4
Lochcarron (GB) ..... 28 D 3
Lochearnhead (GB) ... 30 D 1
Lochem (NL).......... 77 F 5
Loches (F) .... 44 C 5
Lochgelly (GB).........31 E 1
Lochgilphead (GB).... 30 B 1
Lochinver (GB)........ 28 D 2
Lochmaben (GB).......31 E 3
Lochmaddy (GB) ..... 28 B 3
Łochów (PL)..........119 E 5
Lochranza (GB)....... 30 B 2
Lockenhaus (A) ...... 97 G 3
Lockerbie (GB).........31 E 3
Löcknitz (D).......... 83 G 4
Locmariaquer (F) .... 42 D 3
Locminé (F)........... 42 D 3

Locorotondo (I) ....111 F 4
Locquirec (F)......... 42 C 1
Locri (I) ....113 C 5
Locronan (F) .... 42 B 2
Loctudy (F) .... 42 B 3
Lodè (I) ....112 D 2
Lodève (F) .... 54 A 2
Lodi (I) .... 101 F 4
Løding (N) .... 179 F 4
Lødingen (N) .... 179 G 3
Lodosa (E) .... 59 E 3
Łódź (PL) .... 122 B 2
Loeches (E) .... 64 C 3
Loen (N) .... 188 C 2
Lofallstrand (N) ..... 188 B 4
Lofário (GR) .... 162 D 3
Löffingen (D) .... 94 B 2
Lofsdalen (S) .... 189 H 2
Lofthus (N) .... 188 C 4
Loftus (GB) ....31 H 4
Log (SLO) .... 134 A 1
Logarska dolina (SLO).. 134 C 1
Logatec (SLO) .... 134 B 3
Logodaš (BG) .... 158 A 3
Logroño (E) .... 59 E 3
Logrosán (E) .... 69 H 1
Løgstør (DK) .... 194 D 4
Løgten (DK) .... 195 E 5
Løgumkloster (DK).... 198 B 4
Lohals (DK) .... 198 D 4
Lohberg (D)...........91 H 5
Lohilahti (FIN) ...... 193 G 2
Lohiniva (FIN) .... 180 D 4
Lohja / Lojo (FIN) ... 191 G 5
Lohne (D)............ 85 E 1
Löhne (D) .... 85 E 2
Lohr am Main (D) .... 89 G 2
Lohsa (D) .... 87 E 3
Lohtaja (FIN) .... 185 E 5
Loiano (I) .... 105 H 3
Loimaa (FIN) .... 191 G 4
Loimaan kunta (FIN) . 191 F 4
Loiri (I) ....112 D 1
Loiron-Ruillé (F). ... 43 G 3
Loitz (D) .... 83 F 3
Loja (E) .... 70 C 5
Lojo / Lohja (FIN)... 191 G 5
Lokalahti (FIN) ...... 191 E 4
Lokka (FIN) .... 181 F 3
Løkken (DK) .... 194 D 4
Løkken (N)........... 182 C 5
Lokn'a (RUS)...........6 D 2
Lőkösháza (H) ....131 E 4
Loksa (EST) .... 201 E 1
Lokve (HR)........... 134 C 4
Lokve (SLO) .... 134 A 2
Lokve (SRB)..........141 E 3
L'Olleria (E) .... 73 F 1
Lom (CZ) .... 86 D 5
Lom (N)............. 188 D 2
Lom / Лом (BG) ... 151 E 5
Łomazy (PL) .... 123 G 2
Lombez (F) .... 53 E 3
Lomci (BG) .... 156 D 2
Lomello (I) .... 101 E 5
Lomen (N) .... 188 D 3
Łomianki (PL) .... 122 D 1
Lomma (S) .... 199 F 3
Lommatzsch (D) ..... 86 D 4
Lommel (B) .... 79 E 1
Lomnice
  nad Popelkou (CZ) .. 87 G 5
Lomonosov (RUS)......6 D 1
Lompolo (FIN) .... 180 D 3
Łomża (PL)...........119 F 4
Lonato (I) .... 101 G 4
Loncari (BIH) .... 137 G 3
Lončarica (HR) ...... 135 G 3
Londinières (F) ...... 39 F 3
London (GB) .... 36 C 4
Londonderry /
  Derry (GB) ...... 23 E 2
Long Eaton (GB) ..... 33 E 4

Long Preston (GB) ...... 32 D 1
Long Sutton (GB) ...... 33 G 4
Longá
  (Pelopónnisos) (GR) .. 168 C 3
Longá (Thessalía) (GR) . 161 E 5
Longádes (GR) .... 160 C 5
Longares (E) .... 59 G 5
Longarone (I) .... 103 F 2
Longeau (F).......... 46 D 3
Longford /
  An Longfort (IRL) .. 23 E 4
Longleat House (GB) .... 35 F 3
Longny-au-Perche (F)... 44 C 2
Longobucco (I) ....113 C 2
Longtown (GB) ....31 E 4
Longué (F)............ 43 H 4
Longueville-sur-Scie (F). 39 F 3
Longuyon (F) ....41 E 4
Longwy (F)............41 E 4
Lonigo (I) .... 102 D 4
Löningen (D) .... 84 D 1
Löningen (D) .... 84 D 1
Lonja (HR) .... 135 F 4
Lons-le-Saunier (F)......51 E 1
Lönsboda (S)......... 195 H 5
Lønsdal (N) .... 179 G 5
Loo (EST) .... 201 E 1
Loosdorf (A) .... 97 F 1
Lopar (HR) .... 134 C 5
Lopare (BIH) .... 137 H 4
Lopătari (RO) .... 152 C 1
Lopatica (MK) .... 145 E 2
Lopcombe Corner (GB).. 35 G 3
Lopera (E) .... 70 C 4
Loppa (N) ....176 D 2
Loppi (FIN) .... 191 H 4
Lopud (HR) .... 139 E 4
Łopuszno (PL) .... 122 C 4
Lora (N).............. 188 D 2
Lora del Río (E). ..... 69 H 4
Lorca (E) .... 71 H 4
Lorcé (B) .... 79 E 3
Lorch (Ostalbkreis) (D) .. 89 G 4
Lorch (Rheingau-
  Taunus) (D) ...... 88 D 1
Loreo (I) .... 103 F 5
Loreto (I) .... 107 H 4
Loreto Aprutino (I) ... 109 G 1
Lorgues (F) .... 55 F 2
Lorica (I) ....113 C 2
Lorient (F) .... 42 C 3
Loriga (P) .... 62 D 3
Loriol-sur-Drôme (F) .. 50 D 5
Lormes (F) .... 45 H 4
Loro Ciuffenna (I) ... 106 D 3
Lorquin (F)...........47 G 1
Lörrach (D) .... 94 A 3
Lorrez-le-Bocage (F) .. 45 F 2
Lorris (F) .... 45 F 3
Los (S) .... 190 A 3
Los Alcázares (E) .... 73 G 4
Los Arcos (E) .... 59 E 3
Los Baños
  de Guardias Viejas (E) ..75 H 4
Los Barrios (E).........74 C 4
Los Corrales (E) ...... 58 B 1
Los Cortijos de Abajo (E). 64 B 5
Los Cristianos (E)......67 F 5
Los Dolores (E)....... 73 E 4
Los Gallardos (E) .... 71 G 5
Los Hinojosos (E).... 64 D 4
Los Llanos de Aridane (E) 67 F 5
Los Lobos (E) .... 71 H 5
Los Navalmorales (E). 64 A 4
Los Navalucillos (E).. 64 A 4
Los Palacios
  y Villafranca (E) .. 69 G 5
Los Santos (E)........ 63 G 3
Los Santos
  de Maimona (E) .. 69 F 3
Los Sauces (E).........67 F 5
Los Villares (E) ...... 70 D 4
Los Yébenes (E) ..... 64 B 4
Losar de la Vera (E) .. 63 G 4
Losenstein (A) .... 96 D 2
Losheim (D)........... 88 C 3
Łosice (PL) .... 123 F 1

Loßburg (D) .... 89 E 5
Lossiemouth (GB)....... 29 F 3
Lößnitz (D)........... 86 C 5
Lostwithiel (GB) ..... 34 C 4
Lote (N) .... 188 C 2
Løten (N) .... 189 F 4
Löttorp (S) .... 197 F 4
Loudéac (F) .... 42 D 2
Loudes (F) .... 50 B 4
Loudías (GR) .... 161 F 3
Loudun (F) .... 43 H 5
Loué (F) .... 43 H 3
Loughborough (GB) .. 33 E 4
Loughrea (IRL) ...... 22 D 5
Louhans-
  Châteaurenaud (F).. 50 D 1
Louhisaari (FIN) ..... 191 F 4
Louisburgh (IRL) .... 22 B 4
Loukísia (GR)........ 165 H 3
Loulay (F) .... 48 C 2
Loulé (P) .... 68 C 5
Louny (CZ) ....91 H 2
Lourdes (F) .... 52 D 4
Loures (P) .... 68 A 1
Louriçal (P) .... 62 B 4
Lourinhã (P) .... 62 A 5
Loúros (GR) .... 164 C 2
Lousa (P) .... 68 A 1
Lousã (P) .... 62 C 4
Lousada (P) .... 62 C 1
Louth (GB) .... 33 G 4
Loutrá (Kentrikí
  Makedonía) (GR) .. 161 H 5
Loutrá
  (Nótio Aigaío) (GR) .. 169 G 2
Loutrá
  (Vóreio Aigaío) (GR) .. 167 F 2
Loutrá Aidipsoú / Λουτρά
  Αιδηψού (GR) .. 165 G 2
Loutrá Aridaías (GR) . 161 E 3
Loutrá Elefterón (GR) . 162 B 3
Loutrá Kaítsas (GR) .. 165 E 2
Loutrá Kyllínis (GR) .. 164 C 4
Loutrá Lagkadá (GR) . 161 G 2
Loutrá Smokóvou (GR). 165 E 2
Loutrá Vólvis (GR) ... 161 H 3
Loutrá Ypátis (GR) .. 165 F 2
Loutráki (GR) .... 165 G 4
Loutráki
  (Dytikí Elláda) (GR) . 164 C 2
Loutráki (Thessalía) (GR). 165 H 2
Loutró Elénis (GR) .. 165 G 5
Loutropigí (GR) ..... 165 E 2
Loútsa (Attikí) (GR)... 166 B 4
Loútsa (Ípeiros) (GR) . 164 C 1
Louvain-la-Neuve (B) . 78 D 3
Louviers (F) .... 39 F 5
Louvigné-du-Désert (F). 43 G 2
Lövånger (S) .... 185 E 4
Lovasberény (H) ..... 129 E 2
Lovászpatona (H) ... 128 C 2
Lövberga (S) .... 183 H 4
Loveč / Ловеч (BG).... 158 D 1
Lovere (I) .... 101 G 3
Loviisa / Lovisa (FIN) . 193 E 4
Lovisa / Loviisa (FIN) . 193 E 4
Lovište (HR)......... 138 C 3
Lövö (N) .... 128 B 2
Lovosice (CZ) .... 87 E 5
Lovran / Laurana (HR). 134 B 4
Lovrenc
  na Pohorju (SLO) .. 134 D 1
Lovrin (RO) .... 146 A 5
Lövstabruk (S) ...... 190 C 5
Lovund (N) .... 183 F 1
Low Street (GB) ..... 37 E 1
Löwenberg (D)....... 83 F 5
Lowestoft (GB) ...... 37 F 2
Łowicz (PL) .... 122 C 1
Lož (SLO) .... 134 B 3
Lozarevo (BG) .... 159 H 1
Lozen (Haskovo) (BG) . 163 E 1
Lozen (Sofia-Grad) (BG). 158 B 2
Lozenec (Burgas) (BG). 157 F 5

Lozenec (Jambol) (BG) . 159 H 2
Lozna (SRB) .... 143 E 2
Loznica (BG) .... 156 D 2
Loznica / Лозница (SRB). 137 H 4
Lozovac (HR) .... 136 C 5
Lozovik (SRB) ....141 E 5
Lozoyuela (E) .... 64 C 1
Luanco (E) .... 57 G 1
Luarca (E) .... 57 F 1
Lubaczów (PL) ...... 123 G 5
Lubań (PL) .... 120 C 4
Lubāna (LV) .... 203 G 3
Lübars (D) .... 86 B 2
Lubartów (PL). ...... 123 F 3
Lubasz (PL)..........117 G 5
Lubawa (PL) .... 118 C 3
Lübbecke (D) .... 85 E 2
Lübben (D) .... 87 E 2
Lübbenau (D) .... 87 E 2
Lübbow (D) .... 82 C 5
Lübeck (D) .... 82 C 3
Lubenec (CZ) ....91 H 2
L'ubercy (RUS)........7 G 2
Lubersac (F) .... 49 F 3
Lubicz Dolny (PL) .....117 H 5
Lubień (Kraków) (PL) . 125 G 2
Lubień (Włodawa) (PL). 123 G 2
Lubień Kujawski (PL).. 121 H 1
Lubieszyn (PL)........116 B 3
Lubin (PL) .... 120 D 3
Lublin (PL) .... 123 F 3
Lubliniec (PL) .... 121 H 5
Lubmin (D) .... 83 F 2
Lubniewice (PL)...... 120 C 1
Lubny (UA) ....13 G 1
Luborzyca (PL)....... 125 G 1
L'ubotín (SK) .... 133 F 2
Lubraniec (PL)........118 B 5
Lubrín (E) .... 71 G 5
Lubsko (PL) .... 120 C 2
Lübtheen (D) .... 82 C 4
Lubycza Królewska (PL). 123 H 5
Lübz (D) .... 82 D 4
Luc-en-Diois (F).......51 E 5
Luc-sur-Mer (F) ..... 38 D 4
Lucainena
  de las Torres (E) .... 72 C 5
Lucan (IRL) .... 23 F 5
Lučani (SRB) .... 139 H 1
Lucca (I) .... 105 G 4
Luče (SLO) .... 134 C 2
Lucena (E) .... 70 C 5
Lucena del Cid (E)... 65 H 3
Lucenay-l'Évêque (F). 45 H 5
Lučenec (SK) .... 132 D 4
Luceni (E) .... 59 G 4
Lucera (I) ....110 C 2
Lüchow (D) .... 82 C 5
Luciana (E) .... 70 C 1
Lucito (I) .... 109 H 3
Luc'k (UA)............12 D 1
Lucka (D) .... 86 B 4
Luckau (D) .... 86 D 2
Luckenwalde (D) .... 86 D 2
Luçon (F) .... 48 B 1
Ludbreg (HR) .... 135 F 2
Lüdenscheid (D) .... 84 D 4
Ludești (RO) .... 151 H 3
Ludiente (E).......... 65 H 3
Lüdinghausen (D).... 84 D 3
Ludinovo (RUS).......7 F 3
Ludlow (GB) .... 32 C 5
Ludogorci (BG) ...... 156 D 2
Luduș (RO) .... 147 F 4
Ludvika (S) .... 190 A 5
Ludwigsburg (D) .... 89 F 4
Ludwigsfelde (D) .... 86 D 2
Ludwigshafen (D).... 94 C 3
Ludwigshafen
  am Rhein (D) .... 89 E 3
Ludwigslust (D) ..... 82 D 4
Ludwigsstadt (D) .....91 E 2
Ludza (LV) .... 203 H 4
Lug (BIH) .... 137 F 3
Luga (RUS)............6 D 1
Lugagnano
  Val d'Arda (I) ...... 102 B 5

A B C D E F G H I J K L M N O P Q R S T U V W X Y Z

Lugano (CH).............. 99 F 5
Lugau (D).............. 86 C 5
Lügde (D)............... 85 F 2
Lugnano
  in Teverina (I) .... 108 D 1
Lugo (E)............... 56 D 2
Lugo (I)............... 107 E 1
Lugoj (RO)............. 150 C 1
Lugones (E)........... 57 G 2
Luhačovice (CZ)........ 93 F 4
Luhalahti (FIN)........ 191 G 2
Luhanka (FIN)......... 191 H 2
Luhtapohja (FIN)...... 187 H 5
Luica (RO)............ 152 C 4
Luidja (EST)........... 200 B 2
Luimneach /
  Limerick (IRL)........ 24 C 3
Luino (I).............. 101 E 3
Luíntra (Nogueira
  de Ramuin) (E)....... 56 D 4
Luisenburg (D).........91 F 3
Luka (BIH)............ 139 E 2
Luka (HR)............. 136 B 5
Luka (SRB)............141 G 5
Lukavac (BIH)......... 137 G 4
Lukavica (BIH)........ 135 H 5
Lukovë (AL)........... 144 C 5
Lukovica
  pri Domžalah (SLO).. 134 C 2
Lukovit (BG).......... 155 E 3
Lukovo (MK).......... 144 D 2
Lukovo
  (Kuršumlija) (SRB).... 143 F 1
Lukovo (Zaječar) (SRB). 143 E 3
Lukovo Šugarje (HR) .. 136 B 4
Łuków (PL)........... 123 F 2
Łukta (PL)............118 C 3
Luleå (S)............. 185 E 2
Lüleburgaz (TR)........19 F 1
Lümanda (EST)........ 200 B 4
Lumbarda (HR)........ 138 C 3
Lumbier (E)........... 59 F 2
Lumbrales (E)......... 63 E 2
Lumbres (F)........... 39 H 1
Lumezzane (I)......... 101 G 4
Lumijoki (FIN)........ 185 G 3
Lumina (RO).......... 153 F 4
Lumparland (FIN)..... 191 E 5
Lumsås (DK).......... 198 D 3
Lumsheden (S)........ 190 B 4
Lun (HR)............. 134 C 5
Luna (E).............. 59 G 3
Lunas (F)............. 54 A 2
Lunca (RO)........... 151 G 5
Lunca Bradului (RO).. 147 H 3
Lunca Cernii
  de Jos (RO).......... 150 D 1
Lunca Corbului (RO)... 151 G 3
Lunca de Jos (RO)..... 148 B 4
Lunca Ilvei (RO)...... 147 H 2
Luncavița (RO)........ 153 F 2
Lünd (N)............. 183 E 3
Lund (S)............. 199 F 3
Lunde (N)............ 194 D 1
Lunde (N)............ 188 C 2
Lunden (D)............81 G 2
Lüneburg (D)......... 82 B 5
Lunel (F)............. 54 B 2
Lünen (D)............ 84 D 3
Lunéville (F)..........47 F 1
Lungern (CH)......... 98 D 3
Lungro (I)............113 B 1
Łuniniec (BY).........6 D 5
Lunz am See (A)....... 97 C 4
Luogosanto (I).........112 C 1
Luokė (LT)............ 204 D 2
Luopioinen (FIN)...... 191 H 3
Luosto (FIN)......... 181 E 4
Lupandi (LV)......... 203 H 5
Lupeni (RO).......... 151 E 2
Lupoglav (HR)........ 135 E 3
Lupșanu (RO)......... 152 C 4
Luque (E)............ 70 C 5
Lurbe-Saint-Christau (F). 52 C 2
Lurcy-Lévis (F)....... 50 A 1
Lure (F)..............47 F 3
Lurgan (GB)........... 23 G 3

Luri (F)................ 55 H 2
Lurisia (I)............ 104 C 3
Lury-sur-Arnon (F).... 45 E 5
Lušci Palanka (BIH).... 135 E 5
Lushnjë (AL)......... 144 C 3
Lusi (FIN)............ 193 E 3
Lusignan (F).......... 48 D 1
Lusigny-sur-Barse (F).. 45 H 2
Lusk (IRL)............ 23 G 5
Luso (P).............. 62 B 3
Lussac (F)............ 48 D 4
Lussac-les-Châteaux (F). 49 E 1
Lussan (F)............ 54 C 1
Lustenau (A)......... 94 D 3
Luster (N)............ 188 C 2
Lütjenburg (D)........ 82 B 2
Luton (GB)........... 36 C 3
Lutterberg (D)........ 85 G 4
Lutterworth (GB) ...... 33 E 5
Lutzelbourg (F).........41 G 5
Lützen (D)............ 86 B 4
Lutzerath (D)......... 88 C 1
Lutzmannsburg (A) .... 97 H 3
Lützow (D)............ 82 C 4
Luumäki (FIN)........ 193 F 3
Luupuvesi (FIN)...... 187 E 4
Luusua (FIN)......... 181 F 5
Luvia (FIN).......... 191 E 3
Luxembourg (L)....... 79 F 5
Luxeuil-les-Bains (F) ... 47 F 3
Luynes (F)............ 44 C 4
Luz-Saint-Sauveur (F) .. 52 D 4
Luzaide (E)........... 59 F 1
Lužani (HR).......... 135 G 4
Luzarches (F)......... 39 H 5
Luzech (F)............ 53 F 1
Luzern (CH).......... 99 E 3
Luzy (F).............. 45 H 5
Luzzara (I)........... 101 G 5
Luzzi (I)..............113 C 2
L'viv (UA)............12 D 2
Lwówek (PL)......... 120 D 1
Lwówek Śląski (PL).... 120 C 4
Lychen (D)........... 83 F 5
Lycksele (S).......... 184 C 3
Lydd (GB)............ 37 E 5
Lydney (GB).......... 35 F 1
Lykoporiá (GR)....... 165 F 4
Lykórrachi (GR)...... 160 C 4
Lyme Regis (GB) ...... 35 E 4
Lymington (GB)....... 38 B 1
Lympia (CY).......... 175 E 3
Lyndhurst (GB)....... 38 B 1
Lyness (GB).......... 26 B 4
Lyngdal (N).......... 194 B 2
Lyngseidet (N).........176 B 4
Lyngsnes (N)......... 183 E 3
Lynmouth (GB)....... 34 D 3
Lynton (GB).......... 34 D 3
Lyon (F).............. 50 D 3
Lyons-la-Forêt (F)..... 39 G 4
Lýrkeia (GR)......... 165 F 5
Lysá nad Labem (CZ)... 92 B 2
Łyse (PL)............. 119 E 4
Lysekil (S)........... 195 F 2
Lysi (CY)............. 175 E 3
Lysík (S)............. 189 G 5
Łysomice (PL).........117 H 4
Lysos (CY)............174 B 4
Lyss (CH)............. 98 C 2
Lysvik (S)........... 189 G 5
Łyszkowice (PL)...... 122 C 2
Lytham Saint Anne's (GB). 32 C 2
Lythrodontas (CY)....174 D 4

M
Maalahti / Malax (FIN).. 191 E 1
Maam Cross (IRL) ..... 22 B 5
Maaninka (FIN) .... 187 F 5
Maaninkavaara (FIN) .. 181 G 5
Maanselkä (FIN) ...... 187 F 4
Maardu (EST)......... 201 E 1
Maarianvaara (FIN)... 187 G 5
Maaseik (B).......... 79 E 2
Maasmechelen (B).... 79 E 2
Maassluis (NL).........76 C 5
Maastricht (NL)....... 79 E 2
Määttälänvaara (FIN).. 187 F 1

Mablethorpe (GB)...... 33 G 3
Macael (E)............ 71 G 5
Mação (P)............ 62 C 5
Macclesfield (GB)..... 32 D 3
Macduff (GB).......... 29 H 3
Maceda (E)............ 56 D 4
Macedo de Cavaleiros (P) 63 E 1
Macelj (HR).......... 135 E 2
Macerata (I).......... 107 G 4
Macerata Feltria (I).... 107 F 3
Măceșu de Jos (RO) .... 151 F 5
Machairádo (GR)...... 164 C 5
Machairas (CY).......174 D 4
Macharce (PL).........119 G 2
Machault (F).......... 40 C 4
Machecoul-
  Saint-Même (F)...... 43 F 5
Machliny (PL).........117 E 4
Machrihanish (GB)..... 23 G 1
Machynlleth (GB)..... 32 B 5
Maciejowice (PL)..... 123 E 2
Măcin (RO).......... 153 E 2
Mackenrode (D)....... 85 H 3
Mačkovci (SLO)...... 135 E 1
Macomer (I)..........112 B 3
Mâcon (F)............ 50 D 1
Macotera (E)......... 63 H 2
Macroom (IRL)....... 24 C 4
Macugnaga (I)........ 100 C 3
Mačvanska
  Pričinović (SRB)...... 140 B 4
Madan / Мадан (BG) ... 162 C 2
Madara (BG).......... 157 E 2
Madaras (H).......... 129 F 5
Maddaloni (I)......... 109 H 5
Maderuelo (E)........ 58 C 5
Madesimo (I)........ 101 F 2
Madona (LV)......... 203 F 3
Madonna
  di Campiglio (I)...... 101 H 2
Madrid (E)........... 64 B 2
Madridejos (E)....... 64 C 5
Madrigal de la Vera (E) . 63 H 4
Madrigal
  de las Altas Torres (E).. 63 H 2
Madrigalejo (E)....... 69 H 1
Madrona (E).......... 64 B 1
Madroñera (E)........ 63 G 5
Madžarovo (BG)...... 163 E 1
Maël-Carhaix (F)...... 42 C 2
Maella (E)............ 60 A 5
Mære (N)............ 183 E 4
Maesteg (GB)......... 34 D 2
Mafra (P)............. 68 A 1
Magacela (E)......... 69 G 2
Magallón (E)......... 59 F 4
Magaña (E)........... 59 E 4
Magaz de Pisuerga (E).. 58 A 4
Magdeburg (D)....... 86 A 2
Magenta (I).......... 101 E 4
Maghera (GB)........ 23 F 2
Magherafelt (GB)..... 23 F 2
Magione (I).......... 107 E 4
Maglaj (BIH)......... 137 G 4
Magliano de' Marsi (I) .. 109 F 2
Magliano in Toscana (I). 106 D 5
Magliano Sabina (I) ... 108 D 2
Maglič (SRB)......... 142 D 2
Maglie (I)............111 H 5
Mäglič (BG).......... 159 F 2
Magnac-Bourg (F)..... 49 F 3
Magnac-Laval (F)..... 49 F 2
Magnor (N).......... 189 G 5
Magny-en-Vexin (F).... 39 G 5
Mágocs (H).......... 128 D 4
Magoúla (GR)........ 164 D 5
Măgura (RO)......... 152 C 5
Magura (SRB)........ 143 E 4
Magura (BG)......... 154 C 2
Magyaratád (H)...... 128 D 4
Magyaregregy (H).... 128 D 4
Magyarmecske (H)... 128 D 5
Magyarszék (H)...... 128 D 5
Mahilëŭ (BY)..........7 E 4
Mahlu (FIN).......... 191 H 1

Mahora (E)........... 65 F 5
Mahovo (HR)......... 135 E 3
Mähring (D)...........91 G 3
Maia (P).............. 62 B 1
Măicănești (RO)...... 152 D 1
Maîche (F)............47 G 4
Maida (I).............113 C 3
Maidenhead (GB)..... 35 H 2
Maidstone (GB)....... 36 D 4
Maienfeld (CH)....... 99 G 3
Mäieruș (RO)......... 152 A 1
Maignelay-Montigny (F). 39 H 4
Maijanen (FIN)....... 180 D 4
Maillezais (F)........ 48 C 1
Mailly-le-Camp (F).... 45 H 1
Mainar (E)........... 65 G 1
Mainau (D)........... 94 C 3
Mainburg (D)......... 95 G 1
Maintenon (F)........ 44 D 1
Mainz (D)............ 89 E 2
Maiori (I)............ 109 H 5
Mairena del Alcor (E).. 69 G 5
Maisach (D).......... 95 F 2
Maison-Neuve (F)..... 46 C 2
Maissau (A).......... 97 F 1
Maizières (F)..........41 E 5
Maja (HR)............ 135 E 4
Majdan Królewski (PL). 123 E 5
Majdanpek (SRB)..... 141 F 5
Majšperk (SLO)....... 134 D 2
Makarska (HR)....... 138 C 2
Makce (SRB)......... 141 E 4
Makedonski Brod (MK). 145 E 3
Makó (H)............ 129 H 4
Makov (SK).......... 132 C 1
Makovo (MK)........ 145 F 2
Maków
  Mazowiecki (PL) ......119 E 5
Maków Podhalański (PL). 125 G 2
Makrakómi (GR)...... 165 E 2
Makri (GR)........... 163 E 3
Makrinítsa (GR)...... 165 G 1
Makrochóri (GR)..... 161 F 4
Makryámmos (GR)... 162 C 3
Makrychóri (Anatolikí Make-
  donía kai Thráki) (GR). 162 C 3
Makrychóri
  (Thessalia) (GR)...... 161 F 5
Makrýgialos (GR)..... 161 F 4
Makrygialós (GR)..... 173 F 4
Makryrráchi (GR)..... 165 E 2
Maksamaa / Maxmo (FIN). 185 F 5
Maksniemi (FIN)..... 185 G 2
Malå (S)............. 184 C 2
Mala / Mallow (IRL) ... 24 C 4
Mala Bosna (SRB) .... 140 B 1
Mala Krsna (SRB)......141 E 4
Mala Subotica (HR)... 135 F 2
Mala Vyska (UA).......13 G 2
Malacky (SK)......... 132 A 3
Maładečna (BY).........6 D 1
Málaga (E)............75 E 3
Malagón (E).......... 64 B 5
Malahide /
  Mullach Íde (IRL) ..... 23 G 5
Malaja Višera (RUS).....6 D 1
Malák Porovec (BG)... 152 C 5
Malăk Preslavec (BG).. 152 C 5
Malalbergo (I)....... 106 D 1
Malandríno (GR)..... 165 E 3
Malaucène (F)........ 54 D 1
Malax / Maalahti (FIN). 191 E 1
Malbork (PL).........117 H 2
Malbrouck,
  château de (F).........41 F 4
Malbuisson (F).........47 F 5
Malcesine (I)........ 101 H 3
Malchin (D).......... 83 E 3
Malchow (D)......... 83 E 4
Malčika (BG)......... 156 B 2
Malczyce (PL)........ 121 E 3
Maldegem (B)........ 78 B 1
Maldon (GB)......... 36 D 3
Małdyty (PL).........118 C 2
Malé (I)............. 101 H 2

Male Pijace (SRB)...... 140 C 1
Malechowo (PL).......117 E 2
Malente-
  Gremsmühlen (D)... 82 B 2
Malesherbes (F)...... 45 E 2
Malesína (GR)........ 165 G 3
Malestroit (F)........ 43 E 3
Malgrat de Mar (E)....61 E 3
Mali Iđoš (SRB)...... 140 B 2
Mali Lošinj (HR)...... 136 A 4
Mali Požarevac (SRB).. 140 D 4
Mali Zvornik (SRB).... 137 H 4
Malia (CY)...........174 C 4
Mália / Μάλια (GR).... 170 C 5
Malicorne-sur-Sarthe (F). 43 H 3
Mălini (RO).......... 148 B 2
Malinska (HR)........ 134 B 4
Maliq (AL)........... 144 D 3
Mališevo (SRB)....... 142 D 4
Maliskylä (FIN)...... 185 H 4
Małkinia Górna (PL)...119 F 5
Malko Gradište (BG).. 163 E 1
Malko Šarkovo (BG)... 159 H 3
Malko Tărnovo (BG)... 157 F 5
Mallaig (GB).......... 28 D 4
Mallén (E)............ 59 F 4
Mallersdorf-
  Pfaffenberg (D)........91 F 5
Malles Venosta/ Mals (I). 101 G 1
Mallnitz (A).......... 96 C 4
Mallow / Mala (IRL)... 24 C 4
Mallwyd (GB)........ 32 B 4
Malm (N)............ 183 E 4
Malmberget (S)...... 180 B 4
Malmedy (B)......... 79 F 3
Malmesbury (GB)..... 35 G 2
Malmköping (S)...... 197 F 1
Malmö (S)........... 199 E 3
Malmslätt (S)........ 197 E 2
Malo (I)............. 102 D 4
Malo-les-Bains (F).... 39 H 1
Maloarchangel'sk (RUS)..7 G 4
Małogoszcz (PL)..... 122 C 4
Maloja (CH).......... 99 G 4
Malojaroslavec (RUS)....7 G 2
Małomice (PL)....... 120 C 3
Malomir (BG)........ 159 G 2
Malomirovo (BG)..... 159 H 3
Malorad (BG)........ 154 D 2
Malovăț (RO)........ 150 D 3
Måløy (N)........... 188 B 1
Malpartida de Cáceres (E). 63 F 5
Malpartida
  de Plasencia (E)...... 63 F 4
Malpica
  de Bergantiños (E)... 56 B 1
Malpica do Tejo (P)... 62 D 5
Mals / Malles Venosta (I). 101 G 1
Målsnes (N)...........176 B 4
Malsta (S)........... 190 B 2
Malta (A)............ 96 C 4
Malta (LV)........... 203 G 4
Maltby (GB).......... 33 E 3
Malton (GB)...........31 H 5
Malu cu Flori (RO).... 151 H 2
Malu Mare (RO)...... 151 F 4
Maluenda (E)........ 59 F 5
Malung (S).......... 189 H 4
Malungsfors (S)...... 189 H 4
Malveira (P)......... 68 A 1
Malveira (P)......... 68 A 2
Malvik (N)........... 182 D 5
Malyn (UA)...........13 E 1
Mamarrosa (P)....... 62 B 3
Mamers (F)........... 44 B 2
Mammari (CY)........174 D 3
Mammola (I).........113 C 4
Mamonovo (RUS).......5 H 4
Manacor (E)...........67 F 3
Manacore (I).........110 D 1
Manamansalo (FIN).. 187 E 3
Manastir (BG)........ 162 D 1
Mănăstireni (RO)..... 152 C 4
Mănăstirea
  Humorului (RO)..... 148 B 2
Mănăstireni (RO)..... 147 E 4
Mancha Real (E)...... 70 D 4

Manchester (GB)....... 32 D 3
Manching (D)......... 95 G 1
Manciano (I)......... 106 D 5
Mandal (N)........... 194 C 2
Mandas (I)...........112 C 4
Mandela (I).......... 109 E 2
Mandelieu-
  la-Napoule (F)....... 55 G 2
Manderscheid (D)...... 88 C 1
Mándra (Anatolikí Makedonía
  kai Thráki) (GR)..... 163 F 2
Mándra (Attikí) (GR).. 165 H 4
Mandráki (GR)....... 171 F 2
Mandre (HR)......... 136 A 4
Mandria
  (Óros Ólimpos) (CY) ...174 C 4
Mandria (Páfos) (CY) ...174 B 5
Mandrica (BG)....... 163 E 2
Mandrikó (GR)....... 171 H 3
Manduria (I).........111 G 4
Măneciu-Ungureni (RO). 152 B 2
Manerbio (I)......... 101 G 4
Manětín (CZ)..........91 H 3
Mánfa (H)........... 128 D 5
Manfredonia (I)......110 D 2
Mangalia (RO)....... 153 F 5
Manger (N).......... 188 A 3
Mangualde (P)....... 62 C 4
Maniago (I).......... 103 F 3
Manilva (E)...........74 C 4
Manisa (TR)...........19 G 3
Manises (E).......... 65 H 4
Mank (A)............ 97 F 2
Månkarbo (S)........ 190 B 5
Manlleu (E).......... 60 D 2
Mannersdorf
  am Leithagebirge (A).. 97 H 2
Mannheim (D)........ 89 E 3
Manole (BG)......... 159 E 3
Manoleasa (RO)...... 148 C 1
Manolić (BG)......... 159 H 1
Manoppello (I)....... 109 G 2
Manorhamilton (IRL).. 22 D 3
Manosque (F)........ 55 E 2
Manresa (E).......... 60 D 3
Manschnow (D)...... 87 E 1
Mansfeld (D)......... 86 A 3
Mansfield (GB)....... 33 E 3
Mansilla de las Mulas (E). 57 H 4
Mansle (F)........... 49 E 2
Mantamádos (GR).... 167 F 1
Manteigas (P)........ 62 D 3
Mantes-la-Jolie (F).... 39 G 5
Mantiel (E).......... 64 D 2
Mäntlahti (FIN)...... 193 F 4
Mantorp (S)......... 197 E 3
Mantoúdi (GR)....... 165 H 3
Mantova (I).......... 101 H 5
Mäntsälä (FIN)...... 191 H 4
Mänttä (FIN)........ 191 H 2
Mäntyharju (FIN).... 193 F 3
Mäntyjärvi (FIN)..... 187 E 1
Mäntyluoto (FIN).... 191 E 3
Manzanares (E)...... 71 E 1
Manzanares el Real (E) . 64 B 2
Manzaneda (E)....... 57 E 4
Manzanera (E)....... 65 G 3
Manzat (F)........... 50 A 2
Manziana (I)......... 108 D 2
Maó / Mahón (E)......67 H 2
Maqellarë (AL)....... 144 D 1
Maqueda (E)......... 64 A 3
Maranchón (E)....... 65 E 1
Maranello (I)........ 105 H 3
Marano (I)........... 103 G 3
Marano di Napoli (I)... 109 G 5
Marans (F)........... 48 C 1
Mărășești (RO)....... 152 D 1
Maratea (I)...........110 C 5
Marateca (P)......... 68 B 2
Marathéa (GR)....... 165 E 1
Marathiás (GR)...... 165 E 3
Marathókampos (GR). 167 F 5
Marathónas (GR).... 166 B 4
Marathópoli (GR).... 168 B 3
Márathos (GR)....... 165 G 1
Marathovounos (CY)...174 B 1

237

Marbach am Neckar (D) 89 F4
Mårbacka (S) 189 G5
Marbella (E) 74 D4
Marble Arch Caves (GB) 23 E3
Marburg (D) 85 E5
Marby (S) 183 F5
Marcali (H) 128 C4
Marcaltő (H) 128 C2
Marčana (HR) 134 A5
Mârčevo (BG) 154 D2
March (GB) 33 G4
Marchamalo (E) 64 C2
Marchaux (F) 47 F4
Marche-en-Famenne (B) 79 E4
Marchegg (A) 97 H1
Marchena (E) 69 H5
Marchenoir (F) 44 D3
Marchiennes (F) 40 A2
Marciac (F) 52 D3
Marciana Marina (I) 106 B5
Marcianise (I) 109 G5
Marcigny (F) 50 B2
Marcilla (E) 59 F3
Marcillac-Vallon (F) 53 H1
Marcillat-en-Combraille (F) 49 H2
Marcilly-le-Hayer (F) 45 G2
Marcinkonys (LT) 205 F5
Marckolsheim (F) 47 H2
Marco de Canaveses (P) 62 C1
Marcoule (F) 54 C1
Mardec (BG) 159 G3
Marene (I) 104 C2
Marennes (F) 48 C2
Marentes (E) 57 E2
Mareuil (F) 49 E3
Mareuil-sur-Lay (F) 48 B1
Margate (GB) 37 E4
Margherita di Savoia (I) 110 D2
Marghita (RO) 146 D2
Marginea (RO) 148 B1
Margonin (PL) 117 F5
Marguerittes (F) 54 C2
María (E) 71 G4
Maria Saal (A) 96 D5
Maria Taferl (A) 97 E1
Mariannelund (S) 197 E4
Mariánské Lázně (CZ) 91 G3
Mariazell (A) 97 F2
Maribo (DK) 198 D4
Maribor (SLO) 134 D1
Mariborsko Pohorje (SLO) 134 D1
Mariefred (S) 197 F1
Mariehamn (FIN) 190 D5
Marienberg (D) 86 D5
Marienstedt (D) 82 C4
Mariestad (S) 195 H2
Marignane (F) 54 D3
Marigny-le-Châtel (F) 45 G2
Marigny-Le-Lozon (F) 38 C5
Marija Bistrica (HR) 135 E2
Marijampolė (LT) 205 E4
Marikostinovo (BG) 161 H2
Marín (E) 56 B4
Marina (HR) 138 B2
Marina di Camerota (I) 110 C5
Marina di Campo (I) 106 B5
Marina di Carrara (I) 105 F4
Marina di Castagneto-Donoratico (I) 105 G5
Marina di Gioiosa Ionica (I) 113 C4
Marina di Grosseto (I) 106 C5
Marina di Leuca (I) 114 F1
Marina di Massa (I) 105 F4
Marina di Pietrasanta (I) 105 G4
Marina di Pisa (I) 105 G4
Marina di Ragusa (I) 115 F5
Marina di Ravenna (I) 107 E1
Marina di Torre Grande (I) 112 B3
Marinella (I) 114 B3
Marineo (I) 114 D3
Marines (F) 39 G5
Maringues (F) 50 A2
Marinha Grande (P) 62 A4
Marinka (BG) 157 F4
Marinkainen (FIN) 185 F4
Marino (I) 109 E3
Mărişel (RO) 147 E4
Marismas del Odiel, paraje natural de las (E) 74 A2
Maritsa / Марица (BG) 158 D3
Märjamaa (EST) 200 D2
Marjaniemi (FIN) 185 G2
Marjna Horka (BY) 6 D4
Markaryd (S) 195 G5
Markdorf (D) 94 D3
Market Drayton (GB) 32 D4
Market Harborough (GB) 33 F5
Market Rasen (GB) 33 F3
Market Weighton (GB) 33 F2
Markethill (GB) 23 F3
Markgröningen (D) 89 F4
Marki (PL) 122 D1
Markina-Xemein (E) 58 D1
Märkisch Buchholz (D) 86 D2
Markkleeberg (D) 86 C4
Markneukirchen (D) 91 F2
Markópoulo (Iónia Nisiá) (GR) 164 C4
Markópoulo (Marathónas) (GR) 165 H5
Markópoulo (Vougliaméni) (GR) 165 H4
Markov Monastir (MK) 143 F5
Markovac (Velika Plana) (SRB) 141 E5
Markovac (Vršac) (SRB) 141 E3
Markovo (BG) 157 E3
Markranstädt (D) 86 B4
Markt Erlbach (D) 89 H3
Markt Indersdorf (D) 95 F1
Markt Sankt Florian (A) 96 D2
Marktbreit (D) 89 G2
Marktheidenfeld (D) 89 G2
Marktl (D) 96 B2
Marktoberdorf (D) 95 E3
Marktredwitz (D) 91 F3
Markušica (HR) 137 G2
Marl (D) 84 C3
Marlborough (GB) 35 G2
Marle (F) 40 B4
Marlenheim (F) 47 G1
Marlow (D) 83 E2
Marlow (GB) 35 H2
Marmande (F) 48 D5
Marmári (GR) 166 B4
Marmaris (TR) 19 H4
Mármaro (GR) 167 E3
Marmolejo (E) 70 C3
Marmoutier (F) 47 G1
Marnay (F) 47 E4
Marne (D) 81 G3
Marnitz (D) 82 D4
Marnovo Manastir (MK) 145 F2
Marolles-les-Braults (F) 44 B2
Maróneia (GR) 162 D3
Maroni (CY) 174 D4
Maroslele (H) 129 H4
Marostica (I) 103 E4
Marotta (I) 107 G3
Márpissa (GR) 170 C2
Marquartstein (D) 95 H3
Marquion (F) 40 A3
Marquise (F) 39 G1
Marradi (I) 106 D2
Marraskoski (FIN) 181 E5
Mars-la-Tour (F) 41 E5
Marsaglia (I) 105 E2
Marsala (I) 114 B3
Marsberg (D) 85 F3
Marsciano (I) 107 F5
Marseillan (F) 54 A3
Marseille (F) 54 D3
Marseille-en-Beauvaisis (F) 39 G4
Marsico Nuovo (I) 110 C4
Marske-by-the-Sea (GB) 31 H4
Märsta (S) 197 G1
Marstal (DK) 198 C4
Marstrand (S) 195 F3
Marta (I) 108 C1
Martano (I) 111 H5
Martel (F) 49 G5
Martelange (B) 79 E5
Martfű (H) 129 G3
Marthon (F) 49 E3
Martignacco (I) 103 G3
Martigné-Ferchaud (F) 43 F3
Martigny (CH) 98 C5
Martigny-les-Bains (F) 47 E2
Martigues (F) 54 D3
Martim Longo (P) 68 D5
Martin (SK) 132 C2
Martin Brod (BIH) 136 C4
Martín de la Jara (E) 74 D2
Martín de Yeltes (E) 63 F2
Martina (CH) 99 H3
Martina Franca (I) 111 F4
Martinengo (I) 101 F4
Martinet (E) 60 C2
Martingança (P) 62 A4
Martinniemi (FIN) 185 H2
Martinšćica (HR) 134 B5
Martis (I) 112 B1
Martjanci (SLO) 135 E1
Martofte (DK) 198 C3
Martonvaara (FIN) 187 G5
Martonvásár (H) 129 E2
Martorell (E) 60 D4
Martos (E) 70 D4
Martti (FIN) 181 F4
Marttila (FIN) 191 F4
Marvão (P) 62 D5
Marvejols (F) 50 A5
Marykirk (GB) 29 H5
Marynin (PL) 123 G3
Maryport (GB) 31 E4
Mas-Cabardès (F) 53 H3
Mas de Barberans (E) 60 A5
Mas de las Matas (E) 65 H1
Masegoso de Tajuña (E) 64 D2
Masevaux-Niederbruck (F) 47 G3
Masi (N) 176 D4
Masku (FIN) 191 F4
Maslenica (HR) 136 B4
Maslinica (HR) 138 B2
Maslovare (BIH) 137 F4
Maspalomas (E) 67 G5
Massa (I) 105 G4
Massa Fiscaglia (I) 107 E1
Massa Marittima (I) 106 C4
Massa Martana (I) 107 F5
Massafra (I) 111 F4
Massamagrell (E) 65 H4
Massarosa (I) 105 G4
Massat (F) 53 F4
Masseube (F) 53 E3
Massiac (F) 50 A4
Massiaru (EST) 200 D4
Mastichári (GR) 171 F2
Masty (BY) 6 C5
Masueco (E) 63 F1
Maszewo (Szczecin) (PL) 116 C3
Maszewo (Zielona Gora) (PL) 120 C2
Mátala (GR) 172 D4
Matalascañas (E) 74 A2
Matalebreras (E) 59 E4
Matallana de Torío (E) 57 G3
Mataró (E) 61 E3
Mataruška Banja (SRB) 142 D1
Mătăsari (RO) 151 E3
Matca (RO) 152 D1
Matejče (MK) 143 F5
Matelica (I) 107 G4
Matera (I) 111 E4
Mateševo (MNE) 139 G4
Mátészalka (H) 131 F1
Mateus (P) 62 D1
Matfors (S) 190 B2
Matha (F) 48 D2
Máti (GR) 166 B4
Matignon (F) 43 E1
Matiši (LV) 203 E1
Matka (MK) 143 E5
Matku (FIN) 191 G4
Matlock (GB) 33 E3
Matosinhos (P) 62 B1
Matour (F) 50 C1
Matrei am Brenner (A) 95 G4
Matrei in Osttirol (A) 95 H4
Mattersburg (A) 97 G2
Mattighofen (A) 96 C2
Mattinata (I) 110 D2
Mattmar (S) 183 F5
Mattsee (A) 96 B2
Mattsmyra (S) 190 A3
Matulji (HR) 134 B4
Maubeuge (F) 40 B2
Maubourguet (F) 52 D3
Maubuisson (F) 48 B4
Mauchline (GB) 30 C2
Mauerkirchen (A) 96 B2
Mauguio (F) 54 B2
Maula (FIN) 185 G1
Maulbronn (D) 89 E4
Mauléon (F) 43 G5
Mauléon-Barousse (F) 53 E4
Mauléon-Licharre (F) 52 B3
Maure-de-Bretagne (F) 43 E3
Mauriac (F) 49 H4
Mauron (F) 43 E2
Maurs (F) 49 H5
Mautern in Steiermark (A) 97 E3
Mauterndorf (A) 96 C4
Mauthausen (A) 97 E1
Mauthen (A) 96 B5
Mauvezin (F) 53 E2
Mauzé-sur-le-Mignon (F) 48 C2
Mavréli (GR) 161 E5
Mavrochóri (GR) 160 D4
Mavrokklísi (GR) 163 F2
Mavroléfki (GR) 162 B3
Mavrommáta (GR) 165 E2
Mavrommáti (GR) 168 C3
Mavronéri (GR) 161 G3
Mavrove (AL) 144 C4
Mavrovi Anovi (MK) 144 D1
Mavrovo (MK) 144 D1
Mavrovoúni (Kentrikí Makedonía) (GR) 161 F3
Mavrovoúni (Thessalía) (GR) 165 F1
Maxhütte (D) 91 F5
Măxineni (RO) 153 E2
Maxmo / Maksamaa (FIN) 185 F5
Mayals (E) 60 B4
Maybole (GB) 30 C3
Mayen (D) 88 C1
Mayenne (F) 43 H2
Mayerling (A) 97 G2
Mayet (F) 44 B3
Maynooth (IRL) 23 F5
Mayorga (E) 57 H4
Mayrhofen (A) 95 G4
Mazagón (E) 69 E5
Mazagran (F) 40 C4
Mazamet (F) 53 H3
Mazara del Vallo (I) 114 B3
Mazarakiá (GR) 164 B1
Mazarete (E) 65 E1
Mazarrón (E) 72 D4
Mažeikiai (LT) 204 C1
Mazères (F) 53 F3
Mázi (GR) 160 C5
Mazières-en-Gâtine (F) 48 D1
Mazotos (CY) 175 E4
Mazsalaca (LV) 203 E1
Mazyr (BY) 7 E5
Mazzarino (I) 115 E4
Mazzarò (I) 115 G3
Mcensk (RUS) 7 G3
Mealhada (P) 62 B3
Meaux (F) 40 A5
Mechelen (Malines) (B) 78 C2
Mečka (BG) 152 B5
Meckenbeuren (D) 94 D3
Mêda (P) 62 D2
Međa (SRB) 140 D2
Medak (HR) 136 B4
Mede (I) 100 D5
Medebach (D) 85 E4
Međeđa (BIH) 139 F1
Medelim (P) 62 D4
Medellín (E) 69 G1
Medemblik (NL) 77 E3
Meden Buk (BG) 163 E2
Meden Kladenec (BG) 159 G2
Medeni Poljani (BG) 161 H1
Medgidia (RO) 153 F4
Medgyesegyháza (H) 130 D4
Mediaş (RO) 147 G5
Medicina (I) 106 D1
Medina Azahara (E) 70 B4
Medina de Pomar (E) 58 C2
Medina de Rioseco (E) 57 H5
Medina del Campo (E) 63 H1
Medina-Sidonia (E) 74 B4
Medinaceli (E) 65 E1
Medkovec (BG) 151 E5
Médous, grotte de (F) 52 D4
Médousa (GR) 162 C2
Medovo (BG) 157 F4
Mędrzechów (PL) 122 D5
Medulin (HR) 134 A5
Međumajdam (HR) 135 E4
Meduno (I) 103 G3
Međurečje (SRB) 139 H2
Medveđa (SRB) 143 F3
Medveja (HR) 134 B4
Medviđa (HR) 136 C5
Medvode (SLO) 134 B2
Medyka (PL) 127 G1
Medyn' (RUS) 7 G3
Medzilaborce (SK) 133 H2
Medžitlija (MK) 145 F3
Meerane (D) 86 C5
Meersburg (D) 94 C3
Mefjordbotn (N) 176 A4
Mefjordvær (N) 176 A4
Méga Déreio (GR) 163 E2
Méga Monastíri (GR) 165 F1
Megáli Panagía (GR) 161 H4
Megáli Vólvi (GR) 161 H3
Megálo Chorió (Agathonísi) (GR) 171 G3
Megálo Chorió (Stereá Elláda) (GR) 165 E2
Megálo Chorió (Tílos) (GR) 171 F1
Megalochóri (Attikí) (GR) 165 G5
Megalochóri (Thessalía) (GR) 165 E1
Megalópoli / Μεγαλόπολη (GR) 168 C2
Megálos Prínos (GR) 162 C3
Mégara / Μέγαρα (GR) 165 G4
Megève (F) 51 F2
Megísti (GR) 171 H1
Megyaszó (H) 126 D5
Mehamn (N) 177 F1
Mehedeby (S) 190 B4
Mehikoorma (EST) 201 G4
Mehun-sur-Yèvre (F) 45 E5
Meigle (GB) 29 F5
Meijel (NL) 79 E1
Meilen (CH) 99 E2
Meillant (F) 45 F5
Meimoa (P) 62 D3
Meina (I) 100 D3
Meinerzhagen (D) 84 D4
Meiningen (D) 85 H5
Meira (E) 57 E2
Meiringen (CH) 98 D3
Meisenheim (D) 88 D2
Meißen (D) 86 D4
Meitingen (D) 89 H5
Mel (I) 103 E3
Melalahti (FIN) 187 F3
Mélampes (GR) 172 C3
Melaniós (GR) 167 E3
Melánthi (GR) 160 D4
Melátes (GR) 164 D1
Melbeck (D) 82 B5
Melbu (N) 179 F2
Meldal (N) 182 C5
Meldola (I) 107 E2
Meldorf (D) 81 G3
Melegnano (I) 101 E4
Melenci (SRB) 140 C2
Melendugno (I) 111 H4
Melfi (I) 110 C3
Melgaço (P) 56 C4
Melgar de Abajo (E) 57 H4
Melgar de Fernamental (E) 58 B3
Melhus (N) 182 D5
Melía (GR) 165 F1
Melide (E) 56 C2
Melides (P) 68 B3
Meligalás (GR) 168 C3
Melíki (GR) 161 F4
Melilli (I) 115 G4
Melineşti (RO) 151 F3
Mélisey (F) 47 F3
Mélissa (GR) 162 C3
Melíssi (GR) 165 F4
Melissochóri (GR) 165 G4
Melissópetra (GR) 160 C4
Melito di Porto Salvo (I) 115 H3
Melívoia (GR) 162 C2
Melk (A) 97 F1
Melksham (GB) 35 F2
Mellansel (S) 184 C5
Melle (D) 85 E2
Melle (F) 48 D2
Mellendorf (D) 85 G1
Mellerstain (GB) 31 F2
Mellerud (S) 195 G2
Mellieha (M) 114 C5
Mellilä (FIN) 191 F4
Mellin (D) 86 A1
Mellingen (D) 86 A5
Mellrichstadt (D) 89 H1
Melnica (SRB) 141 F5
Melnice (HR) 134 C5
Melnik (BG) 161 H1
Mělník (CZ) 92 A2
Melpers (D) 85 G5
Melrose (GB) 31 E2
Melsungen (D) 85 G4
Meltaus (FIN) 181 E5
Melton Mowbray (GB) 33 F4
Meltosjärvi (FIN) 180 D5
Melun (F) 45 F2
Melvich (GB) 26 A4
Mélykút (H) 129 F5
Memaliaj (AL) 144 C4
Membrilla (E) 71 E1
Membrío (E) 63 E5
Memmingen (D) 95 E2
Mena (UA) 7 F5
Menaggio (I) 101 E3
Menai Bridge (GB) 32 A3
Menasalbas (E) 64 A4
Menat (F) 50 A2
Mendavia (E) 59 E3
Mende (F) 50 B5
Menden (D) 84 D3
Mendenítsa (GR) 165 F3
Mendrisio (CH) 99 F5
Menen (B) 78 B2
Menesjärvi (FIN) 177 F5
Menetés (GR) 171 F5
Menfi (I) 114 C3
Ménfőcsanak (H) 128 C1
Mengamuñoz (E) 63 H3
Mengara (I) 107 F4
Mengen (D) 94 C2
Mengeš (SLO) 134 C2
Mengíbar (E) 70 D4
Mengiševo (BG) 159 G1
Menídi (GR) 164 D2
Ménigoute (F) 48 D1
Meniko (CY) 174 D3
Mennetou-sur-Cher (F) 45 E4
Mens (F) 51 E5
Mentana (I) 109 E2
Menthon (F) 51 F2
Menton (F) 55 H2
Méntrida (E) 64 B3

A B C D E F G H I J K L M N O P Q R S T U V W X Y Z

A B C D E F G H I J K L **M** N O P Q R S T U V W X Y Z

Meppel (NL) 77 F3
Meppen (D) 84 D1
Mequinenza (E) 60 A4
Mer (F) 44 D3
Merag (HR) 134 B5
Meråker (N) 183 E5
Meran / Merano 101 H2
Merano / Meran (I) 101 H2
Merate (I) 101 F4
Mercatale (I) 107 F3
Mercatale (I) 107 E4
Mercatino Conca (I) ... 107 F3
Mercato San Severino (I) 109 H5
Mercato Saraceno (I) .. 107 E2
Mercéz (SRB) 143 E2
Mercœur (F) 49 G4
Merdrignac (F) 43 E2
Mere (GB) 35 F3
Merei (RO) 152 C2
Méréville (F) 45 E2
Mergozzo (I) 100 D3
Méribel (F) 51 F3
Mérichas (GR) 169 G2
Merichleri (BG) 159 F3
Mérida (E) 69 F1
Mérignac (F) 48 C5
Merijärvi (FIN) 185 G4
Merikarvia (FIN) 191 E2
Mering (D) 95 F2
Merişani (RO) 151 G3
Merkendorf (D) 89 H3
Merkinė (LT) 205 E5
Merklingen (D) 89 G5
Merle, tours de (F) .. 49 G4
Mernye (H) 128 D4
Merošina (SRB) 143 F2
Mers-les-Bains (F) 39 F3
Mersch (L) 79 F5
Merseburg (D) 86 B4
Mersevát (H) 128 C2
Mērsrags (LV) 202 C2
Merthyr Tydfil (GB) ... 35 E1
Mértola (P) 68 D4
Méru (F) 39 H5
Merville (F) 39 H2
Merville-Franceville (F) 38 D5
Méry-sur-Seine (F) 45 H2
Merzig (D) 88 B3
Mesa Geitonia (CY) 174 D5
Mesagne (I) 111 G4
Mesanagrós (GR) 171 H4
Mesão Frio (P) 62 C1
Meschede (D) 85 E4
Mescherin (D) 83 H4
Meschers-sur-Gironde (F) 48 C3
Mešeišta (MK) 145 E2
Mesići (BIH) 137 H5
Mesihovina (BIH) 138 C2
Mesiméri (GR) 161 G4
Meškuičiai (LT) 205 E1
Meslay-du-Maine (F) ... 43 H3
Mesocco (CH) 99 F4
Mesochóra (GR) 164 D1
Mesochóri (Nótio Aigaío) (GR) 171 F5
Mesochóri (Thessalía) (GR) 161 E5
Mesogi (CY) 174 B4
Mesola (I) 103 F5
Mesolóngi / Μεσολόγγι (GR) 164 D3
Mesón do Vento (E) 56 C2
Mesopótamo (GR) 164 C1
Mesoraca (I) 113 C3
Mesótopos (GR) 167 E2
Mespelbrunn (D) 89 F2
Meßdorf (D) 86 A1
Messei (F) 43 H1
Messelt (N) 189 F3
Messina (I) 115 G2
Messíni / Μεσσήνη (GR) . 168 C3
Meßkirch (D) 94 C2
Messlingen (S) 189 G1
Meßstetten (D) 94 C2
Mestá (GR) 167 E4
Mésti (GR) 163 E3

Mestlin (D) 82 D4
Město Albrechtice (CZ) . 93 F2
Mestre (I) 103 F4
Mesvres (F) 45 H5
Mesztegnyő (H) 128 C4
Metajna (HR) 136 B4
Metalika (BIH) 139 F2
Metallikó (GR) 161 G3
Metamórfosi (GR) 161 H4
Metaxádes (GR) 163 E2
Meteliai (LT) 205 E5
Metéora (GR) 160 D5
Methil (GB) 31 E1
Methóni (Pelopónnisos) (GR) 168 B3
Methóni (Kentriki Makedonía) (GR) 161 F4
Metković (HR) 138 D3
Metličina (BG) 157 F2
Metlika (SLO) 134 D3
Metnitz (A) 96 D4
Metóchi (Stereá Elláda) (GR) 166 B3
Metóchi (Thessalía) (GR) 165 G2
Metsäkyla (FIN) 187 F2
Metsäkylä (FIN) 193 F4
Metsämaa (FIN) 191 G4
Métsovo / Μέτσοβο (GR) . 160 D5
Mettingen (D) 84 D1
Mettlach (D) 88 B3
Mettmann (D) 84 C4
Metz (F) 41 E5
Metzervisse (F) 41 F4
Metzingen (D) 89 F5
Meulan (F) 39 G5
Meung-sur-Loire (F) ... 44 D3
Meursault (F) 46 D5
Meuselwitz (D) 86 B4
Mevagissey (GB) 34 C5
Meximieux (F) 50 D2
Meyenburg (D) 83 E4
Meymac (F) 49 H3
Meyrueis (F) 54 A1
Meyzieu (F) 50 D3
Mezdra (BG) 155 E3
Mèze (F) 54 B3
Mézel (F) 55 F1
Mežica (SLO) 134 C1
Mézidon (F) 38 D5
Mézières-en-Brenne (F) . 44 D5
Mézières-sur-Issoire (F) 49 F2
Mézin (F) 52 D1
Mezőberény (H) 130 D3
Mezőcsát (H) 129 H1
Mezőfalva (H) 129 E3
Mezőhegyes (H) 129 H4
Mezőhék (H) 129 H3
Mezőkovácsháza (H) 129 H4
Mezőkövesd (H) 129 H1
Mezőörs (H) 128 D2
Mezőszilas (H) 129 E3
Mezőtúr (H) 129 H3
Mezquita de Jarque (E) . 65 G2
Mezzano (I) 103 E3
Mezzolombardo (I) 101 H3
Mgarr (M) 114 C5
Mia Milia (CY) 175 E3
Miajadas (E) 69 G1
Miastko (PL) 117 E2
Mica (RO) 147 G4
Micăsasa (RO) 147 F5
Michajlov (RUS) 7 H2
Michałkowo (PL) 119 E1
Michalovce (SK) 133 H3
Michałowo (PL) 119 H4
Micheldorf in Oberösterreich (A) 96 D2
Michelstadt (D) 89 F2
Michendorf (D) 86 C1
Michói (GR) 164 D4
Michów (PL) 123 F3
Mickūnai (LT) 205 G4
Mid Yell (GB) 27 G1
Middelburg (NL) 78 B1
Middelfart (DK) 198 C3
Middelharnis (NL) 76 C5

Middlesbrough (GB) 31 G4
Middleton-in-Teesdale (GB) 31 F4
Middlewich (GB) 32 D3
Midhurst (GB) 38 D1
Midleton (IRL) 24 D4
Midsund (N) 188 C1
Miechów (PL) 122 C5
Mięczyn (PL) 123 H4
Miedes de Aragón (E) .. 65 F1
Miedziana Góra (PL) ... 122 D4
Międzybrodzie Bialskie (PL) 125 F2
Międzychód (PL) 116 D5
Międzygórze (PL) 124 B1
Międzylesie (PL) 124 B1
Międzyrzec Podlaski (PL) 123 F1
Międzyrzecz (PL) 120 D1
Międzyzdroje (PL) 116 B2
Miehikkälä (FIN) 193 H4
Miejska Górka (PL) 121 E3
Miélan (F) 52 D3
Mielec (PL) 123 E5
Mielno (PL) 116 D2
Mieluskylä (FIN) 185 H4
Miercurea Ciuc (RO) ... 148 B5
Miercurea Nirajului (RO) 147 H4
Miercurea Sibiului (RO) 147 F5
Mieres (E) 57 G2
Mieroszów (PL) 120 D5
Mierzęcice (PL) 121 H5
Miesbach (D) 95 G3
Mieszkowice (PL) 116 B5
Mietoinen (FIN) 191 F4
Miettila (FIN) 193 G3
Mieżiškiai (LT) 205 F2
Migennes (F) 45 G3
Migliarino (I) 107 E1
Miglionico (I) 111 E4
Miguel Esteban (E) 64 D4
Miguelturra (E) 70 D1
Mihăeşti (Piteşti) (RO) 151 H2
Mihăeşti (Slatina) (RO) 151 H4
Mihai Viteazu (Cluj-Napotica) (RO) 147 F4
Mihai Viteazu (Constanţa) (RO) 153 F3
Mihail Kogălniceanu (RO) 153 F4
Mihăileşti (Bucureşti) (RO) 152 B4
Mihăileşti (Buzău) (RO) 152 C3
Mihajlovac (Negotin) (SRB) 141 G5
Mihajlovac (Smederevo) (SRB) 141 E4
Mihajlovo (Stara Zagora) (BG) 159 F2
Mihajlovo (Vraca) (BG) . 154 D2
Mihalkovo (BG) 162 B1
Mihalţ (RO) 147 F5
Mihályfa (H) 128 C3
Mihályi (H) 128 C2
Mijas (E) 74 B3
Mijoux (F) 51 E1
Mikkelbostad (N) 176 A5
Mikkeli (FIN) 193 F2
Mikkelvik (N) 176 B3
Mikleuš (HR) 135 H3
Mikołajki (PL) 119 E3
Mikoszéplak (H) 128 B3
Mikre (BG) 158 D1
Mikrevo (BG) 161 G1
Mikrí Doxipára (GR) ... 163 F1
Mikrí Mantíneia (GR) .. 168 C3
Mikró Déreio (GR) 163 E2
Mikró Doukáto (GR) 162 D3
Mikró Eleftherochóri (GR) 161 E5
Mikrókampos (GR) 161 G3
Mikrópoli (GR) 161 H2
Mikrothíves (GR) 165 F1
Mikstat (PL) 121 G3
Mikulov (CZ) 93 E5
Mikulovice (CZ) 93 E2
Milagro (E) 59 F3

Miłakowo (PL) 118 C2
Milano (I) 101 E4
Milano Marittima (I) .. 107 F2
Milanovce (SK) 132 B4
Milàs (TR) 19 G4
Mílatos (GR) 170 C5
Milazzo (I) 115 G2
Milcoiu (RO) 151 G2
Milejczyce (PL) 119 G5
Milejewo (PL) 118 C2
Mileševo Dol (PL) 139 G2
Mileševo (SRB) 140 C2
Milestone (IRL) 24 D3
Miletići (HR) 136 B3
Mileto (I) 115 H1
Milevsko (CZ) 92 A4
Milford (GB) 36 B5
Milford Haven / Aberdaugleddau (GB) 25 H5
Milhão (P) 57 F5
Milia (CY) 175 E3
Miliá (Anatolikí Makedonía kai Thráki) (GR) 163 E1
Miliá (Dytikí Makedonía) (GR) 160 D4
Miliá (Ípeiros) (GR) .. 160 D5
Milići (BIH) 137 H5
Milicz (PL) 121 F3
Milín (CZ) 92 A3
Milína (GR) 165 G2
Milis (I) 112 B3
Milişăuţi (RO) 148 B1
Militello in Val di Catania (I) 115 F4
Miljevina (BIH) 139 E2
Millares (E) 65 H5
Millas (F) 53 H4
Millau (F) 54 A1
Millesimo (I) 104 C3
Millford (IRL) 23 E1
Millom (GB) 31 E5
Millport (GB) 30 C2
Millstatt (A) 96 C5
Millstreet (IRL) 24 C4
Milltown Malbay (IRL) . 24 B2
Milly-la-Forêt (F) 45 E2
Milmarcos (E) 65 F1
Milmersdorf (D) 83 G5
Milna (HR) 138 B2
Miločer (MNE) 139 F5
Milohnići (HR) 134 B4
Miłomłyn (PL) 118 C3
Milos (GR) 169 G4
Miloševa Kula (SRB) ... 141 F5
Miłosław (PL) 121 F1
Miłówka (PL) 125 F2
Miltach (D) 91 G5
Miltenberg (D) 89 F2
Milton Keynes (GB) 35 H1
Milutinovac (SRB) 141 G4
Mimizan (F) 52 B1
Mimizan-Plage (F) 52 B1
Mimoň (CZ) 87 F5
Mina de São Domingos (P) 68 D4
Minas de Ríotinto (E) . 69 F4
Minaya (E) 65 E5
Mindelheim (D) 95 E2
Minden (D) 85 F2
Mindin (F) 43 E4
Mindja (BG) 159 F1
Mindszent (H) 129 G4
Minehead (GB) 35 E4
Mineralni Bani (BG) ... 162 D1
Minerbe (I) 102 D5
Minerbio (I) 106 D1
Minervino Murge (I) ... 110 D3
Minglanilla (E) 65 F4
Mingorría (E) 64 A2
Miničevo (SRB) 143 G1
Minkió (FIN) 191 F4
Minkowice Oławskie (PL) 121 F4
Minsk (BY) 6 D4
Mińsk Mazowiecki (PL) . 123 E1
Minsterley (GB) 32 C4
Mintlaw (GB) 29 H3

Mionica (SRB) 140 C5
Mionnay (F) 50 D2
Mioveni (RO) 151 H3
Mira (E) 65 F4
Mira (I) 103 E4
Mira (P) 62 B3
Mira de Aire (P) 62 B3
Mirabella Imbaccari (I) 115 E4
Miraflores (E) 58 C3
Miraflores de la Sierra (E) 64 B2
Miramar (P) 55 G2
Miramar (P) 62 B1
Miramare (I) 107 F2
Miramare, castello di (I) 103 H4
Miramont-de-Guyenne (F) 49 E5
Miranda de Ebro (E) ... 58 D2
Miranda del Castañar (E) 63 G3
Miranda do Corvo (P) .. 62 B4
Miranda do Douro (P) .. 63 F1
Mirande (F) 52 D3
Mirandela (P) 63 E1
Mirandilla (E) 69 F1
Mirandola (I) 101 H5
Mirano (I) 103 E4
Miravci (MK) 145 G2
Mirebeau (F) 44 B5
Mirebeau-sur-Bèze (F) . 46 D4
Mirecourt (F) 47 E4
Mirepoix (F) 53 G4
Mireşu Mare (RO) 147 E2
Miribel (F) 50 D2
Mirkovo (BG) 158 C1
Mirna (SLO) 134 C3
Miroševce (SRB) 143 F3
Miroşi (RO) 151 H4
Mirosławiec (PL) 116 D4
Mirotice (CZ) 92 A4
Mirovice (CZ) 92 A4
Mirovo (BG) 156 C3
Mirow (D) 83 E4
Mirueña de los Infanzones (E) 63 H2
Mirzec (PL) 122 D3
Mišar (SRB) 140 C4
Misi (FIN) 181 E5
Misilmeri (I) 114 C2
Miskolc (H) 126 D5
Mislinja (SLO) 134 D1
Mistelbach (A) 97 G1
Misterbianco (I) 115 F3
Mistretta (I) 115 E3
Místros (GR) 165 H3
Misurina (I) 103 E2
Misvær (N) 179 F4
Míthymna (GR) 167 E1
Mitrašinci (MK) 145 H1
Mitrópoli (GR) 165 E1
Mitsero (CY) 174 D3
Mittelberg (A) 95 F4
Mittelberg (A) 95 E4
Mittenwald (D) 95 F3
Mittenwalde (D) 86 D2
Mittersill (A) 95 H4
Mitterteich (D) 91 F3
Mittweida (D) 86 C4
Mižhir'ja (UA) 12 D3
Mizija (BG) 155 E2
Mizil (RO) 152 C3
Mjadzel (BY) 6 D4
Mjällom (S) 190 C1
Mjöbäck (S) 195 G4
Mjölby (S) 196 D3
Mjøndalen (N) 189 E5
Mladá Boleslav (CZ) ... 92 B2
Mladá Vožice (CZ) 92 B4
Mladé Buky (CZ) 87 G5
Mladenovac / Младеновац (SRB) 140 D5
Mladinovo (BG) 163 E1
Mlado Nagoričane (MK) . 143 F5
Mława (PL) 118 D4
Mlini (HR) 139 E4

Młynary (PL) 118 C2
Mniów (PL) 122 C4
Mnichovo Hradiště (CZ) . 87 F5
Mníšek nad Hnilcom (SK) 133 F2
Mo i Rana (N) 183 G1
Moaña (E) 56 B4
Moate (IRL) 23 E5
Mocejón (E) 64 B4
Móchlos (GR) 173 F3
Möckern (D) 86 B2
Möckmühl (D) 89 F3
Moclín (E) 70 D5
Modane (F) 51 G4
Modbury (GB) 34 D4
Modelo do Minho (P) ... 56 B5
Modelu (RO) 152 D4
Modena (I) 105 H2
Módi (GR) 165 F3
Modica (I) 115 F5
Modigliana (I) 107 E2
Modliborzyce (PL) 123 F4
Mödling (A) 97 G2
Modra (SK) 132 A4
Modran (BIH) 135 H5
Modrava (CZ) 91 H5
Modriča (BIH) 135 H5
Modrište (MK) 145 E1
Modugno (I) 111 E3
Moëlan-sur-Mer (F) 42 C3
Moelv (N) 189 F3
Moen (N) 176 B4
Moena (I) 103 E2
Moers (D) 84 C3
Moffat (GB) 31 E3
Moftinu Mic (RO) 146 D1
Mogadouro (P) 63 E1
Mogente (E) 73 E1
Mogielnica (PL) 122 D2
Mogila (MK) 145 F2
Mogilno (PL) 117 G5
Moglia (I) 101 H5
Mogliano Veneto (I) ... 103 F4
Moglicë (AL) 144 D3
Mogón (E) 71 E3
Mogoş (RO) 147 E5
Mogoşoaia (RO) 152 B4
Moguer (E) 69 E5
Mohács (H) 129 E5
Mohelnice (CZ) 93 E3
Mohill (IRL) 23 E4
Möhkö (FIN) 187 H5
Moholm (S) 195 H2
Mohyliv-Podil's'kyj (UA) 13 E2
Moi (N) 194 B2
Moià (E) 60 D3
Moie (I) 107 G3
Moimenta (P) 57 E5
Moimenta da Beira (P) . 62 D2
Moineşti (RO) 148 C4
Moirans (F) 51 E4
Moirans-en-Montagne (F) 51 E1
Moíres (GR) 172 D4
Mõisaküla (EST) 201 E4
Moisdon-la-Rivière (F) . 43 F3
Moisei (RO) 147 G2
Moisiovaara (FIN) 187 F3
Moisling (D) 82 C3
Moissac (F) 53 E1
Moita (P) 68 B2
Mojácar (E) 72 C5
Mojados (E) 58 A5
Mojkovac (MNE) 139 G3
Mojstrana (SLO) 134 B1
Mokra Gora (SRB) 139 G1
Mokronog (SLO) 134 C3
Mol (B) 78 D2
Mol (SRB) 140 C2
Mola di Bari (I) 111 F3
Moláoi (GR) 169 E4
Molat (HR) 136 A4
Mold / YrWyddgrug (GB) . 32 C3

Moldava nad Bodvou (SK) ..... 133 F 3
Molde (N) .... 188 C 1
Moldova Nouă (RO) ...... 150 C 3
Moldoveni (RO) .... 148 C 4
Moldoviţa (RO) .... 148 A 2
Møldrup (DK) .... 194 D 5
Molètai (LT) .... 205 G 3
Molfetta (I) .... 111 E 3
Molières (F) .... 53 F 1
Molina de Aragón (E) ..... 65 F 1
Molina de Segura (E) .... 73 E 3
Molinella (I) .... 106 D 1
Molinicos (E) .... 71 G 2
Molinos (E) .... 65 H 1
Molins de Rei (E) .... 60 D 4
Moliterno (I) .... 110 D 5
Molitg-les-Bains (F) .... 53 H 5
Molkom (S) .... 195 H 1
Möllbrücke (A) .... 96 C 5
Mollerussa (I) .... 60 B 3
Molliens-Dreuil (F) ..... 39 G 3
Mollina (E) .... 74 D 2
Mölln (D) .... 82 C 4
Mollösund (S) .... 195 F 3
Mölnlycke (S) .... 195 F 3
Mólos (GR) .... 165 F 2
Molpe (FIN) .... 191 E 1
Molsheim (F) .... 47 G 1
Molve (HR) .... 135 F 2
Molveno (I) .... 101 H 3
Mombeltrán (E) .... 63 H 4
Mombuey (E) .... 57 F 5
Momčilgrad /
Момчилград (BG) ... 162 D 1
Momčilovci (BG) ...... 162 C 1
Momino Selo (BG) ..... 159 E 2
Mommark (DK) .... 198 C 4
Momo (I) .... 100 D 4
Mon Idée (F) .... 40 C 3
Monaghan /
Muineachán (IRL) ..... 23 F 3
Monasterace Marina (I) .. 113 C 4
Monasterevin (IRL) ...... 25 F 2
Monasterio
de Rodilla (E) .... 58 C 3
Monastir (I) .... 112 C 5
Monastiráki (Anatolikí
Makedonía
kai Thráki) (GR) ...... 163 E 3
Monastiráki
(Dytikí Elláda) (GR) ... 164 C 2
Monbazillac (F) .... 49 E 5
Moncalieri (I) .... 100 C 5
Moncalvo (I) .... 100 D 5
Monção (P) .... 56 B 4
Moncarapacho (P) .... 68 D 5
Mönchdorf (A) .... 97 E 1
Mönchengladbach (D) .... 84 B 4
Monchique (P) .... 68 B 5
Monclar-de-Quercy (F) .. 53 F 2
Moncofa (E) .... 66 A 3
Moncontour (F) .... 43 E 2
Moncontour (F) .... 43 H 5
Moncoutant (F) .... 48 C 1
Monda (E) .... 74 D 3
Mondariz (E) .... 56 C 4
Mondavio (I) .... 107 G 3
Mondéjar (E) .... 64 C 3
Mondello (I) .... 114 C 2
Mondim de Basto (P) .... 62 C 1
Mondolfo (I) .... 107 G 3
Mondoñedo (E) .... 56 D 1
Mondorf-les-Bains (L) ... 79 F 5
Mondoubleau (F) ...... 44 C 3
Mondovì (I) .... 104 C 3
Mondéjar (E) .... 64 C 3
Mondragon (F) .... 54 C 1
Mondragon /
Arrasate (E) .... 58 D 2
Mondragone (I) .... 109 G 4
Mondsee (A) .... 96 C 2
Moneasa (RO) .... 146 D 4
Monein (F) .... 52 C 3
Monemvasía /
Μονεμβασία (GR) ... 169 E 4
Mónesi di Triora (I) .... 104 C 3
Monesterio (E) .... 69 F 3

Monestier-
de-Clermont (F) ...... 51 E 4
Monestiés (F) .... 53 G 1
Moneygall (IRL) ...... 24 D 2
Moneymore (GB) ..... 23 F 2
Monfalcone (I) .... 103 H 3
Monflanquin (F) ...... 49 E 5
Monforte (P) .... 68 D 1
Monforte de Lemos (E) .. 56 D 3
Monguelfo / Welsberg (I) . 103 E 1
Monheim (D) .... 89 H 4
Mönichkirchen (A) ..... 97 G 3
Monifieth (GB) .... 29 G 5
Monistrol (E) .... 60 D 3
Monistrol-d'Allier (F) ... 50 B 4
Monistrol-sur-Loire (F) .. 50 C 4
Mönkebude (D) .... 83 G 3
Mońki (PL) .... 119 G 3
Monmouth /
Trefynwy (GB) ...... 35 F 1
Monnickendam (NL) ...76 D 4
Monodéndri (GR) ..... 160 C 5
Monódryo (GR) .... 166 B 3
Monólithos (GR) ...... 171 G 3
Monopoli (I) .... 111 F 3
Monor (H) .... 129 F 2
Monor (RO) .... 147 G 3
Monóvar (E) .... 73 E 2
Monpazier (F) .... 49 F 5
Monreal (D) .... 88 C 1
Monreal del Campo (E) .. 65 F 2
Monreale (I) .... 114 C 2
Monroy (E) .... 63 F 5
Monroyo (E) .... 60 A 5
Mons (Bergen) (B) ..... 78 C 3
Møns Klint (DK) ...... 199 E 4
Monsanto (P) .... 63 E 4
Monsaraz (P) .... 68 D 2
Monschau (D) .... 84 B 5
Monségur (F) .... 48 D 5
Monselice (I) .... 103 E 5
Monsols (F) .... 50 C 2
Mönsterås (S) .... 197 E 4
Monsummano Terme (I) . 105 H 4
Mont-Dauphin (F) .....51 G 5
Mont-de-Marsan (F) .... 52 C 2
Mont-Louis (F) .... 53 G 5
Mont-roig del Camp (E) .. 60 B 5
Mont-Saint-Vincent (F) .. 50 C 1
Mont-sous-Vaudrey (F) ..47 E 5
Montabaur (D) .... 88 D 1
Montacute House (GB) .. 38 A 1
Montagnac (F) .... 54 A 3
Montagnana (I) .... 102 D 5
Montagrier (F) .... 49 E 4
Montaigu (F) .... 43 F 5
Montaigu-de-Quercy (F) . 53 E 1
Montaigut (F) .... 50 A 2
Montaione (I) .... 105 H 5
Montal, château de (F) .. 49 G 5
Montalbán (E) .... 65 G 1
Montalbo (E) .... 64 D 4
Montalcino (I) .... 106 D 4
Montalegre (P) .... 56 D 5
Montalieu-Vercieu (F) ...51 E 2
Montalivet-les-Bains (F) . 48 B 3
Montalto
delle Marche (I) ...... 107 H 5
Montalto di Castro (I) .. 108 C 2
Montalto Uffugo (I) .... 113 B 2
Montalvão (P) .... 62 D 5
Montamarta (E) .... 57 G 5
Montana (CH) .... 98 C 4
Montana / Монтана (BG) 154 D 3
Montañana (E) .... 59 G 5
Montánchez (E) .... 69 G 2
Montanejos (E) .... 65 H 3
Montargil (P) .... 68 C 1
Montargis (F) .... 45 F 3
Montastruc-
la-Conseillère (F) ..... 53 F 2
Montauban (F) .... 53 F 2
Montauban-
de-Bretagne (F) ...... 43 E 2
Montbard (F) .... 45 H 4
Montbazens (F) .... 53 G 1

Montbazon (F) .... 44 C 4
Montbéliard (F) .... 47 G 4
Montbenoît (F) .... 47 F 5
Montblanc (E) .... 60 C 4
Montbozon (F) .... 47 F 4
Montbrió del Camp (E) .. 60 B 4
Montbrison (F) .... 50 C 3
Montceau-les-Mines (F) . 50 C 1
Montcenis (F) .... 45 H 5
Montchanin (F) .... 46 C 5
Montcornet (F) .... 40 B 4
Montcuq-en-
Quercy-Blanc (F) .... 53 F 1
Montdidier (F) .... 39 H 4
Monte-Carlo-
Monaco (MC) ...... 55 H 2
Monte da Pedra (P) .... 62 C 5
Monte Redondo (P) .... 62 B 4
Monte San Savino (I) ... 107 E 4
Monte Sant' Angelo (I) ..110 D 2
Monteagudo
de las Vicarías (E) ..... 59 E 5
Montealegre
de Campos (E) ...... 57 H 5
Montealegre
del Castillo (E) ...... 71 H 2
Montebello Ionico (I) ....115 H 2
Montebello Vicentino (I) . 102 D 4
Montebelluna (I) ...... 103 E 3
Montebourg (F) .... 38 B 4
Montecarotto (I) ...... 107 G 3
Montecatini Terme (I) .. 105 H 4
Montecchio
Maggiore (I) .... 102 D 4
Montech (F) .... 53 F 2
Montecorvino Rovella (I). 110 B 4
Montedoro (I) .... 114 D 4
Montefalcone (I) ...... 107 F 5
Montefalcone
di Val Fortore (I) .....110 B 2
Montefalcone
nel Sannio (I) ...... 109 H 3
Montefiascone (I) ...... 108 D 1
Montefiore dell'Aso (I) . 107 H 4
Montefrío (E) .... 70 D 5
Montegallo (I) .... 107 G 5
Montegiorgio (I) ...... 107 G 4
Montegranaro (I) ...... 107 H 4
Montegrotto Terme (I) . 103 E 4
Montejícar (E) .... 71 E 5
Montejo de Tiermes (E) . 58 C 5
Monteleone
di Spoleto (I) ...... 107 G 5
Montélimar (F) .... 50 D 5
Montella (I) .... 110 B 4
Montellano (E) .... 74 C 3
Montelupo Fiorentino (I). 105 H 4
Montemaggiore
Belsito (I) .... 114 D 3
Montemagno (I) ...... 100 D 5
Montemayor (E) ...... 70 B 4
Montemayor de Pililla (E). 58 A 5
Montemor-o-Novo (P) .. 68 C 2
Montemor-o-Velho (P) .. 62 B 3
Montendre (F) .... 48 D 4
Montenegro
de Cameros (E) ...... 58 D 4
Montenero di Bisaccia (I). 109 H 3
Montenero Sabino (I) .. 109 E 2
Montepulciano (I) ...... 107 E 4
Montereale (I) .... 109 F 1
Montereale (I) .... 103 F 3
Montereau-
Fault-Yonne (F) ..... 45 F 2
Monterenzio (I) ...... 106 D 2
Monteriggioni (I) ...... 105 H 5
Monteroni di Lecce (I) .. 111 H 4
Monterosso al Mare (I) . 105 F 3
Monterotondo (I) ...... 109 E 2
Monteroni
Marittimo (I) ...... 106 C 4
Monterroso (E) .... 56 D 3
Monterrubio
de la Serena (E) ...... 69 H 2

Monterubbiano (I) ..... 107 H 4
Montesano
sulla Marcellana (I) ...110 C 5
Montesarchio (I) ...... 109 H 4
Montescaglioso (I) .....111 E 4
Montesilvano Marina (I). 109 G 1
Montesquieu-
Volvestre (F) ...... 53 F 3
Montesquiou (F) ...... 52 D 2
Montevarchi (I) .... 106 D 3
Montfaucon (F) .... 43 G 5
Montfaucon-
d'Argonne (F) ...... 40 D 4
Montfaucon-
en-Velay (F) ...... 50 C 4
Montfort-en-Chalosse (F). 52 B 2
Montfort-l'Amaury (F) .. 45 E 1
Montfort-sur-Meu (F) .. 43 F 2
Montfort-sur-Risle (F) .. 39 E 5
Montgaillard (F) ...... 53 F 4
Montgenèvre (F) ...... 51 G 4
Montgiscard (F) ...... 53 F 3
Montgomery (GB) ..... 32 C 5
Montguyon (F) .... 48 D 4
Monthermé (F) .... 40 C 3
Monthey (CH) .... 98 C 4
Monthois (F) .... 40 C 4
Monthureux-
sur-Saône (F) ....47 E 3
Monti (F) .... 112 C 1
Montichiari (I) .... 101 G 4
Monticiano (I) .... 106 D 4
Montiel (E) .... 71 F 2
Montier-en-Der (F)...... 46 C 2
Montignac (F) .... 49 F 4
Montigny-le-Roi (F) ....47 E 3
Montigny-sur-Aube (F) .. 46 C 3
Montijo (E) .... 69 F 1
Montijo (P) .... 68 B 2
Montilla (E) .... 70 C 5
Montioni (I) .... 106 C 5
Montivilliers (F) ...... 39 E 4
Montjean-sur-Loire (F) .. 43 G 4
Montlhéry (F) .... 45 E 1
Montlieu-la-Garde (F) .. 48 D 4
Montlouis-sur-Loire (F) .. 44 C 4
Montluçon (F) .... 49 H 1
Montluel (F) .... 50 D 2
Montmarault (F) ...... 50 A 1
Montmartin-sur-Mer (F). 38 B 5
Montmédy (F) .... 40 D 4
Montmélian (F) .... 51 F 3
Montmirail (F) .... 40 B 5
Montmirail (F) .... 44 C 3
Montmirey-
le-Château (F) ....47 E 4
Montmoreau-
Saint-Cybard (F) ..... 48 D 3
Montmorillon (F) ...... 49 F 1
Montmort (F) .... 40 B 5
Montodine (I) .... 101 F 4
Montoggio (I) .... 105 E 2
Montoire-sur-le-Loir (F). 44 C 3
Montoito (P) .... 68 D 2
Montorio al Vomano (I). 109 F 1
Montoro (E) .... 70 C 4
Montpellier (F) .... 54 B 2
Montpezat-
de-Quercy (F) ...... 53 F 1
Montpezat-
sous-Bauzon (F) .... 50 C 5
Montpon-Ménestérol (F). 48 D 4
Montpont-en-Bresse (F). 50 D 1
Montréal (F) .... 52 D 2
Montréal (F) .... 53 G 3
Montréal-la-Cluse (F) ...51 E 2
Montredon-
Labessonnié (F) ..... 53 G 2
Montréjeau (F) .... 53 E 4
Montrésor (F) .... 44 D 5
Montresta (I) .... 112 B 2
Montret (F) .... 50 D 1
Montreuil-Bellay (F) ... 43 H 5
Montreux (CH) .... 98 B 4
Montrevault (F) .... 43 G 4
Montrevel-en-Bresse (F). 50 D 1

Montrichard
Val-de-Cher (F) .... 44 D 4
Montrond-les-Bains (F) . 50 C 3
Montrose (GB) .... 29 G 5
Monts-sur-Guesnes (F).. 44 B 5
Montsalvy (F) .... 49 H 5
Montsauche (F) .... 45 H 4
Montségur,
château de (F) ...... 53 G 4
Montseny (E) .... 61 E 3
Montserrat (E) .... 65 H 5
Montserrat,
monestir de (E) ..... 60 D 3
Montsûrs (F) .... 43 H 2
Montuenga (E) .... 64 A 1
Montuïri (E) .... 67 F 3
Monza (I) .... 101 E 4
Monzón (E) .... 60 A 3
Monzón de Campos (E) . 58 A 4
Moordorf (D) .... 81 E 4
Moosburg an der Isar (D). 95 G 1
Mór (H) .... 128 D 2
Mora (E) .... 64 B 4
Mora (P) .... 68 C 1
Mora (S) .... 189 H 4
Mora de Rubielos (E)... 65 H 3
Mora la Nova (E) ...... 60 B 5
Morąg (PL) .... 118 C 2
Mórahalom (H) .... 129 G 5
Moraira (E) .... 66 A 5
Morais (P) .... 63 E 1
Moraítika (GR) .... 164 B 1
Morakovo (MNE) ...... 139 G 4
Moral de Calatrava (E)... 70 D 2
Moraleda
de Zafayona (E) ..... 70 D 5
Moraleja (E) .... 63 E 4
Moraleja de Sayago (E) . 63 G 1
Moraleja del Vino (E) .. 63 G 1
Morales de Rey (E) .... 57 G 4
Morales de Toro (E) .... 63 H 1
Morano Calabro (I) .....113 B 1
Morărești (RO) .... 151 G 2
Morárp (S) .... 199 E 3
Morasverdes (E) .... 63 F 3
Morata de Jalón (E) .... 59 F 5
Morata de Tajuña (E) .. 64 C 3
Moratalla (E) .... 71 H 3
Moravče (SLO) .... 134 C 2
Moravci-v-Slovenskih
Goricah (SLO) ...... 135 E 1
Moravica (BG) .... 156 C 3
Moravica (HR) .... 134 C 4
Moraviţa (RO) .... 150 B 2
Morávka (CZ) .... 93 G 3
Moravská Třebová (CZ). 93 E 3
Moravské Budějovice (CZ). 92 D 5
Moravske Toplice (SLO) . 135 E 1
Moravský Beroun (CZ) .. 93 F 3
Moravský Krumlov (CZ). 92 D 5
Morbach (D) .... 88 C 2
Morbegno (I) .... 101 F 3
Mörbisch (A) .... 97 H 2
Mörbylånga (S) .... 197 E 4
Morcenx (F) .... 52 B 1
Morciano
di Romagna (I) ..... 107 F 3
Morcone (I) .... 109 H 4
Morcote (CH) .... 99 F 5
Mordelles (F) .... 43 F 2
Mordy (PL) .... 123 F 1
Morecambe (GB) ...... 32 C 1
Moreda (E) .... 71 E 5
Morée (F) .... 44 D 3
Morella (E) .... 66 A 1
Moreni (RO) .... 152 A 3
Mores (I) .... 112 B 2
Morestel (F) .... 51 E 3
Moret Loing
et Orvanne (F) ..... 45 F 2
Moreton (GB) .... 35 G 1
Moretonhampstead (GB). 34 D 4
Moreuil (F) .... 39 H 3
Morez (F) .... 51 E 1
Morfasso (I) .... 105 F 2
Mórfio (GR) .... 164 B 1

Morfou (CY) .... 174 C 3
Morgat (F) .... 42 B 2
Morges (CH) .... 98 B 4
Morgex (I) .... 100 B 3
Morhange (F) .... 41 F 5
Mori (I) .... 101 H 3
Morina (SRB) .... 139 H 4
Moritzburg (D) .... 86 A 4
Morjärv (S) .... 185 F 1
Morlaàs (F) .... 52 C 3
Morlaix (F) .... 42 C 1
Mormanno (I) .... 113 B 1
Mormant (F) .... 45 F 1
Mormoiron (F) .... 54 D 1
Mornant (F) .... 50 C 3
Moroeni (RO) .... 152 A 2
Morón de Almazán (E) . 59 E 5
Morón de la Frontera (E) .74 C 2
Morosaglia (F) .... 55 H 3
Morović (SRB) .... 137 H 3
Morpeth (GB) .... 31 G 3
Morro Jable (E) .... 67 H 5
Mörrum (S) .... 199 G 3
Morsbach (D) .... 84 D 5
Mörsil (S) .... 183 F 5
Mörskom /
Myrskylä (FIN) ..... 193 E 4
Morsleben (D) .... 86 A 2
Mortagne-au-Perche (F). 44 C 2
Mortagne-
sur-Gironde (F)...... 48 C 3
Mortagne-sur-Sèvre (F). 43 G 5
Mortágua (P) .... 62 C 3
Mortain-Bocage (F) .... 43 G 1
Mortara (I) .... 100 D 4
Morteau (F) .... 47 F 5
Mortrée (F) .... 44 B 1
Moryń (PL) .... 116 B 5
Morzine (F) .... 51 G 2
Mosbach (D) .... 89 F 3
Mosby (N) .... 194 C 2
Moščenice (HR) .... 134 B 4
Moščenička Draga (HR). 134 B 4
Moschendorf (A) ...... 97 H 4
Moschopótamos (GR).. 161 F 4
Moscou = Moskva (RUS) .7 G 2
Moscow = Moskva (RUS) .7 G 2
Mosina (PL) .... 121 E 1
Mosjøen (N) .... 183 F 1
Mosko (BIH) .... 139 E 4
Moskosel (S) .... 184 D 1
Moskva (RUS) .... .7 G 2
Moslavina
Podravska (HR) ..... 135 H 3
Moşna (RO) .... 149 E 3
Mosonmagyaróvár (H) . 128 C 1
Mosonszolnok (H) .... 128 C 1
Mosqueruela (E) ...... 65 H 2
Moss (N) .... 195 E 1
Mossala (FIN) .... 191 E 5
Mossat (GB) .... 29 G 4
Mössingen (D) .... 89 F 5
Most (BG) .... 162 D 1
Most (CZ) .... 86 D 5
Most na Soči (SLO) .... 134 A 2
Mosta (M) .... 114 C 5
Mostar (BIH) .... 138 D 2
Mosteiro (E) .... 56 B 3
Mosterhamn (N) ...... 188 A 5
Móstoles (E) .... 64 B 3
Mostowo (PL) .... 117 E 2
Mosty (PL) .... 123 G 2
Mostyn (GB) .... 32 C 5
Mostys'ka (UA) .... .12 C 2
Mosvik (N) .... 182 D 4
Moszczenica (PL) ...... 122 B 3
Mota del Cuervo (E) .... 64 D 5
Mota del Marqués (E) ... 57 H 5
Motala (S) .... 196 D 2
Motherwell (GB) ...... 30 D 2
Motilla del Palancar (E) . 65 F 4
Motovun (HR) .... 134 A 4
Motril (E) .... 75 D 2
Motru (RO) .... 151 E 3
Motta di Livenza (I) ... 103 E 4
Motta Sant' Anastasia (I).115 F 3
Motta Visconti (I) ..... 101 E 4

A B C D E F G H I J K L M N O P Q R S T U V W X Y Z

Mottola (I) . . . . .111 F 4
Mouchard (F) . . . . .47 E 5
Moudon (CH) . . . . 98 B 3
Moúdros (GR) . . . . 162 D 5
Mougins (F) . . . . 55 G 2
Mouhijärvi (FIN) . . . . 191 F 3
Mouilleron-en-Pareds (F) . 48 C 1
Moulins (F) . . . . 50 A 1
Moulins-Engilbert (F) . . . 45 H 5
Moulins-la-Marche (F) . . . 44 C 1
Moult (F) . . . . 38 D 5
Mount Bellew (IRL) . . 22 D 5
Mount
  Stewart Gardens (GB) . 23 H 3
Mountain Ash (GB) . . . . . 35 E 2
Mountmellick (IRL) . . . . . 25 E 2
Mountrath (IRL) . . . . 25 E 2
Moura (P) . . . . 68 D 3
Mourão (P) . . . . 69 E 3
Mourenx (F) . . . . 52 C 3
Mouríki (GR) . . . . 165 G 3
Mourmelon-le-Grand (F) . 40 C 5
Mourniés (GR) . . . . 172 B 3
Mourujärvi (FIN) . . . . . . 181 G 5
Mouscron (B) . . . . 78 B 2
Moustiers-
  Sainte-Marie (F) . . . . 55 F 2
Mouthe (F) . . . . .47 F 5
Mouthier (F) . . . . .47 F 5
Mouthoumet (F) . . . . 53 H 4
Moutier (CH) . . . . 98 C 2
Moûtiers (F) . . . . .51 F 3
Moutiers-
  les-Mauxfaits (F) . . . . 48 B 1
Moutoullas (CY) . . . . . .174 C 4
Moutsoúna (GR) . . . . . . 170 C 1
Mouy (F) . . . . 39 H 4
Mouzakaíoi (GR) . . . . . . 164 C 1
Mouzáki (GR) . . . . 165 E 1
Mouzon (F) . . . . 40 D 4
Movila Miresii (RO) . . . 152 D 2
Moviliţa (RO) . . . . 152 C 3
Moville (IRL) . . . . 23 F 1
Moyenneville (F) . . . . . . 39 G 3
Moyuela (E) . . . . 65 G 1
Možajsk (RUS) . . . . .7 F 2
Mozirje (SLO) . . . . 134 C 2
Mrągowo (PL) . . . . .119 E 2
Mrakovica (BIH) . . . . . . 135 F 5
Mramorak (SRB) . . . . . .141 E 4
Mratinje (MNE) . . . . 139 F 3
Mrazovac (BIH) . . . . 135 E 5
Mrčajevci (SRB) . . . . . . 142 D 1
Mrežičko (MK) . . . . 145 G 2
Mrkonjić Grad (BIH) . . . 137 E 4
Mrkopalj (HR) . . . . 134 C 4
Mrocza (PL) . . . . .117 F 4
Mrzeżyno (PL) . . . . .116 C 2
Mrzygłód (PL) . . . . 122 B 5
Mścisław (BY) . . . . .7 E 4
Mšeno (CZ) . . . . 87 F 5
Mszana Dolna (PL) . . . . 125 G 2
Mszczonów (PL) . . . . . . 122 C 2
Mtarfa (M) . . . . .114 C 5
Muccia (I) . . . . 107 G 4
Much (D) . . . . 84 D 5
Much Wenlock (GB) . . . . 32 D 5
Mücheln (D) . . . . 86 B 4
Mucientes (E) . . . . 58 A 5
Muckross House (IRL) . 24 B 4
Mudanya (TR) . . . . .19 G 2
Mudau (D) . . . . 89 F 3
Muel (E) . . . . 59 G 5
Muelas del Pan (E) . . . . 63 G 1
Muff (IRL) . . . . 23 E 1
Muge (P) . . . . 68 B 1
Mügeln (D) . . . . 86 C 4
Muggia (I) . . . . 103 H 4
Mugla (BG) . . . . 162 C 1
Muğla (TR) . . . . .19 H 4
Mugron (F) . . . . 52 C 2
Mugueimes (E) . . . . 56 C 5
Mühlacker (D) . . . . 89 E 4
Mühlbach
  am Hochkönig (A) . . . 96 C 3
Mühlberg (D) . . . . 86 D 3
Mühldorf am Inn (D) . . . 95 H 2

Mühlen Eichsen (D) . . . . 82 C 3
Mühlhausen (D) . . . . 85 H 4
Mühltroff (D) . . . . 86 B 5
Muhniemi (FIN) . . . . . . 193 F 4
Muhos (FIN) . . . . 185 H 3
Muhovo (BG) . . . . 158 C 2
Muineachán /
  Monaghan (IRL) . . . . 23 F 3
Muir of Ord (GB) . . . . . . 29 E 3
Muirkirk (GB) . . . . 30 D 2
Mukačeve (UA) . . . . .12 C 3
Mula (E) . . . . 71 H 3
Mülheim (D) . . . . 84 C 3
Mulhouse (F) . . . . .47 G 3
Mullach Íde /
  Malahide (IRL) . . . . . 23 G 5
Müllheim (D) . . . . 94 A 3
Mullingar / An Muileann
  gCearr (IRL) . . . . 23 E 5
Müllrose (D) . . . . 87 E 2
Mullsjö (S) . . . . 195 H 3
Mulrany (IRL) . . . . 22 B 4
Multia (FIN) . . . . 191 H 1
Muñana (E) . . . . 63 H 3
Münchberg (D) . . . . .91 F 2
Müncheberg (D) . . . . . . 87 E 1
München (D) . . . . 95 G 2
Münchhausen (D) . . . . . 85 E 4
Mundesley (GB) . . . . . . 37 E 1
Mundford (GB) . . . . 33 H 5
Munera (E) . . . . 71 F 1
Mungia (E) . . . . 58 D 1
Muñico (E) . . . . 63 H 3
Muniesa (E) . . . . 65 G 1
Munkebo (DK) . . . . 198 C 3
Munkedal (S) . . . . 195 F 2
Munkfors (S) . . . . 189 H 5
Münnerstadt (D) . . . . . . 89 G 1
Muñogalindo (E) . . . . . . 63 H 3
Munsala (FIN) . . . . 185 F 5
Münsingen (CH) . . . . . . 98 D 3
Münsingen (D) . . . . 89 F 5
Münster (CH) . . . . 99 E 4
Munster (D) . . . . .81 H 5
Münster (D) . . . . 84 D 2
Munster (F) . . . . .47 G 2
Münstertal (D) . . . . 94 A 2
Münzenberg (D) . . . . . . 89 E 1
Münzkirchen (A) . . . . . . 96 C 1
Muodoslompolo (S) . . . 180 C 3
Muonio (FIN) . . . . 180 C 3
Muotkatunturit (FIN) . . 177 F 4
Mur-de-Barrez (F) . . . . . 49 H 5
Mûr-de-Bretagne (F) . . . 42 D 2
Murakeresztúr (H) . . . . 128 B 4
Muráň (SK) . . . . 133 E 3
Murano (I) . . . . 103 F 4
Murat (F) . . . . 50 A 4
Murat-sur-Vèbre (F) . . . 53 H 2
Murato (F) . . . . 55 H 3
Murau (A) . . . . 96 D 4
Muravera (I) . . . . .112 D 5
Murça (P) . . . . 62 D 1
Murchante (E) . . . . 59 F 4
Murcia (E) . . . . 73 E 3
Mureck (A) . . . . 97 G 5
Muret (F) . . . . 53 F 3
Murfatlar (RO) . . . . 153 F 4
Murgeni (RO) . . . . 149 E 5
Murgeşti (RO) . . . . 152 C 2
Murguía (E) . . . . 58 D 2
Muri (CH) . . . . 99 E 2
Murias de Paredes (E) . . 57 F 3
Murighiol (RO) . . . . 153 G 2
Murino (MNE) . . . . 139 H 4
Muriqan (AL) . . . . 142 B 5
Murjek (S) . . . . 180 B 5
Murlough Bay National
  Nature Reserve (GB) . . 23 G 1
Murnau am Staffelsee (D) . 95 F 3
Muro (P) . . . . 55 G 3
Muro de Alcoy (E) . . . . . 73 F 1
Muro Lucano (I) . . . . . . .110 C 4
Murol (F) . . . . 50 A 3
Murole (FIN) . . . . 191 H 2
Muros (E) . . . . 56 B 3
Murowana Goślina (PL) . 121 E 1

Mürren (CH) . . . . 98 D 4
Murrhardt (D) . . . . 89 G 4
Murska Sobota (SLO) . . . 135 E 1
Mursko Središče (HR) . . 135 E 1
Murten (CH) . . . . 98 C 3
Murter (HR) . . . . 136 B 5
Murtosa (P) . . . . 62 B 2
Murtovaara (FIN) . . . . . 187 F 1
Murvica (HR) . . . . 136 B 5
Murviel-lès-Béziers (F) . . 54 A 3
Mürzsteg (A) . . . . 97 F 3
Mürzzuschlag (A) . . . . . 97 F 3
Musina (BG) . . . . 156 B 3
Musninkai (LT) . . . . 205 F 3
Mussalo (FIN) . . . . 193 F 4
Musselburgh (GB) . . . . . .31 E 2
Musselkanaal (NL) . . . . . 77 G 3
Mussidan (F) . . . . 49 E 4
Mussomeli (I) . . . . .114 D 3
Mussy-sur-Seine (F) . . . 46 C 3
Müstair (CH) . . . . 99 H 3
Mustasaari /
  Korsholm (FIN) . . . . 185 E 5
Mustèr / Disentis . . . . . 99 E 3
Mustion as (FIN) . . . . . 191 G 5
Mustion Linna (FIN) . . . 191 G 5
Mustla (EST) . . . . 201 F 4
Mustvee (EST) . . . . 201 G 2
Muszaki (PL) . . . . .118 D 4
Muszyna (PL) . . . . 125 H 3
Muta (SLO) . . . . 134 D 1
Mutala (FIN) . . . . 191 G 3
Mutterstadt (D) . . . . 89 E 3
Mutzschen (D) . . . . 86 C 4
Muurame (FIN) . . . . 191 H 2
Muurasjärvi (FIN) . . . . . 185 H 5
Muurla (FIN) . . . . 191 G 4
Muurola (FIN) . . . . 181 E 5
Muuruvesi (FIN) . . . . . . 187 F 5
Muxía (E) . . . . 56 A 2
Muzillac (F) . . . . 43 E 4
Muzine (AL) . . . . 144 D 5
Muzzana
  del Turgnano (I) . . . . 103 G 3
Myckelgensjö (S) . . . . . 184 C 5
Myjava (SK) . . . . 132 A 3
Mýki (GR) . . . . 162 C 2
Mykínes / Μυκήνες (GR) . 165 F 5
Mykines
  (Færøerne) (DK) . . . . 194 A 4
Mykolaïv (UA) . . . . .12 D 2
Mykolaïv (UA) . . . . .13 G 3
Mýkonos / Μύκονος (GR) . 170 C 1
Myllykoski (FIN) . . . . . . 193 F 4
Myllykylä (FIN) . . . . 191 F 1
Myllymäki (FIN) . . . . . . 191 G 1
Mýloi (GR) . . . . 165 F 5
Mylopótamos (GR) . . . . 169 E 5
Mynämäki (FIN) . . . . . . 191 F 4
Myre (N) . . . . 179 G 2
Myrhorod (UA) . . . . .13 G 1
Mýrina / Μύρινα (GR) . . 162 D 5
Myronivka (UA) . . . . . . .13 F 1
Myrskylä /
  Mörskom (FIN) . . . . . 193 E 4
Myrtiés (GR) . . . . 171 F 2
Mýrtos (GR) . . . . 173 E 4
Myrtou (CY) . . . . .174 D 3
Myrviken (S) . . . . 189 H 1
Mysen (N) . . . . 195 F 1
Mysłakowice (PL) . . . . . 120 D 4
Myślenice (PL) . . . . 125 G 2
Myślibórz (PL) . . . . .116 C 5
Mysłowice (PL) . . . . 122 B 5
Mystrás / Μυστράς (GR) . 168 D 3
Mysusæter (N) . . . . 189 E 2
Myszków (PL) . . . . 122 B 5
Myszyniec (PL) . . . . .119 E 4
Mýtikas (GR) . . . . 164 C 3
Mytilíni / Μυτιλήνη (GR) . 167 F 2
Mytišči (RUS) . . . . .7 G 2
Mólos (GR) . . . . 166 C 2

N

Naamijoki (FIN) . . . . . . 180 D 5
Naantali (FIN) . . . . 191 F 4
Naarajärvi (FIN) . . . . . . 193 F 1

Naarva (FIN) . . . . 187 H 5
Naas / An Nás (IRL) . . . 25 F 1
Nabburg (D) . . . . .91 F 4
Načeradec (CZ) . . . . 92 B 3
Náchod (CZ) . . . . 87 H 5
Nadab (RO) . . . . 146 C 4
Nadarevo (BG) . . . . 156 D 3
Nadarzyn (PL) . . . . 122 D 1
Nádasdladány (H) . . . . . 128 D 2
Naddvik (N) . . . . 188 C 3
Nadela (E) . . . . 56 D 2
Nădlac (RO) . . . . 146 A 5
Nădudvar (H) . . . . .131 E 2
Nadur (M) . . . . .114 B 4
Nadvirna (UA) . . . . .12 D 3
Nærbø (N) . . . . 194 A 1
Nærøy (N) . . . . 183 E 3
Næstved (DK) . . . . 198 D 4
Näfels (CH) . . . . 99 F 2
Náfpaktos /
  Ναύπακτος (GR) . . . . 165 E 3
Náfplio / Ναύπλιο (GR) . 165 F 5
Naggen (S) . . . . 190 A 2
Nagłowice (PL) . . . . 122 C 4
Nagold (D) . . . . 89 E 5
Nagu / Nauvo (FIN) . . . 191 F 5
Nagyalásony (H) . . . . . . 128 C 3
Nagyatád (H) . . . . 128 C 4
Nagybajom (H) . . . . 128 C 4
Nagybaracska (H) . . . . . 129 E 5
Nagycenk (H) . . . . 128 B 1
Nagydobsza (H) . . . . . . 128 C 5
Nagydorog (H) . . . . 129 E 4
Nagyecsed (H) . . . . .131 F 1
Nagygyimót (H) . . . . . . 128 C 2
Nagyhalász (H) . . . . 127 E 5
Nagyharsány (H) . . . . . . 129 E 5
Nagyigmánd (H) . . . . . . 128 D 1
Nagykálló (H) . . . . .131 F 1
Nagykanizsa (H) . . . . . . 128 B 4
Nagykapornak (H) . . . . . 128 B 3
Nagykáta (H) . . . . 129 G 2
Nagykereki (H) . . . . .131 F 2
Nagykónyi (H) . . . . 128 D 4
Nagykőrös (H) . . . . 129 F 3
Nagykörű (H) . . . . 129 H 2
Nagylak (H) . . . . 129 H 5
Nagylengyel (H) . . . . . . 128 B 3
Nagymágocs (H) . . . . . . 129 H 4
Nagymányok (H) . . . . . . 129 E 4
Nagyrábé (H) . . . . .131 E 2
Nagyszakácsi (H) . . . . . 128 C 4
Nagyszénás (H) . . . . . . 129 H 3
Nagyvázsony (H) . . . . . . 128 D 3
Nahe (D) . . . . .81 H 3
Naidăş (RO) . . . . 150 B 3
Naila (D) . . . . .91 F 2
Nailloux (F) . . . . 53 F 3
Nailsworth (GB) . . . . . . 35 F 1
Nairn (GB) . . . . 29 E 3
Najac (F) . . . . 53 G 1
Najdenovo (BG) . . . . . . 159 E 2
Nájera (E) . . . . 58 D 3
Nakkila (FIN) . . . . 191 F 3
Nakło nad Notecią (PL) . .117 F 4
Nakovo (SRB) . . . . 140 D 2
Nakskov (DK) . . . . 198 D 4
Nalbant (RO) . . . . 153 F 2
Nałęczów (PL) . . . . 123 F 3
Näljänkä (FIN) . . . . 187 F 2
Naltijärvi (FIN) . . . . 177 E 5
Namdalseid (N) . . . . . . 183 E 4
Namest nad Oslavou (CZ) . 92 D 4
Namsos (N) . . . . 183 E 3
Namsskogan (N) . . . . . . 183 F 3
Namur (Namen) (B) . . . . 78 D 3
Namysłów (PL) . . . . 121 F 4
Nancy (F) . . . . .47 E 1
Năneşti (RO) . . . . 152 D 1
Nangis (F) . . . . 45 F 2
Nannestad (N) . . . . 189 F 5
Nant (F) . . . . 54 A 2
Nanterre (F) . . . . 39 H 5
Nantes (F) . . . . 43 F 4
Nanteuil-le-Haudouin (F) . 40 A 5
Nantiat (F) . . . . 49 F 2

Nantua (F) . . . . .51 E 2
Nantwich (GB) . . . . 32 D 3
Náousa (GR) . . . . 170 C 1
Náousa / Νάουσα (GR) . 161 E 3
Napoli (I) . . . . 109 G 5
Narberth (GB) . . . . 34 C 1
Narbolia (I) . . . . .112 B 3
Narbonne (F) . . . . 54 A 3
Narbonne-Plage (F) . . . . 54 A 3
Narcao (I) . . . . .112 B 5
Nardò (I) . . . . .111 G 5
Narew (PL) . . . . .119 H 4
Narila (FIN) . . . . 193 F 2
Narkaus (FIN) . . . . 185 H 1
Narni (I) . . . . 108 D 1
Naro (I) . . . . .114 D 4
Naro-Fominsk (RUS) . . . .7 G 2
Narol (PL) . . . . 123 G 5
Närpes (FIN) . . . . 191 E 1
Narta (HR) . . . . 135 F 3
Narthaki (GR) . . . . 165 F 1
Năruja (RO) . . . . 152 C 1
Narva (EST) . . . . 201 H 1
Narva-Jõesuu (EST) . . . 201 H 1
Narvik (N) . . . . .176 A 5
Närv/Sör (S) . . . . 189 H 4
Näsåker (S) . . . . 183 H 5
Năsăud (RO) . . . . 147 G 2
Nasbinals (F) . . . . 50 A 5
Našice (HR) . . . . 135 H 4
Nasielsk (PL) . . . . .118 D 5
Naso (I) . . . . 115 F 2
Nassau (D) . . . . 88 D 1
Nassereith (A) . . . . 95 F 4
Nässjö (S) . . . . 195 H 4
Nastola (FIN) . . . . 193 E 3
Nata (M) . . . .
Natalinci (SRB) . . . . . . 140 D 5
Nattavaara (S) . . . . 180 B 5
Nättraby (S) . . . . 199 H 3
Naucelle (F) . . . . 53 G 1
Nauders (A) . . . . 95 E 5
Nauen (D) . . . . 86 C 1
Naujoji Akmenė (LT) . . . 204 D 1
Naul (IRL) . . . . 23 G 5
Naumburg (D) . . . . 86 B 4
Naunhof (D) . . . . 86 C 4
Naustdal (N) . . . . 188 B 2
Nauvo / Nagu (FIN) . . . 191 F 5
Nava (E) . . . . 57 G 2
Nava de la Asunción (E) . 64 A 1
Nava del Rey (E) . . . . . . 63 H 1
Navacepeda
  de Tormes (E) . . . . . . 63 H 3
Navacerrada (E) . . . . . . 64 B 2
Navaconcejo (E) . . . . . . 63 G 4
Navahermosa (E) . . . . . 64 A 3
Navahrudak (BY) . . . . . . .6 D 5
Navalcán (E) . . . . 63 H 4
Navalcarnero (E) . . . . . . 64 B 3
Navaleno (E) . . . . 58 D 4
Navalmanzano (E) . . . . . 64 A 1
Navalmoral
  de la Mata (E) . . . . . . 63 G 4
Navalperal
  de Pinares (E) . . . . . . 64 A 2
Navaluenga (E) . . . . 64 A 2
Navalvillar de Pela (E) . . 69 H 1
Navamorcuende (E) . . . . 64 A 3
Navan / An Uaimh (IRL) . 23 F 5
Navarredonda
  de Gredos (E) . . . . . . 63 H 3
Navarrenx (F) . . . . 52 C 2
Navarrés (E) . . . . 65 H 5
Navarrete (E) . . . . 58 D 3
Navàs (E) . . . . 60 D 3
Navas de Jorquera (E) . . 65 F 5
Navas de Oro (E) . . . . . . 64 A 1
Navas de San Juan (E) . . 71 E 3
Navas del Madroño (E) . . 63 E 5
Navascués (E) . . . . 59 G 2
Navasfrías (E) . . . . 63 E 3
Navatalgordo (E) . . . . . . 63 H 3
Nave (I) . . . . 101 G 4
Nave Redonda (P) . . . . . 68 B 3
Navelli (I) . . . . 109 F 2

Naveros (E) . . . . 74 B 4
Navia (E) . . . . 57 F 1
Navia de Suarna (E) . . . 57 E 2
Navl'a (RUS) . . . . .7 G 4
Năvodari (RO) . . . . 153 F 4
Náxos (GR) . . . . 170 C 1
Naxxar (M) . . . . .114 C 5
Nay (F) . . . . 52 C 3
Nazaré (P) . . . . 62 A 5
Nazilli (TR) . . . . .19 H 3
Ndrejaj (AL) . . . . 142 C 4
Ndroq (AL) . . . . 144 C 2
Néa Alikarnassós (GR) . . 170 C 5
Néa Anchíalos /
  Νέα Αγχίαλος (GR) . . 165 G 1
Néa Apollonía (GR) . . . 161 H 3
Néa Artáki (GR) . . . . . . 165 H 3
Néa Éfesos (GR) . . . . . . 161 F 4
Néa Epídavros (GR) . . . 165 H 5
Néa Fókaia (GR) . . . . . . 161 H 5
Néa Iraklítsa (GR) . . . . . 162 B 3
Néa Kallikráteia (GR) . . 161 G 4
Néa Kerdýlia (GR) . . . . . 161 H 3
Néa Kíos (GR) . . . . 165 F 5
Néa Koróni (GR) . . . . . . 168 C 3
Néa Mákri /
  Νέα Μάκρη (GR) . . . . 166 B 4
Néa Málgara (GR) . . . . . 161 G 4
Néa Meságkala (GR) . . . 161 F 5
Néa Michanióna (GR) . . 161 G 4
Néa Moudaniá (GR) . . . 161 G 4
Néa Pélla (GR) . . . . 161 F 3
Néa Péramos (Anatolikí
  Makedonía
  kai Thráki) (GR) . . . . . 162 B 3
Néa Péramos
  (Attikí) (GR) . . . . 165 H 4
Néa Plágia (GR) . . . . . . 161 G 4
Néa Poteídaia (GR) . . . . 161 G 4
Néa Roúmata (GR) . . . . 172 B 3
Néa Sánta (Anatolikí Makedonía
  kai Thráki) (GR) . . . . . 163 E 2
Néa Sánta (Kentrikí
  Makedonía) (GR) . . . . 161 G 3
Néa Skióni (GR) . . . . . . 161 H 5
Néa Stýra (GR) . . . . 166 B 4
Néa Tríglia (GR) . . . . . . 161 G 4
Néa Zíchni (GR) . . . . . . 161 H 3
Neagra Şarului (RO) . . . 147 H 3
Neamţ (RO) . . . . 148 B 3
Neápoli (Dytikí
  Makedonía) (GR) . . . . 160 D 4
Neápoli (Kríti) (GR) . . . 173 E 3
Neápoli
  (Pelopónnisos) (GR) . . 169 E 4
Neápoli
  (Vóreio Aigaío) (GR) . . 167 F 2
Neath /
  CastellNedd (GB) . . . . 34 D 2
Nebel (D) . . . . .81 F 1
Nebljusi (HR) . . . . 135 E 5
Nebra (D) . . . . 86 A 4
Neckarelz (D) . . . . 89 F 3
Neckargemünd (D) . . . . 89 E 3
Neckarsteinach (D) . . . . 89 F 3
Neckarsulm (D) . . . . 89 F 3
Nečujam (HR) . . . . 138 B 2
Neda (E) . . . . 56 C 1
Nedelino (BG) . . . . 162 D 2
Nedelišče (HR) . . . . 135 E 2
Nedervetil (FIN) . . . . . . 185 F 5
Nedjalsko (BG) . . . . 159 H 2
Nedstrand (N) . . . . 188 B 5
Neede (NL) . . . . 77 G 5
Neermoor (D) . . . . .81 E 4
Nées Pagasés (GR) . . . . 165 G 1
Nefyn (GB) . . . . 32 A 4
Negorci (MK) . . . . 145 G 2
Negotin /
  Неготин (SRB) . . . . .141 G 5
Negotino (MK) . . . . 145 G 1
Negovanovci (BG) . . . . 150 D 4
Negrar (I) . . . . 101 H 4
Negraşi (RO) . . . . 151 H 3
Negreira (E) . . . . 56 B 2
Nègrepelisse (F) . . . . . . 53 F 2
Negreşti (RO) . . . . 148 D 4

Negreşti-Oaş (RO) ..... 147 F 1
Negru Vodă (RO) .... 153 F 5
Neheim (D) .... 84 D 3
Nehoiu (RO) .... 152 B 2
Neiden (N) .... 177 G 3
Neila (E) .... 58 D 4
Nejdek (CZ) ....91 G 2
Neksø (DK) .... 199 G 4
Nelahozeves (CZ) .... 92 A 2
Nelas (P) .... 62 C 3
Nelidovo (RUS) ....7 E 2
Nellim (FIN) .... 177 G 4
Nelson (GB) .... 32 D 2
Nemakščiai (LT) .... 204 D 3
Neman (RUS) .... 6 B 4
Neméa / Νεμέα (GR) ... 165 F 5
Nemenčinė (LT) .... 205 G 4
Nemesszalók (H) ...... 128 C 2
Nemesvid (H) .... 128 C 4
Németkér (H) .... 129 E 3
Nemours (F) .... 45 F 2
Nemunėlio
   Radviliškis (LT) .... 205 F 1
Nemyriv (UA) ....13 E 2
Nenagh /
   An tAonach (IRL) ..... 24 D 2
Nénita (GR) .... 167 E 4
Nenzing (A) .... 94 D 4
Neo Chorio
   (Akamas) (CY) ......174 B 4
Neo Chorio
   (Kythrea) (CY) ..... 175 E 3
Néo Erásmio (GR) ..... 162 C 3
Néo Iraío (GR) .... 165 F 5
Néo Mikró Chorió (GR) . 165 E 2
Néo Monastíri (GR). ... 165 F 1
Néo Perivóli (GR) .... 165 F 1
Néo Petrítsi (GR) .... 161 G 2
Neochoráki (GR) ...... 165 G 4
Neochóri (Anatolikí Makedonía
   kai Thráki) (GR) ..... 163 F 1
Neochóri (Kardítsa) (GR). 165 E 1
Neochóri
   (Stereá Elláda) (GR) ... 166 B 3
Neochóri (Tríkala) (GR). 165 E 1
Néos Marmarás (GR) .. 161 H 5
Néos Skopós (GR) .... 161 H 3
Nepomuk (CZ) ....91 H 4
Nérac (F) .... 52 D 1
Neráida (Kardítsa) (GR). 165 E 1
Neráida
   (Mavrommáta) (GR) .. 165 E 2
Neratovice (CZ) .... 92 B 2
Nerdvika (N) .... 182 B 5
Nereju (RO) .... 152 C 1
Neresheim (D) .... 89 H 4
Nereta (LV) .... 203 E 4
Nereto (I) .... 107 H 5
Neretva Delta (HR) .... 138 D 3
Nerezi (MK) .... 143 F 5
Nerezine (HR) .... 134 B 5
Nerežišća (HR) .... 138 B 2
Néris-les-Bains (F). ...... 49 H 2
Nerja (E) ....75 F 3
Néronde (F). .... 50 C 2
Nérondes (F). .... 45 F 5
Nerotriviá (GR) ...... 165 H 3
Nerpio (E) .... 71 G 3
Nerva (E) .... 69 F 4
Nervesa
   della Battaglia (I) ..... 103 F 3
Nervi (I) .... 105 E 3
Nes (N) .... 189 E 4
Nes (NL) .... 77 F 2
Nesbyen (N) .... 188 D 4
Nesebăr / Несебър (BG). 157 F 4
Nesjahverfi (IS) ...... 178 D 3
Neskaupstaður (IS) .... 178 D 2
Nesle (F) .... 40 A 4
Nesna (N) .... 183 F 1
Nesoddtangen (N) .... 189 E 5
Nesseby (N). .... 177 G 2
Nesselwang (D) .... 95 E 3
Nestáni (GR) .... 165 F 5
Nestório (GR) .... 160 D 4
Nesvik (N) .... 188 B 5
Netolice (CZ). .... 92 A 5

Netretić (HR). .... 134 D 4
Nettuno (I). .... 109 E 4
Nettuno, grotta di (I)....112 A 2
Neu Darchau (D). ...... 82 C 5
Neu-Isenburg (D) ...... 89 E 1
Neu Lübbenau (D) ..... 86 D 2
Neu-Nagelberg (A). .... 92 B 5
Neu Ulm (D) .... 89 G 5
Neuastenberg (D). ..... 85 E 4
Neubeckum (D). .... 84 D 3
Neubrandenburg (D) .. 83 F 4
Neubukow (D) .... 82 D 3
Neuburg
   an der Donau (D). ... 95 F 1
Neuchâtel (CH) .... 98 C 3
Neuenburg (D)........81 E 4
Neuenbürg (D)........ 89 E 4
Neuenhaus (D)........ 84 C 1
Neuenkirchen (D).......81 H 5
Neuenstadt
   am Kocher (D) ...... 89 F 3
Neuerburg (D) .... 88 B 1
Neufahrn
   in Niederbayern (D) ... 95 H 1
Neufchâteau (B) ...... 79 E 5
Neufchâteau (F)........47 E 2
Neufchâtel-en-Bray (F). 39 G 4
Neufchâtel-sur-Aisne (F). 40 B 4
Neufelden (A). .... 96 D 1
Neuffen (D) .... 89 F 5
Neugersdorf (D) ...... 87 F 4
Neuhardenberg (D) .... 87 E 1
Neuharlingersiel (D) ....81 E 3
Neuhaus (Elbe) (D) .... 82 C 4
Neuhaus (Oste) (D).......81 G 3
Neuhaus am
   Rennweg (D). .... 86 A 5
Neuhaus im Solling (D). . 85 G 3
Neuhaus-
   Schierschnitz (D).......91 E 2
Neuhausen
   am Rheinfall (CH) ... 99 E 1
Neuhofen
   an der Krems (A) ..... 96 D 2
Neuillé-Pont-Pierre (F) .. 44 C 4
Neuilly-le-Réal (F)..... 50 B 1
Neuilly-l'Évêque (F) .... 46 D 3
Neuilly-Saint-Front (F). .. 40 A 5
Neukalen (D) .... 83 E 3
Neukirch (D) .... 87 E 4
Neukirchen (D).......81 G 1
Neukirchen
   am Großvenediger (A) . 95 H 4
Neukloster (D) .... 82 D 3
Neulengbach (A).......97 G 1
Neum (BIH) .... 138 D 3
Neumarkt
   am Wallersee (A) ...... 96 C 2
Neumarkt
   in der Oberpfalz (D)....91 E 4
Neumarkt
   in Steiermark (A) ...... 97 E 4
Neumarkt-Sankt Veit (D). 95 H 1
Neumünster (D).......81 H 3
Neunburg
   vorm Wald (D) ....91 G 4
Neung-sur-Beuvron (F) . 45 E 4
Neunkirchen (A) ...... 97 G 2
Neunkirchen (D) ...... 88 C 3
Neuötting (D)......... 95 H 2
Neupölla (A) .... 97 F 1
Neuruppin (D) .... 83 E 5
Neuschwanstein (D) ... 95 F 3
Neusiedl am See (A). ... 97 H 2
Neuss (D) .... 84 C 4
Neustadt (Dosse) (D) .. 83 E 5
Neustadt (Hessen) (D) . 85 F 5
Neustadt (Holstein) (D). . 82 C 3
Neustadt (Titisee) (D) .. 94 B 2
Neustadt
   am Rübenberge (D) .. 85 F 1
Neustadt an der Aisch (D). 89 H 3
Neustadt
   an der Donau (D)......91 F 5
Neustadt an der Orla (D). 86 B 5

Neustadt
   an der Waldnaab (D) ..91 F 3
Neustadt
   an der Weinstraße (D). 88 D 3
Neustadt bei Coburg (D) .91 E 2
Neustadt-Glewe (D)... 82 D 4
Neustadt in Sachsen (D). 87 E 4
Neustift im Stubaital (A). 95 F 4
Neustrelitz (D) .... 83 F 4
Neuves-Maisons (F)......47 E 1
Neuvic (F) .... 49 H 4
Neuvic (F) .... 49 E 4
Neuville (F) .... 50 D 2
Neuville-aux-Bois (F). .. 45 E 3
Neuville-de-Poitou (F) .. 49 E 1
Neuvy-le-Roi (F) ...... 44 C 4
Neuvy-
   Saint-Sépulchre (F).... 49 G 1
Neuvy-sur-Barangeon (F). 45 E 4
Neuwied (D) .... 88 D 1
Névache (F).............51 G 4
Nevarėnai (LT) .... 204 C 1
Nevel (RUS) ....6 D 3
Nevers (F) .... 45 G 5
Nevesinje (BIH) ...... 139 E 3
Nevestino (BG)........ 158 A 2
Nevlunghavn (N)...... 195 E 1
New Abbey (GB) ...... 30 D 4
New Alresford (GB) ... 35 H 3
New Cumnock (GB) ... 30 D 3
New Deer (GB) .... 29 H 3
New Galloway (GB) ... 30 D 3
New Quay (GB) .... 32 A 5
New Romney (GB) .... 37 E 5
New Ross (IRL) .... 25 F 3
Newark-on-Trent (GB)... 33 F 3
Newbiggin-
   by-the-Sea (GB).......31 G 3
Newborough (GB) .... 32 A 3
Newbridge /
   An Droichead Nua (IRL). 25 F 2
Newburgh
   (Aberdeen) (GB).......31 E 1
Newburgh (Fife) (GB)... 29 H 3
Newbury (GB) .... 35 H 2
Newcastle Emlyn (GB). 34 C 1
Newcastle-
   under-Lyme (GB)...... 32 D 4
Newcastle-
   upon-Tyne (GB).......31 G 4
Newcastle West (IRL)... 24 C 3
Newhaven (GB) .... 36 C 5
Newmarket (GB) ..... 33 H 5
Newmarket (IRL)...... 24 C 4
Newmarket
   on Fergus (IRL) ..... 24 C 2
Newnham (GB) .... 35 F 1
Newport /
   Casnewydd (GB) ... 35 E 2
Newport
   (Isle of Wight) (GB) .. 38 C 1
Newport (Mayo) (IRL) .. 22 B 4
Newport
   (Pembrokes) (GB) ... 25 H 4
Newport
   (Tipperary) (IRL) .... 24 D 2
Newport (Wrekin) (GB).. 32 D 4
Newport-on-Tay (GB)... 29 G 5
Newport Pagnell (GB). . 35 H 1
Newquay (GB) .... 34 B 4
Newry (GB) .... 23 G 3
Newton Abbot (GB)... 34 D 4
Newton-Aycliffe (GB)...31 G 4
Newton Ferrers (GB)... 34 D 5
Newton Stewart (GB).. 30 C 4
Newtonmore (GB) .... 29 F 4
Newtown / Y Drenewydd
   (Powys) (GB) ..... 32 C 5
Newtown
   (Here. And Worc.) (GB). 35 F 1
Newtown
   Saint Boswells (GB)....31 F 2
Newtownabbey (GB)... 23 G 2
Newtownards (GB) .... 23 G 3
Newtownbutler (GB)... 23 E 3
Newtownhamilton (GB). 23 F 3

Newtownstewart (GB) .. 23 E 2
Nexon (F) .... 49 F 3
Neyland (GB) .... 25 H 5
Nibe (DK) .... 194 D 4
Nica (LV) .... 202 A 4
Nicastro (I).......... 113 C 3
Nice (F) .... 55 G 2
Nicgale (Neicgaļs) (LV) . 203 F 4
Nickelsdorf (A)........ 97 H 2
Nicolosi (I)........... 115 F 3
Nicosia (I)........... 115 E 3
Nicotera (I)...........115 H 1
Niculiţel (RO) .... 153 F 2
Nidderau (D) .... 89 F 1
Nideggen (D) .... 84 B 5
Nidzica (PL) ....118 D 4
Niebla (E) .... 69 F 5
Nieborów (PL) .... 122 C 1
Niederalteich (D)......91 H 5
Niederaula (D) .... 85 G 5
Niederbronn-les-Bains (F).41 H 5
Niederelsungen (D) .... 85 F 4
Niederjossa (D) ...... 85 G 5
Niederkrüchten (D) .... 84 B 4
Niederottnang (A) .... 96 C 2
Niederstetten (D) .... 89 G 3
Niederstotzingen (D) .. 89 H 5
Niedrzwica Duża (PL) .. 123 F 3
Niedźwiedzia,
   jaskinia (PL) ...... 124 C 1
Nielisz (PL) .... 123 G 4
Niemcza (PL) .... 121 E 5
Niemegk (D) .... 86 C 2
Niemisel (S) .... 185 E 1
Niemodlin (PL)....... 121 F 5
Nienburg (Saale) (D) ... 86 A 1
Nienburg (Weser) (D) .. 86 B 3
Niepołomice (PL) .... 125 G 1
Nieporęt (PL) .... 122 D 1
Nierstein (D) .... 89 E 2
Niesky (D) .... 87 F 4
Nieszawa (PL)........117 H 5
Nieul (F) .... 49 E 2
Nieuwpoort-Bad (B) ... 78 A 1
Nigríta / Νιγρίτα (GR).. 161 H 3
Niinisalo (FIN) .... 191 F 2
Nijar (F) .... 72 C 5
Nijemci (HR) .... 137 H 2
Nijkerk (NL) .... 77 E 4
Nijmegen (NL) .... 77 E 5
Nijverdal (NL) .... 77 F 4
Níkaia (GR) .... 165 F 1
Níki (GR) .... 160 D 3
Nikifóros (GR) .... 162 B 2
Nikísiani (GR) .... 162 B 3
Nikitari (CY)......... 174 C 3
Nikitas (CY) .... 174 C 3
Nikitas (GR) .... 161 H 4
Nikkaluokta (S) ...... 180 A 3
Nikola Kozlevo (BG) ... 157 E 2
Nikolaevo (Pleven) (BG). 156 A 3
Nikolaevo (Sliven) (BG). 159 G 2
Nikolaiika (GR) ...... 165 E 4
Nikolovo (BG) .... 162 D 1
Nikopol (BG) .... 151 H 5
Nikopol' (UA) ....13 H 2
Nikópoli (GR) .... 164 C 2
Nikšić (MNE) .... 139 F 4
Nilivaara (S) .... 180 B 4
Nilsiä (FIN) .... 187 F 5
Nîmes (F) .... 54 C 2
Nin (HR) .... 136 B 4
Ninove (B) .... 78 C 2
Niort (F) .... 48 D 1
Nípsa (GR) .... 163 E 3
Niš / Ниш (SRB) ..... 143 F 2
Nisa (P) .... 62 D 5
Nisáki (GR) .... 160 A 5
Nisko (PL) .... 123 F 5
Niscemi (I)...........115 E 4
Nitaure (LV) .... 203 E 3
Niton (GB) .... 38 C 1

Nitra (SK) .... 132 B 4
Nitrianske Pravno (SK) . 132 C 3
Nitry (F)............. 45 H 3
Nittedal (N) .... 189 F 5
Nittenau (D) ....91 F 5
Nittendorf (D) ....91 F 5
Nivala (FIN) .... 185 G 4
Nivelles (B) .... 78 C 3
Niwica (PL) .... 120 B 3
Nižyn (UA) ....7 F 5
Nizza Monferrato (I). .. 104 D 2
Njasviž (BY) ....6 D 5
Njivice (HR) .... 134 B 4
Njunis (GR)..........176 B 5
Njurundabommen (S). . 190 B 2
Noailles (F) .... 39 H 4
Noáin (E) .... 59 F 2
Noblejas (E) .... 64 C 3
Nocera Inferiore (I). .. 109 H 5
Nocera Terinese (I).... 113 B 3
Nocera Umbra (I) .... 107 F 4
Noceto (I)........... 105 G 2
Noci (I).............. 111 F 3
Nodeland (N) .... 194 C 2
Nœux (F) .... 39 H 2
Noevci (BG).......... 158 A 1
Nogara (I)........... 101 H 5
Nogaro (F)........... 52 D 2
Nogent (F) .... 46 D 3
Nogent-le-Roi (F) .... 44 D 1
Nogent-le-Rotrou (F). . 44 C 2
Nogent-sur-Seine (F). . 45 G 2
Noginsk (RUS) ....7 G 2
Noguera (E). .... 65 F 2
Nohfelden (D) .... 88 C 2
Noia (E) .... 56 B 3
Noirétable (F). .... 50 B 3
Noirmoutier-en-l'Île (F) . 43 E 5
Noja (E)............. 58 B 2
Nokia (FIN) .... 191 G 3
Nola (I) .... 109 H 5
Nolay (F). .... 46 C 5
Noli (I) .... 104 D 3
Nombela (E) .... 64 A 3
Nomeny (F)...........41 E 5
Nomexy (F)...........47 F 2
Nómia (GR) .... 169 E 4
Nonancourt (F) ...... 44 D 1
Nonant-le-Pin (F) .... 44 B 1
Nonaspe (E) .... 60 A 4
None (I) .... 100 C 5
Nonio (I) .... 100 D 3
Nontron (F) .... 49 E 3
Nonza (F)............ 55 H 3
Nõo (EST) .... 201 F 4
Noordwijk aan Zee (NL) .76 D 4
Noormarkku (FIN)..... 191 F 3
Nora (S) .... 196 C 1
Norberg (S) .... 190 A 5
Norcia (I)............ 107 G 5
Nord Edewecht (D).......81 F 5
Nord-Lenangen (N) ....176 B 3
Nordborg (DK) .... 198 C 3
Nordby (DK) .... 198 B 3
Nordby (DK) .... 198 C 3
Norddeich (D) .... 80 D 4
Nordeide (N) .... 188 B 3
Norden (D) ....81 E 4
Nordenau (D) .... 85 E 4
Nordenham (D) .... 81 F 5
Norderney (D) .... 80 D 3
Norderstedt (D).......81 H 4
Nordfjordeid (N) ..... 188 B 2
Nordfold (N) .... 179 G 4
Nordhalben (D) ....91 E 2
Nordhausen (D) ...... 85 H 3
Nordhorn (D) .... 84 C 1
Nordingrå (S) .... 190 C 1
Nordkapp (N) .... 177 E 1
Nordkjosbotn (N)......176 B 4
Nordli (N) .... 183 F 3
Nordmaling (S) ...... 184 D 5
Nordmark (S) .... 189 H 5
Nordseter (N) .... 189 F 3
Nordurfjörður (IS) .... 178 B 1
Noreña (E) .... 57 G 2

Noresund (N) .... 189 E 5
Norg (NL) .... 77 F 3
Norheimsund (N) ..... 188 B 4
Norra Bergnäs (S) .... 184 C 1
Norra Kvill
   nationalpark (S) .... 197 E 3
Norra Råda (S) .... 189 H 5
Norra Storfjället (S). .... 183 G 1
Norråker (S). .... 183 G 4
Norrby (S) .... 184 C 3
Nørre Aaby (DK) ...... 198 C 3
Nørre Alslev (DK) ..... 198 D 4
Nørre Nebel (DK) ..... 198 B 3
Nørre Snede (DK) ..... 198 C 2
Nørre Vorupør (DK) .. 194 C 4
Norrent-Fontes (F) .... 39 H 2
Norrköping (S) .... 197 E 2
Norrnäs (FIN) .... 191 E 1
Norrsundet (S) .... 190 B 4
Norrtälje (S). .... 190 C 5
Norrviken (S) .... 195 G 5
Norsjö (S) .... 184 D 3
Nort-sur-Erdre (F). ... 43 F 4
Nörten-Hardenberg (D). 85 G 3
North Berwick (GB)....31 E 1
North Walsham (GB) .. 37 E 1
Northallerton (GB)....31 G 5
Northam (GB) .... 34 D 3
Northampton (GB) ... 33 F 5
Northeim (D) .... 85 G 3
Northleach (GB) ..... 35 G 1
Northwich (GB) ...... 32 D 3
Norton (D)...........31 H 5
Nortorf (D).............81 H 3
Norwich (GB) .... 37 E 1
Nosivka (UA)...........7 F 5
Nossebro (S) .... 195 G 3
Nossen (D). .... 86 D 4
Noszlop (H) .... 128 C 2
Noto (I)..............115 G 5
Notodden (N). .... 188 D 5
Notre-Dame-
   de-Bellecombe (F) ....51 F 2
Nottingham (GB) ..... 33 E 4
Nouan-le-Fuzelier (F) .. 45 E 4
Nousiainen (FIN) ..... 191 F 4
Nouvion-
   en-Ponthieu (F) ..... 39 G 3
Nouzonville (F) ...... 40 C 3
Nõva (EST) .... 200 C 2
Nova (H) .... 128 B 3
Nova Breznica (MK) .. 143 E 5
Nová Bystrica (SK) ... 132 D 1
Nová Bystřice (CZ) ... 92 C 5
Nova Crnja (SRB)..... 140 D 2
Nova Gorica (SLO) ... 134 A 2
Nova Gradiška (HR) .. 135 G 4
Nova Kachovka (UA) ...13 H 2
Nova Kamena (BG) ... 152 D 5
Nova Levante (I) ..... 103 E 2
Nová Paka (CZ) ...... 87 G 5
Nova Pazova (SRB) .. 140 C 4
Nová Role (CZ) ....91 G 2
Nová Sedlica (SK) .... 133 H 2
Nova Siri Marina (I)....111 E 5
Nova Topola (BIH) ... 135 G 5
Nova Varoš (SRB). ... 139 H 4
Nova vas (SLO) ...... 134 B 3
Nova Zagora /
   Нова Загора (BG) ... 159 F 2
Novačene (BG) .... 158 C 1
Novaci (MK) .... 145 F 2
Novaci (RO) .... 151 F 2
Novaci (SRB) .... 140 C 5
Novafeltria (I) .... 107 E 3
Nováky (SK)......... 132 C 3
Novales (E) .... 59 H 4
Novalja (HR) .... 136 A 4
Novara (I)........... 100 D 4
Novara di Sicilia (I)....115 G 2
Nové Hrady (CZ) ..... 92 B 5
Nové Město
   na Moravě (CZ) ..... 92 D 3
Nové Město
   nad Metují (CZ) ..... 92 D 2
Nové Město
   nad Váhom (SK)...... 132 B 3

Nové Zámky (SK) ...... 132 **B 4**
Novelda (E) ...... 73 **E 2**
Novellara (I) ...... 102 **C 5**
Noventa Vicentina (I)... 103 **E 5**
Noves (F) ...... 54 **D 2**
Novgorod = Veliki Novgorod (RUS)...6 **D 1**
Novhorod-Sivers'kyj (UA) ...7 **F 5**
Novi Bečej (SRB) ... 140 **C 2**
Novi di Modena (I) ..... 101 **H 5**
Novi Dojran (MK) ... 145 **H 2**
Novi Grad (BIH) ...... 135 **H 5**
Novi Grad / Bosanski Novi (BIH) .. 135 **E 5**
Novi Han (BG) ...... 158 **B 2**
Novi Karlovci (SRB) .. 140 **C 3**
Novi Kneževac (SRB) .. 140 **C 1**
Novi Ligure (I) ...... 104 **D 2**
Novi Marof (HR) ..... 135 **E 2**
Novi Pazar / Нови пазар (BG) ... 157 **E 2**
Novi Pazar / Нови Пазар (SRB) ... 142 **D 3**
Novi Sad / Нови Сад (SRB) ... 140 **C 3**
Novi Šeher (BIH) ..... 137 **F 4**
Novi Senkovac (HR) ... 135 **H 3**
Novi Slankamen (SRB) . 140 **C 3**
Novi Travnik (BIH)...... 137 **F 5**
Novi Vinodolski (HR) ... 134 **C 4**
Novigrad (HR) ...... 136 **B 4**
Novigrad / Cittanova d'Istria (HR). 134 **A 4**
Novigrad Podravski (HR). 135 **F 2**
Novion-Porcien (F)... 40 **C 4**
Novo Brdo (SRB) ...... 143 **F 4**
Novo Delčevo (BG) ... 161 **G 1**
Novo Korito (SRB) ... 143 **G 1**
Novo Mesto (SLO) ... 134 **C 3**
Novo Miloševo (SRB)... 140 **C 2**
Novo Selo (BIH) ...... 135 **H 5**
Novo Selo (MK) ...... 145 **H 1**
Novo Selo (Ruse) (BG) ... 152 **B 5**
Novo Selo (Sofia-Grad) (BG) ... 158 **C 2**
Novo Zvečevo (HR) ... 135 **G 4**
Novohrad-Volyns'kyj (UA)...13 **E 1**
Novomoskovsk (RUS) ...7 **H 3**
Novomyrhorod (UA) ...13 **G 2**
Novoržev (RUS) ...6 **D 2**
Novoselë (AL)...... 144 **B 3**
Novoselec (BG) ...... 159 **G 2**
Novoselo (BG) ...... 150 **D 4**
Novoselycja (UA)...13 **E 3**
Novosil' (RUS) ...7 **G 3**
Novoukraïnka (UA)...13 **G 2**
Novovolyns'k (UA) ...12 **C 1**
Novozybkov (RUS) ...7 **F 4**
Novska (HR) ...... 135 **F 4**
Nový Bor (CZ)...... 87 **F 5**
Nový Bydžov (CZ)... 92 **C 2**
Nový Jičín (CZ)... 93 **G 3**
Novyj Buh (UA) ...13 **G 2**
Nowa Brzeźnica (PL) ... 121 **H 4**
Nowa Dęba (PL) ... 123 **E 5**
Nowa Huta (PL) ... 125 **G 1**
Nowa Karczma (PL) ...117 **G 2**
Nowa Ruda (PL) ... 121 **E 5**
Nowa Sarzyna (PL) ... 123 **F 5**
Nowa Słupia (PL) ... 122 **D 4**
Nowa Sól (PL) ... 120 **C 2**
Nowa Wieś Wielka (PL)...117 **G 5**
Nowe (PL)...117 **H 3**
Nowe Miasteczko (PL). 120 **D 2**
Nowe Miasto (PL) ...118 **D 5**
Nowe Miasto Lubawskie (PL)......118 **C 3**
Nowe Miasto nad Pilicą (PL). 122 **C 2**
Nowe Miasto nad Wartą (PL). 121 **F 2**
Nowe Skalmierzyce (PL) 121 **G 2**
Nowe Warpno (PL)...116 **B 3**
Nowica (PL)...118 **C 2**

Nowogard (PL)...116 **C 3**
Nowogród (PL)...119 **F 4**
Nowogród Bobrzański (PL)..... 120 **C 2**
Nowogrodziec (PL) ... 120 **C 3**
Nowosiółki (PL) ... 123 **H 5**
Nowy Duninów (PL).....118 **B 5**
Nowy Dwór Gdański (PL)...117 **H 2**
Nowy Dwór Mazowiecki (PL) ... 122 **D 1**
Nowy Korczyn (PL)..... 122 **D 5**
Nowy Sącz (PL) ... 125 **H 2**
Nowy Staw (PL)...117 **H 2**
Nowy Targ (PL)... 125 **G 2**
Nowy Tomyśl (PL) ... 120 **D 1**
Nowy Wiśnicz (PL)... 125 **H 1**
Nowy Żmigród (PL) ... 127 **E 2**
Noyant (F) ...... 44 **B 4**
Noyers (F) ...... 45 **H 3**
Noyers-sur-Jabron (F) ... 55 **E 1**
Noyon (F) ...... 40 **A 4**
Nozay (F) ...... 43 **F 4**
Nucet (RO) ...... 146 **D 4**
Nucşoara (RO) ...... 151 **H 2**
Nueil-les-Aubiers (F) ... 43 **G 5**
Nules (E) ...... 66 **A 2**
Nulvi (I)...... 112 **B 1**
Numana (I) ...... 107 **H 3**
Numancia (E) ...... 59 **E 4**
Nummela (FIN) ... 191 **H 4**
Nummi (FIN) ...... 191 **G 4**
Nuneaton (GB) ...... 33 **E 5**
Nunnanen (FIN) ... 177 **E 5**
Nuñomoral (E) ...... 63 **F 3**
Nunspeet (NL) ...... 77 **E 4**
Nuorgam (FIN) ... 177 **F 3**
Nuoro (I)......112 **C 2**
Nur (PL)...... 119 **F 5**
Nurallao (I)......112 **C 4**
Nürburg (D)...... 88 **C 1**
Núria (E) ...... 60 **D 2**
Nurmes (FIN) ... 187 **G 4**
Nurmijärvi (FIN) ... 187 **G 4**
Nurmijärvi (FIN) ... 191 **H 4**
Nurmo (FIN) ...... 191 **F 1**
Nürnberg (D)......91 **E 4**
Nürtingen (D)...... 89 **F 5**
Nus (I) ...... 100 **C 3**
Nusfalău (RO) ...... 146 **D 3**
Nusse (D) ...... 82 **B 4**
Nuštar (HR) ...... 137 **H 2**
Nuttlar (D) ...... 85 **E 4**
Nuttupera (FIN) ...... 185 **F 4**
Nuutajärvi (FIN) ... 191 **G 3**
Nyåker (S)...... 184 **D 5**
Nybergsund (N) ... 189 **G 3**
Nyborg (DK) ...... 198 **D 4**
Nybro (S) ...... 197 **E 5**
Nydrí (GR) ...... 164 **C 3**
Nýřany (CZ)...91 **H 3**
Nyíracsád (H)...... 131 **F 1**
Nyírad (H) ...... 128 **C 3**
Nyíradony (H)...... 131 **F 1**
Nyírbátor (H)......131 **F 1**
Nyírbéltek (H)...... 131 **F 1**
Nyírbogát (H)......131 **F 1**
Nyíregyháza (H) ...... 131 **E 1**
Nyírlugos (H)......131 **F 1**
Nyírmada (H) ...... 127 **F 5**
Nykarleby / Uusikaarlepyy (FIN)... 185 **F 5**
Nykøbing Falster (DK)... 198 **D 4**
Nykøbing Mors (DK) ... 194 **C 4**
Nykøbing S (DK) ... 198 **D 3**
Nyköping (S)...... 197 **F 2**
Nykvarn (S)...... 197 **F 1**
Nyksund (N)...... 179 **G 2**
Nymburk (CZ)...... 92 **B 2**
Nymfaía (GR) ...... 162 **D 2**
Nymfaío (GR) ...... 160 **D 3**

Nynäshamn (S) ...... 197 **G 2**
Nyon (CH) ...... 98 **A 4**
Nyons (F) ...... 54 **D 1**
Nýrsko (CZ)......91 **H 4**
Nyrud (N) ...... 177 **G 4**
Nysa (PL) ...... 121 **F 5**
Nysäter (S) ...... 195 **G 1**
Nyseter (N) ...... 188 **D 2**
Nysted (DK) ...... 198 **D 5**
Nyúl (H) ...... 128 **D 1**
Nyvoll (N)...176 **D 3**

O

O Barco (E) ...... 57 **E 4**
O Bolo (E) ...... 57 **E 4**
O Castro de Caldelas (E). 56 **D 4**
O Corgo (E) ...... 56 **D 2**
O Grove (E) ...... 56 **B 3**
O Porriño (E) ...... 56 **B 4**
Oadby (GB) ...... 33 **F 4**
Oakham (GB) ...... 33 **F 4**
Oancea (RO) ...... 149 **E 5**
Oanes (N) ...... 194 **B 1**
Oban (GB) ...... 28 **C 5**
Obârşia-Cloşani (RO)... 150 **D 2**
Obbola (S) ...... 184 **D 5**
Obdach (A) ...... 97 **E 4**
Obedinenie (BG) ...... 156 **B 2**
Obejo (E) ...... 70 **B 3**
Ober-Grafendorf (A) ... 97 **F 2**
Oberammergau (D)..... 95 **F 3**
Oberau (D)...... 95 **F 3**
Oberaudorf (D) ...... 95 **H 3**
Oberdrauburg (A)...... 96 **B 5**
Obereßfeld (D)...... 89 **H 1**
Obergünzburg (D) ...... 95 **E 3**
Obergurgl (A) ...... 95 **F 5**
Oberhaslach (F)......47 **G 1**
Oberhausen (D) ...... 84 **C 3**
Oberhof (D)...... 85 **H 5**
Oberkirch (D) ...... 88 **D 5**
Oberkirchen (D) ...... 85 **E 4**
Oberkochen (D) ...... 89 **G 4**
Obermarchtal (D) ...... 89 **G 5**
Obernai (F)......47 **G 1**
Obernburg am Main (D)...... 89 **F 2**
Oberndorf am Neckar (D). 89 **E 5**
Oberndorf bei Salzburg (A) ... 96 **B 2**
Obernzell (D) ...... 96 **C 1**
Oberölsbach (D) ...91 **E 4**
Oberprechtal (D)... 94 **B 2**
Oberpullendorf (A) ... 97 **H 3**
Obersontheim (D) ... 89 **G 4**
Oberstaufen (D) ...... 94 **D 3**
Oberstdorf (D) ...... 95 **E 3**
Obertauern (A) ...... 96 **C 4**
Obertraun (A) ...... 96 **C 3**
Oberursel (D) ...... 89 **E 1**
Obervellach (A) ...... 96 **C 4**
Oberviechtach (D) ...91 **G 4**
Oberwart (A) ...... 97 **G 3**
Oberwesel (D) ...... 88 **D 1**
Oberwiesenthal (D) ...91 **G 2**
Oberwölz (A) ...... 96 **D 4**
Oberzeiring (A) ...... 97 **E 4**
Óbidos (P) ...... 62 **A 5**
Obilić (SRB) ...... 143 **E 4**
Obing (D) ...... 95 **H 2**
Objat (F) ...... 49 **F 4**
Objazda (PL)...... 117 **F 1**
Obninsk (RUS) ...7 **G 2**
Obnova (BG) ...... 156 **B 2**
Obojan' (RUS) ...7 **H 5**
Obón (E) ...... 65 **H 1**
Oborín (SK) ...... 133 **H 3**
Oborište (BG) ...... 158 **C 2**
Oborniki (PL)...117 **E 5**
Oborniki Śląskie (PL) ... 121 **E 3**
Obornjača (SRB) ...... 140 **C 2**
Oborovo (HR) ...... 135 **E 3**
Obrenovac / Обреновац (SRB) .... 140 **C 4**

Obretenik (BG)...... 156 **C 2**
Obrež (SRB) ...... 140 **C 4**
Obročište (BG) ...... 157 **F 2**
Obrov (SLO) ...... 134 **B 3**
Obrovac (HR) ...... 136 **C 4**
Obrovac Sinjski (HR) ... 138 **B 1**
Obrowo (PL)...117 **H 5**
Obršani (MK) ...... 145 **F 2**
Obrzycko (PL)...117 **E 5**
Obsteig (A) ...... 95 **F 4**
Obsza (PL) ...... 123 **G 5**
Obudavac (BIH) ...... 137 **G 3**
Obzor / Обзор (BG) ... 157 **F 3**
Očakiv (UA)...13 **G 3**
Ocaña (E) ...... 64 **C 4**
Occhiobello (I) ...... 103 **E 5**
Očevlja (BIH) ...... 137 **G 5**
Ochagavía (E) ...... 59 **G 2**
Ochsenfurt (D)...... 89 **G 2**
Ochsenhausen (D) ... 94 **D 2**
Óchthia (GR) ...... 164 **D 3**
Ochtrup (D)...... 84 **C 2**
Ochtyrka (UA) ...7 **G 5**
Ockelbo (S) ...... 190 **B 4**
Ocland (RO) ...... 148 **A 5**
Ocna Mureş (RO) ...... 147 **F 4**
Ocna Sibiului (RO) ... 151 **F 1**
Ócsa (H) ...... 129 **F 2**
Öcsöd (H) ...... 129 **H 3**
Ödåkra (S) ...... 199 **E 3**
Odârne (D) ...... 156 **A 2**
Odda (N) ...... 188 **B 4**
Odden Færgehavn (DK). 198 **D 3**
Odder (DK) ...... 198 **C 3**
Odeceixe (P) ...... 68 **B 5**
Odeleite (P) ...... 68 **D 5**
Odelzhausen (D) ...... 95 **F 2**
Odemira (P) ...... 68 **B 4**
Ödemiş (TR) ...19 **G 3**
Odense (DK) ...... 198 **C 3**
Odenthal (D) ...... 84 **C 4**
Oderberg (D) ...... 83 **G 5**
Oderzo (I) ...... 103 **F 3**
Odesa (UA) ...13 **G 3**
Ödeshög (S) ...... 195 **H 3**
Odivelas (P) ...... 68 **C 3**
Odobeşti (RO) ...... 152 **D 1**
Odolanów (PL)...... 121 **F 3**
Odolo (I)......101 **H 4**
Odorheiu Secuiesc (RO). 147 **H 5**
Odrinci (BG) ...... 157 **F 2**
Odrowąż (PL)...... 122 **D 3**
Odry (CZ) ...... 93 **F 3**
Odrzywół (PL) ...... 122 **C 3**
Odžaci (SRB) ...... 137 **H 2**
Odžak (BIH) ...... 135 **H 5**
Odžak (MNE) ...... 139 **G 2**
Oebisfelde (D) ...... 86 **A 1**
Oederan (D) ...... 86 **D 5**
Oeiras (P) ...... 68 **A 2**
Oelde (D) ...... 85 **E 3**
Oelsnitz (Plauen) (D)... 86 **C 5**
Oelsnitz (Zwickau) (D)...91 **F 2**
Oesaran (AL) ...... 144 **C 4**
Oettingen in Bayern (D). 89 **H 4**
Oetz (A) ...... 95 **F 4**
Offenbach am Main (D). 89 **E 1**
Offenburg (D) ...... 88 **D 5**
Offida (I) ...... 107 **H 4**
Offranville (F) ...... 39 **F 3**
Ofir (P) ...... 56 **B 5**
Oggiono (I) ...... 101 **E 3**
Ogliastro Cilento (I) ...110 **B 5**
Ogorzelec (PL) ...... 120 **D 5**
Ogošte (SRB) ...... 143 **F 4**
Ogre (LV) ...... 203 **E 3**
Ogrodzieniec (PL)...... 122 **B 5**
Ogulin (HR) ...... 134 **D 4**
Ohaba Lungă (RO) ... 146 **C 5**
Ohlstadt (D) ...... 95 **F 3**
Ohorn (D)...... 87 **E 4**
Ohrdruf (D) ...... 85 **H 5**
Ohrid (MK) ...... 145 **E 2**
Öhringen (D) ...... 89 **F 3**
Oía (GR) ...... 170 **C 3**
Oiartzun (E)...... 59 **E 1**

Oijärvi (FIN) ...... 185 **H 1**
Oikarainen (FIN) ... 181 **E 5**
Oinói (Attikí) (GR) ... 165 **H 4**
Oinói (Dytikí Elláda) (GR). 164 **B 3**
Oinói (Stereá Elláda) (GR). 165 **H 4**
Oinoússes (GR) ...... 167 **F 3**
Oiron, château d' (F) ... 43 **H 5**
Oirschot (NL) ...... 79 **E 1**
Oisemont (F)...... 39 **G 3**
Oisterwijk (NL) ...... 79 **E 1**
Oitti (FIN) ...... 191 **H 4**
Oituz (RO) ...... 148 **C 5**
Oitylo (GR)...... 168 **D 4**
Öja (FIN) ...... 185 **F 4**
Ojakylä (FIN)...... 185 **G 2**
Ojdula (RO) ...... 148 **B 5**
Ojén (E)......74 **D 4**
Ojos Negros (E) ...... 65 **F 2**
Ojrzeń (PL)...... 118 **D 5**
Ojuelos (E) ...... 69 **H 3**
Öjung (S) ...... 190 **A 3**
Okány (H)......131 **E 3**
Okehampton (GB) ...... 34 **D 4**
Oker (D) ...... 85 **H 2**
Oklaj (HR) ...... 136 **C 5**
Oknö (S) ...... 197 **E 5**
Okol (AL) ...... 142 **C 4**
Okonek (PL) ...... 117 **E 3**
Okop (BG) ...... 159 **G 2**
Okorš (BG) ...... 152 **D 5**
Oksa (PL) ...... 122 **C 4**
Oksböl (DK) ...... 198 **B 3**
Oksby (DK) ...... 198 **A 3**
Øksfjord (N) ...176 **D 3**
Okučani (HR) ...... 135 **G 4**
Okulovka (RUS) ...7 **E 1**
Ólafsfjörður (IS) ... 178 **B 1**
Ólafsvík (IS) ...... 178 **A 2**
Olaine (LV) ...... 202 **D 3**
Olargues (F) ...... 53 **H 3**
Olaszliszka (H) ...... 127 **E 5**
Oława (PL) ...... 121 **F 4**
Olazagutía (E)...... 59 **E 2**
Olbernhau (D) ...... 86 **D 5**
Olbia (I)......112 **D 1**
Old Mellifont (IRL) ... 23 **F 4**
Oldcastle (IRL) ...... 23 **E 4**
Oldebroek (NL) ...... 77 **F 4**
Olden (N) ...... 188 **C 2**
Oldenburg (D)...81 **F 5**
Oldenburg in Holstein (D) ... 82 **C 2**
Oldenzaal (NL) ...... 77 **G 4**
Oldervik (N)...176 **B 3**
Oldham (GB) ...... 32 **D 2**
Oldmeldrum (GB) ... 29 **G 3**
Oldsum (D)...81 **F 1**
Olecko (PL) ...... 119 **F 2**
Oleggio (I) ...... 100 **D 4**
Oleiros (E) ...... 56 **C 1**
Oleiros (P) ...... 62 **C 4**
Oleksandrija (UA) ...13 **G 1**
Ølen (N) ...... 188 **B 5**
Olesa de Montserrat (E). 60 **D 3**
Oleśnica (PL)...... 121 **F 4**
Olesno (PL) ...... 121 **G 4**
Oleszyce (PL) ...... 123 **G 5**
Oletta (F) ...... 55 **H 3**
Olette (F) ...... 53 **G 5**
Olevs'k (UA)...13 **E 1**
Ølgod (DK) ...... 198 **B 3**
Olhão (P) ...... 68 **C 5**
Olhava (FIN) ...... 185 **H 2**
Oliana (E) ...... 60 **C 2**
Olib (HR) ...... 136 **A 4**
Oliena (I)......112 **C 3**
Oliete (E) ...... 65 **H 1**
Olite (E) ...... 59 **F 3**
Oliva (E) ...... 66 **A 5**
Oliva de la Frontera (E). 69 **E 3**
Oliva de Mérida (E) ... 69 **G 2**
Olivares de Júcar (E) ... 65 **E 4**
Oliveira de Azeméis (P). 62 **B 2**
Oliveira de Frades (P) ... 62 **C 2**

Oliveira do Bairro (P) .... 62 **B 3**
Oliveira do Douro (P). ... 62 **C 1**
Oliveira do Hospital (P).. 62 **C 3**
Olivenza (E) ...... 69 **E 2**
Olivet (F) ...... 45 **E 3**
Olivone (CH) ...... 99 **F 4**
Olkusz (PL)...... 122 **B 5**
Ollerton (GB) ...... 33 **F 3**
Olliergues (F) ...... 50 **B 3**
Ollilanvaara (FIN) ... 181 **E 5**
Ollioules (F) ...... 55 **E 3**
Öllölä (FIN) ...... 193 **H 1**
Olmedillo de Roa (E) ... 58 **B 4**
Olmedo (E) ...... 64 **A 1**
Olmedo (I)......112 **B 2**
Olmeto (F) ...... 55 **H 5**
Olocau del Rey (E) ... 65 **H 2**
Olofström (S) ...... 199 **G 2**
Olombrada (E) ...... 58 **B 5**
Olomouc (CZ)...... 93 **F 3**
Olonzac (F) ...... 53 **H 3**
Olost (E) ...... 60 **D 2**
Olot (E) ......61 **E 2**
Olovo (BIH) ...... 137 **G 5**
Olpe (D) ...... 84 **D 4**
Olsberg (D) ...... 85 **E 4**
Olshammar (S) ...... 195 **H 2**
Olst (NL) ...... 77 **F 4**
Ølstykke (DK) ...... 199 **E 3**
Olsztyn (PL)...... 118 **D 3**
Olsztynek (PL)...... 118 **D 3**
Olszyna (PL) ...... 120 **C 4**
Oltedal (N) ...... 194 **B 1**
Olten (CH) ...... 98 **D 2**
Olteniţa (RO)...... 152 **C 5**
Olula del Río (E) ... 71 **G 5**
Ólvega (E) ...... 59 **E 4**
Olvera (E)......74 **C 3**
Olympía (GR) ...... 164 **D 5**
Olympiáda (Kentrikí Makedonía) (GR) ..... 161 **H 4**
Olympiáda (Thessalía) (GR) ... 161 **F 5**
Ólynthos (GR) ...... 161 **H 4**
Omagh (GB) ...... 23 **E 2**
Omalós (GR) ...... 172 **B 3**
Oman (BG) ...... 159 **H 2**
Omarčevo (BG) ...... 159 **G 2**
Omarska (BIH) ...... 135 **F 5**
Omegna (I) ...... 100 **D 3**
Omiš (HR) ...... 138 **B 2**
Omišalj (HR) ...... 134 **B 4**
Ommen (NL) ...... 77 **F 4**
Omodos (CY)...174 **C 4**
Omoljica (SRB) ...... 140 **D 4**
Omorfochóri (GR) ... 165 **F 1**
Ömossa (FIN) ...... 191 **E 2**
Omurtag (BG) ...... 159 **G 1**
Oña (E) ...... 58 **C 2**
Oñati (E) ...... 59 **E 2**
Onda (E) ...... 65 **H 3**
Ondara (E) ...... 66 **A 5**
Ondarroa (E) ...... 59 **E 1**
Oneglia (I) ...... 104 **C 4**
Onesse-Laharie (F)... 52 **B 1**
Oneşti (RO) ...... 148 **C 5**
Onich (GB) ...... 28 **D 5**
Onkamo (FIN) ...... 181 **G 5**
Onkamo (FIN) ...... 193 **H 1**
Ontaneda (E) ...... 58 **B 1**
Ontiñena (E) ...... 60 **A 3**
Ontiniente / Ontinyient (E)...... 73 **F 1**
Ontinyent / Onteniente (E)...... 73 **F 1**
Ontur (E) ...... 71 **H 2**
Onuškis (LT) ...... 205 **F 4**
Onzain (F) ...... 44 **D 4**
Oost-Vlieland (NL) ... 77 **F 2**
Oostburg (NL) ...... 78 **B 1**
Oostende (Ostende) (B). ... 78 **A 1**
Oosterbeek (NL) ...... 77 **E 5**
Oosterend (NL) ...... 77 **E 2**
Oosterhout (NL) ...... 78 **D 1**
Oostkamp (B) ...... 78 **B 1**

Oostmalle (B) .... 78 D 1
Ootmarsum (NL) .... 77 G 4
Opaka (BG) .... 156 C 2
Opalenica (PL) .... 121 E 1
Opan (BG) .... 159 F 3
Opatija (HR) ...... 134 B 4
Opatovac (HR) .... 137 H 2
Opatów (PL) .... 123 E 4
Opava (CZ) ...... 93 F 2
Opicina (I) ...... 103 H 4
Opladen (D) .... 84 C 4
Opočka (RUS) ......6 D 3
Opoczno (PL) .... 122 C 4
Opole (PL) .... 121 G 5
Opole Lubelskie (PL) .. 123 E 3
Opovo (SRB) .... 140 D 3
Oppach (D) .... 87 E 4
Oppdal (N) .... 189 E 1
Oppenau (D) .... 88 D 5
Oppenheim (D) .... 89 E 2
Opphaug (N) .... 182 C 4
Opphus (N) .... 189 F 3
Oppido Lucano (I) ......110 D 4
Oppido Mamertina (I)..115 H 2
Oprişor (RO) .... 151 E 4
Ópusztaszer (H) ...... 129 G 4
Opuzen (SRB) .... 138 D 3
Ora / Auer (I) .... 101 H 2
Oradea (RO) ...... 146 C 3
Oradour-sur-Glane (F) .. 49 F 2
Oradour-sur-Vayres (F) .. 49 F 3
Orahova (BIH) ...... 135 F 4
Orahovac (SRB) .... 142 D 4
Orahovica (HR) ...... 135 H 4
Oraiókastro (GR) ..... 161 G 3
Oraison (F) .... 55 E 2
Orajärvi (FIN) ...... 180 D 5
Orange (F) .... 54 C 1
Orani (I) ....112 C 3
Oranienbaum (D) .. 86 B 3
Oranienburg (D) ...... 86 D 1
Oranmore (IRL) ...... 22 C 5
Orašac (HR) ...... 139 E 4
Orašac (SRB) .... 140 D 5
Orasi (MNE) ...... 139 F 4
Orašje (BIH) ...... 137 G 3
Orăştie (RO) ...... 151 E 1
Orăştioara de Sus (RO) .. 151 E 1
Oraşu Nou (RO) .... 147 E 1
Oravainen /
   Oravais (FIN) .... 185 F 5
Oravais /
   Oravainen (FIN) ..... 185 F 5
Oravikoski (FIN) ..... 193 F 1
Oraviţa (RO) ...... 150 C 2
Oravská Lesná (SK) ... 132 D 1
Orba (E) ...... 66 A 5
Ørbæk (DK) ...... 198 C 4
Orbassano (I) ...... 100 C 5
Orbe (CH) ...... 98 B 3
Orbeasca de Jos (RO) .. 151 H 4
Orbec (F) ...... 39 E 5
Orbetello (I) ...... 108 B 1
Orbey (F) ....47 G 2
Örbottyán (H) ...... 129 F 1
Orce (E) ...... 71 F 4
Orcera (E) ...... 71 F 3
Orchies (F) ...... 40 A 2
Orchomenós /
   Ορχομενός (GR) .... 165 G 3
Orchowo (PL) .... 121 G 1
Orcières (F) .....51 F 5
Orcival (F) ...... 50 A 3
Ordes (E) ...... 56 C 2
Ordino (AND) ...... 60 C 1
Ordizia (E) ...... 59 E 2
Orduña (E) ...... 58 D 2
Ordžonikidze (UA) ....13 H 2
Ore (S) ...... 190 A 3
Orea (E) ...... 65 F 2
Orebić (HR) ...... 138 C 3
Örebro (S) .... 197 E 1
Orechovo-Zujevo (RUS) ..7 G 2
Öregcsertő (H) ...... 129 F 4
Öreglak (H) ...... 128 C 4
Öregrund (S) .... 190 C 5
Orellana de la Sierra (E) ... 69 H 1

Orellana la Vieja (E) .... 69 H 1
Oreoí (GR) .... 165 G 2
Orešak (BG) .... 158 D 1
Orestiáda /
   Ορεστιάδα (GR) ..... 163 F 1
Organyà (E) .... 60 C 2
Orgaz (E) .... 64 B 4
Orgelet (F) ....51 E 1
Orgères-en-Beauce (F) .. 44 D 2
Órgiva (E) .... 72 A 5
Orgon (F) .... 54 D 2
Orgosolo (I) ....112 C 3
Orgovány (H) .... 129 F 3
Orhei (MD) .... .13 F 3
Oria (E) .... 71 G 5
Oria (I) ....111 G 4
Oricáin (E) .... 59 F 2
Origny-Sainte-Benoite (F) .. 40 A 3
Orihuela / Oriola (E)... 73 E 3
Orihuela
   del Tremedal (E) ..... 65 F 2
Orikum (AL) .... 144 B 4
Orimattila (FIN) ...... 191 H 4
Oriola / Orihuela (E)... 73 E 3
Oriolo (I) ....111 E 5
Oripää (FIN) .... 191 F 4
Orissaare (EST) ...... 200 C 3
Oristano (I) ....112 B 3
Öriszentpéter (H) .... 128 B 3
Orivesi (FIN) .... 191 G 2
Orizare (BG) .... 157 F 4
Orizovo (BG) .... 159 E 3
Orjahovo (BG) .... 151 F 5
Ørje (N) .... 195 F 1
Orkanger (N) .... 182 C 5
Örkelljunga (S) ...... 195 G 5
Örkény (H) .... 129 F 3
Orlane (SRB) .... 143 E 3
Orlate (SRB) .... 143 E 4
Orléans (F) .... 45 E 3
Orlová (CZ) .... 93 G 3
Orlovat (SRB) .... 140 D 3
Orly (F) .... 45 E 1
Òrma (GR) .... 161 E 3
Ormídeia (CY) .... 175 E 3
Órmos (GR) .... 161 G 4
Órmos Korthíou (GR)... 166 C 5
Órmos Panagías (GR)... 161 H 4
Ormož (SLO) .... 135 G 2
Ormsjö (S) ....183 H 4
Ormskirk (GB) .... 32 C 2
Ormtjernkampen
   nasjonalpark (N)..... 189 E 3
Ormília (GR) .... 161 H 4
Ornans (F) ....47 F 5
Ørnes (N) .... 179 F 5
Orneta (PL) ....118 C 2
Ornós (GR) .... 170 C 1
Örnsköldsvik (S) ..... 184 C 5
Or'ol (RUS) ....7 G 4
Orolik (HR) .... 137 H 2
Orom (SRB) .... 140 C 1
Oron-la-Ville (CH) .... 98 B 3
Oropesa (E) .... 63 H 4
Oropesa del Mar (E)... 66 A 2
Orosei (I) ....112 D 2
Orosháza (H) .... 129 H 4
Oroszlány (H) .... 129 E 2
Oroszló (H) .... 128 D 4
Orounta (CY) ....174 D 3
Orpierre (F) .... 55 E 1
Orpington (GB) ...... 36 C 4
Orreaga /
   Roncesvalles (E)..... 59 F 2
Orrefors (S) .... 197 E 5
Orša (BY) ....7 E 4
Orsa (S) .... 189 H 3
Orsay (F) .... 45 E 1
Orsières (CH) .... 98 C 5
Orsogna (I) .... 109 G 2
Orşova (RO) .... 150 D 3
Ørsta (N) .... 188 C 1
Ørsundsbro (S) ...... 197 F 1
Orta Nova (I) ....110 C 4
Orta San Giulio (I) .... 100 D 3
Ortakoi (CY) ....174 D 3

Orte (I) .... 108 D 1
Orth an der Donau (A) .. 97 H 1
Orthez (F) .... 52 B 3
Ortigueira (E) .... 56 D 1
Ortisei /
   Sankt Ulrich (I) ..... 103 E 2
Ortnevik (N) .... 188 B 3
Orton (GB) ....31 F 5
Ortona (I) .... 109 H 2
Ortrand (D) .... 86 D 3
Örträsk (S) .... 184 D 4
Orubica (HR) .... 135 G 4
Orune (I) ....112 C 2
Orusco de Tajuña (E)... 64 C 3
Orvalho (P) .... 62 C 4
Orvieto (I) .... 107 E 5
Orvinio (I) .... 109 E 2
Orzesze (PL) .... 125 E 1
Orzinuovi (I) .... 101 F 4
Orzoja (BG) .... 151 E 5
Orzysz (PL) ....119 F 3
Os (N) .... 189 F 1
Osa de la Vega (E) .... 64 D 4
Osborne House (GB) ... 38 C 1
Osby (S) .... 195 H 5
Oschatz (D) .... 86 C 4
Oschersleben (D) ..... 86 A 2
Oschiri (I) ....112 C 2
Osečina (SRB) .... 140 B 5
Oseja de Sajambre (E)... 57 H 2
Osen (N) .... 182 D 4
Osera de Ebro (E) .... 59 H 5
Osie (N) ....117 G 3
Osięciny (PL) ....117 H 5
Osieczna (PL) .... 121 E 2
Osiecznica (PL) ...... 120 C 3
Osiek (PL) .... 123 E 5
Osijek (HR) .... 137 G 2
Osilo (I) ....112 B 2
Osimo (I) .... 107 G 4
Osinja (BIH) .... 135 H 5
Osnabrück (D) .... 85 E 2
Ośno Lubuskie (PL) ... 120 C 1
Osoblaha (CZ) .... 93 F 2
Osoppo (I) .... 103 G 2
Osor (HR) .... 134 B 5
Oşorhei (RO) .... 146 C 2
Osorno la Mayor (E)... 58 A 3
Osowiec (PL) ....119 G 3
Osøyro (N) .... 188 B 4
Ospedaletti (I) .... 104 C 4
Ospitaletto (I) .... 101 G 4
Oss (NL) .... 77 E 5
Óssa (GR) .... 161 G 3
Ossa de Montiel (E) ... 71 F 1
Ossiach (A) .... 96 D 5
Ossun (F) .... 52 D 3
Ostaškov (RUS) ....7 G 2
Østby (N) .... 189 G 3
Oster (UA) ....7 F 5
Øster Vrå (DK) ...... 195 E 4
Osterburg (D) .... 82 D 5
Osterburken (D) ..... 89 F 3
Østerby Havn (DK) ... 195 E 4
Østerbybruk (S) ..... 190 C 5
Østerbymo (S) ...... 196 D 3
Österfärnebo (S) .... 190 B 5
Osterfeld (D) .... 86 B 4
Osterhofen (D) ...... 96 B 1
Osterholz-
   Scharmbeck (D).......81 G 5
Osteria del Gatto (I)... 107 F 4
Osterode am Harz (D) .. 85 H 3
Östersund (S) .... 189 H 3
Östersundom /
   Itäsalmi (FIN) ...... 191 H 5
Österväla (S) .... 190 B 5
Osterwieck (D) ...... 85 H 2
Ostffyasszonyfa (H) .. 128 C 2
Östhammar (S) ...... 190 C 5

Ostheim vor der Rhön (D). 89 H 1
Ostia Antica (I) ...... 108 D 3
Ostiglia (I) .... 101 H 5
Östmark (S) .... 189 G 5
Ostra (I) .... 107 G 3
Ostrach (D) .... 94 D 2
Ostrava (CZ) .... 93 G 3
Oštrelj (BIH) .... 136 D 4
Ostritz (D) .... 87 F 4
Ostroh (UA) ....12 D 1
Ostrołęka (PL) ....119 E 4
Ostroróg (PL) ....117 E 5
Ostrov (CZ) ....91 G 2
Ostrov (RO) .... 152 D 5
Ostrov (RUS) ....6 D 2
Ostrów Lubelski (PL) .. 123 G 3
Ostrów
   Mazowiecka (PL).....119 F 5
Ostrów
   Wielkopolski (PL) .... 121 F 3
Ostrowiec-
   Świętokrzyski (PL)... 123 E 4
Ostrowite (PL) ....117 H 5
Ostrožac (Bihać) (BIH) .. 135 E 5
Ostrožac
   (Mostar) (BIH) ...... 138 D 2
Ostrzeszów (PL) ..... 121 G 3
Ostuni (I) ....111 G 4
Osuna (E) .... 69 H 5
Oswestry (GB) ...... 32 C 4
Oświęcim (PL) ...... 125 E 1
Osztopán (H) .... 128 C 4
Otanmäki (FIN) ...... 187 E 4
Otava (FIN) .... 193 F 2
Oţeleni (RO) .... 148 C 3
Oţelu Roşu (RO) ..... 150 D 1
Otepää (EST) .... 201 F 4
Oteren (N) ....176 B 4
Oteşani (RO) .... 151 F 2
Oteševo (MK) ...... 145 E 2
Othery (GB) .... 35 E 3
Otívar (E) ....75 F 3
Otley (GB) .... 33 E 4
Otmuchów (PL) ...... 121 F 5
Otnes (N) .... 189 F 2
Otočac (HR) .... 134 D 5
Otočec (SLO) .... 134 D 3
Otok (HR) .... 137 H 2
Otoka (BIH) .... 135 E 5
Otopeni (RO) .... 152 B 4
Otrokovice (CZ) ...... 93 F 4
Otta (N) .... 189 E 2
Ottana (I) ....112 C 3
Ottaviano (I) .... 109 H 5
Ottenschlag (A) ..... 97 F 1
Ottensheim (A) ...... 96 D 1
Otter Ferry (GB) ..... 30 B 1
Otterburn (GB) ....31 F 3
Otterndorf (D) ....81 G 3
Otternish (GB) ...... 28 B 3
Otterøy (N) .... 183 E 3
Ottersberg (D) ....81 G 5
Otterup (DK) .... 198 C 4
Ottery Saint Mary (GB) .. 35 E 4
Øttevény (H) .... 128 C 1
Ottmarsheim (F) ......47 H 3
Ottobeuren (D) ...... 95 E 2
Ottobrunn (D) .... 95 G 2
Öttömös (H) .... 129 G 4
Ottsjö (S) .... 183 F 5
Ottweiler (D) .... 88 C 3
Otwock (PL) .... 122 D 1
Ouarville (F) .... 44 D 2
Ouchy (CH) .... 98 B 3
Oucques (F) .... 44 D 3
Oud-Beijerland (NL)...76 C 5
Ouddorp (NL) ....76 C 5
Oude Pekela (NL) .... 77 G 3
Oudenaarde (B) ..... 78 B 2
Oudenbosch (NL) .... 78 D 1
Oughterard (IRL) .... 22 C 5
Ouistreham (F) .... 38 D 5
Oulainen (FIN) ...... 185 G 4
Oulchy-le-Château (F) .. 40 A 5

Oulu / Uleåborg (FIN) .. 185 H 2
Oulunsalo /
   Uleåsalo (FIN) .... 185 H 3
Oulx (I) .... 100 A 5
Oundle (GB) .... 33 F 5
Ouranópoli (GR) ..... 162 B 4
Ourém (P) .... 62 B 5
Ourense (E) .... 56 D 4
Ourique (P) .... 68 C 4
Ourol (E) .... 56 D 1
Ourville-en-Caux (F) .. 39 E 4
Oust (F) .... 53 F 4
Outeiro de Rei (E) .... 56 D 2
Outokumpu (FIN) .... 193 G 1
Outomuro (E) .... 56 C 4
Outwell (GB) .... 33 G 4
Ouzouer-le-Marché (F).. 44 D 3
Ouzouer-sur-Loire (F) .. 45 F 3
Ovada (I) .... 104 D 2
Ovanåker (S) .... 190 A 3
Ovar (P) .... 62 B 2
Ovča Mogila (BG) .... 156 B 2
Ovčar Banja (SRB) ... 139 H 1
Ovedskloster (S) ..... 199 F 3
Overath (D) .... 84 C 4
Øverbygd (N) ....176 B 5
Øverhalla (N) .... 183 E 3
Överhörnäs (S) ...... 184 C 5
Overijse (B) .... 78 C 2
Överkalix (S) .... 185 F 1
Överkiminge /
   Ylikiiminki (FIN) .... 185 H 2
Övermark (FIN) ...... 191 E 1
Övertorneå (S) ...... 180 D 5
Överum (S) .... 197 E 3
Oveselu (RO) .... 151 F 3
Ovidiu (RO) .... 153 F 4
Oviedo (E) .... 57 G 2
Ovindoli (I) .... 109 F 2
Øvre Årdal (N) ...... 188 D 3
Øvre Soppero (S).... 180 B 3
Ovruč (UA) ....13 E 1
Oxburgh Hall (GB) ... 33 H 4
Oxelösund (S) .... 197 F 2
Oxford (GB) .... 35 H 1
Oxie (S) .... 199 F 3
Oxýlithos (GR) ...... 166 B 3
Oxýneia (GR) .... 160 D 5
Oy-Mittelberg (D)..... 95 E 3
Oybin (D) .... 87 F 5
Øye (N) .... 188 D 3
Øyer (N) .... 189 F 2
Oyntdartfjørdur
   (Færøerne) (DK)..... 194 A 4
Oyón-Oion (E) .... 59 E 3
Oyonnax (F) ....51 E 1
Øysang (N) .... 194 D 2
Øystese (N) .... 188 B 4
Oyten (D) ....81 G 5
Ozalj (HR) .... 134 D 3
Ożarów (PL) .... 123 E 4
Ożarów
   Mazowiecki (PL).... 122 D 1
Ożbalt (SLO) .... 134 D 1
Ózd (H) .... 126 C 5
Ozieri (I) ....112 C 2
Ozimek (PL) .... 121 G 5
Ozora (H) .... 129 E 3
Ozorków (PL) .... 122 B 2
Ozun (RO) .... 152 B 1

P

Paakkila (FIN) .... 187 G 5
Paalasmaa (FIN) ..... 187 G 5
Paavola (FIN) .... 185 H 3
Pabaiskas (LT) ...... 205 E 2
Pabianice (PL) ...... 122 B 2
Pabiržė (LT) .... 205 E 1
Pabradė (LT) .... 205 G 3
Paceco (I) ....114 B 3
Pacheiá Ámmos (GR) .. 173 F 3
Páchi (GR) .... 165 G 4
Pachino (I) ....115 G 5
Pachna (CY) ....174 C 4
Pachyammos (CY) ....174 B 3
Paço de Sousa (P)... 62 C 1

Paços de Ferreira (P) .... 62 C 1
Pacov (CZ) .... 92 B 4
Pacsa (H) .... 128 C 3
Pacy-sur-Eure (F)..... 39 F 5
Paczków (PL) .... 121 E 5
Pădarevo (BG) ...... 159 H 1
Padasjoki (FIN) ...... 191 H 3
Padej (SRB) .... 140 C 2
Pađene (HR) .... 136 C 5
Paderborn (D) .... 85 E 3
Paderne (P) .... 68 C 5
Padiham (GB) .... 32 D 2
Padina (SRB) .... 140 D 3
Padinska Skela (SRB) .. 140 D 4
Padirac, gouffre de (F) .. 49 G 5
Padornelo (E) .... 57 E 4
Padova (I) .... 103 E 4
Padragkút (H) .... 128 C 3
Padrón (E) .... 56 B 3
Padru (I) ....112 D 2
Padstow (GB) .... 34 C 4
Padul (E) ....75 F 3
Paesana (I) .... 104 B 2
Paestum (I) ....110 B 4
Páfos (CY) ....174 B 4
Pag (HR) .... 136 B 4
Paganico (I) .... 106 D 5
Pagègiai (LT) .... 204 C 5
Pagiriai (LT) .... 205 F 3
Pagny (F) ....41 E 5
Pagóndas (GR) ...... 167 G 5
Pagoúria (GR) ...... 162 D 3
Pagramantis (LT) .... 204 C 3
Páhi (H) .... 129 F 3
Paianía (GR) .... 165 H 4
Paide (EST) .... 201 E 2
Paignton (GB) .... 35 E 4
Paimbœuf (F) .... 43 E 4
Paimio (FIN) .... 191 F 4
Paimpol (F) .... 42 D 1
Painshill (GB) .... 36 C 4
Painswick (GB) ...... 35 F 1
Paisley (GB) .... 30 C 2
Paistunturit (FIN)...... 177 F 3
Pajala (S) .... 180 C 4
Pajęczno (PL) .... 121 F 4
Páka (H) .... 128 B 4
Pakość (PL) ....117 G 5
Pakoštane (HR) ..... 136 B 5
Pakrac (HR) .... 135 G 4
Pakruojis (LT) .... 205 E 1
Paks (H) .... 129 E 4
Palacios de la Sierra (E).. 58 C 4
Palacios
   de Sanabria (E)....... 57 F 4
Palacios del Sil (E) ... 57 F 3
Paladru (I) ....51 E 3
Palafrugell (E) ....61 F 2
Palagiano (I) ....111 F 4
Palagonia (I) ....115 F 4
Palaia (I) .... 105 H 5
Palaiá Epídavros (GR) .. 165 G 5
Palaiá Krovýli (GR) .... 162 D 3
Palaíchori (CY) ....174 D 4
Palaíkastro (GR) ..... 173 F 3
Palaíkythro (CY) ..... 175 E 3
Palaiochóri (GR) ..... 172 B 3
Palaiochóri (Dytikí
   Makedonía) (GR) .... 161 E 5
Palaiochóri (Ípeiros) (GR). 164 C 1
Palaiochóri
   (Pelopónnisos) (GR).. 168 D 3
Palaiokastrítsa /
   Παλαιοκαστρίτσα (GR). 160 A 5
Palaiókastro
   (Chalkidikí) (GR) .... 161 H 4
Palaiókastro (Dytikí
   Makedonía) (GR) ..... 161 E 4
Palaiókastro
   (Sérres) (GR) .... 161 H 2
Palaiókastro
   (Stereá Elláda) (GR).. 165 E 2
Palaiokómi (GR) ..... 161 H 3
Palaiometocho (CY) ...174 D 3
Palaiópoli (GR) ...... 162 D 4
Palaiópyrgos (GR) ... 165 E 3

A B C D E F G H I J K L M N O P Q R S T U V W X Y Z

Pálairos (GR) .... 164 C 2
Palaiseau (F) .... 45 E 1
Palaiópoli (GR) .... 166 C 5
Palamás (GR) .... 165 E 1
Palamós (E) ....61 F 3
Palanga (LT) .... 204 B 2
Palas de Rei (E) .... 56 D 3
Palata (I) .... 109 H 3
Palatítsia (GR) .... 161 F 4
Palatna (SRB) .... 143 E 3
Palau (I) ....112 C 1
Palavas-les-Flots (F) .... 54 B 3
Palazzo del Pero (I) .... 107 E 4
Palazzo Pretorio (I) .. 106 D 2
Palazzo
  San Gervasio (I) ...110 D 3
Palazzolo Acreide (I) ...115 E 3
Palazzolo sull'Oglio (I) . 101 F 4
Palazzuolo sul Senio (I). 106 D 2
Paldiski (EST) .... 200 D 2
Pale (BIH) ....137 G 5
Palena (I) .... 109 G 2
Palencia (E) .... 58 A 4
Paleohóri (GR) .... 161 H 4
Palermo (I) ....114 C 4
Palestrina (I) .... 109 E 3
Palévené (LT) .... 205 F 2
Palež (BIH) .... 137 H 5
Pálháza (H) .... 127 E 4
Páli (H) .... 128 C 2
Paliá Kavála (GR) ..... 162 B 3
Paliano (I) .... 109 E 3
Palić (SRB) .... 140 C 1
Palidoro (I) .... 108 D 3
Palinges (F) .... 50 C 1
Palinuro (I) ....110 C 5
Palioúri (GR) .... 161 H 5
Paliouriá (GR) .... 161 E 5
Paliseul (B) .... 78 D 4
Palivere (EST) .... 200 C 4
Pälkäne (FIN) .... 191 G 3
Pålkem (S) .... 185 E 1
Palládio (GR) .... 165 F 5
Palluau (F) .... 43 F 5
Palma de Mallorca (E) ...67 F 3
Palma del Río (E) ..... 69 H 4
Palma
  di Montechiaro (I) ...114 D 4
Palmadula (I) ....112 A 1
Palmanova (I) .... 103 G 3
Palmela (P) .... 68 B 2
Palmi (I) ....115 H 2
Palo del Colle (I) .....111 E 3
Páloi (GR) .... 171 F 2
Palojoensuu (FIN) ..... 180 C 3
Palokki (FIN) .... 193 G 1
Palomäki (FIN) .... 187 F 5
Palomares del Campo (E). 64 D 4
Palomas (E) .... 69 G 2
Palombara Sabina (I) ... 109 E 2
Palos de la Frontera (E).. 69 E 5
Palotás (H) .... 129 F 1
Pals (E) ....61 F 2
Pålsboda (S) .... 197 E 1
Paltamo (FIN) .... 187 F 3
Paltaniemi (FIN) ...... 187 F 3
Păltiniş (RO) .... 151 F 1
Paluzza (I) .... 103 G 2
Pámfyla (GR) .... 167 F 2
Pamhagen (A) .... 97 H 2
Pamiers (F) .... 53 F 4
Pampäli (LV) .... 202 B 4
Pampilhosa da Serra (P) . 62 B 3
Pampilhosa do Botão (P). 62 B 3
Pampliega (E) .... 58 B 4
Pamplona (E) .... 59 F 2
Panagía (Anatolikí Makedonía
  kai Thráki) (GR) ... 162 C 3
Panagía (Dytikí
  Makedonía) (GR) ... 161 E 5
Panagía (Ípeiros) (GR) . 164 C 1
Panagía (Thessalia) (GR). 160 D 5
Panagia Eleosa (CY) .. 175 G 1
Panagjurište (BG) ..... 158 C 2
Panaitólio (GR) .... 164 D 3
Pancalieri (I) .... 100 C 5
Pančarevo (BG) .... 158 B 2

Pančevo /
  Панчево (SRB) ...... 140 D 4
Panciu (RO) .... 152 D 1
Pancorbo (E) .... 58 C 3
Pâncota (RO) .... 146 C 4
Pandino (I) .... 101 F 4
Pandrup (DK) .... 194 D 4
Panemunis (LT) ..... 205 G 1
Panes (E) .... 58 A 1
Panevėžys (LT) .... 205 F 2
Panga (EST) .... 200 B 3
Pangbourne (GB) ..... 35 H 2
Paničerevo (BG) ...... 159 F 2
Pankakoski (FIN) ..... 187 G 5
Pankow (D) .... 86 D 1
Pannonhalma (H) ..... 128 D 2
Pano Archimandrita (CY).174 C 4
Pano Arodes (CY) ...174 B 4
Pano Deftera (CY) ...174 D 3
Pano Dikomo (CY) ...174 D 3
Pano Lakatameia (CY)...174 D 4
Pano Lefkara (CY) ...174 D 4
Pano Panagia (CY) ...174 B 4
Pano Platres (CY) ...174 C 4
Pano Zodeia (CY) ...174 C 3
Panórama (Anatolikí Makedonía
  kai Thráki) (GR)... 161 H 2
Panórama (Kentrikí
  Makedonía) (GR)... 161 G 4
Panormítis (GR) ..... 171 H 3
Pánormos (Kríti) (GR)... 170 B 5
Pánormos
  (Nótio Aigaío) (GR) .. 166 C 5
Pantánassa (GR) ..... 169 E 4
Päntäne (FIN) .... 191 F 2
Panteleímonas (GR) ... 161 F 5
Pantelimon
  (București) (RO) ... 152 B 4
Pantelimon
  (Constanța) (RO) ... 153 F 3
Pantelleria (I) ....114 A 5
Paola (I) ....113 B 2
Pápa (H) .... 128 C 2
Páparis (GR) .... 168 D 2
Papasidero (I) ....113 B 1
Papenburg (D) ....81 E 5
Pápigko (GR) .... 160 C 5
Papilė (LT) .... 204 D 1
Papilys (LT) .... 205 F 1
Pappádes (GR) .... 165 G 2
Pappádos (GR) .... 167 F 2
Pappenheim (D) ......91 E 5
Parabita (I) ....111 H 5
Paracín (SRB) .... 143 E 3
Paracuellos de Jiloca (E). 59 F 5
Parád (H) .... 129 G 1
Paradeisiá (GR) ..... 168 C 2
Paradela (P) .... 56 C 5
Parainen / Pargas (FIN) . 191 F 5
Parajes (E) .... 57 E 2
Parakálamos (GR) .... 160 C 5
Parákoila (GR) .... 167 F 2
Paralía
  (Dytikí Ellada) (GR) ... 164 D 4
Paralía (Kentrikí
  Makedonía) (GR) ... 161 F 4
Paralía
  (Pelopónnisos) (GR) .. 169 E 3
Paralía Akrátas (GR) ... 165 E 4
Paralía Avdíron (GR) ... 162 C 3
Paralía Kotsikiás (GR)... 165 H 2
Paralía Kýmis (GR) ... 166 B 3
Paralía Saránti (GR) ... 165 G 4
Paralía Skotínas (GR) ... 161 F 5
Paralía Tyroú (GR) ... 169 E 3
Paralímni (CY) ... 175 F 3
Parálio Ástros (GR) ... 168 D 2
Paralovo (SRB) .... 143 E 4
Paramé (F) .... 43 F 1
Páramo del Sil (E) ... 57 F 3
Paramythiá (GR) ..... 164 C 1
Paranésti (GR) .... 162 C 2
Parapótamos (GR) .... 164 B 1
Pârâul Rece (RO) ..... 152 A 2
Paray-le-Monial (F)..... 50 C 1
Parchim (D) .... 82 D 4

Parczew (PL) .... 123 G 2
Pardubice (CZ) .... 92 C 2
Paredes (P) .... 62 C 1
Paredes de Coura (P) ... 56 B 5
Paredes de Nava (E) ... 58 A 4
Pareja (E) .... 64 D 2
Parekklisia (CY) ....174 D 4
Parentis-en-Born (F) ... 52 B 1
Parenzo / Poreč (HR) ... 134 A 4
Párga / Πάργα (GR)..... 164 B 1
Pargas / Parainen (FIN) . 191 F 5
Parikkala (FIN) .... 193 G 2
Paril (BG) .... 161 H 2
Parincea (RO) .... 148 D 4
Paris (F) .... 39 H 5
Parkalompolo (S) ..... 180 C 4
Parkano (FIN) .... 191 F 2
Parla (E) .... 64 B 3
Parlavà (E) ....61 F 2
Parma (I) .... 105 G 2
Parndorf (A) .... 97 H 2
Pärnu (EST) .... 200 D 3
Pärnu-Jaagupi (EST)... 200 D 3
Parola (FIN) .... 191 G 3
Páros / Πάρος (GR) ... 170 C 1
Parpariá (GR) .... 167 E 3
Parsberg (D) ....91 F 5
Pârscov (RO) .... 152 C 2
Parsdorf (D) .... 95 G 2
Partakko (FIN) .... 177 G 4
Partanna (I) ....114 C 3
Partenen (A) .... 95 E 4
Parthenay (F) .... 48 D 1
Parthéni (GR) .... 171 F 1
Partinico (I) ....114 C 2
Partizani (BG) .... 159 H 1
Partizani (SRB) ...... 140 D 5
Partizánske (SK) ..... 132 B 2
Partizanske Vode (SRB). 139 G 1
Partney (GB) .... 33 G 3
Pârvenec (BG) .... 158 D 3
Pârvomaj (BG) .... 161 G 2
Pârvomaj /
  Първомай (BG) ..... 159 E 3
Pas de la Casa (AND) ... 60 C 1
Pas-en-Artois (F) ..... 39 H 3
Pasaia (E) .... 59 E 1
Pasarel (BG) .... 158 B 2
Paşcani (RO) .... 148 C 3
Pasewalk (D) .... 83 G 4
Pasikovci (HR) .... 135 G 4
Pasłęk (PL) ....118 C 2
Pašman (HR) .... 136 B 5
Passais (F) .... 43 G 2
Passau (D) .... 96 C 1
Passignano
  sul Trasimeno (I) ... 107 E 4
Pastavy (BY) ....6 D 4
Pastrana (E) .... 64 D 2
Păstrovo (BG) .... 159 E 2
Pasvalys (LT) .... 205 F 1
Pašvitinys (LT) ...... 205 E 1
Pasym (PL) ....118 D 3
Pásztó (H) .... 129 G 1
Patalenica (BG) ...... 158 C 3
Pătârlagele (RO) ..... 152 C 2
Patay (F) .... 44 D 3
Pateley Bridge (GB) ... 33 E 1
Paterna de Rivera (E)...74 B 4
Paternion (A) .... 96 C 5
Paternò (I) ....115 F 3
Paternopoli (I) ....110 B 3
Patersdorf (D) ....91 G 5
Patiópoulo (GR) ..... 164 D 2
Patitíri (GR) .... 166 A 1
Pátmos (GR) .... 171 E 1
Patos (AL) .... 144 C 3
Pátra / Πάτρα (GR) ... 165 E 4
Patreksfjörður (IS) ... 178 A 2
Patrikí (CY) .... 175 F 2
Patrington (GB) ...... 33 G 2
Pattada (I) ....112 C 2
Patterdale (GB) ....31 E 5
Patti (I) ....115 F 2
Pattijoki (FIN) ...... 185 G 3
Pătulele (RO) .... 150 D 4

Pau (F) .... 52 C 3
Pauillac (F) .... 48 C 4
Paúl (P) .... 62 D 3
Paularo (I) .... 103 G 2
Paulhaguet (F) .... 50 B 4
Păulis (RO) .... 146 C 5
Paullo (I) .... 101 E 4
Păunești (RO) .... 148 D 5
Pavel (BG) .... 156 B 2
Pavel Banja (BG) ..... 159 E 2
Pavia (I) .... 101 E 5
Pavia (P) .... 68 C 1
Pavilly (F) .... 39 F 4
Pavino Polje (MNE) ... 139 G 3
Păvliani (GR) .... 165 F 3
Pavlica (SRB) .... 142 D 2
Pavlikeni (BG) .... 156 B 3
Pavlovce nad Uhom (SK). 133 H 3
Pavlovskij Posad (RUS) .7 G 2
Pavullo nel Frignano (I) . 105 H 3
Paxoí (GR) .... 164 B 1
Payerne (CH) .... 98 C 3
Paymogo (E) .... 68 D 4
Payrac (F) .... 49 F 5
Pazardžik /
  Пазарджик (BG) .... 158 D 3
Pazin / Pisino (HR) ... 134 A 4
Pazo de Irixoa (E)....... 56 C 2
Pčelinovo (BG) .... 159 F 1
Pčelnik (BG) .... 157 F 3
Pcoliné (SK) .... 133 H 2
Peal de Becerro (E) ... 71 E 4
Peć / Pejë (SRB) ..... 139 H 4
Pec pod Sněžkou (CZ)... 87 G 5
Peccia (CH) .... 99 E 4
Peccioli (I) .... 105 G 5
Peceneaga (RO) .... 153 E 2
Pečenjevce (SRB) .... 143 F 3
Pechea (RO) .... 153 E 1
Pecica (RO) .... 146 B 5
Pećigrad (BIH) .... 135 E 5
Pećinci (SRB) .... 140 C 4
Peciu Nou (RO) ...... 150 B 1
Pecka (SRB) .... 140 B 5
Peckelsheim (D) ..... 85 F 3
Pécs (H) .... 128 D 5
Pécsely (H) .... 128 D 3
Pécsvárad (H) .... 129 E 5
Pečurice (MNE) ...... 139 G 5
Pedaso (I) .... 107 H 4
Pedersker (DK) ...... 199 G 4
Pedersöre /
  Pedersören k (FIN) ... 185 F 5
Pedersören k /
  Pedersöre (FIN) ... 185 F 5
Pedoulas (CY) ....174 C 4
Pedrafita
  do Cebreiro (E) ... 57 E 3
Pedrajas
  de San Esteban (E) ... 58 A 5
Pedralba (E) .... 65 H 4
Pedralba
  de la Pradería (E) ... 57 E 5
Pedras Salgadas (P) ... 62 D 1
Pedraza (E) .... 64 B 1
Pedrera (E) .... 70 B 5
Pedro Abad (E) .... 70 C 4
Pedro Bernardo (E) ... 63 H 4
Pedro Muñoz (E) ..... 64 D 5
Pedrógão (P) .... 68 D 3
Pedrógão (P) .... 62 A 4
Pedrógão Grande (P) ... 62 C 4
Pedrola (E) .... 59 G 4
Peebles (GB) ....31 E 2
Peel (GB) .... 30 C 5
Peenemünde (D) ...... 83 G 2
Pefkári (GR) .... 162 C 3
Pefki (GR) .... 165 G 2
Péfkos (GR) .... 160 C 4
Pega (P) .... 63 E 3
Pegalajar (E) .... 70 D 4
Pegau (D) .... 86 B 4
Pegeia (CY) ....174 B 4
Pegli (I) .... 104 D 3
Pegnitz (D) ....91 E 3

Pego (E) .... 66 A 5
Pegognaga (I) .... 101 H 5
Pegolotte (I) .... 103 E 5
Peguera (E) ....67 E 3
Pehčevo (MK) .... 145 H 1
Peine (D) .... 85 H 2
Peio (I) .... 101 H 2
Peïra-Cava (F) .... 55 H 1
Peiraiás / Πειραιας (GR). 165 H 4
Peißenberg (D) .... 95 F 3
Peiting (D) .... 95 F 3
Peitz (D) .... 87 E 2
Pejë / Peć (SRB) ..... 139 H 4
Pelagićevo (BIH) ..... 137 G 3
Pelasgía (GR) .... 165 G 2
Pélekas (GR) .... 160 A 5
Pelendri (CY) ....174 C 4
Peletá (GR) .... 169 E 3
Pelhřimov (CZ) .... 92 C 4
Pelkosenniemi (FIN) ... 181 F 4
Pellegrino Parmense (I). 105 F 2
Pellérd (H) .... 128 D 5
Pellesmäki (FIN) ..... 193 F 1
Pello (FIN) .... 180 D 5
Pelovo (BG) .... 155 E 2
Pelplin (PL) ....117 H 3
Peltosalmi (FIN) ..... 187 E 5
Peltovuoma (FIN) ... 177 E 5
Pélussin (F) .... 50 D 3
Pembroke (GB) ..... 25 H 5
Pembroke Dock (GB) .... 25 H 5
Pen-y-bont /
  Bridgend (GB) .... 34 D 2
Penacova (P) .... 62 B 3
Penafiel (E) .... 58 B 5
Penafiel (P) .... 62 C 1
Penalva do Castelo (P) . 62 D 2
Penamacor (P) .... 62 D 4
Peñaranda
  de Bracamonte (E) .... 63 H 2
Peñaranda de Duero (E). 58 C 5
Peñarroya-
  Pueblonuevo (E) ... 69 H 3
Penarth (GB) .... 35 E 2
Peñas de San Pedro (E).. 71 G 2
Peñascosa (E) .... 71 G 2
Peñausende (E) ...... 63 G 1
Pendine (GB) .... 34 C 1
Penedono (P) .... 62 D 2
Penela (P) .... 62 B 4
Pénestin (F) .... 43 E 4
Penhas da Saúde (P) ... 62 D 3
Penhas Juntas (P) ... 57 E 5
Peniche (P) .... 62 A 5
Penicuik (GB) ....31 E 2
Penig (D) .... 86 C 3
Peníscola /
  Peñíscola (E) ...... 66 B 1
Penkovci (BG) .... 158 A 2
Penkun (D) .... 83 G 4
Penmaenmawr (GB)... 32 B 3
Penne (I) .... 109 G 1
Penne-d'Agenais (F) ... 53 E 2
Penrhyndeudraeth (GB). 32 B 4
Penrith (GB) ....31 E 4
Penryn (GB) .... 34 B 5
Pentageia (CY) ....174 C 4
Pentagioí (GR) .... 165 E 3
Pentakomo (CY) ....174 D 4
Pentálofo (GR) ...... 164 D 3
Pentálofos (GR) ..... 160 D 4
Pénte Vrýses (GR) ... 161 G 3
Pentéli (GR) .... 165 H 4
Penteória (GR) .... 165 F 3
Pentrofoelas (GB) ... 32 B 3
Penzance (GB) .... 34 B 5
Penzberg (D) .... 95 F 3
Pénzesgyőr (H) ..... 128 C 3
Penzlin (D) .... 83 F 4
Pér (H) .... 128 D 1
Pera (CY) ....174 D 4
Pera Chorio (CY) ....174 D 3
Perä-Posio (FIN) ... 187 E 1

Perachóra (GR) .... 165 G 4
Peraía (Pélla) (GR) ... 161 E 3
Peraía
  (Thessaloníki) (GR) ... 161 E 4
Peraleda del Zaucejo (E) . 69 H 2
Peralejos
  de las Truchas (E)..... 65 F 2
Perales de Tajuña (E) ... 64 C 3
Perales del Alfambra (E). 65 G 2
Perales del Puerto (E) ... 63 E 4
Peralta (E) .... 59 F 3
Peralta de Alcofea (E) ... 60 A 3
Peralva (P) .... 68 D 5
Pérama (GR) .... 160 C 5
Pérama /
  Πέραμα (Attikí) (GR). . 165 H 4
Pérama (Iónia Nisiá) (GR). 160 A 5
Pérama (Ípeiros) (GR)... 160 C 5
Pérama (Kríti) (GR) ... 170 B 5
Peranka (FIN) .... 187 F 2
Perast (MNE) .... 139 F 4
Peratáta (GR) .... 164 B 4
Perbál (H) .... 129 E 1
Percy-
  en-Normandie (F)... 38 C 5
Pérdika (Attikí) (GR)... 165 H 5
Pérdika (Ioánnina) (GR). 164 C 1
Pérdika
  (Thesprotía) (GR) ... 164 B 1
Pérdikkas (GR) .... 161 E 3
Peregu Mare (RO) ... 146 B 5
Perejaslav-
  Chmel'nyc'kyj (UA) ....13 F 1
Pereruela (E) .... 63 G 1
Pereslavl'-Zalesskij (RUS) .7 G 1
Peretu (RO) .... 151 G 2
Pergine Valsugana (I) ... 101 H 3
Pergola (I) .... 107 F 3
Perho (FIN) .... 185 G 5
Periam (RO) .... 146 A 5
Periana (E) ....75 E 3
Périers (F) .... 38 B 5
Périgueux (F) .... 49 E 4
Períkleia (GR) .... 161 F 2
Perino (I) .... 101 F 5
Periş (RO) .... 152 B 3
Perişor (RO) .... 151 E 4
Períssa (GR) .... 170 C 3
Peristerá (GR) .... 161 G 4
Peristerona
  (Ammóchostos) (CY) ..174 E 3
Peristerona
  (Lefkoşa) (CY) ....174 D 3
Peristerona (Páfos) (CY).174 B 4
Perívlepto (GR) ..... 165 F 1
Perivóli (Dytikí
  Makedonía) (GR) ... 160 D 5
Perivóli
  (Stereá Elláda) (GR) ... 165 E 2
Perivólia (CY) ... 175 E 4
Perivolia (CY) ... 170 A 5
Perjasica (HR) .... 134 D 4
Perkáta (H) .... 129 E 3
Perković (HR) .... 138 B 2
Perleberg (D) .... 82 D 5
Perlez (SRB) .... 140 D 3
Përmet (AL) .... 144 D 4
Pernå / Pernaja (FIN) ... 193 E 4
Pernaja / Pernå (FIN) ... 193 E 4
Pernarava (LT) ...... 205 E 3
Pernarec (CZ) ....91 H 3
Pernek (SK) .... 132 A 4
Pernes-les-Fontaines (F). 54 D 1
Pernik / Перник (BG) ... 158 B 2
Perniö (FIN) .... 191 G 5
Pernitz (A) .... 97 G 2
Péronne (F) .... 40 A 3
Perosa Argentina (I) ... 100 B 5
Pérouges (F) .... 50 D 2
Perperek (BG) .... 162 D 1
Perperikon (BG) ...... 159 F 4
Perpignan (F) .... 53 H 4
Perrero (I) .... 100 B 5
Perreux (F) .... 50 C 2
Perros-Guirec (F) ... 42 C 1

Persenbeug (A) 97 E2
Pershore (GB) 35 G1
Perstorp (S) 199 F3
Perth (GB) 31 E1
Pertisau (A) 95 G3
Pertoča (SLO) 135 E1
Pertoúli (GR) 164 D1
Pertteli (FIN) 191 G4
Pertuis (F) 55 E2
Pertunmaa (FIN) 193 E3
Pertusa (E) 59 H4
Perućac Vrelo (SRB) ... 139 G1
Perugia (I) 107 F3
Perušić (HR) 134 D5
Peruštica (BG) 158 D3
Péruwelz (B) 78 B3
Pervenchères (F) 44 B2
Pervomajs'k (UA) 13 G2
Pesaro (I) 107 F3
Pescara (I) 109 G1
Pescasseroli (I) 109 G3
Pesceana (RO) 151 F3
Peschici (I) 110 D1
Peschiera del Garda (I) . 101 H4
Pescia (I) 105 G4
Pescina (I) 109 F2
Pescocostanzo (I) 109 G3
Pescolanciano (I) 109 G3
Pescopagano (I) 110 C4
Pescorocchiano (I) 109 E2
Peshkopi (AL) 144 D1
Pesiökylä (FIN) 187 F2
Pesmes (F) 47 E4
Peso da Régua (P) 62 D1
Pesočani (MK) 145 E2
Pesoz (E) 57 E2
Pessáni (GR) 163 E2
Peštani (MK) 145 E2
Peštera (BG) 158 D3
Peştişani (RO) 151 E2
Pestovo (RUS) 7 F1
Pešurići (BIH) 137 H5
Petačinci (SRB) 143 H3
Petäjäskoski (FIN) 185 G1
Petäjävesi (FIN) 191 H2
Petalax (FIN) 191 E1
Petalídi (GR) 168 C3
Pétange (L) 79 E5
Pétas (GR) 164 C2
Peterborough (GB) 33 G4
Peterhead (GB) 29 H3
Peterlee (GB) 31 G4
Petersfield (GB) 35 H3
Petershagen (D) 85 F1
Pétervására (H) 129 G1
Pethelinós (GR) 161 H3
Petilia Policastro (I) . 113 C3
Petina (I) 110 C4
Petite-Rosselle (F) ... 41 F4
Petka (SRB) 143 F4
Petkeljärven
  kansallispuisto (FIN) . 187 H5
Petko Karavelovo (BG) . 156 C2
Petkula (FIN) 181 E3
Petlovača (SRB) 140 B4
Petoúsi (GR) 164 C1
Petra (CY) 174 C3
Petra (E) 67 H2
Pétra (GR) 167 E1
Petralia Sottana (I) .. 115 E3
Petrálona (GR) 161 G4
Petraná (GR) 161 E2
Petrčane (HR) 136 B4
Petrel / Petrer (E) ... 73 E2
Petrer / Petrel (E) ... 73 E2
Petreto-Bicchisano (F) . 55 H5
Petric (BG) 158 C2
Petrič / Петрич (BG) .. 161 G2
Petrijevci (HR) 137 G1
Petrila (RO) 151 E1
Petrína (GR) 168 C2
Petrinja (HR) 135 E4
Petriş (RO) 146 D5
Pétrola (E) 71 H2
Petróna (GR) 164 D2
Petroşani (RO) 151 E1
Petroússa (GR) 162 B2

Petrova (RO) 147 G1
Petrovac (MNE) 139 F5
Petrovac (SRB) 141 E5
Petrovaradin (SRB) 140 C3
Petrovčić (SRB) 140 C4
Petrovec (MK) 143 F5
Petrovice (CZ) 92 A4
Pettenbach (A) 96 D2
Pettigoe (IRL) 23 E3
Petworth (GB) 38 D1
Peuerbach (A) 96 C1
Peura (FIN) 185 G1
Pewsey (GB) 35 G2
Peyrat-le-Château (F) . 49 G3
Peyrehorade (F) 52 B2
Peyrepertuse,
  château de (F) 53 H4
Peyriac-Minervois (F) . 53 H3
Peyrolles-
  en-Provence (F) 55 E2
Peyruis (F) 55 E1
Pézenas (F) 54 A3
Pezinok (SK) 132 A4
Pezoúla (GR) 162 C3
Pfaffenhofen
  an der Ilm (D) 95 G1
Pfäffikon (CH) 99 E2
Pfalzgrafenweiler (D) . 89 E5
Pfarrkirchen (D) 96 B1
Pfeffenhausen (D) 95 G1
Pforzheim (D) 89 E4
Pfreimd (D) 91 F4
Pfronten (D) 95 E3
Pfullendorf (D) 94 C2
Pfullingen (D) 89 F5
Pfunds-Dorf (A) 95 E4
Pfungstadt (D) 89 E2
Phalsbourg (F) 41 G5
Philippeville (B) 78 C4
Philippsreut (D) 91 H5
Piacenza (I) 101 F5
Piadena (I) 101 G5
Piana (F) 55 G4
Piana degli Albanesi (I) . 114 C2
Piancastagnaio (I) 106 D5
Piancavallo (I) 103 F3
Piandelagotti (I) 105 G3
Pianella (I) 109 G2
Piano del Cansiglio (I) . 103 F3
Piano del Voglio (I) .. 105 H3
Pianoro (I) 106 D2
Piansano (I) 108 C1
Pias (P) 68 D2
Piaseczno (PL) 122 D1
Piaski (Lublin) (PL) .. 123 G3
Piaski
  (Mierzeja Wiślana) (PL) . 118 C1
Piątek (PL) 122 B1
Piątnica
  Poduchowna (PL) 119 F4
Piatra (RO) 151 H5
Piatra-Neamţ (RO) 148 B3
Piatra-Olt (RO) 151 G4
Piazza al Serchio (I) . 105 G3
Piazza Armerina (I) ... 115 E4
Piazza Brembana (I) ... 101 F3
Piazzola sul Brenta (I) . 103 E4
Piber (A) 97 F4
Pibeste (F) 52 D4
Pićan (HR) 134 B4
Picassent / Picasent (E) . 65 H5
Picasent / Picassent (E) . 65 H5
Picerno (I) 110 C4
Pickering (GB) 31 H5
Pico (I) 109 F4
Picquigny (F) 39 H3
Piechowice (PL) 120 C4
Piecki (PL) 119 E3
Piedicavallo (I) 100 C3
Piedicroce (F) 55 H4
Piediluco (I) 109 E1
Piedimonte Matese (I) . 109 H4
Piedra,
  monasterio de (E) ... 65 H3
Piedrabuena (E) 70 C1
Piedrafita de Babia (E) . 57 F2

Piedrahíta (E) 63 H3
Piedralaves (E) 64 A3
Piedras Albas (E) 63 E4
Piedratajada (E) 59 G4
Piekoszów (PL) 122 C4
Pieksämäki (FIN) 193 F1
Pielavesi (FIN) 187 E5
Pieniężno (PL) 118 C2
Piennes (F) 41 E4
Pieńsk (PL) 120 C3
Pienza (I) 106 D4
Pierowall (GB) 26 C1
Pierre-Buffière (F) ... 49 F3
Pierre-de-Bresse (F) .. 46 D5
Pierrefitte-Nestalas (F) . 52 D4
Pierrefitte-sur-Aire (F) . 40 D5
Pierrefonds (F) 40 A4
Pierrefontaine-
  les-Varans (F) 47 F4
Pierrefort (F) 50 A5
Pierrelatte (F) 54 C1
Pieskowa Skała (PL) ... 122 B5
Piešťany (SK) 132 B3
Pieszyce (PL) 121 E5
Pietarsaari /
  Jakobstad (FIN) 185 F5
Pietra Ligure (I) 104 D3
Pietralunga (I) 107 F4
Pietraperzia (I) 115 E4
Pietrari (RO) 151 F2
Pietrasanta (I) 105 G4
Pietroasa (RO) 146 D4
Pietroşani (RO) 152 A5
Pieve del Cairo (I) ... 101 E5
Pieve di Bono (I) 101 G3
Pieve di Cadore (I) ... 103 F2
Pieve di Soligo (I) ... 103 F3
Pieve di Teco (I) 104 C3
Pieve Santo Stefano (I) . 107 E3
Pievepelago (I) 105 G3
Pigádi (GR) 165 G2
Pigés (GR) 164 D1
Pigna (I) 104 C4
Pihlajaveden as (FIN) . 191 G1
Pihlava (FIN) 191 E3
Pihtipudas (FIN) 185 H5
Piikkiö (FIN) 191 F4
Piippola (FIN) 185 H4
Piispajärvi (FIN) 187 F2
Pikeliai (LT) 204 C1
Pikérmi (GR) 165 H4
Piła (PL) 117 E4
Pilas (E) 69 F5
Pilat-Plage (F) 48 B5
Pilawa (PL) 123 E2
Piława Górna (PL) 121 E5
Piles (E) 66 A4
Pilica (PL) 122 B5
Pílio (GR) 165 H3
Pilis (H) 129 F2
Pilisszentkereszt (H) . 129 E1
Pilisvörösvár (H) 129 E1
Pilštanj (SLO) 134 D2
Pilviškiai (LT) 204 D4
Pilzno (PL) 127 E1
Piña de Campos (E) 58 A3
Pina de Ebro (E) 59 H5
Pincehely (H) 129 E3
Pińczów (PL) 122 C5
Pineda de la Sierra (E) . 58 C3
Pineda de Mar (E) 61 E3
Pinerolo (I) 100 B5
Pineto (I) 107 H5
Piney (F) 45 H2
Pingeyri (IS) 176 A2
Pinguente / Buzet (HR) . 134 B4
Pingvellir (IS) 178 B3
Pinhal Novo (P) 68 B2
Pinhão (P) 62 B2
Pinheiro (P) 56 C5
Pinhel (P) 63 E2
Pinkafeld (A) 97 G3
Pinneberg (D) 81 H4
Pinnow (D) 87 H2
Pino (F) 55 H2
Pino de la Virgen (E) . 67 E5

Pinofranqueado (E) 63 F3
Pinols (F) 50 B4
Pinos Puente (E) 70 D5
Pinsk (BY) 6 D5
Pintamo (FIN) 187 E2
Pinto (E) 64 B3
Pinzano
  al Tagliamento (I) .. 103 G3
Pinzolo (I) 101 H3
Piobbico (I) 107 F3
Piombino (I) 106 C5
Pione (I) 105 F2
Pionki (PL) 123 E3
Pionsat (F) 49 H2
Piotrków Kujawski (PL) . 118 A5
Piotrków
  Trybunalski (PL) 122 B3
Piove di Sacco (I) 103 E5
Piovene Rocchette (I) . 102 D3
Pipriac (F) 43 E3
Piran / Pirano (SLO) .. 134 A3
Pirano / Piran (SLO) .. 134 A3
Pirdop (BG) 158 C1
Piriac-sur-Mer (F) 43 E4
Pirin (BG) 161 H1
Pirkkala (FIN) 191 G3
Pirmasens (D) 88 D3
Pirna (D) 87 E4
Pirok (MK) 143 E5
Pirot / Пирот (SRB) ... 143 G2
Pirovac (HR) 136 C5
Pirttikoski (FIN) 181 F5
Pisa (I) 105 G4
Pischia (RO) 146 B5
Pisciotta (I) 110 C5
Pişcolt (RO) 146 D2
Piscu Vechi (RO) 151 E5
Písek (CZ) 92 A4
Pisino / Pazin (HR) ... 134 A4
Piskokéfalo (GR) 173 F3
Piškorevci (HR) 135 H4
Pismenovo (BG) 157 F5
Pisodéri (GR) 160 D3
Pisogne (I) 101 G3
Písses (GR) 166 B5
Pissónas (GR) 165 H3
Pissos (F) 52 C1
Pissouri (CY) 174 C5
Pisticci (I) 111 E4
Pistoia (I) 105 H4
Pisz (PL) 119 E3
Piszczac (PL) 123 G1
Piteå (S) 185 E2
Piteşti (RO) 151 H3
Pithiviers (F) 45 E2
Pitigliano (I) 106 D5
Pitlochry (GB) 29 F5
Pitmedden Garden (GB) . 29 H3
Pitomača (HR) 135 G3
Pittenween (GB) 31 E1
Pitvaros (H) 129 H4
Pivka (SLO) 134 B3
Pivnica (HR) 135 G3
Pivnice (SRB) 140 B2
Piwniczna (PL) 125 H2
Pizarra (E) 74 D3
Pizzighettone (I) 101 F5
Pizzo (I) 115 H1
Pizzoli (I) 109 F2
P'jatychatky (UA) 13 G1
Plabennec (F) 42 B1
Plačkovci (BG) 159 F1
Plaisance (F) 52 D2
Pláka
  (Pelopónnisos) (GR) . 169 E3
Pláka
  (Vóreio Aigaío) (GR) . 162 D5
Pláka Litochórou (GR) . 161 F5
Plakiás (GR) 172 C3
Plan-d'Aups (F) 55 E3
Planá (CZ) 91 G3
Plancoët (F) 43 E1
Plandište /
  Пландище (SRB) 141 E3
Planina (Jesenice) (SLO) . 134 B1

Planina
  (Ljubljana) (SLO) ... 134 B3
Planina pri Sevnici (SLO) . 134 D2
Planinica (SRB) 143 G1
Plános (GR) 164 C5
Plas Newydd (GB) 32 A3
Plasencia (E) 63 F4
Plaški (HR) 134 D4
Plăstina (BG) 159 G1
Plasy (CZ) 91 H3
Platamona Lido (I) 112 B1
Platamónas (GR) 162 C2
Platánia (Anatolikí Makedonía
  kai Thráki) (GR) 168 C2
Plataniá
  (Pelopónnisos) (GR) . 162 B2
Plataniá
  (Thessalía) (GR) 165 G2
Platánia (GR) 172 B3
Platanístasa (CY) 174 D4
Platanistása (GR) 166 C4
Platanítis (GR) 165 E3
Plátanos (Chaniá) (GR) . 172 A3
Plátanos (Irákleio) (GR) . 172 D4
Plátanos
  (Thessalía) (GR) 165 F2
Platariá (GR) 164 B1
Plateau-d'Assy (F) 51 G2
Platiána (GR) 164 D5
Platičevo (SRB) 140 C4
Platja d'Aro (E) 61 F3
Platja i
  Grau de Gandia (E) .. 66 A4
Platys Gialós
  (Iónia Nisí) (GR) ... 164 B4
Platys Gialós
  (Mílos) (GR) 169 H3
Platys Gialós
  (Mýkonos) (GR) 170 C1
Platýstomo (GR) 165 E2
Plau am See (D) 83 E4
Plaue (D) 86 B1
Plauen (D) 86 B5
Plav (MNE) 139 H4
Plavča (HR) 134 D5
Plaviņas (LV) 203 F3
Plavna (SRB) 141 G5
Plavnica (MNE) 139 G5
Plavsk (RUS) 7 G3
Playa Blanca (E) 67 H4
Pleaux (F) 49 H4
Pleine-Fougères (F) ... 43 F1
Pleinfeld (D) 91 E5
Plejsy (SK) 133 F3
Plélan-le-Grand (F) ... 43 E3
Plélan-le-Petit (F) ... 43 E2
Pléneuf-Val-André (F) . 43 E1
Plenița (RO) 151 E4
Plentzia (E) 58 D1
Plépi (GR) 169 F2
Plešin (MNE) 142 D2
Plešivec (SK) 133 F3
Plessis Bourré,
  château du (F) 43 H4
Plestin-les-Grèves (F) . 42 C1
Pleszew (PL) 121 F2
Pleternica (HR) 135 H4
Plettenberg (D) 84 D4
Pleumartin (F) 49 E1
Pleumeur-Bodou (F) 42 C1
Pleven (BG) 156 A2
Pleyben (F) 42 C2
Pliego (E) 71 H4
Pliska (BG) 157 E2
Plitvička jezera (HR) . 134 D5
Plitvički Ljeskovac (HR) . 134 D5
Pljevlja / Ужице (MNE) . 139 G2
Ploaghe (I) 112 B2
Ploče (HR) 138 D3
Plochingen (D) 89 F4
Płock (PL) 118 C5
Plodovitovo (BG) 159 G3
Ploemeur (F) 42 C3

Ploërmel (F) 43 E3
Plœuc-sur-Lié (F) 42 D2
Ploieşti (RO) 152 B3
Plomári / Πλωμάρι (GR) . 167 F2
Plombières-les-Bains (F) . 47 F3
Plomin (HR) 134 B4
Plön (D) 82 B3
Plonéour-Lanvern (F) .. 42 B3
Płońsk (PL) 118 D5
Plopeni (RO) 152 B3
Plosca (RO) 151 H5
Płoty (PL) 116 C3
Plouagat (F) 42 D1
Plouaret (F) 42 C1
Plouay (F) 42 C3
Ploubalay (F) 43 E1
Ploudalmézeau (F) 42 B1
Plouescat (F) 42 B1
Plougasnou (F) 42 C1
Plougastel-Daoulas (F) . 42 B2
Plougonven (F) 42 C1
Plouguenast (F) 42 D2
Plouha (F) 42 D1
Plouigneau (F) 42 C1
Ploumanac'h (F) 42 C1
Plouzévédé (F) 42 B1
Plovdiv / Пловдив (BG) . 158 D3
Plumbridge (GB) 23 E2
Plungė (LT) 204 C2
Pl'ussa (RUS) 6 D1
Pluvigner (F) 42 D3
Plužine (BIH) 139 E2
Plužine (MNE) 139 F3
Plymouth (GB) 34 D4
Plympton (GB) 34 D4
Plymstock (GB) 34 D4
Plýtra (GR) 169 E4
Plzeň (CZ) 91 H3
Pniewo (PL) 116 B4
Pniewy (PL) 120 D1
Pobiedziska (PL) 121 F1
Pobierowo (PL) 116 C2
Poboru (RO) 151 G3
Pobrđe (SRB) 142 D3
Počep (RUS) 7 F4
Pöchlarn (A) 97 F1
Počinok (RUS) 7 F3
Počitelj (BIH) 138 D3
Pocking (D) 96 C1
Pocsaj (H) 131 F2
Počuta (SRB) 140 C5
Poda (MNE) 139 H3
Podajva (BG) 152 C5
Podareš (MK) 145 H1
Podari (RO) 151 F4
Podbořany (CZ) 91 H2
Podbrezová (SK) 132 D3
Podčetrtek (SLO) 134 D2
Poddębice (PL) 121 H2
Poděbrady (CZ) 92 B2
Podensac (F) 48 D5
Podersdorf am See (A) . 97 H2
Podgajci Posavski (HR) . 137 H3
Podgarić (HR) 135 F3
Podgora (HR) 138 C3
Podgorač (HR) 135 H4
Podgorac (SRB) 143 F1
Podgorica (MNE) 139 G4
Podgrad (SLO) 134 B3
Podhoroď (SK) 133 H3
Podhum (BIH) 138 C1
Podkoren (SLO) 134 A1
Podkova (BG) 162 D2
Podlejki (PL) 118 C2
Podlugovi (BIH) 137 G5
Podnovlje (BIH) 135 H5
Podochóri (GR) 162 B3
Podogorá (GR) 164 D2
Podolínec (SK) 133 F2
Podol'sk (RUS) 7 G2
Podpeč (SLO) 134 B2
Podrašnica (BIH) 137 E4
Podravski Kloštar (HR) . 135 G3
Podromanija (BIH) 137 H5
Podsreda (SLO) 134 D2
Podsused (HR) 135 E3
Podturen (HR) 135 F1

A
B
C
D
E
F
G
H
I
J
K
L
M
N
O
P
Q
R
S
T
U
V
W
X
Y
Z

A B C D E F G H I J K L M N O P Q R S T U V W X Y Z

Podu Iloaiei (RO) .... 148 D 3
Podu Turcului (RO) .... 148 D 5
Podujevë / Podujevo... 143 E 3
Podujevo /
  Podujevë (SRB) .... 143 E 3
Podunavci (SRB) .... 142 D 2
Poeni (RO) .... 151 H 4
Poggibonsi (I) .... 105 H 5
Poggio Imperiale (I)...110 C 1
Poggio Mirteto (I) ..... 109 E 2
Poggio Renatico (I) .... 106 D 1
Poggio Rusco (I) ...... 101 H 5
Pöggstall (A) .... 97 F 1
Pogoanele (RO) .... 152 D 3
Pogonianí (GR) .... 160 B 5
Pogorzela (PL) .... 121 F 2
Pogradec (AL) .... 144 D 3
Pogrodzie (PL) ....118 C 2
Pohja / Pojo (FIN) ...... 191 G 5
Pohja-Lankila (FIN) ..... 193 G 2
Pohjaslahti (FIN) .... 185 H 1
Pohjaslahti (FIN) .... 191 G 2
Pohlitz (D) .... 87 E 2
Pohořelice (CZ) .... 93 E 5
Poiana Brașov (RO) ..... 152 A 1
Poiana Lacului (RO) .... 151 G 3
Poiana Mare (RO) ..... 151 E 5
Poiana Mărului (RO)... 150 D 2
Poiana Sibiului (RO) ... 151 F 1
Poibrene (BG) .... 158 C 2
Poienari (RO) .... 151 G 2
Poienești (RO) .... 148 D 4
Poienile
  de Sub Munte (RO) ... 147 G 1
Poio de Arriba (E) ...... 56 B 3
Poirino (I) .... 100 C 5
Poissons (F) .... 46 D 2
Poissy (F) .... 39 G 5
Poitiers (F) .... 49 E 1
Poix-de-Picardie (F) .... 39 G 4
Poix-Terron (F) .... 40 C 4
Pojate (SRB) .... 143 E 1
Pojejena (RO) .... 150 B 3
Pojo / Pohja (FIN) ..... 191 G 5
Pokka (FIN) .... 181 E 3
Poklečani (BIH) .... 138 D 2
Pokój (PL) .... 121 F 4
Pokupsko (HR) .... 135 E 4
Pola / Pula (HR) ...... 134 A 5
Pola de Allande (E) .... 57 F 2
Pola de Laviana (E) .... 57 G 2
Pola de Lena (E) ...... 57 G 2
Pola de Siero (E) ...... 57 G 2
Polače (HR) .... 138 D 4
Polack (BY) ....6 D 3
Polán (E) .... 64 B 4
Polanica-Zdrój (PL) ... 121 E 5
Połaniec (PL) .... 123 E 5
Polanów (PL) ....117 E 2
Polcenigo (I) .... 103 F 3
Połczyn-Zdrój (PL) ...116 D 2
Polegate (GB) .... 36 D 5
Polemi (CY) ....174 B 4
Polesella (I) ...... 103 E 5
Polessk (RUS) ....6 B 4
Polgárdi (H) .... 128 D 3
Polhov Gradec (SLO) ... 134 B 2
Policastro Bussentino (I) ...110 C 5
Police (PL) ....116 B 3
Polichnítos /
  Πολιχνίτος (GR) ... 167 E 2
Polička (CZ) .... 92 D 3
Poličnik (HR) .... 136 B 4
Policoro (I) ....111 E 5
Polignano a Mare (I).....111 F 3
Poligny (F) ....47 E 5
Polikraište (BG) ..... 156 C 3
Polis (CY) ....174 B 4
Polistena (I) ....115 H 1
Politiká (GR) .... 165 H 3
Poljana (SLO) ..... 134 C 1
Poljana (SRB) ....141 E 4
Poljana Pakračka (HR) .. 135 F 4
Poljanovo (BG) ..... 159 F 3
Poljčane (SLO) ......134 D 2
Polje (BIH) .... 135 H 5

Poljica (HR) .... 138 C 3
Poljice (BIH)........... 137 G 4
Polkowice (PL) ..... 120 D 3
Polla (I) ....110 C 4
Pölläkkä (FIN) ...... 193 G 1
Pollara, Spiaggia di (I) ..115 F 1
Pöllau (A) .... 97 G 3
Polle (D) .... 85 F 2
Pollença (E) ....67 F 2
Pollfoss (N) .... 188 D 2
Pollos (E) .... 63 H 1
Polmak (N)......... 177 G 3
Polonne (UA) ....13 E 1
Polperro (GB) ...... 34 C 4
Polski Gradec (BG) .... 159 G 3
Polski Trambeš (BG) .. 156 C 2
Poltár (SK) .... 133 E 3
Poltava (UA) ....13 G 1
Põltsamaa (EST).... 201 F 3
Põlva (EST)........ 201 G 4
Polvijärvi (FIN) ..... 187 G 5
Polýdrosos (GR) ... 165 F 3
Polýgyros /
  Πολύγυρος (GR) ... 161 H 4
Polykárpi (GR) ...... 161 E 3
Polykástano (GR) ... 160 D 4
Polýkastro (GR) ..... 161 F 3
Polýmylos (GR) ..... 161 E 4
Polypótamos (GR) ... 166 B 4
Polýrracho (GR) .... 161 E 4
Polzela (SLO) ...... 134 C 2
Pomar de Cinca (E) ... 60 A 3
Pomarance (I) ..... 105 H 5
Pomàrla (RO) ...... 148 B 1
Pombal (P) .... 62 B 4
Pomellen (D) ...... 83 G 4
Pomezí nad Ohří (CZ) ...91 F 3
Pomezia (I) .... 108 D 3
Pomi (RO) .... 147 E 1
Pomiechówek (PL) ..... 122 D 1
Pomigliano d'Arco (I) ... 109 H 5
Pommersfelden (D) ..... 89 H 2
Pomorie /
  Поморие (BG) .... 157 F 4
Pomos (CY) ....174 B 3
Pomoštnik (BG) ..... 159 G 3
Pompei (I) .... 109 H 5
Pómpia (GR) .... 172 D 4
Poncin (F) ....51 E 2
Ponferrada (E) ..... 57 F 3
Poniatowa (PL) ..... 123 F 3
Poniec (PL) .... 121 E 2
Ponikovica (SRB) .... 139 H 1
Pons (F) .... 48 C 3
Ponsacco (I) ...... 105 G 5
Pont-à-Marcq (F) .... 40 A 2
Pont-à-Mousson (F) ....41 E 5
Pont-Audemer (F) .... 39 E 4
Pont-Aven (F) ...... 42 C 3
Pont Canavese (I) ... 100 C 4
Pont-Château (F) ... 43 E 4
Pont-Croix (F) ...... 42 B 2
Pont-d'Ain (F) ...... 50 D 2
Pont-de-Chéruy (F) .... 50 D 3
Pont-de-Dore (F) ... 50 B 3
Pont-de-l'Arche (F) ... 39 F 5
Pont-de-Roide (F) ....47 F 4
Pont-de-Salars (F) ... 53 H 1
Pont-de-Vaux (F) ... 50 D 1
Pont-de-Veyle (F) ... 50 D 2
Pont-d'Ouilly (F) ... 38 D 5
Pont-du-Château (F) ... 50 A 3
Pont-en-Royans (F) ...51 E 4
Pont-l'Abbé (F) ..... 42 B 3
Pont-l'Évêque (F) .... 39 E 4
Pont-Saint-Esprit (F).... 54 C 1
Pont-Saint-Vincent (F) ...47 E 1
Pont-Sainte-Maxence (F) . 39 H 5
Pont-Scorff (F) ...... 42 C 3
Pont-St-Martin (I) ... 100 C 4
Pont-sur-Yonne (F) ... 45 G 2
Pontacq (F) .... 52 C 3
Pontailler-sur-Saône (F) . 46 D 4
Pontão (P) .... 62 B 4
Pontardawe (GB)....... 34 D 1

Pontarddulais (GB)....... 34 D 1
Pontarion (F) ...... 49 G 2
Pontarlier (F) ......47 F 5
Pontassieve (I) ..... 106 D 3
Pontaubault (F) .... 43 F 1
Pontaumur (F) ...... 49 H 2
Pontcharra (F) ....51 F 3
Pontchartrain (F).... 45 E 1
Ponte Arche (I) .... 101 H 3
Ponte Caldelas (E).... 56 B 4
Ponte da Barca (P) ... 56 C 5
Ponte de Lima (P) .... 56 B 5
Ponte de Sor (P)..... 68 C 1
Ponte di Legno (I) ... 101 G 2
Ponte di Piave (I) . 103 F 4
Ponte Leccia (F) ... 55 H 3
Ponte nelle Alpi (I) ... 103 F 3
Ponte San Pietro (I) ... 101 F 4
Ponte Tresa (CH) .... 99 E 5
Pontearedas (E) ..... 56 B 4
Pontebba (I) ...... 103 G 2
Pontecagnano (I) .... 109 H 5
Ponteceno (I) ...... 105 F 2
Pontecesso (E) ...... 56 B 2
Pontecorvo (I) ..... 109 F 4
Pontedecimo (I)..... 105 E 2
Pontedera (I)....... 105 G 5
Pontedeume (E) ..... 56 C 1
Pontefract (GB) ..... 33 E 2
Pontelandolfo (I) .... 109 H 4
Pontevedra (E) ..... 56 B 3
Pontevico (I) ...... 101 G 5
Pontfaverger-
  Moronvilliers (F) ...... 40 C 4
Pontgibaud (F) ...... 50 A 3
Pontigny (F) .... 45 G 3
Pontinia (I) .... 109 E 4
Pontinvrea (I) ..... 104 D 3
Pontivy (F) .... 42 D 2
Pontlevoy (F) ..... 44 D 4
Pontoïrákleia (GR) ... 161 F 2
Pontoise (F) ...... 39 G 5
Pontones (E) ...... 71 F 3
Pontoon (IRL) ...... 22 C 4
Pontorson (F) ..... 43 F 1
Pontremoli (I) ..... 105 F 3
Pontresina (CH) .... 99 G 4
Pontrieux (F) ..... 42 D 1
Pontrilas (GB) ..... 35 E 1
Ponts (F) .... 60 C 3
Pontvallain (F) .... 44 B 3
Pontypool (GB) ..... 35 E 1
Pontypridd (GB) .... 35 E 2
Poole (GB) .... 38 B 1
Pootsi (EST) .... 200 D 4
Popadić (SRB) ..... 140 C 5
Poperinge (B) ...... 78 A 2
Popești (Iași) (RO) ... 148 D 3
Popești (Oradea) (RO) .. 146 D 2
Popești
  (Râmnicu Vâlcea) (RO). 151 F 2
Popești-Leordeni (RO) .. 152 B 4
Popielów (PL) ... 121 F 4
Popinci (BG) ..... 158 D 2
Popinci (SRB) .... 140 C 4
Popoli (I) .... 109 G 2
Popov Most (BIH) .. 139 F 2
Popovac (SRB) .... 143 F 1
Popovača (HR) .... 135 E 3
Popovica (BG) .... 159 E 3
Popovo / Попово (BG) . 156 D 2
Poppenhausen (D) .... 89 G 1
Poppi (I) .... 107 E 3
Poprad (SK) ..... 133 E 2
Popsko (BG) ..... 163 E 1
Porcari (I) ...... 105 G 4
Porchov (RUS) ....6 D 2
Porcuna (E) ..... 70 C 4
Porczyny (PL) .... 121 H 2
Pordenone (I) .... 103 F 3
Pordim (BG) ..... 156 A 2
Poręba (PL) ..... 122 B 5
Poreč / Parenzo (HR) .. 134 A 4
Pori / Björneborg (FIN) . 191 F 3
Porjus (S) .... 180 A 5
Porlock (GB) ..... 34 D 3
Pornainen (FIN) ..... 191 H 4

Pörnbach (D)............ 95 G 1
Pornic (F) .... 43 E 5
Pornichet (F)....... 43 E 4
Poroina Mare (RO) ..... 151 E 4
Porolissum, castrul (RO). 147 E 3
Póros (GR) .... 164 C 3
Póros / Πόρος (GR) ... 165 H 5
Poroszló (H) ...... 129 H 1
Porozina (HR) ..... 134 B 4
Pórpi (GR) .... 162 D 3
Porquerolles (F) .... 55 F 4
Porrentruy (CH) .... 98 C 2
Porretta Terme (I) ... 105 H 3
Porsgrunn (N)...... 195 E 1
Port Askaig (GB) .... 30 A 2
Port Aventura (E) .... 60 C 5
Port-Bail (F) ..... 38 B 4
Port-Barcarès (F) .... 54 A 4
Port Charlotte (GB) ... 30 A 2
Port-Cros (F) ..... 55 F 4
Port d'Alcúdia (E) ...67 F 2
Port d'Andratx (E) ...67 E 3
Port-de-Bouc (F) ... 54 D 3
Port de Pollença (E) ...67 F 2
Port de Sóller (E) ...67 F 2
Port Ellen (GB) .... 30 A 2
Port-en-
  Bessin-Huppain (F)..... 38 C 4
Port Erin (GB) ..... 32 A 1
Port-Eynon (GB) .... 34 D 2
Port Glasgow (GB) ... 30 C 2
Port-Joinville (F) ... 43 E 5
Port-la-Nouvelle (F) ... 54 A 4
Port Láirge /
  Waterford (IRL) ... 25 E 4
Port Laoise /
  Portlaoise (IRL) ... 25 E 2
Port-Leucate (F) .... 54 A 4
Port-Louis (F) ... 42 C 3
Port-Manech (F) ... 42 C 3
Port-Navalo (F) .... 42 D 4
Port of Ness (GB) ... 28 C 1
Port-Saint-Louis-
  du-Rhône (F) ..... 54 D 3
Port Saint Mary (GB) ... 32 A 1
Port-Sainte-Marie (F) ... 52 D 1
Port-sur-Saône (F) ...47 E 3
Port Talbot (GB) .... 34 D 2
Port-Vendres (F) ... 54 A 5
Port William (GB) ... 30 C 4
Porta Westfalica (D) ... 85 F 2
Portadown (GB) .... 23 F 3
Portaferry (GB) .... 23 H 3
Portalegre (P) ... 68 D 1
Portalrubio (E) ... 65 G 1
Portariá (Kentrikí
  Makedonía) (GR) ... 161 G 4
Portariá (Thessalía) (GR). 165 G 1
Portarlington (IRL) ... 25 E 2
Portavadie (GB) ... 30 B 2
Portavogie (GB) ... 23 H 3
Portbou (E) ....61 F 1
Portel (P) .... 68 D 3
Portelo (P) ...... 57 E 5
Portezuelo (E) ... 63 F 4
Portglenone (GB) ... 23 F 2
Porthcawl (GB) ... 34 D 2
Porthmadog (GB) ... 32 A 4
Portici (I) ..... 109 G 5
Portilla de la Reina (E) ... 58 A 2
Portillo (E) ..... 58 A 5
Portimão (P) .... 68 B 5
Portimo (FIN) ... 185 H 1
Portinho (P) .... 68 B 2
Portishead (GB) ... 35 F 2
Portlaoise /
  Port Laoise (IRL) ... 25 E 2
Portman (E) ..... 73 E 4
Portmarnock (IRL) ... 23 G 5
Portnacroish (GB) ... 28 D 5
Portnaguran (GB) ... 28 C 1
Portnahaven (GB) ... 30 A 2
Porto (F) .... 55 G 4
Porto (P) .... 62 B 1
Porto Alto (P) ... 62 B 1
Porto Azzurro (I) ... 106 B 5
Pórto Boúfalo (GR) ... 166 B 4

Pórto Carrás (GR) .... 161 H 5
Porto Ceresio (I) .... 101 E 3
Porto Cervo (I) ....112 D 1
Porto Cesareo (I) ....111 G 5
Porto Cristo (E) ....67 G 3
Porto de Lagos (P) ... 68 B 5
Porto de Mós (P) ... 62 B 5
Porto di Vasto (I) ... 109 H 2
Porto do Barqueiro (E) .. 56 D 1
Porto do Son (E) ... 56 B 3
Porto Empedocle (I)...114 D 4
Porto Ercole (I) ... 108 B 2
Porto Garibaldi (I) ... 107 E 1
Portó Germenó (GR) ... 165 G 4
Pórto Kágio (GR) ... 168 D 4
Porto Moniz (P) ... 68 A 4
Porto Pino (I) ....112 B 5
Pórto Ráfti (GR) ... 166 B 5
Porto Recanati (I) ... 107 H 4
Porto Rotondo (I) ....112 D 1
Porto San Giorgio (I) ... 107 H 4
Porto Sant' Elpidio (I) ... 107 H 4
Porto Santo Stefano (I) . 108 B 1
Porto Tolle (I) ... 103 F 5
Porto Torres (I) ....112 B 1
Porto-Vecchio (F) ... 55 H 5
Portoferraio (I) ... 106 B 5
Portofino (I) ... 105 E 3
Portogruaro (I) ... 103 G 3
Portomaggiore (I) ... 107 E 1
Portomarín (E) ... 56 D 3
Portomouro (E) ... 56 B 2
Portonovo (E) ... 56 B 4
Portopetro (E) ...67 G 3
Portorož /
  Portorose (SLO) ... 134 A 3
Portoscuso (I) ....112 A 5
Portovenere (I) ... 105 F 4
Portpatrick (GB) ... 23 H 2
Portree (GB) ... 28 C 3
Portrush (GB) ... 23 F 1
Portsalon (IRL) ... 23 E 1
Pörtschach
  am Wörther See (A) ... 96 D 5
Portsmouth (GB) ... 38 C 1
Portstewart (GB) ... 23 F 1
Portugalete (E) ... 58 D 1
Portumna (IRL) ... 24 D 2
Poruba (CZ) ... 93 G 3
Porvoo / Borgå (FIN) ... 193 E 4
Porzuna (E) ... 64 B 5
Posada (I) ....112 D 2
Posada (E) ... 69 H 4
Posedarje (HR) ... 136 B 4
Poschiavo (CH) ... 99 G 4
Poseidonía (GR) ... 169 H 2
Poshnjë (AL) ... 144 C 3
Posio (FIN) ... 187 F 1
Positano (I) ... 109 H 5
Pößneck (D) ... 86 A 5
Posta (I) ... 109 E 1
Poșta Câlnău (RO) ... 152 C 2
Postira (HR) ... 138 B 2
Postojna (SLO) ... 134 B 3
Posušje (BIH) ... 138 C 2
Potamia (CY) ... 175 E 3
Potamiés (GR) ... 173 E 3
Potamoí (GR) ... 162 B 2
Potamós (GR) ... 172 A 2
Potamoúla (GR) ... 164 D 2
Potcoava (RO) ... 151 G 4
Potenza (I) ...110 D 4
Potenza Picena (I) ... 107 D 4
Potes (E) ... 58 A 1
Potigny (F) ... 38 D 5
Potlogi (RO) ... 152 A 4
Potoci (BIH) ... 138 D 2
Potočnica (BG) ... 163 E 1
Potok (HR) ... 135 F 4
Potós (GR) ... 162 C 4
Pötrau (D) ... 82 B 4
Potsdam (D) ... 86 C 1
Pottenstein (A) ... 97 G 2
Potters Bar (GB) ... 36 C 3

Pöttmes (D)............ 95 F 1
Potton (GB)........... 33 G 5
Potworów (PL) ..... 122 D 3
Pouancé (F) ... 43 G 3
Pougues-les-Eaux (F).... 45 G 3
Pouilly (F)......... 50 C 2
Pouilly-en-Auxois (F).... 46 C 4
Pouilly-sur-Loire (F) ... 45 F 4
Poúlithra (GR) ... 169 E 3
Poúnta (GR) ... 170 B 2
Pournári (GR) ... 165 F 2
Poussu (FIN) ... 187 F 1
Pouyastruc (F) ... 52 D 3
Pouzauges (F) ... 43 G 5
Považská Bystrica (SK) . 132 C 2
Poveda de la Sierra (E) .. 65 E 2
Povlja (HR) ... 138 C 2
Povljana (HR) ... 136 B 4
Póvoa de Lanhoso (P) ... 56 C 5
Póvoa de Varzim (P)... 62 B 1
Poysdorf (A) ... 93 E 5
Pöytyä (FIN) ... 191 F 4
Poza de la Sal (E) ... 58 C 2
Požaranje (SRB) ... 143 E 4
Požarevac /
  Пожаревац (SRB).....141 E 4
Požega (HR) ... 135 G 4
Požega (SRB) ... 139 H 1
Poznań (PL) ... 121 E 1
Pozo Alcón (E) ... 71 F 4
Pozo Cañada (E) ... 71 F 2
Pozo de Guadalajara (E) . 64 C 2
Pozo Higuera (E) ... 71 H 5
Pozoblanco (E) ... 70 B 3
Pozohondo (E) ... 71 G 2
Pozondón (E) ... 65 F 2
Pozuelo (E) ... 71 G 2
Pozuelo de Calatrava (E). 70 D 2
Pozuelo de Zarzón (E) ... 63 F 4
Pozzallo (I) ....115 F 5
Pozzomaggiore (I) ....112 B 2
Pozzuoli (I) ... 109 G 5
Pozzuolo del Friuli (I) ... 103 G 3
Pra Loup (F) ... 55 F 1
Prabuty (PL) ...117 H 3
Prača (BIH) ... 137 H 5
Prachatice (CZ) ... 92 A 5
Pradelles (F) ... 50 B 5
Prádena (E) ... 64 B 1
Prades (F) ... 53 H 5
Prado del Rey (E) ...74 C 2
Pradoluengo (E) ... 58 C 3
Præstø (DK) ... 199 E 4
Prägraten
  am Großvenediger (A). 95 H 4
Praha (CZ) ... 92 A 2
Prahecq (F) ... 48 D 2
Prahovo (SRB) ...141 G 5
Praia a Mare (I) ...113 B 1
Praia da Barra (P) ... 62 B 2
Praia da Rocha (P) ... 68 B 5
Praia da Tocha (P) ... 62 A 4
Praia da Vieira (P) ... 62 A 4
Praia de Mira (P) ... 62 B 3
Praia de Santa Cruz (P) .. 68 A 1
Praid (RO) ... 147 H 4
Prali (I) ... 100 B 5
Pralognan-la-V. (F) ...51 G 3
Prámanta (GR) ... 164 D 1
Prangins (CH) ... 98 B 4
Prangío (GR) ... 163 F 2
Pranjani (SRB) ... 139 H 1
Prapatnica (HR) ... 138 B 2
Prasiés (GR) ... 170 A 5
Prastío (CY) ... 175 E 3
Prastio Lefkosias (CY) ...174 B 3
Prat de Comte (E) ... 60 D 2
Pratella (I) ... 109 G 4
Prati di Tivo (I) ... 109 F 1
Prato (I) ... 107 E 5
Prato (I) ... 105 H 4
Pratola Peligna (I) ... 109 G 2
Prats de Lluçanès (E) ... 60 D 2
Prats
  de-Mollo-la-Preste (F). 53 H 5
Prauthoy (F) ... 46 D 3

Pravda (BG) . . . . 152 D 5
Pravdinsk (RUS) . . . . .6 B 5
Pravec (BG) . . . . 158 C 1
Pravia (E) . . . . 57 G 1
Praz-sur-Arly (F) . . . . . .51 F 2
Pré-en-Pail (F) . . . . 43 H 2
Pré-Saint-Didier (I) . . . . 100 B 3
Prebold (SLO) . . . . 134 C 2
Précy-sous-Thil (F) . . . . . 45 H 4
Predappio (I) . . . . 107 E 2
Predazzo (I) . . . . 103 E 2
Preddvor (SLO) . . . . 134 B 2
Predeal (RO) . . . . 152 A 1
Predejane (SRB) . . . . 143 G 3
Predești (RO) . . . . 151 F 4
Predoi / Prettau (I) . . . . . 103 E 1
Predošćica (HR) . . . . 134 B 4
Preetz (D) . . . . 82 B 2
Pregarten (A) . . . . 97 E 1
Preiļi (LV) . . . . 203 G 4
Prejmer (RO) . . . . 152 B 1
Preko (HR) . . . . 136 B 5
Preljina (SRB) . . . . 139 H 1
Prelog (HR) . . . . 135 F 2
Prelošćica (HR) . . . . 135 E 4
Přelouč (CZ) . . . . 92 C 2
Premantura (HR) . . . . . . 134 A 5
Prémery (F) . . . . 45 G 5
Premià de Mar (E) . . . .61 G 4
Premilcuore (I) . . . . 107 E 2
Premnitz (D) . . . . 86 B 1
Premuda (HR) . . . . 136 A 4
Prenjas (AL) . . . . 144 D 2
Prenzlau (D) . . . . 83 G 4
Přerov (CZ) . . . . 93 F 4
Prerow (D) . . . . 83 E 2
Preselec (BG) . . . . 159 G 1
Preselenci (BG) . . . . 153 E 5
Preševo (SRB) . . . . 143 F 4
Prešov (SK) . . . . 133 G 2
Pressath (D) . . . . .91 F 3
Pressbaum (A) . . . . 97 G 1
Prestatyn (GB) . . . . 32 B 3
Presteigne (GB) . . . . 32 C 5
Prestfoss (N) . . . . 189 E 5
Přeštice (CZ) . . . . .91 H 4
Preston (GB) . . . . 32 C 2
Prestonpans (GB) . . . .31 E 1
Prestwick (GB) . . . . 30 C 2
Pretoro (I) . . . . 109 G 2
Prettau / Predoi (I) . . . . 103 E 1
Prettin (D) . . . . 86 C 3
Pretzsch (D) . . . . 86 C 3
Preuilly-sur-Claise (F) . . 44 C 5
Préveza / Πρέβεζα (GR) . 164 C 1
Prevršac (BIH) . . . . 135 E 4
Prezid (HR) . . . . 134 C 3
Pribinić (BIH) . . . . 137 F 4
Priboj (BIH) . . . . 137 H 4
Priboj / Прибој (SRB) . . 139 G 2
Příbor (CZ) . . . . 93 G 3
Příbram (CZ) . . . . 92 A 3
Priego (E) . . . . 65 E 2
Priego de Córdoba (E) . . 70 C 5
Priekulė (LT) . . . . 204 B 2
Priekule (LV) . . . . 202 A 4
Prien am Chiemsee (D) . . 95 H 2
Prienai (LT) . . . . 205 E 4
Prievidza (SK) . . . . 132 C 3
Prigoria (RO) . . . . 151 F 2
Prigradica (HR) . . . . 138 C 3
Prijeboj (HR) . . . . 134 D 5
Prijedor (BIH) . . . . 135 F 5
Prijepolje /
Пријепоље (SRB) . . 139 G 2
Prilep (MK) . . . . 145 F 2
Prilike (SRB) . . . . 139 H 2
Priluka (BIH) . . . . 137 E 5
Primel-Trégastel (F) . . 42 C 1
Primišlje (HR) . . . . 134 D 4
Primolano (I) . . . . 103 E 3
Primorsko (BG) . . . . 157 F 5
Primošten (HR) . . . . 138 A 2
Primstal (D) . . . . 88 C 3
Princetown (GB) . . . . 34 D 4

Prinés (GR) . . . . 170 A 5
Prisad (BG) . . . . 157 E 4
Prisad (MK) . . . . 145 F 1
Prishtinë / Priština . . . . 143 E 4
Prisoje (BIH) . . . . 138 C 2
Priština /
Prishtinë (SRB) . . . . . 143 E 4
Pritzerbe (D) . . . . 86 C 1
Pritzier (D) . . . . 82 C 4
Pritzwalk (D) . . . . 83 E 5
Privas (F) . . . . 50 C 5
Priverno (I) . . . . 109 E 4
Privlaka (Vukovar) (HR) . 137 H 2
Privlaka (Zadar) (HR) . . 136 B 4
Prizren (SRB) . . . . 142 D 5
Prizzi (I) . . . . .114 D 3
Prnjavor (BIH) . . . . 135 G 5
Prnjavor (SRB) . . . . 140 B 4
Proaza (E) . . . . 57 G 2
Probištip (MK) . . . . 143 G 5
Probota (RO) . . . . 148 C 2
Probstzella (D) . . . . 86 A 5
Prochod (BG) . . . . 159 H 2
Prochowice (PL) . . . . . . 120 D 3
Próchoma (GR) . . . . 161 F 3
Procida (I) . . . . 109 G 5
Prodromos (CY) . . . . . . .174 C 4
Pródromos (GR) . . . . . . 165 G 4
Produlești (RO) . . . . 152 A 3
Proença-a-Nova (P) . . . 62 C 4
Proevska Banja (MK) . . 143 F 5
Profítis Ilías (GR) . . . . . 170 C 3
Profondeville (B) . . . . . . 78 D 3
Progër (AL) . . . . 145 E 3
Prokópi (GR) . . . . 165 H 3
Prokuplje /
Прокупље (SRB) . . . . 143 F 2
Prolom (BG) . . . . 158 A 2
Prómachoi (GR) . . . . . . 161 E 2
Pronsfeld (D) . . . . 88 B 1
Propriano (F) . . . . 55 H 5
Prosenik (BG) . . . . 157 F 4
Prosílio (GR) . . . . 162 C 2
Prosotsáni (GR) . . . . 162 B 2
Prossedi (I) . . . . 109 F 4
Prostějov (CZ) . . . . 93 E 4
Prostki (PL) . . . . .119 F 2
Proszowice (PL) . . . . 125 G 1
Protokklísi (GR) . . . . 163 F 2
Prötzel (D) . . . . 87 E 1
Prousós (GR) . . . . 164 D 3
Provadija /
Провадия (BG) . . . . 157 F 3
Provatónas (GR) . . . . . . 163 F 3
Provenchères
-sur-Fave (F) . . . . . . .47 G 2
Provins (F) . . . . 45 G 2
Prozor (BIH) . . . . 137 F 5
Pruchnik (PL) . . . . 127 F 1
Prudhoe (GB) . . . . .31 G 4
Prudnik (PL) . . . . 121 F 5
Prüm (D) . . . . 88 B 1
Pruna (E) . . . . .74 C 3
Prundu (RO) . . . . 152 B 5
Prunetta (I) . . . . 105 H 4
Prunișor (RO) . . . . 151 E 3
Pruszcz (PL) . . . . .117 G 4
Pruszcz Gdański (PL) . . .117 H 2
Pruszków (PL) . . . . 122 D 1
Pružany (BY) . . . . .6 C 5
Pryluky (UA) . . . . .7 F 5
Przasnysz (PL) . . . . .118 D 4
Przechlewo (PL) . . . . . . .117 F 3
Przedbórz (PL) . . . . 122 C 4
Przedecz (PL) . . . . 121 H 1
Przemęt (PL) . . . . 120 D 2
Przemków (PL) . . . . 120 D 3
Przemyśl (PL) . . . . 127 G 2
Przesmyki (PL) . . . . 123 F 1
Przeworsk (PL) . . . . 127 F 1
Przybiernów (PL) . . . . . .116 C 3
Przysucha (PL) . . . . 122 D 3
Przytuły (PL) . . . . .119 F 3
Przytyk (PL) . . . . 122 D 3
Psača (MK) . . . . 143 G 5
Psachná (GR) . . . . 165 H 3

Psáka (GR) . . . . 164 B 1
Psará (GR) . . . . 166 D 3
Psarádes (GR) . . . . 160 D 3
Psári (Korinthía) (GR) . . 165 F 5
Psári (Messinía) (GR) . . 168 C 2
Psátha (GR) . . . . 165 G 4
Psathópyrgos (GR) . . . . 165 E 3
Psérimos (GR) . . . . 171 F 2
Psimolofou (CY) . . . . . . .174 D 3
Psínthos (GR) . . . . 171 H 3
Pskov (RUS) . . . . .6 D 2
Psychró (GR) . . . . 173 E 3
Pszczew (PL) . . . . 120 D 1
Pszczyna (PL) . . . . 125 E 1
Ptolemaïda /
Πτολεμαΐδα (GR) . . 161 E 4
Ptuj (SLO) . . . . 135 E 2
Puchberg
am Schneeberg (A) . . . 97 G 2
Púchov (SK) . . . . 132 C 2
Pucioasa (RO) . . . . 152 A 2
Pučišća (HR) . . . . 138 C 2
Puck (PL) . . . . .117 G 1
Puckeridge (GB) . . . . 36 C 3
Puçol / Puzol (E) . . . . . . 65 H 4
Pudarci (BG) . . . . 162 D 1
Pudasjärvi /
Kurenalus (FIN) . . . . 187 E 2
Pudob (SLO) . . . . 134 B 3
Puebla de Alcocer (E) . . 69 H 1
Puebla de Almenara (E) . 64 C 4
Puebla de Beleña (E) . . 64 C 1
Puebla de
Don Fadrique (E) . . . . 71 G 4
Puebla de
Don Rodrigo (E) . . . . . 64 A 5
Puebla de Guzmán (E) . 69 E 4
Puebla de la Calzada (E) . 69 F 1
Puebla de la Reina (E) . . 69 G 2
Puebla de Lillo (E) . . . . . 57 H 2
Puebla de Obando (E) . . . 69 F 1
Puebla de Sanabria (E) . 57 F 4
Pueblica de Valverde (E) . 57 G 5
Puente
de Domingo Flórez (E) . 57 E 4
Puente de Génave (E) . . 71 F 3
Puente de los Fierros (E) . 57 G 2
Puente
de Montañana (E) . . . . 60 B 2
Puente Genil (E) . . . . . . 70 B 5
Puente la Reina (E) . . . . 59 F 2
Puente
la Reina de Jaca (E) . . 59 G 3
Puente Viesgo (E) . . . . . 58 B 1
Puentenansa (E) . . . . 58 A 1
Puerto Castilla (E) . . . . . 63 G 3
Puerto de Béjar (E) . . . . 63 G 3
Puerto de la Cruz (E) . .67 F 5
Puerto de la Encina (E) . .74 C 2
Puerto de la Estaca (E) . .67 E 5
Puerto del Rosario (E) . .67 H 5
Puerto de Mazarrón (E) . 72 D 4
Puerto
de San Vicente (E) . . . . 63 H 5
Puerto Lápice (E) . . . . . . 64 C 5
Puerto Lumbreras (E) . . 71 H 5
Puerto Real (E) . . . . . . .74 A 4
Puerto Serrano (E) . . . . .74 C 3
Puertollano (E) . . . . 70 D 2
Puget-Théniers (F) . . . . 55 G 1
Puhja (EST) . . . . 201 F 3
Puhos (FIN) . . . . 187 E 2
Puhos (FIN) . . . . 193 H 1
Pui (RO) . . . . 151 E 1
Puiești (RO) . . . . 148 D 4
Puig-reig (E) . . . . 60 D 2
Puigcerdà (E) . . . . 60 D 1
Puiseaux (F) . . . . 45 E 2
Puisserguier (F) . . . . 54 A 3
Pujols (F) . . . . 48 D 5
Pukavik (S) . . . . 197 E 1
Pukë (AL) . . . . 142 C 5
Pukiš (BIH) . . . . 137 H 3
Pukkila (FIN) . . . . 191 H 4
Pula (I) . . . . .112 C 4
Pula / Pola (HR) . . . . . . 134 A 5
Pulaj (AL) . . . . 144 B 1
Puławy (PL) . . . . 123 E 3

Pulborough (GB) . . . . . . 38 D 1
Pulkau (A) . . . . 92 D 5
Pulkkila (FIN) . . . . 185 H 4
Pulpí (E) . . . . 71 H 5
Pulsnitz (D) . . . . 87 E 4
Pułtusk (PL) . . . . .119 E 5
Pumpėnai (LT) . . . . 205 F 2
Punat (HR) . . . . 134 C 5
Punghina (RO) . . . . 151 E 4
Punkaharju (FIN) . . . . . . 193 G 2
Punkalaidun (FIN) . . . . . 191 G 3
Punta Ala (I) . . . . 106 C 5
Punta Križa (HR) . . . . . . 134 B 5
Punta Umbría (E) . . . . . . 69 E 5
Puokio (FIN) . . . . 187 E 3
Puolango (FIN) . . . . 187 E 3
Purbach
am Neusiedler See (A) . 97 H 2
Purchena (E) . . . . 71 G 5
Purgstall
an der Erlauf (A) . . . . . 97 E 2
Purkersdorf (A) . . . . 97 G 1
Purmerend (NL) . . . . . . .76 D 4
Purmu (FIN) . . . . 191 H 3
Purullena (E) . . . . 71 E 5
Puševo (BG) . . . . 159 F 1
Púshkin (RUS) . . . . .6 D 1
Püspökladány (H) . . . . . .131 E 2
Pustoška (RUS) . . . . .6 D 3
Pusula (FIN) . . . . 191 G 4
Puszcza
Mariańska (PL) . . . . . 122 C 2
Puszczykowo (PL) . . . . . 121 E 1
Pusztamagyaród (H) . . . 128 B 4
Pusztaszabolcs (H) . . . . 129 E 2
Pusztaszemes (H) . . . . . 128 D 3
Pusztavám (H) . . . . 128 D 2
Putanges-le-Lac (F) . . . 43 H 1
Putbus (D) . . . . 83 F 2
Putgarten (D) . . . . 83 F 1
Putignano (I) . . . . .111 F 3
Putinci (SRB) . . . . 140 C 3
Putineiu
(Alexandria) (RO) . . . . 151 H 5
Putineiu
(Giurgiu) (RO) . . . . . . 152 B 5
Putlitz (D) . . . . 82 D 4
Putna (RO) . . . . 148 A 1
Puttelange (F) . . . . .41 F 5
Putten (NL) . . . . 77 E 4
Puttgarden (D) . . . . 82 C 2
Putyv'l (UA) . . . . .7 G 5
Puumala (FIN) . . . . 193 F 2
Puy du Fou,
grand parc du (F) . . . 43 G 5
Puy-Guillaume (F) . . . . . 50 B 2
Puy-l'Évêque (F) . . . . . . 49 F 5
Puylaurens (F) . . . . 53 G 3
Puymirol (F) . . . . 53 E 1
Puzol / Puçol (E) . . . . . . 65 H 4
Pwllheli (GB) . . . . 32 A 4
Pyce / Ruse . . . . 152 B 5
Pyhäjärvi (FIN) . . . . 185 H 4
Pyhäjoki (FIN) . . . . 185 G 3
Pyhältö (FIN) . . . . 193 F 1
Pyhäntä (FIN) . . . . 187 F 3
Pyhäntä (FIN) . . . . 185 H 4
Pyhäsalmi (FIN) . . . . . . 185 H 4
Pyhäselkä (FIN) . . . . 193 H 1
Pyhätunturi (FIN) . . . . . 181 G 5
Pyhtää / Pyttis (FIN) . . . 193 F 4
Pyla (CY) . . . . 175 E 3
Pyla-sur-Mer (F) . . . . . . 48 B 5
Pylés (GR) . . . . 171 F 5
Pýli (GR) . . . . 164 D 1
Pylío (GR) . . . . 171 F 2
Pylkönmäki (FIN) . . . . . 191 H 1
Pyloroí (GR) . . . . 161 E 5
Pýlos / Πύλος (GR) . . . . 168 B 3
Pyrga Larnakas (CY) . . 175 E 4
Pyrgadíkia (GR) . . . . . . 161 H 4
Pyrgí (Iónia Nisiá) (GR) . 160 A 5
Pyrgí
(Vóreio Aigaío) (GR) . 167 E 4
Pyrgos (CY) . . . . .174 D 4

Pýrgos / Πύργος
(Dytikí Elláda) (GR) . . . 164 D 5
Pýrgos (Pyrgos) (GR) . . . 172 D 4
Pýrgos
(Stereá Elláda) (GR) . . 165 G 3
Pýrgos
(Vóreio Aigaío) (GR) . . 167 G 5
Pýrgos Diroú (GR) . . . . . 168 D 4
Pyrjatyn (UA) . . . . .13 G 1
Pyrsógianni (GR) . . . . . . 160 C 4
Pyrzyce (PL) . . . . .116 C 4
Pyskowice (PL) . . . . 121 H 5
Pythagóreio (GR) . . . . . 167 G 5
Pýthio (GR) . . . . 163 F 2
Pyttis / Pyhtää (FIN) . . . 193 F 4
Pyzdry (PL) . . . . 121 F 1
Póros (GR) . . . . 164 C 4

Q

Qala (M) . . . . .114 B 4
Quakenbrück (D) . . . . . . 84 D 1
Quarré-les-Tombes (F) . . 45 H 4
Quarteira (P) . . . . 68 C 5
Quarto d'Altino (I) . . . . 103 F 4
Quartu Sant' Elena (I) . .112 C 5
Quatretonda (E) . . . . . . 73 F 1
Quedlinburg (D) . . . . . . 86 A 3
Queenborough (GB) . . . 36 D 4
Queensferry (GB) . . . . . 32 C 3
Queluz (P) . . . . 68 A 2
Queralbs (E) . . . . 60 D 2
Querfurt (D) . . . . 86 A 4
Quéribus,
château de (F) . . . . . 53 H 4
Quérigut (F) . . . . 53 G 4
Quero (E) . . . . 64 C 5
Quesada (E) . . . . 71 E 4
Questembert (F) . . . . . . 43 E 3
Quettehou (F) . . . . 38 C 4
Quiberon (F) . . . . 42 D 4
Quickborn (D) . . . . .81 H 3
Quiévrain (B) . . . . 78 B 3
Quillan (F) . . . . 53 G 4
Quillebeuf-
sur-Seine (F) . . . . 39 E 4
Quimper (F) . . . . 42 B 2
Quimperlé (F) . . . . 42 C 3
Quincinetto (I) . . . . 100 C 4
Quincoces de Yuso (E) . . 58 C 2
Quingey (F) . . . . .47 E 5
Quintana (E) . . . . 69 H 2
Quintana
del Puente (E) . . . . 58 B 4
Quintana
Martín Galíndez (E) . . 58 C 2
Quintana Redonda (E) . . 58 D 5
Quintanar
de la Orden (E) . . . . . 64 D 4
Quintanar
de la Sierra (E) . . . . . . 58 D 4
Quintanar del Rey (E) . . 65 F 5
Quintanilha (P) . . . . 57 F 5
Quintanilla
de Onésimo (E) . . . . . . 58 A 5
Quintin (F) . . . . 42 D 2
Quinto (E) . . . . 59 H 5
Quinzano d'Oglio (I) . . 101 F 4
Quiroga (E) . . . . 57 E 3
Quissac (F) . . . . 54 B 2
Qukës (AL) . . . . 144 D 2

R

Raab (A) . . . . 96 C 1
Raabs an der Thaya (A) . 92 C 5
Raahe / Brahestad (FIN) . 185 G 3
Raajärvi (FIN) . . . . 181 F 5
Rääkkylä (FIN) . . . . 193 G 1
Raalte (NL) . . . . 77 F 4
Raanujärvi (FIN) . . . . . . 180 D 5
Raasiku (EST) . . . . 201 E 2
Raate (FIN) . . . . 187 G 2
Raattama (FIN) . . . . 180 D 3
Rab (HR) . . . . 134 C 5
Raba Wyżna (PL) . . . . . 125 G 2
Rabac (HR) . . . . 134 B 4
Rábade (E) . . . . 56 D 2
Rábafüzes (H) . . . . 128 A 3

Rabastens (F) . . . . 53 G 2
Rabastens-
de-Bigorre (F) . . . . . . 52 D 3
Rabat (M) . . . . .114 C 5
Rábaújfalu (H) . . . . 128 C 1
Rabe (SRB) . . . . 140 C 1
Rabiša (BG) . . . . 150 D 5
Rabka (PL) . . . . 125 G 2
Rabrovo (MK) . . . . 145 H 2
Rabrovo (SRB) . . . . .141 E 4
Rača (Kragujevac) (SRB) .141 E 5
Rača (Podujevo) (SRB) . . 143 E 3
Răcăciuni (RO) . . . . 148 C 5
Răcari (RO) . . . . 152 B 3
Răcășdia (RO) . . . . 150 C 2
Racconigi (I) . . . . 100 C 5
Rače (SLO) . . . . 134 D 1
Ráches (GR) . . . . 165 F 2
Răchitoasa (RO) . . . . . . 148 D 4
Rachiv (UA) . . . . .12 D 3
Raciąż (PL) . . . . .118 C 5
Racibórz (PL) . . . . 124 D 1
Račinovci (HR) . . . . 137 H 3
Račišće (HR) . . . . 138 C 3
Râciu (RO) . . . . 147 G 4
Ráckeve (H) . . . . 129 E 2
Racovița (RO) . . . . 151 G 1
Raczki (PL) . . . . .119 G 2
Radalj (SRB) . . . . 137 H 4
Rădăuți (RO) . . . . 148 B 1
Råde (N) . . . . 195 E 1
Radeberg (D) . . . . 87 E 4
Radebeul (D) . . . . 86 D 4
Radeburg (D) . . . . 86 D 4
Radechiv (UA) . . . . .12 D 2
Radegunda (SLO) . . . . . 134 C 2
Radenci (SLO) . . . . 135 E 1
Radenthein (A) . . . . 96 C 5
Radevo (BG) . . . . 159 G 2
Radevormwald (D) . . . . . 84 D 4
Radgoszcz (PL) . . . . 122 D 5
Radicondoli (I) . . . . 105 H 5
Radievo (BG) . . . . 159 F 3
Radimlja (BIH) . . . . 138 D 3
Radiovce (MK) . . . . 143 E 5
Radków (PL) . . . . 120 D 5
Radlje ob Dravi (SLO) . . 134 D 1
Radljevo (SRB) . . . . 140 C 5
Radnevo / Раднево (BG) . 159 F 2
Radnice (CZ) . . . . .91 H 3
Radolevo (SRB) . . . . 140 D 2
Radolfzell
am Bodensee (D) . . . . 94 C 3
Radom (PL) . . . . 122 D 3
Radomir /
Радомир (BG) . . . . . 158 A 2
Radomirci (BG) . . . . 155 E 3
Radomsko (PL) . . . . 122 B 4
Radomyšl' (UA) . . . . .13 E 1
Radomyśl Wielki (PL) . . 123 E 5
Radošina (SK) . . . . 132 B 3
Radoszyce (PL) . . . . 122 C 4
Radotín (CZ) . . . . 92 A 3
Radovan (RO) . . . . 151 F 4
Radovče (MNE) . . . . 139 G 4
Radovec (BG) . . . . 163 F 1
Radovići (MNE) . . . . 139 F 4
Radoviš (MK) . . . . 145 G 1
Radovljica (SLO) . . . . . . 134 B 2
Radovnica (SRB) . . . . . . 143 G 4
Radstadt (A) . . . . 96 C 5
Radstock (GB) . . . . 35 F 2
Raduil (BG) . . . . 158 C 2
Radunci (BG) . . . . 159 F 2
Raduša (MK) . . . . 143 E 5
Radviliškis (LT) . . . . 205 E 2
Radwanice (PL) . . . . 120 D 3
Radymno (PL) . . . . 127 G 1
Radzanów (PL) . . . . .118 C 5
Radziejów (PL) . . . . .117 G 5
Radzymin (PL) . . . . 122 D 1
Radzyń Chełmiński (PL) .117 H 4
Radzyń Podlaski (PL) . . 123 F 2
Raesfeld (D) . . . . 84 C 3
Raffadali (I) . . . . .114 D 4
Rafína (GR) . . . . 166 B 4

Rágama (E) ... 63 H 2
Ragana (LV) ... 203 E 2
Raglan (GB) ... 35 E 1
Raguhn (D) ... 86 B 3
Ragunda (S) ... 190 B 1
Ragusa (I) ... 115 F 5
Rahačoŭ (BY) ... 7 E 4
Rahden (D) ... 85 E 1
Rahlstedt (D) ... 81 H 4
Rain am Lech (D) ... 95 F 1
Räisälä (FIN) ... 181 F 5
Raisio (FIN) ... 191 F 4
Raittijärvi (FIN) ... 176 C 5
Raja Jooseppi (FIN) ... 177 G 5
Rajac (SRB) ... 141 G 5
Rajadell (E) ... 60 D 3
Rajamäki (FIN) ... 191 H 4
Rajcza (PL) ... 125 F 2
Rajec (SK) ... 132 C 2
Rajgród (PL) ... 119 G 3
Rajince (SRB) ... 143 F 4
Raka (SLO) ... 134 D 3
Rakalj (HR) ... 134 B 5
Rakita (BG) ... 158 A 1
Rakitna (SLO) ... 134 B 3
Rakitnica (BG) ... 159 F 2
Rakitnika (HR) ... 135 F 3
Rakitovo (BG) ... 158 C 3
Rakke (EST) ... 201 F 2
Rakkestad (N) ... 195 F 1
Rákóczifalva (H) ... 129 G 3
Rakoniewice (PL) ... 120 D 1
Rákos (H) ... 129 H 4
Rakova Bara (SRB) ... 141 F 4
Rakovac (BIH) ... 135 G 5
Rakovica (BG) ... 150 D 5
Rakovica (HR) ... 134 D 5
Rakovník (CZ) ... 91 H 2
Rakovo (BG) ... 159 G 1
Rakovski / Раковски (BG) ... 159 E 2
Rakvere (EST) ... 201 F 2
Ralja (SRB) ... 140 D 4
Ram (SRB) ... 141 E 4
Ramacca (I) ... 115 F 4
Ramales de la Victoria (E) ... 58 C 1
Ramallosa (E) ... 56 B 3
Ramatuelle (F) ... 55 F 3
Ramberg (N) ... 179 E 3
Rambervillers (F) ... 47 F 2
Rambouillet (F) ... 45 E 1
Rambucourt (F) ... 41 E 5
Râmeţ (RO) ... 147 F 5
Rămetea (RO) ... 147 F 4
Rámia (GR) ... 164 D 1
Râmnicu Sărat (RO) ... 152 D 2
Râmnicu Vâlcea (RO) ... 151 G 2
Ramsau (A) ... 96 C 3
Ramsau bei Berchtesgaden (D) ... 96 B 3
Ramsele (S) ... 183 H 5
Ramsey (Cambs.) (GB) ... 33 G 5
Ramsey (Isle of Man) (GB) ... 30 C 5
Ramsgate (GB) ... 37 E 4
Ramsjö (S) ... 190 A 2
Ramstein-Miesenbach (D) ... 88 D 3
Ramsund (N) ... 179 G 2
Ramundberget (S) ... 189 G 1
Ramvik (S) ... 190 C 1
Ramygala (LT) ... 205 F 2
Ranalt (A) ... 95 F 4
Rânca (RO) ... 151 F 2
Randaberg (N) ... 194 A 1
Randalstown (GB) ... 23 G 2
Randan (F) ... 50 A 2
Randanne (F) ... 50 A 3
Randazzo (I) ... 115 F 3
Randers (DK) ... 194 D 5
Råneå (S) ... 185 F 1
Rangsdorf (D) ... 86 D 2
Raniżów (PL) ... 123 F 5
Rankweil (A) ... 94 D 4
Rannapungerja (EST) ... 201 G 2
Ranovac (SRB) ... 141 E 5
Rantasalmi (FIN) ... 193 F 2

Rantsila / Frantsila (FIN) ... 185 H 3
Ranua (FIN) ... 185 H 1
Raon-l'Étape (F) ... 47 F 2
Rapallo (I) ... 105 E 3
Räpina (EST) ... 201 G 4
Rapla (EST) ... 200 D 2
Rapolano Terme (I) ... 106 D 4
Rapolla (I) ... 110 C 3
Rapperswil (CH) ... 99 E 2
Raptópoulo (GR) ... 168 C 3
Raša (HR) ... 134 B 4
Räsälä (FIN) ... 193 F 1
Rascafría (E) ... 64 B 1
Răscruci (RO) ... 147 F 3
Rasdorf (D) ... 85 G 5
Raseiniai (LT) ... 204 D 3
Raška (SRB) ... 142 D 2
Raslavice (SK) ... 133 G 2
Rasno (BIH) ... 138 D 2
Râşnov (RO) ... 152 A 1
Rasova (RO) ... 153 E 4
Rasovo (BG) ... 151 E 5
Rasquera (E) ... 60 B 5
Rast (RO) ... 151 E 5
Rastede (D) ... 81 H 4
Rastenberg (D) ... 86 A 4
Rastenfeld (A) ... 97 F 1
Rastošnica (BIH) ... 137 H 4
Rastatt (D) ... 89 E 4
Ratekau (D) ... 82 C 3
Rates (P) ... 62 B 1
Rathdowney (IRL) ... 25 E 2
Rathdrum (IRL) ... 25 G 2
Rathenow (D) ... 86 B 1
Rathfriland (GB) ... 23 G 3
Rathkeale (IRL) ... 24 C 3
Rathmelton (IRL) ... 23 E 1
Rathmore (IRL) ... 24 C 4
Rathmullan (IRL) ... 23 E 1
Rathnew (IRL) ... 25 G 2
Ratingen (D) ... 84 C 4
Ratkovac (SRB) ... 142 D 4
Ratkovo (SRB) ... 137 H 2
Rátót (H) ... 128 B 3
Ratten (A) ... 97 F 3
Rattenberg (A) ... 95 G 3
Rattersdorf-Liebing (A) ... 97 H 3
Rattray (GB) ... 29 F 5
Rättvik (S) ... 190 A 4
Ratzeburg (D) ... 82 C 4
Raubling (D) ... 95 H 3
Raucourt-et-Flaba (F) ... 40 D 4
Raudaskylä (FIN) ... 185 G 4
Raudoné (LT) ... 204 D 3
Raufarhöfn (IS) ... 178 C 1
Raufoss (N) ... 189 F 4
Rauha (FIN) ... 193 G 3
Rauland (N) ... 188 C 5
Rauma (FIN) ... 191 E 3
Rauris (A) ... 96 B 4
Rautalampi (FIN) ... 193 E 1
Rautas (S) ... 180 A 3
Rautavaara (FIN) ... 187 F 4
Rautio (FIN) ... 185 G 4
Rautjärvi (FIN) ... 193 G 2
Rauzan (F) ... 48 D 4
Ravanjska (HR) ... 136 B 4
Ravanusa (I) ... 115 E 4
Ravello (I) ... 109 H 5
Ravenna (I) ... 107 E 1
Ravensbrück (D) ... 83 F 5
Ravensburg (D) ... 94 D 3
Ravna Dubrava (SRB) ... 143 G 3
Ravna Gora (HR) ... 134 C 4
Ravna Reka (SRB) ... 143 F 1
Ravne na Koroškem (SLO) ... 134 C 1
Ravnec (BG) ... 159 H 2
Ravnište (SRB) ... 143 E 2
Ravnje (SRB) ... 140 B 4
Ravno (BIH) ... 139 E 3
Ravno Bučje (SRB) ... 143 G 2
Ravnogor (BG) ... 162 B 1

Rawa Mazowiecka (PL) ... 122 C 2
Rawicz (PL) ... 121 E 3
Rawtenstall (GB) ... 32 D 2
Rayleigh (GB) ... 36 D 4
Rayol-Canadel-sur-Mer (F) ... 55 F 3
Râyrinki (FIN) ... 185 G 5
R'azan' (RUS) ... 7 H 2
Ražana (SRB) ... 139 H 1
Ražanac (HR) ... 136 B 4
Razboj (BIH) ... 135 G 5
Razbojna (SRB) ... 143 E 2
Raždaginja (SRB) ... 139 H 3
Razdol (BG) ... 161 G 1
Răzena (BG) ... 159 F 2
Razgrad / Разград (BG) ... 156 D 2
Razlog (BG) ... 161 H 1
Razlovci (MK) ... 143 H 5
Reading (GB) ... 36 B 4
Réalmont (F) ... 53 G 2
Rebais (F) ... 45 G 1
Rebordelo (P) ... 62 B 2
Rebricea (RO) ... 148 D 3
Recanati (I) ... 107 H 4
Recaş (RO) ... 150 B 1
Recco (I) ... 105 E 3
Recea (Braşov) (RO) ... 151 H 1
Recea (Piteşti) (RO) ... 151 H 4
Recea-Cristur (RO) ... 147 F 3
Recey-sur-Ource (F) ... 46 D 3
Rechnitz (A) ... 97 H 3
Rećica (HR) ... 134 D 4
Recke (D) ... 84 D 1
Recklinghausen (D) ... 84 C 3
Recoaro Terme (I) ... 101 H 4
Recuerda (E) ... 58 D 5
Rečyca (BY) ... 7 E 5
Recz (PL) ... 116 D 4
Ręczno (PL) ... 122 C 3
Reda (PL) ... 117 G 1
Redalen (N) ... 189 F 4
Redange (L) ... 79 E 5
Redcar (GB) ... 31 H 4
Redditch (GB) ... 32 D 5
Redhill (GB) ... 36 C 4
Rédics (H) ... 128 B 4
Redon (F) ... 43 E 3
Redondela (E) ... 56 B 4
Redondo (P) ... 68 D 2
Redruth (GB) ... 34 B 5
Rees (D) ... 84 B 3
Reeth (GB) ... 31 G 5
Reftele (S) ... 195 G 4
Regalbuto (I) ... 115 F 3
Regen (D) ... 91 H 5
Regensburg (D) ... 91 F 5
Regenstauf (D) ... 91 F 5
Reggello (I) ... 106 D 3
Reggia di Santu Antine (I) ... 112 B 2
Reggio di Calabria (I) ... 115 G 2
Reggio nell'Emilia (I) ... 105 G 2
Reggiolo (I) ... 101 H 5
Reghin (RO) ... 147 G 4
Regkínio (GR) ... 165 F 3
Reguengos de Monsaraz (P) ... 68 D 2
Rehau (D) ... 91 F 2
Rehburg-Loccum (D) ... 85 F 1
Rehden (D) ... 85 E 1
Rehna (D) ... 82 C 3
Reichéa (GR) ... 169 E 3
Reichenau (CH) ... 99 F 3
Reichenau an der Rax (A) ... 97 G 3
Reichenbach (Niederschlesischer Oberlausitzkreis) (D) ... 87 F 4
Reichenbach (Vogtlandkreis) (D) ... 86 B 5
Reichertshofen (D) ... 95 G 1
Reichshoffen (F) ... 41 H 5
Reigate (GB) ... 36 C 4
Reignier-Esery (F) ... 51 F 2
Reillanne (F) ... 55 E 2
Reims (F) ... 40 B 5
Reinach (CH) ... 98 D 2
Reinbek (D) ... 82 B 4

Reinberg (D) ... 83 F 2
Reine (N) ... 179 E 3
Reinfeld (D) ... 82 B 3
Reinheim (D) ... 89 F 2
Reinli (N) ... 189 E 4
Reinosa (E) ... 58 B 2
Reischenhart (D) ... 95 H 3
Reisjärvi (FIN) ... 185 H 5
Reiss (GB) ... 26 B 4
Reit im Winkl (D) ... 95 H 3
Reitzenhain (D) ... 86 D 5
Rejowiec (PL) ... 123 G 3
Rekovac (SRB) ... 143 E 1
Remagen (D) ... 84 C 5
Rémalard (F) ... 44 C 2
Remeskylä (FIN) ... 185 H 4
Remetea (RO) ... 148 A 4
Remetea Mare (RO) ... 150 B 1
Remetea Mică (RO) ... 146 B 5
Remich (L) ... 79 F 5
Remiremont (F) ... 47 F 3
Remolinos (E) ... 59 G 4
Remoulins (F) ... 54 C 2
Rempstone (GB) ... 33 E 4
Remscheid (D) ... 84 C 4
Rémuzat (F) ... 54 D 1
Rena (N) ... 189 F 3
Renazé (F) ... 43 G 3
Renchen (D) ... 88 D 5
Renda (LV) ... 202 B 3
Rende (I) ... 113 B 2
Rendsburg (D) ... 81 H 2
Rengsdorf (D) ... 84 D 5
Reni (UA) ... 13 F 4
Renko (FIN) ... 191 G 4
Renkum (NL) ... 77 E 5
Rennebu (N) ... 189 E 1
Rennerod (D) ... 84 D 5
Rennes (F) ... 43 F 2
Rennes-les-Bains (F) ... 53 G 4
Rennweg am Katschberg (A) ... 96 C 4
Rensjön (S) ... 180 A 3
Rentína (GR) ... 161 H 3
Renwez (F) ... 40 C 3
Répcelak (H) ... 128 C 2
Repki (PL) ... 123 F 1
Replot (FIN) ... 185 E 5
Repojoki (FIN) ... 177 F 5
Reposaari (FIN) ... 191 E 3
Repvåg (N) ... 177 E 2
Requena (E) ... 65 G 4
Réquista (F) ... 53 H 2
Rerik (D) ... 82 D 3
Resanovci (BIH) ... 136 D 4
Resavica (SRB) ... 141 F 5
Resen (MK) ... 145 E 2
Resende (P) ... 62 C 1
Reșița (RO) ... 150 C 2
Resko (PL) ... 116 C 3
Resna (MNE) ... 139 F 4
Resnik (SRB) ... 140 D 4
Restelica (SRB) ... 142 D 5
Resuttano (I) ... 115 E 3
Reszel (PL) ... 119 E 2
Retford (GB) ... 33 F 3
Rethel (F) ... 40 C 4
Rethem (D) ... 85 F 1
Rethen (D) ... 85 G 2
Réthymno / Ρέθυμνο (GR) ... 170 A 5
Retiers (F) ... 43 F 3
Retortillo de Soria (E) ... 58 D 5
Retournac (F) ... 50 C 4
Rétság (H) ... 129 F 1
Retuerta del Bullaque (E) ... 64 A 5
Retz (A) ... 92 D 5
Reuilly (F) ... 45 E 5
Reus (E) ... 60 C 4
Reusel (NL) ... 78 D 1
Reußenstein (D) ... 89 G 5
Reutlingen (D) ... 89 F 5
Reutte (A) ... 95 F 3
Revel (F) ... 53 G 3
Révfülöp (H) ... 128 C 3
Revigny (F) ... 40 D 5
Revin (F) ... 40 C 3

Řevničov (CZ) ... 92 A 2
Revonlahti (FIN) ... 185 G 3
Rewa (PL) ... 117 G 1
Rewal (PL) ... 116 C 2
Reyðarfjörður (IS) ... 178 D 2
Reykhólar (IS) ... 178 A 2
Reykholt (IS) ... 178 B 2
Reykjahlíð (IS) ... 178 C 2
Reykjavik (IS) ... 178 A 3
Rēzekne (LV) ... 203 G 4
Rezzato (I) ... 101 G 4
Rezzoaglio (I) ... 105 E 2
Rgotina (SRB) ... 141 G 5
Rhade (D) ... 81 G 4
Rhayader (GB) ... 32 B 5
Rheda (D) ... 85 E 3
Rhede (Bocholt) (D) ... 81 E 5
Rhede (Ems) (D) ... 84 C 1
Rheinbach (D) ... 84 C 5
Rheinberg (D) ... 84 B 4
Rheinböllen (D) ... 88 D 2
Rheine (D) ... 84 D 2
Rheinfelden (CH) ... 98 D 1
Rheinfelden (D) ... 94 A 3
Rheinhausen (D) ... 84 C 3
Rheinsberg (D) ... 83 F 5
Rhêmes-Notre-Dame (I) ... 100 B 4
Rhenen (NL) ... 77 E 5
Rheydt (D) ... 84 B 4
Rhinau (F) ... 47 H 2
Rhinow (D) ... 86 B 1
Rho (I) ... 101 E 4
Rhondda (GB) ... 35 E 2
Rhosneigr (GB) ... 32 A 3
Rhossili (GB) ... 34 D 2
Rhüden (D) ... 85 G 2
Rhuthun / Ruthin (GB) ... 32 C 3
Rhyl (GB) ... 32 B 3
Rhynern (D) ... 84 D 3
Rhynie (GB) ... 29 G 3
Riaillé (F) ... 43 F 4
Rial (E) ... 56 B 4
Riaño (E) ... 57 H 2
Rians (F) ... 55 E 2
Rianxo (E) ... 56 B 3
Riaza (E) ... 64 C 1
Riba de Saelices (E) ... 65 E 1
Riba de Santiuste (E) ... 64 D 1
Ribadavia (E) ... 56 C 4
Ribadelago (E) ... 57 E 4
Ribadeo (E) ... 57 E 1
Ribadesella (E) ... 57 H 1
Ribarci (SRB) ... 143 G 4
Ribarica (BG) ... 158 D 1
Ribariće (SRB) ... 142 D 3
Ribarska Banja (SRB) ... 143 F 2
Ribas de Campos (E) ... 58 A 4
Ribčev Laz (SLO) ... 134 B 2
Ribe (DK) ... 198 B 3
Ribeauvillé (F) ... 47 G 2
Ribécourt-Dreslincourt (F) ... 40 A 4
Ribeira de Pena (P) ... 62 D 1
Ribemont (F) ... 40 A 3
Ribera (I) ... 114 C 4
Ribera Brava (P) ... 68 A 4
Ribera de Cardós (E) ... 60 C 1
Ribera del Fresno (E) ... 69 G 2
Ribérac (F) ... 49 E 4
Ribes de Freser (E) ... 60 D 2
Ribiers (F) ... 55 E 1
Ribnica (BIH) ... 137 G 4
Ribnica (Dolenjavas) (SLO) ... 134 B 3
Ribnica (Pivka) (SLO) ... 134 C 3
Ribnica na Pohorju (SLO) ... 134 D 1
Ribniţa (MD) ... 13 F 3
Ribnovo (BG) ... 161 H 1
Ribnitz-Damgarten (D) ... 83 E 2
Říčany (CZ) ... 92 B 3
Riccia (I) ... 109 H 4
Riccione (I) ... 107 F 2
Richelieu (F) ... 44 B 5
Richelsdorf (D) ... 85 G 4
Richmond (GB) ... 31 G 5

Richmond upon Thames (GB) ... 36 C 4
Richtenberg (D) ... 83 E 2
Rickling (D) ... 81 H 3
Ricla (E) ... 59 F 5
Ricobayo (E) ... 63 G 1
Riđica (SRB) ... 137 H 1
Riec-sur-Belon (F) ... 42 C 3
Ried im Innkreis (A) ... 96 C 2
Ried im Oberinntal (A) ... 95 E 4
Riedenburg (D) ... 91 F 5
Riedlingen (D) ... 94 D 2
Riegel am Kaiserstuhl (D) ... 94 A 2
Riegersburg (A) ... 97 G 4
Riego de la Vega (E) ... 57 G 4
Riesa (D) ... 86 D 4
Riesi (I) ... 115 E 4
Riestedt (D) ... 86 A 3
Rietavas (LT) ... 204 C 3
Rietberg (D) ... 85 E 3
Rieti (I) ... 109 E 2
Rieumes (F) ... 53 F 3
Rieupeyroux (F) ... 53 G 1
Rieux-Volvestre (F) ... 53 F 3
Rievaulx Abbey (GB) ... 31 H 5
Riez (F) ... 55 F 2
Riezlern (A) ... 95 E 4
Rīga (LV) ... 202 D 3
Rígaio (GR) ... 165 F 1
Rignac (F) ... 53 G 1
Rignano Flaminio (I) ... 108 D 2
Riihimäki (FIN) ... 191 H 4
Riisipere (EST) ... 200 D 2
Riistavesi (FIN) ... 187 F 5
Rijeka (BIH) ... 137 G 5
Rijeka (HR) ... 134 B 4
Rijeka Crnojevica (MNE) ... 139 F 5
Rijssen (NL) ... 77 F 4
Riksgränsen (S) ... 176 A 5
Rila (BG) ... 158 B 3
Rillo (E) ... 65 G 2
Rillo de Gallo (E) ... 65 E 1
Rilski manastir (BG) ... 158 B 3
Rimavská Sobota (SK) ... 133 G 2
Rimbo (S) ... 197 G 1
Rimini (I) ... 107 F 2
Rimše (LT) ... 205 H 2
Rimske Toplice (SLO) ... 134 D 2
Rincón de la Victoria (E) ... 75 E 3
Rincón de Soto (E) ... 59 F 3
Rindal (N) ... 182 C 5
Ringaskiddy (IRL) ... 24 D 4
Ringe (DK) ... 198 C 4
Ringebu (N) ... 189 E 3
Ringford (GB) ... 30 D 4
Ringkøbing (DK) ... 194 C 3
Ringsaker (N) ... 189 F 4
Ringstad (N) ... 188 B 2
Ringsted (DK) ... 198 D 3
Ringwood (GB) ... 38 B 2
Rinkaby (S) ... 199 G 3
Rinteln (D) ... 85 F 2
Río (E) ... 165 E 4
Rio Maior (P) ... 62 A 5
Rio Marina (I) ... 106 B 5
Riocavado de la Sierra (E) ... 58 C 4
Riogordo (E) ... 75 E 3
Riola Sardo (I) ... 112 B 4
Riolo Terme (I) ... 107 E 2
Riom (F) ... 50 A 2
Riom-ès-Montagnes (F) ... 49 H 4
Riomaggiore (I) ... 105 F 3
Rionero in Vulture (I) ... 110 C 3
Rioseco de Tapia (E) ... 57 G 3
Rioveggio (I) ... 105 H 3
Rioz (F) ... 47 F 5
Ripač (BIH) ... 135 E 5
Ripanj (SRB) ... 140 D 4
Riparbella (I) ... 105 G 5
Ripatransone (I) ... 107 H 5
Ripley (GB) ... 33 E 3
Ripoll (E) ... 60 D 2
Ripon (GB) ... 31 G 5
Riquewihr (F) ... 47 G 2
Riš (BG) ... 159 H 1
Risan (MNE) ... 139 F 4
Risbäck (S) ... 183 G 3

Risca (GB) 35 E2
Riscle (F) 52 D2
Risnes (N) 194 B1
Risør (N) 194 D2
Risøyhamn (N) 179 G2
Rissa (EST) 182 D5
Risti (EST) 200 D2
Ristiina (FIN) 193 F2
Ristijärvi (FIN) 187 F3
Ristilampi (FIN) 181 E5
Ristovac (SRB) 143 F4
Risum (D) 81 G1
Ritíni (GR) 161 F4
Ritoniemi (FIN) 187 F5
Ritsóna (GR) 165 H3
Rittmannshausen (D) . . 85 G4
Riudoms (E) 60 C4
Ríumar (F) 60 B5
Riva del Garda (I) 101 H3
Rivarolo Canavese (I) . . 100 C4
Rive-de-Gier (F) 50 C3
Rives (F) 51 E3
Rivesaltes (F) 53 H4
Rívio (GR) 164 D3
Rivisondoli (I) 109 G3
Rivne (UA) 12 D1
Rivoli (I) 100 B5
Rivolta d'Adda (I) 101 F4
Ríza (GR) 164 D3
Rizário (GR) 161 E3
Rizokarpaso (CY) 175 G1
Rizovoúni (GR) 165 E1
Rjukan (N) 188 D5
Roa (N) 189 E4
Roa de Duero (E) 58 B5
Roadside (GB) 26 B4
Roan (N) 182 D4
Roanne (F) 50 C2
Roata de Jos (RO) 152 A4
Robbio (I) 100 D4
Röbel (D) 83 E4
Robertsfors (S) 185 E4
Robertville (B) 79 F3
Robič (SLO) 134 A2
Robledillo de Gata (E) . . 71 F2
Robledo de Chavela (E) . 64 B2
Robres (E) 59 H4
Rocamadour (F) 49 G5
Rocca di Mezzo (I) 109 E4
Rocca di Papa (I) 109 E3
Rocca San Casciano (I) . 107 E2
Rocca Sinibalda (I) 109 E2
Roccadaspide (I) 110 C4
Roccalbegna (I) 106 D5
Roccalumera (I) 115 G2
Roccamonfina (I) 109 G4
Roccapalumba (I) 114 D3
Roccaraso (I) 109 G3
Roccastrada (I) 106 D5
Roccella Ionica (I) 113 C4
Rocchetta
  Sant' Antonio (I) 110 C3
Rochdale (GB) 32 D2
Rochebonne,
  château de (F) 50 C4
Rochechouart (F) 49 E3
Rochefort (B) 78 D4
Rochefort (F) 48 C2
Rochefort-en-Terre (F) . . 43 E3
Rochefort-Montagne (F). 50 A3
Rochefort-sur-Nenon (F) .47 E5
Rochehaut (B) 78 D4
Rochemaure (F) 50 D5
Rocheservière (F) 43 F5
Rochester (GB) 36 D4
Rochlitz (D) 86 C4
Rociana del Condado (E). 69 F5
Rockenhausen (D) 88 D2
Rocroi (F) 40 C2
Róda (GR) 160 A5
Roda de Isábena (E) . . . 60 A2
Rodacherbrunn (D) 91 E2
Rodavgí (N) 164 C1
Rødberg (N) 188 D4
Rødby (DK) 198 D5
Rødbyhavn (DK) 198 D5

Rødding (DK) 194 C5
Rødding (DK) 198 B3
Rödeby (S) 199 H2
Rodeiro (E) 56 C3
Rødekro (DK) 198 B4
Rodel (GB) 28 B2
Rodellar (E) 59 H3
Roden (NL) 77 D2
Ródenas (E) 65 F2
Rodewisch (D) 86 C5
Rodez (F) 53 H1
Rodi Garganico (I) 110 D1
Rodiezmo (E) 57 G3
Roding (D) 91 G5
Rodítis (GR) 162 D2
Rodna (RO) 147 H2
Rodochóri (GR) 161 E3
Rododáfni (GR) 165 E4
Rodolívos (GR) 162 B3
Rödön (S) 183 G5
Rodópoli (GR) 161 G2
Rodopós (GR) 172 B3
Ródos / Ρόδος (GR) . . . 171 H3
Rodováni (GR) 172 B3
Rodvattnet (S) 184 C5
Rødvig (DK) 199 E4
Roermond (NL) 79 F2
Roeselare (Roulers) (B) . 78 B2
Rogač (HR) 138 B2
Rogača (SRB) 140 D5
Rogačica
  (Gnjilane) (SRB) 143 F4
Rogačica
  (Valjevo) (SRB) 139 G1
Rogalin (PL) 121 E1
Rogaška Slatina (SLO) . 134 D2
Rogatec (SLO) 134 D2
Rogatica (BIH) 137 H5
Rogätz (D) 86 B2
Roggendorf (D) 82 C4
Roggiano Gravina (I) . . 113 B1
Roggosen (D) 87 E3
Rogliano (I) 113 C2
Rognan (N) 179 G5
Rogowo (PL) 117 F5
Rogoznica (HR) 138 A2
Rogoźno (PL) 117 E5
Rohan (F) 42 D2
Rohatyn (UA) 12 D1
Rohožník (SK) 132 A3
Rohr (D) 85 H5
Rohrbach
  in Oberösterreich (A). . 96 D1
Rohrbach-lès-Bitche (F) .41 G5
Rohrbrunn (D) 89 F2
Rohuküla (EST) 200 C2
Roisel (F) 40 A3
Roissy (F) 39 H5
Roja (LV) 202 C2
Rojales / Rojals (E) 73 E3
Rök (S) 195 H3
Rokietnica (PL) 121 E1
Rokiškis (LT) 205 G2
Røkland (N) 179 G5
Rokovci (HR) 137 H2
Rokuan
  kansallispuisto (FIN) . 185 H3
Rokycany (CZ) 91 H3
Røldal (N) 188 C5
Rolfstorp (S) 195 F4
Rolle (CH) 98 B4
Roma (I) 108 D3
Romagnano Sesia (I) . . 100 D4
Roman (BG) 155 E3
Roman (RO) 148 C3
Romana (I) 112 B2
Românaşi (RO) 147 E3
Romangordo (E) 63 G5
Romanija (BIH) 137 H5
Romans-sur-Isère (F) . . . 50 D...
Romanshorn (CH) 99 F1
Rombas (F) 41 F4
Romford (GB) 36 D4
Römhild (D) 89 H1
Romilly-sur-Seine (F) . . . 45 G2
Romny (UA) 7 G5

Romont (CH) 98 C3
Romorantin-
  Lanthenay (F) 44 D4
Romsey (GB) 38 B1
Roncade (I) 103 F4
Ronce-les-Bains (F) 48 B3
Roncegno (I) 102 D3
Roncesvalles /
  Orreaga (E) 59 F2
Ronchamp (F) 47 F3
Ronchi (F) 103 H3
Ronciglione (I) 108 D2
Roncobilaccio (I) 105 H3
Ronda (E) 74 C3
Rønde (DK) 195 E5
Rondeslottet (N) 189 E2
Rondissone (I) 100 C4
Rõngu (EST) 201 F4
Rönnäng (S) 195 F3
Rønne (DK) 199 G4
Ronneburg (D) 86 B5
Ronneby (S) 199 G3
Rønnede (DK) 199 E4
Rönnöfors (S) 183 F5
Ronse (Renaix) (B) 78 B2
Roosendaal (NL) 78 D1
Ropczyce (PL) 127 E5
Roperuelos
  del Páramo (E) 57 G4
Ropinsalmi (FIN) 176 C5
Ropotovo (MK) 145 F1
Roquebillière (F) 55 G1
Roquebrun (F) 54 A3
Roquebrune-
  Cap-Martin (F) 55 H2
Roquecourbe (F) 53 G2
Roquefort (F) 52 C1
Roquefort-sur-Soulzon (F). 54 A2
Roquemaure (F) 54 C1
Roquesteron (F) 55 G2
Roquetaillade,
  château de, ... 48 D5
Roquetas de Mar (E) 75 H3
Roquevaire (F) 55 E3
Rore (BIH) 136 D4
Røros (N) 189 F1
Rorschach (CH) 99 F2
Rørvig (DK) 198 D3
Rørvik (N) 183 E3
Rørvik (N) 182 D5
Ros Comáin /
  Roscommon (IRL) 22 D5
Rosà (I) 103 E4
Rosal de la Frontera (E). 69 E4
Rosans (F) 54 D1
Rosarno (I) 115 H1
Roscoff (F) 42 C1
Roscommon /
  Ros Comáin (IRL) 22 D5
Roscrea (IRL) 25 E2
Rose (I) 113 C2
Rose (MNE) 139 F4
Rosegg (A) 96 D5
Rosen (BG) 157 F4
Rosendal (N) 188 B4
Rosenheim (D) 95 H2
Rosenthal-Bielatal (D) . . 87 E5
Roses (E) 61 F2
Roseto degli Abruzzi (I). 107 H5
Rosheim (F) 47 G1
Roşia (RO) 146 D3
Roşia de Secaş (RO) . . . 147 F5
Rosica (BG) 153 E5
Rosice (CZ) 92 D4
Rosières-en-Santerre (F). 39 H3
Rosignano Marittimo (I). 105 G5
Rosignano Solvay (I) . . 105 G5
Roşiori de Vede (RO) . . . 151 H4
Roskilde (DK) 199 E3
Roskovec (AL) 144 C3
Roslavl' (RUS) 7 F4
Rosmaninhal (P) 63 E5
Rosolina Mare (I) 103 F5
Rosolini (I) 115 F5
Rosoman (MK) 145 G1
Rosporden (F) 42 C3
Ross-on-Wye (GB) 35 F1

Rossano (I) 113 C1
Roßberg (A) 96 D1
Rosscarbery (IRL) 24 C5
Roßdorf (D) 89 E2
Rossell (E) 66 A1
Rosses Point (IRL) 22 D3
Rossio ao Sul do Tejo (P). 62 C5
Rosslare (IRL) 25 F4
Rosslare Harbour /
  Calafort Ros Láir (IRL) . 25 F4
Roßlau (D) 86 B2
Rosslea (GB) 23 E3
Rosson (S) 183 H4
Roßwein (D) 86 D4
Rostock (D) 82 D3
Rostov Veliki (RUS) 7 G1
Rostrenen (F) 42 D2
Rostrevor (GB) 23 G4
Rosvik (N) 179 G4
Rosvik (S) 185 E2
Rosyth (GB) 31 E1
Röszke (H) 129 G5
Rota (I) 74 A3
Rotǎrǎşti (RO) 151 G2
Rotenburg (D) 81 G5
Rotenburg
  an der Fulda (D) 85 G4
Roth (D) 91 E4
Rötha (D) 86 C4
Rothbury (GB) 31 G3
Röthenbach
  an der Pegnitz (D) 91 E4
Rothenburg (D) 87 F3
Rothenburg
  ob der Tauber (D) 89 G3
Rothéneuf (F) 43 F1
Rotherham (GB) 33 E3
Rothes (GB) 29 G3
Rothesay (GB) 30 C2
Rothwell (GB) 33 F5
Rotonda (I) 110 D5
Rotondella (I) 111 E5
Rott (D) 95 F2
Rott am Inn (D) 95 H2
Rottach (D) 95 G3
Rottenbach (D) 89 H1
Rottenburg
  am Neckar (D) 89 F5
Rottenburg
  an der Laaber (D) 95 G1
Rottenmann (A) 96 D3
Rotterdam (NL) 76 D5
Rottne (S) 195 H4
Rottneros (S) 189 G5
Rottweil (D) 94 B2
Rötz (D) 91 G4
Roubaix (F) 40 A1
Roudnice
  nad Labem (CZ) 92 A2
Rouen (F) 39 F4
Rouffach (F) 47 G3
Rougé (F) 43 F3
Rougemont (F) 47 F4
Rougemont-
  le-Château (F) 47 G3
Rouillac (F) 48 D3
Roujan (F) 54 A3
Roulans (F) 47 F3
Roundstone (IRL) 22 B5
Rovaniemi (FIN) 181 E5
Rovato (I) 101 F4
Rovereto (I) 101 H3
Roverud (N) 189 F5
Roviés (GR) 165 G2
Rovigno / Rovinj (HR) . . 134 A4
Rovigo (I) 103 E5
Rovinari (RO) 151 E3
Rovinj / Rovigno (HR) . . 134 A4
Roviśce (HR) 135 F3
Rowy (PL) 117 H2
Royal Leamington
  Spa (GB) 33 E5
Royal Tunbridge
  Wells (GB) 36 D5

Royan (F) 48 C3
Royat (F) 50 A3
Roybon (F) 50 D4
Roye (F) 39 H4
Royère-de-Vassivière (F). 49 G3
Røyrvik (N) 183 F3
Royston (GB) 36 C3
Röyttä (FIN) 185 G1
Rožaje (MNE) 139 H3
Rozalimas (LT) 205 E2
Rózan (PL) 119 E5
Rozay-en-Brie (F) 45 F1
Rožen (BG) 161 H1
Rozino (BG) 158 D1
Rožmitál
  Pod Třemšínem (CZ) . . 92 A4
Rožňava (SK) 133 F3
Rožanstvo (SRB) 139 H1
Rožnov (RO) 148 C4
Rožnov
  pod Radhoštěm (CZ) . . 93 G3
Rozogi (PL) 119 E3
Rozovec (BG) 159 E2
Rozoy-sur-Serre (F) 40 B4
Rozprza (PL) 122 B3
Rótǎrǎşti (RO) 151 G2
Roztoky (CZ) 92 A2
Rozvadov (CZ) 91 G3
Rras (AL) 142 C5
Rrëshen (AL) 144 C1
Rrogozhinë (AL) 144 C2
Rtanj (SRB) 143 F1
Ruabon (GB) 31 G5
Rubbestadneset (N) 188 A5
Rubena (E) 58 C3
Rubeņi (LV) 203 F4
Rubeži (MNE) 139 F4
Rubí (E) 60 D4
Rubí de Bracamonte (E) . 63 H1
Rubiães (P) 56 B5
Rubielos de Mora (E) . . 65 H3
Rubiera (I) 105 H2
Rucǎr (RO) 151 H2
Rucava (LV) 202 A4
Ruciane-Nida (PL) 119 E3
Ruda Śląska (PL) 122 A5
Rudamina (LT) 205 E5
Rudare (SRB) 143 E3
Rudawica (PL) 120 C3
Rüdersdorf bei Berlin (D). 86 D1
Rüdesheim
  am Rhein (D) 88 D2
Rudiškės (LT) 205 E4
Rudiškiai (LT) 205 E1
Rudkøbing (DK) 198 C4
Rudna (PL) 120 D3
Rudna (RUS) 7 E3
Rudna Glava (SRB) . . . 141 F3
Rudnica (MNE) 139 G2
Rudnica (SRB) 142 D2
Rudnik (Kosovska
  Mitrovica) (SRB) 142 D3
Rudnik
  (Kragujevac) (SRB) . . 140 D5
Rudnik
  nad Sanem (PL) 123 F5
Rudo (BG) 139 G2
Rudolphstein (D) 91 F2
Rudolstadt (D) 86 A5
Rudozem (BG) 162 C2
Rue (F) 39 G2
Ruec (BG) 156 D3
Rueda (E) 63 H1
Rueda de Jalón (E) 59 G5
Ruelle-sur-Touvre (F) . . . 49 E3
Ruen Руен (BG) 157 E4
Ruffec (F) 49 E2
Ruffieux (F) 51 E2
Rugby (GB) 33 E5
Rugeley (GB) 32 D4
Rugles (F) 44 C1
Ruhla (D) 85 H5
Ruhland (D) 87 E3
Ruhpolding (D) 95 H3
Ruidera (E) 71 F3
Rüjiena (LV) 203 E1
Ruka (FIN) 181 G5

Ruma / Рума (SRB) 140 C3
Rumboci (BIH) 137 F5
Rumburk (CZ) 87 F4
Rumengol (F) 42 B2
Rumenka (SRB) 140 C3
Rumia (PL) 117 G1
Rumigny (F) 40 C3
Rumilly (F) 51 E2
Rummu (EST) 200 D2
Rumšiškės (LT) 205 F4
Runcorn (GB) 32 C3
Runde (N) 188 B1
Rundvik (S) 184 D5
Runni (FIN) 187 E4
Runtuna (S) 197 F2
Ruokojärvi (FIN) 193 G2
Ruokolahti (FIN) 193 G3
Ruokto (S) 180 A4
Ruoms (F) 54 C1
Ruotsinpyhtää /
  Strömfors (FIN) 193 E4
Ruovesi (FIN) 191 G2
Rupa (HR) 134 B4
Rupea (RO) 147 H5
Rupt-sur-Moselle (F) . . .47 F3
Rus (RO) 147 F2
Rusca Montană (RO) . . 150 D1
Ruscova (RO) 147 G1
Ruše (SLO) 134 D1
Ruse / Русе (BG) 152 B5
Ruşeţu (RO) 152 D3
Ruševo (HR) 135 H4
Rush (IRL) 23 G5
Rushden (GB) 33 F5
Ruski Krstur (SRB) 140 B2
Rusko (FIN) 191 F4
Rusko Selo (SRB) 140 D2
Rusksele (S) 184 C3
Rusnė (LT) 204 B3
Rusokastro (BG) 159 H2
Russborough
  House (IRL) 25 F2
Rüsselsheim (D) 89 E2
Russenes (N) 177 E2
Russi (I) 107 E2
Rust (A) 97 H2
Rustefjelbma (N) 177 G2
Ruswil (CH) 98 D2
Rute (E) 70 C5
Rüthen (D) 85 E3
Ruthin / Rhuthun (GB) . . 32 C4
Rüti (CH) 99 E2
Rutigliano (I) 111 F3
Rutka-Tartak (PL) 119 G1
Rutki-Kossaki (PL) 119 F4
Rutledal (N) 188 B3
Ruukki (FIN) 185 G3
Ruuponsaari (FIN) 185 H5
Ruurlo (NL) 77 F5
Ruvo di Puglia (I) 111 E3
Ruwer (D) 88 B2
Ruynes-
  en-Margeride (F) 50 A4
Ružinci (SRB) 150 D5
Ružomberok (SK) 132 D2
Ry (DK) 194 D5
Ryákia (GR) 161 F4
Rybczewice Drugie (PL) . 123 G4
Rybnik (PL) 125 E1
Rybno (PL) 118 C4
Rychliki (PL) 118 C2
Rychnov
  nad Kněžnou (CZ) . . . 92 D2
Rychnowo (PL) 118 C3
Rychwał (PL) 121 G2
Rychwał (PL) 121 G2
Ryd (S) 195 H5
Ryde (GB) 38 C1
Rydułtowy (PL) 125 E1
Rydzyna (PL) 121 E2
Rye (GB) 36 D5
Rygge (N) 195 E1
Ryglice (PL) 126 D1
Rygnestad (N) 194 C1
Rykene (N) 194 D2
Ryki (PL) 123 E2
Ryl'sk (RUS) 7 G5
Rymań (PL) 116 D2

Rymanów (PL) .... 127 E 2
Rýmařov (CZ) .... 93 E 2
Rymättylä (FIN) .. 191 F 4
Rýmnio (GR) .... 161 E 2
Ryn (PL) ....119 E 2
Rypefjord (N) ....176 D 2
Rypin (PL) ....118 B 4
Rysjedalsvika (N) .. 188 B 3
Rysstad (N) .... 194 C 1
Ryttylä (FIN) ... 191 H 4
Rzásnik (PL) ....119 E 5
Rzeczyca (PL) .... 122 C 2
Rzepin (PL) .... 120 B 1
Rzeszów (PL)......... 127 F 1
Ržev (RUS) ....7 F 2

S

's-Gravendeel (NL) ....76 D 5
's-Heerenberg (NL).. 77 E 5
's-Hertogenbosch (NL).. 77 E 5
Sa Calobra (E)..........67 F 2
Sa Pobla (E) ....67 F 3
Sa Ràpita (E) ....67 F 3
Sääksjärvi (FIN) .... 185 G 5
Saal an der Donau (D)..91 F 5
Saalbach (A) .... 95 H 3
Saales (F) ....47 G 2
Saalfeld (D) .... 86 A 5
Saalfelden
   am Steinernen Meer (A). 96 B 3
Saanen (CH) .... 98 C 4
Saarbrücken (D) .... 88 C 3
Saarburg (D)........... 88 B 2
Sääre (EST) .... 200 B 4
Saarenkylä (FIN) .. 181 E 5
Saari (FIN) .... 193 H 2
Saariharju (FIN) ...... 187 E 1
Saarijärvi (FIN) ... 191 H 1
Saarikoski (FIN) ....176 C 5
Saariselkä (FIN) .. 177 G 5
Saarlouis (D)........... 88 B 3
Saas-Fee (CH) ....98 D 5
Šabac / Шабац (SRB) 140 C 4
Sabadell (E) .... 60 D 3
Săbăoani (RO) .... 148 C 3
Sabaudia (I)........... 109 E 4
Sabbioneta (I) .... 101 G 5
Sabero (E) .... 57 H 3
Sabile (LV) .... 202 B 3
Sabiñánigo (E) ...... 59 H 3
Sabinosa (E)..........67 E 5
Sabiote (E)........... 71 E 3
Šabla (BG) .... 157 G 2
Sablé-sur-Sarthe (F)... 43 H 3
Sables-d'Or-les-Pins (F) 43 E 1
Sabóia (P)........... 68 B 4
Sabres (F)........... 52 C 1
Sabrosa (P) .... 62 D 1
Sabugal (P) .... 63 E 3
Šaca (SK) .... 133 G 3
Sacavém (P) .... 68 A 1
Sacedón (E) .... 64 D 2
Săcel (RO) .... 147 G 2
Săcele (Brașov) (RO).... 152 A 1
Săcele
   (Constanța) (RO)...... 153 F 4
Săceni (RO) .... 151 H 4
Saceruela (E)........... 70 C 1
Sacile (I) .... 103 F 3
Sacoşu Turcesc (RO)... 150 B 1
Sacramenia (E)........ 58 B 5
Săcueni (RO) .... 146 C 2
Sada (E)................. 56 C 1
Sádaba (E) .... 59 F 3
Sădievo (BG) .... 159 G 2
Sadina (BG) .... 156 D 2
Sadovec (BG) .... 155 F 3
Sadovo (BG) .... 157 F 3
Sadovo / Садово (BG).. 159 E 3
Sadu (RO)........... 151 G 1
Sæby (DK) .... 195 E 4
Săedinenie /
   Съединение (BG) .. 158 D 2
Saelices (E) .... 64 D 4
Sælvig (DK) .... 198 C 3
Sævrøy (N)........... 188 A 3
Safara (P) .... 69 E 3

Säffle (S) .... 195 G 1
Saffron Walden (GB) .... 36 D 3
Safonovo (RUS) ....7 F 3
Şag (RO) .... 150 B 1
Šag (RO) .... 146 D 3
Sagard (D) .... 83 F 2
S'Agaró (E) ....61 F 3
Sagiáda (GR) .... 160 B 5
Sagres (P) .... 68 A 5
Sagunt / Sagunto (E).. 65 H 4
Sagvåg (N) .... 188 A 5
Ságvár (H) .... 128 D 3
Sahagún (E).......... 57 H 4
Sahalahti (FIN) ...... 191 G 3
Sahinovići (BIH)...... 137 E 4
Sahl (DK) .... 194 C 5
Sahloinen (FIN) ...... 191 H 2
Šahy (SK) .... 132 C 4
Saignelégier (CH) ...... 98 C 2
Saija (FIN)........... 181 G 4
Saillagouse (F) .... 53 G 5
Saillans (F)........... 50 D 5
Saimaanranta (FIN) .. 193 G 3
Sains (F) .... 40 B 3
Sains-du-Nord (F)...... 40 B 3
Saint Abb's Head National
   Nature Reserve (GB)..31 F 2
Saint-Affrique (F)..... 53 H 2
Saint-Agnant (F) ...... 48 C 2
Saint-Agrève (F).......... 50 C 4
Saint-Aignan (F) ...... 44 D 4
Saint-Aignan-sur-Roë (F). 43 G 3
Saint-Alban-
   sur-Limagnole (F) .... 50 B 5
Saint Albans (GB) .... 36 C 3
Saint-Amand-
   en-Puisaye (F)...... 45 F 4
Saint-Amand-les-Eaux (F). 40 A 2
Saint-Amand-
   Longpré (F) .... 44 C 3
Saint-Amand-
   Montrond (F)...... 49 H 1
Saint-Amans (F) ...... 50 B 5
Saint-Amans-
   des-Cots (F)...... 49 H 5
Saint-Amans-Soult (F)... 53 H 3
Saint-Amant-
   Roche-Savine (F)...... 50 B 3
Saint-Amant-Tallende (F). 50 A 3
Saint-Amarin (F) ......47 G 3
Saint-Ambroix (F) ...... 54 B 1
Saint-Amé (F)..........47 F 3
Saint-Amour (F) ...... 50 D 1
Saint-André-
   de-Cubzac (F)........... 48 C 4
Saint-André-de-l'Eure (F). 39 F 5
Saint-André-
   de-Valborgne (F)...... 54 B 1
Saint-André-les-Alpes (F). 55 F 1
Saint Andrews (GB)....31 E 1
Saint-Anthème (F) ...... 50 B 3
Saint-Antonin-
   Noble-Val (F)........... 53 G 1
Saint-Arnoult-
   en-Yvelines (F)........ 45 E 2
Saint Asaph (GB)........ 32 B 3
Saint-Astier (F) ...... 49 E 4
Saint-Auban (F) ...... 55 G 2
Saint-Aubin-
   d'Aubigné (F) .... 43 F 2
Saint-Aubin-
   du-Cormier (F) ...... 43 F 2
Saint-Aubin-sur-Mer (F). 38 D 4
Saint-Aulaye-
   Puymangou (F) ...... 48 D 4
Saint Austell (GB) .... 34 C 4
Saint-Avold (F)..........41 F 5
Saint-Aygulf (F) ...... 55 G 3
Saint-Béat (F) .... 53 E 4
Saint-Beauzély (F) ...... 53 H 1
Saint-Benin-d'Azy (F) .. 45 G 5
Saint-Benoît-du-Sault (F). 49 F 1
Saint-Benoît-
   sur-Loire (F) .... 45 E 4
Saint-Bertrand-
   de-Comminges (F).. 53 E 4
Saint-Blin (F) .... 46 D 2

Saint-Bonnet-de-Joux (F). 50 C 1
Saint-Bonnet-
   en-Champsaur (F)......51 F 5
Saint-Bonnet-
   le-Château (F) .... 50 C 3
Saint-Brévin-les-Pins (F). 43 E 4
Saint-Briac-sur-Mer (F).. 43 E 1
Saint-Brice-en-Coglès (F). 43 F 2
Saint-Brieuc (F) .... 42 D 1
Saint-Calais (F)........... 44 C 3
Saint-Cast (F) .... 43 E 1
Saint-Céré (F) .... 49 G 5
Saint-Cergue (CH) .... 98 A 4
Saint-Cernin (F) ...... 49 H 4
Saint-Chamas (F)...... 54 D 2
Saint-Chamond (F)...... 50 C 3
Saint-Chély-d'Apcher (F). 50 A 5
Saint-Chély-d'Aubrac (F). 50 A 5
Saint-Chinian (F) ...... 53 H 3
Saint-Ciers-
   sur-Gironde (F)........ 48 C 4
Saint-Cirq-Lapopie (F) .. 53 F 1
Saint-Clair-sur-l'Elle (F).. 38 C 5
Saint-Clar (F) .... 53 E 2
Saint-Claud (F) .... 49 E 2
Saint-Clears (GB) .... 34 C 1
Saint-Cyprien (F) ...... 49 F 5
Saint-Cyprien-Plage (F).. 54 A 5
Saint David's (GB) .... 25 H 4
Saint-Denis (F) .... 39 H 5
Saint-Denis-d'Oléron (F). 48 B 2
Saint-Denis-d'Orques (F). 43 H 3
Saint-Didier-en-Velay (F). 50 C 4
Saint-Dié-
   des-Vosges (F) ....47 G 2
Saint-Dier-d'Auvergne (F). 50 B 3
Saint-Dizier (F) .... 46 D 1
Saint-Donat-
   sur-l'Herbasse (F) .... 50 D 4
Saint-Éloy-les-Mines (F).. 50 A 2
Saint-Émilion (F) ...... 48 D 5
Saint-Étienne (F) ...... 50 C 3
Saint-Étienne-
   de-Baïgorry (F)...... 52 A 3
Saint-Étienne-
   de-Lugdarès (F)...... 50 B 5
Saint-Étienne-
   de-Montluc (F)...... 43 F 4
Saint-Étienne-
   de-Saint-Geoirs (F)....51 E 4
Saint-Étienne-
   de-Tinée (F)...... 55 G 1
Saint-Étienne-
   en-Dévoluy (F)......51 F 5
Saint-Étienne-
   les-Orgues (F)...... 55 E 1
Saint-Fargeau (F) ...... 45 F 4
Saint-Félicien (F)...... 50 C 4
Saint-Firmin (F) ......51 F 5
Saint-Florent (F) ...... 55 H 3
Saint-Florent-le-Vieil (F). 43 G 4
Saint-Florent-sur-Cher (F). 45 E 5
Saint-Florentin (F)...... 45 G 3
Saint-Flour (F) .... 50 A 4
Saint-François-
   Longchamp (F) ....51 F 3
Saint-Fulgent (F)...... 43 G 5
Saint-Galmier (F)...... 50 C 3
Saint-Gaudens (F) ...... 53 E 4
Saint-Gaultier (F)...... 49 F 1
Saint-Genest-
   Malifaux (F) .... 50 C 4
Saint-Gengoux-
   le-National (F)...... 50 C 1
Saint-Geniez-d'Olt-
   et-d'Aubrac (F)...... 53 H 1
Saint-Genis-
   de-Saintonge (F)...... 48 C 3
Saint-Genis-Laval (F)...... 50 D 3
Saint-Genix-
   sur-Guiers (F) ....51 E 3
Saint-Geoire (F) ....51 E 3
Saint-Georges-
   de-Didonne (F)...... 48 C 3
Saint-Georges-
   en-Couzan (F)......... 50 B 3

Saint-Georges-
   sur-Loire (F)........... 43 G 4
Saint-Germain-
   de-Calberte (F) ...... 54 B 1
Saint-Germain-
   des-Fossés (F)......... 50 B 2
Saint-Germain-
   du-Bois (F) ...... 46 D 5
Saint-Germain-
   du-Plain (F) ...... 50 D 1
Saint-Germain-du-Teil (F). 54 A 1
Saint-Germain-
   en-Laye (F) ...... 39 G 5
Saint-Germain-Laval (F). 50 B 3
Saint-Germain-
   Lembron (F) ...... 50 A 3
Saint-Germain-
   les-Belles (F) ...... 49 G 3
Saint-Germain-l'Herm (F). 50 B 3
Saint-Gervais-
   d'Auvergne (F) .... 50 A 2
Saint-Gervais-
   les-Bains (F) ....51 G 2
Saint-Gervais-
   les-Trois-Clochers (F).. 44 B 5
Saint-Gervais-
   sur-Mare (F) ...... 54 A 2
Saint-Géry (F) ...... 53 F 1
Saint-Gildas-de-Rhuys (F). 42 D 4
Saint-Gildas-des-Bois (F). 43 E 4
Saint-Gilles (F)...... 54 C 2
Saint-Gilles-
   Croix-de-Vie (F) ...... 48 E 5
Saint-Gingolph (F) ......51 G 1
Saint-Girons (F) ...... 53 F 4
Saint-Girons-Plage (F).... 52 B 2
Saint-Gobain (F) ...... 40 A 4
Saint-Guénolé (F) ...... 42 B 3
Saint-Guilhem-
   le-Désert (F) ...... 54 A 2
Saint-Haon-le-Châtel (F). 50 B 2
Saint Helens (GB) .... 32 C 3
Saint Helier (GB) .... 38 B 5
Saint-Herblain (F) ...... 43 F 4
Saint-Hilaire (F) ...... 53 G 4
Saint-Hilaire-de-Riez (F). 43 E 5
Saint-Hilaire-
   de-Villefranche (F) .... 48 C 2
Saint-Hilaire-
   des-Loges (F)...... 48 C 1
Saint-Hilaire-
   du-Harcouët (F)...... 43 G 1
Saint-Hippolyte (F)......47 G 4
Saint-Hippolyte-
   du-Fort (F) ...... 54 B 2
Saint-Honoré-
   les-Bains (F)...... 45 H 5
Saint-Hubert (B) ...... 79 E 4
Saint-Imier (CH) ...... 98 C 2
Saint Ives (GB) ...... 33 G 5
Saint Ives (GB) ...... 34 B 5
Saint-Jacques-
   de-la-Lande (F) ...... 43 F 2
Saint-Jacut-de-la-Mer (F). 43 E 1
Saint-James (F) ...... 43 F 2
Saint-Jean-Brévelay (F). 42 D 3
Saint-Jean-Cap-Ferrat (F). 55 H 2
Saint-Jean-d'Angély (F) . 48 C 2
Saint-Jean-
   de-Bournay (F) ...... 50 D 3
Saint-Jean-de-Daye (F).. 38 C 5
Saint-Jean-de-Losne (F). 46 D 5
Saint-Jean-de-Luz (F).. 52 A 3
Saint-Jean-
   de-Maurienne (F) ......51 F 4
Saint-Jean-de-Monts (F). 43 E 5
Saint-Jean-du-Bruel (F).. 54 A 2
Saint-Jean-du-Gard (F).. 54 B 1
Saint-Jean-en-Royans (F).51 E 4
Saint-Jean-
   Pied-de-Port (F) ...... 52 B 3
Saint-Jeoire (F) ....51 F 2
Saint-Jouin-
   de-Marnes (F) ...... 43 H 5
Saint-Juéry (F) ...... 53 G 2
Saint-Julien (F) ....51 E 1
Saint-Julien-Chapteuil (F). 50 C 4

Saint-Julien-
   de-Vouvantes (F).. 43 G 3
Saint-Julien-du-Sault (F). 45 G 3
Saint-Julien-
   en-Genevois (F)........51 F 2
Saint-Julien-l'Ars (F). 49 E 1
Saint-Junien (F) ...... 49 F 2
Saint Just (GB) ...... 34 B 5
Saint-Just-
   en-Chaussée (F)...... 39 H 4
Saint-Just-en-Chevalet (F). 50 B 2
Saint-Rambert (F).. 50 C 3
Saint-Justin (F) ...... 52 C 2
Saint Keverne (GB) ...... 34 B 5
Saint-Lary-Soulan (F)...... 52 D 4
Saint-Laurent-
   de-Chamousset (F) .. 50 C 3
Saint-Laurent-
   de-la-Salanque (F) .... 54 A 4
Saint-Laurent-du-Pont (F).51 E 3
Saint-Laurent-
   en-Grandvaux (F) ......51 E 1
Saint-Laurent-
   les-Bains (F) ...... 50 B 5
Saint-Laurent-Médoc (F). 48 C 4
Saint-Laurent-
   sur-Gorre (F) ...... 49 F 3
Saint-Laurent-sur-Mer (F). 38 C 4
Saint-Léger-
   sous-Beuvray (F) ...... 45 H 5
Saint-Léonard-
   de-Noblat (F) ...... 49 G 3
Saint-Lô (F) ...... 38 C 5
Saint-Louis (F) ......47 H 3
Saint-Loup-
   sur-Semouse (F)......47 F 3
Saint-Loup-
   sur-Thouet (F) ...... 43 H 5
Saint-Luc (CH) ...... 98 D 4
Saint-Lunaire (F) ...... 43 E 1
Saint-Lys (F)...... 53 F 3
Saint-Macaire (F) ...... 48 D 5
Saint-Maixent-l'École (F). 48 D 1
Saint-Malo (F) ...... 43 E 1
Saint-Malo-
   de-la-Lande (F) ...... 38 B 5
Saint-Mamet-
   la-Salvetat (F) ...... 49 H 5
Saint-Mandrier-
   sur-Mer (F)...... 55 E 3
Saint-Marcellin (F) ......51 E 4
Saint Margaret's
   Hope (GB) ...... 26 B 4
Saint-Mars-la-Jaille (F).. 43 G 4
Saint-Martin-
   d'Auxigny (F) ...... 45 E 5
Saint-Martin-
   de-Belleville (F) ......51 F 3
Saint-Martin-
   de-Crau (F) ...... 54 C 2
Saint-Martin-
   de-Londres (F) ...... 54 B 2
Saint-Martin-de-Ré (F). 48 B 2
Saint-Martin-
   de-Seignanx (F) ...... 52 A 2
Saint-Martin-
   de-Valamas (F) ...... 50 C 4
Saint-Martin-du-Canigou,
   abbaye de (F) ...... 53 H 5
Saint-Martin-
   en-Bresse (F)...... 46 D 5
Saint-Martin-Vésubie (F). 55 G 1
Saint-Martory (F) ...... 53 E 4
Saint-Mathieu (F) ...... 49 E 3
Saint-Maurice (CH) ...... 98 C 4
Saint Mawes (GB) ...... 34 B 5
Saint-Maximin-
   la-Sainte-Baume (F) .. 55 E 3
Saint-Médard-
   en-Jalles (F) ...... 48 C 5
Saint-Méen-
   le-Grand (F) ...... 43 E 2
Saint Michael's
   Mount (GB) .... 34 B 5

Saint-Michel (F)........... 40 B 3
Saint-Michel-
   de-Maurienne (F) ....51 F 4
Saint-Michel-
   en-Grève (F) ...... 42 C 1
Saint-Michel-
   en-l'Herm (F) ...... 48 B 1
Saint-Michel-
   Mont-Mercure (F) ..... 43 G 5
Saint-Mihiel (F) ...... 40 D 5
Saint-Nazaire (F) ...... 43 E 4
Saint-Nectaire (F) ...... 50 A 3
Saint Neots (GB) ...... 33 G 5
Saint-Nicolas-
   d'Aliermont (F) ...... 39 F 3
Saint-Nicolas-
   de-la-Grave (F) ...... 53 E 1
Saint-Nicolas-
   de-Port (F)..........47 F 1
Saint-Nicolas-
   du-Pélem (F) ...... 42 D 2
Saint-Omer (F) ...... 39 H 1
Saint-Pair-sur-Mer (F) ... 38 B 5
Saint-Palais (F) ...... 52 B 3
Saint-Palais-sur-Mer (F) . 48 C 3
Saint-Pardoux-
   la-Rivière (F) ...... 49 E 3
Saint-Paul-
   Cap-de-Joux (F) ...... 53 G 2
Saint-Paul-
   de-Fenouillet (F) ...... 53 H 4
Saint-Paul-de-Vence (F). 55 G 2
Saint-Paul-sur-Ubaye (F).51 G 5
Saint-Paul-
   Trois-Châteaux (F) .... 54 C 1
Saint-Paulien (F) ...... 50 B 4
Saint-Pé-de-Bigorre (F). 52 C 4
Saint-Pée-sur-Nivelle (F). 52 A 3
Saint-Péray (F) ...... 50 D 4
Saint-Père-en-Retz (F) . 43 E 4
Saint Peter Port (GB) .... 38 A 4
Saint-Philbert-
   de-Grand-Lieu (F)..... 43 F 5
Saint-Pierre-
   d'Albigny (F) ....51 F 3
Saint-Pierre-
   de-Chartreuse (F) ......51 E 3
Saint-Pierre-
   de-Chignac (F) ...... 49 F 4
Saint-Pierre-d'Oléron (F). 48 B 2
Saint-Pierre-Église (F) ... 38 B 4
Saint-Pierre-le-Moûtier (F). 45 F 5
Saint-Pierre-Quiberon (F). 42 D 4
Saint-Pierre-sur-Dives (F). 38 D 5
Saint-Pois (F) ...... 43 G 1
Saint-Pol-de-Léon (F) .. 42 C 1
Saint-Pol-sur-Ternoise (F). 39 H 2
Saint-Pons-
   de-Thomières (F)...... 53 H 3
Saint-Porchaire (F) ...... 48 C 2
Saint-Pourçain-
   sur-Sioule (F)........... 50 A 1
Saint-Privat (F) ...... 49 G 4
Saint-Quay-
   Portrieux (F) ...... 42 D 1
Saint-Quentin (F) ...... 40 A 3
Saint-Rambert-
   d'Albon (F) ...... 50 D 4
Saint-Rambert-
   en-Bugey (F)..........51 E 3
Saint-Raphaël (F) ...... 55 G 3
Saint-Rémy-
   de-Provence (F) ...... 54 D 2
Saint-Rémy-
   sur-Durolle (F) ...... 50 B 2
Saint-Renan (F) ...... 42 B 1
Saint-Riquier (F) ...... 39 G 3
Saint-Romain-
   de-Colbosc (F) ...... 39 E 4
Saint-Rome-de-Tarn (F). 53 H 1
Saint-Saëns (F) ...... 39 F 4
Saint-Satur (F) ...... 45 F 4
Saint-Saulge (F) ...... 45 G 5
Saint-Sauveur-
   en-Puisaye (F)...... 45 G 4
Saint-Sauveur-
   le-Vicomte (F)........ 38 B 4

Saint-Sauveur-Lendelin (F) .... 38 B 5
Saint-Sauveur-sur-Tinée (F) ..... 55 G 1
Saint-Savin (F) .... 49 F 1
Saint-Savin (F) .... 48 C 4
Saint-Savinien (F) .... 48 C 2
Saint-Seine-l'Abbaye (F) .... 46 D 4
Saint-Sernin-sur-Rance (F) .... 53 H 2
Saint-Servan-sur-Mer (F) .... 43 F 1
Saint-Sever (F) .... 52 C 2
Saint-Sever-Calvados (F). 38 C 5
Saint-Sulpice-les-Feuilles (F) .... 49 F 1
Saint-Symphorien (F) .. 52 C 1
Saint-Symphorien-de-Lay (F) .... 50 C 2
Saint-Symphorien-d'Ozon (F) .... 50 D 3
Saint-Symphorien-sur-Coise (F) .... 50 C 3
Saint-Thégonnec Loc-Eguiner (F) .... 42 C 1
Saint-Trivier-de-Courtes (F) .... 50 D 1
Saint-Trivier-sur-Moignans (F) ..... 50 D 2
Saint-Trojan-les-Bains (F) .... 48 B 2
Saint-Tropez (F) .... 55 G 3
Saint-Vaast-la-Hougue (F) .... 38 C 4
Saint-Valery-en-Caux (F). 39 E 3
Saint-Valery-sur-Somme (F) .... 39 G 3
Saint-Vallier (F) .... 50 D 4
Saint-Vallier-de-Thiey (F) .... 55 G 2
Saint-Varent (F) .... 43 H 5
Saint-Vaury (F) .... 49 G 2
Saint-Véran (F) ...51 G 5
Saint-Vincent (I) ...... 100 C 3
Saint-Vincent-de-Tyrosse (F) .... 52 B 2
Saint-Vivien-de-Médoc (F) .... 48 C 3
Saint-Wandrille-Rançon (F) .... 39 F 4
Saint-Yorre (F) .... 50 B 2
Saint-Yrieix-la-Perche (F). 49 F 3
Sainte-Adresse (F) ...... 39 E 4
Sainte-Anne-d'Auray (F). 42 D 3
Sainte-Croix (CH) ..... 98 B 3
Sainte-Croix-du-Mont (F). 48 D 5
Sainte-Croix-Volvestre (F). 53 F 4
Sainte-Enimie (F) ..... 54 A 1
Sainte-Foy-la-Grande (F). 49 E 5
Sainte-Foy-l'Argentière (F) .... 50 C 3
Sainte-Geneviève-sur-Argence (F) ..... 50 A 5
Sainte-Hélène (F) ..... 48 C 4
Sainte-Hermine (F) ...... 48 C 1
Sainte-Livrade-sur-Lot (F). 53 E 1
Sainte-Lucie-de-Tallano (F) ..... 55 H 5
Sainte-Marie-aux-Mines (F) ....47 G 2
Sainte-Maure-de-Touraine (F) ...... 44 C 5
Sainte-Maxime (F) ..... 55 G 3
Sainte-Menehould (F). 40 D 5
Sainte-Mère-Église (F) .. 38 C 4
Sainte-Sévère-sur-Indre (F) .... 49 G 1
Sainte-Suzanne-et-Chammes (F) ..... 43 H 2
Sainte-Tulle (F) ..... 55 E 2
Saintes (F) .... 48 C 3
Saintes-Maries-de-la-Mer (F) ..... 54 C 3
Saintfield (GB) .... 23 G 3
SaintMonans (GB) ......31 E 1
Saissac (F) .... 53 G 3

Šajkaš (SRB) .... 140 C 3
Šakiai (LT) .... 204 D 3
Sakskøbing (DK) ...... 198 D 4
Saku (EST) .... 200 D 2
Sakula (SRB) .... 140 D 3
Säkylä (FIN) .... 191 F 3
Sala (S) .... 190 B 5
Šal'a (SK) .... 132 B 4
Sala Consilina (I) .... 110 C 4
Sălacea (RO) .... 146 D 2
Salacgrīva (LV) .... 202 D 1
Salakas (LT) .... 205 H 2
Salamajärvi (FIN) ..... 185 G 5
Salamanca (E) .... 63 G 2
Salamína / Σαλαμίνα (GR) .... 165 H 4
Salamiou (CY) ....174 C 4
Salamis (CY) .... 175 F 3
Salantai (LT) .... 204 C 1
Salánti (GR) .... 169 E 2
Salar (E) .... 70 D 5
Sălard (RO) .... 146 C 2
Salardú (E) .... 60 B 1
Salas (E) .... 57 F 1
Salaš (SRB) ....141 G 5
Salas de los Infantes (E). 58 C 4
Salaspils (LV) .... 202 D 3
Sălătrucu (RO) .... 151 G 2
Salbohed (S) .... 190 B 5
Salbris (F) .... 45 E 4
Salcia (RO) .... 151 E 4
Šalčininkai (LT) ...... 205 G 5
Salcombe (GB) .... 34 D 5
Saldaña (E) .... 58 A 3
Saldus (LV) .... 202 B 3
Sale (I) .... 101 E 5
Salem (D) .... 94 C 3
Salemi (I) ....114 B 3
Sälen (S) .... 189 G 3
Salen (Argyll and Bute) (GB). 28 D 5
Salen (Highland) (GB) ... 28 D 5
Salernes (F) .... 55 F 2
Salerno (I) .... 109 H 5
Salers (F) .... 49 H 4
Salgótarján (H) ...... 126 B 5
Sali (HR) .... 136 B 5
Salice Terme (I) ...... 101 E 5
Salies-de-Béarn (F) ..... 52 B 3
Salies-du-Salat (F) ...... 53 E 4
Salignac-Eyvigues (F).. 49 F 4
Salihli (TR) ....19 G 3
Salihorsk (BY) ......6 D 5
Salinas (E) .... 57 G 1
Salindres (F) .... 54 B 1
Salins (F) ....47 E 5
Salisbury (GB) .... 35 G 3
Sălişte (RO) .... 151 F 1
Săliştea de Sus (RO) .... 147 G 2
Salla (FIN) .... 181 G 4
Sallanches (F) ....51 F 2
Sallent (E) .... 60 D 3
Sallent de Gállego (E) .. 59 H 2
Salles-Curan (F) .... 53 H 1
Salles-sur-l'Hers (F) ..... 53 G 3
Salmanovo (BG) .... 157 E 3
Salmerón (E) .... 65 E 2
Salmoral (E) .... 63 H 2
Salmünster (D) .... 89 F 1
Salo (FIN) .... 191 G 4
Salò (I) .... 101 G 4
Salobreña (E) ....75 F 3
Salon-de-Provence (F) .. 54 D 2
Salonta (RO) .... 146 C 3
Salorino (E) .... 63 E 5
Salou (E) .... 60 C 5
Salsbruket (N) .... 183 E 3
Salses-le-Château (F) ... 53 H 4
Salses, fort de (F) .... 53 H 4
Salsomaggiore Terme (I) .... 105 F 2
Saltash (GB) .... 34 D 4
Saltburn-by-the-Sea (GB) ....31 H 4

Saltcoats (GB) .... 30 C 2
Salto (P) .... 56 C 5
Saltoluokta (S) ...... 180 A 4
Saltvik (FIN) .... 190 D 5
Saltzgitter-Lebenstedt (D) .... 85 H 2
Saluggia (I) .... 100 C 4
Saluzzo (I) .... 104 B 2
Salva (RO) .... 147 G 2
Salvacañete (E) .... 65 F 3
Salvagnac (F) .... 53 F 2
Salvan (CH) .... 98 C 4
Salvaterra de Magos (P). 68 B 1
Salvaterra de Miño (E)... 56 B 4
Salvatierra / Agurain (E). 59 E 2
Salvatierra de los Barros (E) .... 69 F 2
Salviac (F) .... 49 F 5
Salzburg (A) .... 96 B 3
Salzgitter-Bad (D) .... 85 H 2
Salzhausen (D) ....81 H 5
Salzkotten (D) .... 85 E 3
Salzwedel (D) .... 82 C 5
Šamac / Bosanski Šamac (BIH). 137 G 3
Samarína (GR) .... 160 C 4
Samatan (F) .... 53 E 3
Sambiase (I) ....113 C 3
Sambir (UA) ....12 C 2
Samboal (E) .... 64 A 1
Sambuca di Sicilia (I)....114 C 3
Samedan (CH) .... 99 G 4
Samer (F) .... 39 G 2
Sámi (GR) .... 164 C 4
Sammatti (FIN) .... 191 G 4
Sammichele di Bari (I)....111 E 3
Samnanger (N) .... 188 B 4
Samobor (HR) .... 134 D 3
Samodreža (SRB) ..... 143 E 3
Samoëns (F) ....51 G 2
Samokov (MK) .... 145 E 1
Samokov / Самоков (BG). 158 B 2
Samorín (SK) .... 132 A 4
Samos (E) .... 56 D 3
Samoš (SRB) .... 140 D 3
Sámos / Σάμος (GR) .... 167 G 5
Samothráki (GR) ...... 162 D 4
Samovodene (BG) ..... 159 F 1
Sampatiki (GR) .... 169 E 3
Samper de Calanda (E). 65 H 1
Sampeyre (I) .... 104 B 2
Samtens (D) .... 83 F 2
Samugheo (I) ....112 C 2
San Adrián (E) .... 59 E 3
San Agustín del Guadalix (E) .... 64 C 2
San Amaro (E) .... 56 C 4
San Andrés del Rabanedo (E) ..... 57 G 3
San Antolín de Ibias (E). 57 E 2
San Antonio Abad / Sant Antoni de Portmany (E). 66 C 4
San Bartolomé de la Torre (E) ...... 69 E 5
San Bartolomé de las Abiertas (E) .... 64 A 4
San Bartolomeo in Galdo (I) ....110 B 2
San Benedetto del Tronto (I) .... 107 H 5
San Benedetto in Alpe (I) .... 106 D 2
San Benedetto Po (I) ... 101 H 5
San Bernardino (CH) .. 99 F 4
San Biagio Platani (I)....114 D 4
San Bonifacio (I) ...... 101 H 4
San Candido / Innichen (I) .... 103 F 1
San Carlos del Valle (E). 71 E 2
San Casciano in Val di Pesa (I) ..... 105 H 4
San Cataldo (I) ....111 H 4
San Cataldo (I) .... 115 E 4
San Cipirello (I) ....114 C 3
San Clemente (E) .... 65 E 5
San Colombano al Lambro (I) .... 101 F 5

San Cosme (E) .... 57 E 1
San Cristóbal de Entreviñas (E) .... 57 G 5
San Cristóbal de la Vega (E) .... 64 A 1
San Damiano d'Asti (I).. 100 C 5
San Daniele del Friuli (I). 103 G 3
San Daniele Po (I) .... 101 G 5
San Demetrio Corone (I).113 C 2
San Donà di Piave (I) ... 103 F 4
San Donaci (I) ....111 G 4
San Emiliano (E) .... 57 G 2
San Esteban (E) .... 57 G 1
San Esteban de Gormaz (E) .... 58 C 5
San Esteban del Molar (E). 57 G 5
San Esteban del Valle (E). 63 H 3
San Fele (I) ....110 C 4
San Felice a Cancello (I). 109 H 5
San Felice Circeo (I) .... 109 E 4
San Felice sul Panaro (I). 105 H 2
San Felices de los Gallegos (E) .... 63 E 4
San Ferdinando di Puglia (I) ....110 D 2
San Fernando (E) ....74 A 4
San Fratello (I) ....115 F 2
San Galgano, abbazia (I) .... 106 D 4
San Gavino Monreale (I).112 B 4
San Gemini (I) .... 107 F 5
San Giacomo / Sankt Jakob (I) .... 103 E 1
San Gimignano (I) ..... 105 H 5
San Ginesio (I) .... 107 G 4
San Giorgio del Sannio (I) .... 109 H 4
San Giorgio Canavese (I). 100 C 4
San Giorgio di Nogaro (I). 103 G 3
San Giorgio Ionico (I)....111 F 4
San Giorgio Piacentino (I) .... 101 F 5
San Giovanni a Piro (I)...110 C 5
San Giovanni di Sinis (I) .112 B 3
San Giovanni in Fiore (I).113 C 2
San Giovanni in Persiceto (I) .... 105 H 2
San Giovanni Lupatoto (I) .... 101 H 4
San Giovanni Rotondo (I).110 C 2
San Giovanni Suergiu (I).112 B 5
San Giovanni Valdarno (I) .... 106 D 3
San Giuliano Terme (I).. 105 G 4
San Giustino (I) .... 107 E 3
San Ildefonso o La Granja (E) .... 64 B 1
San Isidro (E) .... 72 C 5
San Javier (E) .... 73 E 3
San José (E) .... 72 C 5
San Jose / Sant Josep de sa Talaia (E) .... 66 C 4
San Juan de Alicante / Sant Joan d'Alacant (E). 73 E 2
San Juan de la Peña, monasterio de (E) ..... 59 G 3
San Juan de los Terreros (E) ..... 71 H 5
San Juan del Olmo (E)... 63 H 3
San Juan del Puerto (E).. 69 E 5
San Lazzaro di Savena (I) .... 106 D 1
San Leo (I) .... 107 F 3
San Leonardo de Yagüe (E) .... 58 D 4
San Leonardo in Passiria (I) .... 101 H 1
San Lorenzo de Calatrava (E) ...... 70 D 3
San Lorenzo de la Parrilla (E) ..... 65 E 4
San Lorenzo Nuovo (I). 107 E 5
San Lucido (I) .... 113 B 2
San Luis de Sabinillas (E).74 C 4
San Marcello (I) .... 107 G 3
San Marcello Pistoiese (I). 105 H 4
San Marco Argentano (I).113 B 2

San Marco dei Cavoti (I). 109 H 4
San Marco in Lamis (I)...110 C 2
San Marino (RSM) ...... 107 F 3
San Martín de Castañeda (E) ...... 57 E 4
San Martín de la Vega (E). 64 C 3
San Martín de Montalbán (E) .... 64 A 4
San Martín de Valdeiglesias (E) ... 64 A 3
San Martino di Castrozza (I) .... 103 E 2
San Mateo de Gállego (E). 59 G 4
San Mauro Forte (I) ....110 D 4
San Michele all'Adige (I). 101 H 3
San Miguel de Salinas (E). 73 E 3
San Miguel del Arroyo (E). 58 A 5
San Millán de la Cogolla (E) .... 58 D 3
San Millán de Lara (E) .. 58 C 4
San Miniato (I) .... 105 H 4
San Nicolás del Puerto (E) .... 69 H 4
San Nicolo (I) .... 107 E 1
San Nicolò Gerrei (I)....112 C 4
San Pancrazio Salentino (I) ....111 G 4
San Pedro (E) .... 71 G 2
San Pedro de Alcántara (E) ....74 D 4
San Pedro de Latarce (E). 57 H 5
San Pedro de Mérida (E). 69 G 1
San Pedro del Arroyo (E). 63 H 2
San Pedro del Pinatar (E). 73 E 3
San Pedro Manrique (E) .... 59 E 4
San Pellegrino Terme (I). 101 F 4
San Piero a Sieve (I) ... 105 H 4
San Pietro in Casale (I) . 106 D 1
San Pietro Vernotico (I)..111 G 4
San Polo d'Enza (I) .... 105 G 2
San Quirico d'Orcia (I).. 106 D 4
San Rafael (E) .... 64 B 2
San Remo (I) .... 104 C 4
San Roque (E) ....74 C 4
San Roque (E) .... 56 B 2
San Rufo (I) ....110 C 4
San Sadurniño (E) ...... 56 C 1
San Salvador de Cantamuda (E) ..... 58 A 2
San Salvo (I) .... 109 H 2
San Sebastián (Donostia) (E) .... 59 E 1
San Sebastián de la Gomera (E) ....67 F 5
San Sebastiano Curone (I) .... 105 E 4
San Severino Marche (I). 107 G 4
San Severo (I) .... 110 C 2
San Silvestre de Guzmán (E) .... 68 D 5
San Sperate (I) ....112 C 5
San Stefano (BG) ...... 159 H 2
San Telmo (E) .... 69 E 4
San Teodoro (I) ....112 D 2
San Valentino alla Muta / Sankt Valentin auf der Haide (I) ..... 101 G 1
San Vicente de Alcántara (E) ..... 62 D 5
San Vicente de la Barquera (E) .... 58 A 1
San Vicente de la Cabeza (E) ..... 57 F 5
San Vicente del Raspeig (E) ..... 73 F 2
San Vigilio di Marebbe / Sankt Vigil Enneberg (I) .... 103 E 1
San Vincenzo (I) .... 106 C 4
San Vitero (E) .... 57 F 5
San Vito al Tagliamento (I) ... 103 G 3
San Vito Chietino (I) .... 109 H 2
San Vito dei Normanni (I).111 G 4
San Vito di Cadore (I) ... 103 F 2

San Vito lo Capo (I) ......114 B 2
San Vito sullo Ionio (I)...113 C 3
San Vittore del Lazio (I). 109 G 4
Sânandrei (RO) .... 146 B 3
Sanary-sur-Mer (F) ...... 55 E 3
Sancergues (F) .... 45 F 3
Sancerre (F) .... 45 F 4
Sanchidrián (E) .... 64 A 1
Sancoins (F) .... 45 F 5
Sâncraiu de Mureș (RO). 147 G 4
Sancti Petri (E) ....74 A 4
Sancti-Spíritus (E) ..... 63 F 2
Sand (N) .... 188 B 5
Sand (N) .... 189 F 4
Sand in Taufers / Campo Tures (I) ..... 103 E 1
Sandane (N) .... 188 C 2
Sandanski / Сандански (BG) ...... 161 G 1
Sandarne (S) .... 190 B 3
Sandau (D) .... 82 D 5
Sandbach (GB) .... 32 D 3
Sande (D) ....81 F 4
Sande (N) .... 188 B 1
Sande (N) .... 189 E 5
Sande (P) .... 62 C 1
Sandefjord (N) ...... 195 E 1
Sandeid (N) .... 188 B 5
Sandgerði (IS) .... 178 A 3
Sandnes (N) .... 194 A 1
Sandness (GB) .... 27 D 3
Sandnessjøen (N) ..... 183 F 1
Sando (E) .... 63 F 2
Sandomierz (PL) ..... 123 E 4
Sândominic (RO) ...... 148 B 4
Sándorfalva (H) ...... 129 G 4
Sandown (GB) .... 38 C 1
Sandrigo (I) .... 103 E 4
Sandringham House (GB). 33 H 4
Šandrovac (HR) ...... 135 F 3
Sandstad (N) .... 182 C 5
Sănduleni (RO) .... 148 C 4
Sandur (Færøerne) (DK). 194 A 5
Sandviken (S) .... 190 B 4
Sandvikvåg (N) .... 188 B 4
Sandwich (GB) .... 37 E 4
Sandy (GB) .... 33 G 5
Sangarcía (E) .... 64 A 1
Sangaste (EST) .... 201 F 4
Sângeorgiu de Pădure (RO) ...... 147 H 4
Sângeorz-Băi (RO) .... 147 G 2
Sangerhausen (D) ..... 86 A 3
Sangis (S) .... 185 F 1
Sangüesa (E) .... 59 F 3
Sanguinet (F) .... 48 B 5
Saní (GR) .... 161 G 5
Sanica (BIH) .... 136 D 4
Sanitz (D) .... 83 E 3
Sankt Aegyd am Neuwalde (A) ..... 97 F 2
Sankt Andrä (A) .... 97 E 5
Sankt Andreasberg (D). 85 H 3
Sankt Anton am Arlberg (A) .... 95 E 4
Sankt Blasien (D) .... 94 B 3
Sankt Christophen (A).. 97 G 2
Sankt Gallen (A) .... 97 E 3
Sankt Gallen (CH) ..... 99 F 2
Sankt Gallenkirch (A)... 94 D 4
Sankt Georgen am Längsee (A) .... 97 E 5
Sankt Georgen im Attergau (A) .... 96 C 2
Sankt Georgen im Schwarzwald (D) ..... 94 B 2
Sankt Gilgen (A) .... 96 C 3
Sankt Goar (D) .... 88 D 1
Sankt Goarshausen (D).. 88 D 1
Sankt Ingbert (D) ..... 88 C 3
Sankt Jakob / San Giacomo (I) ..... 103 E 1
Sankt Jakob im Rosental (A) .... 96 D 5
Sankt Johann im Pongau (A) .... 96 C 4
Sankt Johann in Tirol (A). 95 H 3

A B C D E F G H I J K L M N O P Q R S T U V W X Y Z

Sankt Lambrecht (A) .... 96 D 4
Sankt Leonhard am Forst (A)........... 97 F 2
Sankt Leonhard im Pitztal (A) .... 95 F 4
Sankt Lorenzen im Lesachtal (A)....... 96 B 5
Sankt Margarethen (D)..81 G 3
Sankt Märgen (D)... 94 B 2
Sankt Michael im Lungau (A)........ 96 C 4
Sankt Michael in Obersteiermark (A) . 97 E 3
Sankt Michaelisdonn (D).81 G 3
Sankt Moritz (CH)..... 99 G 4
Sankt Niklaus (CH) ..... 98 D 4
Sankt Olof (S) .... 199 F 3
Sankt Oswald (A) ..... 96 D 5
Sankt Paul im Lavanttal (A)... 97 E 5
Sankt Peter in der Au Markt (A)... 97 E 2
Sankt Peter-Ording (D)..81 F 2
Sankt-Peterburg (RUS)...6 D 1
Sankt Pölten (A)........ 97 F 1
Sankt Ulrich / Ortisei (I) 103 E 2
Sankt Valentin (A)..... 97 E 2
Sankt Valentin auf der Haide / San Valentino alla Muta ..... 101 G 1
Sankt Veit an der Glan (A). 96 D 5
Sankt Vigil Enneberg / San Vigilio di Marebbe ... 103 E 1
Sankt Vith (B) .... 79 F 4
Sankt Wendel (D)... 88 C 3
Sankt Wolfgang im Salzkammergut (A). 96 C 3
Sanlúcar de Barrameda (E) .....74 A 3
Sanlúcar de Guadiana (E) ...... 68 D 5
Sanlúcar la Mayor (E).... 69 F 5
Sanluri (I) ....112 B 4
Sànmartin (RO) .... 148 B 5
Sânmihaiu Almaşului (RO)...... 147 E 3
Sânmihaiu de Câmpie (RO)... 147 G 3
Sânmihaiu Român (RO). 150 B 1
Sannainen (FIN)........ 193 E 4
Sannazzaro de' Burgondi (I) ... 101 E 5
Sannicandro di Bari (I)...111 E 3
Sannicandro Garganico (I)........110 C 1
Sânnicolau Mare (RO). 146 A 5
Sanniki (PL) .... 122 B 1
Sanok (PL) .... 127 F 2
Sanquhar (GB) .... 30 D 3
Sansepolcro (I) .... 107 E 3
Sanski Most (BIH) .... 135 F 5
Sant' Agata de' Goti (I) 109 H 4
Sant' Agata di Militello (I).115 F 2
Sant' Agata di Puglia (I) .110 C 3
Sant Agustí de Lluçanès (E)........ 60 D 2
Sant' Andrea Frius (I)..112 C 4
Sant Andreu de Llavaneres (E)....61 E 3
Sant' Angelo dei Lombardi (I)......110 B 3
Sant' Angelo in Vado (I). 107 F 3
Sant' Angelo Lodigiano (I)..... 101 E 5
Sant' Antioco (I).........112 B 5
Sant Antoni de Calonge (E) ....61 F 3
Sant Antoni de Portmany / San Antonio Abad (E) . 66 C 4
Sant' Antonio di Gallura (I)..........112 C 1
Sant Boi de Lluçanès (E). 60 D 2
Sant Carles de la Ràpita (E)... 66 B 1
Sant Celoni (E) ....61 E 3
Sant Cugat del Vallès (E) .... 60 D 4

Sant Esteve d'En Bas (E) ..61 E 2
Sant Feliu de Guíxols (E). .61 F 3
Sant Francesc de Formentera (E)..... 66 D 5
Sant Hilari Sacalm (E) ...61 E 3
Sant Hipòlit de Voltregà (E) .... 60 D 2
Sant Joan d'Alacant / San Juan de Alicante (E) .... 73 F 2
Sant Joan de les Abadesses (E) .. 60 D 2
Sant Josep de sa Talaia / San Jose (E) .... 66 C 4
Sant Julià de Lòria (AND) . 60 C 1
Sant Llorenç de Morunys (E)........ 60 C 2
Sant Lluís (E)...........67 H 2
Sant Mateu (E) .... 66 A 1
Sant Miquel (E) .... 66 D 4
Sant' Onofrio (I)........115 H 1
Sant Pau de Segúries (E) .61 E 2
Sant Pere de Rodes, monestir de (E)........61 F 2
Sant Pol de Mar (E)......61 E 3
Sant Quirze de Besora (E).......... 60 D 2
Sant Quirze Safaja (E) .. 60 D 3
Sant Ramon (E) .... 60 C 3
Sant Sadurní d'Anoia (E) .... 60 D 4
Sant Salvador de Toló (E) 60 B 2
Santa Amalia (E) ...... 69 G 1
Santa Ana (E) .... 71 G 2
Santa Bàrbara (E) ..... 60 B 5
Santa Bárbara de Casa (E) .... 69 E 4
Santa Catarina da Fonte do Bispo (P) . 68 D 5
Santa Caterina di Pittinuri (I).........112 B 3
Santa Caterina Valfurva (I) .... 101 G 2
Santa Caterina Villarmosa (I) ....115 E 3
Santa Cesarea Terme (I) .111 H 5
Santa Coloma de Farners (E)..........61 E 3
Santa Coloma de Queralt (E) .... 60 C 4
Santa Colomba de Somoza (E) ...... 57 F 4
Santa Comba (E) ...... 56 B 2
Santa Comba Dão (P) .. 62 C 3
Santa Comba de Rossas (P)....... 57 E 5
Santa Croce di Magliano (I) ....110 B 2
Santa Cruz de la Palma (E)........67 E 5
Santa Cruz de la Sierra (E) .... 69 G 1
Santa Cruz de la Zarza (E)........ 64 C 3
Santa Cruz de Moya (E).. 65 G 3
Santa Cruz de Mudela (E). 71 E 2
Santa Cruz de Tenerife (E).67 F 5
Santa Cruz del Retamar (E) ...... 64 B 3
Santa Elena (E)......... 71 E 4
Santa Eufemia (E) .... 70 B 2
Santa Eufemia Lamezia (I)...........113 C 3
Santa Eulalia (E)..... 65 G 2
Santa Eulàlia (E)..... 69 E 1
Santa Eulalia de Oscos (E). 57 E 2
Santa Eulalia del Río (E) . 66 D 4
Santa Fe (E).......... 70 D 5
Santa Fiora (E) .... 106 D 3
Santa Gertrude (I)..... 101 H 2
Santa Giusta (I) ....112 B 3
Santa Kurutze Kanpezu (E)..... 59 E 2
Santa Lucia del Mela (I)..115 G 2
Santa Luzia (P)..... 68 C 4
Santa Magdalena de Pulpis (E) .... 66 A 1

Santa Margalida (E) .....67 F 2
Santa Margarida do Sàdão (P) .... 68 C 3
Santa Margherita (I)....112 B 5
Santa Margherita di Belice (I)...........114 C 3
Santa Margherita Ligure (I) ..... 105 E 3
Santa Maria Capua Vetere (I)..... 109 G 4
Santa Maria da Feira (P) . 62 B 2
Santa María de Huerta (E). 65 E 1
Santa María de Nieva (E) . 71 G 5
Santa Maria de Valverde (E)...... 57 G 5
Santa Maria degli Angeli (I) .... 107 F 4
Santa María del Campo (E)........ 58 B 4
Santa María del Campo Rus (E).... 65 E 4
Santa Maria del Páramo (E)...... 57 G 4
Santa Maria della Versa (I) .... 101 E 5
Santa María la Real de Nieva (E)... 64 A 1
Santa Maria Maggiore (I). 100 D 3
Santa-Maria-Siché (F) .. 55 H 5
Santa Marina de Valdeón (E)...... 57 H 2
Santa Marina del Rey (E). 57 G 3
Santa Marinella (I) ..... 108 C 2
Santa Marta (E) ..... 69 F 2
Santa Marta de Penaguião (P)..... 62 D 1
Santa Marta de Tormes (E) ..... 63 G 2
Santa Ninfa (I) ....114 C 3
Santa Olalla (E)....... 64 A 3
Santa Olalla del Cala (E). 69 F 4
Santa Pau (E)..........61 E 2
Santa Pola (E) ..... 73 F 2
Santa Ponça (E).......67 E 3
Santa Severa (I) ..... 108 C 2
Santa Sofia (I) ..... 107 E 2
Santa Sofia d'Epiro (I) ...113 C 2
Santa Susanna (E)...61 E 3
Santa Teresa di Riva (I) ..115 G 2
Santa Teresa Gallura (I)..112 C 1
Santa Uxía de Ribeira (E). 56 B 3
Santa Venera (M).......114 C 5
Santaella (E) ..... 70 B 5
Santaliestra y San Quílez (E)... 60 A 2
Sàntămăria-Orlea (RO) . 151 E 1
Santana (P) ..... 68 A 4
Sântana (RO)... 146 B 4
Santana da Serra (P)..... 68 C 5
Santander (E) ..... 58 B 1
Santanyí (E)............67 F 3
Santarcangelo di Romagna (I) ..... 107 F 2
Santarém (P)..... 68 B 1
Santas Martas (E) ..... 57 H 4
Sant'Elia a Pianisi (I)... 109 H 3
Sant'Elpidio a Mare (I) .. 107 H 4
Santeramo in Colle (I) ...111 E 4
Santes Creus, monestir (E)........... 60 C 4
Santesteban / Doneztebe (E) ..... 59 F 1
Santhià (I) .... 100 D 4
Santiago de Alcántara (E)...... 62 D 5
Santiago de Compostela (E) .... 56 B 2
Santiago de la Espada (E). 71 F 3
Santiago de la Ribera (E). 73 E 3
Santiago del Campo (E). 63 F 5
Santiago do Cacém (P) .. 68 B 3
Santiago do Escoural (P)..... 68 C 2
Santibáñez de Béjar (E).. 63 G 3
Santibáñez de la Peña (E). 58 A 2
Santibáñez de la Sierra (E). 63 G 3

Santibáñez de Vidriales (E)........ 57 G 4
Santillana del Mar (E)... 58 B 1
Santiponce (E) .... 69 G 5
Santisteban del Puerto (E) .... 71 E 3
Santo Domingo de la Calzada (E) .... 58 D 3
Santo Domingo de Silos (E)........... 58 C 4
Santo Estêvão (P) ...... 68 B 1
Santo Estêvão (P) ..... 62 D 3
Santo-Pietro-di-Tenda (F). 55 H 3
Santo Stefano d'Aveto (I). 105 E 2
Santo Stefano di Cadore (I) ...... 103 F 2
Santo Stefano di Camastra (I) ....115 E 2
Santo Stefano Quisquina (I)..........114 D 3
Santo Stino di Livenza (I). 103 F 4
Santo Tirso (P) ...... 62 B 1
Santo Tomé (P) ..... 71 E 4
Santoméri (GR) ..... 164 D 4
Santoña (E) ..... 58 C 1
Santu Lussurgiu (I) .....112 B 3
Santurtzi (E).......... 58 D 1
Sanxenxo (E)...... 56 B 3
Sanza (I) ....110 C 5
São Bartolomeu de Messines (P)...... 68 C 5
São Brás de Alportel (P). 68 C 5
São Cristóvão (P)....... 68 C 2
São Domingos (P)..... 68 B 3
São Gregório (P) ...... 56 C 4
São Jacinto (P) ...... 62 B 2
São João da Madeira (P). 62 B 2
São João da Pesqueira (P). 62 D 1
São João de Tarouca (P). 62 D 2
São João dos Caldeireiros (P) ... 68 D 4
São José da Lamarosa (P). 68 B 1
São Leonardo (P)..... 69 E 3
São Manços (P)..... 68 D 2
São Marcos da Serra (P). 68 C 5
São Marcos do Campo (P). 68 D 3
São Martinho das Amoreiras (P)..... 68 C 4
São Martinho do Porto (P)..... 62 A 5
São Matias (P)..... 68 D 3
São Miguel de Machede (P)..... 68 D 2
São Pedro da Torre (P)... 56 B 4
São Pedro de Moel (P).. 62 A 4
São Pedro do Sul (P)..... 62 C 2
São Romão (P)..... 62 D 3
São Teotónio (P) ..... 68 B 4
São Vicente da Beira (P). 62 D 4
Saorge (F) ..... 55 H 5
Sapanca (TR).........19 H 1
Săpânţa (RO)..... 147 H 1
Sapareva Banja (BG). 158 B 2
Sapataria (P) ..... 68 A 1
Sappada (I) ..... 103 F 2
Sappee (FIN)..... 191 H 3
Sapri (I) ....110 C 5
Säräisniemi (FIN)..... 187 E 2
Saraiu (RO) ..... 153 E 3
Saraja (BG)..... 158 D 2
Sarajärvi (FIN)..... 187 E 1
Sarajevo (BIH)..... 137 G 5
Sarakíniko (GR)..... 165 H 3
Saramon (F) ..... 53 E 3
Saranci (BG)..... 158 C 1
Sarandë (AL)..... 144 C 5
Sarantáporo (GR) ..... 161 E 5
Saray (TR).......19 G 2
Sarayköy (TR)......19 H 3
Šarbanovac (SRB) ..... 143 F 1
Sarbinowo (Debno) (PL).116 B 5
Sarbinowo (Koszalin) (PL).116 D 2
Sárbogárd (H).........129 E 3
Sarcelles (F)............ 39 H 5

Sardara (I) ....112 B 4
Sardínia (GR)........... 164 D 2
Sardoal (P)........... 62 C 5
S'Arenal (E).............67 F 3
Sarengrad (HR)......... 137 H 2
Sarentino / Sarntal (I) .. 102 D 2
Sargans (CH) .... 99 F 3
Sari-d'Orcino (F) ..... 55 G 4
Sariá (GR) .... 171 F 4
Sarichioi (RO) .... 153 F 3
Sariñena (E)........... 59 H 4
Sarkad (H).............131 E 3
Sarkadkeresztúr (H)....131 E 3
Sárkeresztes (H)....... 129 E 2
Sárkeresztúr (H)....... 129 E 3
Särkisalmi (FIN) .... 193 G 2
Särkisalo / Finby (FIN). 191 G 5
Šarkovo (BG).......... 159 H 3
Sarlat-la-Canéda (F).... 49 F 5
Sarmaşu (RO) .... 147 G 4
Sármellék (H) ..... 128 C 3
Sarmizegetusa (RO).... 150 D 1
Sarmizegetusa Regia (RO) ..... 151 E 1
Särna (S) ..... 189 G 3
Sarnaki (PL) ..... 123 G 1
Sarnano (I)..... 107 G 5
Sarnen (CH) ..... 99 E 3
Sarnevo (BG)..... 159 F 2
Sárnica (BG)..... 162 B 1
Sarnico (I) ..... 101 F 4
Sarno (I) ..... 109 H 5
Sarnówka (PL) ..... 121 E 3
Sarntal / Sarentino (I) .. 102 D 2
Sarny (UA) ....12 D 1
Sárö (S) ..... 195 F 4
Sarón (E) ..... 58 B 1
Sarone (I) ..... 103 F 3
Saronída (GR)..... 165 H 5
Saronno (I) ..... 101 E 4
Sárosd (H) ..... 129 E 3
Sárospatak (H) ..... 127 E 5
Sarpsborg (N) ..... 195 F 1
Sarracín (E) ..... 58 B 3
Sarral (E) ..... 60 C 4
Sarralbe (F)..... 41 G 5
Sarre-Union (F) ..... 41 G 5
Sarrebourg (F)..... 47 G 1
Sarreguemines (F) ...41 G 5
Sárrétudvari (H) .....131 E 2
Sarria (E) ..... 56 D 3
Sarrión (E) ..... 65 G 3
Sarroch (I) ....112 C 5
Sars-Poteries (F) ..... 40 B 3
Sarsina (I) ..... 107 E 3
Sarstedt (D)..... 85 G 2
Sárszentmiklós (H) ..... 129 E 3
Sarteano (I) ..... 107 E 5
Sartène (F) ..... 55 H 5
Sárti (GR) ..... 162 B 5
Sartilly-Baie-Bocage (F). 43 F 1
Sarule (I)..............112 C 3
Săruleşti (Buzău) (RO).. 152 C 1
Săruleşti (Râmnicu Vâlcea) (RO). 151 F 3
Sárvár (H)..... 128 B 2
Sarvsjö (S) ..... 189 H 1
Sarzana (I) ..... 105 F 3
Sarzeau (F) ..... 42 D 4
Sarzedas (P) ..... 62 D 4
Sasa (MK) ..... 143 G 5
Sásca Montană (RO) ..... 150 C 3
Sascut (RO) ..... 148 D 5
Sásd (H) ..... 128 D 4
Sasnava (LT) ..... 205 E 4
Sassari (I) ....112 B 2
Sassello (I) ..... 104 D 3
Sassenage (F)..... 51 E 4
Sassenberg (D) ..... 85 E 2
Sassenheim (NL)..... 76 D 4
Sassetta (I) ..... 106 C 4
Saßnitz (D)..... 83 F 2
Sasso Marconi (I)..... 105 H 3
Sassoferrato (I) ..... 107 F 4
Sassoleone (I) ..... 106 D 2

Sassuolo (I) .... 105 H 2
Sástago (E) ..... 59 H 5
Sátão (P) ..... 62 D 2
Satchinez (RO) ..... 146 B 5
Säter (S) ..... 190 A 5
Satillieu (F) ..... 50 C 4
Sątoczno (PL) ..... 119 E 2
Satolas (F) ..... 50 D 3
Sátoraljaújhely (H) ..... 127 E 5
Šatov (CZ) ..... 92 D 5
Satovca (BG) ..... 162 B 1
Satow (D) ..... 82 D 3
Sátres (GR) ..... 162 C 2
Satrup (D) ..... 81 H 1
Sattel (CH) ..... 99 E 2
Sattledt (A) ..... 96 D 2
Satu Mare (RO) ..... 147 E 1
Satulung (RO) ..... 147 E 2
Saúca (E) ..... 64 D 1
Sauda (N) ..... 188 B 5
Sauðárkrókur (IS) ..... 178 B 1
Sauerlach (D) ..... 95 G 2
Sauga (EST) ..... 200 D 3
Saugues (F) ..... 50 B 4
Sauland (N) ..... 188 D 5
Saulieu (F) ..... 45 H 4
Saulkrasti (LV) ..... 202 D 2
Sault (F) ..... 54 D 1
Saulx (F) .....47 F 3
Saulxures-sur-Moselotte (F)......47 F 3
Saumur (F) ..... 43 H 4
Saundersfoot (GB) ..... 34 C 1
Sauris di Sopra (I) ..... 103 F 2
Sauveterre-de-Béarn (F). 52 B 3
Sauveterre-de-Guyenne (F) ..... 48 D 5
Sauveterre-de-Rouergue (F) ..... 53 G 1
Sauvo (FIN) ..... 191 F 5
Sauxillanges (F)..... 50 A 3
Sauze d'Oulx (I) ..... 100 A 5
Sauze-Vaussais (F) ..... 48 D 2
Sauzon (F) ..... 42 D 4
Sava (I) ....111 G 4
Savália (GR) ..... 164 D 5
Sävar (S) ..... 185 E 4
Săvârşin (RO) ..... 146 D 5
Savelli (I) ....113 C 2
Savenay (F) ..... 43 E 4
Săveni (RO) ..... 148 C 1
Saverdun (F) ..... 53 F 3
Saverne (F) .....41 G 5
Savigliano (I)..... 104 C 2
Savignac-les-Églises (F) ..... 49 F 4
Savignano Irpino (I) .....110 B 3
Savignano sul Rubicone (I) ..... 107 F 2
Savigny-sur-Braye (F) .. 44 C 3
Saviñán (E) ..... 59 F 5
Savines-le-Lac (F) .....51 F 5
Savino Selo (SRB) ..... 140 B 2
Savitaipale (FIN) ..... 193 F 3
Šavnik (MNE) ..... 139 F 3
Savognin (CH) ..... 99 G 4
Savona (I) ..... 104 D 3
Savonlinna (FIN) ..... 193 G 2
Savonranta (FIN) ..... 193 G 1
Sävsjö (S) ..... 195 H 4
Savudrija (HR) ..... 134 A 3
Savukoski (FIN) ..... 181 F 4
Sawbridgeworth (GB) ..... 36 C 3
Sax (E) ..... 73 E 2
Saxmundham (GB) ..... 37 E 2
Saxnäs (S) ..... 183 G 3
Sayatón (E) ..... 64 D 3
Säynätsalo (FIN) ..... 191 H 2
Säyneinen (FIN) ..... 187 F 5
Scaër (F) ..... 42 C 2
Scăeşti (RO) ..... 151 F 4
Scafa (I) ..... 109 G 2
Scafati (I) ..... 109 H 5

Scalasaig (GB)........... 30 A 1
Scalby (GB).............31 H 5
Scalea (I).............113 B 1
Scalloway (GB)........ 26 D 1
Scandiano (I) .... 105 G 2
Scanno (I)............ 109 G 3
Scansano (I) .... 106 D 5
Scânteia (Iaşi) (RO) ..... 148 D 3
Scânteia (Slobozia) (RO)... 152 D 3
Scanzano Jonico (I) ....111 E 5
Scarborough (GB)....... 33 F 1
Scardovari (I)........ 103 F 5
Scarinish (GB)........ 28 B 5
Scarriff (IRL) .... 24 D 2
Ščekino (RUS)........7 G 3
Ščepan Polje (MNE) . 139 F 2
Scey-sur-Saône (F) .....47 E 3
Schachendorf (A) .... 97 H 3
Schaffhausen (CH) .... 99 E 1
Schafstädt (D) ...... 86 B 4
Schagen (NL)........76 D 3
Schaprode (D) ...... 83 F 2
Scharbeutz (D)....... 82 C 3
Schärding (A) ...... 96 C 1
Scharnitz (A)....... 95 F 4
Scheeßel (D).......81 H 5
Scheggia (I)........ 107 F 4
Scheibbs (A)........ 97 F 2
Scheifling (A) ...... 97 E 4
Scheinfeld (D) ...... 89 H 2
Schenefeld
  (Pinneberg) (D) ....81 H 4
Schenefeld
  (Steinburg) (D)...81 H 3
Scherfede (D) .... 85 F 3
Schermbeck (D) .... 84 C 3
Scheßlitz (D)....... 91 E 3
Scheveningen (NL)...76 C 4
Schiedam (NL)......76 C 5
Schieder (D) .... 85 F 2
Schierling (D) ....91 F 5
Schiermonnikoog (NL) .. 77 F 2
Schiers (CH)....... 99 G 3
Schifferstadt (D) .... 89 E 3
Schilpario (I) ...... 101 G 3
Schiltach (D) ...... 89 E 5
Schiniás (GR)....... 166 B 4
Schio (I)........ 102 D 4
Schirmeck (F)......47 G 1
Schirnding (D) ....91 F 3
Schitu (RO) .... 152 B 4
Schitu Duca (RO) ... 149 E 3
Schitu Goleşti (RO)... 151 H 2
Schitul Sihla (RO) ... 148 B 3
Schkeuditz (D).... 86 B 4
Schkölen (D).... 86 B 4
Schladming (A) ..... 96 C 3
Schlagbrügge (D)... 82 C 3
Schlanders / Silandro (I). 101 H 2
Schlangenbad (D)..... 88 D 1
Schleching (D) ...... 95 H 3
Schleiden (D) ...... 84 B 5
Schleiz (D) ...... 86 B 5
Schleswig (D).......81 H 2
Schleusingen (D)..... 89 H 1
Schlieben (D) ...... 86 D 3
Schliersee (D)....... 95 G 3
Schlitz (D) .... 85 G 5
Schlotheim (D)...... 85 H 4
Schluchsee (D)...... 94 B 3
Schlüchtern (D) ..... 89 G 1
Schluderbach /
  Carbonin (I) ... 103 F 2
Schluderns / Sluderno (I). 101 G 1
Schlüsselfeld (D) ..... 89 H 2
Schlutup (D) ...... 82 C 3
Schmalkalden (D)..... 85 H 5
Schmallenberg (D)...... 85 E 4
Schmidmühlen (D)...91 F 4
Schmilka (D) ...... 87 E 5
Schmölln
  (Altenburger Land) (D). 86 B 5
Schmölln (Uckermark) (D). 83 G 4
Schnackenburg (D)... 82 D 5
Schnaittenbach (D)...91 F 4
Schneeberg (D)...... 86 C 5
Schneverdingen (D)......81 H 5

Schönau
  im Schwarzwald (D) .. 94 A 3
Schönberg (Freyung-
  Grafenau) (D) ....91 H 5
Schönberg (Nordwestmec-
  klenburg) (D) ...... 86 B 5
Schönberg (Plön) (D)... 82 B 2
Schönberg
  im Stubaital (A) ...... 95 G 4
Schönebeck (D)....... 86 B 2
Schöneck (D).......91 F 2
Schönecken (D)..... 88 B 1
Schönewalde (D)...... 86 D 3
Schongau (D)....... 95 F 3
Schöningen (D)...... 86 A 2
Schönmünzach (D) ... 89 E 5
Schönsee (D).......91 G 4
Schönthal (D).......91 G 4
Schönwald
  im Schwarzwald (D).. 94 B 2
Schönwalde
  am Bungsberg (D) ... 82 C 2
Schoonhoven (NL)...76 D 5
Schopfheim (D) ..... 94 A 3
Schöppenstedt (D).... 85 H 2
Schoppernau (A)..... 94 D 4
Schorndorf (D)...... 89 E 4
Schortens (D).......81 E 4
Schotten (D)....... 89 G 4
Schramberg (D)..... 89 E 5
Schrems (A)........ 92 B 5
Schrobenhausen (D) .... 95 F 1
Schröcken (A)....... 95 E 4
Schrozberg (D)..... 89 G 3
Schruns (A) ...... 94 D 4
Schuls / Scuol (CH)... 99 H 3
Schüttorf (D)....... 84 C 1
Schwaan (D)....... 82 D 3
Schwabach (D).......91 E 4
Schwäbisch
  Gmünd (D) ...... 89 G 4
Schwäbisch Hall (D)... 89 G 4
Schwabmünchen (D) ... 95 F 2
Schwaigern (D) ..... 89 F 3
Schwalenberg (D)... 85 F 3
Schwalmstadt-
  Treysa (D)......... 85 F 5
Schwalmstadt-
  Ziegenhain (D)... 85 F 5
Schwandorf (D).......91 F 4
Schwanebeck (D).... 86 A 2
Schwanenstadt (A)..... 96 D 3
Schwanewede (D)....81 F 5
Schwarmstedt (D)... 85 G 1
Schwarza (D) ...... 86 A 5
Schwarzach
  im Pongau (A) ..... 96 C 4
Schwarzenbach
  an der Saale (D)...91 F 2
Schwarzenbek (D).... 82 B 4
Schwarzenberg (D)... 86 C 5
Schwarzenburg (CH).. 98 C 3
Schwarzenfeld (D).....91 F 4
Schwarzheide (D) ... 87 E 3
Schwarzsee (CH).... 98 C 3
Schwaz (A)....... 95 G 4
Schwechat (A) ..... 95 G 4
Schwedt (D) ...... 83 G 5
Schweich (D)....... 88 C 2
Schweinfurt (D) ..... 89 H 2
Schweinitz (D)...... 86 D 3
Schwelm (D)....... 84 C 4
Schwendi (D) ..... 94 D 2
Schwenningen (D).... 94 B 2
Schwerin (D)....... 84 D 3
Schwerte (D)....... 84 D 3
Schwetzingen (D).... 89 E 3
Schwyz (CH)....... 99 E 3
Sciacca (I)........114 C 4
Scicli (I)........115 F 5
Ščigry (RUS) ....7 H 4
Scilla (I)........115 H 2
Ścinawa (PL)...... 121 E 3
Scoarţa (RO)...... 151 E 2
Scole (GB)........ 37 E 2
Sconser (GB)..... 28 C 3
Scopello (I)........ 100 D 3

Scordia (I)..............115 F 4
Scornicești (RO)....... 151 G 3
Ščors (UA)........7 F 5
Scorzè (I) .... 103 E 4
Scourie (GB)....... 28 D 1
Scrabster (GB)....... 26 B 4
Scrioaştea (RO)....... 151 H 4
Ščučyn (BY).......6 C 5
Scunthorpe (GB)........ 33 F 2
Scuol / Schuls (CH)... 99 H 3
Seaca de Pădure (RO).. 151 E 4
Seaford (GB)....... 36 D 5
Seaham (GB)........31 G 4
Seaton (GB)....... 35 E 4
Seaton Delaval (GB)....31 G 4
Sebecevo (SRB)...... 142 D 3
Sebeş (RO)....... 147 F 5
Sebež (RUS).......6 D 3
Sebiş (RO)....... 146 C 4
Sebnitz (D)....... 87 E 4
Sečanj (SRB)...... 140 D 3
Secemin (PL)...... 122 C 4
Seckau (A)....... 97 E 4
Seclin (F) .... 40 A 2
Secondigny (F)....... 48 D 1
Sečovce (SK)...... 133 G 3
Šečovská Polianka (SK). 133 G 3
Secu (RO)...... 148 B 3
Secuieni (RO)....... 148 D 4
Secusigiu (RO)....... 146 B 3
Seda (LT)....... 204 C 1
Sedan (F)....... 40 D 4
Sedano (E)....... 58 B 2
Sedbergh (GB).......31 F 5
Sedgefield (GB).......31 G 4
Sedico (I)........ 103 E 3
Sedilo (I)........112 C 3
Sedini (I)........112 B 1
Sedlare (SRB)....... 143 E 4
Sedlčany (CZ)....... 92 A 3
Sedlec-Prčice (CZ)... 92 B 4
Šeduva (LT)....... 205 E 2
Sędziszów (PL)...... 122 C 5
Sędziszów
  Małopolski (PL).... 127 E 1
Seebach (F)........41 H 5
Seebenau (D)....... 82 C 5
Seeboden (A) ..... 96 C 5
Seebruck (D)....... 95 H 2
Seefeld in Tirol (A) ... 95 F 4
Seehaus (A)....... 96 D 3
Seehausen (Aland) (D).. 82 D 5
Seehausen
  (Magdeburg) (D)..... 86 A 2
Seeheim (D)....... 89 E 2
Seelisberg (CH).... 99 E 3
Seelow (D)....... 87 E 1
Seewalchen
  am Attersee (A) ..... 96 C 2
Seewiesen (A) ..... 97 F 3
Sefkerin (SRB)...... 140 D 3
Segarcea (RO)....... 151 F 4
Segesd (H)....... 128 C 4
Segesta (I)........114 B 3
Seget Donji (HR)....... 138 B 2
Segl Maria / Sils ..... 99 G 4
Segni (I)........ 109 E 3
Segonzac (F)....... 48 D 3
Segorbe (E)....... 65 H 4
Segovia (E)....... 64 B 1
Segré (F)....... 43 G 3
Segura (P)....... 63 E 4
Segura de la Sierra (E).. 71 F 3
Segura de León (E)... 69 F 3
Segura de los Baños (E). 65 G 1
Sehnde (D)....... 85 G 2
Seia (P)....... 62 D 3
Seiches-sur-le-Loir (F).. 43 H 4
Seierstad (N)....... 183 E 3
Seifhennersdorf (D)..... 87 F 4
Seignelay (F)....... 45 G 3
Seilhac (F)....... 49 G 4
Seinäjoki (FIN)..... 191 F 1

Seini (RO)............. 147 E 1
Seirijai (LT)....... 205 E 5
Seissan (F) ...... 53 E 2
Seitenstetten Markt (A). 97 E 2
Seixal (P)....... 68 A 2
Seixo (O Tomiño) (E) .. 56 B 4
Sejny (PL)........119 G 2
Sékoulas (GR)....... 165 E 5
Šekovići (BIH)....... 137 H 4
Selanovci (BG)....... 151 F 5
Selargius (I)........112 C 5
Selb (D).......91 F 2
Selbekken (N)....... 182 C 5
Selbu (N)....... 182 D 5
Selby (GB)....... 33 F 2
Selce (HR)....... 134 C 4
Selçuk (TR).......19 G 3
Seleuş (RO)....... 146 C 4
Selevac (SRB)....... 140 D 5
Selfoss (IS)....... 178 B 3
Selianítika (GR)....... 165 E 4
Seligenstadt (D) ..... 89 F 2
Selínia (GR)....... 165 H 4
Selinunte (I)........114 B 3
Selishtë (AL)....... 144 D 1
Selje (N)....... 188 B 1
Seljord (N)....... 188 D 5
Selkirk (GB).......31 E 2
Sella Nevea (I)....... 103 H 2
Sellasía (GR)....... 168 D 3
Selles-sur-Cher (F) .... 44 D 4
Sellía (GR)....... 172 C 3
Sellières (F).......47 E 5
Sellin (D)....... 83 F 2
Sellye (H)....... 128 D 5
Selm (D)....... 84 D 3
Selmsdorf (D)....... 82 C 3
Selna (HR)....... 135 H 4
Selommes (F)....... 44 D 3
Selongey (F)....... 46 D 4
Seløy (N)....... 183 E 1
Selsey (GB)....... 38 C 1
Selters (D)....... 89 F 1
Seltz (F).......41 H 5
Selva / Wölkenstein (I). 103 E 2
Selvino (I)....... 101 F 3
Semeliškès (LT)....... 205 F 4
Semelci (HR)....... 137 G 2
Semenic (RO)....... 150 C 2
Semerdžievo (BG)..... 152 B 5
Semič (SLO)....... 134 C 3
Semily (CZ)....... 87 G 5
Seminara (I).......115 E 4
Semizovac (BIH)....... 137 G 5
Semmering-Kurort (A).. 97 G 3
Semproniano (I)....... 106 D 5
Semur-en-Auxois (F) .. 45 H 4
Semur-en-Brionnais (F). 50 C 2
Sena (E)....... 60 A 3
Sénas (F)....... 54 D 2
Sencelles (E).......67 F 2
Senden (D)....... 89 G 5
Sendim (P)....... 63 F 1
Senec (SK)....... 132 A 4
Seneffe, château de (B).. 78 C 3
Senez (F)....... 55 F 2
Senftenberg (D)....... 87 E 3
Senigallia (I)....... 107 G 3
Senise (I)........110 D 5
Senj (HR)....... 134 C 5
Senje (SRB)....... 143 E 1
Senlis (F)....... 39 H 5
Sennecey-le-Grand (F). 50 D 1
Sennen (GB)....... 34 B 5
Sennestadt (D)....... 85 E 2
Sennik (BG)....... 159 E 1
Sennori (I)........112 B 1
Sennybridge (GB)....... 34 D 1
Senohrad (SK)....... 132 D 4
Senokos (BG)....... 157 F 2
Senonches (F)....... 44 C 2
Senones (F).......47 G 2
Senorbì (I)........112 C 4
Senovo (BG)....... 156 D 2

Senožeče (SLO)....... 134 B 3
Sens (F)....... 45 G 2
Senta / Сента (SRB).. 140 C 1
Šentilj v Slovenskih
  goricah (SLO)...... 134 D 1
Šentjernej (SLO)....... 134 D 3
Šentjur (SLO)....... 134 D 2
Sépeaux-
  Saint-Romain (F) ...... 45 G 3
Šepetivka (UA).......13 E 1
Sepino (I)....... 109 H 4
Sępólno Krajeńskie (PL).117 F 4
Šepreuş (RO)....... 146 C 4
Septemvri (BG)....... 158 C 3
Septemvrijci (BG)....... 151 E 5
Sepúlveda (E)....... 64 B 1
Sequeros (E)....... 63 F 3
Seraing (B)....... 79 E 3
Seravezza (I)....... 105 G 4
Šerbănești (RO)....... 151 G 4
Sercaia (RO)....... 151 H 1
Sered' (SK)....... 132 B 4
Seredžius (LT)....... 205 E 3
Seregélyes (H)....... 129 E 3
Seregno (I)....... 101 E 4
Serfaus (A)....... 95 E 4
Sergijev Posad (RUS)...7 G 2
Seriate (I)....... 101 F 4
Šerići (BIH)....... 137 H 4
Sermaize-les-Bains (F).. 46 D 1
Sermide (I)....... 101 H 5
Sermoneta (I)....... 109 E 3
Sernancelhe (P)....... 62 D 2
Serock (PL)........119 G 4
Serón (E)....... 71 F 5
Serón de Nágima (E).. 59 E 5
Seròs (E)....... 60 A 4
Serpa (P)....... 68 D 4
Serpuchov (RUS)....7 G 2
Serra (E)....... 65 H 4
Serra de Outes (E)..... 56 B 3
Serra San Bruno (I)....113 C 4
Serrabone, prieuré de (F). 53 H 5
Serracapriola (I)....... 110 B 3
Serramanna (I)....... 112 B 4
Serravalle Scrivia (I).. 105 E 2
Serres (F).......51 E 5
Sérres / Σέρρες (GR).. 161 H 2
Serrières (F)....... 50 D 4
Sersale (I)........113 C 4
Sertã (P)....... 62 C 4
Servia (GR)....... 161 E 4
Servian (F)....... 54 A 3
Servigliano (I)....... 107 E 3
Sesa (E)....... 59 H 4
Seseña (E)....... 64 B 3
Sesimbra (P)....... 68 A 2
Sesma (E)....... 59 E 3
Sessa Aurunca (I)....... 109 G 4
Sesta Godano (I)....... 105 F 3
Šestanovac (HR)....... 138 C 2
Sestino (I)....... 107 E 3
Sesto / Sexten (I)....... 103 F 1
Sesto Calende (I)....... 100 D 3
Sesto Fiorentino (I)..... 105 H 4
Sestola (I)....... 105 H 3
Sestri Levante (I)....... 105 E 3
Sestriere (I)....... 100 A 5
Sestrimo (BG)....... 158 C 3
Sestrunj (HR)....... 136 B 5
Sestu (I)........112 C 5
Sesvete (HR)....... 135 E 2
Séta (GR)....... 165 H 3
Šeta (LT)....... 205 F 3
Setcases (E)....... 60 D 2
Sète (F)....... 54 B 3
Setenil
  de las Bodegas (E)......74 C 3
Setermoen (N).......176 A 5
Settimo Torinese (I).... 100 C 5
Settle (GB)....... 32 D 1
Setúbal (P)....... 68 B 2

Seulo (I)........112 C 4
Seurre (F)....... 46 D 5
Sevenoaks (GB)....... 36 D 4
Sever do Vouga (P)..... 62 B 2
Sévérac-d'Aveyron (F)... 54 A 1
Seveso (I)....... 101 E 4
Sevettijärvi (FIN)..... 177 G 3
Sevilla (E)....... 69 G 5
Sevilleja de la Jara (E) ... 63 H 5
Sevlievo /
  Севлиево (BG)....... 159 E 1
Sevnica (SLO)....... 134 D 2
Sevojno (SRB)....... 139 H 1
Sévrier (F).......51 F 2
Sevsk (RUS).......7 G 4
Sexten / Sesto (I)....... 103 F 1
Seyches (F)....... 49 E 5
Seyda (D)....... 86 C 2
Seyðisfjörður (IS)....... 178 D 2
Seyne (F)....... 55 F 1
Seyssel (F).......51 E 2
Sežana (SLO)....... 134 A 3
Sézanne (F)....... 45 G 1
Sezimovo Ústí (CZ)... 92 B 4
Sezze (I)....... 109 E 4
Sfântu Gheorghe (RO).. 152 B 1
Sfântul Andrei (RO)... 153 E 5
Sferracavallo (I)........114 C 2
Sforzacosta (I)....... 107 G 4
Shaftesbury (GB)....... 38 A 1
Shanklin (GB)....... 38 C 1
Shap (GB).......31 F 5
Sheerness (GB)....... 36 D 4
Sheffield (GB)....... 33 F 3
Shefford (GB)....... 36 C 3
Shëmri (AL)....... 142 D 5
Shëngjin (AL)....... 144 C 1
Shënmëri (AL)....... 144 C 2
Shepshed (GB)....... 33 E 4
Shepton Mallet (GB) ... 35 F 3
Sherborne (GB)....... 38 A 1
Shercock (IRL) ..... 23 F 4
Sheringham (GB)....... 37 E 1
Shiel Bridge (GB)....... 28 D 4
Shieldaig (GB)....... 28 C 3
Shijak (AL)....... 144 C 2
Shipston-on-Stour (GB). 35 G 1
Shkodër (AL)....... 142 B 5
Shoreham (GB)....... 38 C 1
Shrewsbury (GB)....... 32 C 4
Shrewton (GB)....... 35 G 3
Shupenzë (AL)....... 144 D 1
Sianów (PL)........117 E 2
Siátista (GR)....... 160 D 4
Šiauliai (LT)....... 205 E 2
Sibari (I)........113 C 1
Sibbhult (S)....... 199 G 2
Sibbo / Sipoo (FIN)... 191 H 4
Šibenik (HR)....... 136 C 5
Sibinj (HR)....... 135 H 4
Sibiu (RO)....... 151 G 1
Sicienko (PL)........117 G 2
Sicignano
  degli Alburni (I)....... 110 C 4
Sick (I).......81 G 5
Sicula (RO)....... 146 C 4
Sićuraj (HR)....... 138 C 3
Sideby (FIN)....... 191 E 2
Sidensjö (S)....... 184 C 5
Siderno (I)........113 C 4
Sidári / Σιδάρι (GR).. 160 A 5
Sidiró (GR)....... 163 E 2
Sidirókastro (GR)....... 161 H 2
Sidmouth (GB)....... 35 E 4
Siebenlehn (D)....... 86 D 4
Siedlce (PL)....... 123 F 1
Siedlec (PL)....... 120 D 1
Siegburg (D)....... 84 C 5
Siegen (D)....... 85 E 5
Siegsdorf (D)....... 95 H 3
Siemiany (PL)........118 C 3
Siemiatycze (PL)....... 123 G 1
Siena (I)....... 105 H 5

A B C D E F G H I J K L M N O P Q R **S** T U V W X Y Z

Sieniawa (PL) ... 123 F5
Sieniawka (PL) ... 120 B4
Siennica (PL) ... 123 E1
Sieppijärvi (FIN) ... 180 D4
Sieradz (PL) ... 121 H3
Sieraków (PL) ... 116 D5
Sierakowice (PL) ... 117 G2
Sierck-les-Bains (F) ... 41 F4
Sierentz (F) ... 47 G3
Sierninghofen (A) ... 96 D2
Sierpc (PL) ... 118 C5
Sierra de Fuentes (E) ... 63 F5
Sierra de Yeguas (E) ... 74 D2
Sierra Nevada (Pradollano) (E) ... 72 A5
Sierre (CH) ... 98 C4
Sievi (FIN) ... 185 G4
Sievin as (FIN) ... 185 G4
Siewierz (PL) ... 121 H5
Sigean (F) ... 54 A4
Sigerfjord (N) ... 179 G2
Siggjarvåg (N) ... 188 A5
Sighetu Marmaţiei (RO) ... 147 F1
Sighişoara (RO) ... 147 H5
Siglufjörður (IS) ... 178 B1
Sigmaringen (D) ... 94 C2
Signy-l'Abbaye (F) ... 40 C4
Sígri (GR) ... 167 E2
Sigtuna (S) ... 197 F1
Sigüenza (E) ... 64 D1
Sigulda (LV) ... 203 E2
Siikainen (FIN) ... 191 F2
Siikajoki (FIN) ... 185 G3
Siilinjärvi (FIN) ... 187 F5
Sijarinska Banja (SRB) ... 143 F3
Sikås (S) ... 183 G5
Síkinos (GR) ... 170 C2
Siklós (H) ... 128 D5
Sikovuono (FIN) ... 177 F4
Sikyóna (GR) ... 165 F4
Šilai (LT) ... 205 F2
Šilalė (LT) ... 204 C2
Silandro / Schlanders (I) ... 101 H2
Silba (HR) ... 136 A4
Silbaš (SRB) ... 140 B3
Şile (TR) ... 19 G1
Silen (BG) ... 163 E1
Siles (E) ... 71 F3
Siliqua (I) ... 112 B5
Silistra / Силистра (BG) ... 152 D4
Siliваşu de Câmpie (RO) ... 147 G4
Silivri (TR) ... 19 G1
Siljan (N) ... 195 E1
Siljansnäs (S) ... 190 A4
Silkeborg (DK) ... 194 D5
Silla (E) ... 65 H5
Sillamäe (EST) ... 201 G1
Sillé-le-Guillaume (F) ... 43 H2
Silleda (E) ... 56 C3
Sillian (A) ... 95 H5
Silloth (GB) ... 31 E4
Silnowo (PL) ... 117 E3
Šilo (HR) ... 134 C4
Sils (E) ... 61 E3
Sils / Segl Maria (CH) ... 99 G4
Siltakylä (FIN) ... 193 F4
Šilutė (LT) ... 204 C3
Silvalen (N) ... 183 E1
Silvaplana (CH) ... 99 G4
Silvares (P) ... 62 D4
Silves (P) ... 68 B5
Silvi Marina (I) ... 109 G1
Silz (A) ... 95 H4
Simancas (E) ... 58 A5
Şimand (RO) ... 146 B4
Šimanovci (SRB) ... 140 C4
Símantra (GR) ... 161 G4
Simaság (H) ... 128 B2
Simav (TR) ... 19 H2
Simaxis (I) ... 112 B3
Simbach (D) ... 95 H1
Simbach am Inn (D) ... 96 B2
Simeonovgrad (BG) ... 159 F3
Simeria (RO) ... 151 E1
Şimian (RO) ... 150 D3
Šimići (BIH) ... 135 F5
Simitli (BG) ... 161 G1

Simlångsdalen (S) ... 195 G5
Şimleu Silvaniei (RO) ... 147 E3
Simmerath (D) ... 84 B5
Simmern (D) ... 88 D2
Simnas (LT) ... 205 E5
Simo (FIN) ... 185 G2
Simola (FIN) ... 193 G3
Simonfa (H) ... 128 D4
Simonsbath (GB) ... 34 D3
Simonswald (D) ... 94 B2
Simontornya (H) ... 129 E3
Simópoulo (GR) ... 164 D5
Simrishamn (S) ... 199 G3
Sinaia (RO) ... 152 A2
Sinalunga (I) ... 107 E4
Sinarcas (E) ... 65 G4
Şinca Veche (RO) ... 151 H1
Sindel (BG) ... 157 F3
Sindelfingen (D) ... 89 F4
Sindi (EST) ... 200 D3
Sındırgı (TR) ... 19 G3
Sineşti (Râmnicu Vâlcea) (RO) ... 151 F3
Sineşti (Slobozia) (RO) ... 152 C4
Sinettä (FIN) ... 181 E5
Sineu (E) ... 67 F2
Singen (D) ... 94 C3
Sini Vir (BG) ... 157 E2
Siniscola (I) ... 112 D2
Sinj (HR) ... 138 B2
Sinopoli (I) ... 115 H2
Sinsheim (D) ... 89 F3
Sint-Niklaas (B) ... 78 C1
Sint-Oedenrode (NL) ... 79 E1
Sint-Truiden (Saint-Trond) (B) ... 78 D2
Sintautai (LT) ... 204 D4
Sintra (P) ... 68 A1
Sinzig (D) ... 84 C5
Sion (CH) ... 98 C4
Šipanska Luka (HR) ... 138 D4
Šipka (BG) ... 159 E1
Šipovo (BG) ... 158 D1
Sipoo / Sibbo (FIN) ... 191 H4
Sipote (RO) ... 148 D2
Šipovo (BIH) ... 137 E4
Sippola (FIN) ... 193 F4
Šiprage (BIH) ... 137 F4
Sira (N) ... 194 B2
Siracusa (I) ... 115 G4
Siret (RO) ... 148 B1
Sirevåg (N) ... 194 A2
Şiria (RO) ... 146 C3
Širig (SRB) ... 140 C3
Siritovci (HR) ... 136 C5
Sirkka (FIN) ... 180 D3
Sirma (N) ... 177 F3
Sirmione (I) ... 101 G4
Široka Läka (BG) ... 162 C5
Široki Brijeg (BIH) ... 138 D2
Široko Polje (HR) ... 137 G2
Sirolo (I) ... 107 H3
Siruela (E) ... 70 B1
Širvintos (LT) ... 205 F3
Sisak (HR) ... 135 E4
Šišan (HR) ... 134 A5
Sisante (E) ... 65 E5
Šišenci (BG) ... 150 D5
Síses (GR) ... 170 B5
Sişeşti (RO) ... 150 D3
Šišljavić (HR) ... 134 D4
Šišmanci (BG) ... 159 E3
Sissa (I) ... 101 G5
Sissonne (F) ... 40 B4
Şiştarovăţ (RO) ... 146 C5
Sisteron (F) ... 55 E1
Sistiana (I) ... 103 H3
Siteía (GR) ... 173 F3
Sitges (E) ... 60 D4
Sitovo (BG) ... 152 D5
Sittard (NL) ... 79 E2
Sittensen (D) ... 81 H4
Sittingbourne (GB) ... 36 D4

Siuntio / Sjundeå (FIN) ... 191 G5
Siuro (FIN) ... 191 G3
Siurua (FIN) ... 185 H2
Sivac (SRB) ... 140 B2
Šivačevo (BG) ... 159 F2
Sivasli (TR) ... 19 H3
Six-Fours-les-Plages (F) ... 55 E3
Siziano (I) ... 101 E4
Sizun (F) ... 42 B2
Sjenica (SRB) ... 139 H2
Sjenićak Lasinjski (HR) ... 134 D4
Sjøåsen (N) ... 183 E4
Sjöbo (S) ... 199 F3
Sjøholt (N) ... 188 C1
Sjötorp (S) ... 195 H2
Sjoutnäset (S) ... 183 G3
Sjøvegan (N) ... 176 A5
Sjulsmark (S) ... 185 E4
Sjundeå / Siuntio (FIN) ... 191 G5
Sjusjøen (N) ... 189 F3
Skåbu (N) ... 189 E3
Skadovs'k (UA) ... 13 H3
Skælskør (DK) ... 198 D4
Skærbæk (DK) ... 198 B4
Skafidiá (GR) ... 164 D5
Skaftafell (IS) ... 178 C3
Skagaströnd (IS) ... 178 B1
Skage (N) ... 183 E3
Skagen (DK) ... 195 E3
Skaidi (N) ... 177 E2
Skaill (GB) ... 26 C3
Skaistgirys (LT) ... 205 E1
Skała (PL) ... 121 G5
Skála (Iónia Nisiá) (GR) ... 164 C4
Skála (Nótio Aigaío) (GR) ... 171 E1
Skála (Pelopónnisos) (GR) ... 168 D3
Skála (Stereá Elláda) (GR) ... 165 G3
Skála (Vóreio Aigaío) (GR) ... 167 E2
Skála Eresoú (GR) ... 167 E2
Skála Kalliráchis (GR) ... 162 C3
Skála Oropoú (GR) ... 165 H4
Skála Rachoníou (GR) ... 162 C3
Skaland (N) ... 176 A4
Skalavik (Færøerne) (DK) ... 194 A5
Skalbmierz (PL) ... 122 C5
Skålevik (N) ... 194 C2
Skalica (BG) ... 159 G2
Skalica (SK) ... 132 A3
Skalité (SK) ... 132 C1
Skalochóri (Dytikí Makedonía) (GR) ... 160 D4
Skalochóri (Vóreio Aigaío) (GR) ... 167 E2
Skamnélli (GR) ... 160 C5
Skandáli (GR) ... 162 D5
Skanderborg (DK) ... 198 C2
Skånevik (N) ... 188 B5
Skänninge (S) ... 196 D2
Skäpiškis (LT) ... 205 G2
Skara (S) ... 195 G2
Skaramagkás (GR) ... 165 H4
Skåre (S) ... 195 G1
Skárfeia (GR) ... 165 F2
Skärhamn (S) ... 195 F3
Skarnes (N) ... 189 F5
Skarplinge (S) ... 190 C4
Skarsvåg (N) ... 177 E1
Skarszewy (PL) ... 117 G2
Skärvången (S) ... 183 F4
Skaryszew (PL) ... 122 D3
Skarżysko-Kamienna (PL) ... 122 D4
Skattungbyn (S) ... 190 A3
Skatval (N) ... 182 D5
Skaudvilė (LT) ... 204 D3
Skaulo (S) ... 180 B4
Skaun (N) ... 182 D5
Skawa (LV) ... 203 H4
Skawina (PL) ... 125 G1
Skee (S) ... 195 F1
Skegness (GB) ... 33 G3
Skei (N) ... 188 C2

Skei (N) ... 182 C5
Skela (SRB) ... 140 C4
Skelleftaå (S) ... 185 E3
Skelleftehamn (S) ... 185 E3
Skelmersdale (GB) ... 32 C2
Skender Vakuf / Kneževo (BIH) ... 137 E4
Skepastó (GR) ... 161 H3
Skerries (IRL) ... 23 G5
Ski (N) ... 189 F5
Skíathos (GR) ... 165 H2
Skibbereen (IRL) ... 24 B5
Skibby (DK) ... 199 E3
Skibotn (N) ... 176 C4
Skiemonys (LT) ... 205 G3
Skien (N) ... 194 D1
Skierniewice (PL) ... 122 C2
Skillingaryd (S) ... 195 H4
Skiniás (GR) ... 165 E4
Skinnarbu (N) ... 188 D5
Skinnskatteberg (S) ... 190 A5
Skipagurra (N) ... 177 G2
Skipton (GB) ... 32 D2
Skive (DK) ... 194 D5
Skivjane (SRB) ... 142 D4
Skjeberg (N) ... 195 F1
Skjelvik (N) ... 179 F5
Skjern (DK) ... 198 B2
Skjerstad (N) ... 179 F4
Skjervøy (N) ... 176 C3
Skjolden (N) ... 188 C2
Skjønhaug (N) ... 189 F5
Sklavopoúla (GR) ... 172 A3
Sklíthro (GR) ... 165 G1
Škłoŭ (BY) ... 7 E4
Skobelevo (BG) ... 159 E3
Skočivir (MK) ... 145 F2
Skoczów (PL) ... 125 E2
Skodje (N) ... 188 C1
Škofja Loka (SLO) ... 134 B2
Škofljica (SLO) ... 134 C2
Skog (S) ... 190 C1
Skog (S) ... 190 B3
Skógafoss (IS) ... 178 B3
Skogar (IS) ... 178 B3
Skoghall (S) ... 195 G1
Skogstorp (S) ... 197 E1
Skoki (PL) ... 117 F5
Skoklosters slott (S) ... 197 F1
Skollenborg (N) ... 189 E5
Skópelos (GR) ... 165 H2
Skopí (GR) ... 173 F3
Skopiá (GR) ... 165 F2
Skopje (MK) ... 143 F5
Skopós (GR) ... 161 E3
Skopun (Færøerne) (DK) ... 194 A5
Skórcz (PL) ... 117 G3
Skorenovac (SRB) ... 140 D4
Skorovatn (N) ... 183 F3
Skorped (S) ... 184 C5
Škorpilovci (BG) ... 157 F3
Skotína (GR) ... 161 F2
Skotterud (N) ... 189 F5
Skoúra (GR) ... 168 D3
Skoúrta (GR) ... 165 H4
Skoútari (GR) ... 161 H3
Skoutári (GR) ... 168 D4
Skoutáros (GR) ... 167 E1
Skövde (S) ... 195 H2
Skrá (GR) ... 161 F2
Skrad (HR) ... 134 C4
Skradin (HR) ... 136 C5
Skreia (N) ... 189 F4
Skriaudžiai (LT) ... 205 E4
Skrolsvik (N) ... 176 A4
Skrunda (LV) ... 202 B3
Skudeneshavn (N) ... 194 A1
Skujene (LV) ... 203 E3
Skuleskogens nationalpark (S) ... 190 C1
Skull (IRL) ... 24 B5
Skultuna (S) ... 197 E1
Skuodas (LT) ... 204 C1
Skurup (S) ... 199 F4
Skuteč (CZ) ... 92 D3

Skutskär (S) ... 190 B4
Skvyra (UA) ... 13 F1
Skwierzyna (PL) ... 116 C5
Skýdra (GR) ... 161 F3
Skylloura (CY) ... 174 D3
Skýros (GR) ... 166 C2
Sládečkovce (SK) ... 132 B4
Sládkovičovo (SK) ... 132 A4
Sladun (BG) ... 163 F1
Slagelse (DK) ... 198 D3
Slagnäs (S) ... 184 C2
Slakovac (SRB) ... 141 E4
Slancy (RUS) ... 6 C1
Slane (IRL) ... 23 F4
Slangerup (DK) ... 199 E3
Slănic (RO) ... 152 B2
Slănic-Moldova (RO) ... 148 C5
Slano (HR) ... 138 D4
Slaný (CZ) ... 92 A2
Šlapanice (CZ) ... 93 E4
Slapy (CZ) ... 92 A3
Slatina (BIH) ... 135 G5
Slatina (HR) ... 135 G3
Slatina (RO) ... 151 G4
Slatina (Bor) (SRB) ... 141 G5
Slatina (Čačak) (SRB) ... 142 D1
Slatina-Timiş (RO) ... 150 D2
Slatine (HR) ... 138 B2
Slatino (MK) ... 143 E5
Slatinski Drenovac (HR) ... 135 G4
Šlaŭharad (BY) ... 7 E3
Slavejno (BG) ... 162 C1
Slavičín (CZ) ... 93 G4
Slavkov u Brna (CZ) ... 93 E4
Slavkovica (SRB) ... 140 C5
Slavonice (CZ) ... 92 C5
Slavonski Brod (HR) ... 135 H4
Slavonski Kobaš (HR) ... 135 G5
Slavonski Šamac (HR) ... 137 G3
Slavotin (BG) ... 154 C2
Slavovica (BG) ... 156 A2
Slavuta (UA) ... 12 D1
Sława (PL) ... 120 D2
Sławatycze (PL) ... 123 H2
Sławno (PL) ... 117 E2
Sławoborze (PL) ... 116 D3
Sleaford (GB) ... 33 F4
Šlesin (PL) ... 121 G1
Sliedrecht (NL) ... 76 D5
Sliema (M) ... 114 C5
Sligeach / Sligo (IRL) ... 22 D3
Sligo / Sligeach (IRL) ... 22 D3
Sliven / Сливен (BG) ... 159 G2
Slivnica (BG) ... 158 B1
Slivo Pole (BG) ... 152 B5
Šljivovica (SRB) ... 139 G1
Slobozia (RO) ... 152 D3
Słomniki (PL) ... 122 C5
Slonim (BY) ... 6 C5
Sloten (NL) ... 77 E3
Slough (GB) ... 36 B4
Sloup (CZ) ... 93 E4
Slovac (SRB) ... 140 C5
Slovenj Gradec (SLO) ... 134 C1
Slovenska Bistrica (SLO) ... 134 D2
Slovenská Kajňa (SK) ... 133 G2
Slovenské Ďarmoty (SK) ... 132 D4
Slovenske Konjice (SLO) ... 134 D2
Slovenské Nové Mesto (SK) ... 133 G3
Slovinci (HR) ... 135 F4
Słubice (PL) ... 120 B1
Słuck (BY) ... 6 D5
Sluderno / Schluders (I) ... 101 G1
Sluis (NL) ... 78 B1
Šluknov (CZ) ... 87 E4
Slunj (HR) ... 134 D4
Słupca (PL) ... 121 G1
Słupsk (PL) ... 117 F1
Smålandsstenar (S) ... 195 G4
Smaljavičy (BY) ... 6 D4

Smârdioasa (RO) ... 152 A5
Smarhon (BY) ... 6 D4
Šmarje (SLO) ... 134 A3
Šmarje pri Jelšah (SLO) ... 134 D2
Šmarješke Toplice (SLO) ... 134 D3
Šmartno (SLO) ... 134 C2
Smedby (S) ... 197 E5
Smědeč (CZ) ... 92 A3
Smederevo / Смедерево (SRB) ... 141 E4
Smederevska Palanka / Смедеревска Паланка (SRB) ... 141 E5
Smedjebacken (S) ... 190 A5
Smeraldo, grotta dello (I) ... 110 A4
Smigáda (GR) ... 163 E2
Śmigiel (PL) ... 121 E2
Smila (UA) ... 13 G1
Smilčić (HR) ... 136 B5
Smilde (NL) ... 77 F3
Smilec (BG) ... 158 D2
Smiljan (BG) ... 162 C2
Smilgiai (LT) ... 205 E2
Smiltene (LV) ... 203 F2
Smjadovo (BG) ... 159 H1
Smojmirovo (MK) ... 145 H1
Smokovljani (HR) ... 138 D3
Smolenice (SK) ... 132 A3
Smolensk (RUS) ... 7 E3
Smoljan / Смолян (BG) ... 162 C1
Smørhamn (N) ... 188 B2
Smygehamn (S) ... 199 F4
Snagov (RO) ... 152 B3
Snaith (GB) ... 33 E2
Snåsa (N) ... 183 E4
Sneek / Snits (NL) ... 77 E3
Sneem (IRL) ... 24 B4
Śniadowo (PL) ... 119 H4
Snihurivka (UA) ... 13 G2
Snillfjord (N) ... 182 C5
Snina (SK) ... 133 H2
Snits / Sneek (NL) ... 77 E3
Šnjegotina Velika (BIH) ... 135 G5
Soave (I) ... 101 H4
Soběslav (CZ) ... 92 B4
Sobieszewo (PL) ... 117 H2
Sobieszów (PL) ... 120 C4
Sobotka (CZ) ... 87 F5
Sobótka (PL) ... 121 E4
Sobra (HR) ... 138 D4
Sobrado dos Monxes (E) ... 56 C2
Sobral da Adiça (P) ... 69 G3
Sobral de Monte Agraço (P) ... 68 A1
Sobrance (SK) ... 133 H3
Sobreira Formosa (P) ... 62 C4
Søby (DK) ... 198 C4
Sočanica (SRB) ... 142 D3
Soccia (F) ... 55 H4
Sochaczew (PL) ... 122 C1
Sochaux (F) ... 47 G4
Sochós (GR) ... 161 H3
Socka (SLO) ... 134 A2
Socodor (RO) ... 146 B4
Socol (RO) ... 150 B3
Socovos (E) ... 71 G3
Socuéllamos (E) ... 64 D5
Sodankylä (FIN) ... 181 E4
Söderåkra (S) ... 197 E5
Söderbärke (S) ... 190 A5
Söderfors (S) ... 190 B5
Söderhamn (S) ... 190 B3
Söderköping (S) ... 197 E2
Söderskog (S) ... 199 F3
Södertälje (S) ... 197 F1
Sodražica (SLO) ... 134 C3
Sodupe (E) ... 58 C1
Soest (D) ... 85 G2
Soest (NL) ... 77 E4
Sofádes (GR) ... 165 E1
Sofia / София (BG) ... 158 B1
Sofiero (S) ... 199 E3
Sofikó (GR) ... 165 G5
Sögel (D) ... 81 E5
Sogliano al Rubicone (I) ... 107 E2
Soglio (CH) ... 99 G4

Sogndal (N)........... 188 C 3
Søgne (N)............. 194 C 2
Soham (GB)........... 33 G 5
Soignies (B)........... 78 C 3
Şoimi (RO)............ 146 C 4
Soini (FIN)............ 191 G 1
Soinlahti (FIN)........ 187 E 4
Soissons (F)........... 40 A 4
Söjtör (H)............. 128 B 3
Söke (TR)............. 19 G 3
Sokna (N)............. 189 E 4
Sokobanja (SRB)...... 143 F 1
Sokol (BG)............ 152 C 5
Sokolac (BIH)......... 137 H 5
Sokółka (PL)........... 119 H 3
Sokolov (CZ)........... 91 G 2
Sokołów Małopolski (PL). 123 F 5
Sokołów Podlaski (PL).. 123 F 1
Sokoły (PL)............ 119 G 4
Sola (N)............... 194 A 1
Solana de los Barros (E). 69 F 2
Solana del Pino (E)..... 70 D 3
Solares (E)............ 58 B 1
Solberg (S)............ 184 C 5
Solčava (SLO)......... 134 C 1
Sol'cy (RUS)............ 6 D 2
Solda / Sulden (I)...... 101 G 2
Sölden (A)............. 95 F 4
Soldeu (AND).......... 60 C 1
Solec Kujawski (PL).... 117 G 4
Solec nad Wisłą (PL)... 123 E 3
Solec-Zdrój (PL)....... 122 D 5
Solenzara (F).......... 55 H 5
Solesmes (F).......... 43 H 3
Solesmes (F).......... 40 A 3
Solevåg (N)........... 188 C 1
Solf (FIN)............. 191 E 1
Solferino (I).......... 101 G 4
Solignac (F).......... 49 F 3
Solignac-sur-Loire (F).. 50 B 4
Solihull (GB)......... 33 E 5
Solin (HR)............ 138 B 2
Solina (PL)........... 127 F 2
Soline (HR)........... 136 A 5
Solingen (D).......... 84 C 4
Söll (A)............... 95 H 3
Sollana (E)........... 65 H 5
Sollefteå (S)......... 183 H 5
Sollenau (A).......... 97 G 2
Sollentuna (S)........ 197 G 1
Sóller (E)............. 67 F 2
Sollerön (S).......... 189 H 4
Søllested (DK)........ 198 D 4
Solliès-Pont (F)....... 55 F 3
Solnečnogorsk (RUS)... 7 G 2
Solnik (BG).......... 157 F 3
Solofra (I)........... 109 H 5
Soloi (CY)............ 174 C 3
Solosancho (E)........ 63 H 3
Solothurn (CH)........ 98 D 2
Solre-le-Château (F)... 40 B 3
Solrød (DK).......... 199 E 3
Solsona (E)........... 60 C 2
Solt (H)............. 129 F 3
Soltau (D)............ 81 H 5
Soltvadkert (H)....... 129 F 4
Solunto (I)............ 114 D 2
Sölvesborg (S)........ 199 G 3
Solvorn (N)........... 188 C 3
Soma (TR)............. 19 G 3
Somberek (H)......... 129 E 5
Sombernon (F)........ 46 C 4
Sombor (SRB)......... 137 H 1
Şomcuta Mare (RO).... 147 F 2
Someren (NL).......... 79 E 1
Somero (FIN)......... 191 G 4
Sõmeru (EST)........ 201 F 2
Sommaroøy (N)........ 176 A 4
Sommatino (I)......... 115 E 4
Sömmerda (D)......... 86 A 4
Sommesous (F)........ 45 H 1
Sommières (F)........ 54 B 2
Somogyszob (H)....... 128 C 4
Somogyviszló (H)..... 128 D 5
Somolinos (E)......... 64 D 1
Sompolno (PL)........ 121 G 1
Son Servera (E)........ 67 G 2

Soncillo (E)........... 58 B 2
Soncino (I)........... 101 F 4
Søndeled (N)......... 194 D 2
Sønder Felding (DK)... 198 B 2
Sønderborg (DK)...... 198 C 4
Sønderby (DK)........ 198 C 4
Sondershausen (D).... 85 H 4
Søndersø (DK)....... 198 C 3
Sondrio (I)............ 101 F 3
Sonneberg (D)......... 91 E 2
Sonnewalde (D)....... 86 D 3
Sonogno (CH)........ 99 E 4
Sonsbeck (D)......... 84 B 3
Sonseca (E).......... 64 B 4
Sonta (SRB).......... 137 H 1
Sonthofen (D)........ 95 E 3
Sontra (D)........... 85 G 4
Sopeira (E).......... 60 B 2
Sopilja (BIH)......... 139 E 2
Sopište (MK)......... 143 F 5
Šoporňa (SK)......... 132 B 4
Sopot (BG)........... 158 D 2
Sopot (PL)........... 117 H 1
Sopot (SRB)......... 140 D 5
Sopotnica (MK)....... 145 E 3
Şopotu Nou (RO)...... 150 D 2
Sopron (H).......... 128 B 1
Sora (I)............. 109 F 3
Soragna (I).......... 101 G 5
Søråker (S).......... 190 C 1
Sørarnøy (N)........ 179 F 4
Sorbas (E).......... 72 C 5
Sore (F)............ 52 C 1
Söréd (H).......... 128 D 2
Soresina (I)......... 101 F 4
Sörfors (S)......... 184 D 4
Sorga (D)........... 85 G 5
Sorgono (I)......... 112 C 3
Sorgues (F)......... 54 C 1
Soriano
  nel Cimino (I)..... 108 D 2
Soriano (E).......... 59 E 4
Sørkjosen (N)....... 176 C 3
Sørland (N)......... 179 E 4
Sorø (DK).......... 198 D 3
Soroca (MD)......... 13 G 1
Soroní (GR)......... 171 H 3
Sørreisa (N)........ 176 A 4
Sorrento (I)......... 109 H 5
Sørrollnes (N)...... 176 A 5
Sorsakoski (FIN)..... 193 F 1
Sorsele (S)......... 184 C 2
Sörsjön (S)......... 189 G 3
Sorso (I)........... 112 B 1
Sort (E)............ 60 B 2
Sortino (I).......... 115 E 4
Sorunda (S)......... 197 G 2
Sørvær (N)......... 176 C 1
Sørvågen (N)....... 179 E 3
Sørvagur
  (Færøerne) (DK).. 194 A 4
Sörvattnet (S)...... 189 G 3
Sos del Rey Católico (E). 59 G 3
Soses (E)........... 60 A 4
Sosnovyj Bor (RUS)... 6 C 1
Sosnowica (PL)...... 123 G 2
Sosnowiec (PL)...... 122 B 5
Sospel (F).......... 55 F 2
Šoštanj (SLO)....... 134 C 2
Šostka (UA)......... 7 G 5
Sota seter (N)....... 188 D 2
Sotillo de la Adrada (E). 64 A 3
Sotin (HR)........... 137 H 2
Sotira (CY)......... 175 F 3
Sotíra (GR)......... 161 E 3
Sotkamo (FIN)...... 187 F 4
Soto de los Infantes (E). 57 F 2
Soto de Luiña (E).... 57 F 1
Soto de Sajambre (E). 57 H 2
Soto del Barco (E)... 57 G 1
Sotogrande (E)....... 74 C 4
Sotopalacios (E)..... 58 B 3

Sotrondio (E)........ 57 G 2
Sottomarina (I)...... 103 F 5
Sottrum (D).......... 81 G 5
Sottunga (FIN)...... 191 E 5
Sotuélamos (E)...... 71 F 1
Soúda / Σούδα (GR)... 170 A 5
Souesmes (F)........ 45 E 4
Soufflenheim (F)..... 41 H 5
Souflí / Σουφλί (GR)... 163 F 2
Souilgia (GR)....... 172 B 3
Sougné-
  Remouchamps (B).. 79 E 3
Souillac (F)......... 49 G 5
Souilly (F)......... 40 D 5
Soulac-sur-Mer (F)... 48 B 3
Soulaines-Dhuys (F).. 46 C 2
Soulinári (GR)....... 168 C 3
Soulópoulo (GR)..... 160 C 5
Soultz-Haut-Rhin (F).. 47 G 3
Soultz-sous-Forêts (F).. 41 H 5
Souni-Zanakia (CY)... 174 C 4
Soúnio (GR)......... 166 B 5
Souppes-sur-Loing (F).. 45 F 2
Sourdeval (F)....... 43 G 1
Soure (P).......... 62 B 4
Sournia (F).......... 53 H 4
Sourotí (GR)........ 161 G 4
Soúrpi (GR)......... 165 G 2
Sousceyrac (F)...... 49 G 5
Sousel (P).......... 68 D 1
Soustons (F)........ 52 B 2
Soutelo (E)........ 56 C 3
South Molton (GB)... 34 D 3
South Queensferry (GB). 31 E 1
South Shields (GB)... 31 G 4
Southam (GB)....... 33 E 5
Southampton (GB)... 38 C 1
Southborough (GB)... 36 D 5
Southend (GB)...... 23 H 1
Southend-on-Sea (GB). 36 D 4
Southport (GB)..... 32 C 2
Southsea (GB)..... 38 C 1
Southwell (GB)..... 33 F 3
Southwold (GB)..... 37 E 2
Souvála (GR)....... 165 H 5
Souvigny (F)........ 50 A 1
Sovata (RO)........ 147 H 4
Soverato (I)........ 113 C 3
Soveria Mannelli (I).. 113 C 3
Sovetsk = Tilsit (RUS)... 6 B 4
Søvik (N).......... 188 C 1
Sozopol / Созопол (BG). 157 F 4
Sozópoli (GR)....... 161 G 4
Spa (B)............ 79 E 3
Spaichingen (D)..... 94 C 2
Spakenburg (NL)..... 77 E 4
Spalding (GB)...... 33 G 4
Spandau (D)........ 86 C 1
Spangenberg (D).... 85 G 4
Spáre (LV)......... 202 B 2
Spárta (GR)........ 165 G 4
Spárti / Σπάρτη (GR).. 168 D 3
Spárto (GR)........ 164 C 2
Spas (AL).......... 142 D 5
Spas-Demensk (RUS).. 7 F 3
Spas-Klepiki (RUS).... 7 H 2
Spasovo (Dobrič) (BG). 153 F 5
Spasovo
  (Stara Zagora) (BG). 159 E 2
Spáta (GR)......... 165 H 4
Spean Bridge (GB)... 28 C 3
Spello (I).......... 107 F 5
Spennymoor (GB).... 31 G 4
Sperchiáda (GR).... 165 E 2
Sperlonga (I)....... 109 F 4
Spétses (GR)....... 169 E 2
Speyer (D)......... 89 E 3
Spezzano Albanese (I). 113 C 1
Spezzano della Sila (I). 113 C 2
Spiddal (IRL)....... 22 C 5
Spiekeroog (D)...... 81 E 3
Spielfeld (A)........ 97 F 5
Spiez (CH)......... 98 D 3
Spijkenisse (NL)..... 76 C 5
Spílaia Diroú (GR)... 168 D 4
Spílaio Límnon (GR). 165 E 4

Spíli (GR)........... 172 C 3
Spilia (CY)......... 174 C 4
Spilimbergo (I)...... 103 G 3
Spilsby (GB)........ 33 G 3
Spinazzola (I)....... 110 D 3
Spincourt (F)........ 41 E 4
Spindlerův Mlýn (CZ). 87 G 5
Spionica Donja (BIH). 137 G 3
Špišić Bukovica (HR). 135 G 3
Spišská Kapitula (SK). 133 F 2
Spišská Nová Ves (SK). 133 F 2
Spital am Pyhrn (A).. 96 D 3
Spittal an der Drau (A). 96 C 5
Spitz (A)........... 97 F 1
Spjelkavik (N)...... 188 C 1
Split (HR).......... 138 B 2
Splügen (CH)....... 99 F 4
Spodnji Brnik (SLO).. 134 B 2
Spodsbjerg (DK).... 198 D 4
Špoģi (Špogi) (LV)... 203 G 4
Špola (UA)......... 13 F 2
Spoleto (I)........ 107 F 5
Spornitz (D)........ 82 D 4
Spotorno (I)........ 104 D 3
Spremberg (D)...... 87 E 3
Spresiano (I)....... 103 F 3
Sprikutova (LV)..... 203 H 4
Springe (D)........ 85 G 2
Spuž (MNE)........ 139 G 4
Squinzano (I)....... 111 G 4
Srbac (BIH)........ 135 G 5
Srbica (SRB)....... 142 D 4
Srbobran /
  Србобран (SRB)... 140 C 2
Srđevići (BIH)...... 137 E 5
Srebărna (BG)...... 152 D 5
Srebrenica (BIH).... 137 H 5
Srebrenik (BIH)..... 137 G 3
Sredec (BG)........ 159 F 2
Sredec / Средец (BG). 159 H 2
Središče ob Dravi (SLO). 135 E 2
Središte (BG)....... 152 D 5
Srednje (BIH)....... 137 G 5
Srednogorci (BG)... 162 C 1
Sredska (SRB)...... 143 E 5
Srem (PL).......... 121 F 2
Sremska Kamenica (SRB). 140 C 3
Sremska Mitrovica (SRB). 140 B 4
Sremska Rača (SRB). 137 H 3
Sremski Karlovci (SRB). 140 C 3
Srnetica (BIH)...... 136 D 4
Srnice Donje (BIH).. 137 G 3
Środa Śląska (PL)... 121 E 4
Środa Wielkopolska (PL). 121 F 1
Srpska Crnja (SRB).. 140 D 2
Srpski Brod /
  Bosanski Brod (BIH). 135 H 4
Srpski Itebej (SRB).. 140 D 2
Srpski Miletić (SRB). 137 H 2
Srpsko Sarajevo (BIH). 137 G 5
Stade (D).......... 81 H 4
Stádio (GR)........ 165 F 5
Stadskanaal (NL).... 77 G 3
Stadt Wehlen (D)... 87 E 4
Stadthagen (D)..... 85 F 2
Stadtilm (D)........ 86 A 5
Stadtkyll (D)....... 88 B 1
Stadtlohn (D)....... 84 A 2
Stadtoldendorf (D)... 85 G 3
Stadtroda (D)...... 86 B 5
Stadtsteinach (D)... 91 E 2
Staffanstorp (S).... 199 F 3
Staffin (GB)....... 28 C 3
Stafford (GB)...... 32 D 4
Stágira (GR)....... 161 H 4
Stahle (D)......... 85 F 3
Stahovica (SLO).... 134 C 2
Staicele (LV)...... 203 E 1
Staines (GB)....... 36 C 4
Stainz (A)......... 97 F 4
Stakčín (SK)....... 133 H 2
Stakevci (BG)...... 154 C 2
Stalać (SRB)....... 143 E 1
Stalbe (LV)........ 203 E 2
Stalída (GR)....... 170 C 5
Stall (A).......... 96 B 5

Stalowa Wola (PL)... 123 F 5
Stambolijski (BG)... 158 D 3
Stamford (GB)...... 33 F 4
Stamná (GR)....... 164 D 3
Stamnes (N)........ 188 B 3
Stams (A).......... 95 F 4
Stamsund (N)...... 179 F 3
Stange (N)......... 189 F 4
Stanišić (SRB)..... 137 H 1
Stanišinci (SRB).... 143 E 2
Stanisławów (PL)... 123 E 1
Staňkov (CZ)....... 91 H 4
Stankovci (HR)..... 136 C 5
Stanley (GB)....... 31 G 4
Stános (SRB)....... 164 D 2
Stanós (GR)........ 161 H 4
Stans (CH)......... 99 E 3
Stansstad (CH)..... 99 E 3
Stansted (GB)...... 36 D 3
Stapar (SRB)....... 137 H 1
Staporków (PL)..... 122 C 3
Stapar (SRB)....... 137 H 1
Stara Biała (PL)..... 118 C 5
Stará Boleslav (CZ).. 92 B 2
Stara Kamienica (PL). 120 C 4
Stará Ľubovňa (SK).. 133 F 2
Stara Moravica (SRB). 140 B 2
Stara Novalja (HR).. 136 A 4
Stara Pazova (SRB).. 140 C 3
Stara reka (BG)..... 159 G 1
Stara Turá (SK)..... 132 B 3
Stara Zagora /
  Стара Загора (BG). 159 F 2
Starachowice (PL)... 122 D 4
Staraja Russa (RUS).. 6 D 1
Staravina (MK)..... 145 F 3
Starcevo (BG)...... 162 C 2
Starchiojd (RO)..... 152 B 2
Stare Czarnowo (PL). 116 C 4
Stare Jeżewo (PL).. 119 G 4
Stare Pole (PL)..... 117 H 2
Stare Żukowice (PL). 125 H 1
Stargard Szczeciński (PL). 116 D 3
Stårheim (N)....... 188 B 2
Stari Bar (MNE).... 139 F 5
Stari Dojran (MK)... 145 H 2
Stari Gradac (HR)... 135 G 3
Stari Jankovci (HR). 137 H 2
Stari Log (SLO)..... 134 C 3
Stari Majdan (BIH). 135 F 5
Stari Mikanovci (HR). 137 G 2
Starica (RUS)....... 7 F 2
Starigrad (Hvar) (HR). 138 B 3
Starigrad (Senj) (HR). 134 C 5
Starigrad Paklenica (HR). 136 B 4
Starnberg (D)...... 95 F 2
Staro Orjahovo (BG). 157 F 3
Staro Petrovo Selo (HR). 135 G 4
Staro Selo (BG)..... 158 D 1
Staro Slano (BIH)... 139 E 4
Starodub (RUS)...... 7 F 4
Starogard Gdański (PL). 117 H 3
Starokostjantyniv (UA). 13 E 2
Starosel (BG)....... 158 D 2
Starozreby (PL)..... 118 C 5
Stary Dzierzgoń (PL). 118 B 3
Stary Gostków (PL). 121 H 5
Stary Sącz (PL)..... 125 H 2
Starý Smokovec (SK). 133 E 2
Starzyny (PL)....... 122 B 4
Staszów (PL)....... 122 D 5
Statland (N)....... 183 E 3
Statos-Agios Fotios (CY).174 B 4
Stavanger (N)...... 194 B 1
Stahle (D)......... 85 F 3
Staveley (GB)...... 33 E 3
Stavelot (B)....... 79 E 3
Stavenhagen
  Reuterstadt (D)... 83 E 3
Stavenisse (NL).... 78 C 1
Stavern (N)........ 195 E 1
Stavoren (NL)...... 77 E 3
Stavrochóri (GR)... 173 E 4
Stavrodrómi (GR)... 164 D 4
Stavrós (Imathía) (GR). 161 F 3
Stavrós (Kríti) (GR). 170 A 5

Stavrós (Thessalía) (GR). 165 F 1
Stavrós
  (Thessaloníki)) (GR). 161 H 3
Stavroúpoli (GR).... 162 C 2
Stavrovouni (CY).... 175 E 4
Stavrós (GR)....... 164 C 3
Stavsjo (N)........ 189 F 4
Stawiski (PL)....... 119 F 3
Stawiszyn (PL)..... 121 G 2
Štěchovice (CZ).... 92 A 3
Steckborn (CH)..... 99 F 1
Steeg (A).......... 95 E 4
Steenbergen (NL)... 78 C 1
Steenvoorde (F).... 39 H 1
Steenwijk (NL)..... 77 F 3
Stefan Karadžovo (BG). 159 H 3
Ştefăneşti (RO)..... 148 D 1
Stefáni (Ípeiros) (GR). 164 C 1
Stefáni
  (Stereá Elláda) (GR). 165 H 4
Stefaniná (GR)..... 161 H 3
Stefanovíkeio (GR). 165 F 1
Stege (DK)........ 199 E 4
Stegersbach (A).... 97 G 4
Stegna (PL)........ 117 H 2
Ştei (RO).......... 146 D 4
Steibis (D)........ 94 D 3
Steigen (N)........ 179 F 3
Stein (A).......... 97 F 1
Stein (N).......... 189 F 4
Stein am Rhein (CH). 99 F 1
Steinach (D)....... 91 E 2
Steinach am Brenner (A). 95 G 4
Steinau an der Straße (D). 89 F 1
Steinbach-
  Hallenberg (D).... 85 H 5
Steinborg (N)...... 188 A 3
Steinen (D)........ 188 B 3
Steinfeld (A)....... 96 C 5
Steinfeld (D)....... 85 E 1
Steingaden (D)..... 95 F 3
Steinhaus / Cadipietra (I). 103 E 1
Steinhausen (D).... 94 D 2
Steinheim (Höxter) (D). 85 F 3
Steinheim
  (Unterallgäu) (D). 95 E 2
Steinheim
  am Albuch (D)... 89 G 4
Steinkjer (N)...... 183 E 4
Steinshamn (N).... 182 A 5
Steinsland (N)..... 188 A 4
Stekene (B)........ 78 C 1
Stemnítsa (GR).... 165 E 5
Stenay (F)........ 40 D 4
Stendal (D)........ 86 B 1
Stende (LV)....... 202 B 2
Stení Dírfis (GR)... 165 H 3
Stenlille (D)....... 198 D 3
Stenløse (DK)..... 199 E 3
Stenness (GB)..... 26 B 3
Stenó (GR)........ 165 F 5
Stenudden (S)..... 179 H 5
Stenungsund (S)... 195 F 3
Stepanci (MK)..... 145 F 1
Stepnica (PL)...... 116 B 3
Stepojevac (SRB).. 140 D 5
Sterkrade (D)...... 84 C 3
Stérna (Anatolikí Makedonía
  kai Thráki) (GR). 162 C 2
Stérna
  (Pelopónnisos) (GR). 165 F 5
Sternberg (D)...... 82 D 3
Šternberk (CZ)..... 93 F 3
Stérnes (GR)....... 170 A 5
Sterup (D).......... 81 H 1
Sterzing / Vipiteno (I). 102 D 1
Stevenage (GB).... 36 C 3
Stevrek (BG)....... 159 G 1
Stewarton (GB).... 30 C 2
Steyr (A).......... 96 D 2
Steyrermühl (A).... 96 C 2
Steževo (BG)...... 156 B 2
Stia (I)........... 107 E 3
Stigliano (I)....... 110 D 4

A B C D E F G H I J K L M N O P Q R S T U V W X Y Z

Stigtomta (S) 197 F2
Stiklestad (N) 183 E4
Stilo (I) 113 C4
Štimlje (SRB) 143 E4
Stintino (I) 112 A1
Štip (MK) 145 G1
Stirling (GB) 30 D1
Štirovača (HR) 134 C5
Štitar (SRB) 140 B4
Štítnik (SK) 133 F3
Štivan (HR) 134 B5
Stjärnhov (S) 197 F1
Stjärnsund (S) 196 D2
Stjørdal (N) 182 D5
Stobi (MK) 145 G1
Stockach (D) 94 C2
Stockbridge (GB) 35 G3
Stockelsdorf (D) 82 C3
Stockerau (A) 97 G1
Stockholm (S) 197 G1
Stockport (GB) 32 D3
Stocksbridge (GB) 33 E3
Stockton-on-Tees (GB) ... 31 G4
Stoczek Łukowski (PL) ... 123 E2
Stod (CZ) 91 H4
Stöde (S) 190 B2
Stoeneşti (Piteşti) (RO) . 151 H2
Stoeneşti (Slatina) (RO) . 151 G4
Stoicăneşti (RO) 151 G4
Stojkite (BG) 162 C1
Stoke-on-Trent (GB) 32 D4
Stokite (BG) 159 E1
Stokke (N) 195 E1
Stokkvågen (N) 183 F1
Stokmarknes (N) 179 F2
Stolac (BIH) 139 E3
Stolberg (Harz) (D) 86 A3
Stolberg (Rheinland) (D) . 84 B5
Stolice (SRB) 137 H4
Stolin (BY) 6 D5
Stollberg (D) 86 C5
Stöllet (S) 189 G4
Stolno (PL) 117 G4
Stolpen (D) 87 E4
Stolzenau (D) 85 F1
Stómio (GR) 161 F5
Ston (HR) 138 D3
Stone (GB) 32 D4
Stonehaven (GB) 29 G4
Stonglandet (N) 176 A4
Stopanja (SRB) 143 E2
Stopnica (PL) 122 D5
Storå (S) 196 D1
Stora Blåsjön (S) 183 F3
Stora Skedvi (S) 190 A5
Stora Sundby (S) 197 F2
Stora Sundby (S) 197 E1
Storby (FIN) 190 D5
Stordal (N) 188 C1
Store Heddinge (DK) 199 E4
Store Molvik (N) 177 G1
Storebø (N) 188 A4
Storebro (S) 197 E4
Støren (N) 182 D5
Storfors (S) 195 H1
Storforsen (S) 184 D1
Storforshei (N) 183 G1
Storkow (D) 87 E2
Storlien (S) 183 E5
Stormi (FIN) 191 F3
Stornoway (GB) 28 C1
Storo (I) 101 G3
Storożynec' (UA) 12 D3
Storsjö (S) 189 G1
Storslett (N) 176 C3
Storsteinnes (N) 176 B4
Storuman (S) 183 H3
Storvik (N) 176 D3
Storvik (S) 190 B4
Stotel (D) 81 F4
Stoŭbcy (BY) 6 D5
Stourbridge (GB) 32 D5
Stournaraíika (GR) 164 D1
Stourport (GB) 32 D5
Støvring (DK) 194 D4
Stow-on-the-Wold (GB) ... 35 G1
Stowe Gardens (GB) 35 H1

Stowmarket (GB) 33 H5
Stożer (BG) 157 F2
Strà (I) 103 E4
Strabane (GB) 23 E2
Strachówka (PL) 123 E1
Stracin (MK) 143 G5
Stradalovo (BG) 158 A3
Stradella (I) 101 E5
Stradsett (GB) 33 H4
Straelen (D) 84 B3
Stragari (SRB) 140 D5
Straja (RO) 148 A1
Stråkonice (CZ) 92 A4
Straldža (BG) 159 H2
Stralsund (D) 83 F2
Štramberk (CZ) 93 G3
Stranda (N) 188 C1
Strandebarm (N) 188 B4
Strandhill (IRL) 22 D3
Strandža (BG) 159 H3
Strängnäs (S) 197 F1
Strangford (GB) 23 H3
Strání (CZ) 93 F5
Stranice (SLO) 134 D2
Stranorlar (IRL) 23 E2
Stranraer (GB) 23 H2
Strasbourg (F) 47 H1
Strasburg (D) 83 G4
Strasorelci (BG) 155 E2
Straßburg (A) 96 D4
Straßwalchen (A) 96 C2
Stratford-upon-Avon (GB) . 33 E5
Strathaven (GB) 30 D2
Stratóni (GR) 161 H4
Strátos (GR) 164 D3
Stratton (GB) 34 C3
Straubing (D) 91 G5
Straumen (N) 179 G4
Straumen (N) 183 E4
Straumen (N) 179 F4
Straumsjøen (N) 179 F2
Straumsnes (N) 179 G4
Straupitz (D) 87 E2
Strausberg (D) 86 D1
Straußfurt (D) 86 A4
Straža (SLO) 134 C3
Straža (SRB) 141 E3
Stražica (BG) 156 C3
Strážnice (CZ) 93 F5
Strážný (CZ) 92 A5
Strážske (SK) 133 H2
Štrbské Pleso (SK) 133 E2
Streatley (GB) 35 H2
Street (GB) 35 F3
Strehaia (RO) 151 E3
Strehla (D) 86 D4
Streitberg (D) 91 E3
Strelča (BG) 158 D2
Strelci (BG) 159 E2
Strelec (BG) 156 C2
Stremci (BG) 162 D1
Strenči (LV) 203 F2
Strengberg (A) 97 E2
Strezimirovci (SRB) 143 G3
Strezovce (SRB) 143 F4
Stříbro (CZ) 91 G3
Strjama (BG) 159 E2
Strmac (HR) 135 G4
Strmica (MK) 136 D5
Strmilov (CZ) 92 C4
Strmosten (SRB) 141 F5
Strobl (A) 96 C3
Stroești (RO) 151 F2
Strofyliá (GR) 165 H2
Strojkovce (SRB) 143 F3
Strokestown (IRL) 22 D4
Stromberg (D) 88 D2
Stromeferry (GB) 28 C3
Strömfors /
  Ruotsinpyhtää (FIN) ... 193 E4
Stromness (GB) 26 B3
Strömsbruk (S) 190 B2
Strömsnasbruk (S) 195 G5
Strömstad (S) 195 F1
Strömsund (S) 183 G4

Strongoli (I) 113 D2
Stronie Śląskie (PL) 124 C1
Strontian (GB) 28 C5
Stropkov (SK) 133 G2
Stroud (GB) 35 F1
Stroumpi (CY) 174 B4
Strovlés (GR) 172 B3
Strovolos (CY) 174 D3
Struer (DK) 194 C5
Struga (MK) 144 D2
Struge (SLO) 134 C3
Strumica (MK) 145 H1
Strumień (PL) 125 E1
Strumjani (BG) 161 G1
Stryj (UA) 12 D2
Stryków (PL) 122 B2
Stryn (N) 188 C2
Strzegom (PL) 120 D4
Strzegowo-Osada (PL) 118 D5
Strzelce Krajeńskie (PL) . 116 C5
Strzelce Opolskie (PL) .. 121 G5
Strzelin (PL) 121 E4
Strzelno (PL) 117 G4
Strzyżów (PL) 127 E1
Strzyżowice (PL) 121 H5
Stubbekøbing (DK) 199 E4
Stubičke Toplice (HR) ... 135 E3
Štubik (SRB) 141 G5
Stubline (SRB) 140 C4
Studena (SRB) 143 G3
Studena
  (Haskovo) (BG) 163 F1
Studena (Pernik) (BG) ... 158 B2
Studenci (HR) 138 C2
Studenec (BG) 156 D2
Studenica (SRB) 142 D2
Studénka (CZ) 93 G3
Studina (RO) 151 G5
Studzienice (PL) 117 F2
Stugun (S) 183 G5
Stühlingen (D) 94 B3
Stuhr (D) 81 G5
Stulpicani (RO) 148 B2
Stupari (BIH) 137 G4
Stupava (SK) 132 A4
Stupino (RUS) 7 G2
Stupinigi (I) 100 C5
Sturehov (S) 197 F1
Sturminster
  Newton (GB) 38 A1
Štúrovo (SK) 132 C5
Stuttgart (D) 89 F4
Stykkishólmur (IS) 178 A2
Stylída / Στυλίδα (GR) .. 165 F2
Stylloi (CY) 175 F3
Stýra (GR) 166 B4
Suances (E) 58 B1
Subačius (LT) 205 F2
Subate (LV) 203 F5
Subbiano (I) 107 E3
Subiaco (I) 109 E3
Subijana-Morillas (E) ... 58 D2
Subostrel (BG) 161 G1
Subotica /
  Суботица (SRB) 140 B1
Subotište (SRB) 140 C4
Subtropical
  Gardens (GB) 34 A5
Suceava (RO) 148 B2
Suceviţa (RO) 148 A1
Sucha Beskidzka (PL) 125 F2
Suchań (PL) 116 C4
Suchedniów (PL) 122 D4
Suchiniči (RUS) 7 G3
Suchorze (PL) 117 F2
Suchowola (PL) 119 G3
Süchteln (D) 84 B4
Sucina (E) 73 E3
Suciu de Sus (RO) 147 F2
Sudbury (Derby) (GB) 33 E4
Sudbury (Suffolk) (GB) .. 36 D3
Suddesjaur (S) 184 D1
Süderbrarup (D) 81 H1
Sudża (RUS) 7 G5
Şugag (RO) 151 F1

Suhareka /
  Suva Reka (SRB) 143 E4
Suhindol (BG) 156 B3
Suho Polje (BIH) 137 H3
Suhopolje (HR) 135 G3
Šuica (BIH) 137 E5
Šuici (RO) 151 G2
Suinula (FIN) 191 G3
Suippes (F) 40 C5
Šuja (RUS) 7 H1
Sukeva (FIN) 187 F4
Sukobin (MNE) 139 G5
Sukošan (HR) 136 B5
Sukovo (SRB) 143 G3
Sukth (AL) 144 B2
Šula (MNE) 139 F2
Sulden / Solda (I) 101 G2
Sulechów (PL) 120 D2
Sulęcin (PL) 120 C1
Sulejów (PL) 122 C3
Sulejówek (PL) 122 D1
Sulina (RO) 153 H2
Sulingen (D) 85 F1
Sulitjelma (N) 179 G4
Sulkava (FIN) 193 G2
Sułkowice (PL) 125 G2
Sully-sur-Loire (F) 45 E3
Sulmierzyce (PL) 121 F3
Sulmona (I) 109 G2
Sulz am Neckar (D) 89 E5
Sulzbach (D) 88 C3
Sulzbach an der Murr (D) . 89 F4
Sulzbach-Rosenberg (D) .. 91 F4
Sulzemoos (D) 95 F2
Sumartin (HR) 138 C2
Sumba (Færøerne) (DK) ... 194 A5
Sumburgh (GB) 26 D1
Sümeg (H) 128 C2
Šumen / Шумен (BG) 157 E3
Sumer (BG) 154 D3
Sumiainen (FIN) 191 H1
Sumiswald (CH) 98 D3
Sumony (H) 128 D5
Šumperk (CZ) 93 E2
Sumy (UA) 7 G5
Sund (FIN) 190 D5
Sunde (N) 188 B5
Sunde (N) 182 C5
Sunderland (GB) 31 G4
Sundern (D) 84 D4
Sundom (FIN) 191 E1
Sundsvall (S) 190 B2
Sungurlare (BG) 159 H1
Suni (I) 112 B3
Sunja (HR) 135 F4
Sunnansjö (S) 190 A5
Sunndalsøra (N) 188 D1
Sunne (S) 189 G5
Sunne (S) 183 G5
Sunnemo (S) 189 H5
Suntaži (LV) 203 E3
Suodenniemi (FIN) 191 F3
Suolahti (FIN) 191 H1
Suolijoki (FIN) 185 G1
Suomenlinna (FIN) 191 H5
Suomenniemi (FIN) 193 F3
Suomusjärvi (FIN) 191 G4
Suomussalmi (FIN) 187 F2
Suomutunturi (FIN) 181 F5
Suonenjoki (FIN) 193 F1
Suopelto (FIN) 185 H5
Super-Besse (F) 50 A3
Super Molina (E) 60 D2
Supetar (HR) 138 B2
Supetarska Draga (HR) ... 134 C5
Supino (I) 109 F3
Suplac de Barcău (RO) ... 146 D2
Supraśl (PL) 119 H4
Supuru de Jos (RO) 147 E2
Surahammar (S) 197 E1
Suraia (RO) 152 D1
Šurany (SK) 132 B4
Suraž (RUS) 7 F4

Surbo (I) 111 H4
Surčin / Сурчин (SRB) ... 140 C4
Surdegis (LT) 205 F2
Surdulica (SRB) 143 G4
Surgères (F) 48 C2
Súria (E) 60 D3
Surnadalsøra (N) 182 C5
Sursee (CH) 98 D2
Survilliers (F) 39 H5
Susa (I) 100 B5
Susak (HR) 136 A4
Sušara (SRB) 141 E3
Susch (CH) 99 G3
Susek (SRB) 140 B3
Suseni
  (Miercurea Ciuc) (RO) . 148 A4
Suseni (Piteşti) (RO) ... 151 H3
Sušice (CZ) 91 H4
Süßen (D) 89 G5
Susurluk (TR) 19 G2
Susz (PL) 118 B3
Süteşti (RO) 152 D2
Sutinske Toplice (HR) ... 135 E2
Sutivan (HR) 138 B2
Sutjeska (BIH) 137 G5
Sutjeska (SRB) 140 D3
Sutomore (MNE) 139 F5
Sutri (I) 108 D2
Sutterton (GB) 33 G4
Sutton (GB) 36 C4
Sutton Coldfield (GB) ... 33 E5
Sutton-in-Ashfield (GB) . 33 E3
Sutton-on-Sea (GB) 33 G3
Suure-Jaani (EST) 201 E3
Suva Reka /
  Suhareka (SRB) 143 E4
Suvainiškis (LT) 205 G1
Suvereto (I) 106 C4
Suvodanja (SRB) 140 C5
Suvodol (MK) 145 E1
Suvorovo (BG) 157 F2
Suwałki (PL) 119 G2
Suzdal' (RUS) 7 H1
Suzzara (I) 101 H5
Svaljava (UA) 12 C3
Svalöv (S) 199 F3
Svaneke (DK) 199 G4
Svanstein (S) 180 D5
Svanvik (N) 177 H3
Svappavaara (S) 180 B4
Svärdsjö (S) 190 A4
Svarstad (N) 195 E1
Svartå (S) 195 H1
Svartevatn (N) 194 B1
Svätý Jur (SK) 132 A4
Svedala (S) 199 F3
Sveg (S) 189 H2
Švékšna (LT) 204 C2
Svelgen (N) 188 B2
Svelvik (N) 189 E5
Svenčionys (LT) 205 H3
Svendborg (DK) 198 C4
Svenljunga (S) 195 G4
Svenstavik (S) 189 H1
Sveštari (BG) 156 D1
Sveti Bogorodica,
  manastir (BG) 157 F5
Sveti Filip i Jakov (HR) . 136 B5
Sveti Ivan Žabno (HR) ... 135 F3
Sveti Ivan Zelina (HR) .. 135 E3
Sveti Juraj (HR) 134 C5
Sveti Nikola (MNE) 144 B1
Sveti Nikole (MK) 143 F5
Sveti Petar na moru (HR) . 136 B5
Sveti Rok (HR) 136 C4
Sveti Stefan (MNE) 139 F5
Sveti Vlas (BG) 157 F4
Svetlahorsk (BY) 7 E5
Svetlen (BG) 156 D2
Svetlogorsk (RUS) 5 H3
Svetozar Miletić (SRB) .. 137 H1
Svežen (BG) 159 E2
Sviby (EST) 200 C2
Svidník (SK) 133 G2
Švihov (CZ) 91 H4
Svilajnac (SRB) 141 E5

Svilengrad /
  Свиленград (BG) 163 E1
Svingvoll (N) 189 E3
Sviniţa (RO) 150 C3
Svinoy (Færøerne) (DK) .. 194 B4
Svištov / Свищов (BG) ... 151 H5
Svitavy (CZ) 92 D3
Svitlovods'k (UA) 13 G1
Svođ (SRB) 143 G3
Svode (BG) 158 C1
Svoge (BG) 158 B1
Svolvær (N) 179 F3
Svorkmo (N) 182 C5
Svoronáta (GR) 164 B4
Svrljig (SRB) 143 G2
Swadlincote (GB) 33 E4
Swaffham (GB) 33 H4
Swalmen (NL) 79 F2
Swanage (GB) 38 B1
Swanley (GB) 36 D4
Swanlinbar (IRL) 23 E3
Swansea / Abertawe (GB) . 34 D2
Swarzędz (PL) 121 F1
Świdnica
  (Wałbrzych) (PL) 121 E4
Świdnica
  (Zielona Gora) (PL) ... 120 C2
Świdwin (PL) 116 D3
Świebodzice (PL) 120 D4
Świebodzin (PL) 120 C1
Świecie (PL) 117 G4
Świecko (PL) 120 B1
Świeradów-Zdrój (PL) 120 C4
Świerzawa (PL) 120 D4
Świerzno (PL) 116 C2
Święta Lipka (PL) 119 E2
Swindon (GB) 35 G2
Swinford (IRL) 22 C4
Świnoujście (PL) 116 B2
Swords (IRL) 23 G5
Syčovka (RUS) 7 F2
Syców (PL) 121 F3
Sykaminiá (GR) 167 F1
Sykäräinen (FIN) 185 G5
Syke (D) 81 G5
Sykiá (GR) 171 F1
Sykkylven (N) 188 C1
Sylling (N) 189 E5
Sylt-Ost (D) 81 F1
Syltefjord (N) 177 H2
Sými (GR) 171 H2
Synod Inn (GB) 32 A5
Syötekylä (FIN) 187 E1
Syre (GB) 26 A5
Syrianochori (CY) 174 C3
Sysmä (FIN) 191 H3
Sysslebäck (S) 189 G4
Syväjärvi (FIN) 181 E4
Syvde (N) 188 B1
Sývota (GR) 164 B1
Syyspohja (FIN) 193 G3
Szabadbattyán (H) 129 E3
Szabadszállás (H) 129 F3
Szadek (PL) 121 H3
Szalkszentmárton (H) 129 F3
Szamocin (PL) 117 F5
Szamotuły (PL) 117 E5
Szany (H) 128 C2
Szarvas (H) 129 H3
Százhalombatta (H) 129 E2
Szczawno-Zdrój (PL) 120 D4
Szczebrzeszyn (PL) 123 G4
Szczecin (PL) 116 B4
Szczecinek (PL) 117 E3
Szczekociny (PL) 122 B5
Szczerców (PL) 121 H3
Szczucin (PL) 122 D5
Szczuczyn (PL) 119 F3
Szczurkowo (PL) 118 D1
Szczurowa (PL) 125 H1
Szczyrk (PL) 125 F2
Szczytna (PL) 121 F3
Szczytno (PL) 118 D3
Szécsény (H) 126 B5
Szederkény (H) 129 E5
Szeged (H) 129 G4

Szeghalom (H) ....131 E 3
Szegvár (H) .... 129 G 4
Székely (H) .... 127 F 5
Székesfehérvár (H) .. 129 E 2
Székkutas (H) .... 129 H 4
Szekszárd (H) ...... 129 E 4
Szendrő (H) .... 126 D 5
Szentendre (H) ..... 129 F 1
Szentes (H) .... 129 G 4
Szentgotthárd (H) .. 128 A 3
Szentlászló (H) .... 128 D 5
Szentlőrinc (H) .... 128 D 5
Szenyér (H) .... 128 C 4
Szepietowo-Stacja (PL)..119 G 2
Szerencs (H) .... 127 E 5
Szigetszentmiklós (H).. 129 F 2
Szigetújfalu (H) ... 129 E 2
Szigetvár (H) ...... 128 D 5
Szikszó (H) .... 126 D 5
Szilvásvárad (H) ... 126 C 5
Szil (H) .... 128 C 2
Szklarska Poręba (PL) .. 120 C 4
Szlichtyngowa (PL) .. 120 D 2
Szolnok (H) .... 129 G 2
Szőlősgyörök (H) ... 128 D 3
Szombathely (H) .... 128 B 2
Szprotawa (PL) ..... 120 C 3
Szreńsk (PL) .... 118 C 4
Sztabin (PL) ....119 G 3
Sztum (PL) ....117 H 3
Szubin (PL) ....117 F 5
Szydłów (PL) .... 122 D 5
Szydłowiec (PL) .... 122 D 3
Szymbark (PL) ...... 126 D 2
Szypliszki (PL).......119 G 2

T
Taastrup (DK) ...... 199 E 3
Tab (H) .... 128 D 3
Tabanovce (MK) .... 143 F 5
Tábara (E) .... 57 G 5
Tabasalu (EST) ..... 200 D 1
Taberg (S) .... 195 H 3
Tabernas (E) .... 72 B 5
Tabivere (EST) ..... 201 E 3
Taboada (E) .... 56 D 3
Tábor (CZ) .... 92 B 4
Tábua (P) .... 62 C 3
Tabuaço (P) .... 62 D 1
Tabuenca (E) .... 59 F 5
Täby (S) .... 197 G 1
Tác (H) .... 129 E 3
Tachov (CZ) ....91 G 3
Tadcaster (GB) ..... 33 E 2
Taebla (EST) .... 200 C 2
Tafalla (E) .... 59 F 3
Tafjord (N) .... 188 D 1
Ţaga (RO) .... 147 F 3
Taggia (I) .... 104 C 4
Tagliacozzo (I) .... 109 F 2
Taglio di Po (I) .... 103 F 5
Tahal (E) .... 71 G 5
Tahkvuori (FIN) .... 187 F 5
Tain (GB) .... 29 E 2
Tain-l'Hermitage (F).... 50 D 4
Taipadas (P). ...... 68 B 2
Taipalsaari (FIN) ... 193 F 3
Taivalkoski (FIN) ... 187 F 1
Taivassalo (FIN) ... 191 F 4
Täkač (BG) .... 157 E 2
Takácsi (H) .... 128 C 2
Takovo (SRB) ...... 139 H 1
Taktikoúpoli (GR) .. 165 G 5
Tala (CY) ....174 B 4
Talarrubias (E) .... 69 H 1
Talaván (E) .... 63 F 5
Talavera de la Reina (E).. 63 H 4
Talavera la Real (E) .. 69 F 2
Talayuela (E) ...... 63 G 4
Talayuelas (E) ..... 65 G 4
Taldom (RUS) ....7 G 1
Talgarth (GB) ...... 35 E 1
Talla (I) .... 107 E 3
Tallard (F) ....51 F 5
Tällberg (S) .... 190 A 4
Tallinn (EST) ...... 200 D 1
Talloires-Montmin (F)..51 F 2

Tallow (IRL) .... 24 D 4
Talluskylä (FIN). ... 187 E 5
Tállya (H) .... 127 E 5
Tălmaciu (RO). .... 151 G 1
Talmont-Saint-Hilaire (F).. 48 B 1
Tal'ne (UA) ....13 F 2
Talsi (LV) .... 202 B 2
Talvik (N) ....176 D 3
Tamames (E) ...... 63 F 3
Támara de Campos (E) .. 58 A 4
Tamarinda (E) ......67 G 2
Tamarite de Litera (E) .. 60 A 3
Tamási (H) .... 128 D 4
Tamsweg (A) .... 96 D 4
Tamsalu (EST) ..... 201 F 2
Tampere (FIN) ..... 191 G 3
Tamworth (GB) .... 33 E 4
Tana Bru (N) ...... 177 G 2
Tanágra (GR) ...... 165 H 4
Tandådalen (S) .... 189 G 3
Ţăndărei (RO) ..... 153 E 3
Tandragee (GB) .... 23 F 3
Tandsbyn (S) ...... 190 A 1
Tandsjöborg (S) ... 190 A 3
Tanganheira (P) ... 68 B 4
Tangerhütte (D) ... 86 B 1
Tangermünde (D) .. 86 B 1
Tanhua (FIN) ...... 181 F 4
Taningies (F) ....51 F 2
Tanlay (F) .... 45 H 3
Tann (D) .... 85 G 5
Tännäs (S) .... 189 G 1
Tänndalen (S) ..... 189 G 1
Tannheim (A) ..... 95 E 3
Tannila (FIN) ...... 185 H 2
Tanvald (CZ) .... 87 G 5
Taormina (I) ....115 G 3
Tapa (EST) .... 201 F 2
Tapia de Casariego (E).. 57 E 1
Tápiószecső (H) ... 129 F 2
Tápiószele (H). .... 129 G 2
Tápiószentmárton (H).. 129 G 2
Tapolca (H) .... 128 C 3
Tapolcafő (H) ...... 128 C 2
Tar (HR) .... 134 A 4
Taracena (E) .... 64 C 2
Tarancón (E) .... 64 D 3
Taranto (I) ....111 F 4
Tarare (F) .... 50 C 2
Taraš (SRB) .... 140 C 2
Tarašča (UA) ....13 F 1
Tarascon (F). ...... 54 C 2
Tarascon-sur-Ariège (F) . 53 F 4
Tarazona (E) .... 59 F 4
Tarazona
   de la Mancha (E) .... 65 F 5
Tarbert (IRL) ...... 24 B 3
Tarbert
   (Argyll and Bute) (GB) . 28 B 2
Tarbert
   (Western Isles) (GB) .. 30 B 2
Tarbes (F) .... 52 D 3
Tarbet (GB) .... 30 C 1
Tarcento (I) .... 103 G 3
Tarčin (BIH) .... 137 G 5
Tardets-Sorholus (F) . 52 B 3
Tardienta (E) ...... 59 H 4
Tärendö (S) .... 180 C 4
Targon (F) .... 48 D 5
Târgoviște (RO) ... 152 A 3
Târgoviște /
   Търговище (BG) .... 156 D 3
Târgu Bujor (RO) .. 153 E 1
Târgu Cărbunești (RO) . 151 F 3
Târgu Frumos (RO).. 148 D 3
Târgu Jiu (RO) ..... 151 E 2
Târgu Lăpuș (RO).. 147 F 2
Târgu Logrești (RO) . 151 F 3
Târgu Mureș (RO).. 147 G 4
Târgu Neamț (RO).. 148 B 3
Târgu Ocna (RO)... 148 C 5

Târgu Secuiesc (RO)... 148 B 5
Târgușor (RO)...... 153 F 4
Tarhos (H).........131 E 3
Tarifa (E) ....74 C 5
Tarján (H) .... 129 E 1
Tărlişua (RO) ...... 147 G 2
Tărlungeni (RO) ... 152 B 1
Tarm (DK) .... 198 B 2
Tarmstedt (D) ....81 G 5
Tarna Mare (RO)... 147 E 1
Tärnaby (S) .... 183 G 2
Tărnăveni (RO) .... 147 G 5
Tarnobrzeg (PL) ... 123 E 5
Tarnogród (PL) .... 123 G 5
Tarnos (F) .... 52 A 2
Târnova (RO) ...... 146 C 4
Tarnów (PL) .... 125 H 1
Tarnowo Podgórne (PL) . 121 E 1
Tarnowskie Góry (PL) .. 121 H 5
Tarouca (P) .... 62 D 2
Tarp (D) ....81 G 1
Tarporley (GB) ..... 32 C 3
Tarquinia (I) ...... 108 C 2
Tarragona (E) ..... 60 C 4
Tarrasa / Terrassa (E) .. 60 D 3
Tàrrega (E) .... 60 C 3
Tårs (DK) .... 198 D 4
Tarsia (I) ....113 B 1
Tartas (F) .... 52 B 2
Tartu (EST) .... 201 F 3
Tarvasjoki (FIN) ... 191 F 4
Tarvisio (I) .... 103 H 2
Täsch (CH) .... 98 D 5
Tåsjö (S) .... 183 H 4
Tăşnad (RO) .... 146 D 2
Tassin (F) .... 50 D 3
Tata (H) .... 129 E 1
Tatabánya (H) ..... 129 E 1
Tataháza (H) ...... 129 F 5
Tătăranu (RO) ..... 152 D 1
Tătărăştii de Jos (RO).. 151 H 4
Tătărăştii de Sus (RO) .. 151 H 4
Tatarbunary (UA) ...13 F 4
Tatárszentgyörgy (H).. 129 F 3
Tau (N) .... 194 B 1
Tauberbischofsheim (D). 89 G 2
Taucha (D) .... 86 C 4
Taufers im Münstertal /
   Tubre .... 101 G 2
Taufkirchen (D) .... 95 H 1
Taujėnai (LT) ...... 205 F 3
Taulé (F) .... 42 C 1
Taunton (GB) ...... 35 E 4
Taunusstein-Neuhof (D). 89 E 1
Tauplitz (A) .... 96 D 3
Tauragė (LT) .... 204 C 3
Tauragnai (LT) ..... 205 G 2
Taurene (LV) ...... 203 F 2
Taurianova (I) .....115 H 4
Tauste (E) .... 59 G 4
Tăuţii-Măgherăuş (RO). 147 F 2
Tauves (F) .... 49 H 3
Tavankut (SRB) .... 140 B 1
Tavannes (CH) ..... 98 C 2
Tavarnelle (I) ..... 105 H 5
Tavastila (FIN) .... 193 F 4
Tavaux (F) .... 46 D 5
Taverna (I) ....113 C 4
Tavernelle (I) ..... 107 E 5
Tavernes (F). ...... 55 E 2
Tavernes
   de la Valldigna (E).... 66 A 4
Tavira (P) .... 68 D 5
Tavistock (GB) ..... 34 D 4
Tavronítis (GR) .... 172 B 3
Tavşanlı (TR) ....19 H 2
Taxenbach (A) ..... 96 B 4
Tayinloan (GB) .... 30 B 2
Taynuilt (GB) ...... 28 D 5
Tayport (GB) ...... 29 E 3
Tāža (BG) .... 159 E 2
Tázlár (H) .... 129 F 4
Tazones (E) .... 57 H 1
Tczew (PL) ....117 H 2
Teaca (RO) .... 147 G 3
Teano (I) .... 109 G 4
Teba (E) ....74 D 3

Tebay (GB) ....31 F 5
Techendorf (A)...... 96 C 5
Techirghiol (RO) ... 153 F 5
Tecklenburg (D). ... 84 D 2
Tecuci (RO) .... 152 D 1
Teeriranta (FIN) ... 187 F 1
Teféli (GR) .... 172 D 4
Tegel (D). .... 86 D 1
Tegelen (NL) ...... 79 F 1
Tegernsee (D) ..... 95 G 3
Teggiano (I) ....110 C 5
Téglás (H) ....131 E 1
Teguise (E) ....67 H 4
Teignmouth (GB) .. 35 E 4
Teijo (FIN) .... 191 G 5
Teisendorf (D) ..... 96 B 2
Teisko (FIN) .... 191 G 2
Teiuş (RO) .... 147 F 5
Teixeiro (E) .... 56 C 2
Teixoso (P) .... 62 D 3
Tekeriš (SRB) ..... 140 B 4
Tekija (SRB) ....141 G 4
Tekirdağ (TR) ....19 G 2
Telavåg (N) .... 188 A 4
Telč (CZ) .... 92 C 4
Telde (E) ....67 G 5
Telese (I) .... 109 H 4
Telford (GB) .... 32 C 4
Telfs (A) .... 95 F 4
Telgte (D) .... 84 D 2
Teliš (BG) .... 155 E 3
Tellingstedt (D) .....81 G 2
Telšiai (LT) .... 204 C 1
Telti (I) ....112 C 1
Teltow (D) .... 86 D 1
Tembleque (E) .... 64 C 4
Temerin /
   Темерин (SRB) .... 140 C 2
Temmes (FIN) ..... 185 H 3
Tempio Pausania (I) ..112 C 1
Templemore (IRL) .. 24 D 2
Templewo (PL) .... 120 C 1
Templin (D) .... 83 F 5
Temse (B) .... 78 C 2
Temska (SRB) ..... 143 G 2
Temvria (CY) ....174 C 3
Tenala (FIN) ...... 191 G 5
Tenby /
   Dinbych-y-pysgod (GB). 34 C 2
Tence (F) .... 50 C 4
Tende (F) .... 55 H 1
Tendilla (E) .... 64 D 2
Tenja (HR) .... 137 H 2
Tenneville (B) ..... 79 E 3
Tenterden (GB) .... 36 D 5
Teolo (I) .... 103 E 4
Teovo (MK) .... 145 F 1
Tepasto (FIN) ..... 180 D 3
Tepelenë (AL) ..... 144 C 4
Teplá (CZ) ....91 G 3
Teplice (CZ) .... 87 E 5
Tepsa (FIN) .... 181 E 4
Ter Apel (NL) ..... 77 G 3
Teramo (I) .... 107 H 5
Terchová (SK) ..... 132 B 2
Terebeşti (RO) .... 146 D 2
Terebovlja (UA) ....12 D 2
Teremia Mare (RO) .. 146 A 5
Terena (P) .... 68 D 2
Teresin (PL) .... 122 C 1
Terespol (PL) ...... 123 H 1
Terezino Polje (HR) .. 135 G 3
Tergnier (F) .... 40 A 4
Terjärv (FIN) ...... 185 G 5
Terlizzi (I) ....111 E 3
Termas
   de Monfortinho (P) .. 63 E 4
Terme Luigiane (I) ..113 B 2
Termini Imerese (I) ..114 D 2
Terminillo (I) ...... 109 E 1
Termoli (I) ....110 B 1
Terneuzen (NL) .... 78 C 1
Terni (I) .... 109 E 1
Ternitz (A) .... 97 G 2

Ternopil (UA) ....12 D 2
Terpezița (RO) .... 151 E 4
Terpsithéa (GR) ... 165 E 3
Terracina (I) ...... 109 F 4
Terråk (N) .... 183 E 2
Terralba (I) ....112 B 4
Terranova di Pollino (I) ..110 D 5
Terranuova Bracciolini (I). 106 D 3
Terras de Bouro (P) .. 56 C 5
Terrassa / Tarrasa (E) .. 60 D 3
Terrasson-Lavilledieu (F). 49 F 4
Terrenoire (F) ..... 50 C 4
Terriente (E) ...... 65 F 3
Teruel (E) .... 65 G 3
Tervakoski (FIN) ... 191 H 4
Tervel /Тервел (BG) .. 152 D 5
Tervete (LV) ...... 202 C 4
Tervo (FIN) .... 187 E 5
Tervola (FIN) ...... 185 G 1
Tervuren (B) ...... 78 C 2
Terzaga (E) .... 65 F 2
Tešanj (BIH) ...... 137 F 4
Teşila (RO) .... 152 B 2
Teslić (BIH) .... 137 F 4
Teslui (RO) .... 151 H 3
Tessin (D) .... 83 E 3
Tessy-Bocage (F) .. 38 C 5
Tét (H) .... 128 C 2
Tetbury (GB) ...... 35 F 2
Teterow (D) .... 83 E 3
Teteven (BG) ...... 158 D 1
Tetiïv (UA) ....13 F 2
Tetouo (RO) ...... 151 F 3
Tetovo (BG) .... 152 B 5
Tetovo (MK) ...... 143 E 5
Tetrákomo (GR) ... 164 D 1
Tettnang (D) ...... 94 D 3
Teuchern (D) ...... 86 B 4
Teufen (CH) .... 99 F 2
Teulada (I) ....112 B 5
Teupitz (D) .... 86 D 5
Teuva (FIN) .... 191 E 1
Tevel (H) .... 129 E 4
Tewkesbury (GB) .. 35 F 1
Tezze (I) .... 103 F 3
Thale (D) .... 86 A 3
Thalfang (D) ...... 88 C 2
Thalgau (A) .... 96 B 2
Thalheim (D) ...... 86 C 5
Thalmässing (D) ...91 E 5
Thalwil (CH) ...... 99 E 2
Thame (GB) .... 35 H 1
Thann (F) ....47 G 3
Thannhausen (D) .. 89 H 5
Thaon (F) ....47 F 2
Tharandt (D) ...... 86 D 4
Tharsis (E) .... 69 E 4
The Mumbles (GB) .. 34 D 2
The Pleasance (GB) . 29 G 5
Theologos (GR) ... 162 C 3
Théoule-sur-Mer (F).. 55 G 2
Thérma (Anatolikí Makedonía
   kai Thráki) (GR)..... 162 D 4
Thermá (Kentrikí
   Makedonía) (GR) .... 161 H 3
Thérma
   (Vóreio Aigaío) (GR) .. 167 F 5
Thermes
   de Chassenon (F) .. 49 E 3
Thérmi (Kentrikí
   Makedonía) (GR) .... 161 G 4
Thermí
   (Vóreio Aigaío) (GR) .. 167 F 5
Thermísia (GR) .... 169 E 2
Thérmo (GR) ...... 164 D 3
Thermopýles (GR).. 165 E 3
Thérouanne (F) .... 39 H 2
Thespiés (GR) ..... 165 G 4
Thesprotikó (GR) .. 164 C 1
Thessaloníki /
   Θεσσαλονίκη (GR) .. 161 G 3
Thetford (GB) ..... 33 H 5
Theux (B) .... 79 E 3
Thèze (F) .... 52 C 3

Thiaucourt-Regniéville (F).41 E 5
Thiberville (F). .... 39 E 5
Thiéblemont-
   Farémont (F) ..... 46 C 1
Thiendorf (D) ..... 86 D 4
Thiene (I) .... 102 D 4
Thiers (F) .... 50 B 2
Thiesi (I) ....112 B 2
Thiessow (D). ..... 83 F 2
Thionville (F).......41 E 4
Thíra / Θήρα (GR) .. 170 C 3
Thiron-Gardais (F) .. 44 C 2
Thirsk (GB) ....31 G 5
Thisted (DK) ...... 194 C 4
Thíva / Θήβα (GR) .. 165 G 4
Thiviers (F) .... 49 F 3
Thizy-les-Bourgs (F). 50 C 2
Thoissey (F) .... 50 D 2
Tholey (D) .... 88 C 3
Thollon (F) ....51 G 1
Tholó (GR) .... 168 B 2
Tholopotámi (GR) .. 167 E 4
Tholós (GR) .... 161 H 3
Thomastown (IRL) .. 25 E 3
Thônes (F) ....51 F 2
Thonon (F) ....51 F 1
Thorens-Glières (F)..51 F 2
Thorikó (GR) ...... 166 B 5
Þórlákshöfn (IS) ... 178 B 3
Thorne (GB) .... 33 F 2
Thornhill (GB) ..... 30 D 3
Þórshöfn (IS) ...... 178 D 1
Thouarcé (F) ...... 43 H 4
Thouars (F) .... 43 H 5
Thouría (GR) ...... 168 C 3
Thrapston (GB) .... 33 F 5
Threshfield (GB) ... 32 D 1
Thueyts (F) .... 50 C 5
Thuin (B). .... 78 C 3
Thuir (F) .... 53 H 5
Thum (D) .... 86 C 5
Thun (CH). .... 98 D 3
Thüringen (A) ..... 94 D 4
Thurles / Durlas (IRL).. 24 D 3
Thursby (GB) ....31 E 4
Thurso (GB) .... 26 B 4
Thury-Harcourt (F). 38 D 5
Thusis (CH) .... 99 F 3
Thyborøn (DK) .... 194 C 4
Țibana (RO) ...... 148 D 3
Tibro (S) .... 195 H 2
Țicleni (RO) ...... 151 E 3
Tidaholm (S) ...... 195 H 3
Tidö (S) .... 197 F 1
Tiefenbronn (D) ... 89 E 4
Tiefencastel (CH) .. 99 G 3
Tiefensee (D) ...... 86 D 1
Tiel (NL) .... 77 E 2
Tielt (B) .... 78 B 2
Tienen (B) .... 78 D 2
Tiengen (D) .... 94 B 3
Tiercé (F) .... 43 H 4
Tierga (E) .... 59 F 5
Tierp (S) .... 190 C 5
Tigharry (GB) ..... 28 B 3
Tighina (MD).......13 F 3
Tighnabruaich (GB) .. 30 B 2
Tigkáki (GR) ...... 171 F 2
Tignes (F) ....51 G 3
Tihany (H) .... 128 D 3
Tiistenjoki (FIN) ... 191 F 1
Tíjola (E) .... 71 G 5
Tikkakoski (FIN) ... 191 H 1
Tikkala (FIN) ...... 193 H 1
Tilburg (NL) .... 78 D 1
Tilbury (GB) .... 36 D 4
Tileagd (RO) ...... 146 D 3
Tillberga (S) ...... 197 F 1
Tillières-sur-Avre (F). 44 C 1
Tilly-sur-Seulles (F). 38 D 5
Tilsit (RUS) ....6 B 4
Timi (CY) ....174 B 4
Timișești (RO) .....148 B 4
Timișoara (RO) ... 150 B 1
Timmendorfer Strand (D). 82 D 4
Timoleague (IRL) .. 24 C 5
Timrå (S) .... 190 B 1

A B C D E F G H I J K L M N O P Q R S T U V W X Y Z

A B C D E F G H I J K L M N O P Q R S T U V W X Y Z

Tinahely (IRL) .... 25 F 2
Tinca (RO) .... 146 C 2
Tinchebray (F) .... 43 G 1
Tineo (E) .... 57 F 2
Tinglev (DK) .... 198 B 4
Tingsryd (S) .... 195 H 5
Tingstäde (S) .... 197 G 3
Tingvoll (N) .... 182 B 5
Tinnoset (N) .... 188 D 5
Tínos (GR) .... 166 D 5
Tiñosillos (E) .... 64 A 1
Tintagel (GB) .... 34 C 4
Tinténiac (F) .... 43 F 2
Tiobraid Árann /
 Tipperary (IRL) .... 24 D 3
Tione di Trento (I) .... 101 H 3
Tipasoja (FIN) .... 187 F 4
Tipperary /
 Tiobraid Árann (IRL) .... 24 D 3
Tipu (EST) .... 201 E 3
Tiranë (AL) .... 144 C 2
Tirano (I) .... 101 G 2
Tiraspol (MD) .... 13 F 3
Tire (TR) .... 19 G 3
Tírig (E) .... 66 A 1
Tiriolo (I) .... 113 C 3
Tirrenia (I) .... 105 G 4
Tirschenreuth (D) .... 91 F 3
Tirstrup (DK) .... 195 E 5
Tíryntha (GR) .... 165 F 5
Tiševica (BG) .... 155 E 3
Tismana (RO) .... 151 E 2
Tisno (HR) .... 136 C 5
Tišnov (CZ) .... 92 D 4
Tisovec (SK) .... 133 E 3
Tisvildeleje (DK) .... 199 E 3
Tiszaalpár (H) .... 129 G 3
Tiszacsege (H) .... 130 D 1
Tiszaföldvár (H) .... 129 G 3
Tiszakécske (H) .... 129 G 3
Tiszalök (H) .... 127 E 5
Tiszalúc (H) .... 126 D 5
Tiszaörvény (H) .... 129 H 1
Tiszaroff (H) .... 129 H 2
Tiszasüly (H) .... 129 H 2
Tiszasziget (H) .... 129 G 5
Tiszaújváros (H) .... 130 D 1
Tiszavasvári (H) .... 131 E 1
Titaguas (E) .... 65 G 4
Titel (SRB) .... 140 C 3
Titisee-Neustadt (D) .... 94 B 2
Tito (I) .... 110 C 4
Titran (N) .... 182 C 4
Tittmoning (D) .... 96 B 2
Titu (RO) .... 152 A 3
Tivat (MNE) .... 139 F 4
Tiveden
 nationalpark (S) .... 195 H 2
Tivenys (E) .... 60 B 5
Tiverton (GB) .... 35 E 3
Tivissa (E) .... 60 B 5
Tivoli (I) .... 109 E 3
Tjæreborg (DK) .... 198 B 3
Tjällmo (S) .... 197 E 2
Tjeldsto (N) .... 188 A 3
Tjentište (BIH) .... 139 F 2
Tjøme (N) .... 195 E 1
Tjong (N) .... 179 E 5
Tjørnuvik
 (Færøerne) (DK) .... 194 A 4
Tjøtta (N) .... 183 F 1
Tkon (HR) .... 136 B 5
Tlačene (BG) .... 155 E 3
Tlmače (SK) .... 132 C 4
Tłuchowo (PL) .... 118 B 5
Tłuszcz (PL) .... 123 E 1
Tobarra (E) .... 71 H 2
Tobermore (GB) .... 23 F 2
Tobermory (GB) .... 28 C 5
Toberonochy (GB) .... 30 B 1
Toblach / Dobbiaco (I) .... 103 F 1
Tocha (P) .... 62 B 3
Tochni (CY) .... 174 C 4
Tocina (E) .... 69 G 4
Todi (I) .... 107 F 5
Todireni (RO) .... 148 D 2

Todmorden (GB) .... 32 D 2
Todor Ikonomovo (BG) .... 157 E 2
Todorići (BIH) .... 137 E 5
Todtmoos (D) .... 94 A 3
Todtnau (D) .... 94 A 3
Töfsingdalen
 National park (S) .... 189 G 2
Toft (GB) .... 27 G 2
Tofte (N) .... 195 E 1
Toftir
 (Færøerne) (DK) .... 194 A 4
Toftlund (DK) .... 198 B 4
Tohmajärvi (FIN) .... 193 H 1
Toholampi (FIN) .... 185 G 4
Toichío (GR) .... 160 D 3
Toijala (FIN) .... 191 G 3
Toivakka (FIN) .... 193 E 2
Toivala (FIN) .... 187 F 5
Tojšići (BIH) .... 137 H 4
Tokačka (BG) .... 162 D 2
Tokaj (H) .... 127 E 5
Tokarnia (PL) .... 122 C 4
Toledo (E) .... 64 B 4
Tolentino (I) .... 107 G 4
Tolfa (I) .... 108 C 2
Tolga (N) .... 189 F 1
Tolkmicko (PL) .... 118 B 2
Tollarp (S) .... 199 F 3
Tølløse (DK) .... 198 D 3
Tolmezzo (I) .... 103 G 2
Tolmin (SLO) .... 134 A 2
Tolna (H) .... 129 E 4
Toló (GR) .... 165 F 5
Tolosa (E) .... 59 E 1
Tolosa (P) .... 62 C 5
Tolox (E) .... 74 D 3
Tolva (FIN) .... 181 G 5
Tolve (I) .... 110 D 4
Tomar (P) .... 62 B 5
Tomaševac (SRB) .... 140 D 3
Tomašica (BIH) .... 135 F 5
Tomaszów
 Lubelski (PL) .... 123 H 5
Tomaszów
 Mazowiecki (PL) .... 122 C 3
Tombebœuf (F) .... 49 E 5
Tomelilla (S) .... 199 F 3
Tomelloso (E) .... 64 D 5
Tomeşti (RO) .... 150 D 1
Tomintoul (GB) .... 29 F 4
Tomislavgrad (BIH) .... 138 C 2
Tømmervåg (N) .... 182 B 5
Tompa (H) .... 129 F 5
Tomra (N) .... 188 C 1
Tona (E) .... 60 D 3
Tonara (I) .... 112 C 3
Tonbridge (GB) .... 36 D 5
Tondela (P) .... 62 C 3
Tønder (DK) .... 198 B 4
Tongeren (B) .... 79 E 2
Tongue (GB) .... 26 A 4
Tonnay-Boutonne (F) .... 48 C 2
Tonnay-Charente (F) .... 48 C 2
Tonneins (F) .... 52 D 1
Tonnerre (F) .... 45 H 3
Tönning (D) .... 81 G 2
Tønsberg (N) .... 195 E 1
Tonstad (N) .... 194 B 1
Tootsi (EST) .... 200 D 3
Topana (RO) .... 151 G 3
Topčii (BG) .... 156 D 2
Topczewo (PL) .... 119 G 5
Töpen (D) .... 91 F 2
Topeno (FIN) .... 191 G 4
Topla (SLO) .... 134 C 1
Toplet (RO) .... 150 D 2
Topli Dol (SRB) .... 143 G 2
T'oploje (RUS) .... 7 G 3
Toploú (GR) .... 173 F 5
Topola (SRB) .... 140 D 5
Topolčani (MK) .... 145 F 2
Topol'čany (SK) .... 132 B 3
Topólia (GR) .... 172 B 3
Topolog (RO) .... 153 F 3
Topolovăţu Mare (RO) .... 150 C 1
Topoloveni (RO) .... 151 H 3

Topolovgrad /
 Тополовград (BG) .... 159 G 3
Topolovnik (SRB) .... 141 E 4
Topolovo (BG) .... 162 C 1
Toponár (H) .... 128 D 4
Toporu (RO) .... 152 A 5
Topraisar (RO) .... 153 F 5
Toprzyny (PL) .... 118 D 1
Topusko (HR) .... 135 E 4
Torà (E) .... 60 C 3
Torano Castello (I) .... 113 B 2
Torbole (I) .... 101 H 3
Torcello (I) .... 103 F 4
Torchiarolo (I) .... 111 G 4
Torcy (F) .... 45 F 1
Tordera (E) .... 61 E 3
Tordesillas (E) .... 63 H 1
Tordesilos (E) .... 65 F 2
Tore (GB) .... 29 E 3
Töre (S) .... 185 F 1
Töreboda (S) .... 195 H 2
Torella del Sannio (I) .... 109 H 3
Torelló (E) .... 60 D 2
Toreno (E) .... 57 F 3
Torgau (D) .... 86 C 3
Torgelow (D) .... 83 G 4
Torhout (B) .... 78 B 2
Torigni-les-Villes (F) .... 38 C 5
Torija (E) .... 64 D 2
Torino (I) .... 100 C 5
Torla (E) .... 59 H 2
Tormac (RO) .... 150 B 1
Törmänen (FIN) .... 177 G 5
Törmänmäki (FIN) .... 187 F 3
Tormos (E) .... 59 G 4
Tornal'a (SK) .... 133 E 4
Tornavacas (E) .... 63 G 4
Tornio (Torneå) (FIN) .... 185 G 1
Tornjoš (SRB) .... 140 C 2
Tornyiszentmiklós (H) .... 128 B 4
Toro (E) .... 63 H 1
Toróni (GR) .... 161 H 5
Toropec (RUS) .... 7 E 2
Toros (BG) .... 158 D 1
Torpo (N) .... 188 D 4
Torpoint (GB) .... 34 D 4
Torpshammar (S) .... 190 B 1
Torquay Torbay (GB) .... 35 E 4
Torquemada (E) .... 58 A 4
Torralba de Calatrava (E) .... 70 D 1
Torrão (P) .... 68 C 3
Torre Annunziata (I) .... 109 H 5
Torre Beretti (I) .... 100 D 5
Torre Canne (I) .... 111 F 3
Torre de Dona Chama (P) .... 57 E 5
Torre de Juan Abad (E) .... 71 E 2
Torre de la Higuera (E) .... 74 A 2
Torre de Moncorvo (P) .... 63 E 1
Torre de' Passeri (I) .... 109 G 2
Torre del Bierzo (E) .... 57 F 3
Torre del Campo (E) .... 70 D 4
Torre del Greco (I) .... 109 H 5
Torre del Mar (E) .... 75 E 3
Torre dell'Impiso (I) .... 114 B 2
Torre Faro (I) .... 115 G 2
Torre Orsaia (I) .... 110 C 5
Torre-Pacheco (E) .... 73 E 3
Torre Pèllice (I) .... 100 B 5
Torrebaja (E) .... 65 G 3
Torreblanca (E) .... 66 A 2
Torrecaballeros (E) .... 64 B 1
Torrecampo (E) .... 70 C 3
Torrecilla en Cameros (E) .... 58 D 5
Torrecillas de la Tiesa (E) .... 63 G 5
Torredembarra (E) .... 60 C 4
Torredonjimeno (E) .... 70 D 4
Torregrossa (E) .... 60 B 3
Torreira (P) .... 62 B 2
Torrejón de Ardoz (E) .... 64 C 2
Torrejón de la Calzada (E) .... 64 C 2
Torrejón el Rubio (E) .... 63 F 5
Torrejoncillo (E) .... 63 F 4
Torrejoncillo del Rey (E) .... 64 D 3
Torrelacárcel (E) .... 65 G 2
Torrelaguna (E) .... 64 C 2

Torrelapaja (E) .... 59 E 5
Torrelavega (E) .... 58 B 1
Torrellano (E) .... 73 F 2
Torrelobatón (E) .... 57 H 5
Torrelodones (E) .... 64 B 2
Torremaggiore (I) .... 110 C 2
Torremejía (E) .... 69 F 2
Torremocha (E) .... 69 G 1
Torremolinos (E) .... 75 E 3
Torrent (E) .... 65 H 5
Torrente de Cinca (E) .... 60 A 4
Torrenueva (E) .... 71 E 2
Torreperogil (E) .... 71 E 3
Torres del Río (E) .... 59 E 3
Torres Novas (P) .... 62 B 5
Torres Vedras (P) .... 68 A 1
Torrevieja (E) .... 73 E 3
Torri del Benaco (I) .... 101 H 4
Torridon (GB) .... 28 D 3
Torriglia (I) .... 105 E 2
Torrijas (E) .... 65 G 3
Torrijo de la Cañada (E) .... 59 F 5
Torrijos (E) .... 64 A 3
Tørring (DK) .... 198 C 3
Torrita di Siena (I) .... 107 E 4
Torroella de Montgrí (E) .... 61 F 2
Torrox (E) .... 75 F 3
Torsås (S) .... 197 E 5
Torsby (S) .... 189 G 5
Torshälla (S) .... 197 E 1
Tórshavn
 (Færøerne) (DK) .... 194 A 4
Torsminde (DK) .... 194 C 5
Törtel (H) .... 129 G 3
Tórtoles de Esgueva (E) .... 58 B 4
Tortolì (I) .... 112 D 3
Tortoman (RO) .... 153 F 4
Tortona (I) .... 101 E 5
Tortorici (I) .... 115 F 2
Tortosa (E) .... 60 B 5
Tortosendo (P) .... 62 D 3
Toruń (PL) .... 117 H 5
Torup (S) .... 195 G 4
Torvaja (EST) .... 201 F 4
Tørvikbygd (N) .... 188 B 4
Torvinen (FIN) .... 181 E 4
Toržok (RUS) .... 7 F 2
Torzym (PL) .... 120 C 1
Tosbotn (N) .... 183 F 2
Toscolano-Maderno (I) .... 101 G 4
Tosno (RUS) .... 6 D 1
Tossa de Mar (E) .... 61 F 3
Tostedt (D) .... 81 H 4
Totana (E) .... 71 H 4
Tôtes (F) .... 39 F 4
Tótkomlós (H) .... 129 H 4
Totnes (GB) .... 34 D 4
Tótvázsony (H) .... 128 D 3
Toucy (F) .... 45 G 3
Toul (F) .... 47 E 1
Toulon (F) .... 55 E 2
Toulon-sur-Arroux (F) .... 50 C 1
Toulouse (F) .... 53 F 2
Toumpítsi (GR) .... 165 E 5
Tourcoing (F) .... 40 A 1
Tourlída (GR) .... 164 D 3
Tournai (Doornik) (B) .... 78 B 3
Tournan-en-Brie (F) .... 45 F 1
Tournay (F) .... 52 D 3
Tournoël, château de (F) .... 50 A 2
Tournon-d'Agenais (F) .... 53 E 1
Tournon-Saint-Martin (F) .... 49 F 1
Tournon-sur-Rhône (F) .... 50 D 4
Tournus (F) .... 50 D 1
Tourouvre-au-Perche (F) .... 44 C 1
Tours (F) .... 44 C 4
Toury (F) .... 45 E 2
Toužim (CZ) .... 91 G 3
Tovariševo (SRB) .... 137 H 2
Tovarnik (HR) .... 137 H 2
Towcester (GB) .... 33 F 5
Töysä (FIN) .... 191 G 1
Trá Lí / Tralee (IRL) .... 24 B 3
Trabanca (E) .... 63 F 1

Trabazos (E) .... 57 F 5
Traben-Trarbach (D) .... 88 C 2
Trabia (I) .... 114 D 2
Trabotivište (MK) .... 143 H 5
Tracheiá (GR) .... 165 G 5
Trachíli (GR) .... 166 B 3
Trachonas (CY) .... 174 D 3
Trachoni (CY) .... 175 E 3
Tracino (I) .... 114 A 5
Trafaria (P) .... 68 A 2
Trafoi (I) .... 101 G 2
Tragacete (E) .... 65 F 3
Traiguera (E) .... 66 A 1
Traisen (A) .... 97 F 2
Traiskirchen (A) .... 97 G 2
Traismauer (A) .... 97 F 1
Trakai (LT) .... 205 F 4
Trakošćan (HR) .... 135 E 2
Tralee / Trá Lí (IRL) .... 24 B 3
Trallwng /
 Welshpool (GB) .... 32 C 4
Tramagal (P) .... 62 C 5
Tramariglio (I) .... 112 A 2
Tramatza (I) .... 112 B 3
Tramonti di Sopra (I) .... 103 F 2
Tramore (IRL) .... 25 E 4
Tranås (S) .... 196 D 3
Trancoso (P) .... 62 D 2
Tranebjerg (DK) .... 198 C 3
Tranemo (S) .... 195 G 4
Tranent (GB) .... 31 E 2
Trani (I) .... 111 E 2
Trånkovo (BG) .... 159 F 2
Transtrand (S) .... 189 H 3
Trapani (I) .... 114 B 2
Trappstadt (D) .... 89 H 1
Trasacco (I) .... 109 F 3
Trassem (D) .... 88 B 2
Traun (A) .... 96 D 2
Traunkirchen (A) .... 96 C 2
Traunreut (D) .... 95 H 2
Traunstein (D) .... 95 H 2
Traupis (LT) .... 205 F 2
Trautenfels (A) .... 96 D 3
Travemünde (D) .... 82 C 3
Travnik (BIH) .... 137 F 4
Trawniki (PL) .... 123 G 3
Trbovlje (SLO) .... 134 C 2
Trbuk (BIH) .... 137 G 4
Trbušani (SRB) .... 139 H 1
Trebbin (D) .... 86 D 2
Trébeurden (F) .... 42 C 1
Trebisacce (I) .... 113 C 1
Trebišov (SK) .... 133 G 3
Trebnje (SLO) .... 134 C 3
Třeboň (CZ) .... 92 B 5
Trebsen (D) .... 86 C 4
Trebujena (E) .... 74 A 3
Trecastagni (I) .... 115 G 3
Trecate (I) .... 100 D 4
Tredegar (GB) .... 35 E 1
Tredozio (I) .... 107 E 2
Treffort-Cuisiat (F) .... 51 E 1
Treffurt (D) .... 85 H 4
Treffynnon /
 Holywell (GB) .... 32 C 3
Trefynwy /
 Monmouth (GB) .... 35 F 1
Tregaron (GB) .... 32 B 5
Trégastel (F) .... 42 C 1
Tregnago (I) .... 101 H 4
Tregony (GB) .... 34 C 5
Tréguier (F) .... 42 D 1
Trehörningsjö (S) .... 184 C 5
Treia (D) .... 81 G 2
Treia (I) .... 107 G 4
Treignac (F) .... 49 G 3
Treis Vrýsses (GR) .... 163 E 2
Trelissick Garden (GB) .... 34 B 5
Trelleborg (DK) .... 198 D 3
Trelleborg (DK) .... 198 D 3
Tremestieri (I) .... 115 G 2
Tremetousia (CY) .... 175 E 3
Tremezzo (I) .... 101 E 3
Tremp (E) .... 60 B 2
Trenčianske Teplice (SK) .... 132 B 2
Trenčín (SK) .... 132 B 2
Trendelburg (D) .... 85 F 3
Trenta (SLO) .... 134 A 2
Trento (I) .... 101 H 3
Treppeln (D) .... 87 E 2
Trepuzzi (I) .... 111 G 4
Trescore Balneario (I) .... 101 F 4
Tresenda (I) .... 101 G 3
Tresfjord (N) .... 188 C 1
Tresjuncos (E) .... 64 D 4
Trešnjevica (SRB) .... 143 E 1
Trespaderne (E) .... 58 C 2
Třešť (CZ) .... 92 C 4
Trets (F) .... 55 E 3
Tretten (N) .... 189 E 3
Treuchtlingen (D) .... 89 H 4
Treuen (D) .... 86 B 5
Treuenbrietzen (D) .... 86 C 2
Treungen (N) .... 194 D 1
Trevélez (E) .... 72 A 5
Trèves (F) .... 54 A 1
Trevi (I) .... 107 F 5
Trévières (F) .... 38 C 4
Treviglio (I) .... 101 F 4
Trevignano Romano (I) .... 108 D 2
Treviño (E) .... 58 D 2
Treviso (I) .... 103 F 4
Trévoux (F) .... 50 D 2
Trewithen (GB) .... 34 C 5
Trezzo sull'Adda (I) .... 101 F 4
Trgovište (SRB) .... 143 G 4
Trhové Sviny (CZ) .... 92 B 5
Triánta (GR) .... 171 H 4
Triaucourt-
 en-Argonne (F) .... 40 D 5
Tribanj Krušćica (HR) .... 136 B 4
Triberg
 im Schwarzwald (D) .... 94 B 2
Tribsees (D) .... 83 E 3
Tricarico (I) .... 110 D 4
Tricase (I) .... 111 H 5
Tricesimo (I) .... 103 G 3
Trichiana (I) .... 103 E 3
Trie-sur-Baïse (F) .... 52 D 3
Trieben (A) .... 97 E 3
Trier (D) .... 88 B 2
Trieste (I) .... 103 H 4
Trifels (D) .... 88 D 3
Trifeşti (RO) .... 148 D 2
Trigrad (BG) .... 162 B 1
Trigueros (E) .... 69 E 4
Triigi (EST) .... 200 B 3
Trijueque (E) .... 64 D 2
Tríkala / Τρίκαλα
 (Thessalía) (GR) .... 165 E 1
Tríkala (Kentrikí
 Makedonía) (GR) .... 161 F 3
Tríkala
 (Pelopónnisos) (GR) .... 165 F 4
Tríkeri (GR) .... 165 G 2
Tríklino (GR) .... 164 D 2
Trikomo (CY) .... 175 F 3
Trilj (HR) .... 138 C 2
Trillevallen (S) .... 183 F 5
Trillo (E) .... 64 D 2
Trílofo (GR) .... 165 E 2
Trim (IRL) .... 23 F 5
Trindade (P) .... 63 E 1
Třinec (CZ) .... 93 H 3
Tring (GB) .... 35 H 1
Trinità d'Agultu (I) .... 112 C 1
Trinitapoli (I) .... 110 D 2
Trino (I) .... 100 D 5
Triora (I) .... 104 C 3
Trípoli / Τρίπολη (GR) .... 165 F 4
Triponzo (I) .... 107 F 5
Triptis (D) .... 86 B 5
Trittau (D) .... 82 B 4
Trittenheim (D) .... 88 C 2
Trivento (I) .... 109 H 3

Trjavna / Трявна (BG) .. 159 F1
Trnava (SK) 132 A4
Trnova Poljana (BIH) .. 136 D5
Trnovo (BIH) 139 E2
Trnovo ob Soči (SLO) .. 134 A2
Troarn (F) 38 D5
Trofa (P) 62 C1
Trofa (P) 62 B1
Trofaiach (A) 97 E3
Trofors (N) 183 F2
Trogir (HR) 138 B2
Troia (I) 110 C2
Troina (I) 115 F3
Trois-Ponts (B) 79 E3
Troisdorf (D) 84 C5
Trojan / Троян (BG) 158 D1
Trojane (SLO) 134 C2
Trojanovo (BG) 159 H2
Trojanski manastir (BG) 158 D1
Trollhättan (S) 195 F2
Tromsø (N) 176 B4
Trondheim (N) 182 B5
Tronö (S) 190 B3
Troo (F) 44 C3
Trooditissa (CY) 174 C4
Troon (GB) 30 C2
Trópaia (GR) 165 E5
Tropea (I) 115 H1
Tropojë (AL) 142 C4
Trosa (S) 197 F2
Trostberg (D) 95 H2
Trostjanec' (UA) 7 G5
Troulloi (CY) 175 E3
Trouville-sur-Mer (F) . 39 E4
Trowbridge (GB) 35 F2
Troyes (F) 45 H2
Trpanj (HR) 138 C3
Trpezi (MNE) 139 H3
Trpinja (HR) 137 H2
Trsa (MNE) 139 F3
Tršić (SRB) 137 H4
Trstenik (HR) 138 B2
Trstenik (Kraljevo) (SRB) 143 E2
Trstenik (Priština) (SRB) 143 E4
Trsteno (HR) 139 E4
Trstín (SK) 132 A3
Trubčevsk (RUS) 7 F4
Trubia (E) 57 G2
Trubjela (MNE) 139 F4
Truchas (E) 57 F4
Truchtersheim (F) 47 H1
Trujillo (E) 63 G5
Trun (F) 38 D5
Truro (GB) 34 B5
Trușești (RO) 148 C1
Truskava (LT) 205 F3
Trutnov (CZ) 87 G5
Truva (TR) 19 F2
Trygóna (GR) 160 D5
Trýpi (GR) 168 D3
Tryškiai (LT) 204 D1
Tržac (BIH) 134 D5
Trzcianka (PL) 117 E5
Trzciel (PL) 120 D1
Trzcińsko-Zdrój (PL) .. 116 B5
Trzebiatów (PL) 116 C2
Trzebiel (PL) 120 B2
Trzebieszów (PL) 123 F1
Trzebież (PL) 116 B3
Trzebinia (PL) 125 F1
Trzebnica (PL) 121 E3
Trzciewiec (PL) 117 G4
Trzemeszno (PL) 121 G1
Tržič (SLO) 134 B2
Tsada (CY) 174 B4
Tsagaráda (GR) 165 G1
Tsamantás (GR) 160 B5
Tsangári (GR) 164 C1
Tsepélovo (GR) 160 C5
Tseri (CY) 174 D3
Tsotíli (GR) 160 D4
Tsoukaládes (GR) 164 C2
Tsoútsouros (GR) 173 E4
Tuam / Tuam (IRL) 22 C5
Tuam / Tuaim (IRL) 22 C5
Tubbercurry (IRL) 22 C4
Tubilla del Agua (E) .. 58 B2

Tübingen (D) 89 F5
Tubre / Taufers
  im Münstertal (I) 101 G2
Tučepi (HR) 138 C2
Tuchan (F) 53 H4
Tuchola (PL) 117 G3
Tuchomie (PL) 117 F2
Tuchów (PL) 125 H1
Tuczno (PL) 116 D4
Tudela (E) 59 F4
Tudela de Duero (E) ... 58 A5
Tudor Vladimirescu (RO) 153 E1
Tudora (RO) 148 C2
Tudu (EST) 201 F2
Tudulinna (EST) 201 G2
Tufeni (RO) 151 H4
Tufești (RO) 153 E3
Tuffé Val de
  la Chéronne (F) 44 C3
Tuheljske Toplice (HR) 134 D2
Tuhkakylä (FIN) 187 F4
Tui (E) 56 B4
Tuineje (E) 67 H5
Tüja (LV) 202 D2
Tukums (LV) 202 C3
Tula (RUS) 7 G3
Tulach Mhór /
  Tullamore (IRL) 23 E5
Tulare (SRB) 143 F3
Tulcea (RO) 153 F2
Tul'čyn (UA) 13 F2
Tuliszków (PL) 121 G2
Tulla (IRL) 24 C2
Tullamore /
  Tulach Mhór (IRL) 23 E5
Tulle (F) 49 G4
Tullgarns slott (S) ... 197 F2
Tullins (F) 51 E4
Tulln an der Donau (A) 97 G1
Tullow (IRL) 25 F2
Tulovo (BG) 159 F2
Tulppio (FIN) 181 G3
Tulsk (IRL) 22 D4
Tumba (S) 197 G1
Tuohikotti (FIN) 193 F3
Tuoro sul Trasimeno (I) 107 E4
Tupilați (RO) 148 C3
Tura (H) 129 F1
Turalići (BIH) 137 H5
Turba (EST) 200 D2
Turbe (BIH) 137 F4
Turburea (RO) 151 F3
Turceni (RO) 151 E3
Turckheim (F) 47 G2
Turda (RO) 147 F4
Turégano (E) 64 B1
Turek (PL) 121 G2
Turenki (FIN) 191 H4
Turgeliai (LT) 205 G4
Turgutlu (TR) 19 G3
Türi (EST) 201 E3
Turi (I) 111 F3
Turia (RO) 148 B5
Turija (BIH) 137 G4
Turija (SRB) 140 C2
Turinge (S) 197 F1
Turis (E) 65 H5
Turja (SRB) 141 F4
Turjak (SLO) 134 C3
Türje (H) 128 C3
Túrkeve (H) 129 H3
Turku / Åbo (FIN) 191 F4
Turmiel (E) 65 E1
Turnberry (GB) 30 C3
Turnhout (B) 78 D1
Türnitz (A) 97 F2
Turnov (CZ) 87 F5
Turnu Măgurele (RO) ... 151 H5
Turnu Ruieni (RO) 150 D2
Túrony (H) 128 D5
Turośl (PL) 119 E3
Turre (E) 71 H5
Turriers (F) 55 F1
Turriff (GB) 29 H3
Tursi (I) 111 E5
Turț (RO) 147 E1

Turtola (FIN) 180 D5
Turzovka (SK) 132 C1
Tuscania (I) 108 C2
Tuse (DK) 198 D3
Tušilović (HR) 134 D4
Tušovica (SRB) 159 H1
Tuszyn (PL) 121 H2
Tutin (SRB) 139 H3
Tutova (RO) 148 D5
Tutrakan (BG) 152 C5
Tuttlingen (D) 94 C2
Tuturano (I) 111 G4
Tutzing (D) 95 F2
Tuulos (FIN) 191 H3
Tuupovaara (FIN) 193 H1
Tuusniemi (FIN) 187 F5
Tuusula (FIN) 191 H4
Tuxford (GB) 33 F3
Tuzi (MNE) 139 G4
Tuzla (BIH) 137 G4
Tuzsér (H) 127 F5
Tvărdica (BG) 159 F1
Tvedestrand (N) 194 D2
Tver (RUS) 7 F2
Tverečius (LT) 205 H3
Tvøroyri
  (Færøerne) (DK) 194 A5
Tvrdošín (SK) 132 D2
Tvrdošovce (SK) 132 B4
Twardogóra (PL) 121 F3
Twimberg (A) 97 E4
Twist (D) 84 C1
Twistringen (D) 81 F5
Tychowo (PL) 117 E3
Tychy (PL) 125 F1
Tyczyn (PL) 127 F1
Tydal (N) 183 E5
Tyin (N) 188 B5
Tykocin (PL) 119 G4
Tympáki (GR) 172 D4
Tymvou (CY) 162 C2
Týn nad Vltavou (CZ) .. 92 A4
Tyndaris (I) 115 F2
Tyndrum (GB) 28 D5
Tynemouth (GB) 31 G5
Tynkä (FIN) 185 G4
Tynset (N) 189 F2
Tyresö (S) 197 G1
Tyringe (S) 199 F3
Tyristrand (N) 189 E5
Tyrnävä (FIN) 185 H3
Týrnavos /
  Τύρναβος (GR) 161 F5
Tyrós (GR) 169 E3
Tysse (N) 188 B4
Tyssebotn (N) 188 B3
Tyssedal (N) 188 B4
Tyszowce (PL) 123 H4
Tytuvėnai (LT) 204 D2
Tywyn (GB) 32 A5
Tzanáta (GR) 164 C4
Tzermiádo (GR) 173 E3

U

Ub (SRB) 140 C5
Úbeda (E) 71 E4
Überlingen (D) 94 C3
Ubľa (SK) 133 H2
Ubli (HR) 138 C4
Ubli (MNE) 139 F4
Ubrique (E) 74 C3
Uchte (D) 85 F1
Uckange (F) 41 E4
Uckfield (GB) 36 C5
Uclés (E) 64 D3
Uda (RO) 148 C2
Udbina (HR) 136 C4
Udbyhøj (DK) 195 E5
Uddevalla (S) 195 F2
Uddheden (S) 189 G5
Uden (NL) 79 E1
Udine (I) 103 G2
Udovo (MK) 143 G1
Udvar (H) 129 E5
Uebigau (D) 86 D3
Ueckermünde (D) 83 G3

Uelzen (D) 82 B5
Uetersen (D) 81 H4
Uetze (D) 85 G1
Uffenheim (D) 89 H3
Ugāle (LV) 202 B2
Ugao (SRB) 139 H3
Ugărčin (BG) 158 D1
Ugento (I) 111 H5
Ugijar (E) 72 A5
Ugine (F) 51 F3
Uglič (RUS) 7 G1
Ugljan (HR) 136 B5
Ugljane (HR) 138 C2
Ugljevik (BIH) 137 H3
Ugrinovci (SRB) 140 D5
Uguniemi (FIN) 193 H2
Uherské Hradiště (CZ) . 93 F4
Uherský Brod (CZ) 93 F4
Uhingen (D) 89 G4
Uhlířské Janovice (CZ) 92 B3
Uhrsleben (D) 86 A2
Uhrusk (PL) 123 H3
Uig (GB) 28 C3
Uimaharju (FIN) 187 H5
Uithoorn (NL) 76 D4
Uithuizen (NL) 77 G2
Ujazd (Kędzierzyn-
  Koźle) (PL) 121 G5
Ujazd (Opatów) (PL) ... 123 E4
Ujazd (Tomaszów
  Mazowiecki) (PL) 122 C2
Ujejsce (PL) 121 H5
Újfehértó (H) 131 E1
Újhartyán (H) 129 F2
Újiráz (H) 131 E3
Újkígyós (H) 130 D4
Ujście (PL) 117 E4
Ujué (E) 59 F3
Ukkola (FIN) 187 H5
Ukmergé (LT) 205 F3
Ulanów (PL) 123 F5
Ulcinj (MNE) 139 G5
Uleåborg / Oulu (FIN) . 185 H2
Uleåsalo /
  Oulunsalo (FIN) 185 H3
Ulefoss (N) 194 D1
Uleila del Campo (E) .. 71 G5
Ülenurme (EST) 201 F3
Ulëzë (AL) 144 C1
Ulfborg (DK) 194 C5
Ulič (SK) 133 H2
Ul'janovka (UA) 13 F2
Uljma (SRB) 141 E3
Ullånger (S) 190 C1
Ullapool (GB) 28 D2
Ullared (S) 195 G4
Ullava (FIN) 185 G4
Ulldecona (E) 66 B1
Üllés (H) 129 G4
Üllő (H) 129 F2
Ulm (D) 89 G5
Ulmen (D) 88 C1
Ulmeni (Baia Mare) (RO) 147 E2
Ulmeni (Călărași) (RO) 152 C4
Ulog (BIH) 139 E2
Ulricehamn (S) 195 G3
Ulrichsberg (A) 96 D1
Ulriksdals slott (S) .. 197 G1
Ulsberg (N) 189 E1
Ulsta (GB) 27 G2
Ulsteinvik (N) 188 B1
Ulverston (GB) 31 E5
Ulvik (N) 188 C4
Ulvila (FIN) 191 F3
Ulvsjö (S) 189 H3
Umag / Umago (HR) 134 A4
Umago / Umag (HR) 134 A4
Uman' (UA) 13 F2
Umbertide (I) 107 F4
Umbukta (N) 183 G1
Umčari (SRB) 140 D4
Umeå (S) 184 D4
Umhausen (A) 95 F4
Umin Dol (MK) 143 F5
Umka (SRB) 140 D4
Umljanović (HR) 136 D5

Unari (FIN) 181 E4
Uncastillo (E) 59 G3
Undersåker (S) 183 F5
Undredal (N) 188 C2
Uneča (RUS) 7 F4
Unešić (HR) 136 C5
Úněšov (CZ) 91 H3
Ungheni (MD) 13 E3
Ungheni (Pitești) (RO) 151 H4
Ungheni
  (Târgu Mureș) (RO) ... 147 G4
Ungilde (E) 57 F5
Unguraș (RO) 147 F3
Unhais da Serra (P) ... 62 D3
Unhošt (CZ) 92 A2
Unichowo (PL) 117 F2
Uničov (CZ) 93 E3
Uniejów (PL) 121 H2
Unije (HR) 134 B5
Unirea (Alba Iulia) (RO) 147 F4
Unirea (Craiova) (RO) . 151 E4
Unisław (PL) 117 G4
Unna (D) 84 D3
Unnaryd (S) 195 G4
Unquera (E) 58 A1
Unterach (A) 96 C3
Unterhaching (D) 95 G2
Unterkulm (CH) 98 D2
Unterschleißheim (D) .. 95 G2
Unterwasser (CH) 99 F2
Unterweißenbach (A) ... 97 E1
Upavon (GB) 35 G2
Upesgriva (LV) 202 C2
Úpice (CZ) 87 H5
Upinniemi (FIN) 191 H5
Uppingham (GB) 33 F4
Upplands-Väsby (S) 197 G1
Uppsala (S) 190 C5
Upton (GB) 35 F1
Upyna (LT) 204 D2
Uraiújfalu (H) 128 C2
Uras (I) 112 B4
Urbania (I) 107 F3
Urbe (I) 104 D2
Urbino (I) 107 F3
Urda (E) 64 B5
Urdos (F) 52 C4
Urechești (RO) 148 D5
Urepel (F) 52 A4
Urfahr (A) 96 D1
Urfeld (D) 95 F3
Uri (I) 112 B2
Uriage (F) 51 E4
Uricani (RO) 151 E2
Urjala (FIN) 191 G3
Urk (NL) 77 E3
Urla (TR) 19 G3
Urlați (RO) 152 B3
Urlingford (IRL) 25 E3
Urnäsch (CH) 99 F2
Urnes (N) 188 C3
Uroševac / Ferizaj (SRB) 143 E4
Urovica (SRB) 141 G5
Urshult (S) 195 H5
Urșilor, peștera (RO) . 146 D4
Urszulin (PL) 123 G3
Ururi (I) 110 B3
Ury (F) 45 F2
Urziceni (Buzău) (RO) . 152 C2
Urziceni
  (Satu Mare) (RO) 146 D1
Urzicuța (RO) 151 F5
Usagre (E) 69 G3
Uşak (TR) 19 H3
Ušće (SRB) 142 D2
Usedom (D) 83 G3
Usingen (D) 89 E1
Usk (GB) 35 E1
Uskoplje (BIH) 139 E4
Üsküdar (TR) 19 G1
Uslar (D) 85 G3
Ussat (F) 53 F4
Ussé, château d' (F) .. 44 B4
Usséglio (I) 100 B4
Ussel (F) 49 H3
Usseln (D) 85 E4
Ustaoset (N) 188 D4

Ustaritz (F) 52 A3
Uster (CH) 99 E2
Ústí nad Labem (CZ) ... 88 E5
Ústí nad Orlicí (CZ) .. 92 D3
Ustibar (BIH) 139 G2
Ustikolina (BIH) 139 F2
Ustiprača (BIH) 139 F2
Ustka (PL) 117 E1
Ustrem (BG) 159 G3
Ustronie Morskie (PL) . 116 D2
Ustrzyki Dolne (PL) ... 127 G2
Ustrzyki Górne (PL) ... 127 G3
Ususău (RO) 146 C5
Utajärvi (FIN) 185 H3
Utåker (N) 188 B3
Utbjoa (N) 188 B5
Utebo (E) 59 G4
Utelle (F) 55 G1
Utena (LT) 205 G2
Utiel (E) 65 G4
Utne (N) 188 C4
Utrecht (NL) 77 E5
Utrera (E) 69 G5
Utrillas (E) 65 G1
Utsjoki (FIN) 177 F3
Uttendorf (A) 96 B2
Uttendorf (A) 95 H4
Uttoxeter (GB) 32 D4
Utvik (N) 188 C2
Uurainen (FIN) 191 H1
Uusikaarlepyy /
  Nykarleby (FIN) 185 F5
Uusikaupunki (FIN) 191 E4
Uvac (SRB) 139 G2
Uvdal (N) 188 D4
Užava (LV) 202 A2
Uzdin (SRB) 140 D3
Uzdowo (PL) 118 C4
Uzel (F) 42 D2
Uzerche (F) 49 G3
Uzès (F) 54 C1
Užhorod (UA) 12 C3
Užice / Ужице (SRB) ... 139 H1
Uzundžovo (BG) 159 F3
Uzunköprü (TR) 19 F2
Uzyn (UA) 13 F1

V

Vaajakoski (FIN) 191 H2
Vääkiö (FIN) 187 F2
Vaala (FIN) 187 E3
Vaalajärvi (FIN) 181 E4
Vaalimaa (FIN) 193 F4
Vaals (NL) 79 F3
Vaaraslahti (FIN) 187 E5
Vaasa / Vasa (FIN) 185 E5
Vaasa / Vanha (FIN) ... 185 E5
Vaassen (NL) 77 F4
Vabalninkas (LT) 205 F1
Văbel (BG) 151 H5
Vabre (F) 53 H2
Vác (H) 129 F1
Văcărești (RO) 152 A3
Vacha (D) 85 G5
Väddö (S) 190 C5
Vadheim (N) 188 B3
Vado Ligure (I) 104 D3
Vadsø (N) 177 G2
Vadstena (S) 195 H2
Vadu Izei (RO) 147 F1
Vaduz (FL) 99 G2
Væggerløse (DK) 198 D5
Vafaîika (GR) 162 C2
Vafiochóri (GR) 161 F3
Våg (N) 128 C2
Vågaholmen (N) 179 E5
Vågåmo (N) 189 E2
Våge (N) 188 B4
Vägeva (EST) 201 F3
Vaggeryd (S) 195 H4
Vágia (GR) 165 G4
Vagioniá (GR) 172 D4
Vagney (F) 47 F3
Vagos (P) 62 B3
Vagur (Færøerne) (DK) . 194 A5

A B C D E F G H I J K L M N O P Q R S T U V W X Y Z

A
B
C
D
E
F
G
H
I
J
K
L
M
N
O
P
Q
R
S
T
U
V
W
X
Y
Z

Vähäkyrö (FIN) . . . . 191 F 1
Vahto (FIN) . . . . 191 F 4
Vaiano (I) . . . . 105 H 4
Vaida (EST) . . . . 201 E 2
Vaihingen an der Enz (D) . 89 F 4
Väike-Maarja (EST) . . . . . 201 F 2
Väike-Rakke (EST) . . . . . . 201 F 3
Vailly-sur-Aisne (F) . . . . . . 40 B 4
Vailly-sur-Sauldre (F) . . . . 45 F 4
Vainikkala (FIN) . . . . 193 G 3
Vainupea (EST) . . . . 201 F 1
Vainutas (LT) . . . . 204 C 3
Vaisaluokta (S) . . . . 179 H 4
Vaison-la-Romaine (F) . . 54 D 1
Vaiste (EST) . . . . 200 D 3
Vajszló (H) . . . . 128 D 5
Vajta (H) . . . . 129 E 3
Vajzë (AL) . . . . 144 C 4
Vakarel (BG) . . . . 158 C 2
Väkosel (BG) . . . . 162 B 1
Vaksdal (N) . . . . 188 B 4
Vál (H) . . . . 129 E 2
Val-de-Reuil (F) . . . . 39 F 5
Val-d'Isère (F) . . . . 51 G 3
Val-Thorens (F) . . . . 51 G 3
Vålådalen (S) . . . . 183 F 5
Valadares (P) . . . . 62 B 1
Valalta (HR) . . . . 134 B 2
Valamen (FIN) . . . . 193 G 1
Valandovo (MK) . . . . 145 H 2
Valareña (E) . . . . 59 F 4
Valaská Belá (SK) . . . . . . 132 C 2
Valašské Meziříčí (CZ) . . 93 G 3
Valax (FIN) . . . . 193 E 4
Valberg (F) . . . . 55 G 1
Vålberg (S) . . . . 195 G 1
Valbiska (HR) . . . . 134 B 5
Valbo (S) . . . . 190 B 4
Valbondione (I) . . . . 101 F 3
Valbonë (AL) . . . . 142 C 4
Valbonnais (F) . . . . 51 E 4
Vălča Poljana (BG) . . . . . 159 H 3
Vălcani (RO) . . . . 146 A 5
Vălčedrăm (BG) . . . . 151 E 5
Vălčidol (BG) . . . . 157 F 2
Vălčin (BG) . . . . 159 H 1
Valdagno (I) . . . . 101 H 4
Valdahon (F) . . . . 47 F 4
Valdaj (RUS) . . . . 7 E 1
Valdecaballeros (E) . . . . . 69 H 1
Valdecabras (E) . . . . 65 E 3
Valdecarros (E) . . . . 63 H 2
Valdedios (E) . . . . 57 G 1
Valdefuentes (E) . . . . 69 G 1
Valdeganga (E) . . . . 65 F 5
Valdelinares (E) . . . . 65 H 2
Valdelacasa de Tajo (E) . 63 H 5
Valdemărpils (LV) . . . . . . 202 B 2
Valdemarsvik (S) . . . . 197 F 3
Valdemeca (E) . . . . 65 F 3
Valdemorillo (E) . . . . 64 B 2
Valdemoro (E) . . . . 64 B 2
Valdenoceda (E) . . . . 58 C 2
Valdepeñas (E) . . . . 71 E 2
Valdepeñas de Jaén (E) . 70 D 5
Valderas (E) . . . . 57 H 4
Valderiès (F) . . . . 53 G 2
Valdestillas (E) . . . . 58 A 5
Valdeverdeja (E) . . . . 63 H 5
Valdevimbre (E) . . . . 57 G 4
Valdezcaray (E) . . . . 58 D 3
Valdieri (I) . . . . 104 B 3
Valdobbiadene (I) . . . . . . 103 E 3
Vale de Açor (P) . . . . 68 D 4
Vale de Cambra (P) . . . . . 62 B 2
Vale de Estrela (P) . . . . . . 62 D 3
Vale de Prazeres (P) . . . . 62 D 4
Valea Argovei (RO) . . . . . 152 C 4
Valea Ierii (RO) . . . . 147 E 4
Valea Lui Mihai (RO) . . . 146 D 2
Valea Mare Pravăţ (RO) . 151 H 2
Valea Mărului (RO) . . . . . 153 E 1
Valea Nucarilor (RO) . . . 153 G 2
Valea Sării (RO) . . . . 152 C 1
Valea Stanciului (RO) . . . 151 F 5

Valea Ursului (RO) . . . . . . 148 D 4
Valeggio sul Mincio (I) . 101 H 4
Valença do Minho (P) . . . 56 B 4
Valençay (F) . . . . 44 D 5
Valence (F) . . . . 50 D 4
Valence-d'Agen (F) . . . . . 53 E 1
Valence-d'Albigeois (F) . . 53 H 2
Valence-sur-Baïse (F) . . . . 52 D 2
Valencia (E) . . . . 65 H 4
Valencia de Alcántara (E) . 62 D 5
Valencia de Don Juan (E) . 57 G 4
Valencia de las Torres (E) . 69 G 3
Valencia del Ventoso (E) . 69 F 3
Valenciennes (F) . . . . 40 A 2
Văleni (RO) . . . . 151 H 4
Vălenii de Munte (RO) . . 152 B 2
Valensole (F) . . . . 55 E 2
Valentano (I) . . . . 108 C 1
Valentigney (F) . . . . 47 G 4
Valenza (I) . . . . 100 D 5
Våler (N) . . . . 189 F 4
Valeria (E) . . . . 65 E 4
Valfabbrica (I) . . . . 107 F 4
Valga (EST) . . . . 201 F 5
Valgorge (F) . . . . 50 C 5
Valgrisenche (I) . . . . 100 B 3
Valguarnera (I) . . . . 115 E 4
Valhelhas (P) . . . . 62 D 3
Valimitika (GR) . . . . 165 E 4
Valjevo / Ваљево (SRB) . 140 C 5
Valjok (N) . . . . 177 F 3
Valjunquera (E) . . . . 60 A 5
Valka (LV) . . . . 203 F 1
Valkeakoski (FIN) . . . . . . 191 G 3
Valkeala (FIN) . . . . 193 F 3
Valkenburg (NL) . . . . 79 E 2
Valkenswaard (NL) . . . . . . 79 E 1
Valkininkai (LT) . . . . 205 F 5
Valkla (EST) . . . . 201 E 1
Vall d'Alba (E) . . . . 66 A 2
Vall de Uxó /
    La Vall d'Uixó (E) . . . . 65 H 4
Valladolid (E) . . . . 58 A 5
Vallata (I) . . . . 110 C 3
Vallbo (S) . . . . 183 F 5
Valldal (N) . . . . 188 D 1
Valldemossa (E) . . . . 67 E 2
Valle (N) . . . . 194 C 1
Valle Castellana (I) . . . . . 107 G 5
Valle de Abdalajís (E) . . . 74 D 3
Valle de Cabuérniga (E) . 58 A 1
Valle de la Serena (E) . . . 69 G 2
Valle de Matamoros (E) . 69 F 3
Valle Mosso (I) . . . . 100 D 4
Valleberga (S) . . . . 199 F 4
Vallehermoso (E) . . . . 67 E 5
Vallejera de Riofrío (E) . . 63 G 3
Vallentuna (S) . . . . 197 G 1
Valleraugue (F) . . . . 54 B 1
Vallet (F) . . . . 43 F 5
Valletta (M) . . . . 114 C 5
Vallgrund (FIN) . . . . 185 E 5
Valloire (F) . . . . 51 F 4
Vallombrosa (I) . . . . 106 D 3
Vallon-en-Sully (F) . . . . . 49 H 1
Vallon-Pont-d'Arc (F) . . . 54 C 1
Vallorbe (CH) . . . . 98 B 3
Vallorcine (F) . . . . 51 G 2
Vallouise (F) . . . . 51 F 4
Vallsta (S) . . . . 190 B 3
Vallter 2000 (E) . . . . 60 D 1
Valma (EST) . . . . 201 F 3
Valmiera (LV) . . . . 203 E 2
Valmojado (E) . . . . 64 B 3
Valmont (F) . . . . 39 E 4
Valmontone (I) . . . . 109 E 3
Várda (GR) . . . . 164 D 4
Valmorel (F) . . . . 51 F 3
Valongo (P) . . . . 62 B 1
Valoria la Buena (E) . . . . 58 A 4
Valøya (N) . . . . 182 D 3
Vardø (FIN) . . . . 191 E 5
Valožyn (BY) . . . . 6 D 4

Valpaços (P) . . . . 56 D 5
Valpalmas (E) . . . . 59 G 4
Valporquero,
    cueva de (E) . . . . 57 G 3
Valpovo (HR) . . . . 137 G 1
Valprato Soana (I) . . . . . . 100 C 4
Valras-Plage (F) . . . . 54 A 3
Valréas (F) . . . . 54 D 1
Vals-les-Bains (F) . . . . 50 C 5
Valsamáta (GR) . . . . 164 B 4
Valsavarenche (I) . . . . 100 B 4
Valset (N) . . . . 182 C 4
Valsjöbyn (S) . . . . 183 F 4
Valtotópi (GR) . . . . 161 H 3
Valtournenche (I) . . . . . . 100 C 3
Valu lui Traian (RO) . . . . 153 F 4
Valun (HR) . . . . 134 B 5
Valvasone (I) . . . . 103 G 3
Valverde (E) . . . . 59 F 4
Valverde (E) . . . . 67 E 5
Valverde de Júcar (E) . . . 65 E 4
Valverde de Leganés (E) . 69 E 2
Valverde del Camino (E) . 69 F 4
Valverde del Fresno (E) . . 63 E 3
Valýra (GR) . . . . 168 C 3
Vamberk (CZ) . . . . 92 D 2
Vámhus (S) . . . . 189 H 3
Vámosmikola (H) . . . . . . 129 E 1
Vámosoroszi (H) . . . . 127 G 5
Vámospércs (H) . . . . 131 F 2
Vámosszabadi (H) . . . . . . 128 D 1
Vampula (FIN) . . . . 191 F 4
Vamvakoú
    (Pelopónnisos) (GR) . 168 D 3
Vamvakoú
    (Thessalía) (GR) . . . . 165 F 1
Vanassaare (EST) . . . . 201 F 3
Vânători (RO) . . . . 147 H 5
Vânători-Neamţ (RO) . . . 148 B 3
Vanda / Vantaa (FIN) . . . 191 H 4
Vandellòs (E) . . . . 60 B 5
Vändra (EST) . . . . 201 E 3
Vandžiogala (LT) . . . . 205 E 3
Väne (LV) . . . . 202 B 3
Vangaži (LV) . . . . 202 D 3
Vangsnes (N) . . . . 188 C 3
Vangsvik (N) . . . . 176 A 4
Vânju Mare (RO) . . . . 150 D 4
Vannäs (S) . . . . 184 D 4
Vannavålen (N) . . . . 176 B 3
Vannes (F) . . . . 42 D 3
Vantaa / Vanda (FIN) . . . 191 H 4
Vanttauskoski (FIN) . . . . 181 E 5
Vaour (F) . . . . 53 G 1
Vara (S) . . . . 195 G 3
Varades (F) . . . . 43 G 4
Varakļāni (LV) . . . . 203 G 3
Varallo (I) . . . . 100 D 3
Varangerbotn (N) . . . . . . 177 G 2
Varano de Melegari (I) . . 105 F 2
Varaždin (HR) . . . . 135 E 2
Varaždinske Toplice (HR) . 135 E 2
Varazze (I) . . . . 104 D 3
Várbica (Haskovo) (BG) . 159 E 3
Vărbica
    (Veliko Tărnovo) (BG) . 156 C 3
Vărbilău (RO) . . . . 152 B 2
Vărbjane (BG) . . . . 157 E 2
Vărbovka (BG) . . . . 156 B 3
Vărbovo (BG) . . . . 163 E 1
Vârciorog (RO) . . . . 146 D 3
Varde (DK) . . . . 198 B 3
Vardim (BG) . . . . 156 B 2
Vardomb (H) . . . . 129 E 4

Vardun (BG) . . . . 159 G 1
Varel (D) . . . . 81 F 4
Varellaíoi (GR) . . . . 166 B 4
Väréna (LT) . . . . 205 F 5
Varengeville-sur-Mer (F) . 39 F 3
Varenna (I) . . . . 101 E 3
Varennes-
    en-Argonne (F) . . . . . . 40 D 5
Varennes-sur-Allier (F) . . 50 A 1
Varennes-
    sur-Amance (F) . . . . . 47 F 2
Vareš (BIH) . . . . 137 G 5
Varese (I) . . . . 101 E 3
Varese Ligure (I) . . . . 105 F 3
Vârfu Câmpului (RO) . . . 148 B 1
Vârfurile (RO) . . . . 146 D 5
Vårgårda (S) . . . . 195 G 3
Vargas (E) . . . . 58 B 1
Varhaug (N) . . . . 194 A 1
Variaş (RO) . . . . 146 B 5
Variku (EST) . . . . 200 C 2
Varilhes (F) . . . . 53 F 4
Váris (GR) . . . . 161 E 4
Varkaus (FIN) . . . . 193 F 1
Várkiza (GR) . . . . 165 H 5
Vărlezi (RO) . . . . 153 E 1
Varmahlíð (IS) . . . . 178 B 2
Varmo (I) . . . . 103 G 3
Varna (SRB) . . . . 140 B 4
Varna / Варна (BG) . . . . 157 F 3
Värnamo (S) . . . . 195 H 4
Varnhem (S) . . . . 195 G 2
Varniai (LT) . . . . 204 D 2
Várpalota (H) . . . . 128 D 2
Varpaisjärvi (FIN) . . . . . . 187 F 5
Vars (F) . . . . 51 G 5
Vârşag (RO) . . . . 147 H 4
Vărşec (BG) . . . . 154 D 3
Vârşolţ (RO) . . . . 147 E 3
Varthólomió (GR) . . . . . . 164 D 4
Vartius (FIN) . . . . 187 G 3
Vârtoapele de Sus (RO) . 151 H 4
Vârtop (RO) . . . . 151 E 4
Värtsilä (FIN) . . . . 193 H 1
Varvara (BG) . . . . 103 E 4
Varvarin (SRB) . . . . 143 E 1
Várvölgy (H) . . . . 128 C 3
Varzi (I) . . . . 101 E 5
Varzy (F) . . . . 45 G 4
Vasa (CY) . . . . 174 C 4
Vasa / Vaasa (FIN) . . . . . 185 E 5
Vasaráperä (FIN) . . . . 187 F 1
Vasarás (GR) . . . . 168 D 3
Vásárosnámény (H) . . . . 127 F 5
Vaşcău (RO) . . . . 146 D 4
Vasil Levski (BG) . . . . 159 F 3
Vasil Levski (BG) . . . . 159 E 2
Vasileia (CY) . . . . 174 D 2
Vasilevo (BG) . . . . 157 G 2
Vasiliká (Kentrikí
    Makedonía) (GR) . . . . 161 G 4
Vasiliká
    (Stereá Elláda) (GR) . . 165 G 2
Vasiliká
    (Vóreio Aigaío) (GR) . 167 F 2
Vasilikó (GR) . . . . 164 C 3
Vasilikó (GR) . . . . 165 H 3
Vasilikós (GR) . . . . 164 C 5
Vasilís (GR) . . . . 165 F 1
Vasilópoulo (GR) . . . . . . 164 C 5
Vašda (E) . . . . 63 H 4
Vaškai (LT) . . . . 205 F 1
Vaski (LV) . . . . 202 C 3
Vaskijärvi (FIN) . . . . 191 F 4
Vaskio (GR) . . . . 191 G 4
Vaskivesi (FIN) . . . . 191 G 2
Vasknarva (EST) . . . . 201 G 2
Vaslui (RO) . . . . 149 E 4
Vassieux-en-Vercors (F) . 51 E 4
Vassy (F) . . . . 38 C 5
Västanfjärd (FIN) . . . . . . 191 F 5
Västenbäck (S) . . . . 190 B 1

Väster Haninge (S) . . . . . 197 G 1
Västerås (S) . . . . 197 F 1
Västervik (S) . . . . 197 F 3
Vasto (I) . . . . 109 H 2
Vasvár (H) . . . . 128 B 3
Vasyl'kiv (UA) . . . . 13 F 1
Vát (H) . . . . 128 B 2
Vaţa de Jos (RO) . . . . . . 146 D 5
Vatan (F) . . . . 45 E 5
Vaterá (GR) . . . . 167 F 2
Vátheia (GR) . . . . 168 D 4
Vathý
    (Iónia Nisiá) (GR) . . . 164 C 3
Vathý
    (Nótio Aigaío) (GR) . . 171 E 2
Vathý
    (Stereá Elláda) (GR) . . 165 H 3
Vathýlakkos (GR) . . . . . . 161 E 4
Vathýs (GR) . . . . 171 F 2
Vatili (CY) . . . . 175 E 3
Vatin (SRB) . . . . 141 E 3
Vatne (N) . . . . 188 C 1
Vatra Dornei (RO) . . . . . 147 H 2
Vatra Moldoviţei (RO) . . 148 A 2
Vattholma (S) . . . . 190 C 3
Vau i Dejës (AL) . . . . 142 C 5
Vaucouleurs (F) . . . . 47 E 1
Vaŭkavysk (BY) . . . . 6 C 5
Vauvert (F) . . . . 54 C 2
Vauvillers (F) . . . . 47 E 3
Vaux-le-Vicomte,
    château de (F) . . . . . 45 F 2
Vávdos (GR) . . . . 161 G 4
Växjö (S) . . . . 195 H 5
Våxtorp (S) . . . . 195 G 5
Vayrac (F) . . . . 49 G 4
Veberöd (S) . . . . 199 F 3
Vecbebri (LV) . . . . 203 E 3
Vechta (D) . . . . 85 E 1
Vecinos (E) . . . . 63 G 2
Veckelax /
    Vehkalahti (FIN) . . . . 193 F 4
Vecpiebalga (LV) . . . . 203 F 3
Vecsés (H) . . . . 129 F 2
Vecumnieki (LV) . . . . 202 D 4
Vedea (RO) . . . . 151 G 3
Vedelago (I) . . . . 103 E 4
Veendam (NL) . . . . 77 G 3
Veenendaal (NL) . . . . 77 E 5
Veere (NL) . . . . 78 B 1
Vega de Espinareda (E) . 57 F 3
Vega de Valcarce (E) . . . 57 E 3
Vegadeo (E) . . . . 57 E 1
Vegarienza (E) . . . . 57 G 3
Vegårshei (N) . . . . 194 D 2
Vegas del Condado (E) . . 57 H 3
Veghel (NL) . . . . 79 E 1
Veguellina de Órbigo (E) . 57 G 4
Vehkalahti /
    Veckelax (FIN) . . . . . . 193 F 4
Vehmaa (FIN) . . . . 191 F 4
Vehmersalmi (FIN) . . . . . 193 F 1
Veidnesklubben (N) . . . . 177 F 2
Veikkola (FIN) . . . . 191 H 5
Veinge (S) . . . . 195 G 5
Veiros (P) . . . . 68 D 1
Veiviržėnai (LT) . . . . 204 C 2
Vejen (DK) . . . . 198 B 3
Vejer de la Frontera (E) . 74 B 4
Vejle (DK) . . . . 198 C 3
Vekilski (BG) . . . . 157 E 2
Vela Luka (HR) . . . . 138 B 3
Velada (E) . . . . 63 H 4
Velagići (BIH) . . . . 136 D 4
Velayos (E) . . . . 64 A 2
Velbert (D) . . . . 84 C 4
Velburg (D) . . . . 91 H 4
Velde (N) . . . . 183 E 4
Velden
    (Nürnberger Land) (D) . 91 H 4
Velden
    am Wörther See (A) . . 96 D 5
Veldhoven (NL) . . . . 79 E 1
Velena (LV) . . . . 203 F 2

Velence (H) . . . . 129 E 2
Velenje (SLO) . . . . 134 C 2
Veles (MK) . . . . 145 F 1
Velešta (MK) . . . . 144 D 2
Velestíno (GR) . . . . 165 F 1
Vélez Blanco (E) . . . . 71 G 4
Vélez de Benaudalla (E) . 75 F 4
Vélez-Málaga (E) . . . . 75 E 3
Vélez Rubio (E) . . . . 71 G 4
Veli Iz (HR) . . . . 136 B 5
Veli Lošinj (HR) . . . . 136 A 4
Veličani (BIH) . . . . 139 E 3
Veliés (GR) . . . . 169 E 4
Velím (H) . . . . 135 G 4
Velika Drenova (SRB) . . . 143 E 2
Velika Gorica (HR) . . . . . 135 E 3
Velika Jablanica (SRB) . . 139 H 4
Velika Jamnička (HR) . . . 135 H 4
Velika Kladuša (BIH) . . . 134 D 4
Velika Kopanica (HR) . . . 135 H 4
Velika Kruša (SRB) . . . . . 142 D 5
Velika Mučna (HR) . . . . . 135 F 2
Velika Plana
    (Kragujevac) (SRB) . . 141 E 5
Velika Plana (Niš) (SRB) . 143 E 2
Velike Lašče (SLO) . . . . . 134 C 3
Veliki Bastaji (HR) . . . . . 135 G 3
Veliki Gaj (SRB) . . . . 141 E 3
Veliki Grđevac (HR) . . . . 135 F 3
Veliki Izvor (SRB) . . . . . . 143 G 1
Veliki Novgorod (RUS) . . . 6 D 1
Veliki Popović (SRB) . . . 141 E 5
Veliki Preslav (BG) . . . . . 156 D 3
Veliki Prolog (HR) . . . . . . 138 D 3
Veliki Radinci (SRB) . . . . 140 C 3
Veliki Raven (HR) . . . . . . 135 F 3
Veliki Tabor (HR) . . . . . . 134 D 2
Veliki Trnovac (SRB) . . . . 143 F 4
Veliki Zdenci (HR) . . . . . 135 F 3
Velikije Luki (RUS) . . . . . . 7 E 3
Veliko Gradište (SRB) . . 141 E 4
Veliko Orašje (SRB) . . . . 141 E 5
Veliko Tărnovo / Велико
    Търново (BG) . . . . . . 159 F 1
Velilla del Río Carrión (E) . 58 A 2
Velimlje (MNE) . . . . 139 F 3
Vélines (F) . . . . 48 D 5
Velingrad /
    Велинград (BG) . . . . 158 C 3
Veliž (RUS) . . . . 7 E 3
Veljun (N) . . . . 134 D 4
Velká Bíteš (CZ) . . . . 92 B 4
Velká Bystřice (CZ) . . . . . 93 F 3
Velká nad Veličkou (CZ) . 93 F 5
Vel'ké Kapušany (SK) . . . 133 H 3
Velké Meziříčí (CZ) . . . . . 92 D 4
Vel'ké Ripňany (SK) . . . . 132 B 3
Vel'ké Úľany (SK) . . . . . . 132 A 4
Velkua (FIN) . . . . 191 F 4
Vel'ký Krtíš (SK) . . . . 132 D 4
Vel'ký Meder (SK) . . . . . . 132 B 5
Vellahn (D) . . . . 82 C 4
Velletri (I) . . . . 109 E 3
Vellinge (S) . . . . 199 E 3
Vélos (GR) . . . . 166 B 3
Velpke (D) . . . . 85 H 1
Velten (D) . . . . 86 C 1
Velventós (GR) . . . . 161 E 4
Velyka Lepetycha (UA) . . 13 H 2
Vemdalen (S) . . . . 189 H 1
Vemdalsskalet (S) . . . . . . 189 H 1
Véménd (H) . . . . 129 E 5
Vemhån (S) . . . . 189 H 2
Venaco (F) . . . . 55 H 4
Venafro (I) . . . . 109 G 3
Venarey-les-Laumes (F) . 45 H 4
Venaria Reale (I) . . . . 100 C 5
Vénčan (BG) . . . . 157 E 3
Vence (F) . . . . 55 G 2
Venda Nova (P) . . . . 56 C 5
Vendas Novas (P) . . . . . . 68 C 2
Vendel (S) . . . . 190 C 5
Vendeuvre (F) . . . . 45 H 2
Vendôme (F) . . . . 44 C 3
Venec (Burgas) (BG) . . . . 159 H 2
Venec (Šumen) (BG) . . . . 157 E 2
Veneheitto (FIN) . . . . 185 H 3

Venezia (I) ... 103 F4
Vengjaneset (N) ... 188 B4
Venialbo (E) ... 63 G1
Venjan (S) ... 189 H4
Venlo (NL) ... 79 F1
Vénna (GR) ... 162 D3
Vennesla (N) ... 194 C2
Vennesund (N) ... 183 E2
Venosa (I) ... 110 D3
Venray (NL) ... 79 F1
Venta (LT) ... 204 D1
Venta Nueva (E) ... 57 F2
Ventas de Huelma (E) ... 75 F2
Ventimiglia (I) ... 104 B4
Ventnor (GB) ... 38 C1
Ventspils (LV) ... 202 A2
Venturina (I) ... 106 C4
Vera (E) ... 71 H5
Vera (N) ... 183 E4
Verbania-Pallanza (I) ... 100 D3
Verberie (F) ... 39 H4
Verbicaro (I) ... 113 B1
Verbier (CH) ... 98 C5
Verčane (SRB) ... 140 D5
Vercel-Villedieu (F) ... 47 F4
Vercelli (I) ... 100 D4
Verchnjadzvinsk (BY) ... 6 D3
Verchn'odniprovs'k (UA) ... 13 H1
Verdalsøra (N) ... 183 E4
Verden (D) ... 81 G5
Verdikoússa (GR) ... 161 E5
Verdun (F) ... 40 D5
Verdun-sur-Garonne (F) ... 53 F2
Verdun-sur-le-Doubs (F) ... 46 D5
Verenci (BG) ... 159 G1
Vereşti (RO) ... 148 C2
Verfeil (F) ... 53 F2
Vergato (I) ... 105 H3
Vergína (GR) ... 161 F4
Vergt (F) ... 49 E4
Verín (E) ... 56 D5
Verl (D) ... 85 E2
Vermand (F) ... 40 A3
Vermenton (F) ... 45 G3
Vermosh (AL) ... 142 C4
Verneşti (RO) ... 152 C2
Vernet-les-Bains (F) ... 53 H5
Verneuil-sur-Avre (F) ... 44 C1
Vernon (F) ... 39 G5
Vernoux-en-Vivarais (F) ... 50 D5
Verny (F) ... 41 E5
Véroia / Βέροια (GR) ... 161 F4
Veroli (I) ... 109 F3
Verona (I) ... 101 H4
Verran (N) ... 182 D4
Verrès (I) ... 100 C3
Versailles (F) ... 45 E1
Versmold (D) ... 85 E2
Verteillac (F) ... 49 E4
Vértesboglár (H) ... 129 E2
Vertus (F) ... 40 B5
Verucchio (I) ... 107 F2
Verviers (B) ... 79 E3
Vervins (F) ... 40 B3
Verzuolo (I) ... 104 B2
Verzy (F) ... 40 B5
Vesanto (FIN) ... 187 E5
Vescovato (F) ... 55 H3
Vése (H) ... 128 C4
Veselec (RO) ...
Veselí nad Lužnicí (CZ) ... 92 B4
Veselí nad Moravou (CZ) ... 93 F5
Veselie (BG) ... 157 F5
Veselinovo (BG) ... 159 G2
Vesilahti (FIN) ... 191 G3
Vesivehmaa (FIN) ... 191 H3
Veskoniemi (FIN) ... 177 G5
Vesoul (F) ... 47 F3
Véssa (GR) ... 167 E4
Vestby (N) ... 189 E5
Vestbygda (N) ... 194 B2
Vesterø Havn (DK) ... 195 E4
Vestertana (N) ... 177 F2
Vestmanna (Færøerne) (DK) ... 194 A4
Vestnes (N) ... 188 C1
Vestone (I) ... 101 G4

Vestre Jakobselv (N) ... 177 G2
Veszprém (H) ... 128 D3
Veszprémvarsány (H) ... 128 D2
Vésztő (H) ... 131 E3
Veteli (FIN) ... 185 G5
Vetlanda (S) ... 196 D4
Vetovo (BG) ... 152 B5
Vetralla (I) ... 108 D2
Vetren (Burgas) (BG) ... 157 E4
Vetren (Pazardžik) (BG) ... 158 C2
Vetren (Stara Zagora) (BG) ... 159 F2
Vetrino (BG) ... 157 E2
Vetriolo Terme (I) ... 101 H3
Vetschau (D) ... 87 E3
Veules-les-Roses (F) ... 39 F3
Veulettes-sur-Mer (F) ... 39 E3
Veurne (B) ... 78 A1
Vevey (CH) ... 98 B4
Vévi (GR) ... 161 E3
Veynes (F) ... 51 E5
Veyre (F) ... 50 A3
Veyrier (F) ... 51 F2
Vezdemarbán (E) ... 57 H5
Vézelay (F) ... 45 G4
Vézelise (F) ... 47 E2
Vézénobres (F) ... 54 B1
Vézins-de-Lévézou (F) ... 53 H1
Vezzani (F) ... 55 H4
Vezzano (I) ... 101 H3
Viadana (I) ... 101 G5
Viana (E) ... 60 D3
Viana do Alentejo (P) ... 68 C3
Viana do Bolo (E) ... 57 E4
Viana do Castelo (P) ... 56 B5
Vianden (L) ... 79 F4
Vianen (NL) ... 76 D5
Viareggio (I) ... 105 G4
Vias (F) ... 54 A3
Vibo Valentia (I) ... 115 H1
Viborg (DK) ... 194 D5
Vibraye (F) ... 44 C3
Vic (F) ... 60 D3
Vič (SLO) ... 134 C1
Vic-en-Bigorre (F) ... 52 D3
Vic-Fezensac (F) ... 52 D2
Vic-le-Comte (F) ... 50 A3
Vic-sur-Aisne (F) ... 40 A4
Vic-sur-Cère (F) ... 49 H4
Vicdessos (F) ... 53 F4
Vicebsk (BY) ... 7 E3
Vicenza (I) ... 103 E4
Vichy (F) ... 50 B2
Vico (F) ... 55 G4
Vico del Gargano (I) ... 110 D1
Vico Equense (I) ... 109 H5
Vicovu de Jos (RO) ... 148 A1
Vicovu de Sus (RO) ... 148 A1
Victoria / Rabat (M) ... 114 B4
Victoria (RO) ... 151 G1
Vidago (P) ... 56 D5
Vidareidi (Færøerne) (DK) ... 194 B4
Vidauban (F) ... 55 F3
Viddal (N) ... 188 C1
Videbæk (DK) ... 194 C5
Videle (RO) ... 152 A4
Videm (SLO) ... 134 C3
Vidiáki (GR) ... 165 E5
Vidigueira (P) ... 68 D3
Vidin / Видин (BG) ... 150 D5
Vidnava (CZ) ... 93 E5
Vidra (RO) ... 147 E4
Vidreres (E) ... 61 E3
Vidrovan (MNE) ... 139 F3
Vidsel (S) ... 184 D1
Viduklė (LT) ... 204 D3
Viechtach (D) ... 91 G5
Viechtwang (A) ... 96 D2
Vieira de Leiria (P) ... 62 A4
Vieira do Minho (P) ... 56 C5
Vieja, cueva de la (E) ... 72 D1
Viekšniai (LT) ... 204 D1
Vielha (E) ... 60 B1
Vielle-Aure (F) ... 52 D4
Vielmur-sur-Agout (F) ... 53 G2
Vielsalm (B) ... 79 E4

Vienenburg (D) ... 85 H2
Vienne (F) ... 50 D3
Vieremä (FIN) ... 187 E4
Viernheim (D) ... 89 E3
Vierraden (D) ... 83 G5
Viersen (D) ... 84 B4
Vierumäki (FIN) ... 193 E3
Vierzon (F) ... 45 E4
Viešintos (LT) ... 205 E2
Viešvilė (LT) ... 204 D3
Vietas (S) ... 179 H4
Vieste (I) ... 110 D1
Vietri di Potenza (I) ... 110 C4
Vietri sul Mare (I) ... 109 H5
Vieux-Boucau-les-Bains (F) ... 52 A2
Vievis (LT) ... 205 E2
Vif (F) ... 51 E4
Vig (DK) ... 198 D3
Vigeland (N) ... 194 C2
Vigeois (F) ... 49 G4
Vigevano (I) ... 101 E4
Viggiano (I) ... 110 D5
Vignanello (I) ... 108 D2
Vigneulles (F) ... 41 E5
Vignola (I) ... 105 H3
Vignole Borbera (I) ... 105 E2
Vignory (F) ... 46 D2
Vigo (E) ... 56 B4
Vigo di Fassa (I) ... 103 E2
Vigone (I) ... 100 B5
Vigonza (I) ... 103 E4
Vihanti (FIN) ... 185 G3
Vihiers (F) ... 43 H5
Vihtavuori (FIN) ... 191 H1
Vihteljärvi (FIN) ... 191 G3
Vihti (FIN) ... 191 H4
Viiala (FIN) ... 191 G3
Viiksimo (FIN) ... 187 G3
Viimsi (EST) ... 200 D1
Viinijärvi (FIN) ... 193 G1
Viiratsi (EST) ... 201 E3
Viitasaari (FIN) ... 185 H5
Vijciems (LV) ... 203 F2
Vik (IS) ... 178 B3
Vik (N) ... 194 D2
Vik (N) ... 183 E2
Vik (N) ... 188 C3
Vika (S) ... 190 A4
Vikajärvi (FIN) ... 181 E5
Vikedal (N) ... 188 B5
Vikersund (N) ... 189 E5
Vikeså (N) ... 194 B1
Vikevåg (N) ... 194 B1
Vikingstad (S) ... 197 E2
Vikoč (BIH) ... 139 F2
Viksdalen (N) ... 188 B2
Viksjö (S) ... 190 B1
Viksta (S) ... 190 C5
Vila Baleira (P) ... 68 A4
Vila Boim (P) ... 69 E2
Vila de Cruces (E) ... 56 C3
Vila de Rei (P) ... 62 C5
Vila do Bispo (P) ... 68 B5
Vila do Conde (P) ... 62 B1
Vila Fernando (P) ... 69 E1
Vila Flor (P) ... 63 E1
Vila Franca das Naves (P) ... 62 D2
Vila Franca de Xira (P) ... 68 B5
Vila Fresca de Azeitão (P) ... 68 B5
Vila Nova da Barquinha (P) ... 62 B5
Vila Nova de Cerveira (P) ... 56 B5
Vila Nova de Famalicão (P) ... 62 B1
Vila Nova de Foz Côa (P) ... 63 E2
Vila Nova de Gaia (P) ... 62 B1
Vila Nova de Milfontes (P) ... 68 B4
Vila Nova de Paiva (P) ... 62 D2
Vila Nova de Poiares (P) ... 62 C3
Vila Nova de Santo André (P) ... 68 B3
Vila Nova de São Bento (P) ... 68 D4
Vila Pouca de Aguiar (P) ... 62 D1

Vila Praia de Ancora (P) ... 56 B5
Vila Real (P) ... 62 D1
Vila-real / Villarreal (E) ... 66 A2
Vila Real de Sto António (P) ... 68 D5
Vila-rodona (E) ... 60 C4
Vila-seca (E) ... 60 C4
Vila Velha de Ródão (P) ... 62 D5
Vila Verde (P) ... 56 B5
Vila Verde da Raia (P) ... 56 D5
Vila Verde de Ficalho (P) ... 69 E4
Vila Viçosa (P) ... 68 D2
Vilada (E) ... 60 D2
Viladamat (E) ... 61 F2
Viladrau (E) ... 61 E3
Vilafamés (E) ... 66 A2
Vilafranca (E) ... 65 H2
Vilafranca del Penedès (E) ... 60 D4
Vilagarcía de Arousa (E) ... 56 B3
Vilaka (LV) ... 203 G1
Vilalba (E) ... 56 D2
Vilaller (E) ... 60 B2
Vilamarxant (E) ... 65 H4
Vilāni (LV) ... 203 G4
Vilanova (E) ... 57 E1
Vilanova d'Alcolea (E) ... 66 A2
Vilanova de Arousa (E) ... 56 B3
Vilanova de Sau (E) ... 61 E2
Vilanova i la Geltrú (E) ... 60 D4
Vilar de Barrio (E) ... 56 D4
Vilar Formoso (P) ... 63 E3
Vilches (E) ... 71 E3
Vilejka (BY) ... 6 D4
Vilhelmina (S) ... 183 H3
Vília (GR) ... 165 E4
Vilina Vlas (BIH) ... 137 H5
Viljakkala (FIN) ... 191 G2
Viljandi (EST) ... 201 E3
Vilkakrūgs (LV) ... 203 H4
Vilkaviškis (LT) ... 204 D4
Vilkija (LT) ... 205 E3
Vilkyškiai (LT) ... 204 C3
Villa Bartolomea (I) ... 102 D5
Villa del Prado (E) ... 64 A3
Villa del Río (E) ... 70 C4
Villa Literno (I) ... 109 H4
Villa Minozzo (I) ... 105 G3
Villa Potenza (I) ... 107 G4
Villa Reale, giardini della (I) ... 105 G4
Villa San Giovanni (I) ... 115 G2
Villa Santa Maria (I) ... 109 G3
Villa Santina (I) ... 103 G2
Villa Vomano (I) ... 107 H5
Villablanca (E) ... 68 D5
Villablino (E) ... 57 F2
Villabona (E) ... 59 E1
Villabrágima (E) ... 57 H5
Villabuena del Puente (E) ... 63 H1
Villacañas (E) ... 64 C4
Villacarriedo (E) ... 58 B1
Villacarrillo (E) ... 71 E3
Villach (A) ... 96 D5
Villacidro (I) ... 112 B4
Villada (E) ... 57 H4
Villadiego (E) ... 58 B3
Villadossola (I) ... 100 D3
Villaescusa de Haro (E) ... 64 D4
Villafáfila (E) ... 57 G5
Villaflores (E) ... 63 H2
Villafranca (E) ... 59 F3
Villafranca de los Barros (E) ... 69 F2
Villafranca de los Caballeros (E) ... 64 C5
Villafranca del Bierzo (E) ... 57 E3
Villafranca di Verona (I) ... 101 H4
Villafranca in Lunigiana (I) ... 105 F3
Villafranca Montes de Oca (E) ... 58 C3
Villafranca Piemonte (I) ... 100 B5
Villafranca Tirrena (I) ... 115 G2

Villafranco del Guadalquivir (E) ... 69 G5
Villafrati (I) ... 114 D3
Villafrechós (E) ... 57 H5
Villafruela (E) ... 58 B4
Villafuerte (E) ... 58 B4
Villagarcía del Llano (E) ... 65 F5
Villager de Laciana (E) ... 57 F2
Villaggio Mancuso (I) ... 113 C3
Villaharta (E) ... 70 B3
Villahermosa (E) ... 71 F2
Villahoz (E) ... 58 B4
Villaines-la-Juhel (F) ... 44 C1
Villala (FIN) ... 193 G1
Villalba de Guardo (E) ... 58 A2
Villalba de la Sierra (E) ... 65 E3
Villalba de los Barros (E) ... 69 F2
Villalba del Rey (E) ... 64 D3
Villalcázar de Sirga (E) ... 58 A3
Villalengua (E) ... 59 F5
Villalgordo del Marquesado (E) ... 65 E4
Villalón de Campos (E) ... 57 H4
Villalonga (E) ... 66 A5
Villalpando (E) ... 57 H5
Villalpardo (E) ... 65 F5
Villamañán (E) ... 57 G4
Villamanrique (E) ... 71 F2
Villamanrique de la Condesa (E) ... 69 F5
Villamartín (E) ... 74 B3
Villamartín de Campos (E) ... 58 A4
Villamartín de Don Sancho (E) ... 57 H3
Villamassargia (I) ... 112 B5
Villamayor de Campos (E) ... 57 H5
Villamayor de Gállego (E) ... 59 G5
Villamayor de Santiago (E) ... 64 D4
Villandraut (F) ... 52 C1
Villanova Monteleone (I) ... 112 B2
Villanubla (E) ... 58 A5
Villanueva de Alcardete (E) ... 64 D4
Villanueva de Alcorón (E) ... 65 E2
Villanueva de Algaidas (E) ... 70 C5
Villanueva de Argaño (E) ... 58 B3
Villanueva de Bogas (E) ... 64 C4
Villanueva de Cameros (E) ... 58 D4
Villanueva de Córdoba (E) ... 70 C3
Villanueva de Franco (E) ... 71 E2
Villanueva de Gállego (E) ... 59 G4
Villanueva de Huerva (E) ... 59 G5
Villanueva de la Concepción (E) ... 75 E3
Villanueva de la Fuente (E) ... 71 F2
Villanueva de la Jara (E) ... 65 E4
Villanueva de la Reina (E) ... 70 D4
Villanueva de la Serena (E) ... 69 G1
Villanueva de la Sierra (E) ... 63 F4
Villanueva de la Vera (E) ... 63 G4
Villanueva de las Torres (E) ... 71 E5
Villanueva de los Castillejos (E) ... 69 E5
Villanueva de los Infantes (E) ... 71 E2
Villanueva de San Carlos (E) ... 70 D2
Villanueva del Arzobispo (E) ... 71 E3
Villanueva del Campo (E) ... 57 H5
Villanueva del Duque (E) ... 70 B3
Villanueva del Fresno (E) ... 69 E3
Villanueva del Rey (E) ... 69 H3
Villanueva del Río y Minas (E) ... 69 G4
Villanueva del Trabuco (E) ... 75 E3

Villány (H) ... 129 E5
Villaquejida (E) ... 57 G4
Villaquilambre (E) ... 57 G3
Villar de Cañas (E) ... 64 D4
Villar de Domingo García (E) ... 65 E3
Villar de Peralonso (E) ... 63 F2
Villar del Arzobispo (E) ... 65 G4
Villar del Rey (E) ... 69 E1
Villarcayo (E) ... 58 C2
Villard-de-Lans (F) ... 51 E4
Villardeciervos (E) ... 57 F5
Villardefrades (E) ... 57 H5
Villarejo de Fuentes (E) ... 64 D4
Villarejo de Salvanés (E) ... 64 C3
Villarente (E) ... 57 H3
Villares de la Reina (E) ... 63 G2
Villares del Saz (E) ... 65 E4
Villargordo del Cabriel (E) ... 65 F4
Villaricos (E) ... 71 H5
Villarino de los Aires (E) ... 63 F1
Villarmayor (E) ... 63 G2
Villarquemado (E) ... 65 G2
Villarramiel (E) ... 57 H5
Villarreal / Vila-real (E) ... 66 A2
Villarrín de Campos (E) ... 57 G5
Villarrobledo (E) ... 64 D5
Villarroya de la Sierra (E) ... 59 F5
Villarroya de los Pinares (E) ... 65 H2
Villarrubia de los Ojos (E) ... 64 C5
Villarrubia de Santiago (E) ... 64 C3
Villars-les-Dombes (F) ... 50 D2
Villars-sur-Ollon (CH) ... 98 C4
Villars, grottes de (F) ... 49 E3
Villarta de San Juan (E) ... 64 C5
Villasalto (I) ... 112 C4
Villasana de Mena (E) ... 58 C2
Villasandino (E) ... 58 B3
Villasante (E) ... 58 B3
Villasarracino (E) ... 58 A3
Villaseco de los Reyes (E) ... 63 F1
Villasequilla (E) ... 64 B4
Villasimius (I) ... 112 C5
Villasor (I) ... 112 B5
Villatobas (E) ... 64 C4
Villatoya (E) ... 65 G5
Villaverde del Río (E) ... 69 G4
Villaviciosa (E) ... 57 H1
Villaviciosa de Córdoba (E) ... 70 B3
Villaviciosa de Odón (E) ... 64 B3
Villavieja de Yeltes (E) ... 63 F2
Villé (F) ... 47 G2
Ville-en-Tardenois (F) ... 40 B5
Ville-sur-Tourbe (F) ... 40 C5
Villebois-Lavalette (F) ... 49 E3
Villedieu-les-Poêles-Rouffigny (F) ... 38 C5
Villefagnan (F) ... 48 D2
Villefort (F) ... 54 B1
Villefranche-d'Albigeois (F) ... 53 G2
Villefranche-de-Lauragais (F) ... 53 F3
Villefranche-de-Lonchat (F) ... 48 D4
Villefranche-de-Rouergue (F) ... 53 G1
Villefranche-du-Périgord (F) ... 49 F5
Villefranche-sur-Cher (F) ... 44 D4
Villefranche-sur-Mer (F) ... 55 H4
Villefranche-sur-Saône (F) ... 50 D2
Villel (E) ... 65 G3
Villemur-sur-Tarn (F) ... 53 F2
Villena (E) ... 73 E1
Villenauxe-la-Grande (F) ... 45 G1
Villeneuve (F) ... 53 G1
Villeneuve (F) ... 54 C2
Villeneuve-d'Ascq (F) ... 40 A2
Villeneuve-de-Berg (F) ... 50 C5

A
B
C
D
E
F
G
H
I
J
K
L
M
N
O
P
Q
R
S
T
U
V
W
X
Y
Z

A B C D E F G H I J K L M N O P Q R S T U V W X Y Z

Villeneuve-de-Marsan (F) . 52 C 2
Villeneuve-
l'Archevêque (F) .. 45 G 2
Villeneuve-sur-Lot (F) ... 53 E 1
Villeneuve-sur-Yonne (F). 45 G 3
Villeréal (F) .... 49 E 5
Villers-Bocage (F) .... 39 H 3
Villers-Bocage (F) .... 38 C 5
Villers-Bretonneux (F).... 39 H 3
Villers-Cotterêts (F) ..... 40 A 5
Villers-devant-Orval (B) . 78 D 5
Villers-Farlay (F)........47 E 5
Villers-la-Ville (B)........ 78 C 3
Villers-le-Lac (F) ....47 F 5
Villers-sur-Mer (F)...... 38 D 4
Villersexel (F)..........47 F 4
Villerupt (F)............41 E 4
Villerville (F)........... 39 E 4
Villetta Barrea (I) .... 109 G 3
Villiers-Saint-Georges (F). 45 G 1
Villingen (D) .... 94 B 2
Villnöß / Funes (I) ...... 103 B 2
Villoldo (E)........... 58 A 3
Villoria (E) .... 63 H 2
Villotta (I) .... 103 F 3
Vilnius (LT)........... 205 G 4
Viľnohirs'k (UA).......13 H 1
Vilppula (FIN) .... 191 G 2
Vilsbiburg (D).......... 95 H 1
Vilshofen
an der Donau (D).. 96 C 1
Vilusi (MNE)........... 139 F 4
Vilvoorde (B)......... 78 C 2
Vimercate (I) .... 101 E 4
Vimianzo (E) .... 56 B 2
Vimieiro (P)........... 68 D 2
Vimioso (P) .... 57 F 5
Vimmerby (S) .... 197 E 4
Vimpeli (FIN) .... 185 G 5
Vimperk (CZ) .... 92 A 5
Vinac (BIH)........... 137 E 4
Vinadio (I) .... 104 B 3
Vinaixa (E) .... 60 B 4
Vinaròs (E) .... 66 B 1
Vinay (F)...........51 E 4
Vinça (F) .... 53 H 5
Vinča (SRB) .... 140 D 4
Vinchiaturo (I) .... 109 H 4
Vinci (I) .... 105 H 4
Vindeln (S)........... 184 D 4
Vinderup (DK) .... 194 C 5
Vindsvik (N)........... 188 B 5
Vinga (RO) .... 146 B 5
Vingåker (S)........... 197 E 2
Vingelen (N) .... 189 F 1
Vingrom (N) .... 189 E 3
Vinhais (P) .... 57 E 5
Vinica (MK) .... 145 G 5
Vinica (SLO) .... 134 D 4
Viničani (MK) .... 145 F 1
Viniste (BG) .... 154 C 2
Vinjesvingen (N) .... 188 C 4
Vinkovci (HR) .... 137 H 2
Vinni (EST)........... 201 F 2
Vinnycja (UA).........13 E 2
Vinsternes (N)........... 182 B 5
Vinstra (N) .... 189 E 2
Vintileasca (RO)........ 152 C 1
Viñuelas (E) .... 64 C 2
Vinuesa (E) .... 58 D 4
Vipava (SLO) .... 134 B 3
Vipiteno / Sterzing (I) .. 102 D 1
Vir (BIH) .... 138 C 2
Vir (HR) .... 136 B 4
Vira (HR) .... 138 B 3
Vire Normandie (F)...... 38 C 5
Vireši (LV)........... 203 F 2
Vireux-Wallerand (F).... 40 C 3
Virgen (A)........... 95 H 4
Virginia (IRL) .... 23 E 4
Virieu (F)...........51 E 5
Virieu-le-Grand (F)...... 51 E 2
Virkkala (FIN) .... 191 G 5
Virkkula (FIN) .... 181 G 5
Virmutjoki (FIN) .... 193 G 3
Virolahti (FIN) .... 193 F 4

Virovitica (HR) .... 135 G 3
Virpazar (MNE)........ 139 F 5
Virrat (FIN) .... 191 G 2
Virsbo (S) .... 190 A 5
Virserum (S) .... 197 E 4
Virtasalmi (FIN) .... 193 F 2
Virton (B) .... 79 E 5
Virtsu (EST) .... 200 C 3
Viru-Nigula (EST)....... 201 F 1
Vis (HR) .... 138 B 3
Visaginas (LT)......... 205 H 2
Visby (S) .... 197 G 4
Visé (B) .... 79 E 3
Visegrad (BIH) .... 137 H 5
Visegrád (H) .... 129 F 1
Viserba (I) .... 107 F 2
Viseu (P) .... 62 C 2
Viseu de Jos (RO) ...... 147 G 1
Viseu de Sus (RO) ...... 147 G 1
Vișina (RO) .... 151 G 5
Vișina Nouă (RO) ...... 151 G 5
Višnja Gora (SLO) ...... 134 C 3
Višnjica (SRB) .... 140 D 4
Viso del Marqués (E) .... 71 E 2
Visoko (BIH) .... 137 G 5
Višovgrad (BG) .... 156 B 3
Visp (CH) .... 98 D 4
Víssani (GR) .... 160 C 5
Visselhövede (D) ....81 H 5
Vissenbjerg (DK) .... 198 C 3
Vissiniá (GR) .... 160 D 3
Visso (I) .... 107 G 5
Vistabella
del Maestrazgo (E) .... 65 H 3
Vistheden (S) .... 185 E 2
Vištytis (LT) .... 204 D 4
Visuvesi (FIN) .... 191 G 2
Visz (H) .... 128 D 3
Vitaby (S) .... 199 F 3
Vitanesti (RO) .... 152 A 5
Vitanovac (SRB) .... 142 D 1
Viterbo (I) .... 108 D 2
Vitez (BIH) .... 137 F 5
Vitigudino (E) .... 63 F 2
Vitina (BIH) .... 138 D 3
Vitina (SRB) .... 143 E 4
Vítkov (CZ) .... 93 F 3
Vítoli (GR) .... 165 E 2
Vitolište (MK) .... 145 F 2
Vitomirești (RO) .... 151 G 3
Vitomirica (SRB) .... 139 H 4
Vitoria-Gasteiz (E)....... 58 D 2
Vitovlje (BIH) .... 137 F 4
Vitré (F)........... 43 G 2
Vitrey-sur-Mance (F) .....47 E 3
Vitriola (I) .... 105 G 3
Vitrolles (F) .... 54 D 3
Vitry-en-Artois (F)....... 40 A 2
Vitry-le-François (F)..... 46 C 1
Vitsand (S) .... 189 G 5
Vittangi (S) .... 180 B 4
Vitte (D) .... 83 F 2
Vitteaux (F) .... 46 C 4
Vittel (F)...........47 E 2
Vittoria (I)...........115 F 5
Vittorio Veneto (I) ...... 103 F 3
Vittoriosa / Birgu (M)....114 C 5
Vittsjö (S) .... 195 G 5
Vitznau (CH) .... 99 E 3
Viù (I)........... 100 B 4
Vivaro (I) .... 103 F 3
Viveiro (E) .... 56 D 1
Vivel del Río Martín (E) .. 65 G 1
Viverols (F)........... 50 B 3
Viveros (E) .... 71 F 2
Viviers (F)........... 50 D 5
Vivonne (F) .... 49 E 1
Vizela (P) .... 62 C 1
Vizille (F)...........51 E 4
Vižinada (HR) .... 134 A 4
Viziru (RO) .... 153 E 3
Vizovice (CZ) .... 93 F 4
Vizsoly (H) .... 127 E 5
Vizzavona (F) .... 55 H 4
Vizzini (I) ....115 F 4
Vlachává (GR)......... 161 E 5

Vlachiótis (GR) .... 168 D 3
Vlachogiánni (GR)....... 161 E 5
Vlachokerasiá (GR)...... 168 D 2
Vlachomándra (GR) ..... 165 E 3
Vlachópoulo (GR)...... 168 C 3
Vladaja (BG) .... 158 B 2
Vlădeni (RO) .... 148 D 2
Vlădești (RO) .... 151 H 2
Vladičin Han (SRB) ..... 143 G 4
Vladievci (MK) .... 145 H 1
Vladila (RO) .... 151 G 5
Vladimir (RUS) ....7 H 1
Vladimirci (SRB) .... 140 C 4
Vladimirescu (RO)...... 146 B 5
Vladimirovac (SRB)..... 140 D 3
Vladimirovo (MK) ...... 145 H 1
Vladinja (BG) .... 156 A 3
Vlăduleni (RO) .... 151 G 4
Vlagtwedde (NL)....... 77 G 3
Vlăhița (RO) .... 148 A 5
Vlahovo (BG) .... 162 C 1
Vlasenica (BIH) .... 137 H 5
Vlašim (CZ) .... 92 B 3
Vlasina Okruglica (SRB). 143 G 4
Vlasotince (SRB) .... 143 G 3
Vlásti (GR) .... 160 D 4
Vlčany (SK) .... 132 B 4
Vlieland (NL)........ 76 D 2
Vlissingen (NL) .... 78 B 1
Vlkolínec (SK) .... 132 D 2
Vlorë (AL) .... 144 B 4
Vlotho (D) .... 85 F 2
Vlychó (GR) .... 164 C 3
Vobbia (I) .... 105 E 2
Voćin (HR) .... 135 G 3
Vöcklabruck (A) .... 96 C 2
Vodeničane (BG)....... 159 H 2
Vodice (Rijeka) (HR) .... 134 B 4
Vodice (Šibenik) (HR).... 136 C 5
Vodňany (CZ) .... 92 A 5
Vodnjan /
Dignano (HR) .... 134 A 5
Voe (GB) .... 27 G 2
Vogatsikó (GR) .... 160 D 4
Vogelsdorf (D) .... 86 D 1
Voghera (I) .... 101 E 5
Vogošća (BIH) .... 137 G 5
Vohenstrauß (D) ....91 F 4
Vohringen (D) .... 89 G 5
Vöhma (EST) .... 201 E 3
Vöhringen (D) .... 89 G 5
Voikka (FIN) .... 193 F 3
Voikoski (FIN) .... 193 F 3
Voila (RO) .... 151 H 1
Voineasa (RO) .... 151 F 2
Voinești (RO) .... 148 D 3
Voiron (F)...........51 E 3
Voiteur (F)...........47 E 5
Voitsberg (A) .... 97 F 4
Vojakkala (FIN) .... 185 G 1
Vojens (DK) .... 198 B 4
Vojka (SRB) .... 140 C 4
Vojnić (HR) .... 134 D 4
Vojnik (SLO) .... 134 D 2
Vojnika (RO) .... 159 H 2
Vojnjagovo (BG) .... 158 D 2
Vojska (SRB) .... 141 E 1
Vojtanov (CZ) ....91 F 2
Voka (EST) .... 201 G 1
Volary (CZ) .... 92 A 5
Volda (N) .... 188 C 1
Voldės (A) .... 95 G 4
Volendam (NL)....... 77 E 4
Volissós (GR) .... 167 E 3
Volkach (D) .... 89 H 2
Völkermarkt (A) .... 97 E 5
Völklingen (D) .... 88 C 3
Volkmarsen (D) .... 85 F 4
Volkovija (MK) .... 144 D 1
Volmunster (F)..........41 G 5
Voločys'k (UA).........12 D 2
Volodymyr-
Volyns'kyj (UA).......12 C 1
Volokolamsk (RUS).......7 F 2
Volonne (F) .... 55 E 1
Vólos / Βόλος (GR) ..... 165 G 1
Volpiano (I) .... 100 C 5
Volta Mantovana (I) .... 101 G 4

Volterra (I) .... 105 H 5
Voltri (I) .... 104 D 3
Volturara Appula (I) .....110 D 2
Voluntari (RO) .... 152 B 4
Volvic (F) .... 50 A 2
Volx (F) .... 55 E 2
Volyně (CZ) .... 92 A 4
Vonešta Voda (BG) ..... 159 F 1
Vónitsa (GR) .... 164 C 2
Vonnas (F) .... 50 D 2
Vonyarcvashegy (H).... 128 C 3
Voorschoten (NL)......76 D 4
Voorst (NL) .... 77 F 5
Voorthuizen (NL) ...... 77 E 4
Vopnafjörður (IS) ...... 178 D 1
Vörå / Vöyri (FIN) ...... 185 F 5
Vorau (A) .... 97 G 3
Vorchdorf (A) .... 96 D 2
Vorden (NL)........ 77 F 5
Vordernberg (A) .... 97 E 3
Vorderriß (D) .... 95 G 3
Vordingborg (DK) ...... 198 D 4
Vorë (AL) .... 144 C 2
Voreppe (F)...........51 E 4
Vorey (F) .... 50 B 4
Vornicení (RO) .... 148 C 1
Voroklini (CY) .... 175 E 4
Vorona (RO) .... 148 C 2
Voroneț (RO) .... 148 B 2
Vorsfelde (D) .... 85 H 1
Vorța (RO) .... 146 D 5
Võru (EST) .... 201 G 4
Vorupør (HR) .... 198 A 2
Voss (N) .... 188 B 4
Võsu (EST) .... 201 F 1
Vothylakas (CY) .... 175 G 2
Votice (CZ) .... 92 B 3
Votonósi (GR) .... 160 D 5
Vouchorína (GR) ...... 160 D 4
Voúdia (GR) .... 169 H 4
Vouillé (F)........... 49 E 1
Voukoliés (GR) .... 172 B 3
Vouliagméni /
Βουλιαγμένη (GR) ... 165 H 5
Vouni (CY) ....174 C 4
Voutás (GR) .... 165 G 2
Vouvant (F) .... 48 C 1
Vouvray (F) .... 44 C 4
Vouzela (P) .... 62 C 2
Vouziers (F) .... 40 C 4
Voves (F) .... 44 D 2
Vovoúsa (GR) .... 160 D 5
Vóyri / Vörå (FIN) ...... 185 F 5
Voz (N) .... 134 B 4
Vozarci (MK) .... 145 F 1
Voznesens'k (UA) ....13 G 2
Vrå (DK) .... 194 D 4
Vráble (SK) .... 132 B 4
Vraca / Враца (BG) ..... 154 D 3
Vračev Gaj (SRB) ....141 E 4
Vrachnéika (GR) .... 165 E 4
Vrådal (N) .... 194 D 1
Vrana (HR) .... 134 B 5
Vranduk (BIH) .... 137 F 4
Vrani (RO) .... 150 B 2
Vrani Kon (BG) .... 159 G 1
Vranilovci (BG) .... 159 E 1
Vranino (BG) .... 157 G 2
Vranja (HR) .... 134 B 4
Vranje (SRB) .... 143 F 4
Vranjska Banja (SRB) ... 143 G 4
Vranov
nad Topľou (SK) .... 133 G 2
Vransko (SLO) .... 134 C 2
Vranštica (MNE) .... 139 G 3
Vrástama (GR) .... 161 H 4
Vrata (RO) .... 150 D 4
Vratarnica (SRB) .... 143 G 1
Vratnica (MK) .... 143 E 5
Vravróna (GR) .... 166 B 4
Vražogrnac (SRB) ...... 143 G 1
Vrbanja (HR) .... 137 H 3
Vrbas / Врбас (SRB) .... 140 B 2
Vrbaška (BIH) .... 135 G 4

Vrbljani (BIH) .... 136 D 4
Vrbnik (HR) .... 134 C 4
Vrbno
pod Pradědem (CZ) . 93 F 2
Vrboska (HR) .... 138 B 3
Vrbové (SK) .... 132 B 3
Vrbovec (HR) .... 135 E 3
Vrbovsko (HR) .... 134 C 4
Vrchlabí (CZ) .... 87 G 5
Vrčin (SRB) .... 140 D 4
Vrdnik (SRB) .... 140 C 3
Vreden (D) .... 84 C 2
Vrela (SRB) .... 142 D 4
Vrelo (RO) .... 134 D 5
Vrelo (SRB) .... 143 F 2
Vreoci (SRB) .... 140 D 5
Vresse-sur-Semois (B) ... 78 D 4
Vrésthena (GR) .... 168 D 3
Vreta kloster (S) .... 197 E 2
Vrgorac (HR) .... 138 D 3
Vrhnika (SLO) .... 134 B 2
Vrhpolje (BIH) .... 135 F 5
Vrísa (GR) .... 167 F 2
Vrlika (HR) .... 136 D 5
Vrnjačka Banja (SRB) ... 143 E 2
Vrnograč (BIH) .... 135 E 4
Vrontádos (GR) .... 167 E 3
Vrontamás (GR) .... 168 D 3
Vronteró (GR) .... 160 D 3
Vrontoú (GR) .... 161 E 4
Vrosína (GR) .... 160 C 5
Vrouchás (GR) .... 170 D 5
Vrpolje (Šibenik) (HR) . 138 A 2
Vrpolje
(Slavonski Brod) (HR). 137 G 2
Vršac / Вршац (SRB) ....141 E 3
Vršani (BIH) .... 137 H 3
Vrsar (HR) .... 134 A 4
Vrsi (HR) .... 136 B 4
Vrtoče (BIH) .... 136 C 4
Vrutok (MK) .... 145 E 1
Vrýses (GR) .... 170 A 5
Vrysiá (GR) .... 165 F 1
Vsetín (CZ) .... 93 G 4
Vučitrn (SRB) .... 143 E 3
Vučje (SRB) .... 143 F 3
Vučkovica (SRB) .... 142 D 1
Vukan (BG) .... 158 A 1
Vukosavlje (BIH) .... 135 H 5
Vukovar (HR) .... 137 H 2
Vulcan (RO) .... 151 E 2
Vulcana-Băi (RO) ...... 151 H 2
Vulpești (RO) .... 151 H 3
Vultureni (RO) .... 147 F 3
Vulturești (RO) .... 151 G 3
Vuohijärvi (FIN) .... 193 F 3
Vuokatti (FIN) .... 187 F 4
Vuolijoki (FIN) .... 187 E 4
Vuollerim (S) .... 184 D 1
Vuonislahti (FIN) ...... 187 G 2
Vuoskojaure (S) .... 180 A 3
Vuostimo (FIN) .... 181 F 4
Vuotso (FIN) .... 181 E 3
Vurpăr (RO) .... 147 G 5
Vylkove (UA)..........13 G 4
Vyróneia (GR) .... 161 G 2
Vyrytsa (RUS) ....7 E 1
Vysoké Mýto (CZ) ..... 92 D 3
Vyšší Brod (CZ) .... 96 D 1
Vytína (GR) .... 165 E 5
Vyzítsa (GR) .... 165 G 1
Vyžnycja (UA)..........12 D 3

W

Waalwijk (NL)........76 D 5
Waasmunster (B)........ 78 C 2
Wabern (D) .... 85 F 4
Wąbrzeźno (PL)........117 H 4
Wąchock (PL) .... 122 D 4
Wachow (D) .... 86 C 1
Wächtersbach (D)....... 89 F 1
Waddesdon Manor (GB). 35 H 1
Wadebridge (GB) .... 34 C 4
Wädenswil (CH)....... 99 E 2
Wadlew (PL) .... 122 B 3
Wadowice (PL)......... 125 F 1

Wadowice Górne (PL) .. 123 E 5
Wagenfeld (D) .... 85 E 1
Wageningen (NL) ...... 77 E 5
Waging am See (D)...... 96 B 2
Wagrain (A) .... 96 C 4
Wągrowiec (PL).........117 F 5
Wahlstedt (D)............81 H 3
Waiblingen (D)......... 89 F 4
Waidhaus (D)...........91 G 4
Waidhofen
an der Thaya (A) .... 92 C 5
Waidhofen
an der Ybbs (A) .... 97 E 2
Waidring (A) .... 95 H 3
Waischenfeld (D).........91 E 3
Waizenkirchen (A) ...... 96 D 1
Wakefield (GB) .... 33 E 2
Wałbrzych (PL) .... 120 D 4
Walchensee (D) .... 95 F 3
Walchsee (A) .... 95 H 3
Wałcz (PL) .... 117 E 2
Wald (CH) .... 99 F 2
Wald-Michelbach (D) .. 89 E 3
Waldbröl (D) .... 84 D 5
Waldeck (D) .... 85 F 4
Waldenbuch (D) .... 89 F 5
Waldenburg (D) .... 86 C 5
Waldfischbach-
Burgalben (D)....... 88 D 3
Waldheim (D) .... 86 C 4
Waldkappel (D) .... 85 G 4
Waldkirch (D) .... 94 A 2
Waldkirchen (D).........91 H 5
Waldkraiburg (D) .... 95 H 2
Waldmünchen (D).........91 G 4
Waldsassen (D) ....91 F 3
Waldshut (D) .... 94 B 3
Walenstadt (CH) .... 99 F 2
Waliły-Stacja (PL).......119 H 4
Walim (PL) .... 121 E 5
Wallasey (GB) .... 32 C 3
Walldorf (D) .... 89 E 3
Walldürn (D) .... 89 F 3
Wallenfels (D) ....91 E 2
Wallersdorf (D) .... 95 H 1
Wallerstein (D) .... 89 H 4
Wallingford (GB) .... 35 H 2
Walsall (GB) .... 32 D 5
Walsrode (D)...........81 H 5
Walsum (D) .... 84 C 3
Waltershausen (D) ...... 85 H 4
Walton-
on-the-Naze (GB) ... 37 E 3
Waltrop (D) .... 84 D 3
Wanderup (D)...........81 G 1
Wandlitz (D) .... 86 D 1
Wanfried (D) .... 85 G 4
Wangen im Allgäu (D)... 94 D 3
Wangenbourg (F)........47 G 1
Wangerland-
Hooksiel (D)...........81 F 4
Wangerooge (D) ....81 E 3
Wängi (CH) .... 99 F 2
Wanna (D)...........81 G 3
Wantage (GB) .... 35 G 4
Wanzleben (D) .... 86 A 2
Wapno (PL)...........117 F 5
Warburg (D) .... 85 F 3
Wardenburg (D) ....81 F 5
Ware (GB) .... 36 C 3
Waregem (B) .... 78 B 2
Waremme
(Borgworm) (B) ... 78 D 3
Waren (D) .... 83 E 4
Warendorf (D) .... 84 D 2
Warin (D) .... 82 D 3
Warka (PL) .... 122 D 2
Warkworth (GB)..........31 G 3
Warlubie (PL) .... 117 H 3
Warmensteinach (D) ...91 F 3
Warminster (GB) .... 35 F 3
Warnemünde (D) .... 82 D 2
Warrenpoint (GB) ...... 23 G 4
Warrington (GB) .... 32 C 3
Warstein (D) .... 85 E 3

Warszawa (PL) .... 122 D 1
Warszów (PL) .... 116 B 2
Warta (PL) .... 121 H 2
Warth (A) .... 95 E 4
Warwick (GB) .... 33 E 5
Washington (GB) .... 31 G 4
Wasilków (PL) .... 119 G 4
Wąsosz (PL) .... 121 E 3
Wasselonne (F) .... 47 G 1
Wassen (CH) .... 99 E 3
Wassenaar (NL) .... 76 D 4
Wassenberg (D) .... 84 B 4
Wasseralfingen (D) .... 89 G 4
Wasserbillig (L) .... 79 F 5
Wasserburg am Inn (D) .... 95 H 2
Wassertrüdingen (D) .... 89 H 4
Wassigny (F) .... 40 B 3
Wassy (F) .... 46 D 2
Wasungen (D) .... 85 H 5
Watchet (GB) .... 35 E 3
Waterford / Port Láirge (IRL) .... 25 E 4
Waterloo (B) .... 78 C 2
Waterville (IRL) .... 24 A 4
Watford (GB) .... 36 C 4
Watton (GB) .... 33 H 4
Wattwil (CH) .... 99 F 2
Waulsort (B) .... 78 D 4
Wavre (Waver) (B) .... 78 D 3
Waxweiler (D) .... 88 B 1
Węchadłów (PL) .... 122 C 5
Wedel (D) .... 81 H 4
Weener (D) .... 81 E 5
Weert (NL) .... 79 E 1
Weferlingen (D) .... 86 A 2
Wegberg (D) .... 84 B 4
Wegeleben (D) .... 86 A 2
Weggis (CH) .... 99 E 3
Węgierska Górka (PL) .... 125 F 2
Węgliniec (PL) .... 120 C 3
Węgorzewo (PL) .... 119 E 2
Węgorzyno (PL) .... 116 D 3
Węgrów (PL) .... 123 E 1
Wegscheid (D) .... 96 C 1
Wehr (D) .... 94 A 3
Weibersbrunn (D) .... 89 F 2
Weichshofen (D) .... 95 H 1
Weida (D) .... 86 B 5
Weiden in der Oberpfalz (D) .... 91 F 3
Weikersheim (D) .... 89 G 3
Weil der Stadt (D) .... 89 F 4
Weilburg (D) .... 89 E 1
Weilheim (D) .... 95 F 3
Weilheim an der Teck (D) .... 89 F 5
Weimar (D) .... 86 A 4
Weinfelden (CH) .... 99 F 1
Weingarten (D) .... 94 D 3
Weinheim (D) .... 89 E 3
Weinsberg (D) .... 89 F 3
Weismain (D) .... 91 E 3
Weißbriach (A) .... 96 C 5
Weißenbach am Lech (A) .... 95 E 3
Weißenberg (D) .... 87 F 4
Weißenburg in Bayern (D) .... 91 E 5
Weißenfels (D) .... 86 B 4
Weißenhorn (D) .... 89 G 5
Weißenkirchen in der Wachau (A) .... 97 F 1
Weißensee (D) .... 86 A 4
Weißenstadt (D) .... 91 F 3
Weißkirchen in Steiermark (A) .... 97 E 4
Weißwasser (D) .... 87 F 3
Weitra (A) .... 92 B 5
Weiz (A) .... 97 E 4
Wejherowo (PL) .... 117 G 1
Weldon (B) .... 33 F 5
Wellin (B) .... 78 D 4
Wellingborough (GB) .... 33 F 5
Wellington (GB) .... 35 E 3
Wellington Bridge (IRL) .... 25 F 4
Wells (GB) .... 35 E 2
Wells-next-the-Sea (GB) .... 33 H 4

Wels (A) .... 96 D 2
Welsberg / Monguelfo (I) .... 103 E 1
Welshpool / Trallwng (GB) .... 32 C 4
Weltenburg (D) .... 91 F 5
Welwyn Garden City (GB) .... 36 C 3
Welzheim (D) .... 89 G 4
Welzow (D) .... 87 E 3
Wem (GB) .... 32 C 4
Wemding (D) .... 89 H 4
Wemyss Bay (GB) .... 30 C 2
Wenden (D) .... 85 H 2
Wengen (CH) .... 98 D 3
Wenns (A) .... 95 F 4
Werben (D) .... 82 D 5
Werdau (D) .... 86 C 5
Werder (D) .... 86 C 1
Werdohl (D) .... 84 D 4
Werfen (A) .... 96 C 3
Werl (D) .... 84 D 3
Werlte (D) .... 81 E 5
Wermelskirchen (D) .... 84 C 4
Wermsdorf (D) .... 86 C 4
Wernberg (D) .... 91 F 4
Werne (D) .... 84 D 3
Werneck (D) .... 89 G 2
Werneuchen (D) .... 86 D 1
Wernigerode (D) .... 85 H 3
Wertach (D) .... 95 E 3
Wertheim (D) .... 89 F 2
Werther (D) .... 85 E 2
Wertingen (D) .... 89 H 5
Wesel (D) .... 84 C 3
Wesenberg (D) .... 83 F 4
Wesendorf (D) .... 85 H 1
Wesselburen (D) .... 81 G 2
Wessobrunn (D) .... 95 F 2
West Auckland (GB) .... 31 G 4
West Bridgford (GB) .... 33 E 4
West Kilbride (GB) .... 30 C 2
West Linton (GB) .... 31 E 2
West Looe (GB) .... 34 C 4
West Mersea (GB) .... 37 E 3
West-Terschelling (NL) .... 77 E 4
Westbury (GB) .... 35 F 2
Westendorf (A) .... 95 H 3
Westenholz (D) .... 85 G 1
Westerburg (D) .... 84 D 5
Westerholt (D) .... 81 E 4
Westerland (D) .... 81 F 1
Westerlo (B) .... 78 D 2
Westernbödefeld (D) .... 85 E 4
Westerstede (D) .... 81 E 4
Westhofen (D) .... 89 E 2
Weston Park (GB) .... 32 D 4
Weston-super-Mare (GB) .... 35 E 2
Westport / Cathair na Mart (IRL) .... 22 B 4
Wetherby (GB) .... 33 E 2
Wetlina (PL) .... 127 F 3
Wetter (D) .... 84 D 4
Wetteren (B) .... 78 C 2
Wettin (D) .... 86 B 3
Wettringen (D) .... 84 D 2
Wetwang (GB) .... 33 F 1
Wetzikon (CH) .... 99 E 2
Wetzlar (D) .... 85 E 5
Wexford / Loch Garman (IRL) .... 25 F 3
Weyer (A) .... 97 E 2
Weyhausen (D) .... 85 H 1
Weyhill (GB) .... 35 G 2
Weymouth (GB) .... 38 A 1
Weyregg am Attersee (A) .... 96 C 2
Whaley Bridge (GB) .... 32 D 3
Whitburn (GB) .... 30 D 2
Whitby (GB) .... 31 H 5
Whitchurch (GB) .... 32 C 4
Whitebridge (GB) .... 29 E 4
Whitehaven (GB) .... 30 D 5
Whitehead (GB) .... 23 G 2

Whiteness (GB) .... 26 D 1
Whithorn (GB) .... 30 C 4
Whitland (GB) .... 34 C 1
Whitley Bay (GB) .... 31 G 3
Whitstable (GB) .... 37 E 4
Whittlesey (GB) .... 33 G 4
Wiązów (PL) .... 121 F 4
Wiązowna (PL) .... 122 D 1
Wick (GB) .... 26 B 4
Wickford (GB) .... 36 D 4
Wicklow / Cill Mhantáin (IRL) .... 25 G 2
Wicko (PL) .... 117 F 1
Widawa (PL) .... 121 H 3
Widnes (GB) .... 32 C 3
Więcbork (PL) .... 117 F 4
Wiedenbrück (D) .... 85 E 3
Wiefelstede (D) .... 81 F 4
Wiehe (D) .... 86 A 4
Wiejce (PL) .... 116 D 5
Wiek (D) .... 83 F 1
Wielbark (PL) .... 118 D 3
Wieleń (PL) .... 116 D 5
Wielichowo (PL) .... 121 E 2
Wieliczka (PL) .... 125 G 1
Wielopole Skrzyńskie (PL) .... 127 E 1
Wieluń (PL) .... 121 H 4
Wien (A) .... 97 G 1
Wiener Neudorf (A) .... 97 G 2
Wiener Neustadt (A) .... 97 G 2
Wieruszów (PL) .... 121 G 3
Wierzbica (Chełm) (PL) .... 123 G 3
Wierzbica (Radom) (PL) .... 122 D 3
Wies (A) .... 97 F 5
Wiesau (D) .... 91 F 3
Wiesbaden (D) .... 89 E 1
Wieselburg (A) .... 97 E 2
Wiesenburg (D) .... 86 C 2
Wiesensteig (D) .... 89 G 5
Wiesentheid (D) .... 89 H 2
Wiesenttal (D) .... 91 E 3
Wiesing (A) .... 95 G 3
Wiesloch (D) .... 89 E 3
Wiesmath (A) .... 97 G 3
Wiesmoor (D) .... 81 E 4
Wigan (GB) .... 32 C 2
Wigton (GB) .... 31 E 4
Wigtown (GB) .... 30 C 4
Wijewo (PL) .... 120 D 2
Wijhe (NL) .... 77 F 4
Wil (CH) .... 99 F 2
Wildalpen (A) .... 97 E 3
Wildbad im Schwarzwald (D) .... 89 E 4
Wildeshausen (D) .... 81 F 5
Wildon (A) .... 97 F 4
Wilfersdorf (A) .... 97 H 1
Wilga (PL) .... 123 E 2
Wilhelmsburg (A) .... 97 F 2
Wilhelmshaven (D) .... 81 F 4
Wilhering (A) .... 96 D 1
Wilkau-Haßlau (D) .... 86 C 5
Willebroek (B) .... 78 C 2
Willemstad (NL) .... 76 D 5
Willingen (D) .... 85 E 4
Williton (GB) .... 35 E 3
Wilmslow (GB) .... 32 D 3
Wilnsdorf (D) .... 85 E 5
Wilsdruff (D) .... 86 D 4
Wilster (D) .... 81 G 3
Wilton (GB) .... 35 G 3
Wiltz (L) .... 79 E 4
Wimborne Minster (GB) .... 38 B 1
Wimereux (F) .... 39 G 1
Wincanton (GB) .... 35 F 3
Winchcombe (GB) .... 35 G 1
Winchelsea (GB) .... 36 D 5
Winchester (GB) .... 35 H 4
Windeck (D) .... 84 D 5
Windermere (GB) .... 31 E 5
Windischeschenbach (D) .... 91 F 3
Windischgarsten (A) .... 96 D 3
Windsbach (D) .... 89 H 3
Windsor (GB) .... 36 B 4

Winkleigh (GB) .... 34 D 3
Winklern (A) .... 96 B 5
Winnenden (D) .... 89 F 4
Winnigstedt (D) .... 85 H 2
Winnweiler (D) .... 88 D 3
Winschoten (NL) .... 77 G 2
Winsen (Aller) (D) .... 85 G 1
Winsen (Elbe) (D) .... 81 H 4
Winsford (GB) .... 32 D 3
Wińsko (PL) .... 121 E 3
Winsum (NL) .... 77 G 2
Winterberg (D) .... 85 E 4
Winterswijk (NL) .... 77 G 5
Winterthur (CH) .... 99 E 2
Wintzenheim (F) .... 47 G 2
Wipperfürth (D) .... 84 D 4
Wisbech (GB) .... 33 G 4
Wischhafen (D) .... 81 G 3
Wishaw (GB) .... 30 D 2
Wisła (PL) .... 125 E 2
Wislica (PL) .... 122 D 5
Wismar (D) .... 82 D 3
Wiśniowa (PL) .... 127 E 1
Wissant (F) .... 39 G 1
Wissembourg (F) .... 41 H 5
Wissen (D) .... 84 D 5
Wisznice (PL) .... 123 G 2
Witham (GB) .... 36 D 3
Withernsea (GB) .... 33 G 2
Witkowo (PL) .... 121 F 1
Witney (GB) .... 35 G 1
Witnica (PL) .... 116 C 5
Witten (D) .... 84 D 3
Wittenberg (D) .... 86 C 2
Wittenberge (D) .... 82 D 5
Wittenburg (D) .... 82 C 4
Wittichenau (D) .... 87 E 3
Wittingen (D) .... 85 H 1
Wittlich (D) .... 88 C 2
Wittmund (D) .... 81 E 4
Wittstock (D) .... 83 E 5
Witzenhausen (D) .... 85 G 4
Wiżajny (PL) .... 119 G 1
Władysławowo (PL) .... 117 G 1
Włocławek (PL) .... 117 H 5
Włodawa (PL) .... 123 H 2
Włodowice (PL) .... 122 B 5
Włoszakowice (PL) .... 121 E 2
Włoszczowa (PL) .... 122 C 4
Wöbbelin (D) .... 82 D 4
Woburn (GB) .... 36 B 3
Wodynie (PL) .... 123 E 1
Wodzisław (PL) .... 122 C 5
Wodzisław Śląki (PL) .... 125 E 1
Woensdrecht (NL) .... 78 C 1
Woerden (NL) .... 76 D 5
Wœrth (F) .... 41 H 5
Wohlen (CH) .... 99 E 2
Woippy (F) .... 41 E 5
Wojcieszków (PL) .... 123 F 2
Wojcieszów (PL) .... 120 D 4
Wojnicz (PL) .... 125 H 1
Woking (GB) .... 36 C 4
Wokingham (GB) .... 35 H 2
Wola Krzysztoporska (PL) .... 122 B 3
Wolanów (PL) .... 122 D 3
Wolbrom (PL) .... 122 B 5
Wołczyn (PL) .... 121 G 4
Woldegk (D) .... 83 F 4
Wolfach (D) .... 89 E 5
Wolfegg (D) .... 94 D 3
Wolfen (D) .... 86 B 3
Wolfenbüttel (D) .... 85 H 2
Wolfhagen (D) .... 85 F 4
Wolfratshausen (D) .... 95 G 2
Wolfsberg (A) .... 97 E 5
Wolfsburg (D) .... 85 H 1
Wolgast (D) .... 83 G 3
Wolin (PL) .... 116 B 3
Wölkenstein / Selva (I) .... 103 E 2
Wolkersdorf im Weinviertel (A) .... 97 G 1
Wöllersdorf (A) .... 97 G 2
Wollersheim (D) .... 84 B 5
Wollin (D) .... 86 C 2

Wolmirstedt (D) .... 86 A 2
Wolnzach (D) .... 95 G 1
Wołomin (PL) .... 122 D 1
Wołów (PL) .... 121 E 3
Wolsingham (GB) .... 31 G 4
Wolsztyn (PL) .... 120 D 2
Wolvega (NL) .... 77 F 3
Wolverhampton (GB) .... 32 D 5
Wolverton (GB) .... 35 H 1
Woodbridge (GB) .... 37 E 2
Woodhall Spa (GB) .... 33 G 3
Woodstock (GB) .... 35 H 1
Wooler (GB) .... 31 F 2
Worb (CH) .... 98 D 3
Worbis (D) .... 85 H 4
Worcester (GB) .... 32 D 5
Wörgl (A) .... 95 H 3
Workington (GB) .... 30 D 4
Worksop (GB) .... 33 E 3
Workum (NL) .... 77 E 3
Wörlitz (D) .... 86 C 3
Wormerveer (NL) .... 76 D 4
Wormhout (F) .... 39 H 1
Worms (D) .... 89 E 2
Wörrstadt (D) .... 89 E 2
Wörth am Main (D) .... 89 F 2
Wörth am Rhein (D) .... 89 E 4
Wörth an der Donau (D) .... 91 G 5
Worthing (GB) .... 38 D 1
Woźniki (PL) .... 121 H 5
Wragby (GB) .... 33 F 3
Wrecsam / Wrexham (GB) .... 32 C 4
Wręczyca Wielka (PL) .... 121 H 4
Wrexham / Wrecsam (GB) .... 32 C 4
Wriezen (D) .... 87 E 1
Wrocław (PL) .... 121 E 4
Wronki (PL) .... 117 E 5
Wroughton (GB) .... 35 G 2
Września (PL) .... 121 F 1
Wschowa (PL) .... 120 D 2
Wulfen (D) .... 84 C 3
Wullowitz (A) .... 96 D 1
Wünnenberg (D) .... 85 E 3
Wünsdorf (D) .... 86 D 2
Wunsiedel (D) .... 91 F 3
Wunstorf (D) .... 85 F 1
Wuppertal (D) .... 84 C 4
Würzburg (D) .... 89 G 2
Wurzen (D) .... 86 C 4
Wusterhausen (D) .... 83 E 5
Wusterwitz (D) .... 86 B 1
Wustrow (Bad Doberan) (D) .... 82 D 3
Wustrow (Nordvorpommern) (D) .... 83 E 2
Wuustwezel (B) .... 78 D 1
Wydminy (PL) .... 119 F 2
Wyk auf Föhr (D) .... 81 F 1
Wymondham (GB) .... 33 H 4
Wyrzysk (PL) .... 117 F 4
Wysoka (PL) .... 117 F 4
Wysokie (PL) .... 123 F 4
Wysokie Mazowieckie (PL) .... 119 F 4
Wyszków (PL) .... 119 E 5
Wyszogród (PL) .... 122 C 1

Xàbia / Jávea (E) .... 66 A 5
Xanten (D) .... 84 B 3
Xánthi / Ξάνθη (GR) .... 162 C 2
Xàtiva (E) .... 73 F 4
Xeresa (E) .... 66 A 4
Xert (E) .... 66 A 1
Xerta (E) .... 60 B 5
Xertigny (F) .... 47 F 2
Xerókampos (GR) .... 173 F 4
Xino Neró (E) .... 161 E 3
Xinzo de Limia (E) .... 56 D 4
Xirokámpi (GR) .... 168 D 3
Xirókampos (Ípeiros) (GR) .... 164 D 1
Xirókampos (Nótio Aigaío) (GR) .... 171 F 1

Xirolímni (GR) .... 161 E 4
Xixona (E) .... 73 F 2
Xubia (E) .... 56 C 1
Xunqueira de Ambía (E) .... 56 D 4
Xylaganí (GR) .... 162 D 3
Xylofagou (CY) .... 175 F 4
Xylókastro / Ξυλόκαστρο (GR) .... 165 F 4
Xylópoli (GR) .... 161 G 3
Xylóskalo (GR) .... 172 B 3
Xylotymvou (CY) .... 175 E 3
Xyniáda (GR) .... 165 F 2

Y Drenewydd / Newtown (Powis) (GB) .... 32 C 5
Yablanitsa (BG) .... 158 B 1
Yalova (TR) .... 19 G 2
Yanguas (E) .... 59 E 4
Yarmouth (GB) .... 38 B 1
Ybbs an der Donau (A) .... 97 E 2
Ýdra / Ύδρα (GR) .... 169 F 2
Yebra (E) .... 64 D 3
Yecla (E) .... 73 E 1
Yenne (F) .... 51 E 3
Yeovil (GB) .... 38 A 1
Yepes (E) .... 64 C 4
Yerville (F) .... 39 F 4
Yesa (E) .... 59 G 3
Yeste (E) .... 71 G 3
Ylakiai (LT) .... 204 C 1
Ylämaa (FIN) .... 193 G 3
Ylämylly (FIN) .... 193 G 1
Yläne (FIN) .... 191 F 4
Yli-Ii / Överijo (FIN) .... 185 H 2
Yli-Kärppä (FIN) .... 185 H 1
Yli-Muonio (FIN) .... 180 C 3
Yli Nampa (FIN) .... 181 E 5
Yli-Olhava (FIN) .... 185 H 2
Ylihärmä (FIN) .... 185 F 5
Ylikiiminki / Överkiminge (FIN) .... 185 H 2
Ylistaro (FIN) .... 191 F 1
Ylitornio (Övertorneå) (FIN) .... 185 F 1
Ylivieska (FIN) .... 185 G 4
Ylläsjärvi (FIN) .... 180 D 4
Ylöjärvi (FIN) .... 191 G 3
York (GB) .... 33 E 1
Youghal (IRL) .... 24 D 4
Yoxford (GB) .... 37 E 2
Ypäjä (FIN) .... 191 G 4
Ypáti (GR) .... 165 G 2
Ypéreia (GR) .... 165 F 1
Yport (F) .... 39 E 4
Yppäri (FIN) .... 185 G 3
Ypsonas (CY) .... 174 C 5
Ýpsos (GR) .... 160 A 5
Yssingeaux (F) .... 50 C 4
Ystad (S) .... 199 F 4
Ytterhogdal (S) .... 190 A 2
Yttermalung (S) .... 189 H 4
Yuncos (E) .... 64 B 3
Yunquera (E) .... 74 D 3
Yunquera de Henares (E) .... 64 C 2
Yverdon-les-Bains (CH) .... 98 B 3
Yvetot (F) .... 39 F 4
Yvoir (B) .... 78 D 3
Yvoire (F) .... 51 F 1
Yzeure (F) .... 50 A 1

Zaanstad (NL) .... 76 D 4
Žabalj (SRB) .... 140 C 3
Zabar (H) .... 126 C 5
Žabari (SRB) .... 141 E 5
Zabárdo (BG) .... 162 C 1
Ząbki (PL) .... 122 D 1
Ząbkowice Śląskie (PL) .... 121 F 4
Zablaće (HR) .... 138 A 1
Žabljak (Pljevlja) (MNE) .... 139 F 3

A B C D E F G H I J K L M N O P Q R S T U V W X Y Z

A B C D E F G H I J K L M N O P Q R S T U V W X Y Z

Amsterdam 266	Den Haag 282	Helsinki...........297	Milano...........311	Sevilla 329
Antwerpen........268	Dijon 283	Istanbul...........297	Monaco	Sofia.............330
Athína 269	Dresden 284	København 298	Monte-Carlo ...312	Stockholm 331
Barcelona.........270	Dublin 285	Lausanne 299	München 313	Strasbourg........332
Basel 271	Dubrovnik 286	Leipzig............299	Nantes...........314	Stuttgart..........333
Belfast 272	Düsseldorf........287	Liège 300	Napoli 315	Torino 334
Berlin 273	Edinburgh 288	Lille..............301	Nice 316	Toulouse..........335
Bern 274	Essen 289	Lisboa 302	Nürnberg 317	Venezia 336
Bordeaux 275	Firenze 290	Liverpool 303	Oslo 318	Warszawa........337
Bratislava 276	Frankfurt-	London 304	Palermo 319	Wien.............338
Bremen...........277	am-Main 291	Luxembourg......306	Paris 320	Zagreb............340
Brugge 278	Genève 292	Lyon..............307	Porto 324	Zürich 341
Bruxelles/	Genova 293	Madrid 308	Praha 325	
Brussel........279	Göteborg 294	Manchester 309	Roma.............326	
Bucureşti 280	Hamburg 295	Marseille..........310	Rotterdam 327	
Budapest 281	Hannover 296		Salzburg 328	

AMSTERDAM

0   1,2 km

(▲ △) **Noordwijk** aa

Noor

(▲) **Katwijk** aan Ze

Katwijk

(▲) **Wassena**

(▲) **SCHEVENINGEN**

De Kieviet

(Ⓟ) **DEN HAAG**
('S-GRAVENHAGE)

Kijkduin

Voorbu

Loosduinen

Rijswijk

Monster   Poeldijk

Harwich

's-Gravenzande

Kingston-upon-Hull

**Hoek van
Holland**

Naaldwijk   De Lier

Westerlee

Maasdijk   Honselersdijk

Maasland

Europoort

Maasvlakte 2

IJSSELMEER
MARKERMEER
AMSTERDAM
HAARLEM
UTRECHT
ROTTERDAM
LEIDEN
DELFT
HILVERSUM
Den Helder
De Schooten
Oosterland
Stevinsluizen
(Wieringen)
Hippolytushoef
Koudum
Molkwerum
Julianadorp
Breezand
Gelderse Buurt
Amstelmeer
Wieringermeer
Wieringerwerf
Stavoren
Warns
Bakhuizen
Rijs
Sondel
Nijemirdum
Oudemirdum
Groote Keeten
Anna Paulowna
Callantsoog
't Zand
't Zwanenwater
Slootdorp
Wieringerwaard
Middenmeer
Polder
Schagerbrug
St.-(Zijpe)
Maarensvlotbrug
Schagen
Barsingerhorn
Kolhorn
Medemblik
Petten
Hondsbosse Zeewering
St.-Maarten
Burgervlotbrug
Winkel
Opperdoes
Zijdewind
Dirkshorn
(Harenkarspel)
Nieuwe-Niedorp
Twisk
Onderdijk
Andijk
Camperduin
Groet
Warmenhuizen
Oudkarspel
Hoogwoud
Abbekerk
Midwoud
Wervershoof
(Drechterland)
Enkhuizen
Sijbekarspel
Opmeer
(Noorder-Koggenland)
Zwaagdijk
Hoogkarspel
Nibbixwoud
Bovenkarspel
(Stede-Broec)
Schoorl
Langedijk
Spanbroek
Wadway
Wognum
Westwoud
Zwaag
De Streek
Bergen
Koedijk
Broek op L.
Obdam
Heerhugowaard
Spierdijk
Blokker
Hem
Venhuizen
Markerwaarddijk
Urk
Bergen aan Zee
St.-Pancras
Hensbroek
Berkhout
(Wester-Koggenland)
Schellinkhout
Oosterleek
Wijdenes
Oterleek
Egmond aan Zee
Egmond a/d Hoef
Oudorp
Ursem
Avenhorn
Hoorn
Heiloo
Alkmaar
Schermer
Schermerhorn
Scharwoude
NOORD-HOLLAND
Ketelbrug
Egmond-Binnen
Grootschermer
Swifterbant
Limmen
Castricum aan Zee
Akersloot
Graft
De Rijp
Westbeemster
De Beemster
Oosthuizen
(Zeevang)
Middenbeemster
West-Graftdijk
Oost-Graftdijk
Alkmaarder-meer
Castricum
Uitgeest
Houtribsluizen
Lelystad
OOSTELIJK
Heemskerk
Edam
Volendam
Krommenie
Jisp
Wormer
Wormerveer
Wijk aan Zee
Beverwijk
Zaandijk
Purmerend
Lelystad Haven
Oostvaardersdijk
Newcastle
Assendelft
Velsertunnel
Purmerland
Ilpendam
Marken
Kerkbuurt
Velsen
Westzaan
Koog a/d Z.
Broek in Waterland
Monnickendam
Gouwzee
Oostvaardersplassen
Aviodrome
FLEVOLAND
IJmuiden
Zaanstad
Oostzaan
Landsmeer
Zuiderwoude
De Vaart
Almere-Buiten
Nationaal Park Zuid-Kennemerland
Driehuis
Santpoort
Zaandam
Uitdam
Bloemendaal
Spaarndam
Coentunnel
Zunderdorp
Overveen
Almere
Schellingwoude
IJmeer
Bloemendaal aan Zee
Haarlemmerliede
IJ-Tunnel
Durgerdam
Almere-Stad
ZUIDELIJK-FLEVOLAND
Zwanenburg
Trekkersveld
Harderwijk
Zandvoort
Aerdenhout
Heemstede
Osdorp
Vijfhuizen
Badhoevedorp
Cruquius
Diemen
Duivendrecht
Muiden
Muiderberg
Almere-Haven
Almere-Hout
Gooimeer
Hoge Vaart
Zeewolde
Amstelveen
Weesp
Hollandse Brug
Naarden
Huizen
Stichtse Brug
Vogelenzang
Bennebroek
Hoofddorp
Schiphol
Ouderkerk
Amsterdam Zuidoost
Eemmeer
Horst
De Zilk
Hillegom
Haarlemmermeer
Abcoude
Nigtevecht
Bussum
Nederhorst den Berg
Laren
Blaricum
Eem
Spakenburg
Noordwijkerhout
Keukenhof
Nieuw-Vennep
polder
Aalsmeer
Uithoorn
Baambrugge
Vreeland
't Gooi
Eemnes
Bunschoten
Lisse
Abbenes
Rijsenhout
Westeinder Plassen
Kudelstaart
Vinkeveense Plassen
's-Graveland
Kortenhoef
Eembrugge
Nijkerk
Sassenheim
Voorhout
Leimuiden
Vinkeveen
Loenen
Oud-Loosdrecht
Nieuw-Loosdrecht
Baarn
Voorthuizen
Kaag
Warmond
Kagerplassen
Oude-Wetering
Aarkanaal
Kromme Mijdrecht
Wilnis
Loosdrechtse Plassen
Soestdijk
Hoevelaken
Terschuur
Rijnsburg
Braassemermeer
Langeraar
Nieuwveen
Mijdrecht
(De Ronde Venen)
Nieuwer-ter-Aa
Breukelen
Breukeleveen
Lage Vuursche
Soest
Hoogland
Oegstgeest
Roelofarendsveen
(Kaag en Braassem)
Noordeinde
Tienhoven
Hollandsche Rading
Maartensdijk
Amersfoort
Barneveld
Hoogmade
Woubrugge
Ter Aar
Noorden
(Stichtse Vecht)
Maarssen
Soestduinen
Bilthoven
Den Dolder
Leiderdorp
Koudekerk
Nieuwkoop
Nieuwkoopse Plassen
Kockengen
Westbroek
Oud-Zuilen
Bosch en Duin
Centrum
Achterveld
Leusden-Zuid
Alphen a/d Rijn
De Haar
Haarzuilens
Soesterberg
De Bilt
Voorschoten
Zoeterwoude
Rijndijk
Kamerik
Meije
Zegveld
Vleuten
De Meern
Woudenberg
Renswoude
ZUID-HOLLAND
Hazerswoude-Dorp
Zwammerdam
Bodegraven
Woerden
Harmelen
Leidsche Rijn
Zeist
Stompwijk
Benthuizen
Boskoop
Nieuwerbrug
(Bodegraven-Reeuwijk)
Bunnik
Kromme Rijn
Maarn
Scherpenzeel
Ederveen
Leidschendam
Reeuwijk Dorp
Linschoten
Odijk
Driebergen-Rijsenburg
Doorn
Maarsbergen
Overberg
Zoetermeer
Waarder
Montfoort
Hollandse IJssel
Nieuwegein
Houten
Nationaal Park Utrechtse Heuvelrug
Veenendaal
Waddinxveen
Reeuwijk
Driebruggen
Reeuwijkse Plassen
Oudewater
IJsselstein
Werkhoven
Langbroek
Leersum
Amerongen
Moerkapelle
Pijnacker
Bleiswijk
Gouda
Benschop
Lopikerkapel
Schalkwijk
Vianen
Cothen
Wijk bij Duurstede
Elst
Rhenen
Zevenhuizen
Polsbroekerdam
Hagestein
Berkel en Rodenrijs
Moordrecht
Gouderak
Haastrecht
Polsbroek
Vlist
Lopik
Maurik
Eck en Wiel
Bergschenhoek
(Zuidplas)
Stolwijk
Cabauw
Lexmond
Rijswijk
Lienden
Hillegersberg
Nieuwerkerk
Schoonhoven
Jaarsveld
Hei- en Boeicop
Everdingen
Culemborg
Beusichem
Ommeren
Kesteren
Krimpenerwaard
Berkenwoude
Bergambacht
Ammerstol
Langerak
Ameide
(Zederik)
Meerkerk
Nieuwpoort
Zijderveld
Asch
Zoelen
Rijnkanaal

ANTWERPEN

0 560 m

Antwerpen city map

Hoek van Holland

GENT ST. NIKLAAS
HULST

LINKEROEVER

ZANDVLIET STABROEK
ROTTERDAM BREDA
GOES BERGEN OP ZOOM

TURNHOUT
EINDHOVEN
LIÈGE HASSELT

MAS
Felixhuis
Hessenhuis
Begijnhof
Huis van Roosmalen
Zuiderpershuis
MHKA
Volkshuis « Help U Zelve »
FotoMuseum
ZUID
De vijf werelddelen
Koninklijk Museum voor Schone Kunsten
Nieuw Gerechtshof
Bolivarplaats
Gillisplaats
Lambermontplaats
Marnixplaats

KATHEDRAAL
St-Jakobskerk
Opera
Astrid
Centraal
Diamant
Aquatopia
Dierentuin
Diamondland

BORGERHOUT

STADSPARK
Plantin

KONING ALBERT PARK

WIJK ZURENBORG

BERCHEM

STUIVENBERGPLEIN

Park
Spoor Noord

KIELPARK

BOELAARPARK

A 112
R 1

BRUXELLES/BRUSSEL
MECHELEN

Regional map

Terneuzen
Lamswaarde
Prosperpolder
Berendrecht
Stabroek
Kapellen
Maria-ter-Heide
Oostmalle
Beerse
Oud-Turnho...

Vogelvaarde
Graauw
Doel
Hoevenen
Brasschaat
Westmalle
Malle
Vlimmeren
Vosselaar
N 12

Zaamslag
Ter Hole
Nieuw-Namen
Kieldrecht
Ekeren
St.-Job-in-'t-Goor
Zoersel
Wechelderzande
Gierle
Tielen
N 19
Kasterle

Spui
Axel
Hulst
Clinge
Meerdonk
Grote Geule
Petroleumhaven
Schoten (ANVERS)
Schilde
Lille
R 10

Absdale
De Klinge
Kallo
Verrebroek
ANTWERPEN
Oelegem
Poederlee
Lichtaart
Ten Aard

Heikant
Paal
Melsele
Zwijndrecht
Deurne
Halle
Zandhoven
Vorselaar
Grobbendonk
Herentals
Geel

Zuiddorp
Koewacht
St.-Gillis-Waas
Beveren
Wijnegem
Wommelgem
Massenhoven
Pulle
Bouwel
O.L.V. Olen

Overslag
Kemzeke
Vrasene
Borgerhout
Berchem
Borsbeek
Ranst
Emblem
Nijlen
Olen

Wachtebeke
Moerbeke
St-Pauwels
Nieuwerkerken-Waas
Hoboken
Mortsel
Broechem
Herenthout

St.-Niklaas (St. Nicolas)
Belsele
Haasdonk
Kruibeke
Wilrijk
Boechout
Kessel
Bevel
Grobbendonk

Sinaai
De Ster
Bazel
Hemiksem
Edegem
Kontich
Lier (Lierre)
Berlaar
Itegem
Morkhoven

Zevenneren
Eksaarde
Temse (Tamise)
Schelle
Aartselaar
Lint
Waarloos
Koningshooikt
Zoerle-Parwijs
Olen

Lokeren
Waasmunster
Hamme
Steendorp
Wintam
Niel
Reet
Rumst
Duffel
St.-Katelijne-W (MALINES)
Heist-op-den-Berg
Hulshout

GENT GAND
Zele
Grembergen
Ruisbroek
Boom
Willebroek
Walem
Beerzel
Westmeerbeek
Herselt

Dendermonde (Termonde)
Baasrode
St.-Amands
Puurs
Breendonk
Tisselt
Leest
Bonheiden
Booischot
Aarschot

MECHELEN
Muizen
Rijmenam
Keerbergen
Begijnendijk
Langdorp
Zichem

SCHELDE
Rupel
Nete
Albert Kanaal

ATHÍNA

0 2 km

KORINTHOS · ELEFSINA · ATTIKI ODOS · FILI · AG.-TRIADA · THESSALONIKI LAMIA

ACHARNÉS · A. LIÓSSIA · SKA · KIFISIÁ · IRÁKLIO · MAROÚSSI · PETROÚPOLI · N. LIÓSSIA · N. IONÍA · N. IÓNIA · FILOTHÉI · HALÁNDRI · DAFNÍ · E 94 · PERISTÉRI · PSIHIKÓ · N. PSIHIKÓ · HOLARGÓS · HAÍDARI · MICHELIN · EGÁLEO · G. VARVÁRA · AKRÓPOLI · KAISARIANÍ · NÍKEA · KALITHÉA · MOSHÁTO · N. SMIRNI · ÓROS YMITTÓS · ILIOÚPOLI · ARGIROÚPOLI · PEIRAIÁS · Averoff · PALEÓ FÁLIRO · AMFITHÉA · KALAMÁKI ALIMOS

GLYFÁDA, SOÚNIO, VOULIAGMÉNI · VOULIAGMÉNI, SOÚNIO

N. ÉVVOIA / N. ΕΥΒΟΙΑ

N. SKÝ / N. ΣΚΥ

Chalkida / Χαλκίδα

Thíva / Θήβα

ATHÍNA / ΑΘΗΝΑ

PEIRAIÁS / ΠΕΙΡΑΙΑΣ

ATTIKI / ΑΤΤΙΚΗ

Glyfáda / Γλυφάδα

Vouliagméni / Βουλιαγμένη

Lávrio / Λαύριο

Akr. Soúnio / Ακρ. Σούνιο

Kárystos / Κάρυστος

N. Kéa / Ν. Κέα

BARCELONA

TERRASSA / TARRASA   GIRONA   PUIGCERDÀ / VIC

0 — 1750 m

TERRASSA / TARRASA
MATARÓ

Temple del Sagrat Cor
Parc Creueta del Coll
Parc Güell
Hospital de Sant Pau
SAGRADA FAMILIA
CASA MILÀ
Monestir Santa Maria de Pedralbes
Ciutat Universitària
Catedral
Arenas de Barcelona (Museu del Rock)
Parc de la Ciutadella
Parc Zoologic
VILA OLÍMPICA
LA BARCELONETA
MAR MEDITERRANIA
Palau Sant Jordi
Castell de Montjuic
Estadi Olímpic Lluis Companys
Auditori Sot del Migdia
Fira de Mostres Montjuïc-2

VALLBONA
SANTA COLOMA DE GRAMENET
NOU BARRIS
SANT ANDREU
SANTA ADRIA DE BESÒS
BADALONA
TIBIDABO
VALLVIDRERA
COLLSEROLA
SARRIÀ
SANT GERVASI DE CASSOLES
SANT JUST DESVERN
LES CORTS
SANTS
MONTJUÏC

Poble Espanyol . . . . E
Museu Nacional d'Art de Catalunya . . . . M⁴
Museu d'Arqueològia . . . . M⁵
Teatre Grec . . . . T¹
Fundació Joan Miró . . . . W
Pavelló Mies van der Rohe . . . . Z

N

CASTELLDEFELS   CASTELLDEFELS SITGES   CASTELLDEFELS SITGES   BALEARES, GENOVA

Sabadell
Mataró
Badalona
BARCELONA
L'Hospitalet
Sant Cugat del Vallès
Montcada i Reixac
Cerdanyola
Rubí
Martorell
Molins de Rei
Sant Feliu
Sant Boi
Gavà
Castelldefels
Vilafranca del Penedès
Sant Sadurní d'Anoia
Esparreguera
Olesa de Montserrat
El Prat de Llobregat
El Masnou
Premià de Mar
Vilassar de Mar
Montgat
Argentona
Mollet
Montmeló
Ripollet
La Llagosta
Sant Vicenç dels Horts
Viladecans

Costa de
D O R

BASEL

0 ___ 200 m

N

City map labels

KARLSRUHE, FREIBURG IM B., WEIL AM RHEIN

MULHOUSE

KANNENFELD-PARK

JOHANNESKIRCHE

ST. JOHANNS-PARK

MESSE

CLARAMATTE

KONGRESS-ZENTRUM

St. Antonius-Kirche

Skulpturhalle

Peterskirche

Fischmarktpl.

Café Spitz

Theodorskirche

Botanischer Garten

Pharmazie-Historisches Museum

Andreaspl.

Naturhistorisches Museum

Spalentor

Holbeinbrunnen

Marktpl.

Museum der Kulturen

Jüdisches Museum der Schweiz

Gemsberg

Heuberg

Spalenberg

Münster

Unterer Heuberg

Barfüsserpl.

Musikmuseum

Historisches Museum Basel

Antikenmuseum

Cartoon-museum

Museum für Gegenwartskunst

Basler Papiermühle

Spielzeug Welten Museum

Fastnachtsbrunnen

Schweizerisches Architekturmuseum

KUNSTMUSEUM

St-Alban-Berg

PAULUSKIRCHE

Haus zum Kirschgarten

SCHÜTZENMATT-PARK

VIVARIUM

ZOOLOGISCHER GARTEN

ROSENFELDPARK

CHRISTOPH MERIAN PARK

OBERWIL / BELFORT

REINACH

KUTSCHENMUSEUM

DELEMONT, BERN, LUZERN, ZÜRICH

MULHOUSE, BELFORT

ZÜRICH, BERN, LUZERN

GRENZACH

MUSEUM TINGUELY

Unterer Rheinweg

Oberer Rheinweg

Mittlere Rheinbrücke

Rhein Sprung

Wettsteinbr.

Regional map labels

BASEL

St. Louis

Huningue

Allschwil

Binningen

Birsfelden

Muttenz

Pratteln

Münchenstein

Reinach

Liestal

Lörrach

Weil a. Rh.

Riehen

Grenzach-Wyhlen

Rheinfelden

Bad Säckingen

Laufenburg

Waldshut-Tiengen

Zurzach

Brugg

Baden

Wettingen

BASEL-LAND

Schopfheim

Todtmoos

SCHAFFHAUSEN

RHEIN

Goetheanum

BELFAST

FERNILL HOUSE PEOPLE'S MUSEUM — ZOOLOGICAL GARDENS, CASTLE — ULSTER FOLK AND TRANSPORT MUSEUM — CARRICKFERGUS LONDONDERRY/DERRY

0   200 m
0   200 yards

CLIFTON HOUSE

Sinclair Seamen's Church

St Anne's Cathedral

War Memorial

Oh Yeah Music Centre

Black Box Theater

Custom House

Albert Memorial Clock Tower

Lagan Lookout Center

CASTLECOURT SHOPPING CENTRE

Tesco

ST GEORGE'S PARISH

Linen Hall Library

LINEN WAREHOUSE

Waterfront Hall

ROYAL BELFAST ACADEMICAL INSTITUTE

Church House

City Hall

NORTH OF COURTS OF JUSTICE

Grand Opera House

Donegall Sq.

ST-GEORGE'S MARKET

YORKSHIRE HOUSE

GREAT VICTORIA

Crown Liquor Saloon

St Malachy's Church

ULSTER HALL

GOLDEN MILE

NORTH OF IRELAND SPORTS GROUND

University

Queen's University

Palm House

ELMWOOD HALL

Ulster Museum

Tropical Ravine Botanic

FRIAR'S BUSH GRAVEYARD

Botanic Gardens

NEWCASTLE

DUBLIN — LISBURN

ANTRIM MOUNTAINS

Benmore or Fair Head

Murlough Bay

Torr Head

Runabay Head

Ballypatrick Forest

Cushendun

Knocknacarry

Glendun

Ossian's Grave

Cushendall

Glenariff or Waterfoot

Red Bay

Garron Point

Glenariff Forest Park

Waterfalls

Big Trosk

Dungonnell Dam

Collin Top

Carnlough

Carnlough Bay

Glenarm

The Sheddings

Carnagee

Feystown

Carnalbanagh Sheddings

Ballygalley Head

Carncastle

Ballygalley

Drains Bay

Slemish Mountain

LARNE

Agnew's Hill

Moorfields

Shoptown

Kilwaughter

Millbrook

Larne

Isle of Muck

Portmuck

Mullaghboy

Millbay

Island Magee

Ballyboley Forest

Magheramorne

The Gobbins

Glynn

Larne Lough

Ballyeaston

Glenoe

Five Corners

Ballynure

Ballycarry

Black Head

Ballyclare

Doagh

Straid

Milebush

Whitehead

Antrim

Parkgate

Woodburn

Eden

Templepatrick

Mossley

Monkstown

Carrickfergus

Patterson's Spade Mill

Greenisland

Belfast Lough

Lyle

Hyde Park

Whiteabbey

Helen's Bay

Grey Point

Bangor

Groomsport

Newtownabbey

Squires Hill

Holywood

Crawfordsburn

Cookstown

Coagh

Newport Trench

Aldergrove

Ardmore Point

BELFAST AIRPORT

The Diamond

NORTH-DOWN

Cultra

Stormont Parliament House

Tullyhogue

Kilsally

Ardboe

Killycolpy

Nutt's Corner

Clady

Crumlin

Divis

Craigantlet

Six Road Ends

NEAGH

Gartree Point

Rams Island

Glenavy

Legoniel

BELFAST

Stormont

Dundonald

Scrabo Hill

Newtownards

Stewartstown

Mountjoy

Washing Bay

Lough Beg

Stoneyford

Hannahstown

Newtownbreda

Comber

Newmills

Coalisland

Aughamullan

CRAIGAVON

Ardmore Point

Aghalee

Dunmurry

Moneyreagh

Mount Stewart Gardens

Temple of the Winds

Dungannon

Maghery

Milltown

Charlestown

Derrytrasna

Aghagallon

Maghaberry

Lambeg

Lisburn

Drumbeg

Lagan Valley

Carryduff

Ballygowan

Lisbane

Ardmillan

Moygashel

Laghey Corner

Peatlands

Derryadd

Soldierstown

Magheralin

Drumbo

Grey Abbey

Wildfowl and Wetlands Trust

Nendrum Monastery

Mahee Island

The Argory

Derrykeevan

Derryanvil

Moira

Mazetown

B23

The Temple

Baileysmill

Rowallane Gardens

Balloo Cross Roads

Kircubbin

Strangford Lough

Moy

Charlemont

Tullyroan

Drummanor

Dollingstown

Taughblane

Hillsborough

Boardmills

Lisburn

Annahilt

Saintfield

Raffrey

Derryboye

Islandmore

Benburb

Ardress House

Drumannor

Lurgan

Waringstown

Kilntown

Donaghcloney

Wells Cross

Clare

Dromore

Ballykee

The Spa

Ballynahinch

Crossgar

Killyleagh

Blackwatertown

Aghinlig

Loughgall

Craigavon

Portadown

Moyallan

Lawrencetown

Blackskull

Waringsford

Dromara

Slieve Croob

Listooder

Delamont

Audley's Castle

Armagh

Richhill

Kilmore

Clare

Seapatrick

Dromore

Ballyalton

Castle Ward

Milford

Hamiltonsbawn

Tandragee

Gilford

Banbridge

Loughinisland

Inch Abbey

Saul

Churchtown

Leslie Hill

Killeen

Laurelvale

Scarva

Corbet Milltown

BANBRIDGE

Kilkinamurry

Legananny

Dolmen

Quoile Countryside Centre

Downpatrick

Struell Wells

Markethill

Gosford Forest Park

Eleven Lane Ends

Poyntz Pass

Loughbrickland

Katesbridge

Lowtown

Annadorn

Ballyhornan

BERLIN

0   1 km

BERLIN-TEGEL

Flughafen Tegel

A 111 / E 26

Hohenzollernkanal

VOLKSPARK JUNGFERNHEIDE
Jungfernheideteich

Heckerdamm

SIEMENSSTADT

AB. DR. CHARLOTTENBURG

Schlossgarten
SCHLOSS CHARLOTTENBURG
SCHLOSSPARK CHARLOTTENBURG

M16
M13

WEST-END

Funkturm
Messegelände

Halensee

Hubertussee
Delbrückstr.

Königsallee

PREUSSEN PARK

AB. KR. WILMERSDORF

HEIDELBERGER PL.

SCHMARGENDORF

VOLKSPARK WILMERSDORF

Kurt-Schumacher-Damm
Saatwinkler Damm

Hollän0erstraße

VOLKSPARK REHBERGE
GOETHEPARK

Gedenkstätte Plötzensee
Maria Regina Martyrum

WESTHAFEN

Westhafenkanal

JUNGFERNHEIDE

TIERGARTEN
FRITZ-SCHLOSS-PARK

Spree

Neuer See

TIERGARTEN

ZOOLOGISCHER GARTEN

LIETZENSEE PARK
Lietzensee

Kurfürstendamm

WEDDING

GESUNDBRUNNEN

VOLKSPARK HUMBOLDTHAIN

SCHÖNHAUSER ALLEE

PANKOW

WEISSENSEE

ERNST-THÄLMANN-PARK

Volkspark Friedrichshain

EUROPA-SPORT-PARK BERLIN

MONBIJOU-PARK   Alexanderplatz

PERGAMONMUSEUM
NEUES MUSEUM
Unter den Linden
Brandenburger Tor
Pl. der Republik
Str. des 17. Juni

FRANKFURTER TOR

Berlin-Museum
JÜDISCHES MUSEUM
WALDECK-PARK

TEMPODROM
Ida-Wolff-Platz

Deutsches Technikmuseum

KREUZBERG

Landwehrkanal

TREPTOW

Platz der Luftbrücke

VOLKSPARK HASENHEIDE
Hasenheide

NEUKÖLLN

M13 Bröhan Museum
M16 Sammlung Berggruen

A 100 173

BERLIN

POTSDAM

Sanssouci

Spandau
Staaken

Reinickendorf
BERLIN-TEGEL

Pankow
Weißensee
Hohenschönh.

Marzahn

Hellersdorf
Neuenhagen

Lichtenberg

Treptow

Köpenick

Steglitz
Zehlendorf

BERLIN-BRANDENBURG

Strausberg

Erkner

BERN

0   150 m

N

BIEL/BIENNE

SOLOTHURN, BASEL, ZÜRICH

SOLOTHURN, BASEL, ZÜRICH

LANGNAU, LUZERN, THUN, INTERLAKEN

LANGNAU, LUZERN, THUN, INTERLAKEN

LANGNAU, LUZERN, THUN, INTERLAKEN

MURTEN, NEUCHÂTEL, AARBERG

GENÈVE, LAUSANNE, FRIBOURG, AARBERG

LÄNGGASSE

GROSSE SCHANZE

Botanischer Garten

Kunstmuseum

KURSAAL SCHÄNZLI

Rosengarten

NYDEGGKIRCHE

Nydeggbrücke

Französische Kirche

Kornhauspl.

Rathaus

Nydeggasse

Heiliggeist-Kirche

Käfigturm

Bärenplatz

Marktgasse
Zeitglockenturm

Kramgasse

Gerechtigkeitsgasse

Bern Show

Bundeshaus

Einsteinhaus

Münster

Erlacherhof

Junkerngasse

Bärenpark

Einsteinhaus

Münsterplatz

Plattform

Bundes-terrasse

CASINO

KLEINE SCHANZE

MATTENHOF

Schweizerisches Alpines Museum

Kunsthalle

Aare

KIRCHENFELD

Helvetiaplatz

Bernisches historisches Museum

Museum für Kommunikation

Naturhistorisches Museum

ENGLISCHE KIRCHE

SULGENBACH

THUN, BELP

Vue des Alpes

Cernier Dombresson

Fontaines Savagnier

Boudevilliers

Valangin

Peseux

NEUCHÂTEL

Auvernier

Hauterive

Marin-Epagnier

Cortaillod

Cudrefin

la Sauge

Portalban

Chabrey

Salavaux

Vallamand

Villars-le-Gd

Avenches

Faoug

Courgevaux

Dompierre

Domdidier

Courtion

Courtepin

Payerne

Mannens

Noréaz

FRIBOURG

Bieler See

St. Petersinsel

la Neuveville

le Landeron

St. Blaise

Gampelen

Ins

Müntschemier

Treiten

Fräschels

Kerzers

Mt Vully

Sugiez

Môtier

Murten

Lac de Moret

Gempenach

Salvenach

Liebistorf

Gurmels

Ulmiz

Gümmenen

Mühleberg

Frauenkappelen

Wohlen

Niederwangen

Flamatt

Wünnewil

Überstorf

Oberbalm

Niederscherli

Zimmerwald

Schwarzenburg

Rohrbach

Tafers

Tentlingen

Lyss

Aarberg

Seedorf

Radelfingen

Münchenbuchsee

Kirchlindach

Meikirch

Murzelen

Zollikofen

Bolligen

Ostermundigen

BERN

Köniz

Muri

Gurten

Belp

Kehrsatz

Münsingen

Wichtrach

Kiesen

Steffisburg

Burgdorf

Hindelbank

Bäriswil

Krauchthal

Hasle

Ramsei

Trachselwald

Lützelflüh

Rüegsau

Sumiswald

Lüderenalp

Wasen

Affoltern

Huttwil

Eriswil

Dürrenroth

Häusernmoos

Weier

Ahorn

Langnau

Trub

Trubschachen

Bärau

Signau

Schüpbach

Röthenbach

Eggiwil

Schangnau

Hohgant

Innereriz

BORDEAUX

0 — 200 m

LES CHARTRONS

LA BASTIDE

VIEUX BORDEAUX

MÉRIADECK

PEY-BERLAND

Darwin

Jardin botanique

Parc aux Angéliques

Jardin public

Petit Hôtel Labottière
Muséum d'histoire naturelle
Palais Gallien
Cité mondiale
Cours Xavier Arnozan
CAPC- Musée d'Art contemporain
Monument aux Girondins
Esplanade des Quinconces
Basilique St-Seurin
Site archéologique de St-Seurin
MAISON DU VIN DE BORDEAUX
Notre-Dame
Hôtel Acquart
Grand Théâtre
Place de la Bourse
Miroir d'eau
Cours de l'Intendance
Hôtel Pichon
Passage Sarget
Musée national des Douanes
Bordeaux Patrimoine mondial
Porte Dijeaux
Pl. Gambetta
Square Vinet
Pl. St-Pierre
M. des Arts décoratifs
Centre Jean-Moulin
Galerie des Beaux-Arts
St-Bruno
HÔTEL DU DÉPARTEMENT
CITÉ MUNICIPALE
Palais Rohan
St-André
Tour Pey-Berland
Porte Cailhau
Pl. du Palais
BORDEAUX MONUMENTAL
Musée des Beaux-Arts
St-Paul-les-Dominicains
Maison de Jeanne de Lartigue
Hôtel de Région
Espl. Charles de Gaulle
Musée d'Aquitaine
PALAIS DES SPORTS
Porte de Bourgogne
Tribunal de grande instance
ÉCOLE NATIONALE DE LA MAGISTRATURE
Porte de la Grosse Cloche
Flèche St-Michel
Pl. Duburg
St-Michel
CENTRE ANDRÉ MALRAUX
THÉÂTRE PORT DE LA LUNE
Pl. des Capucins
Abbatiale Ste-Croix
I.U.T. MONTAIGNE
Porte d'Aquitaine
Musée des Compagnons du Tour de France
St-Jean

GARONNE
Pont de Pierre

Cimetière de la Chartreuse

Inset map

St-Aubin-de-Médoc
Blanquefort
MICHELIN
St-Loubès
St-Michel-de-Fronsac
St-Médard-en-Jalles
Ste-Eulalie
St-Sulpice-et-Cameyrac
Bassens
Eysines
Bruges
Carbon-Blanc
Le Bouscat
Lormont
Yvrac
Montussan
Beychac-et-Caillau
BORDEAUX
Caudéran
Cenon
Artigues-près-B.
Pompignac
Mérignac
BORDEAUX-MÉRIGNAC
Floirac
Talence
Bouliac
Carignan-de-Bordeaux
Sallebœuf
Pessac
Bègles
Camarsac
Gradignan
Villenave-d'Ornon
Latresne
Créon
Cénac

BRATISLAVA

0   2 km

BRNO, PRAHA

RAČA
VAJNORY
VÝCHODNÉ NÁDRAŽIE
TRNAVA TRENČÍN
NITRA

LAMAČ
DÚBRAVKA
KRASŇANY
Račianska
Vajnorská
JURAJOV DVOR
TRNÁVKA
NOVÉ MESTO
KRAMÁRE
KOLIBA
Kamzík 440
Vajnorská
Rožňavská
cesta
KUTIKY
VINOHRADY
Brnianska
Pražská
Vajnorská
Trnavská
Trnavská cesta
ŠTRKOVEC
OSTREDKY
HORSKÝ PARK
Sancová
Račianska
POŠEŇ
SLÁVIČIE ÚDOLIE
Karloveská
Ružinov
KARLOVA VES
NIVY
Gagarinova
PRIEVOZ
STARÉ MESTO
Karadžičova
Prievozska
Most SNP
VRAKUŇA
Nábr. gen. L. Svobodu
DUNAJ
Einsteinova
Malý Dunaj
Slovnaftská
PODUNAJSKÉ BISKUPICE
WIEN
E 65
E 58
COLNICA
E 58
DVORY
cesta
PETRŽALKA
DUNAJ
svornosti
Bratská
Panonska
Panonska
Kutlíkova
ÖSTERREICH
LÚKY
Pajštúnska
BERG
KITTSEE
Dolnozemská cesta
EISENSTADT
GYÖR, BUDAPEST

KOMÁRNO
E 575

BREMEN

0   1 km

BREMERHAVEN

A 27 / E 234

WORPSWEDE

LILIENTHAL

Oslebshauser Heerstr.
OSLEBSHAUSER PARK
GRÖPELINGEN

Trupe
Truperdeich
Truperdeich
Wümme

BORGFELD

Maschinenfleet
Waller Feldmarksee
Kleine Wümme
Harjes Wettern
Alte Wettern
Clats Wettern

Torfkanal

Holler Fleet

Borgfelder Allee

Werfthafen
SPACE PARK

Kuhgraben
Kuhgrabensee

A 27 / E 234

Freihafen
Hochschulring
Hochschulring

Stadtwaldsee

HAFEN

Heerstraße
Bremerhavener Str.
Nordstraße

WALLER PARK

Osterfeuerberger Ring
Hemmstraße

Universitätsallee
Universität

BÜRGER
PARK

HORN-LEHE

Weser
Europahafen
Holz- und Fabrikenhafen

WOLTMERSHAUSEN

Neustädter Hafen

Achterstr.
Leher Heerstr.
Am Oberneulander Heerstr.

Oberneulander Landstr.

FINDORFF

SCHWACHAUSEN

BOTANISCHER GARTEN

ACHTERDIEK-PARK

A 27 / E 234

CONGRESSCENTRUM
MESSEHALLE

Focke Museum

NEUE VAHR

Senator-Apelt-Straße

Auf dem Bohlenkamp

NEUSTADTS-ANLAGEN

Kurfürstenallee
Kurfürstenallee
Richard-Boljahn-Allee
Kurt-Schumacher-Allee

A 281

Warturmer Heerstr.

ALTE NEUSTADT

Bismarckstraße
Humboldtstraße

Ludwig-Roselius-Allee

HUCHTING

Ochtum

A 281

Kleine Weser

Osterdeich
Osterdeich
Hamburger Str.
Hastedter Osterdeich

Sebaldsbrücker Heerstr.

SCHLOSSPARK

HUCKELRIEDE

Werdersee

NEUSTADT
CITY AIRPORT BREMEN

HABENHAUSEN

HEMELINGEN

OSNABRÜCK

OSNABRÜCK, HAMBURG, HANNOVER

HAMBURG, HANNOVER

Rastede (20)
Nuttel
Südende
Loy
Neuenfelde
Meyenburg
Lange Heide

Teufelsmoor
Sandhsn.
Hüttenbusch
Ostertimke
Oldendorf

Borbeck
Wahnbek
Ipwegermoor
Schwanewede
Eggestedt
Heilshorn
Pennigbüttel
Neu St. Jürgen
Kirchtimke
Brümmerhof

Neuenkruge
Huntorf
Rekum
Farge
Löhnhorst
Osterholz-Scharmbeck
Worpswede (50)
Ostendorf
Tüschendorf
Westertimke
Tarmstedt
Steinfeld

OLDENBURG
Berne
Ganspe
Lemwerder
Vegesack
Burglesum
Scharmbeckstotel
Ritterhude
St. Jürgensland
Grasberg
Wilstedt
Vorwerk
Winkeldorf

Neuenhuntorf
Harmenhausen
Bardewisch
Altenesch
Trupermoor
Lilienthal
BREMEN
Oberneuland
Fischerhude
Ottersberg

Hude
Bookholzberg
Schönemoor
Deichhausen
Gröpelingen
Horn-Lehe
Osterholz
Oyten
Sagehorn
Bassen

Delmenhorst
Stuhr
Huchting
Oldenburg

Ganderkesee
Falkenburg
Stuhr
Dreye
Mahndorf
Achim (20)

Naturpark
Weyhe

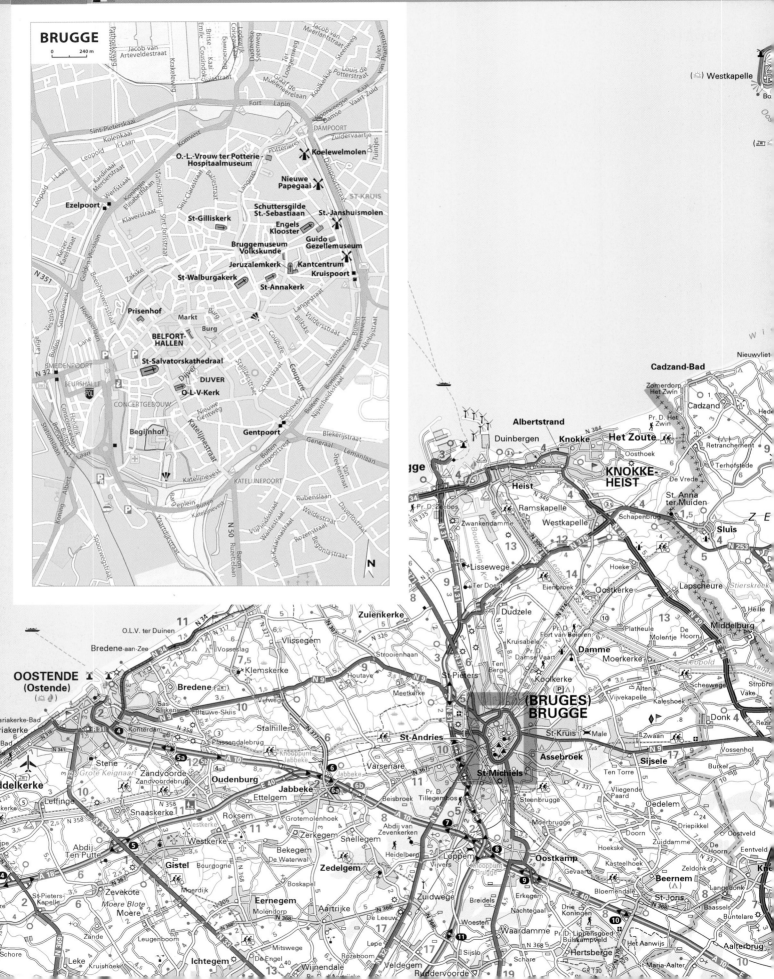

BRUGGE

0   240 m

Jacob van Aertveldestraat
Jacob van Maerlantstraat

O.-L.-Vrouw ter Potterie - Hospitaalmuseum
Koelewelmolen
Nieuwe Papegaai
DAMPOORT
ST-KRUIS
Ezelpoort
Schuttersgilde St.-Sebastiaan
St.-Janshuismolen
St-Gilliskerk
Engels Klooster
Guido Gezellemuseum
Bruggemuseum Volkunde
Jeruzalemkerk
Kantcentrum
St-Walburgakerk
Kruispoort
St-Annakerk
Prisenhof
Markt
Burg
BELFORT-HALLEN
St-Salvatorskathedraal
SMEDENPOORT
BEURSHALLE
Dijver
DIJVER
O-L-V-Kerk
CONCERTGEBOUW
Begijnhof
Gentpoort
KATELIJNEPOORT

N

Westkapelle

Cadzand-Bad
Zomerdorp Het Zwin
Cadzand
Nieuwvliet

Albertstrand
Duinbergen
Knokke
Het Zoute
KNOKKE-HEIST
Oosthoek
Retranchement
Terhofstede
De Vrede
St. Anna ter Muiden
Heist
Ramskapelle
Westkapelle
Schapenbrug
Sluis
Pr. D. Zeebos
Zwankendamme
Hoeke
Lapscheure
Heille
Lissewege
Ter Doest
Eienbroek
Oostkerke
Middelburg
Zuienkerke
Dudzele
Platheule
Molentje
De Hoorn
O.L.V. ter Duinen
Vlissegem
Strooienhaan
Damme
Moerkerke
Bredene-aan-Zee
Vosseslag
Houtave
St-Pieters
Ten Berge
Koolkerke
Vijvekapelle
Kaleshoek
Scheewege
Vake
Klemskerke
Meetkerke
OOSTENDE
(Ostende)
Bredene
Donk
St-Kruis
Male
Zwaan
Vossenhol
Mariakerke-Bad
Mariakerke
Sas Slijkens
Blauwe-Sluis
Stalhille
(BRUGES) BRUGGE
Assebroek
Sijsele
Burkel
Stene
Konterdam
Plassendalebrug
St-Andries
Varsenare
St-Michiels
Ten Torre
Oedelem
Middelkerke
Zandvoorde
Zandvoordebrug
Oudenburg
Jabbeke
Beisbroek
Pr. D. Tillegembos
Steenbrugge
Moerbrugge
Ten Putte
Leffinge
Snaaskerke
Ettelgem
Roksem
Pr. D. Fort van Beieren
Zevenkerken
Loppem
Oostkamp
Kasteelhoek
Zeldonk
Wilskerke
Westkerke
Grotemolenhoek
Snellegem
Bekegem
Heidelberg
Vijvers
Oostveld
Eentvelde
St-Pieters-Kapelle
Abdij Ten Putte
Gistel
Bourgogne
De Waterval
Zerkegem
Zedelgem
Loppem
Oostkamp
Hoekske
Beernem
St-Joris
Zevekote
Moerdijk
Boskapel
Zuidwege
Erkegem
Bloemendale
Baassels
Moere
Moere Blote
Leugenboom
Aartrijke
De Leeuw
Nachtegaal
Drie Koningen
Waardamme
Pr. D. Lippensgoed Bulskampveld
De Aanwijs
Aalterbrug
Zande
Leke
Kruishoek
Mitsweg
De Engel
Rozeboom
Sijslo
Hertsberge
St-Maria-Aalter
Ichtegem
Wijnendale
Molendorp
Veldegem
Schare
Ruddervoorde
Woesten

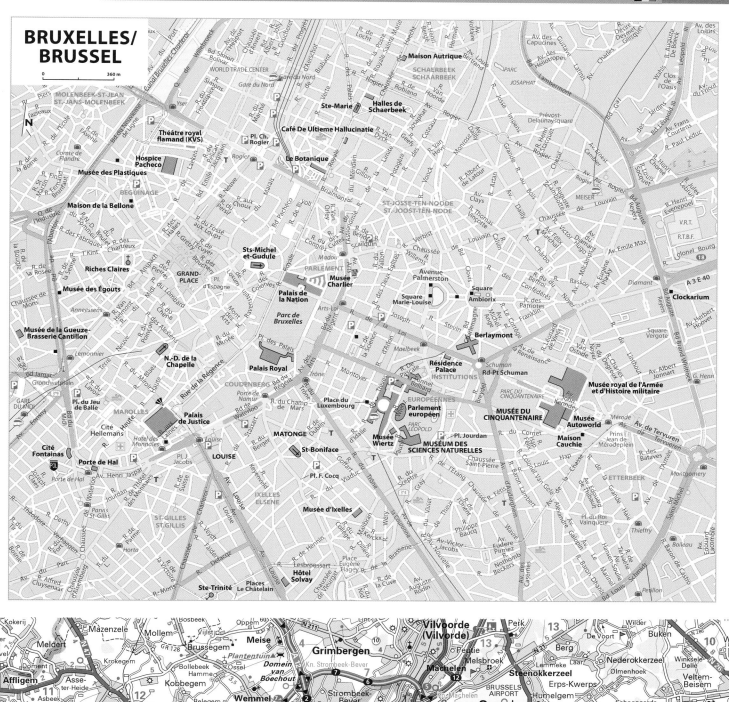

BRUXELLES/
BRUSSEL

0   360 m

MOLENBEEK-ST-JEAN
ST-JANS-MOLENBEEK

WORLD TRADE CENTER

Maison Autrique

SCHAERBEEK
SCHAARBEEK

PARC
JOSAPHAT

Gare du Nord

Théâtre royal
flamand (KVS)

Pl. Ch.
Rogier

Ste-Marie

Halles de
Schaerbeek

Hospice Pacheco

Café De Ultieme Hallucinatie

Musée des Plastiques

Le Botanique

Maison de la Bellone

ST-JOSSE-TEN-NOODE
ST-JOOST-TEN-NODE

MEISER

V.R.T.

Riches Claires

Sts-Michel
et-Gudule

PARLEMENT

Musée Charlier

R.T.B.F.

Musée des Égouts

GRAND-
PLACE

Palais
de la Nation

Square
Marie-Louise

Square
Ambiorix

Clockarium

Musée de la Gueuze-
Brasserie Cantillon

N.-D. de la
Chapelle

Parc de
Bruxelles

Berlaymont

Square
Vergote

Square
Hoover

Palais Royal

COUDENBERG

Résidence
Palace

Rd-Pt Schuman

Musée royal de l'Armée
et d'Histoire militaire

GARE
DU MIDI

Rue de la Régence

INSTITUTIONS

Pl. du Jeu
de Balle

MAROLLES

Palais
de Justice

EUROPÉENNES

PARC DU
CINQUANTENAIRE

MUSÉE DU
CINQUANTENAIRE

Musée
Autoworld

Cité
Hellemans

MATONGE

Place du
Luxembourg

Parlement
européen

PARC
LÉOPOLD

Maison
Cauchie

Cité
Fontainas

Porte de Hal

St-Boniface

Musée
Wiertz

MUSÉUM DES
SCIENCES NATURELLES

Pl. Jourdan

ETTERBEEK

LOUISE

Pl. F. Cocq

IXELLES
ELSENE

Musée d'Ixelles

ST-GILLES
ST-GILLIS

Hôtel
Solvay

Ste-Trinité

Places
Le Châtelain

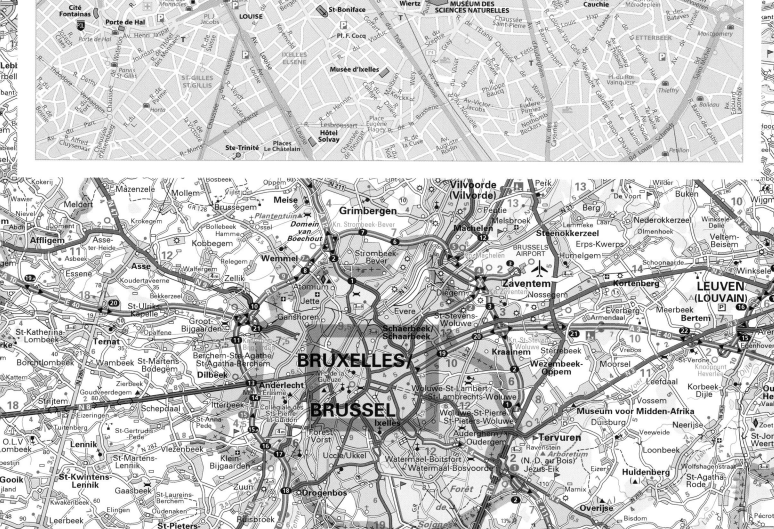

Vilvoorde
(Vilvoorde)

Meise

Grimbergen

Machelen

Steenokkerzeel

Erps-Kwerps

BRUSSELS
AIRPORT

Affligem

Asse

Wemmel

Strombeek-
Bever

Zaventem

Kortenberg

LEUVEN
(LOUVAIN)

Atomium

Jette

Diegem

Nossegem

Everberg

Meerbeek

Bertem

St-Ulriks-
Kapele

Ganshoren

St-Stevens-
Woluwe

Groot-
Bijgaarden

Kraainem

Sterrebeek

Wezembeek-
Oppem

Ternat

Berchem-Ste-Agathe/
St-Agatha-Berchem

Schaerbeek/
Schaarbeek

BRUXELLES/

Dilbeek

Anderlecht

Woluwe-St-Lambert/
St-Lambrechts-Woluwe

Museum voor Midden-Afrika

BRUSSEL

Ixelles

Woluwe-St-Pierre/
St-Pieters-Woluwe

Forest/
Vorst

Auderghem/
Oudergem

Tervuren

Klein-
Bijgaarden

Uccle/Ukkel

Watermael-Boitsfort
Watermaal-Bosvoorde

Jezus-Eik

Huldenberg

Lennik

Drogenbos

Overijse

Forêt

BUCUREȘTI

0 ——— 300 m

Curtea Veche	C	Imobilul Tehnoimport	L
Banca Națională	D	Pasajul Macca-Vilacrosse	E
Biblioteca Universitară	F	Pasajul Hanul cu Tei	N
Caru' cu Bere	K	Palatul Șuțu/Muzeul Municipiului București	S

Academiei (Str.)	2	Gabroveni (Str.)	7
Benjamin Franklin (Str.)	3	Schitul Dărvari (Str.)	8
Covaci (Str.)	4	Smârdan (Str.)	9
Culmea Veche (Str.)	5	Șelari (Str.)	12
Edgar Quinet (Str.)	6	Stavropoleos (Str.)	13

BUDAPEST

DEN HAAG
SCHEVENINGEN

0   280 m

N

NOORDZEE

De Pier
Zeekant
Oostduinpark
Harstenhoekweg
Sea Life Scheveningen
Kurhaus
Groningsestraat
Zwolsestraat
Museum Beelden aan Zee
CASINO
POL
Harstenhoekweg
Bosschestraat
Stevinstraat
BELGISCH PARK
Circustheater
SCHEVENINGEN
Muzee Scheveningen
Badhuisweg
Gentsestraat
Doornikstraat
DUTTENDEL
Van Alkemadelaan
Obelisk
Nieuwe Duinweg
Parklaan
Brusselselaan
Pompstationsweg
Maurits de Brauwweg
KLEIN ZWITSERLAND
Oude Waalsdorperweg
Crest
Landscheidingsweg
Groenendaal
Buurtweg

Strandweg
Jacob
Vijzelstraat
Westbroekpark
Het Kanaal
Haringkade
DUINZIGT
Van Kijfhoeklaan
Stalpertstraat
Van
Ruychrocklaan
DUINBOS
Oosterbeek

VAN STOLKPARK
Van Stolkpark
Van Alkemadelaan
Ruychrocklaan
Goeilijfstraat
G
Clingendael
Van

De Haven
Voor haven
2e Haven
Lelykade
Dr. Aletta Jacobsweg
Madurodam
B.M.Teldersweg
HUBERTUSPARK
Koninginnegracht
Oostduin Arendsdorp
ROSARIUM
Jozef Israelsplein
Paul Gabrielstraat
BENOORDENHOUT
Leidsestraatweg

STATENKWARTIER
Professor
SCHEVENINGSCHE BOSCHJES
Kerkhoflaan
Delistraat
Riouwstraat
ARCHIPELBUURT
Celebesstraat
Malakkastraat
Burgemeester Patijnlaan
POL
Scheldkade
Javastraat
Nassauplein
Jan van Nassaustraat
's-Gravenweg
Haagsche Bos

NEDERLANDS CONGRES CENTRUM
Fotomuseum Den Haag
GEM
Het Catshuis
Zorgvliet
Gemeentemuseum Den Haag
Museon
Omniversum
President Kennedylaan
Jacob Catslaan
Vredespaleis
Groot Hertoginnelaan
Museum Mesdag
Museum voor Communicatie
Prins Hendrikpl.
Mauritskade
Zuid-Hollandlaan
Koekamp
BEZUIDENHOUT
Letterkundig Museum & Kinderboekenmuseum
Prinses Irenepad
CENTRAAL STATION

RIOOLGEMAAL
BOSJES VAN POOT
HOUTRUST-HALLEN
Kanaalweg
Houtrustweg
Pres. Kennedylaan
DUINOORD
Conradkade
Suezkade
Laan van Meerdervoort
Prins Hendrikstraat
Piet Heinstraat
Hogewal
Noordeinde
Kazernestraat
Lange Voorhout
Lange Vijverberg
MAURITSHUIS
Korte Vijverberg
Zwartepad
Bezuidenhout
Juliana van Stolberglaan

VLAARDINGEN
Segbroeklaan
Thomsonlaan
Sportlaan
Mezenlaan
Koningspl.
Witte De Withstraat
Vondelstraat
Spuistraat
Spuiplein
Bernhardviaduct
Laurens

Laan van Meerdervoort
Valkenboskade
Weimarstraat
REGENTESSEKWARTIER
Westeinde
Gedempte Gracht
Nieuwe Haven
Schedeldoekshaven
Schenkkade
A12

NAALDWIJK, DELFT VLAARDINGEN   WATERINGEN   VOORBURG   AMSTERDAM GOUDA, UTRECHT

Katwijk aan Zee
Katwijk a/d Rijn
Valkenburg
Rijnsburg
Warmond
Kagerplassen
Braassemermeer
Oude Wetering
LEIDEN
Oegstgeest
Leiderdorp
Koudekerk
Langeraar
Nieuwveen
Mijdrecht
(De Ronde Venen)
Nieuwer-ter-Aa
Roelofarendsveen
(Kaag en Brassem)
Woubrugge
Hoogmade
Noorden
Noordeinde
Nieuwkoop
Kockengen
De Haar

Wassenaar
De Kievit
Voorschoten
Zoeterwoude
Rijndijk
Hazerswoude-Dorp
Stompwijk
Benthuizen
Boskoop
Alphen a/d Rijn
Meije Zegveld
Zwammerdam
Bodegraven
(Bodegraven-Reeuwijk)
Nieuwerbrug
Waarder
Driebruggen
Woerden
Harmelen
Linschoten
Kamerik
Haarzuilens

SCHEVENINGEN
DEN HAAG
('S-GRAVENHAGE)
Kijkduin
Voorburg
Loosduinen
Rijswijk
Leidschendam
Zoetermeer
Waddinxveen
Moerkapelle
Reeuwijk
Reeuwijk-Dorp
Waarder
Reeuwijkse Plassen
Oudewater
Montfoort

Harwich
Monster
Poeldijk
Wateringen
Nootdorp
Pijnacker
Bleiswijk
Zevenhuizen
A12-E30
Moordrecht
Gouderak
Gouda
Haastrecht
Vlist
Polsbroek
Lopik

Kingston-upon-Hull
's-Gravenzande
Hoek van Holland
Naaldwijk
De Lier
Honselersdijk
Schipluiden
DELFT
Berkel en Rodenrijs
Bergschenhoek
Hillegersberg
Nieuwerkerk
Zuidplas
Moordrecht
Ouderkerk
Krimpen a/d IJ.
Schoonhoven
Bergambacht
Ammerstol
Groot Ammers
Nieuwpoort
Streefkerk
Goudriaan

Maasvlakte
Maasvlakte 2
Europoort
Maassluis
Vlaardingen
Maasland
Maasdijk
Westerlee
Overschie
Schiedam
ROTTERDAM
Capelle
Krimpen a/d L.
Lekkerkerk
Bleskensgraaf
Molenaarsgraaf

Oostvoorne
Brielle
Rozenburg
Pernis
Zwartewaal
Kinderdijk
Ridderkerk
Alblasserdam

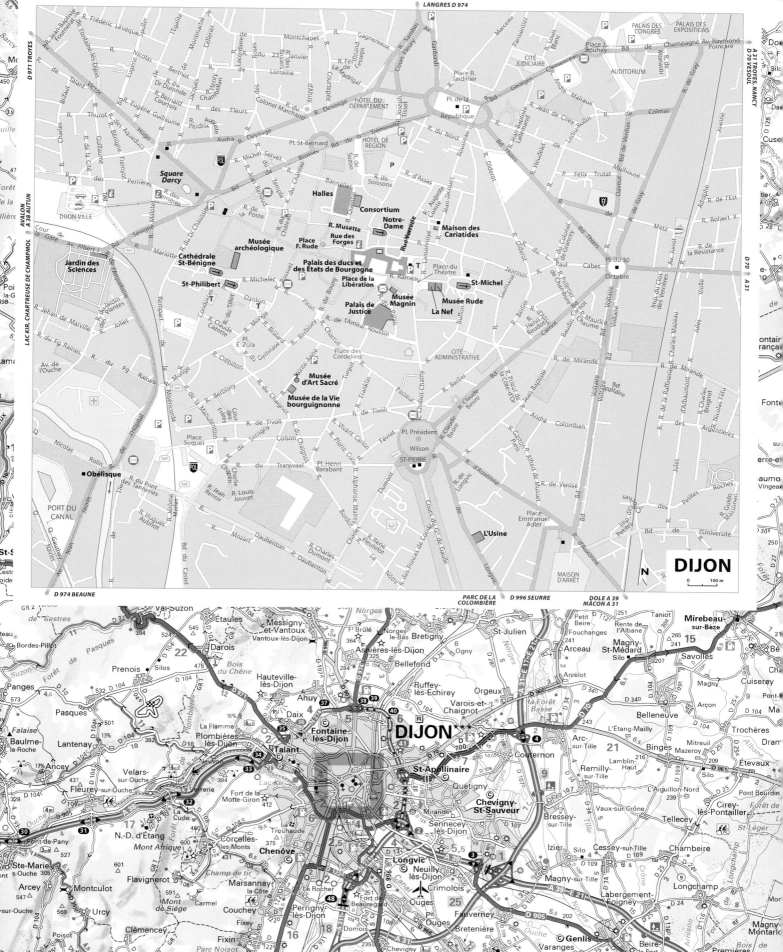

DIJON
0   100 m

N

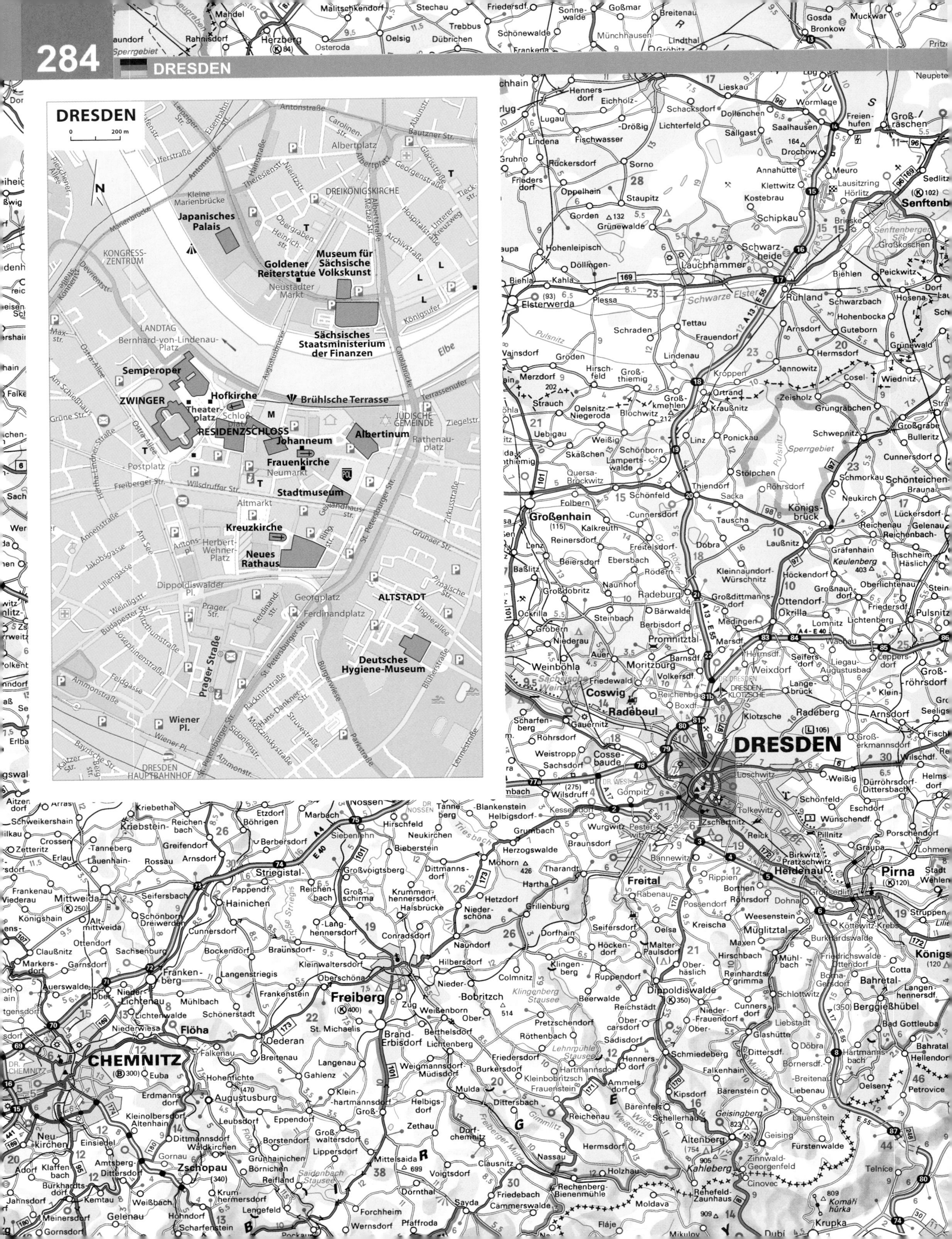

DRESDEN

0 200 m

N

Japanisches Palais
Goldener Reiterstatue
Museum für Sächsische Volkskunst
Sächsisches Staatsministerium der Finanzen
KONGRESS-ZENTRUM
LANDTAG
Bernhard-von-Lindenau-Platz
Semperoper
ZWINGER
Hofkirche
Theaterplatz
RESIDENZSCHLOSS
Johanneum
Brühlsche Terrasse
Albertinum
JÜDISCHE GEMEINDE
Frauenkirche
Neumarkt
Stadtmuseum
Altmarkt
Kreuzkirche
Neues Rathaus
ALTSTADT
Deutsches Hygiene-Museum
Wiener Pl.
DRESDEN HAUPTBAHNHOF
Prager Straße

DREIKÖNIGSKIRCHE
Albertplatz
Neustädter Markt
Postplatz
Wilsdruffer Str.
Ferdinandplatz
Georgplatz

DRESDEN
Senftenberg
Elsterwerda
Großenhain
Radeburg
Coswig
Radebeul
Königsbrück
Ruhland
Lauchhammer
Moritzburg
Pirna
Heidenau
Freital
Freiberg
CHEMNITZ
Mittweida
Hainichen
Nossen
Zschopau
Flöha
Augustusburg
Altenberg
Dippoldiswalde
Glashütte
Königstein

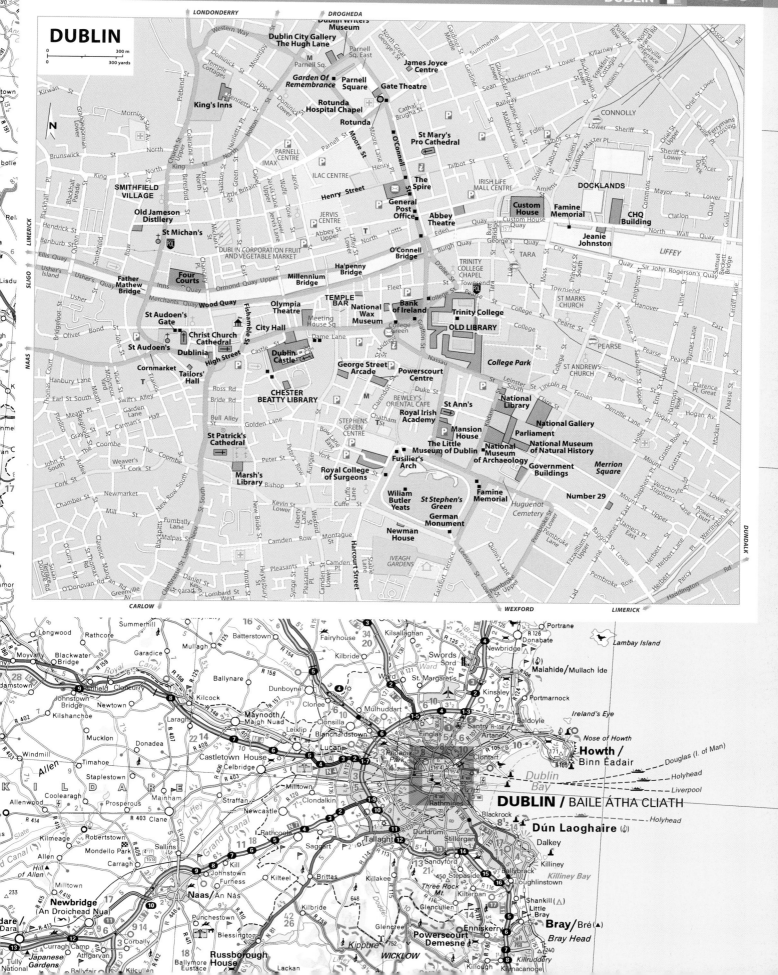

DUBLIN

300 m
300 yards

LONDONDERRY · DROGHEDA

Dublin Writers Museum
Dublin City Gallery The Hugh Lane
James Joyce Centre
Garden Of Remembrance
Parnell Square
Gate Theatre
King's Inns
Rotunda Hospital Chapel
Rotunda
St Mary's Pro Cathedral
CONNOLLY
SMITHFIELD VILLAGE
The Spire
Old Jameson Distllery
St Michan's
Henry Street
General Post Office
Abbey Theatre
Custom House
Famine Memorial
CHQ Building
DOCKLANDS
Four Courts
Father Mathew Bridge
Millennium Bridge
Ha'penny Bridge
O'Connell Bridge
Jeanie Johnston
LIFFEY
TARA
TRINITY COLLEGE CHAPEL
St Audoen's Gate
Olympia Theatre
Wood Quay
TEMPLE BAR
National Wax Museum
Bank of Ireland
Trinity College
OLD LIBRARY
St Audoen's
Christ Church Cathedral
Dublinia
City Hall
High Street
Dublin Castle
College Park
ST ANDREW'S CHURCH
PEARSE
Cornmarket
Tailors' Hall
George Street Arcade
Powerscourt Centre
CHESTER BEATTY LIBRARY
BEWLEY'S ORIENTAL CAFE
St Ann's
National Library
St Patrick's Cathedral
Royal Irish Academy
Mansion House
National Gallery
Parliament
National Museum of Archaeology
National Museum of Natural History
The Little Museum of Dublin
Government Buildings
Merrion Square
Marsh's Library
Royal College of Surgeons
Fusilier's Arch
Famine Memorial
Number 29
Wiliam Butler Yeats
St Stephen's Green
German Monument
Huguenot Cemetery
Newman House
IVEAGH GARDENS

CARLOW · WEXFORD · LIMERICK · DUNDALK

Howth / Binn Éadair
Douglas (I. of Man)
Holyhead
Liverpool
Dublin Bay
DUBLIN / BAILE ÁTHA CLIATH
Dún Laoghaire
Holyhead
Bray / Bré
Naas / An Nás
Newbridge (An Droichead Nua)
Russborough House
Powerscourt Demesne
WICKLOW
KILDARE

DÜSSELDORF

0   500 m

N

Museum Kunst Palast

Hofgarten

Ratinger Tor

Hofgarten

Goethemuseum

Paul-Klee-Platz

Dreischeibenhaus

ALTSTADT

Königsallee

Apollo-Platz

Harold str.

Hauptbahnhof

Düsseldorf Hbf

Stahlwerkstr.

Handelszentrum

Oberbilker Markt

Ellerstraße

Lessingplatz

Oberbilker Allee

Gangelplatz

D-Oberbilk

VOLKSGARTEN

Moorenplatz

Südliche Düssel

Erftplatz

Bilker Allee

Kirchfeldstr.

Fürstenwall

Südring

Rheinbrücke Düsseldorf-Neuss

Rhein

Th. Heuss-Brücke

Theodor-Heuss-Brücke

Reeser Pl.

Johannstr.

Heinrich-Ehrhardt-Straße

Frankenplatz

Golzheimer Pl.

Kennedydamm

Spichernplatz

Münsterplatz

Kolpingplatz

Klever Str.

Jülicher Str.

Grunerstraße

Graf-Recke-Straße

Rochusmarkt

Schillerplatz

Grafenberger Allee

Cranachstraße

Ackerstraße

Birkenstraße

Pl. der Diakonie

Behrenstraße

Höherweg

Erkrather Str.

Ronsdorfer Str.

Lierenfeld

Mörsenbroicher Weg

Vautierstraße

Dominikus-Krankenhaus

Drususstraße

Luegallee

Meerbusch

Luegplatz

Helmut-Hentrich-Platz

Rheinbahnhaus

Belsenplatz

Düsseldorfer Str.

Am Seestern

Lohweg

Hansaallee

Prinzenallee

Heerdter Sandberg

Oberkasseler Str.

Löricker Str.

Brüsseler Str.

Pariser Str.

Quirinstraße

Kaiserswerther Str.

Rheinkniebrücke

Völklinger Str.

Fährstr.

Martinstr.

Bachstr.

Aachener Str.

Volmerswerther Str.

Suitbertusstraße

Frucht-str.

Am Hennekamp

Witzelstr.

Corneliusstraße

Färberstraße

Flügelstr.

Kruppstr.

Ellerstr.

Fichtenstraße

Ronsdorfer Str.

Kettwiger Str.

Karl-Geusen-Straße

Kurthsweg

Offenbacher Weg

Wormser Weg

Bingener Weg

ADAC

POL

Regional map

DUISBURG

MÜLHEIM

KREFEL D

KEMPEN

NETTETAL

VIERSEN

MÖNCHEN-GLADBACH

Rheydt

NEUSS

DÜSSEL-DORF

Ratingen

Mettmann

Wülfrath

VELBERT

Velbert

ELBERFELD

WUPPERT

SOLINGEN

Hilden

Langenfeld

Monheim

Dormagen

Grevenbroich

Erkelenz

Wegberg

Brüggen

Tegelen

Venlo

Naturpark

Hattingen

Sprockhövel

Remscheid

Erkrath

Haan

MASNFIELD TRAQUAIR CENTRE
ROYAL BOTANIC GARDEN
LEITH

Statue Sherlock Holmes
York Place
Picardy Place
Royal Terrace
Calton Hill
REGENT GARDENS

Scottish National Portrait Gallery
James Craig Observatory

Abercromby Place

The Scotch Malt Whisky Society
St Andrew and St George
Buchan House
N° 26
Dundas House
New Register House
General Register House
Café Royal
Old Post Office
Old Calton Cemetery
St Andrew's House
Circular Greek Temple
National Monument
Nelson's Monument
Regent Terrace
Regent Road
Royal High School
Greek Temple

Georgian House
Assembly Rooms
George Street
West Register St.
Princes Street
JENNERS
Scott Monument
East Princes Street Gardens
BALMORAL HOTEL
WAVERLEY CENTRE

CHARLOTTE SQUARE
Floral Clock
Royal Scottish Academy
National Gallery of Scotland
The Edinburgh Dungeon
City Art Centre

West Register House
West Princes Street Gardens
Museum on the Mound
The Real Mary King's Close
Anchor Close
Mowbray House
John Knox House
Canongate Tolbooth
Canongate Church
Museum of Edinburgh - Huntly House
Scottish Parliament
Moray House
Our Dynamic Earth

Gladstone's Land
Mylne's Court
Lady Stair's House
City Chambers
High Street
Tron Kirk
Museum of Childhood
Trinity Church
Jeffrey Street

Ramsay Lodge
Lawnmarket
The Hub
Mercat Cross
Parliament Square
Parliament House
Castle
The Scotch Whisky Experience
St Giles' Cathedral
Castle Hill
Cowgate
Adam House
University Staff Club
Old College

Esplanade
Law Courts
Chambers Street
Grassmarket
Candlemaker Row
NATIONAL MUSEUM OF SCOTLAND
Festival Theatre

King's Stables Road
The Vennel
West Port
Greyfriars Church and Churchyard
Flodden Wall
George Heriot's School
Bistro Square
Student Centre
McEwan Hall
Medical School
CENTRAL MOSQUE & ISLAMIC CENTRE
Appleton Tower

QUARTERMILE
Dugald Stewart Building
George Square
David Hume Tower
Library

West Meadow Park
East Meadow Park

EDINBURGH

0 — 250 m
0 — 250 yards

INTERNATIONAL CONFERENCE CENTRE

PEEBLES
BIGGAR
GALASHIELS
GALASHIELS JEDBURGH

FIRTH OF FORTH

North Berwick
Culross
Grangemouth
Bo'Ness
Inverkeithing
Forth Bridge
South Queensferry
Dalmeny
Leith
Musselburgh
Portobello
Prestonpans
Haddington
Falkirk
Linlithwood
Murrayfield
EDINBURGH
Dalkeith
Bathgate
Livingston
Currie
Loanhead
Dalkeith
Penicuik
Roslin
PENTLAND HILLS
WEST LOTHIAN
MIDLOTHIAN
LAMMERMUIR

ESSEN

N

0   500 m

Top map (Essen city center):

Altendorf · Holsterhausen · Rüttenscheid

Universität Essen · Krupp Hauptverwaltung · Weberplatz · Kreuzeskirche · St. Gertrud Kirche · St. Peter Kirche · St. Barbara Kirche · Kennedyplatz · Limbecker Pl. · Münster · Domschatzkammer · Hirschlandplatz · Heilige Kreuz Kirche · Bismarckplatz · Freiheit · Opernplatz · Steinplatz · St. Michael Kirche · St. Ignatius Kirche · Philharmonie und Saalbau · Opernhaus · Stadtgarten · St. Engelbert Kirche · Jüdische Gemeinde · Museum Folkwang · Rüttenscheider Stern · St. Hubertus Kirche

Key streets: Altendorfer Str. · Friedrich-Ebert-Straße · Hindenburgstraße · Kruppstraße · Bismarckstraße · Hohenzollernstraße · A 40 · A 52

Bottom map (Ruhr region overview):

ENSCHEDE · Hengelo · Losser · Bentheim · Rheine · Gronau

DUISBURG · MOERS · OBERHAUSEN · MÜLHEIM · Dinslaken · Bottrop · GELSENKIRCHEN · Gladbeck · Herten · RECKLINGHAUSEN · Herne · Castrop-Rauxel · Lünen · DORTMUND · Unna · ESSEN · BOCHUM · Witten · Hattingen · HAGEN · Iserlohn · Schwerte · Velbert · Ratingen · Wülfrath · Mettmann

FIRENZE

0   300 m

N

Key labels (city centre map):

FORTEZZA DA BASSO, DELLA FORTEZZA, PAL. DEI CONGRESSI, PAL. DEGLI AFFARI, PORTA AL PRATO, Piazza Adua, Piazza della Stazione, Chiostro Verde, S. Maria Novella, Ognissanti, Palazzo Strozzi, Chiostro d. Scalzo, Sant'Apollonia, Convento e museo di San Marco, Galleria d. Accademia, Opificio d. Pietre dure, SAN LORENZO, Ospedale degli Innocenti, Santissima Annunziata, Museo Archeologico, Santa Maria Maddalena dei Pazzi, DUOMO, Piazza Sant'Ambrogio, Mercato di SantʼAmbrogio, Piazza dei Ciompi, Piazza della Signoria, GALLERIA DEGLI UFFIZI, Piazza di Sta Croce, Santa Croce, Museo Horne, Ponte Vecchio, Museo Galileo, Santa Felicita, Museo Bardini, Giardino Bardini, SANTA MARIA DEL CARMINE, Santo Spirito, Piazza S. Spirito, Piazza dei Pitti, Museo La Specola, Palazzo Pitti, Giardino di Boboli, Forte del Belvedere, Museo delle Porcellane, Giardino delle Rose, Piazzale Michelangelo, San Miniato al Monte, Passeggiata ai Colli, Piazzale D. Isolotto, Porta Romana

Regional map (lower):

Carmignano, Poggio a Caiano, PRATO EST, Sesto Fiorentino, Campi Bisenzio, Signa, Scandicci, FIRENZE, Fiesole, AEROPORTO AMERIGO VESPUCCI, Bagno a Ripoli, Pontassieve, Montelupo Fiorentino, Impruneta

FRANKFURT AM MAIN

0   500 m

N

BOTANISCHER GARTEN

GRÜNEBURGPARK

Palmengarten

Naturmuseum Senckenberg

BOCKENHEIM

MESSE FRANKFURT
CONGRESS CENTER
MESSETURM

GALLUSWARTE

WESTHAFEN

Goethe-Haus

Museum für Moderne Kunst

St. Bartholomäus Kirche

Museum für Angewandte Kunst

Städelsches Kunstinstitut

SACHSENHAUSEN

Henninger Turm

BORNHEIM
Bornheim Mitte

Zoo

GÜNTHERSBURGPARK

ROTHSCHILD PARK

JÜDISCHE GEMEINDE

HAUPTBAHNHOF

Main

WIESBADEN

MAINZ

FRANKFURT A. M.

OFFENBACH

Hanau

Rüsselsheim

Bad Homburg

Oberursel

Langen

Neu-Isenburg

Büdingen

Gelnhausen

Mühlheim

GENÈVE

Scale: 0 — 300 m

Inset map (Genève city centre):

NYON, LAUSANNE

Parc Mon Repos · Sainte-Trinité · LE PRIEURÉ · Palais Wilson · Lac Léman · PARC BEAULIEU · PARC DES CROPETTES · LES PÂQUIS · PORT DES PÂQUIS · TEMPLE DES PÂQUIS · BASILIQUE NOTRE DAME · SAINT-GERVAIS · Rhône · Mausolée du Duc de Brunswick · Île J.-J. Rousseau · Jardin Anglais · Musée Barbier-Mueller · Musée international de la Réforme · Maison Tavel · Musée Rath · Grand Rue · R. des Granges · Place de Neuve · SACRÉ-CŒUR · VIEILLE VILLE · Cathédrale Saint-Pierre · Immeuble La Clarté · ÉGLISE ST-JOSEPH · Place du Bourg-de-Four · Mur des Réformateurs · Bibliothèque universitaire · Musée d'Art et d'Histoire · Museum d'Histoire Naturelle · Cathédrale Orthodoxe Ste-Croix · Petit Palais · Fondation Baur · LES TRANCHÉES · PARC DES CONTAMINES · PLAINPALAIS · Rd-Pt de Plainpalais

EVIAN-LES-BAINS, THONON-LES-BAINS · MONT-BLANC, CHAMONIX, MÉGÈVE

BOURG-EN-BRESSE, BELLEGARDE-SUR-VALSERINE · GEX · ST-JULIEN-EN-GENEVOIS, ANNECY, LYON, GRENOBLE

Surrounding region (main map):

Les Jannez · Combe-Froide · Roche des Trois Commères · Bois-d'Amont · Carroz · Marchairuz · Les Amburnex · Bière · Gimel · St-George · Saubraz · Longirod · St-Oyens · Essertines-sur-Rolle · Pizy · Bougy-Villars · Tartegnin · Rolle · Burtigny · Gilly · Bursins · Luins · Vinzel · Bursinel · St-Cergue · Genolier · Givrins · Begnins · Vich · La Côte · Gland · Dully · Arzier · Le Muids · Bassins · Coinsins · Duillier · Trélex · Bénex · Prangins · Abb. de Bonmont · Gingins · Chéserex · Grens · Signy-Avenex · Borex · Nyon · Promenthoux · Yvoire · La Rippe · Crassier · Eysins · Crans-près-Céligny · Céligny · Messery · Nernier · Chavannes-de-Bogis · Bogis-Bossey · Céligny-Port · Chens-s-Léman · Grilly · Châtaignereaie · Founex · Beauregard · Silo · Douvaine · Commugny · Pré-Claudy · Tougues · Conches · Coppet · Vereitre · Chens-le-Pont · Chilly · Ballaison · Chavannes-des-Bois · Mies · Tannay · Hermance · Collongette · Aubonne · Loisin · Villars-Dame · La Bâtie · Collex-Bossy · Versoix-la-Ville · Chevrens · Anières · Corsier · Veigy-Foncenex · St-Didier · Versoix · Genthod · Collonge-Bellerive · St-Maurice · Gy · Foncenex · Bellevue · Vésenaz · La Capite · Sionnet · Corsinge · Jussy · Prévessin-Moëns · Ferney-Voltaire · Pregny · Chambésy · Vandoeuvres · Choulex · Presinge · La Renfile · Juvigny · St-Genis-Pouilly · Meyrin · GENÈVE · Cointrin · Saconnex · Palais des Nations · Cologny · Ville-la-Grd · Montauban · Armia · Martigny · Thoiry · Fénières · C.E.R.N. · Bourdigny · Chêne-Bougeries · Ambilly · Annemasse · Satigny · Vernier · Peissy · Peney · Loëx · Aïre · Moillesulaz · Chêne-Bourg · Chêne-Thônex · Cranves-Sales · Malval · Dardagny · Russin · Aire-la-Ville · Onex · Lancy · Véssy · Collonges · Vétraz-Monthoux · La Plaine · La Petite Grave · Bernex · Plan-les-Ouates · Carouge · Troinex · Veyrier · Monnetier-Mornex · Arthaz-Pont-N.-D. · Villy · Challex · Mucelle · Cartigny · Lully · Confignon · Saconnex-d'Arve · Pas de l'Échelle · Mornex · La Chapelle · Logras · Farges · Avully · Laconnex · Perly · Certoux · Bardonnex · Croix-de-Rozon · Bossey · Reignier-Ésery · Péron · Chancy · Athenaz · Soral · St-Julien-en-Genevois · Thairy · Landecy · Les Treize Arbres · Marsinge · Esery · Menthières · Crêt de la Goutte · Avusy · Sezegnin · Malagny · Veigy · Songy · Humilly · Feigères · Beaumont · Petit-Pommier · Neydens · Archamps · La Muraz · Cusy · Arculinge · Bellegarde-s-Valserine · Défilé de l'Écluse · Chevrier · Vulbens · Valleiry · Viry · La Côte · Germagny · Éluiset · Blécheins · Moisin · La Forge · Pers-Jussy · Corbonod · Vanchy · Léaz · Raclaz · Vulbens · La Fontaine · Bloux · Bellossy · Vers · Présilly · Chez-Vachoux · Malchamp · Chênex · Faramaz · Longeray · Chevrier · Lanctans l'Écluse · Fort

Crêt de Chalam · Le Reculet · Noire Combe · Hte Crête · Chézery-Forens · L'Eperry · Le Grd Essert · Les Replats · Crêt de Chalam · Col du Sac · Crêt de la Goutte · Pertes de la Valserine · Pougny · Collonges

GENOVA

STAZIONE PRINCIPE

Palazzo del Principe
Commenda San Giovanni di Prè
Palazzo Reale
Galata Museo del Mare
SS. Annunziata del Vastato
Castelletto
Museo Chiossone
Palazzo Doria-Spinola
ACQUARIO
Biosphera
Città dei Bambini
Palazzo San Giorgio
Teatro Carlo Felice
Galleria Mazzini
AIR TERMINAL
Spianata dell'Acquasola
Antichi Magazzini del Cotone
Centro Congressi
Porta Siberia
PORTO ANTICO
S. Lorenzo
Palazzo Ducale
Pza di Ferrari
De Ferrari
S. Stefano
Chiesa del Gesù
BACINO PORTO VECCHIO
BACINO DELLE GRAZIE
Museo di Sant'Agostino
Sant'Agostino
MERCATO ORIENTALE
Piazza Verdi
STAZIONE BRIGNOLE
CORTE LAMBRUSCHINI
Santa Maria Assunta in Carignano
Villa Croce (Museo di Arte Contemporanea)
AVAMPORTO
LA FIERA
Piazzale John Fitzgerald Kennedy
Piazzale Cavalieri di Vittorio Veneto

Mura di S. Bartolomeo
CASTELLO MACKENZIE
FERRARIS

N

0   200 m

Masone
Arenzano
Voltri
Prà
Pegli
Sestri Ponente
GENOVA VOLTRI 13
AEROPORTO CRISTOFORO COLOMBO
Cornigliano Ligure
Sampierdarena
GENOVA
Nervi
Recco
Camogli
Bogliasco
Pieve Ligure
Sori
Ruta
San Martino di Noceto

GÖTEBORG

0   5 km

E 6 ↓   ↓ HELSINGBORG, MALMÖ

HAMBURG

500 m

STELLINGEN · EPPENDORF · HOHELUFT · WINTERHUDE · EPIPHANIAKIRCHE · MATTHÄUSKIRCHE · BARMBEK · HEILANDKIRCHE · ST. SOPHIEN KIRCHE · HARVESTEHUDE · HEILIG GEIST KIRCHE · EIMSBÜTTEL · ST. ELISABETH KIRCHE · UHLENHORST · EILBEK · BAHRENFELD · VOLKSPARK · VOLKSPARK STADION · AUSSENALSTER · BINNENALSTER · OTHMARSHEN · OTTENSEN · ALTONA · Hamburger Kunsthalle · Fernsehturm · Museum für Hamburgische Geschichte · Museum für Kunst und Gewerbe · Sprinkenhof · HAMMERBROOK · Altonaer Museum · HAUPTKIRCHE SANKT TRINITATIS · St. Michaeliskirche · Reeperbahn · St. Pauli · ELBCHAUSSEE · HAFEN · Norderelbe · Elbe

Brokdorf · Freiburg · Glückstadt · Elmshorn · Wischhafen · Krautsand · Drochtersen · Stade · Uetersen · Pinneberg · Quickborn · Norderstedt · Ahrensburg · Bad Oldesloe · Reinfeld · Kaltenkirchen · Buxtehude · Harburg · Wedel · Schenefeld · HAMBURG · Wandsbek · Bergedorf · Reinbek · Schwarzenbek · Geesthacht · Seevetal

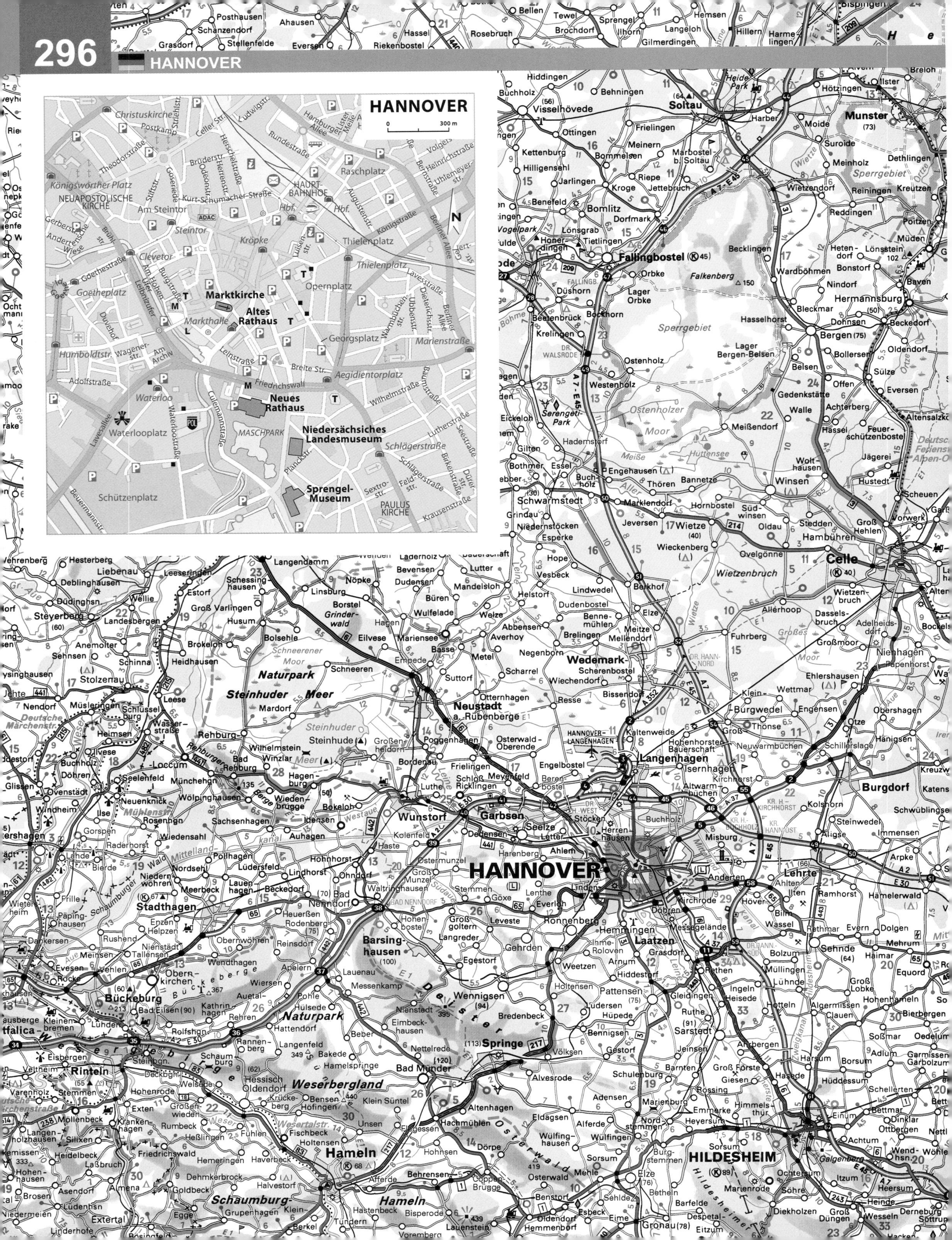

HANNOVER

Scale: 0 — 300 m

Inset city map labels:
Christuskirche, Postkamp, Königsworther Platz, NEUAPOSTOLISCHE KIRCHE, Theodorstraße, Celler Str., Ludwigstr., Hamburger Allee, Lister Meile, Rundestraße, HAUPTBAHNHOF, Raschplatz, Am Steintor, ADAC, Steintor, Hbf., Kröpke, Thielenplatz, Opernplatz, Berliner Allee, Königstr., Marktkirche, Altes Rathaus, Markthalle, Georgsplatz, Marienstraße, Goetheplatz, Humboldtstr., Am Archiv, Leinstraße, Breite Str., Aegidientorplatz, Wilhelmstraße, Adolfstraße, Waterloo, Friedrichswall, Neues Rathaus, Niedersächsisches Landesmuseum, Schlägerstraße, Lutherstr., Waterlooplatz, MASCHPARK, Planckstr., Sprengel-Museum, Schützenplatz, PAULUS KIRCHE, Krausenstraße, Seelstraße

Main map place names (selection):
Soltau, Munster, Visselhövede, Bomlitz, Fallingbostel, Dorfmark, Bergen, Bergen-Belsen, Walsrode, Schwarmstedt, Wietze, Winsen, Celle, Hustedt, Steyerberg, Stolzenau, Naturpark Steinhuder Meer, Neustadt a. Rübenberge, Wedemark, Burgdof, Loccum, Rehburg, Bad Rehburg, Wunstorf, Garbsen, Langenhagen, Hannover-Langenhagen, Burgwedel, Lehrte, Stadthagen, Bückeburg, Rinteln, Barsinghausen, Wennigsen, Springe, Bad Münder, Laatzen, Sehnde, Hildesheim, Hameln, Schaumburg, Weserbergland, Naturpark, Deister, Süntel

HANNOVER

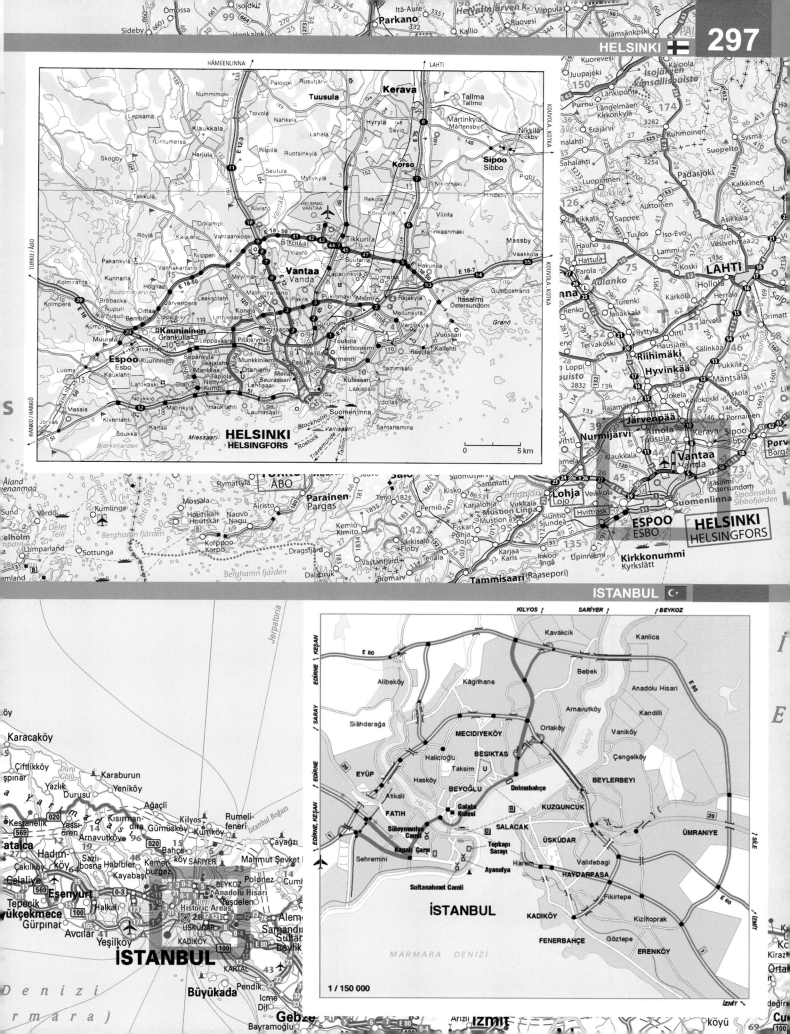

ISTANBUL C·

KØBENHAVN

MALMÖ

Helsingborg

Helsingør

Landskrona

Lund

Hillerød

Fredensborg

Frederiksværk

Tårnby

Dragør

KASTRUP

Amager

Saltholm

Køge Bugt

ØRESUND

0   5   10 km

AARHUS

ODENSE

SJÆLLAND

Roskilde

Ballerup

Holbæk

Kalundborg

Nyborg

Odense

Fredericia

Horsens

Slagelse

Ringsted

Sorø

Køge

Ystad

Trelleborg

Kristianstad

Hässleholm

SKÅNE

FYN

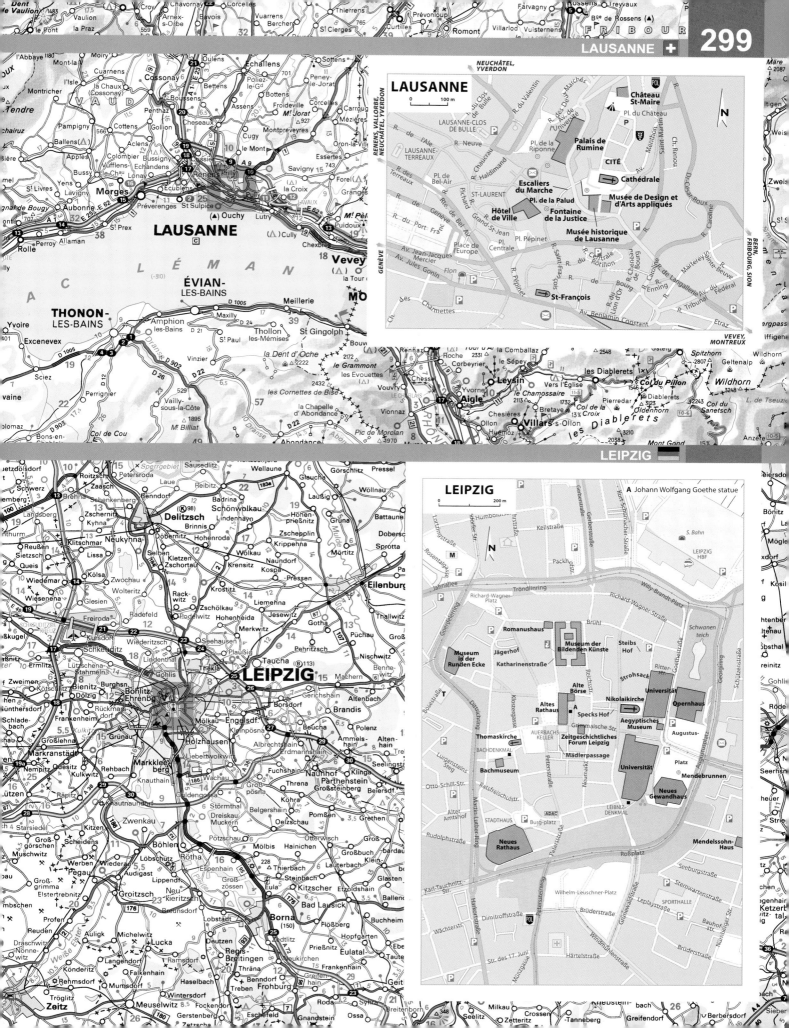

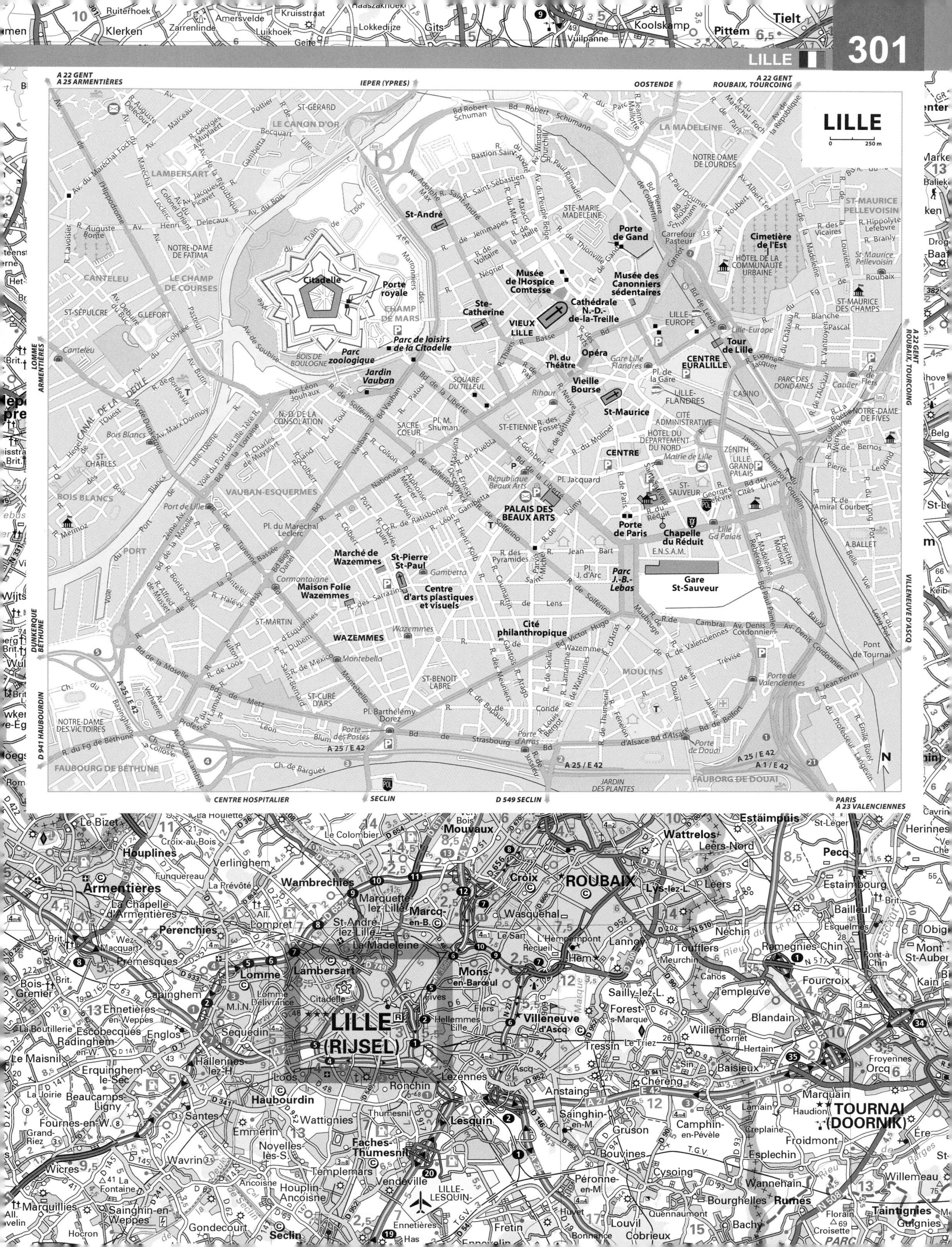

LILLE

0 — 250 m

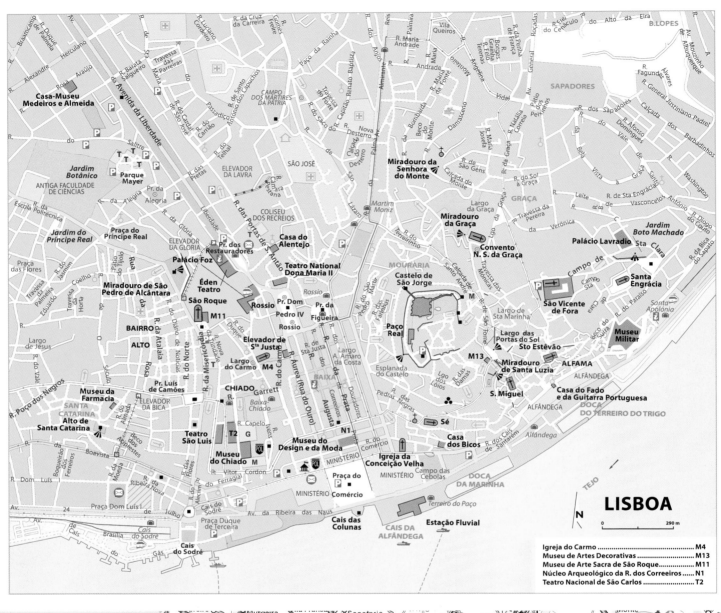

LISBOA

Igreja do Carmo M4
Museu de Artes Decorativas M13
Museu de Arte Sacra de São Roque M11
Núcleo Arqueológico da R. dos Correeiros N1
Teatro Nacional de São Carlos T2

LIVERPOOL

Scale: 0 — 300 m / 0 — 300 yards

Points of interest and features (inset city map):

- Walker Art Gallery
- St George's Hall
- Statue of Eleanor Rigby
- Cavern Walks
- Royal Liver Building
- Cunard Building
- Port of Liverpool Building
- Museum of Liverpool
- Merseyside Maritime Museum
- Tate Liverpool
- ALBERT DOCK
- Beatles Story
- ACC LIVERPOOL
- PIER HEAD
- CHAVASSE PARK
- BLUECOAT ART CENTRE
- LIVERPOOL ONE
- Metropolitan Cathedral of Christ the King
- Liverpool Anglican Cathedral
- Chinese Arch
- CHINATOWN
- CLAYTON SQUARE SHOPPING CENTRE
- Ranelagh Pl.
- ST JOHN'S CENTRE TOWER
- ST JOHN'S GARDEN
- QUEEN SQUARE
- LIME STREET
- CENTRAL
- MOORFIELDS
- JAMES STREET
- Queensway Tunnel
- MERSEY
- N (compass)

Directions / road references:
CROSBY · A65, A59 · PRESTON, M57, M58 · MANCHESTER, M6 · A580 MANCHESTER · ISLE OF MAN, DUBLIN · WALLASEY · BIRKENHEAD · M57 · A57, WARRINGTON · M57, M6 · M62, MANCHESTER · WIDNES

Regional map place names:
Black Combe · Lowick Bridge · Oxen Park · Newby Bridge · Cartmel Fell · Old Hutton · Rise Hill · Dent · Lea Yeat · Dentdale · Broughton-in-Furness · Levens · Endmoor · Birkdale · Scarisbrick · Mawdesley · Coppull · Adlington · Bromley Cross · Tottington · BURY · Bamford · Ainsdale · Burscough · Wrightington · Horwich · BOLTON WEST · Blackrod · Little Lever · Heywood · Royton · Formby · Ormskirk · Skelmersdale · WIGAN · Westhoughton · Aspull · Farnworth · Kearsley · Radcliffe · Whitefield · Middleton · Chadderton · Formby Point · Lydiate · Aughton · Up Holland · Orrell · Ince · Hindley · Atherton · Walkden · Pendlebury · Prestwich · Hightown · Maghull · Rainford · Moss Billinge Bank · Abram · Leigh · Tyldesley · Worsley · Eccles · SALFORD · MANCHESTER · Dublin (Isle of Man) · Douglas (Isle of Man) · Belfast · Blundellsands · Crosby · Litherland · Kirkby · Golborne · Irlam · Urmston · Bootle · New Brighton · ST. HELENS · Knowsley · Haydock · Newton-le-Willows · Winwick · Cadishead · Partington · Stretford · Denton · Liverpool Bay · Wallasey · LIVERPOOL · Roby · Huyton · Prescot · Burtonwood · Fearnhead · Ashton-upon-Mersey · Sale · STOCKPORT · Hoylake · Moreton · BIRKENHEAD · WARRINGTON · Woolston · Broadheath · Gatley · Cheadle · West Kirby · Irby · Port Sunlight · Bebington · Ditton · Gt. Sankey · Grappenhall · Stockton Heath · Altrincham · Hale · Bramhall · Thurstaston · Pensby · Bromborough · Widnes · Speke · Higher Walton · Bucklow Hill · Handforth · Heswall · Eastham · LIVERPOOL JOHN LENNON AIRPORT · Hale · Halton · Daresbury · Stretton · Wilmslow · Point of Ayr · Parkgate · Thornton Hough · Runcorn · Frodsham · Lower Whitley · Knutsford · Alderley Edge · Prestbury · Neston · Willaston · Ellesmere Port · Gt. Budworth · Ollerton · Mostyn · Holywell · Greenfield · Elton · Lach Dennis

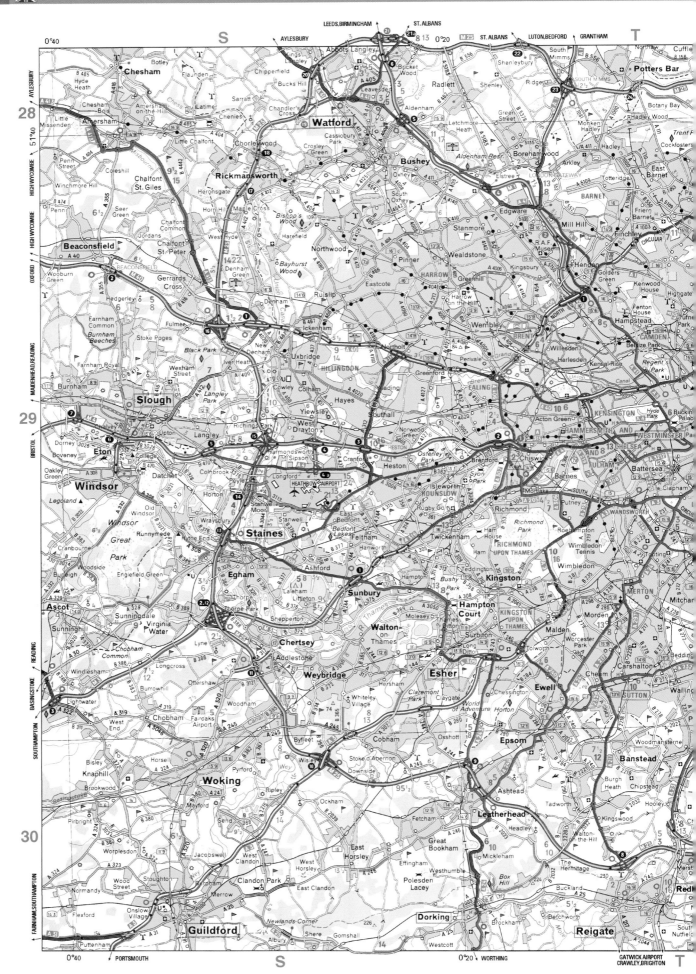

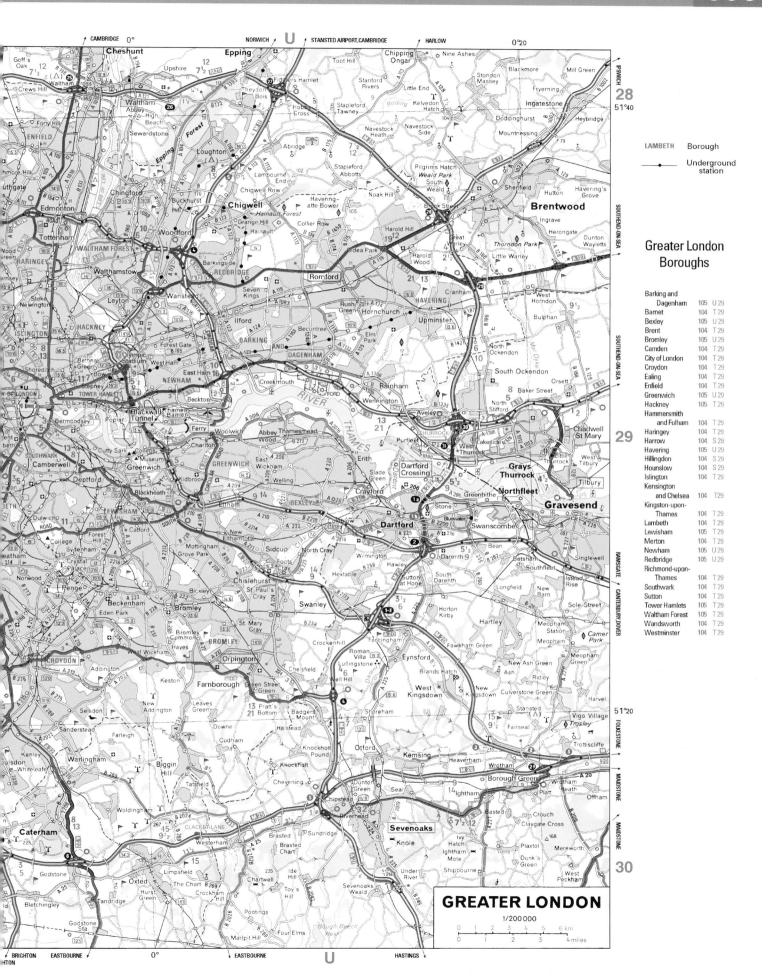

GREATER LONDON

1/200000

LAMBETH Borough
• Underground station

Greater London Boroughs

Barking and Dagenham	105 U 29
Barnet	104 T 29
Bexley	105 T 29
Brent	104 T 29
Bromley	105 U 29
Camden	104 T 29
City of London	104 T 29
Croydon	104 T 29
Ealing	104 T 29
Enfield	104 T 29
Greenwich	105 U 29
Hackney	105 T 29
Hammersmith and Fulham	104 T 29
Haringey	104 T 29
Harrow	104 S 29
Havering	105 U 29
Hillingdon	104 S 29
Hounslow	104 S 29
Islington	104 T 29
Kensington and Chelsea	104 T 29
Kingston-upon-Thames	104 T 29
Lambeth	105 T 29
Lewisham	105 T 29
Merton	104 T 29
Newham	105 U 29
Redbridge	105 U 29
Richmond-upon-Thames	104 T 29
Southwark	104 T 29
Sutton	104 T 29
Tower Hamlets	105 T 29
Waltham Forest	105 T 29
Wandsworth	104 T 29
Westminster	104 T 29

City inset map (LUXEMBOURG)

LIMPERTSBERG
CIMETIÈRE ISRAÉLITE
WEIMERSHOF
Square Édouard André
Chambre de commerce du Grand-Duché
Banque IKB International
Centre national sportif D'Coque
Commission européenne
Banque européenne d'investissement
Cour de justice de l'Union européenne
Cour des comptes
KIRCHBERG
CENTRE EUROPÉEN
Secrétariat général du Parlement européen
Grand Théâtre de la ville de Luxembourg
La Chaise
CHAMP DES GLACIS
Safe & Sorry
Philharmonie
Centre des conférences
Monument R. Schuman
Centre R. Schuman
MUDAM
Pl. de l'Europe
Fort Thüngen
TOUR MALAKOFF
Tour Alcide-de-Gasperi
Pont Vauban
CLAUSEN
Villa Vauban
Pl. W. Churchill
Palais Grand-Ducal
Cathédrale Notre-Dame

LUXEMBOURG
0   230 m
N

Regional map

Malmedy, Büllingen, Naturpark, Weißer Stein 689, Schmidtheim, Müsch
Stavelot, Waimes, Faymonville, Bullingen
Gerolstein, Hillesheim, Dreis, Dockweiler, Oberstadtfeld, Meisburg, Steinborn, Oberkail, Spangdahlem, Landscheid

Parc Naturel, Haute-Sûre
Wiltz (Kiischpelt), Winseler, Pommerloch, Villers-la-Bonne-Eau, Harlange, Kaundorf, Büderscheid, Lipperscheid
Eschweiler, Wilwerwiltz, Stolzembourg, Putscheid, Hoscheid, M. St. Nicolas, Vianden, Obersgegen, Bivels, Geichlingen
Sinspelt, Oberweis, Mettendorf, Bitburg, Binsfeld, Herforst, Speicher, Zemmer, Föhren

Bavigne (lac de la Hte Sûre), Insenborn, Boulaide, Eschdorf, Heiderscheid, Welscheid, Erpeldange, Brandenbourg, Bastendorf, Grenglay, Fouhren, Roth, Naturpark
Hochfels, Tintange, Neunhausen, Arsdorf, Herrenberg, Bettendorf, Reisdorf, Dillingen, Bollendorf, Bollendorf-Pont, Irrel, Niederweis, Helenenberg
Bodange, Martelange, H. Martelange, Rambrouch, Grosbous, Feulen, Ettelbrück, Diekirch, Beaufort, Ermsdorf, Grundhof, Weilerbach, Berdorf, Echternacherbrück, Echternach, Schweich, Kordel, Quint
Perle, Folschette, Vichten, Berg, Mertzig, Schieren, Médernach, Haller, Mullerthal, G. du Loup, Rosport, Ralingen, Ehrang
Heinstert, Attert, Oberpallen, Redange, Noerdange, Useldange, Bissen, Cruchten, Nommern, Christnach, PETITE SUISSE LUXEMBOURGEOISE, Osweiler, Born, Trierweiler, TRIER
Nobressart, Tontelange, Beckerich, Saeul, Brouch, Lintgen, Larochette, Heffingen, Consdorf, Scheidgen, Mompach, Waldrach
Arlon (Aarlen), Eischen, Steinfort, Tuntange, Hollenfels, Bour, Ansembourg, Bourglinster, Junglinster, Reuland, Godbrange, Bech, Berbourg, Wasserbillig, Oberbillig, Konz
Koerich, Kehlen, Steinsel, Lorentzweiler, Gonderange, Biwer, Weckern, Manternach, Mertert, Langsur
Kopstal, Walferdange, Hostert, Roodt, Rodenbourg, Gonderange, Machtum, Wellen, Nittel, Tawern, Wiltingen
LUXEMBOURG, Senningen, Niederanven, Flaxweiler, Grevenmacher, Söst, Saarburg
Capellen, Mamer, Bertrange, Strassen, Hamm, Schuttrange, Canach, Oberdonven, Ahn, Wormeldange, Wincheringen, Trassem
Kleinbettingen, Autelbas, Dippach, Leudelange, Hesperange, Moutfort, Oetrange, Greiveldange, Ehnen, Beurig, Zerf
Messancy, Schouweiler, Reckange-s-Mess, Mondercange, Bous, Stadtbredimus, Palzem, Merzkirchen
Athus, Bascharage, Sanem, Bettembourg, Frisange, Weiler-la-Tour, Dalheim, Remich, Bech-Kleinmacher, Nennig, Schwebsange, Orscholz, Britten
Longwy, Pétange, Differdange, Soleuvre, Belvaux, Schifflange, Esch-s-Alzette, Kayl, Dudelange, Mondorf-les-Bains, Wellenstein, Remerschen, Mettlach
Mont-St Martin, Herserange, Rédange, Zolwerknapp, Hussigny-Godbrange, Rumelange, Évrange, Burmerange, Perl, Schengen, Apach, Merzig
Longuyon, Villerupt, Audun-le-Tiche, Ottange, Volmerange-les-Mines, Roussy, Contz, Sierck, Waldwisse, Hilbringen
MEURTHE-, Kanfen, Forêt de Garche, Beyren, Borg, SAARLAND

LYON

MADRID (City Center)

Espacio culturales Conde Duque
Palacio de Liria
Museo ABC
MALASAÑA
CENTRO CULTURAL CLARA DEL REY
Plaza Dos de Mayo
Museo Municipal
Museo del Romanticismo
Plaza Alonso Martínez
PL. STA. BARBARA
Plaza de Colón
Museo de Cera
TORRE DE MADRID
EDIFICIO ESPAÑA
Museo Cerralbo
Plaza de España
CHUECA
Museo Arqueológico Nacional
SALAMANCA
PALACIO DEL SENADO
Gran Vía
Palacio de Buenavista
La Encarnación
Jardines de Sabatini
Plaza del Callao
Gran Vía
Pl. de Cibeles
Palacio de Linares
Puerta de Alcalá
Palacio Real
Teatro Real de la Opera
Plaza de Oriente
Las Descalzas Reale
Real Academia de Bellas Artes de San Fernando
Teatro de la Zarzuela
Palacio de Comunicaciones
Museo Nacional de Artes Decorativas
BANCO DE ESPAÑA
Museo Naval
Campo del Moro
JARDINES LEPANTO
Plaza de la Armería
Plaza de la Villa
Torre de los Lujanes
Plaza de la Puerta del Sol
Plaza de la Provincia
PALACIO DEL CONGRESO
MUSEO THYSSEN-BORNEMISZA
Bolsa de Madrid
H. Ritz
Casón del Buen Retiro
Catedral N.S. de la Almudena
Plaza Mayor
Iglesia Arzobispal Castrense
Casa de Cisneros
San Miguel
Palacio de Sta Cruz
H. PALACE
MUSEO DEL PRADO
Parque del Buen Retiro
LA CHOPERA
Jardines de las Vistillas
San Pedro
Capilla del Obispo
San Isidro
Plaza de la Paja
San Andrés
Real Basílica de San Francisco el Grande
PARQUE DE LA CORNISA
EL RASTRO
CaixaForum
Real Jardín Botánico
PARQUE DALIEDA DE S. FRANCISCO
LA LATINA
LAVAPIÉS
CENTRO DE ARTE REINA SOFÍA
Museo Nacional de Antropología
ATOCHA
OBSERVATORIO ASTRONÓMICO

MADRID

0 — 300 m

MADRID (Regional map)

Colmenarejo
Las Matas
El Goloso
Universidad
Belvis de J.
Daganzo de Arriba
Meco
Las Rozas de Madrid
El Pardo
Mingorrubio
Valdelatas
Alcobendas
ADOLFO SUÁREZ MADRID BARAJAS
Camarma de Esteruelas
Majadahonda
Fuencarral
Paracuellos de J.
Ajalvir
Alcalá de Henares
Villanueva del Pardillo
Aravaca
Barajas
Los Berrocales del Jarama
Torrejón de Ardoz
Pozuelo de Alarcón
Casa de Campo
San Fernando de Henares
Boadilla del Monte
Coslada
Mejorada del Campo
Alcorcón
Villaviciosa de Odón
MADRID
Rivas-Vaciamadrid
Arganda del Rey
Leganés
Getafe
Móstoles
Fuenlabrada
Pinto
Parque Regional
WARNER BROS
Parla
R. Manzanares del Rey
Tajuña

N

DIRECTION DU PORT
Docks de la Joliette
FRAC
Pl. Marceau
Saint-Lazare
Musée des Beaux-arts
Pl. de la Joliette
Palais Longchamp
Pl. J.-P. Guesde
Porte d'Aix
Gare St-Charles
Musée Grobet-Labadié
Muséum d'histoire naturelle
SNCM
CITÉ DE LA MUSIQUE
Longchamp
GARE MARITIME
Anc. Cath. de la Major
Centre de la Vieille Charité
HÔTEL DE LA RÉGION
ST-THÉODORE
LES CARMES
Hôtel-Dieu
JOLIETTE
Cath. de la Major
LE PANIER
Musée d'Histoire de Marseille
NOAILLES
St-Vincent de Paul (Les Réformés)
Musée Regards de Provence
Montée des Accoules
Préau des Accoules
Pl. Daviel
Alcazar
Mémorial de la Marseillaise
MUCEM
Maison diamantée
Hôtel de Cabre
Grand-Rue
St-CANNAT
CENTRE BOURSE
La Canebière
Pl. du Marché des Capucins
Palais des Arts
Villa Méditerranée
St-Laurent
Musée des Docks romains
Port antique
M1
Noailles
ST-MICHEL
Palais du Pharo
Fort St-Jean
Quai du Port
St-Ferréol
Pl. J.
Parc du Pharo
Mémorial des camps de la mort
Vieux-Port-Hôtel de Ville
Q. de la Fraternité
Opéra
VIEUX-PORT
STE-TRINITÉ
N.-D.-du-Mont-Cours Julien
Théâtre de la Criée
Q. de Rive Neuve
Pl. Thiars les Arcenaulx
ST-CHARLES
Cours Julien
N.-D. du Mont
Cours Honoré-d'Estienne-d'Orves
Musée Cantini
Musée de Santons Marcel Carbonel
Palais de Justice
Préfecture
ST-SACREMENT
Fort St-Nicolas
Basilique St-Victor
Jardin P. Puget
Estrangin Préfecture
Cours Pierre Puget
ST-JEAN-BAPTISTE
ST-LAMBERT
N.-D. DE LOURDES
ST-JOSEPH
Pl. Castellane
Notre-Dame de la Garde
ROUCAS-BLANC
SAINT-FRANÇOIS D'ASSISE
SACRÉ-COEUR
PARC DU 26E CENTENAIRE

MARSEILLE
0   300 m

Palais de la Bourse-Musée de la Marine et de l'Economie de Marseille .. M1

Ensuès-la-Redonne
Val-de-Ricard
Niolon★
La Vesse
Anse de l'Estaque
St-Joseph
Le Merlan
Plan-de-Cuques
N.-D. du Château
Crx de Garlaban
Pont-de-l'Etoile
Méjean
Les Figuières
La Madrague-de-la-Ville
St-Louis
A507:fin 2017
St-Jérôme
Les Olives
Allauch★
Carry-le-Rouet
Le Rouet-Plage
Madrague-de-Gignac
Rade de Marseille
La Rose
St-Julien
St-Just
Les Trois-Lucs
Camoins-les-Bains
Napollon
★★★ **MARSEILLE**
Île Ratonneau
Le Frioul
St-Barnabé
La Valentine
Aubagne
Île Pomègues
Châu d'If
Prado Carénage
La Pomme
La Bastidonne
Île Pomègues
Cap Caveaux
Rade d'Endoume
Plages du Prado
St-Marcel
St-Menet
La Penne-sur-Huveaune
Le Charrel
Carnoux-en-Provence
Îles du Frioul
Bonneveine
La Pointe-Rouge
Ste-Marguerite
St-Loup
La Capélette
Le Cabot
PARC NATIONAL
Roquefort-la-Bédoule
Mazargues
Mt St-Cyr
St-Cyr
La Gélade
Les Fourniers
Les Barles
La Madrague-de-Montredon
Montredon
Le Redon
La Panouse Vaufrèges
Mt Carpiagne
Camp militaire
Mt Rose
Marseilleveyre
Col de la Gineste
Forêt de la Gardiole
Ste-Croix
Cap Croisette
Callelongue
Logisson
Col de Cassis
Mt de la Saoupe
Île Tiboulen
Les Goudes
CALANQUES
Cassis
Port-Miou
N.-D. de Bon-Voyage
Sormiou
DES
Morgiou
Cal. de Port-Miou
Île Maire
Bec Sormiou
Cap Morgiou
★★★ Cap
Île Planier
Cal. de Sormiou
Grotte Cosquer

MILANO

0 — 300 m

Arco della Pace
Arena
Parco Sempione
Torre Branca
Acquario civico
Triennale Design Museum Pal. d'Arte
San Simpliciano
S. Marco
CASTELLO SFORZESCO
PINACOTECA DI BRERA
Giardini Pubblici Indro Montanelli
Planetarium
Museo Civico di Storia naturale
GAM
PAC
CENACOLO
Pal. Litta
Teatro dal Verme
Piccolo Teatro
Gallerie d'Italia
Teatro alla Scala
Palazzo Marino
Museo Poldi Pezzoli
Casa di Manzoni
Museo Bagatti Valsecchi
Pal. Castiglioni
Palazzo Berri-Meregalli
Villa Necchi Campiglio
S. Maria delle Grazie
Museo Civico Archeologico
S. Maurizio
S. Fedele
S. Carlo al Corso
S. Babila
S. Maria d. Passione
PINACOTECA AMBROSIANA
Galleria V. Emanuele II
Pza Cordusio
Pal. della Ragione
DUOMO
S. Ambrogio
Museo della Scienza e della Tecnologia Leonardo da Vinci
S. Satiro
Museo del Duomo
S. Gottardo in Corte
Conservatorio G. Verdi
S. Pietro in Gessate
S. Giorgio al Palazzo
S. Alessandro
Torre Branca
S. Antonio Abate
S. Lorenzo Maggiore
Ca' Granda Università
S. Nazaro
Teatro Carcano
Museo Diocesano
Sant' Eustorgio
Porta Ticinese
S. Cristoforo
Teatro Franco Parenti

PORTA GENOVA
PORTA VITTORIA

Nerviano
Barbaiana
Pogliano Milanese
Rho
Cornaredo
Sedriano
Vittuone
Bareggio
Settimo Milanese
Cesano Boscone
Corsico
Romano Banco
Assago
Trezzano sul Naviglio
Buccinasco
Pero
Novate Milanese
Bollate
Cormano
Cusano Milanino
Bresso
Balsamo
Sesto San Giovanni
Cologno Monzese
Cologno Nord sul Naviglio
Brugherio
Cernusco sul Naviglio
Gorgonzola
Bussero
Pioltello
Segrate
Vimodrone
Rodano
Melzo
Peschiera Borromeo
San Donato Milanese
Chiaravalle Milanese
San Giuliano Milanese

MILANO
Castello Sforzesco
Duomo
S. Ambrogio
LINATE

MONTE-CARLO

0   250 m

N

MER MÉDITERRANÉE

St-Sauveur-sur-Tinée
St-Martin-Vésubie
La Colmiane
La Bollène
Rimplas
La Roche

VENTIMIGLIA
MENTON
A 8 MENTON
A 8
MENTON
MONTE-CARLO BEACH

A8/E74
NICE
LA TURBIE
A8 NICE, EZE
CAP-D'AIL

Hameau de Sillet
N.-D. des Car
Thiéry
LES MONEGHETTI
Mont des Mules
AUREILLA
BORDINA
LA ROUSSA
FAUSSIGNANA
ST-ROMAN
TÉNAO
MONTE CARLO COUNTRY CLUB
MONTE-CARLO SPORTING-CLUB
LARVOTTO
Plage du Larvotto

MONTE-CARLO
Casino Monte-Carlo
Port
Jardin Exotique
MONACO
Palais princier
Musée océanographique
FONTVIEILLE
STADE LOUIS II
Jean-Charles Rey
Pointe St Martin
Roseraie Princesse Grace
Parc paysager
HÉLIPORT
Port du Cap-d'Ail

VILLEFRANCHE-S-MER

NATIONAL
PARC
Cime du Diable
Les Merveilles
Cime de la Nauque
L'Authion
MERCANTOUR
Col de Turini
Turini
Peira-Cava
Moulinet
Col de Brouis
Breil-s-R
Lucéram
Col de Braus
St-Roch
Sospel
Olivetta-San-Michele
L'Escarène
Castillon
Col de Castillon
Peille
Ste-Agnès
Blausasc
Gorbio
Peillon
Roquebrune-
L'Annonciade
La Turbie
Beausoleil
MENTON
Cap-Martin
Cap Martin
MONTE-CARLO ★★★
MONACO ★★★
La Condamine
Cap-d'Ail
Èze
Èze-Bord-de-Mer
Beaulieu-sur-Mer
Villefranche-sur-Mer
St-Jean-Cap-Ferrat
Cap Ferrat ★★
NICE ★★★
NICE CÔTE-D'AZUR
Col de Vence
Baou de St-Jeannet
Tourrettes-sur-Loup
Vence
St-Paul-de-Vence
La Colle-sur-Loup
Cagnes-s-M.
St-Laurent-du-Var
Cros-de-Cagnes
Villeneuve-Loubet
Biot
Vallauris
ANTIBES ★★
Marineland
Aquasplash
Valbonne
Sophia-Antipolis
Carros
Colomars
Falicon
Gattières
St-Jeannet
CÔTE D'AZUR

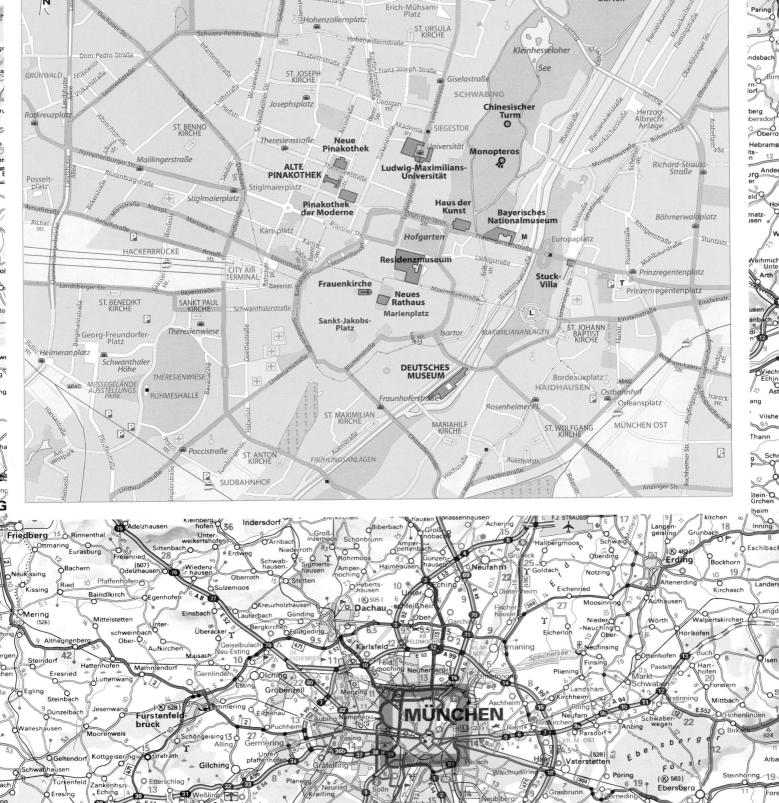

MÜNCHEN

0   500 m

N

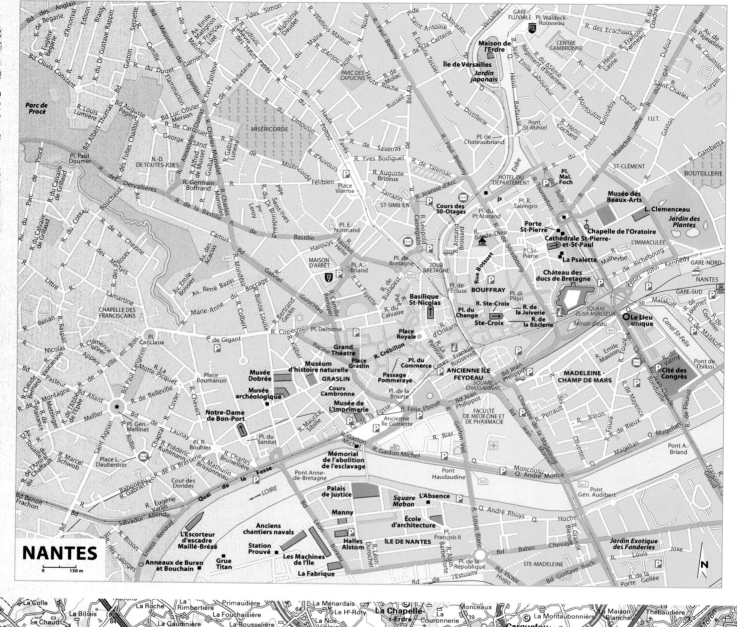

NANTES

0   150 m

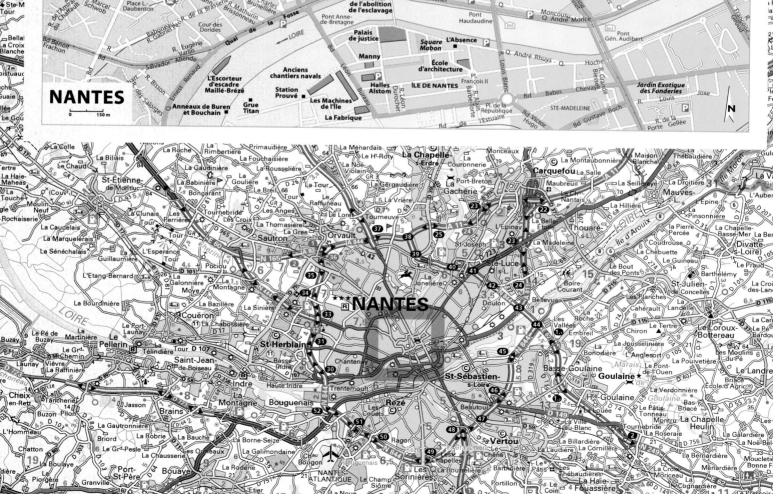

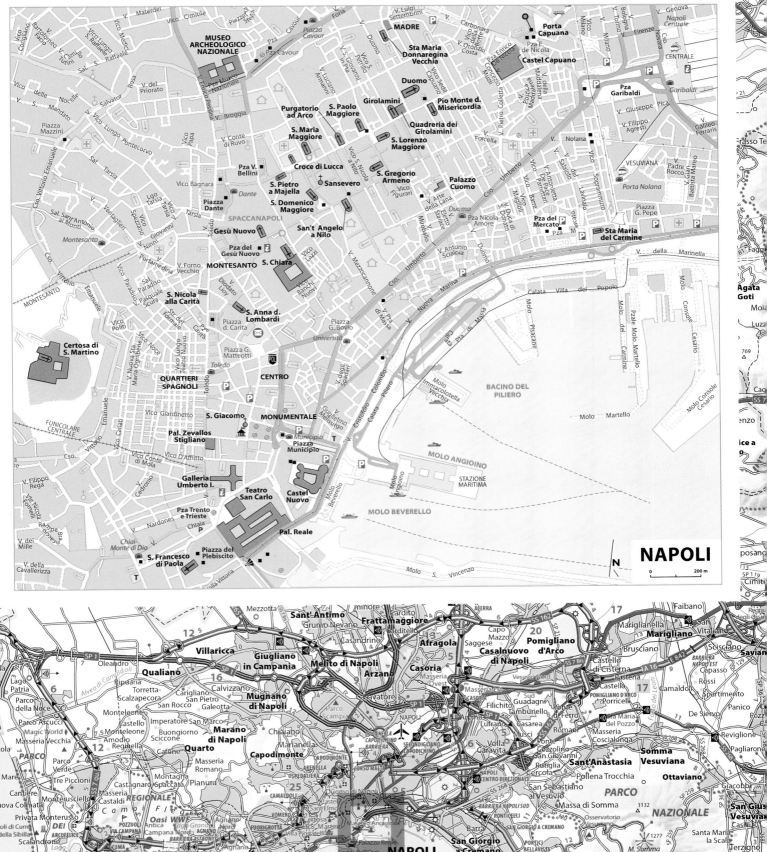

NAPOLI

N

0   200 m

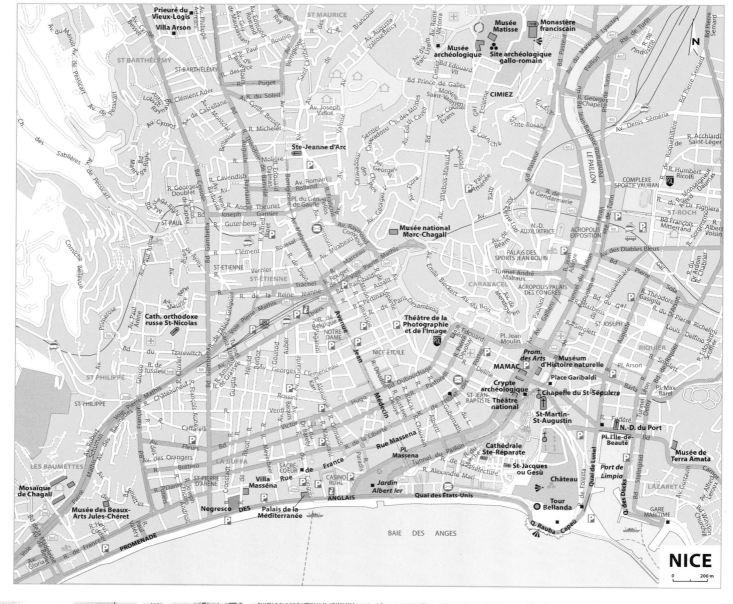

NICE

0   200 m

BAIE DES ANGES

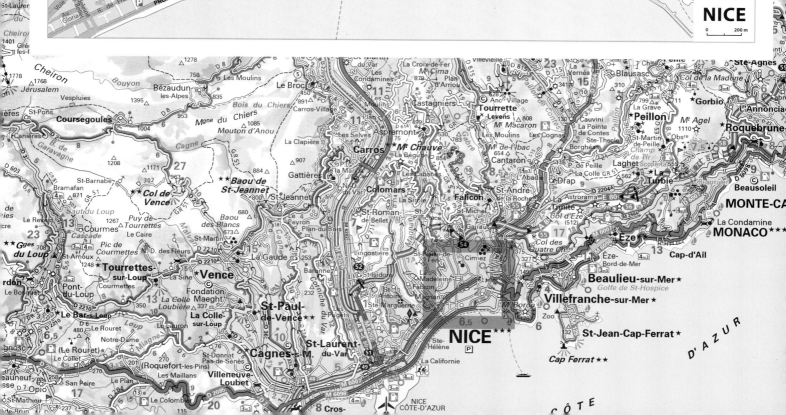

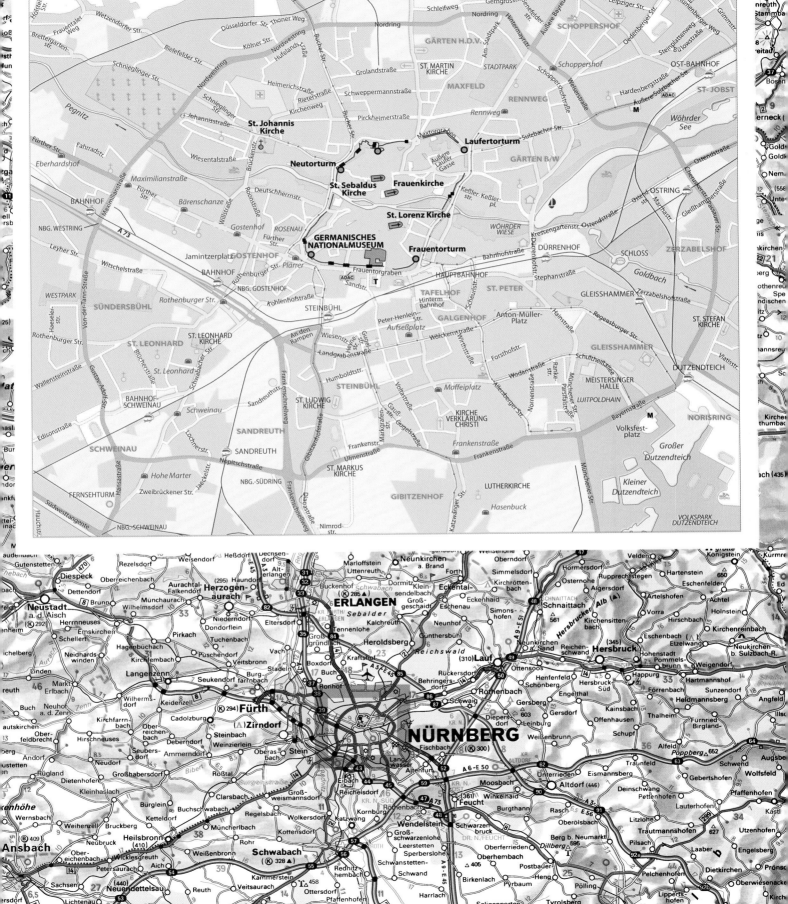

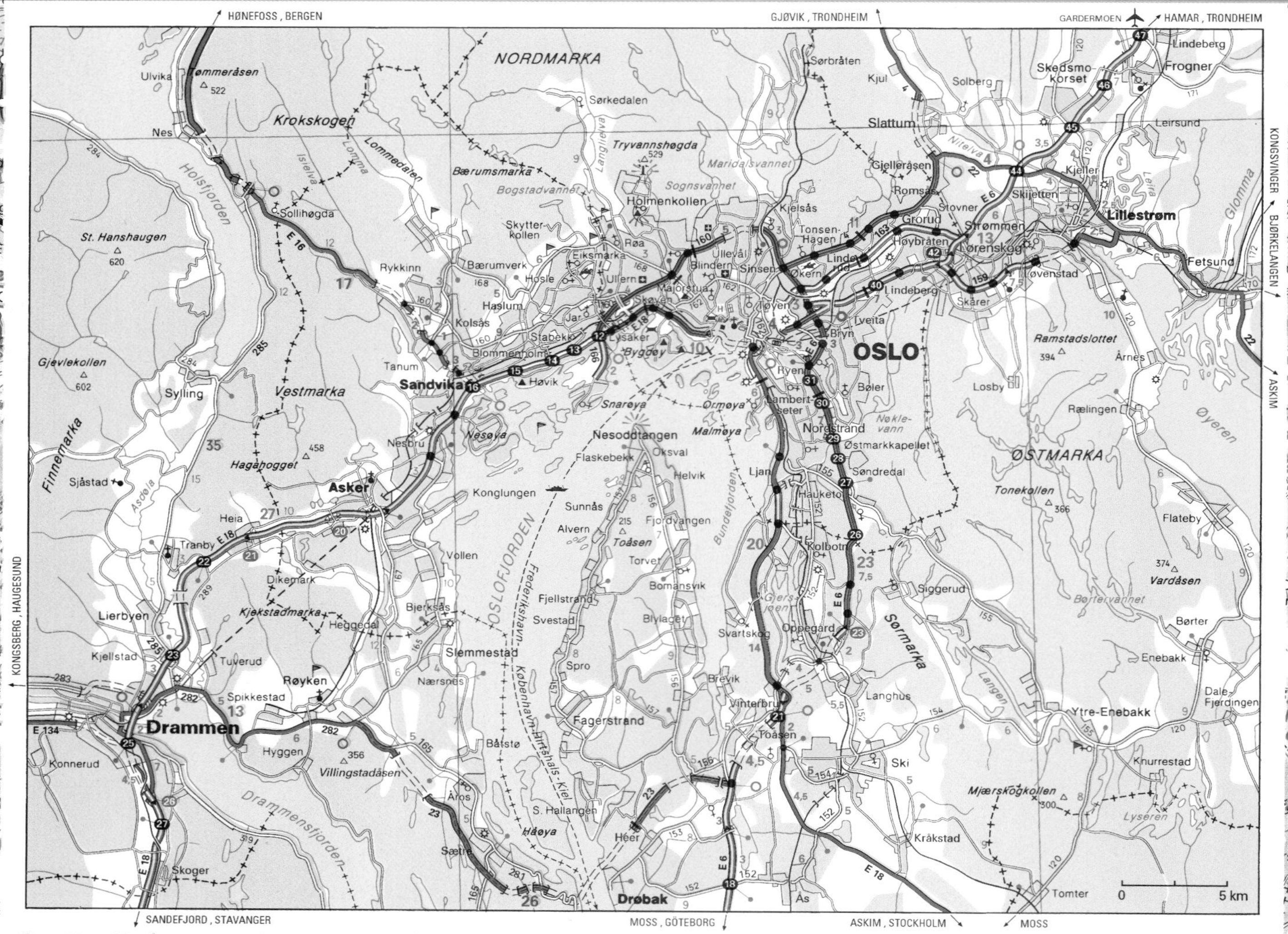

HØNEFOSS, BERGEN   GJØVIK, TRONDHEIM   GARDERMOEN ✈ HAMAR, TRONDHEIM

NORDMARKA

OSLO

Sandvika

Asker

Drammen

OSLOFJORDEN

ØSTMARKA

Lillestrøm

Drøbak

SANDEFJORD, STAVANGER   MOSS, GÖTEBORG   ASKIM, STOCKHOLM   MOSS

0   5 km

Hemsedal

Hamar   Elverum

Gjøvik

Ringsaker

BUSKERUD

Hønefoss

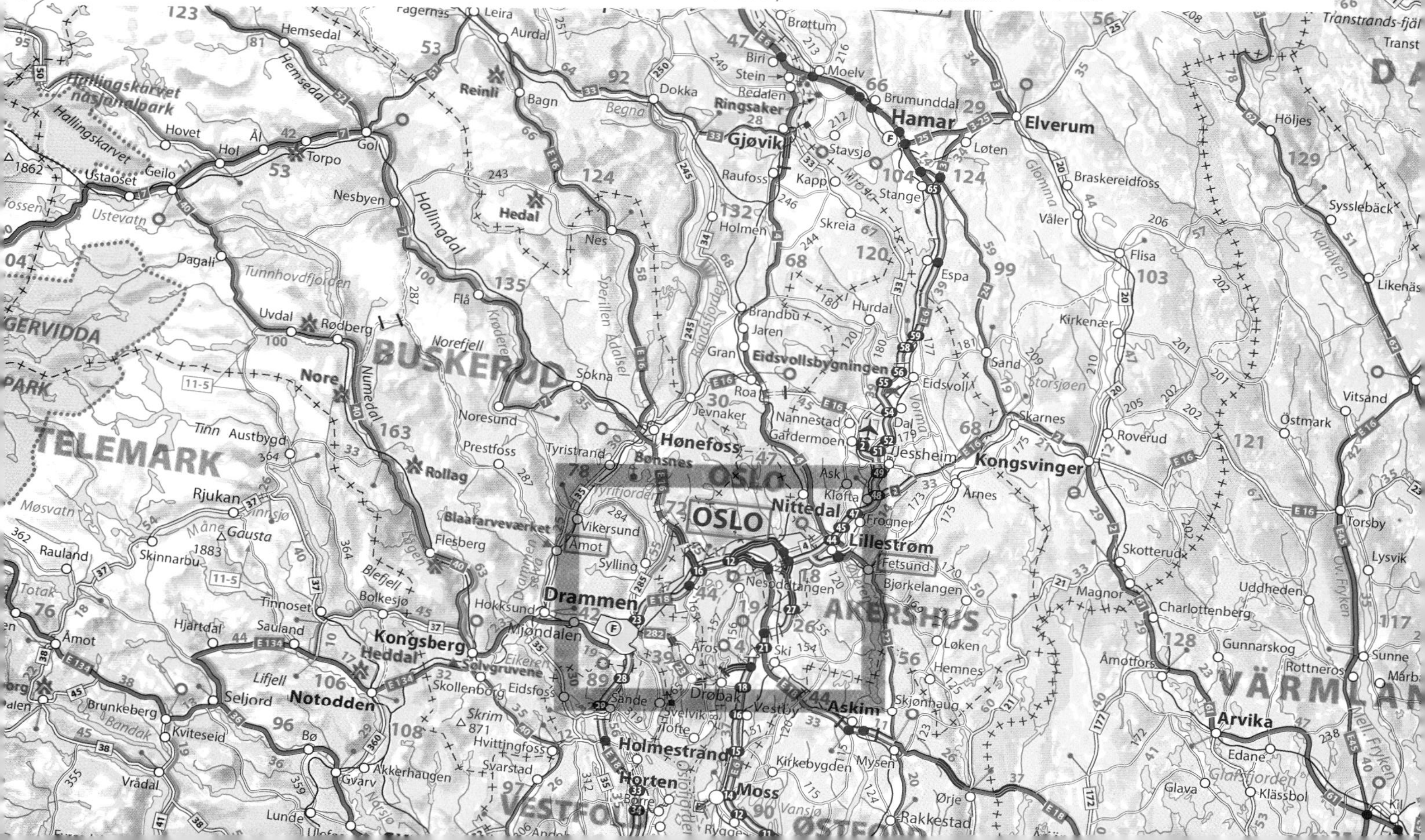

OSLO

Drammen

Kongsvinger

TELEMARK

Kongsberg

Notodden

AKERSHUS

Lillestrøm

Askim

Arvika

VESTFOLD

Moss

ØSTFOLD

VÄRMLAND

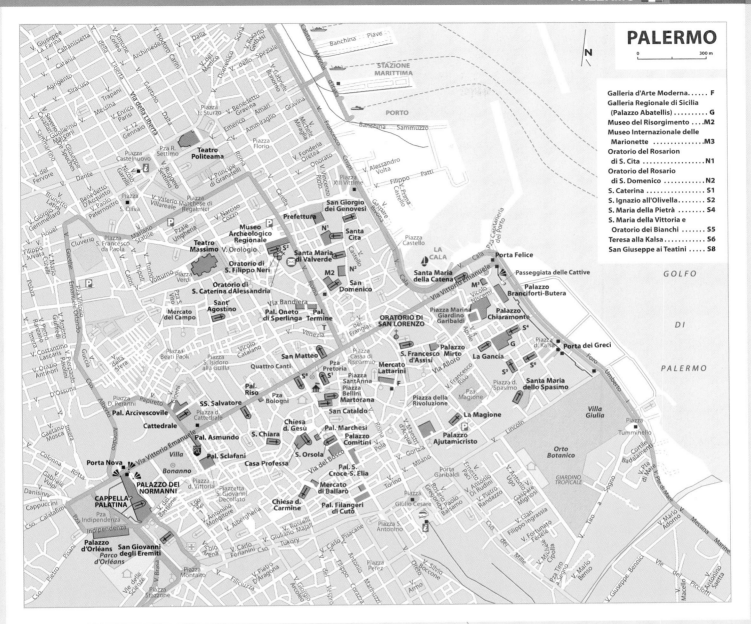

PALERMO

0   300 m

Galleria d'Arte Moderna......	F
Galleria Regionale di Sicilia (Palazzo Abatellis)	G
Museo del Risorgimento M2	
Museo Internazionale delle Marionette M3	
Oratorio del Rosarion di S. Cita	N1
Oratorio del Rosario di S. Domenico	N2
S. Caterina	S1
S. Ignazio all'Olivella	S2
S. Maria della Pietrà	S4
S. Maria della Vittoria e Oratorio dei Bianchi	S5
Teresa alla Kalsa	S6
San Giuseppe ai Teatini	S8

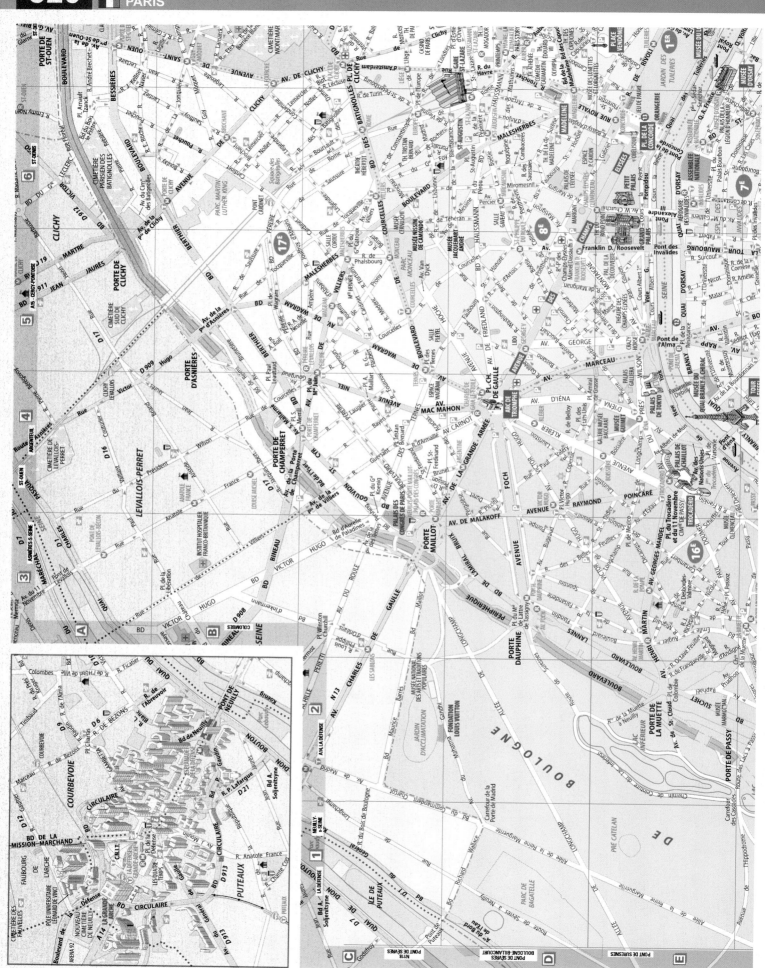

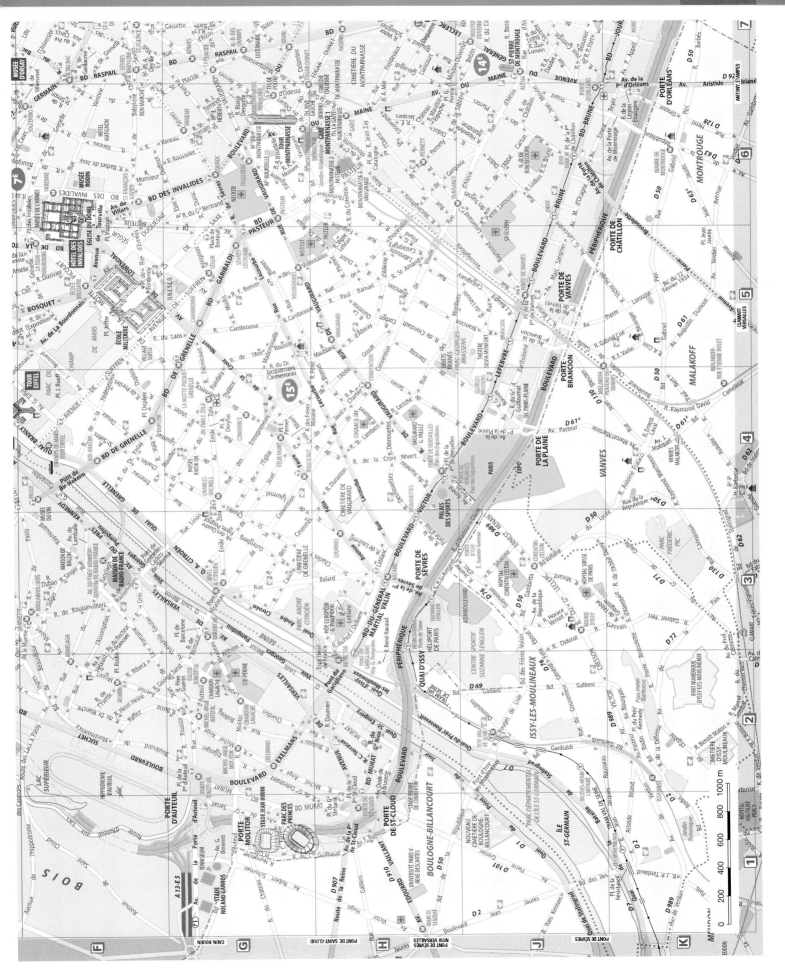

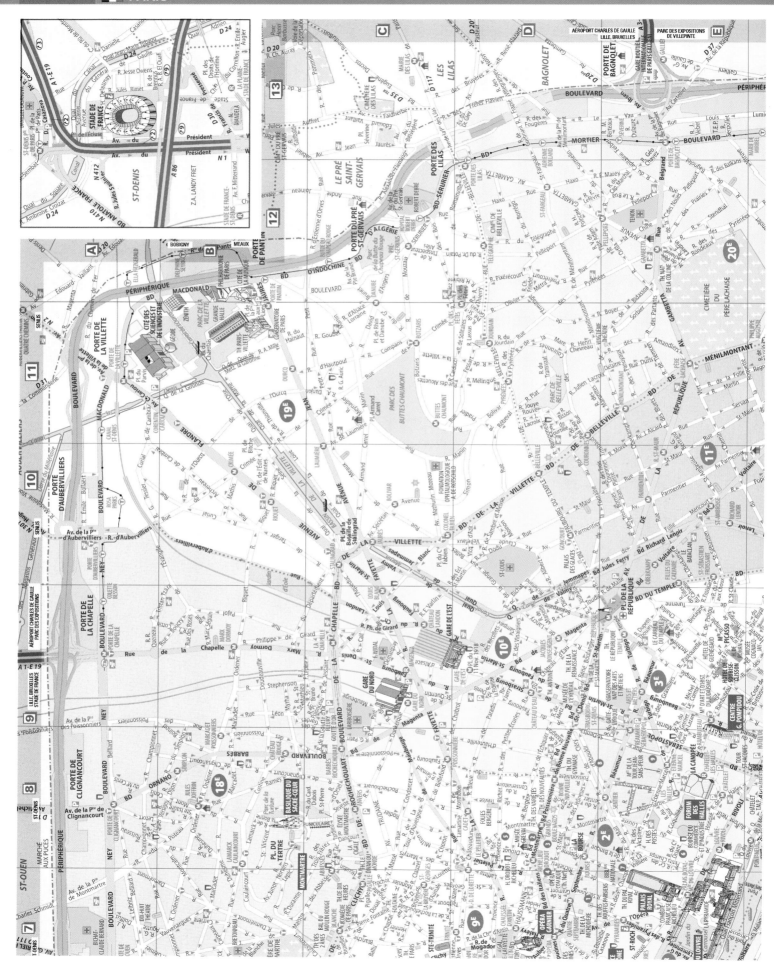

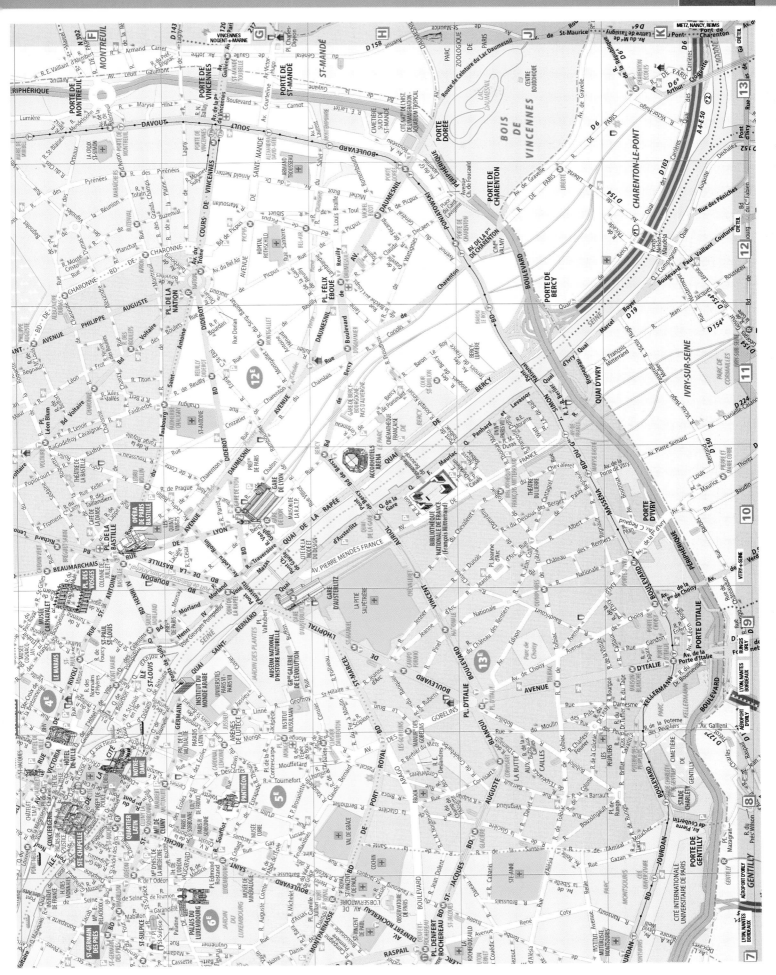

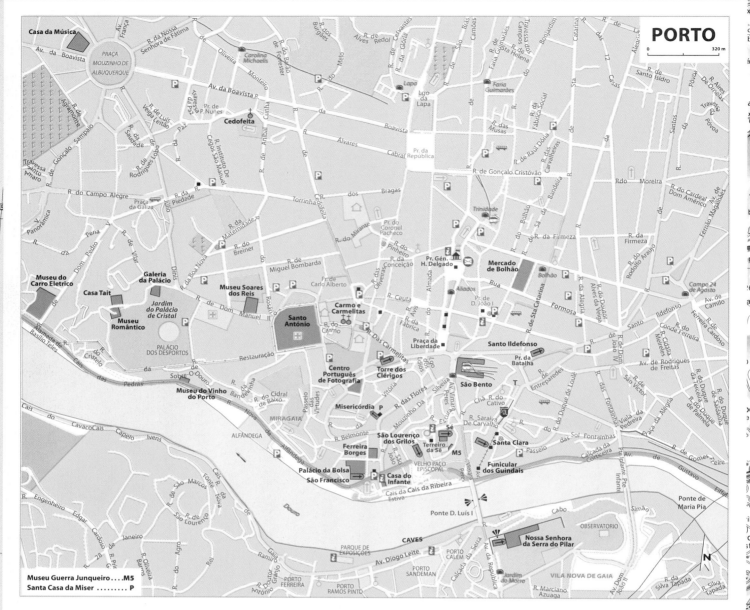

PORTO

0 ___ 320 m

Museu Guerra Junqueiro....M5
Santa Casa da Miser ....P

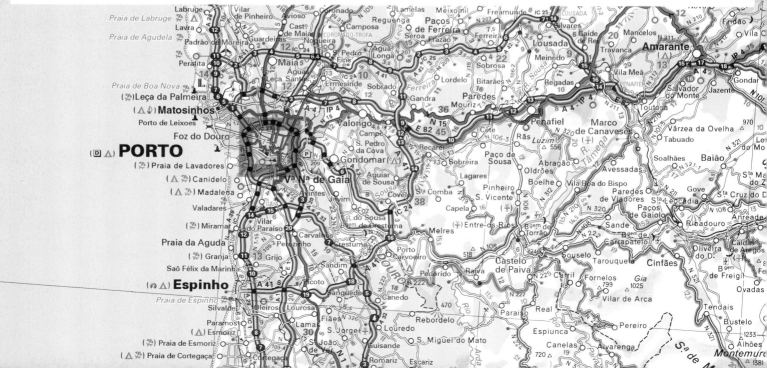

PRAHA

0 — 2 km

STATENICE · HOROMĚŘICE · PŘEDNÍ KOPANINA · NEBUŠICE · SUCHDOL · SEDLEC · LYSOLAJE · BOHNICE · ČIMICE · DOLNÍ CHABRY · DÁBLICE · ČAKOVICE · KBELY · LETŇANY · LETECKÉ MUZEUM · KOBYLISY · STŘÍŽKOV · PROSEK · TRÓJA · LIBEŇ · VYSOČANY · HLOUBĚTÍN · KYJE · VOKOVICE · DEJVICE · BUBENEČ · HOLEŠOVICE · KARLÍN · HRDLOŘEZY · MALEŠICE · ŠTĚRBOHOLY · VELESLAVÍN · STŘEŠOVICE · HRADČANY · PRAŽSKÝ HRAD · JOSEFOV · ŽIŽKOV · LIBOC · BŘEVNOV · SV. MIKULÁŠE · KARLŮV MOST · STARÉ MĚSTO · NOVÉ MĚSTO · VINOHRADY · VRŠOVICE · STRAŠNICE · DOLNÍ MĚCHOLUPY · HOSTIVAŘ · HORNÍ MĚCHOLUPY · RUZYNĚ · MOTOL · MALÁ STRANA · OLŠANSKÉ HŘBITOVY · ŘEPY · KOŠÍŘE · SMÍCHOV · VYŠEHRAD · NUSLE · MICHLE · ZÁBĚHLICE · PETROVICE · HÁJE · CHODOV · KŘESLICE · STODŮLKY · JINONICE · RADLICE · PODOLÍ · KRČ · KAČEROV · OPATOV · ÚJEZD · HLUBOČEPY · BRANÍK · HOLYNĚ · MALÁ CHUCHLE · HODKOVIČKY · LHOTKA · LIBUŠ · KUNRATICE · ŠEBEROV · OŘECH · SLIVENEC · VELKÁ CHUCHLE · MODŘANY

Kladno · Slaný · Beroun · Karlštejn · PRAHA · Kutná Hora · Kolín · Poděbrady · Nymburk · Rakovník · Křivoklát · Dobříš · Benešov

ROMA

0 520 m

Top map (city center)

VITERBO · TERNI · MUSEO NAZ. DI VILLA GIULIA · GALLERIA NAZ. D'ARTE MODERNA · S. COSTANZA · FIRENZE

GALLERIA BORGHESE
VILLA BORGHESE
Vle Giuseppe Mazzini
Pincio · Il Pincio · Piazza Napoleone I
Santa Maria del Popolo
Piazza del Popolo
FLAMINIO
Porta Pinciana
Piazzale Brasile
Santa Maria dei Miracoli
PRATI
Villa Médicis
Trinità dei Monti
Santa Maria della Vittoria
AULA OTTAGONA
Terme di Diocleziano
Museo dell'Ara Pacis
Mausoleo di Augusto
PIAZZA DI SPAGNA
Santa Susanna
Santa Maria degli Angeli
MUSEI VATICANI
Giardini Vaticani
CASTEL SANT'ANGELO
Fontana del Tritone
Palazzo Barberini
Piazza della Repubblica
Roma Termini
PIAZZA S. PIETRO
PALAZZO ALTEMPS
San Luigi dei Francesi
FONTANA DI TREVI
Giardino del Quirinale
San Carlo alle Quattro Fontane
Sant'Andrea al Quirinale
PALAZZO MASSIMO ALLE TERME
Sant'Agnese in Agone
PIAZZA NAVONA
PANTHEON
Pal. del Quirinale
Piazza d. Esquilino
Pal. della Cancelleria
S. Ignazio
SANTA MARIA MAGGIORE
Santa Prassede
Palazzo Farnese
Sant'Andrea della Valle
Santa Maria Sopra Minerva
GESÙ
Piazza Venezia
FORI IMPERIALI
P.za Campo dei Fiori
Area Sacra
VILLA FARNESINA
Vittoriano
Santa Maria in Aracoeli
PALAZZO DEI CONSERVATORI
PALAZZO NUOVO
FORO ROMANO
San Pietro in Vincoli
Domus Aurea
GIANICOLO
Palazzo Corsini
Tempio di Apollo Sosiano
Teatro di Marcello
PALAZZO SENATORIO
PIAZZA DEL CAMPIDOGLIO
S.S. Cosma e Damiano
Tempio di Venere e Roma
TRASTEVERE
ISOLA TIBERINA
Tempio della Fortune Virile
Pza d. Bocca della Verità
Arco di Giano
Arco di Constantino
COLOSSEO
Sta Maria in Trastevere
Chiesa di San Pietro in Montorio
San Benedetto in Piscinula
S. Crisogono
Tempio di Vesta
PALATINO
San Clemente
Piazza di S. Giovanni in Laterano
Scala Santa
Santa Cecilia in Trastevere
Santa Maria in Cosmedin
CIRCO
Ss. Giovanni e Paolo
Pal. Lateranense
Battistero
SAN GIOVANNI IN LATERANO
Villa Doria Pamphilj
Santa Sabina
MASSIMO
Santo Stefano Rotondo
MTE. CELIO
VILLA CELIMONTANA
Circo Massimo
MTE. AVENTINO
PARCO DI PORTA CAPENA
Porta San Paolo
TERME DI CARACALLA
Piramide di Caio Cestio

FIUMICINO · SAN PAOLO FUORI LE MURA · PIRAMIDE DI CAIO CESTIO · E.U.R., FIUMICINO · NAPOLI · CATACOMBE, VIA APPIA ANTICA

Bottom map (regional)

Madonna di Bracciano · Isola Farnese · GUIDONIA · Tivoli
La Storta · Il Pino · Settebagni · Guidonia
Spizzichino · La Giustiniana
Ottavia · San Onofrio
ROMA · Città del Vaticano · Villa d'Este · Villa Adriana · TIVOLI
Corviale · Torre Nova

ROTTERDAM

SEVILLA

0 _____ 280 m

N

Monasterio de la Cartuja-Centro Andaluz de Arte Contemporáneo

OMNIMAX

San Lorenzo
Nuestro Padre Jesús del Gran Poder
Plaza de Sta Isabel
S. Marcos
CONVENTO DE STA ISABEL
Convento de Santa Paula

Plaza de Gavidia
Plaza de la Concordia
Plaza de la Encarnación
Metropol Parasol
PALACIO DE LAS DUEÑAS
JARDINES DEL VALLE

Plaza Duque de la Victoria
MUSEO DE BELLAS ARTES
Plaza del Museo

Palacio de Lebrija
Plaza Cristo de Burgos
Convento S. Leandro
Casa de Pilatos

La Magdalena
Capilla de S. José
El Salvador
Plaza del Salvador
Plaza de Pilatos

Caja de Ahorros S. Fernando
Museo del Baile Flamenco
BARRIO DE SANTA CRUZ

Plaza Nueva
Ayuntamiento
Plaza San Francisco

Monumento a la Tolerancia
Castillo de San Jorge
El Carmen
La Real Maestranza

Palacio Arzobispal
Santa María La Blanca
Plaza Poeta Luis Chamizo

Plaza del Altozano
Capilla de los Marineros
TRIANA
Sta Ana

TEATRO DE LA MAESTRANZA
Catedral
GIRALDA
Hospital de los Venerables
Plaza de Sta Cruz
Plaza de los Refinadores

PUERTO

Iglesia-Hospital de la Caridad
Torre de la Plata
REAL ALCÁZAR
Jardines del Alcázares
Palacio de Carlos V
LABERINTO

Torre del Oro
Puerta de Jerez
H. Alfonso XIII

Plaza de Cuba
Universidad Antigua Fábrica de Tabacos
Prado de S. Sebastián

Palacio de San Telmo
JARDINES DE S. TELMO
JARDINES DEL PRADO DE S. SEBASTIÁN

Plaza de España

SEVILLA

Llerena
Guillena
Gerena
Brenes
La Estación
La Trinidad
La Campana

Aznalcóllar
Torre de la Reina
Alcalá del Río
El Rosal Alto
Carmona

El Indiano
Los Encinares de Sanlúcar la Mayor
La Rinconada
San José de la Rinconada
Necrópolis romana
Zahariche
Argamasil

Albaida del Aljarafe
Valencina de la Concepción
Santiponce
Ruinas de Itálica
La Jarilla
El Caudal
Virgen del Rocío
Sta Clara

Olivares
Salteras
Castilleja de la Cuesta
Camas
Sta Catalina
Matasanos

Sanlúcar la Mayor
Villanueva del Ariscal
Gines
San Pablo
La Cierva
Alcaudete
Sto Domingo
La Gloria

Castilleja del Campo
Carrión de los Céspedes
Espartinas
Tomares
Torreblanca de los Caños
Sta Genoveva
Los Claveles
El Balcón de los Alcores
El Viso del Alcor
El Álamo

Huévar
Umbrete
Bormujos
S. Juan de Aznalfarache
Montequinto
Las Encinas
Mairena del Alcor
La Iglesia

Benacazón
Mairena del Aljarafe
Gelves
Cast
Gandul
Neblines
Porcún
El Palomar

Bollullos de la Mitación
Palomares del Río
Bellavista
Alcalá de Guadaíra
A 92
Marchena

Pilas
Aznalcázar
Coria del Río
La Alegría
Granja Asunsema
Torrelengua
Paradas

Santuario de Cuatrovitas
Almensilla
Tobalina
Marchenilla

La Puebla del Río
Dos Hermanas
Mirabel
Menjíllar
Arahal

Villamanrique
Colinas
La Corchuela
Matallana
Las Monjas

SOFIA
СОФИЯ

200 m

N

SLIVNICA / СЛИВНИЦА — A — B — VRACA / ВРАЦА — C — D

Pont des Lions
Львов Мост

Marché "des femmes"

St-Cyrille-et-St-Méthode

Mosquée des Bains

Georgi S. Rakovski

Pirotska
Пиротска

Synagogue

Halles

Mosquée des Bains

Bains centraux

Ste-Petka-des-Selliers

Palais présidentiel

CUM

Pl. Battenberg

Amphithéâtre romain

Tombe d'Ivan Vazov

Place de L'Indépendance

Rotonde St-Georges

Ancien siège du parti communiste

Ancien palais royal

OPÉRA NATIONAL

Ste-Sophie

Mon¹ Vasil Levski

Sáborna
Съборна

Ste-Nedelja

Banque de Bulgarie

Grande mosquée

St-Nicolas

St-Alexandre-Nevski

Galerie nationale des Arts étrangers

Académie nationale des Beaux-Arts

Jardin municipal

MUSÉE ARCHÉOLOGIQUE

Tour jaune

Palais du Synode

Bibliothèque nationale

Parc Oboriște

Mon¹ Stefan Stambolov

ASSEMBLÉE NATIONALE

Uiljam Gladston

Théâtre Ivan-Vazov

Maison Ivan Vazov

Pl. Narodno Sábranie
Пл. Народно Събрание

Université St-Clément d'Ohrid

Uiljam

Gladston

Pl. Slavejkov
Пл. Славейков

Georgi S. Rakovski

Mausolée du Prince Alexandre Iᵉʳ de Battenberg

Pont des Aigles
Орлов Мост

Maison Pejo Javorov

Evlogi

Georgiev

Vasil Levski Stadion

Jardin de Boris

Palais national de la Culture

Parc Sud

PERNIK / ПЕРНИК
VITOŠA / ВИТОША

MUSÉE NATIONAL DE LA TERRE ET DE L'HOMME

BOJANA, MUSÉE NATIONAL D'HISTOIRE

BURGAS / БУРГАС — VARNA / ВАРНА — PLOVDIV / ПЛОВДИВ

SOFIA
СОФИЯ

SOFIA

SOFIA-GRAD

PERNIK
ПЕРНИК

Pernik
Перник

Radomir
Радомир

Zemenski man.

Botevgrad
Ботевград

Etropole
Етрополе

Mogenski

UPPSALA, LULEÅ 18° NORRTÄLJE 18°30

VÄSTERÅS, OSLO 59°30

Rätan 315 99 Alby Ljungan 47/89 Torpshammar Timrå 233 Häggdånger
Karolinerleden Söråker
Stöde Alnö

Håtuna ARLANDA Lunda
Sigtuna Märsta 181 Frösunda Kårsta Riala
Husby-Ärlinghundra Skånela Orkesta Morsta E18 189 Sättra
Håbo-Tibble Näshagen Rosersberg Lindholmen Vada Stångberga Roslags-Kulla
Bro Norrsunda Mark m Karby Össeby-Garn Broilsta Rumsättra
Löwenströmska-lasarettet Hammarby Gröndal 188 Brottby Norrbacka N. Ljusterö
Lässa Västra Ryd Uplands-Väsby Ormsta Angarn Österåker Väsbystrand
Brunna Ed Frestaby Vallentuna Åkersberga Fågelarö S. Ljusterö
Kungsängen Bollstanäs Byle 187 Näs Svinninge Resarö Grundvik
Kallhäll Norrviken Rydbo Trälhavet Saxarfjärden
Björknäs 150 151 152 153 Edsberg Ensta Östra Ryd Bogesund Vaxholm Oskar-Fredriksborg Grinda
Tibble Rotebro Täby 183 Enebyberg Tynningö Värmdö Boda
Sollentuna 154 172 173 Roslags-Näsby Askrikefjärden Värmdölandet Kopparmora
Jakobsberg Danderyd Djursholm Kummelnäs Evlinge
Järfälla Barkarby Uriksdal Morby Brevik Gustavsberg Hemmesta
Munsö Hässelby Spånga Stocksund Lidingö Boo Trälmora Ingarö
Vällingby Solvalla Sundbyberg Haga Millesgården Kil Fruvik Skeppsdalström
Bromma Solna Östermalm Baggens Farstalandet Mörtnäs
Ekeby Stenhamra Angby STOCKHOLM Boo 16 222 Ingarö Skalsmara
Drottningholm Nockeby Alvik Skansen Nacka Fisksätra Brunn Enkärret
Lovö Essingen Södermalm Saltsjöbaden Gåsö Eknäs
Turholm Hammargården Långholmen Årsta Älta
Ekerön Älvnäs Malarhöjden Hägersten Enskede Tyresö Erstaviken Mörtviken
Narsta 152 153 Alvsjö Orby Stureby Skarpnäck Sköndal
Skarholmen 151 Segeltorp Enskede Strängsund Skogås Brevik
Sturehov Hallunda 147 148 Vårby Stuvsta Farsta Skrubba Nämndöfjärden
Botkyrka 146 Fittja Alby Högdalen Strångsund 17 Handen
Salem Huddinge Magelungen Tyresta nationalpark
Södertälje E20 E4 145 Tullinge Länna Ekedal
Salem Ronninge Tumba Onsången
144 Uttran Vårsta
141 E20 143 142 Pershagen
142 0 5 10 km

NORRKÖPING, MALMÖ 18° NYNÄSHAMN 18°30

VÄSTMANLANDS LÄN Fjärdhundra Örsundsbro Rimbo 102 Norrtälje
Storå Surahammar Skultuna Tillberga Knivsta 184 191 E18 25 Kapellskär
Lindesberg Hallstahammar Skoklosters 142 143 144 Märsta 181 189 94 Ångsö nationalpark
Nora Kolsva 130 133 141 Enköping 147 Sigtuna 72 Wira bruk STOCKHOLMS
Kölbäck Tidö Bålsta 68 Vallentuna 188 LÄN
Köping Kungsör Torshälla Jäder 147 Upplands- 176 185 Åkersberga
Frövi Fellingsbro Skogstorp 134 Strängnäs Väsby Sollentuna 173 Täby
Arboga Stora Sundby Eskilstuna Drottningholm Lidingö
Örebro Ålberga Gripsholms Sturehov Boo STOCKHOLM
SÖDERMANLANDS Styckebruk Mariefred Turinge 146 Tumba
LÄN Malmköping Nykvarn Södertälje Jordbro Tyresö
Kumla Pålsboda Vingåker Elen Stjärnhov Järna 141 Västerhaninge
Hallsberg Katrineholm Bettna Gnesta Sorunda Ösmo Nynäshamn
Stjärnsund Eriksberg Runtuna Trosa Vagnhärad Tullgarn Mysingen

STRASBOURG

0   100 m

N

QUARTIER ALLEMAND

Parc des Contades

St-Pierre-le-Jeune
Palais du Rhin
Pl. de la République
BIBLIOTHÈQUE NATIONALE
St-Paul

St-Pierre-le-Jeune (protestant)
HÔTEL D'ANDLAU
Hôtel des Deux-Ponts
Place Broglie
Hôtel de Klinglin
ÉVÊCHÉ
Musée Tomi Ungerer
Pl. de l'Université
Palais universitaire

GARE CENTRALE
Pl. de la Gare
ST-JEAN-BAPTISTE
Pl. St-Pierre-le-Jeune
Pl. du Vieux-Marché-aux-Vins
Pl. de l'Homme de Fer
L'AUBETTE
Pl. Kléber
Pl. des Étudiants
Pl. du Temple Neuf
Pl. du Marché-Neuf
Ancienne pharmacie du Cerf
Maison Kammerzell
CATHÉDRALE NOTRE-DAME
Pl. du Château
St-Guillaume
ÉCOLE SUP. DES ARTS DÉCORATIFS

ST-JEAN
TOUR DU BOURREAU
St-Pierre-le-Vieux
R. du Bain-aux-Plantes
Pl. B. Zix
CITÉ ANCIENNE
Pl. Gutenberg
Pl. de la Cathédrale
Palais Rohan
Pont Ste-Madeleine
STE-MADELEINE

STE-AURÉLIE
AUDITORIUM
Pl. Hans Jean Arp
É.N.A.
PETITE FRANCE
Ponts couverts
Pont St-Martin
HÔTEL DE LA CHAMBRE DE COMMERCE
Musée de l'Œuvre Notre-Dame
Musée historique
Pl. du Marché-aux-Cochons-de-Lait
Pl. de Zurich

Musée d'Art moderne et contemporain
Barrage Vauban
HÔTEL DU DÉPARTEMENT
Pl. H. Dunant
Pl. des Moulins
St-Thomas
Ancienne douane
Pont du Corbeau
Cour du Corbeau
Pl. des Orphelins

St-Nicolas
ST-LOUIS
ST-NICOLAS
Maison de Pasteur
Musée alsacien
KRUTENAU

HARAS NATIONAL
Pl. de l'Hôpital
Hospices
CITÉ ADMINISTRATIVE

STRASBOURG

Kehl

Molsheim

Schiltigheim
Hœnheim
Bischheim

Marlenheim

Lingolsheim
Ostwald
Illkirch-Graffenstaden
STRASBOURG ENTZHEIM INTERNATIONAL

Willstätt
Kork
Neumühl
Kehl

Renchen
Appenweier
Offenburg

STUTTGART

0   500 m

N

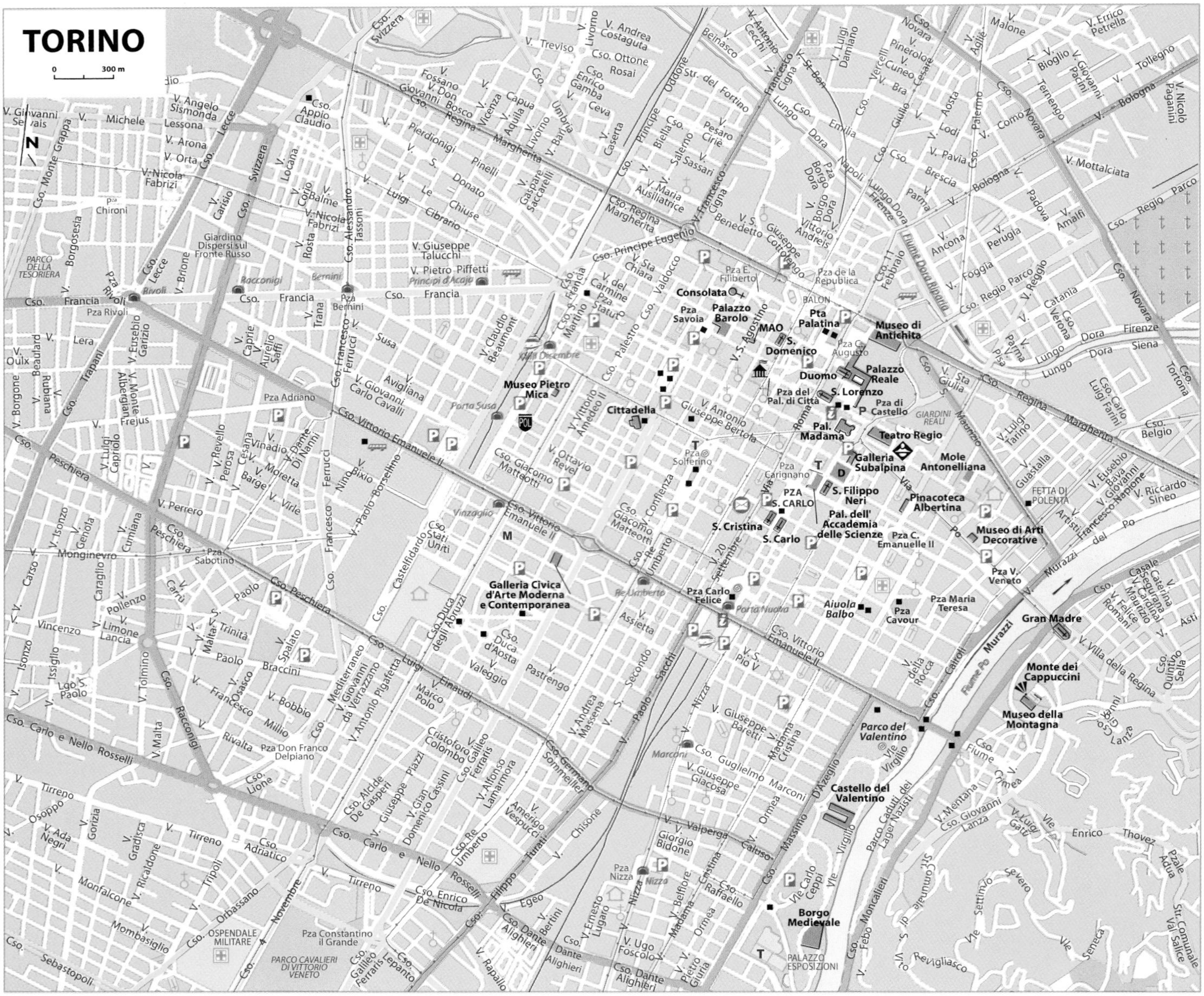

TORINO

0   300 m

N

Major landmarks and labels:
- Consolata
- Palazzo Barolo
- Palazzo Savoia
- MAO
- Pta Palatina
- Museo di Antichità
- S. Domenico
- Duomo
- S. Lorenzo
- Palazzo Reale
- Museo Pietro Mica
- Cittadella
- Pal. Madama
- Teatro Regio
- Galleria Subalpina
- Mole Antonelliana
- Pza Solferino
- Pza Carignano
- S. Filippo Neri
- Pinacoteca Albertina
- S. Carlo
- PZA S. CARLO
- S. Cristina
- Pal. dell' Accademia delle Scienze
- Museo di Arti Decorative
- Pza C. Emanuelle II
- Galleria Civica d'Arte Moderna e Contemporanea
- Pza Carlo Felice
- Porta Nuova
- Aiuola Balbo
- Pza Cavour
- Pza Maria Teresa
- Gran Madre
- Monte dei Cappuccini
- Museo della Montagna
- Parco del Valentino
- Castello del Valentino
- Borgo Medievale
- Palazzo Esposizioni
- Ospedale Militare
- Pza Constantino il Grande
- Parco Cavalieri di Vittorio Veneto
- Parco della Tesoriera
- Giardino Dispersi sul Fronte Russo
- Porta Susa

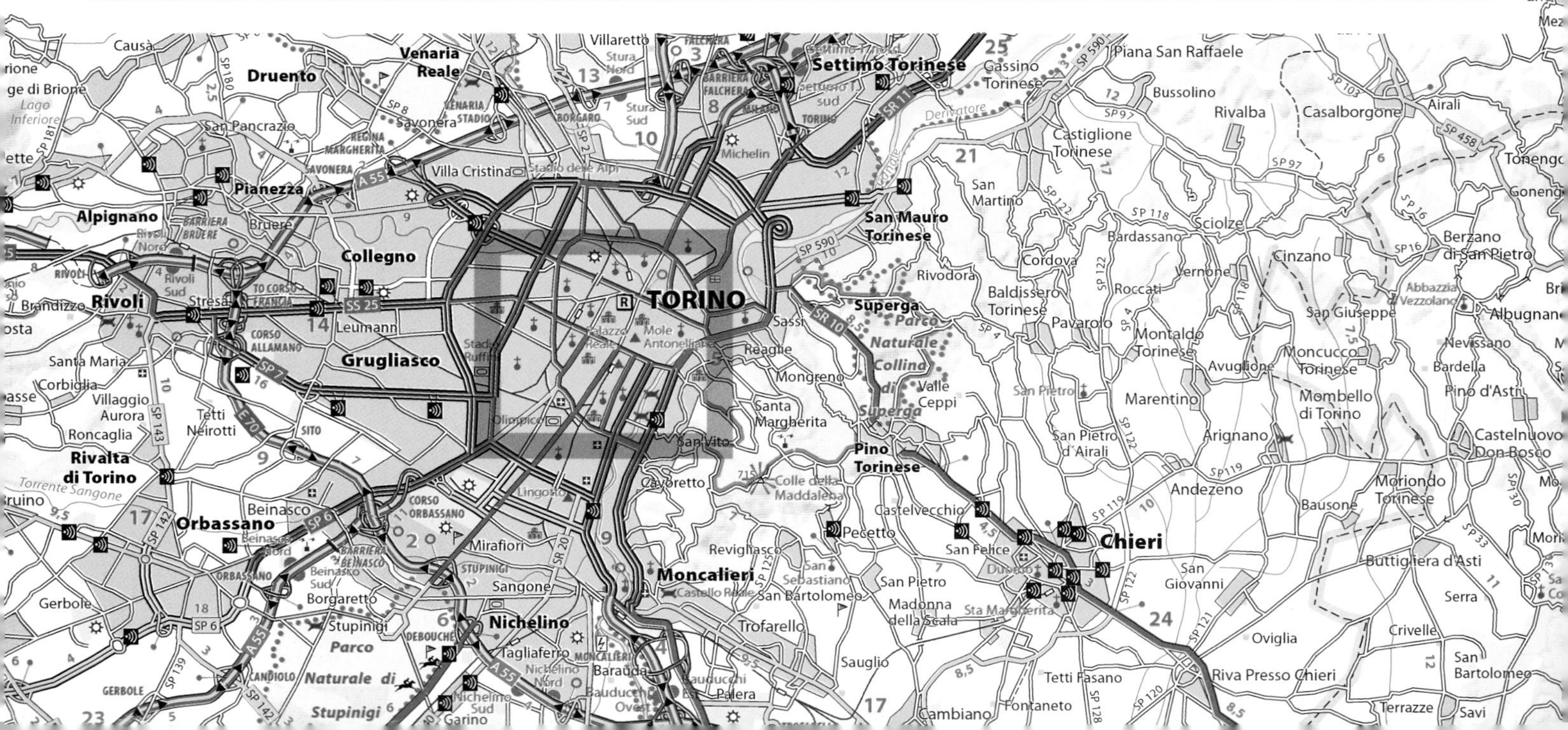

Surrounding area (lower map):
- Druento
- Venaria Reale
- Settimo Torinese
- Piana San Raffaele
- Gassino Torinese
- Bussolino
- Castiglione Torinese
- Pianezza
- Alpignano
- Collegno
- San Mauro Torinese
- Rivoli
- Grugliasco
- TORINO
- Superga
- Parco Naturale Collina di Superga
- Rivalta di Torino
- Orbassano
- Pino Torinese
- Chieri
- Moncalieri
- Nichelino
- Beinasco
- Mirafiori
- Stupinigi
- Parco Naturale di Stupinigi
- Ivrea
- Fioriano

TOULOUSE

0   150 m

N

BASILIQUE ST-SERNIN
Musée St-Raymond
Collège de l'Esquila
Bibliothèque
Chapelle des Carmélites
N.-D.-du-Taur
Hôtel Le Grand Balcon
Capitole
Pl. du Capitole
Donjon
Les Jacobins
R. d'Alsace-Lorraine
Hôtel de Bernuy
Pl. Salengro
St-Jérôme
R.J.-Chalande
Musée du Vieux-Toulouse
Tour Pierre-Séguy
Pl. St-Georges
Tour de Serta
Musée des Augustins
N.-D.-de-la-Daurade
HÔTEL D'ASSÉZAT
Pl. St-Étienne
Cathédrale St-Étienne
Hôtel de Fumel
R. Croix-Baragnon
Pont Neuf
R. Malcousinat
N.-D.-la-Dalbade
Hôtel de Clary
Hôtel Béringuier-Maynier
Musée Paul-Dupuy
R. Pharaon
Pl. Montoulieu
GARONNE
Jardin Royal
Grand Rond
Pont St-Michel
Palais de Justice
Muséum d'histoire naturelle
Jardin des Plantes
Monument de la Résistance

MATABIAU

Labastide St-Pierre
Montbartier
Campsas
Canals
St-Rustice
Grenade
St-Jory
Bruguières
Gagnac
St-Alban
Castelginest
Pechbonnieu
St-Loup-Cammas
Aucamville
L'Union
Blagnac
TOULOUSE BLAGNAC
Colomiers
Pibrac
Tournefeuille
Plaisance-du-Touch
Cugnaux
Portet-s-Garonne
Ramonville St-Agne
Vieille Toulouse
Castanet-Tolosan
Escalquens
Balma
Verfeil
Francarville

TOULOUSE ★★★

VENEZIA

0   300 m

N

CANALE DELLE SACCHE

CANALE DELLE FONDAMENTE

CANALE DI SAN MARCO

CANALE DELLA GIUDECCA

MESTRE

Fondamenta Contarini
Fondamenta de le Capuzine
Fondamenta de la Sensa
Fondamenta dei Ferali
Fondamenta di Cannaregio
C. Larga Piave
Campo di Sant'Alvise
Campo del Ghetto Nuovo
Fondamenta de la Misericordia
Sacca Della Misericordia
Fondamente Nuove
Campo dell'Abbazia
C. Larga dei Botteri
Fondamenta Nuove
Campo S. Giustina

S. Giobbe
Scuola Spagnola
PARCO SAVORGNAN
S. Marcuola
PAL. LABIA
Campo S. Geremia
S. Geremia e S. Lucia
Pal. Vendramin Calergi
Fondaco dei Turchi
Fondaco del Megio
Riva di Biasio
Ca'Pesaro
CA'D'ORO
Scuola Grande di S. Marco
S. Maria d. Miracoli
S. Zanipolo
San Francesco della Vigna
STAZIONE MERCI
San Giacomo dall'Orio
Fabbriche Vecchie
Teatro Malibran
Piazzale Roma
Pzale Roma
Campo S. Polo
Fabbriche Nuove
Fond. Querini-Stampalia
SCUOLA GRANDE DI S. GIORGIO DEGLI SCHIAVONI
SANTA MARIA GLORIOSA DEI FRARI
Crosera
Pal. Bernardo
Teatro Goldoni
Mercerie
Darsena Grande
SCUOLA GRANDE DI SAN ROCCO
Rio Terà del Pensieri
Fondamenta de le Procuratie
Pal. Pisani Moretta
Ca'Foscari
Pal. Grassi
Scala del Bovolo
SAN MARCO
S. Zaccaria
MUSEO STORICO NAVALE
Campo Sta Margherita
Ca'Rezzonico
S. Stefano
PIAZZA S.MARCO
S. Giovanni in Bragora
Riva degli Schiavoni
Fondamenta della Tana
PALAZZO DELLO SPORT
Scuola Grande dei Carmini
Campo S. Biagio
PALAZZO DUCALE
La Fenice
Campo Sta Barnaba
Calle Lunga de S. Barnaba
S. Sebastiano
GALLERIE D. ACCADEMIA
Punta della Dogana – Centro di Arte Contemporanea
San Giorgio Maggiore
Fondamenta Zattere ai Ponte Longo
Coll. P. Guggenheim
Ca'Dario
Santa Maria della Salute
Squèro di S. Trovaso
Gesuati
CANALE DI SAN MARCO
Mulino Stucky
Fondamenta S. Biagio
Fondamenta del Pte Piccolo
CANALE DELLA GIUDECCA
Fondamenta de le Convertite
Campo del Cosmo
Ramo Corte Grandi
Fondazione Giorgio Cini
CANALE DI SAN MARCO
Canal Grande
PALAZZO LOREDAN

MESTRE
Collalto
Vallonga
Barriera
Susegana
Santa Lucia di Piave
Cittadella
Mareno
Campolongo
San Felice
Ramera
Monticano
Cimetta
Borgo di Sopra
Fontanelle
Codogne
Portobuffolè
Cornizza
Rivarotta
Ghirano
Pozzo

Fucina
Zigaragai
Cavino
Luneo
Spinea
Mira
Malpaga
Mirano
Dolo
Borbiago
La Casona
Oriago
Molin Rotto
Chiesa Gambara
Piazza Vecchia
Trivignano
Olmo
Maerne
Zelarino
Rossignago
MIRANESE
MESTRE-CENTRO
CASTELLANA
MIRA ORIAGO
Porto Marghera
Moranzani
Malcontenta
Fusina
Marocco
Dese
TERRAGLIO
Bazzera Nord
Carpenedo
Favaro Veneto
Campalto
BARRIERA VENEZIA MESTRE
Marghera
MESTRE
VENEZIA
Tronchetto
La Giudecca
San Clemente
VENEZIA
San Marco
Palazzo Ducale
Lido
San Lazzaro degli Armeni
Lido di Venezia
DESE MARCON
MARCO POLO BELLUNO
Ca' Noghera
AEROPORTO MARCO POLO
Tessera
Mazzorbo
Torcello
Burano
Sant'Erasmo
Murano
Punta Sabbioni
Ca' Savio
Lio Piccolo
Acqualandia
Cavallino
Porto di Piave Vecchia
Malamocco
Laguna Veneta

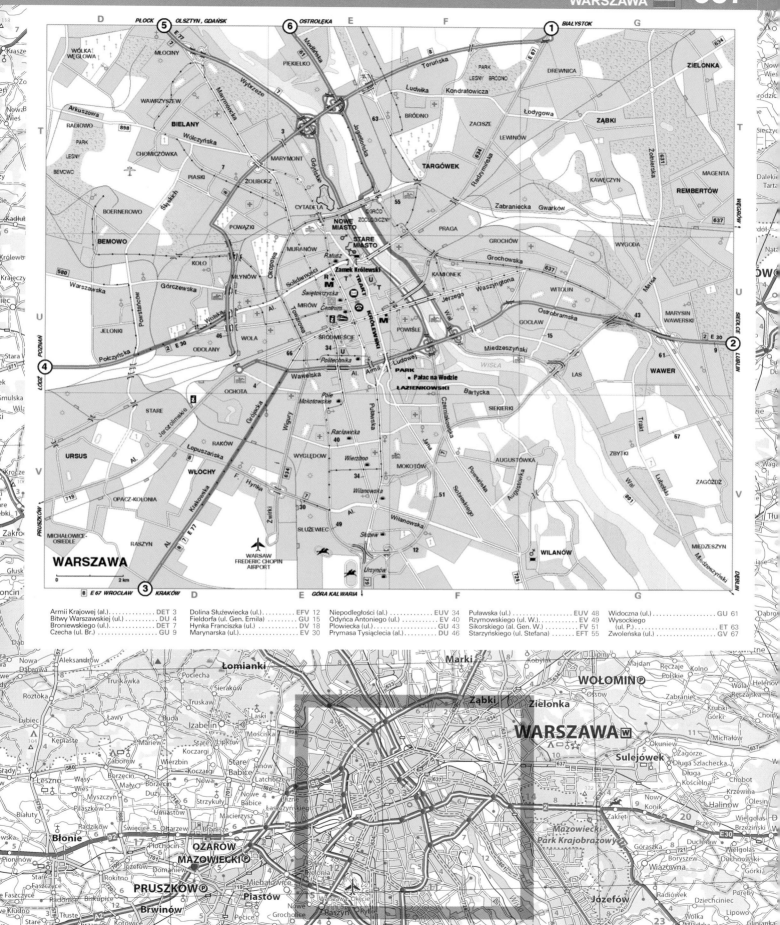

WARSZAWA

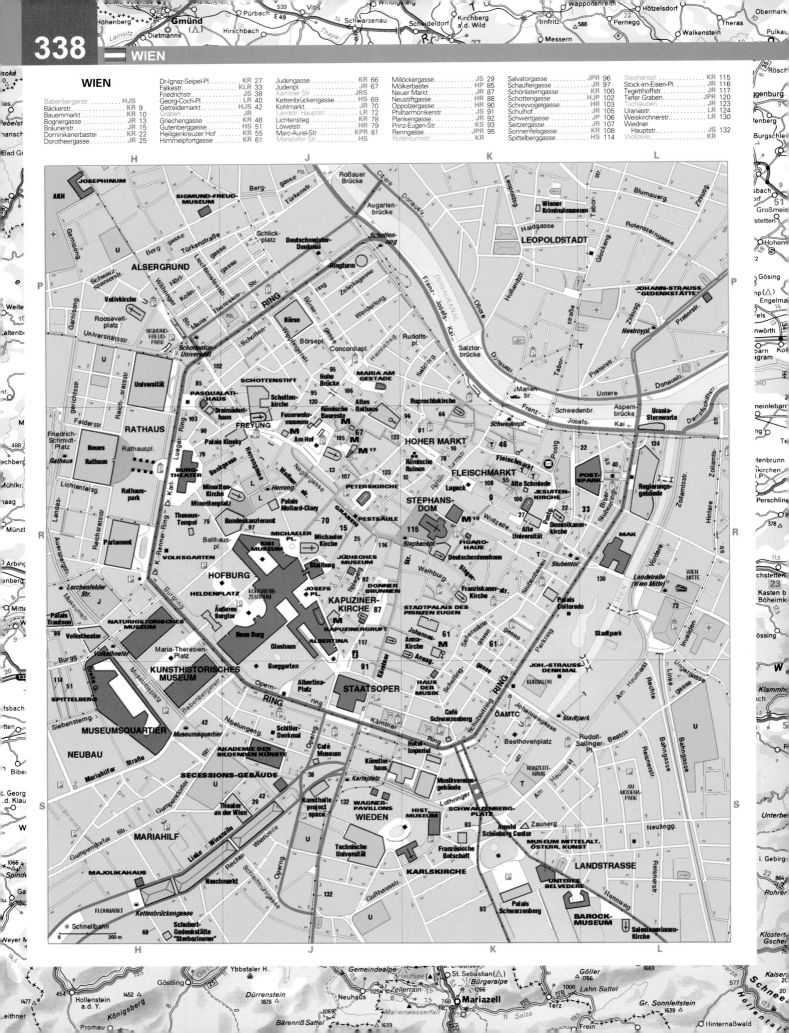

ZÜRICH (inset city map)

0 — 200 m

Museum für Gestaltung
Schweizerisches Landesmuseum
HAUPTBAHNHOF
Bahnhofplatz
Löwenplatz
Jules Verne
SCHIPFE
Lindenhof
AUGUSTINER-KIRCHE
Weinplatz
Sankt Peterskirche
Zunfthaus «Zur Meisen»
Fraumünster
WOHNMUSEUM
Paradeplatz
Bahnhofstrasse
SCHANZENGRABEN
Stadthausanlage
Bürkliplatz
KONGRESSGEB.
General-Guisan-Quai
ARBORETUM
LIEBFRAUENKIRCHE
EIDG. TECHN. HOCHSCHULE
Niederdorfstrasse
PREDIGER-KIRCHE
Froschaugasse
Niederdorfstrasse
Neumarkt
Spiegelgasse
Rathaus
Grossmünster
KUNSTHAUS
OBERDORF
Wasserkirche
FRANZÖSISCHE KIRCHE
Bellevueplatz
Sechseläutenplatz
STADELHOFEN
Stadelhoferplatz
OPERNHAUS
Zürichsee
N

Surrounding region (road map)

Neustadt, Donaueschingen (694), Oberbränd, Hüfingen, Blumberg, SCHAFFHAUSEN, Neuhausen, SCHAFFHAUSEN, Stühlingen, Eglisau, Bülach, Kloten, BADEN, Wettingen, Dietikon, Schlieren, Wohlen, Bremgarten, ZÜRICH, Dübendorf, Adliswil, Thalwil, Küsnacht, Affoltern, Horgen, Meilen, Wädenswil, Rapperswil, Baar, Cham, Zug, Einsiedeln, Küssnacht, Weggis, LUZERN, Emmen, Hochdorf, Schwyz, Brunnen, Glarus, Näfels, Mollis, Wattwil, Rüti, Uznach, WALENSEE, Weesen, Churfirsten, Unterwasser

Conduire en Europe

Les tableaux d'information suivants indiquent les principaux règlements routiers communiqués au moment de la rédaction de cet atlas (15.05.16) ; la signification des symboles est indiquée ci-dessous, ainsi que quelques notes supplémentaires.

 Limitation de vitesse en kilomètres/heure s'appliquant aux :

Autoroutes		Routes à une seule chaussée
Routes à chaussées séparées		Agglomérations urbaines
Autoroute payante avec vignette		Jeu d'ampoules de rechange
Taux maximum d'alcool toléré dans le sang. On ne doit pas considérer ceci comme acceptable ; il n'est JAMAIS raisonnable de boire et de conduire.		Âge minimum du conducteur
		Port de la ceinture de sécurité à l'avant et à l'arrière
Âge minimum des enfants admis à l'avant.		Câble de remorquage
Gilet de sécurité		Port du casque pour les motocyclistes et les passagers
Triangle de présignalisation		Allumage des codes jour et nuit
Trousse de premiers secours		Pneus cloutés
Extincteur		Pneus hiver obligatoires en condition de circulation hivernale

Documents nécessaires obligatoires à tous les pays : certificat d'immatriculation du véhicule ou certificat de location, assurance responsabilité civile, plaque d'identification nationale. Il est vivement conseillé de se renseigner auprès de l'Automobile Club.

Driving in Europe

The information panels which follow give the principal motoring regulations in force when this atlas was prepared for press (15.05.16). An explanation of the symbols is given below, together with some additional notes.

Speed restrictions in kilometres per hour applying to:

Motorways	Single carriageways
Dual carriageways	Urban areas
Toll road with compulsory vignette/sticker	Whether a spare bulb set must be carried
Maximum permitted level of alcohol in the bloodstream. This should not be taken as an acceptable level - it is NEVER sensible to drink and drive.	Minimum age for drivers
	Whether seatbelts are compulsory for the driver and all passengers in both front and back seats
Minimum age for children to sit in the front passenger seat.	Tow rope
Reflective jacket	Whether crash helmets are compulsory for both motorcyclists and their passengers
Whether a warning triangle must be carried.	Whether headlights must be on at all time
Whether a first aid kit must be carried	Studded tyres
Whether a fire extinguisher must be carried	Winter tyres compulsory in wintry driving conditions

Documents required for all countries: vehicle registration document or vehicle on hire certificate, third party insurance cover, national vehicle indentification plate. You are strongly advised to contact the national Automobile Club for full details of local regulations.

Autofahren in Europa

Die nachfolgenden Tabellen geben Auskunft über die wichtigsten Verkehrsbestimmungen in den einzelnen Ländern dieses Atlasses (Stand 15.05.16) die Erklärung der Symbole sowie einige ergänzende Anmerkungen finden Sie im Anschluß an diesen Text.

Geschwindigkeitsbegrenzungen in km/h bezogen auf:

Autobahnen		Straßen mit einer Fahrbahn
Schnellstraßen mit getrennten Fahrbahnen		Geschlossene Ortschaften
Gebührenpflichtige Autobahn mit Vignette		Mitführen eines Satzes von Glühbirnen als Reserve
Promillegrenze: Es sei darauf hingewiesen, daß auch die kleinste Menge Alkohol am Steuer das Fahrvermögen beeinträchtigt		Mindestalter für Kfz-Führer
		Anschnallpficht vorne und hinten
Mindestalter, ab welchem Kinder vorne sitzen dürfen.		Abschleppseil
Sicherheitsweste		Helmpflicht für Motorradfahrer und Beifahrer
Mitführen eines Warndreiecks		Abblendlicht vorgeschrieben (Tag und Nacht)
Mitführen eines Verbandkastens		Spikereifen
Mitführen eines Feuerlöschers		Winterreifen bei Winterwetter gesetzespflichtig

Notwendige und vorgeschriebene Dokumente in allen Staaten: Fahrzeugschein oder Mietwagenbescheinigun, Internationale grüne Versicherungskarte, Nationlitätskennzeichen. Es empfiehlt sich, genauere Informationen bei den jeweiligen Automobilclubs einzuholen.

Autorijden in Europa

In de tabellen hierna staan de voornaamste verkeersregels medegedeeld bij het opstellen van deze Atlas (15.05.16); de betekenis van de symbolen is hieronder beschreven met enkele toelichtingen.

⏱ Snelheidsbeperkingen in km/uur op:

🏍 Autosnelwegen

🏁 Wegen met één rijbaan

🏁 Wegen met gescheiden rijbanen

🏙 Binnen de bebouwde kom

🏁 Betalende autosnelweg met vignet

💡 Reservelampen verplicht

🔘 Minimum leeftijd bestuurder

🍷 Maximum toegestaan alcohol-gehalte in het bloed. Dit dient niet beschouwd te worden als een aanvaardbaar gehalte; het is NOOIT verstandig om te rijden na gebruik van alcohol.

Autogordel, verplicht voor- en achterin

🔧 Sleepkabel

👶 Minimum leeftijd voor kinderen voorin het voertuig.

Valhelm verplicht voor motorrijders en passagiers

Dimlichten verplicht zowel nachts als overdag

🦺 Reflecterend vest

🔺 Gevarendriehoek verplicht

⚙ Spijkerbanden

➕ EHBO-pakket verplicht

Winterbanden verplicht bij winterse verkeersomstandig-heden

🧯 Brandblusapparaat

Vereiste documenten in alle landen:
kentekenbewijs van het voertuig of huurcertificaat, verzekering burgerlijke aansprakelijkheid, plaat land van herkomst.
Het verdient aanbeveling informatie in te winnen bij de automobielclub.

Guidare in Europa

I riquadri informativi che seguono forniscono le principali norme di circolazione, in vigore al momento della redazione di questo atlante (15.05.16); la spiegazione dei simboli viene data di seguito, insieme ad alcune annotazioni supplementari.

⏱ Limiti di velocità in chilometri/ora riferiti a:

🏍 Autostrade

🏁 Strade a carreggiata unica

🏁 Strade a carreggiata doppia

🏙 Aree urbane

🏁 Autostrada a pedaggio con contrassegno autostradale

💡 Assortimento di lampadine di ricambio

🍷 Tasso massimo di alcol tollerato nel sangue. Tale tasso non dovrebbe essere considerato come accettabile; non è MAI sensato guidare dopo aver bevuto.

🔘 Età minima del guidatore

Uso delle cinture di sicurezza per i sedili anteriori e posteriori

👶 Età minima richiesta, affinché i bambini possano sedere davanti

🔧 Cavo di traino

Uso del casco per i motociclisti ed i passeggeri

🦺 Giubbotto di sicurezza

Si devono tenere gli anabba glianti sempre accesi

🔺 Triangolo di presegnalazione

⚙ Pneumatici chiodati

➕ Cassetta di pronto soccorso

Pneumatici invernali obbligatori in condizioni di circolazione invernali

🧯 Estintore

Documenti obbligatori in tutti i paesi:
carta di circolazione del veicolo oppure certificato di autonoleggio, assicurazione e carta verde, targa d'identificazione nazionale.
E' vivamente consigliato rivolgersi all' Automobile Club.

Conducir en Europa

Los siguientes cuadros informativos recogen las principales reglamentaciones automovilísticas que nos han sido comunicadas en el momento de la redacción de este atlas (15.05.16); el significado de los símbolos, junto con algunas notas complementarias, se indica más abajo.

⏱ Límites de velocidad en kilómetros/hora que se aplican en:

🏍 Autopistas

🏁 Carreteras con calzada única

🏁 Carreteras con calzadas separadas

🏙 Zona urbanas

🏁 Autopista de pago mediante viñeta

💡 Juego de lámparas de recambio

🍷 Máximo permisible de alcohol en sangre. Este máximo no debe considerarse como un nivel aceptable; NUNCA es aconsejable beber si se conduce.

🔘 Edad mínima del conductor

Cinturón de seguridad delante y detrás

🔧 Cable de remolque

👶 Edad mínima de los niños para viajar en los asientos delanteros.

Casco protector para motociclistas y pasajeros

🦺 Chaleco reflectante

Luces encendidas día y noche

🔺 Triángulo de señalización de peligro

⚙ Neumáticos con clavos

➕ Botiquín de primeros auxilios

Neumáticos de invierno obligatorios en condiciones de circulación invernales

🧯 Extintor

Documentación obligatoria en todos países:
certificado de matriculación del vehículo o certificado de aquiler, seguro de responsabilidad civil, placa de identificación del país.
Recomendamos informarse en el Automóvil Club.

Conduzir na Europa

Os quadros de informação seguintes indicam as principais regras rodoviárias em vigor no momento da redacção deste Atlas (15.05.16); o significado dos simbolos está indicado abaixo assim como algumas notas suplementares.

⏱ Limites de velocidade em km/h que se aplicam em:

🏍 Auto-estradas

🏁 Estradas com uma única faixa de rodagem

🏁 Estradas com faixas de rodagem separadas

🏙 Aglomerações urbanas

🏁 Auto-estrada com portagem com estampilha fiscal

💡 Jogo de lâmpadas sobressalentes

🍷 Taxa máxima de alcoolémia tolerada no sangue. Não é considerada au tável; nunca é razoável beber e conduzir.

🔘 Idade mínima do condutor

Uso do cinto de segurança à frente e atrás

👶 Idade mínima das crianças admitidas à frente

🔧 Cabo de reboque

Uso do capacete para os motociclistas e acompanhantes

🦺 Colete reflector

Acender luzes médias dia e noite

🔺 Triângulo de pré-sinalização

⚙ Uso de pneus com pregos

➕ Estojo de primeiros socorros

Pneus de inverno obrigatórios em condições de circulação de inverno

🧯 Extintor

Documentos obrigatórios em todos os países:
certificado de registo de propriedade ou certificado de aluguer - seguro de responsabilidade civil - Placa de identificação nacional.
Aconselha se pedir informações junto do automóvel clube.

Code	Country	🛣	🛣🛣	🛤	🏙	🍷	●	#	△	✚	🔧	💡	✎	⊘	2	◐	Age	●	●	Period	❄	□
(A)	ÖSTERREICH	130		100	50	0,5	●		●	●	○						18	●	●	01/10 31/05	❄	●
(AL)	SHQIPËRIA	110	90	80	40	🚫	●		●	●							18	●	●		❄	○
(AND)	ANDORRA			70	40	0,5	●	10	●	○	○						18	●	●			○
(B)	BELGIQUE, BELGIË	120	120	90	50	0,5	●		●	○	○						18	●	●	01/11 31/03		
(BG)	BALGARIJA, БЪЛГАРИЯ	130		90	50	0,5	●	12	●	●							18	●	●		❄	
(BIH)	BOSNA I HERCEGOVINA	130	100	80	60	0,3	●	12	●	●	○	●	●				18	●	●		❄	❄
(BY)	BELARUS', БЕЛАРУСЬ	110		90	60	🚫	●	12	●	●							18	●	●			
(CH)	SCHWEIZ, SUISSE, SVIZZERA	120	100	80	50	0,5	●		●	●	○						18	●	●	24/10 30/04		
(CY)	KÝPROS, KIBRIS	100		80	50	0,5	●	10	● x2		○	○					18	●	●			
(CZ)	ČESKÁ Republika	130		90	50	🚫	●		●	●							18	●	●		❄	❄
(D)	DEUTSCHLAND			100	50	0,5	●		●	●							18	●	●		❄	❄
(DK)	DANMARK	130		80	50	0,5	●		●	●							18	●	●	01/11 15/04		
(E)	ESPAÑA	120	100	90	50	0,5	●		●	○							18	●	●			
(EST)	EESTI	110		90	50	0,2	●		● x2	●							18	●	●	15/10 15/04	❄	
(F)	FRANCE	130	110	90	50	0,5	●	10	●	●	○						18	●	●	15/11 31/03		
(FIN)	SUOMI, FINLAND	120	100	80	50	0,5	●		●	●	○						18	●	●	01/11 31/03	❄	
(FL)	LIECHTENSTEIN			80	50	0,8	●		●	●							18	●	●			○
(GB)	UNITED KINGDOM	112	112	96	48	0,8	●		●	○							17	●	○			○
(GR)	ELLÁDA, ΕΛΛΑΔΑ	130		90	50	0,5	●	12	●	●							18	●	●		❄	
(H)	MAGYARORSZÁG	130	110	90	50	🚫	●	12	●	●							17	●	●		❄	
(HR)	HRVATSKA	130	110	90	50	0,5	●	12	●	●	○	●					18	●	●		❄	
(I)	ITALIA	130	110	90	50	0,5	●	12	●	●							18	●	●	15/11 15/03	❄	
(IRL)	IRELAND, ÉIRE	120	100	80	50	0,5	●		○	○							17	●	○			○
(IS)	ÍSLAND		90	80	50	0,5	●		●	●							17	●	●	01/12 15/04		○
(L)	LUXEMBOURG	130		90	50	0,5	●	12	●	●							18	●	●	01/12 31/03	❄	
(LT)	LIETUVA	130	110	90	50	0,4	●	12	●	●							18	●	●	01/11 01/04	❄	
(LV)	LATVIJA		100	90	50	0,5	●		●	●							18	●	●	01/11 30/04	❄	
(M)	MALTA			80	50	0,8	●	11	●	○							18	●	○			○
(MC)	MONACO				50	0,5		○	○	○							18	●	●		❄	
(MD)	MOLDOVA			80	50	🚫	●	12	●	●							18	●	●			○
(MK)	MAKEDONIJA, МАКЕДОНИЈА	130	100	80	50	0,5	●	12	●	●	○	○	●				18	●	●		❄	❄
(MNE)	CRNA GORA, ЦРНА ГОРА		100	80	60	0,3	●	12	●	●							18	●	●			❄
(N)	NORGE	100	100	80	50	0,2	●		●	●							18	●	●	01/11 28/03		○
(NL)	NEDERLAND	130	100	80	50	0,5	●	12	○	●							18	●	○			○
(P)	PORTUGAL	120	100	90	50	0,5	●	12	●	●							18	●	●			○
(PL)	POLSKA	140	120	90	50	0,2	●		●	●							18	●	●		❄	
(RO)	ROMÂNIA	130	100	90	50	🚫	●	12	●	●							18	●	●		❄	❄
(RSM)	SAN MARINO			90	50	0,5	●	12	●	●							18	●	●			●
(RUS)	ROSSIJA, РОССИЯ	110	110	90	60	🚫	●	12	●	●	●						18	●	●			○
(S)	SVERIGE	110	90	90	50	0,2	●		●	○	○						18	●	●	01/10 15/04	❄	○
(SK)	SLOVENSKÁ Republika	130		90	50	🚫	●	10	●	●	○	○	○				18	●	●		❄	
(SLO)	SLOVENIJA	130	110	90	50	0,5	●		●	●	○	○					18	●	●		❄	
(SRB)	SRBIJA, СРБИЈА	120	100	80	50	0,3	●	12	●	●	○	●					18	●	●			
(TR)	TÜRKIYE	120		90	50	0,5	●	12	●	●							18	●	●		❄	
(UA)	UKRAÏNA, УКРАЇНА	130	110	90	60	🚫	●	12	●	●							18	●	●			○

Legend

● Obligatoire / Compulsory / Vorgeschrieben / Verplicht / Obbligatorio / Obligatorio / Obrigatório

○ Recommandé / Recommended / Empfohlen / Aanbevolen / Raccomandato / Recomendado / Recomendado

 Interdit / Prohibited / Verboten / Verboden / Vietato / Prohibido / Proibido

01/10 15/04 — Période d'autorisation / Periode of regulation enforcement / Genehmigungsdauer / Toegelaten perode / Periodo d'autorizzazione / Periodo de autorización / Período de autorização

❄ Pneus hiver obligatoires en condition de circulation hivernale / Winter tyres compulsory in wintry driving conditions / Winterreifen bei Winterwetter gesetzespflichtig / Winterbanden verplicht bij winterse verkeersomstandigheden / Pneumatici invernali obbligatori in condizioni di circolazione invernali / Neumáticos de invierno obligatorios en condiciones de circulación invernales / Pneus de inverno obrigatórios em condições de circulação de inverno

Automobile Club
Automobil Club / Automobielclub / Club del Automóvil / Automóvel clube

(A) Österreich
ÖAMTC
WIEN
☎ : +43 (0)1 711 99 10 200
http:// www.oeamtc.at

ARBÖ
WIEN
☎ : +43 1 891 210
http:// www.arboe.at

(AL) Shqipëria
Automobile Club Albania (ACA)
TIRANÉ
☎ : +355 42 38 70 11
http:// www.aca.al

(AND) Andorra
Automòbil Club d'Andorra (ACA)
ANDORRA la VELLA
☎ : +376 803 400
http:// www.aca.ad

(B) Belgique, België
R.A.C.B
BRUXELLES / BRUSSEL
☎ : +32 2 287 09 11
http://www.racb.com

Touring Club Belgium (TCB)
BRUXELLES / BRUSSEL
☎ : +32 2 233 22 11
http://www.touring.be

(BG) Balgarija/България
Union des Automobilistes Bulgares (UAB)
SOFIA/СОФИЯ
☎ : +359 2 935 79 35
http://www.sba.bg

(BIH)
Bosna i Hercegovina
BIHAMK
SARAJEVO
☎ : +387 33 212 772
http:// www.bihamk.ba

(BY) Belarus'/Беларусь
Belorusskij Klub Avtomototurizma (BKA)
MINSK/МИНCK
☎ : +375 17 222 06 66
http://www.bka.by

(CH)
Schweiz, Suisse, Svizzera
Touring Club Suisse / Schweiz / Svizzero (TCS)
VERNIER
☎ : +41 22 417 27 27
http://www.tcs.ch

Automobil Club der Schweiz / Automobile Club de Suisse (ACS)
BERN
☎ : +41 31 328 31 11
http://www.acs.ch

(CY) Kýpros, Kıbrıs
Cyprus Automobile Association (CAA)
LEFKOSIA/LEFKOŞA
☎ : +357 22 313 233
http://www.caa.com.cy

(CZ) Česká republika
Ústřední automotoklub České republiky (UAMK)
PRAHA 4
☎ : +420 2 611 04 279
http://www.uamk-cr.cz

Autoklub České republiky (ACCR)
PRAHA 1
☎ : +420 222 898 219
http://www.autoklub.cz

(D) Deutschland
ADAC
MÜNCHEN
☎ : +49 89 76 76 0
http://www.adac.de

Automobilclub von Deutschland (AVD)
FRANKFURT am MAIN
☎ : +49 69 660 60
http://www.avd.de

(DK) Danmark
Forenede Danske Motorejere (FDM)
KGS. LYNGBY
☎ : +45 45 27 07 07
http://www.fdm.dk

(E) España
Real Automóvil Club de España (RACE)
MADRID
☎ : +34 91 594 72 75
http://www.race.es

Real Federación Española de Automovilismo (RFE de A)
MADRID
☎ : +34 91 729 94 30
http://www.rfeda.es

(EST) Eesti
Eesti Autospordi Liit (EAL)
TALLINN
☎ : +372 6398 666
http://www.autosport.ee

(F) France
Automobile Club de France
PARIS
☎ : +33 1 43 12 43 12

Fédération Française des Automobiles Clubs et Usagers de la Route
PARIS
☎ : +33 1 56 89 20 70
http://www.automobileclub.org

(FIN) Suomi, Finlande
Autoliitto (AL)
HELSINKI
☎ : +358 9 72 58 44 00
http://www.autoliitto.fi

(FL) Liechtenstein
Automobil club Fürstentums Liechtenstein (ACFL)
TRIESEN
☎ : +423 237 67 67
http://www.acfl.li

(GB) United Kingdom
Automobile Association (AA)
BASINGSTOKE
☎ : +44 870 600 0371
http:// www.theaa.com

Green Flag Motoring Assistance
LEEDS
☎ : +44 (0)845 246 15 57
http://www.greenflag.com

(GR) Elláda/Ελλάς
Automobile and Touring Club of Greece (ELPA)
ATHINA/AΘHNA
☎ : +30 210 606 8800
http://www.elpa.gr

(H) Magyarország
Magyar Autóklub (MAK)
BUDAPEST
☎ : +36 1 345 1 800
http://www.autoklub.hu

(HR) Hrvatska
Hrvatski Autoklub (HAK)
ZAGREB
☎ : +385 1 66 11 999
http://www.hak.hr

(I) Italia
Automobile Club d'Italia (ACI)
ROMA
☎ : +39 6 499 81
http://www.aci.it

Touring Club Italiano (TCI)
MILANO
☎ : +39 2 85 261
http://www.touringclub.it

(IRL) Ireland
Royal Irish Automobile Club (RIAC)
DUBLIN 2
☎ : +353 1 677 51 41
http://www.riac.ie

The Automobile Association Ireland Limited (AA)
DUBLIN
☎ : +353 1 617 99 99
http://www.aaireland.ie

(IS) Ísland
Félag Íslenskra Bifreiðaeigenda (FIB)
REYKJAVÍK
☎ : +354 414 99 99
http://www.fib.is

Icelandic Motorsport Association (LIA)
REYKJAVÍK
☎ : +354 58 89 100
http://www.ais.is

(L) Luxembourg
Automobile Club du Grand Duché de Luxembourg (ACL)
BERTRANGE
☎ : +352 45 00 45
http://www.acl.lu

(LT) Lietuva
Lietuvos Automobilininku Sajunga (LAS)
VILNIUS
☎ : +370 5 210 44 33
http://www.las.lt

Lietuvos Automobiliu Sporto Federacija (LASF)
KAUNAS
☎ : +370 37 350 106
http://www.lasf.lt

(LV) Latvija
Latvijas Automoto Biedriba (LAMB)
RĪGA
☎ : +37 1 6756 6222
http://www.lamb.lv

Latvijas Automobilu Federacija (LAF)
RĪGA
☎ : +37 1 6752 02 96
http://www.laf.lv

(M) Malte
Touring Club Malta (TCM)
MSIDA
☎ : +356 7900 0116
http://www.touringclubmalta.org

(MC) Monaco
Automobile Club de Monaco (ACM) MONACO
☎ : +377 93 15 26 00
http://www.acm.mc

(MD) Moldova
Automobil Club din Moldova (ACM)
CHIŞINĂU
☎ : +373 22 29 27 03
http://www.acm.md

(MK) Makedonija /Македонија
Avto Moto Sojuz na Makedonija
SKOPJE/СКОПЈЕ
☎ : +389 2 318 11 81
http://www.amsm.mk

(MNE) Crna Gora
Auto Moto Savez Crne Gore (AMS)
PODGORICA
☎ : +382 20 234 999
http://www.amscg.org

(N) Norge
Kongelig Norsk Automobilklub (KNA)
OSLO
☎ : +47 21 60 49 00
http://www.kna.no

Norges Automobil-Forbund (NAF)
OSLO
☎ : +47 92 60 85 05
http://www.naf.no

(NL) Nederland
Koninklijke Nederlandse Toeristenbond (ANWB)
DEN HAAG
☎ : +31 70 314 71 47
http://www.anwb.nl

Koninklijke Nederlandse Automobiel Club (KNAC)
DEN HAAG
☎ : +31 70 383 16 12
http://www.knac.nl

(P) Portugal
Automóvel Club de Portugal (ACP) LISBOA
☎ : +351 21 318 01 00
http://www.acp.pt

(PL) Polska
Polski Zwiazek Motorowy (PZM) WARSZAWA
☎ : +48 22 849 93 61
http://www.pzm.pl

Polskie Towarzystwo Turystyczno-Krajoznawcze (PTTK) WARSZAWA
☎ : +48 22 826 57 35
http://www.pttk.pl

(RO) România
Automobil Clubul Român (ACR)
BUCUREŞTI
☎ : +40 21 222 22 22
http://www.acr.ro

(RUS) Rossija/Россия
Russian Automobile Society (RAS-VOA)
MOSKVA/MOCKBA
☎ : +7 495 629 75 40
http://www.voa.ru

Avtoclub assistance Rus (ACAR)
MOSKVA/MOCKBA
☎ : +7 495 925 50 00
e-mail : info@acarus.ru

(RSM) San Marino
Automobile Club San Marino (ACS) DOGANA
☎ : +378 549 90 88 60
http:// www.automobileclub.sm

(SRB) Srbija/Србија
Auto-Moto Savez Srbije (AMSS) BEOGRAD/БЕОГРАД
☎ : +381 11 333 11 00
http://www.amss.org.rs

(S) Sverige
Kungliga Automobil Klubben
STOCKHOLM
☎ : +46 8 678 00 55
http://www.kak.se

Motormännens Riksförbund
STOCKHOLM
☎ : +46 8 690 38 00
http://www.motormannen.se

(SK) Slovenská republika
Autoklub Slovenskej Republiky (AKSR)
BRATISLAVA
☎ : +421 (2) 638 345 67
http://www.aksr.sk

Slovensky Autoturist Klub (SATC)
BRATISLAVA
☎ : +421 (2) 682 492 11
http://www.satc.sk

(SLO) Slovenija
Avto-Moto Zveza Slovenije (AMZS)
LJUBLJANA
☎ : +386 1 530 51 00
http://www.amzs.si

(TR) Türkiye
Türkiye Otomobil Sporlari Federasyonu (TOSFED)
ISTANBUL
☎ : +90 216 465 11 55
http://www.tosfed.org.tr

Turkiye Turing ve Otomobil Kurumu (TTOK)
ISTANBUL
☎ : +90 212 282 81 40
http://www.turing.org.tr

(UA) Ukraïna/Україна
Fédération Automobile d'Ukraine (FAU)
KYIV/КИЇВ
☎ : +380 44 206 78 76
http://www.fau.io

112UA L'VIV/ЛЬВІВ
☎ : +380 32 29 70 112
http://www.112ua.com

Distances

	Amsterdam	Athína/Αθήνα	Barcelona	Basel	Beograd/Београд	Bergen	Berlin	Bilbao	Bordeaux	Bratislava	Bruxelles/Brussel	București	Budapest	Calais	Cherbourg	Clermont-Ferrand	Dublin	Dubrovnik	Firenze	Frankfurt-am-Main	Genève	Genova	Göteborg	Hamburg	Helsinki	Istanbul	København	Köln	Kraków	Kyïv/Київ	Lille	Lisboa	Ljubljana	London
Amsterdam																																		
Athína/Αθήνα	2821																																	
Barcelona	1537	2383																																
Basel	729	2427	1024																															
Beograd/Београд	1729	1095	1985	1276																														
Bergen	1456	3822	2811	1808	2731																													
Berlin	668	2345	1872	869	1254	1485																												
Bilbao	1419	3421	612	1206	2325	2793	1967																											
Bordeaux	1085	3127	570	872	2030	2459	1633	333																										
Bratislava	1241	1659	1844	897	568	2173	695	2121	1775																									
Bruxelles/Brussel	206	2771	1338	539	1680	1578	768	1220	886	1192																								
București	2221	1196	2601	1878	614	3181	1703	2937	2644	1017	2173																							
Budapest	1405	1465	1921	1061	374	2364	887	2257	1970	203	1357	824																						
Calais	367	2970	1325	694	1879	1741	930	1202	868	1390	199	2372	1555																					
Cherbourg	788	3248	1224	867	2148	2162	1336	994	660	1685	589	2666	1850	461																				
Clermont-Ferrand	926	2744	620	529	1647	2265	1344	703	368	1412	727	2262	1588	712	717																			
Dublin	613	3534	1885	1254	2443	2304	1493	1458	1124	1954	762	2935	2119	568	509	1273																		
Dubrovnik	1921	1086	2004	1371	473	2861	1653	2340	2047	1007	1873	969	771	2075	2234	1664	2635																	
Firenze	1372	905	1086	646	1013	2390	1238	1423	1228	871	1182	1623	948	1335	1493	889	1964	641																
Frankfurt-am-Main	448	2382	1331	329	1290	1489	549	1483	1149	802	401	1783	967	602	935	799	1163	1482	973															
Genève	978	2429	773	251	1332	2058	1113	1042	708	1089	692	1942	1267	756	891	325	1316	1350	612	577														
Genova	1206	2253	858	479	1156	2248	1180	1194	999	1014	1016	1766	1091	1195	1264	660	1755	1174	246	805	381													
Göteborg	1083	3031	2427	1424	1940	793	692	2416	2082	1382	1206	2390	1574	1370	1786	1894	1931	2313	1890	1106	1673	1857												
Hamburg	473	2635	1778	814	1543	996	290	1807	1473	985	597	1993	1177	761	1177	1245	1321	1858	1395	497	1063	1247	619											
Helsinki	1770	3154	3265	2263	2063	1363	1329	3104	2770	1656	1894	2102	1719	2058	2474	2543	2619	2635	2500	1794	2511	2572	760	1306										
Istanbul	2695	1099	2957	2241	970	3696	2218	3293	3000	1533	2647	649	1339	2849	3105	2617	3409	1273	1978	2256	2298	2113	2905	2512	2758									
København	777	2726	2121	1119	1635	1108	387	2111	1777	1076	901	2085	1269	1065	1481	1550	1626	1997	1584	801	1367	1552	317	313	952	2599								
Köln	269	2566	1357	493	1475	1411	577	1401	1067	987	213	1968	1152	415	771	823	975	1667	1137	193	742	965	1037	427	1726	2440	732							
Kraków	1224	1857	2255	1252	766	2077	599	2411	2065	427	1300	1100	391	1475	1858	1723	2036	1160	1290	978	1501	1425	1286	882	1281	1731	981	1087						
Kyïv/Київ	1989	2101	3045	2041	1477	2837	1364	3200	2854	1320	2095	902	1117	2258	2661	2512	2818	1886	2067	1767	2290	2202	1778	1642	1298	1547	1741	1902	872					
Lille	287	2883	1252	622	1792	1661	850	1135	801	1304	112	2285	1469	114	505	641	674	1893	1266	510	684	1123	1287	677	1976	2757	982	323	1394	2176				
Lisboa	2251	3550	1251	2037	3157	3626	2799	866	1153	2966	2053	3772	3092	2034	1827	1524	771	3175	2253	2314	1874	2025	3252	2641	3941	4127	2947	2234	3258	4047	1967			
Ljubljana	1235	1626	1456	741	535	2181	995	1792	1499	428	1146	1144	462	1378	1604	1117	1938	649	483	803	803	618	1648	1186	2061	1500	1343	987	838	1582	1235	2623		
London	478	3082	1433	802	1990	1852	1041	1307	973	1502	310	2483	1667	116	122	821	443	2182	1446	708	864	1303	1478	868	2167	2955	1173	522	1585	2368	223	2138	1466	
Luxembourg	412	2567	1152	331	1476	1610	766	1282	948	1026	213	2007	1191	415	734	620	976	1590	975	233	510	803	1236	626	1925	2441	931	204	1193	1982	304	2113	943	523
Lyon	925	2551	638	400	1455	2125	1233	889	555	1238	698	2065	1390	762	815	172	1323	1473	701	696	150	469	1752	1141	2441	2425	1447	719	1620	2410	692	1727	925	871
Madrid	1773	2981	623	1559	2588	3146	2320	398	685	2445	1574	3203	2523	1555	1348	1056	1493	2606	1689	1835	1384	1456	2773	2162	3462	3558	2468	1755	2779	3568	1488	627	2058	1661
Málaga	2315	3355	983	2007	2961	3689	2840	929	1217	2819	2116	3577	2896	2097	1890	1593	2042	2979	2062	2303	1757	1830	3315	2705	4004	3931	3010	2297	3227	4021	2030	610	2432	2203
Marseille	1236	2611	507	667	1514	2466	1544	843	648	1372	1010	2124	1450	1074	1127	477	1635	1532	627	1008	417	395	2104	1494	2944	2485	1799	1031	1808	2569	1004	1674	985	1182
Milano	1060	2116	978	340	1024	2108	1040	1314	1016	882	879	1634	959	1029	1203	633	1630	1042	304	665	320	140	1724	1113	2440	1989	1418	829	1292	2079	959	2145	495	1137
Minsk/Мінск	1768	2595	2901	1898	1504	1904	1143	3070	2736	1203	1874	1369	1144	2037	2440	2368	2597	1913	2047	1624	2147	2182	1107	1421	798	2014	1520	1681	802	584	1953	3901	1606	2145
Moskva/Москва	2472	3312	3607	2604	2220	2391	1847	3774	3440	1907	2578	1762	1848	2740	3144	3074	3301	2629	2753	2330	2853	2914	1656	2125	1107	2909	2224	2385	1503	872	2657	4605	2312	2849
München	831	2035	1363	398	944	1771	587	1604	1258	492	741	1474	657	975	1202	915	1535	1058	652	393	591	632	1238	776	1986	1909	933	577	871	1764	832	2448	411	1083
Nantes	884	3170	893	852	2073	2258	1432	663	329	1698	685	2679	1863	598	325	535	477	2091	1353	947	748	1121	1884	1274	2573	3043	1579	867	1915	2705	599	1484	1544	448
Napoli	1842	844	1557	1116	1483	2860	1708	1893	1698	1341	1652	1237	1418	1805	1963	1359	2434	273	474	1441	1080	713	2360	1865	2999	1301	2055	1605	1776	2590	1734	2724	953	1913
Oslo	1376	3325	2720	1717	2233	499	985	2710	2376	1675	1500	2683	1867	1664	2080	2188	2224	2606	2183	1400	1966	2150	295	912	812	3198	611	1330	1579	2069	1581	3541	1943	1772
Palermo	1847	1131	242	1121	1494	2865	1713	1898	1704	1346	1658	2104	1429	1810	1969	1365	2439	673	479	1446	1086	718	2365	1870	3010	2458	2060	1610	1787	2620	1740	2729	959	1915
Paris	511	2878	1036	506	1787	1885	1059	919	585	1324	312	2306	1489	297	357	425	857	1901	1147	574	541	914	1511	901	2200	2752	1206	493	1542	2332	226	1750	1254	405
Porto	2086	3385	1159	1873	2991	3460	2634	711	999	2801	1887	3607	2927	1868	1661	1370	461	3009	2092	2149	1709	1860	3086	2476	3775	3961	2781	2068	3092	3882	1801	313	2462	1974
Praha	894	1987	1721	719	896	1839	361	1875	1532	337	907	1346	529	1109	1398	1189	1669	1285	1039	517	967	1009	1047	655	1638	1860	742	701	488	1325	1017	2722	623	1217
Rīga	1718	2839	2926	1924	1757	1034	998	2975	2641	1319	1779	1758	1382	1942	2345	2362	2547	2298	2163	1535	2172	2233	477	1265	315	2437	833	1586	962	1055	1859	3806	1722	2095
Roma	1642	1011	1359	916	1283	2660	1508	1693	1499	1141	1452	1893	1218	1605	1763	1159	2234	440	274	1241	881	513	2160	1665	2799	1467	1855	1405	1550	2338	1534	2526	755	1713
Rotterdam	76	2830	1482	684	1739	1487	694	1364	1030	1250	154	2231	1415	316	734	870	563	1931	1328	456	863	1156	1113	502	1802	2703	808	263	1255	2021	233	2195	1253	425
Salzburg	975	1903	1500	535	812	1915	730	1741	1395	386	877	1368	551	1111	1338	1052	1672	926	668	536	728	698	1382	920	1989	1777	1077	721	766	1671	969	2585	279	1220
Sarajevo	1747	1161	2003	1294	305	2687	1402	2340	2046	716	1699	915	537	1901	2158	1664	2461	246	1030	1309	1350	1166	2088	1688	2260	1168	1783	1493	927	1654	1809	3170	551	2009
Sevilla	2247	3376	1004	2029	2983	3621	2794	861	1148	2841	2048	3598	2918	2029	1822	1519	1967	3001	2084	2309	1779	1851	3247	2636	3936	3953	2942	2229	3249	4043	1962	393	2453	2135
Skopje/Скопје	2153	702	2416	1760	429	3155	1677	2752	2459	991	2106	625	798	2307	2564	2076	2868	456	1437	1715	1757	1572	2364	1971	2494	818	2059	1899	1184	1527	2216	3583	958	2416
Sofia/София	2112	800	2374	1659	387	3114	1636	2710	2417	950	2064	389	756	2266	2523	2035	2827	691	1396	1674	1715	1531	2322	1929	2452	568	2017	1858	1143	1290	2174	3541	916	2374
St. Peterburg	2304	3348	3525	2523	2257	1521	1589	3606	3272	1850	2410	2132	1913	2573	2976	2993	3133	2829	2694	2210	2771	2832	1143	1896	391	2946	1303	2217	1458	1243	2489	4437	2253	2681
Stockholm	1427	3376	2771	1769	2285	1027	1037	2761	2427	1726	1551	2735	1918	1715	2131	2200	2275	2657	2234	1451	2017	2202	470	963	292	3249	662	1381	651	1062	1632	3592	1994	1823
Strasbourg	602	2413	1129	141	1322	1698	758	1274	940	856	429	1838	1021	622	849	597	1182	1435	785	217	390	613	1313	702	2158	2286	1008	355	1148	1937	520	2105	789	730
Tallinn	2039	3150	3261	2258	2059	1156	1324	3342	3008	1652	2145	2098	1714	2308	2712	2728	2869	2631	2496	1946	2507	2567	607	1631	5	2748	798	1952	1273	1307	2225	4173	2055	2416
Thessaloníki	2350	503	2612	1957	625	3351	1873	2948	2655	1188	2302	697	994	2504	2760	2272	3064	687	1633	1911	1953	1768	2560	2167	2690	599	2255	2096	1380	1598	2412	3779	1154	2612
Toulouse	1180	2986	329	879	1889	2554	1694	445	245	1747	991	2505	1824	966	900	376	1526	1907	990	1158	685	758	2180	1570	2869	2859	1875	1162	2082	2871	895	1267	1360	1074
Tromsø	3017	4966	4361	3358	3874	1866	2626	4351	4017	3316	3141	3463	3508	3305	3721	3829	3865	4247	3824	3041	3607	3791	1944	2553	1360	4113	2251	2971	2637	2730	3222	5182	3584	3413
Valencia	1878	2724	352	1377	2330	3130	2209	612	779	2188	1679	2946	2266	1664	1442	963	1594	2348	1431	1672	1126	1199	2768	2117	3609	3301	2463	1695	2597	3391	1594	887	1801	1773
Venezia	1308	1865	1236	603	774	2288	1135	1572	1279	631	1142	1383	709	1292	1466	897	1921	792	262	856	583	398	1788	1293	2264	1738	1483	1064	1041	1829	1222	2403	244	1400
Vilnius	1653	2580	2792	1790	1489	1722	1028	2955	2621	1094	1759	1399	1157	1922	2325	2260	2482	2073	1939	1541	2038	2099	925	1306	608	2049	804	1566	737	768	1838	3786	1497	2030
Warszawa	1217	2182	2351	1349	1091	1880	592	2520	2185	653	1323	1201	716	1486	1889	1819	2046	1632	1498	1075	1597	1658	976	870	982	2055	969	1130	296	772	1403	3350	1057	1594
Wien	1156	1702	1799	813	610	2130	652	2036	1690	79	1108	1060	244	1310	1600	1330	1870	961	826	718	1006	961	1338	946	1688	1575	1033	902	465	1364	1218	2881	385	1418
Zagreb	1335	1487	1591	881	396	2271	1067	1927	1634	421	1287	1006	345	1489	1745	1251	2049	607	618	897	938	753	1719	1276	2053	1361	1414	1081	738	1465	1397	2758	139	1597
Zürich	813	2348	1051	86	1192	1854	837	1280	946	817	622	1798	982	775	950	603	1335	1312	588	390	279	416	1469	859	2237	2156	1164	554	1225	2015	705	2111	659	883

Distances
Distances / Entfernungen / Afstandstabel /Distanze / Distancias / Distâncias

Les distances sont comptées à partir du centre-ville et par la route la plus pratique, c'est-à-dire celle qui offre les meilleures conditions de roulage, mais qui n'est pas nécessairement la plus courte.

Distances are calculated from town-centres and using the best roads from a motoring point of view - not necessarily the shortest.

Die Entfernungen gelten ab Stadtmitte unter Berücksichtigung der günstigsten (nicht immer kürzesten) Strecke.

De afstanden zijn in km berekend van centrum tot centrum langs de geschickste, dus niet noodzakelijkerwijze de kortste route.

Le distanze sono calcolate a partire dal centro-città e seguendo la strada che, pur non essendo necessariamente la più breve, offre le migliori condizioni di viaggio.

El kilometraje está calculado desde el centro de la ciudad y por la carretera más práctica para el automovilista, que no tiene porqué ser la más corta.

As distâncias entre as principais cidades são contadas a partir do centro da cidade e pela estrada mais pratica, ou seja, a que oferece melhores condições de acesso, mas que não é necessáriamente a mais curta.

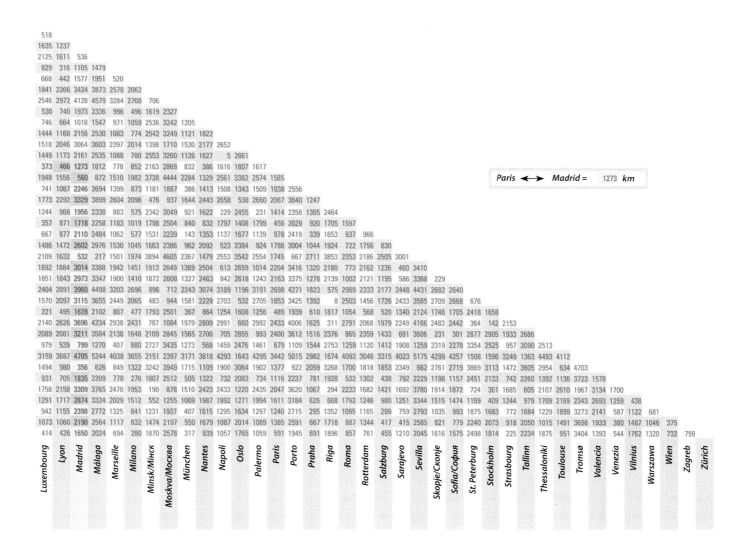

Paris ←→ Madrid = 1273 km

	Luxembourg	Lyon	Madrid	Málaga	Marseille	Milano	Minsk/Мinck	Moskva/Москва	München	Nantes	Napoli	Oslo	Palermo	Paris	Porto	Praha	Riga	Roma	Rotterdam	Salzburg	Sarajevo	Sevilla	Skopje/Скопje	Sofia/София	St. Peterburg	Stockholm	Strasbourg	Tallinn	Thessaloniki	Toulouse	Tromsø	Valencia	Venezia	Vilnius	Warszawa	Wien	Zagreb	Zürich
Lyon	518																																					
Madrid	1635	1237																																				
Málaga	2125	1611	536																																			
Marseille	829	316	1105	1479																																		
Milano	668	442	1577	1951	520																																	
Minsk/Мinck	1841	2266	3424	3873	2578	2062																																
Moskva/Москва	2546	2972	4128	4579	3284	2768	706																															
München	530	740	1973	2336	996	496	1619	2327																														
Nantes	746	664	1018	1547	971	1059	2536	3242	1205																													
Napoli	1444	1168	2156	2530	1083	774	2542	3249	1121	1822																												
Oslo	1518	2046	3064	3603	2397	2014	1398	1710	1530	2177	2652																											
Palermo	1449	1173	2161	2535	1088	780	2553	3260	1126	1827	5	2661																										
Paris	373	466	1273	1812	778	852	2163	2869	832	386	1616	1807	1617																									
Porto	1948	1556	560	872	1510	1982	3738	4444	2284	1329	2561	3382	2574	1585																								
Praha	741	1087	2246	2694	1399	873	1181	1887	386	1413	1508	1343	1509	1038	2556																							
Riga	1773	2292	3329	3899	2604	2096	476	937	1644	2443	2658	538	2660	2067	3640	1247																						
Roma	1244	968	1956	2330	883	575	2342	3049	921	1622	229	2455	231	1414	2358	1305	2464																					
Rotterdam	357	871	1718	2258	1183	1019	1798	2504	840	832	1797	1408	1799	456	2029	920	1705	1597																				
Salzburg	667	877	2110	2484	1062	577	1531	2239	143	1353	1137	1677	1139	978	2419	339	1653	937	966																			
Sarajevo	1486	1472	2602	2976	1530	1045	1663	2386	962	2092	523	2384	924	1798	3004	1044	1924	722	1756	830																		
Sevilla	2109	1632	532	217	1501	1974	3894	4605	2367	1479	2553	3542	2554	1745	667	2711	3853	2353	2186	2505	3001																	
Skopje/Скопje	1892	1884	3014	3388	1942	1451	1913	2649	1369	2504	613	2659	1004	2204	3416	1320	2180	773	2162	1236	460	3410																
Sofia/София	1851	1843	2973	3347	1900	1410	1872	2608	1327	2463	842	2618	1243	2163	3375	1278	2139	1002	2121	1195	586	3368	229															
St. Peterburg	2404	2891	3960	4498	3203	2696	896	712	2243	3074	3189	1196	3191	2698	4271	1823	575	2989	2333	2177	2448	4431	2682	2640														
Stockholm	1570	2097	3115	3655	2449	2065	483	944	1581	2228	2703	532	2705	1853	3425	1392	8	2503	1456	1726	2433	3585	2709	2668	676													
Strasbourg	221	495	1628	2102	807	477	1793	2501	367	864	1254	1608	1256	489	1939	610	1817	1054	568	520	1340	2124	1746	1705	2418	1658												
Tallinn	2140	2626	3696	4234	2938	2431	787	1084	1979	2809	2991	660	2992	2433	4006	1625	311	2791	2068	1979	2249	4166	2483	2442	364	142	2153											
Thessaloniki	2089	2081	3211	3584	2138	1648	2109	2845	1565	2700	705	2855	993	2400	3612	1516	2376	865	2359	1433	691	3606	231	301	2877	2905	1933	2686										
Toulouse	979	539	799	1270	407	880	2727	3435	1273	568	1459	2476	1461	679	1109	1544	2753	1259	1120	1412	1908	1259	2319	2278	3354	2525	957	3090	2513									
Tromsø	3159	3687	4705	5244	4038	3655	2151	2397	3171	3818	4293	1643	4295	3442	5015	2982	1674	4093	3046	3315	4023	5175	4299	4257	1508	1596	3249	1363	4493	4112								
Valencia	1494	980	356	626	849	1322	3242	3949	1715	1109	1900	3064	1902	1377	922	2059	3268	1700	1818	1853	2349	662	2761	2719	3869	3113	1472	3605	2954	634	4703							
Venezia	931	705	1835	2209	778	276	1807	2512	505	1322	732	2083	734	1116	2237	781	1928	532	1302	438	792	2229	1198	1157	2133	742	2260	1136	3723	1578								
Vilnius	1758	2158	3309	3765	2470	1953	190	878	1510	2423	2433	1220	2435	2047	3620	1067	294	2233	1682	1421	1692	3780	1914	1872	724	301	1685	605	2107	2610	1967	3134	1700					
Warszawa	1291	1717	2874	3324	2029	1512	552	1255	1069	1987	1992	1271	1994	1611	3184	626	668	1792	1246	980	1251	3344	1515	1474	1169	409	1244	979	1709	2169	2343	2693	1259	438				
Wien	942	1155	2398	2772	1325	841	1231	1937	407	1615	1295	1634	1297	1240	2715	295	1352	1095	1165	299	759	2793	1035	993	1875	1683	772	1684	1229	1699	3273	2141	587	1122	681			
Zagreb	1073	1060	2190	2564	1117	632	1344	2197	550	1679	1087	2014	1089	1385	2591	667	1718	887	1344	417	415	2585	821	779	2240	2073	918	2050	1015	1491	3656	1933	380	1487	1046	375		
Zürich	414	428	1650	2024	694	280	1870	2578	317	939	1057	1765	1059	591	1945	691	1896	857	761	455	1210	2045	1616	1575	2498	1814	225	2234	1875	951	3404	1393	544	1762	1320	732	799	

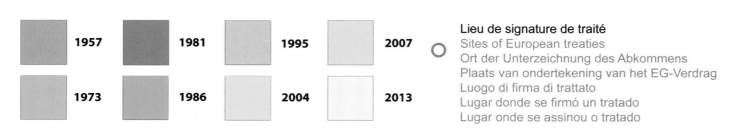

Lieu de signature de traité
Sites of European treaties
Ort der Unterzeichnung des Abkommens
Plaats van ondertekening van het EG-Verdrag
Luogo di firma di trattato
Lugar donde se firmó un tratado
Lugar onde se assinou o tratado

1957   1981   1995   2007

1973   1986   2004   2013

Europe des 28
28 EU Member States / Europa der 28 / Het Europa van de 28
Europa dei 28 / Europa de los 28 / Europa dos 28

Schengen

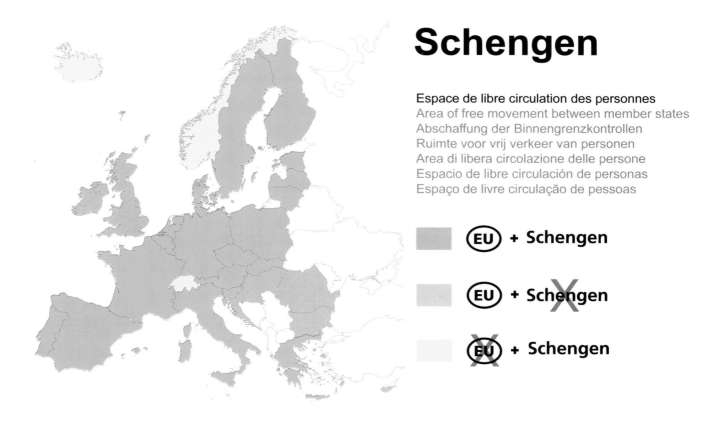

Espace de libre circulation des personnes
Area of free movement between member states
Abschaffung der Binnengrenzkontrollen
Ruimte voor vrij verkeer van personen
Area di libera circolazione delle persone
Espacio de libre circulación de personas
Espaço de livre circulação de pessoas

(EU) + Schengen

(EU) + Schengen

(EU) + Schengen

Euro : €

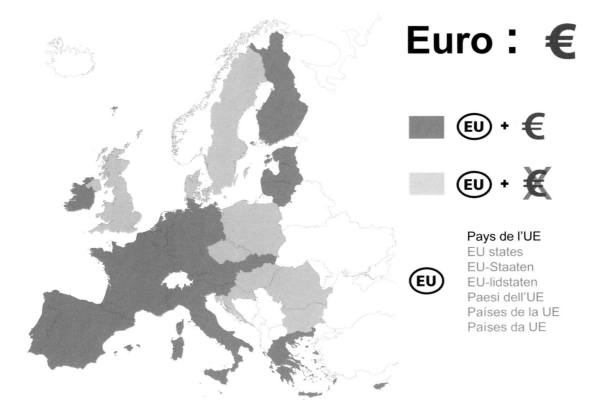

(EU) + €

(EU) + €

Pays de l'UE
EU states
EU-Staaten
EU-lidstaten
Paesi dell'UE
Países de la UE
Países da UE

	(F)	NOM FRANÇAIS	NOM LOCAL	x 1000	km²	h/km²	
	D	ALLEMAGNE	Deutschland	81197	357 170	227	Berlin
	A	AUTRICHE	Österreich	8545	83 879	102	Wien (Vienne)
	B	BELGIQUE	België, Belgique	11231	30 530	368	Brussel/Bruxelles
	BG	BULGARIE	България	7223	111 000	65	Sofia
	CY	CHYPRE	Κύπρος / Kýpros, Kıbrıs	1153	9 250	125	Lefkosia (Nicosie)
	HR	CROATIE	Hrvatska	4238	56 590	75	Zagreb
	DK	DANEMARK	Danmark	5638	43 090	131	København (Copenhague)
	E	ESPAGNE	España	46476	505 940	92	Madrid
	EST	ESTONIE	Eesti	1314	45 230	29	Tallinn
	FIN	FINLANDE	Suomi, Finland	5461	338 420	16	Helsinki/Helsingfors
	F	FRANCE	France	66217	549 087	121	Paris
	GR	GRÈCE	Ελλάδα ,Ellada	10869	131 960	82	Athína (Athènes)
	H	HONGRIE	Magyarország	9863	93 030	106	Budapest
	IRL	IRLANDE	Ireland, Éire	4615	70 280	66	Dublin
	I	ITALIE	Italia	60789	301 340	202	Roma (Rome)
	LV	LETTONIE	Latvija	1993	64 490	31	Riga
	LT	LITUANIE	Lietuva	2932	65 300	45	Vilnius
	L	LUXEMBOURG	Luxembourg, Lëtzebuerg	556	2 590	215	Luxembourg
	M	MALTE	Malta	427	320	1 334	Valletta (La Valette)
	NL	PAYS-BAS	Nederland	16865	41 500	406	Amsterdam
	PL	POLOGNE	Polska	38011	312 680	122	Warszawa (Varsovie)
	P	PORTUGAL	Portugal	10401	92 220	113	Lisboa (Lisbonne)
	RO	ROUMANIE	România	19904	238 390	83	București (Bucarest)
	GB	ROYAUME-UNI	United Kingdom of Great Britain & Northern Ireland	64559	243 610	265	London (Londres)
	SK	SLOVAQUE, République	Slovenská Republika	5418	49 036	110	Bratislava
	SLO	SLOVÉNIE	Slovenija	2061	20 270	102	Ljubljana
	S	SUÈDE	Sverige	9696	447 420	22	Stockholm
	CZ	TCHÈQUE, République	Česká Republika	10525	78 870	133	Praha (Prague)

Sources : Eurostat 2015

![EU]	⊜⊜⊜⊜	⊜ (1 000 000 000 e)	⊜/🯅 (en e)	🕐(GMT)	RÉGIME POLITIQUE	FÊTE NATIONALE
25/03/1957	€	3 025 900,0	37 266	+ 1 (hiver) + 2 (été)	République fédérale	03/10
01/01/1995	€	337 161,8	39 457	+ 1 (hiver) + 2 (été)	République fédérale	26/10
25/03/1957	€	409 407,0	36 453	+ 1 (hiver) + 2 (été)	Monarchie constitutionnelle et parlementaire	21/07
01/01/2007	Leva (BGN)	44 162,3	6 114	+ 2 (hiver) + 3 (été)	République	03/03
01/05/2004	€	17 420,6	15 109	+ 2 (hiver) + 3 (été)	République	01/10
01/07/2013	Kuna (HRK)	43 897,0	10 358	+ 1 (hiver) + 2 (été)	République	25/06
01/01/1973	Danske Krone (DKK)	266 244,5	47 223	+ 1 (hiver) + 2 (été)	Monarchie parlementaire	16/04
01/01/1986	€	1 081 190,0	23 263	+ 1 (hiver) + 2 (été)	Royaume (Monarchie parlementaire)	12/10
01/05/2004	€	20 460,9	15 571	+ 2 (hiver) + 3 (été)	République	24/02
01/01/1995	€	207 220,0	37 945	+ 2 (hiver) + 3 (été)	République	06/12
25/03/1957	€	2 183 631,0	32 977	+ 1 (hiver) + 2 (été)	République	14/07
01/01/1981	€	176 022,7	16 195	+ 2 (hiver) + 3 (été)	République	25/03
01/05/2004	Forint (HUF)	108 747,9	11 026	+ 1 (hiver) + 2 (été)	République	20/08
01/01/1973	€	214 623,0	46 506	GMT (hiver) + 1 (été)	République	17/03
25/03/1957	€	1 636 371,7	26 919	+ 1 (hiver) + 2 (été)	République	02/06
01/05/2004	€	24 377,7	12 232	+ 2 (hiver) + 3 (été)	République	18/11
01/05/2004	€	37 189,7	12 684	+ 2 (hiver) + 3 (été)	République	16/02
25/03/1957	€	52 112,5	93 728	+ 1 (hiver) + 2 (été)	Monarchie constitutionnelle	23/06
01/05/2004	€	8 796,5	20 601	+ 1 (hiver) + 2 (été)	République	21/09
25/03/1957	€	678 572,0	40 236	+ 1 (hiver) + 2 (été)	Monarchie constitutionnelle et parlementaire	27/04
01/05/2004	Złoty (PLN)	427 737,4	11 253	+ 1 (hiver) + 2 (été)	République	03/05
01/01/1986	€	179 378,9	17 246	GMT (hiver) + 1 (été)	République	10/06
01/01/2007	Leu (RON)	160 352,8	8 056	+ 2 (hiver) + 3 (été)	République	01/12
01/01/1973	Pound Sterling (GBP)	2 568 940,8	39 792	GMT (hiver) + 1 (été)	Monarchie constitutionnelle	13/06
01/05/2004	€	78 070,8	14 410	+ 1 (hiver) + 2 (été)	République	01/09
01/05/2004	€	38 543,2	18 700	+ 1 (hiver) + 2 (été)	République	25/06
01/01/1995	Svensk Krona (SEK)	444 235,3	45 816	+ 1 (hiver) + 2 (été)	Monarchie parlementaire	06/06
01/05/2004	Koruna Česká (CZK)	154 738,7	14 702	+ 1 (hiver) + 2 (été)	République	28/10

MICHELIN INNOVE SANS CESSE POUR UNE MEILLEURE MOBILITÉ PLUS SÛRE, PLUS ÉCONOME, PLUS PROPRE ET PLUS CONNECTÉE.

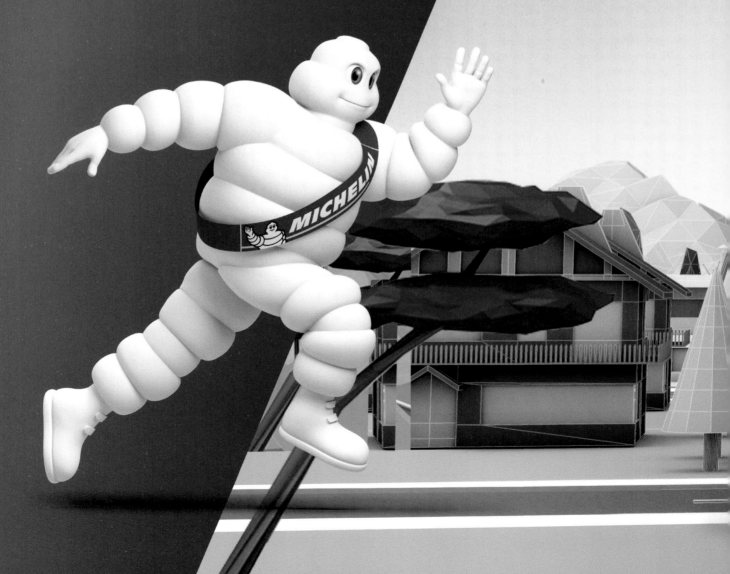

Les pneus s'usent plus vite sur les petits trajets en ville...

?

VRAI !

La fréquence des freinages et des accélérations en ville use davantage vos pneus ! Dans les embouteillages, armez-vous de patience et conduisez en douceur.

La pression des pneus agit uniquement sur la sécurité...

?

FAUX !

Au-delà de la tenue de route et de la consommation de carburant, une sous pression de 0,5 Bar diminue de 8 000 km la durée de vie de vos pneus. Pensez à vérifier la pression environ une fois par mois, surtout avant un départ en vacances ou un long trajet.

Équiper ma voiture avec **2 pneus hiver** me garantit une sécurité maximum...

?

FAUX !

En hiver, en dessous de 7°C notamment, pour une meilleure tenue de route, vos quatre pneus doivent être identiques et changés en même temps.

2 PNEUS HIVER SEULEMENT = la tenue de route de votre véhicule n'est pas optimale.

4 PNEUS HIVER = c'est le choix d'une **meilleure sécurité** dans les virages, en descente et en cas de freinage.

Si vous êtes régulièrement confrontés à la pluie, à la neige ou au verglas, optez pour un pneu de la gamme **MICHELIN Alpin**. Cette gamme vous offre confort et précision de conduite pour affronter les obstacles de l'hiver.

MICHELIN

MICHELIN S'ENGAGE

▶ MICHELIN EST LE **N°1 MONDIAL DES PNEUS ÉCONOMES EN ÉNERGIE** POUR LES VÉHICULES LÉGERS.

▶ POUR **SENSIBILISER LES PLUS JEUNES À LA SÉCURITÉ ROUTIÈRE,** MÊME EN DEUX-ROUES : DES ACTIONS DE TERRAIN ONT ÉTÉ ORGANISÉES DANS **16 PAYS** EN 2015.

QUIZ

1 POURQUOI BIBENDUM, LE BONHOMME MICHELIN, EST BLANC ALORS QUE LE PNEU EST NOIR ?

Le personnage de Bibendum a été imaginé à partir d'une pile de pneus, en 1898, à une époque où le pneu était fabriqué avec du caoutchouc naturel, du coton et du soufre et où il est donc de couleur claire. Ce n'est qu'après la Première guerre mondiale que sa composition se complexifie et qu'apparaît le noir de carbone. Mais Bibendum, lui, restera blanc !

2 SAVEZ-VOUS DEPUIS QUAND LE GUIDE MICHELIN ACCOMPAGNE LES VOYAGEURS ?

Depuis 1900, il était dit alors que cet ouvrage paraissait avec le siècle, et qu'il durerait autant que lui. Et il fait encore référence aujourd'hui, avec de nouvelles éditions et la sélection sur le site MICHELIN Restaurants - Bookatable dans quelques pays.

3 DE QUAND DATE « BIB GOURMAND » DANS LE GUIDE MICHELIN ?

Cette appellation apparaît en 1997 mais dès 1954 le Guide MICHELIN signale les « repas soignés à prix modérés ». Aujourd'hui, on le retrouve sur le site et dans l'application mobile MICHELIN Restaurants - Bookatable.

Si vous voulez en savoir plus sur Michelin en vous amusant, visitez l'Aventure Michelin et sa boutique à Clermont-Ferrand, France :
www.laventuremichelin.com

MICHELIN
Une meilleure façon d'avancer

Édition 2017 par Michelin Travel Partner
© 2017 Michelin , Propriétaires-éditeurs
Société par actions simplifiée au capital de 11 288 880 EUR
27 Cours de l'Île Seguin - 92100 Boulogne-Billancourt (France) - R.C.S. Nanterre 433 677 721

CARTE STRADALI E TURISTICHE PUBBLICAZIONE PERIODICA
Reg. Trib. di Milano N° 80 del 24/02/1997 Dir. Resp. FERRUCCIO ALONZI
The publisher disclaims all liability for the names used to designate certain places, regions
or areas where their use may result in a dispute under international law.
Places have been designated by their most commonly used names in order to make the text easier for readers to understand.

Malgré tout le soin apporté à la réalisation de cet ouvrage, il se peut qu'un exemplaire défectueux ait échappé à notre vigilance.
Dans ce cas, veuillez le rapporter à votre libraire qui vous l'échangera ou contacter :
Michelin Cartes et Plans, 27 cours de l'Île Seguin - F-92105 Boulogne-Billancourt Cedex

While every effort is made to ensure that all information printed in this publication is correct and up-to-date,
Michelin Maps & Guides accepts no liability for any direct, indirect or consequential losses howsoever caused
so far as such can be excluded by law.
Please help us to correct errors and omissions by writing to us at
Michelin Cartes et Plans, 27 cours de l'Île Seguin - F-92105 Boulogne-Billancourt Cedex

Printed in Italy - Nuovo Istituto Italiano Arti Grafiche (NIIAG) - 24126 Bergamo (Italie) – DL : 01/2017

Photo de couverture : Marina Ignatova / Fotolia.com

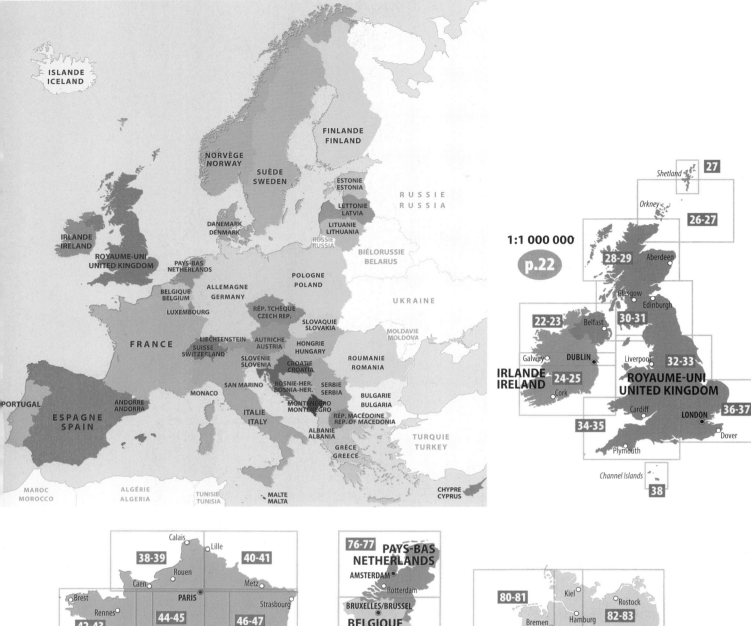

1:1 000 000

p.22

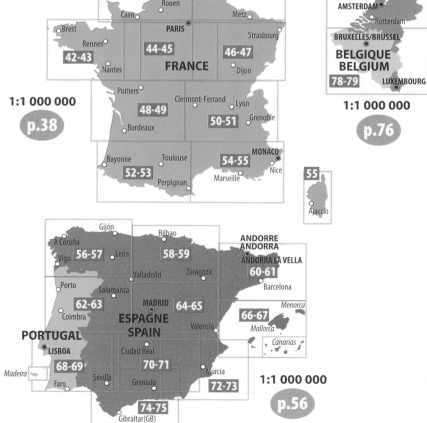

1:1 000 000

p.38

1:1 000 000

p.76

1:1 000 000

p.56

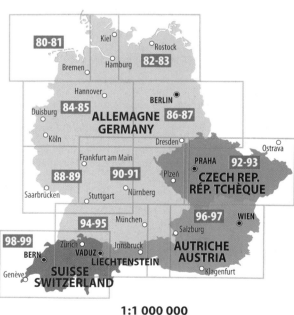

1:1 000 000

p.80